KODANSHA
ENCYCLOPEDIA OF
JAPAN

Distributors
JAPAN: KODANSHA LTD., Tokyo.
OVERSEAS: KODANSHA INTERNATIONAL LTD., Tokyo.
   U.S.A., Mexico, Central America, and South America: KODANSHA INTERNATIONAL/USA LTD.
    through HARPER & ROW, PUBLISHERS, INC., New York.
   Canada: FITZHENRY & WHITESIDE LTD., Ontario.
   U.K., Europe, the Middle East, and Africa: INTERNATIONAL BOOK DISTRIBUTORS LTD.,
    Hemel Hempstead, Herts., England.
   Australia and New Zealand: HARPER & ROW (AUSTRALASIA) PTY. LTD., Artarmon, N.S.W.
   Asia: TOPPAN COMPANY (S) PTE. LTD., Singapore.

Published by Kodansha Ltd., 12-21, Otowa 2-chome, Bunkyo-ku, Tokyo 112 and Kodansha
International/USA Ltd., 10 East 53rd Street, New York, New York 10022.
Copyright © 1983 by Kodansha Ltd.
All rights reserved.
Printed in Japan.
First edition, 1983.

LCC 83-80778
ISBN 0-87011-621-5 (Volume 1)
ISBN 0-87011-620-7 (Set)
ISBN 4-06-144531-6 (0) (in Japan)

Library of Congress Cataloging in Publication Data
Main entry under title:

Kodansha encyclopedia of Japan.

   Includes index.
   1. Japan—Dictionaries and encyclopedias. I. Title:
Encyclopedia of Japan.
DS805.K633 1983   952′.003′21   83-80778
ISBN 0-87011-620-7 (U.S.)

KODANSHA
ENCYCLOPEDIA OF
JAPAN

1

KODANSHA

INTRODUCTION

The *Encyclopedia of Japan* represents the consummation of two decades of efforts by Mr. Shōichi Noma, Honorary President of Kōdansha, Ltd, to further international cultural exchange. These efforts have already borne rich fruit in the founding of Kōdansha International and the many excellent books it has published, as well as in the creation of the Noma African Literature Prize. They now reach a new level of achievement through the completion of this major undertaking.

The *Encyclopedia of Japan* is unique in being the first comprehensive encyclopedia seeking to present the totality of a major world culture in a foreign language. It is probably also unparalleled among works of its type for the close international cooperation it has required. Some 680 Japanese and 524 non-Japanese scholars from 27 nations have contributed articles to it, a few providing more than 100 short articles each. Counting a large number of short articles produced in the Tōkyō office of Kōdansha, about 40 percent of the text was initially produced by Japanese, while the remaining 60 percent was written by foreign scholars. Planning and editing were jointly carried out in Tōkyō and Cambridge, Massachusetts.

The original concept for this encyclopedia was suggested by the New York publisher Mr. Maurits Dekker, and he and Mr. Gen Itasaka of Harvard were the first editors. At the time of completion, Mr. Itasaka was the Editor in Chief, with Mr. Minoru Fujita of Kōdansha the Managing Editor and Mr. Alan Campbell, Dr. Gyō Furuta, and Mr. Takeshi Kokubo the joint executive editors. Two Advisory Committees were created, one in the United States under my chairmanship but including the distinguished English scholar Professor Ronald Dore and three scholars of Japanese birth teaching in American universities, the other in Japan consisting of Japanese scholars under the chairmanship of former president of Hitotsubashi University Mr. Shigeto Tsuru. A staff of up to 25 persons at a single time worked editorially on the *Encyclopedia* in the Tōkyō office, and over the years more than 110 persons, many of them graduate students at Harvard University, were associated with the Cambridge operation to perform the arduous tasks of translating articles from Japanese into English and editing all of the items. The result has been a thoroughly international enterprise, involving mostly Japanese and Americans, but including other non-Japanese, especially those from other English-speaking countries.

This is, of course, not the first encyclopedia on Japan to appear in a foreign language, but it is by far the largest and most comprehensive. The first encyclopedic work of note was the *Dictionnaire de l'histoire et de la géographie du Japon* by E. Papinot, published in 1899 and subsequently in English (*Historical and Geographical Dictionary of Japan*, 1908), which for decades was an indispensable tool for all foreign students of Japanese history. Basil Hall Chamberlain's *Things Japanese* of 1890 was also a treasure house of information on Japan, delightfully presented. These classics have been followed more recently by various other reference works on Japan and major historical encyclopedias in German and French.

All these works, however, are much more narrow in their focus than the *Encyclopedia of Japan* or are now somewhat out of date. It, in contrast, contains the results of the latest scholarship as marshalled by acknowledged experts in each field, and it has 9,417 entries covering 37 categories of information, from such standard ones as history, literature, art, religion, economy, and geography to less obvious fields, such as science, technology, law, women, folklore, plant and animal life, food, clothing, sports, and leisure. Its articles are divided into 123 major presentations of more than 3,500 words each, 1,429 medium-length articles of around 750 to 2,500 words, and 7,865 shorter entries of 50 to 500 words.

The organization and compilation of a work of this magnitude and complexity cannot be briefly described here but deserves a whole separate article. An original proposal for a one-volume encyclopedia grew into an eight-volume work, with approximately 1,000 photographs, maps, and charts, and a ninth index volume, which contains many thousands of names and words mentioned but not given separate entries in the *Encyclopedia* and with Japanese characters included for all proper nouns and other important items for purposes of reference. Many difficult problems had to be solved, such as the question of listing subjects under Japanese terms or their English equivalents, the best English translations for Japanese terms, the correct pronunciation of Japanese names, the division of Japanese words in romanization, the most appropriate use of capitalization, and many other matters that are too complex to allow easy description. Throughout there was the need for consistency in quality, style, and details of orthography. The whole compilation required an extraordinary effort at cooperation on a massive scale across difficult barriers of language. As such, it itself is a notable achievement of international cooperation in scholarship. It is hoped that it will prove itself worthy of the great efforts put into it by providing assistance to people throughout the world who wish to know more about Japan.

The appearance of the *Encyclopedia of Japan* symbolizes the great importance Japan has achieved in world affairs. The non-Western cultural background of Japan makes it less readily accessible to people in other countries and results in a generally weak representation of Japanese matters in encyclopedias and other works of reference in Occidental languages. As the world's second largest economic entity, Japan has become too important to permit such neglect. The other peoples of the world need to know much more about this country and its culture. It is the hope of Kōdansha and the editors and collaborators in this project that, by providing this reliable, comprehensive, and easily available source of information on Japan, they will foster international understanding of this extraordinary country and in this way contribute to fruitful relations between Japan and the rest of the world. They hope to help answer many of the questions foreigners have about Japan and also stimulate their interest and desire to know more. They realize that many imperfections are inevitable in a pioneering enterprise of this sort, and they would welcome corrections and advice from any source. They realize that more and progressively better work is required if the ultimate goal of true international understanding is to be achieved. This encyclopedia they regard as a beginning, not an end. They hope that, by increasing accurate knowledge about Japan in the world, it will help create conditions that will demand its own subsequent improvement and refinement.

September 1983   Edwin O. Reischauer

PUBLISHER'S FOREWORD

Any country that has one language, is surrounded on all sides by the sea, shares no boundary with another nation, and possesses a long history as well will naturally come to have its own characteristic culture and way of life. Japan is such a country. Due to this particular set of geographical circumstances it has had little opportunity to become known to other countries but at the same time has not been faced with the necessity of being known to them. In line with a national character that makes a virtue of not speaking about oneself, Japan's efforts to make itself known to the world have long been extremely limited in comparison with its avid desire to learn about other countries.

However, in recent years our globe has grown smaller with the progress of world civilization and, more particularly, with the rapid advances in transportation and communications since World War II. In the present world where mutual understanding is vital for peace as well as in the economic and cultural spheres, Japan is no longer in the position of being able to overlook any misunderstanding or lack of understanding on the part of other nations.

We at Kōdansha have been aware of the likelihood of such a situation arising for some time and have long contemplated the possibility of publishing an English-language encyclopedia about Japan that would hopefully contribute to an overall understanding of Japan. After a long period of preparation, work on this project commenced in 1974 and, almost ten years later, the *Encyclopedia of Japan* is now finally ready for publication.

Early foreign works about Japan include the "Wajinden" section in the Chinese work *Wei zhi (Wei chih)* dating back to the third century and, in Europe, the reports on Japan written by Jesuit missionaries in the 16th century. Of course numerous fine, scholarly works were written after that, but especially since World War II, Japanese studies has witnessed a spectacular growth and development. Feeling that we should utilize to the fullest the fruits of that development, in the editing of this encyclopedia we have sought the advice and cooperation of scholars throughout the world, and fully half of the contributors to this encyclopedia are non-Japanese. This look at Japanese culture through foreign eyes has provided many new insights and made this an exceptional encyclopedia for Japanese as well as non-Japanese.

Further, in order to introduce Japan as comprehensively and concretely as possible, this work goes beyond history, literature, and art to cover the social sciences, scientific technology, and other topics necessary to present Japan as it is today. Therefore it meets the needs not only of students and scholars in Japanese studies but of all those who feel an interest in or have some particular concern regarding Japan, including businessmen and the general educated public.

This first effort in the world to compile an encyclopedia about Japan in English has entailed various difficulties, but these have now been overcome, and we are proud to present what we feel will be an important work in the advancement of understanding of Japan abroad. All of us involved in the publication of the *Encyclopedia of Japan* will be proud and happy if we are thereby able to contribute even a little to mutual understanding in the world today.

Noma Koremichi
President, Kōdansha, Ltd

September 1983

ADVISORY COMMITTEE

EDITORIAL STAFF

HOW TO USE THIS ENCYCLOPEDIA

General

The *Encyclopedia of Japan* represents a ten-year joint effort by Japanese and Western scholars and editors to provide an up-to-date and sophisticated compilation of knowledge about Japan to the English-speaking world. Only in recent years has such a comprehensive reference work about Japan in English been made possible by the growth of Western interest in and scholarship on Japan. This growth is reflected in the large number (over 500) of Western contributors and the diversity of subjects covered by them. Over half the *Encyclopedia* (some 60 percent of the text) was written in English by Western scholars. At the same time a rapid increase in the number of translators and of English-speaking editors familiar with the Japanese language has made possible the inclusion of many articles by Japanese scholars, particularly on subjects for which no English-speaking author was available. Articles written in Japanese and translated or adapted for the *Encyclopedia* make up the remaining 40 percent of the text, and the number of Japanese contributors is nearly 700. The editors hope that this joint effort will lead to a further breaking down of barriers and to increased cooperation between Japanese and Western scholars.

The *Encyclopedia* covers both historical Japan and Japan in the world today, examining philosophy and science, politics and economics, literature and the arts, food and clothing, and many other subjects. Japan's past and present and its interaction with the West, broadly defined, has also received attention.

The editors have had in mind a wide audience comprising a broad range of interests and levels of knowledge regarding Japan: students, scholars, diplomats, businessmen, and the general public. The challenge thus facing them was that of creating, through the careful selection and preparation of entries, a work that could both introduce Japan to those unfamiliar with it and supply more detailed knowledge for the specialist. To achieve this dual purpose authors of all articles were asked to introduce the topic at a level appropriate for a high-school student and proceed far enough to provide a good starting point for more advanced students with some knowledge of Japan. Authors of articles on more specialized topics were asked to synthesize available knowledge and to indicate the many open-ended questions and areas for further consideration. In all articles basic definitions or explanations have been inserted whenever unfamiliar concepts or Japanese terms are introduced and an effort made to provide sufficient background for the convenience of the general reader.

An important feature of the *Encyclopedia of Japan* is the inclusion of broad introductory or survey articles for most of the major areas into which Japanese culture can be divided. Some of these are of considerable length, for example, the articles on the HISTORY OF JAPAN (almost 70,000 words) and LITERATURE (over 53,000 words). Cross references from these general articles lead the reader to articles of intermediate length on the subordinate topics mentioned in them and directly or indirectly to the many thousands of shorter identification articles that make up the bulk of the *Encyclopedia*.

For the convenience of readers who may wish to use the *Encyclopedia* as an introduction to Japanese culture as a whole or to one of its subdivisions, a list of some of the most important of these general survey articles appears below.

AGRICULTURE
ANIMALS
ART (see also BUDDHIST ART; PAINTING; UKIYO-E; SCULPTURE)
CERAMICS
CLOTHING
COOKING (see also FOOD AND EATING)
ECONOMIC HISTORY
EDUCATION
FILM, JAPANESE
FESTIVALS
FLOWER ARRANGEMENT
HISTORY OF JAPAN
INTERNATIONAL RELATIONS
JAPAN
JAPANESE LANGUAGE
LEGAL SYSTEM
LITERATURE
MANAGEMENT
MARTIAL ARTS
MEDICINE
NATURAL SCIENCES
PLANTS
RELIGION (see also BUDDHISM; CONFUCIANISM; CHRISTIANITY; SHINTŌ; ZEN)
SOCIETY
THEATER, TRADITIONAL (see also BUNRAKU; KABUKI; KYŌGEN; NŌ)
WOMEN IN JAPAN, HISTORY OF

Article Headings

In their effort to reach a wide English-speaking audience the editors have used English for article titles whenever possible. Nevertheless, given the special nature of this encyclopedia it is only natural that many titles are in Japanese. The general rule has been to use English for those topics more likely to be looked up in English by the general reader and Japanese for those topics more likely to be looked up in Japanese. (The latter include topics widely known in the West under their Japanese names as well as topics likely to be looked up only by the specialist, who would expect to find them in Japanese.) For the many articles that did not clearly fall into either of these categories the decision was necessarily an arbitrary one. In such cases, and others where confusion might occur, a cross reference under the title in the other language has been provided (e.g., Japan Current→Kuroshio; Niniroku Jiken→February 26th Incident). Most longer articles have been divided into subsections introduced by headings in boldface type or italics so that the reader who does not wish to read the entire article can easily find information on some subtopic. In the case of some very long articles the major subheadings have been listed at the beginning of the article.

Article Arrangement

All articles are arranged alphabetically. The alphabetization is letter by letter, not the word-by-word alphabetization found in some encyclopedias. In inverted titles (MACARTHUR, DOUGLAS; MUSIC, TRADITIONAL) the letter-by-letter alphabetization continues to the end of the heading regardless of inversion or commas. A consequence of this policy (made necessary by the lack of an established convention regarding the division of romanized Japanese words) is that articles on persons with the same surname are not necessarily grouped together. For example, between MORI ARINORI and MORI SOSEN appear such articles as MORIGUCHI; MORIKAWA KYOROKU; MORIMOTO KAORU; and MORINAGA & CO, LTD. This is also true of articles beginning with the same English word, JAPAN FEDERATION OF RELIGIONS appearing after JAPANESE AMERICANS and JAPANESE SPANIEL rather than being grouped with other articles beginning with the word Japan. The abbreviation of Saint (St.) is alphabetized as if spelled out. Numbers are also alphabetized as if spelled out: MARCH 15TH INCIDENT appears before MARCH INCIDENT; "441st" is alphabetized "four forty first." When two or more articles have identical titles, proper nouns appear first, followed by common nouns. The order followed for identical proper nouns is persons, places, and things.

The system of spelling for Japanese words adopted in this encyclopedia uses *m* instead of *n* before *p, b,* and *m.* This has an obvious effect on alphabetical arrangement: readers should look for *kampaku, shimbun,* and Jimmu rather than the *kanpaku, shinbun,* and Jinmu of many recent publications. Another matter that affects the alphabetical placement of Japanese personal names is the inclusion or omission of the *no* found in ancient names (e.g., Fujiwara no Sadaie). The policy of this encyclopedia is to include the *no* in the names of persons born before 1193 and to omit it in all later names except where Japanese common usage includes it, as in Kamo no Mabuchi. In article titles and throughout the *Encyclopedia,* Japanese, Chinese, and Korean personal names are given surname first, the normal order used in those languages (e.g., Mishima Yukio rather than Yukio Mishima or Mishima, Yukio).

Cross References

The *Encyclopedia* contains two types of cross references: entry-heading cross references and textual cross references. The former (which appear among the alphabetical entry listings in boldface type followed by an arrow pointing to a different title in smaller type) tell the reader that the topic in question is treated under the latter title. Textual cross references are words that appear in SMALL CAPITALS within the text of an article. The small capitals are an indication that the *Encyclopedia* contains an article whose title either consists of those words or begins with those words (usually the former). For example, in the sentence "The family's fortunes were established by TOKUGAWA IEYASU, who founded the TOKUGAWA SHOGUNATE," the words in small capitals indicate actual article titles. In "He fought at the Battle of SEKIGAHARA," the cross reference is to SEKIGAHARA, BATTLE OF. These textual cross references are selective rather than all-inclusive. In other words, all topics in small capitals appear as articles in the *Encyclopedia,* but not all possible topics are so indicated, and the reader should not assume that there is no article on a person or topic not put in small capitals. As general policy, articles on Japanese place names (most important place names have articles) are seldom cross-referenced, and articles on persons and other topics are often not cross-referenced unless they are felt to be immediately relevant to the subject being discussed. Cross references to a subsection within an article take the form "see JAPAN: geological structure," in which the words following the colon indicate a subheading.

Bibliographies

Many articles are followed by suggestions for further reading in English, Japanese, and occasionally other languages. Some of the longer bibliographies are grouped under subtopics but most are arranged alphabetically by author. The names of Japanese authors are given in Japanese order (surname first) for works in Japanese and in Western order for works in English, but the principle of alphabetization by surname is unaffected. Publishers' names are included only for certain categories of Japanese reference works and collected texts which often have confusingly similar titles. For an annotated bibliography of works on Japanese history in Japanese, see the article DISCIPLINE OF JAPANESE HISTORY, A GUIDE TO RESEARCH.

No attempt has been made to give English translations of the titles of Japanese works in the bibliographies that follow articles. When Japanese works are mentioned in the text of an article, however, English translations of their titles are usually given in parentheses. When such an English title is printed in italics, it is the title of an actual English translation of the work. When it appears in roman type, it is merely a literal translation of the Japanese title for the reader's information.

Author's Signatures

Names of authors are given in full after the articles or sections of articles written by them. Most articles that appear without a signature were researched and written by members of the *Encyclopedia* editorial staff. In general the names of Japanese authors are given in the normal Japanese order (surnames first) and those of Western authors surname last. However, a number of Japanese authors who publish widely in English preferred to have their names given in the Western order. In order to avoid confusion in these cases, the surnames of all authors are printed in SMALL CAPITALS.

Romanization

The system of romanization for Japanese used in this encyclopedia is the Hepburn or Standard system, the romanization found in most English-language publications on Japan. The *Encyclopedia* follows the older Hepburn practice of using *m* instead of *n* before *p*, *b*, or *m*. Long vowels are indicated by macrons on all words, including well-known place names (Tōkyō, Ōsaka). An apostrophe is used to distinguish syllable-final *n* from *n* at the beginning of a syllable (e.g., *ken'in* "seal of approval" vs *kenin* "vassal"). Japanese vowels are pronounced much as in Spanish or Italian and Japanese consonants much as in English, except that *g* is always pronounced as in "go," never as in "gender." Long vowels are pronounced the same as short vowels but drawn out to approximately double their length. Dipthongs are pronounced as combinations of short vowels. For more on the sound system of Japanese, see the article JAPANESE LANGUAGE.

There is a lack of common agreement on the division of Japanese into individual words in romanization, particularly the many compound words and phrases borrowed from Chinese. The principle followed in this encyclopedia was to divide words so as to make sense and grammatical relationships clear, while at the same time keeping individual words short enough to grasp easily. In some cases the same nominalizing suffix may be spelled as a separate word in one expression and as part of a longer word in another, depending on its grammatical function (e.g., *nihonshi* "Japanese history" vs *gendai nihon shi* "history of modern Japan"). For more on romanization, see ROMANIZATION RULES in the index volume.

Chinese words and names are given in the official *pinyin* system, followed in parentheses by the more familiar spelling that is still to be found in many English-language publications. In most cases this familiar spelling is in the Wade-Giles system. However, for some well-established place names, the more familiar Chinese post office system (the one often used on maps) is followed. A few personal names are given in a dialect spelling that has become established in English (e.g., Chiang Kai-shek, Sun Yat-sen). The system of romanization used for Korean is the McCune-Reischauer system. Sanskrit words are transliterated in the system most widely used in English-language publications.

Illustrations

The *Encyclopedia* contains some 1,000 illustrations in the form of photographs, maps, diagrams, graphs, charts, and tables. In addition to the maps of Japan as a whole in the article JAPAN and the historical and interpretive maps to be found in many articles, there is a map for each of Japan's 47 prefectures in or near the respective article. In the latter, cities, towns, and villages of over 10,000 population are included, as well as some smaller communities of cultural importance. The designation as city, town, or village is an administrative one and may not reflect actual size, i.e., a town may be larger than a city. Railroads in existence as of 1980 have been included on most maps; national highways are shown but not all local ones. The major sources for these maps were 1980–83 publications by the Geographic Survey Institute, a Japanese government bureau.

Dates

Dates prior to Japan's adoption of the Western calendar on 1 January 1873 have been converted from the old Japanese lunar civil calendar. Every effort has been made to give precise conversions, taking into account the discrepancy between the beginning of the year in the lunar calendar and that in the Western solar calendar. Thus the Western dates given in this encyclopedia will sometimes differ from those found in most standard Japanese reference works, as these sometimes assign a date at the beginning or end of the lunar year to the wrong solar year. When data for precise conversion were not available or when the context called for it, the Japanese dates were included along with the Western ones. For an explanation of Japanese dates, see CALENDAR, DATES, AND TIME.

Money

In references to money or value prior to the establishment of the yen monetary system in 1871, values are given in the monetary or nonmonetary units (e.g., measures of rice) in use at the time. Because of the wide fluctuations in value, no attempt has been made to give modern yen or dollar equivalents for these units. For the period 1871 to 1945 most money values are stated in yen. However, because of the great difference between the value of the pre-World War II yen and the postwar yen, no dollar equivalents are given. Post-1945 values are given in both yen and US dollars. Dollar figures are based on the dollar value of the yen in the year in question. For information on these values, see YEN.

Weights and Measures

Japan has used the metric system officially since 1959, and weights and measures are given in metric units throughout the *Encyclopedia*. As a rule these are followed by the US equivalents in parentheses. Whenever traditional weights and measures are mentioned, approximate metric and US equivalents are given. For information on the traditional units, see WEIGHTS AND MEASURES.

Population and Other Figures

Figures for the populations of Japanese prefectures, cities, towns, and villages are based on the 1980 Japanese census. All other figures have been made as up-to-date as possible, dates being indicated in parentheses. Sales figures and other data for Japanese business firms are based on information provided by the companies themselves.

HISTORICAL PERIODS USED IN THIS ENCYCLOPEDIA

Yamato	ca 300–710
Asuka	latter part of the 6th century to 710
Nara	710–794
Heian	794–1185
Fujiwara	894–1185
Rokuhara	1167–1185
Kamakura	1185–1333
Muromachi	1333–1568
Nambokuchō	1336–1392
Sengoku	1467–1568
Azuchi-Momoyama	1568–1600
Edo	1600–1868
Meiji	1868–1912
Taishō	1912–1926
Shōwa	1926–

ABBREVIATIONS USED IN THIS ENCYCLOPEDIA

a	acre
AB	Artium Baccalaureus, Bachelor of Arts
AD	anno Domini, year of our Lord
AM	ante meridiem, before noon
AM	Artium Magister, Master of Arts
art.	article
b	born
BA	Bachelor of Arts
BC	before Christ
BS	Bachelor of Science
bu	bushel
C	Centigrade
ca	circa
cc	cubic centimeter
cg	centigram
Ch	Chinese
chap.	chapter
cm	centimeter
Co	Company
cu	cubic
d	died
DC	District of Columbia
E	East
ed	editor(s), edited
e.g.	*exempli gratia*, for example
Eng	English
et al	*et alii*, and others
etc	et cetera
F	Fahrenheit
fl	*floruit*, flourished
fl oz	fluid ounce
ft	foot
gal	gallon
gm	gram
gr	grain
ha	hectare
i.e.	*id est*, that is
in	inch
Inc	incorporated
J	Japanese
Jr	Junior
kg	kilogram
kl	kiloliter
km	kilometer
Kor	Korean
l	liter
lat	latitude
lb	pound
long	longitude
Ltd	Limited
m	meter
MA	Master of Arts
Mfg	Manufacturing
mg	milligram
mi	mile
ml	milliliter
mm	millimeter
Mt.	Mount, Mountain
N.	North
NE	Northeast
no.	number
NW	Northwest
oz	ounce
p	page

para.	paragraph
PhD	Philosophiae Doctor, Doctor of Philosophy
PM	post meridiem, afternoon
pop	population
Port	Portuguese
pp	pages
pt	pint, part
qt	quart
r	reigned, ruled
repr	reprinted
rev ed	revised edition
S	South
SE	Southeast
ser	series
Skt	Sanskrit
sq cm	square centimeter
sq ft	square foot
sq in	square inch
sq km	square kilometer
sq m	square meter
sq mi	square mile
sq yd	square yard
Sr	Senior
supp.	supplement
SW	Southwest
tr	translator, translated
trad	traditionally
vol	volume
vs	verses
W	West
yd	yard

A

abacus

(soroban). A portable manual calculator widely used in Japan. It has a rectangular frame with a varying number of vertical bamboo rods. On the present-day Japanese abacus each rod is strung with five wooden beads. The top horizontal row of beads is separated from the other four by a crossbar. Rods to the left of a chosen point designate units, tens, hundreds, and so forth, and rods to the right of that point designate decimal places. The cleared position is with the four beads below the crossbar all down, and the one bead above the crossbar up. To indicate one, move up a single bead below the crossbar on the unit rod. To indicate two, move another up; three, the third up; and four, the fourth. To indicate five, bring the bead above the crossbar down and also move all beads below the crossbar down. Six is shown by leaving the upper bead for five in its down position, and raising one bead below the crossbar up. For seven, raise another lower bead up, for eight, another, and for nine, the last. Thus, all digits from zero to nine can be represented on a single rod. To represent 10, put one on the ten rod, and clear the unit rod; 100, one on the hundred rod, and so forth. Thus base-ten numbers can be represented, with one numeral on each rod.

The abacus varies in size from those small enough to fit in the pocket to large demonstration models used for teaching. The average abacus is from 20 to 30 centimeters (8 to 12 in) in length and from 7 to 12 centimeters (3 to 5 in) in width.

A seven-bead abacus (two beads above the crossbar and five below) was imported from China during the 16th century. By the mid-1700s, when commercial activities flourished, use of the abacus along with reading and writing was taught to the general populace. A Japanese abacus with one upper and five lower beads was used from the Meiji period (1868–1912). In 1926 abacus arithmetic *(shuzan)* became part of the curriculum in the seventh and eighth grades. It was added to the elementary school curriculum in 1938, at which time the present five-bead model was introduced. The abacus is also taught in accounting and business courses in vocational senior high schools.

Although small electronic calculators are widely used today, many commercial and banking institutions still depend on the abacus. The Japanese believe learning the abacus develops children's ability to handle figures, and special schools (JUKU) just for abacus lessons flourish throughout the country. Highly skilled abacus users can carry out computations in their heads.

abalones

(awabi). In Japanese *awabi* is the common name for large marine snails of the class Gastropoda and family Haliotidae. Ten species of *awabi* are distributed in the coastal waters of Japan. Of these, three large species, namely the *madakaawabi* (giant abalone or *madaka* abalone; *Haliotis gigantea*), *megaiawabi* (megai abalone; *H. sieboldii*), and *kuroawabi* (Japanese abalone; *H. discus*), are important to Japan's fishing industry. The first two species occur in the warm current regions of Japan and the Korean peninsula. Some giant abalones attain a shell length of 30 centimeters (12 in). The *kuroawabi* has an exceptionally wide breeding distribution, extending as far as the coast of the Shandong (Shantung) Peninsula, while the convergent pinto abalone *(H. kamtchatkana)* ranges in distribution as far as the northwestern coast of North America. The small *tokobushi (H. aquatilis)* is a common species found in the warm currents of Japan and is used for food. As part of the growing shellfish farming industry, abalones are now actively bred in large saltwater tanks until they reach a shell length of about 3 centimeters (1.2 in). They are then released into the sea and cultivated. *HABE Tadashige*

The Japanese have known the abalone since ancient times. Judging from Jōmon period archaeological remains and shell mounds, it

Abashiri

Ice floes outside Abashiri harbor in the early spring.

is clear that prehistoric man in Japan ate abalone and utilized its shell for various purposes. The earliest mention of *awabi* in Japanese literature appears in the MAN'YŌSHŪ, the oldest extant anthology of Japanese verse, completed in the latter half of the 8th century. The *awabi* was pressed into service as a poetic image for similes or conceits describing a parallel between one-sided love and the univalve (single) shell of the abalone. This elaborate parallel was often repeated and became a fixed conceit in the practice of the Japanese WAKA (31-syllable poem). Thus the abalone has long been associated with unrequited love, a notion that is still reflected in a current proverb. In marriage customs of early modern Japanese society, clams (bivalved or double shelled) were served at weddings, whereas abalone was considered an inauspicious or taboo food on such occasions. Whole, dried *awabi* was exported to China for many years because the powdered shell of the abalone as well as the meat was said to be effective for treating eye diseases in ancient China. Although *awabi* was shunned at weddings, it has long been an auspicious symbol when used as NOSHI, flattened, dried strips of the flesh fastened to offerings to the gods *(kami)*. The *noshi* used today derive from this practice but consist of elaborately folded paper figures employed in gift giving on celebratory occasions. As a food, abalone is eaten by the Japanese boiled or as *mizugai,* that is, eaten raw with a dip made of sweet *sake (mirin),* soy sauce, and vinegar.

SAITŌ Shōji

Abashiri

City in northeastern Hokkaidō on the coast of the Sea of Okhotsk. Abashiri has been a flourishing fishing port since the beginning of the 19th century; the catch includes salmon, trout, mackerel, squid, and crabs. The harbor is closed every winter from January to March because of ice floes. Its principal industries are food processing, dairy farming, and lumber. The main agricultural products are potatoes, legumes, and beets. Part of the city is located within Abashiri Quasi-National Park, which has several lakes, a museum, and the MOYORO SHELL MOUND, a Jōmon-period (ca 10,000 BC–ca 300 BC) archaeological site. There is a maximum security prison here. Pop: 44,777.

Abashiri, Lake

(Abashiriko). In the city of Abashiri, northeastern Hokkaidō. The water is a mixture of fresh and salt water; the lake bottom consists of

stagnant black mud. Pond smelt is the principal catch. Area: 34 sq km (13 sq mi); circumference: 44 km (27 mi); depth: 16 m (52 ft).

Abe Akira (1934–)

Novelist. Born in Hiroshima Prefecture. A graduate of Tōkyō University, where he majored in French literature, he worked in radio and television production until 1971 when he became a full-time professional writer. Abe writes in the tradition of the I-NOVEL (watakushi shōsetsu), and his major concern is the depiction of events from his own life and the lives of his family. Two of his most highly regarded works are *Miseinen* (1968, The Adolescent), a collection of short stories, and *Shirei no kyūka* (1970, Commander on Leave), his first major novel.

Abe family

1. Influential family (UJI) of ancient Japan, based in Iga Province (now part of Mie Prefecture). Little credence can be given to the statement in the chronicle *Nihon shoki* (720) and the 9th-century genealogy *Shinsen shōjiroku* that the progenitor of the Abe was Prince Ōbiko no Mikoto, son of the legendary 8th emperor Kōgen. Nonetheless, many prominent men of the early historical period bore the name Abe; and both the general ABE NO HIRAFU and the poet ABE NO NAKAMARO are said to have descended from this famous family.

2. A family claiming descent from a certain Abi (the pronunciation of the name later changed to Abe), elder brother of the chieftain Nagasunehiko, who resisted the conquest of Yamato by the legendary emperor JIMMU. By the middle of the Heian period (794–1185) they had achieved great power in northern Honshū. See ABE NO YORITOKI.   *KITAMURA Bunji*

Abe Isoo (1865–1949)

Socialist and Christian educator. A member of the Meiji-period (1868–1912) group of Japanese reformers who were led to socialism through Christianity, he participated in the birth of many of the organizations and societies that formed the basis of the Japanese socialist and labor movements. Abe always professed a gradualist vision of social reform and change and maintained these beliefs even while many of his fellow activists were becoming more radical.

Born in the Fukuoka domain (now Fukuoka Prefecture), he graduated from Dōshisha University (Kyōto), where under the influence of NIIJIMA JŌ, he became a Christian. After serving briefly as a minister in Okayama Prefecture, he went to the United States in 1891 to study at the Hartford School of Theology. There he was drawn to Christian socialism, and, returning to Japan in 1895, he devoted himself to social reform and teaching at middle schools.

In 1903 he became a professor at Waseda University, where he was an energetic promoter of baseball as a student sport. He also founded the SHAKAI SHUGI KENKYŪKAI (Society for the Study of Socialism) with KATAYAMA SEN, KŌTOKU SHŪSUI, and Murai Tomoyoshi (1861–1944). The organization was the parent of Japan's first officially proclaimed socialist party, the SHAKAI MINSHUTŌ (Socialist Democratic Party), formed in 1901. Abe was responsible for writing the manifesto, but the party was outlawed by the authorities two days after its formation. Abe was opposed to the Russo-Japanese War (1904–05) and, like many who shared his political and moral views, voiced his opinions through publication and other activities. He published the magazine *Shin kigen* (New Era) in 1905 with KINOSHITA NAOE and ISHIKAWA SANSHIRŌ and helped to revive the newspaper HEIMIN SHIMBUN in 1907. After the arrest and execution of Kōtoku Shūsui for an alleged plot to assassinate the emperor Meiji (see HIGH TREASON INCIDENT OF 1910), however, he disassociated himself from those radicals advocating direct and violent action to overthrow the state and joined the more moderate elements of the socialist and labor movements.

In 1921 Abe became one of the founders of the Japan Fabian Society and three years later was chosen its chairman. About the same time he also formed the Seiji Kenkyūkai (Political Study Association) with such socialist leaders as ŌYAMA IKUO and KAGAWA TOYOHIKO.

Abe was also active in the labor movement, participating in such organizations as the YŪAIKAI, the precursor of Japan's first major trade union association, the Japan Federation of Labor (SŌDŌMEI). He served as adviser to the Yūaikai and wrote many articles for its journal. At the time of the 1926 split in the Sōdōmei between the left and moderate factions, Abe sided with the moderates and assisted in the organization of their political party, SHAKAI MINSHUTŌ (Socialist People's Party). Chosen chairman, he resigned from his post at Waseda. He was elected to the Diet in the elections of 1928 and 1932.

In order to strengthen the socialist movement and present a stronger front in the face of a darkening political horizon, in 1932, together with ASŌ HISASHI and other leftist elements in the party, he decided to form the SHAKAI TAISHŪTŌ (Socialist Masses Party). Abe was again chosen chairman. As the Shakai Taishūtō began drifting to the right, notably in the late 1930s, Abe felt uncomfortable, and in 1940 he and others resigned to form a new party, calling it the Kinrō Kokumintō (Nationalist Labor Party). It was hoped that the party would continue the moderate social-democratic tradition, but it was outlawed by the government soon after its formation. In 1940 Abe resigned from the Diet. After World War II, he served as an adviser to the newly formed Nihon Shakaitō (JAPAN SOCIALIST PARTY) until his death.

▬ ——Abe Isoo, *Shakai shugisha to naru made* (1932). Katayama Tetsu, *Abe Isoo den* (1958). Takano Zen'ichi, *Abe Isoo: Sono chosaku to shōgai* (1964).   *Charles M. MERGENTIME*

Abe Jirō (1883–1959)

Philosopher; critic; educator. Born in Yamagata Prefecture; graduate of Tōkyō University, where he majored in philosophy. In 1922, after teaching at several Tōkyō colleges, he became professor of aesthetics at Tōhoku University in Sendai and achieved acclaim as a scholar. He was a follower of the noted early 20th-century novelist NATSUME SŌSEKI; his own writing reflects careful study of Western philosophy. Abe was much influenced by German idealism and introduced Neo-Kantian philosophy to Japan. Among his important early works is *Santarō no nikki* (1914–15, Santarō's Diary), a collection containing diary entries, essays, and short stories, which was looked on as something of a minor classic by Japanese young people for many years. After his retirement, Abe founded the Nihon Bunka Kenkyūjo (Japanese Culture Research Institute) with personal funds. Other notable works include *Tokugawa jidai no geijutsu to shakai* (1931), a study of Edo-period (1600–1868) art and society.

Abekawa

Also known as Abegawa. River in Shizuoka Prefecture, central Honshū, originating in the Minobu Mountains and flowing south through the Shizuoka Plain to the city of Shizuoka, where it flows into Suruga Bay. There are numerous landslides at the riverhead. Hot springs are found at the upper reaches, where *wasabi* (horseradish) is produced. Tea plantations are located on the mountain slopes in the drainage basin. The river is the main source of water for irrigating the fertile Shizuoka Plain. Length: 51 km (32 mi); area of drainage basin: 567 sq km (219 sq mi).

Abe Kōbō (1924–)

Novelist and playwright of international recognition, and without doubt one of the most outstanding Japanese literary personalities in the second half of the 20th century. One of the main themes of his novels and plays is the alienation of modern man in urban society. Frequently writing in the style of the absurd, Abe is an observant commentator on contemporary life.

Life —— Abe Kōbō (given name Kimifusa) was born on 7 March 1924 in Tōkyō, where his father, a physician hired by the Manchurian School of Medicine in Mukden (now Shenyang), was back on a research assignment. Abe was scarcely a year old when the family returned to Mukden, where he lived until the age of 16. The concept of the *furusato* (hometown), so deeply ingrained in most Japanese, seems to have no place in Abe's life, as he himself admits. In official family documents he is registered as a native of the northern island of Hokkaidō, where he indeed lived for several years, but the place where he was born (Tōkyō), the place where he was brought up (Mukden), and the place of his family's origin (Hokkaidō) have little connection. "I am," says Abe, "a man without a hometown."

In 1941 Abe was sent to Tōkyō for schooling and military training. His academic achievements were not outstanding, and his attitude toward World War II was at best equivocal: revulsion against fascism and militarism mixed with an understandable desire to participate in the national effort.

Abe turned to medicine early, not because he was particularly interested in this discipline, but because he could think of nothing else to do and because his family pressured him in this direction. In 1943 he enrolled as a medical student at Tōkyō University, where he specialized in gynecology. The studies bored him, and he was unsuccessful in his examinations. Nevertheless, he subsequently passed after he informed his professor of his intent not to practice. Abe's study of medicine undoubtedly lends an element to his writing that would otherwise not be present, particularly in such science fiction works as *Daiyon kampyōki* (1959; tr *Inter Ice Age 4,* 1970) and *Ningen sokkuri* (1967, The Image of Man).

Abe married while still a student. His wife, Machi, is an accomplished artist and stage designer, and the couple lead independent parallel careers. Machi has provided illustrations of the highest artistry for many of Abe's works.

Abe decided to pursue literature rather than medicine as a career even before graduating from medical school; he published stories during the late 1940s and early 1950s that drew comparison with Kafka's because of their theme of metamorphosis. He continues to be a prolific, innovative writer and enjoys a wide following in Japan as well as abroad.

Works——The twin themes of alienation and loss of identity are central to almost all of Abe's prose works; both are dealt with in contemporary culture and apply not only to Japan, though that is invariably the setting of his works, but also to modern industrial society in general. In this sense, Abe is less specifically Japanese in his approach to modern social problems than such other giants of modern Japanese fiction as TANIZAKI JUN'ICHIRŌ, KAWABATA YASUNARI, or MISHIMA YUKIO. Yet in another sense Abe is very Japanese; he is not fluent in any foreign language, and his contact with foreign literature has always been through Japanese translations.

From his early novels on, Abe has been consistently preoccupied with the stultifying effect of urban isolation on modern man. In *Suna no onna* (1962; tr *The Woman in the Dunes,* 1964), for example, a schoolteacher who is an amateur insect collector leaves the city to hunt for beetle specimens in an outlying area of sand dunes. He becomes trapped at the bottom of a deep pit where a woman is living and is held captive by villagers who eke out a meager existence among the shifting sands, constantly battling the encroaching dunes to keep from being buried. At first he resists captivity, but ultimately he realizes that what had seemed a prison of sand offers a kind of freedom he had never known before in the city. This discovery is conveyed through the symbolism of the sexual liberation that he experiences in his sandy prison.

A similar escape from urban life and its stifling effects is presented in *Hako otoko* (1973; tr *The Box Man,* 1974), a kind of novel of the absurd in which the protagonist cuts himself off from his fellow men by taking up residence in a box that provides an anonymity and freedom denied him in everyday life. In *Tanin no kao* (1964; tr *The Face of Another,* 1966), the hero endeavors to fashion a new identity by concealing his "real" self with a mask that hides his badly scarred face. In all three of these novels the heroes are alienated from contemporary life, the result of smothering urbanization.

One of Abe's favorite literary devices is the turnabout or inversion of roles. The hunter becomes the hunted; the aggressor the victim. In *Woman in the Dunes,* the insect collector who catches beetles and pins them to a board for classification is himself caught by the villagers, incarcerated in a hole in the sand, and observed in much the same fashion as he had observed his specimens. The inversion of roles is strikingly demonstrated in the way a beetle sought by the collector habitually eludes its predators. The insect lures a pursuer farther and farther into the desert until the chaser is overcome by fatigue and thirst. Then the beetle takes over the role of predator, devouring its prey. The analogy with the insect collector's fate is obvious. Similarly, in *Moetsukita chizu* (1967; tr *The Ruined Map,* 1969) a detective who sets out to trace a missing husband not only fails to find the man he seeks, but in fact ends up losing his own identity.

Another recurrent element in Abe's writing is the city, the modern urban agglomeration—impersonal, stifling, and ugly. Modern man is lost there, in a labyrinth—Abe uses this word frequently—the key to which he is eternally seeking but never finds. The frustration of life under such conditions is overwhelming and emasculating. Man is reduced to mere object; he becomes lost in the maze of the city and ceases to exist because he cannot be seen. For Abe contemporary life is isolated and lonely. Dangerous as well as destructive, urban living is something to flee from, for it crushes man and renders him impotent. In *The Woman in the Dunes,* the hero physi-

cally withdraws from the city; in *The Ruined Map,* by losing his identity he turns away from the city; in *The Box Man,* he rejects the city by secluding himself in a box.

Abe is as serious a playwright as he is a novelist, and heads a theater group that produces his dramatic works. The high quality of their productions has won considerable acclaim. In his play *Tomodachi* (1967; tr *Friends,* 1971), Abe is again preoccupied with loneliness and the city. The protagonist, a young man living alone, is invaded by a large family who claim they have come to rescue him from solitude. Over his objections they insist, absurdly, on the will of the majority and systematically proceed to deprive him of all he has.

Abe is not just a contemporary writer and playwright, he is a true modern in the sense that he deals with the problems of modern life; his writings have universal appeal because the problems they deal with are universal.

■——Works by Abe: *Abe Kōbō zensakuhin* (1972–73). *Bō ni natta otoko* (1969), tr Donald Keene as *The Man who Turned into a Stick* (1975). *Daiyon kampyōki* (1959), tr E. Dale Saunders as *Inter Ice Age 4* (1970). *Mikkai* (1977), tr Juliet W. Carpenter as *Secret Rendezvous* (1979). *Suna no onna* (1962), tr E. Dale Saunders as *The Woman in the Dunes* (1964). *Tanin no kao* (1964), tr E. Dale Saunders as *The Face of Another* (1966). *Moetsukita chizu* (1967), tr E. Dale Saunders as *The Ruined Map* (1969). *Tomodachi* (1967), tr Donald Keene as *Friends* (1971). *Hako otoko* (1973), tr E. Dale Saunders as *The Box Man* (1974). Works on Abe: William Currie, "Abe Kōbō's Nightmare World of Sand," in Kinya Tsuruta and Thomas E. Swann, ed, *Approaches to the Modern Japanese Novel* (1976). Takano Toshimi, *Abe Kōbō ron* (1971).

E. Dale SAUNDERS

Abe Masahiro (1819–1857)

Daimyō of the Fukuyama domain (now part of Hiroshima Prefecture) and senior councillor (*rōjū*) of the Tokugawa shogunate between 1843 and 1857. As chief senior councillor (*rōjū shuseki*) from 1845 to 1855 he was responsible for the shogunate's drastic change of diplomatic policy toward Western nations.

When Commodore Matthew PERRY arrived in 1853 with demands that Japan end its policy of seclusion, Abe took the unprecedented step of soliciting opinions from the daimyō and other officials, Confucian scholars, and even the imperial court. Abe's attempt to achieve national unity failed, however, for the replies were mostly vague and gave the shogunate no clear mandate. Moreover, he had set a dangerous precedent by allowing the imperial court and certain prominent daimyō to participate in the shogunate's decision-making process.

Under renewed pressure from Perry, he concluded a treaty of friendship with the United States (see KANAGAWA TREATY). Similar pacts with Great Britain, Russia, and the Netherlands followed shortly. Abe's policy was attacked by TOKUGAWA NARIAKI of the Mito domain (now part of Ibaraki Prefecture) and others who thought the shogunate should adopt a stiffer posture and attempt to "expel the barbarians." His domestic policies also met opposition, notably from II NAOSUKE, and Abe resigned his position as chief senior councillor in 1855. He remained influential within the shogunate until his death, however, urging the employment of talented men, seeking to modernize the army and navy, and establishing a shogunate school for Western studies.

Abe Nobuyuki (1875–1953)

General and politician; prime minister (1939–40). Born in Ishikawa Prefecture, he graduated from the Military Academy and the Army War College. Abe served as chief of the Military Affairs Bureau (Gummukyoku) and army vice-minister before being appointed minister of state in 1930 to carry out the duties of the ailing war minister UGAKI KAZUSHIGE. Put on the inactive list in 1936, three years later he was asked to form a cabinet after the resignation of HIRANUMA KIICHIRŌ. Abe stressed the overriding authority of cabinet decisions and sought to end the SINO-JAPANESE WAR OF 1937–1945 and to maintain strict neutrality in the growing European conflict. Unable to obtain the cooperation of either the political parties or the military, he resigned in January 1940. Three months later he was sent to Nanjing (Nanking) as a special envoy to advise the puppet regime of WANG JINGWEI (Wang Ching-wei) set up by the

Japanese and to negotiate a treaty ensuring Japan's military and economic rights in occupied China. He was appointed governor-general of Korea in 1944. After World War II Abe was listed as a war criminal by the Supreme Commander for the Allied Powers (SCAP) but was never indicted.

Abe no Hirafu (fl mid-7th century)

General of the Yamato court. The chronicle *Nihon shoki* (720) records that during the reign of Empress SAIMEI Abe was sent on three occasions between 658 and 660 to subdue the EZO tribesmen of northern Japan. It is said that he made his way along the Japan Sea coast with a fleet of 180 ships, going as far north as Shiribeshi, a place that some scholars locate in present-day Hokkaidō. In 663, during the reign of Emperor TENJI, Abe led an expeditionary force to defend the Korean kingdom of PAEKCHE from conquest by its neighbor SILLA. The Japanese were routed, however, by the combined forces of Silla and the Chinese Tang (T'ang) dynasty in the great naval battle of HAKUSUKINOE. Abe was later appointed commander of DAZAIFU, the military headquarters in Kyūshū, in anticipation of a retaliatory invasion from the continent. KITAMURA Bunji

Abe no Munetō (fl mid-11th century)

Warrior of Mutsu Province (now Aomori, Iwate, Miyagi, and Fukushima prefectures) late in the Heian period (794–1185); son of ABE NO YORITOKI and younger brother of ABE NO SADATŌ. During the EARLIER NINE YEARS' WAR (1051–62), Munetō defeated the forces of the court in the Battle of Torinomi Palisade (1057), but when Sadatō was killed at Kuriyagawa Palisade in 1062, Munetō and his surviving brothers surrendered. Taken to Kyōto, Munetō was exiled to Iyo Province (now Ehime Prefecture) in 1064 and later to Dazaifu in Chikuzen Province (now part of Fukuoka Prefecture); the date and place of his death are unknown. G. Cameron HURST III

Abe no Nakamaro (698–770)

Poet and Chinese government official of the 8th century. In 717, with KIBI NO MAKIBI and the priest GEMBŌ, he accompanied a Japanese embassy to Tang (T'ang) China as a student. His companions returned to Japan in 735, but Nakamaro remained in the Chinese capital, Chang'an (Ch'ang-an), where he took a Chinese name and accepted an official post. An able administrator, he also established a high literary reputation and was befriended by such famous poets of the day as Li Bo (Li Po; 701–763) and Wang Wei (701–761). In 753 he attempted to return to Japan with the embassy of FUJIWARA NO KIYOKAWA but was shipwrecked and soon found himself back in China, where he eventually became an important regional military governor (he served as governor-general [Ch: *duhu* or *tu-hu*] of Vietnam). He died in Chang'an after 54 years' absence from home. In Japan, Nakamaro is best remembered for a *waka* poem, included in the anthology HYAKUNIN ISSHU, that expresses his longing for his native land. KITAMURA Bunji

Abe no Sadatō (1019–1062)

Local magnate in Mutsu Province (now Aomori, Iwate, Miyagi, and Fukushima prefectures) late in the Heian period (794–1185). With his father, ABE NO YORITOKI, he fought against the court in the EARLIER NINE YEARS' WAR (1051–62). In the Battle of Torinomi Palisade (1057) Sadatō destroyed the forces of Minamoto no Yoriyoshi (988–1075), but in 1062 Yoriyoshi, with the aid of the Kiyohara family of neighboring Dewa Province (now Akita and Yamagata prefectures), defeated and killed him at Kuriyagawa Palisade. The Kiyohara succeeded the Abe as hegemons of the northeast, only to be crushed in turn by MINAMOTO NO YOSHIIE in the LATER THREE YEARS' WAR (1083–87). G. Cameron HURST III

Abe no Yoritoki (?–1057)

Local magnate in Mutsu Province (now Aomori, Iwate, Miyagi, and Fukushima prefectures) late in the Heian period (794–1185); father of ABE NO SADATŌ and ABE NO MUNETŌ. The Abe were local commanders in charge of aborigines (the so-called *fushū*) who had submitted to the court. By Yoritoki's time the family controlled six districts of Mutsu, but he sought to extend their rule further. He invaded neighboring territories and refused to pay taxes to the cen-

tral government. In 1051 the court dispatched Minamoto no Yoriyoshi (988–1075) and his son MINAMOTO NO YOSHIIE to suppress him. The campaign, known as the EARLIER NINE YEARS' WAR (1051–62), succeeded only after great difficulties and frequent reverses. Yoritoki was killed in the Battle of Torinomi Palisade in 1057, but his sons continued their resistance for another five years. G. Cameron HURST III

Abe Shigetaka (1890–1939)

Educator. Born in Niigata Prefecture, he graduated from Tōkyō University and was a professor there from 1934. Abe introduced empirical, statistical methods in educational research to Japan. He used American methods in his extensive research and proposed various educational reforms. Among his works is *Kyōiku kaikaku ron* (1937, Educational Reform). SUGIYAMA Akio

Abe Shinnosuke (1884–1964)

Newspaperman and critic. Born in Saitama Prefecture. After graduation from Tōkyō University he embarked on a busy journalistic career, starting with the *Manshū nichinichi shimbun*, a Japanese-language daily published in Manchuria. He became the chief editor and director of the *Ōsaka mainichi shimbun* (later the MAINICHI SHIMBUN). After leaving the *Mainichi*, he gained popularity for his incisive political criticism, consisting mainly of sketches of statesmen. He acted as the chairman of the board of Nippon Hōsō Kyōkai (NHK; Japan Broadcasting Corporation) from 1960 until his death. GOTŌ Kazuhiko

Abe Shōō (ca 1653–1753)

Specialist in *honzōgaku* (traditional pharmacognosy), who traveled around Japan collecting animal, plant, and mineral specimens of medicinal value. Born in Morioka (now in Iwate Prefecture). He first studied medicine and later pharmacognosy. He collected medicinal materials by order of the Tokugawa shogunate and advised local districts about the cultivation of sugarcane, cotton, and other crops. He also cultivated medicinal plants in Edo (now Tōkyō). SUZUKI Zenji

Abe Tadaaki (1602–1675)

Daimyō of the Edo period (1600–1868). Born into a FUDAI daimyō family (i.e., a daimyō family who had been vassals of the Tokugawa before the latter's rise to power), Tadaaki as a child entered the service of the future shōgun TOKUGAWA IEMITSU as a page and companion. He was rapidly promoted and handsomely rewarded; in 1633 he was appointed *wakadoshiyori* (junior councillor), a rank subordinate only to that of *rōjū* (senior councillor), and then, in the same year, he was appointed *rōjū*. In 1639 Tadaaki was named lord of Oshi Castle in northern Musashi Province (now Saitama Prefecture) with an assessed income of 50,000 *koku* (see KOKUDAKA). In 1663, his holdings were assessed at 80,000 *koku*. With the *rōjū* MATSUDAIRA NOBUTSUNA, Tadaaki ably assisted Iemitsu and his successor, TOKUGAWA IETSUNA. He was known for his integrity and administrative skills; it was at his suggestion that *rōnin* (masterless *samurai*) were not expelled from Edo (now Tōkyō) after the abortive coup d'etat of 1651 (see KEIAN INCIDENT), but were provided with useful employment.

Abe Tomoji (1903–1973)

Novelist; critic; translator. Born in Okayama Prefecture, Abe studied English literature at Tōkyō University. He associated with many writers, including FUNAHASHI SEIICHI, IBUSE MASUJI, and KITAGAWA FUYUHIKO. His first book, *Koi to Afurika* (1930), was a collection of short stories. With *Shuchiteki bungakuron* (On Subjective Literary Criticism), published in the same year, Abe emerged as one of the strongest opponents of the rising proletarian literary movement. In 1936 he completed his major novel, *Fuyu no yado*, which depicts Japanese intellectuals as suffering from skepticism and unable to deal with the looming threat of militarism. Abe was in Java during World War II and traveled to Europe, China, and Russia after the war. He continued to write liberal, political novels and also translated works by Byron, Shakespeare, Melville, the Brontës, and Austen. James R. MORITA

Abe Yoshishige (1883–1966)

Philosopher and educator. Born in Ehime Prefecture, Abe studied philosophy at Tōkyō University. Early in his career he became a disciple of NATSUME SŌSEKI and wrote literary criticism from an idealist point of view. He introduced Kantian philosophy to Japan.

After two years of study at the University of Heidelberg in Germany, he became a professor at Keijō University in Seoul in 1926. He became principal of the First Higher School in 1940. There he maintained his liberal educational policies even under wartime conditions.

After World War II he served briefly as minister of education in the SHIDEHARA KIJŪRŌ cabinet. He was a leading figure in the various postwar educational reforms. He urgently requested the US Education Mission to Japan not to enforce any policies disregarding Japan's traditions and circumstances. He was also opposed to Japanese rearmament and spoke out for the peace movement.

In 1947, Abe became head of the Peers' School (see GAKUSHŪIN UNIVERSITY) and served in that capacity for almost 20 years. He established the financial independence of this school, which was no longer under the administration of the Imperial Household Ministry, and founded Gakushūin University in 1949.

Abe also advised his friend, the publisher Iwanami Shigeo (1881–1946), about projects for the Iwanami Shoten publishing house. His works include a two volume work about Western philosophy, *Seiyō kodai chūsei tetsugaku shi* (1917), and a biography of Iwanami, *Iwanami Shigeo den* (1957).   *KURAUCHI Shirō*

Abiko

City in northwestern Chiba Prefecture, central Honshū, located between the river Tonegawa and the marshland known as TEGANUMA. Abiko developed as a POST-STATION TOWN on the Mito Kaidō, a highway that connected Tōkyō and Mito. It is now a satellite city of Tōkyō, with some horticulture, mainly flowers. The Teganuma marsh is a part of the prefectural park. Pop: 101,061.

Abō Pass

(Abō Tōge). Located on the border between Nagano and Gifu prefectures, central Honshū. It abuts such peaks as YAKEDAKE. Located within the Chūbu Sangaku National Park. A bus road built through this pass in 1934 is a major tourist route in this area famous for its rugged mountain scenery. The HIRAYU HOT SPRING is found at the western end. Altitude: 1,812 m (5,943 ft).

abortion

(datai). Although the Penal Code carries a penalty of from one year or less of penal servitude to life imprisonment for the illegal performance of an abortion, the act has largely been decriminalized under the EUGENIC PROTECTION LAW. This law, enacted in 1948, made legal the termination of a pregnancy for medical, eugenic, economic, or ethical reasons. Recently, the government proposed an amendment to eliminate economic reasons as a justification for abortion, but it was rejected by the Diet because of protests by feminists and also by doctors, who profit from the current law. See also FAMILY PLANNING.   *SAWANOBORI Toshio*

Abugawa

River in Yamaguchi and Shimane prefectures, western Honshū, flowing from the Abu Mountains to the Sea of Japan at the city of Hagi. It has been harnessed for electric power by the Abugawa Dam at the village of Kawakami. The area in the vicinity of the gorge called CHŌMONKYŌ, a stretch of spectacular precipices and crags extending for some 12 km (7 mi) in the middle reaches of the river, has been designated a prefectural natural park. Length: 82 km (51 mi).

Abukumagawa

River in Fukushima and Miyagi prefectures, northern Honshū, flowing north from Sambon'yaridake, a mountain in the Nasu Volcanic Zone, to the Pacific Ocean at Sendai Bay. It passes between the Abukuma and the Ōu mountains and through the cities of Kōriyama and Fukushima. It is the second longest river in the Tōhoku region after Kitakamigawa. Length: 196 km (122 mi); area of drainage basin: 5,480 sq km (2,115 sq mi).

Abukuma Mountains

(Abukuma Sanchi). A range of mountains running north to south mainly in eastern Fukushima Prefecture, northern Honshū. At the northern end is the lower part of the river Abukumagawa in Miyagi Prefecture, and at the southern end is the lower part of the river Kujigawa in Ibaraki Prefecture. The mountains are an elevated peneplain with an average height of 300–500 m (984–1,640 ft). The highest peak is Ōtakineyama (1,193 m; 3,913 ft), a monadnock.

Aburatsubo

Resort area in the city of Miura, western Miura Peninsula, eastern Kanagawa Prefecture, central Honshū. Named Aburatsubo ("oil bottle") because of its shape and the unruffled waters of the bay. Aburatsubo has a yacht harbor, swimming areas, an aquarium, and the Marine Biological Station of Tōkyō University.

abuse of right

(kenri ran'yō). The exercise of rights by a property owner beyond reasonable social limits; prohibited by the CIVIL CODE, article 1, paragraph 3. In 1947 the Civil Code was amended to establish a prohibition against abuse of right, the principle of PUBLIC WELFARE, and the principle of fidelity and good faith. The theory of the prohibition of abuses of rights, however, had been acknowledged judicially and academically since the 1920s, when it became clear that the 19th-century theory of the free exercise of rights could not be applied to the differing social conditions of the 20th century. A prohibition of the abuse of ownership rights had become particularly necessary. The German Civil Code prohibits the exercise of rights with the sole purpose of inflicting injury upon another. The Japanese Civil Code, however, considers the objectively improper use of a right to be an abuse of right, regardless of the subjective intent of the rightholder.

A property owner whose property has been obstructed by another can demand the removal of the obstruction. However, an abuse of that right of demand is not permitted. For example, if a person builds a structure without authorization on land owned by another but the interference with the owner's rights is minimal, causes only slight damage, and would require great expense to remove, case precedent since 1925 holds that the property owner cannot demand the removal of the obstruction. He may only seek monetary compensation for damages from the party who caused the obstruction. Sometimes, abuses of rights may become tortious behavior toward another person. For example, if an owner of land significantly cuts off the sunlight from a neighbor's house by constructing a building, it has been held by the court that even where there is no statutory illegality, the landowner will bear liability for compensation for damages in tort to the party whose sunlight has been blocked. See also OWNERSHIP RIGHTS; PROPERTY RIGHTS.   *KAWAI Takeshi*

Abutsu Ni (?–1283)

(Abutsu the Nun). WAKA poet, author of the poetic travel diary *Izayoi nikki* (Diary of the Waning Moon). Adopted daughter of Taira no Norishige, the sometime governor of Sado Province (now part of Niigata Prefecture), she served at court as lady-in-waiting to the princess later known as ex-Empress Anka Mon'in, and was called variously Anka Mon'in no Shijō and Anka Mon'in Emon no Suke. She became a nun on the death of her husband in 1275. While still a court lady, she had had several children by different men, and around 1250 at about the age of 30, she had met and become the secondary wife of FUJIWARA NO TAMEIE (1198–1275). She bore him two sons, of whom the elder, REIZEI TAMESUKE (1263–1328), became founder of the Reizei branch of the family. As son and heir of the great FUJIWARA NO SADAIE (Fujiwara no Teika; 1162–1241) and head of the foremost poetic family at court, Tameie was an extremely influential if not particularly gifted poet, and his heir Tameuji (1222–86) had also already become an important figure in court circles. Abutsu worked to obtain for her own children, especially Tamesuke, a share of her husband's land, property, and poetic prestige, and an open dispute over this inheritance broke out after Tameie's death. For complex reasons, Abutsu decided to bring one aspect of her son's case before the military court of the shōgun, and to plead her cause she made the arduous journey to the shogunal capital at Kamakura in 1277 (or, according to some sources, 1279). Her hopes for a speedy decision were in vain, however, for the military government was preoccupied with the threat of an imminent Mongol invasion, and a ruling of the military court in favor of Tamesuke was not made until 1291. Tamesuke had also been ordered by the Kyōto court to hand over to the senior Nijō branch of the family valuable poetic documents inherited by Tameie that had been in Abutsu's custody. There is strong evidence that Tamesuke complied only in part, handing over only the least important documents and adding to them a number of clever forgeries, while retaining the most precious and authoritative manuscripts for himself and his descendants and thereby "certifying" the poetic legitimacy of his line. On the other hand, in the late 13th and 14th centuries the appearance from Nijō sources of spurious documents attributed to Teika suggests that the Nijō faction was conscious of having been duped by Tamesuke and that it retaliated by manufacturing forgeries of its own to compensate for the precious materials still securely in the possession of its Kyōgoku–Reizei opponents. All of these developments had major consequences for the history of Japanese classical poetry, which might have followed a quite different course had it not been for Abutsu's actions.

Although her historical significance is far greater than her intrinsic importance as a poet and author, Abutsu, who was a woman of character and intelligence, was an accomplished if not gifted poet. Imperial anthologies beginning with the *Shoku kokinshū* (1265, Collection of Ancient and Modern Times Continued) contain 48 of her poems, and her *Izayoi nikki* is a minor classic. The latter is a poetic travel diary recounting her reasons for going to Kamakura, describing the sights and experiences of the journey, and recording correspondence and poetic exchanges with friends and relatives during the early part of her stay in the shogunal capital. It concludes with a 151-line CHŌKA (long poem) and envoy, setting forth her grievances in verse. In addition, the work contains 116 short poems, of which 86 are by Abutsu. She is also generally accepted as the author of *Utatane no ki* (Record of a Nap), a fragmentary account of events in the year 1238. Her *Yoru no tsuru* (The Night Crane) is a short treatise on poetics in the form of a letter believed to have been written from Kamakura to her son Tamesuke at his request. Based entirely on the teachings of Sadaie and Tameie, it shows that Abutsu considered herself a legitimate authority and custodian of the family poetic tradition.

📖 ——Abutsu Ni, *Izayoi nikki,* tr Edwin O. Reischauer, in Edwin O. Reischauer and Joseph K. Yamagiwa, *Translations from Early Japanese Literature* (1951). Robert H. Brower and Earl Miner, *Japanese Court Poetry* (1961).
Robert H. Brower

academic degrees

(gakui). The 1953 Ministry of Education ordinance on academic degrees officially established only the master's degree *(shūshi)* and doctor's degree *(hakushi)* as legitimate academic degrees. It made no provision for the bachelor's degree *(gakushi),* which in Japan is regarded more as a title than a recognized degree.

The academic-degree system was instituted by the Academic Degree Order (Gakuirei) of 1887. Prior to World War II, the doctorate was the only degree conferred, and was awarded by the minister of education. Later, with the revision of the law in 1920, the right of colleges and universities to confer degrees was recognized by the government.

The master's degree was instituted as part of the educational reform that followed World War II. It is awarded to those who have completed an integrated course of study at an advanced level and generally requires two years of research work beyond the bachelor's degree. The doctor's degree is awarded to those who have completed academic course work at the highest level, usually involving extensive research and the presentation of a thesis.

Of the total of 88,884 doctorates awarded in Japan between 1957 and 1980, 68.5 percent were given by national universities and 22.5 percent by private institutions. About half of all master's degrees were earned in the field of engineering, and half of all doctorates in medicine. *Amano Ikuo*

academic freedom

(gakumon no jiyū). A civil right guaranteed by article 23 of the 1947 CONSTITUTION of Japan. It refers to the freedom of academicians to engage in research and present their findings. It also provides the right to teach one's beliefs and to disagree with established views or government authorities. Academic freedom is unique to institutions of higher learning and thus is accorded only to those within such institutions. Academic freedom was not mentioned in the Meiji

Constitution of 1889, and it was always under threat of actual or attempted interference by the government, particularly in the 1930s when the ultranationalist ideology of a uniquely Japanese political system based on the imperial institution (see KOKUTAI) prevailed. Since World War II, this newly acquired constitutional right, along with the expansion of UNIVERSITY AUTONOMY, has provided scholars with unprecedented freedom of academic activity.

The students' share of these rights has been more limited than that of teachers and scholars. This narrow interpretation was a reflection of continued public acceptance of the traditionally passive relationship of student to instructor as well as the government policy on education, which lacked a full understanding of the concept of freedom of learning. However, widespread student movements in the late 1960s expanded the rights of students to academic freedom and participation in university decision making. *Hiroshi Itoh*

accent in the Japanese language

In Japanese the system of accent (phonetic characteristics that give prominence to one syllable of a word or phrase) is one of pitch accent: words are differentiated with regard to the place where pitch drops.

Accent in the Modern Standard Language —— The Japanese words for "oyster," "fence," and "persimmon" are identical as far as their consonants and vowels are concerned (all three *kaki*) but differ in pitch: *káki ga, kakí ga, kakí gá* (given here with the case marker *ga*). The acute accent here indicates high pitch: the vowels so marked are higher in pitch than the unmarked vowels by a small but perceptible amount, ranging from a semitone to a major third. Not all combinations of high and low pitch are possible; for example, no word has a high-low-high melody. The place, if any, at which pitch drops determines which syllables are high pitched and which low pitched: the syllables are high pitched up to the drop in pitch, if any, and low thereafter, except that the first syllable is low if the second is high. The contribution that a word makes to the melody of phrases in which it appears can thus be indicated by a mark at the place, if any, at which it contributes a drop in pitch: *ka¹ki* "oyster," *kaki¹* "fence," *kaki* "persimmon." In dictionaries, separate symbols are often used to indicate the place where pitch rises and the place where pitch falls (e.g., *ka⌐ki⌐ ga*); however, the symbol for rise in pitch is superfluous, since the location of the rise is predictable.

For any given number of syllables that can make up a Japanese word, there are accentless words of that number of syllables—words that contribute no drop in pitch to the pronunciation—and there are words with first syllable accent, words with second syllable accent, etc, that is, words contributing a drop in pitch at the end of their first syllable, words contributing a drop in pitch at the end of their second syllable, etc. Modern Japanese has both long and short syllables. A short syllable consists of either a short vowel alone or a consonant plus a short vowel; thus the word *atama¹* "head" consists of three short syllables. A long syllable contains one of the following: a long vowel or a diphthong or a syllable-final consonant (either a nasal, as in *sense¹i* "teacher," or the onset of a double consonant, as in *gappei* "merger"). A long syllable consists of two moras *(onsetsu),* a short syllable of only one mora. In other words, a long syllable consists of what would make up a short syllable plus additional material that counts as the equivalent of another short syllable. A long syllable counts as two units and a short syllable as one unit in the scansion of classical Japanese poetry; the common classical Japanese verse forms involve lines of five and seven moras. The common practice of referring to *hiragana* and *katakana* (see KANA) as "syllabic scripts" and translating the Japanese word *onsetsu* as "syllable" is unfortunate, since an *onsetsu* may make up less than a syllable and each *kana* symbol represents a mora rather than a syllable.

Both the syllable and the mora play roles in the Japanese accent system. A long syllable, like a short syllable, provides only one place where accent can occur; for example, while there are words such as *shi¹nnen* "new year" and *sense¹i* "teacher," in which a drop in pitch occurs after the first mora of a long syllable, no words display such a melody as *shin¹nen* or *sensei¹,* in which the second mora of a long syllable is high pitched and the following mora low pitched. The syllable is the unit that bears the accent, the mora the unit in which length and distance are measured. These roles of syllable and mora are illustrated in the rule for accent in recent loanwords: put accent on the syllable containing the third from last mora, e.g., *sokura¹tesu* "Socrates," *poke¹tto* "pocket," *mara¹son* "marathon," *washi¹nton* "Washington."

Accent in the Japanese language

Regular Accent Correspondences in Two-Syllable Nouns							
	Kyōto		Kagoshima	Tōkyō		Aomori	
cow	*ushi*	= *úshí gá*	falling	*ushi*	= *ushí gá*	*ushi*	= *ushi ga*
bridge	*ha'shi*	= *háshi ga*	falling	*hashi'*	= *hashí ga*	*hashi*	= *hashi ga*
flower	*ha'na*	= *hána ga*	level	*hana'*	= *haná ga*	*hana'*	= *haná ga*
chopsticks	*'hashi*	= *hashi gá*	level	*ha'shi*	= *háshi ga*	*ha'shi*	= *háshi ga*
window	*'mado'*	= *madó ga*	level	*ma'do*	= *mádo ga*	*ma'do*	= *mádo ga*

The various parts of speech differ with regard to the range of accentual distinctions they allow. Nouns exhibit the maximum possible range of accentual distinctions; for example, among three-syllable nouns one finds unaccented (*sakana* "fish"), first syllable accent (*ma'kura* "pillow"), second syllable accent (*koko'ro* "heart"), and third syllable accent (*atama'* "head"). Postpositions *(joshi)* show accent distinctions when combined with an unaccented noun: *sakana ma'de* "to the fish," *sakana kara'* "from the fish," *sakana' shika* "only the fish." These postpositions act alike when combined with an accented noun: *ma'kura made* "to the pillow," *ma'kura kara* "from the pillow," *ma'kura shika* "only the pillow." This reflects the fact that in Japanese there can be only one drop in pitch per phrase; both the noun and the postposition potentially contribute accents, but only the first accent potentially present in a phrase is actually pronounced: *ma'kura* + *ma'de* = *ma'kura made*. There are no basically unaccented postpositions (that is, postpositions that do not exhibit an accent when used in a context in which an accent that it contributed could be manifested), though there is an accentual type not found in nouns, i.e., preaccented postpositions such as *shika*, which contribute an accent on the final syllable of a preceding unaccented noun, e.g., *gakusei* + *'shika* = *gakuse'i shika* "only the student." Verbs and adjectives show only a two-way accent distinction: if a verb or adjective root contributes an accent, the place of that accent is predictable. The place of that predictable accent, however, depends on the particular inflectional form: *kakure'ru, kaku'reta* "hides" (intransitive), "hid." Derived verb forms share the accentedness or unaccentedness of the basic verb, though the accent will necessarily be on a different syllable: *kakurerare'ru, kakurera'reta* "is/was subjected to (someone) hiding."

Superimposed on the Japanese accentual system is an intonational system, consisting of various modifications of pitch that mark the function of the sentence (question, exclamation, etc) or emphasize parts of it. While the intonational systems of English and Japanese agree in many details (e.g., in both languages, questions may be marked by a rise in pitch at the end), the interaction of the intonational system with the pitch accent system in Japanese is very different from that of the intonational and stress systems of English. For example, the interrogative rise in pitch in Japanese affects only the final syllable regardless of where the accent is, whereas in English the last stressed syllable of a question is on a low pitch and the rise in pitch extends over that syllable and all subsequent syllables. As a result of such differences, certain Japanese speech melodies are liable to misinterpretation by foreigners; for example, in Japanese a fall in pitch followed by rise on the final syllable is simply an accent combined with the question intonation, but the melody is often identical with the English intonation that conveys irritation.

Accent in Dialects——Accent is the domain in which Japanese dialects show the greatest diversity. It is also the domain in which Japanese dialects have been studied in the most detail. Extensive surveys directed by such scholars as Hirayama Teruo, Kindaichi Haruhiko, TŌJŌ MISAO, and Shibata Takeshi have yielded impressive compilations of data covering in remarkable depth not only the four main Japanese islands but also the whole Ryūkyū Archipelago and many other remote places.

The accentual system of the Japanese standard language is identical to that of the Tōkyō dialect and differs in only minor respects from the accentual systems of the dialects of most of eastern and northern Honshū (the area from Aichi and Gifu prefectures eastward, except for the area from Ibaraki Prefecture to central Miyagi, in which accentual distinctions have been lost entirely), of western Honshū (from Okayama and Tottori prefectures westward), and of northeastern Kyūshū (Ōita and Fukuoka prefectures). Strikingly different accentual systems are found in central Honshū, in western Kyūshū, and in the Ryūkyū Islands.

In Kansai dialects (the area from Mie through Hyōgo Prefecture, as well as most of Shikoku), there are more accentual distinctions

than in the standard language: words differ not only with regard to where there is a drop in pitch but also with regard to whether the word begins on a high or on a low pitch. Moreover, the place at which pitch drops generally differs from that in eastern Honshū. In western Kyūshū (specifically, an area taking in most of Saga, Nagasaki, Kumamoto, and Kagoshima prefectures), there are fewer accentual distinctions than in the standard language: a word of any length imposes either a falling or a level melody on any phrase that it begins. The chart gives illustrations of the regular correspondences between the accentual systems of Kyōto (a typical Kansai dialect), Kagoshima (western Kyūshū), Tōkyō, and Aomori (northern Honshū); acute accent, as before, indicates high pitch, and ' is used not only to mark a drop in pitch but also to indicate those Kyōto words that begin on a low pitch. The popular misconception that pitches in Kyōto are those of Tōkyō turned upside down is fostered by such examples as the words for "bridge" (*hashi*: high-low in Kyōto, low-high in Tōkyō) and "chopsticks" (*hashi*: low-high in Kyōto, high-low in Tōkyō). Since Kyōto draws more accentual distinctions than Tōkyō does, its pitches, of course, could not be simply an inversion of those of Tōkyō.

History of Japanese Accentual Systems——The modern Kyōto accentual system is very close to that recorded in the RUIJU MYŌGI SHŌ, an extensive word list compiled in Kyōto in approximately 1100, in which the pitch of each syllable is indicated by traditional Chinese tone marks. The *Ruiju myōgi shō* distinguished five accentual types among two-syllable nouns, whereas modern Kyōto distinguishes only four and modern Tōkyō three. Of the nouns that in modern Kyōto have the high-low melody, approximately half (including "bridge") were recorded as high-low and the other half (including "flower") were recorded as low-low. Virtually without exception, in modern Aomori and the rest of northern Honshū, as well as in northeastern Kyūshū, those nouns recorded in the *Ruiju myōgi shō* as high-low are unaccented and those recorded as low-low have second syllable accent, though no distinction between those two types is made elsewhere in Honshū. The regularity of this correspondence among geographically distant dialects provides strong evidence that the various dialects are descendants of an ancestral language that made the accentual distinctions recorded in the *Ruiju myōgi shō*, with subsequent phonetic changes wiping out various distinctions and changing the manifestation of the different accentual types in the various dialects. Similarly, with few exceptions, words with falling melodies in western Kyūshū have a high pitched first syllable in the *Ruiju myōgi shō* and those with level melodies a low pitched first syllable. The western Kyūshū accentual system can thus be seen to have arisen from a system like that of the *Ruiju myōgi shō* through phonetic changes in which pitch differences after the first syllable were lost and only the pitch of the first syllable remained distinctive. The northernmost dialects of the western Kyūshū accent region exhibit what may well be the most conservative form of western Kyūshū accent: the falling melody differs from the level only in the first syllable, which is high pitched for the falling melody and low pitched for the level, with all subsequent syllables low pitched. The different realizations of the falling melody in other dialects would then have arisen through phonetic changes in which the high pitch on the first syllable shifted toward the end of the phrase, i.e., to the second syllable in Nagasaki and to the next to last syllable in Kagoshima.

If the ancestral Japanese accentual system is in fact something close to that of the *Ruiju myōgi shō*, then extensive parallel changes must have taken place independently in eastern Honshū (e.g., in Tōkyō) and western Honshū (e.g., in Hiroshima), namely a shift of accent toward the end of the phrase. This is not implausible, in view of the existence of numerous other accent shifts in the history of Japanese dialects, as in the case just discussed of the shift of high pitch in the development of local variants of the falling melody in western Kyūshū.

■■ ——Bernard Bloch, "Studies in Colloquial Japanese I: Inflection" and "Studies in Colloquial Japanese III: Derivation of Inflected Words," in Roy A. Miller, ed, *Bernard Bloch on Japanese* (1970). Hirayama Teruo, *Nihongo onchō no kenkyū* (1957). Hirayama Teruo, *Zenkoku akusento jiten* (1960). Okuda Kunio, *Accentual Systems in Japanese Dialects* (1975). Tokugawa Munemasa, "Towards a Family Tree for Accent in Japanese Dialects," tr James D. McCawley in *Papers in Japanese Linguistics* (1972).

James D. McCawley

accounting and auditing

Bookkeeping methods used in keeping financial records of business transactions and in preparing statements concerning the assets, liabilities, and operating results of a business. The term also denotes certain theories, behavioral assumptions, measurement rules, and procedures for collecting and reporting useful information concerning the activities and objectives of an organization.

Early History of Japanese Accounting —— There is evidence that some methods of accounting were used in Japan even before the 7th century. Modern methods have been developed mainly since the 16th century. Account books, first mentioned in 1520, are extant from 1615. Sophisticated single-entry systems developed many supplementary books. The double-entry method was known from books but not practiced until the end of Japan's isolation in the mid-19th century, when translations and European accountants introduced modern bookkeeping.

The Meiji period (1868–1912) saw accelerated modernization of accounting. When Japan transferred the Hong Kong mint's old equipment to Ōsaka in 1871, a Portuguese chief accountant kept the books in English and they were later translated into Japanese. The Portuguese accountant stayed in Japan until 1878, drafting an accounting system for the government and for teaching accounting.

More significant was the contribution of Alexander Allan Shand, an Englishman hired by the Japanese MINISTRY OF FINANCE (MOF) in 1872 to write a guide to bank bookkeeping, which was published in Japanese in 1873. The first Japanese limited-liability joint-stock company and the first bank both followed his system. Shand, who was greatly influenced by the American banking system, remained as an adviser and teacher until 1877. The MOF taught courses using his book; Shand's system spread to other banks and, by the 1890s, to large-scale commercial and industrial firms.

FUKUZAWA YUKICHI, the noted educator, played a major role in modernizing and Americanizing accounting. He translated a standard American accounting text in the mid-1870s, introducing both single- and double-entry methods. Accounting was included in the curriculum of Keiō Gijuku (now KEIŌ UNIVERSITY), an institution of higher learning founded by Fukuzawa. To adapt the Sino-Japanese numerical system, which required characters for thousand, hundred, and ten, Fukuzawa introduced the zero and nine numerals. In 1878 Arabic numerals and horizontal writing first appeared.

Another notable teacher, Whitney, the proprietor of Bryant, Stratton and Whitney Business College in Newark, New Jersey, (the first two were authors of the aforementioned book translated by Fukuzawa), reached Japan in 1875 and taught at its first commercial school, later Hitotsubashi University. He remained five years and wrote a textbook for his course.

The German model of accounting succeeded the Anglo-American models after the MINISTRY OF JUSTICE appointed the German Karl F. H. ROESLER to codify commercial law. His code, finally approved in 1899, prescribed account books and their preservation for 10 years. Corporate directors were to prepare financial statements for statutory auditors, but rules were not detailed. Asset valuation was vague, permitting firms to adjust profits and limit disclosure.

The Professionalization of Accounting —— The relative absence of foreign investment in Japan before the 20th century limited demands for disclosure. It was only after losses to foreign investors, stemming from the abrupt price decline of a major company involving accounting malpractice, that the government was forced to recognize accounting as a profession in 1909, although professional accountants had appeared in the 1890s. In 1927, when there were two or three hundred accountants, this recognition became law, and the title of "public accountant" was given to professional school and college accounting graduates.

In 1934 the Ministry of Commerce and Industry (Shōkōshō) issued rules for financial statements and, shortly after the beginning of World War II, the army and navy ministries issued manuals for munitions factories' statements. The Planning Board (Kikakuin), established in 1937 to control the wartime economy, published tentative financial standards for all manufacturers in 1941.

Japan's defeat in 1945 led to an American-influenced revolution in accounting. Disarmament required the dissolution of the ZAIBATSU, the giant financial and industrial combines which had dominated the wartime economy. The skimpy reports submitted by these companies to the Occupation authorities indicated that additional regulations were necessary. On the basis of a draft prepared by Murase Gen, a new set of regulations was prepared to replace the Planning Board's standards.

During the Occupation, the ECONOMIC STABILIZATION BOARD recruited Japanese accounting professors, businessmen, and bureaucrats for a committee to investigate accounting systems. This committee eventually became the Business Accounting Council (BAC) of the MOF; it issued a statement of accounting principles based upon a work by American accountants. The SECURITIES EXCHANGE LAW and the Certified Public Accountants Law, both passed in 1948, reflected American influence. After the Occupation, the COMMERCIAL CODE was repeatedly amended to conform to these laws. The code's corporate sections, revised in 1952, were modeled on Illinois state law.

Later the need for international coordination exerted some impact. Japan was among the seven executive members of the Conference of Asian and Pacific Accountants in 1951 and a founding member of the International Accounting Standards Committee in 1973. American and international influences contributed to a fairer Japanese Generally Accepted Accounting Principles (GAAP) and to greater disclosure.

Sources of Accounting Principles —— Until 1974 the Commercial Code and the Securities Exchange Law contained inconsistent definitions of accounting terms. The two laws have separate but somewhat overlapping jurisdictions and independent regulatory mechanisms. The code, regulating over one million firms, is administered by the Ministry of Justice; the exchange law covers corporations listed on the STOCK EXCHANGES or planning to issue securities in excess of ¥100 million. The exchanges themselves have added disclosure requirements for over-the-counter stocks, different sets of requirements for their first and second section stocks, and standards for disclosing changes in depreciation and inventory valuation methods.

The MOF regulates 3,000 firms under the Securities Exchange Law. Its Securities Bureau provides ADMINISTRATIVE GUIDANCE, reviewing reports and even on occasion forcing the dismissal of independent auditors. BAC issues opinions on accounting and auditing principles, always labeling them "interim" and never "final," in recognition of GAAP's continuous development. The Japanese Institute of Certified Public Accountants (JICPA) publishes an ethics code and cooperates with the MOF in developing GAAP.

The Commercial Code is administered by the Ministry of Justice with the assistance of the Legislative Council of the ministry. The code recognizes the private entrepreneur, uncommon because of high personal taxes, and three corporate forms—the unlimited liability partnership, limited partnership with general and limited partners, and limited-liability joint-stock corporation (*kabushiki kaisha*). The code requires all corporations to publish a balance sheet and to file a business report, income statement, and proposed earnings distribution at the firm's office and (by tax regulation) with the tax authorities.

The Accounting Profession in Japan —— Professional quality and quantity largely determine the effectiveness of accountants. In 1978, the JICPA had less than 6,000 members (the United States, with twice Japan's population and GNP, had 150,000 CPAs, with about 80 percent practicing).

One of the reasons for the small number of CPAs in Japan is the restrictive system of professional certification. The Certified Public Accountants Law provides for three progressively difficult examinations. College graduates are exempted from the preliminary exam in liberal arts subjects. To become a Junior CPA, a candidate must pass all seven subjects, ranging from economics to accounting theory in the intermediate examination. College professors and PhDs are exempt from tests in their fields of specialization. After additional courses and three years of experience, the final examination may be taken. Between 1949 and 1974, only 7 percent of 75,220 candidates passed the intermediate examination; 17 percent of 18,828 candidates passed the final. Currently about 300 people become CPAs annually.

Only 2,000 of the 25,000 public accountants registered under the 1927 law became CPAs after the adoption of the new law. Those who did not become CPAs are still allowed to practice publicly, but they cannot do audits or certify financial statements under the Securities Exchange Law. Foreign CPAs residing in Japan are allowed to practice if their national requirements resemble Japan's and if they pass a test on Japanese accounting. Foreign accounting firms, especially American, have established branches in Japan.

Japanese CPAs originally operated individually, but a 1966 law established audit corporations with unlimited liability, consisting of five or more CPAs. Unlike the practice in the United States, most of these organizations are not named after their principals. Tohmatsu, Awoki & Co, an exception, had 80 partners, 360 professionals, 11 Japanese offices, and several international offices in 1978. About 40 audit corporations conduct and sign most MOF-required audits. The MOF, preferring them for their joint responsibility, independence, and competence, is seeking further consolidation.

A CPA can become a tax agent merely by applying. The 20,000 members of the Japan Federation of Tax Agents Associations, founded under a 1951 law, passed an examination or presented qualifications. They prepare tax returns and often perform bookkeeping services for small firms. An audit corporation cannot file a tax return, and if one of its directors serves as tax agent for a firm, it cannot be that firm's auditor.

Corporate accounting employees generally possess little formal training, and job rotation prevents them from staying long in any one department. They do receive on-the-job training and are encouraged to take classes. Bookkeeping practices which employ bound slips instead of account books currently take three forms: the one-slip (a general slip), used by single proprietors; the three-slip, employing cash receipt and payment in addition, used in financial firms; and the five-slip, adding purchase and sales slips, the method that is most adaptable to complex firms.

Auditing Practices——Forms of auditing vary with company size. Corporations with capital of ¥100 million or less require one or more statutory auditors. Corporations capitalized at over ¥100 million still depend on statutory auditors but with increased powers. The Commercial Code requires both a statutory auditor's report and an independent audit for all companies exceeding ¥1 billion capitalization. Foreign companies listed on the Tōkyō Stock Exchange must meet the requirements of their home country and must also be audited by a Japanese accountant.

At the annual meeting, stockholders elect statutory auditors (excluding directors and employees) and determine their compensation. A Japan Statutory Auditors Association, working closely with the Ministry of Justice, drafts auditing standards. The auditors receive documents only shortly before the annual meeting, a practice that allows for only perfunctory study. Lack of qualifications also limits the utility of the auditors, who are nonetheless jointly liable for any damages to the corporation due to their negligence.

The Securities Exchange Law requires the filing of reports with the MOF, stock exchanges, and corporate offices. These reports must contain a complete company profile, including stock history, a list of directors and their histories, and the status of employees. In addition, the condition of the business, its fixed assets, planned investments, production capacity, results and plans, sales and backorders, a cash flow statement, forecast, and, finally, an independent financial audit with detailed schedules of assets and liabilities must be included in the report. The MOF can require additional data and examine company records, and the firm may request the MOF to withhold "secret" information from the public.

Corporate fund sources—predominantly banks and retained earnings—have also influenced auditing. Firms seeking capital from overseas must meet foreign standards. The BAC requires every professional auditor to abide by its nonbinding auditing standards and work rules. The JICPA issues detailed auditing notes and guidelines. Normal procedures resemble American auditing, although there is no independent confirmation of cash and certain payables and receivables. The auditor must be independent, with no material interest in the firm. The auditor may not have been an employee of the firm in the previous year or of a government agency regulating the firm in the past two years.

The BAC has established four options for audit opinions: unqualified; qualified because of inconsistency or nonconformity with GAAP or with the law; adverse; and disclaimer. About 70 percent of audits are unqualified; most of the remainder are qualified, primarily because of nonconformity with GAAP. Less than 0.5 percent are adverse opinions and disclaimers.

Consolidation——Traditionally, parent financials, which are still issued, dominate reportage, allowing income shifts with subsidiaries to "smooth" profit. After debating 10 years, MOF required for fiscal 1977 minimal audited consolidation of all subsidiaries owned over 50 percent by parent companies. Parent companies still need report only dividends and investment and not equity share of earnings in other affiliates in which their ownership is 50 percent or less. Tax effect accounting is not compulsory. Ownership exceeding 50 percent requires inclusion of irrelevant activities, e.g., manufacturers' financing subsidiaries, private railways' retail stores and hotels. Subsidiaries in which parent control is impossible (bankruptcy, liquidation) or temporary, or cases in which affiliates are immaterial are exempt. Actually, a parent with less than 50 percent ownership can exercise control thanks to stock held by its close allies.

MOF provided as optional the American method of reporting equity in undistributed profits for subsidiaries in which the parent owns 20–50 percent of the equity. Most firms followed the minimal requirement but an increasing number of firms are using equity accounting. About 20 firms registered with SEC, including some of Japan's largest, employed American equity method and tax allocation as required by S-1. Some S-12 registrants, though not required, followed the same method. It is expected that MOF will require equity accounting in the near future.

Balance Sheets——Japanese balance sheets place assets on the left and liabilities and shareholders' equity on the right. Assets are divided into current (cash, receivables, inventory), fixed, and deferred. Notes receivable, converted from accounts receivable, are substantial and often discounted. Tax regulations provide a 1 to 2 percent reserve for doubtful receivables, based on business classification and not experience. This reserve may exceed accounting requirements, but if it is above the tax limit, the excess is restored to taxable income. Inventories are priced at the lower of cost or market value. Tax law permits an inventory price fluctuation reserve based on closing inventory for first-in, first-out inventories, which most firms take.

Fixed assets include plant and equipment, usually depreciated by the declining balance method using tax rates and charged to regular expenses. Substantial special depreciation of equipment costs is deducted before taking further special depreciation, and both are charged to nonoperating expenses. Land, which was not depreciated but revalued several times during the 1950s, is reported at extremely low values and constitutes a "hidden reserve." Noncurrent assets (investments and loans) are reported at the lower of acquisition cost or market value and constitute a hidden reserve because of the market rise. They are tapped when income proves insufficient. Treasury stock, permissible but rare, is an asset.

Liabilities include current, long-term, reserves, and minority interests. Firms prefer short-term loans (often exceeding long-term debt) because the banks roll over short-term debt and charge a lower short-term prime rate. As economic expansion decelerated in the 1970s, companies reduced their debts. The current liabilities category also includes accounts payable, accrued expenses, customers' advances, and taxes payable.

Tax-deductible reserves are included as liabilities. The overseas market development reserve, a percentage of gross exports, must be restored to income equally over five succeeding years. The reserve for loss on overseas investments, 10 to 100 percent of investments in less developed countries, must be restored to income equally over five years after a five-year grace period. Many industries are permitted special reserves. Nondeductible reserves, once a hiding place for profits, lost popularity after the JICPA required disclosure.

Long-term liabilities include bonds, long-term debt, and employees' severance benefits. The latter, based on length of service and latest wage rate, is granted between the ages of 55 and 60. Companies usually follow tax regulations which permit a 50 percent liability reserve, assuming separation of all employees at fiscal year-end. Long-term liabilities may include substantial employee deposits.

Stockholders' equity encompasses capital, capital surplus, and retained earnings. Common stock, issued and outstanding at par value (usually ¥50, but sometimes ¥500 per share), constitutes capital. Corporations used to distribute authorized capital as rights issues at par to stockholders, but this practice has become rare. Stock options are nonexistent, possibly because the difference between the option and current stock price is individually taxable as gift income. Dividends return a percentage (usually 10–15 percent) of par value, which is often lower than the market price. Companies selling stock close to market value transfer the excess over par value to capital surplus, from which free distribution is transferred to capital. Stock dividends, however, are transferred from retained earnings. Companies must contribute 10 percent of dividends to the legal reserve until 25 percent of capital par value is reached. The legal reserve may only reduce a deficit or be capitalized, after which it must be rebuilt. The ordinary surplus consists of voluntary reserves, unappropriated previous earnings, and current income.

Income Statements —— Income statements disclose net sales, which is gross sales less returns and discounts, except for firms with frequent returns. Firms generally prefer the cash to the accrual method. Gross profit is net sales less the cost of sales. Operating income is gross profit less expenses (sales, general, and administrative, including the enterprise tax). Interest received, dividends, and some capital gains less nonoperating expenses (usually interest paid) constitute nonoperating income, which, added to operating income, totals ordinary income. Net income before reserves and income taxes includes ordinary income and extraordinary income (extraordinary credits less extraordinary expenses, e.g., the losses occasioned in selling seconds). Reserve reversals then establish pretax income. Net income is calculated by deducting income taxes, minority interests in consolidated subsidiaries, and the amortization of goodwill.

While only foreign-denominated long-term receivables and payables may be translated at historical rates, the statements usually follow the monetary/nonmonetary approach by translating at current rates and recognizing immediately any losses or gains. The consolidated statement of retained earnings reports the beginning annual balance; deducts legal reserve transfers, cash dividends, fees for directors and auditors; and adds current net income.

Tax Accounting —— Corporate and individual taxpayers use blue or white tax forms. The blue form is preferable because it carries privileges, such as loss carry-forward and carry-backward and deductible reserves and allowances. Use of this form is granted only when proper books are kept and is revocable in the event of malpractice, with a heavy retroactive penalty assessed. A corporation capitalized at ¥50 million or more is investigated by a regional tax inspector. These inspectors, who are assigned a large number of cases, concentrate on such questionable items as entertainment. Adjustments, however minor, are common.

Tax calculation begins with reported pretax income. Reserves, depreciation, entertainment, and donations exceeding taxable incomes are restored. The corporation may not deduct over 105 percent of the previous year's entertainment amount or ¥4 million plus 0.025 percent of the paid-in capital. Donations, with few exceptions, are restricted to 1.25 percent of taxable income plus 0.25 percent of capital and capital surplus. The enterprise tax paid and corporate dividends, already taxed, are then deducted. The prefecture levies the enterprise tax at 12 percent of this total.

Transfers of technology overseas—55 percent of revenues for knowledge, 20 percent for patents—and special depreciations are deducted from taxable income. The corporate tax is then calculated, at 30 percent for net dividends (dividends declared less dividends received) and at 40 percent for the balance. The local governments levy an inhabitants' tax on this sum of 17.3 percent (5.2 percent prefectural and 12.1 percent municipal). Corporate income tax payments permit a 10 percent maximum credit for research. The effective combined corporate tax rate is 53 to 54 percent. Recent budget deficits have increased regulatory stringency and restricted deductions. See also FINANCIAL REPORTING; CORPORATE FINANCE; TAXES; TAX ACCOUNTING; TAX LAW; BANKING SYSTEM; AUDITING STANDARDS.

📖 Aoki Shigeo, ed, *Nihon kaikei hattatsushi: Wagakuni kaikeigaku no seisei to tembō* (1976). Robert J. Ballon, Iwao Tomita, and Hajime Usami, *Financial Reporting in Japan* (1976). Coopers & Lybrand, *Japan* (1977). Daiwa Securities Co, Ltd, *Memorandum on Consolidated Financial Statements* (1977). Donald A. DuBois and Kyōjirō Someya, "Accounting Development in Japan," *The Accountant* (5 May 1977). Zen'ichi Ishikawa, *Major Accounting Differences Between the United States and Japan* (1976). Kōjirō Nishikawa, "The Early History of Double-Entry Bookkeeping in Japan," in A. C. Littleton and B. S. Yamey, *Studies in the History of Accounting* (1956). Price Waterhouse, *Doing Business in Japan* (1975).   *Paul H. ARON*

Acheson statement

A major policy statement concerning the Far East made by United States Secretary of State Dean G. Acheson on 12 January 1950 before the National Press Club in Washington, DC. Discussing military policy in the Far East, he said that the US defense line was along a perimeter defined by the Aleutian archipelago, Japan, Okinawa, and the Philippines. He stated that the United States would make a direct response to any threats to Japan or the Philippines, two countries with which the United States had particularly close ties. Ach-

eson added that countries beyond the perimeter that he had defined, if attacked, must first expect to defend themselves, but could hope for help from other countries under the terms of the United Nations Charter.

Acheson's statement was generally taken to indicate that the United States had abandoned Korea and Taiwan. The Korean War started in June 1950, and it is often claimed that the North Koreans had been encouraged by the Acheson statement in their decision to attack the South.

achievement tests

(gakuryoku tesuto). Standardized scholastic tests have been employed in Japan on the prefectural level as part of the entrance examinations for public high schools since 1948 and for all national and prefectural universities since 1979. Achievement testing was conducted on the national level in primary and middle schools by the Ministry of Education between 1961 and 1966, but the practice was discontinued in 1967 because of public opposition.

HIDANO Tadashi

Achilles Corporation

(Akiresu). Formerly called Kohkoku Chemical Industry Co, Ltd. Manufacturer and vendor of Achilles-brand products, including urethane and rubber products, footwear, and resin. Founded in 1947. In 1981 its share of the domestic market for footwear was 20 percent, for rubber boats 50 percent, and for polyurethane synthetic leather 30 percent. The firm has a nationwide computer-connected network of 40 sales bases. It has a joint venture company in the United Kingdom (Achilles Foam Board Co), a subsidiary company in the United States (Kohkoku U.S.A., Inc), and business offices in Hong Kong and Amsterdam. Total sales for the fiscal year ending October 1981 were ¥79.3 billion (US $342.7 million) and capitalization was ¥6.5 billion (US $28.1 million). The head office is in Tōkyō.

acupuncture

(hari). Ancient East Asian medical technique which consists of puncturing the body at designated points with special needles; together with *kyū* (MOXA TREATMENT), it has been practiced for over 2,000 years in East Asia. Acupuncture is said to have originated in China or India. Since its introduction to Japan in the 6th century, it has been popularly regarded as an effective means of medical treatment and health maintenance.

The ancient Asian concept of disease varies greatly from that of modern Western medicine. Physical health was considered to be a condition that permitted the person to conduct his life in a normal fashion, and disease was considered to be the result of an imbalance caused by the strain of internal and external stress. Traditional medicine is posited on the belief that therapeutic treatment consists in correcting that imbalance. *Hari* and *kyū* are both used to achieve this end. The practitioner of traditional medicine determines the condition and degree of the strain in patients by examining rheological change in their bodies. The major *kampō* (Chinese medicine) examination includes checking the pulse, abdominal muscle tone, and condition of the skin and underlying tissues. See also MEDICINE: traditional medicine.

Acupuncture consists of inserting very fine gold, silver, or stainless steel needles (0.1–0.3 mm [0.004–0.012 in] in diameter, 3–9 cm [1.2–3.5 in] in length) into the skin and underlying tissues at specific points *(keiketsu).* After the needles are inserted to an appropriate depth (about 0.1–90 mm or 0.004–3.5 in), they may be removed immediately, left *in situ* for 5–15 minutes, twirled, or moved up and down 2–3 millimeters (0.079–0.118 in). The acupuncturist decides the size and kind of needle, the depth and direction of insertion, and the method of handling the needles after puncture according to the physical strength of the patient and the tissue condition at the points to be punctured. There are many methods of applying acupuncture, established after centuries of practical experience and theorizing. The most effective method still remains undetermined, requiring further scientific research.

In the Western world, acupuncture began attracting attention in the 1940s, but it was not until the 1970s that its analgesic effects were fully recognized. It is hoped that physiological research on acupuncture will lead to a better understanding of the general mechanisms of pain.

SHIROTA Fumihiko

Adachi Buntarō (1865–1945)

Anthropologist and physician. Born in Izu Province (now part of Shizuoka Prefecture). Graduated from Tōkyō University School of Medicine in 1894. Adachi studied anatomy in Germany and became professor at Kyōto University. He was the first to carry out comparative anatomical studies of the Japanese and other peoples. He wrote a study in German on the physical characteristics of the Japanese in 1928.

Adachi Kagemori (?–1248)

Warlord of the early part of the Kamakura period (1185–1333). Born in Sagami Province (now part of Kanagawa Prefecture), Adachi was politically influential as the maternal grandfather of Hōjō Tsunetoki (1224–46) and HŌJŌ TOKIYORI, the fourth and fifth Kamakura regents (shikken). As reward for his father's military aid in founding the Kamakura shogunate, the shōgun MINAMOTO NO SANETOMO in 1218 appointed Kagemori vice-governor (suke) of Dewa Province (now Yamagata and Akita prefectures) in charge of the strategic fortifications at Akita (AKITAJŌ). The post was hereditary in the Adachi family until their destruction in 1285. In 1247 Kagemori joined with Tokiyori to destroy the powerful MIURA FAMILY, rivals of the HŌJŌ FAMILY, in the HŌJI CONFLICT.

Adachi Kenzō (1864–1948)

Politician. Born in Higo Province (now Kumamoto Prefecture); graduated from the Kumamoto domain school, Seiseikō. Adachi worked as a reporter during the Sino-Japanese War of 1894–95 and founded several newspapers in Korea. In 1895 he was implicated in the assassination of Queen MIN, an incident that greatly inflamed anti-Japanese sentiment in Korea, but was eventually acquitted. In 1902 he was elected to the Diet. Known for his skillful conduct of election campaigns, he was subsequently reelected 14 times and enjoyed a successful career as a member of the RIKKEN DŌSHIKAI (later known as the KENSEIKAI and the RIKKEN MINSEITŌ), holding the posts of minister of communications and home minister under several administrations. With the occurrence of the MANCHURIAN INCIDENT in 1931, Adachi decided to cooperate with the militarists in their call for a "national unity" cabinet, a decision that led to the collapse of the second WAKATSUKI REIJIRŌ cabinet, in which he was home minister. He withdrew from the Rikken Minseitō in 1931 and the following year formed the ultranationalistic KOKUMIN DŌMEI party with NAKANO SEIGŌ. After serving as councillor in the second KONOE FUMIMARO cabinet (1940), he retired from politics.

Adachi Tadashi (1883–1973)

Businessman and business community leader. Born in Tottori Prefecture. Graduated from Tōkyō Higher Commercial School (now Hitotsubashi University). Adachi joined Mitsui & Co, but switched to Ōji Paper Co in 1907 at the invitation of FUJIWARA GINJIRŌ. He became president in 1942, retiring in 1946. Although purged in 1947 by the Occupation authorities, he staged a comeback in 1950 and served in a variety of positions, including the chairmanships of the National Association of Commercial Broadcasters in Japan and the Japan Productivity Center and the presidency of the Japan Chamber of Commerce and Industry. SHINOMIYA Toshiyuki

Adachi Ward

(Adachi Ku). One of the 23 wards of Tōkyō. In the Edo period (1600–1868) one of the important POST-STATION TOWNS on the highway Ōshū Kaidō. During World War II plants and factories were concentrated here. Today it is rapidly becoming a residential area. Pop: 619,668.

Adams, William (1564–1620)

English mariner resident in Japan in the early 17th century; also known as Miura Anjin (Miura Pilot) from the location, on Miura Peninsula, near Edo (now Tōkyō), of the estate granted him by TOKUGAWA IEYASU.

Adams was born in Gillingham, Kent, and apprenticed as a shipwright. In 1598 he sailed as a pilot in a Dutch fleet, and after a series of mishaps his disabled ship, the LIEFDE, reached Kyūshū in April 1600. He was befriended by Ieyasu, who employed him as commercial agent, informant, pilot, shipbuilder, and interpreter. Adams thus became a man of influence and renown, owning a large estate with some 80 servants and traveling around the country on official business.

With the encouragement of Ieyasu, Adams wrote letters to the Dutch and the English, inviting them to trade with Japan. When the Dutch arrived in 1611, he acted as their interpreter and agent; he later helped the English merchants, although his efforts on their behalf were not always appreciated by his fellow countrymen, who regarded him as a "naturalised Japanner." He made several commercial voyages from Japan by junk, trading in Okinawa, Cochin China, and Siam.

Adams's influence notably waned after the death of his patron Ieyasu in 1616. He died in or near the port town of Hirado (the site of the English and Dutch trading posts) on 16 May 1620, leaving a Japanese wife and two children. An annual festival is held in his honor at Hemi, the site of his Miura estate, although the monuments there are probably the tombs of his wife and children and not of Adams himself. His adventurous life has been the subject of several books in both English and Japanese, most recently James Clavell's novel Shōgun (1976).

■——C. J. Purnell, ed, The Log-Book of William Adams, 1614–1619 (1916). P. C. Rogers, The First Englishman in Japan (1956). Michael COOPER

Adatarasan

Volcanic mountain group in northern Fukushima Prefecture, northern Honshū, part of the Nasu Volcanic Zone. Consisting of the mountains Kimenzan, Minowayama (the highest; 1,718 m or 5,635 ft), Tetsuzan, and Adatarayama, the group extends 10 km (6 mi) north to south. Located within the Bandai–Asahi National Park, Adatarasan has numerous hot springs and ski areas.

administered prices

(kanri kakaku). Prices that are unilaterally set by oligopolistic enterprises rather than determined by supply and demand, or competition in the free market. In the late 1960s, there were a number of mergers between big firms in such key Japanese industries as steel and automobiles, which intensified business concentration. As a result, relations between the oligopolistic market and administered prices came under public scrutiny, and the government considered possible antitrust actions. However, there have been very few prosecutions of price cartels in Japan because even in such oligopolistic industries as oil, petrochemicals, paper and pulp, and nonferrous metals, the market price responds seasonally to supply and demand. In trying to implement antitrust measures, only on such items as toothpaste, cosmetics, hand soaps, and cameras has the government been able to ban the system of resale price maintenance, the practice of requiring the distributors of a manufacturer's product to sell at certain prices, or at not less than minimum prices.

Recently, however, public concern has focused on different types of administered prices. In contrast to relatively stable wholesale prices, the price of agricultural products has been subject to great increases because of import restrictions. Retail and service prices have also risen. These consumer price rises resulted from government attempts to regulate competition in order to protect small businesses. ADACHI Tetsuo

Administrative Court

(Gyōsei Saibansho). A special court, separate from the judicial system, with jurisdiction only over administrative cases, instituted under the CONSTITUTION of 1889. Also called the Court of Administrative Litigation. Article 61 of the 1889 constitution stated that no regular court of law could assume jurisdiction over any suit "which relates to rights alleged to have been infringed by the illegal measures of the administrative authorities, and which shall come within the competency of the Court of Administrative Litigation specially established by law." ITŌ HIROBUMI, the principal drafter of the constitution, gave two main reasons for the establishment of the Administrative Court: first, to ensure the independence of the administrative branch from the judicial courts, it should have the power to decide suits arising from administrative measures; second, administrative cases should be adjudicated by "men well versed in administrative affairs."

The Administrative Court sat in Tōkyō and consisted of a president and 15 to 20 counselors, all appointed in the name of the emperor. Although judges could receive appointments, ordinarily men from high administrative positions were given preference. Appointments ran until members reached retirement age.

Jurisdiction of the court extended to the following kinds of cases: taxes and administrative fees; refusals or revocations of licenses; public works; disputes over boundaries between public and private lands; local police administration; and miscellaneous cases as determined by law. The court could not deal with cases involving discretionary powers of administrators, but only with alleged excesses involving those powers or violations of the rights or duties of individuals. The Administrative Court was abolished with the enactment of the 1947 constitution, article 76 of which provides that the whole judicial power is vested in the courts and that "no extraordinary tribunal shall be established."

——H. S. Quigley, *Japanese Government and Politics* (1932).

John M. MAKI

administrative guidance

(*gyōsei shidō*). A method employed by agencies of the Japanese government to obtain the adherence of individuals and enterprises to policies or practices deemed desirable by the government. Such guidance is not legally binding, although informal sanctions are sometimes imposed on those who do not voluntarily cooperate; it must be confined to the duties and functions of the agency concerned; and where matters fall within the purview of the ANTIMONOPOLY LAW, the guidance must accord with one of the laws which specifically allow for exemptions to that statute.

Bureaucrats in Japan have traditionally exercised broad administrative powers, usually drafting and implementing legislation designed to carry out major national goals and objectives. This was particularly true during the post-World War II reconstruction in the 1950s, when Japan embarked upon an extensive program of industrial development. Special legislation enacted during this period authorized government ministries to directly determine investment plans for such industries as petroleum refining, shipbuilding, and the merchant marine, and to bring about the rationalization of other industries.

The economic affairs ministries were given more general responsibility for guiding the economy in desired directions. In addition to officially sanctioned administrative decisions, the responsible agencies also resorted to the practice of administrative guidance without specific legal authority. This practice is not unique to Japan, although it has probably been more widely accepted there as a style of government administration than in other democracies. Some observers hold that the Japanese case is not much different from the dynamic of official suggestion and voluntary compliance increasingly initiated by bureaucrats and government leaders in other modern managed economies.

The MINISTRY OF INTERNATIONAL TRADE AND INDUSTRY (MITI) has made extensive use of administrative guidance, especially after Japan began the progressive liberalization of trade and investment controls in 1964. Prior to this time, the government had been able to implement INDUSTRIAL POLICY by controlling allocations of foreign exchange for capital equipment and technology imports (see FOREIGN EXCHANGE CONTROL). After restrictions on the use of foreign exchange were lifted, MITI sought new methods for implementing the government's industrial policies. The INDUSTRIAL STRUCTURE COUNCIL, an advisory committee of MITI, drafted a law which would have given MITI comprehensive authority to initiate producer specialization, set appropriate investment levels, and promote mergers and groupings. Opposed by the MINISTRY OF FINANCE, the Fair Trade Commission, and sectors of the business establishment, the legislation was rejected by the Diet in 1962 and 1963. As a consequence, administrative guidance was increasingly relied upon to implement measures designed to control "excess competition," encourage new industries and the rationalization of others, bring about adjustments in output in response to changes in the economy or market conditions, administer emergency price controls, and fine-tune the performance of Japanese industry.

Administrative guidance also has been used to implement "voluntary" restrictions on Japanese exports, such as those negotiated under orderly marketing agreements with the United States and other countries. These restrictions generally have required MITI to decide, through administrative guidance, the exact production and export allocation that will be assigned to each manufacturer or exporter of the commodity involved when these firms, as is often the case, are unable to agree among themselves.

Administrative guidance may consist of direction, requests, warnings, suggestions, or encouragement. In addition, the huge number of directives, notifications, and opinions emanating from the economic affairs ministries often constitute administrative guidance in a broad sense. Numerous ad hoc and informal channels are used for the communication of guidance. It is often conveyed in the form of recommendations from a *shingikai*, or MINISTERIAL DELIBERATIVE COUNCIL.

These *shingikai* became the main vehicle for indirectly implementing industrial policy in the 1960s. MITI's Industrial Structure Council, with 20 or more supporting subcommittees, is perhaps the most influential of these councils, which exist in many government agencies. They are made up of representatives of industry, trade associations and business organizations, banking and financial interests, academics, and other groups. They meet to discuss and pass on actions usually proposed by government officials with responsibility for the issue at hand.

MITI and other administrative agencies prefer to exercise their guidance through persuasion, advice, and inducement. These inducements include special loans from the government and quasi-governmental development banks; tax credits and accelerated write-offs; and subsidies, particularly for research and development in infant industries or those whose expansion is considered to be in the national interest.

On occasion, however, failure to comply may result in the denial of these and other inducements. A particularly important power is MITI's ability to organize administrative guidance cartels when falling demand calls for the shared cutback of output in an industry. A firm in an established, prospering industry may be in a position to ignore administrative guidance, but in weaker industries there are strong incentives for voluntary compliance. In two famous cases more direct sanctions were applied. In 1965, SUMITOMO METAL MINING CO, LTD, violated a steel industry agreement to cut production in order to stabilize prices, and MITI interrupted the supply of coking coal to Sumitomo in response. As it turned out, the demand for steel increased sharply before the company felt the effect of this sanction. A similar case in 1966 involved IDEMITSU KŌSAN CO, LTD, a leading Japanese oil company, which failed to abide by the industry association consensus. This case, incidentally, illustrates that not all guidance is forced upon the private sector; here and in other instances, it has been initiated at the request of the industry.

The effectiveness of administrative guidance, never very great, has in fact been diminishing. MITI, for example, has had a long string of guidance failures, mainly in cases where there was little consensus between the government and the private sector or between the various ministries or government agencies involved. Most notable were the unsuccessful attempt to promote mergers in the Japanese automotive industry in the late 1960s; the proposed paper producers' merger, which was finally aborted by the Fair Trade Commission; and ongoing efforts to consolidate the number of producers in the computer industry.

Administrative guidance has come under increasing attack from domestic and foreign critics since the early 1970s. The reduced dependence on government aid and protection of many of the now fully developed industries has made them critical of government interference, particularly that of MITI, and less susceptible to informal pressures. Resistance to guidance has increased as a result.

There have also been legal challenges that could result in strict limitations on the use of guidance. Foremost among these was the charge brought by the Fair Trade Commission in February 1974 that the Japan Petroleum Association (representing the entire industry), along with 12 oil-refining companies and 17 of their executives, violated the Antimonopoly Law by entering into a series of agreements regarding the production volume and selling price of refined petroleum products. The resulting indictment by the Supreme Public Prosecutor's Office in May 1974 caused a sensation in Japan because it was the first time that an industry had been indicted for illegal cartel agreements since the law was enacted in 1947.

The Tōkyō High Court handed down its landmark ruling on the case on 26 September 1980. It found the defendants not guilty on the charge of collaborating on production adjustments, but guilty on the charge of price fixing. The court held that the production adjustments were overseen and approved by MITI under the provisions of the 1962 Petroleum Industry Law, which empowers the ministry to work out and publish annual supply-demand programs for the industry and to obtain production schedules from each refiner. The law also requires MITI to take the lead in dealing with crisis situations, such as the one caused by the formation of OPEC in 1973, at the time the violations were alleged to have occurred.

The same reasoning did not apply, however, to the matter of the price agreements. The court dismissed the oil industry's argument that it had been following MITI's administrative guidance. The ruling held, in effect, that a basic economic law, the Antimonopoly Law, takes precedence over administrative guidance, and therefore the formation of a cartel at MITI's direction, but not sanctioned under the antimonopoly statute, constitutes an illegal restraint of trade.

■——Eleanor M. Hadley, *Antitrust in Japan* (1970). Dan Fenno Henderson, *Foreign Enterprise in Japan: Laws and Policies* (1973). Imai Ken'ichi, "Japan's Industrial Organization," *Japanese Economic Studies* (Spring-Summer 1978). Chalmers Johnson, "MITI and Japanese International Economic Policy," in Robert A. Scalapino, ed, *The Foreign Policy of Modern Japan* (1977). Eugene J. Kaplan, *Japan: The Government-Business Relationship* (1973). Nakamura Hideichirō, "Japan, Incorporated and Postwar Democracy," *Japan Economic Studies* (Spring-Summer 1978). Philip H. Trezise with Suzuki Yukio, "Politics, Government, and Economic Growth in Japan," in Hugh Patrick and Henry Rosovsky, ed, *Asia's New Giant: How the Japanese Economy Works* (1976). Ueno Hiroya, "Conception and Evaluation of Japanese Industrial Policy," *Japanese Economic Studies* (Winter 1976–77). M. Y. Yoshino, *Japan's Managerial System: Tradition and Innovation* (1968). *Eugene J. KAPLAN*

administrative law

(*gyōsei hō*). The rubric of administrative law in Japan as elsewhere covers the bundle of legal theories and principles that define the organization and functions of the executive branch of government (see GOVERNMENT, EXECUTIVE BRANCH), the administrative process, and direct JUDICIAL REVIEW of governmental actions. These principles in Japanese administrative law derive primarily from continental, especially German, notions and find their sources in academic writings, statutory provisions, judicial decisions, and to some extent administrative custom and practice. Although there is no code or basic statute as in the substantive (civil, criminal, and commercial) or procedural (criminal and civil) codes or the CONSTITUTION, the statutory materials are numerous and diffuse. They include the Cabinet Law (Naikaku Hō), the National Administrative Organization Law (Kokka Gyōsei Soshiki Hō), the Administrative Case Litigation Law (Gyōsei Jiken Soshō Hō), various statutes concerning the civil service, local government and the police, and social and economic regulatory legislation.

Despite the continuing influence of continental ideas under the 1947 constitution, there has been a major shift away from the continental view of the separation of powers doctrine as reflected in the Meiji Constitution of 1889. Under the Meiji Constitution the cabinet was responsible solely to the emperor and not to the Diet. Also, the judicial courts were denied jurisdiction to hear direct appeals from administrative decisions. Instead, the 15-member ADMINISTRATIVE COURT, located in Tōkyō, was established with limited jurisdiction as the exclusive forum to adjudicate appeals from administrative decisions. Despite this adherence to a strict separation of the executive from the legislative and judicial branches, there were limited checks in that the Diet had control of the budget and the judicial courts ruled on the validity of executive decisions in ordinary civil and criminal cases.

In contrast, the postwar constitution is premised on the "dual" sovereignty of the legislature and the courts. The cabinet and through it the ministries are accountable to the Diet. There is express provision for judicial review. Since Japanese courts, with few exceptions, conduct *de novo* trials in cases involving direct administrative appeals, there is, at least theoretically, less deference to administrative decisions under Japanese law than in the United States, where generally the scope of judicial review is limited.

The central organizing concept of Japanese administrative law is the notion of "administrative acts" (*gyōsei kōi; Verwaltungsakt; acte administratif*), which derives from scholarly theory and parallels the concept of juristic acts (*hōritsu kōi*) in the CIVIL CODE. An administrative act is defined as the exercise of public power based on law by an administrative body that affects private persons in a concrete fashion. As such, an administrative act is the scholarly equivalent to the statutory term "administrative disposition" (*gyōsei shobun*), or simply "disposition" (*shobun*). An administrative act must have statutory authority. It has binding effect (*kōsokuryoku*) and is not reversible even by the issuing agency, except through prescribed legal procedures. Although there is some scholarly disagreement over the exact parameters of the definition of the term, the concept of administrative acts covers most if not all formal administrative actions.

Typical administrative acts or dispositions include the various types of governmental approval (*kyoka, ninka, menkyo*), decisions (*kettei, saitei, shinketsu*), orders (*meirei*), prohibitions (*kinshi*), acknowledgments (*kakunin*), and public notices (*kōnin, tsūchi, kokuji*). It should be noted, parenthetically, that there is a conspicuous lack of uniformity in statutory terminology used to designate various types of administrative actions. Separate statutes employ different terms to describe the same function. One government study has found, for instance, that at least 10 separate terms were used to designate an administrative "hearing."

Academic theory further defines administrative acts as either discretionary acts (*sairyō kōi*) or mandatory acts (*kisoku kōi*). The distinction depends upon the degree to which, by statutory scheme or necessity, the agency has discretion in exercising its authority.

These concepts are primarily organizing principles that provide a structure to administrative law. They also have functional importance, however, in the area of JUDICIAL REVIEW. Japanese courts have generally construed their power to review administrative appeals narrowly, limiting their jurisdiction to appeals from actions formalized as administrative acts or dispositions. Thus review is denied in instances where the challenged governmental action does not have "direct and concrete legal effect" upon the party bringing suit. (See, for example, *Tōfukuin* v. *Minister of Health and Welfare*, 22 Minshū 3147 [Sup. Ct., 3rd P.B., Dec. 24, 1968].) Consequently, judicial review is not obtainable in cases of ADMINISTRATIVE GUIDANCE (*gyōsei shidō*), that ubiquitous form of state direction based on a suggested course of conduct and voluntary compliance. Similarly, actions subject to the free discretion of an agency are considered to be nonreviewable. It should be noted, however, that in the latter instance ordinarily the courts make a *de novo* determination of the facts, and if the decision is not supported, they may hold that there has been an abuse of discretion or, by construing the particular statute, find the action in question "exceeded the scope of discretion."

Finally, underlying all Japanese principles of administrative law is a basic dichotomy between private and public law. One manifestation of this division was the prewar debate led by HOZUMI YATSUKA and MINOBE TATSUKICHI as to the proper scope of the state's liability under the Civil Code for tortious damages. Another is the judge-made doctrine that contracts entered into in violation of regulatory (*torishimari*) statutes (such as the FOREIGN EXCHANGE AND FOREIGN TRADE CONTROL LAW), as opposed to mandatory (*kyōkō*) statutes, remain valid between the parties. (See *Bank of Okinawa* v. *Tōkai Electric Construction K.K.*, 129 Minshū 1029 [Sup. Ct., 3rd P.B., July 15, 1975].) *John O. HALEY*

administrative litigation

(*gyōsei soshō*). Procedure whereby a court makes an examination and decision concerning an objection to an action by a government agency or disputes about legal relationships under administrative law. In response to significant public interest in these administrative cases, the Administrative Litigation Law (Gyōsei Soshō Hō) was enacted in 1962.

Administrative litigation is divided into four types. (1) Appeal litigation or other exercises of public power; these include requests for the nullification of a tax assessment, the reversal of the dismissal of a complaint petition, the invalidation of decisions or dispositions, or a finding of illegal failure to act as where applications for business licenses have been shelved. (2) Litigation between concerned parties, in regard to legal relationships based on public law; these cases include litigation to confirm the status of public employees or to demand losses resulting from the exercise of eminent domain. (3) Class action litigation, which is filed in order to rectify administrative illegalities for the benefit of the common public, for example, a case where voters dispute the validity of an election. (4) Institutional litigation between national or public institutions; an example would be the case of the head of a local government demanding the nullification of an illegal resolution by the assembly.

Among the four types of litigation, suits to nullify dispositions are the most prevalent. Such suits must be filed, in principle, within three months from the date of knowledge of the disposition. When a suit for nullification is filed, execution of the action is not suspended. If there is concern that there would be difficulty in recovering the damages incurred in the execution or continuation of the action, the plaintiff may ask the court to suspend the execution. This order is granted when urgently necessary to avoid future difficulty and where it appears plausible that the plaintiff will win the litigation. When it is thought that a suspension of execution will create serious obstacles in administrative operations, the prime minister may object and nullify the suspension. Where it is clear that a government agency action or decision is illegal, the court must nullify it by court decision. However, in special situations where nullification would lead to extraordinary damage to the public interest, the court may decide to dismiss the suit.

Administrative Management Agency

(Gyōsei Kanri Chō). Agency of the national government. It provides advice on managerial and organizational problems, assists in organizational planning, and coordinates agency reorganizations. It formulates plans for improving administrative efficiency in government offices and reducing the size and complexity of the bureaucracy in order to achieve bureaucratic reform. It also collects and compiles statistical information on the organization and size of the Japanese government and receives public complaints concerning the management and policies of the government. Established in 1948, it is administratively attached to the PRIME MINISTER'S OFFICE. It is headed by a director-general, appointed by the prime minister, who is usually one of the ministers of state.

The Commission for Administrative Management and Inspection, which is attached to the agency, advises the agency on measures for bureaucratic reform. The commission was established in 1965 to help implement reform measures that were outlined in the 1964 report of the Provisional Council on Administrative Reform. See BUREAUCRACY.   *Daniel A.* METRAUX

administrative procedure

Legal procedure followed in order to ensure that administrative acts of government agencies (e.g., the granting or revocation of licenses, permits, and registrations) conform to the law and are conducted fairly. There are two types of administrative procedure. The first concerns acts that suspend or terminate previously granted rights and privileges, such as the revocation of a business license or an operator's permit. The second concerns the granting of such rights and privileges or the approval of the plans and regulations of a government agency. The opportunity for those affected by administrative acts to represent their interests is generally granted through the holding of a public hearing. A public announcement of the hearing is made, and concerned parties are notified of the date and purpose of the hearing. The parties are allowed to make written and oral statements, submit evidence, and present expert testimony.

The Meiji Constitution, in effect until the end of World War II, provided administrative courts for the adjudication of complaints concerning administrative acts. These courts, along with the right to petition government agencies for redress, provided after-the-fact relief. The 1947 constitution eliminated administrative courts and placed complaints of administrative injustice under civil court jurisdiction. Under the influence of United States law, provisions were made for ADMINISTRATIVE LITIGATION.

There are, however, few established provisions for prior hearing and review of regulations and administrative acts. As the character of administrative acts increases in technical complexity, the need for ensuring fairness through prior review has become more apparent. A number of nations have enacted administrative procedure laws to provide for such review, but Japan has yet to do so.   *ARA* Hide

administrative scrivener

(gyōsei shoshi). A legal functionary who is employed in the business of drafting, on behalf of the public, documents which are to be submitted to government and other public offices and documents which evidence rights and duties or facts. Persons eligible to become administrative scriveners are attorneys, patent agents, certified public accountants, tax agents, persons who have been employed in administrative affairs as public officials for a long period of time and

persons who have passed the administrative scrivener's examination. An eligible person becomes an administrative scrivener upon enrollment on the membership list maintained by the Administrative Scriveners' Association. There are presently some 5,000 administrative scriveners in Japan. Administrative scriveners are often utilized in the drafting of documents for the establishment of a company, applications for building permits, informal dispute settlement agreements, and contracts. Generally the fees for these services are low.
KOJIMA Takeshi

Adogawa

River in Shiga Prefecture, central Honshū, flowing from northeastern Kyōto to Lake Biwa. It runs between the Hira Mountains and the Tamba Highlands in its upper reaches and forms a wide delta in its lower reaches. Small *ayu* (sweetfish) are caught at the mouth of the river. Length: 44 km (27 mi).

adoption

(yōshi). Adoption has been widely practiced in Japan for at least 1,300 years. Both the rationale for adoption and the wide variety of adoptive practices can best be understood in the perspective of the household system (IE). The primary purpose of Japanese adoption has been to ensure household continuity. The practices persisted even after radical changes in the CIVIL CODE affected the post-World War II household.

"Adoption" generally refers to a variety of different practices. Adoption can be practiced to provide homes for orphans, illegitimate children, and foundlings, or to provide children for childless couples. These practices, which focus primarily on the welfare of the child, characterize adoption in the United States and Britain, where it is a relatively recent institution.

A different type of adoption is that for the purpose of providing an heir. Not principally aimed at providing for the welfare of children, this kind of adoption is concerned with carrying on a line and transmitting property when no natural child exists as the heir. Such adoption was common in ancient Greece and Rome, as well as in China and India, and made the adoptee into a fictive son (or daughter).

Japanese adoption falls more closely into the latter category, but with significant differences. In Japan, adoption was practiced to carry on the household *(ie)* and to ensure succession over time. Japanese adoption was also practiced for the benefit of establishing connections between homes, even when a natural son did exist, and thus had economic and political overtones as well.

By the Edo period (1600–1868) the household *(ie)* was fixed as the basic social unit because it was the production unit responsible for the payment of revenues. The house was both a group of people who existed in a particular generation, and the "house" as an institution over time. It included the property and professional enterprise of the group, as well as the house name (and code), the ancestors, and genealogy. The status of houses varied greatly, from the *daimyō*, or nobility who had the highest status, to the vast majority of the population, who were peasant farmers.

The continuation of the house (and its property, ancestors, "name," and professional enterprise) was extremely important, and so succession became a main goal of house members. By the Edo period the Japanese did not practice joint inheritance (for example, dividing the property among all children, or establishing a joint family which would include all the brothers). Rather the house was passed on intact, and only one person (the *kachō*, or household head) succeeded to the property in each generation. The wife of the *kachō* held a position parallel to the successor, since she was entered in the genealogy and became a house ancestor along with him. Thus there were only two adults (a married couple) in the household in each generation. The household was thus distinct from a "family" and its genealogy did not record genealogical relationships, but rather the historic tables of organization of the house. Thus the adoptee was also recorded in the genealogy and no distinction was made between the latter and the house "son."

Characteristics of Japanese Adoption —— Certain characteristics of Japanese adoption thus distinguish it from adoption in countries such as England and the United States.

1. The house, rather than the individual adoptee, is the primary focus. The latter is adopted for the purpose of carrying on the house and its professional enterprise.

2. Japanese adoptees are not foundlings, but usually close relatives. Their natal families are known and relationships continue between the two houses.

3. The age of adoption in Japan is older than in the United States. In 1952, for example, in 180,000 cases of adoption, 150,000 adoptees were adults.

4. The Japanese adoptee is given full legal rights as a natal or "real" child. No legal distinction is made between the "real" and adoptive child.

A variety of adoption practices exist. These include the adoption of a male who is married to the household daughter (the *muko yōshi*, or adopted husband) and the adoption of either a male or female child. Even a married couple can be adopted *(fūfu yōshi)*, although this means that another household succession line will end, and is therefore an extreme situation. A younger brother or grandchild can also be adopted. In these cases, adoption changes the generation of the adoptee, moving him into the correct generation for succession.

The position of the adopted husband, who must adapt to the mores of a group over whom he is also supposed to occupy a position of authority, is frequently depicted in folklore and proverbs. The difficult position of the adopted husband illustrates one of the ways in which Japanese adoption is similar to marriage, for the adopted husband is really in a position akin to the young bride coming into a house and, traditionally, occupying the lowest position. The adopted husband has a better situation because he comes into the house as the head, and is also the breadwinner; nevertheless, he may be henpecked by both his wife and her mother. The situation of the adopted husband is a common topic in modern literature, for example, in Futabatei Shimei's *Sono omokage* (1906; tr *An Adopted Husband,* 1919). Other problems of adoption are depicted in Natsume Sōseki's *Michikusa* (1915; tr *Grass on the Wayside,* 1969) and Shimazaki Tōson's *Ie* (1910–11; tr *The Family,* 1976).

Adoption in Historical Perspective——Japanese adoption is first mentioned in documents of the Nara period (710–794). A distinctly Japanese flavor for adoption had already developed by then, for the practice clearly violated the Chinese-derived legal codes of that time. Such violations included younger brother adoption and the adoption of people of a different surname. During the Kamakura period (1185–1333) the rationale for adoption changed, so that males were adopted even when "real sons" existed to form beneficial household alliances. During this period the preferred adoptions were, in order, grandchild, younger brother, and other relatives. During the Edo period adoptive practices became highly elaborated, and detailed distinctions of status were made. The word for adoption *(yōshi)* was limited to males and the word *yōjo* came into use for females. Many terms still common for *yōshi* came into use. These included *muko yōshi* (adoptive husband) and *kyū yōshi* ("emergency" *yōshi,* presumably made so by the death of the household head). The practice of "provisional" or "temporary" adoption also appeared, in which an adoption was made for an interim period, for example, when a household head had died, leaving a successor who was still only a child. In such cases conflicts could arise if the temporary successor did not vacate after the interim. Adoption also became a way of making alliances between prestigious households.

Succession practices among the *samurai* class *(bushi)* of the Edo period are illustrated by a study of 3,000 sons of *bushi* households during the period 1599–1794. Of these sons, 23.6 percent succeeded their households, 16.6 percent established "new" households (i.e., branches or *bunke),* while 22 percent were adopted out. Seventeen percent died young and 19 percent stayed in the house but did not succeed. These figures demonstrate the high incidence of adoption, which is almost the same as the rate of natal succession. They also indicate that competence must have been highly valued, since nearly as many sons stayed in the house but did *not* succeed, as did succeed.

Adoption in Modern Japan——When Japan entered the modern period, the Meiji Civil Code defined adoption in a way that was remarkably similar to past practices. Not until the new Civil Code (enacted during the Occupation in 1948) were substantial changes made in the household system, and these were far wider-reaching for marriage than for adoption. Emphasis was placed on the rights of the individual as opposed to the house. Parental power over the child was weakened, and adoption (at least on paper) was established as an institution for the welfare of the child.

It is difficult to assess the impact of this legislation, however, because of the gap between the legislation and actual practices, which still do not conform to the code in many respects, and because

of a lack of nationwide statistics on current adoption practices. In rural areas where the house possesses either land or a business to carry on or both, adoption seems to be continuing. For example, in postwar village studies Nakane (1967) reports that as many as one-third of the households in her village sample are succeeded by adoption. Befu (1962) and Beardsley et al (1959) put the figure at one-fourth of the households.

Elite families in big business and politics also continue to practice adoption in order to carry on the family name or to create alliances with other families. Among the postwar prime ministers, for example, Yoshida Shigeru was adopted. Kishi Nobusuke and Satō Eisaku were brothers; but Kishi, the older brother, was adopted in order to succeed to his mother's natal Kishi household, and the younger brother, Satō Eisaku, succeeded to the natal Satō home.

Urban Adoption——Adoption among middle and lower white- and blue-collar families in urban Japan is still an open question. Since these families generally have no land or businesses to pass on to their heirs, "succession" for such people may be different from that in the rural or elite household. Rather than adopting an older son in order to continue a house "line," they may choose to send their children to prestigious universities, a decision which will in turn ensure that the children will hold positions which are similar to (or better than) those of their fathers. Succession practices among urban merchants and small-industry families are also unknown. It seems possible that they, too, may adopt to continue their house enterprise. However, virtually no research has been carried out on adoption in urban Japan.

Foundlings——In Japan foundlings are usually brought up by relatives, and adoption of children who have no relatives is extremely difficult, because their social backgrounds are unknown. However, in 1973 a book by Dr. Kikuta Noboru, *Watashi ni wa korosenai* (I Can't Kill), called for a change of adoption laws to allow foster parents to register adopted children as their natural children. Kikuta argued that this was necessary for unwed mothers who did not wish to register their children as illegitimate because of the difficulty these children encounter in finding marriage partners. The proposed law would register a baby as that of the foster parents, preventing it from being traced to the natural mother. Both the fostering of such children and the kind of sealed record system which it would produce would be similar to current practices in the United States. If such a law were enacted one could foresee a set of problems other than those of the henpecked adopted husband emerging in Japan. These might include the problem, common in US adoption, of the search for the "real" parents of adoptees, the dilemma of whether to tell adopted children the truth about adoption; and the authenticity of the adoptive parents versus the "natural" parents. At present these problems do not exist in Japanese adoption, and it is difficult to foresee whether they will become a part of the social scene in Japan.

■——R. K. Beardsley et al, *Village Japan* (1959). Harumi Befu, "Corporate Emphasis and Patterns of Descent in the Japanese Family," in R. J. Smith and R. K. Beardsley, *Japanese Culture: Its Development and Characteristics* (1962). Futabatei Shimei, *Sono omokage* (1906), tr Buhachirō Mitsui and Gregg M. Sinclair as *An Adopted Husband* (1916). Kikuta Noboru, *Watashi ni wa korosenai* (1973). Nakane Chie, *Kinship and Social Organization in Rural Japan* (1967). Shimazaki Tōson, *Ie* (1910–11), tr Cecilia Segawa as *The Family* (1976). Takeuchi Toshimi, "Yōshi," in *Nihon shakai minzoku jiten,* vol 4 (1960).   Jane BACHNIK

adultery

(kantsūzai). Until the 1947 revision of the Penal Code, Japan's adultery laws punished women far more severely than men. Under the present code, however, adultery is no longer a criminal act. Under the earlier code, an adulterous woman and her partner were liable to punishment of no more than two years penal servitude, following complaint by the husband. In certain rare cases a wife was granted divorce or damage payments because of her husband's adultery.

Consistent with the principle of sexual equality in the postwar CONSTITUTION, the Diet declared adultery by either husband or wife no longer a criminal offense. It was reasoned that even if a husband's act of adultery were made punishable by law, most wives would not have sufficient economic resources to maintain themselves independently, and this fact would prevent them from filing complaints against their husbands. Thus, even if the act of adultery by the husband were made punishable, actual equality between husband and wife would not be achieved. Behind this reluctance to

Advertising

	Advertising Expenditure by Medium (in millions of US dollars)						
	Newspaper	Magazine	Radio	Television	Direct mail	Export advertising	Total
1960	190.0	27.8	49.4	107.8	103.3	5.0	483.3
1965	342.5	53.3	44.7	308.3	181.9	24.7	955.6
1970	736.9	116.1	95.8	679.1	411.4	60.6	2,100.0
1975	1,378.7	225.7	202.8	1,417.8	858.8	85.6	4,169.5
1980	3,125.2	565.0	515.6	3,476.7	2,114.3	251.4	10,048.1

NOTE: For the years 1960 through 1970, $1 = ¥360; for 1975, $1 = ¥296.80; for 1980, $1 = ¥226.74. For further information on rates of exchange and conversion table, see YEN.
SOURCE: Dentsū, Inc, *Dentsū kōkoku nenkan* (annual): 1981.

criminalize a husband's act of adultery also lay the traditional tolerance of husbands' extramarital sexual affairs. Adultery is still considered grounds for DIVORCE. *SAWANOBORI Toshio*

adult, legal definition of

In Japan adulthood *(seinen)* is legally defined as the age at which a person becomes entitled to manage his own affairs. The CIVIL CODE (art. 3) specifies 20 years as the age of adulthood. For the emperor, the crown prince, and the eldest grandson of the emperor in direct line, however, the age of adulthood is 18.

Persons who have not reached the age of adulthood are termed minors *(miseinensha)*. A minor, if he marries, is in certain respects regarded as an adult. For example, he may take legal action independently, without the consent of a parent or guardian, and may exercise parental authority over his own children.

Upon reaching adulthood, one gains the right to vote, the power to execute contracts, and the freedom to perform acts that affect one's personal status, such as becoming an adoptive parent or marrying without parental approval. One may also qualify as a notary public or a patent agent *(benrishi)*. *OKA Takashi*

advertising

Japan has the world's second largest advertising industry, with expenditures in 1979 of ¥2.1 trillion (US $9.6 billion). At about 1 percent of Japan's gross national product (GNP), advertising expenditures are roughly equal to those for national defense. On a per capita basis they were approximately ¥16,000 (US $76) in 1978. Computed this way, however, Japanese expenditures are relatively low among industrialized nations, ranking 13th as of 1976.

The major media—newspapers, magazines, television, and radio—typically account for 76 to 78 percent of advertising revenues. Television, with 36 percent in 1979, has been the dominant medium since 1974, when it surpassed newspapers. An average of 10 minutes per hour was devoted to advertisements on the commercial stations. Newspapers, with 31 percent, allocated about 40 percent of their space to advertising, and consistently earn more from advertising than from circulation revenue.

In 1979, 100 firms spent more than ¥608 billion (US $2.8 billion) on advertising and promotion. The largest spender, an automobile firm, spent ¥29 billion (US $132 million). Among the 10 firms with the heaviest expenditures were 2 automobile companies, 4 manufacturers of household appliances and electronics equipment, 3 personal care and household cleaning product firms, and a retail chain. Of the 100 largest advertisers, 13 spent less than 1 percent of sales on advertising and 5 spent more than 8 percent. Food and beverages were the most heavily advertised items (accounting for 18 percent of advertising in the four major media), followed by personal care and household cleaning products (7 percent).

In 1979 there were 4,002 advertising agencies, almost half of which were located in either Tōkyō or Ōsaka. Among these were 11 of the world's 50 largest agencies, including the largest, DENTSŪ, INC. These same 11 received 59 percent of all advertising revenue, and each employed more than 350 people. Most agencies were quite small: 92 percent employed fewer than 30 persons.

Large agencies plan advertising campaigns, conduct market and advertising research, create the advertisements, and select and buy media time or space; they may also provide the ancillary services of sales promotion, public relations, outdoor and direct mail advertising. The largest agencies continue to be deeply involved with media content and form. Smaller agencies tend to concentrate on one or two services, deal with smaller clients, and handle only regional or specialized media.

History —— Advertising in some form is probably as old as commercial enterprise. The earliest reference in Japan to what seems to be a signboard dates from 833. Pictorial documentation of these SIGNBOARDS, or *kamban,* came much later, in 1487, when they were already widespread. The shop curtain (NOREN) with its trademark-like symbol became common in urban areas during the Genroku era (1688–1704). The growing commercialization of the Edo period (1600–1868) brought forth more aggressive forms of promotion, such as handbills and advertisements bound into popular books.

Nonetheless, advertising as a modern industry had to await the development of mass media and a broadly based commercial economy. Those conditions began to emerge in the Meiji period (1868–1912). The first newspaper ad placed by a Japanese firm in a Japanese language newspaper appeared in 1867. With the development of a commercial, nonpolitical press in the 1890s, producers and merchants found a relatively inexpensive substitute for personal selling. FUKUZAWA YUKICHI, an inveterate modernizer and publisher of the newspaper JIJI SHIMPŌ, entered advertising history as an advocate of advertising's positive functions and a determined critic of fraudulent claims.

Newspapers, advertising, and advertising agencies were all introduced to Japan from the West. As in the United States, the agency in Japan began as a space broker, seeking out clients for newspapers. In the United States the agency evolved instead as the representative of the advertiser. In Japan, the agency maintained its close relationship to the media. This early difference accounts for much of the continuing difference in industry structure in the two countries.

The first documented agency, Kōhōdō, was founded in 1886. In the next decade and a half, dozens of agencies sprang up, many of them under the auspices of newspapers. In 1892 an existing news wire service added an advertising agency and changed its name to Teikoku Tsūshinsha. Its growth demonstrated the potential of this combination, and it was widely imitated, most successfully by the Nihon Dempō Tsūshinsha (Dentsū), which was founded in 1907. Local papers eventually became quite dependent upon these firms, which simultaneously provided them with news and revenue.

Competition among newspapers and agencies was intense, with rate slashing and client stealing. Large urban papers often preferred to solicit advertising directly, bypassing the agency. They, however, were plagued by nonpaying advertisers. Trying to attain some measure of stability, Ōsaka agencies and newspapers organized guildlike structures in 1916; Tōkyō agencies and newspapers followed suit in 1923. Participating newspapers agreed to accept advertising only from member agencies—an exclusiveness still characteristic of newspaper advertising.

By 1924 newspaper circulation stood at 6.3 million, or one paper for every two households. Advertising lineage increased from 46 million in 1913 (73 papers) to 208 million in 1926 (116 papers) to 257 million in 1936 (105 papers). Revenues from advertising accounted for an estimated 40 percent of newspaper income as early as 1905.

Mass circulation magazines had begun to provide a new ad medium by 1900, with such magazines as *Taiyō* claiming monthly circulations of 300,000. The real heyday of magazines, though, came in the 1920s and 1930s. In 1937, 71 magazines achieved a combined circulation of 72 million.

Media and agency concentration was already pronounced by the 1920s. Large agencies, such as Dentsū, Hakuhōdō, and Mannensha, dominated the larger accounts and relationships with the major urban dailies. In this period, the agencies operated as space brokers, providing no services to advertisers other than access to media.

From 1937 on, war-induced shortages of consumer goods and paper for newsprint diminished advertising expenditures. Advertising space fell from 257 million lines in 1936 (105 papers) to 165 million lines in 1941 (79 papers), and declined another 42 percent the following year. From 1942 to 1945, to cite the example of one paper, the ASAHI SHIMBUN cut its advertisement space sevenfold.

Postwar History —— The advent of commercial broadcasting in 1951, aggressively promoted by Dentsū's head YOSHIDA HIDEO, and the recovery of the Japanese economy set the stage for advertising's impressive postwar growth. The high economic growth levels of the 1960s put disposable income into the hands of consumers eager to buy, making television advertising an indispensable tool for manufacturers eager to bring their new products to consumers' attention. Under these conditions, advertising revenues grew at nominal average annual rates of 16 percent, from ¥211 billion (US $590 million) in 1961 to ¥344 billion (US $1 billion) in 1965 to ¥756 billion (US $2 billion) in 1970.

Meanwhile, agencies had been evolving, offering new kinds of services to the advertiser. Agencies had looked to the United States for concepts, techniques, services, and forms of organization. One by one, in the middle and late 1950s, they introduced what they had learned, though often only after adapting these new techniques to conform to the existing industry structure. Agencies took up marketing; they built creative divisions, taking over from advertisers the task of creative planning and execution. The position of account executive was created and its occupants made responsible for keeping the advertiser satisfied and directing agency services on his behalf. From the mid-1960s, sales promotion divisions became a feature of these new "full service agencies." Then, in the late 1960s, Japanese agencies began to move beyond the American model, incorporating functions that are performed by other kinds of firms in the United States. Agencies designed and managed exposition pavilions, organized street festivals, produced television specials, and designed urban shopping complexes; they promoted sports events and shaped national celebrations. They worked with media to create new forms (the magazine-book, or "mook") and to provide new services (direct distribution). Such total integration of these functions into the services and purposes of an advertising agency is unique to Japan and may explain why essays on "advertising culture" have such relevance to the Japanese.

In 1971 advertising's share of the GNP dropped below 1 per cent. After the OIL CRISIS OF 1973 advertisers were heard to complain that traditional methods of advertising were losing their effectiveness: consumers were no longer buying every newly advertised product. However, since the low point of 1975, advertising revenues have once again grown more rapidly than the GNP, at a nominal average rate of 14 percent.

Industry Structure —— While Japanese agencies have expanded their services to advertisers, they have not abandoned their original function of media representative. This has had certain consequences on industry structure. First and foremost, it has meant that those advertisers, including competitors, seeking access to a particular medium have had to call upon the services of the agency or agencies that can offer that access. It is thus possible for an agency to obtain as clients all the major producers in an industry. One agency, Dentsū, has utilized this feature of the industry to make itself the preponderant force in Japanese advertising, with 24 percent of the market. Two other agencies, Hakuhōdō and Daikō, between them take another 13 percent; the top five together account for 42 percent.

Once established, the competitive strength of the large agencies has had self-perpetuating mechanisms: (1) greater resources, both financial and personal, available to provide more diversified and innovative services to clients; (2) greater dependence of the media on a continued good relationship with the large agencies; and (3) greater dependence of advertisers on the large agencies for access to the most desirable media.

In contrast, the American agency, as representative of the advertiser, has been constrained from handling competitive products and firms. With any one agency able to acquire as clients only one firm or product line per industry, the advertising industry is characterized, at the top, by several agencies basically similar in size and service offerings. The largest controls less than 2 percent of the market. (The American agency is used as a comparison because, as

it followed its clients abroad in the 1960s, it became a model throughout the industrialized world. That the Japanese industry has not entirely adopted this model has made the Japanese structure anomalous among developed countries.)

A second consequence flows from the fact that, historically, the Japanese agency had close relationships with some media and weaker ties with others. As a result, advertisers became accustomed to using one agency for one set of media and another agency for a different set. As services in addition to media buying began to be provided by agencies, most advertisers extended this custom of split accounts to the new services. In contrast, the American agency typically handles all aspects of the advertising campaign for its assigned brands: planning, creative execution, media selection and buying, and any relevant research.

Some advertisers have attempted to adopt the American system. However, the strong agencies' grip on the most desirable television time and newspaper space virtually requires major advertisers to give at least some of their business to those agencies. Advertisers find that having agencies compete over at least part of the total advertising package stimulates those agencies to provide better services.

The industry, in spite of the many influences from abroad, is still not an international one. With the exception of the joint venture McCann-Hakuhōdō, foreign-based agencies have not done particularly well in Japan, a distinct contrast to the success of American agencies elsewhere in the world. Conversely, Japanese-based agencies have only a minimal presence in foreign markets.

Financing —— An advertising agency does not require major fixed capital investment. However, substantial working capital is necessary as the Japanese agency typically pays the medium two to six months before it is paid by the advertiser, the agency acting in effect as a source of trade credit for its clients. The agency obtains these funds from its own resources or from bank borrowing. No agency is publicly held; there is some exchange of stock with various media.

Future Prospects —— For the next few years, the advertising industry will probably retain most of its current features. The decline of the centralized print media and the growth of local papers and magazines may fragment media buying, to the detriment of large, central agencies. Manufacturers' increased marketing sophistication will lead them to demand more from the agencies, in the form of demonstrated effectiveness or new kinds of services or both.

Long-run predictions are both more radical and more uncertain. Major change will certainly accompany the predicted telecommunications revolution, which will link home computers and television screens to central data bases and other homes and businesses. Experimentation on prototype systems is already under way. When fully developed, these systems will have an impact on shopping and retail distribution, forcing innovation in all forms of sales promotion, including advertising. The media, too, will undoubtedly undergo major change: the period of mass media as we know it may be drawing to a close. Although the full impact of these developments may not be felt for several decades, each move toward the "wired nation" will be certain to have incremental effects on the advertising industry.

■ —— *Advertising Age*, two annual issues on US agencies and international agencies, published in the spring. *Dentsū kōkoku nenkan* (annual; partial translation available in *Dentsu's Japan Marketing/Advertising*). Kiyono Kazuto, ed, *Kōkoku dairiten gaidobukku* (annual). Uchikawa Yoshimi, *Nihon kōkoku hattatsu shi* (1976).

Meredith WADDELL

advertising agencies

(*kōkoku dairiten*). The first advertising agency in Japan was established in 1873. The first agencies developed as representatives of early newspapers, seeking patrons for the advertising space made available in the new medium. After the advent of mass-circulation magazines around the turn of the century, agencies added these periodicals to their business, but the advertising market was limited in size until after World War II, and growth was slow. The industry expanded rapidly in the postwar period in conjunction with the rapid growth of the Japanese economy and the proliferation of media and promotional outlets. Since the 1960s, agencies have begun to offer clients combined marketing services that include market research, merchandising, and sales promotion.

In 1979 there were 4,002 advertising agencies in Japan. Most of these were quite small; 92 percent had fewer than 30 employees. On the other hand, DENTSŪ, INC, the largest agency, handled close to one-fourth of the total advertising business, and the top five agencies controlled 42 percent of the market. Thus Japanese advertising exhibits aspects of both oligopoly and dual structure (the coexistence of a small number of giant firms with large numbers of small- and medium-size enterprises), characteristics of the Japanese economy as a whole.

Because Japanese advertising agencies developed as sales representatives of the media rather than as marketing representatives for clients, many agencies handle the accounts of firms that compete within an industry. This has contributed to the concentration of advertising sales at certain agencies, since all companies seeking to advertise in the outlets represented by these agencies are compelled to use them. Some advertising interests have advocated the reform of the industry through introducing the account-executive system used in the United States and elsewhere. Adoption of this system would give advertising clients more complete service, it is argued, since comprehensive media strategies could be provided, and the agencies could offer marketing advice in the commodity development stage. Under such a system, agencies could, of course, no longer represent competing enterprises.

One of the reasons the shift to the account-executive system has not been achieved is that there are few marketing specialists at Japanese agencies. Some 44 percent of advertising employment is made up of sales representatives, while marketing specialists constitute only 3 percent of the total. Under these circumstances it is difficult for an agency to handle the full range of a client's advertising needs. The training of specialists in creative and marketing areas will be necessary before the advertising agencies can adopt the account-executive system. *Yamanaka Seigō*

adzuki beans → azuki

Aeba Kōson (1855–1922)

Novelist and theater critic. Real name Aeba Yosaburō. Born in Edo (now Tōkyō). In 1874 he began working for the newspaper *Yomiuri shimbun* as a typesetter and proofreader and was eventually promoted to the editorial staff. Encouraged by his mentor Takabatake Ransen (1838–85), then a fashionable journalist, he polished his writing skills. Later associated with TSUBOUCHI SHŌYŌ and other writers who introduced him to Western literature, he published novels and adaptations from American and European literary works. Aeba's writing reflects his interest in and study of the great 17th-century novelist Ihara SAIKAKU. His most representative novel is *Tōsei shōnin katagi* (1886). In 1889 he left the *Yomiuri*, took a job with another newspaper, the *Asahi shimbun*, and continued to write *kabuki* theater reviews as well as articles on Edo literature. *James R. Morita*

aesthetics

Aesthetics as a clearly defined field of study was introduced from the West in the Meiji period (1868–1912), but a considerable amount of writing on the nature of art existed before then, especially in the fields of poetry and drama, and to a lesser extent in painting, calligraphy, music, the tea ceremony, flower arrangement, and landscape gardening. The authors were mainly artists who wished to hand down the secrets of their art to those following in their footsteps. Consequently their remarks tended to be pedagogic in purpose, intuitive in approach, and technical in vocabulary, often lacking a philosophical frame of reference and a logical analysis of aesthetic problems. Yet in many cases they were able to give coherence to their ideas by stressing spiritual discipline and relating them to training in Buddhism, Confucianism, or Shintō.

Historical Trends —— Before and during the Heian period (794–1185), conceptions of art were very much influenced by Chinese aesthetic ideas contained in the Confucian classics. Toward the end of the period Japanese artists for the first time began producing manuals on music, dance, and landscape gardening, but these seldom included original speculations on the nature of art. The only exception was in the domain of literature, which soon asserted its independence from Chinese models. The writings of KI NO TSURAYUKI (d 945), FUJIWARA NO KINTŌ (966–1041), and other poet-critics, though indebted to Chinese poetics for general conception and terminology, propagated a distinctly national literary taste. Women writers of the Heian court, such as MURASAKI SHIKIBU (fl ca 1000) and SEI SHŌNAGON (fl late 10th century), through their essays, diaries, and prose fiction, also expressed a penchant for a type of beauty uniquely their own. The feminine aesthetic sensibility came to permeate many spheres of life not directly connected with art. At the Heian court (in what is now Kyōto), the center of Japan's cultural life during this period, aesthetics rather than ethics sometimes seemed the prime force in motivating human behavior.

Medieval writings on art were characterized by an especially strong tendency to merge art with religion. Again literary figures led the way, with FUJIWARA NO TOSHINARI (1114–1204), KYŌGOKU TAMEKANE (1254–1332), and the Zen monk SHŌTETSU (1381–1459) writing some of the most influential treatises on poetics. Koma Chikazane (1177–1242) in music, Prince Son'en (1298–1356) in calligraphy, ZEAMI Motokiyo (1363–1443) and KOMPARU ZENCHIKU (1405–70?) in the Nō drama, Murata Jukō (d 1502) in the tea ceremony, and Ikenobō Sen'ō (fl 1532–54) in flower arrangement also produced valuable writings on the essence of their respective arts. Common to these writings was the belief that ultimately all arts were one and in harmony with Buddhist teachings. Accordingly they emphasized spiritual training as preliminary to technical mastery of their arts. In their view, art was a means by which to glimpse a higher reality that was invisible to the ordinary eye. Inevitably their ideas pointed toward symbolism of one kind or another.

In the Edo period (1600–1868) aesthetic thinking became more diverse in its basic assumptions. Remarks by YAGYŪ MUNENORI (1571–1646) on martial arts, by Tosa Mitsuoki (1617–91) on painting, and by BASHŌ (1644–94) on HAIKU express a number of traditional ideas on art, albeit with contemporary modifications. On the other hand, the promotion of Neo-Confucianism by the Tokugawa shogunate gave rise to more pragmatic theories of art, such as those formulated by HAYASHI RAZAN (1583–1657), KUMAZAWA BANZAN (1619–91), and Andō Tameakira (1659–1716). Scholars of KOKUGAKU (National Learning), notably MOTOORI NORINAGA (1730–1801) and HIRATA ATSUTANE (1776–1843), rejected Confucian views and advocated ideas of art derived from Shintō classics. Many writings on art, especially on JŌRURI and KABUKI, also emerged that had little to do with Buddhism, Confucianism, or Shintō. By and large aesthetic thought in the Edo period was more humanistic than in previous ages, emphasizing the role of emotion in both the artist's creation and the spectator's appreciation.

General Characteristics —— A distinctive feature of premodern aesthetic thought in Japan was the tendency to value symbolic representation more highly than realistic delineation. To premodern thinkers, mimesis meant not an imitation of outward appearance but a suggestion of inner essence, for true reality lay under the physical surface. In their opinion, the prime value of art was in making visible the invisible mysteries of nature and man. Hence the artist ideally became one with his subject and felt its inner life himself, instead of scrutinizing it objectively from a distance. Western-type realism developed slowly in Japan for this reason.

Another characteristic feature was the lack of any strong attempt to admit the unsightly into what was considered art. By and large premodern concepts of mimesis assumed a selective presentation of the beautiful and discouraged the artist from dealing with the humble and vulgar aspects of human experience. Consequently the artist tended to choose nature for his subject, avoiding the depiction of everyday occurrences in the lives of common people. This penchant, originating in the taste of the Heian court aristocracy, weakened somewhat in later centuries, but no premodern Japanese notion of art came close to those Western aesthetic theories that insisted on art's ability to create beauty out of mundane or ugly materials.

Predictably, elegance was one of the main types of beauty favored in premodern aesthetics, as the Heian court taste for grace and refinement exerted a lasting impact on the later cultural tradition. Such important aesthetic concepts as OKASHI, FŪRYŪ, YŪGEN, and *iki* (see IKI AND SUI) all included a connotation of elegance, though each had other semantic implications as well and represented a different overall outlook. The traditional predilection for elegant beauty discouraged the emergence of a more forceful, masculine type of beauty in Japanese culture.

Another quality highly valued in premodern Japanese aesthetics was impermanence, an appreciation of the evanescent, which could be considered a variation of elegance, for exquisite beauty is fragile and apt to perish easily. Buddhism, with its emphasis on life's mutability, merged with it and provided philosophical depth. Such aesthetic ideals as *aware* (and its later elaboration, MONO NO AWARE), *yūgen*, WABI, and SABI, which were cherished by artists over the centuries, all had perishability as part of their meaning. The desire for immortality through art, often seen in the Western cultural tradition, is seldom observed among premodern Japanese artists.

Simplicity, also valued by the Japanese, was a corollary to the concept of mimesis, which stressed symbolic representation. The mystery of nature could never be presented through description; it could only be suggested, and the terser the suggestion, the greater its effectiveness. An artistically created void, either in time or in space, thus became an important idea in aesthetic speculations. Concepts like *wabi, sabi*, MA, YOJŌ, and SHIBUI were all inclined toward simplicity in their basic implications, uniformly showing distaste for ornate beauty. Simplicity also meant naturalness, or lack of artifice, in artistic expression. In premodern Japanese aesthetics the distance between art and nature was considerably shorter than in its Western counterpart.

Modern Aesthetics —— Western aesthetics was introduced to Japan by NISHI AMANE (1829–97), MORI ŌGAI (1862–1922), and others in the early Meiji period. Today's Japanese term for aesthetics, *bigaku*, was coined by NAKAE CHŌMIN (1847–1901) around 1883. Tōkyō University established a course in aesthetics in 1886, with a Western scholar as its first instructor. Inevitably, early Japanese specialists in the field were all students of Western, especially German, aesthetics, who paid little attention to their native tradition. The trend began to change when KUKI SHŪZŌ (1888–1941) and Ōnishi Yoshinori (1888–1959) pioneered in philosophical studies of premodern Japanese aesthetic thought. Today the gap is narrower, although it still exists, between academic aestheticians who are primarily interested in defining the nature of beauty through Western methodologies and professional critics who try to appraise individual works of art according to traditional criteria. A synthesis of Japanese and Western aesthetics still remains the ultimate challenge for both those groups.

🖾 ——Donald Keene, *Landscapes and Portraits* (1971). Ōnishi Yoshinori, *Bigaku* (1960–61). Makoto Ueda, *Literary and Art Theories in Japan* (1967). Yamazaki Masakazu et al, *Nihonjin no biishiki* (1974). Yasuda Ayao, *Nihon no geijutsuron* (1965, 1972).

Makoto UEDA

Africa and Japan

Although Japan is a member of the Afro-Asian community, it has tended to put more emphasis on relations with the advanced nations of Europe and North America, as well as with Asia and Latin America, than with the nations of Africa. Japanese interest in Africa remains relatively low, due mainly to the fact that possibilities for political, economic, and cultural cooperation remain unrecognized in many cases.

In the 1880s and the 1890s Japan saw Africa fall prey to the Western imperialist powers, a development that reinforced Japan's sense of urgency in its efforts to maintain its own independence. As Japan moved into the ranks of imperialist powers, it was argued that the country should develop an interest in the African continent. Japan's first diplomatic mission in Africa was established in 1918 in Capetown, Union of South Africa. This was followed by missions in Port Said and Alexandria (Egypt) and Mombasa (Kenya). The first trade and friendship agreement was signed with Ethiopia in 1927. The Japanese Ōsaka Shōsen Kaisha shipping lines opened up an East African route in 1926 that led to expanded trade between Japan and that area. This was followed in 1933 by a similar connection with West Africa, which received attention as a new market for Japanese textiles.

Trade relations between Africa and Japan were temporarily severed during World War II, but were slowly resumed in the postwar years. In the period 1960–70, trade with Africa accounted for 8 percent of Japan's exports and 5 percent of imports. Trade with the Republic of South Africa comprised one-third of this figure, a fact of great concern to the other African nations.

Japanese diplomatic relations with Africa developed during the 1960s through negotiations in Paris and New York. Actual establishment of Japanese diplomatic bases in Africa, however, was slow to develop. By the end of the 1960s Japan had established diplomatic relations with almost all the African nations, but there were permanent consulates and embassies in only half that number. In the 1970s permanent facilities increased as Japan made a strong push toward establishing local contact in Africa. This is evident in figures for permanent diplomatic missions for the years 1957 (4), 1960 (5), 1970 (15), 1975 (18), and 1978 (22). Leading African visitors to Japan have included the Ethiopian emperor Haile Selassie, who came to Japan in 1956, and Mobutu Sese Seko, president of Zaire, in 1971. In 1970 the Japanese government sent a goodwill group to Africa with the objectives of establishing personal ties with Black Africa,

strengthening economic assistance, promoting technical assistance, and promoting cooperation in the development of natural resources on a basis of mutual interest.

Recent years have brought stronger African demands for solutions to the problems of colonialism and racial discrimination. As a result, Japan was forced to change its traditional stance of advising African nations to be more trusting toward the former colonial powers. When resolutions denouncing South Africa's apartheid policies were brought before the United Nations, Japan generally abstained, declaring that the true solution did not lie in political sanctions toward South Africa. This view was at odds with that of the members of the Organization of African Unity (OAU), and Japan, along with the other advanced nations, including the United States and Great Britain, came under fire for continuing political and economic relations with South Africa. In October and November of 1974, however, Foreign Minister Kimura Toshio visited Ghana, Nigeria, Zaire, Tanzania, and Egypt, the first visit to Africa by a Japanese foreign minister. This coincided with a move away from a diplomatic policy centered on the great powers toward one which placed increased importance on the opinions of the Third World countries. By this move Japan sought a stance which would emphasize dialogue, understanding, and cooperation in relations with the African nations.

South African policies and economic nationalism remain two issues of crucial importance to the nations of Africa. After Kimura's 1974 visit, Japan took a much more severe position on South Africa, demanding a quick end to apartheid policies in that country. Japan also made known its support for anticolonial movements in Africa. After Rhodesia's unilateral declaration of independence, Japan refused to recognize white minority rule and expressed hopes for a peaceful solution to the problem of self-determination. It faithfully observed the mandatory sanctions toward Rhodesia adopted by the United Nations in 1966 and 1968.

Japan has also taken a sympathetic position toward African expressions of economic nationalism, and economic and technical assistance for Africa has been expanded. Japan's Official Development Assistance (ODA) for Africa, which amounted to US $20 million in 1973, grew to US $280 million by 1978, and Japan now lists almost 40 African nations as recipients of technical assistance. In addition, Japan has granted economic assistance loans to 17 nations and has contributed to the opening of the African Development Fund (AfDF) in 1972. Japan Overseas Cooperation Volunteers have been stationed in a number of African nations including Morocco, Tunisia, Ghana, Liberia, Kenya, Ethiopia, Tanzania, Zambia, Malawi, Senegal, and Uganda.

Up to now Japan has tended to emphasize trade more than assistance, using the example of its own development to encourage self-reliance on the part of other nations. Thus, it has concentrated on improving existing channels of assistance and putting them to wider use. In recent years, however, Japan has moved closer toward a stance of positive cooperation and assistance as evidenced, for example, by the Kilimanjaro Area Development Project in Tanzania.

🖾 ——Eiji Fukunaga, *Japan's Position Toward Africa: Documentary Compilation on Recent Moves* (1975), pamphlet. Matsumoto Shigeharu, Yoneyama Toshinao, and Itani Jun'ichirō, *Afurika handobukku* (1983). Urano Tatsuo, *Afurika kokusai kankei* (1975).

URANO *Tatsuo*

Afro-Asian Conferences

(Ajia Afurika Kaigi). Name given to a number of meetings held to promote the ideas of sovereignty, equality, and solidarity among the nations of Africa and Asia, beginning with the Afro-Asian Conference held in Bandung, Indonesia, in April 1955. Official representatives of 29 countries attended the Bandung Conference, and Japan, as one of the Asian participants, sent Takasaki Tatsunosuke (1885–1964) as its representative. A second Afro-Asian Conference was scheduled to be held in Algiers in 1965, but several circumstances, including Sino-Soviet tensions, disagreements among the African nations, and a coup d'etat in the host country of Algeria led to a cancellation.

There have also been several Afro-Asian meetings on the people's level. Japan was one of the participants in the forerunner for such gatherings, the Asian Relations Conference held in New Delhi, India, in 1947, and the Japanese-Asian Solidarity Committee (presently the Afro-Asian Solidarity Committee) created after this conference sent delegates to five Afro-Asian Peoples' Solidarity Conferences in later years. These were held in Cairo, Egypt (December 1957 to January 1958); Conakry, Guinea (1960), Moshi, Tanganyika (1963); Winneba, Ghana (1965); and Cairo (1972). The 1963 conference opened with renewed tensions between the Soviet Union and China, and the 1972 conference was limited to participation by pro-Soviet nations. In the Japanese committee, a pro-Soviet faction took control after driving out the pro-Chinese members in the late 1960s. Today, there are two committees, pro-Soviet and pro-Chinese, in Japan.   URANO Tatsuo

afterlife

(ano yo, literally, "that world"; shigo no sekai "the world after death"; yomi no kuni "the land of darkness"). The traditional, fundamental Japanese belief about life after death has been that the spirit of the dead gradually loses individuality and finally after the 33rd anniversary of death (32nd by Western count), merges with the spirit of the ancestors and resides in mountains, especially holy mountainous areas such as Kumano, Yoshino, Tateyama, Hakusan, and Osorezan that are held to be the abodes of the gods (see YAMA NO KAMI). The spirit then keeps watch over the living, visits kinsmen over the NEW YEAR holidays, and at the summer BON FESTIVAL comes to protect the rice crop (see TA NO KAMI). An exceptional individual, especially if he has died a tragic (or violent) death, is believed to become a vengeful god (onryō or GORYŌ) who needs to be revered properly if he is to be placated.

Buddhists modified this traditional view, introducing such notions as metempsychosis (Skt: saṃsāra; J: rinne)—different realms of being into which the dead might be reborn: hell (J: jigoku) or the realms of hungry demons (J: gaki), beasts (J: chikushō), the demons called asura (J: ashura), human beings (J: ningen), or divine beings (J: ten). These notions were accompanied by a moral-religious imperative regarding the way to live and exerted a tremendous influence from the latter half of the Heian period (794–1185) and especially from the Kamakura period (1185–1333) on. At the same time, belief in rebirth in AMIDA Buddha's Pure Land also became popular. These notions could be not only morally demanding but also liberating for those for whom life was harsh. Illustrated accounts of hell and of the realm of gaki were made (see JIGOKU-ZŌSHI). The monk Genshin's Ōjōyōshū (984–985) vividly describes the torments of various hells in contrast to the bliss of the Pure Land. The Jūō-gyō (full title Jizō bosatsu hosshin innen jūō-gyō), a Chinese-influenced pseudo-sutra, describes the passage of the dead into the other world.

These representations of the afterlife took hold of the popular imagination during the Kamakura period. It was believed that during the 49 days after death—the period of intermediate existence (Skt: antarā-bhava; J: chūu)—the dead passed through mountains, crossed a river (J: Sanzu no Kawa; the degree of difficulty depending upon his conduct on earth), and after being judged by the lord Emma (Skt: Yāma) or the Ten Lords (J: Jūō) was assigned to a realm for the next life. Around this idea developed various customs, such as clothing the dead in a shirt on which were written passages from a sutra or a mantra (holy word or phrase) or putting money in the casket for traveling expenses. Pure Land Buddhist terms like ōjō, literally, "to go and be born" (i.e., in the Pure Land of the Blessed) and jōbutsu, literally, "to attain Buddhahood" (i.e., in the Pure Land), became synonyms for dying and were used by people of other Buddhist sects. Although Amida's Pure Land was most popular, the "Pure Land" could be that of Śākyamuni Buddha (Nichiren sect) or of Mahāvairocana Buddha (Shingon sect), the Tusita heaven of the bodhisattva Maitreya (J: MIROKU), or the Potalaka of the bodhisattva Avalokiteśvara (J: KANNON).

Among the cognoscenti, these notions counted for little; Buddhists considered life to be śūnya (devoid of substance, empty) and believed that life and death alike should be accepted with equanimity. The Shintō theologian MOTOORI NORINAGA held that one should accept the notion of the dark underworld (yomi) as described in the 8th-century chronicle KOJIKI and not beautify or moralize death artificially. During the period of warrior ascendancy (i.e., the 12th to 19th centuries) some warriors held that the true spirit of the samurai (BUSHIDŌ) lay in his readiness to die rather than to suffer dishonor.

According to surveys taken in the 1970s, fewer than 10 percent of the Japanese people believe in the afterlife.

📖——Yanagita Kunio, Yamamiya kō (1947).

TSUCHIDA Tomoaki

After the Banquet case

Case in which the right of privacy was first formally recognized in Japanese constitutional law. A Tōkyō district court decided on 28 September 1964 that MISHIMA YUKIO in his novel Utage no ato (1960; tr After the Banquet, 1963) had violated the privacy of ARITA HACHIRŌ, the unsuccessful Socialist candidate in the 1959 Tōkyō gubernatorial election. The timing of its 1960 serialization in the magazine Chūō kōron precluded impact on election results.

The court sustained Arita's claim of privacy violation, awarding him ¥800,000 ($2,200), the largest compensation for mental distress given in a defamation or privacy suit between 1945 and the mid-1970s. While on appeal, the dispute was settled by compromise on 28 November 1966. The fame of both the politician and the novelist made this one of the most discussed cases in Japan's history; but the work was far from a vulgar exposé, and some litterateurs alleged violation of literary freedom. The historical significance of the decision, welcomed by most jurists, lay in its establishment of a new right of privacy in Japan and guidelines for determining the infringement of privacy (see PRIVACY, RIGHT TO).

The right of privacy was judicially defined as "the legal right and assurance that one's private life will not be wantonly opened to the public." This right is guaranteed under article 13 of the 1947 constitution, which requires that "all of the people shall be respected as individuals." The right is violated, as in Arita's case, if fear exists that the reader will take the work as factual or similar to the facts of a person's private life, if the average man would not want the matters at issue publicized, or if material about the person in the work is not generally known.

📖——Lawrence W. Beer, "Defamation, Privacy, and Freedom of Expression in Japan," Law in Japan: An Annual 5 (1972). Mishima Yukio, Utage no ato (1960), tr Donald Keene as After the Banquet (1963).

Lawrence W. BEER

Aganogawa

River in Fukushima and Niigata prefectures, northern Honshū. It has its source in three rivers: the Nippashigawa, originating in Lake Inawashiro; the Agagawa (or Ōkawa), originating in the south Aizu Mountains; and the Tadamigawa, which originates in the lake called Ozenuma. It flows west through the Niigata Plain and enters the Sea of Japan at the city of Niigata. Three dams were constructed after World War II, and a coastal industrial district is presently being developed. In 1965 the waters of the Aganogawa were found to be contaminated with methyl-mercury pollutants (see POLLUTION-RELATED DISEASES). The water is utilized for irrigation. The river basin has been designated a prefectural natural park. Length: 168 km (104 mi).

Agano ware

(agano-yaki). Pottery produced near the mountain Fukuchiyama in northern Kyūshū from the early 17th century. Most prized by connoisseurs is the Old Agano ware produced from 1602 to 1632 under the supervision of the Korean potter Chon'gye (J: Sonkai; also known as Agano Kizō; d 1654) and his family for the tea-loving Hosokawa family, lords of Kokura (now part of Fukuoka Prefecture) until their fief was changed to Higo (now Kumamoto Prefecture) in 1632. The products were mainly tea utensils and pieces for everyday use with relatively thick, creamy, white ash glazes and dark brown iron glazes that resembled Old KARATSU WARE and TAKATORI WARE, which were from geographically contiguous areas. Although Agano Kizō left with his lord in 1632, the Agano Sarayama kiln was maintained by his branch families. The main innovations were the introduction of RAKU WARE in the early 18th century and a characteristic bluish green copper glaze in the late 18th century. The 18th- and 19th-century pieces are more colorful and decorative than earlier pieces, but thicker and less well modeled. Today, as a result of archaeological research, some old-style kilns have been reconstructed and the once almost extinct tradition of Agano ware is being revived.

Frederick BAEKELAND

Agata no Inukai no Tachibana no Michiyo (?–733)

A court lady during the reigns of six sovereigns at the end of the Yamato period (ca 300–710) and beginning of the Nara period (710–794). Also known as Tachibana no Michiyo. First married to the imperial prince Minu, she was the mother of TACHIBANA NO MOROE, later a high-ranking court official. By her second husband, FUJIWARA NO FUHITO, the statesman and compiler of the TAIHŌ CODE, she bore a daughter who came to exercise great authority as Empress KŌMYŌ. Her marriage connections and the power of her children made her a woman of considerable influence in the court. One of her poems is included in the 8th-century anthology *Man'yōshū,* and the so-called Shrine of Lady Tachibana at the temple Hōryūji in Nara is said to have been donated by her.

agatanushi

The head of an *agata,* a political unit smaller than a *kuni* (province) in the *kuniagata* system of local administration instituted by the YAMATO COURT (ca 4th century–ca mid-7th century). It is believed that *agatanushi* were originally the hereditary chieftains of small tribal states *(buzoku kokka)* whose position the court acknowledged with this designation *(nushi* means "chief"). Tribal chieftains of larger territories were given the title KUNI NO MIYATSUKO. These two posts stood in no hierarchical relationship, however, for both were directly subordinate to the court. In the late 7th century the KOKUGUN SYSTEM of administration superseded the *kuniagata* system, and the title *agatanushi* was adopted under the RITSURYŌ SYSTEM as one of·the *kabane* status ranks (see UJI-KABANE SYSTEM).

KITAMURA Bunji

Agatsumagawa

River in northern Gumma Prefecture, central Honshū, originating near the Torii Pass on the border with Nagano Prefecture and flowing east to empty into the river Tonegawa near the city of Shibukawa. Its waters were strongly acid because of their volcanic sources, and a neutralization plant was built at the town of Kusatsu in 1964. It is an important source of hydroelectric power. Length: 74 km (46 mi); area of drainage basin: 1,356 sq km (523 sq mi).

Agawa Hiroyuki (1920–   )

Novelist. Born in Hiroshima. Upon graduation from Tōkyō University he was drafted into the Imperial Navy. One of the "first wave" of new writers who appeared at the start of the post-World War II era, Agawa made his debut as an ardent follower of SHIGA NAOYA with the short story "Nennen saisai" (1946), about a soldier who returns to Hiroshima from war to find it destroyed by the atomic blast. Many of his stories reflect his experiences as a naval·officer during the Pacific War. Other notable works include *Haru no shiro* (1952, Spring Castle), for which he received the Yomiuri Literary Prize in 1952, and *Yamamoto Isoroku* (1964–65; tr *The Reluctant Admiral: Yamamoto and the Imperial Navy,* 1980), a much acclaimed biography of the admiral who planned the attack on Pearl Harbor. In 1979 Agawa received the Japan Academy Prize.

Agechirei

(Land Requisition Orders). An ordinance issued in 1843 by MIZUNO TADAKUNI decreeing the return of certain lands to the shogunate or *daimyō.* Part of his program known as the TEMPŌ REFORMS, the ordinance was intended to consolidate Tokugawa house lands that had been dispersed over the years. It designated all lands within 10 *ri* (40 km; 25 mi) of Edo (now Tōkyō) and 5 *ri* (20 km; 12 mi) of Ōsaka as TENRYŌ, or land under direct shogunal control. Private holdings within the designated areas were to be restored to the shogunate and the fief holders transferred to other lands. The order immediately incurred criticism, most vocally from Tokugawa Nariyuki, the powerful daimyō of Wakayama, who had already been antagonized by Tadakuni's earlier prohibition of domainal commercial monopolies, a measure he feared would jeopardize his own lucrative transportation monopoly. Tadakuni was forced to rescind the ordinance, and two days later he resigned from office.

age, legal definition of

In present-day Japan, legal age is reckoned from the date of birth, and is calculated according to the Western calendar. The Law concerning the Counting of Age (1902) includes the date of birth, while the related provision in the CIVIL CODE excludes it. In many cases, attainment of a particular age is deemed a condition for the obtaining of legal capacities, qualifications, rights and duties. Some of the most important of these are as follows. The parent or guardian of a child must provide for the education of that child from 6 years of age through 15 (School Education Law, art. 22). A child who has reached 15 may independently make a will and enter into an employment contract. An adoptive child of 15 or over may no longer be required to furnish the consent of a parent or guardian instead of his own.

However, there are still cases in which the permission of the family court is required.

Women reach the age of eligibility to marry at 16, men at 18. A minor who has reached the age of eligibility to marry, however, still requires parental consent to do so. A married minor is the same as an adult with respect to legal relations with others. Accordingly, for instance, such a person may, without the agreement of his statutory agent, independently perform valid juristic acts. Furthermore, upon attaining the age of 20, the person is free of parental authority and obtains the right to vote.

OKA Takashi

Agency of Industrial Science and Technology

(Kōgyō Gijutsu In). Government research institution of the MINISTRY OF INTERNATIONAL TRADE AND INDUSTRY (MITI). Located in Tōkyō. It was established in 1948 to promote industrial technology. Its activities include conducting experiments and research on mining; performing geological surveys; establishing standards for weights and measures; preserving devices used to maintain those standards, such as the prototype of the kilogram and the device for measuring the ohm; and enforcing industrial standards. Under this agency are 16 research centers, including the National Research Laboratory of Metrology, the GEOLOGICAL SURVEY OF JAPAN, and the National Chemical Laboratory for Industry.

Ageo

City in eastern Saitama Prefecture about 34 km (21 mi) north of Tōkyō. Ageo developed as a POST-STATION TOWN on the NAKASENDŌ, one of the major highways during the Edo period (1600–1868). It was long known for its wheat and sweet potatoes, but since World War II it has become a center for the automobile, nonferrous metal, and machine industries. More recently the city has become a residential district for workers commuting to Tōkyō. Pop: 166,244.

Ago Bay

(Ago Wan). Inlet of the Pacific Ocean on the coast of Shima Peninsula, eastern Mie Prefecture, central Honshū. Part of the Ise–Shima National Park, the bay is also known for its pearl industry, begun by MIKIMOTO KŌKICHI in 1883. There is the National Pearl Research Institute on Kashikojima, an island in the western part of the bay.

agrarian nationalism → nōhon shugi

agricultural cooperative associations

(nōgyō kyōdō kumiai; abbreviated nōkyō). The first agricultural cooperative associations in Japan, called *sangyō kumiai* (production unions), were established in 1900. The associations were established as credit unions, sales and purchase cooperatives, and cooperative farming unions in rural communities. These cooperatives were disbanded in 1943, but the movement was revived in 1947 and has flourished throughout the post–World War II period.

Prewar Cooperatives —— An unusual characteristic of the history of agricultural cooperatives in Japan is that they were developed with the strong support and encouragement of the government and large landowners. The establishment of agricultural credit unions was first proposed in the Diet in 1891 by SHINAGAWA YAJIRŌ and HIRATA TŌSUKE who were influenced by European approaches to agriculture. In 1897 the Ministry of Agriculture and Commerce drafted enabling legislation, which was passed by the Diet and implemented in 1900. The organization of cooperatives was considered a means for modernizing Japanese agriculture and adapting it to a capitalist economy. It was expected that cooperatives would bring about a rationalization of land usage and the integration of rural capital into national financial networks. The system of home rule in the prefectures would also be strengthened, since local government authorities would license and regulate the cooperatives.

A central organization was formed in 1905 under the name Dai Nihon Sangyō Kumiai Chūōkai (Dai Nihon was dropped from the name in 1909). By 1910, 7,308 cooperatives had been formed and membership stood at 437,588. Nearly 60 percent of all towns and villages had been organized.

Prefectural federations were established early in the Taishō period (1912–26), completing a three-tiered, pyramidal structure of the associations (local, prefectural, and national bodies). Sales cooperatives, centered on rice sales, grew rapidly at this time, and they gained increased importance as nationwide markets were consolidated in the aftermath of the RICE RIOTS OF 1918 and the general economic crisis of the early 1920s. TENANT FARMER DISPUTES reflected a breakdown in the system of LANDLORDISM, and the government passed numerous measures to regulate and modernize agriculture. By 1924, just under half of all farms belonged to the cooperatives, of which there were 14,517 individual units and 200 federations. Total membership stood at 3.7 million, of which about 75 percent were farmers, with the bulk of the remainder being merchants and small manufacturers.

The early part of the Shōwa period (1926–) was characterized by the consolidation of the national networks of cooperative organizations, including federations of financial associations and of sales cooperatives for rice, raw silk, and citrus fruits. After the SHŌWA DEPRESSION, cooperatives figured in government recovery plans and organizational activity was intensified. Efforts were launched to enlist all farm households in the associations, and by 1942 membership had risen to 9.2 million in 15,229 local cooperatives and 247 prefectural federations.

The sangyō kumiai were disbanded in 1943, when the wartime government established the centrally controlled Nōgyōkai (Agricultural Association) in their place. Much of the organizational structure of the cooperatives was revived after the war, however, and a number of prewar institutions (such as the NŌRIN CHŪKIN BANK) have survived.　　　　　　　　　　　　　　　　John JUNKERMAN

Postwar Cooperatives —— Postwar agricultural cooperatives (called *nōgyō kyōdō kumiai*, or *nōkyō*) were established to bring the advantages of collective organization to small farmers, both as producers and consumers. They were formed under the provisions of a special law enacted in 1947 as part of the Allied Occupation reforms.

The basic principles of the Japanese cooperative movement, which were embodied in the 1947 law, derive from those of the Rochdale Society of Equitable Pioneers, the world's first organized cooperative movement. The Rochdale Society was established in England in 1844, and its principles were adopted in 1937 as the guiding code of the international cooperative movement. Following this lead, Japanese cooperatives adhere to the following principles: freedom of membership; democratic administration; nonprofit business management and the return of surplus funds to members; equality in the distribution of returns from investment; the maintenance of a fund for the education of cooperative members; and the promotion of joint activities between cooperatives.

The cooperative movement engages in various forms of economic and other activities to fulfill its purposes. These include the marketing of products, large-scale purchases, the extension of credit, mutual aid insurance, and joint production, as well as training, guidance, and agricultural administration to improve the effectiveness of cooperative activities. The movement has a pyramidal structure with three tiers: individual cooperatives at the local level, prefectural federations at the regional level, and national federations at the top. At the very top of the structure is the Zenkoku Nōgyō Kyōdō Kumiai Chūōkai, a coordinating body for all cooperatives. There is an additional subdivision into comprehensive and specialized cooperatives. The former undertake all of the above-mentioned activities, while the latter include both associations for certain types of agriculture (dairy farming, fruit growing, and sericulture, for example) and associations for specialized activities (press information, publications, and health and welfare). There are few specialized associations in Japan and they have relatively little power.

Agricultural cooperatives had a nationwide membership of 7.8 million in 1977; this membership represented 5.2 million farming households, or an effective organization rate of 100 percent. As such, the cooperative movement can be counted as one of the giant organizations of Japan. The business operations of the national federations in 1976, for instance, ranked sixth in comparison to the large general trading companies; the Nōrin Chūkin Bank ranked second in total deposits among all banks in the nation in 1978; and from early in their existence the cooperative mutual aid societies had the highest long-term mutual aid holdings of the insurance world.

At the same time, the cooperatives are facing a number of serious problems. Most threatening to their future is the narrowing of the agricultural base by the progressive urbanization of the country. Because of the spread of cities and the urban economy, many cooperative members are taking on side employment or leaving agriculture altogether. The associations are increasingly faced with a choice between maintaining their status as occupation-based cooperatives

with membership limited to full-time farmers or broadening their charters to become regional organizations with their rosters open to part-time farmers and nonfarmers.

A second problem is that rice farming, which has provided a stable base for the business operations of cooperatives, now suffers from surplus production. The adjustment of rice production levels could jeopardize the financial solvency of the cooperatives.

A third major problem is the consequence of the organizational rationalization that has taken place in recent years. Spurred by the consolidation of town and village administrations, individual cooperatives on the local level have undergone mergers with neighboring cooperatives. This tendency has been reinforced by the centralization and modernization of the nation's DISTRIBUTION SYSTEM, and the pace of such mergers has increased since 1965. Some local cooperatives have become so large that their power rivals that of the prefectural federation, causing a rethinking of the three-tiered structure of the movement.

None of these problems will be simple to resolve. A restructuring of the cooperatives to allow them to continue to fulfill their original purpose may well be necessary for the sake of farmers, farm villages, agriculture, and the nation as a whole.

—— Aono Bunsaku, *Nōkyō: Soshiki to hito to senryaku* (1976). Ie no Hikari Kyōkai, *Kyōdō kumiai jiten* (1966). Suda Yūji, *Nōkyō* (1978). Tachibana Takashi, *Nōkyō: Kyodai na chōsen* (1979). Zenkoku Nōkyō Chūōkai, *Nōkyō dokuhon* (1960). Zenkoku Nōkyō Chūōkai, *Nōkyō nenkan* (annual).　　　　　　*KAWAMOTO Akira*

agricultural rites

(*nōkō girei*). Rites and ceremonies connected with the growth cycle of cultivated food plants. The Old World centered its rites around wheat cultivation, and New World societies concentrated on corn-raising rites, but in Japan, as in the rest of East Asia, agricultural rites have focused on rice growing. Rice transplanting has been the central agricultural activity in Japan, since rice is the staple food crop.

Sowing of rice grain in spring is followed by transplanting of rice seedlings during the rainy season in early summer, with harvest taking place in the fall. Rice cultivation rites tend to center around these important stages. Accordingly, there are ceremonies for encouraging growth during sowing and transplanting, supplications for rain and insect removal, and harvest rites. Both sowing and harvest rites involve the arrival and departure of the TA NO KAMI, the traditional guardian deity of the rice fields. According to folk religious beliefs, during spring sowing the *ta no kami* travels from the sky, the mountains, or the farmhouse to dwell in the fields and watch over the growth of the rice plants until the autumn harvest, whereupon the deity leaves the fields and returns to his former residence.

When the rice seeds are sown, a tree branch inserted in the rice-seedling bed serves as the resting place for the *ta no kami*, symbolizing that trees are the dwelling places (*yorishiro*) of deities. At harvest time, farmhouses set up offerings of rice sheaves, *daikon* (see RADISHES), rice, and glutinous rice (*mochigome*) on the *kami-dana* (see SHINTŌ FAMILY ALTARS) and in the alcove, main room, garden entrance, and storeroom to honor the *ta no kami*. In farming districts in northern Kyūshū, the head of the family gathers leftover rice plants into sheaves and brings them to the house on the day the *ta no kami* is believed to leave the rice paddies to return to the farmhouse. In an earthen-floored room (*doma*) of the house, he sets up a mortar and builds an altar to display the rice sheaves along with bean-studded rice (*sekihan*) and fish as offerings for the *ta no kami*. This practice stems from the belief that the *ta no kami* actually dwells within the rice plants themselves, an idea that was also widespread in Europe's wheat-raising culture, where a "grain spirit" was thought to reside in the wheat plants. Such agricultural beliefs and ceremonies belong to the so-called last sheaf type of farming rites.

On farms in central Japan along the Sea of Japan, the head of the household dons his finest clothes and goes out to the fields to greet the *ta no kami*. He guides the god back to the house for a bath, after which the deity is feted at a ceremonial banquet. The deity is thus anthropomorphized and treated as an honored guest.

Seedling-transplanting (*taue*) ceremonies also consist of rites for the *ta no kami* and take place on two occasions before and after the actual transplanting of the rice shoots. On both occasions offerings of *mochigome*, seaweed, *sake*, fish, and rice are placed on a bed of leaves in a corner of the field or in the house. The offerings always include three bundles of rice seedlings which, like the tree branch in the seed-sowing ceremonies and sheaves in the harvest rites, function as the resting place for the *ta no kami*.

Agricultural rites

One of the ceremonial observances for rice transplanting *(taue)*. The farmer offers beans and rice, seaweed, dried fish, and *sake* to the paddy god and prays for a good harvest. The offering is placed at the paddy's *minakuchi*, or irrigation duct, from which the observance takes its name, Minakuchi Matsuri (Minakuchi Ceremony). Aomori Prefecture, late May.

Rites to encourage the growth of the plants, such as those for rain supplication and insect dispersal, take place between transplanting and harvest. Rain supplication *(amagoi)* rites may take the form of either setting a fire on a hillside or sprinkling water from a sacred place into the rice beds. Rites to drive away insects may consist of chasing harmful pests to the borders of the village, to a river, or to the sea. The observance of both types of rites has declined in recent years.

In addition to the rites mentioned, an elaborate body of ceremonies preceding plant cultivation has developed in Japan. Such rites, which occur during the early to middle part of January, the off-season for rice cultivating, require the farmer to go out to the fields and symbolically perform seed and shoot planting and harvesting. They are a form of imitative magic whereby the celebrants anticipate a fruitful harvest in the coming year (see NEW YEAR). Interestingly enough, these winter rites go beyond rice plants to include grains like barley, Italian millet, and *hie* (another variety of millet) as well as *daikon* and pumpkin. This suggests that there was formerly a variety of agricultural rites in Japan for produce other than rice.

Such rites have lapsed considerably in modern times but have not entirely disappeared. In western Japan, after harvesting barley the villagers assemble to give thanks for a successful crop. Another annual event is the Jūgoya, festivities held on 15 August according to the lunar calendar in celebration of the full moon. The moon receives the name *imo meigetsu* ("taro full moon") in connection with the offerings of *satoimo* (taro) made at this time. This rite probably originated in thanksgiving ceremonies for the taro harvest.

The Okinawa and Amami island chains to the southwest of Japan have developed their own rites, which show marked differences from those in Honshū, Shikoku, and Kyūshū. While in those three islands, rites accompanying transplanting are as important as those surrounding sowing and harvesting, such rites are rarely seen in the southwest islands. Similarly, while rice cultivation rites are paramount on the Japanese mainland, the southwest islands place great emphasis on rites for barley, millet, taro, and sweet potatoes. In the Amami Islands, for instance, summer rites include those for *hie* and millet in addition to rice, while winter rites center on the taro and sweet potato. In Okinawa spring is the time for barley cultivation rites; summer includes harvest rites for rice and *hie;* and fall and winter rites tend to concentrate on the sowing of rice seed and the harvesting of sweet potatoes.

There are a number of other basic differences between agricultural rites in the two regions. Ceremonies in the southwest islands place little emphasis on the *ta no kami.* Further, rites on the Japanese mainland tend to take place within the individual family, but rites in the southwest islands involve the entire hamlet, which selects priestesses according to patrilineal descent groups or from bilateral kin groups. These contrasts reflect differences in the historical, cultural, and social backgrounds of the two areas but at the same time hint at the diversity which characterizes Japanese culture in general.

ITŌ Mikiharu

agriculture

Prior to the Meiji Restoration of 1868, as much as 80 percent of the population of Japan was engaged in farming. Although Japan has always had a great variety of crops in relation to its size, rice has always been overwhelmingly dominant as the main crop. Animal husbandry has remained relatively undeveloped; instead the emphasis has always been on improving productivity per unit of land area in rice and other plant crops. Highly labor-intensive farming methods were developed as a result of the limited acreage allotted to each farm household. These agricultural characteristics gave rise to farming practices and folk customs that in turn profoundly affected the nature of Japanese culture as a whole. After the Meiji Restoration, Japan adopted a policy of changing its traditional agriculture-centered social and economic structure to one centered more on commerce and industry. The proportion of farmers to the total population, the proportion of acreage under cultivation to the total area of the country, and the relative importance of agriculture in the total economy have all declined, while the importation of foodstuffs has increased. The country's tendency toward urbanization has led to a cultural transformation, as agricultural practices have changed, and many of the events and customs of Japanese rural life have begun to lose their meaning. *TSUKUBA Hisaharu*

HISTORY OF AGRICULTURE

Many things are still unknown about the origins of Japanese agriculture, but it is clear that it began about 2,000 years ago with the cultivation of RICE. The rice plant and other important crops were introduced from abroad; very few wild plants have been cultivated in Japan. Efforts by scholars to trace the route that brought the rice plant to Japan have resulted in a variety of inconclusive theories. There is a corresponding lack of knowledge about the first cultivation of other imported crops, although it is certain that the variety of crops gradually increased. In addition to rice, the crops that have been cultivated in Japan since ancient times include wheat, barley, *awa* (Italian millet), *hie* (another variety of millet), SOYBEANS, AZUKI, *daikon* (see RADISHES), and CUCURBITS. In the 16th century, prior to the national seclusion policy adopted by the Tokugawa shogunate, trading ships from European countries often visited Japan and introduced many new foods.

Agriculture and Political Power —— The oldest farm tools were made of wood or stone; later the introduction of the technology of iron manufacturing from the continent made possible the use of iron farm tools. Consequently the yield per unit of area increased, much wasteland was brought under cultivation, and rapid progress in agriculture was made for the first time. The production and use of convenient iron farm tools was initially restricted to those who had access to the technology. These few were able to cultivate large areas of highly productive fields, and they became powerful families. It is presumed that one such family established dominance in struggles for power in ancient Japan and thus became the rulers of the Yamato court. This family then discontinued direct participation in agriculture and set up a tax system to collect part of the farmers' produce to finance their court. By the time of the Nara (710–794) and Heian (794–1185) periods, the ruling class—the imperial family, court nobles, and Buddhist priests—devoted themselves mainly to learning and arts. Ignorant and somewhat disdainful of the workings of agriculture, they made no effort to stimulate agricultural science, and virtually no books were written on the subject for centuries.

From the end of the Heian period, however, influential families emerged in the provinces and assumed increasing political power. These families of the military class accumulated wealth through agricultural production. Taking control of the government in the Kamakura period (1185–1333), they showed greater concern about agriculture than former rulers and encouraged improvements.

Around the beginning of the Edo period (1600–1868) the first Japanese agricultural treatise, volume seven of the military chronicle known as the SEIRYŌKI, was written. In the early part of the Edo period a number of agricultural books were published, the most famous being MIYAZAKI YASUSADA's NŌGYŌ ZENSHO (1696).

Edo Period —— The conditions of Japanese agriculture changed dramatically during the Edo period. With the emergence of a large number of cities and towns, predominant among them Edo (now Tōkyō) and Ōsaka, the percentage of the population not engaged in agriculture increased, and farmers were required to produce more and more. Intensive farming methods were adopted and the output of labor increased. Although hard work was lauded as a virtue, more than half of the rice produced was collected as land tax, and farmers were frequently left with insufficient amounts for their own needs. They made do with wheat, barley, or millet. Agricultural output was increased with endeavors in three major areas in the Edo period: reclaimed lands, fertilizers, and plant breeding. In the latter half of the period the development of *shinden* (reclaimed rice fields) was expedited through the digging of irrigation channels. Some of the irrigation systems and embankments constructed then still exist and demonstrate that a high standard of engineering had been attained by that time. The same technology was also used to build urban waterworks, but the details of their construction are not known. Fertilizers were beneficial in converting wasteland into fertile fields and increasing the yield of existing farms. It was common practice in ancient times to bury leaves and grasses as compost, but a faster method was needed to meet the demand for crops in the Edo period, and human feces became the main source of fertilizer. With the development of towns, this disposal method for human waste proved to be advantageous for both rural and urban communities. Though genetics did not exist then, experiments over a period of time bore new varieties of crops with excellent qualities, especially in the case of rice. One benefit of breeding was that new varieties led to higher yields without increasing the demand for labor. The cultivation of crops for direct sale in the marketplace also flourished in the Edo period, and this brought agriculture and commerce closer together. Continued peace kept city streets alive with people at night, and a great quantity of oil was consumed for light. Lamp oil was pressed from rapeseed, and the strained residue was utilized as fertilizer. This is one example of the many ways rural and urban areas became interdependent.

Modern Era —— During Japan's drive toward modernization after the Meiji Restoration (1868), in agriculture as in other areas European and American practices were studied closely. However, since the natural condition of the land in Japan is quite different from the West, mere transplantation of foreign technology often did not work as well in agriculture as in other sciences. For example, although strenuous efforts were made at the beginning of the Meiji period (1868–1912) to import new crops, fruit trees, flowers, domestic animals, and farm tools, with few exceptions these experiments failed. In many cases these vegetables and fruit trees that yielded major foods in Europe and America were damaged by blight and insects in Japan. As a result, emphasis was shifted back to rice as the main crop and the development of intensive farming methods. Japanese farms remained relatively small. When applicable, however, new scientific knowledge and new technologies were adopted enthusiastically. Elucidation of the physiology of plants and the composition of soil, for example, resulted in the development of chemical fertilizers which gradually replaced natural additives; especially widespread was the use of ammonium sulfate containing nitrogen. Plant breeding flourished with the development of new varieties by hybridization. Since the introduction and employment of these technologies required facilities beyond the capacity of most farmers, agriculture experimental stations were built by the state to conduct most of the plant breeding of important crops. Fertilizers were in great demand, and they became highly profitable commodities. A number of manufacturers grew into major corporations.

🔲 ——Furushima Toshio, *Nihon nōgyō gijutsu shi* (1954). Nakai Nobuhiko, *Nihon no nōgyō* (1969). Nōgyō Hattatsu Shi Chōsakai, ed, *Nihon nōgyō hattatsu shi*, 10 vols (Chūō Kōron Sha, 1953–58). Sunaga Shigemitsu, *Nihon nōgyō gijutsu ron* (1977). Tsukuba Hisaharu, *Nihon nōgyō gijutsu shi* (1959).   TSUKUBA Hisaharu

AGRICULTURAL MODERNIZATION

While much has been said about the industrial accomplishments of the Japanese "economic miracle," the equally impressive rationalization and modernization of agriculture has been largely a "quiet revo-

lution." Many of the highly publicized technological breakthroughs of the so-called green revolution had close parallels in Japan at an earlier time. In the post-World War II period, the most significant changes include the introduction of millions of farming machines; the hybridization of crops, especially rice; and the development of one of the world's largest and most advanced agricultural chemical industries.

One of the most important aspects of this revolution has been a sharp drop in the proportion of the working population engaged in agriculture from nearly 50 percent in 1945 to below 10 percent by the late 1970s. The latter figure approaches that of most Western European nations and is well below that of the Soviet Union. The decline in Japan's farming population did not lead to a decline in output per unit of land; on the contrary, both land and labor productivity have increased steadily. The average yield per area of land in Japan is among the highest in the world. Heavy investments in machinery, high-yield crop strains, and chemicals have made it possible for Japanese farmers to attain one of the highest levels of labor productivity. Perhaps the most surprising result of the agricultural revolution has been the surplus production of rice and the emergence of marketing and storage problems not unlike those involving wheat in the United States, though on a much smaller scale.

Land Reform and Migration —— Of all the reform programs that followed the conclusion of World War II, the LAND REFORMS OF 1946 were perhaps the most successful in bringing about basic and far-reaching changes in Japan. A sweeping redistribution of land largely eliminated tenancy by 1949 and resulted in about 90 percent of cultivated land being farmed by its owner. Confiscated land was sold to the new owners at very low prices with long-term, low-interest mortgages. Postwar food shortages, high prices, an active black market in rice, and general inflation all worked to the advantage of Japan's farmers. In most cases they were able to pay off the debts on their new land with relative ease and to begin investing the capital that was needed for the rationalization of agriculture. The government aided farmers by establishing price support programs, especially for rice (see RICE PRICE CONTROLS). It also gave strong support to agricultural technical schools, experimental stations, and extension programs throughout the rural areas. AGRICULTURAL COOPERATIVE ASSOCIATIONS played important roles through the extension of low-interest loans and the development of group marketing at the village level. The end result was a relatively affluent farming population with the education, incentive, and access to capital needed to purchase the new crop strains and fertilizers to increase yields, as well as the machinery to ease labor demand and increase capacity and flexibility.

Japan began to experience labor shortages by the late 1950s after the beginning of rapid economic growth. The demand for labor in the urban-industrial centers resulted in a growing exodus of people from rural areas, especially younger people. The farm population declined by a third between 1960 and 1975, leading to serious and chronic labor shortages in the agricultural sector. It seems quite unlikely that Japanese agriculture could have succeeded without the spread of machines, chemicals, and other labor-saving devices that paralleled the explosive growth of manufacturing and commerce. A large part of the present agricultural labor force is over 45 years of age, part-time farmers are numerous, and well over half the labor force is female. About 5 percent of new entrants into the labor force choose farming (see the section on farmland within this article).

Postwar Changes in Farming —— Changes in the rural areas of Japan since the mid-1950s have been extraordinary. There has been a dramatic improvement in the standard of living of the Japanese farmer, manifested at the most graphic level by the brightly roofed farmhouses that dot the countryside. Most Japanese farmhouses also have the same high diffusion rates for color TVs, washers, refrigerators, and other appliances found in most urban homes. Another outstanding feature of modernization has been in the area of mechanization. Traditional draft animals and plows have been replaced by power cultivators and tractors. Virtually all land is now cultivated by machine. Traditional methods of hand harvesting are rapidly giving way to power harvesters and combines. In addition, threshers, hullers, pumps, and other machines, including pickup trucks, are in wide use. Portable vinyl greenhouses are an integral part of Japan's agrarian revolution.

The most interesting and widely used machine is the single-axle (or walking) power cultivator. This hand tractor, sometimes referred to as the "iron buffalo" in Asia, had a major impact on Japanese agriculture; it is an outstanding example of the country's potential

Agriculture ——— Terrace farming

A farming couple tend their plots of sweet potatoes on the rugged coast of southwestern Ehime Prefecture, Shikoku. Terrace farming has long been practiced throughout Japan in order to exploit the limited amount of arable land most effectively.

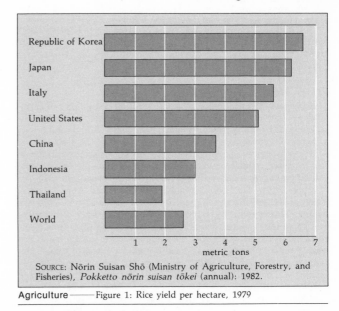

SOURCE: Nōrin Suisan Shō (Ministry of Agriculture, Forestry, and Fisheries), *Pokketto nōrin suisan tōkei* (annual): 1982.

Agriculture ——— Figure 1: Rice yield per hectare, 1979

Agriculture ——— Table 1

			Agricultural Machinery in Use			
	Power cultivators	Riding tractors	Power rice-planting machines	Power reapers	Combines	Farm trucks
1965	2,490,000	18,900	—	—	—	418,000
1968	3,030,460	124,280	—	—	—	864,290
1971	3,201,400	267,210	46,160	582,070	84,190	1,015,070
1974	3,374,910	339,030	434,550	1,218,230	217,070	1,198,870
1977	3,182,370	832,280	1,247,250	1,579,340	525,120	1,372,690
1980	2,752,000	1,471,000	1,746,000	1,619,000	884,000	—

SOURCE: Prime Minister's Office, Statistics Bureau, *Japan Statistical Yearbook* (annual): 1976 and 1981.

for explosive change and growth. The number of these hand tractors grew from 85,000 in 1955 to 2.5 million in 1965, and was close to 3.5 million by 1974. Though they are smaller in horsepower, these machines numbered more than the total tractors in the Soviet Union in the mid-1970s. As demonstrated by its obvious popularity, the hand tractor has become an indispensable piece of farming equipment in Japan. The prototype of the present hand tractor was introduced to Japan from Switzerland and modified to fit the needs of wet-field rice cultivation. One of its most interesting features is its interchangeable wheels: lugged-metal wheels for use in wet-paddy fields and rubber-tired wheels for dry-land cultivation. It can be fitted with special attachments to power a wide range of equipment, including hoes, plows, pumps, threshers, and sprayers. Walking tractors are economical in terms of fuel and are relatively easy and inexpensive to operate and maintain. In recent years, small- and medium-size all-purpose riding tractors have been substituted, with the number of these in operation increasing from about 20,000 in 1965 to 1,471,000 in 1980. The combined total for walking and riding tractors was over 4.2 million in 1980.

During the 1970s an explosive growth in mechanization took place in the harvesting and the planting and transplanting of rice and other crops. Power harvesters increased sharply from 582,070 in 1971 to 1,619,000 in 1980. Corresponding figures for combines were 84,190 in 1971 and 884,000 in 1980. According to Japan's Statistics Bureau, the number of motor-driven rice-planting machines rose from 46,160 in 1971 to 1,746,000 in 1980. In addition, power sprayers and dusters each numbered about 1.5 million units. Rice production in Japan is nearing a state of total mechanization, though some technical problems remain, especially in the area of planting and transplanting. The agricultural machinery industry and experimental stations are continuing their efforts to improve the design and efficiency of planting and transplanting machines. With the new machines, higher-yielding strains, and heavy applications of chemicals (fertilizers, pesticides, and insecticides), Japan's total rice crop

increased from about 8.6 million metric tons (9.5 million short tons) in 1950 to over 11.8 million metric tons (13 million short tons) in 1975. Per capita consumption of rice has declined, and the government is now concerned with problems of overproduction and surplus storage. Government planners are trying to find ways to reduce the size of Japan's rice crop in order to bring it into closer balance with consumer demand. Farmers are being encouraged, and in some cases subsidized, to convert their rice fields to other crops. With Japan's new affluence and changing dietary habits, the rationalization of agriculture has led to high growth rates in the production of meat and dairy products. The production of fresh fruits and vegetables has also increased dramatically as the proportion of grain and grain by-products in the Japanese diet continues to decline.

Japan's traditional labor-intensive agriculture has been transformed into a highly mechanized and capital-intensive system in less than a generation. It remains one of the most productive systems in the world and much of its new technology serves as a model for other developing Asian nations. Some problems and questions remain for the future. Production costs, especially for rice, are very high, and Japanese agriculture requires heavy subsidies, as is true for most Western nations. Most farms are too small in scale for the maximum utilization of land and capital, and operating units should be larger. When and how Japanese farms will reach a more rational size remains a question for the future.

■ ——— Association of Agricultural Relations in Asia, *Equipment for Agricultural Modernization of Japan* (1969). Council for Industry Planning, *Japanese Agriculture Fifteen Years Hence (1980)* (1969). Robert B. Hall, Jr, *Japan: Industrial Power of Asia* (1976). Yūjirō Hayami et al, *A Century of Agricultural Growth in Japan: Its Relevance to Asian Development* (1975). International Society for Educational Information, Inc, *Atlas of Japan: Physical, Economic and Social* (1970). Japan Institute of International Affairs, *White Papers of Japan, 1974/75* (1976). Kazushi Ohkawa, B. Johnson, and H. Kaneda, ed, *Agriculture and Economic Growth: Japan's Experience* (1970). Oriental Economist, ed, *Japan Economic Yearbook* (annual). Statistics Bureau, Prime Minister's Office, *Japan Statistical Yearbook* (1982). The Tsuneta Yano Memorial Society, *Nippon: A Chartered Survey of Japan, 1978/79* (1978).   Robert B. HALL

FARMLAND

The primary factors determining the amount and quality of farmland are climate, topography, geological features, and soil. The Japanese CLIMATE is generally mild, with heavy rainfall and a long growing season, except in Hokkaidō and a part of the alpine zones. The southwestern region is frequently hit by typhoons peculiar to the monsoon climate and is susceptible to damage by flooding caused by strong winds and heavy rains. In the areas facing the Sea of Japan and in the Tōhoku region, agriculture and social and economic activities are also limited by heavy snow accumulations in winter. Topographically, Japan is small but extends far latitudinally, and mountain ranges run in all directions, causing a remarkable variation in temperature from the southern to the northern end and from the plains to highlands. Land is used for single to triple cropping; a great variety of crops is grown and growing methods are diverse. The mountains account for 71 percent of the land, and farmland constitutes only 14.8 percent of the total land area.

Japan abounds in VOLCANOES and most fields have been reclaimed from volcanic ash, which is highly acidic and has low productivity. Iron and aluminum oxide absorb phosphoric acid, resulting in a tendency toward phosphoric acid deficiency. Therefore, fertilizers and composting are required to neutralize the soil. Paddy fields are located primarily in alluvial plains, where irrigation water from rivers supplies various nutrients and freshwater weeds provide atmospheric nitrogen to make the paddies fertile. But there are many old paddy fields that have lost iron and generated hydrogen sulfide, which damages the roots of the rice plant.

The total area under cultivation in 1980 was 5.5 million hectares (13.6 million acres), of which 56 percent was paddy fields and 44 percent other fields. In Japanese agriculture there used to be "three invariable figures," which were the number of farm households, the acreage of land under cultivation, and the number of agricultural laborers. These three figures did not change significantly until recently. They were maintained at a level of 5.5 million households, 6 million hectares (14.8 million acres), and 14 million people, except during World War II and the subsequent land reform period. This ratio, however, crumbled rapidly during the period of high economic growth after 1955, and as of 1980 the figures stood at 4.7 million households, 5.5 million hectares (13.6 million acres), and 7.0 million people. These figures reflect a drop in the share of agriculture in the national economy. The characteristics of Japanese agriculture—improving productivity by labor-intensive paddy-field farming and using surplus farm labor as temporary help in other industries—have been undermined by high economic growth. The "agriculture-first" spirit of labor (see NŌHON SHUGI) has been abandoned, and the idea that there should be an income balance, not only between agriculture and other industries but also among various sectors of agriculture, has prevailed. The results are accelerating trends toward a rural exodus, part-time farming, and working away from home (DEKASEGI). The mechanization of agriculture and formation of major production districts have resulted in a movement toward mass production. However, the extraordinarily high price of land has impeded the development of mass operations which require enlarging the scale of farming. The problem of the ownership of farms must be solved before the industry can grow.

In 1980 there was a total of 4.7 million farm households, of which 13.4 percent farmed full-time and 86.6 percent farmed part-time. Of the part-time farm households, the number of households primarily engaged in farming, or first-class farm households, was 1 million and the number mainly engaged in other jobs, or second-class farm households, was 3 million. The number of farm households classified below by the area of cultivated land represents those of prefectures other than Hokkaidō, where it is cold, agriculture consists mainly of field crops and dairy farming, and the scale and operation are different than in other regions. Farm households outside of Hokkaidō totaled 4.5 million in 1980, of which households with cultivated land under 0.5 hectares (1.2 acres) numbered 1.9 million (42.3 percent); households with cultivated land of 0.5–1.0 hectares (1.2–2.5 acres) numbered 1.3 million (28.7 percent); households with cultivated land of 1.0–1.5 hectares (2.5–3.7 acres) numbered 652,000 (14.4 percent); and households with cultivated land of 1.5 hectares (3.7 acres) or more numbered 663,000 (14.6 percent).

Agriculture ——— Hand tractor

A hand tractor being used to cultivate a drained rice paddy. The rubber-tired wheels used for dry-land cultivation that are seen here can be replaced by lugged metal wheels when working in wet-paddy fields.

These figures indicate that the overwhelming majority are paddy farmers, who at the same time hold side jobs. This is due to the fact that both the recent progress in labor-saving techniques in rice-plant cultivation and farming by contract have made it possible to carry on agriculture as a side job. In fact, the development of extensive moonlighting has solved the problem of poverty that has plagued Japanese farmers. The ratio of dependency on agriculture of a farm household (agricultural income/income of a farm household × 100) was under 50 percent in 1965 and dropped further to 21.1 percent in 1980. As a result, the average farmer's income surpassed other workers' incomes: the average annual total income for a farming family (including *dekasegi* income, grants, and subsidies) in 1980 was ¥5.6 million (US $24,697), or ¥1.14 million (US $5,028) higher than other workers'. The total annual income per capita in agriculture was ¥1.27 million (US $5,600), or ¥157,700 (US $695) more than other workers'.   KAWAMOTO Akira

PLANT CROPS

Over 400 species of crop plant are cultivated in Japan; of these over half are food crops and the rest are industrial and forage crops. Japan's food crops are notably rich in variety. For example, 120 different species of vegetables are grown, more than in France (about 100 species) or the United States (about 90 species). In addition, there are 85 species of fruit trees, 14 species of pulse (pea and bean crops), 13 species of cereal, 7 species of tuber, 5 fungi, and 4 water plants grown commercially. This broad variety is partially due to the wide range of CLIMATE in Japan, from the cold regions of the north to the subtropical zone in the south. A more important reason is that the Japanese have introduced many foreign food crops. Although Japan has an abundance of common flora, indigenous crops are few. They include FUKI (butterbur), *wasabi* (Japanese horseradish), *udo* (salad plant), and *mitsuba* (*Cryptotaenia japonica*) among vegetables; *kuri* (Japanese chestnut), *kaki* (persimmon), and *nashi* (Japanese sand pear) among fruits; and *hakka* (mint) and *mitsumata* (*Edgeworthia papyrifera*) among industrial crops. Because of the small number of indigenous plants, the Japanese have been introducing food crops from the Chinese continent for over 2,000 years. Several European food crops that reached China by way of the SILK ROAD were also introduced to Japan. Many more European and American food crops were introduced after the Meiji Restoration of 1868, and most of the main European and American food crops are now grown in Japan, usually on extremely limited acreage.

The most important of all crops in Japan is RICE, the nation's staple food. Of the total area of 5.5 million hectares (13.6 million acres) under cultivation in Japan as of 1980, paddies occupied 3 million hectares (7.4 million acres), and produced 10 million metric tons (11 million short tons) of unpolished rice. WHEAT AND BARLEY were also introduced from China sometime in the 3rd or 4th century and grown as staple foods auxiliary to rice, often in paddies that were drained after the rice had been harvested. Until 1960 a total area of 1.5 million hectares (3.7 million acres) was devoted to wheat and barley, and annual production amounted to 3.6 million metric

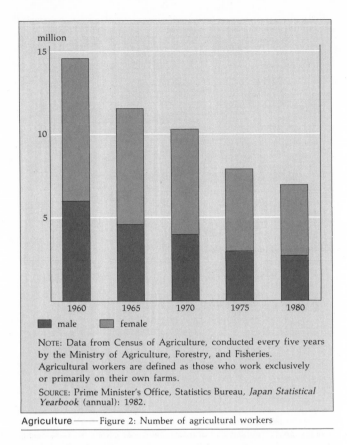

Agriculture——Figure 2: Number of agricultural workers

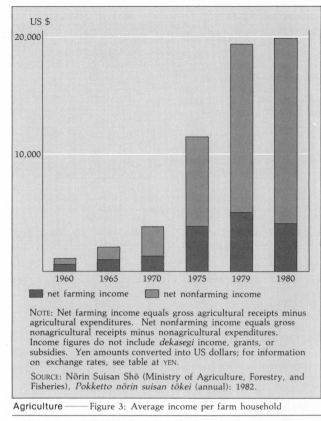

Agriculture——Figure 3: Average income per farm household

tons (4 million short tons). Because of the small acreage of Japan's family farms and their resultant inefficiency, large quantities of inexpensive wheat and barley have been imported from the United States since then, and their cultivation as secondary crops in paddies has largely been discontinued. Imports of millet and buckwheat have also increased, and domestic production is almost nonexistent. In 1980 sweet corn (maize) was grown on 34,000 hectares (84,000 acres), and green feed corn on 112,000 hectares (277,000 acres), but corn was rarely grown as a grain crop. About 320,000 metric tons (352,000 short tons) of pulses were produced, of which SOYBEANS accounted for about 174,000 metric tons (191,400 short tons), satisfying only 4 percent of the domestic demand. As with cereal crops other than rice, pulse cultivation was in a state of decline; one exception was the AZUKI bean, of which the annual crop of about 100,000 metric tons (110,000 short tons) has been maintained.

Among vegetables, RADISHES *(daikon)* are produced in greatest abundance, followed by Chinese cabbage, as shown in Table 2. In addition to the crops shown in the table, numerous leaf and root vegetables are grown for pickling purposes and are an important element in traditional Japanese meals. As the habit of eating Western food has become widespread, the cultivation of cabbage, onions, cucumbers, tomatoes, lettuce, and cauliflower has increased. Traditional Japanese vegetables include Welsh onion *(negi)*, scallion *(rakkyō)*, taro *(satoimo)*, great burdock *(gobō)*, lotus root *(renkon)*, arrowhead *(kuwai)*, Chinese yam *(nagaimo)*, butterbur *(fuki)*, bamboo shoots *(takenoko)*, and Japanese horseradish *(wasabi)*.

In 1980 fruit trees were being grown on about 408,000 hectares (1,010,000 acres) throughout the country; the principal types are shown in Table 3. The most important fruit is the mandarin orange (see MIKAN), which grows in the warm areas of central and western Japan. This is a tangerinelike fruit of excellent quality which was developed in Japan about 300 years ago from a mutation of a variety of orange introduced from China. The second most important orchard fruit is the apple, which was introduced mainly from the United States in the Meiji period (1868–1912) and is grown from central to northern Honshū. Apple and mandarin orange production thus divides the area of Japanese fruit tree cultivation into northern and southern zones. Fruits indigenous to Japan, the chestnut, persimmon, and Japanese sand pear, occupy the 3rd, 5th, and 6th places, respectively, in terms of area under cultivation. The chestnut, persimmon, Japanese plum, and walnut are grown in farmyards for household consumption as well as in orchards. Most of the Japanese fruits, including mandarin oranges, apples, GRAPES, and

PEACHES, are produced for eating fresh and are rarely processed. In warm places of Japan many kinds of citrus fruits are grown. Tropical fruits such as pineapples, bananas, and papayas are grown in limited quantities from Kagoshima to Okinawa. In cooler regions, berries can be grown, but commercial growing is not highly developed.

MUSHROOMS such as *shiitake, enokitake, hiratake,* and *nameko* are cultivated artificially and are in much demand. White mushrooms introduced from Europe are also grown. Green TEA is grown on about 61,000 hectares (150,000 acres), producing about 100,000 metric tons (110,000 short tons) a year. Rush used in making the TATAMI (floor mats) for traditional Japanese-style rooms is grown on about 10,000 hectares (25,000 acres) of paddies, mainly in western Japan. Konjak tuber *(konnyaku)* to be processed for food is cultivated in mountainous areas, with an annual production of about 100,000 metric tons (110,000 short tons). TOBACCO, sugar beets, and sugarcane are also grown, but production is decreasing, as is production of such industrial crops as sesame, rape, and flax. Industrial plants indigenous to Japan are mint, *urushi* (the Japanese LACQUER TREE), and two materials for Japanese paper, *mitsumata* and *kōzo* (paper mulberry; *Broussonelia kajinoki*). Many medicinal herbs are also grown, including ginseng *(chōsen ninjin)*, digitalis, Chinese bellflower (KIKYŌ), rhubarb, senega, and PEONIES. The Japanese INDIGO plant *(tadeai)* is grown for traditional dyes, and dyer's saffron *(benibana)* is produced in small amounts for traditional cosmetics. Mulberry trees for silk production are grown on about 120,000 hectares (300,000 acres) throughout the country. A major cash crop before World War II, silk is now declining gradually. Feed crops for livestock such as orchard grass, Italian rye grass, ladino clover, and alfalfa are grown on 788,000 hectares (1.95 million acres). Corn is the feed crop grown in most quantity, followed by sorghum and sunflowers. Most of these crops are temperate grasses introduced after the Meiji Restoration (1868) or tropical grasses introduced more recently.

📖——Hoshikawa Kiyochika, *Shokuyō sakumotsu* (1980). Nōrin Suisan Shō, *Pokketto nōrin suisan tōkei* (1982).

Hoshikawa Kiyochika

LIVESTOCK

Farmers engaged in animal husbandry in Japan are relatively few, and herd size per family is small; the total area devoted to grassland (about 788,000 hectares or 1.95 million acres) and to growing feed crops (about 975,000 hectares or 2.41 million acres) is also small.

Agriculture —— Table 2

Production of Principal Vegetables, 1980

Crop	Production (metric tons)	Area planted (hectares)
Japanese white radish (daikon)	2,689,000	72,500
Chinese cabbage	1,616,000	38,500
Cabbage	1,545,000	42,700
Onion	1,152,000	28,200
Cucumber	1,018,000	25,300
Tomato	1,014,000	19,300
Watermelon	975,700	33,000
Eggplant	618,700	21,500
Carrot	599,100	24,100
Welsh onion (negi)	538,900	23,800
Taro (satoimo)	458,300	31,700
Lettuce	380,900	18,400
Spinach	352,100	23,800
Green corn	311,900	30,400
Melon	263,900	13,100
Pumpkin and squash	252,000	16,200
Great burdock (gobō)	249,000	13,900
Strawberry	193,300	11,900
Turnip	193,100	7,680
Sweet pepper	161,400	4,730

NOTE: For statistical purposes, the Ministry of Agriculture, Forestry, and Fisheries classifies watermelon, melon, and strawberry as vegetables.
SOURCE: Nōrin Suisan Shō (Ministry of Agriculture, Forestry, and Fisheries), Nōgyō hakusho fuzoku tōkeihyō (annual): 1981.

Agriculture —— Table 3

Production of Principal Fruits, 1980

Fruit	Production (metric tons)	Area planted (hectares)
Mandarin orange (mikan)	2,892,000	139,600
Apple	960,100	51,200
Japanese sand pear (nashi)	484,600	19,900
Watson pomelo (natsumikan)	366,200	15,600
Grape	323,200	30,300
Persimmon (kaki)	265,200	29,400
Peach	244,600	16,500
Hassaku orange	210,300	9,420
Iyokan orange	91,400	7,670
Japanese plum (ume)	64,000	15,900
Pineapple	56,200	3,200
Chestnut (kuri)	47,000	44,100
Navel orange	35,300	3,800
Plum	27,900	2,950
Cherry	15,100	2,780
Loquat	14,200	2,420
Occidental pear	11,200	851

SOURCE: Nōrin Suisan Shō (Ministry of Agriculture, Forestry, and Fisheries), Nōgyō hakusho fuzoku tōkeihyō (annual): 1981. Nōrin Suisan Shō, Poketto nōrin suisan tōkei (annual): 1982.

The high temperatures and humidity of the Japanese summer cause excessive growth of grass; the low temperatures and dryness of the winter cause excessive drying. Grass is harvested abundantly in summer, but high-quality hay is difficult to obtain. Many areas have volcanic-ash soils unsuitable for growing leguminous plants such as alfalfa. These conditions create a low self-sufficiency rate for livestock feed, and the limited amount of grazing land also causes high fixed material costs and labor costs. As a result of all these factors, livestock production costs are high.

Animal bones among the articles unearthed from archaeological sites reveal that the Japanese ate animal flesh in ancient times, but the animals were caught by hunters rather than raised as livestock. The livestock introduced from the Asian mainland were employed as a source of muscle power rather than of food, and domestic fowl were kept as pets. Horses were valued mainly for their military role during the many centuries of samurai ascendancy. In ancient times milk was drunk for medicinal purposes at the imperial court, but consumption of products of four-footed beasts was strictly prohibited after the introduction of Buddhism to Japan in the 6th century AD. In the Meiji period (1868–1912), the consumption of animal products began under the influence of the West, but was small in volume. During the agricultural depression that lasted from the end of the Taishō period (1912–26) through the early years of the Shōwa period (1926–), farmers found they could maintain their farms successfully under unfavorable conditions by raising livestock. As a result, animal husbandry was encouraged nationwide, but livestock was still used primarily for work and as a source of manure, i.e., as an auxiliary to crop farming.

After World War II, the shortage of rice and the increased consumption of wheat flour led to increased consumption of milk, meat, and eggs. This increase has continued ever since at a rate of about 10 percent yearly. In response to this trend, the number of farmers raising livestock also increased; at the same time, the mechanization of agriculture released domestic animals from their work functions and these animals began to be raised for their products. After reaching a peak in the 1950s, the number of livestock-raising households gradually decreased as inexperienced farmers dropped out. In the years of high economic growth from about 1960, however, animal husbandry expanded again as a highly specialized branch of agriculture, with a rapid rise in the average number of animals per farm. For example, the average number of hogs raised by a farming family, in 1960 as low as 2.4, had by 1981 increased to 80, and broiler chickens had reached the level of 15,000 per operation. This reflects yearly increases of about 10 percent in the total number of animals raised and total livestock production, matching Japan's annual increases in consumption.

Native breeds are found in a few species such as CATTLE, HORSES, goats, rabbits, and domestic fowl (see CHICKEN, JAPANESE), but all of Japan's stocks of hogs and sheep were introduced from foreign countries after the Meiji Restoration of 1868. However, Japanese breeders are constantly seeking improvements, and activities are carried on intensively, so the productivity of Japanese livestock is quite high. Horses have a long history in Japan as draft animals, but the mechanization of agriculture has caused a decrease in their number; in 1981 only about 24,000 remained, the majority being racehorses. Cattle, too, were long used as draft animals. In recent years the breeding of dairy cattle has increased, with 2.1 million head and an annual yield of about 6.6 million metric tons (7.3 million short tons) of milk in 1981. Beef cattle have increased to about 2.3 million, yielding about 471,000 metric tons (518,000 short tons) of meat. The present demand for beef far exceeds domestic production, and about 174,000 metric tons (191,000 short tons) were imported in 1980. Hogs numbered 10 million with a yield of 1.4 million metric tons (1.5 million short tons) of pork in 1981, but about 109,000 metric tons (120,000 short tons) were still imported. Chickens raised for egg-laying numbered 165 million in 1981 with an annual production of 2 million metric tons (2.2 million short tons) of eggs. Sheep, goats, rabbits, and mink are also raised, but in quite limited numbers. Quails are raised in small numbers for eggs and meat, and other birds such as ducks and turkeys are even less common.

—— Naitō Motoo, Chikusan daijiten (Yōkendō, 1978).

NAITŌ Motoo

FARMING TECHNIQUES

Farming techniques in Japan have shown a wide range of responses to varying conditions in each region of the country and in different historical periods. Current conditions are best described by examining recent developments in the areas of rice planting, dry field farming, irrigation, land improvement, animal husbandry, horticulture, breeding, agricultural implements, fertilizers, agricultural chemicals, and control of plant diseases and insect pests.

Rice Planting —— Rice cultivation is thought to have originated in the area encompassing the eastern part of India, Burma, Thailand, and the southern part of China, perhaps in the period from 10,000 BC through 4000 BC. In Japan, rice cultivation was introduced to the northern Kyūshū area in the Yayoi period (ca 300 BC–ca AD 300), to the Kinki (Nara–Kyōto) area in the 1st century AD, to the Kantō (Tōkyō) area in the 3rd century AD, and to Hokkaidō in 1885. The northern limit for rice planting in Japan is considered to be the vicin-

Agriculture —— Table 4

			Livestock Raised (in thousands of animals)				
	1950	1955	1960	1965	1970	1975	1981
Dairy cattle	198	421	824	1,289	1,804	1,787	2,104
Beef cattle	2,252	2,636	2,340	1,886	1,789	1,857	2,281
Hogs	608	825	1,918	3,976	6,335	7,684	10,065
Horses	1,071	927	673	322	137	43	24
Goats	413	533	561	325	161	111	62
Chickens Layers	16,545	45,715	52,153	120,197	169,789	154,504	164,716
Broilers				18,279	53,742	87,659	131,252

SOURCE: Prime Minister's Office, Statistics Bureau, *Japan Statistical Yearbook* (annual): 1982.

ity of Abashiri in Hokkaidō, and the highest altitude for rice planting is about 1,200–1,600 meters (3,900–5,200 ft) above sea level in the piedmont areas of Nagano and Yamanashi prefectures.

Weather conditions in July and August are critically important to the growth of rice plants, particularly because of their effects on the duration of sunshine and atmospheric and water temperatures. For this reason rice planting techniques differ considerably from region to region in Japan. In Hokkaidō and Tōhoku, the coldest regions, farmers must be extremely careful to avoid problems arising from cool summer weather. Protected rice nurseries and growth control techniques are utilized to keep the average temperature above 17°C (63°F) during the plant's panicle formation stage, thus avoiding damage from floral impotence, and to maintain a temperature of 10°C (50°F) when the plants ripen, thus avoiding damage from delayed growth. These measures have ensured abundant harvests at low cost. In the warm and humid areas of southwestern Japan, where the water temperature in the paddy field sometimes rises to 30°–40°C (86°–104°F) in summer, and typhoons are frequent in early autumn, special strains of rice with high levels of thermosensitivity are grown, and the harvest is finished by the middle of August. In the areas where the average atmospheric temperature is 17°C (63°F), double-cropping of rice plants is practiced. Rice production in Japan is now thoroughly mechanized at all stages from the transplanting of young seedlings to tending and harvesting.

Dry Field Farming —— Since the Edo period (1600–1868), landowners have placed special emphasis on rice growing in their efforts to improve farmland and develop better varieties of plants. Dry field farming techniques, therefore, were less advanced than their paddy field counterparts, except for some industrial crops. Since 1959, however, the development of dry field farming technology has received a new impetus from the government's farming promotion policy. As with rice, each region of Japan has its own special type of dry field farming. The most representative form is seen in Hokkaidō, where dry fields account for 73 percent of the total cultivated area (1980). Since the severely cold Hokkaidō winter precludes winter crops, the main products are feed crops (corn, oats, rye, soybeans, beets, and turnips), followed by pulses (soybeans, snap beans, and AZUKI beans), potatoes, sugar beets, and wheat. The average scale of operation per farming family in Hokkaidō is the largest in Japan. Soybeans, cereals, and vegetables are abundantly cultivated in the Tōhoku region, where the temperature is low and the growing period for summer crops is short. Dry field agriculture in central Honshū is characterized by truck farming operations with heavy production of vegetables; sweet potatoes, potatoes, and soybeans are cultivated in some areas. In Kyūshū, where the climate is mild, rains frequent, and the soil volcanic ash with low productivity, dry field farming centers on sweet potatoes, wheat, barley, buckwheat, Italian millet, tobacco, and sugarcane, with vegetables cultivated intensively in some areas. In Shikoku and the islands of the Inland Sea, where terraced fields have developed, a mild climate and long sunlight hours encourage the cultivation of sweet potatoes, potatoes, tobacco, vegetables, and fruit trees, although the operating area of each farming family is small. In the dune areas along the Sea of Japan, where there is great variation between daytime and nighttime temperatures, the late raising and forced culture of vegetables (watermelons, squashes, tomatoes, Chinese yams, and onions) is practiced. As previously mentioned, each region has developed its own production techniques for dry field farming and has attained fairly high levels of productivity through such practices as crop rotation, double-cropping (with spring and summer or summer and autumn crops),

and triple-cropping (with spring, summer, and autumn crops). Thoroughly mechanized farming systems featuring a wide variety of machines, both small and large, have also been developed and put into use; in the case of wheat in Hokkaidō, such systems have reduced average work hours by more than 30 percent.

Irrigation —— Rice paddies in Japan total some 3.1 million hectares (7.66 million acres), accounting for 8.2 percent of the country's entire land area, and the quantity of water used for paddy-rice cultivation reaches 56 billion metric tons (61.7 billion short tons) annually. This huge amount of water is brought to the paddies from lakes, rivers, reservoirs, and wells by means of dams, floodgates, waterways, tunnels, siphons, pumps, water taps, and various other irrigation facilities. These facilities have been created to ensure the supply of adequate quantities of water at the appropriate time in the course of the rice plants' growth. Dry fields, which measure some 2.4 million hectares (5.9 million acres) in area, require 1 billion metric tons (1.1 billion short tons) of water annually. In areas specializing in outdoor cultivation of vegetables, greenhouse horticulture, and fruit raising, highly advanced irrigation techniques have produced excellent results with such crops as sweet peppers, tomatoes, cucumbers, eggplants, okra, and taros. Sprinklers and other equipment are used extensively. Special irrigation techniques are essential for greenhouse cultivation of cucumbers, tomatoes, sweet peppers, melons, grapes, and flowers; some greenhouse irrigation systems operate automatically, receiving vital clues from changes in soil moisture, temperature, and relative humidity.

Land Improvement —— Land improvement works in Japan include land reclamation, dredging, securing of irrigation water, irrigation of dry fields, drainage, improvement of soils, and land readjustment. The creation of new areas of arable land through reclamation was actively promoted in the years during and after World War II, a period of chronic food shortages in Japan. As a result, some 400,000 hectares (990,000 acres) of new farmland were created. One of Japan's largest reclamation projects is in HACHIRŌ-GATA, a giant lagoon in Akita Prefecture, where construction of embankments for reclamation, begun in 1957, was completed in 1966. Of the lagoon's original 22,000 hectares (54,000 acres), 17,200 hectares (42,500 acres) have been reclaimed and divided into standardized sectors of 60 hectares (150 acres) for mechanized cultivation. Improvement of Hachirōgata's soil, including elimination of salt and adjustment of acidity, is also being carried out systematically.

Various kinds of hydrologic projects to upgrade irrigation facilities in both paddy and dry field areas are currently underway. Land improvement projects, which once centered on paddy fields, are now extended to dry fields as well. Drainage operations have been planned to eliminate excess groundwater, with pumps and underdrainage systems used to improve land productivity in low and moist areas. For improvement of soils, soil dressing is being conducted on paddies in peat-bog areas as well as on exhausted and polluted paddies, while soil-improving agents and trace elements are applied to dry fields. Japanese agricultural and horticultural activities have long been hampered by the limited areas and often irregular shapes of arable land plots. Therefore, adjustment and realignment of arable land have received top priority in the government's plans to improve agricultural structure and in land consolidation projects, and have contributed greatly to the rise in agricultural productivity.

Animal Husbandry —— Animal husbandry in Japan once depended heavily on stall feeding rather than grazing because of the country's limited amount of open space and heavy precipitation.

After World War II, however, increased demand for dairy products and the widespread use of agricultural machinery radically changed the nature of Japan's livestock industry. The emphasis is now on raising domestic animals for meat and other foodstuff purposes, not for working purposes. Dairy cattle, beef cattle, pigs, and chickens are now bred on a massive scale. Breeding of hardy and highly productive varieties and strains suitable for mass production is being conducted; a variety of techniques, including sperm freezing, artificial insemination, and embryo transfer, is being developed and put to use, while qualitative improvement of domestic animals is being promoted through genetic research. The improvement of barns is also being emphasized; it is making great contributions in extending the life span of animals and increasing both the productivity of animals and the quality of livestock products. To cope with the adverse environmental effects of animal excrement accumulated in and near breeding areas, excrement-processing techniques have been developed and put into use.

Horticulture —— In the Edo period (1600–1868), cultivation of commercial crops on a large scale in paddies and dry fields was prohibited. Commercial and horticultural crops, therefore, were cultivated on a very small scale around houses and on newly developed land. It was only in the Meiji period (1868–1912) that large-scale commercial cultivation of fruit trees and vegetables was begun. In parallel with the development of the Japanese economy in later years, horticulture grew rapidly with the help of plant strains introduced from foreign countries. The Meiji government encouraged the introduction of apples, pears, grapes, oranges, and peaches, and played an important part in the subsequent popularization of fruit tree cultivation. Recent improved techniques in fruit growth control have led to reductions in production costs and work hours. Ripening-period controlling agents, crop-thinning agents, and coating agents are being developed and utilized. To make agricultural work easier, dwarf fruit trees are grown, and development of grafting stocks and better pruning techniques has been promoted. Mechanization of fruit tree cultivation is also underway.

Disease-resistant and highly productive hybrid varieties of many fruits and vegetables are grown to ensure a steady year-round supply of produce. Mass cultivation of virus-free strawberry plants has enabled healthy seedlings to be supplied to cultivators in great numbers; for tomatoes and melons, tests for resistance to fruit splitting have led to production of fruits of excellent quality. New, improved varieties of flowering plants and trees have been developed, especially of such popular flowers as chrysanthemums, lilies, camellias, and azaleas. New techniques for propagating seedlings and controlling growth rates, flowering periods, and dormant periods of flowering plants have also been introduced.

New Varieties —— In the Edo period, plant breeding was carried out close to the place of cultivation, and varieties with outstanding qualities were selected and improved by diligent farmers (RŌNŌ). In the Meiji period, introduction and trial cultivation of high-quality plants originating in Western countries were encouraged by the government in the course of its agricultural promotion program. As cross-breeding techniques based on the principles of genetics were introduced in the Taishō period (1912–26), propagation and widespread distribution of imported plants and their varieties by the pure-line selection process was replaced by improvement of varieties by cross-breeding. At present, breeding projects are conducted for a very wide range of plants, with most of the work done at national and public research stations. Breeding experiments with domestic animals and silkworms are also conducted at national and public research institutes. The main characteristics sought are higher yield, disease resistance, insect resistance, and longer storage life; widely used breeding methods include hybridization, mutation breeding by radiation, breeding by tissue culture and by utilization of haploids or polyploids. Breeding operations at national and public research stations start with the crossing of existing varieties, followed by selection in the first and later generations, physiological character tests, regional adaptation tests, and productivity tests. Lineages with excellent qualities are registered as new varieties after they are screened and cleared by a selecting committee. They are then propagated in great numbers and supplied to cultivators. The rights of breeders are protected by the Seedlings Law (Shubyō Hō). National and prefectural breeding organizations have been formed and are engaged in the introduction of new genetic material from both domestic and foreign sources as well as the preservation of traditional strains.

Agricultural Implements —— The principal agricultural implements in premodern Japan were cultivating tools which employed human or animal power. Implements for processing did not develop notably in the Edo and Meiji periods. Japanese farmers, for example, consistently depended on the SEMBAKOKI ("thousand-toothed rice thresher") for hulling rice. Remarkable progress in agricultural implements, especially processing implements, however, was made after World War I, as internal combustion engines and electric engines were introduced and power equipment for processing came into use. Since World War II, the use of mechanized agricultural equipment, especially for rice planting, has become general. Agricultural implements now widely used include power tillers, tractors, mechanical sprayers and sprinklers, power reapers, threshers, combines, dryers, hullers, pumping and draining machines, milkers, and many others. These implements assist in a wide variety of agricultural operations, including rice planting, dry field farming, mass raising of domestic animals, and mechanized cultivation-harvesting operations in large-scale farming. Selection, processing, packaging, and storage operations also have been mechanized, as have been processing and packing facilities for livestock products. Another innovation, the development of controlled-environment farming using hothouses and cloches, has made year-round cultivation of many crops possible.

Fertilizers —— In premodern Japan, various types of animal manures (human excrement, dried fish, shellfish, bird droppings) and plant manures (straw, dried leaves, seaweed, rice bran, rapeseed cakes, *sake* dregs) were used as fertilizers. With the growth of the chemical fertilizer industry since the Taishō period, production and use of ammonium sulfate, urea, nitrolime, ammonium nitrate, ammonium chloride, superphosphate of lime, fused phosphatic fertilizers, and potassium sulfate have increased rapidly. As the nation's plant improvement activities were directed toward development of varieties that would respond well to fertilizers, and as cultivation methods emphasized dense planting practices with heavy doses of fertilizers, the traditional manures were largely replaced by chemical fertilizers. At present, nitrogenous, phosphatic, and potash fertilizers, and mixed fertilizers of such trace elements as magnesium, manganese, molybdenum, boron, and zinc are produced and applied in large quantities. Crop growth control is facilitated by modifying the quantities of nutrient amounts. In paddy fields, bauxite, pyrite, and limonite fertilizers are applied to revitalize exhausted soils, and bentonite shales are used to prevent seepage of water.

Agricultural Chemicals —— As a result of the trend toward dense planting practices with heavy applications of fertilizers and year-round cultivation in greenhouses and other structures, the use of chemical crop protection and growth-controlling agents has grown markedly. These chemicals include fungicides, insecticides, nemacides, fumigating agents, raticides, herbicides, growth-regulating agents, repellents, and wetting agents. New distribution techniques, including spraying from the air, have been perfected, enabling farmers to cover large areas in very limited time. As the use of agricultural chemicals has increased, examination of their toxicity and residual effects on human bodies has become a standard practice. An Agricultural Chemicals Control Law (Nōyaku Shiyō Hō), designed to prevent hazards to people and domestic animals, has been enacted, and safety regulations limiting time and frequency of use are now in effect. Guidance and instructions for use are provided by government agricultural officials.

Plant Diseases and Insect Pests —— The wide range of climate zones in Japan causes the appearance of plant diseases and insect pests on crops to differ in different regions. The national and prefectural governments are constantly engaged in detecting early danger signals and issue warnings of disease outbreaks and insect infestations as well as periodic reports on blight and insect conditions. Preventive measures taken by farmers on the basis of these warnings and reports include cultivation-related methods (use of blight-resistant varieties, crop rotation, and fallow periods; suspension of cultivation during blight-prone periods; rationalization of fertilizer application); ecological prevention (eradication of bacilli and extermination of intermediate hosts); physical prevention (disinfection of soil and protection of seeds); and chemical prevention (disinfection of soil and seedlings; use of insecticides, fungicides, and so forth). In recent years the importance of biological prevention methods has been particularly stressed in order to minimize pollution by agricultural chemicals. Examples of biological prevention of insect pests include the use of natural enemies and elimination of the reproductive capacity of the insects. An example of the latter method involves *urimibae* (a kind of fly) on Kumejima, an island in Okinawa Prefecture.

Conclusion —— Japanese farming techniques have made remarkable progress since 1945 through the full use of the results of basic research, application and development activities at national and pub-

Agriculture———Table 5

Self-Sufficiency Rates for Major Farm Products
(in percentages)

	1960	1965	1970	1975	1977	1978	1979	1980
Cereals (including animal feed)	83	61	48	43	39	38	35	29
Animal feed	63	55	38	34	30	29	28	28
Staple food grains[1]	90	80	79	76	76	75	73	60
Rice	102	95	106	110	114	111	107	87
Wheat	39	28	9	4	4	6	9	10
Barley and naked barley	107	73	34	10	9	14	17	15
Pulses	44	25	13	9	8	9	8	7
Soybeans	28	11	4	4	3	5	4	4
Vegetables	100	100	99	99	98	97	97	97
Fruits and nuts	100	90	84	84	85	79	86	81
Meat	91	90	89	77	77	80	80	81
Beef	96	95	90	81	75	73	69	72
Pork	96	100	98	86	87	90	90	87
Eggs	101	100	97	97	97	97	98	98
Milk and milk products	89	86	89	82	87	89	87	86
Sugar	18	30	23	16	19	23	24	28
Overall farm products	91	83	79	76	76	75	74	70
Total foodstuffs (including fishery products)[2]	93	88	83	79	78	77	76	77

[1] Rice, wheat, barley, and naked barley.

[2] Calculated with the assumption that rice supply and demand are equal.

NOTE: The self-sufficiency rate equals domestic production divided by total consumption, multiplied by 100. Rates for overall farm products and total foodstuffs are based on total value (wholesale prices); all other figures based on volumes.

SOURCE: Nōrin Suisan Shō (Ministry of Agriculture, Forestry, and Fisheries), *Nōgyō hakusho fuzoku tōkeihyō* (annual): 1981.

lic research institutions, Japanese farmers' commitment to increased production, and the nation's abundant agricultural resources. Agricultural technology has been instrumental in raising farmland productivity and overcoming various natural hazards, and will continue to develop to further meet domestic demands for foodstuffs.

■———Nihon Nōgyō Kenkyūjo, ed, *Sengo nōgyō gijutsu hattatsu shi* (1969–71). Nōgyō Hattatsu Shi Chōsakai, ed, *Nihon nōgyō hattatsu shi*, 10 vols (1954–61). *Hōjō Yoshio*

GOVERNMENT AGRICULTURAL POLICY

From the Meiji Restoration (1868) until the LAND REFORMS OF 1946 immediately after World War II, Japan had a tenant-farming system under which landowners collected high amounts of rent in kind. In the early Meiji period, landowners played an important role in the maintenance and development of agriculture, since it was difficult for tenants to accumulate capital. Following the stabilization of Japanese capitalism after 1897, however, landowners rapidly lost their role in production. The government took over this role, providing support and guidance to agriculture through subsidies, low-interest loans, and other measures, while new techniques developed by government experimental and research institutes were introduced in agricultural operations through education and guidance centers. Even today, with the tenant-farming system abolished and nearly all former tenants now independent farmers, this characteristic has remained the same, with government involvement intensified and diversified.

Agricultural policy and administration immediately after World War II focused on the resolution of problems associated with land reform. After 1955 economic recovery was dramatic, and rapid growth began in about 1960 when a national INCOME-DOUBLING PLAN was adopted. This policy placed top priority on commerce, industry, and urban development, while neglecting the development of agriculture and farming villages. The result was a sharp increase in urban industrial income and stagnation in agricultural income. In order to cope with the situation, the Basic Agriculture Law (Nōgyō Kihon Hō) was promulgated in 1961 to attain high productivity by correcting unfavorable agricultural conditions. Its concrete objec-

tives were fostering of self-supporting owner-farmers, selective expansion of production, and structural improvements in agricultural labor productivity. In short, the new policy emphasized rationalization aimed at attaining the standards of European agriculture under the high economic growth conditions in Japan.

The law, however, did not fundamentally change the framework of the policy which preceded it. It was characterized by excessive emphasis on rice production and income elevation measures based on price manipulation. Among the programs mandated by the law were various subsidized projects, the promotion of large-scale single-crop farming, and the encouragement of highly mechanized modern agricultural practices using large machines aimed at agricultural land readjustment. These measures, however, were doomed to failure. One reason was that the high labor productivity of manufacturing industries could not be expected in agriculture. Another reason was that the rapid development of manufacturing and subsequent urbanization brought a sharp rise in the price of land, reducing the availability of agricultural land and preventing the development of large-scale, industrial farms. Instead, households turned increasingly to outside employment. The development of highly productive agriculture capable of international competition was deemed impossible, unproductive operations were abandoned, and an international division of labor based on the active import of low-priced agricultural products from foreign countries gained much popularity.

After the OIL CRISIS OF 1973, when the United States hinted at the strategic use of food exports in retaliation against the Organization of Petroleum Exporting Countries (OPEC), Japan made a quick turnabout and reemphasized the necessity of attaining self-sufficiency in food. This goal, however, cannot be attained in a short time. Self-sufficiency rates, except that of rice, which in most years is greater than 100 percent, have in fact been decreasing during recent decades. The nation's overall self-sufficiency in agricultural products stood at 91 percent in 1960, dropped to 79 percent in 1970, and fell again to 70 percent in 1980. Self-sufficiency in grains—both staple grains and animal feed grains—dropped from 83 percent to 48 percent and then to 29 percent in the same years, and this decline is likely to continue. Japan may be said to have transferred its food warehouses to foreign countries. See also FOOD SUPPLY.

Present Problems —— Five vital problems face Japanese agricultural policy and administration. First, despite land reforms, small farms still predominate, and the large-scale operations that the Basic Agriculture Law attempted to promote are still rare. Second, the acreage and availability of farmland have decreased. Even excellent farmland has given way to urban and industrial development. Third, overproduction of rice has seriously strained government finances and has pushed the food control system toward the brink of collapse. Japan's agricultural policy, designed to maintain agriculture and farming villages as the cornerstone of a capitalist society by manipulating rice prices, has had to face the necessity, since 1970, of making the control of rice production the primary means of coping with chronic overproduction of the staple food. Fourth, depopulation of farming communities and an increase in nonfarming households have had drastic consequences in farming villages and for individuals, resulting in the stagnation and disruption of agricultural production systems. Finally, although the importance of self-sufficiency in food has been reaffirmed, the government's present subsidy policy sustains low-productivity agriculture, while large-scale, independent operations are stalemated and cooperative operations make little progress. Japanese agricultural policy is now sorely pressed to solve the above problems. Since the problems are not exclusively agricultural but concern the Japanese economy and society as a whole, they should be tackled in a comprehensive manner.

KAWAMOTO Akira

Agriculture, White Paper on

(Nōgyō hakusho). An annual report submitted by the government to the Diet in accordance with provisions of the Basic Agriculture Law (Nōgyō Kihon Hō, 1961). The document provides public information concerning recent economic developments in agriculture and the government measures already taken in regard to them. The government is explicitly required to include its views on trends in agricultural productivity and in rural standards of living. The views of the Agricultural Administration Council (Nōsei Shingikai) must be incorporated in these judgments. Finally, the report informs the Diet and the public of the government's intentions with respect to future policy and legislation.

Michael W. DONNELLY

Aguinaldo, Emilio (1869–1964)

Filipino nationalist leader of the Philippine Revolution, and president of the Philippine Republic, 1899–1901. Born in the town of Kawit, Cavite Province. He became town headman of Kawit and a leader of the underground organization Katipunan in the mid-1890s. Joining the revolt against the Spaniards led by Andres Bonifacio in 1896, he quickly assumed leadership and eliminated Bonifacio in May 1897. The Pact of Biak-na-bato with the Spaniards in December called for an end to the revolt and stipulated Aguinaldo's exile to Hong Kong, where he and others secretly prepared another revolt. Returning home at the outbreak of the Spanish-American War, he declared Philippine independence on 12 June 1898, established the Constitutional Republic of the Philippines in the town of Malolos, and was inaugurated as its president on 23 January 1899. These developments were ignored by the United States in concluding the Paris Peace Treaty with Spain in December 1898, leading to fighting between American and Filipino forces that ended with Aguinaldo's capture in March 1901; he was forced to swear allegiance to the United States and retired from public life. Aguinaldo's attempts to buy arms from Japan and Japanese concern for the Philippine Revolution created rumors that Japan supported Aguinaldo's forces. No significant support came from the Japanese government, however, with the exception of the moral support provided by the presence of army and naval intelligence officers, and civilian intelligence experts such as Sakamoto Shiroo. Aguinaldo had sent Mariano Ponce and Faustino Lichauco to Japan to seek aid, which eventually came from a group of Asian nationalists who arranged the shipment of arms and munitions from Japan. The first ship, Nunobiki maru, was sunk in July 1899, and the second effort was aborted in January 1900. Apart from an unsuccessful campaign for the presidency of the autonomous commonwealth government established by the United States in 1935, Aguinaldo remained in retirement until World War II.

With the occupation of the Philippines by the Japanese in 1942, Aguinaldo hailed Prime Minister TŌJŌ HIDEKI's promise of "in-

Agriculture —— Agricultural modernization

A combine being used to harvest rice on land in Akita Prefecture reclaimed from the lagoon Hachirōgata. Formerly the second largest lake in Japan, this area is now one of the prefecture's major agricultural districts and features large-scale farming using modern agricultural techniques.

Aichi Canal

The Aichi Canal and the reservoir Sōri Ike (top).

dependence with honor." He encouraged cooperation with the Japanese occupation in a radio message on 6 February 1942 and appealed to US General Douglas MACARTHUR on Corregidor, urging him to surrender in the face of Japanese military supremacy. He collaborated with the Japanese military government as a member of the Preparatory Committee for Philippine Independence and of the Council of State that supported the puppet republican government declared on 14 October 1943. Although he hoped to attain a leading role in the new government, the old general was bypassed by Japanese authorities. He was indicted for collaboration but the charges were dropped in an amnesty, and in his late years he returned to quiet retirement, more a historical than a political figure.

YOSHIKAWA Yōko

Aichi Canal

(Aichi Yōsui). Canal in Gifu and Aichi prefectures, central Honshū, extending from the river Kisogawa in southern Gifu Prefecture to the southern tip of the Chita Peninsula in Aichi Prefecture. The completion of this canal in 1961 brought irrigation to the uplands of the Chita Peninsula for the first time. It supplies water to both farms and factories, but with the rapid development of the area surrounding Nagoya in recent years the amount used to supply water to housing units has increased dramatically. Length: 112 km (69 mi).

Aichi Machine Industry Co, Ltd

(Aichi Kikai Kōgyō). A manufacturer, principally of automobile engines, transmissions, and small-size commercial vehicles. It also

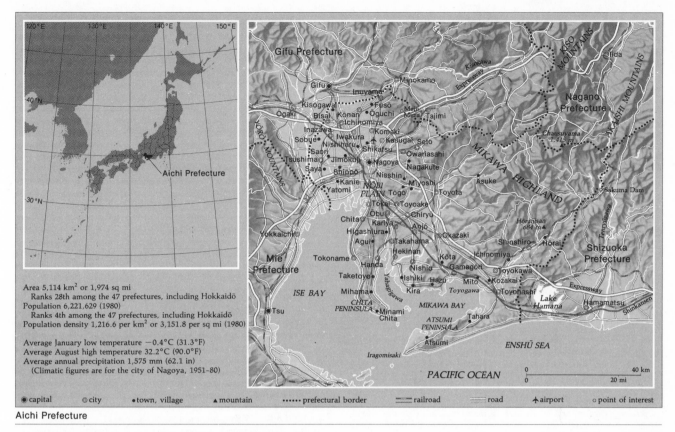

Area 5,114 km² or 1,974 sq mi
  Ranks 28th among the 47 prefectures, including Hokkaidō
Population 6,221,629 (1980)
  Ranks 4th among the 47 prefectures, including Hokkaidō
Population density 1,216.6 per km² or 3,151.8 per sq mi (1980)

Average January low temperature −0.4°C (31.3°F)
Average August high temperature 32.2°C (90.0°F)
Average annual precipitation 1,575 mm (62.1 in)
  (Climatic figures are for the city of Nagoya, 1951–80)

◉ capital   ◎ city   • town, village   ▲ mountain   ••••• prefectural border   ══ railroad   ══ road   ✈ airport   ○ point of interest

Aichi Prefecture

produces machine tools. Established in 1943 when the aircraft division of Aichi Tokei Denki became independent of its parent firm, it started production of automobiles after World War II and in 1965 became affiliated with the NISSAN MOTOR CO, LTD, whose popular small-size cars it produces on consignment. Sales for the fiscal year ending March 1982 totaled ¥194.7 billion (US $808.8 million) and the company was capitalized at ¥3.2 billion (US $13 million). The head office is in Nagoya.

Aichi Prefecture

(Aichi Ken). Located in central Honshū; bordered by Gifu and Nagano prefectures to the north, Shizuoka Prefecture to the east, the Pacific Ocean to the south, and Mie Prefecture to the west. The eastern section is largely covered by the Mikawa Highland. To the west, on the Nōbi Plain, lies the city of NAGOYA, which contains over one-third of the prefecture's entire population. Principal rivers are the KISOGAWA and YAHAGIGAWA.

In feudal times the prefecture was composed of the two provinces of Mikawa and Owari. During the 16th century three warlords from these provinces succeeded in unifying the country: ODA NOBUNAGA, TOYOTOMI HIDEYOSHI, and TOKUGAWA IEYASU.

In the modern age the prefecture has seen a steady growth in the size and number of industrial cities. Located at the center of Japan's main industrial belt, it has become one of the major industrial centers of Japan, ranking fourth among all prefectures in annual production. Textiles, and more recently, steel, chemicals, automobiles, and ceramics are its leading industries. Lumber also continues to be a major industry. Farm products include rice, vegetables, and chickens. Area: 5,114 sq km (1,974 sq mi); pop: 6,221,629; capital: Nagoya. Other major cities include TOYOHASHI, TOYOTA, ICHINOMIYA, and OKAZAKI.

Aichi Steel Works, Ltd

(Aichi Seikō). A member of the Toyota group engaged in production and sale of special steel materials and forged steel products. It is a leader in the manufacture of spring steel and stainless angles. The company was established as the steel manufacturing department of TOYODA AUTOMATIC LOOM WORKS, LTD, in 1934, and became independent in 1940 as Toyoda Steel Works, Ltd. The company adopted its present name in 1945. It supplies 40 percent of its

structural alloy steel, springs, and forged products for automobile manufacture to other members of the Toyota group and exports spring steel to about 60 countries. In 1981 the company's annual sales stood at ¥143.2 billion (US $654 million) and capitalization was ¥6.0 billion (US $27.4 million). The head office is located in Tōkai, Aichi Prefecture.

Aikawa

Town on the island of Sado off the coast of northwestern Honshū; administratively part of Niigata Prefecture. Aikawa developed as a mining town under the jurisdiction of the TOKUGAWA SHOGUNATE when gold was discovered in 1601. With the decline in mining, its population, once as high as 100,000 in the early 1600s, decreased. The old mining commissioner's (Sado bugyō) office and the annual mine festival in July are popular tourist attractions. Pop: 12,721.

Aikawa Yoshisuke (1880–1967)

Also known as Ayukawa Gisuke. Businessman and founder of the Nissan zaibatsu, a major financial and industrial combine before World War II. Born in Yamaguchi Prefecture, he graduated from Tōkyō University and later studied malleable cast iron technology in the United States. In 1910 he established the Tobata Foundry in Kyūshū, which later grew into NISSAN MOTOR CO, LTD, the manufacturer of Datsun automobiles. In 1928 he took over Kuhara Mining, formerly run by his brother-in-law KUHARA FUSANOSUKE, and turned it into a holding company with the name Nihon Sangyō (Nissan). Taking advantage of a major stock market boom after the MANCHURIAN INCIDENT of 1931, he took over 148 of Nissan's subsidiaries and turned the company into a powerful zaibatsu, next in size to MITSUI and MITSUBISHI. The combine flourished, expanding its heavy industry and chemical production to fulfill military contracts. Aikawa moved Nissan to Manchuria in 1937 and reorganized it as the Manchuria Heavy Industry Company, of which he served as president. After World War II the Nissan group was dissolved by the Occupation forces, and Aikawa was forced to resign all of his positions. With the lifting of the purge restrictions, he turned to politics and was elected to the House of Councillors in 1953. In 1956 he established the Japan Small and Medium Enterprises Political League and became its president.   UDAGAWA Masaru

aikidō

One of the Japanese MARTIAL ARTS; a system of pure self-defense derived from the traditional weaponless fighting techniques of *jūjutsu* (see JŪDŌ) in its employment of immobilizing holds and twisting throws whereby an attacker's own momentum and strength are made to work against him.

The art of unarmed, hand-to-hand fighting was at an early date transmitted to Japan from the Asian mainland, and a large number of traditional schools of *jūjutsu*, the forerunner of *jūdō*, had long existed in Japan prior to the Meiji period (1868–1912). Some schools claimed ancient origins from as early as the 14th century; they are said to have developed among the warrior class *(bushi)* and to have been transmitted by successive masters over many generations down to modern-day martial arts experts. In 1882 KANŌ JIGORŌ established his KŌDŌKAN gymnasium in Tōkyō and introduced modern *jūdō*. In developing his own style of modernized self-defense, Kanō left out certain blows and manipulative holds found in traditional *jūjutsu*. Takeda Sōkaku (1860–1943), a martial arts devotee trained in KENDŌ (swordsmanship) and SŌJUTSU (spear techniques), utilized these neglected techniques in teaching the *daitō aiki* system of *jūjutsu*, which he taught mainly in Hokkaidō and Tōhoku (northern Honshū) in the Meiji and Taishō (1912–26) periods.

Ueshiba Morihei (1883–1969), a student of Takeda from Wakayama Prefecture, is credited with the modern systematization of *aikidō*. After much schooling in the various martial arts, Ueshiba drew upon Takeda's teachings and his own religious experiences as a convert to the ŌMOTO sect of Shintō in formulating the basic skills of *aikidō* self-defense as distinct from *jūjutsu* or *jūdō*. He built his first *aikidō* practice center in Tōkyō in 1927. *Aikidō* received public recognition in 1959 when Waseda University instituted it as a course in the athletic department curriculum and established a university club for its practice. Since the 1960s *aikidō* has rapidly gained in popularity throughout Japan and in many countries of the world. Since it is primarily a self-defense system and does not require great physical strength, *aikidō* has attracted many women and elderly practitioners.

Jūjutsu traditionally employed four major techniques *(waza)*: throws *(nagewaza)*, holds and locks *(katame waza)*, joint manipulation *(kansetsu waza)*, and blows to vulnerable pressure points *(atemi waza)*. Of the various schools, the *daitō aiki jūjutsu* school stressed techniques for deflecting blows and checking offensive attacks. *Aikidō* incorporated these teachings, primarily stressing joint manipulation techniques for dealing with armed or unarmed attackers. The *aikidō* student restrains an attacker through locks and holds by manipulating the opponent's joints, usually the wrists, elbows, and shoulders. By meeting rather than blocking a blow, he or she can redirect the flow of an opponent's *ki* (Ch: *qi* or *ch'i*; sometimes translated as mind or positive energy force), dissipate it, and, through joint manipulation, turn it against the opponent until he or she is thrown or pinned.

Practice usually takes an established form, or *kata*: one partner takes the offensive role dealing blows or holds and the other partner deflects these using various *aikidō* moves. Since two persons cannot practice defensive techniques against each other, *aikidō* does not lend itself to a contest situation. However, in the Tomiki form of *aikidō* "free-fight" *(randori)* matches, points are scored for defensive technique by contestants who alternate in taking the role of the attacker, who attempts to touch the opponent with a rubber knife. In the practice hall, students are tested and awarded various levels of rank in a process similar to that of *jūdō* and the other martial arts.

TOMIKI Kenji

Aikoku Fujinkai

(Patriotic Women's Association). Founded in 1901 by OKUMURA IOKO to aid and comfort Japanese soldiers and their families. With charter members from wealthy and prominent circles, the group gained the patronage of the imperial family. For a long time it was the largest women's group in Japan; its membership expanded dramatically during the Russo-Japanese War of 1904–05, and by 1919 it reached over 1 million. As it began another major membership drive in the 1930s, boosting its numbers to over 3 million, friction developed with the army-sponsored women's group DAI NIPPON KOKUBŌ FUJINKAI, which had more direct community ties. In 1942 the two rival organizations and other women's groups were merged by the government to form the DAI NIPPON FUJINKAI.

Aikidō

A throw in an *aikidō* "free-fight" *(randori)* match; the man being thrown (in the role of assailant) holds a rubber knife.

Aikoku Kōtō

(Public Party of Patriots). Political society founded in Tōkyō in January 1874 by ITAGAKI TAISUKE, GOTŌ SHŌJIRŌ, ETŌ SHIMPEI, and other former *samurai* along with a number of *gōnō* (rich farmers). Spearheading the FREEDOM AND PEOPLE'S RIGHTS MOVEMENT, it petitioned the government to establish a national assembly representing former samurai, merchants, and rich peasants. Because of Etō's central role in the SAGA REBELLION one month later, the society feared government suppression and quickly disbanded. In May 1890 Itagaki revived the Aikoku Kōtō with the intention of merging it with the Daidō Kurabu, the Daidō Kyōwakai, and other political groups. That September, soon after the first national election, he accomplished this merger with the formation of the Rikken Jiyūtō, which in turn was replaced by a second Jiyūtō in March 1891.

Aikokusha

(Society of Patriots). One of Japan's first political coalitions; formed by ITAGAKI TAISUKE in February 1875 to associate his RISSHISHA with other local groups in the FREEDOM AND PEOPLE'S RIGHTS MOVEMENT. The group, which had fewer than 50 members, was dissolved the following month when Itagaki accepted the promise made by ŌKUBO TOSHIMICHI at the ŌSAKA CONFERENCE OF 1875 that the government would soon draft a constitution. When no constitution was presented by October of that year, Itagaki withdrew from the government and in September 1878 revived the Aikokusha to promote his goals. Two years later, at the group's fourth assembly, attended by 114 delegates representing 96,900 members of 27 affiliated societies in 24 prefectures, the group decided to rename itself the LEAGUE FOR ESTABLISHING A NATIONAL ASSEMBLY in recognition of its primary aim. This league and thus the Aikokusha were direct predecessors of the JIYŪTŌ (Liberal Party), which Itagaki founded in October 1881.

Aikyōjuku

Private school founded near the city of Mito, Ibaraki Prefecture, by the agrarian nationalist TACHIBANA KŌZABURŌ in April 1931. Its two-and-a-half-year course for primary school graduates and its youth-group lectures focused on mathematics, bookkeeping, natural history, farm management, and other relatively nonideological subjects; regular talks were also given on the importance of village community life and traditional rural virtues, themes emphasized by the school's name, which was literally "Academy for the Love of One's Community." Self-denial, brotherhood, and hard work in the fields were demanded of the students, who never numbered more than 23. When it was discovered that Tachibana and several students were implicated in the MAY 15TH INCIDENT of 1932, the school was closed. It reopened in June but survived only until March 1933.

Ainu

The term Ainu is now used to refer to an indigenous people of Hokkaidō and adjacent islands as a single integrated population,

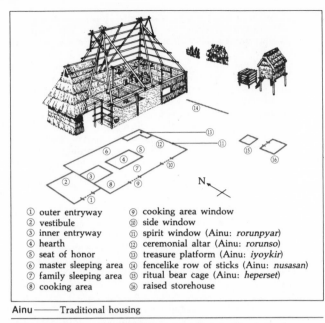

① outer entryway
② vestibule
③ inner entryway
④ hearth
⑤ seat of honor
⑥ master sleeping area
⑦ family sleeping area
⑧ cooking area
⑨ cooking area window
⑩ side window
⑪ spirit window (Ainu: *rorunpyar*)
⑫ ceremonial altar (Ainu: *rorunso*)
⑬ treasure platform (Ainu: *iyoykir*)
⑭ fencelike row of sticks (Ainu: *nusasan*)
⑮ ritual bear cage (Ainu: *heperset*)
⑯ raised storehouse

Ainu——Traditional housing

Restoration drawing of typical 19th-century Ainu dwelling in the Saru region of south central Hokkaidō.

although formerly a number of ethnically distinct groups were recognized. (Originally *ainu* meant man [human being or male] in the Ainu language of Hokkaidō.) The gradual integration of the separate so-called Ainu groups resulted from collective resistance to encroachment by Japanese and other neighboring populations. In 1878 these integrated groups came to be officially referred to in Japanese as *kyūdojin* (former indigenous people). This in turn accelerated the growth among them of a strong group identity.

It is generally assumed that the Ainu were the people referred to as the Emishi or Ezo in ancient Japanese documents, but identification of the Ezo with the ancestors of the Ainu is not clear. The designation Emishi of the Nara (710–794) and Heian (794–1185) periods was subsequently changed to Ezo and whether or not they were the same as either the Mishihase or the "hairy people" (i.e., people referred to by Chinese characters with that literal meaning) of even earlier documents has also not been established, for these terms Emishi, Ezo, Mishihase, and "hairy people" were used by the Japanese in the ancient and premodern periods as general terms to refer to the peoples in the northern part of Japan.

At present, many Ainu live under Japanese jurisdiction in Hokkaidō. Although the number is unknown, many of their ancestors also existed in the northern part of Honshū during much of the Edo period (1600–1868) and at least a few hundred live today in southern Sakhalin in the USSR. Formerly, they also lived in the southern Kuril Islands, along the lower reaches of the Amur, and in southern Kamchatka. As early as 1884 the inhabitants of the northern Kurils were removed to the island of Shikotan by order of the Japanese government; numbering fewer than a hundred (96 people) at the time, they have since been completely assimilated. After World War II some people of the South Kuril Islands (Etorofu and Kunashiri), who have been generally considered to be part of the eastern Hokkaidō Ainu, as well as some from Sakhalin, were removed to Hokkaidō when the Japanese were evacuated. Ainu place names on Honshū are reminders of their ancestors' former presence there.

Population. Treated as aliens by the Japanese and reduced by disease and a low birthrate since the turn of the century, the total number of persons identifying themselves as Ainu in 1979 was 24,160 in Hokkaidō, of whom 47.8 percent were in the Hidaka district of south central Hokkaidō. In a special survey conducted in 1804 the count included at least 23,797—the total number in Hokkaidō and Sakhalin. By 1902 the number had dropped to 17,374, and in one sample village in Hidaka 5 percent of the marriages were with Japanese. By 1927 mixed marriages had increased to 36 percent, of which roughly half were between offspring of mixed marriages, while the Ainu population count remained unchanged. During the next four decades the mixed population had increased to 88 percent and mixed marriages to 43 percent. Possibly more significant is the drop in the number of unmixed births: from approximately 70 percent in 1902 to zero by 1957, and the total unmixed population is said to have dropped to an estimated total of fewer than 200 by 1980.

Origins. The Ainu have frequently been referred to as Caucasoid (Europoid) or Australoid, but such speculations are based largely upon occasional striking resemblances in facial features, beard fullness, and body hairiness. Recent intensive skeletal, anthropometric, serological, and other genetic studies demonstrate closer racial ties with some of the neighboring Tungusic, Altaic, and more especially Uralic populations of Siberia.

Physical characteristics. Although relatively short-limbed in proportion to trunk length and of medium stature (160–162 cm), Ainu males are generally lean and lack the characteristic amounts of subcutaneous fatty tissue of populations adapted to Arctic and other severely cold environments such as the Eskimo and Paleoasiatic Siberians. Adequate series of unmixed Ainu are no longer obtainable for comparative purposes, but mixed Japanese–Ainu samples statistically corrected for hybridization reveal significant serological and other genetic similarities with the Uralic and other peoples of the Taiga-forest regions of Siberia and more distant relationships with the populations of Oceania, Southeast Asia, and Northern Europe (see JAPANESE PEOPLE, PHYSICAL CHARACTERISTICS OF). The skeletal structure is relatively heavy, and in general the morphology intermediate between that of the Jōmon-period and recent Japanese, with the long bones flattened laterally. The head is relatively long (dolicho- to mesocephalic) with a mean cephalic index range of 77 to 79 percent. The most characteristic facial features are the relatively flat face, deeply sunken eyes with sockets relatively square with rounded corners, a markedly sloping forehead and heavy protruding supraorbital ridges. The mid-facial region and lower jaw are broad and heavy; the nose is broad with deep nasal root depression. Head hair is usually abundant, slightly wavy, and generally black with varying degrees of reddish tinge. Moustache, beard, and body hair are also abundant, and graying is not uncommon. Skin color varies from light to light brown and eyes are usually dark brown with up to 10 percent mixed and, rarely, grayish to gray-blue. In spite of these descriptions, a precise distinction between the Japanese and the Ainu cannot be made from the standpoint of physical anthropology.

Lifestyle and economy. Since the commencement of the Meiji period (1868) there has been a gradual shift toward Japanese housing, clothing, food, and other aspects of family life and economy, with traditional dress and religious objects reserved for ceremonial occasions. There has also been a gradual shift from hunting, fishing, and gathering of wild plants to agriculture and commercial marine fishing and, with the initiation of compulsory education, an emphasis on the use of Japanese by the younger generations.

Among the Hokkaidō Ainu, dress for males was a calf-length coatlike garment made of *attush,* a woven textile of shredded and softened inner elm bark fibers, with a woven belt, and in winter a short sleeveless deerskin jacket. Female clothing was similar but ankle-length. Both were decorated with appliqué of linear and curvilinear designs of cotton material in most cases. Their ceremonial garments were generally of either *attush* or cotton, but the appliqué decorations were of cotton. Women also wore a decorated headband and men a front- and back-pointed headpiece. Footwear *(keri)* were moccasin-like sandals of salmon skins, deerhide, or inner walnut bark and, in winter, U-shaped snowshoes of bent willow twigs or grape vines. Formerly a striking feature of all women was a tattooed "moustache" circling the mouth. Started at puberty and completed before marriage, the tattoo was both a sign of preparedness for marriage and a guarantee of acceptability among adults. Tattooing of crosshatch designs on both arms up to the elbows and on the backs of both hands was even more convincing evidence.

Dwellings were rectangular and pole-framed, with small openings in the ceiling and miscanthus or bamboo-leaf thatched roofs and walls, a short, slightly raised ridge with step-thatched roof on both sides and ends, and a doorway protected by a skin or woven hanging and outer thatch baffle. One window, on the eastern side, served for religious purposes. There were windows on other sides as well. Floors were formerly earthen with a raised mat-covered wooden section for sitting and sleeping. They were usually covered throughout with miscanthus leaves and mats. An open fire hearth pit in the center, with smoke vents below both ends of the ridge, was used for cooking and heating. The hearth was important on ceremonial occasions. Near the house there was usually a fence-like row of sticks with wood shavings attached; among these were usually forked sticks with attached skulls of bear, deer, and other animals through whose spirits messages could be sent to the world of spirit deities. Behind the house was a small, thatched hut on poles for storage of dried fish and other provisions.

Dugout canoes similar to those of the Jōmon period of prehistoric Japan and to craft still found in parts of Borneo were used in coastal waters and on lakes. The simple convex bow was used in hunting, with the arrows poison-tipped for larger game. Salmon were speared during their up-river runs, and trout and other river fish were usually trapped or caught with nets made of inner bark fiber. Today, rice and dry crop cultivation, commercial fishing, netting and gathering of cuttlefish, kelp, sea urchins, and shellfish have generally replaced traditional hunting, fishing, and gathering. Game animals such as bear, deer, rabbit, weasel, and other small mammals were formerly important. While men engaged traditionally in hunting and fishing, women gathered wild fruits, nuts, and leafy plant foods or dug for bulbous roots and tubers with antlers or digging sticks.

Social organization. Possibly the most unusual feature of Ainu social organization is the bilineal descent system: males tracing descent through male descent groups (patrilineages) symbolized by different nontotemic animal crests *(itokpa)* and females tracing descent through comparable matrilines symbolized by hereditary chastity belts *(ponkut* or *upsor)*. Mate selection was customarily made by either individual preference or with parental assistance. The bride usually moved to the husband's home, but upon the death of either spouse the house was customarily burned. When burning of houses was prohibited by Japanese law, a small symbolic hut was built to take its place. Village communities *(kotan)* of several to less than 20 houses were located strategically along river banks or near game trails to take advantage of food and water resources.

Language and folktales. Although three major dialects have been recognized (Hokkaidō, Sakhalin, and Kuril), the relationship of Ainu to other languages has not been clearly established. Its phonemic and agglutinative structures are similar to those of the Paleoasiatic languages of northeastern Siberia, but vocabulary and various aspects of grammar are said to resemble those of Southeast Asian and Oceanic languages. There is a rich folklore including poems of epic character *(yukar)* and stories with formalized expressions in prose and poetry, although there is no system of writing. Songs range from impromptu to highly stylized ones, which are sung at work and for pleasure, at festivals, on ceremonial occasions and so on. (See AINU LANGUAGE.)

Religion, music, and dance. Ainu religious beliefs focus on the existence of a distant world composed of the spirit essences of all former earthly beings and inanimate objects subject to the same spirit forces *(kamuy)* which control the visible universe: wind, rain, hail, and, above all, fire *(fuchi)*. Homage must be paid to the spirits of ancestors and their assistance propitiated. Shamans call upon spirit animals, especially bears, foxes, and weasels, to serve as guides, to carry messages, or play tricks. During special three-day-long communal bear festivals *(i-omante),* the spirit of a sacrificed bear can carry messages to the ancestral spirits of a *kotan.* Shaving-tufted prayer sticks *(inau)* are used daily in the home or on the trail. Individual or group dancing was often accompanied by the music of five-stringed instruments. Among other musical instruments there have been drums and the Jew's harp.

🔲 ——M. Inez Hilger, *Together with the Ainu* (1971). Kindaiti Kyosuke, *Ainu Life and Legends* (1941). George Montandon, *La civilisation ainu* (1937). S. Takakura, "The Ainu of Northern Japan: A Study in Conquest and Acculturation," *Transactions of the Philosophical Society of Philadelphia* 50.4 (1960). Watanabe Hitoshi, "The Ainu," in M. G. Biccheri, ed, *Hunters and Gatherers Today* (1972). S. Watanabe et al, "Anthropological and Genetic Studies of the Ainu," *Japan Committee for the International Biological Program,* vol 2, pt 3 (1975).

KŌNO Motomichi and Gordon T. BOWLES

Ainu language

The language originally spoken by the Ainu people of northeastern Asia. There is evidence that the Ainu language was originally spoken in the Tōhoku region of northern Honshū, Hokkaidō, the Kuril Islands, and Sakhalin. Although no record remains of the Tōhoku Ainu dialect, traces can be found in local place names. Partial descriptions of the Kuril dialect can be found in Russian sources, and in the work of the Japanese scholar TORII RYŪZŌ, whose *Les Aïnou des Iles Kouriles* (1903) was an early contribution to the field. A more recent study was done by Murayama Shichirō (b 1908), who translated works by Polish and Russian scholars into Japanese in his *Kita Chishima ainugo* (1971, The Ainu Language of the Northern Kurils).

The last of the Kuril Ainu were removed to Hokkaidō before World War II, and after the war most of the Sakhalin Ainu were repatriated to Hokkaidō, too, so that today the Ainu language is spoken only on that island.

Ainu Studies —— The Ainu language is no longer in daily use, and few living persons have actually spoken Ainu as their primary means of daily communication. Linguists first became interested in the language at the turn of the century, but then only two major dialect groups of Ainu were left: those of Hokkaidō and Sakhalin. These two groups differ and are virtually mutually unintelligible. Both can be subdivided into many minor dialects, of which the Hokkaidō group is the better recorded.

Linguistic studies of Ainu began with the British missionary, John BATCHELOR (1854–1944). Some years later the Japanese scholar KINDAICHI KYŌSUKE (1882–1971) began his studies of Ainu epics *(yukar),* which resulted in several great works on the grammar of the epic and translations not only of the *yukar* but also of other genres of Ainu oral literature. Chiri Mashiho (1909–61), an Ainu, was encouraged by Kindaichi to take up Ainu studies, but unlike his mentor, Chiri concentrated on the colloquial language. He compiled a three-volume etymological dictionary and wrote a number of books and articles on place name etymologies and a variety of other subjects relating to both the Hokkaidō and Sakhalin groups.

At the time Kindaichi and Chiri were conducting their research, fluent speakers of Ainu were already hard to find, and later such scholars as Tamura Suzuko (b 1934) and Murasaki Kyōko (b 1937) had to limit their studies to single informants. These informants are now dead, and although a few old speakers are left, soon these too will have vanished. There is a current revival of interest in the Ainu language among the younger generation of Ainu. Several Ainu language study groups have been started in Hokkaidō with both Ainu and Japanese participants, and the Japanese government is showing a growing concern not only to preserve but to learn from Ainu culture.

Phonology —— The Ainu language has a very simple phoneme inventory. Like Japanese it has only five vowels (/i/, /e/, /a/, /o/, and /u/) and even fewer consonants than Japanese, only 12: the plosives /p/, /t/, /k/, the affricate /c/, the sibilant /s/, the glottal fricative /h/, the liquid /r/, the nasals /m/ and /n/, the semivowels /y/ and /w/, and the glottal plosive /'/.

The syllabic structure is quite simple. For the Hokkaidō dialect it is *CV(C)* (C=consonant, V=vowel), and in Sakhalin, *CV(V)(C);* the vowels must be identical. There are no consonant clusters, no diphthongs, and in the Hokkaidō dialects, no long vowels. /c/, /h/, and /'/ in Hokkaidō Ainu and /p/, /t/, /k/, /r/, /c/, and /'/ in Sakhalin do not appear as final consonants nor do /y/ and /t/ appear before /i/, and /w/ does not precede /u/ and /i/. When syllables are combined, a somewhat complicated system of sound changes occurs in both Hokkaidō and Sakhalin dialect groups.

A pitch accent system is found in most Hokkaidō dialects, but in Sakhalin Ainu, there is instead an opposition between short and long (double) vowels.

Syntax and Grammar —— Ainu word order is similar to that of Japanese. Both are so-called SOV (subject-object-verb word order) languages. In both languages a modifier generally precedes the modified word, and in both it is possible to omit the subject or object or both if it can be inferred from the context. There are also postpositions in Ainu as in Japanese, and some types of verb combinations resemble each other. Unlike Japanese, however, Ainu does not express the objective and dative case by postpositions. In many cases where Japanese would use postpositions, Ainu employs prefixed verbs. Another difference is that in negative statements in Ainu the negation comes before the verb, while in Japanese negatives are suffixed to the verb.

Affixing is one of the distinctive aspects of the Ainu language. By adding prefixes and suffixes very long words can be produced, often so long that they correspond to whole sentences in English or Japanese. There are reflexive prefixes, prefixes expressing mutuality, instrumentality, direction, locative, intensity, etc. (E.g., *yáyko'uwepeker,* "to worry"—from: *yay:* oneself, *ko:* toward, *u:* mutually, *(w)e:* thereby, *pekér:* clear up, make bright.) Also grammatical person is expressed by prefixing. (E.g., *Ku'áni ka cép ka ku é* [I-too-fish-too-I-eat] "I, too, eat fish." *To'ún pe en koré* [That-thing-me-give] "Give me that!") Pronominal affixes appear in the nominative and the objective–dative cases, and only the first and second and the indefinite person are marked. There is no affix for the third person. Pronouns also exist, but they are only used for emphasis.

Suffixes are used after verbs to express causativity, transitivity, or plurality of actor or action. (E.g., *é:* "eat," *ére* "cause to eat"; *hosípi* "go home [sing.]," *hosíppa:* "go home [plur.]."

Ainu nouns do not distinguish gender, case, or number, but some nouns have in addition to their conceptual form a "belonging" form, which expresses that the noun in question is owned by, or is part of, somebody or something. (E.g., *sík* [eye(s)]; *sikíhi* [somebody's eye(s)]; *menóko sikíhi* [the girl's eye(s)].) Only nouns in specific semantic groups have a belonging form; a relationship of possession or belonging between two nouns that have no belonging form is expressed by an attributive particle placed between them. The above examples are taken from the Shizunai dialect of Hokkaidō Ainu, and although specific affixes and lexicon may differ from dialect to dialect, the overall structure is very similar for the Hokkaidō group.

Vocabulary —— There are many compounds and derivatives, and this feature has sometimes been pointed to as a resemblance to the polysynthetic languages. In addition, Ainu is extremely rich in words for natural phenomena.

The number system shows some rather special features. The etymology of the word for 5 (*'asíknep*) has generally been assumed to be "hand," and for 10 (*wánpe*) is probably "both." According to Kindaichi the numbers 6 to 9 correspond to the difference between those numbers and 10. Numbers above 20 are counted by the vicenary system: 40 is "two 20," 60 is "three 20," and 50 is "with 10, three 20," that is "10 more will make 60."

Most of the Japanese loanwords in Ainu relate to objects introduced by the Japanese. In the reverse direction a number of Ainu loanwords exist in Japanese. In the Tōhoku region and more especially in Hokkaidō many place names are of more or less obvious Ainu origin. Two examples are Noboribetsu from *nupúr* (mud) and *pét* (river), and Wakkasakanai from *wákka* (water), *sak* (none), and *náy* (swamp).

Ainu Literature —— Although the Ainu have no written language, their epics, songs, and stories have been orally transmitted from generation to generation, preserving classical forms of speech, which have disappeared from the colloquial language.

The *yukar* (hero epics) form the essence of Ainu literature. A typical *yukar* consists mainly of stock phrases and descriptions, and since the choice of these as well as the framework of the epic is left to each individual reciter to determine, the same story is never repeated exactly, not even when the narrator is the same person. One telling equals one story with the plot remaining the same. The *yukar* are told in the first person with the narrator identifying himself with one or more beings; not necessarily human. The particular melody or tone of voice indicates which "first person" is telling the story at any particular moment. Often the *yukar* are of extraordinary length, some continuing for several hours; others may even extend over several evenings.

Starting in 1928 an Ainu woman and transmitter of *yukar*, Kannari Matsu, spent several years writing down in romanized script all the Ainu epics and songs she could remember. These were translated into Japanese by Kindaichi and published in a nine-volume collection (*Yūkarashū*, 1959–70).

Recently an English translation of *yukar* has been published (Donald Philippi, *Songs of Gods, Songs of Humans*, Tōkyō University Press, 1979).

Affinities —— The origin and affinities of the Ainu language have been much discussed, but there is no consensus. Many similarities exist between Japanese and Ainu which naturally reflect mutual linguistic influences resulting from centuries of close contact between the Ainu and Japanese people. This is seen not only in loanwords and place names, but also in phonology and to some extent grammar, and while the number of Ainu speakers has been dwindling, the influence of the Japanese language on Ainu pronunciation and word formation has been extremely strong. The question of a genetic relationship to other languages also remains in doubt, although a number of theories have been proposed. Until sounder evidence is produced, however, Ainu will continue to be grouped with certain other languages of northeastern Asia either as Paleosiberian or as Paleoasiatic.

■ ——Chiri Mashiho, *Chiri Mashiho chosakushū* (Heibonsha, 1973–75). Chiri Mashiho, *Bunrui ainugo jiten*, 3 vols (1953–62).

Hattori Shirō, ed, *Ainugo hōgen jiten* (1964). Kindaichi Kyōsuke and Chiri Mashiho, *Ainu gohō gaisetsu* (1936). Murasaki Kyōko, *Karafuto ainugo* (1976–79). *Kirsten* REFSING

Ainu music

Ainu music, like other aspects of AINU culture, is distinct from that of Japan as a whole; but it has been influenced by Japanese music. Among the many types of Ainu song the oldest is the *yukar*, long epics about the totemic gods and ancestral heroes of the race. The former are called *kamui-yukar*, the latter *oina;* there are also other subtypes. *Yukar* were traditionally sung on festive and ritual occasions by both men and women; they may be performed solo or by an ensemble and some have short refrains for a chorus. Apart from *yukar*, the two main kinds of Ainu song are *upopo* (festival songs) and *rimse* (group dance-songs). The former are performed sitting down, to the accompaniment of rhythmical taps on a chest; the latter are sung antiphonally, are faster, and have partly meaningless repeated texts. Another kind of dance-song is the *tapkar,* a slow stamping dance, performed solo by men. The Ainu also have work songs, especially for brewing *sake (sake-haw)* and for pounding flour at the bear ceremony, lullabies *(ihumke)* characterized by a special high trilling, and many songs which incorporate imitations of animals or birds—as does *yukar* itself.

Ainu musical instruments include a straw whistle *(wakka-kukutu* or *chi-rekte-kuttar);* a coiled-bark horn *(kosa-bue),* now extinct; a whistle to lure deer; a wide, flat skin drum *(kaco)* used to accompany shamanistic chant *(tusu);* a guimbarde *(mukkuri),* a five-string zither *(tonkori)* formerly played only on Sakhalin; and a type of lute formerly played in the Kurils.

Ainu music shows affinities with the music of China, of the Gilyak people of Sakhalin, and even of certain Amerindian and Eskimo groups. It also sheds some light on ancient Japanese and Northeast Asian musical practices. After the Sakhalin and Kuril Islands Ainu were moved to Hokkaidō at the end of World War II, their culture and music began to disappear, and in recent years Ainu music as a whole has been in decline.

■ ——Nippon Hōsō Kyōkai, ed, *Ainu dentō ongaku* (1965, repr 1972). Donald L. Philippi, *Songs of Gods, Songs of Humans* (1979). *David B.* WATERHOUSE

Aioi

City in southwestern Hyōgo Prefecture, western Honshū, located on the Inland Sea. Originally a fishing village, Aioi developed as a POST-STATION TOWN on the highway San'yōdō. Since the establishment of a shipbuilding industry in 1907, it has become an industrial center. On the third Sunday in May the city holds the Peiron Festival, a boat-racing festival. Pop: 41,498.

aircraft industry → aviation

airports

Commercial airports in Japan are classified by the government into three categories based on size and use. Class 1 consists of Japan's three international airports: Tōkyō International Airport (Haneda), Ōsaka International Airport, and NEW TŌKYŌ INTERNATIONAL AIRPORT (Narita). Class 2 comprises the major domestic airports, of which there are 24 in major urban areas, and class 3 denotes domestic airports located outside major urban areas, of which there are 46 scattered throughout the nation. Besides these, there are 6 airports used jointly by commercial airlines and either Japan's Defense Agency or the American military. Of these 81 commercial and semicommercial airports, 20 have facilities for jet passenger aircraft. Most class 1 and 2 airports are under the supervision of the Ministry of Transport, while class 3 airports are managed by the prefectural governments.

Until the opening of Narita Airport in 1978, Haneda and Ōsaka International were the two major airports in Japan. Although both have 3,000-meter (10,000-ft) main runways, they have very limited areas (408 hectares or 1,008 acres for Tōkyō, 317 hectares or 783 acres for Ōsaka) and poor terminal facilities in proportion to the number of passengers served. Since they are also located near densely populated residential areas, noise has been a serious problem for residents in the vicinity. As a result of a lawsuit filed by area residents, Ōsaka International Airport is required to suspend flight operations between 10 PM and 7 AM, limit the number of aircraft operating per hour, extend financial assistance to area residents for the installation of sound-proofing, and provide compensation to residents forced to move out of the area. Similar measures have been taken at Haneda.

To alleviate the overcrowded conditions at Haneda, Narita Airport was built to handle international flights. It was finally opened in 1978 after a lengthy delay resulting from strong and persistent opposition by local farmers, supported by radical students. There are similar plans to build a new international airport in Ōsaka Bay to serve the Kansai (Ōsaka–Kyōto–Kōbe) area, but planning has been delayed by the strong opposition of local residents.

The maintenance of airports is carried out under the government's Special Account for Airport Improvement. Landing fees and a tax on aircraft fuel are the primary sources of revenue for the airports. Airport operations are governed by the Airport Law of 1952, which follows standards and guidelines established by the International Civil Aviation Organization. *Masui Ken'ichi*

Aisin Seiki Co, Ltd

Manufacturer and seller of automotive components. It also produces and distributes beds, sewing machines, and knitting machines. Founded in 1949, it is a member of the Toyota group. In 1969 it established Aisin–Warner, Ltd, as a joint-venture project with Borg-Warner Corporation of the United States. It received the Deming Prize for superior quality control in 1972. The company has 9 overseas offices, and 10 subsidiaries and affiliates in the United States, Mexico, Panama, Brazil, Belgium, West Germany, England, Singapore, Australia, and Taiwan. Sales for the fiscal year ending March 1982 totaled ¥247.9 billion (US $1.0 billion), of which automotive parts accounted for 94 percent and home appliances and other products for 6 percent. The company was capitalized at ¥9.0 billion (US $37.4 million) in the same year. Corporate headquarters are located in Kariya, Aichi Prefecture.

Aizawa Seishisai (1782–1863)

Scholar of the MITO SCHOOL, a nationalist school of Confucian study. Born in Hitachi Province (now Ibaraki Prefecture); given name Yasushi. He became a pupil of FUJITA YŪKOKU, a noted Neo-Confucian scholar. Aizawa served TOKUGAWA NARIAKI, the lord of the Mito domain (now part of Ibaraki Prefecture), and helped reform his government. He also helped establish a new domain school, Kōdōkan, and was influential in shaping the domain's policies during the politically tumultuous period toward the end of the Tokugawa shogunate. His book on national policy, *Shinron*, inspired many proimperial activists of the day. *Suzuki Eiichi*

Aizawa Tadahiro (1926–   )

Amateur archaeologist known for his discovery of the first paleolithic STONE TOOLS to be recognized in Japan. Born in Tōkyō. A socially withdrawn child who developed an early interest in ancient artifacts, Aizawa spent most of his free time roaming the countryside collecting shards of pottery and stone implements. In the fall of 1946, while peddling sundries in the outskirts of the city of Kiryū, Gumma Prefecture, he came across some obsidian chips and tools in a partly exposed stratum of red clay, part of the so-called KANTŌ LOAM. This loam had previously been considered sterile, most archaeologists believing that human occupation of Japan had begun in the Jōmon period (ca 10,000 BC–ca 300 BC). Aizawa's discovery led to a full-scale investigation of the now famous IWAJUKU SITE by Sugihara Sōsuke (b 1913) and Serizawa Chōsuke (b 1919) in 1949. This event, which led to the rapid identification of other sites, confirmed that PALEOLITHIC CULTURE existed in Japan more than 30,000 years ago.

Aizu Basin

(Aizu Bonchi). In western Fukushima Prefecture, northern Honshū. Bounded by the Ōu Mountains on the east and the Echigo Mountains on the west. A rich agricultural region producing rice and vegetables, it is also known for its lacquer ware and manufacture of communications equipment, cameras, and watches. Major cities are AIZU WAKAMATSU and KITAKATA. Area: approximately 300 sq km (114 sq mi).

Aizu, Battle of → Boshin Civil War

Aizu Hongō ware

(aizu-hongō-yaki). Ceramics made in and around Hongō, the most prolific ceramic production area in the Tōhoku region, near Aizu Wakamatsu in Fukushima Prefecture. Production dates back to 1645, when the MINO WARE potter Mizuno Genzaemon was called to the Aizu domain to make tea-ceremony wares for the local *daimyō*. Work was at first folk-style stoneware made of reddish brown, gritty clay. The rims or shoulders were covered with slip glazes and glossy black overglazes, or with off-white glazes with a gray-green or blue tinge. A well-known traditional product of this type, the *nishin-bachi*—a slab-molded rectangular container for making salted herring—is still made, though it is now usually used as an ashtray.

In the early 1800s porcelain production developed quickly under the patronage of the domainal government. Underglaze-blue porcelains (including *sake* flasks with distinctive geometrical designs on the neck) were most typical of 19th-century Aizu Hongō work, the folk-style stonewares having been relegated to second place. This flourishing porcelain industry was practically destroyed in 1868 when many potters fought for the Tokugawa shogunate in the Boshin Civil War. At the end of the century the industry was revived to meet the demand for electrical insulators and for other commercial products. Today in Hongō both stoneware and porcelain are mass-produced as well as handmade. *David Hale*

Aizu nōsho

(Aizu Book of Agriculture). One of the earliest Japanese agricultural treatises. Written in 1684 by Sase Yojiemon (1630–1711), a rich farmer of the Aizu domain (now part of Fukushima Prefecture), and revised and expanded by his adopted son, Sase Rin'emon. It covers a wide range of agricultural topics, such as techniques for cultivation and irrigation, methods of rice planting and weed removal, and various types of farm implements. *Aizu nōsho* is noteworthy because, unlike other agricultural treatises of the time, it was based primarily not on Chinese works but on the author's own experience.

Aizu Wakamatsu

City in western Fukushima Prefecture, northern Honshū. The most important city in the Aizu Basin. Established as a castle town of the Aizu domain in 1592, much of the city burned in the BOSHIN CIVIL WAR accompanying the Meiji Restoration (1868). Famous for its lacquer ware, the city also produces *sake*, textiles, lumber, and furniture. There is an emerging electronics industry. Tourist attractions include the remains of Wakamatsu Castle, Higashiyama Hot Spring, and IIMORIYAMA, the hill where the BYAKKOTAI, a band of youths, died in a last desperate effort to save the Tokugawa shogunate. Pop: 114,534.

Aizu Yaichi (1881–1956)

Also known as Shūsō Dōjin. TANKA poet, art historian, and calligrapher. Born in the city of Niigata. Graduated from Waseda University where he later became professor of art history. Aizu composed several *tanka* collections, such as *Nankyō shinshō* (1924), which show his attraction to the vigorous style of the late 8th-century anthology, the MAN'YŌSHŪ. He is also remembered for his distinctive style of calligraphy. In 1951 he received the Yomiuri Literary Prize for his collected poems, *Aizu Yaichi zen kashū*.

Ajikawa

Also known as Ajigawa. Canal in the city of Ōsaka, Ōsaka Prefecture, central Honshū. It links the river Yodogawa with Ōsaka Bay. The Ajikawa was constructed in the late 17th century by Kawamura Zuiken (1617–99), a wealthy merchant, engineer, and builder of canals. During the Edo period (1600–1868) it was used for transporting rice and other products to markets in Ōsaka. Its many piers service vessels importing petroleum and coal.

Ajinomoto Co, Inc

Largest manufacturer of L-monosodium glutamate (MSG) and amino acid products in the world. The company's well-known trademark for MSG is Aji-no-moto. MSG was discovered by IKEDA KIKUNAE in 1907 and commercial production was undertaken by Suzuki Saburōsuke in 1908, a year after Ikeda established the company. This unique food seasoning was placed on commercial sale in 1909. The company is now one of Japan's highly diversified food manufacturers as well as a leading international manufacturer of amino acid products for pharmaceutical preparations, foodstuffs, and feed additives. The international activities of the company began in 1917 with the establishment of an office in New York. In 1982 the company had 19 major affiliates and offices in 17 countries and manufacturing facilities in 8 countries. Ajinomoto's joint ventures with leading overseas companies operating in Japan are Knorr Foods Co, Ltd, and Ajinomoto General Foods, Inc. Sales for the fiscal year ending March 1982 totaled ¥393.1 billion (US $1.6 billion), of which processed food, coffees, and soft drinks accounted for 35 percent; seasonings 26 percent; cooking oils and vegetable proteins 23 percent; and amino acids 9 percent. In the same year exports accounted for 7 percent, and the company was capitalized at ¥18.3 billion (US $76 million). Corporate headquarters are in Tōkyō.

ajisai → hydrangea, Japanese

Akabane Kōsaku Bunkyoku

(Akabane Manufacturing Branch). A government-operated factory established in the Akabane section of Tōkyō early in the Meiji period (1868–1912). Beginning with equipment donated by the former Saga domain (now Saga and Nagasaki prefectures), the factory adopted technology from Europe and manufactured steam boilers and light machinery for both government and private enterprises. It was transferred to the Ordnance Department of the Navy Ministry in 1883.

Akabira

City in central Hokkaidō, on the river Sorachigawa. First settled in 1891, Akabira became an important mining town after the opening of a railway line to the ISHIKARI COALFIELD in 1913. Since 1960 many mines have closed down, and active measures are being taken to promote new industries. Pop: 25,467.

Akabori Shirō (1900–   )

Biochemist known for his extensive research on the synthesis of amino acids. Born in Shizuoka Prefecture, he graduated from Chiba Medical College (now a part of Chiba University) and studied chemistry at Tōhoku University. He studied in Germany and the United States and became professor at Ōsaka University after his return. In 1958 he became the first director of Ōsaka University's Institute for Protein Research and, in 1960, university president. He also served as managing director of the Institute of Physical and Chemical Research. He received the Order of Culture in 1965.

Akaezo fūsetsu kō

(Report on the Ezo Lands). A report presented to the Tokugawa shogunate in 1783 by the physician and scholar KUDŌ HEISUKE concerning Russia's southeast advance toward Japan's sparsely populated northern frontier regions, then called EZO. In the work he advised the shogunate to engage in official trade with Russia as a means of averting possible aggression. He also noted the vast potential for enriching Japan through agriculture, colonization, and mining in Ezo. *Akaezo fūsetsu kō* was a forerunner of works like *Kaikoku heidan* (1786) by HAYASHI SHIHEI and *Keisei hisaku* (1798) by HONDA TOSHIAKI, which attacked the shogunate's NATIONAL SECLUSION policy more forcefully.

Akagisan

Conical double volcano northeast of Maebashi, Gumma Prefecture, central Honshū. At the summit there are two crater lakes, Ono and Kono. The western slopes are relatively level, providing excellent farming land. The mountain is part of the Akagi Prefectural Park. Height: 1,828 m (5,996 ft).

Akahata

(Red Flag). Newspaper; principal organ of the JAPAN COMMUNIST PARTY. It is the oldest extant party newspaper in Japan, having been launched in 1928 under the name *Sekki* before the party was legally recognized. In 1935 it was suppressed, but resumed publication immediately after Japan's defeat in 1945. Two years later it was renamed *Akahata*. (*Sekki* and *akahata* are two different pronunciations of the same Chinese characters meaning "red flag.") During the Korean War, publication was temporarily suspended by the Supreme Commander for the Allied Powers (SCAP), Douglas MacArthur, a move that was seen as symbolic of the general repression of communist activities. *Akahata* resumed publication in 1952, following the San Francisco Peace Treaty. In 1959 a Sunday edition was added to the regular daily edition, and the format was changed to have a more general appeal. With a circulation of 3,550,000, it has considerable impact on public opinion in Japan.

Akahata Incident → Red Flag Incident of 1908

akahon → kusazōshi

Akai Electric Co, Ltd

(Akai Denki). Manufacturer of high-fidelity audio and video equipment. Established in 1929, Akai is well known worldwide. In 1969 the company perfected the cross field head as well as the high-quality GX (glass and crystal ferrite) head, and it later developed the world's first portable video tape recorder, using ¼-inch tape, for the consumer market. In 1978 Akai adopted the video home system (VHS) format in the home video market; it expects an increasing volume of sales in this field in the future. Other future plans call for an increased share in domestic markets and expansion in the US market. Akai has overseas subsidiaries in the United States, Australia, England, France, West Germany, Sweden, Denmark, Norway, Canada, and the Philippines. Sales for the fiscal year ending November 1981 totaled ¥90.5 billion (US $404.5 million), of which tape decks comprised 27 percent, other audio products 38 percent, and VTRs 35 percent. For that same year, the export ratio was 92 percent and the company was capitalized at ¥3.2 billion (US $14.3 million). Company headquarters are located in Tōkyō.

Akaishidake

Mountain on the border of Nagano and Shizuoka prefectures, central Honshū; a major peak of the AKAISHI MOUNTAINS in the JAPANESE ALPS. The name Akaishi ("red stone") derives from the reddish hue of quartzite rocks found near its peak. It is popular with experienced mountain climbers. Height: 3,120 m (10,234 ft).

Akaishi Mountains

(Akaishi Sammyaku). Mountain range on the border of Shizuoka, Yamanashi, and Nagano prefectures, central Honshū; extending about 120 km (74 mi) north to south, confined on the east by the river Fujikawa and on the west by the river Tenryūgawa. The southernmost of the three ranges that form the JAPANESE ALPS, this range is often called the Southern Alps and most of its peaks are included in the SOUTHERN ALPS NATIONAL PARK. Some of its peaks are KITADAKE (3,192 m; 10,470 ft), Ainotake (3,189 m; 10,460 ft), KOMAGATAKE (2,966 m; 9,728 ft), AKAISHIDAKE (3,120 m; 10,234 ft), and Nōtoridake (3,026 m; 9,925 ft).

Akai tori

(Red Bird). Children's literary magazine published from July 1918 to October 1936 (publication was temporarily halted from March 1929 to January 1931). Founder and editor SUZUKI MIEKICHI called on numerous established writers to help modernize and improve the quality of children's literature and turned *Akai tori* into one of the most important juvenile publications of its day. It had the backing of intellectuals and educators as well as virtually the entire Japanese literary world. Among the many writers and poets who contributed to its pages were such prominent figures as MORI ŌGAI, SHIMAZAKI TŌSON, NOGAMI YAEKO, AKUTAGAWA RYŪNOSUKE, and KITAHARA HAKUSHŪ. *Akai tori* marked a high point in the actualization of the ideals of children's literature. In general intent it aimed to present stories and tales which were rich in artistic value and written with careful attention to the juvenile sensibility. Thematically, the works published in it reflected sympathy for the democratic humanism of the Taishō period (1912–26) and stressed individuality and a respect for children. *Akai tori* is noted for having pioneered the concept of soliciting contributions by child readers. The success of *Akai tori* spawned other children's magazines; its peak circulation exceeded 30,000. Other writers who participated in its publication include OGAWA MIMEI, SAIJŌ YASO, KUME MASAO, and UNO CHIYO.

Theodore W. GOOSSEN

Akakura Hot Spring

(Akakura Onsen). Located at the foot of the mountain Myōkōsan in southwestern Niigata Prefecture, central Honshū. An earthy, carbonated spring; water temperature 55–60°C (131–140°F). The resort is known for its ski area. Shin Akakura Hot Spring is nearby.

Akama Shrine

(Akama Jingū). Shintō shrine in the city of Shimonoseki, Yamaguchi Prefecture, dedicated to the spirit of the boy emperor ANTOKU (1178–85), who drowned along with many of the Taira family when they suffered a crushing defeat by the rival Minamoto family in the naval engagement at nearby Dannoura. Antoku's remains were recovered and buried within the precincts of a nearby Buddhist temple at Akamagaseki (now Shimonoseki). In 1191 Emperor GO-TOBA renamed the temple Amidaji and ordered the construction of a memorial hall in its precincts where prayers could be offered for the repose of the soul of Antoku, his predecessor. In 1875 the government ordered that the temple be converted to a Shintō shrine, which was called Akama Shrine. Among its many treasures is an early manuscript of the 13th-century *Tale of the Heike* (HEIKE MONOGATARI), known as the *Nagato-bon*. The regular annual festival is held on 7 October, but the shrine is better known for the colorful festival called the Senteisai, which is held annually on 23–25 April to pay reverence to the deceased emperor. *Stanley WEINSTEIN*

Akamatsu family

Warlords of the Muromachi period (1333–1568); descendants of the Murakami Genji branch of the MINAMOTO FAMILY. In 1336 Akamatsu Norimura (1277–1350) allied himself with ASHIKAGA TAKAUJI and was made military governor *(shugo)* of Harima Province (now part of Hyōgo Prefecture, west of Kyōto). He and his heirs later extended their control south and west to Settsu, Mimasaka, and Bizen provinces (now parts of Hyōgo and Okayama prefectures). From the end of the 14th century, the Akamatsu were one of the four families eligible to head the Board of Retainers (Samurai-dokoro) of the Muromachi shogunate. But in 1441 AKAMATSU MITSUSUKE rebelled and assassinated the shōgun ASHIKAGA YOSHINORI and was in turn destroyed by the YAMANA FAMILY and the HOSOKAWA FAMILY. The Akamatsu later regained power in Harima, Mimasaka, and Bizen, but they finally lost their domains in 1521 after being defeated by their vassals, the URAGAMI FAMILY.

Akamatsu Katsumaro (1894–1955)

Political activist. Born in Yamaguchi Prefecture. He helped to form the political study group SHINJINKAI during his senior year at Tōkyō University. After graduation in 1919 he worked as a journalist for the *Tōyō keizai shimpō* until he joined the staff of the Nihon Rōdō Sōdōmei (Japan Federation of Labor) in 1921 and supported its radical wing. The following year he joined the newly organized JAPAN COMMUNIST PARTY, but after the government's suppression of the party in 1923 he became a theorist for the Sōdōmei's right wing. In 1926 he helped to form the SHAKAI MINSHŪTŌ (Socialist People's Party), becoming its secretary-general in 1930. After the MANCHURIAN INCIDENT of 1931 he began to espouse state socialism and in 1932 organized the Nihon Kokka Shakaitō (Japan State Socialist Party) to promote such goals. In 1933 he helped to create the KOKUMIN KYŌKAI (National Association) and in 1937 was elected to the Diet on its slate. In July of that year he helped to organize the more nationalistic Nihon Kakushintō (Japan Reform Party) and became its head. Shortly afterward he engaged in special military missions in China on orders from General ISHIWARA KANJI. During World War II he headed the planning section of the IMPERIAL RULE ASSISTANCE ASSOCIATION. After the war he was barred by the Occupation authorities from political office and remained politically inactive until his death.

Akamatsu Mitsusuke (1373–1441)

Warlord of the Muromachi period (1333–1568). He was an influential figure in the Muromachi shogunate, serving as military governor *(shugo)* of five provinces in central Honshū, including Harima (now part of Hyōgo Prefecture). In 1441 (Kakitsu 1), angered by the attempts of the shōgun ASHIKAGA YOSHINORI to reallocate some of his lands, Mitsusuke invited him to a banquet in Kyōto and assassinated him. Shogunal forces led by YAMANA SŌZEN attacked and defeated Mitsusuke later that year, forcing him to commit suicide. These events are known collectively as the Kakitsu Incident.

Akame, 48 Falls of

(Akame Shijūhattaki). Waterfalls located on a small tributary of the river Nabarigawa, in the southern part of the city of Nabari, Mie Prefecture, central Honshū. Contrary to the name, there are more than 50 waterfalls in all. Noted for their natural beauty and for spring and autumn foliage. A hiking course and camping grounds are located in the vicinity of the falls.

Akan, Lake

(Akanko). In eastern Hokkaidō. Located west of the mountain Oakandake within Akan National Park. Created by an eruption of Oakandake, the lake is shaped like an irregular triangle. Caldera cliffs covered with primeval forests extend on its eastern side. The Akankohan Hot Spring is located on its southern bank. Islands created by lava flows dot the lake. It is the starting point for climbs up Meakandake and Oakandake. Fishing includes pond smelt, trout, crucian carp, and carp. Area: 12.7 sq km (4.9 sq mi); circumference: 26 km (16.1 mi); depth: 36.6 m (120.0 ft); altitude: 419 m (1,374 ft).

Akan National Park

(Akan Kokuritsu Kōen). Situated in eastern Hokkaidō, the park is set in rugged mountain terrain with volcanoes, some of which are active; subarctic forests; and numerous caldera lakes. The largest lake in the area is Lake KUTCHARO in the north; the area surrounding Lake AKAN in the southwest contains the volcanic cones of MEAKANDAKE (1,503 m; 4,930 ft) and OAKANDAKE (1,371 m; 4,497 ft). To the east lies Lake MASHŪ, the second major lake, which has a transparency depth of 35.8 m (117.4 ft), the greatest in the world. The forests consist largely of Japanese beech *(buna)*, Yeddo spruce *(ezomatsu)*, Sakhalin fir *(todomatsu)*, and pine. The strangest natural phenomena are the *marimo* in Lake Akan, which are designated a Special Natural Monument. These balls of algae *(Aegagropila)*, 2–15 cm (0.8–5.9 in) in diameter, rise to the water's surface because of photosynthesis in the early part of the day and sink at night. The park area was once inhabited by AINU, and Ainu "tourist villages" are still found there. Two famous hot spring resorts are Akankohan by Lake Akan and Kawayu by Lake Kutcharo. Area: 875 sq km (337.8 sq mi).

Akasaka Detached Palace

(Akasaka Rikyū). Distinguished example of late Meiji period Western-style architecture; located in Minato Ward, Tōkyō. Designed by Katayama Otokuma (1854–1917), with the palace at Versailles and the Louvre in Paris serving as his models, it was built in 1909 as a residence for the crown prince. Constructed at enormous cost and 10 years in the making, it was symbolic of the Meiji government's desire to demonstrate Japan's attainment of equality with the West. Most of the building materials and furnishings were imported. KURODA SEIKI was among the many collaborating artists whose works decorate the interior. When the palace's importance in the history of Japanese architecture was recognized in the late 1960s, a plan was presented for its restoration, and in 1974 it was converted into an official state guesthouse for visiting foreign dignitaries.

WATANABE Hiroshi

Akashi

City in southern Hyōgo Prefecture, western Honshū. A castle town during the Edo period (1600–1868), Akashi originally developed as a

POST-STATION TOWN on the highways San'yōdō and Shikoku Kaidō. It is now a heavy industry center, with textile, steel, and machinery plants built on reclaimed land, and a major transportation center for the Inland Sea area. Much of the coastal beauty, celebrated in poems in the 8th-century *Man'yōshū* and other literary works, has been lost. Pop: 254,873.

Akashi Strait

(Akashi Kaikyō). Narrow strait in the Inland Sea between Awaji-shima Island and the city of Akashi in Hyōgo Prefecture. It links Ōsaka Bay and the Harima Sea and provides the shortest route between Honshū and Shikoku. After the opening of railway lines its role was taken over by the sea route between Uno and Takamatsu, but plans are now being implemented to span the strait with bridges. It is noted for its strong currents and abundant marine life. Deepest point: 135 m (443 ft).

Akazome Emon (ca 957–1041)

Court lady, WAKA poet. She served Rinshi, wife of the powerful FUJIWARA NO MICHINAGA, and perhaps later Rinshi's daughter, Empress Shōshi (JŌTŌ MON'IN). Married to Ōe no Masahira (952–1012), a provincial official, she had two children, and was the grandmother of the famous scholar ŌE NO MASAFUSA (or Tadafusa; 1041–1111). She became a nun in her late years.

Akazome Emon was one of the foremost women court poets of her day and was ranked by critics of the medieval period on a par with her famous contemporary, Lady IZUMI SHIKIBU. However, her characteristically bland verses lack the passionate intensity of Izumi Shikibu's. The relatively large number of 92 of her poems are found in imperial anthologies, beginning with the SHŪI WAKASHŪ (ca 1000, Collection of Gleanings). Her personal anthology, *Akazome Emon shū*, contains more than 600 poems. Akazome Emon is also traditionally credited with having written at least part (chapters 1–30?) of the important historical tale EIGA MONOGATARI (mid-11th century; tr *A Tale of Flowering Fortunes*, 1980). *Robert H. Brower*

akebi

Akebia quinata. A deciduous, woody vine of the family Lardizaba-laceae which grows wild in mountainous areas of Honshū, Shikoku, and Kyūshū; it is also found in Korea and China. Its new spring shoots are edible. The alternate leaves are compound with five oblong leaflets. Light purple flower clusters appear in the spring, consisting of several small male flowers and one to three larger female flowers 2.5–3 centimeters (1 in) across. The flower consists of three petal-like sepals. The fruit is oblong and light purple in color. When ripe it splits longitudinally, revealing black seeds enclosed in white flesh that is sweet and edible. The Japanese name *akebi* may represent an older pronunciation of *akemi* ("opening fruit"). The vines of a three-leaved variety, *mitsuba akebi (Akebia trifoliata)*, are used in basket making and other handicrafts. The *akebi* was introduced to Europe and the United States in the 19th century, and has been successfully cultivated in public and private gardens. See also MUBE. *Matsuda Osamu*

Akechi Mitsuhide (?–1582)

Also known as Koretō Hyūga no Kami. One of the principal captains of and the assassin of the hegemon ODA NOBUNAGA. A man of obscure origins, Mitsuhide first appears in a reliable source in 1569 as one of Nobunaga's military and administrative deputies in Kyōto; for the next three years he occupied the difficult position of intermediary between Nobunaga and the shōgun ASHIKAGA YOSHI-AKI. Between 1570 and 1573 Mitsuhide also took part in Nobunaga's campaigns in Ōmi (now Shiga Prefecture), to the east of Kyōto, and was awarded Sakamoto Castle and two districts in that province. After distinguishing himself in a series of other campaigns, Mitsuhide was in 1580 assigned Tamba Province (now part of Kyōto and Hyōgo prefectures), Kyōto's immediate hinterland, which he had conquered for Nobunaga. That same year he was appointed one of two special commissioners to conduct a province-wide cadastral survey in Yamato Province (now Nara Prefecture), and in 1581 he performed a similar task in Tango Province (now the northern part of Kyōto Prefecture); thus he became an important agent in the implementation of Nobunaga's comprehensive new land policy, the prelude to the destruction of medieval patterns of landholding (see KENCHI). In 1582, however, he turned against Nobunaga and destroyed him in the HONNŌJI INCIDENT. What real or imagined slight incited Mitsuhide to treason remains a matter of conjecture; in any case, he failed to seize the hegemony and, defeated 11 days later by TOYOTOMI HIDEYOSHI in the Battle of YAMAZAKI, was killed in flight by marauding peasants.

Despite his undistinguished family background, Mitsuhide was a highly cultivated man. In particular, he was an accomplished amateur of the tea ceremony and of linked verse *(renga)*, associating with some of the most renowned masters of these arts, notably the Sakai tea man TSUDA SŌGYŪ and SATOMURA JŌHA, the last of the serious *renga* poets. The *daimyō* and *waka* poet HOSOKAWA YŪSAI was also his intimate; but he rejected Mitsuhide's appeal to take his side after Nobunaga's death. *George Elison*

Aki

City in southeastern Kōchi Prefecture, Shikoku, located on Tosa Bay. Aki is the political, economic, and cultural center of southeastern Kōchi, with convenient transportation to Kōchi, the prefectural capital. Forestry is a thriving industry in the nearby mountains, and on the Aki Plain rice and vegetables are grown. The coast is known for its fishing. Special products of the city include tiles and cutlery. Pop: 25,024.

Akiba Shrine

(Akiba Jinja). Shintō shrine dedicated to Kagutsuchi no Kami, the deity of fire, located on Akihasan, a mountain in the Shūchi district of Shizuoka Prefecture. Although the shrine and the mountain are designated by the same Chinese characters, the shrine is known by one reading *(akiba)* and the mountain by another *(akiha)*.

Founded in the early 8th century, the shrine was believed to afford protection from calamities related to fire. Before the separation of Shintō and Buddhism in 1868, the shrine was closely associated with Akibadera, a Buddhist temple enshrining the bodhisattva KANNON, believed to be the original Buddhist prototype *(honji;* see HONJI SUIJAKU) of the Shintō deity Kagutsuchi. Veneration of this shrine, also popularly known as Sanjakubō, gradually spread throughout eastern Japan in the Edo period (1600–1868) and resulted in many branch shrines throughout Japan. The shrine is noted for its Fire Festival *(himatsuri)*, held annually on 15 and 16 December. Among its treasures are more than 150 swords donated by patrons of the shrine in accordance with the legend that the deity Izanagi used his sword to kill the fire god worshiped here. *Stanley Weinstein*

Akigawa

City in northwestern Tōkyō Prefecture at the confluence of the rivers Akigawa and Tamagawa. Formerly a rural village, Akigawa is now a residential suburb of Tōkyō. Part of the city is located in the Hamura–Kusabana Hills Prefectural Natural Park. Pop: 42,805.

Akihito, Crown Prince (1933–   )

Eldest son of Emperor HIROHITO. He spent much of the wartime period in the mountain resort of Karuizawa. With the surrender and peace in 1945 he returned to Tōkyō and to his studies at Gakushūin High School (Peers' School). At the same time he began his study of the English language and of Western culture under Elizabeth Gray VINING. His coming-of-age ceremony and his investiture as heir to the Japanese throne took place in 1952, the year that he graduated from high school. For the next four years the crown prince attended Gakushūin University. Like his father, he developed an interest in marine biology and began to specialize in ichthyology, particularly the classification of Japanese fish.

In 1959 Prince Akihito married Shōda Michiko (see MICHIKO, PRINCESS), a commoner, the daughter of Shōda Eizaburō, the president of a large flour manufacturing company. The courtship and marriage created a stir because this was the first instance of an heir to the imperial throne marrying outside the circle of the traditional court nobility. Prince Akihito and Princess Michiko reside in the Tōgū Palace in Tōkyō. They have three children, of whom the eldest, Prince HIRO, was born in 1960, held his coming-of-age ceremony in 1980, and graduated from Gakushūin University in 1982. Since visiting the United Kingdom for the coronation of Queen Elizabeth II in 1953, Prince Akihito has made numerous state visits, including visits to the United States, Canada, Australia, New Zealand, and countries in Southeast Asia and South America. He regularly receives visiting dignitaries to Japan. Through his study of foreign languages, Japanese and world history, and international affairs, and through his official activities in Japan and visits abroad, Prince Akihito has prepared himself to succeed Emperor Hirohito as the emperor of Japan and to assume the constitutional role of "symbol of the Japanese state and of the unity of the Japanese people."

Martin C. COLLCUTT

Akimoto Matsuyo (1911–   )

Playwright. Born in Kanagawa Prefecture. Making her debut in 1947 with the one-act play *Keijin,* she established herself within the next decade as a major dramatist. Her plays are characterized by a peculiar earthiness, interweaving folklore and legend with vivid evocations of the sorrows and sufferings of those who inhabit the lowest levels of society. Akimoto has also written many popularly acclaimed radio and television dramas. Her important plays include *Hitachibō Kaison* (1964; tr *The Priest of Hitachi,* 1973) and *Kasabuta Shikibu kō* (1969); both are based on popular local legends and depict victims of Japan's rapid modernization.

akirame

(renunciation, resignation). An important behavioral concept in traditional Japanese popular psychology. Until recently the Japanese have tended to emphasize the virtue of enduring pain and deprivation with patience. It was a part of the warrior's code (reflecting the influence of Confucian ethics) which taught the importance of self-control and perseverance. The willingness to endure and suffer the unavoidable in a spirit of resignation also reflected a kind of fatalism derived in part from Buddhistic thought (and perhaps Taoism). This fatalism contained a certain optimism as is expressed in the popular saying, "Pain is followed by pleasure." Like nature, human life, with its pain and hardships, was regarded as basically transient. Because of this almost stoic resignation, many Japanese in the past endured hardships without protest. Historically, many Japanese also accepted their place in a rigidly hierarchical society with a sense of *akirame.* It is interesting that, for some Japanese, *akirame* seems to bring with it a certain self-pity accompanied by a mildly masochistic feeling of gratification.

▬▬——Minami Hiroshi, *Nihonjin no shinri* (1953).

Hiroshi WAGATSUMA

Akishima

City in western Tōkyō Prefecture, east of the confluence of the rivers Akigawa and Tamagawa. It was a silk- and vegetable-producing village before World War II. Because of its proximity to the Japanese army's Tachikawa Air Field, munition plants were relocated here during the war. It is now both a residential and industrial (electronics and glass) city. East Akishima is occupied by an American military base used jointly with the Japanese Self Defense Forces. Pop: 89,343.

Akishinodera

A nonsectarian Buddhist temple in Nara, formerly affiliated with the Seizan branch of the JŌDO SECT. Akishinodera was founded in 780 by the HOSSŌ SECT scholar Zenju. With cells to accommodate over a thousand monks, it was comparable to SAIDAIJI in size. Patronized by the imperial court from the outset, Akishinodera was designated a *chokuganji,* i.e., a temple at which prayers were offered for the well-being of the emperor. In 834, after the introduction of esoteric Buddhism, it was transformed into a SHINGON SECT temple by imperial decree. The monastery was destroyed in 1135 by a fire which left only the *kōdō* (lecture hall) standing. This building was largely restored in the early part of the Kamakura period (1185–1333) and is known today as the *hondō* (main hall). The principal image of worship *(honzon)* is Yakushi Nyorai (the Buddha of healing) carved in the middle part of the Heian period (794–1185). Of particular interest are four images depicting Gigeiten (patron deity of the arts), Bonten (Brahmā), Taishakuten (Indra), and the bodhisattva Gudatsu (Trāñamukta). The heads are notable examples of dry lacquer sculpture made late in the Nara period (710–794).

Lucie R. WEINSTEIN

Akita

Capital of Akita Prefecture located at the mouth of the river Omonogawa, northern Honshū. A fortification called AKITAJŌ was constructed in 733 (its remains can be seen), and from the 1600s the city flourished as a castle town of the SATAKE FAMILY. Akita is the political and cultural center of the prefecture and a part of the so-called Akita Bay Industrial Area. Principal industries are petrochemical, fertilizer, machinery, pulp, and zinc manufacture. The city is also a distribution center for agricultural produce from the Akita Plain. There are four universities in the town, including Akita University, and a prefectural museum and library. A festival of lanterns is held each August. Pop: 284,830.

Akita Incident

An incident early in the Meiji period (1868–1912) in which members of the Akita Risshikai (Self-Help Society of Akita Prefecture) were arrested and subsequently imprisoned for plotting to overthrow the government. Formed in 1880 in response to the FREEDOM AND PEOPLE'S RIGHTS MOVEMENT, the Akita Risshikai was composed of approximately 3,000 farmers and former *samurai* disenchanted with the Meiji government. Setting 16 June 1881 as the target date, the society's president, Shibata Asagorō, planned an attack on wealthy farmers, police headquarters, banks, and district and prefectural offices in Akita in order to obtain money and arms for further revolutionary activities. The plot was prematurely discovered, however, and those involved were imprisoned by the authorities.

Akitajō

One of a series of fortified outposts in Dewa Province (now Akita and Yamagata prefectures) in northeastern Honshū, used between the 8th and 10th centuries for the pacification of EZO tribesmen. Construction began in 733 on a site in what is now the city of Akita to replace an earlier outpost located farther south. In the latter part of the 8th century the governor *(kokushi)* of Dewa moved his headquarters there. The fort was abandoned sometime after the 9th century but was replaced by newer fortifications nearby, for the area long remained strategically important. The only remains of the original structures are parts of a palisade surrounding the keep and the foundation of a temple. Excavations continue at the site at Takashimizuoka, in the city of Akita.

Akita Oil Fields

(Akita Yuden). In western Akita Prefecture, northern Honshū. The oil fields, the largest of which are at Yabase and Sarukawa, rank second after Niigata Prefecture in domestic petroleum output and make up 20 percent of Japan's annual production. An offshore oil field has also been developed in recent years. In 1979, crude oil production was 49,376 barrels (95 million liters).

Akita Plain

(Akita Heiya). Coastal alluvial plain in central Akita Prefecture, northern Honshū. Bounded on the west by the Sea of Japan and on the east by the DEWA MOUNTAINS, it is a major agricultural region with a large annual rice crop. Several oil wells are located north and south of the city of Akita, and the coastal area near Akita is being developed into an industrial and commercial region. Length: 30 km (19 mi); width: 6 km (4 mi).

Akita Prefecture

(Akita Ken). Located in northern Honshū and bounded by Aomori Prefecture on the north, Iwate Prefecture on the east, Miyagi and Yamagata prefectures on the south, and the Sea of Japan on the west. Largely mountainous, its principal ranges include the ŌU MOUNTAINS in the east and the DEWA MOUNTAINS in the center running in a north-south line. Major rivers are the OMONOGAWA and YONESHIROGAWA. The OGA PENINSULA juts out into the Sea of Japan north of the city of AKITA. Lake TAZAWA is located entirely within the prefecture, and Lake TOWADA on its border with Aomori Prefecture. The climate is marked by heavy precipitation, especially in winter; snow sometimes accumulates to depths of 3 m (10 ft).

Under the ancient provincial system (KOKUGUN SYSTEM), Akita

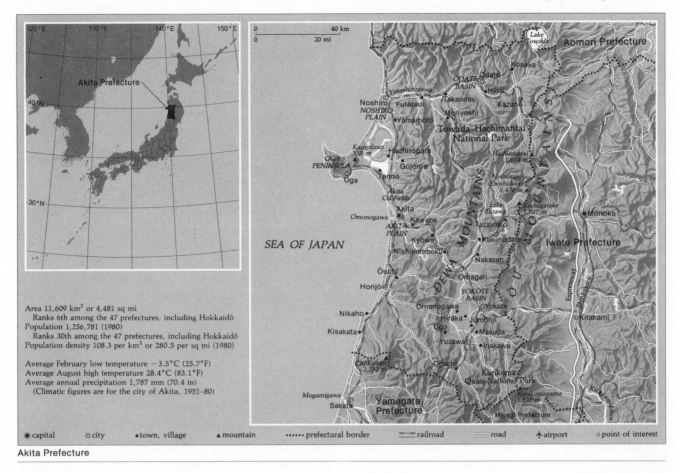

Akita Prefecture

⦿ capital	◎ city	● town, village	▲ mountain	······ prefectural border	▦▦ railroad	▭▭ road	✈ airport	○ point of interest

Area 11,609 km² or 4,481 sq mi
  Ranks 6th among the 47 prefectures, including Hokkaidō
Population 1,256,781 (1980)
  Ranks 30th among the 47 prefectures, including Hokkaidō
Population density 108.3 per km² or 280.5 per sq mi (1980)

Average February low temperature −3.5°C (25.7°F)
Average August high temperature 28.4°C (83.1°F)
Average annual precipitation 1,787 mm (70.4 in)
  (Climatic figures are for the city of Akita, 1951–80)

Prefecture was the Ugo section of Dewa Province. A military outpost, AKITAJŌ, was established in 733 at the present site of Akita. The area was ruled by the SATAKE FAMILY and other *daimyō* during the Edo period (1600–1868).

Its economy has traditionally been dominated by agriculture, especially rice and forestry. It is also a leading producer of petroleum and copper; other minerals include gold, silver, lead, and zinc. *Sake* brewing and the pulp and plywood industries are active. Transportation difficulties caused by its mountainous terrain and snowy winters have long retarded industrial development and led to an outflow of population to urban centers such as Tōkyō and Yokohama. Tourist attractions include TOWADA–HACHIMANTAI NATIONAL PARK, Oga Peninsula, Lake Tazawa, and the mountain KURIKOMAYAMA. There are also numerous hot spring resorts. Area: 11,609 sq km (4,481 sq mi); pop: 1,256,781; capital: Akita. Other major cities include NOSHIRO, YOKOTE, ŌDATE, and KAZUNO.

Akita school

(Akitaha). Also known as Akita *ranga* (Akita Dutch painting). A mid-18th-century school of Japanese painting that flourished in Akita in northern Honshū. Developed by the *daimyō* of Akita, SATAKE SHOZAN (1748–85), and his chief retainer, ODANO NAOTAKE (1749–80), Akita painting was for the most part a judicious mix of naturalistic detail and Western illusionistic methods using traditional Japanese pigments on silk or paper, with an overall surface coating of oil and resin. Compositional interest was focused on the unexpectedly large foreground subject, generally a bird or flower arrangement dramatically modeled in light and shade and frequently juxtaposed against a low-lying, distant landscape in Western perspective.

The style may be said to date from 1773, the year HIRAGA GENNAI (1728–80) traveled to Akita to give advice on the fief's copper mines. While there, Gennai taught the principles of Western painting, which he had learned from the Dutch at Nagasaki, to Shozan, Naotake, and other members of the Akita clan. Shozan provided financial support and actively encouraged his retainers to practice the new style. The three major painters of the school were Shozan, Naotake, and Satake Yoshimi (1749–1800). The early deaths of Shozan and Naotake curtailed the productive period of the Akita school, though some lesser-known artists continued the style for a few more decades.

The main principles of the Akita school are stated in Shozan's essays, "Gahō kōryō" (1778, Art of Painting) and "Gato rikai" (1778, Understanding Painting and Composition). Clearly impressed by the ability of European artists to reproduce texture and form through modeling in light and shade, Shozan and the other Akita artists demonstrated that such methods could be of value to the Japanese artist as well. A particularly notable characteristic of the Akita artists was their dependence on sketchbooks for recording precise observations of flowers, birds, and insects. The scientific studies on which their finished paintings were based might as easily have been employed by naturalists, yet from their rigorous technical standards emerged an inventive art of striking compositional arrangements and exceptional coloristic beauty.

Since the Akita artists were not dependent on painting for a living, few of their pictures were sold on the open art market, and even now few are housed in major museums outside Akita. See also WESTERN-STYLE PICTURES, EARLY.

■ ——Cal French, *Through Closed Doors: Western Influence on Japanese Art* (1977). Naruse Fujio and Sugase Tadashi, "Edo jidai no yōfūga," *Namban bijutsu to yōfūga* (vol 25 of *Genshoku Nihon no bijutsu*; 1970). *Cal* FRENCH

Akitsu

Port town in southern Hiroshima Prefecture, western Honshū, on the Inland Sea. Long known for its *sake* brewing. The town's modern industries, located on reclaimed land, include brick firing, shipbuilding, and sodium sulfide production. Rice, potatoes, mandarin oranges, loquats, and other crops are grown on the surrounding hills. The cultivation of edible oysters and pearl oysters is a major occupation. Pop: 13,857.

Akiyama Saneyuki (1868–1918)

Also called Akiyama Masayuki. Naval officer and architect of modern Japanese naval doctrine. Born in Matsuyama, Iyo Province (now

Ehime Prefecture), of a *samurai* family. Graduating in 1890 from the Naval Academy, Akiyama made an early mark as a widely read, perceptive analyst of naval matters. He was sent to study in the United States (1897–99), where he witnessed the destruction of the Spanish fleet and the American amphibious landings in Cuba as a foreign observer attached to Admiral Sampson's squadron in the Spanish-American War. His subsequent intelligence reports to Tōkyō on American naval technology and doctrine became a classic source of information on the US Navy for Japanese naval planners.

As lieutenant commander, Akiyama was appointed instructor at the Naval Staff College (1902–1903), where his command of a vast range of naval information and his pioneering in certain analytical techniques, like table-top war-gaming, revolutionized instruction at the college and made it an outstanding institution for advanced naval education. During these years Akiyama put together a comprehensive tactical doctrine which integrated both Western and classical Japanese concepts. His doctrine emphasized planning, organization, and morale and envisioned a strategy of attrition whereby an enemy fleet approaching Japan would be weakened in successive assaults by defending naval units.

As a member of the senior staff on the First Fleet under TŌGŌ HEIHACHIRŌ, Akiyama put his genius for tactical planning and organization to stunning effect during the RUSSO-JAPANESE WAR of 1904–05. His seven-stage battle plan was a major element in Tōgō's crushing victory over the Russian fleet at Tsushima in May 1905 (see TSUSHIMA, BATTLE OF) and for several decades following the war was the model for Japan's basic naval strategy in defense of the home islands.

Again instructor at the Staff College (1905–08 and 1912–14), Akiyama exercised a decisive influence in the navy's selection of weapons, tactics, and fleet organization at a time when the fleet was undergoing a period of expansion. As rear admiral in the Navy Ministry by the outset of World War I, he devoted his last years to educating the Japanese public in the importance of maintaining a front-rank navy.

■ ——Bōeichō Bōei Kenshujo Senshishitsu, *Senshi sōsho: Kaigun gunsembi*, vol 1 (1969). Mark Peattie, "Akiyama Saneyuki and the Emergence of Modern Japanese Naval Doctrine," *U.S. Naval Institute Proceedings* (January 1977).   Mark R. PEATTIE

Akiyama Teisuke (1868–1950)

Politician; publisher of the popular Meiji-period newspaper *Niroku shimpō*. Born in Kurashiki, Bizen Province (now Okayama Prefecture). After graduation from Tōkyō University he became a government official, but grew displeased with the exclusive control of the government by men from the former Satsuma and Chōshū domains (now Kagoshima and Yamaguchi prefectures; see HAMBATSU), and resigned. In 1893 he launched the *Niroku shimpō*. The paper went bankrupt in a year and a half but resumed publication in 1900. Its rapidly growing readership made it, along with the YOROZU CHŌHŌ, one of the most important newspapers of the first decade of the 20th century. Akiyama and his newspaper won great popularity, first by carrying out an extensive campaign to expose the injustices of the MITSUI financial combine (ZAIBATSU) and then, in cooperation with the Salvation Army, working to abolish prostitution. He was also active as a member of the Diet, but his vehement attacks on the Katsura cabinet during the Russo-Japanese War (1904–05) gave rise to the rumor that he was a Russian spy, and he was forced to resign his seat. Though the *Niroku shimpō* declined in popularity, Akiyama for the remainder of his life wielded considerable political influence behind the scenes.   KŌUCHI Saburō

Akiyoshidai

Upland in central western Yamaguchi Prefecture, western Honshū. The largest limestone tableland in Japan, it is known for its karst topography. AKIYOSHIDŌ, a lime grotto, is a popular tourist attraction. Average elevation: 300 m (984 ft); area: 130 sq km (50 sq mi).

Akiyoshidō

Also known as Shūhōdō. Limestone cave in the AKIYOSHIDAI upland, western Yamaguchi Prefecture, western Honshū. One of the largest limestone caves in the world, it has a depth of approximately 10 km (6.2 mi), of which 1.5 km (1 mi) is open to tourists. The main passage is 90 m (295 ft) at its widest and 30 m (98 ft) at its highest. The walls of the cave are crystalline limestone. With its rivers, wa-

Akiyoshidai

The Akiyoshidai tableland, covered with the tombstone-like rocks that are one of the peculiar features of karst topography.

terfalls, deep pools, stone pillars, and numerous stalactites and stalagmites, Akiyoshidō is the main tourist attraction of Akiyoshidai Quasi-National Park.

Akiyoshi Toshiko (1929–)

Jazz pianist, band leader, and composer. Highly regarded artist active in American jazz circles. Born in Dairen (Ch: Dalian or Ta-lien; now part of Lüda [Lüta]) in Manchuria. She was inspired by the pianist Hampton Hawes, an American military officer stationed in Japan after World War II. Between 1956 and 1959 she studied at Berklee College of Music in Boston. Akiyoshi settled in California, where together with her husband, Lew Tabackin, she organized a band. She has produced many jazz pieces including the award-winning "Kogun" (The Lost Battalion) of 1974.   ABE Yasushi

Akizuki Rebellion of 1876

(Akizuki no Ran). Rebellion by former *samurai* in Akizuki, Fukuoka Prefecture, on 27 October 1876. Angered by the Meiji government's decrees terminating samurai stipends (see CHITSUROKU SHOBUN) and prohibiting the wearing of swords (HAITŌREI), several hundred warriors of the former Akizuki domain, led by Iso Jun (1827?–76), Miyazaki Kurumanosuke (1835–76), and others, attacked the prefectural office. They planned to combine forces with MAEBARA ISSEI and his men, who revolted simultaneously at Hagi, Yamaguchi Prefecture (see HAGI REBELLION). The Akizuki rebels, however, were quickly captured by government troops from the garrison at Kokura. Iso and Miyazaki committed suicide. This armed revolt, sparked by the similarly motivated JIMPŪREN REBELLION in Kumamoto three days earlier, was symptomatic of bitter disaffection in the dispossessed samurai class in the early part of the Meiji period (1868–1912). See also SAGA REBELLION; SATSUMA REBELLION.

Akkadō

Limestone caves in the town of Iwaizumi, eastern Iwate Prefecture, northern Honshū. Said to be the largest group of such caves in Japan. According to a 1961 survey, the total length of the caves was 7.6 km (4.7 mi); the longest single cave, 2.3 km (1.4 mi); the widest, 17 m (56 ft); the highest, 25 m (82 ft); with a total of 54 branch caves. Primitive oceanic life such as the *horaanagokai (Nerillidae)* inhabits the caves. The cave is open to the public to a distance of 500 m (1,640 ft) from its entrance.

Akō

City in southwestern Hyōgo Prefecture, western Honshū, located on the Inland Sea. Akō developed as a castle town in the Edo period (1600–1868). The town was early known for its salt and cotton, but salt production ended in 1971. Today the major industries are textiles, steel, chemicals, and brick. Akō has long been associated in the popular imagination with the FORTY-SEVEN RŌNIN INCIDENT (1703), in which a band of local retainers avenged the death of their lord; a festival is held at the castle site on 14 December to commemorate the event. The coastal area is part of the Inland Sea National Park. Pop: 51,046.

Akogiura

Also known as Akogigaura. Coastal area in the city of Tsu, Mie Prefecture, central Honshū. Located on Ise Bay, it is famous for its scenic coastal views and its association with the ISE SHRINE. Because of its religious affiliation, the coast is regarded as sacred and there has been a historic prohibition against any fishing or hunting. Also known for NŌ chanting. Part of Isenoumi Prefectural Natural Park, and today the location of several bathing beaches.

Akō Incident of 887

(Akō Jiken or Akō no Fungi). A test of strength between Fujiwara no Mototsune (836–891) and Emperor UDA on the latter's accession in 887. Mototsune expected to be reconfirmed as regent (kampaku), a post he had held under Uda's father, Emperor Kōkō (830–887; r 884–887). But the edict drafted by Uda's favorite, Tachibana no Hiromi (837–890), named Mototsune akō (the title of an ancient Chinese regent), a designation that, he claimed, implied a purely nominal post with no real functions. It was, he insisted, an attempt to deprive him of power. Because of Mototsune's influence in the court, Uda had no choice but to rescind the edict and reappoint him as kampaku. It was not until Mototsune's death in 891 that Uda was able to free himself of Fujiwara REGENCY GOVERNMENT.

G. Cameron HURST III

Akō Incident of 1703 → Forty-Seven Rōnin Incident

Akune

City in northwestern Kagoshima Prefecture, Kyūshū. Principal industries are farming and fishing; it is particularly noted for its citrus fruits. Akune Hot Spring and a beautiful seacoast make this a popular tourist area. Pop: 29,524.

Akutagawa Ryūnosuke (1892–1927)

Short-story writer, poet, and essayist; noted for his virtuoso style in finely crafted stories that explore the underside of human nature. Born in Tōkyō, he was the eldest son of Niihara Toshizō. Soon after his birth his mother, Fuku, went insane. Subsequently he was adopted as a son by his maternal uncle, Akutagawa Michiaki. In his boyhood Akutagawa was puny, frail, and hypersensitive, but always distinguished himself at school. A voracious reader, he accumulated a formidable knowledge not only of Chinese and Japanese classics but of Western literature as well. He was fascinated by such writers as Ibsen, Anatole France, Mérimée, Poe, Baudelaire, and Wilde. He also profited from study of some established Japanese novelists, especially the two great literary men of the time: MORI ŌGAI (1862–1922) and NATSUME SŌSEKI (1867–1916). While majoring in English literature at Tōkyō University, he began to publish a series of remarkable stories. The material for these stories came from 12th- and 13th-century collections of Japanese tales, but they are given sharp twists of modern psychological insight and rendered in a finely polished style.

"Hana" (1916; tr "The Nose," 1961), for example, portrays a high-ranking Buddhist priest who is troubled by the gigantic proportions of his nose. While outwardly calm, he suffers deeply from embarrassment. The priest stumbles on an esoteric treatment that succeeds in shrinking his nose to ordinary size. The transformation, however, unexpectedly invites derision, now more open and unsparing. One morning, much to his relief, he wakes up to discover his nose returned to its former monstrous size. "Now, nobody will laugh at me any more," he sighs to himself as his long dangling nose sways in the morning breeze. Natsume Sōseki, in a letter to Akutagawa, praised "Hana" for its refined humor, polished style, and fresh subject matter. The outstanding novelist of the day, Sōseki added that if Akutagawa could write 20 or 30 stories like this one, he would be a most unique writer, a prophecy that was to prove true.

For his graduation thesis in 1916, Akutagawa wrote an essay on William Morris. After a brief teaching job at the Naval Engineering School, he decided to devote full time to writing. In 1918, he married Tsukamoto Fumiko. These early years were the most productive of Akutagawa's career; he published some of his most

accomplished works, including "Imogayu" (1916; tr "Yam Gruel," 1952), "Hankechi" (1916; tr "A Handkerchief," 1930), "Hōkyōnin no shi" (1918; tr "The Martyr," 1952), and "Kumo no ito" (1918; tr "The Spider's Thread," 1930). The best story from this period is "Jigokuhen" (1918; tr "Hell Screen," 1948), a macabre tale of an eccentric artist who values art over life. Yoshihide, the most renowned artist of his time, is commissioned by his feudal lord to paint the agonies of hell on a screen. Subjecting his models to every conceivable torture, Yoshihide finishes the screen except for the final scene. In order to complete it, he requests the lord to stage an actual burning of a carriage with a beautiful court lady trapped inside. The lord grants Yoshihide's request. The lady inside, however, turns out to be the artist's only daughter, who had previously spurned the lord's amorous advances. Yoshihide hangs himself, leaving behind the finished screen, which is universally acclaimed as a masterpiece.

Akutagawa, firmly established in literary circles by 1918, was regarded as a major opponent of NATURALISM (shizen shugi), which dominated Japanese literature in the early 1900s by thriving on sordid confessions. For the next four years, 1919 to 1922, he continued to write stories as before, borrowing material from old tales and giving them a complex modern interpretation dressed in a delicately textured prose. Representative works dating from this middle period include: "Nankin no Kirisuto" (1920, "Christ in Nanjing [Nanking]"), "Toshishun" (1920; tr "Tu Tze-chun," 1930), "Shūzanzu" (1921; tr "The Painting of an Autumn Mountain," 1962), and "Yabu no naka" (1922; tr "In a Grove," 1952). This period of maturation saw changes in his works such as the disappearance of humor and the erosion of art's authority over life while they continued to portray the disturbing complexities of human existence. "Yabu no naka," which provided the basic plot for KUROSAWA AKIRA's brilliant film RASHŌMON (1950), shows precisely how complex life can be. The story comprises seven different versions of a rape-murder incident involving a young samurai, his wife, and a marauding bandit. The first four accounts of the incident provide circumstantial information, while the couple and the brigand give conflicting, self-glorifying accounts of what really happened in the grove. Most critics agree that the absence of absolute truth is the theme of this puzzling story. Another interpretation is that with the bandit as a catalyst, the couple are forced to face new, unpleasant truths about themselves.

The final period of his literary career, 1923 to 1927, was marred by deteriorating health. Akutagawa's writing underwent some profound transformations. Gone were his superbly constructed period pieces. He wrote not only about contemporary life, but also about his own life, thinly disguised, though he had once frowned on confessional writing. The most significant change was that he lost his desire to be a storyteller. Much of the work in this period was autobiographical in tone; some even resembled embellished diary entries. Despite worsening health, he engaged in a celebrated literary dispute with TANIZAKI JUN'ICHIRŌ (1886–1965), in which Akutagawa upheld lyricism as the primary value in the novel and discredited the role of structure. The most significant fictional work from this final period is Kappa (1927; tr Kappa, 1970), a satirical tale about amphibious elves known as KAPPA, who appear in Japanese folklore. The narrator accidentally falls into the subterranean world of the kappa. At first everything there seems the reverse of human activities: a baby kappa can refuse to be born and it is always the she-kappa who captures her mate. The world of the kappa is no utopia; it has thievery, unemployment, exploitation, war, censorship, and suicide. However, the solutions to some of these problems are quite unorthodox—for example, the unemployed are eaten. Fascinated but weary, the narrator returns to human society, only to find himself committed to a mental hospital. He claims, however, that he still enjoys occasional visits from his old kappa friends, who tell him that his doctor, not he, is the one who suffers from a mental disorder. "Haguruma" (1927; tr "Cogwheel," 1965), another of his late works, is a terrifying account of an extraordinarily sensitive mind that is gradually losing its hold on reality and breaking down. This plotless work is dominated by bizarre, clear images—such as a translucent cogwheel turning in midair—that give rise to paranoia.

Physically and mentally exhausted, Akutagawa committed suicide in 1927 at the age of 35, leaving behind approximately a hundred beautifully wrought stories in a manner not unlike the way the hero of "Hell Screen" had left his masterpiece.

Akutagawa once said that "life is an Olympic Games sponsored by a group of lunatics." If life was sick and irrational to him, art represented a rational tool to control it. At first he felt secure in that world of art that he had created with the aid of precisely defined words, intricate plots, and predictable psychological analysis. However, the raw forces of life began to erode the walls of his world. His art and health failing, he often dreaded that the seed of his mother's insanity would one day sprout in him. In the end Akutagawa took an overdose of Veronal, as if he wanted to take revenge on and destroy whatever rationality was left in him. Eight years after his death, the Akutagawa Prize (see LITERARY PRIZES), to be awarded to outstanding works by promising new writers, was established in his honor. It is one of the most highly coveted and prestigious awards for literature in Japan.

■ ——Works by Akutagawa: *Akutagawa Ryūnosuke zenshū,* 11 vols (Kadokawa, 1967–69). *Tales Grotesque and Curious,* tr Glenn W. Shaw (1930). *Rashōmon and Other Stories,* tr Takashi Kojima (1952). *Japanese Short Stories,* tr Takashi Kojima (1961). *Exotic Japanese Stories: The Beautiful and the Grotesque,* tr Takashi Kojima and John McVittie (1964). *Kappa* (1926–27), tr Geoffrey Bownas (1970). *Aru ahō no isshō* (1927), tr Will Petersen as *A Fool's Life* (1971). Works on Akutagawa: Howard Hibbett, "Akutagawa Ryūnosuke and the Negative Ideal," in Albert Craig and Donald Shively, ed, *Personality in Japanese History* (1970). Kinya Tsuruta, "Akutagawa Ryūnosuke and I–Novelists," *Monumenta Nipponica* 25.1–2 (1970). Kinya Tsuruta, "The Theme of Death in Akutagawa Ryūnosuke," *Literature East and West* 15.4–16.2 (1971–1972). Kinya Tsuruta, "Akutagawa's 'In a Grove,' " in Katsuhiko Takeda, ed, *Essays on Japanese Literature* (1977). Makoto Ueda, "Akutagawa Ryūnosuke," in Makoto Ueda, *Modern Japanese Writers* (1976). Beongcheon Yu, *Akutagawa: An Introduction* (1972).   Kin'ya TSURUTA

akutō

(bands of evildoers). A manifestation of social disturbance during the Kamakura (1185–1333) and Nambokuchō (1336–92) periods. The term occurs in official documents from the 1220s onward, its use becoming frequent after the mid-13th century. These lawless groups included not only ordinary brigands, looters, and pirates, but also estate stewards (JITŌ) and local landholders (MYŌSHU) who banded together for such purposes as the forcible seizure of rents and other wealth from estate (SHŌEN) proprietors. The Kamakura shogunate, feeling threatened by the emergence of these refractory groups, called them *akutō* and took steps against them, but it was forced to call on some of them for aid in the national defense when the MONGOL INVASIONS OF JAPAN loomed over the horizon in the 1270s. Many *akutō,* however, used this opportunity to make raids on estates and seize tax rice. Some even built their own fortifications. Historians have interpreted the appearance of these groups as a sign of a breakdown in local order, and some believe that the *akutō* evolved into the local lords (KOKUJIN) of the Muromachi period (1333–1568).

Alcock, Rutherford (1809–1897)

First British minister to Japan. After serving as British consul in Shanghai and other ports along the South China coast, in 1858 Alcock was appointed British consul general in Japan. Arriving in Edo (now Tōkyō) in 1859, he soon pressed for the opening of trade between Britain and Japan and for shogunal protection of Westerners from Japanese radicals eager to expel them and overthrow the Tokugawa shogunate. Later that year he was appointed minister to Japan. In 1862 he returned to London and wrote an account of his experiences in Japan, *The Capital of the Tycoon,* published in 1863. Returning to Edo the following year, he arranged for British, American, French, and Dutch ships to bombard and destroy shore batteries of the Chōshū domain (now Yamaguchi Prefecture) that had attacked Western ships passing through the Shimonoseki Strait (see SHIMONOSEKI BOMBARDMENT). Differences with Foreign Secretary Lord Russell led to his recall to London in 1864. He served as British minister at Beijing (Peking) from 1865 until his retirement in 1871.

alcoholic beverages in Japanese society

The number of people in Japan who drink alcoholic beverages is estimated to be some 50 million, or about half of the entire population. Alcoholic beverages are an integral part of many social and business activities in Japanese life, and many traditional rites and customs include the consumption of Japanese *sake* (rice wine).

The earliest mention in writing of alcoholic beverages in connection with the Japanese is in the section on Japan in the Chinese historical work WEI ZHI *(Wei chih).* According to this record, which

refers to the 3rd century AD, the inhabitants of YAMATAI (the ancient Japanese state) were fond of liquor and drank at funeral ceremonies while they sang and danced. Other ancient sources that mention the use of alcohol are the Japanese regional accounts known as FUDOKI; these record the existence of establishments called *sakadono* and *sakaya* where *sake* was produced. The earliest anthology of Japanese poetry, the MAN'YŌSHŪ (compiled 8th century, but including much older poems) contains many poems treating the subject of liquor. Particularly noteworthy are 13 poems by ŌTOMO NO TABITO praising *sake,* and YAMANOUE NO OKURA's "Dialogue on Poverty" ("Hinkyū mondō"), in which a poor man sips on *sake* dregs mixed with hot water. Although the *sake* of these records was a beverage made from rice, we do not know precisely what kind of beverage it was. A rice wine resembling the present-day *sake* probably came into existence during the Nara period (710–794).

In Japanese tradition there are rice wine deities similar to the Greek god Bacchus. The chronicle NIHON SHOKI (compiled in 720) reports, for example, how people venerated the wine deity Ōmiwa no Kami during the reign of the legendary emperor SUJIN. Shrines dedicated to deities of wine included the ŌMIWA SHRINE (in what is now Nara Prefecture) as well as Matsuo Shrine and Umemiya Shrine in Kyōto. The three deities of these shrines are known as the Sanshujin (Three Wine Deities). The leaves of the sacred cryptomeria *(sugi)* tree at the Ōmiwa Shrine were used to make ball designs which eventually became trademarks for *sake* brewers. Even today, when new *sake* is produced, it is customary to fashion these balls and hang them from the eaves of breweries.

By the time the RITSURYŌ SYSTEM was instituted in the late 7th century, the court had set up a Sake Production Bureau (Sake no Tsukasa) within the palace, which made rice wine for the court. It was the work of selected women known as *ietoji* to pound the rice to be used for this *sake* and decide how it would be distributed. Women also took part in *sake* banquets. After the beginning of the Nara period, *sake* production moved to Buddhist temples, which then evidently sold the liquor to people in surrounding areas. Several temples, notably Kongōji in Kawachi (in what is now Ōsaka Prefecture), achieved reputations as *sake* producers.

In rural areas people produced their own *sake* for the New Year and other festivals, selling any leftover product. During the Edo period (1600–1868), the commercial production of *sake* flourished, and towns in the KINKI REGION such as Ikeda, Itami, and Nada became famous as *sake* production centers. Previously people had made *sake* throughout the year, but the *sake* industry began to produce only at selected times of the year. The period from the beginning of January to the start of February was considered the best season. *Sake* production became the responsibility of men known as *sakatōji,* many of whom came from the north of Honshū to work in the Kinki region during the winter. The best *sake* was given the name *kudarizake;* this was transported in casks on special ships (see KAISEN) to the shogunal capital of Edo (now Tōkyō) and stored in earthenware pots *(kame).* The introduction of casks made of cryptomeria wood facilitated transport and allowed removal to more distant areas. Beginning in the Muromachi period (1333–1568) and on into the Edo period, a clearer and tastier *sake (seishu)* began to be preferred over the previous cloudy *sake (nigorizake).* In some rural areas people still prefer *nigorizake.*

Sake was indispensable on ceremonial occasions such as the New Year, festivals, weddings, and funerals. The Japanese traditionally made an offering of rice wine to the deities during festivals. Following the festival, there was a banquet called NAORAI where the participants drank the *sake* offered to the deities. On secular occasions, the upper classes served special *machizake* ("waiting *sake*") to guests.

Although in ancient times there were fewer occasions on which alcoholic beverages were drunk, people evidently drank large amounts when they did drink. *Jōgo* (strong drinker) was a term of admiration, and *geko* (weak drinker) a label of scorn. In the Edo period, with the loosening of restrictions as to when liquor might be drunk, drinking contests known as *sakegassen* became a leisure activity. At the same time, the drinking of liquor became a common form of socializing and of entertaining, as at drinking establishments known as *chaya.*

Another difference between premodern and modern drinking habits is reflected in the size of *sake* cups: earlier cups were quite large and one cup was passed around to guests, beginning with the person in the highest social position, but present-day cups are quite small and are intended for individual use.   Ōtō Tokihiko

In present-day Japan it is customary to offer both traditional *sake* and Western alcoholic beverages on public occasions such as New Year's parties, congratulatory occasions, eulogizing ceremonies, weddings, and religious rites. When people return home after work they often enjoy a drink before or after dinner; this is known as the *banshaku* (evening cup). Others join coworkers at a bar or cabaret or at one of the many kinds of typically Japanese small drinking establishments. These are known by generic names such as *akachō-chin* (red lantern), *izakaya* (sit and drink), and *nawanoren* (rope curtain), but all of them are similar in offering both Japanese and Western beverages along with light meals at cheap prices. Many people drink at *yatai,* a kind of movable, roofed stall on wheels which is set up or pulled along the streets at night. These usually offer some particular food, such as noodles or chicken on skewers, along with *sake.* When a group stops at several places during an evening, it is called *hashigozake* (ladder drinking). A general term for the business of providing food, drink, and entertainment, including such traditional establishments as *geisha* houses, is *mizu shōbai* (literally, "the water trade"). Many important discussions in the business and financial world take place over drinks.

A custom in existence since ancient times is for the bride and groom to exchange three cups of *sake* three times in succession in the ceremony known as *sansankudo* ("three-three nine times"). Members of the wedding party also partake of *sake.* At banquets, there is a custom known as *kenshū,* in which one guest pours a cup of *sake* and offers it to another guest, whereupon that person uses the same cup to make a return offering.

In contrast to ancient times, drinking among women in the Edo period and up until World War II was limited mainly to professional entertainers and others who served at banquets. It was considered virtuous for women to abstain from alcohol. With the growth in popularity of social drinking after the war, however, women who drank beer or whisky increased in number.

At present, the Japanese enjoy several varieties of alcoholic beverages. *Seishu* or clear sake is the most representative type of domestic liquor, but other native beverages include *shōchū* (distilled spirits), *doburoku* (unrefined *sake*), *shirozake* (white *sake*), and imitation *sake.* Popular Western alcoholic beverages include beer, whiskey, wine, and brandy. Western drinks were introduced to Japan during the Muromachi period when wines were brought from Portugal. Beer production had its start in 1873, and with the introduction of beer halls on the Ginza in Tōkyō in 1899, beer drinking began to rival *sake* drinking in popularity.

The peak year for the consumption of alcohol in Japan before World War II was 1919; this record was broken in 1953. Consumption figures for 1973 were six times those for 1919. Before the war, *seishu* accounted for 60 percent of consumption figures, and beer 20 percent. Recent years have seen a reverse trend; as of the late 1970s beer accounted for 60 percent and *seishu* had dropped to 30 percent.

TSUCHIDA Mitsufumi

Alexander, Wallace McKinney (1869–1939)

American businessman who worked to improve Japanese-American relations. Born of American parents on the island of Maui, Hawaii; educated at Yale (BA, 1892). Engaged in several businesses, including sugar and shipping in Hawaii, he took an interest in the welfare of his employees, many of whom were Japanese. When relations between the United States and Japan deteriorated over the question of Japanese immigration in the early 1900s, he founded the Japanese-American Relations Committee with Japanese entrepreneur SHIBUSAWA EIICHI and others to promote trade and cultural exchange and to facilitate immigration of Japanese laborers to the United States.

Alien Land Acts

The Alien Land Acts passed by the state of California in 1913 and 1920, as well as similar acts passed by most other far-western states, were efforts to stop the acquisition of agricultural land by Japanese immigrants. Alien land acts had been passed in the late 19th century in several states and the District of Columbia, but these acts were aimed at all aliens—chiefly nonresident aliens or corporations—and usually permitted individual holdings. Discussion of similar legislation occurred again in the late 1970s, for example in Missouri, spurred by fears that oil-rich nonresident Arabs would buy much land. The California acts of 1913 and 1920 and those modeled on them aimed at only one kind of alien, the "alien ineligible to citizen-

ship," that is, Asian immigrants who from 1870 to 1952 were ineligible for naturalization.

The passage of the 1913 act, under the leadership of California's governor, Hiram W. Johnson, precipitated an international crisis between the United States and Japan. It led President Woodrow Wilson to dispatch his secretary of state, William Jennings Bryan, to California in a vain attempt to dissuade the legislature from insulting Japan. The law, once passed, had little real effect, since its intentions could be legally evaded in two ways. Land-leasing and sharecropping contracts of up to three years' duration were permitted under the 1913 statute. Thus many Japanese who wished to enter agriculture leased their land instead of purchasing it, while many would-be agriculturalists, desiring more permanent tenure, purchased land in the name of their American-born children. They, as citizens of the United States, had rights to hold land and other property under the United States Constitution that could not be infringed upon by any state legislature. The 1920 California act made leasing and sharecropping by "aliens ineligible to citizenship" illegal.

The ineffectiveness of the California legislation—and the pattern elsewhere was similar—is shown by the statistics of Japanese land tenure. In 1909 Japanese farmers in California owned about 17,000 acres (6,800 hectares) and leased or sharecropped nearly 140,000 acres (56,000 hectares). By 1919, after six years of the Alien Land Act, Japanese owned about 75,000 acres (30,000 hectares) and leased or sharecropped nearly 385,000 (156,000) more. This acreage represented less than 1 percent of the arable land in California, but the approximately 35,000 Japanese agriculturalists produced a crop worth $67 million annually, about 10 percent of the market value of California's produce. Most of the Japanese farmers worked holdings of less than 8 hectares (20 acres), quite small by American standards.

Despite their ineffectiveness in inhibiting the growth of Japanese-American agriculture, these land laws served as a psychological deterrent. In California the laws stayed on the books until they were declared unconstitutional in a state court decision (*Fujii* v. *State of California,* 1952). All such laws were made moot that same year by the federal Immigration and Nationality Act, which abolished the status of "aliens ineligible to citizenship."

——Roger Daniels, *The Politics of Prejudice: The Anti-Japanese Movement in California and the Struggle for Japanese Exclusion* (1978). Dudley O. McGovney, "The Anti-Japanese Laws of California and Ten Other States," *California Law Review* 35 (1947). Douglas W. Nelson, "The Alien Land Movement of the Late Nineteenth Century," *Journal of the West* 9 (1970). *Roger* DANIELS

alien registration

(gaikokujin tōroku). Registration of personal identity is required of residents in Japan who do not hold Japanese citizenship; required by the Alien Registration Law (Gaikokujin Tōroku Hō, 1952). The law requires these residents to apply for such registration to the mayor or headman of the village, town, or city (in the case of a large city, the head of the ward) where they live and to present a passport and copies of a photograph within 90 days from the date of entry into Japan. The information required on the application form includes the applicant's name, date and place of birth, sex, nationality, occupation, port of entry, passport number, and address while in Japan. Excused from this requirement, under the provisions of the Immigration Control Order (Shutsunyūkoku Kanri Rei), are holders of provisional landing permits, port-of-call landing permits, and transit landing permits for tourist purposes. Violators of the Alien Registration Law are subject to penal servitude or imprisonment of up to one year.

Upon registration by the local government official, registrants are issued a Certificate of Alien Registration that must be renewed every three years or whenever visa status changes. Each registrant, excluding children under the age of 14, is required to carry this certificate at all times and to present it upon demand to police officers, maritime safety officials, railway police officers, or other public officials. See also FOREIGNERS IN JAPAN; FOREIGNERS, LEGAL STATUS OF.

KOTANI Kōzō

aliens → foreigners, legal status of

Allied Council for Japan

(ACJ; J: Tainichi Rijikai). A four-power body charged with advising the Supreme Commander for the Allied Powers (SCAP) on the implementation of the surrender terms for Japan. It was established along with the FAR EASTERN COMMISSION (FEC) at Moscow on 27 December 1945 by the foreign ministers of the United States, the United Kingdom, and the USSR, with the concurrence of China. Its membership consisted of the supreme commander, or his deputy, as chairman (and as US member) and of representatives of the USSR, China, and a member representing jointly the United Kingdom, Australia, New Zealand, and India. The supreme commander's decisions were controlling, and he acted as the sole executive authority of the Allied powers in Japan. The council met 162 times from early 1946 to the end of the Occupation in 1952. In its early years it held a number of lengthy and tense sessions, particularly in regard to the failure of the Soviet Union to repatriate rapidly the large numbers of Japanese military and civilian personnel in Manchuria at the end of the war. It also took up the problems of demilitarization, land reform, and the purge of military and civilian officials. In its last four years the council continued to meet regularly but held few substantive discussions.

📖——W. MacMahon Ball, *Japan—Enemy or Ally?* (1949). William J. Sebald, *With MacArthur in Japan* (1965). *Richard B. FINN*

All Nippon Airways Co, Ltd

(Zen Nippon Kūyu). Airline company. Principally an operator of domestic lines, although it operates international flights irregularly on a charter basis. It handles over 50 percent of the domestic passenger traffic, a share larger than that of JAPAN AIR LINES CO, LTD, which engages chiefly in international flights. The parent company was the Nippon Helicopter Transport Co, established in 1952. This company merged with Far Eastern Airlines in 1958, adopting its current name. Using the slogan "Let's cover the skies all over Japan," All Nippon Airways consolidated its position as the leading airline in domestic flights, expanding its network of routes, switching to jet engines, and selling tickets on a credit basis for the convenience of passengers. It initiated overseas flights in 1971 with a route to Hong Kong. Since then, irregular flights have been undertaken to Manila, Bangkok, Singapore, Kuala Lumpur, Djakarta, Bali, Khabarovsk, Beijing (Peking), and Shanghai. Annual revenue for the fiscal year ending March 1982 totaled ¥397.4 billion (US $1.7 billion) and the company was capitalized at ¥43 billion (US $178.6 million). Corporate headquarters are in Tōkyō.

Alps Electric Co, Ltd

(Arupusu Denki). Manufacturer of various types of electronic parts, including tuners, switches, variable resistors, and keyboards. It was established in 1948. With the widening of markets for such equipment as televisions and tape recorders, the company grew rapidly. It has subsidiary manufacturing companies in South Korea, Taiwan, and Brazil. It also produces automobile stereos through a subsidiary firm. Sales for the fiscal year ending March 1982 totaled ¥180.5 billion (US $750 million), the company's export ratio was 31 percent, and capitalization stood at ¥6.8 billion (US $28.2 million). Corporate headquarters are in Tōkyō.

ama

Sea divers who catch fish and shellfish and gather seaweed. At present, women *ama* are more common in central Japan, while men predominate in the northeastern and southwestern regions of the country. This is the only area in the Japanese fishing industry in which women are directly involved. The *ama* fish principally for *awabi* (ABALONE), *sazae* (wreath shell), *tengusa* (agar-agar), and *egonori* (a kind of seaweed). The gathering of pearl oysters by *ama* in Ago Bay (Mie Prefecture) and other locations is a relatively new trend, having been initiated in the beginning of the 20th century.

There are three methods employed by male *ama*, depending on the local tradition. One is for the *ama* to dive directly into the sea. Another is to use a long stick to gather seaweed while standing in a boat. The third involves the use of a glass-bottomed boat, from which the *ama* brings the abalone up with a long spear. Female *ama* use floating wooden tubs, in which they place the shellfish they catch by diving. Ordinarily, women *ama* work three sessions of approximately two hours each a day. The average diving depth is 9–11 meters (about 30–35 ft), but some divers go to a depth of 27–36 meters (about 90–120 ft). In order to increase the speed of the descent, the *ama* attaches a weight to her body, and for the ascent, she has a lifeline tied around her waist. The lifeline is pulled up by a

man (usually her husband) in a boat. The *ama*'s method of diving was recorded by Chinese observers in Japan in the 3rd century (see WEI ZHI [*Wei chih*]), and, according to the 10th-century procedural code ENGI SHIKI, the *awabi* used in the enthronement ceremony of the emperor was gathered by *ama*. The existence of *ama* is also mentioned in chronicles and anthologies compiled in the 8th century such as the KOJIKI, NIHON SHOKI, FUDOKI, and MAN'YŌSHŪ. The place names Azumi and Atsumi, which are found in various parts of Japan, are said to derive from the name of the chief family of Amabe (*ama* clan; see BE) in ancient Japan.

Amache Relocation Center

A wartime relocation facility for Japanese Americans located near Granada, Powers County, Colorado. The center was in operation from 27 August 1942 until 15 October 1945. It held a maximum of 7,318 persons at any one time; in all, 10,295 persons were confined there. Internees came from northern, central, and southern California. See also JAPANESE AMERICANS, WARTIME RELOCATION OF; WAR RELOCATION AUTHORITY.

📖——M. Paul Holsinger, "Amache," *Colorado Magazine* 41 (1964). *Roger DANIELS*

amae

Amae, which can be translated "dependency wishes," is the noun form of a commonly used Japanese verb, *amaeru,* which has no true equivalent in English but refers to the desire to depend upon the love, patience, and tolerance of others. *Amaeru* can be translated as "to play baby," "to behave like a spoiled child," "to coax," or "to coquet," although in Japanese it derives from the same root as the adjective for "sweet" (*amai*) and possesses an aura of sweetness and permissiveness not conveyed by the pejorative tone of translations into English.

Amae is a central concept in the writings of psychiatrist Doi Takeo (b 1920) concerning how language reflects culture. He defines *amaeru* as the desire "to presume upon another's love," "to bask in another's indulgence," or "to indulge in another's kindness." It arises from feelings of helplessness and the need to be loved and, stated in Freudian terminology, expresses the longing for restoration of the lost quasi-union of mother and child. Doi holds that it is a key to understanding the psychodynamics of Japanese culture, which is relatively tolerant of dependency feelings and relations.

Usages of Amae —— In its narrowest usage in ordinary Japanese speech, *amae* refers specifically to the dependency feelings that an infant entertains toward its mother, i.e., its desire to cling to her and be loved passively as well as its unwillingness to be separated from her. Generally speaking, however, the term is applied to a child only after the age of approximately one year. Japanese society views infantile *amae* as not only a basic need but also very appealing, or "cute" (*kawaii*); and the mother is expected to reciprocate by gratifying (*kawaigaru* or *amayakasu*) the child. Observers of Japanese child-rearing practices note that the psychological boundaries between mother and child are less distant than in the American family, for example, and that interdependence rather than independence is emphasized.

Since the parent-child relationship is reflected in many adult relationships such as husband-wife, teacher-pupil, and leader-follower (OYABUN-KOBUN) in Japanese society, *amae* tends to be prolonged and diffused throughout adult life; and the word is also used to describe the way in which one party, typically the subordinate member, may presume upon the familiarity of a relationship to impose upon the other. It is the hope of the one who "depends" (*amaeru*) that his or her dependency is simultaneously the other's delight, and the goal of such behavior is validation of those expectations. *Amae* behavior is frequently nonverbal, as though a tacit understanding exists between the parties involved and articulation of feeling would cast a pall over their interaction. The degree of manipulative behavior involved may vary but Japanese provides other vocabulary such as *nedaru* (to importune), *toriiru* (to take in) and *kobiru* (to seduce) to describe actions arising from ulterior motives. *Amae* may receive approbation as childlike, cute, or coquettish or be rejected as childish, infantile, or self-centered. Rejection of *amae* leads to resentment (*urami*), and repeated frustration may lead to ambivalence and anxiety and be a cause of neurosis.

Used in its broadest sense, *amae* is represented by the stock phrases, *okotoba ni amaeru* ("taking you at your word") and *goshin-setsu ni amaeru* ("availing myself of your offer"). These are amenities used in accepting favors. They suggest that, although etiquette normally requires reticence and self-effacement, there are occasions when one unabashedly imposes upon a friend or even a stranger. Underlying this license is a recognition that the majority of human relations rest upon a shared calculation of self-interests and that to be overly conscientious in asking and receiving favors—as well as exacting in granting them—is unfriendly and standoffish (mizukusai). Give and take lubricates human interaction and leads to social harmony, although at times it can lead to a collusion of interests (nareai) and may come under censure as self-serving amae.

Doi Takeo on Amae——One of Japan's pioneers in psychiatric medicine, Doi Takeo first began focusing on amae during the early years of his clinical practice in the 1950s. He observed that, whereas Japanese patients possessed in the word amae a means for expressing and accepting their dependency wishes, foreign patients were able to admit to such wishes only after much time, anxiety, and constriction. He was intrigued by this fact, as well as by the phenomenon that Western European languages lack an equivalent word.

Doi concluded that whereas Japanese society encourages and institutionalizes dependency feelings, Western cultures often fail to recognize them or they even ignore them in an unquestioning faith in the self-reliance of "rugged individualism." Only in the writings of Michael Balint on "passive object love" could Doi find a Western psychiatrist attempting to define amae.

In his clinical work, Doi found that Japanese neurotics were frequently inhibited in their desire to amaeru and that their recovery was predicated upon their ability to recognize both their deep-seated desire and their ambivalence about its possible gratification.

In his writings, especially his best selling Amae no kōzō (1971; tr Anatomy of Dependence, 1973), he uses amae to elucidate aspects of Japanese society. He sees it as the core of a constellation of amae-related words and feelings and as the key to understanding the traditional Japanese dilemma between obligations (giri) and feelings (ninjō). In Doi's definition, Japanese-style ninjō is the art of knowing how to amaeru and how to respond to the call of amae in others; giri, or social obligations, exists to be pervaded by ninjō (see GIRI AND NINJŌ).

Amae also explains for Doi the centrality of the mother-child relationship in Japanese society; the importance attached to the ability to "merge" (tokekomu) with others; less distinct notions of subject and object, self and other; differently defined concepts of privacy and individual rights; a dislike for cut-and-dried logic and businesslike relationships; the high degree of nonverbal communication; and the strong aesthetic orientation of the culture.

📖 ——Doi Takeo, Amae no kōzō (1971), tr John Bester as Anatomy of Dependence (1973). Doi Takeo, Sōseki no shinteki sekai (1969), tr William Tyler as The Psychological World of Natsume Sōseki (1976). Douglas Mitchell, Amaeru: Expression of Reciprocal Dependency Needs in Japanese Politics and Law (1976). Helmut Morbasch and William Tyler, "Some Japanese-Western Linguistic Differences Concerning Dependency Needs: The Case of Amae," in Rom Harre, ed, Life Sentences (1976).   William J. TYLER

Amagasaki

City in southeastern Hyōgo Prefecture. Situated on Ōsaka Bay and with river access to Kyōto, Amagasaki has been an important port since the 8th century. It was a castle town under the Matsudaira family during the Edo period (1600–1868). In modern times its proximity to Ōsaka has made Amagasaki a major industrial center. Electrical goods, chemicals, machinery, metals, ceramics, petroleum, and foodstuffs are the principal industries. Pollution and land subsidence are receiving government attention. The remains of Tano, a Yayoi-period (ca 300 BC–ca AD 300) settlement, are located here. Pop: 523,657.

Amagi

City in central Fukuoka Prefecture, Kyūshū. Amagi developed as a POST-STATION TOWN on the Bungo Kaidō, a regional highway, and as a market center for agricultural produce. Today it is known for its lumber, beer, rubber tires, and chemical fertilizer industries. It is particularly famous for its tie-dyed fabrics, Amagi shibori. Pop: 42,864.

Amagi Pass

(Amagi Tōge). Located along the Shimoda highway, central Izu Peninsula, Shizuoka Prefecture, central Honshū. A toll road including the new Amagi Tunnel runs through this pass. The surrounding land is covered with cedar groves, and the cultivation of wasabi (Japanese horseradish) is also carried out in this area. YUGASHIMA HOT SPRING is found on the northern side. The pass is famous as part of the setting of Kawabata Yasunari's Izu no odoriko (The Izu Dancer). Altitude: 800 m (2,624 ft).

Amagisan

Mountain group in central Izu Peninsula, Shizuoka Prefecture, central Honshū. The group consists of volcanic peaks belonging to the FUJI VOLCANIC ZONE and includes many plateaus. The mountains form an important part of the Fuji–Hakone–Izu National Park. The hot springs at Yugashima and Yugano are popular. Principal peaks include: Manjirōdake (1,300 m; 4,264 ft), Manzaburōdake (1,406 m; 4,612 ft), and Tōgasayama (1,197 m; 3,926 ft).

amagoi → rain, rituals for

Amako family

Daimyō of the Sengoku period (1467–1568); descendants of the KYŌGOKU FAMILY of the Uda Genji branch of the MINAMOTO FAMILY. In 1392 Amako Mochihisa became deputy military governor (shugodai) of Izumo Province (now part of Shimane Prefecture) and established himself at Toda Gassan Castle. His grandson Tsunehisa (1458–1541) extended his power into Aki and Bingo provinces (now Hiroshima Prefecture), thus coming into conflict with the ŌUCHI FAMILY and the MŌRI FAMILY. After the death of Tsunehisa's grandson Haruhisa (1514–62?) the Amako declined, and their power was destroyed when Haruhisa's son Yoshihisa (d 1610) was defeated and captured by Mōri forces in 1566. Not long afterward, Yoshihisa's kinsman Amako Katsuhisa (1553–78) attempted to revive the family's fortunes with the aid of their loyal retainer YAMANAKA SHIKANOSUKE; as a vassal of the hegemon ODA NOBUNAGA, Katsuhisa enjoyed a brief success but committed suicide under siege by the Mōri in 1578.

amakudari

The practice of reemploying former bureaucrats in private-sector positions after their retirement from government work. At times the term also applies to the movement of ex-bureaucrats into politics or service with public corporations, as well as to the movement of retiring private-sector executives from larger to smaller firms. Literally, amakudari means "descent from heaven," in recognition of the elite status that bureaucrats have traditionally held in Japanese society.

Although the practice of amakudari can be traced to the period before World War II, it became most prevalent during the late 1960s and early 1970s. Amakudari grows out of complementary public- and private-sector motivations: the desire of bureaucrats, forced to retire at 47–55 years of age with relatively modest financial pensions, for second careers and the desire of private corporations for access to government contacts and information, which they can obtain from ex-bureaucrats. Most ex-bureaucrats serve the organizations they join in advisory rather than direct administrative capacities.

Former bureaucrats are concentrated most heavily in such highly regulated industries as banking, steel, and transportation. There is some variation by ministry in the types of positions they assume. Ministry of International Trade and Industry officials generally "descend" into big business, and Finance Ministry officers into public corporations, banks, and politics. Education and foreign affairs bureaucrats are compelled by lack of connections to rely mainly on their own auxiliary organs for positions. See also BUREAUCRACY.   Kent E. CALDER

Amakusa

Town on Shimoshima, one of the Amakusa Islands off the coast of southern Kyūshū; administratively a part of Kumamoto Prefecture. Primarily known as a fishing port, it also produces clay for porcelain. During the 17th century many Japanese Christians hid in the area to avoid persecution by the Tokugawa shogunate (see KAKURE KIRI-

SHITAN); a church has been built in memory of those who died in the SHIMABARA UPRISING, a rebellion of Christians in 1637. The town is located within the UNZEN–AMAKUSA NATIONAL PARK. Pop: 6,513.

Amakusa Islands

(Amakusa Shotō). Island group approximately 10 km (6 mi) west of Kumamoto Prefecture, Kyūshū, with the Yatsushiro Sea to the east, the Amakusa Sea to the west, and the Shimabara Peninsula to the north. The group consists of more than a hundred large and small islands; the main islands are Amakusa Kamishima and Amakusa Shimoshima. All the Amakusa Islands are hilly with little level land. Wheat and sweet potatoes are cultivated on the slopes of these hills, and because the winter climate is mild, flowers and mandarin oranges are cultivated on some of the islands. There is offshore fishing, and pearls, shrimp, and yellowtail are cultivated in the inlets. Underground resources include coal, building stone, and clay for pottery. The islands form part of the UNZEN–AMAKUSA NATIONAL PARK. Tourist attractions include the numerous relics of early Christians who lived here. The islands are connected with Kyūshū by the Five Amakusa Bridges. Area: 877 sq km (339 sq mi).

Amakusa Sea

(Amakusa Nada). Arm of the East China Sea off the Amakusa Islands and the western coast of Kumamoto Prefecture, western Kyūshū. Bounded on the north by the Nagasaki Peninsula and on the south by the island Kami Koshikijima.

Amakusa Shirō → Shimabara Uprising

Amami Islands

(Amami Shotō). Group of islands between Kyūshū and the Okinawa Islands; part of Kagoshima Prefecture. Includes the islands of AMAMI ŌSHIMA, KIKAISHIMA, TOKUNOSHIMA, OKINOERABUJIMA, and YORONJIMA. In ancient days the Amami Islands belonged to the Ryūkyū kingdom in Okinawa. In 1609 they came under the control of the SHIMAZU FAMILY and after the Meiji period (1868–1912) were administered by Kagoshima Prefecture. In 1946 they were placed under American military rule along with Okinawa, reverting to Kagoshima Prefecture in 1953. The islands are chiefly agricultural, the main crop being sugarcane. Other produce includes bananas and pineapples. Ōshima *tsumugi* (pongee) is a special local product. Tourism is also being developed. Combined area: 1,237 sq km (477 sq mi).

Amami Ōshima

Also known as Ōshima. Island 400 km (248 mi) southwest of Kyūshū, largest of the AMAMI ISLANDS. It is under the administration of Kagoshima Prefecture. The main city is Naze. The island is hilly with little level land and surrounded by coral reefs. Subtropical, the island is the home of the black rabbit of Amami *(Amami no kurousagi)* and the *habu,* a poisonous snake. About 40 percent of the island is arable; the principal agricultural products are sugarcane, sweet potatoes, pineapple, and other fruits. The principal industries are sugar refining and the production of Ōshima *tsumugi* (pongee). Area: 710 sq km (274 sq mi); pop: 85,598.

Amanohashidate

Sandbar in western Wakasa Bay near Oku Tango Peninsula, northwestern Kyōto Prefecture, central Honshū, within the Wakasa Bay Quasi-National Park. Known for the beauty of its gnarled pine trees set against the ocean. Along with Matsushima and Itsukushima, it is one of the "three most famous views in Japan" (Nihon Sankei). Length: approximately 3 km (2 mi); width: 20–170 m (66–558 ft).

Amanojaku

Also known as Amanojakko or Amanosagume. 1. A supernatural creature described in various folktales who acts contrary to the desires of others and is skilled at impersonation. In the tale of the

Amakusa Islands

Four of the Five Amakusa Bridges, joining the Amakusa Islands with Kyūshū. The large island in the foreground is Nagaurajima. The island partially visible at top center is Amakusa Kamishima.

Amami Ōshima —— Elevated storehouses (takakura)

The *takakura* is an ancient type of traditional storehouse still found in the Amami and Izu islands. Shown is a group of *takakura* in the village of Yamato on Amami Ōshima. The storage area (not visible in the photograph) is a platform, atop the pillars and immediately under the roof, where crops can be kept away from dampness.

maiden Uriko (URIKOHIME) it impersonates the girl and attempts to marry in her stead. It is thought to have assumed features of the myth of Amanosagume, a female deity who in the ancient chronicle KOJIKI (712) is said to have persuaded the god Amewakahiko, who had descended to the land of Izumo, to kill a pheasant sent as an emissary from the heavens. 2. In common parlance, a person whose statements or actions perversely contradict accepted notions or the express desires of others. 3. In Buddhist art, the creature or creatures trampled underfoot by the guardian deity groups Niō and Shitennō.

Amanokaguyama → Yamato Sanzan

Amano Tameyuki (1860–1938)

Economist and educator. After graduating from Tōkyō University in 1882, he joined ŌKUMA SHIGENOBU in establishing Tōkyō Semmon Gakkō (now Waseda University), where he taught politics and economics and later became a professor. He joined the political party RIKKEN KAISHINTŌ and was elected to the House of Representatives in the first general election held in Japan (1890). After losing the next election, he returned to Waseda University, where he became the dean of the School of Business in 1904. From 1898 to 1907 he was editor-in-chief of the magazine TŌYŌ KEIZAI SHIMPŌ. In his

Amanohashidate

This pine-covered sandbar, whose name literally means "bridge of heaven," separates Miyazu Bay (left) and the lagoon Asokai.

later years he founded Waseda Jitsugyō, a secondary commercial school and became its principal. His *Keizai genron* (1886) was the first book on the principles of economics published in Japan that adhered to J. S. Mill's laissez-faire economic theories.

YAMADA Katsumi

Amano Teiyū (1884–1980)

Philosopher and educator; noted for his studies of Kant and advocacy of democracy in education.

Amano was born in Kanagawa Prefecture. After graduating from the First Higher School and Kyōto University, he went to Germany and studied philosophy at the University of Heidelberg in 1923–24. On his return to Japan he was appointed to the faculty of Kyōto University, where he developed his theory of human morality. In 1937 he published *Dōri no kankaku* (The Sense of the Right), a highly controversial book that was denounced by military and right-wing groups for its antiwar theme and eventually suppressed by the government.

In the post–World War II period, he was involved in educational reform. He was a member of the Japanese committee that dealt with the first of the UNITED STATES EDUCATION MISSIONS TO JAPAN and of the EDUCATION REFORM COUNCIL (Kyōiku Sasshin Iinkai). After serving as principal of the First Higher School, he was named minister of education in the YOSHIDA SHIGERU cabinet from 1950 to 1952. During his tenure he criticized the left-wing tendencies then prevalent in educational circles and stressed the necessity of moral education in the schools (see KOKUMIN JISSEN YŌRYŌ). He also worked for implementation of the school lunch program and passage of the law requiring the government to underwrite a portion of compulsory education expenses. After retiring as minister of education he founded Dokkyō University. From 1955 to 1963, he served as chairman of the CENTRAL COUNCIL FOR EDUCATION (Chūō Kyōiku Shingikai).

KURAUCHI Shirō

Amano Tōkage (fl 1180–1203)

General of the early part of the Kamakura period (1185–1333). Originally based in Izu Province (now part of Shizuoka Prefecture), Tōkage joined MINAMOTO NO YORITOMO in 1180 and fought under him in the Battle of Ishibashiyama, the first engagement of the TAIRA–MINAMOTO WAR. Toward the end of the war, he helped Yoritomo's brother Noriyori (d 1193) to destroy the remnants of Taira power in Kyūshū. When Yoritomo established his regime at Kamakura in 1185, Tōkage was made military commander in Kyūshū; in about 1195, after his term of office, he returned to Kamakura and became a monk. In 1203, on the orders of the shogunal regent HŌJŌ TOKIMASA, Tōkage assassinated HIKI YOSHIKAZU, the father-in-law of the shōgun MINAMOTO NO YORIIE, who had been plotting to overthrow the HŌJŌ FAMILY. His subsequent career is unknown.

Amaterasu Ōmikami

(Great Divinity Illuminating Heaven). The principal female deity of SHINTŌ mythology, identified with the sun and regarded as the pro-

genitrix of the imperial line. According to the chronicle *Kojiki* (712) she was born from Izanagi when he used water to purify his left eye after a visit to the netherworld; according to the *Nihon shoki* (720) she was born after intercourse between IZANAGI AND IZANAMI. In both accounts she was assigned to rule the High Celestial Plain (TAKAMAGAHARA). Deeply offended by the misdeeds of her younger brother SUSANOO NO MIKOTO, Amaterasu hid herself in a cave *(ama no iwaya)*, leaving the universe in complete darkness and chaos. Lured out of the cave by the feigned merrymaking of the myriad divinities, she shone forth again and order was restored. The divinities associated with her in these accounts were later claimed as ancestors by some of the great families (UJI) of early Japan. Later she dispatched her grandson NINIGI NO MIKOTO to pacify the Japanese islands, having given him the sacred mirror, sword, and jewels that became the IMPERIAL REGALIA; his great-grandson became the first emperor, JIMMU. This legend illustrates how the Amaterasu cult of the Sun Line *uji* (i.e., the imperial line) became predominant over other *uji* cults.

Amaterasu is worshiped at the Inner Shrine (Naikū) of the ancient ISE SHRINE, the central shrine of the Shintō religion. Although the shrine has had changing fortunes in the course of its history, it was directly linked to the imperial line and gradually became a center of popular devotion and, from the 17th century onward, the object of mass pilgrimages (OKAGE MAIRI). The solar, shamanistic, and feminine characteristics of this divinity make her of particular importance in Japanese religion. Because of the solar character of the principal Buddha Mahāvairocana (J: DAINICHI) of the KEGON SECT and the SHINGON SECT, systematic associations between Amaterasu and this Buddha were attempted throughout the medieval period (13th–16th centuries), although the Ise Shrine resisted these syncretic unions. Such associations were more widely accepted by the Buddhist side of syncretism than by its Shintō side; nevertheless, they were of extreme importance in the religious and political worlds (see SYNCRETISM; RYŌBU SHINTŌ). For some time during the medieval period the Ise Shrine was in competition for popularity with the nearby KUMANO SANZAN SHRINES, which had as their animal messenger the three-legged crow, a solar symbol in China and elsewhere.

Allan G. GRAPARD

Amatsu Kominato

Town in southern Chiba Prefecture, central Honshū. Located on the Bōsō Peninsula, Kominato serves as a base for fishing in the Pacific Ocean. The area is associated with NICHIREN, the founder of the Nichiren sect, and an important temple of the sect, Tanjōji, is situated in the town. Other attractions are TAINOURA, a sea bream hatchery, and KIYOSUMIYAMA, the mountain where Nichiren studied and prayed. Pop: 9,479.

Amenomori Hōshū (1668–1755)

Scholar of Neo-Confucianism (SHUSHIGAKU). Born in Ōmi Province (now Shiga Prefecture), he studied under KINOSHITA JUN'AN in Edo (now Tōkyō). In 1689, on his teacher's recommendation, he entered the service of the *daimyō* of Tsushima, an island domain (now part of Nagasaki Prefecture) situated between Korea and Kyūshū. Proficient in Korean and Chinese, he distinguished himself by his tactful handling of diplomatic relations with Korea. As a scholar, he was an orthodox follower of the doctrines of Zhu Xi (Chu Hsi; J: Shushi) and concerned himself primarily with the proper conduct of individuals in society and the moral relationship between emperor and subject. This latter concern prompted him to criticize ARAI HAKUSEKI's designation of the shōgun as king *(kokuō)* in official documents addressed to Korea (see SHUGŌ INCIDENT).

American Depositary Receipts

(ADR). Certificates traded in US securities markets that represent a stated number of shares of the common stock of a non-US corporation. The ADR was devised in the 1920s to overcome problems of transfer, foreign exchange, and the exercise of shareholder rights inherent in the American ownership of non-US securities. In more recent times the ADR has served as the principal instrument by which the common stock of Japanese corporations has been marketed to American investors. The typical arrangement is for an issuing Japanese corporation to appoint a bank in the United States as depositary and a bank in Japan as custodian. Upon the issuer's deposit of its common-stock shares with the custodian, the depositary issues an equivalent number of American Depositary Receipts to securities firms in the United States for ultimate sale to investors. The depositary has the additional responsibilities of forwarding dividend payments, informing the ADR-holder of voting and other rights, and providing a means to exercise these rights. The ADR-holder may sell the ADRs directly on a US stock exchange or, subject to certain conditions, arrange to sell the underlying securities on a Japanese exchange. The first ADR issue by a Japanese corporation was the sale by SONY CORPORATION in June 1961 of 2 million shares, represented by 200,000 ADRs priced at US $17.50 each.

Gary E. ROBERTSON

Amerika Hikozō → Hamada Hikozō

Amerika Mura

Popular name for Mio, a hamlet in the town of Mihama, Wakayama Prefecture, central Honshū. Situated on the western tip of the Kii Peninsula, Amerika Mura ("American Village") is known as the home of emigrants returning from the United States and Canada. The residents, who have retained their Western way of life, live by farming, fishing, or seasonal work found outside the prefecture.

Amida

A Buddha of cardinal importance in the Mahāyāna tradition who presides over the Western Paradise of the Pure Land (J: Jōdo); central to the evolution of PURE LAND BUDDHISM in East Asia. The term Amida or Amita is the Japanese pronunciation of the Chinese transliteration of the Sanskrit titles for this Buddha (Skt: Amitābha, immeasurable light; Amitāyus, immeasurable life). Of the Mahāyāna texts that refer to Amida, the Larger *Sukhāvatī-vyūha* (J: *Dai muryōju kyō*) is the major sutra of Pure Land Buddhism. It details the career of the bodhisattva Dharmākara (the future Amida), which is strikingly analogous to that of the historical Śākyamuni (J: Shaka). As a bodhisattva, Amida made 48 vows to satisfy every conceivable need of mankind, vows which were fulfilled and accomplished, whereupon he achieved Buddhahood and brought to realization his Pure Land. These 48 vows are collectively called the Primal Vow of Amida, although the term is used frequently to refer to the 18th vow, which states that he would not have become a Buddha unless all sentient beings who place sincere trust in him and invoke his name would be born in his Pure Land.

Amida is immensely popular in East Asian Buddhism. When Chinese Buddhism was at its zenith in the Tang (T'ang) period (618–907), Amida statues were the most commonly found images of the Buddha, as is evident in the Longmen (Lung-men) cave temples in Henan (Honan) Province. In Japanese Buddhism, statues of Amida also outnumbered other Buddha images in the Nara (710–794) and subsequent periods.

Amida worship can be classified into three general types. First is Amida as the object of contemplative practice as found in early sects such as the TENDAI SECT and the SHINGON SECT. Second is Amida regarded as a savior who welcomes the dying into his Pure Land, thereby promising eternal life; this was the popular Pure Land belief in China and especially during the Heian period (794–1185) in Japan. Third is Amida as the salvific power which affirms the value of human life and the Buddhahood of all beings, even the lowliest of sinners. This tradition, taught by HŌNEN and SHINRAN in the Kamakura period (1185–1333), stresses the recitation of the NEMBUTSU (*Namu Amida Butsu*: "I place my faith in Amida Buddha"), which is at the same time the call of Amida Buddha to the authentic life and the human response to that call, both of which are to be realized here and now.

In the visual arts Amida is usually portrayed with the bodhisattvas KANNON (Skt: Avalokiteśvara) and Seishi (Skt: Mahāsthāmaprāpta), one on each side. In the paintings called RAIGŌZU he is shown as descending to receive the dying faithful. Many Amida halls (*amidadō*) were built for the worship of Amida, the most famous of which is the Hōōdō of the temple BYŌDŌIN at Uji.

Taitetsu UNNO

Amino Kiku (1900–)

Novelist. Born in Tōkyō. Graduate of Japan Women's University, where she majored in English literature. She began writing in the early 1920s and became a follower of novelist SHIGA NAOYA, whose unique style of autobiographical or personal fiction, known in Japanese as *watakushi shōsetsu* (see I-NOVEL), she admired and imitated. Amino's reputation rests on moving fictionalized accounts of her unhappy life as a divorced working woman. A collection of early short stories is *Kisha no naka* (1940, On the Train). Other works include *Sakura no hana* (1961, Cherry Blossoms), a short-story collection, and *Yureru ashi* (1961–62, Trembling Reed), a long autobiographical novel. In 1967 she received the Yomiuri Literary Prize for *Ichigo ichie* (1967, Once in a Lifetime).

Ami school

(Amiha). School of painting that arose during the 15th century in Kyōto, after the devastation of the ŌNIN WAR (1467–77) brought about the artistic collapse of the major metropolitan Zen temples, which had been centers of artistic activity. The Ami-school painters emerged outside the Zen monasteries and revitalized the Muromachi INK PAINTING tradition during the politically unstable Sengoku period (1467–1568).

During the first half of the 15th century, the Ashikaga shōguns patronized the artist-monks of the most influential Zen Buddhist establishments of the day, the GOZAN monasteries. But in addition, each shōgun was served by a number of *dōbōshū* ("comrades"), individuals privately employed by the shōgun as curators of Chinese paintings in the shogunal collection, experts for repairing and authenticating works of art, and masters of NŌ drama, INCENSE CEREMONY, FLOWER ARRANGEMENT, and *renga* (see RENGA AND HAIKAI) poetry. These *dōbōshū* all incorporated into their names the Chinese characters "*ami*," from the name of the Buddha Amida. The earliest record of such names involves Buddhist painters of the late 13th century connected with Pure Land Buddhism—most likely the JI SECT. Some of the Muromachi-period (1333–1568) Ami artists were outcasts (*kawaramono* or the "riverbank riffraff") who were picked up by the shōgun. Among the better-known early Ami artists were Zen'ami, the master garden-designer, Ryūami, the flower-arranger, and Chōami, the craftsman of minor arts. But the so-called Ami school consists of three generations of Ami painters: NŌAMI (1397–1471), GEIAMI (1431–85), and SŌAMI (ca 1455–1525).

Nōami, also known as Shinnō, was the curator of art objects in the shōgun's collection. His many talents included *renga* poetry composition (his poems are included in the anthologies *Chikurinshō* [1476] and *SHINSEN TSUKUBASHŪ*) and ink painting. The first recorded date for Nōami's activities as a painter is 1465. In 1467 SESSHŪ TŌYŌ went to China with Nōami's painting of the *Eight Views of the Xiao and Xiang* (Eight Views of the Hsiao and Hsiang). Two colophons were inscribed on this painting by Chinese scholars, one of them the noted literatus Jin Shi (Chin Shih). The original painting was lost, but it is reported that Sōami, Nōami's grandson, had copied it. Although there are numerous paintings traditionally attributed to Nōami, these are of questionable provenance; the most widely accepted attribution is the *White-Robed Kannon* (Byakue Kannon, 1468). Painted in ink on silk, with an inscription by the artist himself, it blends the Chinese academic styles of Xia Gui (Hsia Kuei) and Ma Yuan (Ma Yüan) of the Southern Song (Sung) dynasty (1127–1279). Shortly after 1468 Nōami left Kyōto for Yamato in order to escape the destruction of the Ōnin War, and he died at Hase in 1471.

Geiami was called *kokkō* or *kokushu* (national master), as was his son Sōami. The earliest reference to Geiami as a painter is from 1458, when he presented a fan to the shōgun as a New Year's gift. In 1478 Kenkō SHŌKEI came to Kyōto from Kamakura to study painting under him. A long prose and poem composition by the monk-painter Shōju Ryūtō (1428–98) of the Kenninji monastery describes Geiami at work on his screen painting of the *Four Seasons*. In 1480, at the age of 50, Geiami painted *Viewing a Waterfall* in Xia Gui's style in ink and color as a farewell gift to Shōkei, who was about to return to Kamakura, where he transmitted Geiami's style to the next generation of painters at the Kenchōji monastery, Kamakura. Keison, Kōetsu, Kōboku, and Myōden were some of the known members of the Kamakura branch of the Ami school who followed Shōkei.

Geiami's son Sōami, also called Shinsō, is probably the best recorded of the three Ami artists, as his activities are frequently mentioned in the voluminous *Onryōken nichiroku*, the diary of the monks of SHŌKOKUJI temple. In addition to his various other activities, as curator of the shogunal collection he authenticated Chinese paintings and often wrote labels on scrolls, identifying their authorships and subject matter. As a painter he developed two distinct styles of painting: one, continuing the "hard-edge" Xia Gui style of painting as Geiami and Nōami had done, and the other, the "soft style" of painting, synthesizing the soft and cursive brushwork elements of the Chinese Southern Song painter Muqi (Mu-ch'i; J: MOK-KEI) and the rich ink washes and dots of the Chinese Mi style as well as some features of Korean paintings. He also integrated some of the compositional elements of the YAMATO-E tradition into his soft style. The soft style of Sōami was emulated by a number of important painters of the early 16th century, including KANŌ MOTONOBU. Among Sōami's direct followers were Tan'an Chiden, a young ceramist turned painter, and a certain Zean.

A major artistic contribution of the Ami painters was their work on connoisseurship. As curators of the art objects in the shogunal collection, they were responsible for two major documents on Chinese paintings in Japan during the Muromachi period: Nōami's *Gyomotsu on'e mokuroku,* an inventory of selected Chinese paintings in the collection, and the *Kundaikan sō chōki,* a connoisseur's manual known through various later copies, traditionally attributed to either Nōami or Sōami. The latter work is divided into two parts; the first classifies a list of Chinese painters into three qualitative grades, the second gives instruction on the proper way to display art objects in a *toko* (decorative alcove) or a *tana* (the adjoining shelves), and comments on various types of Chinese lacquerwork, ceramics, and bronzes.

Although the Ami school did not continue past the end of the 16th century, it was undoubtedly influential in providing new directions for the course of Japanese painting, particularly for secular art in the late 16th and early 17th centuries. The painting style of SŌTA-TSU and the RIMPA artists of the Edo period (1600–1868) was much influenced by the Ami school.

——Matsushita Takaaki and Tamamura Takeji, *Josetsu, Shūbun, San'ami,* vol 6 of *Suiboku bijutsu taikei* (Kōdansha, 1974).
Yoshiaki SHIMIZU

amma

Method of massage derived from Chinese medical practice; the term also refers to its practitioners. The earliest records regarding *amma* are found in the TAIHŌ CODE (701), which provided for the establishment of a Medical Bureau (Ten'yakuryō), among whose officials were *amma* responsible for administering massage. The massage style practiced by *amma* of that time included various methods that are common today, as well as methods for setting bones that combined massage with techniques from the martial arts. ACUPUNCTURE was also involved, though it is not known how this differed from the ordinary form of acupuncture, if at all. During the Edo period (1600–1868) various schools appeared, such as Hanaokaryū, Tōdōryū, and Ishizakaryū, and practitioners were often protected by domainal lords. It was probably at this time that *amma* therapy came to be performed largely by the blind. In the Meiji period (1868–1912), partly because of the introduction of Western medical practice, *amma* were no longer regarded as physicians. Nevertheless, *amma* survives today as both an occupation and a massage technique. See also SHIATSU; ZATŌ.
INAGAKI Shisei

Amō statement

(Amō *seimei*). A declaration concerning Japan's East Asia policy made by Amō Eiji (1887–1968), chief of the Information Bureau of the Ministry of Foreign Affairs, at a meeting with the press on 17 April 1934. Amō asserted that Japan would maintain a close relation with China and Manchukuo (the puppet state set up in Manchuria by the Japanese) and reject all interference from other countries. He contended that relations between Japan and China were to be handled by those two countries alone. Any moves by other nations to supply China with arms or economic or technical assistance for political purposes would have a divisive effect on relations between China and Japan, and hence could not be ignored by Japan. This statement, which could have been interpreted as a kind of Asian Monroe Doctrine issued by Japan, provoked a strong reaction from several countries, including the United States, which immediately issued a denunciatory statement. Under the guise of a reinterpretation of its content, the Japanese government withdrew the Amō statement in an attempt to maintain peaceful relations with the United States.

Amur River Society

(Kokuryūkai; literally, Black Dragon Society). Ultranationalist association that from 1901 to 1945 promoted Japanese expansion on the Asian continent and conservative values in Japan. An offshoot of the ultranationalist society GEN'YŌSHA, it was founded in 1901 by UCHIDA RYŌHEI with the initial aim of driving Russia out of the East Asian sphere south of the Amur River. The river was regarded by Uchida and many other Japanese nationalists as the northeast Asian perimeter of Japan's national defense. The society published its own journal, *Kokuryū* (later *Ajia jiron*), dispatched agents trained at its own school to gather intelligence on Russian activities in Siberia and Manchuria, and pressured government leaders to adopt a strong foreign policy. Espousing PAN-ASIANISM, it supported such Asian revolutionaries as SUN YAT-SEN and Emilio AGUINALDO in the early 1900s. At the time of the Russo-Japanese War (1904–05), the annexation of Korea (1910), and the SIBERIAN INTERVENTION (1918–22), it sent its own members to engage in covert political activities. During the late 1920s and early 1930s, the society turned its attention to domestic issues, attacking liberal and leftist currents of thought and calling for an emperor-centered national reconstruction.

Composed primarily of descendants of former *samurai* from Kyūshū, the society never had more than several dozen members at one time and never received official government approval of its activities. Yet the close ties of such leading members as TŌYAMA MITSURU to all ranks of the military, several high officials in government ministries, and powerful businessmen gave it far greater influence than most other ultranationalist groups. The society was disbanded by the OCCUPATION authorities in 1945.
FUJIMURA Michio

Anami Korechika (1887–1945)

Army general and army minister at the end of World War II. Native of Ōita Prefecture. Graduated from the Army Academy in 1905. He was appointed to the position of army minister in the SUZUKI KAN-TARŌ cabinet in April 1945. At the 14 August imperial conference to discuss the surrender terms of the POTSDAM DECLARATION Anami insisted on fighting to the end. He killed himself that night, after the imperial decision to surrender was made. His suicide was partly responsible for the failure of an attempted coup d'etat by young army officers intent on continuing the war. *HATA Ikuhiko*

Anan

City in southeastern Tokushima Prefecture, Shikoku; situated on the river Nakagawa. Formerly known as a rice-producing area, the city has rapidly been industrialized, with chemical plants and thermoelectric generating plants on Tachibana Bay at the mouth of the Nakagawa. Pop: 61,253.

Anan Coast

(Anan Kaigan). South of the city of Anan, southeastern Tokushima Prefecture, Shikoku. Characterized by its numerous sea cliffs, sea caves, and tiny islets, and one of the centers of Muroto–Anan Coast Quasi-National Park. Location of numerous breeding places of the loggerhead turtle or *akaumigame (Caretta caretta).*

anarchism

(museifu shugi). Although the Chinese Taoist philosophies of Laozi (Lao-tzu) and Zhuangzi (Chuang-tzu), as well as that of the Japanese thinker ANDŌ SHŌEKI, have anarchistic elements, anarchism rooted in Western philosophy was first introduced to Japan by KŌTOKU SHŪSUI (1871–1911) and ŌSUGI SAKAE (1885–1923). Before them, the ideas of Kropotkin and Bakunin had been introduced to Japan, mixed with socialist and communist philosophies (see MODERN PHILOSOPHY). In 1882 the TŌYŌ SHAKAITŌ (Oriental Socialist Party), based on the principles of anarchism, was founded by TARUI TŌKICHI (1850–1922). It was forced to dissolve within one month. Later developments of anarchism revolved around the figure of Kōtoku Shūsui. He had supported parliamentarism in his *Nihon shakaishugi shinzui* (1903, Essence of Japanese Socialism), but in 1906, after coming under the influence of anarcho-syndicalist thought while traveling in the United States, he advocated direct action by the proletariat to overthrow the power structure. After Kōtoku's execution in 1911 for involvement in the HIGH TREASON INCIDENT

OF 1910, the leadership of the anarchist movement was passed on to Ōsugi Sakae, an advocate of Kropotkin, who stressed the need for a revolution by the proletariat. However, through his study of Bakunin, Ōsugi was led to criticize, in 1922, the Bolshevik Revolution in Russia. A serious controversy with YAMAKAWA HITOSHI and other socialists ensued, and Ōsugi eventually embraced anarchism. This anarchist movement, in conjunction with syndicalism, greatly influenced the proletariat movement at one point, but gradually declined, especially after Ōsugi's death in 1923. Besides the anarchist movement which advocated the violent overthrow of the government, one should mention the nonviolent anarchist philosophy of ISHIKAWA SANSHIRŌ (1876–1956), based on Christianity and humanism.

Takahashi Ken'ichi

ancestor worship

Whether or not "worship" is the right word to apply to the practice, there is no question that the Japanese regularly conduct rites on behalf of the souls of the dead of their households. Sutras are recited before Buddhist family altars (BUTSUDAN) that contain memorial tablets *(ihai)* for the individual dead, and on which candles and incense are burned and flowers and food are offered. These practices have a long history in Japan, and while they owe much to the institutions and ceremonies of China and Korea, it seems likely that veneration of the spirits of the dead formed an important element of pre-Buddhistic religious practice in Japan.

Be that as it may, since the firm establishment of Buddhism in Japan, and at least since the 7th century, ceremonies intended to comfort the dead, to solicit their beneficence and prevent vengeful acts by them, and to secure their safe passage into paradise have been conducted by emperor, noble, warrior, commoner, and untouchable alike. The idiom is almost purely Buddhist at some periods of history, heavily Shintō at others, but most commonly a syncretic amalgam of the two. But since the middle of the 17th century domestic ancestral rites have been inextricably linked to the fortunes of the Buddhist temple and its clergy. By 1665 the domainal lords *(daimyō)* were required by the central government to establish a household registry system. Partly in order to ascertain that Christianity had been completely eradicated, every household was required to register as a parishioner (DANKA) of a Buddhist temple, whose priests would then certify the accuracy of the annual enumeration of its members (see TERAUKE). Among the many responsibilities of the temple was the overseeing of the performance of ancestral rites by its parishioners, and these remain their chief source of revenue today.

The state has frequently intervened to shape and exploit the ancestral rites in Japan. From the Meiji Restoration in 1868 to the end of World War II in 1945, the government was at great pains to construct a link between ancestor worship and filial piety on the one hand, and imperial loyalty on the other. The concept was by no means entirely new, having its roots far back in Japanese history, but the rhetoric was. The theoreticians of this effort maintained that filial piety and loyalty to the emperor were one and the same. Thus, as the father was the head of the house, so the emperor was the head of the national family. All Japanese were thus claimed to be united by ties of kinship. These formulas have long since passed from the scene, but the basic outlines of the ancestral rites remain unblurred.

When a person dies the Buddhist priest is asked to devise an appropriate posthumous name, which is incised on the face of the memorial tablet. On the 49th day after death (see below) the tablet is placed with others in the altar in the main room of the family home of the deceased. Since tablets are made for all persons who at the time of death are regular residents of the house, the altar's population is not at all, strictly speaking, exclusively ancestral in character. To be sure, it includes the ascendant parental generations, the former heads of the house and their wives, but also found there are tablets for unmarried siblings of the heads, children of the present head and his wife, and a variety of other kinsmen who for one reason or another have no other altar in which their tablet could be placed appropriately. In effect, the tablets in the altar of any given house are those of all of its deceased members.

Ceremonies are held and offerings made to the dead of the household on a number of occasions. They may conveniently be categorized in terms of their objectives. Those intended to venerate the collectivity of the ancestors are the New Year, 1–3 January; the vernal and autumnal equinox (HIGAN), approximately 21 March and 23 September; and the Festival of the Dead (see BON FESTIVAL), 13–16 July (in some localities 13–16 August). In addition to these calendrical dates, offerings are made to the household dead every morning and every evening, when they are customarily given the first serving of rice and tea.

Other occasions are designed to comfort the spirit of the individual dead. Ideally these rites are held on the first seven weekly anniversaries of death, a 49-day period during which the new tablet is kept on a low table below the altar. It is then placed in the altar with the other tablets, but special rites are observed for it on the 100th day after death and on the 1st, 3rd, 7th, 13th, 17th, 23rd, 27th, 33rd, and 50th anniversaries of death (the several sects of Buddhism specify other series). In addition, for periods of a few or several years, depending largely on the importance of the deceased and the religiosity of the living, an individual tablet will be singled out for veneration on the monthly death-day *(meinichi)* as well (for a person who died on 8 May, the eighth of every month).

Two features of the system are of considerable importance to an understanding of the whole. First, there is a very strong emphasis on the individual. His or her posthumous Buddhist name appears on the face of the tablet, as does the name in life on the obverse. At the ceremonies directed to the individual, one of the principal offerings is the person's favorite food, and on many occasions he or she will be addressed directly by name or kin term. The living may report to the dead, informing them of family fortune and misfortune, and important events in the lives of their descendants. Upon occasion, particularly at times of dire distress, they will be appealed to for help, and when the living feel that they have failed a parent or an elder sibling they may well apologize to his or her spirit. In more than one sense, then, the spirits of the dead remain in their households.

The second important feature of the system has to do with another issue altogether, for one of the major purposes of the ancestral rites is to move the soul of the newly dead from its ritually polluting, still earthbound state, into the purified collectivity of the long dead ancestors of the house and community. A deceased person is referred to as *hotoke* (Buddha) and most of the rites are Buddhist, as we have seen. But as memories of the individual fade, and as those who knew the person themselves die, the soul becomes more and more remote from the living descendants. At the 33rd or 50th (far more rarely at the 100th) anniversary of death, a transition is marked that obliterates the individual altogether. In some parts of Japan, the posthumous and real-life names are shaved from the tablet and it is burned, cast into the sea, or left in a temple or at the grave by the head of the household. The tablet thus disposed of, he may go to a Shintō shrine and place a stone by the gateway, saying, "The Buddha has become a god" *(hotoke wa kami ni nari . . .).* From that anniversary of his or her death—known as *tomurai age* or *toikiri* (the final rites)—the individual has merged with the collectivity of deities that protect the community and its residents, and no further rites are directed to it alone.

There is a great deal of evidence to support the view that until recent times the ancestors were a powerful force for social control within the household. It is almost equally clear that their power in this regard is now much attenuated. Yet the ancestral rites remain the one occasion on which most Japanese perform what may safely be termed activities of a religious character. The ceremonies may be less and less elaborate, but the dead are not abandoned by the living. Buddhist altars are still found in almost every home.

Nevertheless, a shift of great importance has begun to occur. Since the reforms of the post–World War II period, the household (IE) has ceased to be a legal entity and the nuclear family has emerged as a dominant domestic form. The ancestors were until recently the ancestors of the house, in which descent was reckoned patrilineally. The collection of tablets in the altar, accordingly, represented the kin of the household head, but the family is now a far more restricted unit, and as a consequence the relationship between the dead and the living is defined very differently. Today, children still tend to have memorial tablets made for their parents, and recent surveys have shown that a husband and wife may well have an altar (or its equivalent) in which they venerate the parents of both. Such bilaterality is not entirely unprecedented, but it is likely to become increasingly common as the nuclear family ideal continues to displace the older ideal of the corporate household.

🔲——Aruga Kizaemon, "Nihon ni okeru senzo no kannen," in Kitano Seiichi and Okada Yuzuru, ed, *Ie—Sono kōzō bunseki* (1959). Hirai Atsuko, "Ancestor Worship in Yatsuka Hozumi's State and Constitutional Theory," in Edmund Skrzypczak, ed, *Japan's Modern Century* (1968). William H. Newell, ed, *Ancestors* (1976), contains several articles on Japan. David W. Plath, "Where the Family of God Is the Family," *American Anthropologist* (1964). Robert J. Smith, *Ancestor Worship in Contemporary Japan* (1974). Takeda Chōshū, *Sosen sūhai* (1961).   Robert J. SMITH

An Chung-gŭn (1879–1910)

(J: An Jūkon). Korean nationalist who assassinated the Japanese statesman ITŌ HIROBUMI. The son of a well-to-do provincial family, he was baptized a Catholic at age 15 and then traveled to Seoul and Shanghai where he engaged in Western studies. In 1905, just as he settled into supervising his family's trade business in the port of Chinnamp'o, Japan took over responsibility for Korea's foreign affairs (see KOREAN-JAPANESE CONVENTION OF 1905). With the business threatened by Japanese competition, he sold it and established a school to prepare Koreans in Western skills needed for the nation's defense. He also participated in Korean nationalist activities in Vladivostok, but both these endeavors proved futile in the face of Japan's growing interference in Korea's domestic administration. Focusing his wrath and frustration upon Itō Hirobumi, who in 1906 had become resident general of Japan's advisory administration in Korea, An shot him at a railway station in Harbin, Manchuria, on 26 October 1909. He was executed in 1910 and became a permanent hero to the Korean people.   C. Kenneth QUINONES

Ancient Learning → Kogaku

ando

(literally, "undisturbed possession"). Formal confirmation by a lord of his vassals' rights of proprietorship, governance, or usufruct over real property; one of the principal bases of the lord-vassal relationship in medieval Japan. The most common type was *honryō ando,* the confirmation of a family's hereditary tenure of an estate, granted by the shōguns of the Kamakura (1185–1333) and Muromachi (1333–1568) periods to warriors who became their direct vassals *(go-kenin).* It was usually in the form of an official document *(andojō). Ando,* in the sense of ratification by shogunal authorities, was generally required to formalize the sale or other transfer by a vassal of land or proprietary rights (see YUZURIJŌ).

Andō Hiroshige → Hiroshige

Andō Hirotarō (1871–1958)

Scholar of agriculture and agricultural technologist. Born in Hyōgo Prefecture. After graduation from Tōkyō University in 1895, he entered the Agricultural Experiment Station of the Ministry of Agriculture and Commerce and made many contributions to the study of damage to crops due to cold weather and frost as well as to the improvement of various rice plant varieties. He was director of the Agricultural Experiment Station of the Ministry of Agriculture and Forestry for 21 years from 1920, while serving also as professor of Tōkyō University. Having made excellent improvements in technology in his youth and having been a nationwide leader in experimental research in his later years, he made major contributions in the field of Japanese agricultural technology. He was the author of *Nihon kodai inasakushi zakkō* (1951). He was awarded the Order of Culture in 1956.   KATŌ Shunjirō

andon → lanterns

Andō Nobumasa (1820–1871)

Daimyō of the Iwaki Taira domain (now part of Fukushima Prefecture) and senior councillor *(rōjū)* of the Tokugawa shogunate from 1860 to 1862. When the great elder *(tairō)* II NAOSUKE was assassinated in 1860 (see SAKURADAMONGAI INCIDENT), Andō and KUZE HIROCHIKA assumed leadership of the senior council. Andō was a skilled administrator and attempted to strengthen the shogunate's position politically and economically as well as diplomatically in its dealings with the Western powers. He reorganized Japan's monetary system and carried out other economic reforms to check the rapid inflation caused by the new foreign trade. He hoped to counter the antiforeign, pro-imperial movement by uniting the court and the shogunate (see MOVEMENT FOR UNION OF COURT AND SHOGUNATE), and in 1862 he effected the marriage of Princess KAZU, sister of Emperor KŌMEI, to the shōgun TOKUGAWA IEMOCHI. This act so incensed a group of imperial loyalists that they tried to assassinate him (see SAKASHITAMON INCIDENT). Although Andō survived this attempt, his efforts to strengthen the shogunate failed. Control of the shogunate passed into hands more favorably disposed toward the court and toward the large domains of Satsuma (now Kagoshima Prefecture) and Chōshū (now Yamaguchi Prefecture). Andō was forced to resign (1862) and was placed under house arrest for the next four years. He stood on the side of the shogunal loyalists in the Boshin Civil War which accompanied the Meiji Restoration of 1868. After their defeat he was again placed under house arrest, but was soon pardoned by the new Meiji government.

Andō Shōeki (1703?–1762)

Physician and thinker unique in the pre-Meiji history of Japanese thought for advocating a thoroughgoing egalitarianism. Shōeki was completely unknown until his works were discovered around 1899 by the philosopher KANŌ KŌKICHI. Much about his life is still unknown. It appears that he practiced medicine in the town of Hachinohe (in present-day Aomori Prefecture), although he does not seem to have been a native of the town. Shōeki's chief works, SHIZEN SHIN'EIDŌ and *Tōdō shinden,* were probably written or published around 1752–55.

Many of his followers lived in Hachinohe; professions represented among them included physician, Shintō priest, *daimyō* retainer, and merchant. He also had a few followers in Matsumae (in present-day Hokkaidō), Edo (now Tōkyō), Kyōto, Ōsaka, and Nagasaki. Though some contended that Shōeki's followers constituted a secret society aimed at revolutionary activities, it was more likely that they were a group formed for spiritual training and religious activities.

Shōeki's thought was introduced to Japanese readers by Kanō in the period before World War II, but it was only after the war, when critical examination of traditional thought became popular that Shōeki became widely known in Japan. Shōeki was interesting because he was unique in his opposition to the feudal class system. The translation into Japanese of a work by Egerton Herbert NORMAN that compared Shōeki to similar thinkers in world history was particularly influential in enhancing Shōeki's reputation.

Shōeki said that because all men are equal, each man should work to grow his own food *(chokkō).* That is, the natural order of human society is for people to feed and clothe themselves through engaging in agricultural labor, for men and women to join together on equal terms in monogamous bonds, and for them to give birth to and raise the next generation. Shōeki called this ideal society the "natural world" *(shizen no yo).* In opposition to this he placed the existing society or the "legal world" *(hōsei),* that is, the world of man-made laws and institutions. Through these laws the social distinction between upper and lower class is born, and the emperor and feudal lords can live in luxury, without laboring, by stealing and devouring the fruits of the labor of others. Those of lower social rank become envious and revolt, trying to raise themselves to a higher position. Shōeki said that because there is a differentiation between upper and lower classes, thievery and revolt continue and other evils fill society; he called for a return to the "natural world." He criticized all established fields of learning and such religions as Confucianism and Buddhism as being fundamentally mistaken in their justification of this differentiation.

Forming the theoretical foundation for this kind of social thought was Shōeki's own particular metaphysical view of nature. According to this, there is truth in action *(katsushin)* at the source of all things; the *katsushin* is manifested in the forward and backward movement of the elements *(ki;* Ch: *qi* or *ch'i)* of wood, fire, metal, and water, which together form the eight elements *(hakki).* The harmonious creation and action of all things is carried out through the synergy *(gosei)* of these elements opposing and supplementing each other in their interactions. In opposition to this synergy is the concept of dichotomy *(nibetsu),* or the placing of value distinctions such as upper and lower or good and bad, the process by which people of the "legal world" throw into disorder the harmony of the "natural world." This theory of the eight elements and synergy adds Shōeki's own interpretation to the Chinese concepts of *yin and yang* (J: *in* and *yō)* and the five natural elements so as to reconstitute them as the principles of creation and activity. In regard to heaven *(ten;* Ch: *tian* or *t'ien)* and earth *(chi;* Ch: *di* or *ti),* Shōeki considered these in terms of revolution *(ten;* Ch: *zhuan* or *chuan)* and stasis *(chi* or *tei;* Ch: *ding* or *ting*)—movement and rest—and maintained that mankind embodied the movement and rest of the universe in microcosm. In the same way that movement and rest (heaven and earth) create all things, so mankind performs activities which bring forth crops and descendants in accordance with the laws of synergy: this is the natural state of mankind.

Shōeki's theory of medicine was based on the Chinese medicine of the Jin (Chin; 1125–1234) and Yuan (Yüan; 1279–1368) dynasties and had much in common with the doctrines of the Zhu Xi (Chu Hsi) school (see SHUSHIGAKU) of Confucianism, as, for example, in regard to the laws of the natural world and of human society as being one. Shōeki often said, "Man is an individual at the same time that he embodies all of humanity" (*hito wa bambannin ni shite ichinin nari*). Along with being an expression of his egalitarianism, this also indicates that Shōeki's concern was directed to the way of life of the individual. Just as in the doctrines of Zhu Xi the morality of the individual is thought to be the standard in judging various social and political problems, so too Shōeki thought that the key for solving social problems was the development of a sound mind and body in the individual.

Consequently, although there was sharp criticism in Shōeki's thought of the various decadent phenomena of society that have been produced by class differentiation, there were no concrete plans for social reformation. Further shortcomings can be found in that Shōeki made no provisions for mutual cooperation and solidarity, or for those unable to be self-sufficient.

▬——Bitō Masahide, ed, *Shizen shin'eidō, Tōdō shinden,* excerpted in *Nihon koten bungaku taikei,* vol 97 (Iwanami Shoten, 1966). Bitō Masahide, ed, *Andō Shōeki,* in *Nihon shisō taikei,* vol 45 (1977). Kanō Kōkichi, *Andō Shōeki* (1928). Naramoto Tatsuya, ed, *Tōdō shinden* (Iwanami Bunko, 1966-67). E. H. Norman, "Ando Shoeki and the Anatomy of Japanese Feudalism," *Transactions of the Asiatic Society of Japan,* 3rd ser, 2 (1949). Watanabe Daitō, *Andō Shōeki to shizen shin'eidō* (1930).   *Bitō Masahide*

Anegawa, Battle of

(Anegawa no Tatakai). A major engagement fought on 30 July 1570 (Genki 1.6.28) near the river Anegawa in northern Ōmi Province (now Azai Chō, Shiga Prefecture). The allied armies of the emergent hegemon ODA NOBUNAGA and the future shōgun TOKUGAWA IEYASU defeated the combined forces of ASAI NAGAMASA, the *daimyō* of northern Ōmi, and Asakura Kagetake (d 1575), a general in the service of the daimyō ASAKURA YOSHIKAGE of Echizen (now part of Fukui Prefecture). Two months previously, Nobunaga had invaded Echizen, but was forced to withdraw when Asai, his brother-in-law, turned against him, threatening his rear. When Rokkaku Yoshikata (1521–98) of southern Ōmi also took the field against Nobunaga, his lines of communication were cut, and he was wounded by gunfire during the retreat to his castle town of Gifu. Nobunaga then directed a counteroffensive at Odani Castle, Asai's stronghold. The battle lines were drawn at the Anegawa, some 7 kilometers (4.4 mi) from the castle, when Asakura's forces came to Asai's assistance, creating a combined army variously estimated at some 13,000 men (in the chronicle SHINCHŌ KŌ KI) or more than 20,000 (by Nobunaga at the time). Nonetheless, Nobunaga carried the day, largely through the efforts of Ieyasu, who led the van. Since Kinoshita Tōkichirō (later called TOYOTOMI HIDEYOSHI) also participated in this campaign, it thus involved all three of Japan's great unifiers. Nobunaga failed to capture Odani Castle on this occasion, but his victory broke the cordon that had barred his way to the strategic Kyōto-Ōsaka area.   *George ELISON*

anemone, Japanese

(*shūmeigiku*). *Anemone japonica* or *Anemone hupehensis* var. *japonica*. Also known as *kibunegiku*. A large perennial herb of the buttercup family (Ranunculaceae), thought to be of Chinese origin, which grows wild in mountainous and hilly areas throughout Japan and is also cultivated as an ornamental. Height about 70 centimeters (about 28 in). The ternate compound leaves grow on long stalks from the root; the leaflets are ovate with 3–5 lobes. In autumn, branched flower stalks grow from the upper part of stems and produce pinkish purple double flowers about 5 centimeters (2 in) across. Numerous garden varieties have been developed and the cut flowers are highly popular. See also ICHIRINSŌ; YUKIWARISŌ.

Matsuda Osamu

Anesaki Masaharu (1873–1949)

Scholar of religion and literary critic who laid the foundation for modern religious scholarship in Japan. Pen name Anesaki Chōfū. Born in Kyōto Prefecture. After graduating from the philosophy department of Tōkyō University in 1896, he studied in Germany, England, and India. Early in his career he was closely associated with the writer TAKAYAMA CHOGYŪ and became well known as a critic, writing many essays and reviews. In 1904 he was appointed professor at his alma mater and in 1905 founded the first university department for the study of religion in Japan. He insisted upon an empathetic approach to religion, free of sectarian bias. Anesaki lectured on Japanese culture at Harvard University (1913–15) as well as in France (1919). As the director of the Tōkyō University Library, he devoted himself to reconstructing and restoring collections destroyed in the TŌKYŌ EARTHQUAKE OF 1923. His study of early Christians in Japan is still a standard reference work; two of his major works, *Nichiren: the Buddhist Prophet* (1916) and *History of Japanese Religion* (1930), helped introduce Japanese religion to Western readers.   *Suzuki Norihisa*

anglerfishes

(*ankō*). General name for bottom-dwelling saltwater fish of the class Osteichthyes, order Lophiiformes, family Lopliidae. In Japan the *hon'ankō* (*Lophius litulon*), 1.5 meters (59 in) long, and the *kutsuankō* (*Liphiomus setigerus*), 1 meter (39 in) are caught for food. The body is soft, and the head and mouth large. The fish moves the tip of its first dorsal spine, which looks like a baited fishing rod, to lure small fish and eat them. It inhabits continental shelf areas off Japan and is caught by trawling. Its liver is considered a delicacy and its meat is exported to France and other countries.

In premodern times the common people, especially of Edo (now Tōkyō), greeted the arrival of winter by eating *ankō* served in a pot.

Abe Tokiharu and Saitō Shōji

Anglo-Japanese Alliance

(Nichiei Dōmei). A military alliance between Great Britain and Japan, concluded in 1902 and lasting until 1923. It played a major role in political and military developments in the Far East, especially until the close of World War I, and helped mark Japan's emergence as a major power in the region.

Background——The Anglo-Japanese Alliance was a partnership between two nations remarkably compatible in many ways. Though they were far apart geographically and at different stages of political and economic development, they were both modern, industrialized states with similar ambitions and attitudes. Both had strong navies in East Asian waters, and they shared a concern with protecting their interests on the Asian mainland in the face of Russian expansion in Manchuria and northeast China, which had been intensifying with implicit French support in the period following the Boxer Rebellion of 1900. Japan's leaders, however, were divided over priorities. One faction within the Japanese government, led by ITŌ HIROBUMI, felt that the first priority was to reach an accommodation with Russia whereby Japan would acknowledge Russia's paramount position in Manchuria in return for recognition of Japanese hegemony over Korea. Another faction, led by YAMAGATA ARITOMO and Prime Minister KATSURA TARŌ, argued that Japanese interests would be better served by an alliance with Britain, which would strengthen Japan's hand in any military confrontation with Russia, and it was this policy that ultimately prevailed.

Original Agreement and Revisions——The treaty of alliance was signed in London on 30 January 1902. It was to continue in force for a period of five years and provided for joint action in the event of encroachment against either of the allies by Russia in concert with any fourth power. The two nations affirmed their recognition of each other's special interests and privileges in China, as well as of Japan's special interests in Korea. Thus Japan succeeded in isolating Russia militarily in the Far East, while the British assured themselves of Japanese cooperation in maintaining a balance of power among those nations vying for economic and political advantages in China. Later in the same year the allies held military-naval talks in Yokosuka and London in which they worked out a plan for major joint operations; in due course this plan became one of the key elements in Japan's defense policy.

The provisions of the treaty did not come into full effect during the RUSSO-JAPANESE WAR of 1904–05, since the Russians fought alone. However, while the peace negotiations were in progress at Portsmouth, New Hampshire, in August 1905, the alliance was revised and extended for 10 years. This extension was followed by further military-naval discussions in 1906–07. Taken together, they reassured Japan against the possibility of a Russian war of revenge and enabled Britain to reduce its naval strength in Chinese waters by relying on the Japanese fleet. Britain later tacitly accepted Japan's establishment of a protectorate over Korea.

The alliance was again renewed prematurely in 1911. By this time Britain was growing disenchanted with it, suspecting the Japanese of using it for their own advantage in China. However, Britain was anxious to avoid the expenditure on its navy that would be needed if the alliance were to lapse as scheduled in 1915. To provide against this, the alliance was renewed for 10 years in July 1911, but with a considerably narrowed scope. Britain had implicitly accepted Japan's annexation of Korea in the previous year, but Japan acknowledged that the alliance did not imply any British obligation to aid Japan against the United States. Understandably, many in Japan felt that the value of the alliance was diminished by this provision. Moreover, the original focus of the alliance, the Russian threat in East Asia, had largely ceased to exist.

Growing Dissatisfaction ——— Japan joined the Allies in World War I, though not under obligation to do so according to the terms of the British alliance. Some Japanese statesmen did, however, use the alliance as a pretext for entering the war. Japanese campaigns against German-leased territory in China and Germany's Pacific islands were among the first Allied victories of the war. The Japanese navy willingly carried its operations farther and farther afield in the Pacific, then into the Indian Ocean, and finally to the Mediterranean in response to British pleas for naval assistance.

In Britain, however, disillusionment with the alliance was rising at the time, not because Japan had failed to fulfill its obligations, but rather because of political and commercial tensions stemming from the war. Britain disapproved of some of Japan's actions in China, and was also anxious lest Japan take over British markets in the Pacific and Indian oceans while British merchants were temporarily inactive.

After the war, large segments of British opinion came to feel an aversion to the prewar alliance system, which, it was fashionable to believe, had largely caused the war's outbreak in 1914, and wanted to end the Japanese alliance. On the other hand, the key members of the postwar cabinet, Lloyd George and Lord Curzon, wished to continue it. The Japanese, for their part, argued that the alliance had nothing to do with the prewar alliance system and were distrustful of Anglo-American internationalism.

The alliance was also coming under attack from outside. It was condemned by an indignant China, which felt that the recognition of Japanese claims in Shandong (Shantung) at the Paris Peace Conference of 1919 had resulted partially from the alliance. It was also widely attacked in the United States, which became bitterly critical of Japan's expansion in China and of its naval ambitions. For the same reasons, Canada strongly advocated termination of the alliance, even though the other dominions of the British empire were ready to maintain it.

Termination ——— The issue of renewing or abandoning the alliance was brought to a head in private discussions held at the time of the WASHINGTON CONFERENCE in 1921. Britain and Japan both realized that in the altered circumstances of the postwar period they would need the naval, financial, and political cooperation of the United States to maintain security in the Pacific. Presented with the opportunity of joining in a treaty with the United States, they both embraced it with enthusiasm, even though it meant abandoning the alliance. In effect, Britain and Japan gave up their fairly precise contract in favor of the ambiguous FOUR-POWER TREATY (signed 13 December 1921, effective 17 August 1923) with the United States and France, whose provisions for consultations were never enforced. KATŌ TOMOSABURŌ, the chief Japanese delegate and an advocate of naval expansion, wrote at the time, "What has governed my thinking at the conference has been the need to improve the bad relations which have until now existed between Japan and the United States. That is, I should like as far as possible to set to rights the many anti-Japanese opinions in America." One of the factors in this anti-Japanese sentiment was the continued existence of the alliance. So the Japanese, like the British, found it convenient to discard the alliance in exchange for the benefits they received from other aspects of the Washington settlement.

These considerations were not fully understood by the general public in Japan. Successive Japanese foreign ministers had held that the alliance was the "marrow" of their country's foreign policy. It had protected Japan during years of rapid economic growth, and while some said that Japan did not get enough from the alliance, its governments by and large felt that the nation had benefited considerably. Thus the termination of the alliance in August 1923 was something of a psychological blow for the Japanese. Despite arguments that "the alliance was being merged into something new and more effective," the people remained skeptical. Japan was to remain without allies until the conclusion of the TRIPARTITE PACT with Germany and Italy in 1940.

For two decades the Anglo-Japanese Alliance was an essential element in the Far Eastern policies of its signatories. It enabled Japan to challenge Russian expansion successfully without fear of French intervention and to realize its own expansionist aims in Korea. It helped Britain to advance its interests in China while reducing the expenses involved. It also won great prestige for Japan, as it was the first modern alliance between an Asian nation and an advanced Western nation, even if it was not so much an equal treaty as a pact between a junior and a senior partner. In 1902 Japan was still a growing country, while Britain was a major world power. By 1923 the gap had narrowed, and Japan had unquestionably become the major Pacific power. In this transition the alliance with Britain had played no small part.

———Kajima Morinosuke, *Nichiei gaikō shi* (1957). Kuroha Shigeru, *Nichiei dōmei no kenkyū* (1968). P. C. Lowe, *Great Britain and Japan, 1911–15* (1969). I. H. Nish, *The Anglo-Japanese Alliance, 1894–1907* (1966). I. H. Nish, *Alliance in Decline, 1908–23* (1972). Tsunoda Jun, *Manshū mondai to kokubō hōshin* (1967).

Ian NISH

Anglo-Japanese Commercial Treaty of 1894

(Nichiei Tsūshō Kōkai Jōyaku). Signed in London by the Japanese ambassador to Great Britain, AOKI SHŪZŌ, and the British foreign secretary, John W. Kimberley, on 16 July 1894, the treaty was Japan's first important success in its efforts to remove inequities imposed by the Western powers in 1858 (see ANSEI COMMERCIAL TREATIES). Effective on 17 July 1899, the agreement ended British extraterritorial rights and partly restored Japan's rights of tariff autonomy. Following this example, other Western powers soon concluded similar agreements. Japan's control of tariffs was fully restored in 1911, when the treaty was replaced by another concluded by Foreign Minister KOMURA JUTARŌ. See also UNEQUAL TREATIES, REVISION OF.

Anglo-Japanese relations → United Kingdom and Japan

animals

The Japanese islands are inhabited by Southeast Asiatic tropical animals, Korean and Chinese temperate-zone animals, and Siberian subarctic animals. Japan's fauna includes many species and relicts not found in neighboring areas. Some of these relicts are found on Honshū, but a larger number inhabit the Ogasawara Islands and the islands south of Kyūshū, which have long been separated from the Asian continent. Most such animals are on the verge of extinction because of the limited area of their habitats.

Descriptions of animals inhabiting Japan are given in this article, but scientific names have been omitted where there are independent articles for the animals. For titles of such articles, see the lists at the end of this article.

Overall Characteristics ——— In zoogeographic terms, the sea south of central Honshū belongs to the Indo-Western Pacific region, and the sea north of central Honshū belongs to the Northern Pacific region. The Indo-Western Pacific region is part of the tropical kingdom, abounds in bright coral fish, sea snakes, and turtles, and is also inhabited by the dugong and the black finless porpoise. The Northern Pacific region is part of the northern kingdom, which extends along the southern coast of the Aleutian Islands and the west coast of the United States down to California, and is inhabited by such animals as the fur seal, Steller's sea lion, and Baird's beaked whale. Finally, Hokkaidō, which largely faces the Okhotsk Sea in the Arctic region, is occasionally visited by animals indigenous to the Arctic region, such as the walrus.

Pryer's woodpecker *(noguchigera)*
Sapheopipo noguchii
Island of Okinawa
Wingspread 155 mm

Japanese crested ibis *(toki)*
Nippoina nippon
Island of Sado
Wingspread 410 mm

Japanese mole (Azuma *mogura)*
Mogera wogura
Northern Honshū
Body length 12 cm, tail 2 cm

Japanese giant salamander *(ō sanshōuo)*
Megalobatrachus japonicus
Honshū
Maximum length with tail 1.2 m

Japanese shrew mole *(himizu)*
Urotrichus talpoides
Honshū, Shikoku, Kyūshū
Body length 10 cm, tail 4 cm

Yambaru *kuina*
Rallus okinawae
Island of Okinawa
Body length 30 cm

Iriomote cat (Iriomote *yamaneko)*
Mayairulus iriomotensis
Island of Iriomotejima
Body length 60 cm

Amami spiny mouse *(togenezumi)*
Tokudaia osimensis
Island of Amami Ōshima
Body length 13 cm, tail 10 cm

Amami rabbit *(Amami no kurousagi)*
Pentalagus furnessi
Islands of Amami Ōshima and Tokunoshima
Body length 45 cm

Okinawa habu *(habu)*
Trimeresurus flavoviridis
Island of Okinawa
Length 2 m

Animals——Examples of some species native to Japan

In the zoogeographical division of the Japanese islands by land animals, the Ryūkyū Islands south of Amami Ōshima are sometimes regarded as part of the Oriental region extending from the Malayan Peninsula to India and sometimes as a transition zone from this region to the Palaearctic region; the area north of Yakushima off the southern tip of Kyūshū is considered part of the Palaearctic region. The Ryūkyū Islands are inhabited mostly by tropical animals, such as the flying fox, crested serpent eagle, variable lizard, and butterflies of the family Danaidae. In mainland Japan (Honshū, Shikoku, and Kyūshū) and Hokkaidō, which belong to the Palaearctic region, two predominant groups of animals are known: animals common to deciduous forests of Korea and central and northern China, such as the raccoon dog, sika deer, Japanese crested ibis, Mandarin duck, and hairstreak; and animals of boreal coniferous forests of Siberia, such as the brown bear, pika, hazel grouse, common lizard, and nine-spined stickleback.

Of these animals, those of the Korean and the Chinese group are mostly confined to the Japanese mainland and those of the Siberian group to Hokkaidō. Consequently, it is common to include the mainland in the Manchurian subregion of the Palaearctic region and Hokkaidō in the Siberian subregion. However, the geological history of the Japanese islands, marked by repeated separation and reunion with the Asian continent, is exceedingly complex, giving rise to a corresponding complexity of animal migration and, as a result, noncontinuous distribution: the fauna of Japan differ slightly from those found in corresponding areas of the continent and not a few species are endemic to Japan. Insects of the order Grylloblattodea found only in Japan, the Soviet Union, and Canada; the Himalayan water shrew, distributed in the Japanese mainland, southern China, Taiwan, Southeast Asia, and the Himalayas but not in northern China or Korea, although they are both nearer to Japan; and the eastern barbastelle, distributed in the noncontiguous regions Hokkaidō and Honshū, western China and the Himalayas, and the Caucasus, may perhaps be relicts of species that migrated in the remote past. The distribution of the Japanese serow is analogous when the genus as a whole is considered. The Japanese mainland is inhabited by many endemic species such as the Japanese macaque, Japanese dormouse, copper pheasant, Japanese giant salamander, and primitive dragonfly (Epiophlebia superstes). The Ryūkyū Islands, which are presumed to have separated from the continent long before the mainland, are inhabited by a number of endemic genera, such as Pryer's woodpecker, and the Amami spiny mouse. The Amami rabbit and Iriomote cat belong to endemic genera, but also have characteristics which differ from the standards of higher taxonomic ranks and may be said to be living fossils.

Other examples of living fossils are found in the deep sea and include the slit shell, horseshoe crab, and frilled shark. The giant spider crab, the largest crustacean in the world; the Japanese giant salamander, the largest amphibian of the Recent epoch; and the ōgusokumushi (genus Bathynomus), one of the largest species of the order Isopoda, are also noteworthy Japanese aquatic animals.

There are also many forms of Asian land salamanders, dragonflies, and cicadas. Large swallowtail butterflies number eight species in the mainland alone, a remarkable phenomenon for such a small area of land in the temperate zone.

For the protection of animals feared to be on the verge of extinction, countermeasures such as the conservation of habitats, artificial breeding, and feeding have been reviewed by the ENVIRONMENT AGENCY and some proposals have already been implemented. In order to protect game animals, birds, reptiles, amphibians, freshwater fish, and insects, the agency started a survey of the status of animal populations in 1979 which it plans to repeat every five years to monitor changes.

Mammals——About 110 kinds of land mammals inhabit Japan. With the extinction of the wolf of Hokkaidō before 1900 and the Japanese wolf of the mainland about 1905, the only living large carnivores that present a threat to people and domestic animals are the brown bear in Hokkaidō and Himalayan black bear in the mainland. Ungulates are limited to three forms of shika (sika deer) in the mainland, Tsushima, and Hokkaidō, the kamoshika (Japanese serow) and inoshishi (Japanese wild boar) in the mainland, and the small, primitive Ryūkyū inoshishi (Liukiu wild boar) of the Ryūkyū Islands. The Japanese serow inhabits high, steep mountains in isolation or in pairs and appears also in the alpine zone above 2,400 meters (7,900 ft). This is a relict with a related species inhabiting only Taiwan.

Mammals of medium or small size worth mentioning are: the hibernating tanuki (raccoon dog), which is distributed throughout the mainland, Hokkaidō, Korea, and China; the ten (yellow marten; Martes melampus), which inhabits the mainland and Tsushima and is covered with beautiful chrome yellow fur; the musasabi (giant flying squirrel; Petaurista leucogenys), which inhabits the mainland and grows to about 80 centimeters (32 in) in length; and the saru (Japanese macaque), which inhabits the mainland and Yakushima. The raccoon dog, despite being a canid, climbs trees and eats the fruit of the loquat and persimmon. Of all the monkeys of the world, Japanese monkeys are found the furthest north. Among fruit bats, those with the northernmost habitats in the world are two species of ōkōmori (flying foxes) in the Ryūkyū and Ogasawara Islands.

The Ryūkyū Islands are inhabited by rare endemic species such as the arboreal kenaganezumi (bristled rat; Rattus legatus), which grows to 60 centimeters (24 in) in length, and the terrestrial togenezumi (Amami spiny mouse; Tokudaia osimensis), which has a dense coat of short spines. The rarest are the Amami no kurousagi (Amami rabbit), inhabiting the islands of Amami Ōshima and Tokunoshima, and the Iriomote yamaneko (Iriomote cat). The Amami rabbit is a remnant of the subfamily Palaeolaginae that flourished in the Tertiary period, and the Iriomote cat is a remnant of the tribe Metailurini that flourished in the Miocene period in China and is quite different from the leopard cat of the tribe Felini found in Tsushima, Taiwan, China, and elsewhere.

Small mammals inhabiting the mainland include: numerous kinds of bats; the kawanezumi (Himalayan water shrew; Chimarrogale platycephala); the kayanezumi (harvest mouse; Micromys minutus), which makes a spherical nest in tall grass; the okojo (stoat; Mustela erminea), which inhabits high mountains; house mice, and rats. The himehimizu (furry snouted shrew mole), inhabiting high mountains, and the himizu (Japanese shrew mole), inhabiting low mountains, are endemic genera and closely allied to the American shrew mole (genus Neurotrichus) in the mountain region of the western United States. The yamane (Japanese dormouse) lives in trees in mountain regions, hibernates rolled into a ball, and remains undisturbed even when rolled around. This genus appears to have been widely distributed on the Eurasian continent, and fossils of the same genus have been unearthed from the Pliocene and Lower Pleistocene in Europe.

Endemic species commonly found in cultivated fields and on plains in the mainland include the akanezumi (Japanese field mouse; Apodemus speciosus), the hatanezumi (Japanese vole; Microtus montebelli), the Azuma mogura (Japanese mole), and the jinezumi (dzinezumi shrew; Crocidura dsinezumi); in Hokkaidō are found species that also inhabit the continent, including the yukiusagi (snow hare), the shimarisu (chipmunk; Tamias sibiricus), the Ezo yachinezumi (red backed vole; Clethrionomys rufocanus), and the ōashi togarinezumi (big-clawed shrew; Sorex unguiculatus).

The rarest marine mammal inhabiting Japan is the dugong of the Ryūkyū Islands. They were once plentiful in the sea around the Yaeyama Islands, but in recent years are seldom found. The sunameri (black finless porpoise; Neomeris phocaenoides), only 1 to 1.8 meters (3.3 to 5.9 ft) long, is found in large numbers along the coast of Honshū in south central Japan and sometimes swims up large rivers. The ashika (Japanese sea lion; Zalophus japonicus) is endemic to the coast of the mainland, but it is feared to be on the verge of extinction.

Birds——There is no endemic genus among the 490 species inhabiting Hokkaidō and Honshū; the only endemic genera in any part of Japan are those represented by the following species: the meguro (Bonin honeyeater; Apalopteron familiare), and the extinct Ogasawara mashiko (Bonin grosbeak; Chaunoproctus ferreorostris) of the Ogasawara Islands, and the noguchigera (Pryer's woodpecker) of Okinawa, all of which are native to islands far from the Asian continent. The Pryer's woodpecker inhabits dark jungles and bamboo forests and lives on fallen nuts of the chinquapin, berries, and insects.

There are not so many endemic species of birds as mammals and the only ones in the mainland are the yamadori (copper pheasant) with tail feathers reaching one meter (3.33 ft), the black karasubato (Japanese wood pigeon; Columba janthina), the aogera (Japanese green woodpecker) with red cheeks, and the seguro sekirei (Japanese wagtail) with a black back. The komadori (Japanese robin) lives in mountainous terrain—its chirp is like a horse's neigh, hence the name (literally, "horse bird")—and the nojiko (Japanese yellow bunting; Emberiza sulphurata) lives in forest or grassy areas; both breed only in Japan and can be classified as endemic species, but migrate to southern China, the Philippines, and other places in winter.

Endemic species of the outer islands of Japan include the following: the *akakokko* (Izu Island thrush) in the Izu Islands and Yakushima; the *akahige* (Liukiu robin; *Erithacus komadori*), which has a rufous body, in the Ryūkyū Islands; the *rurikakesu* (Lidth's jay; *Garrulus lidthi*), which has bright chestnut and blue markings, in Amami Ōshima; the Amami *yamashigi* (Amami woodcock; *Scolopax mira*), also in Amami Ōshima; the Ryūkyū *karasubato* (Liukiu wood pigeon; *Columba jouyi*), on Okinawa and neighboring islands; the mysterious Miyako *shōbin* (Miyako kingfisher; *Halcyon miyakoensis*), only one of which has been caught on the island of Miyakojima; and the flightless rail, Yambaru *kuina* (*Rallus okinawae*), first observed by zoologists in 1981, which inhabits dense brushland in the northern part of the island of Okinawa.

Among sea birds seldom seen outside Japan are: the *ahōdori* (short-tailed albatross; *Diomedea albatrus*), of which about 100 individuals remain on the island of Torishima at the southern extremity of the Izu Islands and about 12 in the Senkaku Islands; the *umineko* (black-tailed gull) which breeds on the coasts of Hokkaidō and Honshū; and the *kammuri umisuzume* (Japanese auk; *Synthliboramphus wumizusume*) which breeds in the mainland and the Izu Islands.

Birds which are common, though not endemic, include the following: the *tanchō* (Japanese crane), which breeds in Hokkaidō; the *toki* (Japanese crested ibis; *Nipponia nippon*), of which only several individuals remain, on the island of Sado; the beautiful *oshidori* (mandarin duck), which makes its nest in hollows of trees at water's edge; the *karugamo* (spotbill duck), which is found all over Japan throughout the year; the *sashiba* (gray-faced buzzard eagle), which breeds in the mainland and migrates to the Malayan Peninsula in large flocks in autumn; the *kumataka* (Hodgson's hawk eagle), which inhabits steep mountains on the mainland and is used for hawking; the giant *shimafukurō* (fish owl; *Ketupa blakistoni*) in Hokkaidō; the *kijibato* (eastern turtledove; *Streptopelia orientalis*) and the *hiyodori* (brown-eared bulbul; *Hypsipetes amaurotis*), which live all over Japan; the sweet-voiced *uguisu* (bush warbler); the *kibitaki* (narcissus flycatcher; *Ficedula narcissina*) with a bright lemon breast; the *sankōchō* (black paradise flycatcher; *Terpsiphone atrocaudata*) with long tail feathers; the *yamagara* (varied tit; *Parus varius*), which is trained to perform acrobatics; and the *mejiro* (Japanese white-eye; *Zosterops japonica*), which sucks nectar from flowers. Other birds worthy of mention are: the *onaga* (azure-winged magpie; *Cyanopica cyana*), which is distributed intermittently in the Iberian Peninsula and East Asia; the giant *ōwashi* (Steller's sea eagle; *Haliaeëtus pelagicus*), which migrates to Hokkaidō in the winter; the *umiu* (Temminck's cormorant; *Phalacrocorax filamentosus*), which is used for fishing; the *hototogisu* (cuckoo), of which four species are found in the mainland alone; the *akashōbin* (ruddy kingfisher; *Halcyon coromanda*), which has carmine plumage; the *raichō* (ptarmigan); the *iwahibari* (alpine accentor; *Prunella collaris*), which inhabits high mountains above 2,400 meters (7,900 ft) in Honshū; and the *kiji* (common pheasant), which is found throughout the mainland.

Reptiles and Amphibians —— About 73 species of reptiles and about 40 species of amphibians inhabit Japan. Of the reptiles, 14 species are marine, inhabiting the sea along the coasts of the Ryūkyū and Ogasawara Islands. Five species of marine turtles are found, including the *taimai* (hawksbill turtle) and the *osagame* (leatherback turtle; *Dermochelys coriacea*). Only the *akaumigame* (ridley) and *aoumigame* (green turtle) land on Japanese beaches and lay eggs. The green turtle lives on seaweeds; its meat is tasty and its eggs are edible.

Other marine reptiles are sea snakes that prefer warm seas: the Erabu *umihebi* (sea krait) is found as far north as the coast of the mainland, and the *seguro umihebi* (yellow-bellied sea snake; *Pelamis platurus*) further north to the coast of Hokkaidō.

Of the land reptiles, about half the species are endemic to Japan. The *ishigame* (pond turtle), the *tokage* (skink), the *kana hebi* (lizard), four species of rat snakes (genus *Elaphe*), and the *shiromadara* (colubrid snake; *Dinodon orientalis*), which is marked with black and white, are all endemic and inhabit the mainland. Unlike the mammals and resident birds, many of these live as far north as Hokkaidō. Among the reptiles in the Ryūkyū Islands, 19 species are endemic including the Kishinoue *tokage* (Kishinoue's skink; *Eumeces kishinouyei*), which often grows to a length of 33 centimeters (13 in) and is the largest of all the skinks and lizards in Japan; the Kuroiwa *tokagemodoki* (panther gecko; *Eublepharis kuroiwae*), a gecko resembling a skink; the arboreal, big-eyed Iwasaki *sedakahebi* (snaileater; *Pareas iwasakii*), said to live exclusively on snails; and the *habu* (Okinawa habu), which is deadly poisonous, aggressive, and

extremely dangerous. The *mamushi* (Haly's viper) is the only poisonous snake in the mainland and is far smaller, slower in motion, and less dangerous than the Okinawa habu. The Haly's viper is distributed extensively on the Asian continent in addition to mainland Japan and Hokkaidō. The Takachiho *hebi* (Japanese xenodermin snake; *Achalinus spinalis*), which lives on earthworms and is nocturnal, is a relict that is distributed intermittently in the mainland and the eastern part of China, and the Amami Takachiho *hebi* (*A. werneri*) is endemic to the Ryūkyū Islands.

Among the Japanese amphibians, only about half of the frogs and toads (order Salientia) are endemic, while 15 out of the 16 species of the tailed amphibians (order Caudata) are endemic. Of the 18 species of Asian land salamanders (family Hynobiidae), 12 inhabit Japan. On the mainland are found nine species of two genera including the Kasumi *sanshōuo*, which inhabits ponds in the lowlands, and the Hakone *sanshōuo*, which inhabits mountain streams; one species is found in Tsushima, and two species of different genera in Hokkaidō. Only the *kitasanshōuo* (Siberian salamander; *Salamandrella keyserlingii*), which is a species of Hokkaidō and inhabits swamps, is distributed extensively on the continent, while the others are endemic to Japan. The *ō sanshōuo* (Japanese giant salamander), which grows to a length of 1.2 meters (47 in) and to a weight of over 10.5 kilograms (23 lb), is the largest living amphibian in the world; it belongs to the family Cryptobranchidae, which is different from the family of the above salamanders. It inhabits streams in the mountains of Honshū and Shikoku and emerges from underwater holes to hunt water animals by night. In the Tertiary period this family was widely distributed over Eurasia and North America, but is today a living fossil with the only other species of the same genus inhabiting China and a species of another genus inhabiting the United States.

The red-bellied *imori* (Japanese newt) is indigenous to the mainland and the Ryūkyū Islands and is commonly found in still water. The grotesque *iboimori* (crocodile salamander; *Tylototriton andersoni*) of the Ryūkyū Islands usually conceals itself under fallen leaves in dark, humid places.

Of the frogs and toads in the mainland, endemic species include the following: the *mori aogaeru* (Japanese arboreal rhacophorid; *Rhacophorus arboreus*), which lays eggs on trees near the water; the *kajikagaeru*, which inhabits mountain streams and has long been kept as a pet for its charming voice; the *tagogaeru* (*Rana tagoi*), which inhabits rock caves in mountainous regions; the beautifully colored *ishikawa-gaeru* (*Rana ishikawae*), whose body is covered with conical pustules and inhabits the Ryūkyū Islands; and the *ottongaeru* (*Rana subaspera*), with spiny first fingers on the forelegs.

Other Characteristic Animals —— Important freshwater fish include: the *ayu* (sweetfish), the king of Japanese river fish; the *iwana* (charr; *Salvelinus pluvius*), inhabiting mountain streams; the *moroko* (*Gnathopogon elongatus*), inhabiting rivers on plains; the *wakasagi* (*Hypomesus olidus*), inhabiting lakes and swamps; the *koi* (carp) distributed intermittently in Europe and East Asia; the *funa* (crucian carp) distributed widely throughout the world; the *medaka* (Japanese killifish; *Oryzias latipes*); and the *dojō* (loach; *Misgurnus anguillicaudatus*). More than ten species of the beautiful *tanago* (bitterling; *Acheilognathus moriokae*) inhabit rivers and swamps in northern Japan and lay eggs in the gills of such shellfish as the *karasugai* (*Cristaria plicata*); many of these are endemic species on the verge of extinction, such as the *miyako tanago* (*Tanakia tanago*), in rivers on the Kantō Plain. The *mahaze* (goby) is found along the coast from Hokkaidō down to Kyūshū, and the *tobihaze* (mudskipper; *Periophthalmus cantonensis*) is found in the western part of Tōkyō Bay and along the coasts of South Asia, Australia, and Africa.

In southern Japan, brightly colored coral fish such as the *chōchōuo* (butterfly fish; *Chaetodon collare*) and the *tsubameuo* (*Platax pinnatus*) are found. In the Ryūkyū Islands there is an even wider variety of coral fish, including butterfly fish that exist symbiotically with the sea anemone, such as the *kumanomi* (anemone fish; *Amphiprion bicinctus*), demoiselles such as the *suzumedai* (*Chromis notatus*), parrot fish such as the *hibudai* (*Scarus ghobban*), and beautiful wrasses such as the *hiregurobera* (*Ledidaplois hirsutus*); the huge *nishikiebi* (spiny lobster; *Panulirus ornatus*) grows to a length of 55 centimeters (22 in). In the Inland Sea lives the *namekujiuo* (lancelet; *Branchiostoma belcherii*).

Rare species live in the deep waters of Sagami Bay and Suruga Bay, including the *mitsukurizame* (Japanese goblin shark; *Scapanorhynchus owstoni*), which is elsewhere found only in the sea south of Australia and off the coast of Portugal; the *rabuka* (frilled shark; *Chlamydoselachus anguineus*), which is elsewhere found only off

Norway, northwestern Africa, and California in North America; the *okinaebisugai* (Beyrich's slit shell), which is considered a living fossil; and the giant *takaashigani* (giant spider crab) with extended legs over 3 meters (10 ft) wide. The Japanese goblin shark is a representative of the family Scapanorhynchidae, the frilled shark is the only species of the suborder Chlamydoselachoidei, and the giant spider crab belongs to a genus endemic to Japan.

The *kabutogani* (horseshoe crab) lives along the coast of the Inland Sea and is a remnant of the class Xiphosura, which flourished from the Permian through the Cretaceous period of the Mesozoic era; elsewhere only four species of horseshoe crab belonging to three genera of the same class are found along the east coast of the United States and the coast of Southeast Asia.

Insects —— Many endemic species of insect inhabit Japan. Among them are the *gifuchō*, related to the swallowtails; the *usubashirochō*, a species of Apollo butterfly; the *tsumajiro urajanome* (speckled-wood, *Lasiommata interrupta*), and the *hikagechō (Lethe sicelis)*, relatives of the wood nymphs; the Fuji *midori shijimi* (hairstreak), a relative of the blue butterflies; the *yamamayuga* (Japanese oak silk-moth; *Antheraea yamamai*), a relative of the moths; and the genus *Damaster*, a relative of the ground beetles, living on snail flesh. In the Ryūkyū Islands there are many milkweed butterflies of the South Seas group, including the *ōgomadara* with a 12 centimeter (4.7 in.) wingspread; its relative, the *asagimadara*, is found as far north as Hokkaidō. In the mainland there are many swallowtails of the South Seas group, with eight species of genus *Papilio* alone. On the other hand, the high mountains are inhabited by alpine butterflies of the Siberian group. The large-sized, violet *ōmurasaki*, considered a representative Japanese butterfly, is found also in Korea and China and is not endemic to Japan.

Apart from butterflies, there are many other insects, including 180 species of dragonflies (there are about 20 species of the genus *Sympetrum*), such as the *oniyamma* with a body length of 7.5 centimeters (3 in) and the scarlet *shōjōtombo (Crocothemis servilia)*; there are 20–30 species of cicadas, as well as numerous long-horned grasshoppers and crickets. Fireflies are also plentiful, with about 25–30 species in all of Japan.

The *garoamushi* (grylloblattids; *Galloisiana nipponensis*), which lives under stones in mountainous regions, and the *mukashitombo*, a dragonfly that spends seven to eight years in the larva stage in mountain streams, are noted living fossils. The *mukashitombo* is a remnant of an animal that flourished more than 190 million years ago in the Triassic period; only two species are now known, one each in Japan and the Himalayas.

■ —— *Check-list of Japanese Birds* (Gakushū Kenkyūsha, 1974). Imaizumi Yoshinori, ed, *Genshoku Nihon honyū rui zukan* (Hoikusha, 1960). Nakamura Kenji et al, ed, *Genshoku Nihon ryōsei hachū rui zukan* (Hoikusha, 1963). Okada Yō, ed, *Shin Nihon dōbutsu zukan* (Hokuryūkan, 1965).   IMAIZUMI Yoshinori

Animals in Japanese Culture

Animals in Japanese Culture —— Because of the distinct seasonal elements in the climate of the archipelago, the Japanese are keenly aware of changes in season. As in the case of plants, the lives of animals through the course of a year have provided a "natural calendar" and offered themselves as subjects for works of art. In the images and ideas the Japanese entertain about animals, there are clear signs of the influence that Chinese culture exercised on the native culture of early Japan. Japanese perspectives on animals have been affected largely by two factors: natural and environmental conditions, and traditional and imported cultural influences.

The Japanese archipelago extends some 2,100 kilometers (1,300 mi) from north to south and encompasses a variety of climates. Ocean and offshore currents also cause significant variations in temperature from season to season. The Japanese are sensitive to the changes in nature accompanying these distinct seasonal shifts, and animals and flowers provide the imagery used in artistic and poetic descriptions of the seasons. In addition, since the cultivation of rice became central to the economy in ancient Japan, an awareness of the life cycle of plants and animals has been used as a form of natural almanac.

Many of the beliefs and views held in Japan about various animals stem from native traditions, from Buddhist sources, and from the classic works of Chinese literature. Such traditional animal symbols as cranes and turtles (for felicity and long life) and swallows (for faithful return, i.e., the return of spring) were adopted from the Chinese by the Japanese ruling class, which was eager to emulate things Chinese at the beginning of the ancient period. It was not

until the latter half of the medieval period (13th–16th centuries) that a truly Japanese set of animal symbols evolved. In addition, up until the late 19th century, the vast majority of Japanese did not eat meat or slaughter four-legged animals; they relied chiefly on fish for animal protein. These views derived mainly from Buddhist teachings. Finally, the Japanese view of animals includes the role played by the JIKKAN JŪNISHI, or the sexagenary cycle of the ancient Chinese calendrical system. The cycle is broken down into subcycles of 12 years, each year of which is represented by an animal. Even today the Japanese think of the date of their birth in terms of the year in the sexagenary cycle ("the year of the dragon," "the year of the tiger," and so forth) in addition to the date according to the Gregorian calendar and the imperial reign date.

Agriculture and Animals —— Although Japanese culture has been primarily agriculturally oriented through most of its history, before the introduction of rice cultivation in the Yayoi period (ca 300 BC–ca AD 300), hunting and gathering were central. There was thus a gradual transition from the hunting of birds and animals to obtain meat in the ancient period, to the hunting of animals to protect fields and crops from damage. In ancient times, the wild boar, deer, serow, rabbit, raccoon dog, and wolf inflicted much damage. Deer and wild boar traveled in herds that trampled fields. To prevent such damage, early farmers banded together to build stone walls and moats, to set traps, and to organize group hunting expeditions. With a decrease in the bird and animal population in premodern times, the hunting task shifted to professional hunters.

Birds proved such a constant threat to crops that even today a special ceremony to drive away birds *(torioi)* is conducted in some localities. Bird hunting by professional bird hunters also took place in premodern Japan. However, with the exception of FALCONRY *(takagari)*, which became a symbol of political power, hunting was limited, and a "hunting culture" as understood in cultural anthropology did not develop.

Nor did an indigenous "herding culture" develop. Animal husbandry played a minor role in early Japan and was limited to the raising of wild boars (until the middle of the 8th century), cows, and chickens. None of the animals that have been raised since then (including the horse, cow, goat, hare, chicken, duck, goose, and honeybee) were domesticated in Japan; rather, they were all imported as domesticated animals. Cows and horses were introduced from the Korean peninsula, and the Japanese thus learned how to raise animals, use them in farm work, and utilize their manure for fertilizer, but these were grafts onto the indigenous farm culture and never represented more than a secondary factor.

The same can also be said about fishing. Although it was natural for the Japanese, surrounded by the ocean, to use fish, shellfish, sea plants, and other marine animals as a major source of animal protein, fishing and the cultivation of marine products never became more than a supplement to farming. Fishing did not exert a decisive influence on the basic character of Japanese culture.

Animals in Contemporary Japan —— From the above discussion, it is understandable that a peculiarly Japanese view of animals did not develop. It is also possible to say that the idea of animals being indispensable to human life (a concept basic to both hunting and herding cultures) is rather weak in Japan. Animal imagery, such as that surrounding sheep, deer, rabbits, and horses in the West, did not develop in any powerful or pervasive way in Japan.

Since ancient times the Japanese have made nature—animals and plants—the subject of poetry and art. The majority of Japanese consider this to be an expression of the Japanese "love of nature." Nevertheless, it was only in the 20th century that a genuine concern for the life and welfare of animals developed and conservation efforts gained broad popular support.

The following animal entries are contained in this encyclopedia:
Mammals —— BATS; BEARS; CATS; CATTLE; DEER, JAPANESE; DOG, JAPANESE; DORMOUSE, JAPANESE; FLYING SQUIRRELS; FOXES; HORSES; JAPANESE SPANIEL; JAPANESE TERRIER; KAMOSHIKA; KAWAUSO; MARINE MAMMALS; MOLES; MONKEYS; RABBITS; RATS AND MICE; TANUKI; TOSA DOG; WEASELS; WHALES; WILD BOAR; WILDCATS; WOLF, JAPANESE.
Birds —— BUSH WARBLER; CHICKEN, JAPANESE; CRANES; CROWS; CUCKOOS; GEESE; GULLS; HAWKS AND EAGLES; HERONS; KITE, BLACK; KOMADORI; LARKS; MANDARIN DUCK; PHEASANTS; PLOVERS; PTARMIGAN; RAILS; REED WARBLERS; SHRIKES; SPARROWS; SWALLOWS; THRUSHES; WAGTAILS; WILD DUCKS; WOODPECKERS.
Fishes —— ANGLERFISHES; AYU; BONITO; CARP; CATFISHES; CRU-

CIAN CARP; EEL, JAPANESE; GLOBEFISHES; GOBIES; GOLDFISH; HER-RING; MACKEREL; SALMONS; SAMMA; SARDINES; SEA BREAM; TUNA; WHITEBAIT; YELLOWTAIL.

Reptiles and Amphibians —— FROGS; IMORI; SALAMANDERS; SNAKES; TOKAGE; TURTLES.

Arthropods —— ANTS; BEES AND WASPS; BUTTERFLIES; CICADAS; CRABS; CRICKETS; DRAGONFLIES; FIREFLIES; GOLD BEETLE; HORSE-SHOE CRAB; KIRIGIRISU; SHRIMPS, PRAWNS, AND LOBSTERS; SPIDERS.

Others —— ABALONES; EARTHWORMS; JELLYFISH; LEECHES; OC-TOPUSES; SEA CUCUMBERS; SEA URCHINS; SHELLFISH; SQUID AND CUTTLEFISH.

◣ ——Kamo Giichi, *Kachiku bunkashi* (1973). Saeki Arikiyo, *Ushi to kodaijin no seikatsu* (1967). Saitō Shōji, *Nihonjin to shoku-butsu to dōbutsu* (1975). Suehiro Yasuo, *Sakana no shunka shūtō* (1968). *SAITŌ Shōji*

animism

Belief in the existence of a spiritual life in natural objects, natural phenomena, and the universe itself that is capable of exercising an influence on human beings. The Japanese have apparently believed in spirits called *chi, mi,* or TAMA—which, although not clearly defined, were associated with natural phenomena—since prehistoric times, when they lived by hunting and gathering. The chronicle KOJIKI and the poetry anthology MAN'YŌSHŪ (both 8th century) re-fer to the sun god Ōhirumemuchi, the moon god Tsukiyomi, the mountain god Yamatsumi, and the ocean god Wadatsumi. There was also a belief in such *tama* as *kodama* (the spirit of the trees), *kotodama* (the spirit of words), and *kunitama* (the spirit of the na-tion). On the other hand, gods given individual designations and characteristics were called *kami* or *mikoto*. Examples of these are AMATERASU ŌMIKAMI, ŌKUNINUSHI NO MIKOTO, and so on. These gods and less clearly defined spirits were thought to have control over natural and human phenomena and were collectively referred to as the *yaoyorozu no kami* (literally, "the eight million gods"). Later these spirits of nature and personalized gods combined to form an account of the origin and descent of the gods as presented in the *Kojiki* and NIHON SHOKI, reflecting the process of the political uni-fication of individual clans into a nation. These animistic beliefs have continued to endow the Japanese relationship to nature with a particular spiritual quality. See also RELIGION; SHINTŌ; NATURE IN JAPANESE RELIGION. *FUJITA Tomio*

Anjō

City in central Aichi Prefecture; located 30 km (19 mi) southeast of the city of Nagoya. Before World War II its main activity was rice cultivation utilizing the MEIJI CANAL for water, but more recently it has become a satellite city of Nagoya. There is a growing machine industry. Pop: 123,842.

Ankokuji Ekei (?–1600)

Buddhist warrior-monk of the Azuchi–Momoyama period (1568–1600). Born in the province of Aki (now part of Hiroshima Prefec-ture), he became abbot of the monastery Ankokuji in that province in 1579. A resourceful and worldly monk, Ekei acted as mediator between Mōri Terumoto (1553–1625), the powerful overlord of western Honshū, and the emergent hegemon TOYOTOMI HIDEYO-SHI, when the latter besieged Terumoto's castle at Takamatsu in 1582. Ekei served in Hideyoshi's invasion of Korea in 1592 (see INVASIONS OF KOREA IN 1592 AND 1597) and under his patronage made extensive repairs on Ankokuji as well as on the temple Tōfu-kuji in Kyōto, where he became chief abbot in 1598. He also re-ceived a fief assessed at 60,000 *koku* (see KOKUDAKA) in Iyo Province (now Ehime Prefecture). In 1600, with other commanders loyal to Hideyoshi's heir, Ekei fought under ISHIDA MITSUNARI against TOKUGAWA IEYASU in the epoch-making Battle of SEKIGA-HARA. After Ieyasu's decisive victory, Ekei fled to Kyōto but was soon captured and beheaded.

Anna Incident

(Anna no Hen). A conspiracy at the time of the abdication of Em-peror Reizei (r 967–969) in 969 (Anna 2) whereby the FUJIWARA FAMILY eliminated the influential minister Minamoto no Takaakira

(914–982), second son of the late emperor DAIGO and the chief ob-stacle to the political ambitions of Fujiwara no Saneyori (900–970). A Fujiwara ally, Minamoto no Mitsunaka (913–997), reported the existence of a plot to depose Crown Prince Morihira and elevate Takaakira's son-in-law, Prince Tamehira. Takaakira was disgraced, banished to Kyūshū, and replaced by Saneyori's brother Morotada (920–969). Crown Prince Morihira was put on the throne as Em-peror En'yū (r 969–984), with Saneyori as his regent. Thus the Fuji-wara consolidated their control of the court and established their REGENCY GOVERNMENT as a permanent institution. It was at this time, because of Mitsunaka's services, that the Seiwa Genji branch of the MINAMOTO FAMILY began its own rise to power.

G. Cameron HURST III

Annaka

City in southwestern Gumma Prefecture, central Honshū. Situated on the river Usuigawa, in premodern times Annaka was a POST-STATION TOWN and a castle town on the Nakasendō, a major high-way. Its principal industry is zinc refining. Isobe Hot Spring is lo-cated in the western section of the city. Annaka is also known as the onetime home of NIIJIMA JŌ, a Christian educator and founder of Dōshisha University. Pop: 43,094.

annual events → festivals

Anotsu

Former seaport in Ise Province (now the city of Tsu in Mie Prefec-ture). From the 11th century it was the seat and chief naval base of the Ise Heishi branch of the TAIRA FAMILY, who later achieved po-litical dominance under TAIRA NO KIYOMORI. In the Muromachi period (1333–1568) Anotsu flourished as a major entrepôt of the TALLY TRADE with Ming China; with Hakata (see HAKATA MER-CHANTS) and BŌ NO TSU, it was one of the three principal ports of Japan. Anotsu Harbor was rendered useless for shipping by an earthquake in 1498, but the town prospered throughout the Edo period (1600–1868) as a stopping place for pilgrims traveling to the ISE SHRINE.

Anrakuan Sakuden (1554–1642)

Prelate of the JŌDO SECT (Pure Land sect) of Buddhism; devotee of the tea cult; connoisseur of camellias; dilettante poet; and presumed compiler of the collection of anecdotes known as the *Seisuishō* (Laughs to Wake You Up), a major progenitor of the popular Edo-period (1600–1868) genre called *hanashibon* (books of humorous stories).

Details concerning Sakuden's birthplace, lineage, and most as-pects of his early and middle years are still the subject of scholarly speculation and controversy. It has been conjectured that he was between 7 and 10 years old when he was placed in the Jōonji, a temple of the Pure Land sect in Mino Province (now Gifu Prefec-ture), where he began his novitiate under Sakudō Bunshuku (d 1609). At the age of 11 he was sent to the Zenrinji in Kyōto, main seat of the Seizan branch of the sect. Here he received further edu-cation and religious training under Chikū Hoshuku (d 1586), a dis-tinguished priest renowned for his skill in explaining the *Jōdo hen mandara* (a mandala depicting the Pure Land of Amida). Records indicate that Sakuden, too, became adept at this form of religious instruction, or *mandara etoki*, as it was popularly called. Around the age of 25 he set out for the western provinces, where he is thought to have spent the next 15 years as a sermonizing priest.

In 1594, at the age of 41, Sakuden was appointed chief priest of the temple Shōbōji in Sakai. In 1596 he succeeded his former teacher, Sakudō, as chief priest of the Jōonji when the latter was appointed head of the temple Ryūshōji in the city of Gifu in Mino Province. Upon Sakudō's death in 1609, Sakuden assumed charge of the Ryūshōji for a brief period, but declined an opportunity to succeed him. He returned, instead, to the Jōonji, where he remained until 1613, the year he was appointed 55th abbot of the Seiganji in Kyōto, main temple of the Seizan Fukakusa branch of the Pure Land sect. In 1619 he was granted imperial sanction to wear the "purple robe" *(shie)*, the highest honor available to an ecclesiastic; and in 1623, the year of his retirement at the age of 70, he was twice summoned to the palace by Emperor Go-Mizunoo (r 1611–29) to deliver a discourse on the Pure Land mandala.

Retiring to a pavilion and tea arbor within the precincts of the Seiganji, which he called the Anrakuan (Hermitage of Peace and Comfort), Sakuden spent the remainder of his life amusing himself with poetry, tending his collection of camellias, and entertaining friends and visitors. It was here that he apparently prepared a manuscript of the *Seisuishō* for eventual presentation (1628) to Itakura Shigemune (1588–1656), the shōgun's deputy in Kyōto. The *Seisuishō* consists of more than 1,000 anecdotes loosely grouped within 42 thematic rubrics. Although Sakuden's preface indicates that the collection derives from a record he had kept of stories he had "heard" from the time he was a young priest, many of them seem to have been adapted from accounts in earlier written sources, both Buddhist and secular. An endorsement by Shigemune states that he first heard Sakuden recount some of these stories around the year 1615 and found them so amusing that he urged Sakuden to compile them into a book. Two other works definitely known to have been written by Sakuden survive: *Hyakuchinshū* (Collection of One Hundred Camellias), a quaint descriptive catalogue of the varieties of camellias known to him; and a personal register later designated as *Sakuden oshō sōtōbikae* (Memorandum of the Correspondence of the Priest Sakuden). Extant in Sakuden's own handwriting, this compilation records his correspondence in verse—essentially KYŌKA ("mad verse") and *hokku* (opening stanza of a linked-poem chain known as *renga*; see RENGA AND HAIKAI)—with an impressive number of distinguished personages. These included the *haikai* poet MATSUNAGA TEITOKU, the illustrious landscape architect and tea votary KOBORI ENSHŪ, the poet-novelist KARASUMARU MITSUHIRO, and the preeminent *waka* poet of the day, KINOSHITA CHŌSHŌSHI.

🔲——Miles K. McElrath, Jr, "The *Seisuishō* of Anrakuan Sakuden: Humorous Anecdotes of the Sengoku and Early Edo Periods," PhD dissertation, University of Michigan (1971). Sekiyama Kazuo, *Anrakuan Sakuden: Hanashi no keifu* (1967). Suzuki Tōzō, *Anrakuan Sakuden nōto* (1973).   Miles K. MCELRATH

Ansei commercial treaties

(Ansei *gokakoku jōyaku*; literally, "Ansei five-power treaties"). Trade agreements concluded between the Tokugawa shogunate and the United States, Russia, the Netherlands, Great Britain, and France in 1858 (Ansei 5), only five years after Commodore Matthew PERRY ended Japan's policy of NATIONAL SECLUSION. The treaty with the United States (the HARRIS TREATY) served as the model for the treaties with the other nations. These treaties opened several Japanese cities, including Kanagawa (later changed to nearby Yokohama), Niigata, Hyōgo (now Kōbe), Hakodate, Nagasaki, Edo (now Tōkyō), and Ōsaka, to trade; provided for the exchange of diplomatic representatives; assigned living and recreational areas for foreign residents; set tariff rates; and sanctioned extraterritoriality. These unequal arrangements drew Japan, for the first time in 250 years, into a network of economic and political relationships with the West.

II NAOSUKE, the great elder (*tairō*) of the shogunate, signed the treaties without imperial sanction. This act incensed antishogunate radical activists, who opposed any dealings with the West. The shogunate attempted to eliminate its critics (see ANSEI PURGE) but was constrained to adopt a more conciliatory posture after Ii was assassinated in 1860. Dominated by the radicals, the imperial court was forced to issue several antiforeign edicts between 1862 and 1864; and the political turmoil in Japan induced the Western powers to postpone full implementation of the trade agreements. Finally, on 20 November 1865 (Keiō 1.10.3), a squadron of nine foreign warships forgathered in Hyōgo Bay to demand the prompt opening of Hyōgo and imperial ratification of the treaties. Dismayed by the prospect of a foreign war and under strong pressure from the shogunate, the court, after two days of vehement debate, granted its approval.

Unfavorable tariff rates and extraterritoriality were to be major impediments to Japan's commercial development and national self-esteem, and the amendment of the Ansei treaties remained an important diplomatic issue throughout the Meiji period (1868–1912). See also UNEQUAL TREATIES, REVISION OF.

Ansei Purge

(Ansei no Taigoku). The term refers to the widespread purge, occurring from 1858 to 1860 (Ansei 5–7), of political leaders and court nobles who opposed the TOKUGAWA SHOGUNATE's policies. The purge was carried out by *tairō* (great elder) II NAOSUKE as soon as he assumed office in June 1858. His assassination in March 1860 at the hands of outraged followers of the purge's victims signaled the end of the purge. Ostensibly a reaffirmation of shogunate authority in the face of open challenge, the Ansei Purge represented a vendetta by Ii against his enemies; it culminated in utter failure and served to hurry the shogunate's demise in 1867.

Shogunate decision-makers faced a crisis when Commodore Matthew PERRY arrived in 1853 demanding the opening of Japan to diplomatic and trade relations. The KANAGAWA TREATY (1854) opened up the ports of Shimoda and Hakodate for supplies but made no provision for trade. Townsend HARRIS, coming in 1856 as the first United States consul, intensified the pressure on the shogunate to abandon its policy of NATIONAL SECLUSION. The Second Opium War then raging in China gave a fillip to Harris's warning that if the Japanese did not conclude a commercial treaty with the United States, they could presently anticipate much worse from the British and French. Shogunate leaders had to settle with Harris or risk greater danger later. They devised a treaty (HARRIS TREATY) that would gradually open several ports to trade, but important segments of opinion, notably TOKUGAWA NARIAKI, the *daimyō* of the collateral house of Mito (now part of Ibaraki Prefecture), and SHIMAZU NARIAKIRA, the daimyō of Satsuma (now Kagoshima Prefecture), who both hoped for a stronger role in national affairs, continued to reject any plan to deal with the West. The court nobility at Kyōto mostly agreed.

Meanwhile, a seemingly peripheral issue began to assume major proportions because of the crisis atmosphere brought about by American demands. The 13th Tokugawa shōgun, Iesada (1824–58), was sickly and incompetent. In the absence of a son he would have to be succeeded by a collateral relative. Two candidates were brought forward: the 12-year-old Tokugawa Yoshitomi (1846–66) of the Kii collateral house who was supported by Ii Naosuke, and TOKUGAWA YOSHINOBU (formerly called Hitotsubashi Yoshinobu), the able son of Tokugawa Nariaki.

Thus the two problems of foreign relations and shogunal succession became intertwined and inseparable. The pro-Yoshinobu forces launched a campaign in Kyōto early in 1858 to secure the court's approval of Yoshinobu as the new shōgun. This campaign nearly succeeded because first, the nobles opposed signing a trade treaty, and second, Yoshinobu was Nariaki's son and Nariaki was renowned as an opponent of opening the country.

To counter such machinations in Kyōto, Ii Naosuke was named great elder. Ii signed a treaty with Harris on 29 July without securing imperial approval. Immediately afterward he had Yoshitomi (later TOKUGAWA IEMOCHI) succeed as the 14th shōgun. He then began to suppress those who had supported Yoshinobu: Tokugawa Nariaki was placed under domiciliary confinement, leading daimyō were forced to retire (Shimazu Nariakira had already died), antiforeign court nobles were dismissed from office, and antiforeign proimperial activists like HASHIMOTO SANAI and YOSHIDA SHŌIN were executed. All told, more than 100 were involved in the purge. Retaliation was swift: on 24 March 1860 Ii was murdered by *samurai* from Mito and Satsuma (SAKURADAMONGAI INCIDENT).

One may view the Ansei Purge on three levels: first, as a means of coping with domestic political strife; second, as a specific response to American demands for international accommodation; and on the highest level of generalization, as a form of interaction with the Western powers when Japan was moving onto the stage of world history. Viewed from any of the three levels, the Ansei Purge was a dismal failure. As an effort to settle an internal Japanese political dispute it only brought more trouble. Ii had to acquiesce in Harris's demand for a treaty, though neither the court nor a vocal minority of daimyō wanted Japan's seclusion broken. Secondly, as a response to the need to accommodate American pressure for a treaty, Ii was making a reluctant bid to buy time. He had the treaty signed, but then tried to undermine its implementation. Finally, that Japan should enter modern world history through the instrumentality of the Ansei Purge constituted a long-term misfortune. The purge reinforced tradition just when a trend for wider daimyō participation in shogunate affairs was evolving. It is hard to escape the conclusion that Ii Naosuke's attempt to impose his will at this time of crisis and change ran counter to Japan's needs as well as to the evolutionary tendencies in Japanese politics. The purge therefore marked a step backward and affected the nature of the MEIJI RESTORATION when it came a decade later.

—— Edwin B. Lee, "Ii Naosuke's Attempt to Save the Tokugawa Shogunate," *Studies on Asia* VIII (1967). Conrad D. Totman, "The Struggle for Control of the Shogunate (1853–58)," *Papers on Japan* (East Asian Research Center, Harvard University, 1961). Kawakita Nobuo, *Bakumatsu no seisō* (1968). Yamaguchi Muneyuki, *Bakumatsu seiji shisōshi kenkyū* (1968).   *George M. WILSON*

Antarctic research

After a pioneering expedition in 1912, Japan's Antarctic research got its real start in 1957, when the Shōwa Station was established and wintering-over research expeditions became possible. In the early 1980s Japan had two stations, Shōwa and Mizuho, to conduct virtually all areas of Antarctic research.

History of research expeditions. In January 1912 the Shirase party, Japan's first successful Antarctic research expedition, under First Lieutenant SHIRASE NOBU, penetrated the ice belt in the Ross Sea in the *Kainan maru* (204 gross tons) and landed on the Ross Ice Shelf in the Bay of Whales. The party traveled over the ice shelf to a latitude of 80°05' S. It is credited with the discovery of Kainan Bay and Ōkuma Bay, and it explored the coast of the northeastern limit of the Ross Sea, which is now known as the Shirase Coast.

Japanese Antarctic Research Expedition (JARE). After a long period of no research or exploration by Japanese in the Antarctic, Japan participated in the international scientific exploration of the Antarctic during the International Geophysical Year of 1957–58, establishing the Japanese Antarctic Research Expedition as an officially sponsored national project. In January 1957, the Shōwa Station was established on an ice-free area of the Ongul Islands at the northeastern edge of Lützow–Holm Bay in eastern Queen Maud Land, and wintering-over research expeditions were started. The next year the boat was prevented from approaching the base by thick pack ice, and a wintering-over party could not be left there. After this failure, starting with the third expedition in 1958–59 all expeditions have succeeded in ferrying supplies to the base by helicopter, thus making it possible to keep wintering-over parties at the base continuously. Shōwa Station was closed temporarily in February 1962 because of the aging of the ice-breaker expedition ship *Sōya* (4,860 tons displacement) and other factors.

Research conducted at Shōwa Station at that time included observations pertaining to upper atmosphere physics, including auroras and cosmic rays; meteorological observations; geological and geomorphological studies of exposed rock formations near the coast and of the Yamato Mountains; glaciological research; and ecological studies of life on the continent. Also, the first JARE was accompanied by an oceanographical research vessel, the *Umitaka maru;* since then oceanographical research navigation has been carried out on several occasions.

Shōwa Station was reopened in January 1966, with a new research organization and the newly built research icebreaker *Fuji* (8,570 tons displacement). In 1968–69 an inland expedition was made from Shōwa Station to the South Pole in snow vehicles, covering a round-trip distance of 5,200 kilometers (3,231 mi). Other new areas of research since the reopening of the base have included studies of the water intake and output of the ice sheet behind Shōwa Station, probing of auroras with rockets, and the discovery of a large number of meteorites. The first wintering-over party consisted of 11 men. Since that time the number has gradually increased to the present level of 32. The scale of the base and its facilities have developed greatly in the last 20 years.

Present status and special features of Antarctic research. The headquarters of the Japanese Antarctic Research Expedition is formally part of the Ministry of Education and has as members high officials and appropriate specialists in related ministries, such as the Ministry of Transport and the Ministry of Construction. It is charged with the responsibility for overall planning. The detailed planning and execution of the expeditions is the responsibility of the National Institute of Polar Research and the Japanese Antarctic Research Expedition, which is organized by the institute. In addition, Japan's Antarctic research is conducted under the framework of the Scientific Committee on Antarctic Research (SCAR), part of the nongovernmental International Council of Scientific Unions, of which Japan is a member, and in accordance with the provisions of the international governmental Antarctic Treaty.

Shōwa Station and Mizuho Station. The main base for Japanese Antarctic research is Shōwa Station, built on exposed rock 15 meters (49 ft) above sea level on the East Ongul Island, a small island about 5 kilometers (3 mi) off the coast of Antarctica. Shōwa Station is located at 69°00' S, 39°35' E. The average annual temperature is −10°C (14°F). Routine observations include surface meteorological observations, aerological observations, observations of auroras and geomagnetism, ionospheric observations, tidal observations, seismological observations, and geodesy. Other research projects include observations of upper atmosphere physics by means of rockets, artificial satellite telemetry, and VLF intensity recorders; research in biology, medical sciences, geochemistry, and other environmental sciences; research in earth sciences including geology, geomorphology, and solid earth geophysics; and research on ice and snow.

Mizuho Station was built on the ice sheet at 70°42' S, 44°18' E, at an altitude of 2,170 meters (7,118 ft) above sea level starting in 1970. The average annual temperature at Mizuho Station is −34°C (−29°F). Year-round observations have been conducted at Mizuho Station starting in 1976. These include observations of ice and snow, the atmosphere, and the upper atmosphere, and are normally carried out by 4- or 5-man teams stationed at Mizuho.

The observational programs at Shōwa Station and Mizuho Station are carried out by teams normally staffed with 16 scientists and 16 technicians and general assistants. In addition, a summer party of 10 men conducts oceanographical and other observations on board the icebreaker *Fuji* and also does surveying and geological surveying during the short summer field season.

Japan's Antarctic research is characterized by comprehensive activities in virtually all the areas of Antarctic research with a heavy emphasis on observations of upper atmosphere physics.

—— Hans-Peter Kosack, *Die Polarforschung* (1967). Kusunoki Hiroshi et al, ed, *Nankyoku* (1973). Yoshida Yoshio, "Geography in the Japanese Antarctic," in *Geography in Japan* (1976).
                                        YOSHIDA Yoshio

anti-Christian edicts

(kinkyōrei). Anti-Christian directives of the Azuchi–Momoyama (1568–1600) and Edo (1600–1868) periods. Although the Catholic mission in Japan had to confront occasional hostility and even persecution on an individual and local basis from its inception in 1549, and the Jesuit missionaries were several times banned from the capital city of Kyōto (by imperial decree in 1565), the fragmented political condition of Japan in the Sengoku period (1467–1568) facilitated the religion's regional spread, especially in Kyūshū, where CHRISTIAN DAIMYŌ such as ŌMURA SUMITADA compelled the populace of their domains to turn Christian, destroying Buddhist temples and Shintō shrines. The situation changed as the process of Japan's reunification advanced under TOYOTOMI HIDEYOSHI, whose edicts against Christianity were the first by an effective national authority.

Hideyoshi moved against Christianity immediately upon completing his conquest of Kyūshū. His motive is explained clearly in the notice he issued in Hakata (now Fukuoka) on 23 July 1587 (Tenshō 15.6.18), condemning forced conversions as "unreasonable beyond words and outrageous" and making an elaborate comparison between Christians and adherents of the Honganji branch of the Buddhist True Pure Land sect (JŌDO SHIN SECT), a remarkably cohesive organization that in the 16th century developed into a religious monarchy encompassing whole provinces, competing with secular daimyō, and implacably opposing Hideyoshi's predecessor as a national unifer, ODA NOBUNAGA, in a 10-years' war (1570–80). Hideyoshi asserted that the Jōdo Shin sect had patently been "harmful to the realm" before it was put under control, but he found the Christians' activities "even more undesirable by far." The notice was followed a day later by a decree in which Hideyoshi declared that "Japan is the Land of the Gods," that the Christians' destruction of shrines of the native traditions "is something unheard of in previous ages," that "to corrupt and stir up the lower classes is outrageous," and that the Jesuit missionaries, held culpable for these outrages, must leave Japan "within 20 days"; Portuguese traders were specifically exempted from this antimissionary directive. Factors that probably contributed to Hideyoshi's proclamation of intent to expel the "BATEREN" (padres) were his awareness of the Jesuits' absorption of judicial sovereignty over Nagasaki, the terminus of the Portuguese trading ships in 1580, and his concern over the number and the zeal of their converts among his entourage, including such prominent daimyō as GAMŌ UJISATO, KONISHI YUKINAGA, KURODA YOSHITAKA, and TAKAYAMA UKON.

Although some Christian churches were destroyed, no missionaries left Japan permanently as a result of these edicts. They were not strictly enforced, possibly because Hideyoshi did not want to jeopardize the trade with the Portuguese. Christianity, however, had been stamped a subversive religion, and this determination led, in the aftermath of the SAN FELIPE INCIDENT of 1596, to Hideyoshi's renewed proscription of Christian missionaries and the death of the TWENTY-SIX MARTYRS of Japan on 5 February 1597 (Keichō 1.12.19).

The mission was given a temporary reprieve under the third of Japan's great unifiers, TOKUGAWA IEYASU, and reached its numerical peak, some 300,000 Japanese Christians, in the first decade of the 17th century. By 1612, however, Ieyasu too had turned against the Catholic missionaries and their converts. The immediate background of the anti-Christian directives issued by the Tokugawa shogunate (1603–1867) in that year and applied in its direct domains (TENRYŌ) was the MADRE DE DEUS INCIDENT and the Okamoto Daihachi Incident, a bribery and misfeasance scandal involving Okamoto Daihachi, the Christian secretary of Honda Masazumi (1565–1637), a rōjū (senior councillor) of the shogunate, and the Christian daimyō ARIMA HARUNOBU. The broader context was the shogunate's suspicion of divided loyalties among the Christians and mistrust of the designs of Catholic powers toward Japan, together with the realization, brought about by the establishment of a Dutch trading factory in Hirado three years previously, that the toleration of Catholic missionaries was not a prerequisite of trade with Europeans. The Protestant Dutch cast aspersions upon the activities of their Catholic religious enemies, trading rivals, and political foes; but they did not proselytize for their own faith.

The shogunate's anti-Christian rationale was elaborated in the Statement on the Expulsion of the Bateren, drafted by the Zen monk Konchiin SŪDEN at Ieyasu's behest and dated Keichō 18.12.23 (1 February 1614). Upon repeating that "Japan is in its origins the Land of the Gods," the statement asserts that the Christians aim to make that land into "their own possession" by means of their "pernicious doctrine" (jahō), that they "contravene governmental regulations, traduce Shintō, calumniate the True Law, destroy righteousness, corrupt goodness"—in short, subvert society—and must therefore be suppressed. From this year there followed a general persecution of Christianity in Japan, with the missionaries being forced out of the country or into subterranean activity and their converts pressured to apostatize or be martyred.

By 1616 the shogunate was ordering daimyō to "exert all effort to eliminate this religion among the populace, down to the last peasant and below"; by 1663 a clause requiring the strict prohibition of Christianity "in all provinces and localities" was incorporated in the BUKE SHOHATTO (Laws for the Military Houses). From 1640 to 1792 the shogunate's table of organization included an Office of the Inquisition (Shūmon Aratame Yaku) charged with the scrutiny of suspected Christians (see SHŪMON ARATAME). The anti-Christian element was one of the most prominent constituents of the policy and ideology of NATIONAL SECLUSION. Notwithstanding the elaborate apparatus of the persecution, however, Christianity was not eradicated but driven underground, where it survived in a gradually deteriorating form as a syncretic folk religion among the so-called KAKURE KIRISHITAN (crypto-Christians) until the edicts were voided by the Meiji government's declaration of religious freedom in 1873. See also CHRISTIANITY.

▬——Asao Naohiro, Sakoku, vol 17 of Nihon no rekishi (Shōgakukan, 1975). Charles Boxer, The Christian Century in Japan, 1549–1650 (1951). George Elison, Deus Destroyed: The Image of Christianity in Early Modern Japan (1973). Iwao Seiichi, Sakoku, vol 14 of Nihon no rekishi (Chūō Kōron Sha, 1971). Matsuda Kiichi, Kinsei shoki Nihon kankei Namban shiryō no kenkyū (1967).

George ELISON

Anti-Comintern Pact

Also known as the Tripartite Anti-Comintern Pact (Sangoku Bōkyō Kyōtei). A treaty signed by Japan, Germany, and Italy to oppose the foreign activities and interests of the Soviet Union. Japan and Germany initially concluded the pact in Berlin on 25 November 1936, and Italy joined them as an equal partner on 6 November 1937. The signatories committed themselves to exchanging information on Comintern activities and to collaborating closely on preventive measures. A secret supplementary protocol identified the Soviet Union as the signatories' common enemy and stipulated in general terms that if the Soviet Union without provocation should attack or threaten to attack any of them, the others would consult with one another and undertake "no measure which would tend to ease the situation of the Soviet Union." The signatories also secretly agreed to conclude with the Soviet Union no political treaties opposed to the spirit of the pact without mutual consent. The treaty, drawn up

largely through the efforts of the Japanese military attaché ŌSHIMA HIROSHI and Hitler's diplomatic adviser Joachim von Ribbentrop, marked the first step toward an alliance between Japan and Germany. In 1939 Hungary, Spain, and the Japanese puppet state of MANCHUKUO signed the pact, and in 1941 the treaty was renewed for another five years. See also GERMANY AND JAPAN.

Antimonopoly Law

(Dokusen Kinshi Hō; popular abbreviation of Shiteki Dokusen no Kinshi Oyobi Kōsei Torihiki no Kakuho ni Kansuru Hōritsu, Law concerning the Prohibition of Private Monopoly and Preservation of Fair Trade). Japan's first antimonopoly law enacted in 1947 as part of the economic democratization of Japan begun under the Allied OCCUPATION. The law, "by prohibiting private monopolization, unreasonable restraint of trade, and unfair business practices, . . . aims to promote free and fair competition, to stimulate the initiative of entrepreneurs, to encourage business activities of entrepreneurs, to heighten the level of employment and people's real income, and thereby to promote the democratic and wholesome development of the national economy as well as to assure the interests of consumers in general."

The development of the antimonopoly law in Japan since its inception may be divided into three periods that reflect varying degrees of enforcement. The first period, from 1947 to 1952, was marked by strict enforcement, due largely to the vigorous support of the Occupation. The second period, from 1952 until the mid-1960s, was marked by more relaxed enforcement. Two reasons may be suggested. The first was a 1952 amendment to the law that eliminated the per se illegality of cartels and other provisions dissolving all businesses above certain size limits (see ZAIBATSU DISSOLUTION); the second was a shift in Allied strategy regarding Japan during the Korean War. In the third period, from the mid-1960s until the present, the law has been enforced with renewed vigor. Among factors contributing to renewed enforcement are steady inflation, rising consumerism, the liberalization of trade and capital transactions, and a shift in Japan's national economic policy goal from high growth toward welfare. Furthermore, the year 1977 saw another amendment to the law, this time strengthening its antimonopoly provisions and providing for stricter enforcement.

Although the interpretation and enforcement of the law reflects to a large extent the influence of the American antitrust laws after which the Japanese law was modeled, there are substantive and procedural differences. For example, the private suit for damages has yet to play a large role in enforcement of the law. Similarly, there have been very few criminal prosecutions under the law. Enforcement of the law is left primarily to the jurisdiction of an administrative agency, the Fair Trade Commission (FTC).

Substantively, the three main areas of regulation under the law are private monopolization, unreasonable restraint of trade, and unfair business practices. The major features of the law in these three areas, as they have developed since its enactment in 1947, will be discussed below.

Private Monopolization—— 1. *Definition.* "Private monopolization" is defined in section 2(5) of the law as "business activities by which any entrepreneur, individually, by combination or conspiracy with other entrepreneurs, or in any other manner, excludes or controls the business activities of other entrepreneurs, thereby causing, contrary to the public interest, a substantial restraint of competition in any particular field of trade." Section 2(1) of the law defines "entrepreneur" as any "person who carries on a commercial, industrial, financial, or any other business."

2. *Exclusion.* Business activities of an entrepreneur that exclude those of other entrepreneurs may take various forms. For example, predatory pricing, exclusive-dealing contracts, and other activities that have the effect of stifling competition constitute "exclusion" under the private monopolization sections of the law.

In the SNOW BRAND MILK PRODUCTS CO, LTD, case of 1956, two dominant manufacturers of dairy products conspired with a dominant financial institution and a federation of farmers' cooperatives in Hokkaidō to reduce competition substantially. The financial institution was persuaded to issue loans to dairy farmers only on condition that they agreed not to supply milk to competitors of the two manufacturers. This conspiracy resulted in great injury to the business of other dairy-product manufacturers and a significant reduction in competition. The FTC found this conspiracy an act of private monopolization and so held against the two manufacturers.

3. *Control.* For the purposes of the law's regulation of private monopolization, "control" may be either direct or indirect. The use of power or authority by a stronger entrepreneur to direct, restrict, or prohibit the activities of a weaker entrepreneur is direct control. Such direct control is often exercised through stockholding, restrictive covenants, and financial pressure, but there are other means.

Indirect control is more difficult to define. Indirect control will usually be found in a rigidly structured oligopolistic situation where a leading firm may cause other firms to raise their prices simply by exerting pressure on its own distributors and retailers. The Noda Soy Sauce Co (now KIKKŌMAN CORPORATION) case of 1957 illustrates the manner in which indirect control is exerted. There, the leading manufacturer of soy sauce directed its retailers to charge a "suggested" retail price and enforced this resale price through coercive means. Because of the oligopolistic structure of this industry and a particular problem in product differentiation, smaller competing soy sauce manufacturers had no choice but to engage in resale price maintenance lest their market share be substantially reduced.

Although the Noda case does not suggest that mere parallel price behavior is indicative of control, it does suggest that there may be indirect control where the coercive measures applied by a leading firm to its distributors compel parallel behavior by competitors.

4. *Public interest and particular field of trade.* Under article 2(5) of the law, private monopolization may be found when the conduct of an entrepreneur is such that it causes a substantial restraint of competition contrary to the public interest in a particular field of trade. Each of these elements must be present for conduct to fall within the law's prohibition of private monopolization. The first element, "substantial restraint of competition" is determined qualitatively rather than quantitatively. Nevertheless, quantitative measures such as market share are useful in determining whether competition has been substantially restrained. As a rule of thumb, an entrepreneur with a 25 percent market share is likely to be subject to close scrutiny for possible violations of the law.

As to the second element, "contrary to the public interest," there are two major schools of thought. The prevailing view of the FTC, courts, and legal scholars is that the public interest under the law is the maintenance of free competition for its own sake. In this view, the public interest is harmed whenever free competition is substantially restrained in any market for any reason. On the other hand, there is another view that finds favor among MINISTRY OF INTERNATIONAL TRADE AND INDUSTRY officials and business groups and holds that the public interest under the law is broader than merely the maintenance of free competition. In this view, the public interest is to be determined by a balancing of various interests within the economy. Thus, an entrepreneur who causes substantial restraint of competition while achieving some useful social end, such as environmental protection or the maintenance of the balance of payments, would not fall within the prohibitions of the law. Currently the former view, with its narrower definition of public interest, dominates the decisions of the courts and the FTC.

The third element, a "particular field of trade," is difficult to define precisely. Like the definition of "market" under American antitrust law, the definition of a field of trade depends on the particular facts of a given case. The most important criteria are geographic area, kinds of customers, and the nature of the product.

5. *Regulation of stock acquisitions and mergers.* Section 10(1) of the law is a general prohibition of the acquisition by a company or companies of the stock of another company where the effect of such acquisition will be to restrain competition. This prohibition is reinforced in section 10(2) by a reporting requirement for companies whose business is other than financial, that have assets exceeding ¥2 billion, and hold the stock of another company. In a like manner, section 15(1) prohibits mergers where the effect of the merger will be to restrain competition substantially. Further, sections 15(2) and 15(3) require that a report be filed with the FTC prior to the merger and that no merger be effected until a fixed period of time has elapsed from the date of receipt of the report.

These provisions were strengthened by the 1977 amendments to the law that set upper limits on the stock one company might hold in another. Thus, under section 9(2) any company (other than a financial company such as a bank or insurance firm) whose capital exceeds ¥10 billion or whose assets amount to more than ¥30 billion may not acquire or hold the stock of another company if the value of the acquired stock exceeds the value of the capital or the net assets, whichever is higher, of the acquiring company. However, section 9(2) also provides for exemptions to this general prohibition of

stockholding by giant companies. Moreover, companies holding excess stocks at the time of the amendment are exempted for a period of 10 years from the time of the amendment. Section 13 regulates interlocking directorates, and section 14 regulates the acquisition of stock by individuals.

Furthermore, the 1977 amendments enable the FTC to take direct measures, such as the dissolution of large enterprises to restore competition, when it finds a "monopolistic situation" in an industry. The term "monopolistic situation" is, unlike "private monopolization," precisely defined under the law. Section 2(7) sets out the following elements of a "monopolistic situation": control of a 50 percent market share by a single entrepreneur or a combined 75 percent market share by two entrepreneurs; difficult market entry; substantial price increases combined with either abnormally high prices or great inefficiency on the part of entrepreneurs. Where a monopolistic situation exists, the FTC is empowered under section 8(4) to order the offending entrepreneur to divest itself of a portion of its business provided that divestiture will not reduce the international competitiveness of Japanese enterprise or cause an increase in costs and provided that competition cannot be sufficiently restored by other means.

Unreasonable Restraint of Trade —— 1. *Definition.* Section 2(6) of the law defines an "unreasonable restraint of trade" as follows: "The term 'unreasonable restraint' as used in this law means such business activities, by which entrepreneurs by contract, agreement, or by other concerted activities mutually restrict or conduct their business activities in such a manner as to fix, maintain, or enhance prices, or to limit production, technology, products, facilities, or customers, or suppliers, thereby causing, contrary to the public interest, a substantial restraint of competition in any particular field of trade." Under this definition, "unreasonable restraint of trade" is essentially the activity of a cartel. It should be noted that the prohibition of cartels applies only to horizontal agreements among competitors. Case law has interpreted the definitional requirement that restrictions be mutual to parties to the agreement to mean that a vertical agreement such as that between seller and purchaser does not fall within the purview of the prohibition of "unreasonable restraint of trade."

2. *Proof of a cartel.* In making a case for an "unreasonable restraint of trade" the most difficult element is the establishment of proof that an agreement has been entered into by the parties. Cartel agreements are very often tacit agreements as to price, quantity, etc; and even when material evidence in the form of contracts, letters, or business records exists, it is often very difficult to secure. Generally, to make a case for an unreasonable restraint of trade, the FTC must show that there is evidence of a communication of intent between the parties and that the subsequent conduct of the parties with regard to price has been uniform. As to the first element of the FTC's case, circumstantial evidence of communication between the parties is acceptable proof of the cartel's existence, provided that the subsequent conduct of the parties can then be shown to be uniform.

3. *Trade associations and unreasonable restraints of trade.* Section 8 of the law applies the prohibition of "unreasonable restraint of trade" to trade associations. Trade associations are associations formed by competitors within an industry, ostensibly for the purpose of rationalization of the industry through such measures as product standardization and quality control. Such trade associations exist in most Japanese industries. Without regulation, the activities of these trade associations would be scarcely distinguishable from those of cartels. Thus section 8 of the law requires that every trade association file a report of its existence with the FTC.

4. *Exemptions.* The law itself and other related laws contain provisions that permit the formation and existence of cartels under certain circumstances. Section 24(3) creates an exception for "depression cartels" where prices have fallen below the average cost of production and the threat to the survival of the industry may not be overcome by rationalization. Section 23(4) creates an exception for "rationalization cartels" to effect advances in technology or quality. Thus, under section 23(4) competitors who wish, for example, to share a commonly owned transportation or research facility may apply to the FTC for approval and, upon receiving approval, proceed with the project.

5. *International cartels.* The prohibition of international cartels is provided for in section 6 of the law. The wording of this section, however, does not prohibit the actual formation of an international cartel but rather the act of entering into an agreement or contract that creates such a cartel. Several recent cases involving agreements between Japanese and foreign entrepreneurs have raised difficult is-

sues under this section of the law. The viability of this section is somewhat questionable.

Unfair Business Practices—— 1. *Definition.* Section 2(9) of the law reads as follows: "The term 'unfair business practices' as used in this law shall mean any act coming under any one of the following paragraphs which tends to impede fair competition and which is designated by the Fair Trade Commission: unduly discriminating against other entrepreneurs; dealing at undue prices; unreasonably inducing or coercing customers of a competitor to deal with oneself; trading with another party on such conditions as will restrict unjustly the business activities of the said party; dealing with another party by unwarranted use of one's bargaining position; . . . "

The effect of section 2(9) is not to regulate entrepreneurial activity directly but rather to authorize the FTC to designate business practices within the framework of section 2(9). Under this enabling provision the FTC has promulgated two kinds of designation, general and specific. Specific designations govern conduct in specific industries. Industries that have been subject to specific designations include soy sauce, rubber footwear, oleomargarine, bottled foods, and newspapers. The general designations are promulgated by the FTC and apply to all industries. A discussion of the general designations follows.

2. *Discriminatory acts.* General Designations 1, 2, 3, and 4 deal with discriminatory acts by one or more entrepreneurs. Of these, 1 and 4 are the most important. General Designation 1 prohibits refusals to deal, or boycotts. A refusal to deal by a single entrepreneur is generally assessed on a case-by-case basis while a group refusal to deal or a boycott borders on per se illegality. General Designation 4 prohibits price discrimination for the same product according to location or customers. The legality of price discrimination under General Designation 4 is evaluated under the rule of reason, that is, the challenged discrimination must effect a substantial restraint of competition.

3. *Unreasonable price settings.* General Designation 5 prohibits the supplying of goods at unreasonably low prices or the receipt of goods at unreasonably high prices. To determine whether a price demanded by a supplier is unreasonably low, an examination of whether or not the price is lower than the supplier's cost of production or acquisition must be made. Nevertheless, in some cases a price may be unreasonably low, albeit above cost, if it is considerably less than the industry markup.

4. *Unreasonable coercion and inducement.* General Designation 6 makes it an unfair business practice to induce or coerce customers by offering undue advantages or threatening undue disadvantages. Of these two activities—inducement and coercion—the former has had greater significance in terms of the law's enforcement. Until the enactment of the Law to Prevent Excessive Premiums and Unreasonable Representations (Futō Keihinrui Oyobi Futō Hyōji Bōshi Hō) in 1961, General Designation 6 was the prime means of preventing the offering of excessive premiums and the use of false and misleading advertising.

5. *Unreasonable restrictions.* General Designations 7 and 8 regulate restrictive agreements between entrepreneurs. The common restrictive agreements falling under this designation include agreements pertaining to resale price maintenance, exclusive dealing, tie-in arrangements, and territorial and customer restrictions.

Resale price maintenance is a per se violation of the law in the absence of prior FTC approval. That is to say, resale price maintenance is permitted for products approved by the FTC. However, the list of products approved by the FTC for resale price maintenance is growing smaller.

Exclusive dealing is not a violation of the law unless the exclusive dealing arrangement is made between a manufacturer occupying a dominant market position and several distributors or retailers in a way that deprives the manufacturer's competitors of access to market distribution channels. A tie-in clause is also illegal in the absence of some justifiable reason for the tie-in. However, the number of cases in which a tie-in clause has been held illegal is small. Restrictions on customers have been found to be illegal in several cases where large manufacturers have limited the retailers to whom wholesalers may sell.

6. *Abusive use of economic power.* The abusive use of economic power by a powerful entrepreneur toward less powerful entrepreneurs is prohibited by General Designation 10. Examples of abusive conduct are unwarranted delays in payment to subcontractors for supplies delivered to the manufacturer. As the example above suggests, General Designation 10 is a unique part of the anti-

monopoly law in that its motivating concern is not the preservation of fair competition. General Designation 10 is designed to protect the small entrepreneur against the privations of large entrepreneurs whatever the effect on the large manufacturer's activities or competition.

Enforcement Procedures—— 1. *FTC proceedings.* Primary enforcement of the law is left to the FTC. A violation may be brought to the attention of the FTC in one of three ways. First, a private citizen may report information he considers a violation of the law to the FTC. The FTC must then investigate and decide whether to initiate an action. Second, the Prosecutor General must report to the FTC any violations of which he is aware. Third, the FTC may initiate an investigation *ex officio.* Of these three means of commencing an investigation, the first is by far the most common.

If the results of the investigation indicate that a violation has been committed, the FTC may either recommend to the violator that he cease his illegal behavior and, if this recommendation is accepted, hand down a decision without a hearing, or it may institute formal proceedings against the violator. In most cases, the FTC first makes a recommendation and then, depending on whether the recommendation is accepted, institutes formal proceedings. These proceedings are conducted in an adversary manner with administrative law judges presiding. During the course of the proceedings, the respondent may accept the statement of facts and application of the law as presented by the FTC and propose to eliminate the violations. If the respondent's proposal is in turn accepted by the FTC, what is referred to as a "consent decision" is handed down. Otherwise the proceedings will continue and a formal decision will be handed down. There is no difference in the legal effect of these different types of decision.

2. *Judicial review.* After the decision of the FTC, a party dissatisfied with that decision may bring an appeal directly to the Tōkyō High Court. The High Court then reviews the findings of the FTC as to the correctness of the commission's application of the law. No new findings of fact are made by the High Court unless the facts as found by the FTC are totally without evidentiary support. After the decision of the High Court an appeal may be taken to the Supreme Court.   MATSUSHITA Mitsuo

antiwar movement → peace movement

Antoku, Emperor (1178–1185)

The 81st sovereign *(tennō)* in the traditional count (which includes several nonhistorical emperors); reigned 1180–85; son of Emperor Takakura (1161–81; r 1168–80) and Tokushi (Kenrei Mon'in, 1155–1213?), a daughter of TAIRA NO KIYOMORI, the powerful leader of the military house of Taira (Heike or Heishi). The accession of Kiyomori's grandson to the throne in 1180 marked the zenith of the Taira hegemony over Japan; only a month after his enthronement, however, there occurred the first skirmishes of the TAIRA–MINAMOTO WAR (1180–85), in which the Minamoto destroyed the regime of the Taira. Their power declining, the Taira abandoned Kyōto in 1183, taking Antoku with them to the western provinces. The rival emperor GO-TOBA was installed in his place in the capital city. Antoku met his end with the final defeat of the Taira in the naval battle of DANNOURA (1185), when Kiyomori's widow, Tokiko (Nii no Ama), "plunged into the sea with the young emperor in her arms." She also carried with her the sword and the jewels that, with the sacred mirror, constituted the three IMPERIAL REGALIA. But the classic imperial loyalist history JINNŌ SHŌTŌ KI (1339–43) insists that the jewels "floated to the surface of the sea" and that the sword lost was a replica, the original being preserved in the Atsuta Shrine in Nagoya.   George ELISON

ants

(ari). In Japanese, *ari* is the common name for insects, other than bees and wasps, of the order Hymenoptera, family Formicidae. Of the several thousand species known worldwide, about 160 species of six subfamilies have been identified in Japan. Among these are the *ōhariari (Brachyponera chinensis),* the *amimeari (Pristomyrmex pungens),* the *togeari (Polyrhachis lamellidens),* and the *ōari (genus Camponotus).* Also notable are the *samuraiari (Polyergus samurai),* which do not gather their own food or raise their own young, and

the *kuroyamaari (Formica fusca japonica)*, which work for the *samuraiari* as slaves. Leaf-cutting ants (genus *Atta*), army ants, and driver ants are not found in Japan. NAKANE Takehiko

There are very few popular beliefs and legends about ants in Japan. No mention of ants is found in the earliest Japanese collections of myths and legends, compiled in the 8th century, or in the *Honzō wamyō*, a 10th-century dictionary of natural history. A few references to the ant are found in the *Makura no sōshi* (ca 1000) and *Tsurezuregusa* (ca 1330). In the Meiji period (1868–1912), two stories dealing with ants appear in Lafcadio HEARN's *Kwaidan*, both of which probably derive from Chinese sources. SAITŌ Shōji

Anzai Fuyue (1898–1965)

Poet. Real name Anzai Masaru. Born in Nara Prefecture. Anzai attracted attention as a poet with his first collection of prose poems, *Gunkan Mari* (1929, The Battleship Mari), published while he was living in Dairen (Ch: Dalian; now part of Lüda). He is regarded as an avant-garde poet of the 1930s who, along with KITAGAWA FUYUHIKO, helped establish prose poetry in Japan. His poems are noted for their conciseness and rich imagery. In later years he was active as a film critic. His poetry is collected in *Anzai Fuyue zen shishū* (1966).

Aōdō Denzen (1748–1822)

Western-style artist known especially for copperplate etching, an art in which he followed the initiative of his contemporary SHIBA KŌKAN. Real name Nagata Zenkichi. Born in Iwashiro Province (now part of Fukushima Prefecture), the second son of a family of well-to-do merchants. Although Denzen had studied painting since childhood, the decisive moment in his career did not come until 1794, when he was summoned to the court of MATSUDAIRA SADANOBU, lord of the castle town of Shirakawa and former regent to the shōgun. A screen painting by Denzen had so impressed Sadanobu that he ordered the then 47-year-old artist to study with TANI BUNCHŌ. In 1796, Denzen was appointed official painter to Sadanobu and in the following year was sent to Edo (now Tōkyō). There Denzen mastered the technique of copperplate etching. A few years later Sadanobu bestowed on him the name Aōdō ("Hall of Asia and Europe"), underscoring Denzen's interest in European and Asian art styles. Denzen produced a number of etchings of superb technical quality, chiefly domestic or foreign landscapes and architectural views; he also produced some maps and anatomical drawings.

📖——Cal French, *Through Closed Doors: Western Influence on Japanese Art* (1977). Cal FRENCH

aohon → kusazōshi

Aoi Bunko → Aoi Library

Aoi Festival

(Aoi Matsuri). The festival of the KAMO SHRINES in Kyōto; held on 15 May. Its name derives from the leaves of the *aoi* plant (*Asarum caulescens*), which decorate the headgear of the participants and the oxcarts in the procession; the eaves of many houses along the path of the procession are also decorated in the same way. It is said to have originated sometime in the 7th century. On the morning of the festival, the participants gather at the Kyōto Imperial Palace, dressed like nobles in the late part of the Heian period (794–1185). The procession makes its way across Aoi Bridge to Shimo-Gamo Jinja, one of the two Kamo Shrines. After rites are conducted, the procession moves to Kami-Gamo Jinja, the other shrine further north, where a similar ceremony is held. It then returns to the palace in the evening. Like the two other great Kyōto festivals, the GION FESTIVAL and the JIDAI FESTIVAL, the Aoi Festival draws great crowds. ŌTŌ Tokihiko

Aoi Library

(Aoi Bunko). Also known as the Shizuoka Library (Shizuoka Bunko). A collection of books and documents of the TOKUGAWA SHOGUNATE and its various departments and schools housed in the Shizuoka Prefecture Central Library in the city of Shizuoka. The collection contains several thousand Dutch, French, German, and English books from various departments of the Tokugawa shogunate, including the BANSHO SHIRABESHO, as well as Chinese and Japanese books from private collections and from the SHŌHEIKŌ, the shogunate academy. The library contains such books as François Halma's Dutch-French dictionary (1708), on which the HARUMA WAGE (1796), the first Dutch-Japanese dictionary, was based, and some 100 Japanese manuscripts, among them the official Tokugawa record of its relations with the Dutch. Theodore F. WELCH

aoki

(Japanese laurel). *Aucuba japonica*. An evergreen shrub of the dogwood family (Cornaceae) that grows wild in forested areas of Kyūshū, Shikoku, and Honshū from the Kantō district westward. It grows well in semishaded areas and is tolerant of urban pollution. It is widely cultivated in gardens. With a height of about 2 meters (6.5 ft), it is valuable as a firebreak or windbreak. The leaves are alternate, thick, elliptical, glossy and 10–15 centimeters (4–6 in) long. The *aoki* bears tiny green to purple brown flowers, male and female on separate trees (dioecious), in spring, and the female trees bear coral-colored fruits from autumn through spring. Horticultural varieties include those with narrow leaves and those with mottled leaves. Its leaves were roasted and used as a folk remedy for boils and wounds.

The *aoki* was described by C. P. Thunberg (1743–1828), a Swedish botanist who came to Japan in the latter half of the 18th century; he gave it the Latinized name *aucuba* after *aokiba*, then a Japanese vernacular name for the plant. MATSUDA Osamu

Aoki Kon'yō (1698–1769)

Confucian and WESTERN LEARNING scholar. According to most accounts, Kon'yō was born in Edo (now Tōkyō), the son of a tradesman. He studied Confucianism with ITŌ TŌGAI in Kyōto. In 1719–20 he came to the attention of the Edo magistrate ŌOKA TADASUKE, who recommended him for service to the shōgun TOKUGAWA YOSHIMUNE. In 1739 Kon'yō was given a position supervising the official archives. The following year Yoshimune ordered him to take up Western studies. He first studied under Dutch officials who were temporarily in Edo and reportedly later traveled to Nagasaki to continue his studies. In 1747 he was appointed Confucian scholar of the shogunate's Judicial Council (Hyōjōsho) and in 1767 became head of the Momijiyama Bunko, the shogunal library. His book *Banshokō* (1735, Studies on the Sweet Potato) urged the cultivation of that easily grown tuber to alleviate famine and earned him the nickname of Sweet Potato Professor (Kansho Sensei). Other works include *Oranda kaheikō* (1745, Notes on Dutch Currency) and *Oranda moji ryakkō* (1746, Notes on the Dutch Language).

Aoki Mokubei (1767–1833)

Potter and BUNJINGA painter. Real name Aoki Sahei. Born in Kyōto to a family of successful Gion-district restaurateurs. At an early age he studied with the great scholar and seal carver Kō Fuyō (1722–84). He also went to Ise to study metalwork and later tried his hand at seal carving. After discovering the *Taoshuo* (*T'ao-shuo*; J: *Tōsetsu*), a six-volume book on Chinese ceramics first published in China in 1774, which he read at the home of the literatus Kimura Kenkadō (1736–1802), he began to study pottery under OKUDA EISEN (1753–1811). He made remarkable progress and soon became famous for his reproductions of classic Chinese-style ceramics, including polychrome enamel, blue-and-white ware, and celadon, intended mainly for the *sencha* tea ceremony. He established two kilns: one at Kasugayama in Kanazawa, where he had been invited by the lord of Kaga, and another at Awata in Kyōto. In his later years Mokubei turned increasingly to painting in the *bunjinga* style. He painted not for the public but for personal enjoyment and for that of his friends, who included such Kyōto literati as RAI SAN'YŌ (1781–1832) and Shinozaki Shōchiku (1781–1851). He produced mainly landscapes, generally in a tall, narrow, hanging-scroll format in ink, reddish brown ocher, and indigo, which were much admired by TANOMURA CHIKUDEN (1777–1835). Mokubei's characteristically vibrant landscapes, such as *Autumn Landscape* (1824), employ dry texture strokes and a wash that frequently lends fluidity to the land forms interacting with the atmosphere around them. Louisa CUNNINGHAM

Aoki Shigeru

Umi no sachi (Gifts of the Sea). Oil on canvas. 70 × 181 cm. 1904. Ishibashi Museum of Art, Kurume, Fukuoka Prefecture.

Aoki Shigeru (1882–1911)

Western-style painter identified with the romantic school. Born in the city of Kurume, Fukuoka Prefecture. In 1899 he left middle school and went to Tōkyō, intending to become a painter. He entered the Fudōsha, a school operated by Koyama Shōtarō (1857–1916), and the following year enrolled in the Tōkyō Bijutsu Gakkō (now Tōkyō University of Fine Arts and Music), where he studied under KURODA SEIKI (1866–1924) and FUJISHIMA TAKEJI (1867–1943). He also read extensively in the fields of history, literature, and philosophy. In 1903, while still a student at the Tōkyō Bijutsu Gakkō, he was greatly influenced by the English pre-Raphaelites and became deeply interested in ancient Indian and Japanese legends. This led to his two series *Yomotsu Hirasaka* (Pass to the Land of the Dead) and *Jaimini,* which were entered in the eighth HAKUBAKAI exhibition and took first place. His paintings were characterized by a distinctive romanticism that was then common in literary circles. In the summer of the year of his graduation, he stayed on the coast of Chiba Prefecture with his lover Fukuda Tane and a friend, SAKAMOTO HANJIRŌ (1882–1969), and painted several masterpieces. One of them, *Umi no sachi* (Gifts of the Sea), created a sensation because of its depiction of vigorous nude fishermen hauling in their catch. His numerous seascapes are also regarded as among the best of impressionistic works of the period. In 1907 he exhibited his *Wadatsumi no Iroko no Miya* (Palace under the Sea) at the Tōkyō Industrial Exposition. Although its portrayal of the meeting of the mythic figures Yamasachi Hiko and Toyotama Hime was highly acclaimed by NATSUME SŌSEKI (1867–1916) and others, it was poorly received by his fellow artists and given third (last) place. Discouraged by this event and by the death of his father that year, Aoki returned to Kurume. To support his family he traveled around Kyūshū purveying his talents but was afflicted with tuberculosis in 1910 and hospitalized in the city of Fukuoka as a charity case. He died the following year. His remains were buried on Mt. Keshikeshi (Keshikeshisan), in the suburbs of Kurume, in accordance with a letter he left behind. His works, many of which are held by the Bridgestone Museum of Art, were highly acclaimed after his death and a memorial was erected on the mountain in 1948.

TAKUMI Hideo

Aoki Shūzō (1844–1914)

Diplomat prominent in the effort to revise the Unequal Treaties contracted between Japan and the Western powers in the 1850s. Born into a *samurai* family of the Chōshū domain (now Yamaguchi Prefecture), he studied Western science and medicine. On the eve of the Meiji Restoration (1868) he was sent by his domain to study law in Germany. During his long career Aoki was foreign minister in the cabinets of YAMAGATA ARITOMO and MATSUKATA MASAYOSHI and ambassador to Germany, the United States, and Great Britain, as well as privy councillor and special consultant on revising the Unequal Treaties. As foreign minister, he assumed responsibility for

the ŌTSU INCIDENT (1891), an assassination attempt on the visiting Russian crown prince, and resigned. In 1894, as minister to England, he assisted Foreign Minister MUTSU MUNEMITSU in renegotiating Japan's treaty with Britain (see ANGLO-JAPANESE COMMERCIAL TREATY OF 1894). This action set the pattern for later revisions of treaties with other Western nations (see UNEQUAL TREATIES, REVISION OF).

Aomori

City on Aomori Bay, northern Honshū; capital of Aomori Prefecture. Since the establishment of harbor facilities in 1624, Aomori has been an important shipping and fishing center. The city is the terminal for ferry service to Hokkaidō via the Seikan (Aomori–Hakodate) ferry as well as for the Tōhoku and Ōu National Railway lines. It is also the gateway to the Towada–Hachimantai National Park. Industries include lumber, food products, metal, and machinery. The Asamushi and Sukayu hot springs are located here. The NEBUTA FESTIVAL (1–7 August) and a museum commemorating the artist MUNAKATA SHIKŌ draw visitors. Pop: 287,605.

Aomori Prefectural Museum

(Aomori Kenritsu Kyōdokan). A collection of archaeological and ethnographical material with a section illustrating the recent history of Aomori; opened in 1973. Jōmon-period (ca 10,000 BC–ca 300 BC) pottery vessels, stone implements, and figurines are in the archaeological section; the ethnographical section, in addition to the usual farming and fishing gear, includes a number of *oshirasama* (local gods represented by colorfully draped sticks of wood).

Laurance ROBERTS

Aomori Prefecture

(Aomori Ken). Located at the northern tip of Honshū, and bounded on the north by Tsugaru Strait, on the east by the Pacific Ocean, on the south by Iwate and Akita prefectures, and on the west by the Sea of Japan. The western and central portions are dominated by the Dewa and Ōu mountains respectively, while the eastern area is relatively level, with some hills at the foot of the Ōu Mountains. The TSUGARU PENINSULA on the west and the SHIMOKITA PENINSULA on the east jut out from the northern coast, cradling Mutsu Bay. Major rivers include the IWAKIGAWA in the west and OIRASEGAWA in the east. The latter is fed by Lake Towada, located on the common border with Akita Prefecture. The climate is marked by short summers and long cold winters, with heavy snowfall in the western section. Like Hokkaidō, it is largely free from the rainy season common to the rest of Japan.

Inhabited at an early date, the western part of this region formed the Tsugaru district, and the eastern region the Nambu district. These were combined in 1871 into the prefecture of Hirosaki; later the name was changed to Aomori.

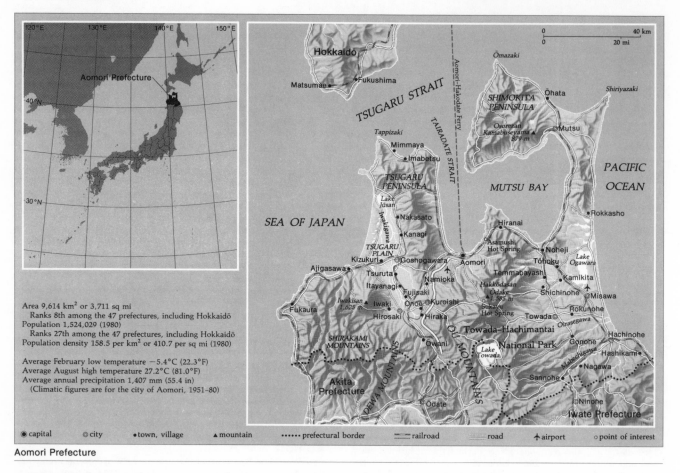

Aomori Prefecture

Area 9,614 km² or 3,711 sq mi
  Ranks 8th among the 47 prefectures, including Hokkaidō
Population 1,524,029 (1980)
  Ranks 27th among the 47 prefectures, including Hokkaidō
Population density 158.5 per km² or 410.7 per sq mi (1980)

Average February low temperature −5.4°C (22.3°F)
Average August high temperature 27.2°C (81.0°F)
Average annual precipitation 1,407 mm (55.4 in)
  (Climatic figures are for the city of Aomori, 1951–80)

The economy has traditionally been dominated by agriculture, forestry, and fishing. The entire prefecture is famous as a leading producer of rice, grains, and apples. Horses were formerly bred in great numbers, but since the end of World War II, have gradually been replaced by diary cattle and other livestock. Aomori's fisheries produce large amounts of mackerel, pike, and squid. Industry has developed slowly because of the prefecture's remote location, and has traditionally been connected with agricultural products and lumber, but in recent years there has been a growth of modern industries centered on the city of HACHINOHE. Lacquer ware continues as a traditional industry in the cities of Aomori and HIROSAKI. Aomori also is important as the transportation gateway to Hokkaidō, with the Aomori–Hakodate railroad ferry serving as the principal link. An undersea railway tunnel connecting Mimmaya on the Tsugaru Peninsula with the southern tip of Hokkaidō was under construction in 1982; completion was expected in 1986.

Traditional festivals such as the Nebuta (or Neputa) Festival of the cities of Aomori and Hirosaki attract visitors from throughout the country. OSOREZAN, a volcano on the Shimokita Peninsula, is famous as a center of traditional Japanese shamanism. Major tourist areas include Towada–Hachimantai National Park and numerous hot spring resorts. Area: 9,614 sq km (3,711 sq mi); population: 1,524,029; capital: Aomori. Other major cities include Hirosaki, Misawa, and Towada.

Aonodōmon

Tunnel in northern Ōita Prefecture, northeastern Kyūshū. Reputedly dug single-handedly through an almost impassable area in the gorge known as YABAKEI by the priest Zenkai over a 30-year period in the middle of the Edo period (1600–1868). Location of Kyōshūhō, a famous scenic area and the best sightseeing spot of Yabakei with fantastically shaped rocks along the river Yamakunigawa. Length: 185 m (607 ft); width: approximately 3.6 m (11.8 ft).

Aono Suekichi (1890–1961)

Critic. Born in Niigata Prefecture. Graduate of Waseda University. While working as a newspaper reporter, he became a staff member in 1923 of Japan's first so-called proletarian literary magazine, *Tane maku hito*, contributing essays on social and political issues. Active as a member of the Communist Party, he turned to literary criticism around 1925 and became the central figure of *Bungei sensen,* the successor to *Tane maku hito.* In a treatment of Marxist literary theory, *Shizen seichō to mokuteki ishiki* (1926), he elaborated on the ideas of Lenin's essay *What Is to Be Done?* stressing that writers needed to be conscious of the proletarian cause. This work exerted considerable influence on Japanese socialist writing of the late 1920s. After the POPULAR FRONT INCIDENT of 1938, he was forced to be less active in literary and social movements. Following World War II, he became president of the Japan Writers' Association (Nihon Bungeika Kyōkai), and was active in the postwar rebirth of the JAPAN P.E.N. CLUB. His principal works include *Shirabeta geijutsu* (1925) and *Tenkanki no bungaku* (1927), both works of literary criticism, and his memoirs, *Bungaku gojūnen* (1957).

Aoshima

Island approximately 1.2 km (0.7 mi) south of the city of Miyazaki, Miyazaki Prefecture, southeastern Kyūshū. It is connected with the mainland at low tide. The unique coastal configuration created by the erosive action of the waves on the island's sandstone and marlstone has given it the name Ogre's Washboard. The rocks are designated as a natural monument. Two hundred twenty-six species of subtropical plants are found on the island. It is part of the Nichinan Coast Quasi-National Park. The area of the island is 0.04 sq km (0.02 sq mi).

Aoto Fujitsuna (fl mid-13th century)

Legendary warrior and wise man of the Kamakura period (1185–1333). A retainer of the shogunal regent (shikken) HŌJŌ TOKIYORI, he served as a judge of the High Court (Hikitsuke) and became famous for his sound decisions. A well-known example of his sagacity is recounted in the 14th-century military chronicle TAIHEIKI. While crossing the river Namerigawa at Kamakura after dark, he dropped 10 *mon* (copper coins) and then spent 50 *mon* buying torches with which to search for them. When people laughed at his expenditure of 50 *mon* to recover 10 *mon,* he explained that the loss of 10 *mon* was harmful to the national economy, whereas the 50 *mon* spent would be usefully circulated among the people, causing no loss at all. This anecdote, often repeated in popular literature of the Edo period (1600–1868), is doubtless apocryphal; indeed, it is not certain whether Fujitsuna ever lived.

Aoyama Gakuin University

(Aoyama Gakuin Daigaku). A private, coeducational university located in Shibuya Ward, Tōkyō. Founded as a school for girls in 1874 by a group of young Japanese Christians and Robert S. Maclay, an American Methodist missionary. In 1883 the school was renamed Tōkyō Eiwa Gakkō (Tōkyō Anglo-Japanese School) and expanded with funds provided by the Methodist Church in America. In 1894 the school adopted its present name, Aoyama Gakuin, and in 1904 became a college. University status was granted in 1948. In keeping with its original spirit, the school strives to instill in the students a strong Christian character, and is known for the high level of its English language and literature instruction. The university has affiliated schools from kindergarten through senior high school and a two-year junior college for women. It maintains faculties of letters, economics, business management, law, science, and engineering and is known for its Economic Research Institute and Institute of Business Research. Night courses are offered in all departments except science and engineering. Enrollment was 12,843 in 1980.

Aoyama Tanemichi (1859–1917)

Internist. Born in Edo (now Tōkyō). A graduate of Tōkyō University, Aoyama studied at the University of Berlin and was named professor at Tōkyō University in 1887. In 1894 Aoyama went to Hong Kong to study the bubonic plague that had broken out there; he himself was infected. He also did work on beriberi and other diseases. Aoyama was head of the clinic attached to Tōkyō University and of its medical faculty, and director of the Institute for Infectious Diseases after it was placed under the jurisdiction of the Ministry of Education. He greatly influenced internal medicine and medical education in Japan. NAGATOYA Yōji

apples

(ringo). *Malus pumila.* The cultivation of apples in Japan began early in the Meiji period (1868–1912), when 75 American varieties and 106 French varieties were introduced. At the outset lack of knowledge of the plant's optimum growing conditions caused repeated failures, but it was later found that places with a cool climate and little rainfall in summer were most suitable for apple cultivation; and the prefectures of Aomori, Nagano, Hokkaidō, Iwate, Yamagata, Akita, and Fukushima became the main centers of production. In addition to the Iwai (American Summer Pearmain), Asahi (McIntosh Red), Kōgyoku (Jonathan), Kokkō (Rall's Janet), Golden Delicious, and Delicious strains introduced from abroad, the Mutsu, Fuji, and Tsugaru, which were developed in Japan after World War II, are now widely grown. Although a wide range of early- to late-ripening varieties are cultivated, a great majority of Japan's production consists of late-ripening varieties. Only about 10 percent of the total crop is processed. NAGASAWA Katsuo

apprentice system

(totei seido). The traditional Japanese apprentice system, which evolved among handicraft artisans, became socially and economically significant during the Edo period (1600–1868). Such a master-apprentice relation had already existed in medieval guilds (ZA), but in many cases, the apprentice (totei) was a bondman rather than hired help. With the formation of merchant guilds (KABUNAKAMA) in the Edo period, the arrangement became formalized, resulting in a contractual relationship that mutually bound the individual master (oyakata) and the hired apprentice. Regulations governing this relation were observed by all *kabunakama.*

Before being formally indentured, the youth had to pay a formal visit (memie) to the master, who then paid "advance money" (tetsuke) to his parents. A formal agreement (shōmon) was drawn up; it was worded in terms of service for a designated length of time, and the oyakata very often requested a statement of guarantee from the apprentice's parents and relatives. The apprentice was usually 10 to 12 years old, and his term of indenture, about 10 years, although this was later shortened. He lived with the oyakata and his

family, and in the process of learning his trade, he not only helped his master without any financial compensation but also performed household chores. Not a few young boys left or ran away before their terms of service were over. As a safeguard against negligence or breach of contract, the oyakata could resort to what was called kagyō-gamae and forbid the apprentice—no matter how qualified—from practicing his trade.

When an apprentice had completed his term of service, he was given a set of tools by the oyakata. He was now ready to set up shop on his own and, if he succeeded in obtaining membership in the artisan's guild, he himself could become an oyakata. Later, as the number of artisans increased, a limit was set on the number of members, making it difficult to become an oyakata. Many artisans were forced to travel from place to place and suffer great hardships. Some were obliged to work at their master's shop as wage earners. With the dissolution of the *kabunakama* in the Meiji period (1868–1912), the apprentice system declined. In some fields, however, as in iron-casting, it remained until recent times. MIYAMOTO Mataji

April 16th Incident

(Yon'ichiroku Jiken). Nationwide arrest of 600 to 700 suspected communists, which took place in 1929 after the police found a Japan Communist Party membership list and broke its code. Most of those arrested were party members who had escaped apprehension in the MARCH 15TH INCIDENT a year earlier. Approximately half of the arrested suspects were tried and found guilty, as were such important party leaders as ICHIKAWA SHŌICHI, Nabeyama Sadachika (1901–79), and Mitamura Shirō (1906–64), who were arrested on 28–29 April. Consequently, the Japan Communist Party suffered a severe setback, from which it recovered only after World War II. See also COMMUNISTS, PUBLIC TRIAL OF.

aquariums

(suizokukan). Of the some 450 aquariums in the world in 1979, about 100 were located in Japan. Most of these are located near the seacoast; geographically they range from subtropical Okinawa in the south to Hokkaidō in the north, and their range of marine specimens is correspondingly broad.

Japan's first aquarium was built in 1882 on the grounds of the Ueno Zoological Gardens in Tōkyō. Its display tanks contained specimens of goldfish, carp, and various other freshwater fish, as well as the giant salamander (*Megalobatrachus japonicus*), a species unknown outside Japan. It also exhibited sea anemones and some other saltwater specimens. In 1890 a larger aquarium was built at Ueno Park in Tōkyō in connection with the Third NATIONAL INDUSTRIAL EXHIBITION. By the end of the 19th century, a total of seven public aquariums had been built at university-affiliated marine laboratories. These were all located at the seashore and equipped with fish tanks of the so-called open system, in which seawater was pumped through the aquarium once and then discarded. It was necessary to release the specimens and close the aquarium in the winter when water temperature fell. At the time only the municipal aquarium in the city of Sakai in Ōsaka Prefecture used the closed system, in which water is continuously recirculated; it housed specimens year-round, maintaining the water temperature with electric heaters. In 1954 a large commercial aquarium was opened to the public at Enoshima, Kanagawa Prefecture. With specimens from all corners of the world and up-to-date facilities that included pneumatic water pumping, it served as a model for a number of aquariums in Japan. HIROSAKI Yoshitsugu

Arabian Oil Co, Ltd

(Arabia Sekiyu). Japan's largest crude oil producer; granted an oil concession by Saudi Arabia in 1957 and Kuwait in 1958 in the offshore area of the Saudi Arabia–Kuwait Divided Zone. The company was established in 1958 by YAMASHITA TARŌ with the support of the Japanese government and business leaders in an effort to explore overseas oil resources. The company succeeded in discovering the Khafji Oil Field in 1960 and the Hout Oil Field in 1963. Since then these two oil fields have been the mainstays of the company, and the crude oil produced from them, namely Khafji crude and Hout crude, has been sold mainly to the Japanese market but also exported to Southeast Asia and Brazil. The company's refining plant at Ras al-Khafji (capacity: 30,000 barrels per day) produces naphtha, diesel oil, and fuel oil. The company has been serving as a bridge between

Japan and Saudi Arabia and Kuwait, strengthening cultural exchange and friendly relations between them and Japan and promoting local development. In the fiscal year ending in December 1981 annual sales totaled ¥546 billion (US $2.5 billion), of which crude oil accounted for 94 percent and oil products 6 percent. Paid up capital as of 1981 was ¥25 billion (US $114.2 million), 20 percent of which was held by the governments of Saudi Arabia and Kuwait (10 percent each) and the remainder by leading Japanese companies and numerous individuals. The head office is in Tōkyō.

Arahata Kanson (1887–1981)

Journalist and activist in the socialist and labor movements. Born Arahata Katsuzō, the son of a small caterer to *geisha* houses in Yokohama, Kanagawa Prefecture, he joined a foreign company upon graduation from primary school in 1901. In 1903 he was baptized a Christian and began an apprenticeship in the Yokosuka Naval Arsenal. His work there and reading of antiwar pamphlets by KŌTOKU SHŪSUI, SAKAI TOSHIHIKO, and other leading socialists converted him in 1904 to socialism, persuading him to leave the arsenal, enter the socialist SHAKAI SHUGI KENKYŪKAI group, and join the movement opposed to the Russo-Japanese War (1904–05). He also established a branch of the socialist association HEIMINSHA in Yokohama. After the war he wrote for the *Heimin shimbun, Hikari,* and numerous other socialist publications; his account of the ASHIO COPPER MINE INCIDENT is considered a classic of Japanese journalism. In June 1908 he and his wife, KANNO SUGA, were arrested for involvement in the RED FLAG INCIDENT OF 1908. After his release in 1910 he joined Sakai and ŌSUGI SAKAE in their literary service agency BAIBUNSHA and from 1912 put out the monthly *Kindai shisō* (Modern Thought). Under the influence of these friends he espoused anarchist syndicalism in articles written for the revived *Heimin shimbun* and other short-lived socialist publications.

Over the next few years his interest in the labor movement and recent trends in European socialism drew him closer to the more revolutionary politics now advocated by Sakai and YAMAKAWA HITOSHI. In 1918 he was arrested for writing articles that transgressed the PRESS LAW OF 1909. Upon release six months later he formed the Labor Unions Research Group and in 1920 initiated contact with the young workers' association YŪAIKAI. In January 1922 he joined Yamakawa in publishing the influential left-wing magazine *Zen'ei* (Vanguard). In July 1922 he helped to found the JAPAN COMMUNIST PARTY and was sent that November on secret Comintern missions to Beijing (Peking) and Moscow. In November 1923 he returned to Japan a dedicated communist free of his former syndicalist convictions. He found the party in complete disarray because of government suppression, and his efforts to revive it took him to Shanghai in January 1925 to confer with other Japanese and Comintern agents. In March 1926 he was jailed for his party membership. That December he was appointed chairman of the party's disciplinary committee. After gaining release from jail the following month, he found his views sharply criticized as "bourgeois" by FUKUMOTO KAZUO and left the party to join the socialist RŌNŌHA (Labor-Farmer faction) and help Yamakawa and Sakai to publish its magazine *Rōnō* from December 1927. But for a brief attempt in 1935 to persuade the Musantō (Proletarian Party) to adopt more left-wing policies, his political activities from 1927 to 1945 were generally devoted to socialist periodicals such as *Zenshin* (Advance) and *Senku* (Pioneer). In December 1937 he was jailed in the massive government crackdown on its critics (see POPULAR FRONT INCIDENT). Released in April 1939, he spent the war years under house arrest, writing and translating.

After World War II Arahata took an active part in the labor movement, serving on numerous labor committees and being elected the first chairman of the National Trade Union of Metal and Engineering Workers. He also helped to found the JAPAN SOCIALIST PARTY, joining its Central Committee in 1947 and winning election to the Diet on its slate in 1946 and 1947. In 1948 his opposition to the party's approval of postal, tobacco tax, and train fare increases led him to leave its ranks. After a vain attempt to create a new socialist party he was defeated in the 1949 election. In 1951 he failed to reorganize the old Rōnōha group and withdrew from active involvement in the labor and socialist movements.

Throughout his career Arahata wrote numerous essays, novels, and historical studies, but his autobiography, *Kanson jiden* (1947; revised 1975), is his most famous work. He also translated extensively, mostly works on the socialist and labor movements in Japan, Britain, and czarist Russia. In recognition of his literary achievements he received several awards, most notably the Mainichi Publication Award (Mainichi Shuppan Bunkashō) in 1960.

■ ——Collected works: *Arahata Kanson chosakushū,* 10 vols (Heibonsha, 1976–77).   Charles M. MERGENTIME

Arai

City in central Niigata Prefecture, central Honshū. Arai developed as a POST-STATION TOWN and market town. In 1935 a chemical plant producing vinyl chloride and acetic acid was set up, and since then the city has become the center of a thriving electrical appliance and precision instrument industry. Pop: 28,574.

Arai Hakuseki (1657–1725)

Confucian scholar, historian, poet, geographer, and statesman. Influential adviser to the Tokugawa shōguns during the second decade of the 18th century. Born to a *samurai* family of obscure origins in the service of a small domain in Kazusa Province (now part of Chiba Prefecture). In his late adolescence (1677) Hakuseki suffered the trauma of becoming a RŌNIN (masterless samurai) when his father, who held a position of some importance in the domain, was dismissed for involvement in a factional dispute. It was at this point that Hakuseki took up the serious study of Confucianism, possibly attracted by its ideal of a meritocracy of upright men; for the remainder of his life this ideal continued to reverberate through his relations with samurai society. Hakuseki reentered samurai service as a Confucian tutor, serving the family of HOTTA MASATOSHI from 1682 to 1691 and in 1694 becoming personal tutor to Tokugawa Tsunatoyo, who later ruled as TOKUGAWA IENOBU, the sixth Tokugawa shōgun. During Ienobu's rule from 1709 to 1712 and that of his young son Tokugawa Ietsugu (1709–16) from 1713 to 1716, Hakuseki served as a key adviser to the shōguns and their chamberlain MANABE AKIFUSA, achieving perhaps greater political influence than any other scholar in Japanese history. Although he received honorary titles and an income that eventually reached 1,000 *koku* (see KOKUDAKA), he remained behind the scenes, with no formal position in the shogunate itself, and was completely dependent for his influence on his personal relationship with the shōgun and Manabe. This situation both colored his political program and put limits on its achievement.

Hakuseki's political program envisioned the transformation of the shogunate, which had taken definitive shape during the rule of the third shōgun, TOKUGAWA IEMITSU, from a military government into a Confucian kingship guided by an upright adviser. In many ways this program was consonant with the trend toward concentration of power in the hands of the shōgun and his immediate associates that had begun during the rule of the fifth shōgun, TOKUGAWA TSUNAYOSHI. What set Hakuseki's program apart from this general trend was its ideological coloration, most apparent in his effort to revise the existing ranks, titles, and rituals symbolizing shogunal authority. For the shogunate as a whole this revision went unrealized; but on the occasion of the Korean embassy of 1711 Hakuseki did succeed in changing the shōgun's title in the diplomatic correspondence from "great ruler" (*taikun*) to "king" (*kokuō*) and in adopting the ritual and appurtenances appropriate to that title. (The significance of the change was that it placed the shōgun on an equal level with the king of Korea diplomatically; it was never used officially within Japan.) Hakuseki's ideological reforms did not survive his period of influence. They were criticized on the one hand as usurping prerogatives of the imperial court at Kyōto and on the other as undermining the martial foundations of the shogunate. Other efforts of Hakuseki to overhaul shogunate policy, however, had a more lasting effect. The most notable were reform of the currency, reorganization and limitation of the foreign trade at Nagasaki (see SHŌTOKU NAGASAKI SHINREI), and improvement of the judicial system.

As a scholar Hakuseki is known for the encyclopedic range of his interests. A significant number of his scholarly works are essentially ideological in aim, written to provide the intellectual underpinnings of his political program. Virtually all of his historical works belong to this category: HANKANPU (1702), a history of the *daimyō* houses; *Koshitsū* (1716), a study of the myths and early history of Japan; *Tokushi yoron* (1712–24), a history of Japan from the Heian period (794–1185) down to the start of the Edo period (1600–1868). He also wrote extensively on linguistics, military affairs, and geography. His best-known geographical work is *Seiyō kibun* (1715), an account of the West based on his interrogations of the Italian Jesuit Giovanni

Battista SIDOTTI. In his own time Hakuseki was noted as a poet in Chinese; today his most widely read work is probably his autobiography, *Oritaku shiba no ki* (ca 1716).

As a student of the scholar KINOSHITA JUN'AN, Hakuseki is nominally assigned to the Zhu Xi (Chu Hsi) school of Japanese Confucianism (SHUSHIGAKU), but his primary interest lay in the political and historical rather than the metaphysical or textual dimensions of Confucianism. He can more meaningfully be categorized as a nativist, as opposed to a sinophile, Confucian scholar. Hakuseki, while maintaining a commitment to Confucianism as a universal system, was primarily concerned with Japanese politics and history. He avoided use of the terms "central" (*chū;* Ch: *zhung* or *chung*) or "civilized" (*ka;* Ch: *hua*) in reference to China, argued in *Koshitsū* against the monogenetic origin of civilization, and attempted, on the occasion of the Korean embassy, to assert Japan's international qualifications as a Confucian state.

▇——*Arai Hakuseki zenshū* (Kokusho Kankō Kai, 1905–06). Arai Hakuseki, *Oritaku shiba no ki* (ca 1716), tr Joyce Ackroyd as *Told Round a Brushwood Fire* (1980). Kurita Mototsugu, *Arai Hakuseki no bunchi seiji* (1952). Matsumura Akira, Bitō Masahide, and Katō Shūichi, ed, *Arai Hakuseki,* in *Nihon shisō taikei,* vol 35 (Iwanami Shoten, 1975). Miyazaki Michio, *Arai Hakuseki no kenkyū* (1958; rev ed, 1969). Kate NAKAI

Arai Ōsui (1846–1922)

Christian community leader. Born to a *samurai* family of the Sendai domain (now Miyagi Prefecture), Arai studied at the domainal school. In 1866 he was sent by the domainal government to study at the SHŌHEIKŌ, the Tokugawa shogunate's academy for Confucian studies in Edo (now Tōkyō), but, dissatisfied with its curriculum, he studied instead with the Confucian scholar YASUI SOKKEN. Learning of the shogunal army's defeat in the Battle of TOBA–FUSHIMI (1868), the first battle of the BOSHIN CIVIL WAR, Arai returned to Sendai. With Tamamushi Sadayū (1823–69), a former teacher, he helped to form a coalition of northeastern domains (ŌUETSU REPPAN DŌMEI) loyal to the shogunate. When Sendai capitulated to the imperial armies, Arai joined the shogunal naval forces led by ENOMOTO TAKEAKI, which resisted for several months in Hakodate. While there, he studied Christianity with NIKOLAI, the Russian Orthodox prelate in Hokkaidō.

In 1871 Arai was invited by MORI ARINORI, the new minister to the United States, who had heard of his interest in Christianity, to accompany him to that country. Mori entrusted Arai to Thomas Lake HARRIS, an unorthodox Christian utopian and leader of the Brotherhood of the New Life in Brocton, New York, with whom Mori had previously studied. Arai was to remain for nearly 30 years in Harris's community, which moved to California in 1875. Proving himself a creative and penetrating thinker, he was Harris's most devoted disciple and became the spiritual mainstay of the brotherhood after Harris's retirement in 1892. His sudden decision to return to Japan in 1899 came as a serious blow to the community.

Arai's motive for returning home was a desire to propagate Harris's teachings among the Japanese. He refused to join any religious organization, preferring to await an opportunity to found his own community. He also refused gainful employment, lived in abject poverty, and never married. By 1903 Arai's teachings had attracted a number of university students and several leading intellectuals of the time. In that year one of his followers built for him a simple house in Tōkyō. This house, named the Kenwasha, was large enough to accommodate 20 students and to serve as a base for his evangelical activities. Although Arai's students were few, one of them, the reformer TANAKA SHŌZŌ, played a significant role in awakening the public conscience. In taking a courageous stand on behalf of the beleaguered villagers of Yanaka in the ASHIO COPPER MINE INCIDENT, Tanaka was supported in no small measure by the friendship and faith of his teacher. At about that time Arai began writing what he claimed to be God's message to mankind. He published a series of pamphlets entitled *Goroku* (Sayings), which he distributed to his friends and associates. His ministry consisted of reading passages from the *Goroku* at meetings and giving individual instruction to those who sought it. After Arai's death, his collected writings were published as *Ōsui kōroku* (5 vols, 1930–31) by Nagashima Tadashige, one of his disciples. HAYASHI Takeji

Arakawa

River in Saitama and Tōkyō prefectures, central Honshū, originating in the Kantō Mountains and flowing through the Kantō Plain into Tōkyō Bay. A multipurpose dam was constructed on the upper reaches creating Lake Chichibu. The lower reaches are known as the SUMIDAGAWA. To prevent floods, the Arakawa Canal was constructed in 1930 on the lower reaches, splitting the river's course into two. NAGATORO, the gorge on its upper reaches, is a popular scenic spot. Length: 177 km (110 mi); area of drainage basin: 3,130 sq km (1,208 sq mi).

Arakawa Toyozō (1894–   )

Potter in the Shino–Oribe (see MINO WARE) tradition. Born in Tajimi, Gifu Prefecture, in the middle of the district where the Shino and Oribe kilns once stood. He studied painting in Kyōto but in 1922 decided to study ceramics under Miyanaga Tōzan (1868–1941). In 1930 he began working as an assistant to KITAŌJI ROSANJIN, making ceramics for a restaurant that Rosanjin was managing. That same year Arakawa found the ruins of the Mutabora kiln, the greatest of the Shino-ware kilns, near Ōkaya in Gifu Prefecture (formerly Mino Province). Until this discovery it had been assumed that Shino, Oribe, Setoguro, and Kiseto wares had been made in Seto, Aichi Prefecture, rather than in Mino. In fact, production in Mino began in the late 16th century, when potters from Seto moved there to escape the devastation of civil war and ended in the early 17th century, when the potters inexplicably returned to Seto. Other Shino, Seto, and Oribe kiln sites were subsequently discovered by other ceramic specialists as well as by Arakawa, inspiring him to undertake the arduous task of reinventing the original Shino, Seto, and Oribe techniques. Arakawa built a Shino-type kiln directly on the remains of the old Mutabora kiln and began producing teabowls, tea-ceremony freshwater jars, and other Shino-ware pieces with the characteristic thick, rich, translucent white glaze and lively, underglaze iron-oxide painted designs. So successful were his efforts that the Japanese government designated him one of the LIVING NATIONAL TREASURES in 1955. Robert MOES

Arakawa Ward

(Arakawa Ku). One of the 23 wards of Tōkyō. Many retail shops and small- and medium-sized enterprises are located here. It has metal machinery, furniture, leather, and confectionery industries. Pop: 198,104.

Arakida Moritake (1473–1549)

RENGA AND HAIKAI poet of the late part of the Muromachi period (1333–1568); considered, along with YAMAZAKI SŌKAN, to be the father of *haikai*. Members of his family had for many generations served as priests at the Ise Shrine, and he himself became chief priest there at age 69. He studied with the *renga* poets SŌGI, SŌCHŌ, and INAWASHIRO KENSAI. Though Moritake's *renga* were included in many collections, he was known chiefly for his *haikai*, which were written before conventions of *haikai* composition became fixed. His hundred-link sequence *Dokugin hyakuin* (1530) and the thousand-link sequence *Tobiume senku* (1540, also called *Moritake senku*) contributed to the establishment of *haikai* as a major genre equal to *renga*. The radical Danrin poets (see DANRIN SCHOOL) later hailed him and Sōkan as their predecessors.

Arakida Reijo (1732–1806)

(also known as Arakida Rei). Writer of the 18th century particularly known for her poetry and historical fiction. Both her father and her childless uncle, by whom she was later adopted, were Shintō priests of the ISE SHRINE. The Arakida family had for generations been known for its literary accomplishments, and early on she was encouraged in her pursuit of learning. As a young woman she took up *renga* (see RENGA AND HAIKAI) poetry, remaining active in *renga* circles to the end of her life. She also achieved fame for her mastery of WAKA, HAIKU, and verse written in Chinese. She is chiefly remembered, however, for her historical novels. In 1768 she produced a collated text of the UTSUBO MONOGATARI, a Heian-period (794–1185) romance, and in 1771 she wrote her two best-known historical novels, *Ike no mokuzu* and *Tsuki no yukue*. The first of these traces 200 years of history, beginning with the reign of Emperor Go-Daigo (r 1318–39), and the second takes place during the struggle between the Taira and the Minamoto families in the late 11th century. Although both set in an age of war, these novels focus on the lives of court aristocrats rather than on the exploits of warriors or statesmen. Arakida's style reflects a rather self-conscious imitation of the writings of the great Heian-period women writers, MURASAKI SHIKIBU and SEI SHŌNAGON. She also produced collections of short stories, travel diaries, and historical works of a scholarly nature. It is generally agreed that her novels are more remarkable for their erudition and echoes of the cadences and nuances of Heian prose than for their actual literary merits.

Araki Sadao (1877–1966)

Ultranationalist general and politician. Native of Tōkyō; graduate of the Army Academy. After fighting in the Russo-Japanese War of 1904–05, he graduated from the Army War College in 1907. From 1914 he held posts in the General Staff Office. He was a military attaché in Russia during World War I and took part in the SIBERIAN INTERVENTION of 1918. From 1928 to 1929 he served as principal of the Army War College and through his ringing calls for a revival of the Japanese spirit and his opposition to Russian communism won fervent support among the young officers. After Araki was appointed chief of the Army Educational Administration in August 1931, these and other young officers joined with rightist ideologues to attempt a coup d'etat (see OCTOBER INCIDENT). Intended in part to make Araki prime minister, the plot was discovered and suppressed. To soothe the insurgent officers, Araki was named army minister in the INUKAI TSUYOSHI and SAITŌ MAKOTO cabinets. He aroused great resentment in the General Staff Office by favoring ideological rather than technological reforms in the army and by replacing all of its major department heads with members of the ultranationalist Imperial Way faction (KŌDŌHA), of which he was a leader. Although promoted to full general in 1933, Araki lacked sufficient political power to implement his proposals for expansion of the army and military confrontation with the Soviet Union. Frustrated by his inaction, in 1936 junior Kōdōha officers staged an armed rebellion in central Tōkyō (see FEBRUARY 26TH INCIDENT); because Araki had given them his tacit support, he was forced to retire from active duty. In 1938, as minister of education in the first KONOE FUMIMARO cabinet, he promoted military instruction at all educational levels. Tried as a class-A war criminal after World War II, Araki was sentenced to life imprisonment. He was paroled in 1954 because of ill health and later pardoned.

Araki Sōtarō (?–1636)

Merchant and international trader of Nagasaki. Born into a *samurai* family in Higo Province (now Kumamoto Prefecture), he moved to Nagasaki in about 1588 and became a trader. In the late 16th century he was licensed to engage in the VERMILION SEAL SHIP TRADE overseas, and early in the 17th century Araki led several commercial expeditions to Southeast Asia, in particular to Annam (now central Vietnam) and Siam (now Thailand). In Annam he won the trust and friendship of a branch of the royal Nguyen family and married a princess whom he brought back to Japan in 1619. His ships, popularly known as *arakibune*, were large wooden vessels characterized by high cabins at bow and stern and two main masts with sails of woven reeds and of canvas. For protection from pirates they flew flags bearing the initials of the Dutch East India Company.

Ara Masahito (1913–1979)

Literary critic. Born in Fukushima Prefecture. Graduate of Tōkyō University, where he majored in English literature. After World War II, Ara became a widely influential critic as a founder and member of *Kindai bungaku*, a progressive literary magazine he launched with HIRANO KEN, ODAGIRI HIDEO, and others in 1946. A humanist, he was influenced in his youth by the Marxist movement of the 1930s. Later, in his criticism of prewar and wartime literature, he raised the question of what the intellectual's role in society should be. The first critic in Japan to apply Freudian theory to literature, he was noted for a series of ground-breaking studies on the outstanding early 20th century novelist, NATSUME SŌSEKI. He also published introductory books on James Joyce and T. S. Eliot and translations of works by Nathaniel Hawthorne and Emily Brontë. His principal works include *Daini no seishun* (1946), a collection of critical essays, and *Sōseki kenkyū nempyō* (1974), an annotated chronology of Sōseki's life, which won the Mainichi Book Award.

Arao

City in northwestern Kumamoto Prefecture, contiguous with the city of Ōmuta in Fukuoka Prefecture. Arao developed as a coal-mining town with the large-scale exploitation of the MIIKE COAL MINES early in the Meiji period (1868–1912). Since the closure of the mines after World War II, most of its residents commute to work in Ōmuta. Principal products are chemicals, pears, oranges, and *nori* (a kind of seaweed). Pop: 61,487.

Araragi

A leading TANKA poetry magazine launched in 1908 by ITŌ SACHIO and followers of the poet MASAOKA SHIKI. It succeeded an earlier magazine, *Ashibi,* which ceased publication that same year, as the official organ of the Negishi Tanka Society. Itō wanted the magazine to reflect his traditionalist view that the best source for poetic inspiration was the MAN'YŌSHŪ, the great 8th-century anthology of Japanese verse. Younger poets like SHIMAKI AKAHIKO and SAITŌ MOKICHI soon pressed for changes as the *tanka* took new directions, and convinced Itō to include critical essays, pieces on Western art theories, translations, and works by opposing schools. Shimaki took over after Itō's death and went even further in shedding the magazine's conventional image. New poets such as ORIKUCHI SHINOBU and Oka Fumoto (1877–1951), as well as the women poets Imai Kuniko (1890–1948) and Sugiura Suiko (1885–1960), were introduced. By 1915 the magazine was one of the most influential organs in *tanka* circles. Saitō succeeded as editor and was followed by TSUCHIYA BUMMEI. *Araragi,* still an influential poetry magazine, has continued over the years to emphasize the Man'yō style and realistic description.

Arashi Kanjūrō (1903–1980)

Actor. Born in Kyōto. Originally a KABUKI actor, Arashi began acting in silent films in 1927 and went on to a long-term career as a period-film actor. Through his roles as swordsman and sleuth in two period-film movie series, respectively titled *Kurama Tengu* and *Umon torimonochō,* Arashi became a box-office star. By the end of World War II, he had appeared in some 100 films. His leading role as the emperor Meiji in the postwar motion picture *Meiji tennō to nichiro daisensō* (1957, The Emperor Meiji and the Great Russo-Japanese War) won him great popularity with moviegoers. In the early 1960s, Arashi began playing mainly supporting roles. He has appeared in numerous period-films and modern movies.

SHIRAI Yoshio

Arashiyama

Also known as Ranzan. Hill in the western section of the city of Kyōto. Favored early on as a recreational area by the Kyōto nobility, Arashiyama is known for its cherry blossoms and autumn foliage. Arashiyama Park includes the river Hozugawa, the bridge Togetsukyō, several temples, inns, and restaurants. Height 375 m (1,230 ft).

arbitration

(*chūsai*). Method of dispute resolution in which both parties agree to submit to a decision (arbitral award) made by an arbitrator of their own choice. The Code of Civil Procedure (Minji Soshō Hō) recognizes arbitration as a legitimate device for dispute resolution and gives the arbitral award the same *res judicata* effect as the judgment of a court. An arbitration agreement is valid only when made in regard to a legal matter which the parties may dispose of freely. The arbitrator himself determines the procedure to be followed unless the parties agree otherwise. The arbitrator is not generally bound by substantive law in making an award but must always hear both parties' sides, and the award must be reasonable and not contrary to public policy. If any of these requirements is violated, the award can be set aside by a court, but the court is not allowed to review the merits of the award.

In order to enforce an arbitral award by a civil execution proceeding, an execution judgment (*exequatur*) must be obtained from a court through a formal action in which the court can only review the procedural requirements of arbitration. The arbitrator may be a private person or body or a public agency. Under some statutes, certain public agencies are given the power to act as arbitrators for settling specific kinds of dispute such as building contract disputes, pollution disputes, or labor disputes. Arbitration is rarely used except for maritime business matters and international trade. In these two areas, the Japan Shipping Exchange and Japan International Commercial Arbitration Association are active as permanent arbitral tribunals with their own rules of procedure. See also DISPUTE RESOLUTION SYSTEMS OTHER THAN LITIGATION.   *Taniguchi Yasuhei*

archaeology

Japanese archaeologists are very active and well supported, and a great deal is known about the prehistory of the Japanese islands. In fact, Japan is one of the most intensively studied archaeological regions in the world. Compared to ongoing archaeological work in other countries, the rate of research in Japan is nothing short of astounding. Excavations are required prior to large public works and construction projects, and Japanese archaeologists investigate and report thousands of sites annually. Some 300,000 archaeological sites were located throughout the country by 1980, or approximately two for every square mile of land, and every year some 8,000 new sites are being opened.

These sites are intensively studied by a corps of approximately 2,000 professional archaeologists affiliated with national, prefectural, or municipal government agencies. Courses in archaeology are available at most universities, and degree programs and graduate training are available at more than ten universities. Two major journals are devoted to archaeology and there are also innumerable regional and specialized series. Indeed, the field has become so large that most Japanese archaeologists now specialize in some particular region or time period.

As a scholarly discipline, Japanese archaeology has several distinctive features. In part this is because it has always been a rather insular field pursued almost exclusively by researchers with only limited contacts with archaeology in other parts of the world. Japanese archaeologists have thus developed distinctive conceptual and procedural approaches for the study of the past. For instance, in most Japanese universities archaeology is considered a highly specialized branch of Japanese history. This affiliation has reinforced the insular nature of the field and has meant that Japanese archaeologists have brought to their work a historic or particularistic approach rather than the social scientific approach taken in some other countries. Traditional Japanese archaeology has focused on problems of cultural chronology and artifact typology, but problems of wider methodological and theoretical significance are increasingly being addressed in recent years.

Archaeological research in Japan has considerable governmental and popular support. By law, responsibility for the preservation of prehistoric sites and the supervision of archaeological research rests with the Agency for Cultural Affairs (Bunkachō), an organ of the Ministry of Education. Prehistoric sites and remains are considered to be a part of the national cultural heritage equal in importance to historic monuments. The agency is nominally charged with the identification and preservation of cultural properties (see CULTURAL PROPERTIES LAW), but in its allocation of research funds and control of retrieval and preservation standards it places a major emphasis on the active research of prehistoric sites. Most of this research is actually carried out by regional specialists employed by prefectural or municipal boards of education. The first chapter of any city or prefectural history is invariably devoted to the prehistoric period, and publication of both popular and scholarly reports on prehistoric research is supported by local governments. Local groups are thus directly involved in the prehistory of their own area, with student and amateur archaeological groups active in all parts of the country. Important prehistoric sites in an area are frequently incorporated into parks or museums and constitute a point of considerable local pride (see IDOJIRI ARCHAEOLOGICAL HALL).

The development of archaeology in Japan reflects the intellectual milieu in which the prehistoric materials were collected and offers insights into the distinctive conceptual and methodological features of the modern discipline.

Prehistoric Archaeology—— *Early period.* Prehistoric sites and remains are so abundant in Japan that they could not possibly go unnoticed. The earliest Japanese references to such sites are found in the *Hitachi fudoki*, a regional geography (see FUDOKI) compiled in AD 713, which describes one of the SHELL MOUNDS in what is now Ibaraki Prefecture. Such sites were not, however, at that time recognized as a source of information about the past. Japanese historians of the Nara period (710–794) had adopted the Chinese approach to history, and they recorded native Japanese legends and myths in the style of the Chinese chronicles and then used these written records to interpret the ancient past and its unusual relics. The major chronicles compiled during the Nara period, the KOJIKI (712) and the NIHON SHOKI (720), proved very useful in that respect; they provided a rough time scale and described supernatural events and beings that could be considered responsible for all odd, old objects found in Japan. Thus, until the beginning of the Edo period (1600–1868), literate Japanese understood the past strictly in terms of events described in the *Kojiki* and *Nihon shoki*.

During the Edo period, many Japanese came to realize that the artifacts found throughout Japan were the products of past human activity rather than of supernatural events, and rational explanations for such artifacts were in accord with the orthodox Neo-Confucian thought of the period. The great Confucian scholar ARAI HAKUSEKI (1657–1725), for example, believed that stone arrowheads had been left behind by non-Japanese human groups mentioned in the early chronicles. Herbalists and other students of nature also realized that STONE TOOLS were man-made; Matsuoka Gentatsu (1669–1746) encountered stone points while searching for medicinal plants. He thought they were AINU arrowheads carried south by large migratory birds wounded by the northern hunters. The realization that they were man-made did not, however, render the artifacts especially interesting or worthy of careful study in the view of most scholars in this period.

Some Edo-period Japanese, however, did find ancient artifacts intriguing, although very few understood that they were a record of the past. Early 19th-century rock collectors, most notably KIUCHI SEKITEI (1724–1808), assembled, categorized, and described large collections of stone tools; their interest rarely went any further. One scholar who did understand the potential of ancient artifacts for the study of the past was Tō Teikan (1732–97). His study of protohistoric HANIWA funerary sculptures, together with a consideration of early historical records, led him to question the events and chronology recorded in the *Kojiki* and *Nihon shoki*.

The potential impact of such work and the development of a true archaeological investigation of the past was blocked by at least three factors. First, very few scholars, especially those of the National Learning school (KOKUGAKU), were willing to question the historical and religious sanctions which supported the imperial line. Second, the traditional Japanese conception of nature, with its lack of a clear division between the human and natural spheres, made it difficult to focus on man-made objects as a field worthy of study unto itself. Finally, the premodern Japanese, with their Chinese model of historiography, were unable to conceive of a period without written records or to realize that objects themselves could form a record of past events. Thus, during the premodern period, interest in strange old artifacts and the ancient past developed out of a number of intellectual trends; however, none of these sources gave rise to a discrete scholarly discipline.

Modern period. An American biologist, Edward S. MORSE (1838–1925), brought a new era to Japanese archaeology when he came to Japan to study mollusks in 1877. Shortly after his arrival, he recognized that a deposit of seashells near Ōmori railroad station in Tōkyō was a prehistoric shell midden similar to ones he had excavated in New England. After accepting a teaching post at Tōkyō University, Morse led an excavation of the ŌMORI SHELL MOUNDS and visited many other middens with his students. His report on the Ōmori remains appeared as volume 1 of the Tōkyō University Science Department memoirs in 1879, and shortly thereafter he returned to the United States. Several of his students and others, however, had become very interested in his work. They had grasped the idea of a prehistoric past and the technique of excavation as a source of both artifacts and information about the past.

With the recognition of an archaeological record of Japan's history, the last decades of the Meiji period (1868–1912) saw a flurry of archaeological activity. An anthropological museum and a department of archaeology were opened at Tōkyō University, several organizations were formed to conduct archaeological research, and a number of journals were founded to report on the series of excavations that followed the work at Ōmori. These early excavations lacked modern controls so that only the grossest cultural variations were apparent at that time. If the research of this period can be said to have a central issue, it was the ethnic identity of the creators of the ancient artifacts. TSUBOI SHŌGORŌ (1863–1913) represented one school that linked prehistoric remains with a semi-mythical non-Ainu group called the Koropokkuru (or Koropokguru). By the end of the Meiji period, however, most scholars had come to believe that the Ainu were responsible for Stone Age remains.

Starting around 1915, a number of Japanese archaeologists came to realize the importance of careful excavation in prehistoric research. Carefully controlled excavation and the resulting recognition of prehistoric cultural diversity were characteristic of the Taishō period (1912–26). Of course, once different cultural assemblages had been perceived, archaeologists were faced with the problem of explaining them, and this became the focus of the research of that period. TORII RYŪZŌ (1870–1953) led a school that saw little time depth in the remains and believed instead that different assemblages were made by contemporaneous but geographically separate prehistoric groups. Gradually, though, it became clear through the careful stratigraphic excavations of archaeologists like Matsumoto Hikoshichirō (1887–1975) that different kinds of pottery dated from different periods. In 1937 YAMANOUCHI SUGAO (1902–70) laid out a general chronological framework for the study of the Jōmon period, which he believed to have begun around 3000 BC, although modern radiocarbon dates have been obtained for JŌMON POTTERY from before 10,000 BC. The old "Ainu theory" was also put to rest during this period by physical anthropological research and the general recognition that it was too simple to explain the rich prehistoric diversity by then recognized in Japan.

Once Yamanouchi's framework was found to be useful, Japanese archaeologists refined and expanded it and then set about applying it to previously unexplored areas of the country. This work led to the recognition of the earliest Jōmon period, but after paleolithic stone artifacts were identified at the IWAJUKU SITE in 1949, an entirely new set of chronological problems was presented to Japanese archaeologists. Chronological studies culminated in the publication of the six-volume summary of Japanese prehistory Nihon no kōkogaku in 1965.

In recent years, Japanese archaeologists have organized to meet the challenge of extensive site surveys and large excavations in areas threatened by industrial construction, urban sprawl, and new transportation routes. Although subject to tight schedules and bureaucratic bottlenecks, the large excavations required by these projects have revealed cultural details which are beginning to flesh out the chronological skeleton established earlier. At the same time, some Japanese archaeologists are moving beyond chronological studies and have begun specific investigations of prehistoric lifeways and society; the questioning of traditional methods and analytical concepts has been resulting in more objective, problem-oriented research. See also HISTORY OF JAPAN: prehistory.

—— Saitō Tadashi, Nihon kōkogaku shi (1974).   Peter BLEED

Protohistoric Archaeology

Protohistory refers to the times immediately preceding recorded history; the protohistoric period in Japan is considered here to roughly encompass the Yayoi period (ca 300 BC–ca AD 300) and the earlier part of the Kofun period (ca 300–710). Some written passages thought to refer to Japan are present in ancient Chinese writings. For example, the word wo (see WA) in the section entitled "Hainei beijing" (Hai-nei pei-ching) in the Chinese geographical book Shanhai jing (Shan-hai ching; thought to have been compiled during the Qin [Ch'in] and Han dynasties) and in a work entitled Lunheng (Lun-heng) written by Wang Chong (Wang Ch'ung) in the 1st century, refers to the Japanese archipelago or part of it; and the word woren (wo-jen) in the geographical section of the Han shu, completed in the latter half of the 1st century, refers to the inhabitants of the Japanese archipelago. Later Chinese historical books also used the terms woren and woguo (wo-kuo) to describe the Japanese islands and their inhabitants. However, these records are fragmentary or based on hearsay, and it is impossible to reconstruct the history of this period solely through historical materials. It is thus essential to make full use of such archaeological materials as site remains and artifacts. See also HISTORY OF JAPAN: protohistory.

Early period. The oldest record we have concerning protohistoric period artifacts is the late-11th-century history Fusō ryakki by the priest Kōen, which mentions the discovery of a bronze bell (DŌTAKU) in AD 668. This report reveals that the ceremonial use of dōtaku had already been forgotten by the 7th century but that it was nevertheless correctly identified as a taku (hand bell). Records also remain of several dōtaku discoveries after 668. However, the various speculations about them, such as the theory appearing in the Nihon sandai jitsuroku in 901 (see RIKKOKUSHI), that they were the treasure bells of Asoka, a 3rd-century BC king of India, show that scientific study of the bells did not occur until much later.

In fact, the systematic collection and study of ancient artifacts did not begin until late in the Edo period (1600–1868), when active re-

search efforts developed out of antiquarian interests. For example, Kamei Nammei (1743–1814), a scholar of the Fukuoka domain (now part of Fukuoka Prefecture) compared a gold seal (see KAN NO WA NO NA NO KOKUŌ NO IN) discovered in 1784 in modern Fukuoka Prefecture with the seal impressions collected in a Ming-dynasty (1368–1644) work, the Jigu yinpu (Chi-ku yin-p'u), and concluded that it was the seal given to a regional Japanese king by the Chinese emperor Guangwu (Kuang-wu) as recorded in the 4th- to 5th-century Chinese chronicle, Hou Han shu. Kamei's treatise on the subject, Kin'inben, illustrated the historical importance of this gold seal.

Another scholar, Aoyagi Tanenobu (1766–1835), studied the burial jars and funeral goods (see PREHISTORIC BURIALS) discovered in Mikumo, Chikuzen Province (now Fukuoka Prefecture) in 1835; his detailed diagrams and records are notable as some of the earliest Japanese archaeological reports. With the discovery of molds for casting bronze spearheads, Aoyagi also advanced the idea that weapon-like bronze artifacts—previously thought to have been imported—were actually locally made ceremonial goods (see BRONZE WEAPONS).

It was also in the Edo period that the first systematic investigation of the tomb mounds (KOFUN) took place. According to legend, several of these were connected with imperial personages of the historical period, and accounts of their pillage can be seen in records as early as the 13th-century Aoki no sanryō ki. However, the first formal excavations of tomb mounds were carried out by TOKUGAWA MITSUKUNI (1628–1700), the daimyō of the Mito domain (now part of Ibaraki Prefecture), in 1692. In order to investigate the historical background of a stone inscription concerning the chieftain ruler (KUNI NO MIYATSUKO) of Nasu (now part of Tochigi Prefecture), Mitsukuni excavated the Kami Samuraizuka and Shimo Samuraizuka tombs in Nasu, first measuring the mound surfaces and drawing diagrams of their shapes. The fact that Mitsukuni reburied the excavated artifacts and restored the tomb mounds after making his records and diagrams deserves special note as a landmark in the advance of scholarship.

A record containing the names, sizes, and locations of some 200 tomb mounds in Fukusato (now Okayama Prefecture) was also compiled in the early Edo period, but such scholarly excavations and distribution surveys were not carried out on a regular basis. In other cases, studies of tomb mounds were stimulated by the increasing destruction of tombs through pillage or land reclamation. Records left by han (daimyō domain) scholars on the occasion of tomb destruction include Kuwayama kofun shikō, written by Saitō Sadanori (1774–1830) in 1822 about the Kuwayama tomb in what is now Yamaguchi Prefecture, and Chikugo shōshi gundan, written in 1856 by Yano Kazusada (1794–1879), who also described the tombs and murals he found during a survey of historical sites in the Kurume domain (now part of Fukuoka Prefecture). Such works are still of great value for scholars today.

Also worthy of note are the work of GAMŌ KUMPEI (1768–1813) and his associates, who surveyed tombs in the Kyōto-Ōsaka-Nara region and produced a treatise on the structural evolution of ancient tombs based on observations of mound shapes, and the work of Philipp Franz von SIEBOLD (1796–1866). Siebold was responsible for introducing Japanese archaeology to the world in his great work of 1832–54, Nippon, based on materials he had received from the medical botanist ITŌ KEISUKE (1803–1901). Thus the foundations for the acceptance and development of modern archaeological methods in the late 19th century were laid during this period.

Late 19th century: postrestoration innovations. Great changes took place in Japanese archaeology after the Meiji Restoration in 1868 and the opening of Japan to the West. Foreign scholars and specialists in many fields came to Japan, among them Edward S. Morse, who conducted the first shell mound excavation in Japan (see the section on prehistoric archaeology above). Using the techniques newly learned from Morse, archaeologists then excavated the MUKŌGAOKA SHELL MOUND at the edge of the Tōkyō University campus in 1884.

The discovery there of an unusual jar was a valuable clue for the defining of the Yayoi period, to which belonged the bronze bells and weapons known from earlier discoveries. Makita Sōjirō was the first to use the term YAYOI POTTERY (in one of his articles), accepting the idea formed by his fellow archaeologists that the jar should be considered distinct from pottery of the Jōmon period (ca 10,000 BC–ca 300 BC). The discovery at other sites of the same kind of jar and of a great quantity of Yayoi pottery together with stone tools at the Atsuta Takakura shell mound in Aichi Prefecture in 1907 led to general agreement that the people who used such pottery belonged to the Stone Age level of prehistory. Torii Ryūzō held that the users of Jōmon pottery were the Ainu and that the users of Yayoi pottery migrated to Japan from the Korean peninsula, finally becoming the ancestors of the modern Japanese.

As for scholarly organization, the Anthropological Association of Tōkyō was founded by Tsuboi Shōgorō of Tōkyō University in 1884, and the Archaeological Society (now the Archaeological Society of Nippon) was organized by MIYAKE YONEKICHI (1860–1929) of the Tōkyō Imperial Household Museum and others in 1896. The former concentrated on prehistoric archaeology, and the latter emphasized the archaeological investigation of the protohistoric and historical periods.

The first archaeology course in Japan was offered at Kyōto University in 1909. The founder of the course, HAMADA KŌSAKU (1881–1938), used the archaeological methods he had learned under Flinders Petrie (1854–1942) in England as the basis for the new program. Since that time, the Kyōto University research group, located as it is in the archaeologically rich Kinai region, has become the center of studies on Japanese protohistory and ancient history. Hamada's 1922 book Tsūron kōkogaku also had a great influence on archaeological methods. Hamada fostered such innovations as organizing interdisciplinary excavation teams and paying close attention to stratigraphy. The first excavation using these new approaches was carried out at the Kō site, Ōsaka Prefecture, in 1917; at that excavation, it was confirmed that Yayoi remains were found on the upper level and therefore postdated Jōmon remains. Hamada agreed with Torii that the users of Yayoi pottery were the ancestors of the modern Japanese; however, he differed from Torii in his recognition of the Jōmon people as also forming part of the Japanese ancestry (see JAPANESE PEOPLE, ORIGIN OF).

In this period William Gowland and Ernest SATOW did important studies on mounded tombs. Satow, an English diplomat, had an interest in ancient remains and conducted field investigations of Kantō region tombs. Through the detail of his illustrated explanations and the accuracy of his quotations from ancient sources, he earned the admiration of Japanese archaeologists and greatly stimulated them. Gowland, an Englishman connected with the Ōsaka Mint, made surveys of the tomb mounds of Ōsaka and Nara during his stay in Japan from 1872 to 1888. His records are assembled in "The Dolmens and Burial Mounds in Japan" (Archaeologia, vol 55, 1897); his accurate descriptions and precise illustrative methods, unknown in Japan at that time, greatly influenced Japanese archaeologists. Gowland's hypothesis that keyhole-shaped tombs are a combination of square and round mounds is still regarded as a novel explanation of their origins. Indeed, the scientific study of tomb mounds is considered to have begun with Gowland.

The scientific excavation of tomb mounds by Japanese scholars was begun by Tsuboi Shōgorō, who excavated the tombs in Ashikaga Park, Tochigi Prefecture, in 1886. He determined the construction dates of the tombs by comparing the excavated materials with records in the 8th-century chronicle Nihon shoki. Thus, tombs where HANIWA funerary sculptures were found were assigned to the period after Emperor Suinin, whose reign records mentioned haniwa production. In cases where beads and gold ear ornaments were found among the grave goods (see BEADS, ANCIENT; EAR ORNAMENTS, ANCIENT), the tombs were assigned to the period before Emperor ŌJIN (late 4th to early 5th century), when it is said that Chinese dress was adopted for the bureaucracy. Such were the dating methods of the Meiji period, in which artifacts and remains were interpreted by being uncritically related to legends in the early chronicles; although excavation techniques were up to date, the interpretive framework of modern protohistoric archaeology had yet to be established.

Early 20th century: typological and chronological studies. In the early 20th century much work was done in the elucidation of the material culture and the relative dating of artifacts of the Yayoi period. Nakayama Heijirō (1871–1956) demonstrated through careful distribution studies that bronze weapons thought to belong to the iron-using Kofun period were buried as grave goods in jar burials and that these jars were of the earlier Yayoi period. Thus, Nakayama interpreted the Yayoi period as a transitional period between the stone- and metal-using ages, that is, a period during which both were used. Then Tomioka Kenzō (1873–1918), a specialist in BRONZE MIRRORS studies at Kyōto University, examined the Handynasty mirrors unearthed with the jar burials at both the Mikumo site and the SUKU SITE in Fukuoka Prefecture. Judging that they

belonged to the end of the Former Han dynasty (206 BC–AD 8), he established the foundations for Yayoi period chronology. His datings were later substantiated by the discovery of Chinese coins minted in AD 14 that were found with Yayoi pottery.

Other work in this area was done by TAKAHASHI KENJI (1871–1929) and UMEHARA SUEJI (b 1893); they both assembled data on, and promoted the typological study of, bronze weapons and bells. Comparing them with similar items from China and the Korean peninsula, they postulated an influence from continental cultures. MORIMOTO ROKUJI (1903–36), who organized the Kōkogaku Kenkyūkai (later the Tōkyō Archaeology Society) in Tōkyō in 1927, was also active in the investigation of YAYOI CULTURE. He demonstrated that it was the product of a primitive system of agriculture based primarily on wet rice technology, and he investigated the shapes of Yayoi vessels from the functional perspective of their use in that agricultural society. From the particular form of distribution of bronze weapons and bells, Morimoto also postulated the existence of opposing spheres of Yayoi culture. Kobayashi Yukio (b 1911), a member of Morimoto's research team, collected data on Yayoi pottery and furthered its typological study by establishing the new concept of "styles" of Yayoi pottery that encompassed sets of contemporaneous pottery shapes.

From 1935 on, the rapid expansion of urban areas throughout Japan resulted in the discovery and investigation of many archaeological sites. The excavation of the KARAKO SITE in Nara Prefecture was especially significant; the many wooden articles found in the Karako Pond mud and identified as the first such items dating from the Yayoi period are valuable for their illustration of the conditions of Yayoi daily life. The Karako site report, written in the main by Kobayashi Yukio, was without doubt the best of all such reports.

Chronological refinement and the detailed study of cultural remains also characterized the kofun studies of this period. It was at this time that the archaeological practice of dating tombs according to the historical periods recorded in the 8th-century chronicle Nihon shoki came under severe criticism from the historian KITA SADAKICHI (1871–1939). He pointed out that Japanese historians had firmly established that the events in the chronicle were described as being older than they actually were and that it was wrong to date the tombs from such events; he also pointed out that the story in the Nihon shoki of haniwa being substitutes for funerary sacrificial victims had been exposed as mere legend and that tombs could not be dated from the presence or absence of haniwa. Kita also rejected the view, drawn from the Nihon shoki and the contemporaneous chronicle Kojiki, that tombs with corridor-style stone chambers represented an earlier type. He instead divided the Kofun period into two parts and, taking into consideration the continental influence on their rise in popularity, placed those tombs in the second half.

In 1912 a six-year excavation of the SAITOBARU TOMB CLUSTER in Miyazaki Prefecture was begun in accordance with the prefectural governor's desire to clarify the myths surrounding the founding of Japan as recorded in the ancient chronicles, but the participation of researchers from Tōkyō University, Kyōto University, and the Tōkyō Imperial Household Museum turned the excavation into a scientific project of unprecedented scale. Information concerning tomb mounds was dramatically increased through this excavation, one example being the discovery of the existence of clay-enclosed coffin facilities (nendokaku). Kobayashi Yukio separately demonstrated that the pit-style stone chambers, which were the main type of early kofun burials, were facilities, like the clay enclosures, for preserving wooden coffins inside. In consequence he rejected the idea of a temporal progression from clay enclosures to stone chambers. Kobayashi also made detailed studies of the position of funerary goods inside and outside the coffins. Later GOTŌ SHUICHI (1888–1960), who had collected data on all types of haniwa, proposed that the origin of these funerary sculptures lay in the desire to reenact graveside ceremonies.

Other scholars were also active in tomb-related dating. Hamada Kōsaku, a participant in the Saitobaru tomb excavations, changed his view that corridor-style stone chambers postdated the introduction of Buddhism after a thorough investigation of the ORNAMENTED TOMBS in Kumamoto Prefecture; he readjusted their dates to the 6th and 7th centuries. Takahashi Kenji studied the imitation stone artifacts found in tombs, taking advantage of his position at the Tōkyō Imperial Household Museum. (At that time tomb mounds were under the supervision of the Imperial Household Agency and their excavation was strictly prohibited. Any articles discovered accidentally had to be handed over to the authorities and were stored in the Tōkyō Imperial Household Museum.) He made clear that these artifacts belonged to tombs yielding *haniwa,* that is, those earlier than ones yielding horse trappings (see HORSE TRAPPINGS, ANCIENT), SUE WARE, and house-shaped stone coffins. Meanwhile, Umehara Sueji found evidence that some of the bronze mirrors deposited in the tombs had been handed down for many generations as heirlooms and therefore could not be used to determine the date of the tomb's construction. However, pointing out that most of the Han-dynasty mirrors occurred together with mirrors from the Wei (220–265) and Jin (Chin; 265–420) dynasties or with locally made mirrors, he hypothesized that the earliest limit for tomb construction matched the era of Wei-dynasty mirror importation.

Furthermore, since Jin- and Wei-dynasty mirrors were buried in large quantities in the tomb mounds of the Kinai (Kyōto-Ōsaka-Nara) region, Umehara reasoned that the 3rd-century polity of YAMATAI, whose queen HIMIKO received many mirrors from China, had to be located in the Kinai area around Kyōto. Hashimoto Masukichi (1880–1956) then countered this opinion, saying that if the mirrors were understood to have been brought from Kyūshū, the Kinai thesis did not hold. Thus the great debate on the location of Yamatai was enjoined.

In concert with typological and chronological studies of tomb goods, scholars studied changes in the shapes of the tombs themselves over time. Although Gotō and Hamada both used contour line maps of the imperial tombs completed around 1935 by the Imperial Household Agency, then responsible for tomb maintenance, in dividing keyhole-shaped tombs into three phases, they developed two different systems of categorization.

In this way the fundamentals of tomb-period research were established in the early 20th century through chronological research based on the datings of continentally derived artifacts and the typological study of various artifacts and related elements. Because of their concentration on comparative artifact studies and methodology, archaeologists made few achievements in relating their findings to the larger picture of culture and society in this period.

Immediate postwar period: academic excavations and research. Protohistoric archaeological activities from 1945 to 1960 centered on the many excavations carried out by universities and other research organizations, and the method of investigation remained much the same as before the war. Yayoi-period research during this period consisted of the excavation of several settlement sites for the purpose of reconstructing the daily life and society of the Yayoi people. The TORO SITE was the first excavation to yield a village composed of PIT HOUSES, with walled pits and paddy remains divided up by raised paths and irrigation ditches; it revealed living conditions in a Late Yayoi (ca 100–ca 300) agricultural settlement of eastern Japan. The excavation of the Itazuke site in Fukuoka Prefecture by Sugihara Sōsuke (b 1913), carried out from 1951 to 1956, revealed that the earliest Yayoi pottery and latest Jōmon pottery existed contemporaneously—both having been found in the same pit house. This raised serious questions concerning the transition from the Jōmon to the Yayoi period.

Meanwhile, research in northern Kyūshū on local tombs of the same style as those on the Korean peninsula resulted in the recognition of a vigorous importation of continental customs and goods during the Yayoi period. Further light was shed on Yayoi life by the work of Kokubu Naoichi (b 1908) and Ono Tadahiro (b 1920). Through excavation of the Hirota site in Kagoshima Prefecture, Kokubu and his associates showed that a special, shellfish-oriented culture thrived during the Yayoi period in the Satsunan Islands south of Kyūshū. Ono investigated the distribution of "highland settlements" *(kōchisei shūraku);* located mainly in the coastal areas of the Inland Sea at altitudes over 100 meters (328 ft), these were occupied during the Middle Yayoi period (ca 100 BC–ca AD 100), probably for defense.

Another important excavation in this period was the five-year excavation (from 1953) of an early Yayoi cemetery at Doigahama, Yamaguchi Prefecture, by Kanaseki Takeo (b 1897) and others. Analysis of the skeletal remains indicated that a large migration, probably from the Korean peninsula, had taken place in the Final Jōmon period (ca 1000 BC–ca 300 BC). The subsequent intermixing of these immigrants with the native Jōmon population was thought to have then produced the Yayoi peoples of western Japan. However, Suzuki Hisashi (b 1912) found the theory of changes resulting from a mixing of populations difficult to accept in the case of eastern Japan and proposed the theory that the Jōmon population east of Aichi Prefecture had been transformed into Yayoi people through the adoption of Yayoi culture rather than through the infusion of new peoples.

Notable artifact research was carried out during this time by Sahara Makoto (b 1932). His bronze bell typology traced changes in handle shape to establish a chronological progression from simple functional handles to highly ornamented ones. Sahara also noted changes in Yayoi-period stone arrowheads, pointing out for the first time that very large, powerful stone arrowheads were being made in great quantity in the central Kinai area during Middle Yayoi. Putting this together with the distribution of highland settlements, he postulated that these indicated the heightening of military activity there and the unification of western Japan by forces centered in the Kinai area. In contrast, the discovery of manufacturing sites of large polished stone axes, adzes, and reaping knives at the Imayama and Tateiwa sites in Fukuoka Prefecture led to the theory that the northern Kyūshū area was one step ahead of the Kinai region in economic organization. They seem to have practiced a division of labor, for the specialized products of northern Kyūshū were traded in large networks, whereas each village in the Kinai area obtained raw materials locally and made their own tools as necessity dictated.

In the area of *kofun* studies, the nationalistic restraints placed on historical research in the 1930s and 1940s were relaxed after the defeat in World War II, and textbooks based on the creation myths of the *Kojiki* and *Nihon shoki* were rewritten to incorporate the findings of modern archaeological studies. However, the archaeologists of the time could not agree on any one interpretation of ancient history. In 1949 Egami Namio (b 1906) presented his unique HORSE-RIDER THEORY concerning the possible invasion of Japan by a continental people who eventually established the YAMATO COURT. It was opposed by Kobayashi Yukio, who pointed out that the use of horse trappings did not occur in Japan until after the mid-Kofun period.

During this postwar period, tomb mound excavations were vigorously carried out, with painstaking research on mound shape, construction, and contents. The work of Kobayashi Yukio was particularly influential. He analyzed the funerary goods of the Ikisan Chōshizuka tomb in Fukuoka Prefecture and subsequently investigated the distribution of bronze mirrors cast from the same mold and buried in tombs throughout the country. In 1952 a number of Wei-dynasty mirrors were excavated from the Tsubai Ōtsukayama tomb in Kyōto Prefecture. Kobayashi included these in his distributional map and hypothesized that the person interred in the tomb either himself played a major role in distributing mirrors (symbols of authority) to regional chieftains or else was the direct descendant of such a person. He drew further conclusions about political power in the country based on his study of mirror distribution. In attempting to prove a progressive chain of hypotheses, Kobayashi's method was a departure from the methods of archaeological argument prevalent up to that time and greatly influenced the next generation of archaeologists.

Recent developments: salvage excavations and tomb preservation. A majority of the large-scale excavations since 1960 has been salvage excavation in response to the threat of site destruction in the wake of intense land development. At the prefectural and municipal levels, special agencies for the excavation of sites were established as needed within the board of education or independently. Organizations were formed for site preservation, and great advances were also made in site investigative techniques. For instance, a system was inaugurated whereby the outdoor work of excavation and the laboratory processing of the resulting artifacts advanced simultaneously.

With large-scale excavation, information concerning the Yayoi period increased rapidly. Archaeologists learned that the *hōkei shūkōbo* (literally, "square, ditched graves") type of prehistoric burial began in the Kinai area and then spread to surrounding areas. They also found previously unknown molds for casting bronze bells in many regions, revealing that bronze goods were manufactured at several centers throughout the country. In addition, paddy field remains were discovered at numerous places; those at the Itazuke site, in particular, raised many questions about the beginnings of Yayoi culture because of the presence of Yūsu-style pottery of the late Jōmon–early Yayoi period.

In order to determine the dynamic changes in society, postwar research on the Yayoi period has focused on comparisons between eastern and western Japan or between the Kinai and northern Kyūshū regions. Questions concerning Yamatai as recorded in the WEI ZHI *(Wei chih),* a Chinese historical work, have also continued to occupy archaeologists. Mizuno Seiichi (1905–71), for example, traced the itinerary of 3rd-century Chinese emissaries through Tsushima and Iki islands in the Tsushima Straits to Matsuura in Saga Prefecture as recorded in the *Wei zhi*. Efforts are also being made at environmental reconstruction with the cooperation of biologists and botanists, and there are many new methods yet to be implemented in the quantitative analysis of cultural remains.

In the area of tomb research, the large keyhole-shaped tombs have been the object of preservation efforts, resulting in fewer large tombs being investigated. Small tombs and tomb clusters of the latest Kofun period, however, have been widely excavated. One such excavation led to the epoch-making discovery of the wall murals at TAKAMATSUZUKA TOMB in Nara Prefecture in 1972. Important work on the beginnings of tomb mound building has been done by Kondō Yoshirō (b 1925), who demonstrated that burials using mounds and having pit-style stone chambers were already occurring in the region centering on Okayama Prefecture in the Late Yayoi period (ca 100–ca 300). He also traced the typological transition from the large Yayoi vessel stands to *haniwa* cylinders. A recent important event was the discovery during cleaning (and subsequent elucidation through x-rays) of an inlaid inscription on the blade of a sword from INARIYAMA TOMB in Saitama Prefecture. Major advances in artifact analysis and preservation have been made in cooperation with physical scientists.

Two new trends in Kofun-period archaeology have appeared since 1960. First, the large-scale excavations preceding construction projects have provided opportunities for clarifying the nature of previously unknown Kofun-period settlement and production sites. Typological studies of HAJI WARE and *sue* ware facilitated by the abundance of excavated materials are being widely carried out, and their integration into a scheme is almost complete. Based on these data, a clearer picture has emerged of the expansion of cultivated land in the Middle-Kofun period and the improvement and availability of iron tools that made it possible. Second, Japanese historians have begun to heed the results of tomb mound research and tried to relate Late-Kofun-period tomb clusters to the territorial spheres of ancient clans (UJI) centering on the Yamato court as known from historical sources. However, doubts have arisen concerning whether imperial tomb mounds should be identified as belonging to the so-called FIVE KINGS OF WA mentioned in the Chinese chronicles, the present basis for Middle-Kofun-period chronology. In order to solve this problem, research has recently tended toward minute typological investigation of ceramics and *haniwa* excavated from the tombs. In other words, recent Kofun-period research has tended toward the investigation of the historical evolution of the period through the use of classical methods. *KANASEKI Hiroshi*

Historical Archaeology

The historic period in Japan is generally accepted as beginning around the Asuka period (latter part of the 6th century to 710) when the Yamato court held sway over the whole country and established its capital in Asuka, the southern part of the Nara Basin. After Japan entered this period, a considerable number of records were written by Japanese, largely in the form of inscriptions, and the ancient chronicles the *Kojiki* and the *Nihon shoki* are fairly accurate for the history of Japan in and after the Asuka period. Thus, historical archaeology in Japan generally concerns the period from the late 7th century through the medieval period up to the present. As such, its sphere of activity overlaps with protohistoric archaeology but is concentrated mainly on the imperial court system, including court, capital, and temple remains.

Early period. Historical archaeology has extremely old roots in Japan, growing out of the study of aristocratic, military, and religious etiquette and precedents called YŪSOKU KOJITSU. This branch of study began in the Heian period (794–1185) and reached its height of popularity during the Edo period (1600–1868). Its most renowned practitioner was Tō Teikan (1732–97), who traveled extensively gathering documents and even wrote on *haniwa* and clothing in his *Shōkōhatsu*. Another important work was *Daidairi zu kōshō*, a detailed description of the Heian palace and capital at HEIANKYŌ (now the city of Kyōto) by Uramatsu Kozen (1736–1804). An earlier work, *Shichidaiji junrei shiki*, written by Ōe Chikamichi (d 1151), describes in detail the seven great temples, such as TŌDAIJI, in Nara. These three treatises have great value for scholars even today. Other studies from the early period concerning old coins, INSCRIPTIONS, tomb mounds, and the like, however, are of less value to modern archaeology.

Late 19th and early 20th century. From the Meiji Restoration (1868) through the first quarter of the 20th century, study concerning the material culture of the early historical periods was not based on the methodology of modern archaeology but on the techniques used by scholars of art history, with a strong orientation toward Buddhist artifacts. A central controversy of this time was that between architectural and textual historians over whether HŌRYŪJI in Nara had been rebuilt or not. Historians of Buddhist architecture led by Sekino Tadasu (1867–1935) contended that the present temple structure was the original, since its style was the same as the contemporaneous Northern Wei style of China. In opposition to this, the historian Kita Sadakichi claimed that it had been rebuilt, arguing that stylistic similarities need not indicate absolute age and referring, furthermore, to the statement in the 8th-century *Nihon shoki* that Hōryūji had burned.

After 1896, the concept of historical archaeology as a separate discipline gained acceptance as a new stress was placed on protohistoric and historic remains by the newly founded Archaeological Society (now the Archaeological Society of Nippon). However, it was not until Hamada Kōsaku introduced European archaeological methods in his *Tsūron kōkogaku* (1922) that scientific site excavation and typological methods began to be used in the field. In the meantime, less than scientific work was done in the chronological classification of sites and artifacts such as tombs, ROOF TILES, BUDDHA TILES, and other Buddhist utensils. At this time, Sekino Tadasu investigated the Heijō capital (HEIJŌKYŌ) and palace in what is now Nara Prefecture without excavating. Using topographical maps and taking into consideration the field configurations, land division methods, and land parcel names he arrived at a general idea of the internal layout of the palace and the grid system of the capital's streets. His findings, published in *Heijōkyō oyobi daidairi kō* (1907), were corroborated by evidence later found in the process of construction work for the preservation of the palace remains.

Formal establishment (1926–1945). During the period 1926–45, the basic theory and concepts of historical archaeology were established; and with the publication of several introductory manuals such as *Bukkyō kōkogaku kōza* (1936–37) and *Nihon rekishi kōkogaku* (1937) and illustrated volumes of artifacts like *Tempyō chihō* (1937), it was increasingly recognized as an independent field of study. Studies of artifact chronologies were widely carried out and excavations of palace and temple sites were conducted on a large scale. Extensive excavations at FUJIWARAKYŌ in ancient Asuka from 1934 to 1941 yielded information on the DAIGOKUDEN and other palace structures.

The Hōryūji controversy continued into this period, and excavations at the site made it clear that the temple had in fact been rebuilt. Limited excavations at temples such as the KUDARADERA REMAINS in Ōsaka Prefecture, the Minami Shiga Haiji and Yukinodera in Shiga Prefecture, and the Kita Shirakawa Haiji and Komadera in Kyōto Prefecture clarified ancient temple architecture. Numerous investigations were also conducted to discover temple sites on the basis of the surface remains of foundation stones, earthen foundation platforms, and roof tiles. These resulted in such reports as *Asuka jidai jiin shi no kenkyū* (1936) and *Kokubunji no kenkyū* (1938) but could offer no more than hypothetical speculations, since they lacked information about subsurface features.

One of the special characteristics of this period was that attention was finally paid to sites other than ancient palaces and temples. Excavations included the pit houses of the common people, Nara-period forts (see TAGAJŌ), and provincial administrative facilities. One notable discovery at this time was the complex of 51 buildings excavated at the Niihari District administrative center in modern Ibaraki Prefecture. Grouped into four clusters, some of the buildings are thought to be storehouses and possibly the district administrator's office.

Postwar period. After World War II, historical archaeology was liberated from the restrictions of nationalistic history and broadened to include all manner of sites and artifacts. Further growth of the field was due to several factors: the realization that interdisciplinary cooperation among architectural historians, specialists in early texts, and archaeologists was necessary; progress in excavation techniques that allowed for the examination of building remains constructed with posts embedded directly in the ground (until then only buildings with foundation stones under the posts had been examined); and the increase in the scale of excavations. *Sue* and *haji* pottery continued to be unearthed in all parts of the country; with progress in chronological studies, comparisons between early historic sites became possible.

Excavations at the Heijō palace site provided much new information about the imperial residence *(dairi)* and the government district. Although the Heijō palace was occupied for only 70 years, it was now learned that many buildings, such as the residences and the imperial audience hall (chōdōin), were moved often within the compound. The discovery of the Naniwa palace site (NANIWAKYŌ), embedded below the city pavements of Ōsaka, also deserves mention.

Further, in contrast to previous investigations which were limited to central temple structures such as the pagoda, main worship hall, and lecture hall, excavations of entire temple precincts, including the priests' residential quarters and the like, began at ASUKADERA, the KAWARADERA REMAINS, and Kōfukuji in Nara Prefecture and SHI-TENNŌJI in Ōsaka Prefecture. These excavations revealed such an array of information that previous theories concerning the course of changes in temple architecture had to be fundamentally revised. Large excavations were also conducted at provincial temples like the Mutsu Kokubunji in Miyagi Prefecture.

New trends in historical archaeology. The phase from 1961 to the present has been a challenging one for Japanese archaeology. Land development projects carried out during the high growth period of the 1960s exposed numerous sites to the danger of destruction. Many archaeologists were called upon to take part in investigations, as shown in the increased number of excavations from 408 in 1961 to 1,975 in 1970 and 7,083 in 1978. This rapid rise in the number of excavations has led to an enormous increase in archaeological information. Those at ASUKA KIYOMIHARA NO MIYA, NAGAOKAKYŌ, and HEIANKYŌ have further illuminated the development of palace architecture, while those at regional government sites, such as forts, administrative centers, and post stations (see EKISEI) have increased our knowledge of provincial government under the Nara-period RITSURYŌ SYSTEM. Excavations at provincial temples (KOKUBUNJI) and numerous smaller regional temples, together with those at commoner settlements and production sites, have yielded a great volume of artifacts and led to a better understanding of conditions in various parts of Japan in different periods.

The sudden increase in excavations and data has brought about a certain amount of confusion, but it has also led to three important by-products: the establishment of the study of wooden tablets (MOKKAN), the discovery of historical paddy field remains, and the birth of medieval archaeology. The discovery in 1961 of 40 wooden tablets with inscriptions at the Heijō palace site was a momentous one for scholars of early Japanese history, for they not only filled in gaps in official chronicles like the *Nihon shoki* and helped to verify their accuracy, but also shed light on the ancient taxation system and the evolution of the Japanese language. The tablets also have great value for historical archaeologists in that the inscriptions reflect the circumstances of deposit and, by extension, the nature of the sites where they are found. Again, a number of them have dates inscribed, making it possible to establish the absolute age of the artifacts with which they were unearthed. In 1978 the Japanese Society for the Study of Wooden Documents (Mokkan Gakkai) was established to facilitate interdisciplinary research by archaeologists and historians.

The discovery of historical paddy field remains is significant in that since the Yayoi period Japan has been an agricultural country primarily dependent on rice cultivation. Through the ages the holders of power always channeled their resources into rice production, and so the study of paddy remains is essential to understanding Japanese history. At first research focused on the reconstruction of the ancient and medieval JŌRI SYSTEM of land division and of the SHŌEN landholding system from surviving evidence of irrigation facilities and paddy boundary paths. Recently, however, progress in excavation technology has resulted in a number of paddy discoveries from the Yayoi to the medieval periods. Many occur together with a settlement and burial ground, making it possible to extrapolate both the overall village structure and rice production capacity.

The third byproduct has been the effort to understand medieval history through archaeology. Until recently, the mainstream of historical archaeology had been Buddhist archaeology, and even after the broadening of research to other kinds of sites and artifacts, it tended to be limited to the Nara and Heian periods. Whatever research that did take place concerning the medieval period was confined to Buddhist ritual implements and burials, and only art historians were interested in medieval ceramics. With the threatened destruction of medieval sites, archaeologists were forced to deal with these too.

The excavation of the ASAKURA FAMILY mansion in Ichijōdani, Fukui Prefecture, begun in 1967, marked the starting point of medieval archaeology. This site is an outstanding example of a daimyō base of the SENGOKU PERIOD (1467–1568). Excavations not only showed the nature of a warlord's residence—completely unknown until then—they also revealed the plan of a medieval castle town.

Artifacts such as the large quantities of Chinese porcelain revealed other aspects of warrior life. Investigations at the Kusado Sengen-chō site in the city of Fukuyama, Hiroshima Prefecture, carried out around the same time, elucidated conditions in a medieval commoner town. Excavations of medieval sites around the country have subsequently gained in popularity, and medieval history, once the exclusive domain of textual scholars, has now been opened for archaeological study. In particular, the great volume of Chinese porcelain being unearthed has necessitated revision of existing conceptions of medieval lifeways and of the cultural and economic intercourse between China and Japan at that time.

KAWAHARA Sumiyuki

archery → kyūdō

archery, mounted → yabusame

Architectural Standards Law

(Kenchiku Kijun Hō). Law enacted in 1950 to protect the lives, health, and property of citizens by establishing minimum standards for building sites, structures, facilities, and use. The main provisions of the law are as follows. (1) In order to construct certain types of building or to construct any building or make large-scale repairs or alterations within city planning areas (all cities, towns, and villages designated by the minister of construction), it is necessary to apply to the city, ward, town, or village for a construction permit. Construction cannot commence until the approval of the construction director is obtained. (2) The law also defines the kinds of building that cannot be constructed in business use areas, industrial areas, or residential areas established by the URBAN PLANNING LAW. The law also limits the height, capacity, and density of buildings. (3) Buildings in fire prevention areas must have a specified type of fireproof construction. (4) Building sites in city planning areas are required to border on a street for two or more meters. (5) In order to promote increased use of buildings and to improve the environment, landowners and other property holders in neighborhoods in cities, towns, and villages may voluntarily conclude a building agreement with regard to the design, use, form, structure, position, and sites of buildings. (6) Administrative offices have the authority to issue corrective orders to remove or to discontinue the construction of buildings that pose a danger to public safety or violate the law. (7) The law sets penalties for those who disobey such orders. Furthermore, the administrative offices can delegate the enforcement of their orders.

It has been argued that full-scale revision of the law is necessary because of the time that has elapsed since its enactment and the emergence of such problems as substantive defects in the law and its ineffectiveness against widespread building violations.

NARITA Yoriaki

architecture, modern

With the Meiji Restoration of 1868, Japan opened its doors to the outside world and devoted its energies to absorbing Western science and technology. The Department of Civil Engineering of the Ministry of Finance, the Department of Architecture and the Department of Railroads of the Ministry of Industry, and the Industrial College (the forerunner of the Department of Engineering at Tōkyō University) were among the leaders. Foreigners were invited as advisers, and of these, Thomas James WATERS and François VERNY were responsible for introducing modern architectural techniques.

At first, traditional Japanese methods of wood construction were combined with Western methods. This was true of the schools built throughout the country after the establishment of a new educational system in 1872. The Kaichi Elementary School (1876) in the city of Matsumoto is an example of early Meiji school architecture.

In 1877 Josiah CONDER arrived in Japan to teach at the Industrial College; he trained many architects, including TATSUNO KINGO and Katayama Tōkuma (1854–1917). The Akasaka Detached Palace by Katayama and the main office of the Bank of Japan by Tatsuno are representative Western-style buildings designed by Japanese at this time.

As part of the general reaction against excessive Westernization in the 1880s, there was rising criticism of overreliance on Western-style architecture. Itō Chūta (1867–1954), an architect and art histo-

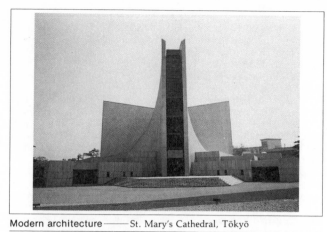

Modern architecture——St. Mary's Cathedral, Tōkyō

Designed by Tange Kenzō. The roof of this structure forms a cross when viewed from above. Completed 1964.

Modern architecture

Recipients of the Architectural Institute of Japan Award
(partial listing)

	Recipient	Work
1949	Taniguchi Yoshirō	Building No. 4 and Student Union Building, Keiō University (Tōkyō); Tōson Memorial Building (Magome, Nagano Prefecture)
1950	Horiguchi Sutemi	Miyuki no Ma (room in the Hasshōkan, an inn in Nagoya)
1951	Antonin Raymond	Reader's Digest Tōkyō Office
1954	Seike Kiyoshi	Various private homes
1955	Murano Tōgo	Hiroshima World Peace Memorial Church
1959	Satō Takeo	Asahikawa City Hall (Hokkaidō)
1960	Sakakura Junzō	Hashima City Hall (Gifu Prefecture)
1961	Maekawa Kunio	Tōkyō Metropolitan Festival Hall
1962	Imai Kenji	Memorial for the 26 Martyred Saints of Japan (Nagasaki)
	Maki Fumihiko	Toyota Memorial Auditorium, Nagoya University
1963	Kikutake Kiyonori	Izumo Shrine Office (Shimane Prefecture)
1964	Urabe Shizutarō	Kurashiki International Hotel (Kurashiki, Okayama Prefecture)
	Yokoyama Kimio	Daikyakuden, a building at the Buddhist temple Taisekiji (Fujinomiya, Shizuoka Prefecture)
	Murano Tōgo	Nissei Hibiya Building (Tōkyō)
1968	Shirai Seiichi	Shinwa Bank Main Office (Sasebo, Nagasaki Prefecture)
1971	Shinohara Kazuo	Various private homes
1974	Okada Shin'ichi	Supreme Court Building (Tōkyō)
1975	Isozaki Arata	Gumma Prefectural Art Museum (Maebashi, Gumma Prefecture)

SOURCE: Architectural Institute of Japan, ed, *Journal of Architecture and Building Science* 92. 117 (1977).

---

rian, was among the first to advocate Asian models for Japanese architecture; he was later responsible for the design of MEIJI SHRINE. After World War I, architects like Frank Lloyd WRIGHT, Antonin RAYMOND, and Bruno TAUT came to Japan, contributing to the reevaluation of traditional Japanese architecture. Through their work Japanese architecture influenced Western architecture, in much the way that *ukiyo-e* had influenced Western painting. The renewed interest in tradition also led to the development by YOSHIDA ISOYA of a new residential style that assimilated traditional SUKIYA-ZUKURI techniques.

At the same time, during the 1920s and 1930s the so-called international style and other European trends influenced Japanese architecture, as evidenced by the Wakasa residence in Tōkyō by HORIGUCHI SUTEMI. The modern architectural movement clashed, however, with nationalistic tendencies in the 1930s, and MAEKAWA KUNIO's design for the Imperial Household Museum was rejected in favor of a more traditionalist entry.

After World War II the activities of Japanese architects increasingly attracted attention overseas. The reconciliation of modern and

traditional architectural forms was one of the major issues during the postwar years. TANIGUCHI YOSHIRŌ designed the building erected as a monument to the writer Shimazaki Tōson, making innovative use of traditional architectural forms, and became in 1949 the first recipient of the Architectural Institute of Japan Award, the most prestigious prize of its kind in Japan. The works of such award-winning architects as MURANO TŌGO and KIKUTAKE KIYONORI reveal the scope and direction of architecture in Japan today. The work of TANGE KENZŌ and, more recently, of ISOZAKI ARATA, has helped to win worldwide recognition for Japanese architecture.

📖——Architectural Institute of Japan, *Nihon kenchiku gakkai kyūjūnen shi,* vol 92 of *Journal of Architecture and Building Science* (1971).
                                                                SEIKE Kiyosi

architecture, traditional domestic

This essay will be a general survey of traditional residential architecture in Japan viewed particularly as a response to the natural environment. The implications of wood as the building material, methods of construction and composition, and traditional concepts of space will be discussed. (For other types of traditional architecture, see BUDDHIST ARCHITECTURE; SHINTŌ ARCHITECTURE.)

Traditional Japan was a primarily agricultural society, centering on activities associated with rice planting. A feeling of cooperation, not an antagonistic relationship, developed between the Japanese and their natural surroundings. Instead of resistance or defense, accommodation and adaptation became the basic stance. Traditional Japanese architecture is characterized by the same attitude toward the natural environment, responding in particular to climatic and geographical conditions.

Japan's climate is distinguished by long, hot, humid summers and relatively short, cold, dry winters, and the Japanese house has evolved accordingly to make the summers more bearable. Since in the past the only relief from the oppressive heat and humidity was found in the cooling movement of air, the choice was toward light and open structures much like those found in Malaysia and other tropical areas. The traditional Japanese house was raised slightly off the ground and the interior opened up to allow for unrestricted movement of air around and below the living spaces. Associated with the heat and humidity of summer were sun and frequent rain. This necessitated a substantial roof structure with long, low overhangs to protect the interior.

With its open structure, the Japanese house is vulnerable to all kinds of intrusion, including dirt, dust, and insects. Noise and lack of privacy are another problem; screens and *shōji* (translucent paper-covered sliding panels) offer a measure of visual privacy to the inhabitants, but for both of these situations, the Japanese have developed appropriate patterns of behavior rather than practical solutions.

Materials and Construction——The choice of building materials has been determined by the climate, wood being preferred to stone. Stone is uncomfortable and unhealthy in hot, humid weather, restricting airflow and closing off the structure; it also requires a longer period of time in preparing materials and in building. In contrast, wood responds more sensitively to the climate, being much cooler and absorbing moisture in summer and not as cold to the touch in winter. Wood is also more suited to withstand earthquakes, an almost daily occurrence in Japan.

The choice of wood and an open structure allows for flexibility in living arrangements according to seasonal changes and the needs of the family. Inner partitions such as *shōji* and *fusuma* (opaque paper-covered sliding panels) can be removed to open up the interior, and except for the roof's supporting columns, a clear space can be exposed.

The actual building of a house was traditionally entrusted to a carpenter *(daiku)*. With specialized skills, the *daiku* was more than a carpenter; he was actually an architect, capable of designing and building an entire structure according to the wishes of the family. The construction of houses by a special occupational group soon led to a standardization of materials and design. There were also social strictures against extravagance in both design and the use of materials. The *daiku* prepared all the supporting columns and beams in his shop area, and in one day erected columns and roof structure with the help of the family or laborers. The position of *daiku* was thus very important, and certain secrets of his craft, such as intricate joinery methods, were closely guarded and passed down through his family. This accounts for the regional variation in building techniques. *Daiku* practiced exclusively in one area and seldom moved about except by order of some authority. For this reason, it is not uncommon to find a very different style of traditional architecture after crossing a mountain pass or another natural barrier.

Apart from the use of wood, the apparently little consideration given toward earthquake protection in the structure itself is striking. Diagonal bracing, for example, is hardly ever seen in walls or roof structure. Rigidity, however, is not the only way for protecting a structure against earthquakes. Wood is flexible and can take more shear and torque for its weight than most other materials. The joinery makes use of the strengths of wood. The walls, consisting essentially of bamboo lattices heavily plastered with clay, are not at all substantial by Western standards but are surprisingly resistant to earthquakes. One room of the traditional house is plastered heavily on four walls in this way, with only a minimal entrance in one. This is directly connected to some of the main supports and helps to strengthen the building. The diagonal was not unknown, for wood diagonal compression braces have been found beneath the plaster walls of a few very old structures, but for some reason it was not used generally. In older structures the joint between a foundation stone and the support post or column was not fixed, so that when the earth moved, the column sometimes simply slid off its foundation stone. After the earthquake, the house could be lifted up and the support placed on another stone with no real damage to the structure.

The wall in a Japanese house is unlike the common wood wall construction found in the United States, where the wall acts as a barrier against the environment and carries structural forces from the rest of the building. In concept the Western wall is not designed to allow for breaks in its system. If an aperture for a door or window is required, elaborate strengthening of surrounding members must be done to make up for the missing parts. It is a continuous system and, if interrupted without proper precautions, can cause failure. The Japanese wall, in contrast, simply fills the required space and allows for virtually any size or type of opening.

Spatial Concepts in Architecture —— A basic spatial concept in Japan is *ma* (written with a Chinese character that is also pronounced *ken* or *aida*). It has no exact English equivalent, variously meaning space, relationship, interval, period, luck, or pause, depending on the context. In architecture the term is applicable to the distance between two posts or the space between two or more walls, rocks in a garden, buildings, people, or anything with a possible relationship.

In constructing a house, the first step is to raise posts and beams until a skeletal structure stable enough to support a roof is completed. The roof is built and the structure is finished, that is, conceptually finished, for the roof now defines a space beneath and between it and the earth. The space has been further organized by the modular placement of the posts and columns. From this point on, design concerns itself with filling in the spaces or intervals between the posts and columns. Two things happen as this filling-in process occurs. First, a relationship is developed between the filled-in wall planes, and subdivisions—rooms—are created. Second, the wall itself alters the relationship of the posts by the kinds of materials used in its construction and its value as a barrier. In both cases, one is adjusting *ma*, or relationships that already exist—a process that lies at the heart of traditional Japanese design. Once the structure is given, design is concerned with the realignment and alteration of already existing relationships. Consequently, in Japanese design the wall has a different conceptual basis than that of Western design. Japanese walls are not defensive. In the West, by contrast, the wall is conceived as defensive, acting as a barrier between two opposing environments, such as winter cold and house warmth.

An important aspect of traditional design is the relationship of the house to its specific environment, particularly the garden; the two are continuous in the mind of a Japanese. The Japanese do not see exterior and interior as two separate entities; in other words, there is no definite point at which exterior ends and interior begins. The lack of barriers in Japanese designs has already been discussed. The Japanese veranda *(engawa)* is a concrete expression of this concept, serving as a transition space from inside to outside. Its function is further expressed by the materials used in its construction. Whereas the floors of the interior of the house are covered with *tatami* mats and the exterior is made of earth and rock, the *engawa* is made of unfinished wood planks, belonging neither to the soft and accommodating interior nor the harsh and more primitive materials on the outside.

The development of the individual spaces within the house was a gradual process of breaking down the larger open space that was available into smaller, more human-scaled spaces. This has already been mentioned with regard to *ma* and the "choosing" of space for a

particular function. In the past the Japanese house was even more open, with no interior screens and only a few fixed walls. The space was large, too large for the individual, and self-standing screens— very often no more than wooden racks draped with fabric—were introduced. Later, folding paper screens came to be used. These, and such furnishings as tables, arm rests, and lamps were placed to designate a space for a specific function—sleeping, eating, or dressing. Individual rooms were later defined by *shōji* and *fusuma*, "sliding doors" that could still be removed to form a single large space.

It would be a misconception to describe the rooms as multipurpose; although they are not as specific as Western rooms, each usually has a special function. In a traditional Japanese house, certain rooms are set aside for members of the family to sleep in, eat in, and so forth.

Unit of Measure —— The module, if it can be called one, since it varied depending on time or place, was the *ken* (written with the same Chinese character as *ma*), or interpost distance. The interpost distance varied from district to district but was generally between 6 and 6.5 feet (1.8 and 1.97 m). It varied since the measurement of *ken* was sometimes center to center of the posts and at other times the inside distance. The interpost distance was eventually standardized at 1.8 meters, however, if only because of the advantage of having a standard *tatami* size (generally 3 by 6 ft; 0.9 by 1.8 m) based on interpost measurement. The important aspect of *ken* is not that it was standardized to all buildings—it was not—but that it became the standard for all other measurements in the building—the columns, beams, ceiling, *shōji*, and so forth, resulting in a harmonious balance of proportion.

The standardization of *ken* also led to the standardization of such construction materials as lumber. Carpenters could focus on the creation of space itself without concern for structure or detailing. The *ken* itself was subordinate to the average human height. The traditional house was designed for a Japanese height of 5.5 feet (1.68 meters), although in aesthetic terms it was designed not for a standing person but for one sitting (seated height is a little more than 36 inches or about 1 meter for a tall Japanese). The garden and the artwork on display are meant to be viewed from a sitting or kneeling position, and the placement of doors, windows, and alcoves is adjusted accordingly.

📖 ——Heinrich Engel, *The Japanese House: A Tradition for Contemporary Architecture* (1964). Edward Sylvester Morse, *Japanese Homes and Their Surroundings* (1972). Seike Kiyoshi, *The Art of Japanese Joinery* (1977). Shin Kenchiku Sha, ed, *A Guide to Japanese Architecture* (rev ed, 1973). SEIKE Kiyosi

Archives and Mausolea Department, Imperial Household Agency

(Kunaichō Shoryōbu). Originally called the Kunaichō Zushoryō, it was established in 1884 as a successor to the ZUSHORYŌ, the imperial archives department that had been created in 701 but had ceased to function by the 11th century. In 1949 it was merged with the Shoryōryō (Bureau of Imperial Mausolea) and given its present name. Besides compiling imperial family records, operating a library, and maintaining the imperial tombs, the department administers the collections of the SHŌSŌIN in Nara. Located within the palace grounds in Tōkyō, it houses some 350,000 items of incomparable rarity, including holographic manuscripts of emperors from the Nara period (710–794) onward as well as Heian-period (794–1185) materials from the Higashiyama collection and the Fushimi collection of the Katsura Detached Palace in Kyōto.

Theodore F. WELCH

Arechi

(Waste Land). Influential post–World War II poetry magazine; originally founded before the war by a small group of Waseda University students led by AYUKAWA NOBUO and Morikawa Yoshinobu (1918–42), it became an important yearly review of modern poetry starting in 1951. The first series of *Arechi*, which took its name from T. S. Eliot's poem, "The Waste Land," appeared briefly between 1939–40. Revived after the war, the second series (1947–48) was published by a group of young poets who best represent the development of modern poetry in the first postwar decade. Collectively known as the *Arechi* poets (though not a coterie per se), the group's central figures were Ayukawa Nobuo and Tamura Ryūichi (b 1923). Adherents included Kitamura Tarō (b 1922), Kuroda Saburō (b 1919), Miyoshi Toyoichirō (b 1920), Nakagiri Masao (b 1919), and,

Ariake Bay

Ariake Bay at low tide.

later, YOSHIMOTO TAKAAKI. Viewing Japan as a "wasteland" in the immediate postwar years and drawing on their wartime experiences, they sought to reestablish the reliability of the language and to reconstruct modern poetry in the postwar era. The third series of *Arechi* took the form of an annual anthology of poetry and criticism, the *Arechi shishū*, published from 1951 to 1958; the group also collaborated on two books: *Shi to shiron* (2 vols, 1953) and *Arechi shisen* (1957).　　　　　　　　　　*Theodore W. GOOSSEN*

Ariake Bay

(Ariake Kai; literally "Ariake Sea"). Inlet of Shimabara Bay, off Nagasaki, Saga, Fukuoka, and Kumamoto prefectures, central western Kyūshū. Not to be confused with Ariake Wan (Ariake Bay), the former name of SHIBUSHI BAY on the southeastern coast of Kyūshū. Known for its large difference in tide levels of as much as 6 m (19.7 ft), this is a shallow sea with a maximum depth of only 20 m (65.6 ft) and mud flats extending 4–6 km (2–4 mi) offshore at low tide. Seaweed *(nori)* and shellfish are produced here, and the shoal areas are being reclaimed. The possibility of coal mining is also being investigated. Two major rivers, the Chikugogawa and Yabegawa, empty into the Ariake Bay. Area: approximately 1,500 sq km (579 sq mi).

Arida

City in northwestern Wakayama Prefecture, central Honshū, located at the mouth of the river Aridagawa. Arida has been famous for its mandarin oranges since the Edo period (1600–1868), and more recently, for its mosquito-repellent incense and herbicides. There is an oil refining industry in the Hatsushima district. The coastal region to the southwest of the city is noted for its beauty. Pop: 35,685.

Aridagawa

River in north central Wakayama Prefecture, central Honshū, flowing west from the Jingamine area of the Kii Mountains to the Kii Channel in the city of Arida. The lower Aridagawa flows through mandarin orange groves. The Futagawa Dam was completed in 1967 for flood control and hydroelectric power. Length: 67 km (42 mi).

Arima Harunobu (1567–1612)

Prominent CHRISTIAN DAIMYŌ of the Azuchi–Momoyama period (1568–1600) and the early part of the Edo period (1600–1868). Lord of the Takaku region of Hizen Province (now part of Nagasaki Prefecture). Harunobu's father, Yoshisada (1521–77), as early as 1563 gave Jesuit missionaries permission to proselytize in the Arima domain, hoping thereby to attract Portuguese traders to his harbor Kuchinotsu; he was baptized André in 1576, but the mission of Arima was persecuted after his death, until in 1580 Harunobu became a Christian, taking the name Protasio. Harunobu's direct inducement to baptism consisted of munitions procured by the Jesuits to help the Arima in the struggle against Ryūzōji Takanobu (1529–84), the powerful daimyō of Saga; in his subsequent career, however, he proved a staunch believer and supporter of Christianity,

the patron of the famed Jesuit *seminario* of Arima, and the lord of a territory that became solidly Christian. He was one of the sponsors of the "Tenshō Embassy" (see MISSION TO EUROPE OF 1582) of Japanese youths to Catholic Europe.

In 1584 Harunobu defeated Ryūzōji in alliance with the great SHIMAZU FAMILY of Kagoshima but fell under their influence; his position as a daimyō was, however, consolidated in 1587, when the national unifier TOYOTOMI HIDEYOSHI, at the conclusion of his victorious Kyūshū campaign against the Shimazu, confirmed the Arima possessions. Harunobu served Hideyoshi in his INVASIONS OF KOREA IN 1592 AND 1597, crossing over to the peninsula in 1592 with the force led by his fellow Christian daimyō KONISHI YUKINAGA. In the climactic struggle which led to the defeat of Konishi and his allies at the Battle of SEKIGAHARA in 1600, Harunobu initially took Yukinaga's side but switched his allegiance in time to permit Arima troops to participate in the reduction of Uto, Yukinaga's fortress in Higo (now Kumamoto Prefecture), in the cause of the future shōgun TOKUGAWA IEYASU. He was accordingly confirmed in his holdings after the Tokugawa victory.

Harunobu was active in the VERMILION SEAL SHIP TRADE in the South China Sea, with disastrous consequences for himself and the Christianity he espoused. In 1608 the crew of one of his ships was involved in an armed squabble in the Portuguese colony of Macao, and a number of Arima's men were killed. Harunobu retaliated by attempting to seize the Portuguese trading vessel that came from Macao to Nagasaki the following year; in the so-called MADRE DE DEUS INCIDENT that followed, the Portuguese ship was blown up. Expecting recognition from the Tokugawa shogunate for this action, Harunobu was enticed by Okamoto Daihachi, a Christian aide of the shogunate's powerful *rōjū* (senior councillor) Honda Masazumi (1565–1637), into the payment of large sums of money, for which Okamoto delivered Ieyasu's letters patent. These proved, however, to be forged. The scandal was exposed in 1612, Okamoto was executed after accusing Harunobu of plotting the murder of the shogunate's Nagasaki *bugyō* (commissioner) Hasegawa Fujihiro (1568–1617), and Arima was first exiled to Kai Province (now Yamanashi Prefecture) and then ordered to commit suicide. In the wake of this sordid affair, both of whose principals were Christians, the shogunate issued the first of its ANTI-CHRISTIAN EDICTS and began to persecute the religion in shogunal domains.

Harunobu's son Naozumi (Dom Miguel; 1586–1641) apostatized and was installed as daimyō in Arima. Unsuccessful in his efforts to force his subjects into abandoning Christianity, he was in 1614 transferred to another fief, Nobeoka in Hyūga Province (now Miyazaki Prefecture). In 1637–38 the old Arima territory became the stage of the SHIMABARA UPRISING.　　　　　　　　　　*George ELISON*

Arima Hot Spring

(Arima Onsen). Located on the northern slope of the mountain ROKKŌSAN, in the city of Kōbe, Hyōgo Prefecture, western Honshū. A common salt spring; maximum water temperature reaches 95°C (203°F). One of the few spas in the Kansai region, it has historically been favored by emperors and Buddhist clergy and is mentioned in many historical and literary works. More recently it has become popular with residents of the Kyōto–Ōsaka–Kōbe metropolitan area.

Arima Ineko (1932–　)

Film star who was popular with Japanese moviegoers from the late 1950s through the early 1960s for her performances in glamorous leading lady roles. Real name Nakanishi Seiko. Born in Ōsaka, she joined the Takarazuka Girls' Operetta Company (TAKARAZUKA KAGEKIDAN) after graduation from high school. She began making films in 1951. In one of her best pictures, *Mitasareta seikatsu* (1962, Full Life), directed by HANI SUSUMU, she played a new type of assertive, independent woman, a part that in many ways resembled her own real-life role as an actress in the Japan of her day. Her other important films include ICHIKAWA KON's *Aijin* (1953, Lovers) and OZU YASUJIRŌ's *Tōkyō boshoku* (1957, Tōkyō Twilight) and *Higambana* (1958, Equinox Flower).　　　　　　*ITASAKA Tsuyoshi*

Arima, Prince (640–658)

(Arima no Miko). Imperial prince of the latter part of the Yamato period (ca 300–710); son of Emperor KŌTOKU (r 645–654) and a potential successor to the throne. After his father's death, he was critical of his aunt Empress SAIMEI (r 655–661) for delegating all authority to her son Prince Naka no Ōe (later Emperor TENJI), and he feigned madness to escape the political intrigues of the late 650s. However, Soga no Akae (623–672), a confidant of Naka no Ōe, duped him into joining an ostensible plot against the government that was actually a trap set by Naka no Ōe to dispose of his rivals. Arima was charged with treason and put to death. Two valedictory poems composed by the young prince shortly before his execution are included in the celebrated 8th-century anthology MAN'YŌSHŪ.

Arima Shinshichi (1825–1862)

Samurai of the Satsuma domain (now Kagoshima Prefecture) who was active in the movement to overthrow the Tokugawa shogunate (1603–1867). In the 1850s, as advisor to the *daimyō* SHIMAZU NARIAKIRA, he spent several years in Edo (now Tōkyō), where he came into contact with other antiforeign, antishogunate radicals. In 1860 he helped to plot the assassination of the great elder *(tairō)* II NAOSUKE but was in Satsuma when it took place (see SAKURADAMONGAI INCIDENT). In 1862, when SHIMAZU HISAMITSU, father of the daimyō of Satsuma, was visiting Kyōto, Arima made plans to organize an antishogunate army there and assassinate high Tokugawa officials. Hisamitsu sent men to persuade Arima and his cohorts to abandon their plans, but they resisted, and Arima and six others were killed in the ensuing fight (see TERADAYA INCIDENT).

Arima Yoriyasu (1884–1957)

Politician. Born in Tōkyō; scion of the Arima family, formerly the *daimyō* family of the Kurume domain (now part of Fukuoka Prefecture). He studied agricultural science at Tōkyō University and taught there for several years. Interested in social reform, he formed the Nihon Nōmin Kumiai (Japan Farmers' Union) together with KAGAWA TOYOHIKO and others. He was elected to the House of Representatives in 1924 as a member of the RIKKEN SEIYŪKAI, and in 1929, after succeeding to the family title of count, he was named to the House of Peers. A confidant of KONOE FUMIMARO, he served as minister of agriculture and forestry in the first Konoe cabinet (1937) and assumed the directorship of the IMPERIAL RULE ASSISTANCE ASSOCIATION in 1940 but resigned after five months in the face of opposition from rightists. He was detained as a war criminal after World War II but was released without being prosecuted. The novelist Arima Yorichika (b 1918) is his third son.

Arisaka Hideyo (1908–1952)

Linguist and historical phonologist of Japanese. Born in the city of Kure, Hiroshima Prefecture; raised in Tōkyō. The son of an engineering professor, he graduated from Tōkyō University in 1931 majoring in linguistics. Primarily because of poor health, Arisaka held no regular academic position; he died at a relatively early age.

Arisaka's most noted contribution to Japanese-language studies was his observation of restrictions on the distribution of the Old Japanese vowels reconstructed by HASHIMOTO SHINKICHI. He suggested that these restrictions could be understood as vestiges of an earlier vowel harmony system. Arisaka was a pioneer also in applying the results of Chinese historical phonology to Japanese, and, conversely, of Japanese historical phonology to Chinese. Much of his work appeared in *Kokugo on'in shi no kenkyū* (1944; rev 1957; Studies in Japanese Historical Phonology).

Arisaka was also involved in the development of structuralist phonological theory. His book *On'inron* (1940, Phonological Theory) was in part a critique of Prague School phonology, though it appeared too soon to take into account the definitive work of that group, Nikolai Trubetskoy's *Grundzüge der Phonologie* (1939). Arisaka's ideas, especially on the application of phonemic theory to historical phonology, were very influential in Japan.

George BEDELL

Arisawa Hiromi (1896–)

Economist; statistician. Born in Kōchi Prefecture and graduated from Tōkyō University, Arisawa later joined the faculty of his alma mater as a specialist in statistics. He went to Germany in the late 1920s and studied the analytical method at the Berlin Business Research Institute. After his return to Japan, Arisawa organized the Sekai Keizai Hihan Kai (World Economy Research Society) and made analytical studies of the world economy. Arisawa, a Marxian economist, was forced to leave Tōkyō University in the Red Purge of 1938. After World War II he returned to the university and formulated an economic recovery plan for the prime minister YOSHIDA SHIGERU; his idea was to concentrate government investment in the two important areas, the steel and coal industries. This plan, known as the *keisha seisan hōshiki* (PRIORITY PRODUCTION SYSTEM), included an attempt to boost coal production to 30 million metric tons (33 million short tons) by 1947. Arisawa's plan was instrumental in the early stage of Japan's postwar economic recovery. After retiring from Tōkyō University, Arisawa became president of Hōsei University. He also served as a member of the Atomic Energy Commission, helping to forge Japan's nuclear power policy. Among Arisawa's academic achievements are his pioneering work in introducing dialectical methods to statistics and his editorship of the *Gendai Nihon sangyō kōza* (1959–60, Lectures on Modern Japanese Industry).

SUGIHARA Shirō

Arishima Takeo (1878–1923)

Novelist, short-story writer, and essayist. Born in Tōkyō of a *samurai* background. His father was a high government official, later turned successful businessman. Arishima first went to one of the mission schools in Yokohama, where he learned English. Later he attended the Peers' School (see GAKUSHŪIN UNIVERSITY). Along with his brothers Arishima Ikuma and SATOMI TON, Arishima is counted among members of the humanist SHIRAKABA SCHOOL, though for the most part he did not share even their extraliterary enthusiasms.

While a student at Sapporo Nōgakkō (Sapporo Agricultural College; now Hokkaidō University), he made a serious commitment to the strain of Christianity preached by UCHIMURA KANZŌ, a modified Calvinism. The commitment lasted until he underwent much soul-searching, reminiscent of many modern protestants in the West. He then espoused a kind of secular humanism, whose central figures included Walt Whitman, Tolstoy, and Prince Kropotkin. His three-and-a-half years' study in the United States at Haverford College and Harvard University put him in touch with socialist and progressive thinkers and gave him a keen understanding of the social and spiritual problems in modern European and American history. The experience apparently also led to his permanent dislocation from the Japanese scene, literary and otherwise, because of the thoroughness with which he absorbed preoccupations and ideas that were only peripheral to contemporary Japanese life and letters.

Not only in *Aru onna* (1919; tr *A Certain Woman,* 1978), his best-known novel, which is essentially a psychological and moral melodrama, but in most of his short fiction and nonfiction, Arishima was transfixed by the Christian and post-Christian dilemmas rooted in a deeply dualistic view of human nature and the world. (Toward the end of his puritanical Christian phase, Arishima summed up his adolescent experience of this dualism in the phrase "the Bible versus sex.") Inspired more perhaps by *Anna Karenina* than by *Madame Bovary,* he placed the burden of his moral message in *Aru onna* on the prototypically late-Romantic heroine: a strong-willed woman in important respects superior to her hypocritical male-dominated society, but afflicted with the fatal flaw of true "passion."

In *Kain no matsuei* (1918; tr *The Descendants of Cain,* 1955), he showed, through the figure of a self-destructive tenant farmer, how God's primal curse lies on both man and nature. Such characters and themes were not well calculated to appeal even to the more Westernized readers in Japan, and they did not. Of Arishima's style, which was erratic though often moving, AKUTAGAWA RYŪNOSUKE remarked that reading it was like listening to Western records on the Victrola: it made him want to hear the real thing.

In "Sengen hitotsu," a manifesto published in 1922, Arishima renounced ownership of a large tenant farm in Hokkaidō which his father had left him. At the same time he despaired of the possibility of playing a progressive role in the "coming revolution" because he was a *"petit bourgeois."* Despite the seeming extremity of his renunciation, the cooperative management consequently instituted by the tenants lasted until recent times. Its survival was in sharp contrast to the short-lived communal experiment of MUSHANOKŌJI SANEATSU.

In 1923 Arishima committed double suicide with his mistress, a married woman who was a reporter for the *Fujin kōron,* a popular women's magazine. He is often treated as an anomalous figure in the literary and intellectual history of the Taishō period (1912–26), one who perhaps had failed to find the right voice before his career

Arita
_____

Ceramics on sale along an Arita street during the annual ceramics fair.

_____

and life were prematurely ended but whose artistic expressions, however flawed, still contain much of interest.

■——*Arishima Takeo zenshū*, 10 vols (Shinchōsha, 1929–30). Arishima Takeo, *Aru onna* (1919), tr Kenneth Strong as *A Certain Woman* (1978). Paul Anderer, "Other Worlds: A Study of Arishima Takeo," PhD dissertation, Yale University (1979). Yamada Akio, *Arishima Takeo: shisei to kiseki* (1973). Yasukawa Sadao, *Arishima Takeo ron* (1967).   William F. Sibley

Arisugawa no Miya Taruhito (1835–1895)

Also known as Taruhito Shinnō (Prince Taruhito). Member of the imperial family (adopted son of Emperor Ninkō, 1800–1846; r 1817–46) and army general after the Meiji Restoration of 1868. In the years preceding the Restoration he was active in the movement to overthrow the Tokugawa shogunate and restore direct imperial rule. He commanded Imperial Army troops against the shogunate forces in the BOSHIN CIVIL WAR (1868–69). After quelling disturbances as governor of Fukuoka Prefecture, he was named to the GENRŌIN (Chamber of Elders) in 1875. Prince Arisugawa again led troops against SAIGŌ TAKAMORI during the SATSUMA REBELLION of 1877 in Kyūshū. He traveled through Europe and the United States in 1882 and was appointed chief of the general staff of the army in 1889.

Arita

Town in western Saga Prefecture, Kyūshū, noted for its porcelain (ARITA WARE). The porcelain industry was introduced to Arita by Yi Sam-p'yong (J: RI SAMPEI) from Korea in 1616 and was later perfected by Sakaida Kakiemon (1596–1666; see KAKIEMON WARE). There are numerous porcelain factories, a museum, and a porcelain inspection station. A month-long ceramic fair is held in May. Pop: 14,673.

Arita Hachirō (1884–1965)

Diplomat and politician. Born on the island of Sado in Niigata Prefecture. Upon graduation from Tōkyō University, he joined the Ministry of Foreign Affairs. Establishing himself as an authority on Asian affairs, Arita rose to the position of vice-minister in 1932. He became minister of foreign affairs in the HIROTA KŌKI cabinet of 1936 and went on to serve in that post in the first KONOE FUMIMARO cabinet and then the HIRANUMA KIICHIRŌ and YONAI MITSUMASA cabinets. He opposed close ties with the Axis powers and advocated friendly relations with the United States, but was forced to make repeated compromises with the increasingly powerful militarist faction in the government.

In 1953 Arita was elected to the Diet as an independent candidate. In 1955 and 1959 he ran unsuccessfully in the Tōkyō gubernatorial race with support from the socialists and other progressive parties, after which he retired from politics. In his late years he brought a suit against the writer MISHIMA YUKIO for invasion of privacy, claiming that Mishima's novel *Utage no ato* (1960; tr *After the Banquet*, 1963) too closely resembled his personal and political life. The matter was settled out of court (see AFTER THE BANQUET CASE).

Arita ware

(*arita-yaki*). Ceramics made in the Arita region in Saga Prefecture, Kyūshū. Also known as Imari ware after the port of Imari, the shipping point for the ware. KAKIEMON WARE, made by successive generations of the Kakiemon family, and NABESHIMA WARE, made at official kilns of the Nabeshima domain, are also classified as Arita ware.

At the beginning of the 17th century, a naturalized Korean potter, RI SAMPEI, discovered clay for ceramics at Izumiyama, Arita, and started the first domestic porcelain production in Japan. Originally an underglaze blue and white porcelain, Arita ware largely changed to a colorful enameled porcelain after Sakaida Kakiemon succeeded in perfecting an enamel overglaze in the 1640s. At first these ceramics were Korean and Chinese in design, but in the Genroku era (1688–1704) more Japanese elements, such as textile design patterns, were added.

Developed under the protection and supervision of the Nabeshima domain, Arita ware was being produced in large quantities by the first half of the 17th century. It spread in use among the nobility, *samurai*, merchants, and commoners, and from the mid-17th to the mid-18th century was exported to Europe by the Dutch East India Company. Quantity production led to a drop in quality from the latter half of the 18th century, and a further blow was dealt by fire in 1828, but factory production began in the Meiji period (1868–1912) and today Arita, along with SETO, is one of the largest ceramic production centers in Japan. See also CERAMICS: Edo-period wares.

Ariwara family

Court nobles of the Heian period (794–1185), descended from two sons of Emperor Heizei (774–824; r 806–809). Emperor SAGA (r 809–823) first granted the surname Ariwara to the children of Takaoka (799–865), the deposed crown prince (see KUSUKO INCIDENT). In 826 Emperor Junna (786–840; r 823–833) granted the name to four sons of Takaoka's brother, Prince Abo (792–842). The most notable member of the family was Prince Abo's son, the poet ARIWARA NO NARIHIRA (825–880), whose descendants prospered throughout the rest of the Heian period.

Ariwara no Narihira (825–880)

WAKA poet of the early part of the Heian period (794–1185). Great-grandson of Emperor Kammu (r 781–806). Narihira held many official posts, but was most famous as a poet and a handsome lover. He is one of the ROKKASEN (Six Poetic Geniuses; the six most renowned poets of the 9th century) and one of the SANJŪROKKASEN (Thirty-Six Poetic Geniuses; the 36 most renowned poets who lived before the 11th century). Eighty-seven of his poems are found in 12 of the 21 *chokusenshū* (poetry collections compiled by imperial order). He has often been mentioned as the author of ISE MONOGATARI (10th century; tr *The Tales of Ise*, 1968). Although this theory is no longer accepted, the majority of the *Ise* tales center on him and more than a third of the poems in the collection were composed by him. The oldest private collection of poetry by Narihira extant is the *Zai Chūjō shū* (Collection of the Middle Captain Ariwara); the copy in question is dated 1450.

In his preface to the KOKINSHŪ, the celebrated early 10th century *waka* collection, KI NO TSURAYUKI (d 945) criticizes Narihira as follows: "As for Ariwara no Narihira, his feelings are too strong; his words, insufficient. It is, so to speak, as if in a faded flower the fragrance were lingering." Tsurayuki was a poet of words, of ideas, not a poet of emotions, like Narihira. In the *Kokinshū* we find many poems that embody Tsurayuki's ideals, but few which, like Narihira's, overflow with passion. A good example is his famous poem:

Tsuki ya aranu	Is there not the same moon?
Haru ya mukashi no	Is not the spring
Haru naranu	The spring of yore?
Waga mi hitotsu wa	While it is only I
Moto no mi ni shite	Who is the same one as before.

(*Kokinshū* 747; and *Ise monogatari*, section 4)

The meaning of the poem is: Although the moon and the scenery are the same as last year, they seem to be different because of the absence of my beloved; only I have not changed, for I love her just as much as I did a year ago. Narihira's importance as a poet is indicated by the fact that the *Ise monogatari*, in which so many of his poems are included, was used throughout the ages as a manual for the study of poetry. Later critics, too, often showed great appreciation for his poetry.

📖 ——Imaizumi Tadayoshi, "Ariwara no Narihira," *Nihon bungaku kōza* II (1950). *Frits Vos*

Ariyoshi Sawako (1931-)

Novelist. Born in Wakayama Prefecture. A graduate of Tōkyō Women's Christian University, where she majored in English literature. Recognized for her persistent emphasis on, and adept handling of, prevailing social issues, Ariyoshi is one of Japan's most popular women writers. Early stories, like *Jiuta* (1956), brought to life the traditional world of Japanese entertainers and artists. In the 1960s and 1970s her work increasingly approached nonfiction as she began dealing with social problems. *Kinokawa* (1959; tr *The River Ki*, 1980), her first long novel, is a sensitive record of four generations of women of Kii Province (now Wakayama Prefecture). She takes a similar vein in *Hanaoka Seishū no tsuma* (1966; tr *The Doctor's Wife*, 1978), an account of the 18th-century surgeon Hanaoka Seishū and his devoted wife. Of her appeal to Japanese readers there can be no doubt; *Kōkotsu no hito* (1972), a novel about problems of the elderly, and *Fukugō osen* (1975, Compound Pollution), a look at pollution in Japan, were both best-sellers.

armed forces, imperial Japanese

Created from the forces of the southwestern domains that overthrew the TOKUGAWA SHOGUNATE in 1867–68, the new imperial Japanese armed forces grew into one of the largest and most powerful military forces in the world before they were abolished in 1945, following Japan's complete defeat in World War II. The founders of the modern armed forces, many of them of *samurai* background, incorporated the organizational principles and training methods of Western military systems and, drawing on the German example in particular, created for the army and the navy prerogatives that were to affect profoundly the history of modern Japan.

Founding of the Imperial Army—— The common slogan of the samurai who overthrew the shogunate and carried out the MEIJI RESTORATION (1868) had been SONNŌ JŌI—restoring the political mandate to the emperor and expelling the "barbarians" who threatened national independence. Antiforeign fever was rapidly cooled, however, in the face of foreign military power, specifically in the KAGOSHIMA BOMBARDMENT, in which British and French warships bombarded the Satsuma domain (now Kagoshima Prefecture) and in the SHIMONOSEKI BOMBARDMENT, in which the Chōshū domain (now Yamaguchi Prefecture) and foreign ships exchanged fire. Samurai activists came to feel acutely that the creation of a modern and centralized army was essential in preserving Japan's independence. Accordingly, the new Meiji government put its first emphasis on the slogan FUKOKU KYŌHEI (Enrich the Nation, Strengthen the Military) and embarked on a wide-scale program to import the technology of advanced Western nations.

The political and military power of the new government was from the start monopolized by Chōshū and Satsuma, the leaders in the restoration movement, and it was at the instigation of a Chōshū man, ŌMURA MASUJIRŌ, the first vice-minister of the new Ministry of Military Affairs, that the effort to found a modern army was begun in 1869. Ōmura had led the reform of Chōshū domainal forces immediately after the humiliation of the Shimonoseki Bombardment. The KIHEITAI militia that he and TAKASUGI SHINSAKU organized from lower-ranking samurai and peasants had destroyed the shogunate forces sent against his domain in the second of the CHŌSHŪ EXPEDITIONS, and from this experience Ōmura had become convinced that peasants, if properly trained, were in no way inferior to samurai in terms of military ability. He therefore sought to found a nationally conscripted army that would include all four classes of people—samurai, farmers, artisans, and merchants.

Instituting a system of conscription required a strong, centralized government, however. This in turn meant that the domainal system would have to be dissolved and the samurai class deprived of their hereditary monopoly over military arms. Ōmura's proposal for universal conscription was strongly resented; and he was murdered by a band of samurai in 1869. But he had laid the groundwork, and under his successor, YAMAGATA ARITOMO, another Chōshū man, the conscription system was finally implemented in 1873 (see CONSCRIPTION ORDINANCE OF 1873).

It should be noted that the conscription system was not particularly welcomed by commoners who were the prime targets of the

draft. Several laws and ordinances provided exemptions for heads of households, first-born sons, only sons, and students. People were also permitted exemption from service through payment for a substitute. Thus, the actual burden fell on the second or third sons of rural families. Uprisings against the system, efforts to avoid induction, and incidents of desertion were common (see KETSUZEI IKKI). In spite of these difficulties, however, universal conscription was put into effect within several years, and by the time of the SATSUMA REBELLION (1877), an uprising of disaffected former samurai, the new army would prove its mettle.

The Prussia of the Far East——It was in part for reasons of convenience and in part because of Ōmura's idealized image of Napoleonic France that the decision was made to organize the new Japanese military on the French model. The navy, however, adopted the British system, since Britain was then the world's premier naval power.

The government invited many French and British military instructors, among them Albert C. du Bousquet and Louis E. Bertin, and offered them high salaries (see FOREIGN EMPLOYEES OF THE MEIJI PERIOD). Textbooks, the names of weapons, and even the issuing of commands were all in foreign languages. Many Japanese were dispatched to foreign countries as students, including a fairly large contingent sent to the United States Naval Academy at Annapolis.

In 1871, just as the adoption of the French system was receiving official confirmation, doubts about France's military powers were raised when it was defeated in the Franco-Prussian War of 1870–71. Yamagata Aritomo and ŌYAMA IWAO, who were in Europe at the time, were impressed by the new Prussian army. They returned to Japan with the belief that the Japanese military system should be modeled on the Prussian system. The power of the pro-French faction in the Ministry of Military Affairs was deeply rooted, however, and it was to take more than 10 years to accomplish this change in policy.

KATSURA TARŌ played a very large part in this transition. He had been sent to France in 1870, but had been unable to begin his studies because of the Prussian occupation of Paris. He consulted with Yamagata and Ōyama and went instead to Berlin, where he remained for three years. Immediately after his return home he was again assigned to Germany, this time as military attaché. He took the opportunity to study carefully its military system, and returned to Japan in 1878. The ARMY GENERAL STAFF OFFICE became independent in December 1878, largely as a result of Katsura's maneuvering.

In 1884 a group of Japanese army officials extended an invitation to Major Klemens W. J. MECKEL, the favorite pupil of Field Marshal Helmuth von Moltke, chief of the Great General Staff of Prussia, to teach at the new Army War College. A total conversion to the Prussian military system was now embarked upon. These events coincided with the decision of Prime Minister ITŌ HIROBUMI to draw up a modern constitution on the Prussian model. It was not unexpected, then, that in due course Japan would be called "the Prussia of the Far East." Indeed, Count Mirabeau's comment that "war was Prussia's national industry" could have applied equally to modern Japan before 1945.

Independence of the Supreme Command—— Of all the aspects of the Prussian military system, the concept of the "independence of the supreme command" was to have the greatest repercussions in Japan. From the institutional perspective the independence of the supreme command could work in two ways: the military command could be given powers equal to those of the military administration, or the military command could be totally independent of the civil government. It was only in Japan that both aspects were fully realized. For even in Prussia, it was only with the rising prestige of the General Staff under von Moltke's leadership and victory in the Franco-Prussian War that the independence of the supreme command was included in the constitution. In Japan, too, both the army and navy ministries had initially been under the *dajō daijin* (grand minister of state), and what later became the Army General Staff Office had been a staff bureau under the army minister charged only with the task of inspecting garrisons (CHINDAI). In fact, at the time of the SAGA REBELLION (1874), Home Minister ŌKUBO TOSHIMICHI had taken command of the expeditionary force, using his full authority as a civil minister. However, during the Satsuma Rebellion criticism was made that such a military system was not conducive to military operations, and military command came to be exercised independently. This practice became institutionalized in 1885, when the DAJŌKAN form of government was abolished and the cabinet system established. It was finally formalized in the Meiji CONSTITUTION of 1889 (see TŌSUIKEN).

The power of the Army General Staff Office was now enlarged and strengthened. Moreover, a provision was made that only active-duty officers would be allowed to hold the posts of service ministers in the cabinet (see GUMBU DAIJIN GEN'EKI BUKAN SEI). During the SINO-JAPANESE WAR OF 1894–1895 and the RUSSO-JAPANESE WAR of 1904–05, the "right of supreme command" was asserted ever more strongly against civil authority.

These developments in Japan were clearly at variance with prevailing trends elsewhere. Even in the Prussian constitution, the military command in principle was required to be assisted by the chancellor, and, while the military command did in fact function independently and interfere increasingly in government, shortly before World War I a number of scholars had begun to object to its independence. Again, in contrast to the army, the German Naval General Staff never succeeded in establishing complete independence of supreme command.

In Japan the Naval General Staff Office became independent in 1893. Soon after, the office of the inspector general of military education, which ranked equal to that of the army minister and the chief of General Staff, was created. Coordination between state affairs and military command, and between politics and military strategy, thus became even more difficult. When the Imperial Headquarters (Daihon'ei), the central command structure, was first established during the Sino-Japanese War of 1894–95, Prime Minister Itō Hirobumi was allowed to attend its meetings at the order of Emperor Meiji. But during the Russo-Japanese War, Prime Minister Katsura Tarō, in spite of his military background, never attended Daihon'ei meetings. When the China War broke out in 1937, Prime Minister KONOE FUMIMARO's request to attend meetings was rejected by the military. Thus did the military exploit its prerogative of supreme command and lead the country recklessly into total war.

Imperial Expansion —— Until about 1870 Japan's armed forces were designed primarily for domestic security. The military leaders of the Meiji government, however, soon began to think in terms of foreign wars. In December 1871, Vice-Minister of Military Affairs Yamagata Aritomo and others issued a joint memorial: "We respectfully submit that the objectives of the Ministry of Military Affairs today exist internally, while the objectives of the future exist externally." In asserting the urgent need for an expansion of military capability, they cited the threat from Russia. This statement may be considered Japan's first national defense policy. There is great significance, too, in the leaders' reference to Russia as the hypothetical enemy, although war with Russia did not become a real possibility until the 1890s, when the two nations came into conflict over their interests in Korea and the Asian continent.

To be sure, already in 1874 some government leaders, including SAIGŌ TAKAMORI, had urged an invasion of Korea in retaliation for "national humiliation" (see SEIKANRON), and an expeditionary force had been sent to Taiwan to chastise aborigines who had murdered Ryukyuan fishermen (see TAIWAN EXPEDITION OF 1874). But it was only after the Satsuma Rebellion that military and national opinion gradually veered toward an expansionist continental policy. Toward this end young Japanese officers were secretly dispatched to China, and the services of adventurers known as TAIRIKU RŌNIN were enlisted. This network of military intelligence was considerably enlarged when KAWAKAMI SŌROKU became a powerful figure in the General Staff.

In spite of Japan's great enthusiasm for foreign military adventures, its armed forces remained small; in 1882 there were only 33,000 soldiers in training, and their equipment remained at a level intended for internal conflict. There was no real provision for general mobilization or logistical support units to sustain a major campaign. Large-scale military expansion and reorganization began in 1884. In the army, field divisions replaced stationary garrisons, and in the navy, mobile squadrons armed with rapid-fire artillery were organized. The size of Japan's military increased by a factor of 2.5 to 3.0.

The economic burden on the Japanese people of a military budget that took up 25 to 30 percent of the national budget was enormous. They were rewarded with victory in the Sino-Japanese War, but the burden of military expenditures became increasingly onerous, as the army sought expansion by 300 percent and the navy, by 400 percent, in preparation for a war with Russia. Japan did indeed win a narrow victory over Russia in 1905, but it then had to prepare for a possible revanchist war. It also felt compelled to expand its naval fleet in order to compete with the growing US Navy.

Reasons for Victory —— Many reasons have been suggested for Japan's victories in the wars with China and Russia. One key reason was that Japan had skillfully maneuvered the timing of the outbreak of hostilities to coincide with the peaking of its planned military strength. The organization and equipment of Japan's military forces were at least equal to that of the enemy in quality, and what Japan lacked in numbers, it could compensate for by making a preemptive attack. In the Russo-Japanese War, for example, the Port Arthur and Baltic fleets of the Russians were made up of new and old battleships of uneven speed and capability. In contrast, Admiral TŌGŌ HEIHACHIRŌ's fleet was composed of ships that had just been completed and that were far superior to Russian ships in speed, maneuverability, and gunnery capability. And, of course, Japan was greatly aided by its proximity to the theater of operations.

At the time of Japan's victories, it was reported that its armies had defeated numerically superior armies. In fact, in the Sino-Japanese War of 1894–95, although China had larger numbers of soldiers, its field forces armed with modern equipment were but a small fraction. As for its navy, apart from two large battleships, the Japanese fleet was actually more powerful. Again, in the Russo-Japanese War, the main strength of the Russian army was located in Europe and the forces which engaged the Japanese directly were only slightly superior numerically.

Of importance also was the difference in training and education. The Japanese General Staff had been thoroughly trained at the new Army War College, while much of the Chinese military was made up of mercenaries. The Russian army consisted mainly of officers of aristocratic background and serfs. Moreover, the Japanese military had the full moral support of the civilian populace. In contrast, both China and Russia were politically unstable, with potentially revolutionary domestic conditions.

Split in a National Defense Policy —— The string of victories naturally heightened the prestige and authority of the military. Generals and admirals were awarded medals and peerages; Admiral Tōgō Heihachirō, Field Marshal Ōyama Iwao, and General NOGI MARESUKE were treated as national heroes. Many young people entered military schools. The army sought to increase its strength by four divisions, and the navy advanced its plan for a HACHIHACHI KANTAI, a fleet that would center on eight battleships and eight cruisers.

Victory in the Russo-Japanese War raised Japan to a position of international importance, but it altered the attitude of the United States, which had hitherto been favorable to Japan. A future conflict between Japan and the United States now became a familiar theme of journalists in both countries. It was against this background that the Japanese military became divided over the issue of strategic priorities. The so-called Advance to the North (hokushinron) group, mainly supported by the army, advocated aggressive action on the Asian continent, using Korea as a base. It saw Russia as the hypothetical enemy. The "Advance to the South" (nanshinron; see SOUTHERN EXPANSION DOCTRINE) group, supported by the navy, called for the extension of Japanese interests in Southeast Asia and the Pacific and saw the United States as the potential enemy. The army and the navy came to fight bitterly over the direction of military operations. In 1907, the Teikoku Kokubō Hōshin (Imperial National Defense Policy) was adopted with imperial approval. It represented a compromise, in which the hypothetical enemy was determined to be "first Russia, then the United States, Germany, and France." The army focused on "taking the offensive against Russian military strength deployed in the Far East" and the navy prepared for "taking the offensive against the US Navy in the Far East."

The policy was redefined in 1918, 1923, and 1936. The ranking of Russia and the United States as hypothetical enemies was altered to meet the changing international situation, but the basic policy of parity between the army and the navy remained the same. Disagreement on the choice between "North or South" became a call for "North and South."

World War I —— In WORLD WAR I (1914–18), Japan reaped the benefits of both belligerency and neutrality. In keeping with its commitments under the ANGLO-JAPANESE ALLIANCE, Japan belatedly entered the war on the Allied side, but it also enlarged its sphere of influence in the Far East and the Pacific Basin and made great profits by monopolizing trade in military materials while the Allies were locked in war with Germany. Military officers were sent to observe the European front, but they do not seem to have understood the revolution in military technology brought about by the conflict. For while new weapons such as tanks and airplanes were being used in vast numbers in Europe, there was not a single tank in the Japanese army, and the few aircraft it possessed had been imported only as samples. The army was not able to break away from the outdated emphasis on infantry.

Delays in modernizing the army were also due to the loss of the hypothetical enemy with the collapse of tsarist Russia in 1917. After World War I, Army Minister UGAKI KAZUSHIGE abolished four divisions, transferring surplus officers to universities and high schools as drill instructors, and worked to establish air and armored forces. This move was very unpopular within the army, and later in 1937, when Ugaki was named by the emperor to form a cabinet, he was successfully opposed by the army. The navy, on the other hand, was able to advance its plans for the Hachihachi Kantai. By the end of World War I, its share of the total national budget had risen to over 30 percent.

The Era of Disarmament——The unprecedented bloodshed in World War I brought calls for pacifism and disarmament. The WASHINGTON NAVAL TREATY OF 1922 fixed the ratio of capital ship tonnage for the United States, Great Britain, and Japan at 10:10:6 and declared a 10-year moratorium on naval construction. The Japanese navy insisted that for national security Japan needed a ratio of 7 against that of 8 of the United States. The Japanese representative in Washington, Admiral KATŌ TOMOSABURŌ, accepted the figure of 7, however, and in this he was supported by the Japanese public.

Public sentiment for disarmament had also been strengthened by the failure of the SIBERIAN INTERVENTION, which had resulted in great loss both in human and financial terms. The number of young men who wanted to enter the military rapidly decreased; in large cities, military personnel preferred not to appear in uniform. It was even rumored that some of the younger officers were reading books on socialism.

Against this background of growing antimilitary sentiment, party politicians worked to strengthen civilian control of the military. HARA TAKASHI and TAKAHASHI KOREKIYO of the RIKKEN SEIYŪKAI party asserted that the General Staff should be abolished and that the right of supreme command should be under the control of the government. Several generals entered the political arena, General TANAKA GIICHI, for example, accepted the presidency of the Seiyūkai. During this era of so-called TAISHŌ DEMOCRACY, the prestige of the military sank to an unprecedented degree and the requirement that service ministers be limited to generals or admirals on the active list was amended to make reserve officers eligible (it was reversed in the 1930s).

The Era of Militarism——The worldwide depression, beginning in 1929, destroyed the international economic order that had been reestablished after World War I and caused a severe crisis in the capitalist system. Germany, Italy, and Japan chose the course of totalitarian government and foreign aggression (see SHŌWA DEPRESSION). In Japan, those who had been disappointed in the international foreign policy of SHIDEHARA KIJŪRŌ called for a hard-line policy and welcomed the military intrusion into government.

The first overt sign of MILITARISM was the MANCHURIAN INCIDENT, a virtual coup d'etat by field grade officers in the GUANDONG (KWANTUNG) ARMY in Manchuria and the central headquarters of the army. Domestically, several aborted coups culminated in the FEBRUARY 26TH INCIDENT of 1936, in which young officers attempted to take over the government. Army discipline of these officers paradoxically led to a larger political role for the military; generals and admirals were now regularly named to form cabinets. It was largely at the instigation of the military that the ANTI-COMINTERN PACT (1936) between Germany, Italy, and Japan and the subsequent TRIPARTITE PACT (1940) were signed.

The China War——For almost 30 years, from the post-Russo-Japanese War era until the second Sino-Japanese War, the size of the Japanese military remained essentially stable. The army had 17 divisions and kept manpower strength at about 250,000, while the navy, which had expanded and modernized, ceased building battleships after the Washington Naval Treaty. When the treaty expired in 1935, however, the signatory countries entered a period of unlimited military expansion. The Imperial Japanese Navy embarked on the construction of warships with a displacement of over 60,000 tons and the development of aircraft carriers. The army, too, demanded military expansion to counter the resurgence of the Far Eastern Army of the Soviet Union. The army and navy regarded each other as rivals, yet at the same time, the service ministries and the high command were continually at odds, making it impossible to arrive at a unified political and military strategy.

The China War broke out in July 1937. The army, which had begun the conflict, assumed that China would soon capitulate, but the Chinese army retreated further into the interior and refused to negotiate for peace. By 1939, almost one million fighting men were tied down on the Asian continent. The war against China, which lacked any clear objective, led to a decline in the morale of Japanese soldiers. The Japanese army, long known for its rigid discipline, perpetrated many atrocities (see NANJING [NANKING] INCIDENT). In occupied areas, Japanese merchants plundered the local economy and earned the hatred of the Chinese people. See also SINO-JAPANESE WAR OF 1937–1945.

In contrast to Japan's initial victories in China, its confrontation with the Soviet Union in the NOMONHAN INCIDENT (1939) on the Mongolian-Manchurian border proved disastrous; Japanese troops were crushed by the mechanized Soviet army. However, the idea of the primacy of spirit over matter that prevailed in the Japanese military at the time did not change even in the face of this overwhelming evidence.

The Pacific War and the Dissolution of the Military——When Japan stood on the brink of the Pacific War three-quarters of a century after the founding of its modern military, it had an army of 2 million men and a naval force with 1.6 million gross tons. These figures represented increases by a factor of 5,000 for the army and a factor of 400 for the navy. Although still bogged down in China and fully aware of the risk of war with the United States and Great Britain, Japan launched its "Advance to the South" to control the resource-rich areas of Malaya, French Indochina, and the Dutch East Indies. In a war between the United States and Japan, the main role would of necessity be played by the navy. As long as the navy did not have confidence, it would be difficult to open hostilities, but by the late 1930s, the Japanese fleet had reached a ratio of 70.6 percent in total tonnage and 94 percent in aircraft carriers as against the American navy. In actual number of ships, moreover, Japan held a slight superiority. Japan decided that, given the differences in the production capabilities of the two nations, any delay in starting hostilities would be only to its disadvantage.

The surprise attack on Pearl Harbor on 7 December 1941 destroyed the main power of the US Pacific Fleet. Within six months Japan had succeeded in occupying Indochina, Malaya, and the Dutch East Indies and pushed far westward into Burma to the Indian frontier and southward to the Solomon Islands. However, following a major defeat at the Battle of MIDWAY in June 1942, Japan found itself on the defensive. By the spring of 1945 most of its cities and industrial facilities had been destroyed by the firebomb raids of B-29 BOMBERS, Hiroshima and Nagasaki were obliterated by atomic bombs, Russian troops moved into Manchuria, and Japan surrendered on 15 August 1945.

To attribute defeat to the enormous gap in scientific technology and material would not be enough. The reasons were more complex; they must include Japan's delay in mobilizing for total war, especially its failure to build up air power, because of its intoxication with initial victories; the lack of cooperation and coordination between the army and the navy; and insufficient exchange of intelligence with the Axis powers. The imperial Japanese forces, which in three generations had become a "nation within a nation," had become victims of their own power. In accordance with the POTSDAM DECLARATION they were abolished on 30 November 1945. See also WORLD WAR II.

🔖——Fujiwara Akira, *Gunjishi* (1961). Hata Ikuhiko, *Gun fashizumu undō shi* (1961).   HATA Ikuhiko

arms and armor

The broad spectrum of Japanese offensive and defensive paraphernalia, including hand weapons, projectiles, various types of body armor, and other battle accessories is collectively known as *bugu* (though specialists make a distinction between *buki* or weapons and *bugu* or armor and accessories). Japanese weapons and armor were often also objects of artistic and symbolic significance.

Legislation controlling the use and possession of weapons in Japan was enacted early in the historical period. According to the TAIHŌ CODE of 701, the criminal and civil codes established during the reign of Emperor MOMMU (r 697–707), only the military were permitted to carry arms; all other weapons were placed under the jurisdiction of the Ministry of Military Affairs (Hyōbushō) and were securely guarded in the imperial armory. With the rise of the warrior class late in the Heian period (794–1185), these early injunctions were gradually ignored, and even the common people carried arms. The widespread, unrestricted possession of arms was curtailed in the

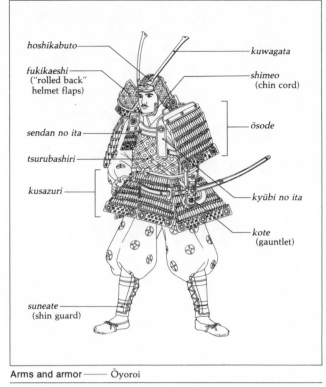

hoshikabuto

fukikaeshi ("rolled back" helmet flaps)

sendan no ita

tsurubashiri

kusazuri

suneate (shin guard)

kuwagata

shimeo (chin cord)

ōsode

kyūbi no ita

kote (gauntlet)

Arms and armor —— Ōyoroi

A 12th-century warrior in a suit of *ōyoroi*. Designed to accommodate maneuvers on horseback, *ōyoroi* consisted of numerous segments joined by colored cords or thongs to ensure flexibility, together with an iron helmet topped by menacing horns. *Ōyoroi* evolved in the 9th century and were not replaced until the introduction of firearms in the 16th.

late 16th century when the national unifier TOYOTOMI HIDEYOSHI deprived all but the SAMURAI of their weapons (see SWORD HUNT). The Tokugawa shogunate (1603–1867) continued to regulate the possession of arms: the carrying of firearms was strictly prohibited and only samurai were permitted to wear two swords, while members of other classes were allowed to wear one short sword, or *wakizashi*. During the two and a half centuries of Tokugawa peace, the symbolic value of weapons increased, and the Japanese sword became the spiritual symbol of BUSHIDŌ, the Way of the samurai. After the Meiji Restoration (1868), the HAITŌREI law was passed in 1876 prohibiting the wearing of swords even by samurai. Thus arms and armor disappeared from daily life, gradually became recognized as art objects, and were avidly sought by connoisseurs and collectors.

Early weapons. Although the distinction between hunting tools and weapons was not yet clear, the earliest objects in Japan that may be tentatively classified as weapons are the stone implements, including axeheads and spearheads, of the prehistoric Jōmon period (ca 10,000 BC–ca 300 BC). Japanese arms changed drastically in the 5th century AD with the introduction of mounted warfare and bronze and iron weapons from the Asian continent. Early bronze weapons included double-edged swords *(tsurugi)*, spearheads, and arrowheads. As iron gradually replaced bronze in the 6th century, a new form of sword, the *tachi*, appeared.

Swords. The *tachi* of this early period, a long sword with a straight blade and a single, unbeveled cutting edge, was often engraved with Chinese inscriptions inlaid in silver along the blade. Often the bronze pommel rings and guards were also decorated with openwork or inlaid ornament. The careful attention paid to decoration suggests that swords were already symbols of martial dignity and were to a certain degree ceremonial in function. In the 7th century, swords with beveled edges appeared; in the middle part of the Heian period (794–1185) the blade received an elegant curve, and the development of the distinctive Japanese sword, whose uniqueness lies equally in functional and aesthetic excellence, was complete. Thereafter, while sword types increased, they retained the essential form developed in the Heian period. See also SWORDS.

Naginata. This weapon, also called *nagamaki,* has a curved blade like a sword, but with a longer and more acutely curved tip, attached to a long wooden handle. The *naginata* saw its greatest use in the Kamakura period (1185–1333). See also NAGINATA.

Spears. There are two types of Japanese spear, identical in function: the *hoko* and the *yari.* The *hoko,* examples of which are preserved in the SHŌSŌIN storehouse in Nara, was in use until the end of the Nara period (710–794). In the *Mōko shūrai ekotoba* picture scrolls, which depict the MONGOL INVASIONS OF JAPAN (1274 and 1281), Mongol footsoldiers are shown using *yari,* although this weapon was not adopted by the Japanese until after the 14th century, along with the use of massed troops in battle.

Bows. First made only from wood or bamboo, by the 9th century bows were made of laminated wood and bamboo. Bows were often lacquered and bound with wisteria vines or cords. Arrows of two, three, and four vanes were used; and while the ancient shafts were about 70 centimeters (28 in) long, by the Edo period (1600–1868) they reached a length of roughly 90 centimeters (36 in). Quivers, also initially of one type, were developed in a variety of forms.

Shields. Designed to ward off arrows, shields were made in great numbers. Although few remain from ancient times, some lacquered ceremonial shields have been preserved at Shintō shrines.

Firearms. Although the word *teppō* (firearms) appears in the text of the 13th-century *Mōko shūrai ekotoba* picture scrolls, the harquebus was not introduced to Japan until 1543, when Portuguese sailors were cast ashore at Tanegashima in what is now Kagoshima Prefecture (see FIREARMS, INTRODUCTION OF). Firearms were immediately adopted and effected a revolution in battle tactics and strategy. The Tokugawa shogunate restricted the production of *teppō* and no advances in design were made. New types of firearm introduced at the end of the Edo period and early in the Meiji period (1868–1912) rendered the harquebus obsolete. Cannons (*ōzutsu* or *taihō*), introduced to Japan shortly after the harquebus, were not used effectively until the early 19th century, when modern foundry technology was imported from the West.

Armor. Unlike the heavy metal-plate armor of the West, Japanese helmets (*kabuto*) and body armor were splendid accoutrements reflecting the unique moral and spiritual traditions of the samurai. In addition to functional utility and decorative beauty, Japanese armor was a symbol that proclaimed, through distinctive forms and colors conspicuously displayed to the enemy, the individual identity of the clan and the glory of its house.

Among the artifacts excavated from ancient burial mounds of the Kofun period (ca 300–710) are examples of helmets and armor based on mainland prototypes. Sculptural representations of these types, the *keikō* and the *tankō,* appear in the HANIWA images from the same period. The *keikō* was a flexible but extremely heavy suit of armor made of long, narrow pieces of iron or bronze joined together edge to edge by cords or strips of leather. The *tankō,* which reached only to the hips, was inflexible and restrictive and made of fitted metal panels riveted together. Two different types of helmet were also found: the *mabisashitsuki kabuto* and the *shōkakutsuki kabuto.* The former had flat, crescent-shaped brims, while the latter were distinguished by a protruding front part like the prow of a ship.

In the 9th century, coincidental with the appearance of the curved-blade sword, a distinctly Japanese style of armor known as *ōyoroi* came into being. *Ōyoroi* were decorated with bright ornaments of gold and silver, their numerous segments joined by cords woven of richly colored threads. Evolving from the *keikō* type of armor, *ōyoroi* were designed to accommodate mounted archers; the warrior's front, back, and left were enclosed in a plate called *kabukidō* and his right was protected by an independent rib shield (*waidate*). Hips and thighs were protected by the *kusazuri,* four panels arranged in tiers and joined by colored laces of strips of leather. The upper part of the chest was guarded on the right by the *sendan no ita* and on the left by the *kyūbi no ita,* both suspended from the shoulders. Arm guards, *ōsode,* completed the armored costume. The helmet, the type known as the *hoshikabuto,* was made of iron and studded with raised decorative rivets. To the left and right were curved panels that swept out and back, forming one continuous piece that hung to the shoulders. The most distinctive decorative element of the helmet, and indeed of the entire suit of armor, was the *kuwagata,* a large, flat metal piece resembling a stylized pair of horns, which rose menacingly from the visor. The breastplate was covered with leather (*tsurubashiri*) which was sometimes painted with images of the Buddhist deity Fudō MYŌŌ (Skt: Acala), one of the Go Dai Myōō, or Five Wisdom Kings, of ESOTERIC BUDDHISM and the special patron of warriors.

Lower-ranking samurai and attendants of the same period wore armor of the *dōmaru* or *haramaki* type. The *dōmaru,* lacking a *wai-*

Arms and armor——— Dōmaru

Detail from one of a pair of six-fold screens entitled *Sieges of Ōsaka Castle,* showing an engagement between Tokugawa (right) and Toyotomi (left) forces. All figures are depicted in *dōmaru* decorated with identifying crests. Colors and gold on paper. Ca 1615. Ōsaka Castle Donjon Collection.

date, was an abbreviated suit of armor enclosing the torso and tied on the right. The *haramaki* was a simpler version secured at the back. By the 14th century, when mounted warfare gave way to battles between massed ranks of foot soldiers, these lighter types of armor gradually replaced the *ōyoroi.*

The introduction of firearms in the 16th century necessitated the development of a new type of armor, the *tōsei gusoku,* many of which had hinged breastplates and back plates fastened on the right. These were modeled on Western armor, perhaps not through necessity so much as fashion, for the samurai taste of the time embraced many foreign (NAMBAN) elements. The distinctive helmets, or *kawarikabuto,* were created in unusual, eye-catching shapes designed to attract attention. Armor produced during the long era of Tokugawa peace, looking to older styles for inspiration, increased in ornamental opulence.

Saddlery. Saddles *(kura),* made of wood and constructed in various styles, are in general classified as either Chinese-style *(karakura)* or Japanese-style *(yamatogura).* The latter are further divided into two types: a formal court saddle, the *suikangura,* used by members of the nobility, and a war saddle, the *gunjingura.* Most saddles were sumptuously decorated with MAKI-E lacquer or inlaid with mother-of-pearl, revealing a high level of artistic craftsmanship. Stirrups *(abumi)* were ring-shaped during the Kofun period, cupshaped *(tsubo abumi)* in the Nara and early Heian periods, and thereafter shaped like an upside-down question mark with the bottom portion extended horizontally *(shitanaga abumi),* a form specifically designed to give sure footing to bowmen. Stirrups were also decorated with mother-of-pearl inlay and *maki-e.*

Miscellaneous weapons. Other implements, some specifically intended to facilitate the apprehension of criminals, included the *sodegarami,* a wooden handle with a double row of barbed prongs designed to catch loose clothing; the *sasumata,* a two-pronged weapon shaped like the horns of a bull, designed to pin a man at the throat; the *jitte,* two parallel steel shafts of unequal length attached to a short handle and used to catch a man's sword and wrench it from his grasp; the *kusarigama,* a sickle attached to a weighted chain and used to entangle the opponent's sword with one end and slit his throat with the other; and the *tetsubō,* an iron stave.

OGASAWARA *Nobuo*

Arms Export, Three Principles of

(Buki Yushutsu Sangensoku). Policy of the Japanese government establishing three specific areas to which the export of arms by Japan is forbidden. They are: communist countries, countries under embargoes mandated by the United Nations, and countries currently, or likely to be in the near future, involved in military conflicts.

During the Korean War (1950–53), when the Japanese defense industry, which had been dismantled after World War II, was reactivated by special procurements made by the United States military, the government passed the Ordnance Manufacturing Law (1953), under which arms trade was permitted (see DEFENSE INDUSTRY). Subsequently, export of weapons and ammunition to Southeast Asia increased, and in 1962 the Ministry of International Trade and Industry, in accordance with the Export Trade Control Order, laid down the regulations mentioned above.

In 1967 Prime Minister SATŌ EISAKU presented these principles to the Diet as the official policy of the government. After the 1973 oil crisis, however, several industries called for a lifting of restrictions as a means of boosting a faltering economy. In February 1976 the MIKI TAKEO cabinet not only refused to allow the export of arms to the three areas but expressed its reluctance to export to other countries as well; it also stated its intention to treat the traffic in related equipment on a par with that of weapons, establishing a new and much more stringent definition of the three principles. Since 1980, efforts both within and outside government have been made to restore some flexibility to Japan's arms policy. MUTSU *Gorō*

Army Academy

(Rikugun Shikan Gakkō). Principal school of the Imperial Japanese Army for the study of military science and the training of officers. First established as the Heigakkō in 1868 in Kyōto, it was later called such names as Heigakusho, Ōsaka Heigakuryō, and Rikugun Heigakuryō. In 1874 the school, then known as the Rikugun Shikan Gakkō, was put under the direct supervision of the Army Ministry and located at Ichigaya, Tōkyō. The first class of students entered the next year. After 1898 it came under the supervision of the newly established Army Educational Administration. The academy was moved to Sagamihara in Kanagawa Prefecture in 1937.

After several changes two programs were put into effect from 1887: a junior course for graduates of the army cadet schools and those who completed the first four years of middle school, and a senior course for officer candidates. Graduates from the academy totaled some 50,000. In 1938 the program for air force officers was established as a separate school. Students spent two years in general course work and basic military studies and two more years in their field of concentration. Upon graduation they were given the rank of apprentice officer. In wartime the course was frequently shortened and the number of students greatly increased. The academy disappeared along with the imperial army after Japan's defeat in World War II. KONDŌ *Shinji*

Army General Staff Office

(Sambō Hombu). Highest organization of the Imperial Japanese Army and, from 1886 to 1889, of the Imperial Japanese Navy. Established in 1878 after the Prussian model, the chief of the General Staff

Office was directly subordinate to the emperor and was in charge of national defense and strategic planning. See also ARMED FORCES, IMPERIAL JAPANESE. *HATA Ikuhiko*

Army Ministry

(Rikugunshō). Central government office that had administrative control over the Japanese army. It was established on 5 April 1872 along with the NAVY MINISTRY to replace the Hyōbushō (Ministry of Military Affairs) of the old imperial administrative system. YAMAGATA ARITOMO was the first to hold the post of minister. The ministry initially had control of both administration and military command, but the latter function was taken over by the ARMY GENERAL STAFF OFFICE, set up in December 1878. At first the ministry head was responsible to the grand minister of state *(dajō daijin)*, but with the establishment of the cabinet system in 1885, he became directly responsible to the emperor. This politically powerful post was usually filled by an army officer on active service (see GUMBU DAIJIN GEN'EKI BUKAN SEI). The ministry was dissolved in December 1945, soon after Japan's defeat in World War II. See also ARMED FORCES, IMPERIAL JAPANESE.

art

Over the centuries, a wide variety of social, economic, political, cultural, and environmental factors have had an influence on the development of Japanese art. However, any attempt to assess these factors and the degree of their influence presents an almost insurmountable problem: those that have had the most noticeable effect on artistic development are also so obvious and basic, and so frequently invoked, that they are close to being clichés. There can be little question about the profound effect that Japanese environmental conditions had on artistic production. The temperate climate and four distinct seasons provided an abundance of seasonal symbols and motifs, such as the plum, the cherry, the maple, and the chrysanthemum, which appear again and again in Japanese art. The Japanese love of nature is reflected in the use of such raw materials as lacquer, wood, bamboo, and paper throughout Japanese architecture. The high humidity and frequent earthquakes and typhoons common to Japan discouraged the use of more permanent materials like stone in architecture and ensured the preference for the more readily mendable and available materials that dominate the Japanese aesthetic.

At the same time, it would be a great mistake to underestimate the profound influence that Japan's proximity to China and continental Asia has had on its artistic development. With Japan's location just 724 kilometers (450 mi) from China and a mere 161 kilometers (about 100 mi) from the Korean peninsula, the periodic influx of artistic traditions from the Asian mainland has unquestionably colored the nature of Japan's artistic production from prehistoric times to the present. The influence of China, whose culture rests at the heart of East Asian creativity, was particularly felt in Japan; Chinese artistic styles and larger segments of Chinese culture, including the great international tradition of Buddhist art, reached Japan either directly or filtered through the Korean peninsula. Even the famous secular style of the Heian court (794–1185) received notable inspiration from continental sources.

In the face of this continuing influence from continental culture, yet another characteristic of Japanese art came to the fore—its ability to absorb continental influences and produce an aesthetic all its own. Despite its proximity to the Asian continent, its position as an isolated island nation enabled Japan to mold enormously varied continental styles into a markedly indigenous expression. In other words, over the years the Japanese have been able to take generations of heterogeneous continental influence and form it into what must be considered a homogeneous whole that is "Japanese."

It is interesting that, despite Japan's contact with and absorption of foreign aesthetics from prehistoric times to the present, Japanese art had little, if any, influence on outside cultures, especially Western cultures, until the last half of the 19th century, when European artists discovered its beauties and developed a passion for *japonaiserie.* Exposure to and consciousness of Japanese art through, for example, Japanese ceramics and woodblock prints played a major role in the development of a modern European painting aesthetic, as well as influencing the aesthetic course of the decorative arts. Since World War II, the study of Japanese art history by Americans and Europeans has made rapid progress, gradually deepening Western recognition and awareness of Japan's great artistic legacy. Present-

day Japanese artists are making an increasingly active contribution to the development of contemporary international art.

The major articles on Japanese art in this encyclopedia include AESTHETICS; ARCHITECTURE, TRADITIONAL DOMESTIC; BONSAI; BUDDHIST ARCHITECTURE; BUDDHIST ART; BUDDHIST SCULPTURE; CALLIGRAPHY; CERAMICS; CRESTS; EMAKIMONO; FLOWER ARRANGEMENT; FOLK CRAFTS; GARDENS; INK PAINTING; INRŌ; LACQUER WARE; MASKS; MODERN PRINTS; NAMBAN ART; NETSUKE; PAINTING; PHOTOGRAPHY; SCREEN AND WALL PAINTING; SHINTŌ ARCHITECTURE; SHINTŌ ART; SHUNGA; SWORDS; TEXTILES; TSUBA; UKIYO-E; and ZENGA. *AKIYAMA Terukazu*

Art Theatre Guild of Japan Co, Ltd

Company engaged in producing, importing, and distributing motion pictures. Established in 1961, it aims to import and distribute foreign films of high artistic value and to produce and distribute Japanese films without suppressing the artistic spirit of the directors. The company has imported such films as the Polish *Matka Joanna od Aniotów* (1961, Mother Joan of the Angels) and the Indian *Pather Panchali* (1955, Little Song of the Road) and distributed films made by Japanese directors such as ŌSHIMA NAGISA and Higashi Yōichi. *SHIRAI Yoshio*

Aruga Kizaemon (1897–1979)

Sociologist. Born in Nagano Prefecture. A graduate of Tōkyō University, he served as professor at Tōkyō University of Education and Keiō University, and as president of Japan Women's University (1965–73). He began as a student of folklore under YANAGI MUNEYOSHI, YANAGITA KUNIO, and ORIKUCHI SHINOBU, later becoming a sociologist. He felt that the cultural and racial characteristics of a people are reflected in the social structures they form out of necessity. In his studies of the social structure of Japanese rural communities, he maintained that there is a close historical and social connection between the landlord–tenant farmer relationship and the rural main family–branch family relationship (see IE). He believed that the vertical kinship relationship found in a clan or large family is the basic form of social relationship in Japanese society, and that it is also found in urban communities and within corporations. He also pointed out that this characteristic Japanese social organization based on the family system reflects the lack of a well-developed social security system. Among his writings are *Nihon kazoku seido to kosaku seido* (1943), *Sonraku seikatsu: Mura to shakai* (1948), and *Aruga Kizaemon chosakushū* (11 vols, 1966–71).

HASUMI Otohiko

asa

Usually referring to hemp (a member of the mulberry family) or ramie (a member of the nettle family), *asa* is a comprehensive term that in its broadest sense includes almost all plant-derived fibers except cotton. Thus it can refer to fibers taken from the inner bark of trees and shrubs such as *fuji* (wisteria), *kōzo, kaji, shina* (types of mulberry), and *bashō* (a fiber-producing plantain), as well as to bast fibers such as hemp, ramie, jute, various nettles, and linen. Of these all but jute and linen have traditionally been used in Japan or Okinawa.

Uncultivated strands of wisteria, mulberry, hemp, and nettle were all probably used in the Jōmon period (ca 10,000 BC–ca 300 BC), their fibers twisted simply by hand. Ramie was brought to Japan from the Asian continent during the Yayoi period (ca 300 BC–ca AD 300) and cultivated for its long, strong, lustrous fibers. Ramie is known in Japanese as *choma* or *karamushi* (China grass). Hemp *(taima),* one of the oldest and most widely used *asa* fibers throughout Japanese history, is sometimes referred to as *hon'asa,* or the original, most basic form of *asa*. Flax was not grown in Japan until modern times. Linen is sometimes called *seiyō asa* (Western *asa*).

Asa fibers are strong, comparatively stiff, and cool. Comfortable in summer, they provide little protection in winter but they were the only fibers available to the general populace until the important introduction of cotton late in the Muromachi period (1333–1568).

Mary DUSENBURY

Asabuki Eiji (1849–1918)

Businessman associated with the MITSUBISHI and MITSUI conglomerates. Born in Bungo Province (now part of Ōita Prefecture), he graduated from Keiō Gijuku (now Keiō University). He joined Mitsubishi Shōkai (later Mitsubishi Corporation) in 1878; in 1891 he became director of Kanegafuchi Bōseki (later KANEBŌ, LTD), a textile company controlled by Mitsui, and revived its fortunes. In 1894 he joined Mitsui and by 1902 was in charge of the entire Mitsui group of enterprises. A liberal and member of the political club KŌJUN-SHA, he worked actively in support of party government.

Asada Gōryū (1734–1799)

Pioneer of modern astronomy in 18th-century Japan. Born in the Kitsuki domain (now part of Ōita Prefecture); son of the Confucian scholar-physician Ayabe Keisai (1676–1750). He succeeded his father as domainal physician in 1767 but soon abandoned the post to pursue his interest in astronomy. He went to Ōsaka and changed his surname. Using Chinese translations of Western scientific works, he studied mathematics, calendar science, and astronomy. Asada improved existing astronomical instruments and formulated several fundamental laws of astronomy. He is credited with having arrived independently at Kepler's third law.

Asada Sōhaku (1815–1894)

Prominent physician in traditional Chinese medicine (kampō). Real name Asada Koretsune. Born in Shinano Province (now Nagano Prefecture), he studied kampō in Kyōto and later practiced in Edo (now Tōkyō). He served as a physician to the shogunal household, and after the Meiji Restoration (1868), to the imperial court. Asada is credited with having systematized kampō, insisting that research and therapy went hand in hand.   YAMADA Terutane

asagao → morning glories

Asahi

City in northeastern Chiba Prefecture, central Honshū. Asahi developed as a market town for agricultural produce from the surrounding area and marine produce from nearby KUJŪKURIHAMA. Although rice is still cultivated, there has been increasing industrialization, centering on the processing of marine products. Pop: 35,721.

Asahi Breweries, Ltd

(Asahi Bīru). A firm that produces and distributes beer, soft drinks, whiskey, and wines. Asahi ranks third, behind Kirin and Sapporo, among Japanese beer brewers. The company also operates restaurants and manufactures pharmaceuticals and glass products. It was founded in 1949 with the splitting up of the Dai Nippon Breweries. Sales for 1981 came to ￥198.4 billion (US $906.2 million), of which 79 percent came from beer, 20 percent from soft drinks, and 1 percent from other sources. The company was capitalized at ￥11 billion (US $50.2 million) the same year. The head office is located in Tōkyō.

Asahi Broadcasting Corporation (ABC)

(Asahi Hōsō). A commercial radio and television broadcasting company serving the greater Ōsaka area. Company offices are located in Ōsaka and the main transmitters in Ikoma, Nara Prefecture. The company began operation as a radio station in 1951, funded by the Ōsaka headquarters of the ASAHI SHIMBUN, one of Japan's largest national daily newspapers. During the next 20 years it went through a number of changes in business and network affiliation. In 1975 it became a major station in the All Nippon News Network (ANN). This network is part of the ASAHI NATIONAL BROADCASTING CO, LTD, which is controlled by Asahi shimbun. ABC programs featuring humor of the Ōsaka area have become popular nationwide.   NAKASA Hideo

Asahi Chemical Industry Co, Ltd

(Asahi Kasei Kōgyō). General chemical firm engaged in manufacture of chemical fibers, petrochemicals, foods, pharmaceutical products, and housing and construction materials. Founded in 1923 as a producer of ammonia, it later began to manufacture rayon, explosives, and artificial flavorings. It assumed its present name in 1946. In the 1960s the company pursued a course of increased diversification, developing its manufacturing operations through an exhaustive use of raw materials and their by-products and through the application of a wide variety of technologies.

Located in Ōsaka, Asahi Chemical leads a group of 200 related companies, including such major firms as Tōyō Jōzō Co, Ltd, and Asahi Organic Chemical Industry Co, Ltd. It has 14 overseas joint-venture companies in 12 nations in Asia, Africa, Central and South America, and Europe. The firm's long-term plans call for developing such growth areas as fermentation, food products, construction materials, and housing, as well as increasing value-added revenue from its line of established products. Sales for the fiscal year ending March 1982 totaled ￥592.4 billion (US $2.46 billion), of which 80 percent came from the sale of textiles, petrochemicals, and chemical products; and 20 percent from fermented products, foods, construction materials, and housing. In the same year the company was capitalized at ￥51.8 billion (US $215.2 million).

Asahi Denka Kōgyō

Chemical company producing various types of goods, including oils, fats, and foodstuffs. Affiliated with the FURUKAWA group, which also includes the FURUKAWA ELECTRIC CO, LTD, and FURUKAWA CO, LTD. Established in 1917, the company first produced caustic soda, hardened oil, margarine, liquid chlorine, and ethylene glycol. After World War II it moved into the petrochemical field. In 1972 it established with Procter and Gamble of the United States a joint-venture company called Procter and Gamble Sun Home for domestic sale of soap and detergents. It has a joint-manufacturing company in Malaysia. Sales for the fiscal year ending March 1982 totaled ￥68.4 billion (US $284.3 million) and the company was capitalized at ￥2.2 billion (US $9.3 million). The head office is located in Tōkyō.

Asahigawa

River in central Okayama Prefecture, western Honshū, flowing south from the Hiruzen Mountains to the Inland Sea. There are many deep gorges and valley basins in its upper reaches, and the broad Okayama Plain is in its lower reaches. The river was once used for transportation; a multipurpose dam has been constructed to harness its waters for agriculture, industry, and other uses. Length: 150 km (93 mi).

Asahi Glass Co, Ltd

(Asahi Garasu). Manufacturer of glass products used in construction, automobiles, television sets, soda compounds, and chemical and ceramic products. A member of the MITSUBISHI group of companies, it is the largest Japanese manufacturer of glass products. Founded in 1907 by Iwasaki Toshiya, it was the first Japanese firm to succeed in the commercial production of plate glass. It quickly established the basis for its current vertically integrated production system by initiating the manufacture of firebrick in 1916 and soda ash in 1917, ensuring its own supply of raw materials for plate glass. In 1944 it merged with Nihon Kasei Kōgyō under the name Mitsubishi Kasei Kōgyō, but assumed its present name after the dissolution of the merger in 1950. It expanded its range of operations after World War II to include the production of safety glass for automobiles, parts for television sets, and halogenous compounds. The company's drawing process for plate glass and ion-exchange membrane electrodialysis process for producing caustic soda have been exported and won praise from specialists abroad. In 1981 total sales were ￥474 billion (US $2.2 billion), of which the sale of glass products accounted for 59 percent, chemical products 37 percent, and ceramics 4 percent. In the same year the export rate was 8 percent and the firm was capitalized at ￥49 billion (US $223.8 million). Corporate headquarters are in Tōkyō.

Asahikawa

City in central Hokkaidō; located on the river Ishikarigawa. Asahikawa developed during the Meiji period (1868–1912) as a government-sponsored farmer-militia (TONDENHEI) settlement. From 1902 it was the home of the Seventh Army division, and today a Self Defense Force division is stationed there. It has developed as an industrial city since World War II, the principal industries being lumber, furniture production, paper pulp, and brewing. There is an airport, and the city is a gateway to Daisetsuzan National Park. Pop: 352,620.

Asahi Mountains

(Asahi Sanchi). Mountain range in central Yamagata Prefecture, northern Honshū, extending about 60 km (37 mi) north to south. Its highest peak is Ōasahidake (1,870 m; 6,134 ft). Largely granite, with many scenic gorges and rushing streams, the mountains have both alpine plants and virgin growth of Japanese beech. Wildlife includes bears, monkeys, and antelopes. Located within the Bandai–Asahi National Park, these peaks are popular with mountain climbers and skiers.

Asahi National Broadcasting Co, Ltd

(Terebi Asahi). A Tōkyō-based commercial broadcasting company serving the Kantō (eastern Honshū) area. Established in 1959 as an educational station with support from the ASAHI SHIMBUN, one of Japan's largest national daily newspapers, and other sources. At the time of founding it was known as Nippon Educational Television (NET). Because of operational problems and because the public-operated Japan Broadcasting Corporation (Nippon Hōsō Kyōkai or NHK) also had an educational network, it switched to general programming in 1973. Funding by *Asahi shimbun* increased over the years, and the firm adopted its present name in 1977. It is affiliated with the All Nippon News Network (ANN), which comprises a total of 10 commercial stations. In 1979 the station caused a stir in the Japanese television world by securing exclusive rights to cover the 1980 Moscow Olympics.   *NAKASA Hideo*

Asahina Yasuhiko (1881–1975)

Pharmacologist. His research in plant chemistry and pharmacognosy, particularly in relation to drugs used in traditional Chinese medicine *(kampō)*, contributed to the development of pharmacology in Japan. Born in Tōkyō, he graduated from Tōkyō University. He studied in Germany and Switzerland and taught at Tōkyō University from 1918 to 1941. He received the Order of Culture in 1943.

Asahi Optical Co, Ltd

(Asahi Kōgaku Kōgyō). Manufacturer of cameras and optical and medical equipment. It uses the trade name Asahi Pentax. Founded in 1938, the firm invented the world's first mechanism for the quick return of a camera mirror in 1954, an invention that ushered in the era of the single-lens reflex camera. Today the company manufactures single-lens reflex cameras of every type and size; it is also planning for increased diversification, chiefly in the field of medical equipment. Its export ratio in 1981 was 72 percent, and it controlled nine overseas subsidiaries. Sales for the fiscal year ending March 1982 totaled ¥57.7 billion (US $240 million) and capitalization stood at ¥5.8 billion (US $24.1 million). Corporate headquarters are in Tōkyō.

Asahi shimbun

One of Japan's oldest and largest national daily newspapers. It began publication in Ōsaka in 1879 as the *Ōsaka asahi shimbun*, a small illustrated paper, with Kimura Noboru as owner, MURAYAMA RYŌHEI as company president and publisher, and Tsuda Tei as managing editor. In 1881 the *Asahi* adopted an all-news format, and, steering an independent course, grew under the astute management of Murayama and UENO RIICHI into an influential commercial daily with a large circulation. The paper branched out to Tōkyō in 1888 as the *Tōkyō asahi shimbun* after buying out the *Mezamashi shimbun,* and took the lead over other national newspaper companies.

At the time of the RICE RIOTS OF 1918, the *Asahi* was critical of the government. The authorities, in turn, found cause to suppress the paper over a minor item said to have injured the emperor's dignity. The softening of editorial policy that followed led many of the reporters on the staff to resign in protest, including noted journalist HASEGAWA NYOZEKAN. Still, the *Asahi* managed to maintain a liberal stance. Though ostensibly middle-of-the-road, it tended in fact to be progressive, and influenced public opinion widely.

Because of its liberal position, the paper's offices were vandalized at the time of the FEBRUARY 26TH INCIDENT. It came under increasingly sharp criticism from the right wing during the 1930s. Prior to World War II, when controls over free speech were tightened and many papers were forced to merge, the Tōkyō and Ōsaka papers joined under the present banner. Owing to a democratization movement within the company, the newspaper was run by officials chosen through company-wide elections for a five-year period following the war, but in 1951 the Murayama and Ueno families again took over management. In 1959 the *Asahi* led the world as the first newspaper

published by facsimile at its Sapporo regional office. Over the years it has become known for its progressive views, cultural orientation, and in-depth coverage of domestic and foreign affairs.

The *Asahi* also publishes the English-language daily, *Asahi Evening News;* Japan's oldest weekly magazine, *Shūkan asahi* (Weekly Asahi, established in 1922); other periodicals; and books. The company has four main offices in Japan, located in Tōkyō, Ōsaka, Nagoya, and Kita Kyūshū, and a branch office in Sapporo. Overseas bureaus are located in Washington, London, Cairo, and Singapore, and offices are maintained in 21 other cities around the world. The *Asahi* carries the Associated Press (AP), Reuter, and Tass wire services, and subscribes to the *New York Times* and *The Times* (London) news services. Circulation: 7.5 million (1980).

Asahi ware

(asahi-yaki). Pottery made at Uji, Kyōto Prefecture, since the early 17th century. The kiln is said to have been one of the seven favorites of tea master KOBORI ENSHŪ (1579–1647). Most products were tea-ceremony wares and reflected the influence of Korean pottery, perhaps by way of KARATSU WARE and HAGI WARE. Asahi ware tends to be heavy, especially the tea bowls, and is made of a coarse, sandy clay. A characteristic mottled pink "deer-spotting" can often be seen on the uneven surface of the clay under a translucent glaze that fires with greenish or bluish tones. Perhaps the best wares were produced from the middle to the end of the 17th century, but, as early pieces were neither dated nor stamped, identification is difficult. The kiln is still in production and is well known for its modern, computer-controlled technology.   *David HALE*

Asai Chū (1856–1907)

Artist name *(gō)* Mokugo; Mokugyo. Western-style painter known for his lyrical watercolors. Born in Edo (now Tōkyō). He studied Japanese-style painting as a child and in 1875 entered the Shōgidō, a school of Western-style painting sponsored by Kunisawa Shinkurō (1847–77), who had returned recently from England. The next year he entered the newly established Technical Fine Arts School (Kōbu Bijutsu Gakkō) and studied with Antonio FONTANESI (1818–82). After Fontanesi returned to Italy, Asai and 10 other classmates, including Koyama Shōtarō (1857–1916), left the school and formed the Jūichijikai (Eleven Character Society). Asai also became a teacher at the Tōkyō Normal School. In 1889 he was instrumental in establishing the Meiji Bijutsukai (Meiji Art Society), Japan's first group of Western-style painters. His most representative works of this period are *Shumpo* (Fields in Spring) and *Shūkaku* (Harvest). He accompanied the Japanese army during the Sino-Japanese War (1894–95) and completed *Ryojun sen'eki sōsaku zu,* based on what he had seen of the battle for Port Arthur (Ch: Lüshun [now part of Lüda]). It won second prize at the fourth Domestic Industrial Exposition held in Kyōto in 1895. He was appointed professor at the Tōkyō Bijutsu Gakkō (now Tōkyō University of Fine Arts and Music) in 1898 and together with KURODA SEIKI (1866–1924) taught Western-style painting. From 1900 Asai studied in France for two years, working mainly in Grez, which he called a "fairyland." Greatly influenced by the impressionists, he completed numerous paintings, including *Gurē no aki* (Autumn at Grez-sur-Loing) in oil and *Fuyu kodachi* (Trees in Winter) and *Gurē no hashi* (Bridge in Grez) in watercolor. After returning to Japan he was appointed professor at the newly opened Kyōto Kōtō Kōgei Gakkō (Kyōto Higher School of Design). He founded the Shōgoin Institute of Western Art in his Kyōto residence in 1903. In 1905 the institute was reorganized as the Kansai Art School. Among artists he trained at the school were Ishii Hakutei (1882–1958), YASUI SŌTARŌ (1888–1955), and UMEHARA RYŪZABURŌ (b 1888). In 1906 he was commissioned by the crown prince to create a design for a tapestry, *Bushi no yamagari* (Hunting in the Mountains). In 1907 when the Ministry of Education's Art Exhibition was inaugurated, he was appointed a judge of the Western-style painting section. Aside from painting, Asai showed brilliant talent in designing and instructed artists in Kyōto in the fields of pottery, lacquer ware, and dyeing.   *TAKUMI Hideo*

Asai family

More properly called Azai. *Daimyō* family of the Sengoku period (1467–1568). The Asai had been in the service of the KYŌGOKU FAMILY of northern Ōmi Province (now Shiga Prefecture) since the mid-1400s, but early in the 16th century Asai Sukemasa (d 1542) turned against his lords and seized their domain. He built a castle at Odani (now Kohoku Chō, Shiga Prefecture) and extended his power by forming alliances with the ASAKURA FAMILY of Echizen (now part of Fukui Prefecture) and the Saitō family of Mino (now part of Gifu Prefecture). Although Sukemasa's grandson ASAI NAGAMASA was married to the sister of the hegemon ODA NOBUNAGA, he fought against Nobunaga in the Battle of ANEGAWA (1570). Defeated, he nonetheless maintained his resistance until he was forced to commit suicide under siege by Nobunaga's forces in 1573, whereupon the Asai became extinct.

Asai Nagamasa (1545–1573)

Sometimes called Azai Nagamasa. Prominent *daimyō* of the Sengoku period (1467–1568); lord of Odani Castle in northern Ōmi Province (now Kohoku Chō, Shiga Prefecture). Although he was married to ODA NOBUNAGA's sister Oichi (ODANI NO KATA), Nagamasa turned against him in 1570; this action forced Nobunaga to break off an invasion of the domains of ASAKURA YOSHIKAGE, whom Nagamasa had joined in the effort to check the emergent hegemon. On 30 July 1570 (Genki 1.6.28) the armies of Nagamasa and Yoshikage were defeated in the Battle of ANEGAWA by the joint forces of Nobunaga and the future shōgun TOKUGAWA IEYASU, but Nagamasa and Yoshikage continued their struggle against Nobunaga. Nagamasa's strategic domains in northern Ōmi became the scene of three years of incessant warfare as Nobunaga moved constantly from one front to another in order to frustrate the attempt of a widespread coalition to encircle and eliminate him. After driving the shōgun ASHIKAGA YOSHIAKI, the coalition's presumed leader, out of Kyōto in the summer of 1573, Nobunaga turned his attention to Nagamasa and Yoshikage, invaded Yoshikage's home base in Echizen Province (now part of Fukui Prefecture), and destroyed him in a swift campaign. Deprived of his indispensable ally and assaulted by the troops of Nobunaga's captain Kinoshita Tōkichirō, Asai Nagamasa committed suicide on 24 September 1573 (Tenshō 1.8.28). Tōkichirō, destined to gain fame later as the national unifier TOYOTOMI HIDEYOSHI, was rewarded with the old Asai domains, and thereby became a daimyō. *George* ELISON

Asai Ryōi (?–1691)

Writer of KANA-ZŌSHI, a kind of popular prose fiction, in the early Edo period. A RŌNIN (masterless *samurai*), he later became a priest at the Honjōji, a temple in Kyōto. Though an erudite, serious scholar, he wrote on a wide variety of subjects in a simple, direct style, aiming to reach as wide an audience as possible. His principal works include the *Tōkaidō meisho ki* (ca 1660, A Record of Famous Spots along the Tōkaidō), a descriptive travel guide; *Otogibōko* (1666) and *Inuhariko* (1692), collections of ghost stories, many of which are adaptations of Chinese and Korean tales; *Kanninki* (1655, Notes on Patience), a didactic treatise; and *Ukiyo monogatari* (ca 1660, Tales of the Floating World), a satirical, episodic account of the life of a bumbling priest named Ukiyobō. In the last work a distinction is first made between the two meanings of the term *ukiyo*—the medieval Buddhist idea of a "world of sadness" and the modern come-what-may idea of the "floating world" that is the central theme of much Edo fiction. It was a precursor of the early works by his contemporary Ihara SAIKAKU (1642–92). Asai also wrote scholarly books, including many commentaries on Buddhist texts and studies of the Japanese classics. He is considered to be Japan's first professional writer.

Asaka

City in southeastern Saitama Prefecture located about 20 km (12 mi) northwest of Tōkyō. Asaka developed as a POST-STATION TOWN during the Edo period (1600–1868). Long associated with the copper-rolling industry, more recently it has become a satellite city of Tōkyō. A US Army camp in Asaka was returned to Japan in 1974, and it currently serves as a base for the Japanese Self Defense Forces. Pop: 90,088.

Asaka Canal

(Asaka Sosui). Man-made irrigation canal in central Fukushima Prefecture, northern Honshū, running from Lake Inawashiro through the Kōriyama and Sukagawa basins. It provides water for irrigation, hydroelectric power, drinking, and industrial purposes. The main canal was opened in 1882 and a new section was completed in 1951. Length (main canal): 95 km (59 mi).

Asaka Tampaku (1656–1737)

Confucian scholar of the Edo period (1600–1868); an early leader of the MITO SCHOOL. Born in the domain of Mito (now part of Ibaraki Prefecture), he studied with SHU SHUNSUI, the refugee scholar from Ming China. Acclaimed for his erudition, especially in history, he was named in 1693 head of the SHŌKŌKAN, the bureau established by TOKUGAWA MITSUKUNI, the *daimyō* of Mito, for the compilation of the monumental history of Japan, DAI NIHON SHI. Although an adherent of the Zhu Xi (Chu Hsi) school of Neo-Confucianism (see SHUSHIGAKU), and on that account a friend of ARAI HAKUSEKI, he corresponded widely with Confucian scholars of other persuasions, including OGYŪ SORAI.

Asakawa Kan'ichi (1873–1948)

Historian. Born in Fukushima Prefecture, he graduated from Tōkyō Semmon Gakkō (now Waseda University). After attending Dartmouth College, he received his PhD in 1902 from Yale University for his study of the TAIKA REFORM. From 1910 to 1942 he taught Japanese and medieval European history at Yale, gaining fame for his comparative studies of feudal institutions in Japan and Europe. Among his numerous English publications is *The Documents of Iriki* (1929; rev ed, 1953), a summary and translation of some 250 documents covering the years 1135 to 1870 in the possession of the Irikiin family of Iriki, Kagoshima Prefecture.

Asakura family

Warrior family of the Muromachi period (1333–1568). Asakura Hirokage (1255–1352) helped the Ashikaga general Shiba Takatsune (1305–67) to defeat NITTA YOSHISADA in 1338 and established himself at Kuromaru Castle in Echizen Province (now part of Fukui Prefecture) as a leading vassal of the SHIBA FAMILY, the military governors (SHUGO) of the area. His son Masakage (1314–72) expanded the Asakura holdings in Echizen, becoming a powerful local lord (KOKUJIN). Asakura Toshikage (or Takakage; 1428–81) took advantage of a succession dispute in the Shiba family to seize all of Echizen. For his services in the ŌNIN WAR (1467–77) the shōgun made him *shugo* of that province in 1471, and he gained the status of a *daimyō*. Toshikage built a large fortification near Ichijōdani (now part of the city of Fukui), and he and his successors transformed Ichijōdani into a cultural center to rival Kyōto. The "house laws" that he established for the governance of his domain were among the best known of their kind (see ASAKURA TOSHIKAGE, 17-ARTICLE CODE OF). The Asakura family line was extinguished in 1573, when the national unifier ODA NOBUNAGA devastated Ichijōdani Castle and Toshikage's grandson ASAKURA YOSHIKAGE committed suicide.

Asakura Fumio (1883–1964)

Western-style sculptor. Born in Ōita Prefecture, he graduated from the Tōkyō Bijutsu Gakkō (now Tōkyō University of Fine Arts and Music) and later taught there. Noted for a disciplined technique and a realistic style of representation, he was a frequent prizewinner in the annual government-sponsored Bunten exhibitions. He received the Order of Culture in 1948. Important works include *Hakamori* (1910, Grave Keeper) and *Ebamu neko* (1942, Cat Consuming Its Prey). His eldest daughter, Asakura Setsu (b 1922), is a painter and designer of stage sets.

Asakura Toshikage, 17-Article Code of

(Asakura Toshikage Jūshichikajō). Also known as Asakura Takakage Jōjō and under other titles; some variants are organized in 16 articles only. A set of household precepts (KAKUN) attributed to Asakura Toshikage (more properly called Takakage; 1428–81), who became military governor (SHUGO) of Echizen Province (now part of Fukui Prefecture) in 1471. The ASAKURA FAMILY continued to rule the province as SENGOKU DAIMYŌ until 1573, when ASAKURA YOSHIKAGE was destroyed by the national hegemon ODA NOBUNAGA. The injunctions are meant to guide successive heads of the Asakura family in their demeanor and the government of their domain. Some of the articles, notably the last two, contain such general maxims as "A well-kept domain is a reflection of the ruler's care" and "To discriminate between right and wrong, good and evil, is what is meant by compassionate judgment." Others are more specific, such as article 14 (15): "Aside from the residence of the Asakura, no other fortified places shall be built in the province. All men of substance

Asamayama

The northern slope of Asamayama as seen from the village of Tsumagoi in Gumma Prefecture.

shall move to [the daimyō's castle town] Ichijōdani; left in the villages shall be [the daimyō's] intendants (DAIKAN) alone." This famous regulation, often cited as ahead of its time, reflects the conditions which prevailed in Japan from the late 16th century onward, rather than the actuality of the Asakura domain in the Sengoku period (1467–1568), and renders the attribution of authorship suspect. If Toshikage indeed compiled these injunctions while he was *shugo* of Echizen (or after he took the tonsure in 1479), then they undoubtedly underwent subsequent redactions at the hands of others. An abbreviated translation is found in George Sansom, *A History of Japan, 1334–1615* (1961).   *George Elison*

Asakura Yoshikage (1533–1573)

Prominent *daimyō* of the Sengoku period (1467–1568); the fifth and last lord of the ASAKURA FAMILY of Echizen Province (now part of Fukui Prefecture). The Asakura displaced the SHIBA FAMILY as military governors (SHUGO) of that province in 1471. Their castle town of Ichijōdani (now part of the city of Fukui), a remote fastness, was transformed into a cultural center that emulated Kyōto in refinement.

Yoshikage became master of this realm in 1548, and his great captain Asakura Norikage (1474–1555) predicted that his would be a period of peace. That period, interrupted by military expeditions into Kaga Province (now part of Ishikawa Prefecture) in 1555 and 1564, came to an end in 1570, when Yoshikage's domains were invaded by ODA NOBUNAGA, and Yoshikage became active in a coalition intent on checking the emergent hegemon. The armies of Yoshikage and his ally ASAI NAGAMASA were defeated, however, by Nobunaga in the Battle of ANEGAWA on 30 July 1570 (Genki 1.6.28), and Yoshikage's fortunes declined. For three years he was able to avoid a decisive encounter, undertaking only occasional sallies. But in 1573, when he again went to Nagamasa's assistance, he was defeated in Ōmi Province (now Shiga Prefecture) and chased back to Echizen by Nobunaga. Abandoning Ichijōdani to the enemy, Yoshikage fled toward the mountains of eastern Echizen, but was betrayed by his kinsman Asakura Kageaki (d 1574) and committed suicide at Rokubō Kenshōji (now the city of Ōno) on 16 September 1573 (Tenshō 1.8.20). Echizen was swept by an organized rising of the Buddhist Jōdo Shin sect (see IKKŌ IKKI) six months later, but it was reconquered by Nobunaga in 1575.   *George Elison*

Asakusa Bunko

(Asakusa Library). Five libraries formed separately during the Edo (1600–1868) and Meiji (1868–1912) periods in the Asakusa section of Tōkyō. The first, also known as the Bokusai Bunko, was the personal collection of Itazaka Bokusai (1578–1655), a physician to the Tokugawa shogunate. Reputedly the first private library in Japan to be opened to the public (1655?), it was destroyed in the great fire of 1657. Three private libraries, all named Asakusa Bunko, were subsequently founded by the *daimyō* Hotta Masamori (1608–51), the Tokugawa vassal Kimura Shigesuke, and the scholar Ōtsuki Joden (1845–1931). The fifth Asakusa Bunko comprised the assembled

collections of Japanese and foreign books in the former Shojakukan Library of the Ministry of Education. Housed in an old rice granary, it was opened to the public in November 1875. Its books have since been dispersed among several libraries, including the Ueno branch of the National Diet Library and the Cabinet Library.

Theodore F. Welch

Asama Hot Spring

(Asama Onsen). Located in the city of Matsumoto, Nagano Prefecture, central Honshū. A simple thermal spring; temperature approximately 50°C (122°F). Established around the beginning of the 17th century by the lords of the Matsumoto domain. Located in an area serving as a base for mountain climbers in the northern Alps (Hida Mountains).

Asamayama

Triple active volcano on the border of Gumma and Nagano prefectures, central Honshū. It has erupted some 50 times in recorded history, causing great damage. On its northern slope there is a rock formation called ONIOSHIDASHI, formed by lava flows at the time of the great eruption of 1783. A volcano observation station belonging to Tōkyō University is located on its eastern slope. Karuizawa, on the southern slope, is a popular summer resort. Part of Jōshin'etsu Kōgen National Park. Height: 2,542 m (8,338 ft).

Asami Keisai (1652–1712)

Scholar of Neo-Confucianism (SHUSHIGAKU). Born in Ōmi Province (now Shiga Prefecture), Keisai initially earned his living as a physician. He became a leading disciple of the Neo-Confucian scholar YAMAZAKI ANSAI in Kyōto, but their relationship was broken off when he disagreed with Ansai's Shintō doctrines (SUIKA SHINTŌ). After Ansai's death, however, Keisai became the most faithful transmitter of his master's teaching. A severe disciplinarian, Keisai severed ties with his students and friends over the slightest omission of *giri* (righteous duty; see GIRI AND NINJŌ). For Keisai, *giri* was the basis of scholarship, indeed of life itself; he praised the FORTY-SEVEN RŌNIN INCIDENT as a display of loyalty. He lived in poverty, steadfastly refusing all offers of official employment, and reportedly never left Kyōto. His treatise SEIKEN IGEN influenced members of the proimperial, antishogunate movement (see SONNŌ JŌI) in the later part of the Edo period (1600–1868).

Asamushi Hot Spring

(Asamushi Onsen). Located in the city of Aomori, Aomori Prefecture, northern Honshū. A weak, common salt spring containing gypsum; water temperature 30–78°C (86–172°F). Facing Aomori Bay, this scenic hot spring is part of the Asamushi–Natsudomari Peninsula Prefectural Natural Park. The resort area surrounding this hot spring, a representative one of the Tōhoku region, features a bathing beach and an aquarium affiliated with Tōhoku University.

Asano Nagamasa (1547–1611)

Military commander and one of the Five Commissioners (Gobugyō) of the Azuchi–Momoyama period (1568–1600); father of ASANO YOSHINAGA. Born in Owari Province (now part of Aichi Prefecture). Nagamasa served as both general and administrator for the hegemon ODA NOBUNAGA and his successor TOYOTOMI HIDEYOSHI. A brother-in-law of Hideyoshi, in 1585 he was appointed senior member of the Gobugyō and was responsible for implementing the military ruler's policy decisions. Two years later he was appointed lord of Obama Castle in Wakasa Province (now part of Fukui Prefecture). After participating in Hideyoshi's invasion of Korea in 1592, he was made *daimyō* of Kai Province (now Yamanashi Prefecture), a domain of moderate size. Although Nagamasa resigned his posts after Hideyoshi's death in 1598, he emerged from retirement to fight with his son Yoshinaga under TOKUGAWA IEYASU in the Battle of SEKIGAHARA (1600).

Asano Sōichirō (1848–1930)

Businessman, founder of the Asano *zaibatsu*, a financial and industrial combine. Born in what is now Toyama Prefecture, Asano moved to Tōkyō in 1871. After attempting a number of other businesses, he made his fortune in coal and coke. In 1884 he bought a government-built cement factory and established the Asano Cement Co (later the NIHON CEMENT CO, LTD). From this base, Asano gradually expanded into many other areas of business, including coal, oil, water power development, shipping, trading, dredge reclamation works, shipbuilding, and iron and steel. Closely linked with YASUDA ZENJIRŌ (1838–1921), a powerful banker, Asano eventually formed the Asano zaibatsu by placing 30 direct subsidiaries and 50 affiliates under the control of Asano Dōzoku Kaisha, a holding company created in 1918.   KOBAYAKAWA Yōichi

Asano Yoshinaga (1576–1613)

Daimyō of the Azuchi-Momoyama period (1568–1600). Son of ASANO NAGAMASA, one of the trusted generals of TOYOTOMI HIDE-YOSHI. With his father, he joined Hideyoshi's ODAWARA CAMPAIGN (1590), in which Hideyoshi was established as hegemon, and the invasion of Korea in 1592 (see INVASIONS OF KOREA IN 1592 AND 1597). For their services, father and son were awarded the province of Kai (now Yamanashi Prefecture). When Hideyoshi's nephew TOYOTOMI HIDETSUGU was suspected of treasonous behavior, Yoshinaga was wrongly accused of complicity by ISHIDA MITSU-NARI and exiled to distant Noto Province (now part of Ishikawa Prefecture) in 1595. Pardoned the following year, he joined the second expedition to Korea in 1597 and fought with KATŌ KIYOMASA at Yolsan (J: Urusan) in one of the most savage battles of the war. Yoshinaga returned to Japan after Hideyoshi's death. In the decisive Battle of SEKIGAHARA (1600) he took the side of TOKUGAWA IEYASU and distinguished himself in the attack on Gifu Castle. He was rewarded with a fief assessed at 376,000 koku (see KOKUDAKA) in Kii Province (now Wakayama Prefecture).

Asanuma Gumi Co, Ltd

Ōsaka-based construction company. Founded in Nara Prefecture in 1892, the company has undertaken construction of many public buildings, such as schools and hospitals. Before World War II the company constructed Japanese military installations and, after the war, American military bases on Okinawa. After the 1950s, the company expanded its business to include civil engineering. In the 1970s it began to build concrete prefabricated houses. The company has a subsidiary firm in Guam. Sales for the fiscal year ending November 1981 totaled ¥134.7 billion (US $602 million), of which the share of architecture and building was 75 percent, civil engineering 24 percent, and real estate 1 percent. The company was capitalized at ¥3.5 billion (US $15.6 million) the same year.

Asanuma Inejirō (1898–1960)

Socialist politician. Born in Miyakejima, Tōkyō Prefecture, he graduated from Waseda University in 1923. While still a student, he joined the fledgling Japan Communist Party and took part in numerous social movements. In 1924 he was sentenced to five months' hard labor for participating in a violent demonstration during the ASHIO COPPER MINE LABOR DISPUTE. Later he helped to form several prewar socialist parties, incuding the RŌDŌ NŌMINTŌ (Labor–Farmer Party). Elected to the House of Representatives on the SHAKAI TAISHŪTŌ (Socialist Masses Party) slate in 1936, he served for 20 years in nine Diets. Immediately after World War II, he helped to organize the JAPAN SOCIALIST PARTY, eventually becoming its secretary-general and chairman. During a visit to Beijing (Peking) in March 1959, he issued the "Asanuma statement," a denunciation of American imperialism as the common enemy of Japan and China, which aroused considerable controversy in Japan. On 12 October 1960 he was stabbed to death by a right-wing youth while giving a speech at a political rally, a televised event seen by thousands. He was a tireless speaker and was known as a pragmatic rather than a rigidly ideological socialist.

Asayama Bontō (1349–ca 1427)

(also known as Bontō An). Renga (linked verse; see RENGA AND HAIKAI) poet and master; Buddhist priest. His lay name was Morotsuna. A household retainer of the Ashikaga family, he served the shōgun Ashikaga Yoshimitsu from an early age, studying linked verse under Yoshimitsu's teacher, the famous NIJŌ YOSHIMOTO. He quickly became one of the outstanding renga poets of the day, and after Yoshimoto's death in 1388 was acknowledged the foremost master of the art. The courtly elegance of his verse was inherited

from Yoshimoto, but Bontō developed it into a distinctively evocative style greatly admired by his contemporaries. He was an influential teacher as well as a poet and critic, numbering among his disciples the famous TAKAYAMA SŌZEI (d 1455). His most important treatise is Bontō anshu hentō sho (1417, Master Bonto's Answers to Questions on Renga).   Robert H. BROWER

Asayama Nichijō (?–1577)

Buddhist priest and political adviser of the Sengoku (1467–1568) and Azuchi–Momoyama (1568–1600) periods. His origins are obscure, and his family name is unknown. He was supposedly born in Asayama, Izumo Province (now part of Shimane Prefecture). In 1532 he went to Kyōto, where he won the favor of Emperor Go-Nara (1496–1557; r 1526–57), who reputedly gave him the name Asayama Nichijō. After the national unifier ODA NOBUNAGA seized control of Kyōto in 1568, Nichijō became his adviser and commissioner of rebuilding (shūzen bugyō), overseeing such projects as the reconstruction of the Imperial Palace. The folowing year Nichijō engaged in a doctrinal dispute with the Jesuit priest Luis FROIS in Nobunaga's presence. Nichijō lost the debate and, embittered by his defeat, became the Jesuits' most implacable enemy and attempted to have them expelled from Japan. Nichijō's excessive hatred of the Jesuits eventually caused him to lose Nobunaga's patronage.

asceticism

The English term "asceticism" can refer to either of two Japanese terms: shugyō or kugyō. Shugyō refers to spiritual exercises undertaken for the attainment of a particular religious goal, and kugyō is a religious practice that makes suffering an effective means to attain a religious goal; kugyō is a category of shugyō. In SHINTŌ, man is understood to be originally pure in nature, and TSUMI (sin) is an adventitious or ritual impurity that may be swept away by a ritual act of cleansing. Under such conditions, there is no need for what is commonly understood as asceticism in the West. In BUDDHISM, man is considered capable of attaining enlightenment by following a set of spiritual exercises, including kugyō. The exercises differ from one sect to another, and the difference is often the sect's distinguishing characteristic, for example, recitation of the NEMBUTSU for the JŌDO SECT and JŌDO SHIN SECT, recitation of the daimoku for the NICHIREN SECT, and zazen (sitting meditation) for the ZEN sect.

Various kinds of self-mortification have been used as spiritual exercises in Japanese religions. Many such practices, known as aragyō (literally, "harsh practices") as well as kugyō, were undertaken as an integral part of esoteric Buddhist (see ESOTERIC BUDDHISM) and mountain religion (SHUGENDŌ; YAMABUSHI) practices. One of the most popular was the waterfall austerities (taki no gyō) in which the practitioner performed ablutions under a waterfall. The austerities of the 12th-century priest MONGAKU at the Nachi waterfall is a famous example of this. In addition, there are fasting (danjiki), constant repetition of the nembutsu, burning parts of the body, and ritual death through burning oneself or drowning, the last mentioned being undertaken in the hope of gaining rebirth in the Pure Land.

Ascetic exercises are still carried on in present-day Japan, although they are generally limited to the TENDAI SECT and the SHINGON SECT. The Tendai practice of sennichi kaihō gyō (thousand-day mountain walking), in which a practitioner walks a circuit of 40 kilometers (25 mi) in the mountains around Mt. Hiei (HIEIZAN) for one thousand nights over a period of seven years, dates from the Heian period (794–1185).

ASEAN and Japan

The Association of Southeast Asian Nations, a regional cooperative organization, was established in August 1967 to protect the stability and security of Southeast Asia from outside intervention and to promote cooperation and mutual aid in economic, social, and cultural spheres. Member nations include Thailand, Indonesia, Malaysia, the Philippines, and Singapore.

The Soviet Union and China criticized the establishment of ASEAN as a "concentration of reactionary powers," but Japan, together with the United States, welcomed the new organization. ASEAN at first limited itself to cooperation in nonpolitical areas. However, with such developments in the early 1970s as President Richard Nixon's visit to China and the end of the Vietnam War, ASEAN moved toward a stronger emphasis on political and security matters. This change in ASEAN's nature can be seen in the declaration on the neutralization of Southeast Asia issued at Kuala Lumpur in November 1971, the Bali Declaration of February 1976, and the conclusion of a treaty of Southeast Asian friendship and cooperation. Japan has consistently supported ASEAN in the belief that the growing unity and development of ASEAN would contribute toward peace and stability in Southeast Asia.

In the first half of the 1970s, relations between Japan and ASEAN were occasionally strained by such economic problems as the controversy over the passage of Japanese oil tankers through the Malacca Strait. With the arrival of the second half of the decade, however, relations between the two parties improved greatly because of Japan's increased concern and cooperation with ASEAN as shown in the landmark Manila speech by Prime Minister FUKUDA TAKEO in August 1978. Japan has made several concrete cooperative proposals to ASEAN, including financial assistance totaling $1 billion for the latter's so-called five major projects as well as financial cooperation in the promotion of cultural exchanges among ASEAN members. Regular meetings between Japan and ASEAN have been held once or twice a year since March 1977 when the first Japan-ASEAN forum was held in Djakarta. Besides the projects mentioned above, ASEAN has addressed the problem of preferential tariffs and worked to create the ASEBEX commodity price stabilization system (modeled after the STABEX—Stabilization of Export Earnings—system established in the West by the 1976 Lomé Treaty to stabilize the export prices of primary products). See also SOUTHEAST ASIA, THE PACIFIC ISLANDS, AND JAPAN.

Matsumoto Saburō

asebi

(Japanese andromeda). *Pieris japonica.* Also known as *ashibi* or *asebo.* An evergreen shrub of the heath family Ericaceae which grows wild in hilly areas of western Honshū, Shikoku, and Kyūshū and is widely cultivated in gardens and parks. It reaches a height of 1.5–3 meters (5–10 ft). The leaves are broad, lance-shaped, leathery and glossy, with serrated margins. In early spring, small, urn-shaped, white flowers appear in terminal clusters at the ends of the branches. Long admired by the Japanese, it is mentioned (as *ashibi*) in ten poems of the 8th-century poetry collection *Man'yōshū.* Many horticultural varieties have been developed over the years, including the *fuiri asebi,* with mottled leaves; the *usubeni asebi,* with pink flowers; the *fukurin asebi,* with white-edged leaves; and the *hime asebi,* a miniature variety. The toxins contained in *asebi* leaves and stems, which benumb cattle eating them, are used in a garden insecticide prepared from the boiled leaves. Similar to the *asebi* but deciduous are such species of the genus *Enkianthus* as the *dōdan-tsutsuji (Enkianthus perulatus),* the *shirodōdan (E. cernuus),* and the *sarasadōdan (E. campanulatus),* which are native to Japan but also cultivated in home gardens. *Matsuda Osamu*

ash-glazed wares → ceramics

Ashibetsu

City in central Hokkaidō, at the confluence of the rivers Sorachigawa and Ashibetsugawa. Its proximity to the ISHIKARI COALFIELD once made Ashibetsu the center of a flourishing coal-mining industry. Today operations are minimal, food processing and lumber being the major industries. Agricultural products include rice and potatoes. The city is within the Furano–Ashibetsu Prefectural Natural Park, which contains the man-made Lake Nokanan. Pop: 32,946.

Ashibetsudake

Mountain in central Hokkaidō; highest peak of the Yūbari Mountains. The steep eastern slope faces the Furano Basin and the western side is separated from the Sorachi Mountains by the valley of the river Ashibetsugawa. With many scenic crags and mountain flora, it is popular with climbers and skiers. Height: 1,727 m (5,665 ft).

Ashida Enosuke (1873–1951)

Educator. Born in Hyōgo Prefecture. Ashida taught from 1904 to 1921 at the elementary school attached to the Tōkyō Higher Normal School. After this period he accepted no official positions; instead, he traveled throughout the country demonstrating his teaching methods. Ashida encouraged students to select their own topics for composition; this was in marked contrast to traditional Japanese methods of teaching composition, which relied upon assigned topics (see SEIKATSU TSUZURIKATA UNDŌ). Ashida was also known for his method of teaching reading, which stressed the motivation of the student. *Sugiyama Akio*

Ashida Hitoshi (1887–1959)

Politician; prime minister in 1948. Born in Kyōto Prefecture, Ashida graduated from Tōkyō University in 1912. In 1932 he resigned from the Ministry of Foreign Affairs in protest over the MANCHURIAN INCIDENT. He joined the RIKKEN SEIYŪKAI (Friends of Constitutional Government Party) and was elected to the Diet in 1932 and in 10 subsequent elections. As head of the JAPAN TIMES from 1933 to 1940, he spoke out against military involvement in political affairs. In October 1945 Ashida joined the first postwar cabinet as minister of health and welfare. A month later, with HATOYAMA ICHIRŌ, he formed the Nihon Jiyūtō (Japan Liberal Party) but in March 1947 organized his own party, the MINSHUTŌ (Democratic Party). In June of that year he became foreign minister in the KATAYAMA TETSU cabinet, and after Katayama's resignation he formed a coalition cabinet in March 1948. During his six-months' tenure as prime minister he denied government employees the right to strike. Implicated in the SHŌWA DENKŌ SCANDAL, he was forced to resign in October 1948, was arrested the following month, and was finally acquitted in 1958. Although Ashida never regained political leadership, he became a prominent member of the Liberal Democratic Party and gained attention as an advocate of Japanese rearmament.

ashide

A decorative style of calligraphy developed during the Heian period (794–1185) in which the shapes and lines of the indigenous Japanese KANA syllabary were rendered as pictures of reeds (hence the name *ashide,* "reed script"), waterfowl, streams, rocks, and other objects associated with waterside scenery. Sketchy under-drawings of marshy scenes were commonly used to decorate the paper used for transcribing poems, and the attempt to cleverly blend the *kana* text into the decorative design on the paper may have inspired the development of *ashide,* which by the late 10th century had become one of several recognized forms of calligraphic script.

The use of the *ashide* calligraphic style as an integral compositional element in a painting or as part of the ornamental background of fine writing paper is known as *ashide-e,* or "reed script painting" and was often employed in the decoration of poetic anthologies or Buddhist sutras, resulting in a complex blend of pictorial and literary associations and allusions in the manner of a rebus. *Ashide-e* designs later came to be employed solely for their playful visual effect as decorative designs on women's embroidered trains, fans, and finely crafted lacquer ware. The number of pictorialized *kana* was quite limited, never including more than half of the over 50 *kana* in the syllabary at the time. Occasionally KANJI (Chinese characters used for writing Japanese) were also depicted in this manner. *Julia Meech-Pekarik*

ashigaru

Foot soldiers of the Muromachi (1333–1568) through Edo (1600–1868) periods. Although their origins can be traced back to the Kamakura period (1185–1333), they first achieved notoriety during the ŌNIN WAR of 1467–77, when miscellaneous soldiery (*zōhyō*), variously called NOBUSHI (armed peasants), AKUTŌ (bandits), and *hayaashi* or *ashigaru* (the "light of foot"), ravaged Kyōto. The court aristocrat and scholar ICHIJŌ KANEYOSHI viewed their emergence as a sign of social overturning (GEKOKUJŌ); and they did indeed overturn the traditional mode of warfare, replacing mounted warriors as the principal force on the battlefield.

Equipped with little or no armor, they were highly mobile; their characteristic weapon was the lance or the bow. The first to systematize *ashigaru* tactics appears to have been the 15th-century general ŌTA DŌKAN. *Ashigaru* played an increasingly crucial role in warfare after the introduction of European firearms in 1543; daimyō and such warlike religious institutions as the temples Negoroji and Honganji organized large units of musketeers (*teppō ashigaru*). The hegemon ODA NOBUNAGA put as many as 3,000 musketeers in the

Ashikaga family —— Genealogy

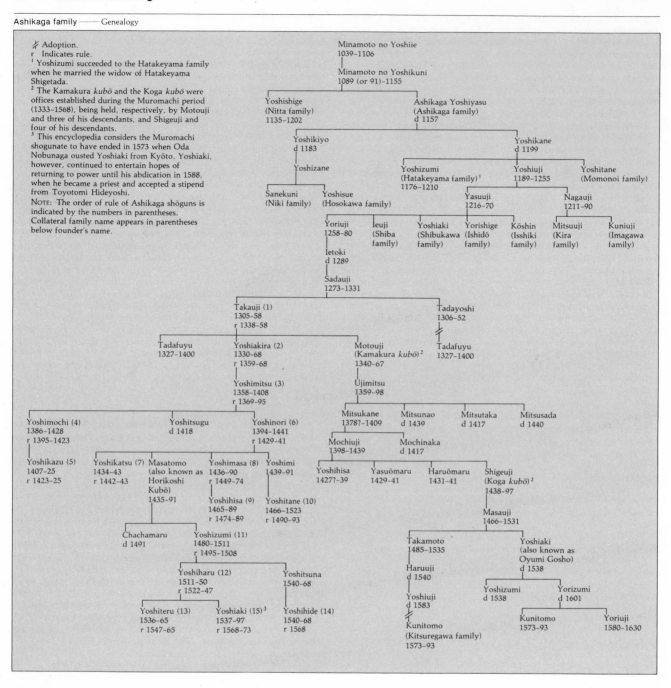

✄ Adoption.
r Indicates rule.
[1] Yoshizumi succeeded to the Hatakeyama family when he married the widow of Hatakeyama Shigetada.
[2] The Kamakura *kubō* and the Koga *kubō* were offices established during the Muromachi period (1333–1568), being held, respectively, by Motouji and three of his descendants, and Shigeuji and four of his descendants.
[3] This encyclopedia considers the Muromachi shogunate to have ended in 1573 when Oda Nobunaga ousted Yoshiaki from Kyōto. Yoshiaki, however, continued to entertain hopes of returning to power until his abdication in 1588, when he became a priest and accepted a stipend from Toyotomi Hideyoshi.
NOTE: The order of rule of Ashikaga shōguns is indicated by the numbers in parentheses. Collateral family name appears in parentheses below founder's name.

Minamoto no Yoshiie
1039–1106

Minamoto no Yoshikuni
1089 (or 91)–1155

Yoshishige
(Nitta family)
1135–1202

Ashikaga Yoshiyasu
(Ashikaga family)
d 1157

Yoshikiyo
d 1183

Yoshikane
d 1199

Yoshizane

Yoshizumi
(Hatakeyama family)[1]
1176–1210

Yoshiuji
1189–1255

Yoshitane
(Momonoi family)

Sanekuni
(Niki family)

Yoshisue
(Hosokawa family)

Yasuuji
1216–70

Nagauji
1211–90

Yoriuji
1258–80

Ieuji
(Shiba family)

Yoshiaki
(Shibukawa family)

Yorishige
(Ishidō family)

Kōshin
(Isshiki family)

Mitsuuji
(Kira family)

Kuniuji
(Imagawa family)

Ietoki
d 1289

Sadauji
1273–1331

Takauji (1)
1305–58
r 1338–58

Tadayoshi
1306–52

Tadafuyu
1327–1400

Yoshiakira (2)
1330–68
r 1359–68

Motouji
(Kamakura *kubō*)[2]
1340–67

Tadafuyu
1327–1400

Yoshimitsu (3)
1358–1408
r 1369–95

Ujimitsu
1359–98

Yoshimochi (4)
1386–1428
r 1395–1423

Yoshitsugu
d 1418

Yoshinori (6)
1394–1441
r 1429–41

Mitsukane
1378?–1409

Mitsunao
d 1439

Mitsutaka
d 1417

Mitsusada
d 1440

Yoshikazu (5)
1407–25
r 1423–25

Yoshikatsu (7)
1434–43
r 1442–43

Masatomo
(also known as Horikoshi Kubō)
1435–91

Yoshimasa (8)
1436–90
r 1449–74

Yoshimi
1439–91

Mochiuji
1398–1439

Mochinaka
d 1417

Yoshihisa (9)
1465–89
r 1474–89

Yoshitane (10)
1466–1523
r 1490–93

Yoshihisa
1427?–39

Yasuōmaru
1429–41

Haruōmaru
1431–41

Shigeuji
(Koga *kubō*)[2]
1438–97

Chachamaru
d 1491

Yoshizumi (11)
1480–1511
r 1495–1508

Masauji
1466–1531

Yoshiharu (12)
1511–50
r 1522–47

Yoshitsuna
1540–68

Takamoto
1485–1535

Yoshiaki
(also known as Oyumi Gosho)
d 1538

Yoshiteru (13)
1536–65
r 1547–65

Yoshiaki (15)[3]
1537–97
r 1568–73

Yoshihide (14)
1540–68
r 1568

Haruuji
d 1540

Yoshizumi
d 1538

Yorizumi
d 1601

Yoshiuji
d 1583

Kunitomo
1573–93

Yoriuji
1580–1630

Kunitomo
(Kitsuregawa family)
1573–93

field; they gained him his great victory in the Battle of NAGASHINO in 1575. His successor as hegemon, TOYOTOMI HIDEYOSHI, is said to have been the son of an *ashigaru*. The "light of foot" formally attained *samurai* status in the Edo period, being ranked as the lowest of that class.
George ELISON

Ashihara Yoshishige (1909–)

Electric company executive; leader of the business community in the Kansai (Ōsaka–Kōbe–Kyōto) area. Born in Kagawa Prefecture and graduated from Kyōto University, Ashihara first worked for the HANKYŪ CORPORATION and later for Kansai Haiden, Inc. After World War II, when the KANSAI ELECTRIC POWER CO, INC, was established, Ashihara became its managing director; he assumed its presidency in 1959. Concerned by the postwar shift of business and economic leadership to Tōkyō, Ashihara helped to create the Kansai Keizai Rengō Kai, a business organization dealing primarily with the interests of the Kansai area, and was its president from 1966 to 1977.
Yui Tsunehiko

Ashikaga

City in southwestern Tochigi Prefecture, central Honshū. It is known historically as the original base of the ASHIKAGA FAMILY, the founders of the Muromachi shogunate (1338–1573). The weaving of Ashikaga *meisen*, a silk fabric, dates to the 8th century. The city now mainly produces tricot, chemicals, and machinery. One may see the remains of the ASHIKAGA GAKKŌ, the largest school in medieval Japan. Pop: 165,756.

Ashikaga family

Warrior family of the 12th to 16th centuries; with the NITTA FAMILY it was one of the two major offshoots of the Seiwa Genji branch of the MINAMOTO FAMILY. The Ashikaga rose to prominence in the 14th century under ASHIKAGA TAKAUJI, who established the MUROMACHI SHOGUNATE (1338–1573). Fifteen shōguns of the Ashikaga family ruled, at least nominally, as hegemons of Japan during two and a half centuries of political and social disorder. The generous patronage that some Ashikaga shōguns lavished on the arts has won them an eminent place in Japanese cultural history.

Origins of the Ashikaga —— The Ashikaga family was founded by Yoshiyasu (d 1157), a grandson of MINAMOTO NO YOSHIIE, the most renowned forebear of the Seiwa Genji. They took the name of their family seat, the Ashikaga estate (shōen) in Shimotsuke Province (now Tochigi Prefecture). Yoshiyasu's son Yoshikane (d 1199) distinguished himself in the service of the Minamoto during the TAIRA–MINAMOTO WAR (1180–85), and in 1189 he accompanied MINAMOTO NO YORITOMO, founder and first shōgun of the Kamakura shogunate (1192–1333), in a campaign of subjugation against the ŌSHŪ FUJIWARA FAMILY in northern Japan.

It was during the time of Yoshikane that the Ashikaga began to intermarry with the HŌJŌ FAMILY, who as shogunal regents (SHIK-KEN) became the real rulers at Kamakura after the death of Yoritomo in 1199. Because of their service to the shogunate and their personal relationship with the Hōjō, during the Kamakura period the Ashikaga extended their influence beyond Shimotsuke into Shimōsa (now part of Chiba and Ibaraki prefectures) and Mikawa (now part of Aichi Prefecture).

Founding of the Muromachi Shogunate —— The Kamakura shogunate was overthrown in 1333 by loyalist forces that rallied to the cause of Emperor GO-DAIGO. Go-Daigo had been seized by Hōjō officials two years earlier for plotting against the shogunate and had been exiled to the Oki Islands in the Sea of Japan (see GENKŌ INCIDENT). His followers continued to resist in the central provinces around Kyōto, and early in 1333 the shogunate dispatched an army from Kamakura under Ashikaga Takauji in an attempt to resolve the problem once and for all. Upon reaching the central provinces, however, Takauji announced his support for the loyalists and seized the shogunate offices in Kyōto. A few weeks later NITTA YOSHI-SADA, leader of the other main branch of the Minamoto and also a vassal of the shogunate, followed Takauji's lead, changed sides, and destroyed the headquarters of the Hōjō-dominated regime in Kamakura.

Go-Daigo returned from exile to Kyōto with the intent of "restoring" direct imperial rule, but his KEMMU RESTORATION lasted scarcely three years and was notably unsuccessful. To a great extent the warrior supporters of the court were divided by a contest between Ashikaga Takauji and Nitta Yoshisada for military hegemony over Japan. Largely as a result of his clash with Yoshisada, Takauji turned against the restoration government in 1335–36, drove Go-Daigo to seek refuge in the mountainous region around Yoshino to the south, and in 1338 established the Muromachi shogunate in Kyōto.

The Ashikaga received their legitimacy from the so-called Northern Court, headed by a branch line of the imperial family that reigned in Kyōto while Go-Daigo and his lineal descendants ruled the Southern Court at Yoshino. The first half-century of the Muromachi period is known also as the age of the NORTHERN AND SOUTHERN COURTS. The imperial schism was brought to an end with the return of the southern emperor to Kyōto in 1392, when the Ashikaga promised to reinstate the practice of alternate succession to the throne by the two rival branches of the imperial family.

During the first half of the period of schism, the Ashikaga were obliged not only to wage war against the supporters of the Southern Court but also to deal with discord within the shogunate itself. So intense did the feuding among the shogunate's leaders become by midcentury that in 1352 Takauji was driven to the point of having his brother ASHIKAGA TADAYOSHI murdered.

Shogunate and Shugo under Yoshimitsu —— The Muromachi shogunate achieved its greatest authority and stability as a governing institution in the late 14th and early 15th centuries under the third shōgun, ASHIKAGA YOSHIMITSU (1358–1408; r 1369–95). By Yoshimitsu's time the Southern Court no longer posed a serious threat. In addition, a number of Ashikaga vassals holding the title of SHUGO or military governor had established territorial domains, often extending over two or more provinces, that were concentrated in the central and western regions of Honshū and the island of Shikoku. Yoshimitsu's success as shōgun lay in his ability to maintain a balance of power between the shogunate and these shugo (known also as SHUGO DAIMYŌ). The principal link between the Ashikaga shōgun and shugo was the office of shogunal deputy (KANREI), held in rotation by the chieftains of three shugo houses collateral to the Ashikaga: the HOSOKAWA, HATAKEYAMA, and SHIBA families.

Yoshimitsu's sons Ashikaga Yoshimochi (1386–1428) and ASHIKAGA YOSHINORI (1394–1441) provided firm leadership in the early 15th century. But even during this time there appeared clear signs of a weakening of the Ashikaga hegemony. The Kantō region, which was administered by the head of a branch line of the Ashikaga who styled himself Kantō KUBŌ (literally, "shōgun of the east"; see KANTŌ KANREI), had never been properly subordinate to the shogunate, and it became necessary during Yoshinori's time to take punitive steps against the kubō Ashikaga Mochiuji (1398–1439) that led to his suicide in 1439. Although the recalcitrant Mochiuji was thus eliminated, there was no one to take his place, and the Kantō region gradually slipped from Ashikaga control. Meanwhile, internal dissension in the form of succession disputes began to plague some of the great shugo houses, including the kanrei houses of Shiba and Hatakeyama. The balance of power between shōgun and shugo, which was the basis of the Ashikaga hegemony, became increasingly precarious.

Decline of the Shogunate —— The ŌNIN WAR, which was fought largely in Kyōto during the decade 1467–77, hastened the end of the Ashikaga hegemony. Portended by the various shugo succession disputes mentioned above, it was precipitated by a dispute within the Ashikaga family itself over the successor to the eighth shōgun, ASHIKAGA YOSHIMASA. In the fighting that ensued, each side was supported by contending factions within the Shiba and Hatakeyama houses. The war finally came to an end in 1477; however, the Ashikaga hegemony had been destroyed and Japan had been plunged into the century of disunion known as the "Warring States" or SEN-GOKU PERIOD.

For the remainder of the Muromachi period the Ashikaga shōguns exercised little power and became in effect the puppets of their leading vassals. Out of the turmoil of the Sengoku period emerged a new class of barons or DAIMYŌ who established territorial domains throughout the country and set the stage for a dynamic process of military unification in the late 16th century. By the time of the first of the great unifiers, ODA NOBUNAGA (1534–82), the Ashikaga shogunate was utterly moribund, and Nobunaga, who tolerated its continuance at least in name for five years after entering Kyōto in 1568 and beginning the major process of unification, finally deposed the 15th shōgun, ASHIKAGA YOSHIAKI (1537–97). Thenceforth, until the early years of the Meiji period (1868–1912), the Ashikaga survived as a minor and totally inconspicuous daimyō family.

The Ashikaga as Patrons of the Arts —— Although the Muromachi period may appear to have been a "dark age" in terms of political and social history, it was also a time of glorious cultural achievement, and the Ashikaga shōguns are remembered for their generous patronage of the arts. The two major spans of cultural flourishing in the Muromachi period were the age of Yoshimitsu in the late 14th and early 15th centuries (see KITAYAMA CULTURE) and the age of Yoshimasa in the late 15th century (see HIGASHIYAMA CULTURE). As the patrons of such arts as the NŌ theater, linked verse (see RENGA AND HAIKAI), monochrome INK PAINTING (which was stimulated especially by the TALLY TRADE and cultural intercourse with China), landscape gardening, and the TEA CEREMONY, the Ashikaga shōguns showed themselves to be far more gifted in the cultural than in the military sphere of medieval rule.

◾ —— John W. Hall, *Government and Local Power in Japan* (1966). George Sansom, *A History of Japan, 1334–1615* (1961). Tanaka Yoshinari, *Ashikaga jidai shi* (1923). H. Paul Varley, *The Ōnin War* (1967). H. Paul Varley, *Imperial Restoration in Medieval Japan* (1971). Watanabe Yosuke, *Muromachi jidai shi* (1948).

H. Paul VARLEY

Ashikaga Gakkō

(Ashikaga School). A major educational facility of the Muromachi period (1333–1568), located in what is now the city of Ashikaga, Tochigi Prefecture. The date of its founding is unknown, and there are several theories about the identity of the original founder, but the most likely candidate is Ashikaga Yoshikane (d 1199), a warrior in the service of the Kamakura shogunate. At its inception it was little more than a library for the use of family members. Only in 1439, when UESUGI NORIZANE installed Kaigen, a monk at the temple Engakuji in Kamakura, as the first director and drew up a set of regulations, was it formally established as a school. Monks made up a large part of the student body, and the curriculum concentrated on Confucian learning, with particular emphasis given to divination studies based on the *Yi jing* (I ching; The Book of Changes). Military science was the other major subject. In this age of turmoil, these were the most important fields of learning for the warrior class, and after graduation, many students became advisers to warriors.

The school reached its zenith during the Sengoku period (1467–1568), especially in the years under the direction of the monk

Kyūka (d 1578), when it is said to have attracted as many as 3,000 students. It continued under the patronage of the Uesugi, Go-Hōjō, and Tokugawa families, but in the middle years of the Edo period (1600–1868) it went into decline, finally closing in 1872. See also ASHIKAGA GAKKŌ ISEKI TOSHOKAN.   Etō Kyōji

Ashikaga Gakkō Iseki Toshokan

(Ashikaga School Historic Site Library). One of Japan's oldest surviving libraries, located in the city of Ashikaga, Tochigi Prefecture. Like the ASHIKAGA GAKKŌ, the school with which it was associated, it is believed to have been founded in the 12th century. By the Muromachi period (1333–1568), it ranked with the KANAZAWA BUNKO as one of the two most highly regarded libraries in Japan, and was particularly noted for its collection of Song (Sung; 960–1279) and Ming (1368–1644) block-printed books. However, during the Edo period (1600–1868) it went into decline, and many of its best holdings were lost. It was closed after the Meiji Restoration of 1868 and, together with other Ashikaga Gakkō property, was preserved by a historic site committee until the end of World War II. Since the war the collection has been housed in a small building on the school site, which also serves as the local public library. More than 2,200 of its old manuscripts and Chinese holdings have been officially designated as National Treasures or Important Cultural Assets.   Theodore F. WELCH

Ashikaga shogunate → Muromachi shogunate

Ashikaga Tadayoshi (1306–1352)

General of the Nambokuchō period (1336–92) and close associate of his elder brother ASHIKAGA TAKAUJI, the first Muromachi shōgun. After helping to restore direct imperial rule by Emperor GO-DAIGO in the KEMMU RESTORATION of 1333, Tadayoshi was made governor (kami) of Sagami Province (now part of Kanagawa Prefecture) and took up residence in Kamakura. In 1335, during an attempted coup d'etat (NAKASENDAI REBELLION) by Hōjō Tokiyuki (d 1353), he killed Go-Daigo's son Prince MORINAGA, who had become an obstacle to Ashikaga ambitions. Turning against Go-Daigo, Tadayoshi and Takauji set up a rival Northern Court in 1336 (see NORTHERN AND SOUTHERN COURTS) and founded the Muromachi shogunate in 1338. In their "dual shogunate" (ryōgosho) system Takauji took charge of military affairs and Tadayoshi of judicial and administrative matters. An able administrator, Tadayoshi at first worked harmoniously with his brother. In 1350, however, because of a longstanding conflict with Takauji's deputy KŌ NO MORONAO, Tadayoshi turned against his brother, proclaimed allegiance to the Southern Court, and raised an army that in the lunar first month of 1351 occupied Kyōto, defeating Takauji's and Moronao's forces (see KANNŌ DISTURBANCE). A month later the brothers were reconciled, the price being Moronao's head, but their concord lasted less than half a year. In the eighth month Tadayoshi fled to Kamakura, but Takauji pursued him there with an army. Again the brothers were ostensibly reconciled; but less than two months later, on 13 March 1352 (Kannō 3.2.26), Tadayoshi died suddenly; it was rumored by poisoning.

Ashikaga Takauji (1305–1358)

A 14th-century military commander and head of a major branch of the Seiwa Genji (a branch of the MINAMOTO FAMILY) who founded the second warrior government in the medieval age, the MUROMACHI SHOGUNATE (1338–1573).

After the accession of Emperor GO-DAIGO to the throne in 1318, the already sizable opposition in Kyōto to the military rule of the Kamakura shogunate (1192–1333) gained new hope that the "Eastern barbarians" in Kamakura would soon be overthrown. Antishogunate plots were uncovered in 1324 and 1331, and, as a result of the second, the emperor himself was seized as a conspirator and exiled to the Oki Islands (see GENKŌ INCIDENT). During Go-Daigo's exile, his supporters, including his son Prince MORINAGA and the redoubtable warrior KUSUNOKI MASASHIGE, kept the loyalists' aspirations alive by harassing the central provinces. Determined to exterminate them, the shogunate in May 1333 (Genkō 3.4) dispatched an army from Kamakura under the command of Ashikaga Takauji. Upon entering the central provinces, Takauji turned traitor, announced his support for Go-Daigo, and attacked and captured the shogunate offices in Kyōto. Within a few weeks, the general NITTA YOSHISADA,

Ashikaga Takauji —— Reputed portrait

Although long considered a likeness of Takauji, scholars have proposed a number of other identifications of this warrior, among them some of Takauji's vassals. Artist unknown. Detail. Colors on silk. 100.3 × 53.3 cm. 14th century. Private collection.

head of another major branch of the Seiwa Genji, also rebelled against the shogunate and destroyed the heart of the regime at Kamakura.

Go-Daigo, returned from exile to Kyōto, set about instituting his cherished dream of direct imperial rule over the country; but his effort proved to be largely a reactionary exercise in futility, and before long his KEMMU RESTORATION was undermined by competition between Takauji and Yoshisada. While Yoshisada ingratiated himself in the service of the emperor, Takauji remained aloof from the new restoration government. In 1335 Takauji was driven, mainly as a result of the machinations of Yoshisada, into rebellion against Go-Daigo. Withdrawing temporarily to Kyūshū, he returned to the central provinces at the head of a newly strengthened army in July 1336 (Engen 1.5), captured Kyōto, and forced Go-Daigo and his remaining followers to flee to Yoshino, south of the capital. Takauji installed Emperor Kōmyō (1322–80; r 1336–48), a member of a rival branch of the imperial family, on the throne and laid the foundations for the Muromachi shogunate in Kyōto, close to the court. Go-Daigo, meanwhile, established a new court at Yoshino. Thus from 1336 to 1392 there existed two competing centers of imperial authority: the Ashikaga-backed Northern Court in Kyōto and the Southern Court of Go-Daigo and his successors at Yoshino (see NORTHERN AND SOUTHERN COURTS).

Takauji received the title of SHŌGUN from the Northern Court in 1338 and thereby became the first in a line of Ashikaga shōguns who ruled Japan, at least nominally, as military hegemons for the next 235 years. Takauji devoted most of his period as shōgun seeking to deal, on the one hand, with the civil war against the supporters of the Southern Court and, on the other hand, with strife within the shogunate itself. The internal strife resulted from antagonism between Takauji's brother ASHIKAGA TADAYOSHI and the vassal chieftains KŌ NO MORONAO and his brother Moroyasu. Tadayoshi succeeded in having the Kō brothers murdered in 1351, but by that time he found himself in opposition to Takauji, who had tended to side with the Kō. Tadayoshi fled to the east but was apparently murdered by Takauji's men early in 1352 (see KANNŌ DISTURBANCE). This brought an end to open conflict within the shogunate, and by the time of his own death six years later, Takauji was able to bequeath to his son and successor as shōgun, Yoshiakira (1330–68; r 1359–68), a fairly stable regime that had overcome its internal rifts and had already eliminated the offensive potential of its external enemy, the Southern Court.

Though he had prevailed over his enemies and brought a measure of stability to Japan in a troubled age, Takauji was vilified by generations of historians and others before World War II for having mistreated Go-Daigo, a rightful emperor. The sentiments of the prewar Japanese toward the Ashikaga chieftain were perhaps most sensationally demonstrated when in 1934 Nakajima Kumakichi (1873–1960), a minister of commerce and industry who was also an amateur historian, was dismissed from his post for having written a book that cast Takauji in a favorable light.

■———George Sansom, *A History of Japan, 1334–1615* (1961). Takayanagi Mitsutoshi, *Ashikaga Takauji* (1955).

H. Paul VARLEY

Ashikaga Yoshiaki (1537–1597)

The 15th and last shōgun of the Muromachi shogunate. Third son of the 12th shōgun, Ashikaga Yoshiharu (1511–50; r 1522–47). At the age of five Yoshiaki was sent to the Buddhist monastery Ichijōin at Nara, where he took the priestly name Kakukei and became abbot in 1562. After his brother Yoshiteru (b 1536; r from 1547) was assassinated in 1565, Yoshiaki renounced the priesthood and sought *daimyō* support for his claim to the succession. He obtained the patronage of ODA NOBUNAGA, who seized control of Kyōto and installed Yoshiaki as shōgun in 1568. As early as the following year, however, Nobunaga began to constrict the shōgun's authority. Yoshiaki, in turn, seems to have intrigued with a coalition of secular and religious lords intent on destroying Nobunaga. By 1573 the differences between the two were irreconcilable. Nobunaga burned the greater part of Kyōto in order to intimidate the shōgun; and when Yoshiaki withdrew to Makinoshima, south of the city, Nobunaga took that supposedly impregnable fortress on 15 August 1573 (Genki 4.7.18) and drove Yoshiaki into exile. Many historians and this encyclopedia call this event the end of the Muromachi shogunate, ignoring the fact that Yoshiaki continued to behave as shōgun. Encouraged by powerful daimyō, he entertained hopes of a return to full honors in Kyōto until the attainment of paramount leadership by TOYOTOMI HIDEYOSHI made Yoshiaki's pretensions unrealistic. Resigned to his fate at last, in 1588 he took the priestly name Shōzan Dōkyū and accepted a stipend from Hideyoshi. The imperial court gave Yoshiaki the honorary rank of *jugō*, entitling him to ceremonial treatment equal to that accorded empresses.

George ELISON

Ashikaga Yoshimasa (1436–1490)

The eighth shōgun of the Muromachi shogunate (1338–1573); ruled 1449–74; son of the sixth shōgun, ASHIKAGA YOSHINORI. Born in Kyōto. After Yoshinori's assassination in 1441, his eldest son, Yoshikatsu (1434–43), became shōgun, but he died two years later. Yoshimasa succeeded him in 1449 (there was no shōgun in the interval). A century after its founding, the Muromachi shogunate had been considerably weakened by conflicts among its own vassals; the capital region was wracked by riots and agrarian disturbances (TSUCHI IKKI), and the national economy was at a standstill. Yoshimasa's rule was also marked by a series of natural calamities, which brought constant famine and disease to all parts of the country in the decade after 1457. In 1467 a succession dispute arose between Yoshimasa's younger brother Yoshimi (1439–91), whom he had designated his successor in 1464, and Yoshihisa (1465–89), the son that his wife, HINO TOMIKO, had unexpectedly borne him a year later; it intensified into a major civil war between their respective supporters. The ŌNIN WAR, which ended inconclusively 10 years later, virtually destroyed the shogunate's authority and inaugurated the century of civil strife known as the SENGOKU PERIOD (1467–1568). A weak ruler, Yoshimasa cared little for affairs of state and devoted most of his time to the arts. On 7 January 1474 (Bummei 5.12.19) he abdicated in favor of Yoshihisa and retired to the Higashiyama section of Kyōto, where he built the famous villa that later became the temple known as GINKAKUJI. Throughout his later life he was an enthusiastic practitioner and patron of poetry, calligraphy, and painting, as well as of the tea ceremony and Nō drama (see HIGASHIYAMA CULTURE).

Ashikaga Yoshimitsu (1358–1408)

Third shōgun of the Muromachi shogunate. Yoshimitsu was 10 when he succeeded his father Yoshiakira (1330–68). He was guided in these early years by the KANREI (shogunate deputy) Hosokawa Yoriyuki (1329–92). Their efforts focused on consolidating the power of the shogunate, refining the HANZEI one-half payment tax-system, regularizing the practice of SHITAJI CHŪBUN, and giving legal recognition to de facto possession of proprietary rights by warriors (ICHIEN CHIGYŌ). In short, by acting as a mediator for competing claims between SHŌEN (private estates) proprietors, *shugo* (military governors), and local warriors, the shogunate succeeded in extending military control over most of the country.

Yoshimitsu next turned to the task of ending the schism between the Southern Court based in Yoshino and the Northern Court in Kyōto. In 1392 he persuaded the emperor of the Southern Court to return to Kyōto, with the understanding that the two lines would alternate; in fact, however, the northern line continued to succeed the throne. (See NORTHERN AND SOUTHERN COURTS.)

The obstreperous military governors still posed a threat; in 1391 Yoshimitsu crushed Yamana Ujikiyo (1344–91; see MEITOKU REBELLION), and in 1399 he destroyed Ōuchi Yoshihiro (1356–1400), *shugo* of several provinces in southwestern Honshū (ŌEI REBELLION). In 1395 he had relinquished the shogunal office to his son Yoshimochi (1386–1428), but he remained in firm control, building a residence in the Kitayama section of Kyōto in the style of the palace of a retired emperor, accumulating civil titles, surrounding himself with artists and learned priests, and living in lavish style (see also KITAYAMA CULTURE).

In 1401 Yoshimitsu established trade relations with China (see TALLY TRADE), entering into a tributary arrangement with the Ming ruler. In a letter to the Ming court he signed himself as "Minamoto, the King of Japan, vassal in the service of the Emperor of China," an act for which he was never quite forgiven by posterity. By means of this "tally trade" Yoshimitsu obtained huge profits and monopolized the import of copper currency.

SHIMADA Jirō

Ashikaga Yoshinori (1394–1441)

The sixth shōgun of the Muromachi shogunate (1338–1573); ruled 1429–41. As the fourth son of ASHIKAGA YOSHIMITSU, he had no expectation of becoming shōgun and at an early age became a Buddhist monk of the Tendai sect with the religious name Gien. He rose to the position of *zasu* (head of the sect) by the late 1420s but returned to secular life on the death of his older brother, the shōgun Ashikaga Yoshimochi, in 1428. Yoshimochi had decreed that his successor should be chosen by lot from among his four brothers, and Yoshinori won the draw. He proved a decisive and overbearing leader determined to restore the shogunate's authority, which had been shaken by regional warlords and the imperial court. He revitalized the judiciary system, strengthened his military organization, and punished or destroyed many of his vassals. His most famous military campaign was against his rebellious kinsman Ashikaga Mochiuji (1398–1439), who controlled the Kantō region as shogunal deputy (Kamakura *kubō*) and was forced to commit suicide in 1439. Yoshinori's dictatorship caused disaffection among his vassals, and he was assassinated by AKAMATSU MITSUSUKE, a military leader of central Honshū.

Ashinoko

Volcanic crater lake in southwestern Kanagawa Prefecture, central Honshū, located within the Fuji–Hakone–Izu National Park. The irregular shoreline of Ashinoko, with views featuring Mt. Fuji (FUJISAN) in the background, makes it popular for tourism. Area: 6.8 sq km (2.6 sq mi); circumference: 18 km (11 mi); depth: 43 m (141 ft).

Ashio

Town in western Tochigi Prefecture, central Honshū. Major copper mining center from early in the Edo period (1600–1868) until 1973, when the mine closed because of a scarcity of ores. In the 1890s the mine was the center of a controversy regarding the pollution of the river Watarasegawa and surrounding rice fields. See ASHIO COPPER MINE INCIDENT; ASHIO COPPER MINE LABOR DISPUTE. Pop: 6,007.

Ashio Copper Mine Incident

(Ashio Dōzan Kōdoku Jiken). The best known of modern Japan's early environmental disasters. Beginning in 1877, the Furukawa Mining Company, headed by FURUKAWA ICHIBEI, expanded its excavation of the Ashio Copper Mine in Tochigi Prefecture, causing acidic pollutants to contaminate the nearby rivers Watarasegawa and Tonegawa. From 1890 floods regularly polluted over 50,000 fertile acres in the north Kantō Plain, threatening the lives and livelihoods of as many as 500,000 people. Local farmers began large-scale protests and petitions; their cause was championed in the Diet by the politicians TANAKA SHŌZŌ and SHIMADA SABURŌ and was supported by a wide range of prominent journalists, socialists, and Christian humanists. In response the government in 1897 directed the Furukawa Mining Company to install expensive pollution controls, but these were not strictly enforced. Furthermore, since flooding continued, the government declared the lands around the village of Yanaka "a flood overflow area" and had the village razed in 1907. In fact, some pollution from the mine continued until its closure in 1972, and in 1974 farmers along the Watarasegawa were awarded the equivalent of US $7 million in the first major case successfully litigated through the government's Environmental Disputes Coordination Commission. The nearly century-long incident illustrates growing Japanese awareness of the ecological, social, and political toll exacted by the government's industrialization policy. See also ENVIRONMENTAL QUALITY; POLLUTION LITIGATION.

Jerry K. FISHER

Ashio Copper Mine labor dispute

(Ashio Dōzan *sōgi*). Labor disturbance of 1907 at the Furukawa Mining Company's Ashio Copper Mine in Tochigi Prefecture. In the previous year some 600 miners, led by the labor organizers Nagaoka Tsuruzō (1864–1914) and Minami Sukematsu (1873–1964), had formed an Ashio branch of the Dai Nihon Rōdō Shiseikai, a miners' union founded by the two men in Hokkaidō, to demand better working conditions, higher wages, and an end to their exploitation under the labor-boss system (HAMBA SEIDO) through which they were paid. Negotiations proving fruitless, violence erupted on 4 February 1907, when miners cut telephone lines and stormed guard towers and other company buildings before being dispersed by local police. Two days later, on 6 February, the miners dynamited the main guard tower and set fire to some 130 buildings. The government declared martial law at the mine and on 7 February sent three militia units to quell the disturbance. Of the 181 miners charged with instigating a riot, 82 were convicted and jailed. Eventually, however, after further troubles at the mine in 1919 and 1921, the miners succeeded in ridding themselves of the labor-boss system. The Ashio riots of 1907 inspired similar disturbances at other mines throughout Japan later in the same year, of which the best known were the BESSHI COPPER MINE LABOR DISPUTES.

Tanaka Akira

Ashio Kōdoku Jiken → Ashio Copper Mine Incident

Ashiya

City in southeastern Hyōgo Prefecture. Situated at the foot of the Rokkō Mountains, commanding a view of Ōsaka Bay and convenient to Kōbe and Ōsaka, Ashiya has been a home to the famous and the rich; the city provided the setting for TANIZAKI JUN'ICHIRŌ's novel *Sasameyuki* (1943–48; tr *The Makioka Sisters*, 1957). ARIMA HOT SPRING is within easy access by a scenic highway. Pop: 81,741.

Ashiya

Town in northern Fukuoka Prefecture, Kyūshū. Located at the mouth of the river Ongagawa on Hibiki Bay, it has been an entrepôt for rice, coal, and salt since ancient times. An American military base was established after World War II, and today it is a base for the Japanese Air Self Defense Force. The town is a part of the Genkai Quasi-National Park. Pop: 18,934.

Ashizurimisaki

Cape in southern Kōchi Prefecture, southwestern Shikoku. It separates Tosa Bay from the Pacific Ocean and is the southernmost point of the island of Shikoku. Along its greatly indented coastline are located an observatory and a lighthouse. Noted for its towering cliffs, its palm trees and other subtropical vegetation, and magnificent scenery, Ashizurimisaki is the main point of interest of ASHIZURI–UWAKAI NATIONAL PARK.

Ashizuri–Uwakai National Park

(Ashizuri–Uwakai Kokuritsu Kōen). The only national park situated on the island of Shikoku. It consists of several small regions scattered about the western side of the island. The chief features are coastal stretches of granite cliffs, sandstone rock formations, coral reefs, and an irregular coastline with many small bays and islets. The focus of the park is the cape of ASHIZURIMISAKI, a narrow promontory at the southernmost tip of the island, famed for panoramic views of the Pacific Ocean and for the temple of Kongōfukuji, first built in 822 by KŪKAI. The area around the cape is rich in subtropical vegetation, such as camellias and banyan trees. The coastline between Minokoshi and Tatsukushi, north of the cape, is noted for its coral reefs and unusual rock formations. Southeast of the city of Uwajima is the Nametoko Gorge, which runs for 12 km (7 mi), with fantastically shaped rocks and waterfalls. The surrounding coastal waters abound in bonito *(katsuo)*. Area: 109 sq km (42 sq mi).

Asia Development Board

(Kōain). Cabinet agency established in December 1938 to coordinate the government's China policy. The SINO-JAPANESE WAR, which had broken out in July 1937, had not been quickly resolved as promised by the military; indeed, it threatened to become a protracted total war. In the fall of 1938 Prime Minister KONOE FUMIMARO decided to set up a separate agency that would coordinate all government activities related to China apart from formal diplomacy, which would continue to be conducted by the Ministry of Foreign Affairs. The prime minister assumed the presidency of the board; he was assisted by four vice-presidents, the ministers of foreign affairs, finance, the army, and the navy. The board opened branch offices in Shanghai, Beiping (Peiping), Zhangjiakou (Kalgan), and Xiamen (Amoy) to supervise the activities of Japanese firms such as the North China Development Company; it also opened a school to train administrators for occupied China. It is thought that the Kōain was set up largely at the instigation of the army, which hoped to outmaneuver the Ministry of Foreign Affairs; and the board did in fact become an instrument of the military. The Kōain was absorbed by the Dai Tōa Shō (Greater East Asia Ministry; see GREATER EAST ASIA COPROSPERITY SPHERE) when that organ was created in November 1942.

Asian Games

(Ajia Taikai). Amateur sports competition among Asian nations held every four years (since 1954) midway between the Olympic games under the auspices of the Asian Games Federation. First held in 1951 in New Delhi. These meets are based on the ideals of the Olympics. The 1951 meet was Japan's first participation in an international meet after the end of World War II. Tōkyō was the site of the third games in 1958 (the second games had been held in 1954). Besides the usual Olympic events, the games include sports particularly popular in Asia, such as badminton, tennis, and table tennis. The origin of these games can be traced back to the Far Eastern Championships held from 1913 to 1938, in which China, Japan, and the Philippines were the major participants. *Takeda Fumio*

Aso

Town in northeastern Kumamoto Prefecture, Kyūshū. Located on the river Kurokawa and part of the ASO NATIONAL PARK, it serves as a base camp for climbing Mt. Aso (Asosan). The area is known for its rice production and animal husbandry. Aso (Uchinomaki) Hot Spring is a popular resort. Pop: 20,655.

Asō Hisashi (1891–1940)

Socialist activist and politician. Born in Ōita Prefecture, he graduated from Tōkyō University. In 1919 he joined the labor group YŪAIKAI and as head of its mining section led several strikes. In 1923 he became secretary of the political office of the Nihon Rōdō Sōdōmei (Japan Federation of Labor; see SŌDŌMEI). In 1926 he helped to form the NIHON RŌNŌTŌ (Japan Labor-Farmer Party) and served as its secretary-general. In 1932 he helped to found the anticommunist SHAKAI TAISHŪTŌ (Socialist Masses Party), became its secretary-general, and in 1936 and 1937 was elected on its slate to

Asosan

A portion of the huge caldera of Asosan with the active crater of Nakadake in the foreground.

the House of Representatives. He began, along with his party, to show sympathy for the military-dominated government and in 1940 became actively involved in the NEW ORDER MOVEMENT of Prime Minister KONOE FUMIMARO.

ason

Also pronounced *asomi*. The second of eight ranks in the system of hereditary titles (KABANE) established in 684 by the emperor TEMMU (see YAKUSA NO KABANE). Initially the rank was bestowed upon 52 clans or lineage groups (UJI) that claimed kinship to the Yamato imperial line. Later it was granted to virtually all prominent clans, and, with the rise of the *ason*-ranked FUJIWARA FAMILY in the late 8th century, *ason* in effect replaced the rank *mahito* as the highest position in the *kabane* system. By the middle of the Heian period (794–1185), with the further decline of the *kabane* system, *ason* had become a general honorific title for court officials of the fourth rank or higher. See also UJI-KABANE SYSTEM.

Aso National Park

(Aso Kokuritsu Kōen). Situated in central Kyūshū, in Ōita and Kumamoto prefectures. The park's most notable feature is the volcano ASOSAN, which has one of the world's largest calderas. The area is also renowned for its hot spring resorts. Asosan is a bleak, sprawling volcano, whose caldera measures 18 km (11 mi) east to west and 24 km (15 mi) north to south. Within this lie five central cones, one of which, Nakadake (1,520 m; 4,986 ft), is still active. The highest of the five is Takadake (1,592 m; 5,222 ft), which affords a fine view over Asosan, as does Aso Hot Spring on the northern slopes of the volcano. Northeast of Asosan lies the extinct volcano KUJŪSAN (1,788 m; 5,865 ft), whose summit is covered with alpine flora and which is thickly wooded on its lower slopes. Northeast of the mountain on Yufudake (1,584 m; 5,196 ft), between Beppu and Kujūsan, is Yufuin Hot Spring, famous for its waters. Both Asosan and Kujūsan have plateaus with good pastures for cattle. Colorful wild Kirishima azaleas *(miyama kirishima)*, found only in Kyūshū, are abundant in early summer. Area: 730.6 sq km (282 sq mi).

Asosan

Volcano in central Kyūshū. The Aso caldera, one of the world's largest, has a circumference of 80 km (50 mi), running about 18 km (11 mi) from east to west and about 24 km (15 mi) from north to south. The so-called Five Peaks of Aso, which are all central cones, are Takadake, Nakadake, Nekodake, Kishimadake, and Eboshidake. The radius of the lava flow created by eruptions of Asosan over the years is about 100 km (62 mi), covering the greater part of the island of Kyūshū. Nakadake still spews out a great volume of volcanic ash, damaging crops in the district. Past eruptions, the most recent being in 1979, have killed a large number of people. Uchinomaki Hot Spring is located within the caldera. There is a driveway and a ropeway to the top of Nakadake. Asosan forms the center of Aso National Park. The highest point is Takadake (1,592 m; 5,222 ft).

Aso Shrine

(Aso Jinja). Shintō shrine in the district of Aso, Kumamoto Prefecture, dedicated to Takeiwatatsu no Mikoto and eleven other deities. One tradition places the establishment of the shrine in 282 BC and another in AD 18; the actual date is unknown. The various deities enshrined here were associated with the ancestors of the Aso clan, the hereditary governors *(kuni no miyatsuko)* of Higo Province (now Kumamoto Prefecture). It was decreed in 1017 that each emperor would make an offering there once during his reign, and the shrine has enjoyed both imperial and popular veneration. Eventually Aso Shrine was designated the first shrine *(ichinomiya)* of Higo. Much of the land that had been granted to the shrine by shōguns and generals was confiscated by TOYOTOMI HIDEYOSHI after his campaign in Kyūshū in 1587. The major festival, a rice-planting ritual known as Mitaue Matsuri, is held annually on 28 July.

Stanley WEINSTEIN

Assembly of Prefectural Governors

(Chihōkan Kaigi). As part of the process of structural reform of the administrative and judicial branches of the government in the early years of the Meiji period (1868–1912), the government leaders ITŌ HIROBUMI and KIDO TAKAYOSHI decided at the ŌSAKA CONFERENCE OF 1875 to hold regular conferences of prefectural governors as a modest start toward a representative assembly. At the first conference, held in June of the same year with Kido presiding, there was debate on the establishment of elected prefectural assemblies. At the second conference, chaired by Itō in July 1878, the governors discussed the so-called SANSHIMPŌ (Three New Laws) regarding prefectural administrative organization, local taxation, and regulations for metropolitan and prefectural assemblies. The third conference, held in February 1880, considered regulations for the establishment of grain reserves (Bikō Chochiku Hō) as well as an amendment to the Sanshimpō. Although the assembly was not conceived as an instrument of representative government, it did play an important part in determining the structure of LOCAL GOVERNMENT in the Meiji period. With the issuance of the 1881 edict promising the establishment of a national parliament within nine years, the Assembly of Prefectural Governors became an advisory body to the Home Ministry and was abolished soon after.

Association of Japanese Geographers

(Nihon Chiri Gakkai). A leading Japanese geographical society formed in 1925 by YAMAZAKI NAOMASA. Its monthly organ, the *Chirigaku hyōron,* launched in March of the same year, publishes articles and research reports on geographical studies in Japan. In recent years the association has published a number of critical studies of Japanese geography, which include *Nihon ni okeru chirigaku* (1976, Geography in Japan) and *Nihon no chiri* (1980, Geography of Japan) as well as several works in English. The number of association members is approximately 2800 (as of 1980), of which one-fourth are affiliated with colleges and universities. General association conferences are held twice a year. *NISHIKAWA Osamu*

assumption of risk

(kiken futan). Term referring to the question whether, in a bilateral contract such as a sales-purchase agreement, the obligations of one party can be terminated when the other party is unable to fulfill his obligations for causes beyond his control. For example, suppose A and B have concluded a contract whereby A agrees to sell something to B for a sum of money, but A's obligation to transfer the item is terminated for reasons not attributable to A. If B's obligation (to pay for the object) is also terminated, A cannot receive payment in return for his obligation, and the obligor bears the risk resulting from the termination of his own obligation. This is called the doctrine of the obligor assuming the risk *(saimusha shugi)*. If, on the contrary, B's obligation continues to exist, and B must pay for the item, even though he does not obtain it, the obligee bears the risk resulting from A's obligation being terminated. This is called the doctrine of the obligee assuming the risk *(saikensha shugi)*.

In general, Japan's CIVIL CODE subscribes to the doctrine of the obligor assuming the risk. If the obligation of one party is terminated for reasons not attributable to either party, the obligation of the other party (B in the example) is also terminated (art. 536). There is, however, an important exception to this doctrine: when the purpose of a contract is the establishment or transfer of real rights to a specific thing and that thing ceases to exist from causes not attributable to the parties concerned, the obligatory duty of the other party does not terminate. Also, in contracts concerned with nonspecific things, as soon as the identity of the thing is fixed, the risk is transferred to the obligee (art. 534). There is, however, strong criticism of this broad adoption of the doctrine of the obligee assuming the risk, and in actual dealings, the doctrine of the obligee assuming the risk is often excluded through special contractual provisions. See also CONTRACTS. *Awaji Takehisa*

Aston, William George (1841–1911)

British diplomat and Japanologist. Born in Northern Ireland. Arriving in Japan in 1864, he worked for the British legation during the late part of the Edo (1600–1868) and the early part of the Meiji (1868–1912) periods, first serving as an interpreter and later as Hyōgo (now Kōbe) consul and secretary to the legation in Tōkyō. He studied the language and culture with Hori Hidenari, a noted National Learning (KOKUGAKU) scholar. In addition to an English translation of the *Nihon shoki* (720; tr *Nihongi*, 1896), an early chronicle of Japanese history, he was the author of a grammar of spoken Japanese as well as such works as *A History of Japanese Literature* (1899) and *Shinto* (1905). He also made a comparative study of the Japanese and Indo-European languages. *Shimada Masahiko*

astronomical observatories

(temmondai). There are three kinds of astronomical observatory and observation facility in Japan: those belonging to national universities, those belonging to institutes for scientific research, and those belonging to amateur astronomers. The only important astronomical observatories staffed by full-time research workers are the Tōkyō Astronomical Observatory, the Kwasan (Kasan) Astronomical Observatory, and the Latitude Observatory of Mizusawa (see MIZUSAWA, LATITUDE OBSERVATORY OF). There are also full-time research workers at the Geographical Survey Institute of the Ministry of Construction (the government agency in charge of geodetic survey astronomy for national land surveying), the Hydrographic Department of the Maritime Safety Agency, and the Ministry of Transport (the editor and publisher of the Japanese ephemeris), but their objectives are the work assigned to their agencies rather than the study of astronomy. The Tōkyō Astronomical Observatory (established in 1878 as an adjunct of Tōkyō University, with its present headquarters in the city of Mitaka, Tōkyō Prefecture) is the largest in Japan; it has five observatories with research departments covering nearly all fields of astronomy except surface observation of the moon and planets and routine tracking observation of latitude. The main observatory of the Kwasan Astronomical Observatory (belonging to Kyōto University) is the Hida Observatory in Gifu Prefecture, where the surface and atmosphere of the moon and planets are studied. The Latitude Observatory of Mizusawa, located at 39° 08′ north latitude in the city of Mizusawa, Iwate Prefecture, which has grown from a temporary latitude observatory established in 1899, has a department to observe the polar motion of the earth and a department to study geophysics. The International Latitude Observation Project Center was once in this observatory and the International Polar Motion Observation Project Center has been there since 1962. The greater part of Japanese private astronomical observatories are ones established by amateur astronomers for their own use; these have become well known for the discoveries of many new comets. See also ASTRONOMY.

📖——Temmon Gaido Henshūbu, ed, *Nihon no temmondai* (1971). *Hirose Hideo*

astronomy

(temmongaku). It was not until the early years of the Meiji period (1868–1912) that astronomy as a branch of science became established in Japan. Prior to that, astronomy was practiced in Japan, but valued chiefly for its use in chronological reckoning (i.e., CALENDAR, DATES, AND TIME). With the Meiji Restoration of 1868 the government began to promote the study of Western astronomy. However, the government's interest remained highly utilitarian, and this emphasis strongly affected early modern astronomical studies in Japan. Today Japanese astronomers are active in celestial physics and radio astronomy as well as classical astronomy.

History of astronomical studies in Japan. The Meiji government at the end of the 19th century encouraged practical astronomical studies, such as those concerned with geodetic surveys and navigation. In 1878 the Ministry of Education established an observatory at Tōkyō University as an educational facility; this also carried out astronomical and weather observations. In 1888 these facilities were integrated with Tōkyō University to form the Tōkyō Astronomical Observatory, the only astronomical observatory in Japan at the time. The moving of this observatory to the Azabu area in Tōkyō coincided with the improvement of techniques for celestial photography, and the photographic observation of the Milky Way and comets was conducted using small telescopes. Major photographs from this time include those of Morehouse's comet taken in 1908 and those of Halley's comet taken at Dairen (Ch: Dalian or Ta-lien; now part of Lüda [Lüta], China) in 1910. Although Hirayama Shin (1867–1945) discovered the asteroids that were later named (498) Tōkyō and (727) Nippon, these efforts were confined to the discovery of individual bodies and did not develop into systematic research.

It was not until after the removal of the Tōkyō Astronomical Observatory to Mitaka on the outskirts of the city in 1924 that astronomical projects began to be carried out actively. In 1927–30 eight asteroids were discovered by Oikawa Okurō (b 1896) and others as the result of observations with a 20-centimeter (8-inch) telescope. At this time astronomical studies were augmented by the installation of a new 65-centimeter (25-inch) refractor, installation of a meridian circle, and an increase in the number of research workers. Position astronomy was the principal field of study because of the comparatively low cost of the equipment required. Japanese achievements in position astronomy include the discoveries of the paths of asteroids by Hirayama Kiyotsugu (1874–1943) and the studies of the movements of artificial satellites by Kozai Yoshihide (b 1928).

The International Latitude Observatory at Mizusawa (see MIZUSAWA, LATITUDE OBSERVATORY OF) was established in 1899 and an International Time Station in Mitaka in 1923. These facilities were instrumental in the discovery by KIMURA HISASHI (1870–1943) of the Z-term in latitude variation and in Miyachi Masashi's (b 1902) detections of latitude variation.

Recent developments. Celestial physics has been active in Western Europe and the United States since the 1930s, but the absence of large telescopes long hindered Japanese astronomers from pursuing the basic observational studies fundamental to work in this area. The Okayama Astrophysical Observatory, equipped with a 188-centimeter (74-inch) reflecting telescope, was established in 1960, and since then studies have advanced greatly. Yamashita Yasumasa (b 1931) and others have published a standard spectral atlas of fixed stars based on observations made with this Okayama telescope; this atlas is highly rated as a basic reference tool.

Since radio astronomy principally developed after World War II, Japanese astronomers were able to participate actively in its establishment as a field of study. One important contribution of Japanese astronomy has been in pioneering electromagnetic radiation observations in the millimeter wavelength range. A millimeter wavelength interferometer consisting of one 45-meter (147-ft) and five 10-meter (32-ft) dishes is in progress; completion is expected in 1984. Fixed-star astronomy and the study of the microcosmos have lagged behind in Japan due to the lack of proper equipment; but study in these areas began in earnest with the completion of the Kiso Observatory equipped with a 105-centimeter (41-inch) Schmidt camera, ranked fourth in the world in size.

Universities training astronomical researchers in Japan are few, the major ones being Tōkyō University, Kyōto University, and Tōhoku University. Positions open to young researchers are limited in number, and this remains one of the major problems of astronomy in Japan, along with the need for new facilities. Attempts have been made to arouse public interest by means of scholarly gatherings such as the international symposium on celestial mechanics that was held in Tōkyō in 1978 in honor of HAGIWARA YŪSUKE, the teacher of many excellent scholars in the field of celestial mechanics. Sponsored by the International Astronomical Union, this symposium gave worldwide recognition to Japanese contributions to astronomy. The major journal of astronomical studies in Japan is *Publications of the Astronomical Society of Japan.* See also ASTRONOMICAL OBSERVATORIES.

📖——Shigeru Nakayama, *A History of Japanese Astronomy: Chinese Background and Western Impact* (1969), focuses on the period up to 1868. *Hirose Hideo*

Asuka

Village in northern Nara Prefecture, central Honshū. Now a quiet rural village, during the 7th century Asuka was the site of several

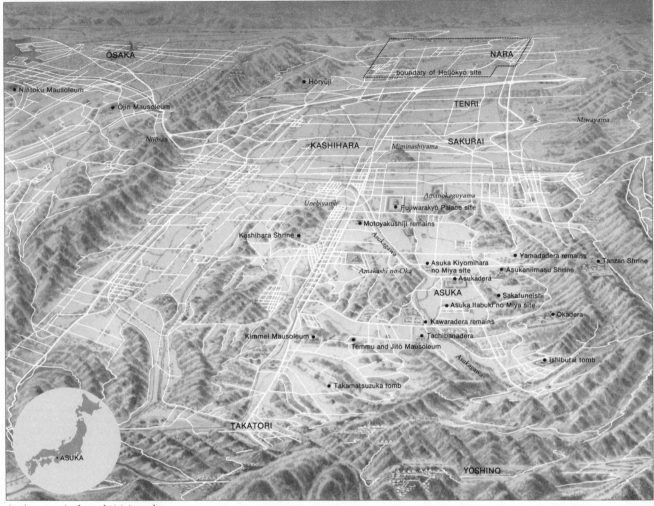

Asuka——Asuka and vicinity today

imperial palaces (see ASUKA PERIOD). There are numerous tombs, shrines, and temples dating from the 5th century and earlier. Asuka was designated a special historical area under a law protecting ancient capitals (Koto Hozon Hō). Pop: 6,987.

Asuka

Name for the region around the present-day village of Asuka, Nara Prefecture; the political and cultural center of Japan during the 6th and 7th centuries before the establishment of the capital at HEIJŌ-KYŌ in 710. Located in the southwest corner of the Yamato Basin some 20–25 kilometers (12.4–15.5 mi) south of the city of Nara, the Asuka region has no precisely defined boundaries but may be considered to include parts of the cities of Sakurai and Kashihara and the town of Takatori. In earlier times, Asuka seems to have denoted a somewhat smaller area, mainly along and to the east of the river Asukagawa, with its southern limit near the temple Tachibanadera.

From about AD 400 the Asuka region was settled largely by branches of the AYA FAMILY, immigrants from Korea. The residences of most Japanese sovereigns before the 8th century—including Emperor JIMMU's legendary Kashihara Palace, the palace ASUKA KIYOMIHARA NO MIYA, and the capital FUJIWARAKYŌ—are recorded as having been either in Asuka or close by, and many of the events described in the chronicle NIHON SHOKI (720) took place in the area.

Except for foundation stones, none of the original palace or temple buildings remain. The Asuka *Daibutsu*, a bronze image of the Buddha cast in 606, is housed in an Edo-period (1600–1868) building on the site of the ancient temple ASUKADERA, where it was the main object of veneration (*honzon*). Asuka came to public attention in 1972 with the discovery of unusual paintings on the walls and ceiling of a stone burial vault excavated at the TAKAMATSUZUKA TOMB.

——Kadowaki Teiji, *Asuka* (rev ed, 1977). Nara National Research Institute of Cultural Properties, *Guide to the Asuka Historical Museum*, tr William R. Carter (1978).   *William R.* CARTER

Asuka culture

(Asuka *bunka*). The culture centering on Asuka (in what is now Nara Prefecture), the site of successive imperial palaces from the mid-6th century to the mid-7th century (not to be confused with the Asuka period, a historical period which in this encyclopedia extends from the latter part of the 6th century to 710). Strongly influenced by Buddhism, which was introduced to Japan in the 6th century (traditionally in either 538 or 552), Asuka culture represented an assimilation of the Chinese culture of the Northern and Southern Dynasties (386–589), transmitted to Japan by Korean immigrants (KIKAJIN).

Chinese and Korean influence is particularly noticeable in much of the architecture and art of the temple HŌRYŪJI, located some distance north of Asuka but usually classified as an example of Asuka Buddhist culture. Representative Asuka pictorial art includes the paintings decorating the doors of the Tamamushi Shrine at Hōryūji and the Tenjukoku Shūchō, an embroidered mandala, at CHŪGŪJI. Greek influence can be seen in the entases of pillars, and Persian influence, in arabesque patterns.

Japanese mastery of the Chinese writing system also dates from this period, as is evidenced in the writing of chronicles and other histories at the order of Prince SHŌTOKU and SOGA NO UMAKO. See also HISTORY OF JAPAN: Asuka history; BUDDHIST SCULPTURE; PAINTING: premodern painting; BUDDHIST ART.

Asukadera

Also known as Moto Gangōji, Hōkōji, or Angoin. The first full-fledged temple complex built in Japan. A small sanctuary still remains on the original site, located in the ASUKA district on the southeast edge of the Yamato plain about 15 miles from Nara. Although this is now a quiet rural region, the traces of ancient palaces and imperial tombs near the temple bear witness to the fact that the Asuka district for centuries was the center of Japanese political and religious life—until 710, when the capital was moved to Nara.

The early history of Asukadera is documented in the 8th-century chronicles NIHON SHOKI and *Shoku nihongi* and in its own temple records. Its founding patron was SOGA NO UMAKO, chief minister to the throne and head of the powerful SOGA FAMILY, which had championed the Buddhist faith throughout the 6th century. Umako was closely associated with Prince SHŌTOKU, and the building of the Asukadera, together with that of the SHITENNŌJI (ca 593) and the HŌRYŪJI (ca 607) temples, marked the stage in the history of Japanese Buddhism when the survival of the faith was no longer threatened and it first became possible to build in great splendor. In the case of Asukadera, aid and counsel from the Buddhist kingdoms of Korea (PAEKCHE, SILLA, and KOGURYŎ) played a vital role in its early history.

The temple was erected soon after a gift of Buddhist relics arrived from Paekche in 588. Accompanying the relics were Korean monks, temple carpenters, a metal founder for the casting of pagoda spires, expert tile workers, and a painter; presumably they set to work with local craftsmen in the construction project. By 592 the main devotional halls *(kondō)* and connecting corridors had been built; in 593 the relics were installed in the foundation of the central pillar of the pagoda; in 596 the pagoda was complete.

According to the *Nihon shoki*, two giant images of the historical Buddha Śākyamuni (Shaka Nyorai) were ordered for the temple in 605 by Soga no Umako on behalf of the empress SUIKO. One of the images was to be in gilt bronze, the other in embroidery. The works were entrusted to the chief engineer and sculptor KURATSUKURI NO TORI, head of the Kuratsukuri family of Buddhist craftsmen. For its time, the casting of so large a bronze statue was an impressive feat of technology. Moreover, this was the first work in Japan known to have served as a *honzon*, or main object of devotion, in a temple hall. A bronze statue 2.75 meters (9 ft) high remains in the temple and the head, at least, is thought to survive from the one described in the *Nihon shoki*. In any event, it is the only remaining artistic relic of the temple's one hundred years of grandeur.

In 596 the temple began its role as a center of Buddhist learning when the first two monks took up residence. One of them was Eji (Kor: Hyecha) from Koguryŏ, who became a teacher of Prince Shōtoku and then his collaborator in the writing of three sutra commentaries. The other was Esō (Kor: Hyechong) from Paekche. The SANRON SCHOOL Buddhist scholar Hyegwan (J: Ekan) arrived in 625. The Japanese monk DŌSHŌ, who returned from Tang (T'ang) dynasty (618–907) China around 660 with relics and a copy of the complete Tripitaka, built two meditation halls at Asukadera. He was the first Japanese to preach the tenets of the HOSSŌ SECT, and several monks who were to distinguish themselves in the Nara period (710–794) studied with him at the temple.

All the ancient buildings disappeared centuries ago, but excavations conducted in 1956–57 disclosed that the original ground plan of the Asukadera was unlike any other yet found in Japan. Its pagoda was surrounded by three *kondō* halls, in contrast to the single *kondō* at Hōryūji or Shitennōji. The same unusual layout has been discovered in ruins in the vicinity of P'yŏngyang, the ancient capital of Koguryŏ, especially at the site called Chŏngan-ni (J: Seiganri). Archaeologists think it possible, however, that this type of building was also employed in Paekche and on the Chinese mainland, even though examples have yet to be found. Elsewhere in the Asukadera, strong Korean influence can be seen in the use of the stone double platform in the east and west *kondō*, in designs on the roof tiles, and in other details of construction.

The naming of this temple is unusually complicated, even though from the time of its founding it has been known informally as Asukadera. In the *Nihon shoki*, its formal name is given as Hōkōji. However, it was also known as GANGŌJI, a name that seems to have been more inclusive and may have referred also to a nearby nunnery (no longer extant). Soon after the capital was transferred to Nara in 710, the Asukadera was also transferred. A new temple was erected in Nara that bore the names both of Gangōji and Asukadera, and the old Asukadera came to be called the Moto (original) Gangōji. The older temple quickly lost its prestige and support, however, and from the early Nara period onward it virtually disappears from historical records. In 1196 an electrical storm caused the pagoda to burn, and thereafter the other buildings must have rapidly deterio-

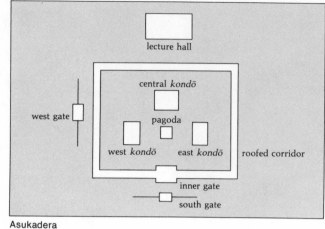

Asukadera

Ground plan of the original main buildings of the temple, discovered during excavations in 1956–57.

rated. Even though the temple became affiliated with the powerful SHINGON SECT, it shared the common fate of other temples in the Asuka district, neglect and poverty. The present *kondō* is a modest building dating from the Kan'ei era (1624–44). The temple now bears the formal name Angoin.

———Nara Kokuritsu Bunkazai Kenkyūjo, *Asukadera hakkutsu chōsa hōkoku*, 5 (1958).   John M. ROSENFIELD

Asukagawa

River in the Nara Basin, Nara Prefecture, central Honshū, originating in the Ryūmon Mountains and emptying into the river Yamatogawa. It flows through such historic sites as the village of Asuka and the city of Kashihara, and many traces of the ancient Asuka culture (mid-6th century to mid-7th century) are found along this river. It is referred to in ancient poems, including the 8th-century anthology *Man'yōshū*. Length: 23 km (14 mi).

Asuka history → history of Japan

Asukai Masaari (1241–1301)

Courtier, WAKA poet, scholar. Grandson of ASUKAI MASATSUNE (1170–1221), who established the family tradition of expertise in classical poetry and also in the court game of kickball (KEMARI). A competent *waka* poet and partisan of the innovating Kyōgoku poetic faction, Masaari had 68 poems included in imperial anthologies, beginning with the *Shoku kokinshū* (1265, Collection of Ancient and Modern Times, Continued). His personal collection, which he entitled *Rinnyoshū* (Collection of Poems as Ugly as the Jealous Woman Next Door), contains more than 1,100 poems. He was also the author of a half dozen autobiographical works, including lyrical diaries and accounts of his travels to Kamakura. He was an assiduous student of the classical literary tradition, and was particularly noted as a student of the KOKINSHŪ and as an authority on the great 11th-century romance, *Genji monogatari* (TALE OF GENJI).

Robert H. BROWER

Asukai Masatsune (1170–1221)

Progenitor of the Asukai branch of the Fujiwara family, courtier, WAKA poet, and expert in the courtly game of kickball (KEMARI). A member of the lesser nobility, Masatsune studied classical poetry with the great Shunzei (FUJIWARA NO TOSHINARI, 1114–1204), and was also a close associate of Shunzei's son Teika (FUJIWARA NO SADAIE, 1162–1241), who succeeded his father as the dominant figure in classical poetry. In 1201 Masatsune was appointed Fellow of the Bureau of Poetry by ex-Emperor Go-Toba and designated one of the six compilers of the eighth imperial anthology *(chokusenshū)*, the SHIN KOKINSHŪ (ca 1205, New Collection of Ancient and Modern Times). The collection contains 22 of his poems, and an additional 110 are included in various later imperial anthologies. His personal anthology, *Asukai shū* (The Asukai Collection, or, written with different characters, The Collection of the Well of Asuka), contains 1,541 poems. He can be classed as one of the better poets of the extraordinarily talented Age of the *Shin kokinshū*, though not in the front rank. He was also regarded as the age's foremost player and teacher of the elegant courtly game of kickball. In keeping with the trend for court families to develop areas of hereditary expertise, Masatsune passed on his training and "trade secrets" to his descendants, who became acknowledged authorities, teachers, and judges of both kickball and classical poetry. The important poetic house which he founded allied itself with the dominant conservative Nijō line of Teika's descendants in the 14th century, and gradually moved to the fore as the latter became increasingly quarrelsome and debilitated. *Robert H. Brower*

Asuka Kiyomihara Code

(Asuka Kiyomihara Ritsuryō). The earliest law code of Japan to be divided into criminal laws *(ritsu)* and administrative regulations *(ryō)*. Compilation of the code began in 681, in the reign of Emperor TEMMU, and it was promulgated in 689 under Temmu's widow and successor, Empress JITŌ. It is named for the ASUKA KIYOMIHARA NO MIYA, the imperial residence from 672 to 694. The administrative section of the code is totally lost and may never have been completed; much of the criminal section, however, can be reconstructed from passages in the chronicle NIHON SHOKI (720). It clearly served as the model for the TAIHŌ CODE, which superseded it in 702. See also LEGAL SYSTEM: history of Japanese law; TAIKA REFORM; RITSURYŌ SYSTEM. *Kitamura Bunji*

Asuka Kiyomihara no Miya

(Asuka Kiyomihara Palace). Residence of Emperor TEMMU and Empress JITŌ from 672 to 694. Probably the largest palace in Japan up to that time, it is thought to have been located in the present-day village of Asuka, Nara Prefecture. The *Nihon shoki* (720) mentions that the palace complex included a hall of state (DAIGOKUDEN) and a full complement of administrative offices; archaeological findings suggest that it had an elaborate drainage system and unusually shaped stone fountains, one of them a model of the Mt. Sumeru (J: Shumisen) of Buddhist mythology. A semiurban capital district *(kyō)* grew up around the palace, and the new Capital Office (Kyōshiki) was established to govern it. Ōtomo no Miyuki (d 701), who had helped Temmu to win the throne in the JINSHIN DISTURBANCE of 672, celebrated the building of the palace in a poem preserved in the 8th-century anthology *Man'yōshū*: "Our great king, god that he is, has turned into a splendid capital the marshy fields where chestnut horses, belly-deep, once trudged." After Temmu's death in 686, his widow and successor, Empress Jitō, ruled from Asuka Kiyomihara no Miya for eight years before moving the capital in 694 to FUJIWARAKYŌ, about 2.5 kilometers (1.5 mi) to the northwest. *William R. Carter*

Asuka period (latter part of 6th century to 710)

A subdivision of the Yamato period (ca 300–710), variously dated but centered in the reign (593–628) of Empress SUIKO. First used at the beginning of the 20th century by historians of art and architecture, the term in its narrow sense designates the years from Suiko's accession (593) to the TAIKA REFORM (645), a period characterized by the adoption of continental art forms and technology from Korea. In this scheme it is followed by the Hakuhō period, centered in the reign (672–686) of Emperor TEMMU and extending from 645 to the establishment of the capital at Heijōkyō (now the city of Nara) in 710, a period marked by direct cultural and technological influences from Tang (T'ang) China. The Asuka period in its broadest sense designates the years from the introduction of Buddhism (traditionally 538 or 552) to 710. In the past, political historians often limited the Asuka period to the years 593–622, when Prince SHŌTOKU served as regent for Suiko and began to create a centralized, bureaucratic state on the Chinese model; but today there is a tendency to use the broader definition. Because the term "Asuka period" is so imprecisely defined and easily misunderstood, historical writings more commonly refer instead to a specific year-name (NENGŌ) or to the reign of a specific sovereign. See also PERIODIZATION.

■——Ueda Masaaki et al, *Asuka saikō* (1979).
William R. Carter

Asukata Ichio (1915–)

Politician; chairman of the JAPAN SOCIALIST PARTY since December 1977. Born in Yokohama, he graduated in 1937 from Meiji University Law School and represented many labor unions. In December 1945 he helped to reorganize the Japan Socialist Party. After serving on the Yokohama City Council and in the Kanagawa Prefectural Assembly, he was elected in 1953 to the House of Representatives, where for 10 years he effectively opposed the government on defense and diplomatic issues. Elected mayor of Yokohama in 1963, the following year he formed the National Association of Progressive Mayors and encouraged citizen participation in local affairs. Since his election as chairman of the Japan Socialist Party, he has sought to unite its various factions and cooperate with other opposition parties against the ruling Liberal Democratic Party. He was reelected to the House of Representatives in 1979.

Atagawa Hot Spring

(Atagawa Onsen). Located in the town of Higashi, Izu Peninsula, eastern Shizuoka Prefecture, central Honshū. A common salt spring; water temperature 32–100°C (90–212°F). Located in a scenic area, this hot spring is a popular tourist spot featuring such attractions as a banana-tree park, a crocodile park, and an orchid experimental station, which utilize the heat of the hot spring.

Atago Shrine

(Atago Jinja). Shintō shrine on ATAGOYAMA, a mountain located in Ukyō Ward, Kyōto. It is now divided into two shrines. The main shrine *(hongū)* is dedicated to Izanami no Mikoto, mother of the fire god; Wakumusubi no Kami, a deity of agriculture; and three other deities. The subsidiary shrine *(wakamiya)* is dedicated to the fire god, Kagutsuchi no Mikoto, and two other deities. From the outset, Atago Shrine was closely associated with a Buddhist temple on Atagoyama, the Hakuunji, which was dedicated to a particular Japanese manifestation of the bodhisattva JIZŌ (Shōgun Jizō) believed to guarantee victory on the battlefield. The Shintō deities of the Atago Shrine, viewed as Japanese incarnations (HONJI SUIJAKU) of Jizō, were called Atago Daigongen, and were thought to protect the capital, prevent fires, and look after the well-being of warriors. The shrine attracted many pilgrims, and numerous subsidiary Atago shrines were built throughout Japan. After the official separation of Shintō and Buddhism in 1868 (see SHINTŌ AND BUDDHISM, SEPARATION OF), the Buddhistic designation Atago Daigongen was changed to Atago Jinja, following the removal of the Buddhist symbols. Pilgrims climb the mountain on 31 July to buy talismans for protection from fire to install in their homes. The annual festival is held on 28 September. *Stanley Weinstein*

Atagoyama

Mountain to the northwest of the city of Kyōto; one of the Tamba Mountains. The ATAGO SHRINE is located at its summit. Takao and Kiyotaki at its base are noted for their autumn foliage. Height: 924 m (3,031 ft).

Atami

City in eastern Shizuoka Prefecture, central Honshū, on the Izu Peninsula. Overlooking Sagami Bay and surrounded by mountains on three sides, it is noted for its mild climate and numerous hot springs. Atami developed as a resort town in the 8th century. The construction of the Tanna Tunnel in 1934 and the Tōkaidō Shinkansen (the super-speed railway) in 1964 have made it one of the most frequented resorts in Japan. A part of FUJI–HAKONE–IZU NATIONAL PARK, Atami has easy access to JIKKOKU PASS, the island of HATSUSHIMA, and the Nishikigaura coast. There is a plum festival in January, a fireworks display in early August, and in the fall a festival honoring OZAKI KŌYŌ, a scene from whose novel *Konjiki yasha* (1897–1903, tr *The Golden Demon*, 1905) took place in Atami. Pop: 50,082.

atomic bomb

A bomb that obtains its destructive energy from chain reactions of fissionable materials. The first atomic bomb used against human targets was dropped at 8:15 AM, 6 August 1945 on Hiroshima, Japan, a city of approximately 350,000 people. Three days later a second bomb was dropped at 11:02 AM over Nagasaki, population 270,000. (These population estimates are based on the 1944 census. There are various other estimates; e.g., see ATOMIC BOMB RELATED DISEASE.) Survivors of these atomic bombings are known in Japanese as *hibakusha*.

Historical Background —— Nuclear fission was discovered by European scientists in 1938. A year later, fearing that Nazi Germany might develop an atomic bomb, Albert Einstein (1879–1955) sent a letter to President Franklin Delano ROOSEVELT urging him to initiate an American atomic weapons program. After some delay, the $2 billion Manhattan Project was launched in 1942. The project engaged as many as 125,000 people at one time to produce uranium 235 and plutonium 239, both fissionable materials, at Oak Ridge, Tennessee, and at Hanford, Washington. In addition, thousands of scientists were mobilized at Los Alamos, New Mexico, to produce the bomb itself.

Although historians are still debating whether the use of the bombs against Japan resulted from a series of specific decisions, or from the momentum of the project and the pressure of the war, the minutes of the Military Policy Committee meeting held in May 1943 describe the first documented discussion on the possible targets as follows: "The point of use of the first bomb was discussed and the general view appeared to be that its best point of use would be on a Japanese fleet concentration in the Harbor of Truk. General W.D. Styer suggested Tokio [sic], but it was pointed out that the bomb should be used where, if it failed to go off, it would land in water of sufficient depth to prevent easy salvage. The Japanese were selected as they would not be so apt to secure knowledge from it as would the Germans."

On 12 April 1945, less than a month before the defeat of Germany, Harry S. TRUMAN became president following Roosevelt's death. On 31 May 1945, there was a meeting of the Interim Committee, which had been set up to advise President Truman on future atomic energy policy. The minutes describe its conclusion: "After much discussion concerning various types of targets and the effects to be produced, the Secretary expressed the conclusion, on which there was general agreement, that we could not give the Japanese any warning; that we could not concentrate on a civilian area; but that we should seek to make a profound psychological impression on as many of the inhabitants as possible. At the suggestion of Dr. James Bryant Conant, the Secretary agreed that the most desirable target would be a vital war plant employing a large number of workers and closely surrounded by workers' houses." It was also confirmed in the same meeting that two bombs to be available in early August should be used. On 13 June, the targets of Kokura, Niigata, and Hiroshima were chosen; Nagasaki was added later.

By this time there were indications that the Japanese were seeking to end the war. Evidence of this is found in ex-Prime Minister KONOE FUMIMARO's cable to the Soviet Union on 12 July which expressed a desire to end the war swiftly. Joseph Stalin showed the cable, which had already been intercepted and decoded by the United States, to Truman on 18 July during the Potsdam Conference. In the meantime, Truman had received the expected news that the first atomic bomb test conducted in Alamogordo, New Mexico, on 16 July had been successful.

The POTSDAM DECLARATION was issued on 26 July with no mention of the United States' willingness to approve Japan's emperor system upon Japan's surrender despite the belief of Joseph Clark GREW, then acting secretary of state, that such an indication of willingness would probably persuade the Japanese to accept the terms of surrender.

By early August the two bombs were on the South Pacific island of Tinian, assembled and ready for use. The decision was made to drop a bomb over Hiroshima on the first clear day, which turned out to be 6 August. The second bombing, which had been scheduled for Kokura on 11 August, was moved up to 9 August by Colonel Paul Tibbetts, commander of the 509th Composite Squadron, in view of the weather forecast.

The official American justification for the use of the two atomic bombs is that it ended the war early, thus saving many American lives which would have been lost if an invasion of the Japanese mainland had been attempted. However, some historians have contended that the decision to use the bombs was influenced by several postwar considerations, most important being the American desire to demonstrate the power of the bomb to the Soviet Union.

Destructive Power of the Atomic Bomb —— The bomb dropped on Hiroshima was 3 meters (9.8 ft) long and 0.7 meters (2.3 ft) in diameter, weighing 4 metric tons (4.4 short tons). Only 1 kilogram

Atomic bomb —— Hiroshima

Scene near the hypocenter of the blast. The ruins of the Industry Promotion Hall at right have been preserved as the Atomic Bomb Dome.

(2.2 lb) of the 10 to 30 kilograms of uranium 235 used in the bomb actually fissioned, producing the TNT equivalent of 13 kilotons of explosive power. The Nagasaki bomb, which used plutonium 239, was 3.5 meters (11.5 ft) long and 1.5 meters (4.9 ft) in diameter, weighing 4.5 metric tons (5 short tons). The explosive power was equivalent to 22 kilotons of TNT. Although the bomb dropped on Nagasaki had greater explosive power, Nagasaki sustained less damage than Hiroshima because of differences in the terrain of the two cities and the difference in the location of the hypocenter (the point on the ground above which the bomb exploded).

In both cities, the bombs detonated between 500 and 600 meters (1,640 and 1,970 ft) above ground. The explosion created a massive fireball. The temperature near the point of explosion reached as high as several million degrees centigrade, in comparison with the several thousand degrees reached by a conventional bomb. A mushroom-shaped cloud was observed rising up after the explosion.

Damage from the explosion was due to heat rays (thermal radiation), the blast (expansion of air), and radiation. Approximately 35 percent of the total energy generated by the bomb was transmitted in the form of thermal radiation, 50 percent in the form of blast, and 15 percent in radiation.

Effects of thermal radiation. The temperature at the hypocenter was estimated to be 3,000° to 4,000°C (5,400° to 7,200°F). For comparison, the melting point of an iron bar is approximately 1,500°C (2,700°F). As a result, those who were exposed to heat rays within 1 kilometer (0.6 mi) of the hypocenter in both cities died within a week. Not only their skin, but also their internal organs were ruptured by the heat. People as far away as 3.5 kilometers (2.2 mi) from the hypocenter also suffered skin burns from the heat rays.

Spontaneous combustion and charring of buildings, railroad ties, fences, and other materials occurred within 3 kilometers (1.9 mi) of the hypocenter. Shadows were imprinted on concrete walls, and the surface of granite stones and roof tiles near the hypocenter melted.

Effects of the blast. The air pressure, which reached several hundred thousand millibars near the epicenter (center of explosion), created a blast effect as the surrounding air rapidly expanded. Shock waves, at or above the speed of sound, were followed by a subsonic flow of air.

A theoretical estimate indicates that at the hypocenter the maximum blast pressure was 35 metric tons/sq m (3.6 short tons/sq ft) and the maximum velocity was 440 m/sec (1,400 ft/sec), while at 3 kilometers (1.9 mi) from the hypocenter the pressure was still 1.3 metric tons/sq m (267 lbs/sq ft) and the velocity 30 m/sec (98 ft/sec). Theoretical calculations also show that the explosion height of 600 meters (1,970 ft), which was the general height at which the two bombs exploded, is the height that maximizes the destructive power of the blast through the so-called Mach effect (the interference caused by the reflection of the original shock waves on the ground).

Within 2 kilometers (1.2 mi) of the hypocenter, all wooden structures were obliterated. Although concrete buildings near the hypocenter were severely damaged, those within the rest of the 2 kilometer range generally withstood the pressure, although their interiors were ravaged by fire.

People near the hypocenter were blown into the air, whether they were inside or outside buildings. Many people became trapped

Atomic bomb——Nagasaki

Victims of the bombing in Nagasaki on the day after the blast.

under fallen buildings which later caught fire. Clothes were torn from bodies. Glass and metal pieces from the buildings were embedded in the flesh of the people nearby.

Effects of radiation. The so-called background radiation normally received by human beings is 0.1 rad per year. People receiving 700 rads (lethal dose) or more usually die; half of those who receive 400 rads (semilethal dose) also die. Those who were within one kilometer (0.6 mi) of the hypocenter in Hiroshima and within 1.2 kilometers (0.75 mi) in Nagasaki received at least the semilethal dose.

Approximately 20 percent of the total deaths are attributed to the initial radiation consisting of gamma rays and neutrons emitted within one minute of the explosion. Residual radioactivity was found to result from either the nuclear reaction of neutrons in the initial radiation or the radioactivity of fissioned or unfissioned bomb materials. Those who entered the cities within 100 hours after the bombings received a considerable dose of residual radiation.

Other effects. The fire storms caused by thermal radiation and secondary sources ravaged both cities. They lasted several hours in Hiroshima, burning every combustible object within a 2 kilometer (1.2 mi) radius. Because of the city's hilly terrain, the fire storm in Nagasaki was not as intense. Moisture which condensed on rising ash and dust later came down as rain in both cities. Because of its color this radioactive precipitation is known as "black rain."

Aftereffects of the Atomic Bomb——*Number of deaths.* The figures often quoted of 78,000 deaths in Hiroshima and 27,000 in Nagasaki are now considered to be low estimates. Because there were substantial but undetermined numbers of Koreans and military personnel in both cities, it is even more difficult to arrive at an accurate estimate. According to a 1977 estimate, some 130,000 to 140,000 people died in Hiroshima, and 60,000 to 70,000 people died in Nagasaki by the end of 1945 (there are various other estimates; for example, see ATOMIC BOMB RELATED DISEASE). The total number of casualties of the A-bomb is estimated to be 350,000 in Hiroshima (43,000 were believed to be military personnel) and 270,000 to 280,000 in Nagasaki. The number of people who died by 1950 due to direct exposure to the bomb is estimated at 200,000 in Hiroshima and 140,000 in Nagasaki.

In both cities the death rate within one kilometer (0.6 mi) was close to 100 percent (here too there are slightly different estimates; see ATOMIC BOMB RELATED DISEASES). One half of the total deaths were due to exposure within this range. Between 1.0 and 1.5 kilometers (0.6 to 0.9 mi) the death rate was approximately 50 percent. Between 1.5 and 2.0 kilometers (0.9 to 1.2 mi) it was 20 to 30 percent, and beyond 2 kilometers (1.2 mi) it was less than 5 percent.

Among the total deaths by the end of 1945, 60 percent were from burns caused by thermal radiation and fire, 20 percent from injuries caused by the blast, and 20 percent from radiation-related disturbances. The death rate of 50 percent of the population in Hiroshima and Nagasaki by 1950 was much higher than the death rate in the case of conventional bombing. By comparison, during the March 1945 fire-bombing of Tōkyō, 17 percent of residents died in the Fukagawa area, which received the heaviest casualties. The Dresden and Hamburg bombings show similar or lower rates.

Material loss. In Hiroshima 70,000 of the 76,000 buildings near the hypocenter were destroyed beyond use. More than 50,000 were totally destroyed by either fire or blast. In Nagasaki approximately 18,000 of the 49,000 buildings were unsalvageable, and 13,000 of these were totally destroyed.

According to a conservative estimate, it would have cost ¥1.54 trillion at 1977 values ($6 billion) to replace the major material loss in Hiroshima and ¥640 billion ($2.5 billion) in Nagasaki.

Medical effects. The initial radiation, consisting of gamma rays and neutrons, damaged exposed somatic cells instantly. Radioactive materials in the body created by neutron bombardment release beta rays which affect the blood-producing tissues for an extended period of time.

The tissues of the human body in order of susceptibility to radiation damage are lymphatic tissues and bone marrow, gonadal cells, epithelial cells of the digestive organs, ovarian follicular cells, connective tissues of the skin, bone, liver, spleen, kidney, heart, nerves, brain, and muscle.

The effects of the atomic bombs on human bodies are usually divided into acute effects (those developed by the end of 1945) and late effects (those developed in 1946 and afterward). Although acute effects were caused by the synergetic actions of heat, blast, and radiation, late effects were often due to radiation alone.

In the acute stage, deaths were caused by collapsing buildings, severe burns, and radiation. Those who escaped death but received severe burns or injuries suffered from fever, thirst, and/or vomiting hours after the bombing. They went into shock and almost all died within the first week.

Those who received heavy doses of radiation, even though their burns or injuries were not severe, developed such symptoms as weakness, nausea, vomiting, diarrhea, expectoration and vomiting of blood, bloody discharge from the bowels, and bloody urine. Most of this group died approximately 10 days after the bombing.

Those who managed to survive this initial period later suffered many of the following additional symptoms: headache, delirium, insomnia, epilation (loss of hair), malaise, nosebleed, genital bleeding, bleeding of the gums, bleeding under the skin, fever, inflammation of the skin and the mouth, decrease of white and red blood cells, loss of sperm, and menstrual abnormalities. Later studies have confirmed that the major acute disturbances caused by radiation exposure are epilation, hemorrhage, decrease of white blood cells and blood platelets, and oral and pharyngeal lesions.

Although most of those who lived through the acute stage seemed to regain health, late effects began to appear gradually. After burns due to thermal radiation healed, there remained protuberant scars known as keloids, which occurred in more than half of the burn victims. Since a higher incidence of keloids was observed among the *hibakusha* than among ordinary burn patients, some researchers believe that radiation increases the occurrence of keloids. Once considered symbolic of A-bomb suffering because of its visibility, keloid cases peaked in 1946–47, after which spontaneous regression of protruding scars tended to occur.

Cataracts were the most common eye disorder among the *hibakusha.* A definite correlation between distance/exposure dose and incidence of cataracts has been observed.

A decrease in the production and count of white and red blood cells and platelets, though more frequently observed in the acute period, still persisted among some *hibakusha* even ten years afterward. Leukemia and multiple myeloma, cancers of the blood, were also observed. Leukemia is a typical late effect; although the leukemia incidence peaked in the 1950s, it continues to be higher among *hibakusha* than among the general population. A correlation between its incidence and distance/exposure dose has been observed. Leukemia is also observed among those who entered Hiroshima or Nagasaki immediately after the explosion. Multiple myeloma cases have gradually increased since 1960.

The incidence of malignant tumors among *hibakusha* increased around 1960. A definite correlation between distance/exposure dose and incidence has been reported for thyroid cancer, breast cancer, lung cancer, and salivary gland cancer. Although the correlation has not been established for other forms of cancer, the incidence of various forms of malignant tumors in Hiroshima and Nagasaki is high.

Special development problems occurred in those exposed to the blasts at a young age or *in utero*. Since the actively dividing cells of young people are more sensitive to radiation, special disorders were expected among this group. For example, the height and weight of young *hibakusha* were found to be significantly less than in comparable groups in the general population. A 1960 survey found that 2,310 *hibakusha* in Hiroshima and 1,562 in Nagasaki were exposed to radiation *in utero*. Congenital malformation such as microcephaly (a condition in which the head is abnormally small) and delayed growth and development of head circumference, stature, and body weight were observed among this group. Serious cases of microcephaly are accompanied by mental retardation. Microcephaly was especially marked among those exposed within the first 18 weeks of gestation and its severity tended to increase with exposure dose. Many consider microcephaly a symbol of the *hibakusha*'s suffering.

Although genetic effects of radiation have been established experimentally, no definite research has established that genetic effects due to A-bomb radiation have appeared in the offspring of *hibakusha*. Likewise, premature aging has been observed among irradiated groups in experiments on animals, but it has not been documented among the A-bomb survivors (see also ATOMIC BOMB RELATED DISEASE).

Psychological effects. According to R. J. Lifton's psychological research, after the bomb explosion the *hibakusha* were "immersed in death," although they did not understand what had happened to cause such complete destruction. They saw their families, friends, and colleagues lying dead around them or heard them pleading to be helped. Their ability to survive emotional collapse was due to a mechanism which has been termed "psychic numbing." However, in many cases *hibakusha* were left with a deep sense of guilt because they had had to abandon others in order to save their own lives. As the late effects began to appear, *hibakusha* realized that their encounter with death was not over; when they saw others die long after exposure to radiation, they realized that theirs was a "permanent encounter with death." The normal support structures within the family and the community had also been destroyed, making it even more difficult for the survivors to cope with their situation.

Impact on family and livelihood. The loss of family is symbolized by the expression "A-bomb orphans." Between 4,000 to 5,000 children in Hiroshima and 1,000 in Nagasaki, are estimated to have lost their parents as a result of the bomb. Disintegration of families is reflected in the number of deaths per family. Near the hypocenter, two out of three members died, while one out of three died in the areas affected by fire. More than half of all families lost their main breadwinner.

A 1965 survey showed that both Hiroshima and Nagasaki *hibakusha* have had higher rates of unemployment, job change, and absence from work than non-*hibakusha*. It also showed that among *hibakusha* a higher number of women and older people, who normally do not work, were working as day laborers. These figures reflect the fact that poor health and poverty have continued to plague the *hibakusha*. Evidence also indicates that there are many more social, economic, physical, and emotional problems which affect every aspect of the *hibakusha*'s lives. Furthermore, these problems intensify as the *hibakusha* grow older.

Non-Japanese hibakusha. There were a considerable number of foreigners among the *hibakusha*. For example, one report estimates that 25,000–28,000 Koreans in Hiroshima and 12,000 in Nagasaki became *hibakusha*. Because the Japanese had brought many of these people from Korea, then a Japanese colony, for forced labor, and discriminated against them even after World War II, the plight of the Korean *hibakusha* was worse than that of Japanese *hibakusha*. Those who returned to Korea do not seem to have fared much better.

There are about 1,000 *hibakusha* now living in the United States, according to one estimate. Out of these people approximately 500 have been identified. They are mostly Japanese Americans who were in Hiroshima or Nagasaki in August 1945 living with relatives. Some had decided to go to Japan instead of staying in the relocation camps into which Japanese Americans were gathered during World War II. (See JAPANESE AMERICANS, WARTIME RELOCATION OF.)

Among the prisoners of war from the United States and the Allied nations detained in Nagasaki, approximately 400 became vic-

tims of the bombing, many of whom survived. In Hiroshima there were approximately 20, all of whom died. In addition to American and Korean *hibakusha*, resident foreigners from China, Germany, the Soviet Union, Mongolia, and other Asian countries also became victims of the bombs.

Postwar Developments —— *United States government.* In September 1945 the General Headquarters (GHQ) of the Allied forces in Japan issued a press code which effectively banned the release of any information on the atomic bomb. As a result, the *hibakusha* were not able to learn about what they had experienced, or even to find out through the media how their symptoms should be treated. Japanese research relating to the effects of the A-bomb was also greatly restricted.

In March 1947 a US presidential order established the Atomic Bomb Casualty Commission (ABCC) to study the effects of the atomic bombings. The ABCC studies are responsible for much of the available information on the actual effects of an atomic bomb on a human population. Many of their results have been summarized in this article. However, since the ABCC was a research organ, no medical treatment was offered to the *hibakusha*, who often underwent batteries of tests given by the ABCC doctors. Many *hibakusha* have expressed negative feelings about the ABCC because they felt they had been used as guinea pigs. The ABCC was reorganized in 1975 and became the Radiation Effects Research Foundation. The foundation is now supported jointly by the Japanese and United States governments.

Japanese government. On 10 August 1945 the Japanese government, through the Swiss government, protested the use of the atomic bombs as a violation of the international laws of war. The SAN FRANCISCO PEACE TREATY and the United States–Japan Security Treaty were signed in September 1951. Under article 19 of the Peace Treaty, the Japanese government renounced its right to claim war damages against the United States. It was later made clear that this included the right of *hibakusha* to claim compensation. See also UNITED STATES–JAPAN SECURITY TREATIES.

The War Victim Relief Law of 1942 was administered by the Japanese military until early October 1945, after which the *hibakusha* had to receive treatment at their own expense. In 1957 the Law for Health Protection and Medical Care for the Atomic Bomb Explosion Sufferers (known as the A-Bomb Medical Law) was passed. Since 1957 the law has been gradually amended to give better and broader assistance to the *hibakusha*. It now provides free medical examinations twice a year and medical care for injuries or sickness recognized to be due to the effects of the A-bombs. The expense of medical care not covered by NATIONAL HEALTH INSURANCE is also borne by the government under this law. Approximately 360,000 people have been issued *hibakusha* certificates which enable them to receive the benefits of this law.

A suit was filed by five *hibakusha* against the government to obtain compensation for the damages they received from the A-bombs. In response the Tōkyō District Court ruled in 1963 that since the *hibakusha* have no right of claim against the American government either under domestic or international law, they could not juridically lay the obligation on the Japanese government. However, the court, while recognizing in the only court judgment of its kind that the atomic bombings of Hiroshima and Nagasaki were violations of international laws of war, ruled that the issue of compensation by the Japanese government originates in its responsibility for the outbreak of the war. Subsequently, the Law concerning the Special Measures for Atomic Bomb Sufferers (also known as the Hibakusha Special Welfare Law) was enacted in 1968. The purpose of the law is to promote the welfare of the *hibakusha* through various financial allowances. Although there are seven categories of application under the law, restrictive conditions such as amount of income earned by *hibakusha* make it difficult for them to receive much aid except for funeral expenses. In 1976 approximately one third of those who had been issued *hibakusha* certificates received some aid under the law. The benefits of these two laws also extend to non-Japanese *hibakusha* who live in Japan. Other governments do not offer special assistance to their *hibakusha*.

Local governments. In 1949 the Japanese government issued laws declaring the city of Hiroshima "Peace Memorial City" and Nagasaki "International Cultural City," and both received financial assistance from the national government for reconstruction. Both cities built peace parks and A-bomb museums which have served as centers for the *hibakusha* and other citizens to work for world peace. For many, the memorial cenotaph in the Hiroshima Peace Park is the symbolic grave of loved ones who were never found. The inscription on the cenotaph, "Rest in peace; the mistake shall never be repeated," represents the committment of the Japanese to a permanent peace.

In contrast to the national government, local governments in Hiroshima and Nagasaki have made the relief of *hibakusha* a priority. With help from nonprofit organizations, citizens' groups, doctors, and other individuals, both cities have established A-bomb hospitals, nursing homes, recreational facilities, and special agencies for the welfare of *hibakusha*.

The two cities have held memorial ceremonies for the deceased A-bomb victims every year since 1946 and are actively engaged in promoting world peace. For example, since 1968 the mayors of both cities have sent telegrams of protest to the six nuclear powers every time they conduct a nuclear weapons test. In total, they have sent approximately 400 such telegrams.

Other organizations and individuals. In the period immediately after the bombing, it was the citizens themselves, the city officials, doctors, nurses, policemen, military personnel, and individual volunteers, who played the chief role in helping the *hibakusha*. Doctors and other medical assistants came from nearby areas to help the survivors. Individual doctors and medical institutions, especially in Hiroshima and Nagasaki, have continued to care for *hibakusha* and to conduct research in this relatively unknown area of medical science.

Efforts to understand the realities and effects of the atomic bomb have also been made by universities, government offices, the mass media, teachers, artists, and other individuals. Besides their concern for the welfare of the *hibakusha*, many have become advocates of the abolition of nuclear weapons as a step toward world peace.

Religious leaders and organizations have also been active and have helped to set up orphanages and initiate workshops to help the *hibakusha* cope with their suffering. Traditionally there have been more Catholics in Nagasaki than in any other city in Japan. As a result, they have tried to understand their suffering within the framework of their faith. For example, some interpreted the A-bomb to be an expression of God's anger at the Japanese. For most of them, the atomic bombing was perceived as only the latest incidence of persecution because of their religion (see CHRISTIANITY).

Help also came from abroad. Japanese Americans in Hawaii who had emigrated from Hiroshima donated relief money to the city as early as 1946. The Moral Adoption program which started in 1950 and the Hiroshima Maidens program in 1955 are also examples of attempts to help the survivors of the A-bombs.

Peace movement. The peace movement in Japan "officially" started in 1954 after the LUCKY DRAGON INCIDENT. However, there had existed germs of such movements which did not flourish because of the generally difficult living conditions and the GHQ press code. For example, the Cooperative Conference of Hiroshima Prefectural Women War Victims was held on 10 August 1948; their resolution included a plea for world peace and relief for *hibakusha*, but the word A-bomb was not used because of the GHQ press code.

In response to the Stockholm Appeal of March 1950, signature collection campaigns spread in Hiroshima and Nagasaki. In August of that year peace rallies were held in both cities although they were "illegal" under GHQ policies. Such small-scale activities were continued for a few years until a large-scale signature collection campaign was initiated in 1954 (see also PEACE MOVEMENT; ATOMIC WEAPONS, MOVEMENT TO BAN).

Hibakusha organizations. The primary aid for survivors comes from among themselves. After economic conditions improved and the peace treaty was concluded, self-help organizations were formed by *hibakusha* in Hiroshima and Nagasaki to improve their own economic, social, and medical situation. This also helped them to come out of their shell of self-pity. In 1956, the Japan Confederation of A- and H-bomb Sufferers Organizations (Nihon Gensuibaku Higaisha Dantai Kyōgikai, or Hidankyō) was formed. The Hidankyō unified the objectives and demands of various *hibakusha* organizations, giving a coherent structure to their movement.

Although the *hibakusha* movement became dependent on the peace movement in the late 1950s when the latter gained momentum, after the ideological split of the peace movement in the middle 1960s, the Hidankyō and the *hibakusha* began to take more active roles.

The Message of the Hibakusha——Today the continually expanding arsenal of the nuclear powers contains enough nuclear weapons to destroy the entire world many times over. In comparison with these weapons, the bombs dropped on Hiroshima and Nagasaki seem to be small and insignificant. However, even the

effects of these "small" bombs were so complex and far-reaching that after 35 years there is still no comprehensive picture of what happened.

Realizing the implications for the future of mankind, many *hibakusha* have transcended their bitterness, sorrow, and anger, as well as their poverty and pain, to tell others of their experience. Having daily faced the reality of living with such an experience, the *hibakusha* have developed many valuable insights into the meaning of life and humanity. They have tried to share these insights with the rest of the world through written material, photographs, films, television programs, exhibits, conferences, and demonstrations.

Their efforts represent an attempt to fulfill the responsibilities which many *hibakusha* feel belong to the present generation: the responsibility to share and understand the past, the responsibility to relieve the burdens of those still suffering, and the responsibility to construct a peaceful and more humane world for the future. See also PACIFISM; WORLD WAR II.

▟——Committee for the Compilation of Materials on the Damage of the Atomic Bombs in Hiroshima and Nagasaki, *The Damage by the Atomic Bombings in Hiroshima and Nagasaki and Their After-Effects* (1979). Committee for the Compilation of Materials on the Damage of the Atomic Bombs in Hiroshima and Nagasaki, *Hiroshima and Nagasaki: The Physical, Medical and Social Effects of the Atomic Bombings* (1981). Japan National Preparatory Committee, *A Call From Hibakusha of Hiroshima and Nagasaki, Proceedings of the International Symposium on the Damage and After-Effects of the Atomic Bombing of Hiroshima and Nagasaki* (1978). City of Hiroshima and City of Nagasaki, *To the United Nations* (1976). Martin J. Sherwin, *A World Destroyed* (1973). Robert Jay Lifton, *Death in Life* (1967). *Tadatoshi* AKIBA

atomic bomb related disease

(*gembakushō*). Direct atomic bomb injuries include those caused by the mechanical, thermal, and radiation effects of a nuclear explosion; victims in Hiroshima and Nagasaki suffered such injuries. Radioactive fallout of fission products causes injuries even to people far from the site: An example of this type of injury is the irradiation suffered by some people from the fallout of the Bikini atoll test explosion on 1 March 1954.

Hiroshima and Nagasaki——The first atomic bomb was dropped over Hiroshima on 6 August 1945, and the second above Nagasaki three days later. The Hiroshima bomb was a uranium 235 bomb and released energy equivalent to about 12.5 kilotons of TNT. The Nagasaki bomb, a plutonium 239 bomb, is thought to have been even more powerful. The bombs exploded approximately 580 meters (1,903 ft) and 500 meters (1,640 ft) in the air above Hiroshima and Nagasaki, respectively. The two cities varied in their overall damage because they are topographically different—Hiroshima is situated on a plain, and Nagasaki spreads over a range of hills—and because in the former some 60 percent of the population lived within a 2-kilometer (1.2-mi) radius from the hypocenter, while in the latter only some 30 percent of the population were in a comparable area. At the time of the attack, Hiroshima's population is estimated to have been 245,423; Nagasaki's 195,290 (these are conservative estimates based on the number of recipients of rice rations in the early summer of 1945; there are larger estimates based on 1944 census figures; see ATOMIC BOMB). The number of deaths in Hiroshima by November 1945 due to the atomic bomb is estimated by a survey report dated 1951 to have been about 64,602; the corresponding figure for Nagasaki is estimated by a similar joint survey report dated 1956 to have been about 39,000 (there are various other estimates). The actual number of dead is considered much larger because these statistics do not include military personnel. Hiroshima's total population at the time of the explosion (including commuters and military personnel) is estimated to have been 420,000.

Medical facilities in both cities were almost totally destroyed. First-aid rescue missions for the survivors were manned by military and civilian medical personnel. A full-scale investigation began in September 1945, when a special research committee was organized. A delegation from the committee cooperated with a US research team; in October 1945 the US–Japan Joint Commission was appointed by the United States National Academy of Sciences and the Science Council of Japan to carry out long-term research on radiation effects. In 1947 the Atomic Bomb Casualty Commission (ABCC) was organized and administered with the cooperation of the Japan National Institute of Health. In April 1975, ABCC evolved into the Radiation Effects Research Foundation (RERF), in which Japan and the United States participated as equal partners.

Clinical Course of Sustained Injuries——Tsuzuki Masao (1892–1961), a doctor who studied the clinical course of A-bomb injuries, divided it into four periods: first (early)—within two weeks of the explosion; second (middle)—third to eighth week; third (late)—third to fourth month; and fourth (last)—long-term. In the first period, almost 100 percent of the population within a radius of 500 meters from the hypocenter and approximately 80 percent within 1,000 meters (3,281 ft) died from blast and radiation injuries, burns, and other traumas (there are larger estimates; see ATOMIC BOMB). Symptoms in others included systemic emaciation, anxiety, fever, vomiting, and such hemorrhagic manifestations as mucosal bleeding, hemoptysis, hematemesis, and melena. Epilation and cutaneous hemorrhage were observed in the second period. About half the deaths occurred during the first week, three-fourths by the end of the second week, and the remaining one-fourth during the second period; that is, the victims who were fated to die did so within two months after exposure. In and after the third period, the injuries stabilized or improved to some degree.

Mechanical Injuries——Glass fragments, beams, and roof tiles blown off collapsing buildings caused most mechanical injuries. Direct blast injuries such as perforated eardrums and damaged lungs or intestines were relatively rare. Severe injuries such as fractures were also infrequent, possibly because many crippled victims burned to death. The body areas most commonly affected by mechanical injuries were the head, face, neck, and upper limbs. Lower limb injuries were more frequent in women than men. The most common injuries were contusions and lacerations. Some injuries were complicated by burns and radiation problems. The mechanical injuries healed within a period of 1 week to 2 years, although some victims still have glass fragments embedded in their bodies today; 50 percent of the mechanically injured healed within 4 weeks and 90 percent within 20 weeks.

Even people as far away as 5,000 meters (16,404 ft) from the hypocenter suffered mechanical injuries. The blast pressures generated at ground zero are estimated to have been 4.5–6.7 metric tons (5.0–7.4 short tons) per square meter for the Hiroshima bomb, and 6–8 metric tons (6.6–8.8 short tons) per square meter for the Nagasaki bomb (here again estimates differ).

Burns——The majority of burns were flash burns. The temperature of the hypocenter is estimated to have reached 3,000–4,000°C (5,400–7,200°F), corresponding to the visible and infrared regions of the spectrum. Burn injuries occurred within 0.3 seconds of the explosion, with the greatest intensity of radiant heat lasting 0.5 seconds. In Hiroshima flash burns were observed among people within a radius of approximately 4.5 kilometers (2.8 mi), although few bullae or serious burns were reported beyond 3 kilometers (1.9 mi); flash burns occurring within 2 kilometers (1.2 mi) were for the most part third degree burns. In Nagasaki the distance in which flash burns were observed reached a radius of approximately 4 kilometers (2.5 mi).

The widespread fires caused another type of injury, fire burns. Half the fire burns suppurated. Fifty percent of the flash burns healed by the 4th week, 90 percent by the 18th week, and 95 percent by the 23rd week after the explosion. Five years later an investigation revealed that almost all the protuberant scars known as keloids caused by fire burns had disappeared, while 10 percent of those resulting from flash burns remained.

Burns were observed among approximately 90 percent of the people in Hiroshima who were unshielded and within 4 kilometers of the hypocenter, and among 78 percent of the comparable population in Nagasaki. Some burns have left functional disturbances resulting from contracture of the limbs, as well as psychological sequelae due to facial scars.

Radiation Injuries——The effects of ionizing radiation are the chief characteristics of atomic bomb injuries.

Estimated exposure doses. The severity of radiation injuries depends on the exposure dose, and the Hiroshima bomb emitted more neutrons than the Nagasaki bomb. Exposure doses resulting from residual radioactivity are estimated at approximately 80 rads at the hypocenter in Hiroshima and 50 rads in Nagasaki. Since the intensity of residual radiation rapidly falls off, the actual doses for persons entering the cities after the explosion are lower than these estimated values, and of course the intensity of radiation also decreases as the distance from the hypocenter increases. The effects of radioactive fallout were therefore relatively small. However, victims in Nagasaki's Nishiyama area probably received doses as large as 11

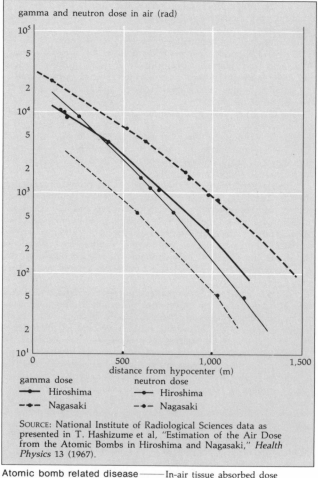

gamma and neutron dose in air (rad)

distance from hypocenter (m)

gamma dose	neutron dose
—•— Hiroshima	—•— Hiroshima
–•– Nagasaki	–•– Nagasaki

SOURCE: National Institute of Radiological Sciences data as presented in T. Hashizume et al, "Estimation of the Air Dose from the Atomic Bombs in Hiroshima and Nagasaki," *Health Physics* 13 (1967).

Atomic bomb related disease——In-air tissue absorbed dose

to 60 rads from fallout irradiation. (It is possible that these estimates may be revised as a result of ongoing studies.)

Acute effects. Acute symptoms among victims surviving three weeks or longer after the A-bomb explosion included vomiting, fever, epilation, purpura, and oropharyngeal ulceration, all of which varied according to the exposure dose. An ABCC survey showed that acute symptoms occurred in 5 to 10 percent of survivors exposed to doses of 50 rads and in 50 to 80 percent of those who received approximately 300 rads.

Late effects. Late effect studies made so far have been largely epidemiological. The incidence of leukemia, in particular, began to increase about three years after exposure to the bomb, reached a peak in 1951, and gradually decreased thereafter. Nevertheless, the present level of incidence is higher than usual. The incidence of acute leukemia among survivors who were under 16 years of age at the time of exposure increased during the first 10 years but has decreased since 1960. Chronic leukemia has been high among survivors who were 30 years and over. In general, the incidence of chronic myeloid leukemia has been higher than normal, especially among the Hiroshima survivors.

The incidence of leukemia rises with an increase in exposure dose, and there has been a difference between the survivors in Hiroshima and those in Nagasaki, probably because the two cities had different patterns of radiation. The incidence of leukemia is high among victims exposed to doses of 20 rads or higher (Hiroshima) and 100 rads or higher (Nagasaki). However, a rising incidence may also be found among those exposed to doses lower than the above levels. No increase in the incidence of leukemia has been observed among children exposed to the bomb *in utero* or whose parents were irradiated.

Other forms of cancer are also found among survivors. A 1960 report revealed that thyroid carcinoma was more frequent among those exposed to the higher doses. The incidence of thyroid carcinoma among them was 6 to 9 times higher than usual for women and 2 to 3 times higher for men. The risk of breast cancer in females exposed to doses of 200 rads or higher has also been 3.6 times higher

Atomic bomb related disease

Clinical Symptoms and Signs of Radiation Injuries				
Degree of severity[1]	1st week	2nd week	3rd week	Approximate mortality and time of death in weeks
Very severe (Group I)	nausea and vomiting (4) fever, apathy, delirium, diarrhea (4) lesions[2] (2) leukopenia (4)	fever (3) emaciation leukopenia (4) anemia hemorrhagic diathesis (1) epilation (1)		100% 1st and 2nd
Severe (Group II)	nausea and vomiting (3) anorexia fatigue	fever (3) leukopenia (2) anemia (1)	anorexia, emaciation, fever, diarrhea, epilation (4) oropharyngeal lesions (4) hemorrhagic diathesis (4) leukopenia (4) anemia (3)	50% 3rd to 6th
Moderately severe (Group III)	gastrointestinal syndrome[3] (3)	leukopenia (2)	anorexia, emaciation, fever, diarrhea, epilation (4~3) oropharyngeal lesions (1~3) hemorrhagic diathesis (1~3) leukopenia (3) anemia (2)	less than 10% 6th or later
Mild (Group IV)	gastrointestinal syndrome (1)	leukopenia (2)	fever (1) epilation (1) oropharyngeal lesions (1) hemorrhagic diathesis (1) leukopenia (1)	none

[1] These descriptive terms were used by the Joint Commission.
[2] These lesions (ulcerations) occurred on all mucous membrane surfaces but were more prevalent in lymphoid areas than elsewhere. The tonsils, pharynx, larynx, nasal passages, and tongue were frequently involved.
[3] Gastrointestinal syndrome includes nausea, vomiting, anorexia, and diarrhea.
NOTE: This classification is presented only as an orientation and there must have been considerable overlap in each category. (4) (3) (2) (1) connote grade of symptoms and signs in order of decreasing severity.
SOURCE: T. Ohkita, "Acute Effects," *Journal of Radiation Research*, Supplement (1975).

than usual; the incidence of breast cancer among female victims is expected to increase because those exposed in their childhood are now reaching the age of carcinogenesis. The rate of mortality from lung cancer during the period 1950–70 among bomb survivors exposed to doses of 200 rads or higher was 1.5 times greater than usual.

In addition, approximately 2.5 percent of the survivors who were within 1 kilometer (0.62 mi) of the hypocenter have developed cataracts, the first proven late effect of the bomb, with subjective symptoms appearing about two years after exposure. A-bomb cataracts often involve spotty or tuff-like turbidness beneath the posterior capsule of the eye lens.

In Hiroshima retarded body weight and height has been observed among survivors who were under 7 years of age at the time of the bombing, but no apparent lag appeared among survivors 12 years of age and older. Young adults exposed to estimated doses of 100 rads or higher were 3 to 5 centimeters (1.2 to 2.0 in) shorter and 3 to 4 kilograms (6.6 to 8.8 lb) lighter than normal. Retarded mental capacity was found in about half of the 60 microcephalic children whose mothers had been exposed to high doses of radiation.

According to an RERF investigation, malignant lymphoma, stomach cancer, salivary gland tumors, and hematalogic disorders other than leukemia were more prevalent among bomb victims. However, birth defects or mortality in the first filial generation, infertility, accelerated aging (including cardiovascular diseases), mortalities other than those caused by malignancies, and altered immunologic functions did not significantly differ from those of the general population. Lymphocyte cultures have revealed that the frequency of chromosome aberrations among bomb survivors is higher than usual and proportional to exposure dose. As yet, the effects of these aberrations on future health is unknown.

Bikini Radiation Injuries—— Radioactive fallout produced by a US thermonuclear test in the Pacific Bikini atoll at around 3:50 AM (JST) on 1 March 1954 inflicted radiation injuries on 23 Japanese fishermen, 239 Marshall Islanders, and 28 Americans, who were all at a great distance from the test site. The Japanese exposed to the fallout, the crew of the *Daigo fukuryū maru (Lucky Dragon V)*, were males aged between 18 and 39.

Exposure to fallout. The crew of the *Daigo fukuryū maru*, a tuna-fishing boat, witnessed a gigantic fireball over the western horizon and heard dull sounds about eight minutes later. At that time their boat was located approximately 190 kilometers (118 mi) east-northeast of the explosion site. White dust began to fall with a light rain around 7:00 AM and continued until around 11:30 AM. The shower was so heavy at one point that the crewmen could not open their eyes or mouths; the dust left on the deck was thick enough to create footprints. Two weeks after the incident, the *Daigo fukuryū maru* returned to its home port in Japan. The crew was eventually sent to a hospital and treated for radiation injuries for about a year. One of them died 206 days after his exposure. No mechanical or burn injuries were involved; the injuries sustained were from radiation alone. (American authorities disputed the cause of this one death, and other figures are sometimes given for the distance of the boat from the explosion site; for example, see LUCKY DRAGON INCIDENT.)

Exposure mode. The fallout on the boat contained 26 nuclides. The presence of uranium 237 suggested that the bomb was of the type which uses natural uranium as its outer component. The radioactive intensity of the fallout at 7:00 AM, 1 March, is estimated at 1.4 Ci/g. The fishing-boat crew received external γ-ray irradiation, internal irradiation from fallout intake, and cutaneous β-ray irradiation from fallout on naked skin. External γ-ray irradiation is considered to have been the main cause of acute symptoms. The two-week doses of γ rays varied but are estimated to have ranged from 170 to 600 rads. Radiochemical analysis of urine and external measurement of thyroid gland radioactivity showed internal irradiation. However, there were no cases of long-term presence of radioactive material in the men examined. The degree of skin injuries led to estimates that local skin exposure doses were roughly 1,000 rads or higher.

Clinical course. The initial general symptoms appearing in the crew included fatigue, nausea, vomiting, and anorexia. Conjunctivitis was observed in all cases. Leukopenia, thrombopenia, and moderate or mild anemia also occurred. The minimum counts of leukocytes were all less than normal: 5 cases at a level of 3,000 per cubic millimeter, 13 cases at a level of 2,000 per cubic millimeter, and 5 cases at a level of 1,000 per cubic millimeter. The minimum count of blood platelets was at a level of 10,000 per cubic millimeter. A few cases showed mild hemorrhagic tendencies. These findings correlated with the condition of the bone marrow. The affected bone marrow ran a course from aplasia to hypoplasia to partial recovery to normalization. As the bone marrow recovered, peripheral blood-cell counts approached normal levels. A temporary decrease in the number of spermatozoa was found, but signs of recovery appeared two years after exposure, and there was no permanent exposure-related sterility.

The main site of injury was the exposed areas of the skin. Working clothes, gloves, and shoes played an unexpected role in protecting the crew from β-ray exposure. Skin injuries developed in this sequence: erythema, edema, bulla, and erosion. Ulceration and necrosis of the head skin were found in two cases. Head epilation recovered after a few months in most instances. Some individuals still show depigmentation, pigmentation, telangiectasia, or atrophy of the skin without, however, signs of carcinogenesis.

Periodic examinations. Examinations have been conducted almost every year on the Bikini victims who started working again after leaving the hospital. Lymphocytic chromosome aberration is higher in the victims and is proportional to external exposure dosage. The effect of this abnormality on their long-term health is unknown. The Bikini survivors now lead almost normal lives. Mild liver dysfunctions are observed in some cases, but it is difficult to correlate them with the radiation exposure.

Thyroid nodules were observed in the majority of the Marshall Islanders who were 10 years or younger at the time of the nuclear test. One of these cases died from acute myelogenous leukemia 18 years after exposure. See also ATOMIC BOMB.

■——A. A. Awa et al, "Cytogenetic Study of the Offspring of Atom Bomb Survivors," *Nature* 218 (1968). Committee for the Compilation of Materials on Damage Caused by the Atomic Bombs in Hiroshima and Nagasaki, *Hiroshima and Nagasaki, The Physical, Medical, and Social Effects of the Atomic Bombings* (1981). R. A. Conrad et al, "A Twenty-year Review of Medical Findings in a Marshallese Population Accidentally Exposed to Radioactive Fallout," Report no. BNL 50424, Brookhaven National Laboratory (1975). T. Hashizume and T. Maruyama, "Physical Dose Estimates for A-Bomb Survivors—Studies at Chiba, Japan," *Journal of Radiation Research,* Supplement (1975). T. Kumatori and K. Miyoshi, "Clinical Studies on Persons Injured by Radioactive Materials," *Diagnosis and Treatment of Radioactive Poisoning* (1963). T. Kumatori et al, *Medical Survey of Japanese Exposed to Fallout Radiation in 1954: A Report after 10 Years* (1965). J. J. Lewis and H. A. Paterson, "Original Signs and Symptoms in Patients Surviving Five Years after Atomic Bomb Exposure under 1,000 Meters," Atomic Bomb Casualty Commission Report no. TR 17–59 (1959). Y. Mikamo et al, "Clinical and Haematological Studies on Bikini Patients," in The Japan Society for the Promotion of Science, ed, *The Research in the Effects and Influences of the Nuclear Bomb Test* (1956). R. W. Miller, "Delayed Radiation Effects in Atomic-Bomb Survivors," *Science* 166 (1969). T. Ohkita, "Acute Effects," *Journal of Radiation Research,* Supplement (1975). A. W. Oughterson and S. Warren, ed, *Medical Effects of the Atomic Bomb in Japan* (1956). Radiation Research Foundation, *The Radiation Effects Research Foundation—A Brief Description* (1978). KUMATORI Toshiyuki

atomic energy, laws concerning

(genshiryoku kankei hō). A special characteristic of Japanese laws concerning atomic energy is that, because of the RENUNCIATION OF WAR clause (art. 9) contained in the 1947 CONSTITUTION, the laws limit the uses of atomic energy to peaceful purposes. The centerpiece of nuclear energy legislation is the Basic Law concerning Atomic Energy (Genshiryoku Kihon Hō, 1955), which contains the three principles that nuclear research, development, and utilization will be for peaceful purposes only, that there will be full public disclosure, and that administration will be autonomous and democratic.

The peaceful uses of nuclear energy are broadly classified into use as a source of power and use of radioactive isotopes. Typical uses of nuclear reactors as power sources are electrical power-generating plants and nuclear-powered ships. In the late 1970s it was planned that nuclear power stations with a total generating capacity of some 30 million kw would be on line in 1985, but it was anticipated that this figure might have to be revised downward in response to local residents' opposition. The basic laws and regulations relating to the use of nuclear energy as a power source include the Law concerning Regulation of Nuclear Raw Materials, Nuclear Fuel Materials, and Nuclear Reactors (Kakugenryō Busshitsu, Kakunenryō Busshitsu Oyobi Genshiro no Kisei ni Kansuru Hōritsu, 1957), and the Cabinet Order concerning the Definition of Nuclear Raw Materials (Kakugenryō Busshitsu Tō no Teigi ni Kansuru Seirei, 1957).

Typical uses of radioactive isotopes are as tracers and as sources of radiation. The relevant laws include the Law concerning Prevention of Radiation Sickness due to Radioactive Isotopes (Hōshasei Dōi Genso Tō ni Yoru Hōshasen Shōgai no Bōshi ni Kansuru Hōritsu, 1957) and the Law concerning Technical Standards for the Prevention of Radiation (Hōshasen Bōshi no Gijutsuteki Kijun ni Kansuru Hōritsu, 1957). Other laws relating to nuclear energy include the Law concerning Compensation for Nuclear Energy Damages (Genshiryoku Songai no Baishō ni Kansuru Hōritsu, 1961), which provides measures for liability for damages to be borne by the proprietors of nuclear reactors, for insurance to cover such liability, and for damages not covered by other damage compensation measures. See also NUCLEAR ENERGY POLICY.   TANSŌ Akinobu

Atomic Energy Research Institute, Japan

(Nihon Genshiryoku Kenkyūjo). Government research corporation with a special status, founded in 1956 to promote the research, development, and utilization of atomic energy. Its services include the basic and applied study of atomic energy; the planning, construction, and operation of nuclear reactors; the training of researchers; and the production and distribution of radioactive isotopes. It maintains research facilities at the Tōkai Research Laboratory (Ibaraki Prefecture), the Takasaki Radiation Chemistry Research Laboratory (Gumma Prefecture), the Ōarai Research Laboratory (Ibaraki Prefecture), and the Radio Isotope Center (Tōkyō).

atomic weapons, movement to ban

International movement for the immediate and complete abolition of nuclear weapons; a response to the nuclear age initiated by the American atomic attacks on Hiroshima and Nagasaki in early August 1945, in the final days of World War II. In Japan, the only country to experience atomic devastation, the antinuclear weapons movement did not congeal into a force of national significance until the mid-1950s, because of difficult living conditions in the period immediately after the war and the restrictions imposed by the Allied Occupation.

America's testing of a hydrogen bomb on Bikini Island in 1954 provided the catalyst. A Japanese fishing vessel called the *Lucky Dragon V* (see LUCKY DRAGON INCIDENT) happened to wander into the radioactive radius just after the blast. Several of the ship's crewmen fell ill, with one even dying from exposure to the radioactive fallout. The incident caused an uproar in Japan. Deep-seated feelings, stemming back to the death and destruction visited on Hiroshima and Nagasaki, were aggravated. The feeling of revulsion associated with the advent and spread of nuclear weapons grew into widespread and often emotional sensitivities that some have called Japan's "nuclear allergy." A small group of housewives in Suginami Ward, Tōkyō, initiated a signature-collecting campaign in May 1954, protesting nuclear-bomb tests and calling for the abolition of all nuclear bombs. What started as a small, localized campaign swept quickly across the country. By the end of the year, more than 20 million signatures had endorsed the protest. The figure eventually exceeded 30 million, probably the largest outpouring of grass-roots protest in Japanese history.

The ban-the-bomb movement started out as a nonpartisan endeavor opposing all nuclear weapons. It thus sidestepped such controversial issues as the UNITED STATES–JAPAN SECURITY TREATIES. But political neutrality proved hard to protect, particularly as reformist parties moved in to organize the massive public outcry into some kind of permanent institutional structure. In September 1955, the Gensuibaku Kinshi Nihon Kyōgikai (Japan Council against Atomic and Hydrogen Bombs, commonly called Gensuikyō) was founded. Gensuikyō sought to abrogate the Security Treaty as part of its efforts to eliminate all nuclear arms. Into this organization entered citizens from all walks of life, including political, religious, intellectual, and labor leaders and the victims of the atomic bombings *(hibakusha)*. The scope of its activities was wide and included support for the *hibakusha*.

Once political parties took organizational control, however, the antinuclear bomb movement turned into an arena of partisan bickering as rival parties attempted to stake out, and extend, their spheres of influence. In 1961 the Democratic Socialist Party left Gensuikyō to form its own organization along with the Liberal Democratic Party, the Kakuheiki Kinshi Heiwa Kensetsu Kokumin Kaigi (National Council for Peace and against Nuclear Weapons; also called Kakkin Kaigi). In 1965 the Japan Socialist Party broke off to establish a third organization, the Gensuibaku Kinshi Nihon Kokumin Kaigi (Japan Congress against Atomic and Hydrogen Bombs; also called Gensuikin). Such divisions have fragmented the antibomb movement, diluting its political influence and diminishing its public prestige.

In spite of the organizational fragmentation and partisan bickering, the antibomb movement as a whole has had a significant impact on a range of public policies, not just in the area of nuclear weapons. It has served as an organizational watchdog for the country's policies on military security. By holding out the threat of, or actually resorting to, demonstrations, sit-ins, protest rallies, local meetings, and political lobbying, and by drawing public attention to sensitive issues through television and press coverage and their own publications, these peace organizations have had a big hand in defining the boundaries of what the government has considered politically permissible. Antibomb groups have organized rallies against the visits of American carriers and submarines suspected of carrying nuclear weapons to Japanese ports. They have participated in protests against the Security Treaty, American military bases, the construction of local atomic energy plants, and proposals to revise article 9 of the constitution. The government's three nonnuclear principles—not to produce, possess, or bring nuclear weapons into Japan—reflect the influence of the antibomb movement.

The antibomb movement has lost some of the early energy that gave it such national prominence during the 1950s and 1960s. However, it is far from moribund, as evidenced by the fact that antibomb groups collected 20 million signatures for a petition calling again for complete disarmament and presented it to the UN Special Session on Disarmament in 1978. But it is probably no longer as potent a political force as it used to be. One reason is that the overall climate of opinion in Japan has been changing, as more and more people express support for the country's Self Defense Forces and the Security Treaty, including America's nuclear umbrella over Japan. Leaders of the antibomb movement remain convinced of the importance of their efforts—perhaps now more than ever before. But the mainstream of public opinion seems to be moving further away from their position, and the complexities of world politics appear to be making their goals increasingly hard to realize. Organizational rifts have not been healed despite recent discussion of reuniting, and partisan conflicts seem no closer to resolution than before.

🕮 ——Arase Yutaka, "Gensuibaku kinshi undō no tōmen suru kadai," *Shisō* (April 1958). Imahori Seiji, *Gensuibaku kinshi undō* (1974). Sakamoto Yoshikazu, "Heiwa undō ni okeru shinri to ronri," *Sekai* (August 1962). Daniel I. OKIMOTO

Atomi Kakei (1840–1926)

Educator and painter; founder of Atomi Girls' School (now Atomi Gakuen Women's University). Born in Ōsaka, the daughter of a poet; original name, Atomi Takino. In her mid-teens, she went to Kyōto to study traditional poetry and painting of the MARUYAMA-SHIJŌ SCHOOL. After operating private schools in both Ōsaka and Kyōto, she went to Tōkyō in 1870 and started a private school with about 80 students ranging in age from 4 to 19, many from the court nobility; enrollment later grew to several hundred. Although both boys and girls were admitted at first, girls' education was increasingly emphasized. The establishment came to be officially known as Atomi Girls' School in 1888, when it moved to a new building in the Koishikawa district. The curriculum, aimed at training girls to be "good wives and wise mothers," centered on the Chinese and Japanese classics, as well as accomplishments such as sewing and the tea ceremony. Kakei remained the school's principal until she was 80 years old. She also taught painting to women at the imperial court and painted court events.

Atsugi

City in central Kanagawa Prefecture, central Honshū. Situated on the west bank of the river Sagamigawa, Atsugi developed as a river port and POST-STATION TOWN in the Edo period (1600–1868). Also a dormitory suburb of Tōkyō. Today it is an important point on the Japanese National Railway, a private railway line, and the Tōmei Expressway. Its principal industries are the production of automobile components, electrical appliances, and rubber goods. Fishing for *ayu* (sweetfish) on the Sagamigawa is a popular pastime; an Ayu Festival is held on the first weekend in August. (In September 1945 Atsugi served as the landing point for the Occupation forces.) Pop: 145,387.

Atsugi Motor Parts Co, Ltd

Automobile parts maker affiliated with the NISSAN MOTOR CO, LTD. Atsugi Motor Parts was established in 1956 as a result of the separation of the Atsugi plant from its parent company, Nissan Motor. It manufactures propeller shafts, clutches, pistons, and suspension parts, of which 90 percent are delivered to Nissan Motor. It has overseas incorporated production plants in Taiwan and Mexico. Sales for the fiscal year ending February 1982 totaled ¥101 billion (US $429.5 million) and the company was capitalized at ¥3.3 billion (US $14.0 million). Corporate headquarters are in Atsugi, Kanagawa Prefecture.

atsuita

A type of heavy brocade (NISHIKI). Originally imported from China, it was named after the thick boards (*atsuita*) around which the cloth was wrapped. The term contrasts with *usuita*, the thin boards around which lighter materials like satin were wrapped. *Atsuita* includes a variety of weaves but the most typical is a six-harness twill of glossed warp and unglossed weft ground with optional, weft-basted patterns in thick glossy silk. It differs from KARA-ORI in the length of the pattern, the number of harnesses for the twill ground, and the character of the designs.

The word *atsuita* also refers to a short-sleeved *kimono* made of such cloth and worn generally by men. In the NŌ theater, it often functions as an undergarment over which a cloak such as the *happi, mizugoromo,* or *sobatsugi* are worn. For old men's roles, *atsuita* costumes have stripes or checks without basted designs. For warrior costumes, short, basted stitches compose triangles, hexagons, or lattice patterns. Alternating blocks of contrasting color or design create rhythmic effects. Supernatural-being roles use bold designs with strong color contrast. Garments with long basted stitches forming a surface design over the geometric ground designs are known as *atsuita kara-ori* and may be worn draped as a cloak over broad divided skirts (*hangiri*).

🕮 ——Fujishiro Tsugio, *Shashin de miru nō no shōzoku* (1972). Japan Society, *Tokugawa Collection: Nō Robes and Masks* (1977). Kitamura Tetsurō, *Nō shōzoku,* no. 46 of *Nihon no bijutsu* (March 1970). Monica BETHE

Atsumi Kiyoshi (1928–)

Comic actor. Real name Tadokoro Yasuo. Born in Tōkyō. In the early 1950s he began working as a comedian in the Asakusa amusement district of Tōkyō. After three years of bad health, he returned to the stage in the late 1950s and also began to appear on television. He made his film debut in Nomura Yoshitarō's *Haikei tennō heika sama* (1963, Greetings, Mr. Emperor). With the phenomenal success of the series created by YAMADA YŌJI, *Otoko wa tsurai yo* (It's Tough Being a Man), beginning in 1969, he became familiar to the public under his role name Tora san. He also appeared in HANI SUSUMU's *Buwana Toshi no uta* (1965, Bwana Toshi).

Itasaka Tsuyoshi

Atsumi Peninsula

(Atsumi Hantō). Located in southern Aichi Prefecture, central Honshū. Bounded on the north by Atsumi Bay and on the south by the Enshū Sea, this long narrow stretch of land extends about 10 km (6 mi) east to west. A great deal of floriculture is carried out here as well as the hothouse cultivation of melons and tomatoes. Iragomisaki, a cape at the southwestern tip of the peninsula, is noted for its spectacular rock formations and lovely beach scenery, and portions of the coastline are included in the Mikawa Bay Quasi-National Park. Area: 200 sq km (77 sq mi).

Atsuta Shrine

(Atsuta Jingū). Shintō shrine in Atsuta Ward, Nagoya, which purportedly holds the sacred sword known as the Kusanagi no Tsurugi ("grass-cutting sword"), one of the three IMPERIAL REGALIA. According to tradition, the shrine was built by the consort of the legendary hero Prince YAMATOTAKERU, whose life was miraculously saved by this sword during his campaign to bring eastern Japan under imperial rule. The shrine began to attract wide attention in 808, when the ritualist Imbe no Hironari protested the shrine's neglect to the court. Soon afterward it was raised to the highest rank and endowed with large estates. From then on, Atsuta Shrine enjoyed the patronage of the imperial court and, from the 15th century, that of the Muromachi and Tokugawa shogunates. Its special status was recognized at the time of Emperor Meiji's accession to the throne in 1868 by the dispatch of imperial envoys to the shrine, an honor otherwise accorded only to the Grand Shrine of Ise. The annual festival date is 5 June. *Stanley* WEINSTEIN

attorneys —➤ lawyers

Attu

The westernmost of the American Aleutians, this bleak and craggy island was the scene during World War II of the first instance of "total sacrifice" *(gyokusai)* by Japanese forces. Having seized Attu on 7 June 1942 (and renamed it Atsutatō), some 2,500 troops under Colonel Yamazaki Yasuyo reportedly fought to the last man before 12,000 American troops recaptured the island on 30 May 1943. In fact, the Americans took 29 prisoners. *Otis* CARY

audiovisual education

Since the end of World War II audiovisual education has been fully developed and widely used in Japan. Although educational silent films were frequently used in classrooms in the 1920s, and in 1933 the government started radio broadcasts for school use extending these two years later to the entire country, the educational significance of audiovisual devices was not yet clearly understood or fully accepted. After World War II, however, audiovisual education was given an enormous boost with the introduction of the theories on audiovisual education of the Americans C. F. Hoban and E. Dale and the US Occupation authorities' encouragement of using films in classrooms.

Recently, there is growing interest in the educational potential of television, radio, tapes, and other electronic media as these devices become more widely available and technically improved. Audiovisual media are used mostly in elementary schools; educational television programs have become very popular, with those produced by Nippon Hōsō Kyōkai (see NHK), the public network, being shown in virtually all elementary schools. Audiovisual facilities are also found in abundance in public halls, youth centers, and educational institutions other than schools. TAKAKUWA *Yasuo*

auditing standards

(kansa kijun). Current Japanese auditing standards were established in 1956 as a tentative statement of the Council of Business Accounting of the Ministry of Finance, although they have been subjected to several revisions since then. The standards have been designed for modernized auditing of financial statements and utilize the test checking process. They presuppose a highly advanced internal control system and its smooth operation. When auditing is conducted at a certain corporation for the first time, special care is taken to determine whether the company has an adequate internal control system that is operating properly. The Japanese auditing standards are divided into three sections: (1) auditing standards in the narrow sense of the term, (2) fieldwork standards, and (3) reporting standards. The first section is composed of general standards and summaries of the fieldwork and reporting standards. The general standards cover auditors' professional competence as well as fairness, due care, and other ethical questions. The summaries of fieldwork standards cover orderliness and timeliness of auditing and decisions on the scope of test checking. The summaries of the reporting standards cover regulations on the scope of the items to be included in the auditors' report, the expression of the auditors' opinion on the financial statements, and other matters. Fieldwork standards deal with ordinary auditing procedures on the premise that there are two types of procedures—ordinary and special. Detailed regulations are provided in the standards on procedures regarding preliminary investigations, auditing procedures for transaction records, and auditing

procedures of items included in financial statements. The standards cover not only financial statements of individual corporations but also interim and consolidated financial statements.

WAKASUGI *Akira*

August First declaration

(Hachiichi *sengen).* Joint appeal by the Central Committee of the Chinese Communist Party and the Chinese Soviet Government calling for a united social and political front of all Chinese to oppose Japan's incursions in North China. Issued on 1 August 1935 at Mo-ergai (Mo-erh-kai) in Sichuan (Szechwan) Province, the declaration proposed that the Communist Party and the ruling Nationalist Party end their civil war and form a coalition government in the interest of national defense. On the same day the Comintern, at the seventh congress in Moscow, issued its own appeal for a united front in China. In December 1935 the Chinese Communist Politburo, meeting at Wayaobao (Wa-yao-pao) in Shaanxi (Shensi), incorporated both August First proposals into a resolution that subordinated class struggle and land reform to the national war effort. The Nationalist government flatly rejected all appeals to cooperate with communists until in the XI'AN (SIAN) INCIDENT of December 1936 its leader, Chiang Kai-shek, was kidnapped and forced to accept a coalition government.

Aung San (1915–1947)

Burmese political leader. A prominent nationalist in the years before World War II, he organized the Burma Independence Army with Japanese assistance in 1942 and later became minister of defense in BA MAW's wartime regime. He was soon disillusioned by Japan's occupation policies and helped to form the Anti-Fascist People's Freedom League, which rose against the Japanese early in 1945. In 1947 he went to London as a Burmese delegate for independence talks with the British government, but on his return to Burma he was assassinated at the instigation of a political rival. See also BURMA AND JAPAN. ŌNO *Tōru*

Australia and Japan

The relationship between Australia and Japan has become of considerable international importance because of the rapid development of trade between the two countries in the 1960s and 1970s. The two economies have become highly complementary, Australia supplying Japan principally with minerals and agricultural products, and Japan supplying Australia largely with manufactured items. This in turn has led to a developing political relationship of great significance in the western Pacific region.

From the late 1950s onward, the discovery and exploitation of vast mineral wealth in Australia coincided with the extremely rapid development of the manufacturing industry in Japan, and this coincidence created opportunities for economic exchange that both countries were quick to seize. By the second half of the 1970s Japan was by far the largest market for Australia's exports and was exceeded only marginally by the United States as the largest source of Australian imports. In the overall trading picture of Japan, Australia loomed less large, though it was nevertheless an important market and a key supply source of certain vital resources, notably iron ore, coal, alumina, bauxite, and wool. The balance of trade was consistently in Australia's favor.

The development of this trade was so rapid that a careful assessment of its broader significance lagged behind its establishment as an accomplished fact. By the early 1970s concern was being expressed on both sides that neither knew enough about the other, except in narrow economic terms, and that some unfortunate historical experiences needed to be lived down.

Historical Background——It is possible to trace contacts between Australia and Japan to shortly before the Meiji Restoration (1868). The first Japanese actually to settle in Australia (a circus proprietor) arrived in Queensland in 1871. By the time the Australian federation was formed in 1901, there were over 3,000 Japanese residents, but the Immigration Restriction Act of 1902, which provided for a dictation test "in a European language," effectively prevented further entry of more than a very few Japanese on short-term visits. The immigration issue provoked disagreement from time to time between the two governments (see AUSTRALIAN IMMIGRATION POLICY

AND JAPAN), and the important part played by Australian Prime Minister William Morris Hughes in successfully combatting the Japanese attempt to have a clause against racial discrimination inserted in the Covenant of the League of Nations was long remembered in Japan.

Before World War II, Britain was by far Australia's largest trading partner. By the mid-1930s, however, a healthy 13 percent of Australia's exports went to Japan, which had become Australia's second-largest export market. Imports from Japan were a much smaller proportion of total imports. This situation was shattered in 1936 by the so-called "trade-diversion episode." A rapid increase in imports of Japanese textiles at the expense of textile imports from Britain led to British pressure upon Australia to reduce Japanese imports, but the Japanese government refused to consider an Australian request for restraint. In May 1936, therefore, Australia unilaterally imposed new and high tariffs on Japanese textiles, which in turn led to discriminatory treatment by Japan against imports from Australia. After it became clear that both sides were being seriously harmed by these policies, it was agreed in 1937 to relax them.

The emotional ties that bound Australia to Britain were still extremely strong, and it is not surprising that Australia should have acceded to a British request largely against its own economic interest. The principle of racial exclusiveness, carried to such lengths by Australia, continued to be an aggravating factor in relations with Japan. In any case, the prevailing perceptions of Japan held in Australia changed from relatively favorable at the turn of the century to increasingly apprehensive and hostile during the 1930s. Full diplomatic relations were not entered into until December 1940, Tōkyō being the second capital (Washington was the first) where Australia set up a legation independent of a British diplomatic establishment.

The logic of events led inexorably to the engagement of both countries on opposite sides of the international armed conflict that broke out on 8 December 1941. During the war, Australian territory was directly threatened by the Japanese armed forces, although a 1942 plan by the Imperial Navy to invade Australia to deny Australian territory to the Americans was vetoed by the army. But the Japanese captured much of New Guinea, bombed Darwin and Broome in northern Australia, and sent midget submarines into Sydney Harbor. Australian forces suffered heavy casualties in the fighting against Japan, and many Australians died as prisoners. Politically the most important consequence of the war from the Australian point of view was that the United States replaced the United Kingdom as the principal guarantor of Australian security (see WORLD WAR II).

Postwar Development——Immediately after the war the general Australian attitude toward Japan remained extremely hostile. Nearly all Japanese-born residents of Australia, who had been interned during the war, were shipped back to Japan. For several years, Japanese wives of Australian servicemen in the BRITISH COMMONWEALTH OCCUPATION FORCE were not permitted to enter Australia. The Australian Labor government was inclined to believe that the emperor should be tried as a war criminal and that strong measures be taken to prevent the revival of Japanese industry. William MacMahon BALL, the Australian who was the British Commonwealth member of the ALLIED COUNCIL FOR JAPAN in 1946 and 1947, was frequently at loggerheads with General Douglas MACARTHUR concerning basic policy for Japan. The Australian government had worked hard, in the face of American determination to monopolize control of the OCCUPATION, for a significant role in the postwar administration of Japan. In the end, Australia provided the largest contingent in the British Commonwealth Occupation Force, centered on Kure, near Hiroshima, and was represented on the Allied Council for Japan and the FAR EASTERN COMMISSION. The role that Australia was allowed to play, however, was limited, to say the least, and far smaller than that initially envisaged by the Australian government. Gradually and often reluctantly, Australian official policy moved to accommodate the more lenient American line toward Japan. The visit to Japan in July 1947 of the Australian foreign minister, H. V. Evatt, seems to have been an early turning point and was followed by a British Commonwealth Peace Conference on the Japanese peace settlement in August. When, at American insistence, further reparations claims on Japan were dropped in May 1949, this completed a process of progressive Australian retreat from major reparations claims.

The government of the Liberal and Country parties under Robert Menzies, which came to power in December 1949, continued to press for restrictions on Japanese rearmament to be written into the peace treaty, but was forced to back down in the face of lack of support from most of the other Allied powers. The ANZUS Pact, signed by Australia, New Zealand, and the United States at the same time as the peace treaty with Japan, served to reassure an Australian government that was becoming more concerned about the possibilities of communist than of Japanese aggression. The Australian Labor Party and sections of the trade union movement, however, maintained their suspicions of Japan and their anxieties about Japanese rearmament well into the 1950s, while the Australian manufacturing industry remained anxious at the prospect of an influx of cheap goods from Japan.

The Growth of Trade——The Agreement on Commerce between the Commonwealth of Australia and Japan, signed in 1957, renewed in 1960, and amended in 1963, was a turning point in relations between the two countries and laid the groundwork for a trade boom of major proportions. The agreement guaranteed both sides most-favored-nation status in respect to tariffs, while also providing that there should be no discrimination in respect of trade between them unless discriminatory measures were applied equally to all third countries. A loophole that enabled Australia to take exceptional measures to protect industries thought to be threatened with disruption by a surge of imports from Japan was closed in 1963, when the agreement was amended by a protocol in which Australia accorded full General Agreement on Tariffs and Trade (GATT) rights to Japan. Other provisions of the agreement related to state trading enterprises and to consultation (both regular and preceding any emergency action); Japan also guaranteed that Australia should have more liberal access to the Japanese market for its exports of wool, wheat, barley, sugar, and other commodities.

The agreement worked as an enormous boost to Australian exports; Japanese exports to Australia also increased, but the balance of trade remained heavily in Australia's favor.

The massive development of Australia's mineral resources, which had not been anticipated when the commerce agreement was signed in 1957, played a key part in the growth of Australian exports to Japan, while Japan's steady economic growth was greatly assisted by the reliability of supply, as well as by the ease of access and relative cheapness, of crucial raw materials from Australia. The effect on the Australian economy was also profound, as it became more broadly based and no longer so heavily dependent on the products of rural industry. Together with other factors that reduced Australia's dependence on the British market and with the increased role of the United States in Australia's trade, the agreement created a framework in which Australia's trading pattern could ultimately be directed away from Europe and toward Asia and the Pacific.

The Relationship in the 1970s——By the early 1970s, although Japan and Australia had become major trading partners, comparatively little had been attempted toward the goal of fostering mutual understanding, so a series of measures to remedy the situation was undertaken by both nations. The Australia, Japan, and Western Pacific Economic Relations Research Project, a continuing program funded by the Australian and Japanese governments to study problems and prospects in the economic relations between the two nations and other nations of the western Pacific region, was inaugurated in 1972 in Canberra and Tōkyō. In April 1976, it brought together the results of three years of research in a report that stressed the complementarity of the two economies and pointed out the beneficial "interdependence" of the trade and investment relationship between them. The report made a number of recommendations for improved policy interchange between the two countries at various levels, and for avoiding violent fluctuations in gains from their economic exchange. It also examined the possibilities for smoother policy communication and discussion among developed and developing countries of the western Pacific area, and it recommended formation of an Organization for Pacific Trade and Development. In 1980, the name of the project was changed to Australia–Japan Research Centre.

A cultural agreement between Australia and Japan, resulting from initiatives taken by the Australian government, was signed in Canberra in 1974. The agreement calls for cultural, educational, and professional exchange and cooperation and covers the establishment of cultural institutions, teaching of language and culture, provision of scholarships, exchange of information about the educational systems of each country, promotion of publications, lectures, concerts, cultural exhibitions, films and recordings, encouragement of translations, access to cultural establishments, mass-media cooperation, tourism, and youth and sporting exchanges. A commission was set up with equal representation from each country to consult on implementation. One particularly significant result of the agreement was a scheme that went into operation in 1978 whereby an Australian scholar lectures on Australian government and politics at three universities in Tōkyō: Tōkyō University, Tsuda College, and Sophia University.

The report of an Australian government committee chaired by Sir John CRAWFORD, which concluded that it was desirable to go beyond the cultural agreement if relations between Australia and Japan were to be deepened, led the government to establish the Australia–Japan Foundation in 1976. The foundation has its headquarters in Sydney and works to promote a closer relationship and greater understanding and interchange between Australia and Japan through nine forms of activity: media, education, travel grants, common-interest-group exchange, research, youth, community liaison, publications, and library support. Its members are drawn from government, business, universities, trade unions, the arts, and sports.

Also in 1976, a Basic Treaty of Friendship and Cooperation between Japan and Australia was signed after several years of complex negotiations. The treaty embodies in formal and symbolic terms the friendship, community of interests, and interdependence that exist between the two countries and establishes a broad framework for further cooperation in specific areas. It also recognizes the two countries' mutual interest in each being a stable and reliable supplier to and market for the other. The agreed minutes to the treaty confirm that the standard of treatment prescribed, on a mutual basis, to nationals and companies as regards their entry and stay and business and professional activities amounts in effect to most-favored-nation treatment.

The liberalization of Australia's immigration policy, undertaken in the early 1970s by the Labor government of Gough Whitlam, though in a sense an extension of changes brought about by previous governments, removed the last vestiges of discrimination on grounds of race from official policy on entry and stay. Since immigration had long been a difficult issue in Australia–Japan relations, the effective demise of the "White Australia" policy naturally contributed to a better understanding. Regular ministerial talks were also instituted by the 1970s, at which a variety of topics, both economic and political, were discussed.

Nevertheless, the disruption of the international economy which followed the 1973–74 oil crisis adversely affected trade between Australia and Japan by reducing Japanese demand. The Australian government meanwhile introduced new controls on the inflow of foreign capital, especially in the mining industry. In an attempt to prevent Japanese buyers operating in cartels from playing separate Australian producers against each other, mineral export pricing decisions were also made subject to Australian government intervention. One effect of these policies was to create uncertainty in Japan about Australia's reliability as a trading partner, especially as policies in a number of areas appeared not to be firm; guidelines were either not clearly spelled out or else were subject to frequent change. When, around 1975, the precise nature of the policies became clearer, they aroused fewer objections from the Japanese. In any case, as time went on, the earlier restrictions on foreign investment in the mining industry were somewhat relaxed, though the emphasis on the need to watch investment and Australia's interests was inherited by later governments.

By the middle and late 1970s the rapid growth of trade that had been a feature of the 1960s was clearly over. At the same time Japanese capital investment in Australia was increasing, though it remained at a much lower level than investment by Australia's traditional suppliers of capital. Adjustments had to be made which caused serious problems, but the two countries appeared gradually to be learning to live with each other's behavior and practices. Controversies over Australian beef exports to Japan in 1974 and over the price paid by Japanese refiners for Australian sugar in 1976–77 were settled by compromises after extended negotiations.

Cutbacks in the Japanese steel industry resulted in substantially reduced demand for Australian iron ore, and this in turn brought into focus the issue of long-term contracts, especially the degree of flexibility that ought to be built into them. Long-term contracts had proved of great value for both sides as a means of regulating the minerals trade, so that the problems now involved were essentially those of adapting a well-tried method to a situation some of whose parameters had shifted.

Other issues included Australia's temporary suspension of uranium mining and export, the high level of protection accorded Australian manufacturing industries, conditions for investment in the motor-vehicle industry in Australia, the position of Australian shipping in carrying cargoes to and from Japan, and the high level of air fares between the two countries. However, despite all these problems, much progress took place during the 1970s in placing the Australia–Japan relationship on a secure footing. Phobias stemming from the past, while not perhaps completely eliminated, had been greatly reduced. A series of public opinion surveys, beginning in 1976, revealed a generally sanguine and in part highly favorable set of attitudes toward Japan, although a residue of caution remained, particularly with the older generation of Australians. Japanese attitudes toward Australia were less well documented, but Japanese visitors to Australia would frequently comment on its enormous land area relative to population and on Japan's dependence on Australian sources of raw materials. Whereas up to the mid-1970s Japanese tended to regard Australia as quintessentially "White," by the 1980s some understanding of the multiethnic nature of recent Australian immigration policy was already in evidence.

It was estimated that in 1980 just over 9,000 Australian schoolchildren were studying the Japanese language in secondary schools throughout the country, while most universities and some colleges of advanced education taught Japanese studies including the language. It was becoming increasingly clear that economic and political relations between the two countries needed to be seen in the context of a much broader set of linkages, between the countries of the western Pacific in particular, which together would constitute a dynamic economic force for the 1980s. The greater economic roles being played by Japan and Australia in the western Pacific economy, together with the relative decline of American influence, the likely emergence of China as a major participant, the presence of the Soviet Union, and the economic growth of several other Northeast and Southeast Asian economies, suggested that Japan and Australia would need to keep their political and economic relationship under constant review.

▧——W. MacMahon Ball, ed, *Australia and Japan: Documents and Readings in Australian History* (1969). E. S. Crawcour, "Barriers to Understanding between Australia and Japan," *Australian Outlook* (December 1977). J. G. Crawford, ed, *Australian Trade Policy 1942–1966: A Documentary History* (1968). Sir John Crawford and Saburo Okita, ed, *Raw Materials and Pacific Economic Integration* (1978). Peter Drysdale and Hironobu Kitaoji, ed, *Australia and Japan: Two Societies and their Interaction* (1980). Peter Drysdale and Kiyoshi Kojima, ed, *Australia–Japan Economic Relations in the International Context: Recent Experience and the Prospects Ahead* (1978). Peter Drysdale and Alan Rix, "Australia's Economic Relations with Asia and the Pacific," *Current Affairs Bulletin* (April 1979). Gordon Greenwood, ed, *Approaches to Asia: Australian Postwar Attitudes and Policies* (1974). Hori Takeaki, *Asu no Gōshū to Nihon to no taiwa* (1976). P. Brian Murphy, "Opening Australian Diplomatic Relations with Japan," *Australian Outlook* (December 1977). Nagasaka Toshihisa, *Kita o muku Ōsutoraria* (1978). The Parliament of the Commonwealth of Australia, *Japan: Report from the Senate Standing Committee on Foreign Affairs and Defence* (1973). The Parliament of the Commonwealth of Australia, *Report of the Ad Hoc Working Committee on Australia–Japan Relations* (1978). D. C. S. Sissons, "1871–1946 nen no Ōsutoraria no nihonjin," *Ijū kenkyū* (March 1974). D. C. S. Sissons, "Manchester v. Japan: The Imperial Background of the Australian Trade Diversion Dispute with Japan, 1936," *Australian Outlook* (December 1976). J. A. A. Stockwin, "Australia's Relations with Japan: Complementarity and Strain," *The Round Table* (April 1975). J. A. A. Stockwin, ed, *Japan and Australia in the Seventies* (1972).

J. A. A. STOCKWIN

Australia–Japan Business Cooperative Committee

A private enterprise organization in Australia concerned with economic relations with Japan. The Australia-Japan Business Cooperative Committee (AJBCC) and its counterpart committee in Japan, the Japan-Australia Business Cooperation Committee, were set up in 1962 as a response to the rapid growth in trade between the two countries which had followed the 1957 Agreement on Commerce. The two committees meet together annually, alternating between Japan and Australia. The AJBCC considers its function to be supplementary rather than a duplication of the efforts of government. It operates entirely under private auspices, with the expenses being met from contributions of member companies. Its membership is representative of a wide range of private industrial, commercial, banking, and rural interests. Its executive confers with government from time to time, particularly with the Australian government's Interdepartmental Committee on Japan.

In the early stages the two committees functioned essentially to establish personal contacts, to break down residual hostilities from World War II, and to educate businessmen in Japan and Australia about the huge trade potential that existed between the two countries. With the passage of time and the accumulation of experience the functions became more specific. At annual meetings of the two committees in the mid-1970s, papers were presented on such issues as monetary and foreign exchange systems, promotion of business links, tariffs and nontariff barriers, trade imbalance, and investment potentials. The AJBCC sponsors two personnel exchange programs, the first consisting of a number of scholarships (to which the Australian government also contributes) enabling Australian students and teachers of Japanese to study in Japan, and the second enabling an exchange of Australian and Japanese high school students.

An important initiative taken at the 1967 AJBCC meeting in Tōkyō led to the foundation of the PACIFIC BASIN ECONOMIC COUNCIL by businessmen of Australia, Japan, the United States, Canada, and New Zealand.

📖——Peter Drysdale, "Japan, Australia and Pacific Economic Integration," *Australia's Neighbours* (November–December 1967).

J. A. A. STOCKWIN

Australian immigration policy and Japan

At the time of Australian federation in 1901, more than 3,000 Japanese were resident in Australia, mostly in the tropical north of the country, many of them in occupations such as pearling. An abrupt halt, however, was brought to further Japanese immigration into Australia by the Immigration Restriction Act of February 1902. The act made immigration dependent on passing a dictation test in a European language (not necessarily English), and this provision was used in such a way as to exclude completely any further immigrants from Japan. (In 1905 the words were changed to "a prescribed language" partly to appease the Japanese government.) The policy derived from the reaction of public opinion in the prefederation Australian colonies to an influx of Chinese during the gold rush period of the 1850s, and later to the introduction of Kanaka laborers into the canefields of Queensland. Feelings of racial superiority mingled with fears of being swamped by other races to produce the policy which came to be known as "White Australia."

The "White Australia" policy was known in Japan as *hakugō shugi*, a term which came to have strongly critical overtones and the use of which, with far less justification, persisted into the 1970s. It was to cause friction in the early decades of the 20th century between the Australian and Japanese governments, with the latter objecting particularly to the fact that the policy of total exclusion placed Japanese on a par with Chinese and other "less advanced" Asian peoples. Japanese still in Australia also suffered from discriminatory legislation of various kinds. Japan and Australia came into direct verbal confrontation at the Versailles Peace Conference of 1919, when William Morris Hughes, Australian prime minister and vociferous "White Australia" advocate, successfully opposed the Japanese attempt to have inserted into the League of Nations Covenant a clause asserting racial equality as a condition of world peace (see VERSAILLES, TREATY OF). Japanese reactions to "White Australia" were, however, largely confined to official protests.

By the 1930s the Japanese population in Australia had declined substantially from its peak at the turn of the century, and World War II reduced it to near the vanishing point, since practically all the Japanese-born residents were deported to Japan after the Allied victory.

"White Australia" persisted in an almost unadulterated form for several years after the war. From 1947, however, a vigorous program of attracting immigrants from European countries was begun, so that between 1947 and 1951 about half a million Europeans had arrived in Australia to take up residence, of whom only about 40 percent were British. Many more were to come in subsequent years. At the same time, however, even Australian servicemen in the Occupation of Japan who had married Japanese women were not allowed to bring them back to Australia, a prohibition that was lifted only in 1952.

The first milestone along the road to the ending of discrimination was passed in 1956 when, for the first time since the Immigration Restriction Act, Asians married to Australians, or who had been resident in Australia for 15 years, became eligible for naturalization. A bigger step was taken in 1966, when the period required for a non-European to become naturalized was reduced to 5 years, and indefinite stay was permitted for non-Europeans deemed to have

skills needed but not available in Australia, though a judgment about assimilability was required to be made about such applicants. The "dictation test" was formally abolished in 1958. Finally, in 1973, after the election of the Labor government of Gough Whitlam, a policy was adopted of nondiscrimination on grounds of race, color, or nationality in the selection of immigrants.

This, however, did not result in a sudden increase in immigrants to Australia from Japan, or indeed from other Asian countries. Permanent and long-term Japanese arrivals in Australia have increased substantially from an average rate of 265 per year in the early 1960s, but their number was only averaging 1,240 in the early 1970s. This can be accounted for by the fact that in depressed economic conditions since 1973, Australia has drastically cut back its intake of immigrants as a whole, occupational eligibility has been consequently narrowed, and the "family reunion" category for long-term entry naturally tends to favor numerically those nationalities already well represented in Australia. Moreover, certain professional associations (such as medical societies) recognize qualifications gained only at a limited number of overseas institutions, which in many cases exclude Japanese institutions. Nevertheless, the statement in the 1977 Immigration Green Paper that "eligibility rules are nondiscriminatory in terms of race, color, nationality, politics, creed or sex" appears to be a reasonably fair expression of the actual situation.

📖——Australian Population and Immigration Council, *Immigration Policies and Australia's Population: A Green Paper* (1977). I. Carter, *Alien Blossom* (1965). D. C. S. Sissons, "Immigration in Australian-Japanese Relations, 1871–1971," in J. A. A. Stockwin, ed, *Japan and Australia in the Seventies* (1972).　　J. A. A. STOCKWIN

Austria and Japan

Austrian-Japanese relations were established in 1869 between the Austro-Hungarian Empire and Japan, nearly ceased during World War I and the interwar period, and became reestablished during the period 1953–55.

Early Austro-Hungarian Relations with Japan——No official diplomatic relations existed in the Edo period (1600–1868), but there was some contact. An instance of unintended contact occurred when Moritz August von Benyowsky, a former Slovakian peer from Austria (later in the Polish military service) was captured by the Russians, exiled to Kamchatka, and then taken prisoner in 1771 by the Japanese, who at that time permitted no foreigner to enter under their NATIONAL SECLUSION law. After his release, he spread his knowledge of East Asia throughout Europe in his frequently reprinted memoirs. A more serious, scientific approach to Japan was made by August Pfizmaier (1808–87), a linguist at the University of Vienna, who in 1847 became the first scholar to indicate the relationship between Japanese and Altaic languages. His translation of RYŪTEI TANEHIKO's *Ukiyogata rokumai byōbu* (1821; tr *Sechs Wandschirme in Gestalten der vergänglichen Welt,* 1847) was the first translation of a Japanese novel into a Western language. It was printed together with a Japanese version, for which *hiragana* (Japanese phonetic) type had been specially made by hand in Vienna. Pfizmaier also translated several Japanese classics, studied the language of the Ainu, and published a great number of articles about Japanese culture. A contemporary of Pfizmaier, the linguist Anton Boller (1811–69), published a monograph in 1858 in which he said that Japanese belonged to the Ural-Altaic language group.

From the Meiji Restoration (1868) to World War I——Neither Pfizmaier nor Boller ever visited Japan, but plans to establish contact with the Japanese had already been made by the Austro-Hungarian government during the early 1850s. They were not, however, realized until 1869, when an official mission signed a trade and shipping treaty with Japan. Because of the inexperience of the new Meiji government, the Austrians were able to gain more favorable terms than the other countries which had come earlier. The treaty, put into force on 1 December 1871, was the last and farthest-reaching of the so-called Unequal Treaties between Japan and the Western powers. Soon afterwards Japan was invited to participate in the World Exhibition held in Vienna in 1873. In April of that year a Japanese delegation headed by SANO TSUNETAMI arrived in Vienna to buy various industrial and agricultural goods needed for the modernization of Japan. Some members of the delegation stayed on after the exhibition and studied in Vienna and other European cities. In June 1873 the IWAKURA MISSION visited Vienna and attempted unsuccessfully to secure a revision of the unequal treaty (see UNEQUAL TREATIES, REVISION OF). In 1897, the treaty of 1869 was succeeded by a new one, to be implemented in August 1899. There was another change in 1912, when yet another bilateral treaty was signed. The Austro-Hungarian mission was upgraded to a legation in March 1883 and finally became an embassy in January 1907; a consulate general had been opened in Yokohama in 1884.

From early on, academic research concerning things Japanese and scientific exchange played an important role in Austrian-Japanese relations. Karl Scherzer and other members of an around-the-world expedition under Admiral Petz collected many facts on Japan and later published them as a handbook for merchants. Junker von Langegg (b 1828), a physician, taught at Kyōto and laid the foundation for what later became Kyōto Prefectural Medical College. Another noted physician, Albrecht von Roretz (1846–84), taught for six years in Nagoya and Yamagata.

Heinrich von Siebold (1852–1908), the younger son of Philipp Franz von SIEBOLD, worked as an interpreter and became a civil servant in the Austro-Hungarian mission in 1872. In 1877, the year that Edward MORSE discovered the ŌMORI SHELL MOUNDS, Siebold, who was also greatly interested in anthropology, excavated seven shell mounds in Ōmori, Tsurumi, and Ōji. Comparing his findings with elements of the Ainu culture, he became aware of the need to study the latter more thoroughly. Together with the geographer Gustav von Kreitner (1848–93), a member of an East Asian expedition from 1877 to 1880 and later consul general in Yokohama, von Siebold traveled to Hokkaidō. His writings on the Ainu culture were the first detailed descriptions in a European language, and von Siebold's collections of cultural artifacts became the basis for the Japanese collection of the Anthropological Museum (Museum für Völkerkunde) in Vienna.

Austria was interested in Japanese techniques in sericulture and sent over several people to investigate them, while the Japanese invited the Austrian Amerigo Hofmann (1875–1945) to help them to overcome problems caused by mountain torrents and forest erosion. His work during the years 1904–09 is known in Japan to this day.

Whereas the Austrian interest in Japan was mainly concentrated on the natural sciences, the Japanese interest in Austria was quite different. ITŌ HIROBUMI, who had visited Vienna with the Iwakura Mission, returned in 1882 to meet and consult with Lorenz von STEIN, a German expert in constitutional law at the University of Vienna. Von Stein's advice to Itō and his group greatly influenced the formulation of the Japanese CONSTITUTION of 1889.

A political highlight of the Austro-Hungarian–Japanese relations was the visit of Crown Prince Franz Ferdinand to Japan in 1893. Diplomatic relations were expanded by the exchange of military and naval attachés during the late 1890s. An Austrian military officer who arrived in 1910, Major Theodor von LERCH, trained a group of Japanese soldiers in skiing near Takada (Niigata Prefecture), thus introducing to Japan a sport which soon became popular.

On the eve of World War I a regular express-shipping service was finally established between Trieste and Kōbe-Yokohama. Austria exported hops, wine, steel, and other goods to Japan and imported such foodstuffs as rice and oils. This early period of friendly diplomatic relations came to an end with the declaration of war and the recall of both ambassadors on 27 August 1914. The cruiser SMS *Kaiserin Elisabeth*, which had brought the crown prince to Japan 20 years earlier, fought side by side with the Germans in 1914 against the Japanese at Qingdao (Tsingtao) and was scuttled by its crew before the fall of that port. Austrian prisoners of war were confined in a camp near Himeji.

Relations between the Wars —— After the war the Austrian Empire, defeated and broken into ethnic divisions, did not reestablish full diplomatic relations with Japan, but the new Austrian Republic was represented by the Swedish ambassador during the years that followed. After 1923 honorary consuls were nominated. Japan, however, reopened its embassy in Austria in 1924, which lasted until Germany's absorption of Austria in 1938. Despite the weakened political relations, academic and cultural exchanges continued. As in the Meiji period, natural scientists such as the botanist Hans Molisch (1856–1937) studied and taught in Japan. Austrian musicians, who had already introduced European music to Japan during the Meiji period, were again invited to give concerts in Japan. Among the Japanese who studied in Austria was the physician and writer SAITŌ MOKICHI, who stayed in Vienna in 1922–23. Oka Masao (b 1898), who had come to Vienna in 1929 to study anthropology, became one of the pioneers of the Viennese school of historic ethnology in Japan. Oka also founded a special school for Japanese studies at the University of Vienna in 1938, which later became the Japanologisches Institut.

Post–World War II Relations —— Diplomatic relations were reestablished on 29 December 1953. Austria reopened a legation in Tō-

kyō in April 1955, and in the same year a foreign trade bureau took post. In November 1955 an exchange of memoranda concerning Austria's neutrality took place between the two countries. Both legations became embassies in November 1957.

From the economic point of view Austria is a minor partner of Japan, although it is noteworthy that Japan has purchased special technical know-how from Austria, such as the LD-process for steel manufacturing. Japan's imports and exports with Austria were nearly equal at the end of the 1960s (never exceeding US $15 million per year in value, which was 0.1 percent of Japan's exports and imports), but during the 1970s the situation rapidly deteriorated for Austria because of Japan's fast-growing export surplus.

The Japan External Trade Organization (JETRO) was prompted by Austria's position as a trusted partner of the Eastern European bloc to open an office in Vienna in October 1968. But the importance of the Viennese post diminished after Eastern European countries opened their doors to foreign firms and trade organizations. Cultural exchange thus was and remains the principal element in Austrian-Japanese relations.

📖 —— Josef Kreiner et al, ed, *Japanforschung in Österreich* (1976). Peter Pantzer, *Japan und Österreich-Ungarn,* Beiträge zur Japanologie, Band 11 (1973).   *Erich* PAUER

Automobile Liability Security Law

(Jidōsha Songai Baishō Hoshō Hō; abbreviation: Jibai Hō). Law enacted in 1955 in response to the rapidly increasing use of the automobile, in order to guarantee compensation for victims of automobile accidents.

The law has three major features. First, heavy liability for damages is imposed on the person who puts the automobile into operation in furtherance of his own interest (usually the owner of the automobile or some other person with the authority to drive the automobile ; however, a person in control of the automobile even without the authority to do so is also included; both the automobile manufacturer and hired driver are excluded). In order to obtain compensation for damages under the Civil Code, the victim must establish that the party causing the injury was negligent (Civil Code, art. 709). However, in the case of automobile accidents, this special statute has shifted the burden to the person in control of the automobile. He will not be able to escape liability for damages unless he can prove that (1) there was no negligence on his part or on the part of the driver; (2) there was negligence on the part of the victim or some third party; and (3) there was no structural defect or functional disorder in the automobile. Thus, liability in relation to automobile accidents has shifted from a liability based on negligence to a heavy liability close to liability without fault.

Second, the law establishes a system of compulsory liability insurance so that even if the party inflicting the injury is without financial resources, the victim is assured of receiving compensation. The maximum amount of the insurance coverage was initially set at ¥300,000 ($833), but has since been raised to ¥500,000 ($1,388) in 1960, ¥1 million ($2,763) in 1964, ¥1.5 million ($4,140) in 1966, ¥3 million ($8,284) in 1967, ¥5 million ($13,952) in 1969, ¥10 million ($36,870) in 1973, ¥15 million ($50,539) in 1975, and ¥20 million ($95,039) in 1978. This reflects the rapid rate of growth of Japan's economy and the increased awareness of human rights and has had a great influence on damages in personal injury cases in general. In addition to compulsory insurance, voluntary insurance for amounts in excess of the mandatory amount is also available.

Third, the law establishes a governmental system to guarantee compensation, whereby the government indemnifies victims of hit-and-run accidents and accidents caused by vehicles that are not covered by mandatory liability insurance. The financial resources for such awards derive from a part of the premiums paid for the compulsory automobile liability insurance.   KATŌ *Ichirō*

automotive industry

The Japanese automobile industry got its start in 1902, when Yoshida Shintarō and Uchiyama Komanosuke, partners in a small company called the Automobile Company (Ōtomōbiru Shōkai) produced a trial car with a two-cylinder, 12-horsepower American engine. In 1904 Yamaha Torao produced a two-cylinder steam automobile in Okayama, and in 1912 Kaishinsha, a company established by Hashimoto Masujirō, produced a car called the Dattogō; both of these were also trial models. Various automobile pioneers continued to make trial models until finally in 1920 Hakuyōsha pro-

Automotive industry——Table 1

Production by Manufacturer, 1980		
	Production	Share (in percentages)
Toyota	3,293,344	29.8
Nissan	2,644,052	23.9
Tōyō Kōgyō	1,121,016	10.2
Mitsubishi	1,104,930	10.0
Honda	956,902	8.7
Isuzu	472,127	4.3
Suzuki	468,683	4.2
Daihatsu	432,374	3.9
Fuji	425,633	3.9
Hino	74,890	0.7
Nissan Diesel	48,121	0.4
Others	812	0.0
Total	11,042,884	100.0

SOURCE: Japan Automobile Manufacturers Association, Inc, *Motor Vehicle Statistics of Japan* (annual): 1981.

duced its Ōtomogō. It had manufactured 250 of these cars by 1923, the largest total production of any make in Japan for those early years.

As can be seen from the above, the earliest trial production of automobiles did not begin much later in Japan than it did in America and Europe. But, despite the many manufacturers in Japan, it was not until much later that the volume of production was large enough to be profitable on a commercial basis. The chief reason was that domestic cars, produced in small quantity, could not compete with the imported cars that flooded into Japan, especially from the United States, just after the TŌKYŌ EARTHQUAKE OF 1923. After the earthquake the Tōkyō city government purchased Model T Fords and rebuilt them as buses (popularly known as Entarō buses), which became a new means of municipal transportation for the destroyed city. Ford and General Motors, with their superior production techniques, marketing, and service systems, established subsidiary companies in Japan in 1925–26 and started assembling trucks and passenger cars from imported parts. After this, the Japanese market was completely taken over by foreign automobiles. It was not until 1933 that annual domestic automobile production surpassed 1,000, while the number of imported cars had already reached 15,000 to 16,000 per year by 1929.

That the Japanese automobile industry was so soon left behind by foreign manufacturers can be attributed mainly to the backwardness and imbalance of Japan's industrial technology at that time, especially since automotive manufacturing involves almost all aspects of the machine-tool industry. Problems were encountered at all stages of the manufacturing process, from the low quality of basic materials such as steel plates and special steels, to underdeveloped techniques and lack of precision in stamping, casting, forging, machining, electroplating, painting, and other operations. Because most of the advanced areas of Japanese industrial technology were related to military production, the country lacked the overall technological development required for auto manufacturing, and many important areas remained underdeveloped. This technological backwardness made the automotive industry a risky investment, and even such established financial and industrial combines (ZAIBATSU) as MITSUI and MITSUBISHI were reluctant to make a genuine commitment to automobile manufacturing, despite strong pressure by the Japanese military authorities for the development of domestic production after World War I.

In the period before World War II, the Japanese automotive industry, under government direction, concentrated on producing trucks for the military. In fact, the Japanese military authorities, who had become aware of the substantial value of motor vehicles for military use during World War I, promulgated the Military Vehicle Subsidy Law (Gun'yō Jidōsha Hojo Hō) in 1918 to promote the development of truck production technology. With the beginning of the Shōwa period (1926–), the promotion of domestic automobile production was intensified in order to accommodate the changing international political situation. While the established *zaibatsu* were still hesitant to enter the industry, new manufacturers arose both as independent businesses and within the new *zaibatsu*, and engaged in automobile production despite numerous technological difficulties.

Among these producers were NISSAN MOTOR CO, LTD, and TOYOTA MOTOR CORPORATION. Nissan, formerly the Automotive Division of the Tobata Foundry Company, obtained the patent for the Datto vehicle and in 1933 became a part of the new Nissan *zaibatsu*. Toyota got its start in 1933 as the Automobile Department of Toyoda Automatic Loom Works, and became an independent corporation in 1936. These two companies were licensed as authorized companies in accordance with the Automotive Manufacturing Industries Law (Jidōsha Seizō Jigyō Hō) of 1935. This act was mainly aimed at protecting and promoting domestic automobile production by providing favorable tax treatment and other incentives for domestic manufacturers, as well as by imposing restrictions on the activities of foreign automobile makers, and the two authorized domestic automobile companies were soon able to enjoy its benefits. As Japan's economy moved onto a wartime footing, foreign auto manufacturers came under strict regulation by the act, leading to the cessation of their production operations in Japan in 1940. The domestic manufacturers focused their production on medium-size trucks in accordance with the military's industrial plans, and at the same time they worked to improve the underdeveloped spare parts industry. Diesel Jidōsha Kōgyō, successor of Tōkyō Jidōsha Kōgyō (now ISUZU MOTORS, LTD), was later added as an authorized auto manufacturer primarily engaged in the production of diesel trucks and buses.

After the beginning of World War II, the domestic makers (including the newly added MITSUBISHI HEAVY INDUSTRIES, LTD, and HINO MOTORS, LTD) provided substantial contributions to the production of military trucks and weapons. After the war, the Occupation authorities allowed these manufacturers to continue some production, principally of trucks, in order to improve the domestic transportation system, but total production in the first year was a mere 20,000 vehicles. Provided an opportunity to recover by the military procurements boom during the Korean War, the domestic automobile manufacturers started to manufacture passenger cars in 1952. In the beginning, most of the demand for passenger cars was from the taxi business, while the demand from private individuals was minimal. Around this time major domestic auto manufacturers began to compete for technical agreements with European automobile manufacturers to improve passenger car manufacturing technology, which had been the least developed area of the industry. As a result, affiliations such as Nissan–Austin, Hino–Renault, and Isuzu–Hillman were born. Transfer of technology from European automakers was not limited to vehicle manufacturers but was also extended to parts manufacturers, in order to refine both the engineering of main component parts and the basic technology relating to the design and production of passenger cars. However, these ties between Japanese and European automakers were temporary, and limited only to transfer of technology for small passenger cars; some domestic makers, such as Toyota and Prince Motor, Ltd, developed their own techniques independently. Also around this time, the government began a policy of support and protection of the domestic auto industry, led by the MINISTRY OF INTERNATIONAL TRADE AND INDUSTRY (MITI). Although it provided no direct financial assistance, it carried out an active program of ensuring favorable allocations of foreign currency to acquire new technology, of restricting vehicle imports and foreign investment, and of helping the auto parts industry to develop with technical assistance and advice.

After 1960, with the Japanese economy in a new period of liberalized trade and high economic growth, the domestic production of passenger cars increased at an unprecedented rate. As the wave of motorization began to sweep the country, several new automobile manufacturers joined the original three passenger car makers from the prewar period. These included Mitsubishi, which had produced trucks during the war and had been split into three companies after the war, two of which had started manufacturing motor vehicles and later merged again; Hino, which had originally manufactured diesel trucks; FUJI HEAVY INDUSTRIES, LTD (maker of the Subaru), which had been an aircraft manufacturer; and Prince. Others included TŌYŌ KŌGYŌ CO, LTD (maker of the Mazda), DAIHATSU MOTOR CO, LTD, and HONDA MOTOR CO, LTD, which had formerly made machinery, three-wheeled cars, and motorcycles. At this point, many new factories were built for the manufacture of passenger cars, with production capacities ranging from upwards of 100,000 vehicles. The parts industry underwent a process of integration and concentration leading to the development of an organized subcontracting system, and nationwide sales networks were strengthened. At the same time, Toyota and Nissan established a full product line policy in response to the widening range of demand. Toyota and Nissan

Automotive industry——Table 2

Motor Vehicle Production and Exports								
	Cars		Trucks		Buses		Total	
	Production	Exports	Production	Exports	Production	Exports	Production	Exports
1955	20,268	2	43,857	907	4,807	322	68,932	1,231
1960	165,094	7,013	308,020	31,028	8,437	768	481,551	38,809
1965	696,176	100,716	1,160,090	90,923	19,348	2,529	1,875,614	194,168
1970	3,178,708	725,586	2,063,883	351,611	46,566	9,579	5,289,157	1,086,776
1975	4,567,854	1,827,286	2,337,632	833,672	36,105	16,654	6,941,591	2,677,612
1980	7,038,108	3,947,160	3,913,188	1,953,685	91,588	66,116	11,042,884	5,966,961

NOTE: Figures for 1980 exclude noncountable knockdown sets.
SOURCE: Nihon Jidōsha Kōgyō Kai (Japan Automobile Manufacturers Association, Inc), *Jidōsha tōkei nempō* (annual): 1980. Japan Automobile Manufacturers Association, Inc, *Motor Vehicle Statistics of Japan* (annual): 1981.

also took the lead in developing "strategic models" such as the Crown, Cedric, Corona, and Bluebird, which were suited to both high-volume production and sales market expansion. The strategies of these two manufacturers were quite successful, and they started to emerge as the giants of the modern Japanese automotive industry.

After 1965, with the advent of an era of free movement of capital, the industry entered a new period. To prepare for the expected invasion of foreign capital led by America's big three automakers, MITI initiated a carefully planned campaign to promote the reorganization of the automobile industry. In 1961 MITI had already announced a plan to strengthen this vital industrial sector by integrating and reorganizing the domestic automobile manufacturers into three groups: makers of mass-production passenger cars, makers of specialty vehicles, and makers of minicars. Despite MITI's efforts, the reorganization was not carried out in the way originally intended because of the differing opinions and expectations on the part of the companies involved. However, some mergers and formations of business groups did occur. Toyota forged agreements with Hino and Daihatsu and thus created its own group. Nissan absorbed Prince in 1966 and established a tie with Fuji Heavy Industries, forming the Nissan Group. These two business groups came to hold 60 percent of the market, showing strong oligopolistic tendencies. Under this situation, other automobile makers gradually began to seek ties with foreign manufacturers, partly at the urging of their banks. Mitsubishi established capital and operational ties with Chrysler Corporation in 1969; this was followed by a capital tie between Isuzu and General Motors Corporation in 1971, and sales and operational ties between Tōyō Kōgyō and the Ford Motor Company the same year.

As a result of these actions, a new structure emerged in the automobile industry consisting of three groups of manufacturers: one group of the two major domestic manufacturers and their affiliates, one group of the three companies associated with foreign manufacturers, and one group of two other independent manufacturers. These last two independent manufacturers are Honda, the world-famous maker of motorcycles that moved into the small car market, and SUZUKI MOTOR CO, LTD, which specializes in motorcycles and minicars.

Beginning around 1968, Toyota and Nissan rapidly increased their exports of automobiles and light trucks. By 1975, they were joined by the quickly expanding Honda company, as well as the manufacturers associated with foreign firms. The Japanese auto industry's competitive strength in world markets can be attributed to several factors, including increases in production scale, improvements in technology due to the introduction of automation and computers, relatively low labor costs vis-à-vis total production costs, and the rising technological level of parts manufacturing. Japanese cars have established a reputation abroad for their high quality and relative ease of maintenance. Furthermore, since the auto industry in Japan is centered on the production of small, fuel-efficient cars because of the country's road conditions and the high cost of gasoline, the Japanese car has proved well suited to the needs of the United States, its biggest market, where a growing demand for second and third cars has coincided with the need to conserve fuel in the wake of the oil crisis of the 1970s.

As of 1977, the two largest producers in Japan each produced over two million vehicles annually, and Toyota passed three million in annual production in 1980; both companies export close to 50 percent of their production. The Japanese auto industry as a whole displays a high degree of dependence on exports, sending 51.1 percent of its total production abroad in 1977 and 54.0 percent in 1980.

However, the precipitous rise in export sales has raised the possibility of import restrictions by countries seeking to maintain a healthy balance of trade. In more recent years, the loss of a competitive edge, due to the rise in value of the yen and the development of small cars by United States manufacturers in order to comply with United States government fuel economy standards, has contributed to a slowdown in Japanese auto exports. Because of this, several Japanese companies plan to produce cars in the United States.

In the brief interval of 25 years, the Japanese automotive industry has been able to increase its annual production one hundredfold, from 111,000 vehicles (including trucks and buses) in 1956 to 11,043,000 vehicles in 1980. The industry accounted for 10 percent of Japan's total manufacturing production in 1977, and followed the food and electrical appliances industries as the third largest in total production. Auto manufacturing employment (including parts manufacturing) totaled 653,000. When employment in related occupations is included, the Japanese auto industry total was approximately 4,500,000, or 10 percent of the nation's entire work force. There are several reasons for this tremendous growth. Among the most important are: the quick and effective adaptation of new technology; the smooth working relations between auto producers, parts workers, and repair and maintenance personnel based on group affiliations; the stable labor–management relations, along with the existence of a skilled labor pool; a highly developed marketing system, with close cooperation between makers and dealers; and effective government regulation, coupled with general government guidance and support.

In the 1970s the social environment of the Japanese auto industry underwent rapid change. Specifically, one may cite the establishment of a recall system to improve auto safety, and the enactment of laws to deal with pollution of metropolitan areas from exhaust fumes (see EXHAUST GAS REGULATION). In general, the Japanese auto industry has responded effectively to the problems of pollution control and safety in part because of the strictness of pollution regulations and the supervision by government agencies of the recall system. It has also dealt with the issue of fuel efficiency by emphasizing the production of small, energy-saving cars, partly because of the imposition of a steep gasoline tax by the government. Yet, as Japan enters a new era of consciousness regarding the consumption of resources and energy, the auto industry will have to make further innovations in technology. It must also clearly identify the role to be played by the automobile in the nation's transportation system and economy as a whole. That is to say, the industry will now have to make a transition from a period of simple quantitative growth to a period of qualitative improvement in response to general and social needs. SHIMOKAWA Kōichi

avatar

(*keshin; gonge*). The form taken by a supernatural being in order to manifest itself in the human world. In Japanese religion both Buddhist and Shintō divinities are believed capable of such visible or even incarnate manifestation. In Buddhism the bodhisattva KANNON (Skt: Avalokiteśvara) is the most celebrated avatar, assuming, according to the LOTUS SUTRA, 33 transformations in order to succor suffering sentient beings. With the Shintō KAMI the idea of the divinity itself assuming animal or bird form should be distinguished from the apparition of a messenger or servant. Thus the fox of Inari, the deer of Kasuga, and the monkey of Sannō are usually taken to be messengers of the divinities, but the snake of the deity Miwa

Aviation

The experimental plane in which Japanese fliers established a world cruising record in 1938.

Myōjin is a transformation of the god himself. The *keshin* forms assumed by the YAMA NO KAMI are especially numerous and diverse. The principal shapes in which he appears are (a) a woman, either old and ugly or young and beautiful; (b) a snake or dragon; (c) a pair of deities, male and female, often with red faces; (d) a four-legged animal such as a deer or bear; (e) a TENGU; (f) an ONI.

For the doctrine that the Shintō *kami* are *keshin* of certain Buddhist divinities, see HONJI SUIJAKU.   *Carmen* BLACKER

aviation

(*kōkū*). The first real progress in the field of aviation in Japan came with the introduction of foreign technology after World War I. Before that, there had been complete dependence upon importation of various types of aviation equipment. Japan soon began to design its own aircraft, featuring many original characteristics, particularly in military planes. After the end of World War II, aviation facilities and technology were converted to peacetime purposes, and the industry is now up to world standards.

The earliest planes. The first plane flights in Japan were made on 19 December 1910 at Yoyogi drill ground in Tōkyō. Captains of the army, Tokugawa Yoshitoshi (1884–1963) and Hino Kumazō (1878–1946), made short demonstration flights in an Henri Farman biplane made in France and a Grade monoplane made in Germany. Although some individuals had made pioneering efforts to develop Japanese airplanes, they were unsuccessful until 1911 when Narahara Sanji (1877–1944) succeeded in flying the first plane made in Japan. Others followed Narahara, but aviation technology was still considerably behind that of the advanced nations of Europe and the United States.

When the Japanese army and navy established air units, they imported various types of equipment from France, Germany, the United States, and the United Kingdom and produced planes under international licensing agreements at military arsenals. After World War I broke out, various types of planes were developed at a rapid pace in Europe, but Japan, although participating in the war, was far removed from the main battlefields in Europe and fell even further behind the progress of the advanced nations in many fields, including aviation technology.

Introduction of foreign technology. In 1919 the army and navy endeavored to modernize their air units drastically, by the army's engagement from France and the navy's from the United Kingdom of large contingents of aviation instructors and by the introduction of various types of new aircraft equipment. At the same time enterprises with large amounts of capital, such as Mitsubishi Shipbuilding Co, Ltd, Kawasaki Shipyard Co, Nakajima Aircraft Co, and Kawanishi Machinery Co, started full-scale development and production of airplanes. In 1923 the first graduates of the Department of Aeronautics at Tōkyō University emerged to form the nucleus of the subsequent Japanese aviation industry.

Rapid progress in the following years was largely due to the introduction of European framemaking techniques and engines: the metal structure technique of Junkers, Dornier, and Rohrbach of Germany; the flying boat technique of Short of the United Kingdom; and engines from Bristol in the United Kingdom, BMW of Germany, and Hispano-Suiza of France.

While Japanese manufacturers were engaged in the production of aircraft under international license, they succeeded in developing their own designs, and in the latter half of the 1920s they delivered so-called "homemade" military airplanes, such as the Mitsubishi shipboard attack plane Model 13 (1924) and the Kawasaki reconnaissance plane Model 88 (1928), which were adopted as standard types. These models displayed the overwhelming influence of foreign engineers and techniques.

While the development and production of various types of planes, most of which were military planes, continued, around 1935 Japanese aeronautical technology began to produce solely Japanese-made planes with features not to be found in European and American aircraft.

Establishment of world records. Japanese-made planes dating from this period were chiefly used as warplanes, since World War II broke out soon afterwards, but they did make some record-breaking flights as civil planes.

The *Kamikaze,* a Mitsubishi high-speed liaison plane owned by the newspaper *Asahi shimbun* and flown by Iinuma Masaaki and Tsukakoshi Kenji, established the first Japanese world record for speed in April 1937 by flying 15,357 kilometers (9,537 mi) from Tōkyō to London via the southern route in 94 hours 17 minutes and 56 seconds, including ground refueling time en route.

In May 1938 an experimental long-range plane, built by the Aeronautical Research Institute of Tōkyō University and piloted by Fujita Yūzō and Takahashi Fukujirō, established a world cruising distance record of 11,651 kilometers (7,235 mi) by flying 19 rounds along a triangular course over the Kantō Plain. No other official record has been set since in Japan.

In August through October 1939 the *Nippon* (a twin-engined transport plane built by Mitsubishi) owned by the newspaper *Mainichi shimbun* and flown by a six-man crew including Captain Nakao Sumitoshi, succeeded in making a round-the-world flight by flying zigzag from Japan to the Aleutian Islands, from North America down to South America, across the Atlantic from South America to Rome, and then back to Tōkyō via the southern route. The actual flight time was 194 hours and the total distance covered was 52,860 kilometers (32,826 mi).

In July 1944 an A26 long-distance plane (a twin-engine plane built by Tachikawa Aeroplane) owned by the newspaper *Asahi shimbun* and manned by five crew members including Captain Nagatomo Shigemitsu, took off from Xinjing (Hsinking; now Changchun or Ch'ang-ch'un) Airport in China and flew a distance of 16,435 kilometers (10,206 mi) along a triangular course in 57 hours and 12 minutes without refueling or landing. This was a far better record than the world record at the time and was not broken until 1962, but it was not recognized as an official record, since it was established during wartime.

Warplanes. In Europe and the United States, heavy fighter planes with relatively high-wing loading capacities and high horsepower engines and with the capability of striking one blow and making a high speed escape were popular. However, among Japanese fighter planes, light varieties with low-wing loading capacities and easy maneuverability in circular flight and the capability of sharp turns were highly rated. In the first half of World War II these flight characteristics contributed appreciably to the early air war victories scored by Japan's army and navy. The representative Japanese fighters were the navy's Model 96 (Mitsubishi, 1936), Model Zero (commonly called Zerosen or ZERO FIGHTER; Mitsubishi, 1940), and *Shiden*-modified (Kawanishi, 1944); and the army's Model 97 (Nakajima, 1937), HAYABUSA (Nakajima, 1941) and *Hayate* (Nakajima, 1944). The *Shiden*-modified and *Hayate,* which appeared in the last stage of the war, were powerful fighters with high-wing loading capacities and high performance and with excellent control and maneuverability features.

The long-distance high-speed reconnaissance planes, called command reconnaissance airplanes by the army, were a type unique to Japan. They had little firepower, but achieved high speed from streamlined fuselages and were able to make secret reconnaissance and photographic reconnaissance flights over wide war areas. The army adopted Models 97 (Mitsubishi, 1937) and 100 (Mitsubishi, 1940), while the navy adopted the *Saiun* (Nakajima, 1944). Flying boats, Kawanishi Models 97 (1937) and 2 (1942), with four engines, gave high-level performance. Japan lacked large strategic bombers such as the B-17 and B-29 of the United States. The number of warplanes produced in the five years from 1941 through 1945 was 30,410 army planes and 31,990 navy planes, totaling 62,400.

Destruction by defeat and revival. With defeat in 1945, Japan was completely prohibited from the production and use of airplanes, and all facilities for aviation research and the production of aircraft were either dismantled or converted to other purposes. This lasted nearly seven years until April 1952, when Japanese aviation activities were finally resumed with the conclusion of the peace treaty. In the seven years of Japanese aviation industry inactivity, the world switched from propeller to jet planes, and aircraft construction changed greatly in all areas, including performance, structure, and equipment.

The Japanese aircraft industry rapidly absorbed new technology through the licensed production of fuselages and engines for new American planes and through the repair and overhaul of a large number of American warplanes stationed in East Asia. Thus in January 1956 a Lockheed T-33A jet trainer, manufactured by Kawasaki Aircraft Company under license, made the first flight of a postwar Japanese-made jet plane; and the Japan Jet Engine Company completed the manufacture of an XJ-3 engine as the first postwar domestic jet engine in July 1956. Meanwhile, facilities for the research and manufacture of airframes and engines were gradually improved and expanded. The first purely domestic airplane was the T1 jet trainer developed and built by FUJI HEAVY INDUSTRIES, LTD; the prototype made its first flight in January 1958. Fuji made the Model A jet, equipped with Bristol Orpheus jet engines made in the United Kingdom, and the Model B, equipped with a domestic J3-3 engine. Fuji made a total of 64 T1 jets, which are used by the SELF DEFENSE FORCES.

The T1 was followed by the YS-11 twin turboprop transport, developed by Nihon Aeroplane Manufacturing Company. The prototype YS-11 made its first flight in August 1962, and a total of 182 planes were built, 76 of which were exported to various countries including the United States. The C-1 jet military transport, developed by KAWASAKI HEAVY INDUSTRIES, LTD; the PS-1 patrol flying boat and US-1 rescue flying boat, developed by Shimmeiwa Industries; and the T-2 supersonic trainer and F-1 supersonic fighter-attack plane, developed by MITSUBISHI HEAVY INDUSTRIES, LTD, are all military planes used by the Self Defense Forces. The success of these companies demonstrates that the Japanese aircraft industry possesses the ability to independently design and build all types of planes, including supersonic class jets.

Of the gross sales of the Japanese aircraft industry, which totaled ¥2,140 billion from 1952, the year of the reopening of Japanese aviation, through 1977, nearly 90 percent was accounted for by the demand for national defense. This is a strikingly high dependence on military demand in comparison with other countries. When production gets under way for the YX PROJECT (target date is 1986), which was started in the autumn of 1978, the existing imbalance may be redressed to some extent by an increase in civil demands.

━━ William Green, *Famous Fighters of the Second World War,* 2 vols (1957–62). Okada Minoru, *Kōkū denshi sōchi* (1972). Bruce Robertson, *Aircraft Making of the World, 1912–1967* (1967).

KIMURA Hidemasa

awabi → abalones

Awa Dance

(Awa Odori). A variation of the Bon dance (BON ODORI) traditionally performed in the city of Tokushima (in Tokushima Prefecture, formerly known as Awa Province) and the surrounding area from 12 August to 15 August during the local observance of the BON FESTIVAL. Groups of men and women parade along the street, dancing and singing the song "Yoshikono-bushi" to the accompaniment of *shamisen,* flutes, and drums. The dance is also known as the "Fool's Dance" (Ahō Odori), referring to the song's refrain, "You're a fool *(ahō)* whether you dance or not, so you might as well dance." This dance is said to have originated when Hachisuka Iemasa (1558–1639) of the Awa domain built a castle in Tokushima and provided *sake* for the townspeople, who became drunk and began to dance.

MISUMI Haruo

Awajishima

Island in the eastern Inland Sea, southeast of Hyōgo Prefecture, central Honshū; the largest island in the Inland Sea. It is a roughly triangular island surrounded by Ōsaka Bay on the east, the Harima Sea on the west, and the Kii Channel on the south. It is surrounded

Awa Dance

by fault shorelines, with little level land but no high mountains. The highest point is Yuzuruhasan (608 m; 1,994 ft). The climate is mild with relatively little precipitation. Agricultural products include flowers, loquats, mandarin oranges *(mikan),* and onions; beef and dairy cattle are raised. Part of the Inland Sea National Park, Awajishima is also a tourist spot with such attractions as the temple ruins of the Awaji Kokubunji and the whirlpools at Naruto. Awaji dolls are a special product. Awajishima is scheduled to be the midpoint on a bridge connecting Honshū and Shikoku. Area: 593 sq km (229 sq mi); pop: 170,220.

Awa maru

A Japanese passenger-cargo ship that was sunk near Okinawa by a United States submarine on 1 April 1945 while proceeding under a World War II safe-conduct agreement with the United States. The United States and Japan earlier had agreed that Japan would provide vessels to transport relief supplies for Allied nationals in various areas of the Pacific under Japanese control, and that the United States would guarantee the immunity of the vessels from Allied attack on both outward and homeward voyages. The *Awa maru,* carrying over 2,000 Japanese passengers and crew on its homeward voyage from Southeast Asia, was only slightly ahead of its prescribed course at the time of the sinking. The United States accepted liability, but settlement was postponed until 1949. Japan waived all claims arising from the incident "in appreciation of the assistance . . . received during the post-surrender period from the Government of the United States of America" (art. 1 of the Agreement for Settlement of the *Awa maru* Claim, signed in Tōkyō on 14 April 1949). At the same time Japan recognized in a separate understanding that OCCUPATION costs and loans, as well as credits extended by the United States, were valid debts owed by Japan.

━━ US, Department of State, *Bulletin,* 15 July 1945. William J. Sebald, *With MacArthur in Japan* (1965). Richard B. FINN

Awano Seiho (1899–)

HAIKU poet. Born Hashimoto Toshio in Nara Prefecture. A major disciple of TAKAHAMA KYOSHI, the leader of the influential HOTOTOGISU (a haiku magazine) coterie. His haiku, while generally faithful to the *Hototogisu* style with its emphasis on a photographic description of landscape, are infused with warm humanity and humor. He published a number of haiku collections, including *Manryō* (1931), *Teihon Seiho kushū* (1947), and *Kōshien* (1972).

Awara

Town in northern Fukui Prefecture, central Honshū. Awara is noted primarily for its hot springs, discovered in 1883. Such sightseeing

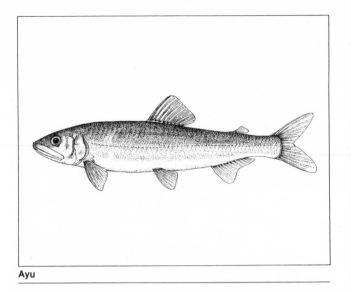

Ayu

areas as TŌJIMBŌ and Lake Kitagata also attract visitors. Principal products are rice, vegetables, and fruit. Pop: 13,608.

aware → mono no aware

Awashima

Island in the eastern Inland Sea, Kagawa Prefecture, Shikoku; one of the Shiwaku Islands and part of the town of Takuma. The island is formed by three mountains joined by sandbars. It is also the site of a national seamen's school. Area: 4 sq km (1.5 sq mi).

Awa Shrine

(Awa Jinja). Shintō shrine in the city of Tateyama, Chiba Prefecture, dedicated to Ame no Futodama no Mikoto, the divine ancestor of the IMBE FAMILY of ritualists. According to the KOJIKI (712, Record of Ancient Matters), this deity played a crucial role in enticing the sun goddess and so-called imperial ancestress, AMATERASU ŌMIKAMI, out of the cave in which she had secluded herself. He later accompanied the grandson of Amaterasu, Ninigi no Mikoto, in his descent to Japan. Tradition has it that the Awa Shrine was built during the reign of the legendary first emperor, Jimmu. It was designated the first shrine *(ichinomiya)* of Awa Province (now part of Chiba Prefecture) in the 8th century (see SHRINES). The Engi Shiki (927, Procedures of the Engi Era) ranked it as an eminent shrine of the nation *(myōjin taisha)*. Today the Awa Shrine is associated with fertility of the soil. The annual shrine festival is celebrated on 10 August. *Stanley WEINSTEIN*

Awataguchi Yoshimitsu (fl 13th century)

Swordsmith of the middle part of the Kamakura period (1185–1333) from Yamashiro (now part of Kyōto Prefecture); member of the Awataguchi (the armorers' district of Kyōto) school of sword making. With Masamune of Sagami (now part of Kanagawa Prefecture), and Yoshihiro of Etchū (now Toyama Prefecture), he was regarded as one of the three great swordsmiths of his time, and the short swords in which he specialized were highly regarded by *daimyō.*

Ayabe

City in central Kyōto Prefecture. Ayabe derives its name from work groups (BE) of naturalized Chinese and Korean immigrants (see AYA FAMILY) who settled in the area in the 400s and engaged in weaving. During the Edo period (1600–1868) it served as a castle town for the Kuki family. In modern times the city's tradition as a textile and sericulture center has been revived; it is the home base of GUNZE, LTD. The headquarters of the Ōmotokyō sect is also located here. A suburb, Kurotani, is famous for its *washi* (Japanese paper). Pop: 42,552.

Aya family

A large and influential group of immigrants (KIKAJIN) and their descendants in ancient Japan. Not strictly a consanguineous "family," most prominent among them were the Yamato no Aya, who settled in Yamato Province (now Nara Prefecture), especially in the ASUKA region. A large part of the original group probably arrived in Japan around 400 AD and was led by Achi no Omi, who, according to the genealogy of the SAKANOUE FAMILY (a branch line), fled with his own and seven other families from the war-torn Korean peninsula. Soon afterward many other immigrants (often called *ayahito*) from Korea settled in Japan at Achi no Omi's behest. Still later immigrants in the 5th and 6th centuries were commonly called *imaki no* (newly arrived) *ayahito.* It seems likely that many if not most of these immigrants were, as Achi no Omi's progeny later claimed, descended from Chinese who had earlier settled in Korea. The character for *aya* is that ordinarily used to designate the Chinese Han dynasty (206 BC–AD 220), but some suggest that the reading *aya* derives from the place name Ara (with variant pronunciations *ana* and *aya*) in southeast Korea. The various branches of the Yamato no Aya became closely allied with the SOGA FAMILY in the middle of the 7th century, and many of its members were prominent in diplomacy, government, military affairs, court ritual, and the support of Buddhism. They also had supervisory functions over those organizations called BE that provided various goods and services. They tended to gravitate to the region of the capital and were less geographically scattered than the HATA FAMILY, also from Korea. *William R. CARTER*

ayame → irises

Ayase

City in central Kanagawa Prefecture, central Honshū. After World War II Ayase, together with the neighboring city of Atsugi, was the site of an American Air Force base. Long a rice-producing area, it is being rapidly urbanized as a residential area and as an industrial center. Pig breeding and market gardening are the main agricultural occupations. Pop: 65,077.

Ayrton, William Edward (1847–1908)

British electrical engineer who contributed significantly to the development of electrical engineering in Japan. In 1873 he accepted an invitation from the Japanese government to teach physics and electrical engineering at Kōbu Daigaku (Engineering College; now part of Tōkyō University), where he remained until 1879. He is credited with having introduced arc lighting to Japan in 1878, when he wired the new central telegraph station.

ayu

(sweetfish). *Plecoglossus altivelis.* An important Japanese freshwater fish of the class Osteichthyes, order Salmoniformes, family Plecoglossidae. It is usually less than 20 centimeters (8 in) in total length and has an adipose fin. Spawned in rivers late in autumn, it descends to the sea and swims upstream early in spring. As fry it feeds on microscopic animals but later it feeds on plankton and as an adult on diatomic algae which it scrapes from rocks on river bottoms with its saw-shaped teeth. It develops a keen sense of territory. Taking advantage of its habit of trying to expel intruders, a special fishing method called *tomozuri* (decoy fishing) is often employed. Cormorants are also used to catch *ayu* (see CORMORANT FISHING). Aquiculture is also practiced. *Ayu* are eaten broiled with salt, fried, or as *ayuzushi* (raw *ayu* with vinegared rice). *ABE Tokiharu*

The sweetfish appears as a good omen in the ancient chronicles *Kojiki* and *Nihon shoki* (8th century) and the *Man'yōshū*, the oldest Japanese poetry anthology (also of the 8th century). It has been a highly valued fish throughout Japanese history, and today is popular as a sport fish. *SAITŌ Shōji*

Ayukawa Nobuo (1920–)

Poet and literary critic. Real name Uemura Ryūichi. Born in Tōkyō. Studied at Waseda University before withdrawing to serve in Japan's armed forces. In 1939 he helped to found the poetry magazine *Arechi,* which had considerable influence in the 1950s. As a central figure of the Arechi coterie, which viewed Japan after the war as a "wasteland," he made a significant contribution to the development of postwar Japanese poetry. Ayukawa has also been an active polemicist who insisted on the poet's social and political responsibility. His works include a critique of modern Japanese poetry, *Gendaishi to wa nani ka* (1949–50), and *Ayukawa Nobuo shishū* (1956), a collection of postwar poems.

Azai family → Asai family

Azai Nagamasa → Asai Nagamasa

azaleas

In Japanese *tsutsuji* is the most general term for evergreen and deciduous azaleas. One evergreen late-blossoming species is called *satsuki* and is distinguished from other azaleas, though it is also referred to as *satsuki tsutsuji*. RHODODENDRONS, like azaleas, are shrubs of the genus *Rhododendron* of the heath family (Ericaceae); they are called *shakunage* in Japanese. Japan is rich in the quantity and variety of wild azaleas, and many horticultural varieties have been developed.

Wild Species of Tsutsuji —— The *yama tsutsuji (Rhododendron kaempferi)* is a half-evergreen shrub that grows in hilly and mountainous areas throughout Japan. Its scarlet flowers open in May or June against the new leaves. There are also white flowered, pinkish purple flowered, and double-flowered varieties. The *mochi tsutsuji (R. macrosepalum)* is an evergreen shrub that grows in hilly areas of central and western Honshū and is also cultivated in gardens. Its hairy leaves and branchlets are a special characteristic. With the new leaves in the spring, light reddish purple flowers open in a rounded cluster. Many horticultural varieties have been developed from this species. The *miyamakirishima (R. kiushianum)* is an evergreen shrub that grows in mountainous areas of Kyūshū. A cluster of these shrubs in flower is a colorful spectacle. The leaves are small and the small flowers are usually magenta or reddish in color. The Unzen *tsutsuji (R. serpyllifolium)* is a small shrub that grows from the Izu Peninsula westward. The branches are thin, and both the flowers and leaves are small. The flowers are pink or white. The *renge tsutsuji (R. japonicum)*, a deciduous shrub that has given rise to a great number of varieties, is generally found in clusters at altitudes of over 1,000 meters (about 3,300 ft). The flowers are usually orange red but scarlet or yellow types also occur. Many horticultural varieties were developed in Europe by crossing this species with *R. molle*, a species of Chinese origin. The *mitsuba tsutsuji (R. dilatatum)* is a deciduous shrub that grows in hilly and mountainous areas of central Honshū. The broad, diamond-shaped leaves usually grow in threes on the branch tips. In early spring it produces deep reddish purple flowers before the leaves appear.

Garden Species of Tsutsuji —— The wild species has long been appreciated in Japan and, since the Kamakura period (1185–1333), has been cultivated as an ornamental; in the Edo period (1600–1868) enthusiasm for azaleas ran particularly high, and many new horticultural varieties were developed.

The Kirishima *tsutsuji (R. obtusum)* is an evergreen with many subspecies whose leaves and flowers vary greatly. The Kurume *tsutsuji (R. obtusum* var. *sakamotoi)* is a species developed in the Kurume region of Kyūshū. The flowers may be single or double, and their colors vary greatly. Some Kurume *tsutsuji* varieties were developed from the *miyamakirishima*. The *ōmurasaki (R. pulchrum)* is an evergreen with leathery, hairy leaves. In the spring two to four white or rose purple flowers open at the tips of the branches. The Ryūkyū *tsutsuji (R. mucronatum)* is an evergreen that reaches a height of about 1.5 meters (5 ft). In early summer one to two groups of white flowers open at the tips of the branches; one subspecies has purple flowers.

The Satsuki —— The *satsuki* or *satsuki tsutsuji (R. indicum)* is an evergreen shrub found growing wild on rocks along rivers in Kyūshū, Shikoku, and western Honshū and is cultivated in home gardens as an ornamental. It grows to a height of 15–90 centimeters (6–35 in). The leaves are linear-lanceolate in shape, with both ends pointed. The *satsuki* resembles the *yama tsutsuji* but has thicker and glossier leaves. In May and June it opens reddish purple flowers 3–5 centimeters (1–2 in) across at the ends of branches. The petals have dark reddish purple blotches on the upper side. In the course of cultivation many varieties have been developed, including white-flowered and double-flowered types. *Satsuki* became popular in the

Edo period when horticultural books listed more than 160 varieties of *satsuki* as distinguished from *tsutsuji*. The number of varieties has now increased to over 500; admirers of *satsuki*, especially potted or in *bonsai*, continue to increase. The name *satsuki* is derived from the old name for the fifth month of the year in the lunar calendar, the approximate time when the plant blossoms.

MATSUDA Osamu

azami → thistles

Azuchi

Town in central Shiga Prefecture, central Honshū, on the eastern shore of Lake Biwa. Its chief occupation is farming. There are many sites of historical interest, including the ruins of AZUCHI CASTLE, built by ODA NOBUNAGA in the 16th century, and Kannonji Castle, the site of the Sasaki family. North of the train station is the temple Kuwanomidera, where the priest Jōe, the son of FUJIWARA NO KAMATARI, is said to have planted mulberry seeds he brought back from Tang (T'ang) China and to have taught the local populace to raise silkworms. Pop: 10,256.

Azuchi Castle

Castle built in Azuchi (in present-day Shiga Prefecture) by the late 16th-century military hegemon ODA NOBUNAGA to defend Kyōto and to consolidate his control over the country. Construction began in 1576 and it took three years to complete. Built on Azuchiyama, a mountain bordering Lake Biwa, its fortifications stretched to the top of the mountain. Azuchi Castle was regarded as the model castle of the age because of its magnificent seven-story donjon *(tenshukaku)*; *daimyō* later copied its architectural style in building their own castles. The layout and building formation represented a transition between the mountain castle and the plains castle. The inner keep had an irregular octagonal base above which alternating square- and octagonal-shaped levels were erected. Inside columns were painted black, gold, and vermilion, and roof tiles were gilded. The inner chambers were decorated with wall paintings by KANŌ EITOKU. The castle was destroyed shortly after Nobunaga's death in 1582.

Azuchi-Momoyama history → history of Japan

Azuchi–Momoyama period

A period of some 30 years (1568–1600) during which first ODA NOBUNAGA and then TOYOTOMI HIDEYOSHI ruled Japan as military hegemons. The name is taken from Nobunaga's AZUCHI CASTLE in Ōmi Province (now Shiga Prefecture) and the location of Hideyoshi's FUSHIMI CASTLE at Momoyama in Yamashiro Province (now part of Kyōto Prefecture). Most historians place the beginning of the period in 1568, when Nobunaga installed the last Muromachi shōgun, ASHIKAGA YOSHIAKI, in office under his control; others place it in 1573, when Nobunaga deposed Yoshiaki and brought the Muromachi shogunate to its definitive end. The end of the period is usually placed in 1600, when TOKUGAWA IEYASU crushed his rivals in the Battle of SEKIGAHARA; but some scholars place it later, in 1603, when Ieyasu received the title of shōgun, or earlier, in 1598, the year of Hideyoshi's death (see PERIODIZATION).

Politically, the Azuchi–Momoyama period was a time of national unification after a century of civil war (see SENGOKU PERIOD). Economically and socially, it saw the establishment of a firm base for centralized feudal rule through the rationalization of landholding (see KENCHI), as well as the growth of commerce, a nationwide money economy, and a thriving urban mercantile class. In the cultural sphere, it was characterized by the decline of Buddhism and the rise of a vigorous secular culture. The architecture and decoration of CASTLES reached their peak of ostentation under the patronage of the hegemons and *daimyō*; the tastes of the merchant townsmen produced major developments in painting, poetry, drama, and the tea ceremony; and Japan was exposed to Western (NAMBAN) culture through contact with European traders and missionaries. See also HISTORY OF JAPAN: Azuchi–Momoyama history.

Azuchi Shūron

(Azuchi Disputation). A formal doctrinal debate between representatives of two Buddhist sects, the JŌDO SECT (or Pure Land sect) and the NICHIREN SECT (or Lotus sect), held on 21 June 1579 (Tenshō 7.5.27) at the behest of the hegemon ODA NOBUNAGA in his castle town of Azuchi. Nobunaga, concerned about the Nichiren sect's general intransigence, combative missionary methods, and growing popularity in Azuchi, ordered the debate after Nichiren zealots disrupted a Jōdo sermon. The Nichiren partisans, called "troublemakers" *(itazuramono)* by Nobunaga, were declared the losers of the contest, and three of their principals, including the aggressive preacher Fuden Nichimon, were executed on the hegemon's orders. Threatened with a general persecution, the main temples of the Nichiren sect acknowledged defeat, swore to abandon their habitual intolerance of other sects, and paid a heavy fine to Nobunaga. By his management of the Azuchi Disputation, Nobunaga showed once again that his unification regime meant to exercise firm control over religious organizations. His action affected not only the Buddhists but the imperial court as well, for Nobunaga had ignored the emperor's traditional role as mediator and ultimate juridical authority in sectarian disputes.   George ELISON

azuki

Also known as adzuki. *Phaseolus angularis,* a bean plant of the family Leguminosae which was introduced from China early in Japan's history and is still widely cultivated. It grows to about 60 centimeters (24 in), with pods about 10 centimeters (4 in) long, containing 8 to 10 beans each. The bean is red, cylindrical, and about 0.5 centimeters (0.2 in) long. It has been cultivated for 2,000 years in the Far East; in Japan, it is boiled with rice on special occasions, red being considered an auspicious color. It is also used for traditional Japanese CONFECTIONS such as *yōkan* (sweet jelly), *shiruko* (sweetened *azuki* bean soup with rice cakes), and *amanattō* (sugared *azuki* beans), which account for 75 percent of total consumption. Annual production is about 100,000 metric tons (110,000 short tons); Hokkaidō is the main growing area.   HOSHIKAWA Kiyochika

Azuma kagami

(Mirror of Eastern Japan). A historical account of the KAMAKURA SHOGUNATE. Its 52 chapters cover the 86 years from 1180, the year of the outbreak of the TAIRA–MINAMOTO WAR, to 1266. Scholars generally attribute authorship to shogunate scribes and archivists, but their names are unknown. Apart from a few letters and documents, the work is written in an awkward form of Chinese, the language of the official histories of the imperial court.

The text is arranged in strictly chronological order, as if the accounts had been written and entered as the events occurred. Japanese scholars have shown, however, that the work in its entirety was written in retrospect sometime between 1266, the last year recorded in the work, and 1301. It has also been shown that the compilers relied heavily on a variety of contemporary, unofficial materials to fill out the entries, especially for the early years when the founders of the shogunate, fighting for their very existence, left few records. These materials include house records of such military families as the Kumagaya and the Kōno; the repositories of such religious institutions as the Tōdaiji, Enryakuji, and Tsurugaoka Hachiman Shrine; diaries and travel accounts of court nobles, including the GYOKUYŌ of KUJŌ KANEZANE, the MEIGETSUKI of FUJIWARA NO SADAIE, and the KAIDŌKI, a travelogue of unknown authorship; and war romances, such as the HEIKE MONOGATARI and the GEMPEI SEISUIKI. The few poems in the work are drawn from the KINKAI WAKASHŪ, an anthology by MINAMOTO NO SANETOMO, the third and the last of the Minamoto shōguns.

Ten of the 86 years spanned by the chronicles have been lost entirely. Moreover, entries for many days and months are missing, or may never have been written. For example, only 190 days are accounted for in the three-year period between 1201 and 1203 (chapters 17–19). The entries also vary considerably in length and fullness. The accounts of the years between 1201 and 1234 (chapters 17–29), for example, are brief and to the point and appear to be summaries of longer original entries. On the other hand, the accounts of the early years, including the years of the Taira–Minamoto War (1180–85), are long and detailed, perhaps because they were drafted in part from the more imaginative war romances. The *Azuma kagami* is a valuable source of information on the political history of the Kamakura period and on early warrior society.

The dozen or so extant editions of the work stem from one of two older editions—the Kanazawa Bunko edition, which circulated in eastern Japan, and the Kikkawa edition, which circulated in western Japan. The Kanazawa edition is the source of most extant editions, including the Hōjō edition, which became famous when TOKUGAWA IEYASU, the founder of the Tokugawa shogunate (1603–1867), used it as a manual of government. The Kikkawa edition, rediscovered in 1911, was compiled in the 16th century for the ŌUCHI FAMILY, who collected historical works and aspired to make the city of Yamaguchi a cultural center to rival ancient Kyōto. There was still a third old edition, the Shimazu, but no copy is known to survive.

——Minoru Shinoda, *The Founding of the Kamakura Shogunate, 1180–1185* (1960). Chitoshi Yanaga, "Source Materials in Japanese History: The Kamakura Period, 1192–1333," *Journal of the American Oriental Society* 59 (1939). Yashiro Kuniji, *Azuma kagami no kenkyū* (1913).   Minoru SHINODA

Azuma Ryōtarō (1893–1983)

Educator; active sports administrator and governor of Tōkyō (1959–67). Born in Ōsaka. After graduating from Tōkyō University with a medical degree in 1917, he studied physiology with Archibald Hill at the University of London. When he returned to Japan he promoted the study of sports physiology as a medical specialty. In 1934 he became professor of medicine at Tōkyō University. After World War II he was employed by the Ministry of Health and Welfare as head of the Medical Affairs Bureau and in 1953 was named president of Ibaraki University. Azuma served as president of several sports organizations, including the JAPAN AMATEUR SPORTS ASSOCIATION from 1947 to 1958. In 1950 he became the first Japanese to serve on the International Olympic Committee. During his second term as governor, Azuma successfully sponsored the 1964 Olympics in Tōkyō.   TAKEDA Fumio

Azumasan

Volcanic mountain group on the border of Fukushima and Yamagata prefectures, northern Honshū; highest peak Nishi Azumasan (2,024 m; 6,639 ft). Almost all these mountains are covered with forests, with old volcanic craters forming lakes and swamps. Located within the Bandai–Asahi National Park.

Azusagawa

River in western Nagano Prefecture, central Honshū. It originates at Yarigatake, the second highest peak in the Hida Mountains, flows through the valley of KAMIKŌCHI, and joins the Naraigawa near the city of Matsumoto, where the river's name changes to Saigawa. There are numerous deep gorges as well as many hot springs. The land along this river forms part of the Chūbu Sangaku National Park. Length: 77 km (48 mi).

B

Baba Keiji (1897–1961)

Scholar of business administration. Born in Ōsaka Prefecture, Baba graduated from Tōkyō University with degrees in engineering and economics. He joined the faculty of his alma mater in 1925 as an associate professor of business administration. Baba's initial research was in industrial economics. In the 1930s, however, influenced by German managerial economics, he became interested in establishing the theoretical bases of management. He believed that the core of management lay in organizational theory, and he read numerous works in this area as well as in the related fields of sociology and psychology. After World War II Baba introduced to Japan the theories of the American scholars C. I. Barnard and H. A. Simon. The influence of the Barnard-Simon school is reflected in Baba's last work, *Keieigaku to ningen soshiki no mondai* (1954, Management and Human Organizational Problems). Baba's many writings are credited with having helped to modernize the postwar Japanese management system. *NODA Kazuo*

Baba Kochō (1869–1940)

Essayist; translator. Real name Baba Katsuya. Born in Kōchi Prefecture; younger brother of BABA TATSUI. While studying at Meiji Gakuin, Tōkyō, he became friendly with the young poet and novelist SHIMAZAKI TŌSON and joined the Bungakukai literary group, in which Shimazaki was a principal member. His own novels and poems were not successful; and they lacked originality. The best of his essays were reminiscences of his association with writers of the late years of the Meiji period (1868–1912). He published translations of works by Daudet, Gorky, Tolstoy, and others. He also taught European languages at Keiō University and was a poetry editor for the newspaper YOROZU CHŌHŌ. *James R. MORITA*

Baba Tatsui (1850–1888)

Political thinker active in the FREEDOM AND PEOPLE'S RIGHTS MOVEMENT in the 1870s and 1880s. The second son of a retainer of the *daimyō* of the Tosa domain (now Kōchi Prefecture), Baba studied English at FUKUZAWA YUKICHI's Keiō Gijuku (now Keiō University) and made two trips to England during the 1870s to study Western law and politics. He took an active part in English social and political life, writing editorials for the London *Examiner* proposing revision of the treaty between Britain and Japan (see UNEQUAL TREATIES, REVISION OF) and essays introducing aspects of Japanese culture to the West. On his return to Japan in 1878 Baba became involved with the people's rights movement; he befriended its leaders, ITAGAKI TAISUKE and GOTŌ SHŌJIRŌ, and with NAKAE CHŌMIN quickly established himself as one of the theoreticians of the movement. In 1881 Baba helped to organize Japan's first national political party, the JIYŪTŌ. As a regular contributor to the *Chōya shimbun* newspaper, he often criticized the leaders of the Meiji government for their reluctance to extend political rights to the Japanese people. In 1885 he was suspected of engaging in antigovernment activities and was arrested. After his release from prison in 1886 he left Japan for political exile in the United States. There he reviewed the progress of the people's rights movement and wrote a long essay in English, *The Political Condition of Japan, Showing the Despotism and Incompetency of the Cabinet and the Aims of the Popular Parties* (1888). He died in Philadelphia. *M. William STEELE*

Baba Tsunego (1875–1956)

Journalist. Born in Okayama Prefecture. Baba left Waseda University before graduating and became an employee of the English-language newspaper the JAPAN TIMES. He later went to the United States and established *The Oriental Economic Review* in 1910 to help mitigate anti-Japanese sentiment in America resulting from the Russo-Japanese War (1904–05). In 1912 publication was discontinued, and Baba returned to his job with the *Japan Times.* He also worked for the KOKUMIN SHIMBUN and, as a critic, wrote many articles expounding the cause of liberalism. From 1945 to 1951 he was president of the YOMIURI SHIMBUN.

Bacon, Alice Mabel (1858–1918)

American teacher of English and a writer on women and life in Japan during the Meiji period (1868–1912). Born in New Haven, Connecticut; daughter of a prominent Congregational clergyman. In 1871 the Japanese government sent five young girls with the IWAKURA MISSION to the United States to be educated. At the request of MORI ARINORI, then Japanese envoy in Washington, Bacon's family sponsored one of the girls, 12-year-old Yamakawa Sutematsu, who lived with them for the next 10 years. Another student was TSUDA UMEKO, who also became a close friend of Alice Bacon during these years.

In June 1888 Yamakawa and Tsuda invited Bacon to Japan. Yamakawa was by then married to General ŌYAMA IWAO (1842–1916), and Tsuda was in charge of English at Joshi Gakushūin in Tōkyō, a school for daughters of the Japanese nobility and a forerunner of Gakushūin University. Bacon taught English at this school until her return to the United States in the fall of the following year.

In 1900 she went again to Japan to assist Tsuda in founding an advanced English language school for women, later known as Tsuda Eigakujuku (now Tsuda College). She also taught at the Tōkyō Women's Higher Normal School (now Ochanomizu Women's University). Until early 1902, when she left Japan for New Haven, she contributed considerably to the development of the school, carrying a heavy teaching load without remuneration.

While in Japan, Bacon observed Japanese life closely and wrote several books. In *Japanese Girls and Women* (1891; revised and enlarged, 1902), she discussed the changes in Japanese women's lives since the beginning of the Meiji period. In 1893 she published *A Japanese Interior,* a collection of her letters to relatives and friends in the United States. *In the Land of the Gods* (1905) is a collection of Japanese folktales. She also edited an American edition of Lieutenant Sakurai Tadayoshi's famous tale of the Russo-Japanese War, *Human Bullets: A Soldier's Story of Port Arthur* (1907). *Shumpei OKAMOTO*

badger → tanuki

badminton

Although badminton was played in Japan in the 1930s, it did not become widely popular until after World War II. In 1946 the Nippon Badminton Association was set up, and All-Japan Championship matches were held starting the next year. In the badminton world championship, held every three years, the Japanese women's team won the Uber Cup three times successively, in 1966, 1969, and 1972. Today, the number of players registered in the Nippon Badminton Association is about 51,000. The number of regular players in the country in the late 1970s was estimated to be 5,000,000. *WATANABE Tōru*

Baibunsha

("Writing for Sale Association"). Organization founded in Tōkyō by SAKAI TOSHIHIKO in 1910 in response to government persecution of socialists following the arrest of KŌTOKU SHŪSUI and others in an alleged plot against the emperor's life (see HIGH TREASON INCIDENT OF 1910). Begun as an agency offering advertising copywriting, translation, ghostwriting, editing, and other literary services, the Baibunsha provided employment for many blacklisted socialists—including ARAHATA KANSON, ŌSUGI SAKAE, YAMAKAWA HITOSHI, and TAKABATAKE MOTOYUKI—and developed into a political club. During World War I it published the magazine *Shin shakai* (New Society) and other socialist writings. In 1919 the association broke up because of ideological disagreements between Sakai and Takabatake, but the latter revived it briefly to publish his new magazine *Kokka shakai shugi* (National Socialism).

bail

(hoshaku). In Japan, as a general rule, a court must grant bail if a defendant so requests, except in the case of certain very serious felonies and other exceptional cases as provided by law; this is called bail as of right. At the time bail is granted, the prosecutor's opinion is heard, and consideration is given to the nature and circumstances of the alleged crime, the probative force of the evidence, and the character and financial resources of the defendant. Bail is set and posted at an amount sufficient to ensure the defendant's appearance. In addition to cash, bail may also be posted in the form of valuable securities or a letter of guarantee from a third party. According to statistics in the late 1970s, release on bail is granted for approximately 50–60 percent of defendants detained in district courts, and for 20–30 percent of defendants in summary courts. The amount of bail is set at between ¥500,000 (US $2,364) and ¥700,000 (US $3,310) in about half of all cases. Release of a suspect on bail at the preinformation stage is not currently permitted in Japan, but there is some support for amending this rule to allow bail in such cases as well. There are no bondsmen in Japan. There is also a system of suspending execution of detention, which is similar to the bail system, whereby the defendant is released in the custody of relatives or a custodial organization of some sort. This system of nonmonetary conditional release has its origins in the legal systems of East Asia. Its use is limited mainly to emergency situations.

Tamiya Hiroshi

baishin

Secondary *(bai)* vassal *(shin),* the vassal of a vassal; also called *matamono.* For example, early in the Kamakura period (1185–1333), the HŌJŌ FAMILY were classified as vassals of the shōgun and thus were *baishin* of the emperor, while vassals of the Hōjō were *baishin* of the shōgun. Most *daimyō* of the Edo period (1600–1868) had two or three *baishin* for every 100 *koku* (1 *koku* = about 180 liters or 5 US bushels; see KOKUDAKA) of rice they received as income from their domains. The vassals of a daimyō, regardless of the size of their stipends, remained *baishin* of the shōgun, in contrast to direct shogunal vassals, who were called *jikisan.*

Baishōron

(The Plum and Pine Discourse). A historical discourse or treatise *(shiron)* in two volumes (or scrolls) probably written between 1352 and 1387 and of unknown authorship. The work begins with a dialogue that takes place at Kitano Shrine in Kyōto on an early spring night in the mid-14th century. For the enlightenment of a crowd of laymen and clergy resting from Buddhist devotions, an aged monk recounts the development of the role of the SHŌGUN and the history of the Kamakura shogunate, in the course of which he touches on the background of the split in the imperial succession into NORTHERN AND SOUTHERN COURTS. Moving into the reign of the emperor GO-DAIGO, he focuses the narration on ASHIKAGA TAKAUJI, from his emergence in the national scene until a time in 1337 when the realm is quiet after the defeat of NITTA YOSHISADA, a follower of Go-Daigo, and the exile of the emperor to Yoshino. At the end of his discourse, the monk praises Takauji and his brother ASHIKAGA TADAYOSHI (1306–52) and explains the name of the work: the prosperity of the shōgun will unfold like plum blossoms, and the longevity of the shogunate will be like the pine. As the title suggests, the dialogue in which all has been narrated is like the breeze through the pines releasing the fragrance of the plum blossoms.

The original text, no longer extant, was probably written by one of the followers of Takauji. The *Baishōron*'s characteristics classify it as a GUNKI MONOGATARI (war chronicle), and it is clearly related to variants of the TAIHEIKI. The version of the *Baishōron* best known until recently is contained in the "Kassembu" (Battle Section) of GUNSHO RUIJŪ, an Edo-period (1600–1868) compendium of classical writing. In addition, there are three main families of older variant texts which are *shahon* ("old, copied books"). In these the dialogue and other literary features distinctive of so-called *kagamimono* ("mirror pieces"), such as the ŌKAGAMI and MASUKAGAMI, are more prominent, but all versions are much more terse and factual than the *Taiheiki,* which by comparison is diffuse and rhetorical. The end of the narrative in the *Baishōron* corresponds roughly to book 18 of the *Taiheiki,* but with only about one-fourth of the latter's textual bulk to that point. With its attention to detail, it has always been acknowledged as a primary historical source, more accurate than the *Taiheiki.*

📖——Yashiro Kazuo and Kami Hiroshi, annotators, *Baishōron, Gen'ishū,* vol 3 of *Shinsen Nihon koten bunko* (1975).

William R. Wilson

Bakan Sensō → Shimonoseki Bombardment

bakemono

Any of various monsters, apparitions, or goblins; preternatural beings in general. *Bakemono* (sometimes called *obake*) are generically termed *yōkai,* as distinguished from GHOSTS or *yūrei,* which typically appear in their original human form to particular persons to whom they bear some specific relation. *Yōkai,* by contrast, may appear in various nonhuman forms, including sounds, fire, or wind, and usually manifest themselves at dusk in a specific place (e.g., a mountain, roadside, body of water, or room), regardless of who is present. TENGU, YAMAMBA, HITOTSUME KOZŌ, and KAPPA are just a few of the types of *bakemono,* which number more than 500. See also ONI.

Inokuchi Shōji

Bakin (1767–1848)

Scholar, critic, diarist, and *haiku* poet. Also known as Takizawa Bakin, Kyokutei Bakin. Real name Takizawa Okikuni. Author of KUSAZŌSHI ("chapbooks") and YOMIHON ("reading books"), two popular genres of Edo-period (1600–1868) prose fiction. Most famous for his historical romance, NANSŌ SATOMI HAKKENDEN (1814–42, Satomi and the Eight "Dogs").

Born in Edo (now Tōkyō) on 4 July 1767, Bakin was the fifth son of a low-ranking *samurai.* Misery, suffering, and the death of family members filled his youth. After a period of drifting, he gave up his samurai status (1788) and lived as a townsman, depending almost entirely on writing for his livelihood. He married (1793) a widow, Aida Ōhyaku, three years his senior, who was the owner of a *geta* (clog) shop in the Iidamachi district of Edo. She bore him three daughters and a son, Sōhaku (1798–1835), who was of weak constitution. Although Bakin himself had irrevocably forsaken his samurai status, he tried his utmost to preserve samurai privileges for Sōhaku and to secure for him the best education possible. Sōhaku's early death meant continued hardship for Bakin as family head. Aside from his writing activities Bakin's major goal was the restoration of the family's fortunes. While at work on *Hakkenden,* he began to lose his eyesight, and went completely blind before finishing the celebrated romance with his daughter-in-law's aid in 1841. He died 1 December 1848.

Bakin's career as an author may be divided into three periods. For more than a decade (1790–1802), after becoming a pupil of SANTŌ KYŌDEN, a popular writer of the day, he wrote mostly *kusazōshi.* Later, after journeying to Nagoya, Kyōto, and Ōsaka, he turned his efforts to *yomihon* and *zuihitsu* (miscellaneous essays) during the years 1803–13, becoming the leading author in Edo. From the time he began publishing *Hakkenden* in periodic installments in 1814 till the end of his life, he devoted himself to long romances, scholarship, correspondence, and his diary.

Bakin is best remembered for his *yomihon,* of which he published more than 30 titles. Next to his masterpiece, *Hakkenden,* his most widely read work is *Chinsetsu yumiharizuki* (1807–11, Crescent Moon: The Adventures of Tametomo), an adventure tale about a historical bowman of legendary skill who strives to restore his family's fortune in the 12th century. Loyalty, filial piety, and the restoration of samurai families like his own were his main themes. His special interest in Chinese and Buddhist philosophy was tempered by a belief in the efficacy of the Japanese gods and a concern for language and style. Underlying his writings is a deeply moral sensibility, seasoned by compassion and a belief in human dignity.

Among his nonfiction writings, his diary is a rich source for information on everyday life in early 19th century Edo. His autobiographical works, *Waga hotoke no ki* (1822, The Lineage of Our House) and *Nochi no tame no ki* (1835, For the Sake of Survival) are important sources for social history. Among his achievements, Bakin is remembered as a pioneering critic of the novel and a historian of developments in Edo-period prose fiction. In *Kinsei mono no hon: Edo sakusha burui* (1834, Edo Authors: The Categories of the Modern Novel) he divides 17th- to 19th-century literature into two broad divisions: an early period, which centered in the Kyōto–Ōsaka area, and a later one, concentrated in Edo. Scholars still accept this view. Bakin remains one of the giants of Japanese literature. By means of his writing in many fields he holds a secure reputation among his countrymen.

■ ——Asō Isoji, *Takizawa Bakin* (1943). Hayashiya Tatsusaburō, ed, *Kasei bunka no kenkyū* (1976). Hora Tomio, Teruoka Yasutaka, Kimura Miyogo, and Shibata Mitsuhiko, ed, *Bakin nikki*, 4 vols (1973). Donald Keene, *World Within Walls* (1976). Mizuno Minoru, *Edo shōsetsu ronsō* (1974). Nakamura Yukihiko and Mizuno Minoru, ed, *Akinari, Bakin* (1977). Leon Zolbrod, *Takizawa Bakin* (1967). Leon M. Zolbrod

bakufu → shogunate

bakuhan system

(*bakuhan taisei;* literally, shogunate [*baku,* from *bakufu*] and domain [*han*] system). The term currently used by most Japanese historians to describe the government and society of the period 1580 to 1868. It is of comparatively recent origin, having come into general use only in the years after World War II. Credit for its acceptance has been given to the institutional historian Itō Tasaburō, whose book *Bakuhan taisei* was published in 1956.

It is a fairly neutral term, suited to scholars of whatever philosophical persuasion, which may account for its popularity. On the one hand, it avoids the problems invited by more abstract descriptions, such as "premodern," "early modern," "later feudalism," and "centralized feudalism." Unlike them, it is confined to a specific period of history in one particular country; it can therefore be used without commitment to any universalistic theory of historical development. On the other hand, when compared with more restricted Japanese terms—"the Tokugawa period," for example, or "the Edo period"—*bakuhan taisei* is very much more accurate, since it recognizes the HAN or domain as well as the Tokugawa *bakufu* (TOKUGAWA SHOGUNATE) and does not confine itself to the shogunal city of Edo (now Tōkyō).

Yet it is still far from ideal, and few scholars employ it without some amplification. The explicit reference to the shogunate, for example, is misleading. The Tokugawa shogunate was not founded until 1603, yet many important elements of government and society associated with the *bakuhan* system were already present as much as two decades earlier. Therefore most analyses of the *bakuhan* system begin around 1580. There is the fact, too, that while the term seems to refer only to the political and administrative system, in which power was divided between the shogunate and the domains, no scholar defines the term without also including economic and social life.

Samurai and Government —— The SAMURAI, who provided the *bakuhan* system with its ruling class, predated the foundation of the Tokugawa shogunate. There had, of course, been samurai, or warriors, in Japan for a very long time, but those of the *bakuhan* system were of rather a special kind. In the first place, most of them had been transformed from part-time to full-time soldiers, trained and equipped for war and for little else. By the beginning of the 17th century they were a self-perpetuating elite, already removed in sympathy from the rest of society, whom they saw as inferior. The next hundred years, in most parts of Japan, saw them physically removed as well, for they were brought in from the countryside to specified quarters in the CASTLE TOWNS. Once there, drawing salaries instead of controlling their own fiefs, they no longer had any independence.

In the second place, there was to be no significant mobilization of troops in Japan between 1638, the year of the SHIMABARA UPRISING, and 1853, when Commodore PERRY's ships sailed into Edo Bay (now Tōkyō Bay), so the members of this ruling class, while they maintained their military trappings—always, for example, keeping swords at their belt—and paid lip service to a mythology of blood and steel (see BUSHIDŌ), were very much more sedentary government servants than warriors. As the shogunate and the domains turned their attention to the administration of their territories, so

they encouraged their samurai to add reading and writing to their skills, and thereafter employed them in a variety of positions ranging from counselor, at one extreme, to clerk or police constable at the other.

In return for their contribution to the government of Japan, which was real enough, and for their readiness to defend Japan from foreign attack, which was rather more problematical, the samurai received a large share of the country's revenue. It was a numerous class, representing, at its peak, as many as 2 million samurai and their families, some 7 percent of the total population; by no means all samurai had official employment, but nevertheless, employed or not, they continued to draw salaries. It must also be noted that this elite was rather less concerned with efficiency than with hereditary rights. For most of the period of the *bakuhan* system, important positions throughout Japan were given to those eligible by birth, rather than to those of the appropriate intellectual capacity.

Although composed for the most part of civil servants, the entire samurai hierarchy was nevertheless organized along prebureaucratic lines, with ties of vassalage linking every man to his lord, and, ultimately to the shōgun, who stood above them all. Above him, of course, was the emperor, but he had no contact with samurai beyond delegating responsibility to their nominal leader, the shōgun. Under the shōgun were two groups of vassals. The first, some 260 in number, were the DAIMYŌ, to whom he entrusted most of the task of provincial administration. They were nominally his vassals, divided into categories of SHIMPAN, FUDAI and TOZAMA, but many, irrespective of their classification, ruled their domains as independent princes. The SANKIN KŌTAI system, which forced them up to Edo each alternate year, obliged them to recognize the shogunate's authority, but otherwise, under normal circumstances, little else was ever required of them. The real Tokugawa vassals were the HATAMOTO ("bannermen") and GOKENIN ("housemen") who made up the Tokugawa *kashindan,* or vassal band. Under them, and also under the various daimyō, came the bulk of the samurai class, who were Tokugawa rear-vassals (BAISHIN)—that is, men who had sworn allegiance to others in turn pledged to the Tokugawa. It was a network in which every samurai was involved, and which, in theory, could facilitate total mobilization in time of crisis.

Farmers and Taxes —— Like the samurai of the *bakuhan* system, the agricultural class (some 80 percent of the population) was a product of the 16th century, for the same pressures which created a professional warrior class also helped form communities devoted entirely to agriculture. Where once the farmer had been a formidable, if intermittent, political force, the late 16th century saw him almost totally separated from the samurai, and deprived of his weapons. In 1588 it was decreed that farmers found with weapons would face severe punishment (see SWORD HUNT), and this was so thoroughly enforced that thereafter their political activities were confined to minor agrarian disturbances (see HYAKUSHŌ IKKI).

While the farmer was thus much more responsive to government than ever before, he was at the same time much freer than he had ever been. This had been effected by the Taikō *kenchi,* a series of cadastral surveys (KENCHI) initiated by TOYOTOMI HIDEYOSHI and subsequently adopted by provincial overlords for their own use. In these surveys, teams of inspectors measured paddies and fields, assessing likely yields (see KOKUDAKA) and carefully noting the name of the person who actually worked the land. Having had his identity noted, each farmer was then personally responsible for paying taxes (NENGU) on the land ascribed to him; this represented an intensification of official control. On the other hand, however, by vesting land ownership in the actual cultivator, the surveys effectively sliced through a number of subsidiary claims, many of which, of some antiquity, would have belonged to those samurai now being moved into castle towns.

To the shogunate and domain governments it was important that agricultural productivity be concentrated in the hands of small farmers, sharing their productivity with neither local overlord, nor landlord nor trader, but instead meeting all their own needs and those of officialdom. If agriculture were organized on these lines, it was thought, the government's share of productivity would be maximized. Therefore farmers had to be guided. To make sure that they husbanded their resources properly, they were offered advice on the minutest details of household management, as, for example, in the famous KEIAN NO OFUREGAKI of 1649. In case they were tempted to drift casually into the status of tenant farmers, the TAHATA EITAI BAIBAI KINSHI REI of 1643 restrained them from selling their land, while 30 years later another law prevented the subdivision of holdings below a certain measure of productivity. Above all, to make sure of a stable agricultural class and therefore a stable tax base, each government forbade its farmers either from taking up other occupations or from moving to any other area.

Townsmen and Commerce —— Some occupational groups within the *bakuhan* system were neither military nor agricultural. To one such group belonged specialist craftsmen, for the most part living in cities and towns and catering to those who, like the samurai, could no longer meet their own needs through their own efforts. They therefore played a vital role in their society, their skills freeing others for different specializations. Nevertheless, it was felt that their contribution was not to be compared to that of either the producers of the nation's food, nor those who watched over its safety. Consequently their social position was not as high, and they were assigned the third position on the social scale, below samurai and farmers.

On the fourth, and lowest, position of accepted society was the much more numerous class of people who made their living in trade, manufacturing, shopkeeping, banking, pawnbroking, and speculating. These were, in short, the merchants and those employed by them, either as assistants or domestic servants. They, too, like the craftsmen, made their living in the cities and towns, selling to the samurai, and to each other, and providing all the facilities of credit and money-changing necessary to urban living. Since tradesmen, merchants, and those employed by them lived in the main centers of population, they were all classified together, in the official mind, under the title CHŌNIN, or townsmen.

The merchants of the *bakuhan* system worked within the confines of an almost totally self-contained economy. Trade with foreign countries, encouraged by Japan's military leaders in the late 16th century, had fallen into disfavour for a variety of reasons, not all of them mercantile. Between 1633 and 1638 a series of edicts sealed Japan off from all but an irreducible minimum of foreign contact and left it with a policy of NATIONAL SECLUSION (Sakoku), unaltered until 1854. Within this restriction, however, the merchants of the *bakuhan* system managed very well. There was, of course, official deprecation of a way of life in which one neither governed nor produced, and which reserved its highest rewards for the cunning and the unscrupulous. Nevertheless, disreputable or not, the merchants and their assistants provided services without which the system—including the *sankin kōtai*—could not possibly have functioned.

Rural Development —— The *bakuhan* system survived for the better part of 300 years, without overt challenge. Historians have often, therefore, been tempted to portray it as a static system. In fact, however, few of its constituent elements were to remain unimpaired; the official ideal of an orderly society in which samurai, farmers, and townsmen applied themselves diligently to their appointed roles, had begun to crumble within a hundred years of the system's foundation.

It was in the villages that the most ominous cracks appeared. Scholars have estimated that, in the course of the 17th century, Japan's agricultural productivity grew by as much as 50 percent, partly because of extensive land reclamation, and partly through more intensive use of land already under-cultivation. Seemingly an innocent development, this nevertheless brought about serious changes, since the governments of the *bakuhan* system, devoted though they were to skimming off all surplus agricultural production in the form of taxation, were to remain officially unaware of it. For one thing, most of the reclaimed land took the form of *hatake*, dry fields, rather than rice paddies and was therefore of little interest to officials to whom rice was still the only crop worth noticing. For another, while governments had been insistent on surveying their domains at the beginning of the 17th century, they grew less assertive when it came to resurveys. By the beginning of the 18th century, surveys were virtually unknown, perhaps because farmers had opposed them so forcefully.

This is not to say that governments ignored agricultural development. In the shogunate and in the domains various reform movements, from the early 18th century onward, tried to assure governments of at least the taxation to which they were legally entitled. They stopped short of fresh surveys, however, choosing instead to emphasize something altogether less contentious, the appointment of honest and capable officials. Accordingly such reforms had only limited success. There was, too, a growing emphasis on UNJŌ, taxes levied on those many products other than rice which farmers were producing in greater quantity. In the 19th century this was to develop into attempts by governments to turn their special products into official monopolies, but these usually encountered

massive noncooperation, ranging from smuggling to outright rebellion.

Increased productivity, and the inability of governments to control it, left an agricultural surplus in the hands of its producers, and the consequences, both for the agricultural community and the elaborate social and political structure built upon it, were severe. There was now every incentive for the farmer to dispose of his surplus for his own profit, at local markets, or at the castle town, or even in the great cities, selling by other than the official commercial channels. Further, access to markets encouraged the farmer to turn away from subsistence and produce goods for sale rather than for his own consumption.

With the appearance of profit, the traditional farming village underwent considerable change. Gone was the farmer of the official ideal, the man who produced everything his family needed, giving up whatever remained as taxes. In his place was a very different figure. By the early 19th century perhaps as many as a quarter of the inhabitants of any given village were likely to be commercially active, buying or processing agricultural products, or else selling to the farmers those things which they had ceased to produce for themselves. Many of the rest would have forsaken subsistence farming for cash crops.

The new opportunities helped some farmers become rich. Others, not so fortunate, failed, borrowed money, and fell into debt, from which not many could escape. In the end, despite the general prohibition, the sale of land became common and with it the appearance of landless agricultural laborers (MIZUNOMI-BYAKUSHŌ). By the end of the *bakuhan* system, as many as half the farmers in Japan were to spend all or part of their time working the land of wealthy landowners (*oyakata*). Many more abandoned agriculture altogether, moving to find employment in towns and cities. Those who remained increasingly expressed their frustration in attacks upon the storehouses of the rich. In general, the countryside of the late *bakuhan* system was very much more prosperous than it had once been, albeit that the prosperity was unequally distributed, but this was of small consolation to the governments of shogunate and domains, which had seen their dream of a placid and easily controlled yeomanry vanish.

Urban Development —— Other dreams were to disappear, too, most notably the dream of a commerce responsive to the needs of government and held in check by it. In the 17th century it did seem as though cooperation between business and government, to their mutual benefit, was a possibility. The earliest entrepreneurs were as much samurai in origin as they were merchants by orientation, and this initial closeness was reinforced by the cordiality with which both sides worked together to build up castle towns and cities. The granting of monopoly status to TOIYA (wholesale dealers) and KABU-NAKAMA (merchant associations) toward the end of the century expressed the conviction of merchants that they could work best under government protection, and of officials that commerce, like the agricultural villages, would function best if it were self-regulating.

By the 18th century, however, disillusionment had set in on both sides. Already government officials were complaining that merchants were doing rather better out of cooperation than governments were, and they made examples of the more immoderately successful. It was also clear that the specially licensed merchant associations were either unable or unwilling to regulate their own activities. This problem surfaced with the issue of price control, the source of considerable anxiety to the shogunate and domains from the 18th century onward. The market price for agricultural products—and more particularly for rice, in which the governments of the period received most of their income—was of particular interest to government officials. A fall in the price of rice effectively reduced samurai income; if such a fall were not accompanied by falls in other commodity prices, samurai income was still further reduced. The 18th and 19th centuries saw both wild fluctuations in the price of rice, and fairly constant rises in prices for other commodities, giving cause for considerable concern. Naturally, in their concern, officials turned to the commercial associations for help, calling on them to supervise the behavior of their members and to adhere to fixed prices. When this proved ineffective, the recriminations began, with officials attributing price fluctuations to the hoarding and speculative buying of greedy merchants. This view was shared outside government, as the growing frequency of UCHIKOWASHI, urban riots in which the main targets were rice-merchants' storehouses, suggests.

For their part, the merchants, too, were uneasy about close relations with officialdom. The national seclusion policy, however, since it precluded participation in any overseas trading ventures, offered no feasible alternative to close contact with governments, central and domainal. At its best, such contact gave protection from competition and an assured income; all too often, however, it was accompanied by pressures for loans, and few merchants could resist lending money to the major political powers. The risks of debt repudiation were considerable, but there nevertheless seemed little alternative use to which capital could be put.

Indeed, the early 19th century gave a great many urban merchants still more cause for disillusion. The rural surplus, and the varieties of village commerce and manufacturing resulting from it, attracted population away from the towns and cities, many of which therefore began to decline. As they declined, so too did the fortunes of established merchants, forced to cope not only with dwindling supplies of labor and raw materials, but with shrinking markets as well. Naturally they turned to their traditional allies and protectors, with complaints and petitions, only to discover that the governments of the *bakuhan* system were now powerless to help them.

Developments in Government

The samurai class, like the urban merchants, failed to adjust to the new realities. When they left the country villages at the beginning of the period to live in urban communities, two totally unforeseen processes were set in motion. One was that village administration, now left to the villagers themselves, became less, not more, responsive to direction from a distant officialdom. Hence the fall in government revenues, and hence, too, the growth of rural commerce. The other was that, since samurai were paid in rice, and since they were denied any share in increased agricultural productivity, they became completely vulnerable to market fluctuations. In their castle towns, therefore, on inelastic incomes, threatened by rising prices (and, let it be said, with something of a taste for city life) but yet able to expect no help from their daimyō, the samurai were easy prey for moneylenders.

They were, too, equally obvious prey for their own daimyō. The daimyō themselves, while threatened by no personal poverty, were nevertheless, as chief executives of their domains, as subject to the pressures of falling income and rising costs as any of their samurai. They, too, borrowed heavily from the mercantile community, but they borrowed even more from their own vassals, constantly, heavily, and with no intention of ever repaying. The samurai had no option but to acquiesce.

Economic problems, therefore, did much to destroy the morale of the samurai class, and much, too, to limit their effective response to military crisis when it eventually came. Economic hardship may have left no outward sign on the government clerk, but it crippled that same man when he was forced to equip himself to repel foreign invaders. It is not to be wondered at, then, that in the 19th century a sense of impending crisis stirred many members of the samurai class into action, particularly within the domains, where for the first time there were consistent demands for better management of domain resources and for more consultation. Nor is it to be wondered at that such demands, in some cases, actually bore fruit, with the appointment to senior office of capable men from the lower ranks of samurai society.

As the 19th century wore on, it became increasingly clear that the *bakuhan* system was a system under severe stress. Once a moderately stable society, it had dissolved into conflict; disturbances in town and country were both more frequent and larger in scale; samurai were restive, and critical of their superiors; the shogunate and domain governments, all financially distraught, were coming to mistrust each other, and in their mistrust had begun to move outside the political conventions. Japan therefore, in the middle of the 19th century, seemed to be on the threshold of some major change. The question is, change of what sort, and how far could it have been accommodated within the existing system? We will never know the answer. The question of institutional change was to be overtaken by the events of the 1850s, when Japan could no longer face its internal problems in isolation. It was not to surface again until one major element of the *bakuhan* system—the Tokugawa shogunate—had been destroyed.

——Harold Bolitho, *Treasures among Men: The Fudai Daimyo in Tokugawa Japan* (1974). Fujino Tamotsu, *Shintei bakuhan taisei shi no kenkyū* (1975). William B. Hauser, *Economic Institutional Change in Tokugawa Japan* (1974). Itō Tasaburō, *Bakuhan taisei* (1956). Kimura Motoi, *Bakuhan taisei shi josetsu* (1961). Thomas C. Smith, *The Agrarian Origins of Modern Japan* (1959). Kozo Yamamura, *A Study of Samurai Income and Entrepreneurship* (1974).

Harold BOLITHO

balance of payments

(kokusai shūshi). A statistical record of all economic transactions between residents of the reporting country and residents of all other countries. By combining certain items that are similar according to some criteria in the balance-of-payments accounts, economists attempt to evaluate various analytical and policy issues raised by the evolution of international transactions.

Definitions and Data Summary

The accompanying table summarizes Japan's balance of payments for the years 1950–78. The merchandise trade balance is the difference between exports and imports. It is one of the most frequently used measures of a country's balance-of-payments performance, but it is only a partial measure. A surplus in the merchandise trade balance indicates an excess of exports over imports, and a deficit in the trade balance implies the opposite. For most years during the 1950s and early 1960s, Japan's merchandise trade balance was in deficit. Since then, surpluses have consistently appeared and have shown a marked tendency to increase over time.

The balance on current account is a second standard indicator of a country's balance-of-payments performance. Like the trade balance, it is still only a partial measure of economic transactions entering the payments accounts, but it is more inclusive in that it combines net merchandise trade, transfer payments, and net invisibles. Transfer payments refer to transactions of goods and services without *quid pro quo,* such as deductions and gifts. Invisible items include expenditures and receipts for transportation of all sorts, insurance premiums and claims, expenditures and receipts for travel by businessmen and tourists, expenditures and receipts relating to investment income, interest on trade credits and loans, and expenditures and receipts of foreign military forces and diplomatic bodies.

Data on Japanese transactions of invisibles for the years available, 1961 to 1978, have shown a consistent trend toward larger and larger deficits. A number of factors account for this phenomenon. First, Japan's net asset position in the world has been quite low. Only in the late 1970s did this begin to change, and it will take building up foreign assets for some time before a perceptible impact on the net invisibles account occurs in the form of earnings on those assets. Second, because of the nature of Japan's imports, many of which are raw materials of various sorts, transportation payments tend to be high relative to transportation items. Third, the Japanese enthusiasm for travel abroad has not been matched by foreign tourism in Japan, a major reason being the comparatively great distance Europeans and Americans must travel in order to reach Japan. Fourth, for years Japan has acquired a wide range of foreign technology via licensing arrangements with foreign firms. While contributing much to the country's domestic economic growth, these licensing arrangements give rise to substantial net payment of fees and royalties to foreigners. See TECHNOLOGY TRANSFER.

Japan's current account balance moved back and forth from modest deficit to modest surplus between 1950 and 1964. This was the period when the balance-of-payments deficit acted as a primary constraint on domestic growth objectives. The current account balance is especially revealing in connection with this matter. Beginning in 1965, Japan's current account has been predominantly in surplus, reflecting the removal, for all intents and purposes, of the previous constraint on domestic economic policies. Only during the OIL CRISIS OF 1973 did Japan's current account swing into deficit in a significant manner. The rapidity with which economic adjustments were made, however, resulted in a return to large current account surpluses in 1976, and thereafter to the present.

The basic balance combines the balance on current account with net long-term capital. Net long-term capital pertains to changes in assets (domestic capital) and liabilities (foreign capital) between residents, private and official, and nonresidents extending over a period of more than one year. Japan's long-term capital account has been very small relative to other payments accounts over the years because the country needed all the domestic capital available for investments at home, and because the government had a policy of tightly controlling the types and amounts of FOREIGN INVESTMENT IN JAPAN. In the late 1970s, policies were substantially relaxed so that long-term capital inflows and outflows became much more active. The recent tendency for Japan to build up its stock of foreign assets has resulted in negative net long-term capital figures. This has been possible as a result of sizable and offsetting current account surpluses.

Balance of payments

Japan's Balance of Payments
(in millions of US dollars)

	Exports	Imports	Merchandise trade balance	Invisibles, net	Balance on current account	Long-term capital, net	Basic balance	Overall balance
1950	829	−526	303	—	476	−4	—	—
1951	1,354	−1,645	−291	—	329	−24	—	—
1952	1,285	−1,692	−407	—	164	−16	—	—
1953	1,249	−2,043	−794	—	−199	−19	—	—
1954	1,606	−2,036	−430	—	−15	−23	—	—
1955	2,002	−2,022	−20	—	−241	−9	—	—
1956	2,476	−2,538	−62	—	−34	−48	—	—
1957	2,839	−3,242	−403	—	−620	−8	—	—
1958	2,870	−2,500	370	—	264	−41	—	—
1959	3,411	−3,047	364	—	361	20	—	—
1960	3,978	−3,711	267	—	143	83	—	—
1961	4,149	−4,707	−558	−383	−982	−11	−993	−952
1962	4,861	−4,460	401	−420	−48	172	124	237
1963	5,391	−5,557	−166	−569	−780	467	−313	−161
1964	6,704	−6,327	377	−784	−480	107	−373	−129
1965	8,332	−6,431	1,901	−884	932	−415	517	405
1966	9,641	−7,366	2,275	−886	1,254	−808	446	337
1967	10,231	−9,071	1,160	−1,172	−190	−812	−1,002	−571
1968	12,751	−10,222	2,529	−1,306	1,048	−239	809	1,102
1969	15,679	−11,980	3,699	−1,399	2,119	−155	1,964	2,283
1970	18,969	−15,006	3,963	−1,785	1,970	−1,591	379	1,374
1971	23,566	−15,779	7,787	−1,738	5,797	−1,082	4,715	7,677
1972	28,032	−19,061	8,971	−1,883	6,624	−4,487	2,137	4,741
1973	36,264	−32,576	3,688	−3,510	−136	−9,750	−9,886	−10,074
1974	54,480	−53,044	1,436	−5,842	−4,693	−3,881	−8,574	−6,839
1975	54,734	−49,706	5,028	−5,354	−682	−272	−954	−2,676
1976	66,026	−56,139	9,887	−5,867	3,680	−984	2,696	2,924
1977	79,333	−62,022	17,311	−6,004	10,918	−3,184	7,734	7,743
1978	95,572	−70,849	24,723	−7,381	16,627	−12,303	4,324	5,650

NOTE: From 1950 to 1960, the Japanese yen was not convertible into other currencies, according to terms stipulated in art. 8 of the IMF Articles of Agreement.

SOURCE: For 1950–60: Bank of Japan, *Hundred-Year Statistics of the Japanese Economy* (July 1966). For 1961–77: Bank of Japan, *Balance of Payments Monthly*.

Economists have found the basic balance measure attractive since it purports to include transactions influenced by general economic forces (trade and investments) or by political or military considerations. Japan's basic balance is reported from 1961 onward. Since the mid-1960s, except for the period immediately surrounding the international oil crisis, the basic balance has tended to be in surplus. This is a further indication that the balance of payments has not acted to constrain Japan's domestic economic performance since 1965.

The overall balance, the final measure displayed, adds to the basic balance net short-term capital, and errors and omissions. Short-term capital transactions are changes in external assets and liabilities other than those arising from official government monetary movements that span a period of less than one year. Errors and omissions are a statistical adjustment factor that compensates for unrecorded transactions that would otherwise cause an "imbalance" between total payments and total receipts in any given period. That is to say, in a statistical sense, the balance of payments must always balance because of its double-entry format. The overall balance does not include changes in liquid assets and liabilities of public entities and authorized foreign exchange banks. Increases in such assets and decreases in liabilities reflect an improvement in the external position of the country, while decreases in assets and liabilities indicate the reverse. Those changes in liquid assets and liabilities are called the balance of monetary movements. This balance is identical in magnitude to the overall balance. Japan's overall balance is reported for the years 1961 through 1977. From 1968 onward, and only except for the oil crisis period of 1973–75, the overall balance has been in surplus, thus indicating the buildup in Japan's external position that has been taking place.

Japan's Balance of Payments in Perspective —— The record of Japan's balance-of-payments performance since the end of World War II is one of growing strength, beginning from a position of substantial international weakness. The recurrent and sometimes worrisome balance-of-payments deficits of the 1950s and early 1960s have given way to chronic surpluses in more recent years. This general trend has persisted even after very substantial changes

in the exchange rate of the Japanese YEN against currencies of other countries whose balance of payments were encountering large deficits.

After World War II, Japan began to rebuild its war-ravaged economy with the aid of loans, primarily from the United States. Japan's poor endowment of natural resources meant that many essential goods had to be imported from abroad. Such import requirements and the country's then very modest ability to earn foreign exchange through exports acted as primary constraints on domestic economic growth until the latter 1960s. If Japan had possessed a substantial backlog of gold and FOREIGN CURRENCY RESERVES, it might have enjoyed more freedom to pursue domestic economic objectives without constant concern about the balance-of-payments performance. Such was not the case, however. Instead, the close connection between changes in the balance of payments and fluctuations in domestic business conditions left a deep impression on Japanese officials concerning their apparent heavy dependence on world markets for the survival and well-being of their country. What astonished foreign observers, in fact, was the very high level of domestic growth Japan was able to achieve and maintain throughout the 1950s and 1960s despite its meager gold and foreign exchange reserves and heavy dependence on imports of goods and capital from abroad (see ECONOMIC HISTORY: contemporary economy).

During the period cited, Japan relied especially heavily on imports from the United States. Such imports consisted of machinery and capital goods not then produced in Japan but essential to new investment, industrial raw materials, and primary agricultural products. A tendency toward a deficit in merchandise trade and services transactions was compensated for by loans from the United States and other countries, and also by expenditures of UNITED STATES ARMED FORCES IN JAPAN. (The last item was especially large during the Korean conflict and the Vietnam War.)

As a result of the recurring balance-of-payments constraint on domestic economic growth, Japan's economic policies emphasized substitution of domestic production for imports wherever possible, along with rapid development of export industries. Policies affecting international capital transactions were also influenced by concern with the country's balance-of-payments position, as well as by the desire to maintain a high degree of independence from foreign influences. Both inward and outward capital transactions were carefully controlled and, accordingly, such transactions grew slowly relative to what might have occurred under more permissive policies.

During 1966–71, Japan's balance-of-payments constraint was replaced by a chronic and growing export surplus that contributed directly and importantly to an exceptionally high rate of growth in gross national product. For the first time the country's stock of foreign exchange reserves began to accumulate to sizable levels. The combination of trends soon evoked strong pressures from abroad for Japan to take appropriate measures to restore balance-of-payments equilibrium.

These fundamental changes in Japan's balance of payments reflected successful efforts to encourage export growth, to reduce import dependence, and to regulate closely the outflow of domestic capital or inflow of capital from foreign sources. On the one hand, TECHNOLOGICAL DEVELOPMENT in manufacturing and in production generally had reduced industrial requirements for imported raw materials, more than offsetting the effects of the all-too-gradual dismantling of official controls on imports and other foreign exchange transactions. On the other hand, Japan's merchandise exports grew rapidly because the domestic industry had been able to achieve a high level of competitive efficiency in producing a wide range of goods for which there were expanding world markets.

In late 1971, with balance-of-payments problems facing Japan, the United States, and various European countries reaching alarming proportions, a new set of international exchange rates was endorsed in the so-called Smithsonian Agreement. The Japanese yen was revalued upward against the US dollar by 16.9 percent. That agreement proved to be unsustainable, however, and ensuing exchange market crises compelled governments to adopt a scheme of generalized floating exchange rates in 1973. Since then, and within the context of such unprecedented events as the quadrupling of petroleum prices in 1973–74 and worldwide inflation and recession in 1974–75, balance-of-payments disequilibria have made the problems of the pre-1971 period seem small by comparison. Japan's balance of payments experienced difficulty briefly during 1973–74—mainly as a result of sharply higher world prices for petroleum, foodstuffs, and other raw materials—but thereafter recovered to the point where record surpluses were established in 1977 and again in 1978.

As might be expected under such conditions, Japan's currency once more appreciated in value against other currencies. Between 1975 and 1978, the yen in fact gained in value against the US dollar by 35.8 percent. But it was not until the first few months of 1979 that the Japanese balance-of-payments surpluses began to show significant signs of moderating. Meanwhile, the announcement of further large increases in world oil prices by oil-producing countries has evoked concern about an escalation of inflation and a slowdown in economic growth throughout the world. What impact such events might have on Japan's balance of payments is not entirely clear. Yet the underlying adaptability and competitive strength of the economy make it unlikely that there will be a return anytime soon to the chronic balance-of-payments difficulties that beset the country during the 1950s and early 1960s. See also FOREIGN EXCHANGE AND FOREIGN TRADE CONTROL LAW; FOREIGN TRADE, GOVERNMENT POLICY ON. Wilbur F. MONROE

Ball, William MacMahon (1901–   )

British Commonwealth member of the ALLIED COUNCIL FOR JAPAN in 1946–47 during the Allied OCCUPATION of Japan (1945–52). Born in Casterton, Victoria, Australia, Ball was head of the Department of Political Science at the University of Melbourne from 1932 until 1968. As representative of Australia, New Zealand, India, and the United Kingdom on the Allied Council, he was critical of many aspects of American Occupation policy. He believed that the Occupation's democratization policies were in general not thoroughgoing enough to ensure permanent social and political change and that the retention of the emperor, though on balance justified, carried with it considerable risks. His most caustic criticism, however, was reserved for the Supreme Commander for the Allied Powers (SCAP) for its treatment of the Allied Council. He felt that the only important area where the council was allowed to have any significant impact on SCAP policy was land reform, where his own ten-point program was in part incorporated. In later years, however, he substantially modified his views on Japan and American policy in

1946–47, admitting that in retrospect some American policies had been more farsighted than those espoused by Australia. See also AUSTRALIA AND JAPAN. J. A. A. STOCKWIN

Bälz, Erwin von (1849–1913)

German physician, resident of Japan from 1876 to 1905. A graduate of the University of Leipzig, Bälz practiced at the university clinic before going to Japan. As physician-in-waiting to the imperial household and professor at Tōkyō University Medical School, he came to know such leaders of the Meiji Restoration as ITŌ HIROBUMI and YAMAGATA ARITOMO. His diary, *Das Leben eines deutschen Arztes im erwachenden Japan* (1931; tr *Awakening Japan: The Diary of A German Doctor,* 1974) is interesting for its observations on these men and its insights into Japan at a time of great change.

Ba Maw (1893–1977)

Burmese statesman who became head of state during the Japanese occupation of Burma in World War II. Educated at Rangoon College, Calcutta University, and Cambridge University, he qualified as a barrister-at-law at Gray's Inn, London, in 1924 and also studied at Bordeaux University, France. Upon his return to Burma in 1924, he served as master of the government high school, Rangoon, and later as lecturer in English at Rangoon College. He also became prominent as a lawyer as a result of his defense of Saya San, the leader of a peasant rebellion. He was named Burma's minister of education in 1932 and of public health in 1934 and became the first prime minister of Burma after its administrative separation from India in 1937. He resigned in 1939 and allied himself with a new generation of radical nationalists working to attain Burmese independence.

Though arrested and imprisoned in 1940, he escaped from jail in April 1942, when Japanese armies were marching toward Upper Burma. When Burma's independence was proclaimed by Japan on 1 August 1943, Ba Maw became head of state and prime minister. After the war he was imprisoned by the Allies in Japan from December 1945 to July 1946. On his return to Burma in 1946, he founded the Mahabama Party, but failed to regain his political reputation. He was detained from August 1947 to July 1948 by the U Nu regime and again from 1966 to 1968 by the Ne Win regime for having contacts with rebels. See also BURMA AND JAPAN. Ōno Tōru

bamboo

(take; sasa). Perennial plants of the family Gramineae which grow wild throughout Japan and are also cultivated for their many uses (see BAMBOO WARE). Over 1,000 species of bamboo are found worldwide, mostly in tropical and subtropical regions; some 400–500 species are found in the subtropical and temperate zones of Japan alone.

Japanese bamboo differs from other varieties in that it forms an extensive rhizome system, its stems do not form clusters, and it has pronounced veinlets connecting the parallel venations on its leaves. The Japanese divide bamboo into taller species, which are known as *take,* and the shorter *sasa,* which are generally no more than 1–2 meters (3–7 ft) in height. The majority of species found in Japan are *sasa,* which are economically less important than *take.* There is no strict taxonomic distinction between the two types, although the stem of the *take* discards its sheath as it grows and that of the *sasa* does not. Some of the most important Japanese species are listed below.

The *mōsōchiku (Phyllostachys pubescens)* is originally from China. It branches extensively and the leaves are small. The hollow woody stems or culms grow to 20 centimeters (8 in) in diameter and 12 meters (39 ft) in height. It is cultivated for its edible shoots *(takenoko);* the culms are used in various kinds of handiwork. A subspecies, the *kikkōchiku,* is favored as an ornamental because of its hexagonal-shaped nodes. The *madake (P. bambusoides)* is also found in China and Taiwan. It is similar to the *mōsōchiku* but has somewhat larger leaves and reaches about 10 centimeters (4 in) in diameter and 20 meters (66 ft) in height. Its sturdy, pliant culm is used for poles and for making the *shakuhachi* (flute). The shoots are edible. An ornamental variety, the *kimmeichiku (P. bambusoides var. castillonis)* has yellow culms. Another variety, the *hoteichiku (P. bambusoides var. aurea)* grows wild in groves in Kyūshū but may have originated in China. It grows to a height of 5–10 meters (16–33 ft), with the lower joints (nodes) narrowly spaced. The *hoteichiku* is used for walking sticks and fishing poles. The *hachiku (P. nigra* var. *henonis),* resembling the *madake* but with thinner leaves, grows to 10 meters (33 ft). A related variety, the *kurochiku (P. nigra),* has a blackish culm and is grown as an ornamental.

The *okamezasa (Shibataea kumasaca),* actually a small *take,* despite its name *(okame + sasa),* grows to a height of 1 meter (3 ft) and is frequently cultivated as an ornamental. The *kanchiku (Chimonobambusa marmorea)* grows to 1–3 meters (3–10 ft) and produces edible shoots from summer to late fall. The *shikakudake (C. quadrangularis),* with a culm that is square in cross section, is grown as an ornamental. The *hōraichiku (Bambusa nana* var. *normalis),* originally from China, is found in warm areas. It has soft leaves and edible shoots; it grows to 2–5 meters (7–16 ft) in height. The *narihiradake (Semiarundinaria fastuosa)* has thin culms with widely spaced joints. The *kumazasa (Sasa albo-marginata)* is usually 50–100 centimeters (20–39 in) tall. The leaves have pale undersides and are edged with white in winter. It is often grown in gardens and used to decorate platters of *sushi* and fresh fish. Many subspecies exist. The *chimakizasa (S. paniculata)* has large, broad leaves, which are used to wrap confections and rice dumplings *(chimaki).* The *chishimazasa (S. kurilensis),* also known as *nemagaridake,* is found in mountainous areas and reaches 3–4 meters (10–13 ft) in height. Its edible shoots are canned or dried. The *suzutake (S. purpurascens)* has purplish-tinged stems and leaves. Its resilient culm is used for making baskets and other objects. The *azumazasa (Sasaella ramosa)* resembles the *kumazasa* but has a straight stem base and thinner leaves. The *medake (Arundinaria simonii)* is found on riverbanks and along seashores, reaching a height of 3–5 meters (10–16 ft). It is cultivated as an ornamental. The *kanzanchiku (Pleioblastus hindsii)* is originally from the Ryūkyū Islands. Its narrow, pointed leaves make it an ornamental plant, and in warm areas it is grown also as a windbreak. The *yadake (Pseudosasa japonica)* grows wild throughout Japan and is also cultivated. It reaches 3–4 meters (10–13 ft) in height; its leaves sometimes grow to 20 centimeters (8 in) long. It has a strong stem, which was formerly used to make arrow shafts.

Sasa species rarely flower. When they do, all the plants in the area flower together and then usually die. *Take* species bloom only once in about 60 years.

📖——Muroi Hiroshi, *Take, sasa no hanashi* (1969). Ueda Kōichirō, *Take to jinsei* (1970). MATSUDA Osamu

bamboo ware

Objects made from this strong, flexible, giant grass are common in Japan and vary widely, from purely utilitarian, everyday articles to highly prized, decorative and artistic craft products. Bamboo has always been much admired in East Asia; along with the plum and the pine, it is one of the three so-called auspicious plants displayed on felicitous occasions. It also symbolizes the Confucian scholar who bends with the wind but does not break. Bamboo grows rapidly and is found in all parts of Japan, though the best variety is said to grow around Beppu in northern Kyūshū, the center of the Japanese bamboo industry.

Tradition has it that bamboo-weaving techniques were first introduced from Korea and China during the 1st century AD. The oldest bamboo objects existing in Japan are in the SHŌSOIN art repository in Nara and date from the 8th century. However, it was not until the 16th century that the artistic potential of bamboo was recognized. Under the influence of the early tea masters like SEN NO RIKYŪ (1522–91), bamboo utensils were used in the tea ceremony and appreciated as works of art. This high regard for bamboo as an art material has continued to the present day; the leading craftsman working in this field, Shōno Shōunsai (1904–74), was designated one of the LIVING NATIONAL TREASURES in 1967.

There are literally hundreds of different uses for bamboo, from fences and blinds to combs and hairpins. From a purely artistic point of view the finest of these artifacts are the vases used in *ikebana* (FLOWER ARRANGEMENT) and known as *hanaike.* Bamboo flower baskets called *hanakago* are also highly regarded. It remains a favorite material for MUSICAL INSTRUMENTS, notably flutes. Important tea-ceremony utensils made of bamboo are the tea whisk, or *chasen,* and the tea spoon, or *chashaku.*

Among the most delightful and uniquely Japanese creations are bamboo bird and insect cages. Children's toys such as tops, kites, and whistles are often made of bamboo. Most common are the many traditional objects for daily life made of bamboo, such as baskets, rakes, umbrellas, fans, buckets, boxes, brooms, chopsticks,

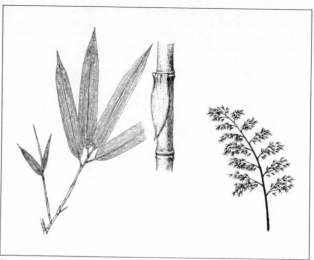

Bamboo——Madake

Bamboo——Chimakizasa

ladles, and towel racks. Bamboo is also used for furniture, such as chairs, benches, and tables.

📖——Robert Austin and Ueda Kōichirō, *Bamboo,* with photographs by Dana Levy (1970). Hugo MÜNSTERBERG

Bancroft, Edgar Addison (1857–1925)

American lawyer and diplomat. Born in Illinois. Bancroft practiced law in Chicago, representing large corporate interests. Appointed ambassador to Japan in 1924, he arrived in Japan a few months after the passage of the United States Immigration Act of 1924, a measure which was used to bar Japanese from immigrating to the United States. Anti-American sentiment was high, but Bancroft won over many Japanese with his ready eloquence and warm personality. Already in frail health, he died after barely eight months of service. The Japanese government honored him with an elaborate funeral and had his body transported in a battleship to San Francisco.

Bandai-Asahi National Park

(Bandai-Asahi Kokuritsu Kōen). Situated in northern Honshū, in Fukushima, Yamagata, and Niigata prefectures. The three separate mountainous zones of the park are characterized by volcanoes, caldera lakes, gorges, ravines, and dense forests, sheltering numerous species of wildlife. In the north the ASAHI MOUNTAINS, dominated by Ōasahidake (1,870 m; 6,134 ft), are noted for their sheer granite slopes and are the habitat of the Japanese serow (KAMOSHIKA), black bear, and flying squirrel. North of these mountains are the Three Mountains of Dewa, sacred to the SHUGENDŌ sect: GASSAN (1,950 m; 6,396 ft), YUDONOSAN (1,504 m; 4,933 ft), and HAGUROSAN (436 m;

1,430 ft). Various species of alpine plant thrive there, including the Japanese black fritillary *(kuroyuri)*.

South of the Asahi Mountains are the Iide Mountains, dominated by Dainichidake (2,498 m; 8,193 ft), with forests of Japanese beech trees *(buna)*. Still further south lies BANDAISAN (1,819 m; 5,966 ft), a volcano that was dormant for over one thousand years until it erupted in 1888, causing the formation of several lakes on its northern slopes. Its dense forests of birch and larch make it an important sanctuary for bird life. On the southern slopes of Bandaisan is Lake INAWASHIRO, situated 514 m (1,686 ft) above sea level. Area of the park: 1,897 sq km (732.2 sq mi).

Ban Dainagon ekotoba

Also known as *Tomo no Dainagon ekotoba*. Late-12th-century EMAKIMONO (illustrated handscroll). The earliest surviving *emaki* depicting a historical incident, it comprises a set of three scrolls, each now in the Sakai Collection in Tōkyō. The story is based on an event in the year 866, when the Ōtemmon, the gate inside the imperial compound in Kyōto, burned mysteriously (see ŌTEMMON CONSPIRACY). Tomo no Yoshio, or Ban Dainagon, the undersecretary of state, accused his political rival Minamoto no Makoto, the minister of the left *(sadaijin)*, of arson. Eventually it was revealed that Yoshio and his son had set the fire, and they and other members of their family were punished with exile. The tale as depicted in the *emaki* is not strict historical fact but rather the embellished version that appears in a number of contemporary manuscripts, including the UJI SHŪI MONOGATARI, where the truth is accidentally revealed in a quarrel between the children of servants.

The first scroll, measuring 31.5 by 827.0 cm (12.4 by 325.6 in), has no text. It opens with a picture of a crowd rushing toward the burning gate, while another gaping crowd appears on the far left side. The movement of the crowds and the individual expressions of the onlookers are rendered with great skill, and the spectacular depiction of the fire is comparable to that in the HEIJI MONOGATARI EMAKI. The second (measuring 31.4 by 849.0 cm [12.3 by 334.3 in]) and third (measuring 31.5 by 918.6 cm [12.4 by 361.7 in]) scrolls each contain two sections of text and two of painting. The first scene in the second scroll shows Makoto's household, where the women wailing indecorously belie their aristocratic surroundings. The second scene shows the crucial fight between the children and then between their parents. The action unfolds in a clockwise motion, a fine example of continuous narrative. The third scroll depicts the investigation of the case and Yoshio's subsequent departure into exile.

The style of this work is characterized by a combination of bright, rich coloring, like that in the GENJI MONOGATARI EMAKI, and lively, fluid drawing, like that in the SHIGISAN ENGI EMAKI. The vivid facial expressions and clever narrative devices are also reminiscent of the *Shigisan engi emaki*. The *Ban Dainagon ekotoba* has traditionally been attributed to Tokiwa Mitsunaga, an artist active in the second half of the 12th century. The attribution is a plausible one, as the work is dated to about 1160–80. The calligraphy of the text has been variously attributed to Fujiwara no Masatsune (1170–1221) and Fujiwara no Norinaga (fl late 12th century).
■——Okudaira Hideo, *Narrative Picture Scrolls*, tr Elizabeth ten Grotenhuis, *Arts of Japan*, vol 5 (1973). Tanaka Ichimatsu, *Ban Dainagon ekotoba*, vol 4 of *Nihon emakimono zenshū* (Kadokawa Shoten, 1961). *Sarah* THOMPSON

Bandaisan

Volcano north of the Inawashiro Basin, northern Fukushima Prefecture, northern Honshū. Its northern slope is called Ura Bandai or the Bandai Kōgen. During an eruption in 1888, lava dammed the Nagasegawa river system to form Lake Hibara, Lake Onogawa, Lake Akimoto, and the swamp called GOSHIKINUMA. There are several hot springs. Part of Bandai–Asahi National Park. Height: 1,819 m (5,966 ft).

Bandō Tsumasaburō (1901–1953)

Film actor. Born in Tōkyō; real name Tamura Denkichi; better known as Ban Tsuma. In 1923 he joined the movie production company founded by MAKINO SHŌZŌ. After his film debut in 1923, he starred in a number of movies. In 1925 he established an independent company, Bandō Tsumasaburō Productions, which enjoyed such success that the film star ONOE MATSUNOSUKE called this period the "Age of Ban Tsuma." He also set up his own studio in Kyōto in 1926, an unusual move for an actor. However, in the talkies era Ban Tsuma's wispy, high voice disappointed his fans; his popularity waned and in 1936 his company folded. He later underwent voice training and performed remarkably in films such as INAGAKI HIROSHI's *Muhō Matsu no isshō* (1943, The Life of Matsu the Untamed). The quintessence of his ability, however, is said to have been in the sweeping swordplay of his silent movies.

ITASAKA Tsuyoshi

banishment

(tsuihō). Term used in premodern Japan for a penal sentence expelling a criminal indefinitely from a designated area, the extent of which depended on the seriousness of the crime. Although reference is made to banishment in ancient Japanese myths, *tsuihō* as a penal category first appeared in the Kamakura period (1185–1333) and was most widely used in the Edo period (1600–1868). Ordinances issued by the Tokugawa shogunate (see KUJIKATA OSADAMEGAKI) defined seven categories of banishment. The lightest of these, *tokoro-barai*, barred the criminal from entering his own village or community, whereas a heavier sentence, Edo *jūri shihō-barai*, forbade the criminal to come within five *ri* (1 *ri* = 3.9 km or 2.4 mi) of Nihombashi, a bridge in central Edo (now Tōkyō). The severest category of banishment excluded the criminal from the 15 provinces around Edo and Kyōto and from the two major highways. In 1734 the shogunate lightened this particular sentence for merchants and farmers, prescribing instead banishment from Edo and the domain where they had committed their crime. Various *daimyō*, against the shogunate's wishes, established their own banishment restrictions. After the Meiji Restoration in 1868, banishment was no longer a penal category. See also PENAL SYSTEM.

bankata

(guards). A term used in the Edo period (1600–1868) to denote *samurai* fighting units, as distinct from samurai administrative units, which were called *yakukata*. More specifically, it referred to select guard units, like the Great Guard (Ōban), whose members were bannermen (HATAMOTO) and housemen (GOKENIN) of the shōgun and whose principal duty was to guard him inside and outside Edo Castle. The guards themselves were called *banshū* or *banshi*.

Conrad TOTMAN

Bankei Yōtaku (1622–1693)

Also known as Bankei Eitaku. Buddhist monk of the RINZAI SECT. Born in what is now the city of Himeji in Hyōgo Prefecture. He lost his father when he was 10 years old. In 1638 he became a monk under Umpo of the temple Zuiōji in Akō and received the name Yōtaku. After Umpo's death, he studied under his disciple Bokuō. Bankei traveled throughout the provinces and in 1650 went to Sūfukuji in Nagasaki to study under the Ming monk Daozhe Chaoyuan (Tao-che Ch'ao-yüan; J: Dōja Chōgen) and received the certification of enlightenment from him. Bankei was widely influential; his disciples were said to number some 50,000. Matsura Shigenobu, *daimyō* of Hirado, Katō Yasuoki, daimyō of Ōshū, and Kyōgoku Takatoyo, daimyō of Marugame were among his lay followers. He traveled throughout Japan and founded the temples Ryūmonji, Nyohōji, and Kōrinji. In his teachings he emphasized the Unborn and Unperishing Buddha Mind (Fushōzen). He rejected the use of KŌAN and always preached to his audience in simple, ordinary language.

banking system

The banking system in Japan is the nation's most important means of channeling individual savings into investment by firms. Banking is more important in Japan than in most industrialized nations, since a larger share of savings is held in banks, and corporations depend far more on borrowing than on stock sales for capital. The current system developed from a variety of historical influences and today is one of the largest in the world.

History of the Banking System——Japanese banking originated with the *ryōgae* (money changers), who first appeared in the 13th century and whose number began to increase significantly at the beginning of the 17th century, when the merchants known as RYŌGAESHŌ appeared. The money changers were located in principal cities, such as Ōsaka, Edo (now Tōkyō), and Kyōto, and in a few regional centers. Activity in Ōsaka was particularly intense, since

Banking system——Financial institutions of Japan

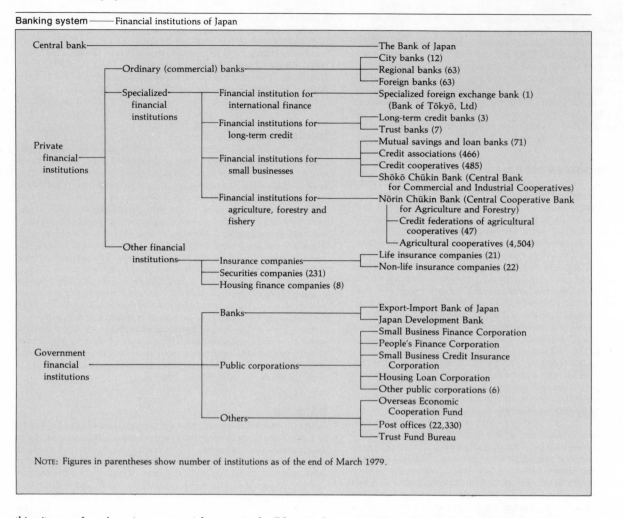

NOTE: Figures in parentheses show number of institutions as of the end of March 1979.

this city was Japan's major commercial center in the Edo period (1600–1868). The *ryōgaeshō* took deposits, extended loans, remitted funds, and exchanged gold and silver. Larger money changers acted as agents of the TOKUGAWA SHOGUNATE and feudal lords.

After the MEIJI RESTORATION of 1868, the *ryōgaeshō* were restricted to dealings in Western silver coins, and many of them soon shut their doors. They were replaced by KAWASE KAISHA (exchange companies). These were the first modern commercial banks in Japan and were organized under the direction of the Tsūshōshi (Bureau of Commerce) to finance commerce and industry. Eight such *kawase kaisha* were established during 1869, their main business activities being the receipt of deposits, issuance of paper currency, extension of loans, handling of remittances, and money changing. After the Tsūshōshi was abolished in 1871, however, many of the *kawase kaisha* began to fail because of the loss of government patronage and a lack of business expertise. Eventually all of the *kawase kaisha* closed, except for the Yokohama Kawase Kaisha, which was reorganized as the Second National Bank in 1874.

While the *kawase kaisha* were in decline, wealthy merchant families, such as the MITSUI and Ono houses, sought to establish private commercial banks. The Meiji government recognized the need for banks, but withheld the necessary permission because it felt that the failure of the *kawase kaisha* would simply be repeated unless institutional reforms were undertaken. In addition, the government recognized the need to replace inconvertible government-issued paper currency with convertible bank notes. Both needs were answered with the introduction of a new banking system, modeled after the NATIONAL BANKS in the United States. A National Bank Ordinance (Kokuritsu Ginkō Jōrei) was issued in December 1872. (It should be noted that a "national bank" was chartered but not owned by the government. The word "national" was borrowed from the United States, where it was used to distinguish nationally chartered banks from state-chartered banks.)

The requirement of specie convertibility was onerous, however, and only four national banks were established before 1876. To facilitate the establishment of more banks, the government revised its regulations in August 1876, abolishing the convertibility require-ment for bank notes and allowing the use of the bonds given as pensions to members of the former *samurai* class as capital for the national banks. These new regulations made the establishment of national banks quite profitable, and their number increased significantly. However, the government soon recognized these revisions to be too lenient, since national banks were issuing notes and their rapid expansion could result in inflation. Restrictions were gradually introduced, and the government suspended permission for new banks after 1879. The total number of national banks established by that year was 153.

During this same period, the government perceived the need to establish a central bank to encourage banking and control the money supply. The BANK OF JAPAN (Nippon Ginkō), based on the European model, was established in 1882 as the central bank. The issue of new bank notes was reserved as the sole right of the Bank of Japan, and the national bank regulations were revised the following year to limit the charters of the national banks to 20 years from their opening of business and to replace their bank notes with notes from the central bank. The national banks were to be reorganized as ordinary banks *(futsū ginkō)* under the newly promulgated Bank Ordinance (Ginkō Jōrei). The new bank regulations were enacted in August 1890 and put into force in July 1893; they comprised 11 articles. By February 1899, virtually all national banks had been dissolved and reorganized as ordinary banks.

Savings banks developed during the same period. In 1874 the government began to encourage savings through the national POSTAL SERVICE network, and in 1880 the first savings bank was established on the model of such banks in Europe and the United States. There were 21 such specialized savings banks by 1883. However, the early savings banks charged high interest for their loans and in many cases suffered from poor management. The government stopped granting permits for new savings banks until the Savings Bank Ordinance (Chochiku Ginkō Jōrei) was enacted in 1890 to regulate their activities.

In the meantime, specialized banks to deal in foreign exchange and long-term financing were also established. The first of these, the YOKOHAMA SPECIE BANK (Yokohama Shōkin Ginkō), was established in 1880 to finance international trade and specie transactions. The government subscribed the capital of this bank and deposited funds with it in order to foster its development. In 1887 further regulations were established to clarify its role as a specialized foreign exchange bank.

The Japanese government also sponsored many long-term credit banks. The first of these, the Nippon Kangyō Bank, was established in 1897 to extend development loans to agriculture and industry. Between 1898 and 1900 agricultural and industrial banks (nōkō ginkō) were established in each prefecture with subsidies from the prefectural government. These banks provided development loans on a regional basis. The HOKKAIDŌ TAKUSHOKU BANK, LTD (Hokkaidō Takushoku Ginkō), was established in 1900 with the specific objective of contributing to the development of Japan's northern main island; it was granted broader lending authority than the other agricultural and industrial banks.

The INDUSTRIAL BANK OF JAPAN, LTD (Nihon Kōgyō Ginkō), was established in 1900 with the objective of providing long-term industrial funds. However, Japanese financial circles were then in turmoil due to the panic of 1900–1901, so the bank postponed opening its doors until 1902. The Industrial Bank provided long-term funds to heavy industry, which developed significantly only after 1905. The bank also borrowed abroad and engaged in trust transactions.

The number of ordinary commercial banks peaked at 1,867 in 1901, after which there was a gradual decrease. The collapse of small and unsound banks accounted for the greater part of the decrease in the beginning, but consolidation of smaller banks also occurred. Full-scale consolidation started with the post–World War I panic of 1920, a financial and business crisis that began a long period of economic stagnation in Japan. There were a number of bank failures at this time. The government revised the bank regulations in 1920 to encourage mergers, and the number of banks decreased by around 100 each year between 1921 and 1926.

The FINANCIAL CRISIS OF 1927 moved the government to promulgate a new Bank Law, which stipulated, among other things, a minimum requirement for bank capital. More than half of the 1,400 ordinary banks existing at the time failed to meet the minimum, and many local small- and medium-sized banks were forced to merge. Thus the number of commercial banks decreased to 683 at the end of 1931 and to 418 at the end of 1936. In February 1942, the Bank of Japan Law (Nippon Ginkō Hō) was enacted to allow the central bank to engage in direct coordination and supply of industrial funds in addition to its role in commercial financing.

Since World War II, the Japanese banking system has changed remarkably. The Bank of Japan Law has been revised again, with a policy board established to democratize policymaking and enhance autonomy. Specialized financial institutions were abolished, so the Nippon Kangyō Bank and the Hokkaidō Takushoku Bank were transformed into ordinary banks. The Industrial Bank of Japan was reorganized as a long-term credit bank in 1952, while the Yokohama Specie Bank was reorganized as the BANK OF TŌKYŌ, LTD (Tōkyō Ginkō), in 1947 and designated a specialized foreign exchange bank in 1954.

Present Banking System —— The Bank of Japan is the central bank (see chart). It issues currency, acts as a lender of last resort, and serves as bank for the government. It also implements MONETARY POLICY, including changes in the official discount rate, open market operations, and changes in reserve requirements.

Ordinary commercial banks rely on savings deposits for lending capital and provide commercial as well as industrial funds. In contrast to the United States, with its state and unit banking system, Japanese commercial banks can operate nationwide through networks of branches. They engage in both short-term commercial banking and long-term financing; long-term loans with a listed maturity of one year or longer comprise about 10 percent of the total loans of all commercial banks, but many short-term loans are rolled over at their maturity, making them de facto long-term loans. Furthermore, Japanese commercial banks are often closely aligned with specific enterprises or ENTERPRISE GROUPS, which obtain their funds from a number of banks but rely on their affiliated bank for the greater part of their borrowing.

The major business of commercial banks consists of receiving deposits, making loans, discounting bills, remitting funds, accepting (i.e., guaranteeing payment of) bills and debts, issuing and accepting letters of credit, accepting securities, paying dividends for enterprises, clearing bills, and safekeeping precious articles. Most of the commercial banks are also licensed to handle foreign exchange transactions.

Commercial banks fall into two categories: city banks (toshi ginkō) and regional banks (chihō ginkō). City banks are generally based in large cities but operate nationwide; they are the giants in Japanese banking. The Bank of Tōkyō is traditionally counted as one of the city banks, though legally it is a specialized foreign exchange bank. Regional banks operate primarily in limited local districts. Their clients are mostly local enterprises, and they generally have surplus funds. As a result, they are lenders in the call loan market (equivalent to the federal funds market in the United States) and allocate more of their funds to bonds than do city banks.

At the end of March 1979, 63 foreign banks operated a total of 84 branch offices in Japan. Since foreign banks operating in Japan must be licensed under the Bank Law just as Japanese commercial banks are, their activities are the same as the indigenous banks. All of the foreign banks operating in Japan are licensed for foreign exchange transactions.

Long-term credit banks were established on the basis of a law enacted in 1952. At present, there are three such banks in Japan: the Industrial Bank of Japan, Ltd (Nippon Kōgyō Ginkō), the LONG-TERM CREDIT BANK OF JAPAN, LTD (Nihon Chōki Shin'yō Ginkō), and the NIPPON CREDIT BANK, LTD (Nippon Saiken Shin'yō Ginkō). The main feature of the long-term credit banks is that they raise funds by floating debentures (see DEBENTURE) and they employ such funds for long-term loans. They are authorized to float debentures up to 20 times the total of their capital and reserves, but they are allowed to accept deposits only from qualified clients.

Trust banks (shintaku ginkō) operate in accordance with the Bank Law, just as commercial banks. However, they differ in the business they conduct: first, the trust banks engage in both banking and trust transactions. Second, they serve as savings institutions for the general public. Since the law requires the separation of trust transactions from commercial banking, trust banks manage trust accounts and banking accounts separately under ADMINISTRATIVE GUIDANCE from the government. At present, only one city bank is engaged in trust transactions, along with seven trust banks.

Mutual savings and loan banks (sōgo ginkō), credit associations (shin'yō kinko), and credit cooperatives (shin'yō kumiai) are financial institutions for small businesses. The mutual banks originated with lottery credit associations (MUJIN) but now operate as ordinary banks. Credit associations and cooperatives are financial institutions originally organized as COOPERATIVE ASSOCIATIONS, but they are usually allowed to accept deposits from and make small loans to nonmembers. They resemble commercial banks in most respects, though they are much smaller in scale.

AGRICULTURAL COOPERATIVE ASSOCIATIONS (nōgyō kyōdō kumiai) are limited to dealings with their members. They are, however, not limited to financial activities but can also purchase and sell goods for their members. Many "agricultural" cooperatives are located in cities. Agricultural cooperatives also organize credit federations that are not allowed to carry out any business other than the granting of credit. At present there are 47 such federations, one in each prefecture.

The Central Cooperative Bank for Agriculture and Forestry (NŌRIN CHŪKIN BANK) is the central institution for cooperative financing. The major activities of the bank are receiving deposits, floating debentures, lending, and remitting funds. Loans are, as a rule, given only to member cooperatives, but surplus funds may be lent to nonmembers with the permission of the MINISTRY OF FINANCE and the MINISTRY OF AGRICULTURE, FORESTRY, AND FISHERIES.

The EXPORT-IMPORT BANK OF JAPAN (Nihon Yushutsunyū Ginkō) was established in 1950 to finance exports, imports, and overseas investment. The bank's main sources of funds are capital subscription by the government's Industrial Investment Special Account (Sangyō Tōshi Tokubetsu Kaikei) and borrowing from the Trust Funds Bureau (Shikin Un'yo Bu). The JAPAN DEVELOPMENT BANK (Nihon Kaihatsu Ginkō) was established in 1951 to provide funds for industrial development. Its primary sources of funds are the same as those of the Export-Import Bank.

There are 10 PUBLIC CORPORATIONS that engage in finance (kōko). Each extends loans to a special sector, such as small business or housing. The main fund sources for these public corporations are capital subscription by the Industrial Investment Special Account and borrowings from the Trust Funds Bureau and from the post office life insurance and annuity accounts. In addition, four of the public corporations can float bonds.

The postal savings system (yūbin chokin seido) is also an important depository of savings. Drawn by the convenience of the national network of post offices (about 22,330), the total amount of postal savings is over 80 percent of total individual deposits in commercial and trust banks combined. These savings, together with the surplus funds of special government accounts, are channeled to the Trust Funds Bureau, which in turn uses the funds for loans to government financial institutions, local governments, and investment in national and local government bonds (see FINANCE, LOCAL GOVERNMENT).

Functions of the Banks——During the period of rapid growth of the Japanese economy, banks played an especially important role in providing financing to enterprises which, because of the shortage of accumulated equity, had to rely on outside capital to fund plant and equipment investment. For example, loans and discounts from banks and other financial institutions provided more than 90 percent of the total net supply of industrial funds in 1965, at the height of the growth period. The city banks, whose large enterprise clients demanded particularly sizable amounts of capital, depended in turn on funds borrowed from smaller banks, credit institutions, agricultural cooperatives, and the central bank. This phenomenon was called the "overloan" position of city banks (see CORPORATE FINANCE).

During the mid-1970s, however, the growth of the Japanese economy stabilized at a moderate level, and the corporate demand for funds eased. On the other hand, the government began to float a sizable amount of national bonds to cover its large budget deficit, and a substantial portion of these bonds were absorbed by city banks (see BONDS, GOVERNMENT). In addition, city banks have gradually begun to lend more to individuals, for such undertakings as housing construction. As a result, the shortage of funds at city banks continues. However, the government is attempting to reduce its deficit, and relatively weak corporate demand for outside funds is expected to continue. Under these conditions, the overloan position of the city banks is likely to subside.

The important role that banks play in financing industrial investment is a reflection of the low level of disposable income of most Japanese households (see CONSUMPTION AND SAVING BEHAVIOR). Although the rate of savings is high, individual deposits are low, and stock and bond purchase is not a feasible form of investment. The Japanese banking system has traditionally engaged in long-term lending, while neither the primary nor secondary securities markets have developed fully (see CAPITAL MARKETS). Moreover, Japanese banks are prohibited by the SECURITIES EXCHANGE LAW from engaging in the underwriting, sale, or distribution of securities (except public bonds and debentures). Trust transactions are also limited, since a bank must obtain a license to engage in trust business, and these licenses are issued only after restrictive conditions are met. Flotation of bank debentures is only allowed to the long-term credit banks and the Bank of Tōkyō, while the number of branches of specialized banks is more restricted than that of commercial banks.

There is little difference in function between the commercial banks, the mutual savings and loan banks, and credit institutions. The homogeneity of these financial institutions sometimes leads to intense competition, especially when demand for funds is slack. One measure taken to cope with this situation has been merger. Two new city banks were formed through mergers: the DAI-ICHI KANGYŌ BANK, LTD (in October 1971, from the Dai-Ichi Bank and the Nippon Kangyō Bank), and the TAIYŌ KŌBE BANK, LTD (in October 1973, from the Taiyō Bank and the Bank of Kōbe). Between 1968 and 1977, there were 112 mergers of smaller financial institutions. Further rationalization to increase efficiency seems to be in order.

📖——T. F. M. Adams and Iwao Hoshii, *A Financial History of the New Japan* (1972). Akashi Teruo and Suzuki Norihisa, *Nihon kin'yūshi* (1957). Katō Toshihiko, *Hompō ginkōshi ron* (1957). Ōkurashō, *Meiji zaiseishi* (1904). Suzuki Hamaji, *Chūshō kigyō kin'yū* (1964). Tōyō Keizai Shimpō Sha, *Kin'yū rokujūnen shi* (1924). Yoshino Toshihiko, *Wagakuni no kin'yū seido* (1973).

NAKAGAWA Kōji

Bank of Japan

(Nippon Ginkō or Nihon Ginkō). The central bank of Japan. It is the only note-issuing bank in the country, and functions as the lender of last resort to the banking system and as the treasurer of the government. Its head office is in Tōkyō, and it has 33 domestic branches, 12 domestic offices, and five overseas offices.

The Bank of Japan was established on 10 October 1882. Its primary objective was to halt the inflation of the early years of the Meiji period (1868–1912), which was particularly virulent after the SATSUMA REBELLION. The inflation was mainly due to the overissue

of nonconvertible bank notes by NATIONAL BANKS and of paper money by the government. MATSUKATA MASAYOSHI, who became finance minister in October 1881, felt it imperative to replace nonconvertible with convertible money and to establish a central bank. This bank was to provide a stable currency, and thus facilitate provision of necessary funds for development of commerce and industry; to reduce interest rates; to serve as a fiscal agent for the government; and to discount foreign exchange bills. After an extensive survey, Matsukata modeled the Japanese central bank after the National Bank of Belgium. The Nippon Ginkō Jōrei (Bank of Japan Regulation) was promulgated in June 1882.

In February 1942 the Bank of Japan was reorganized under the Nippon Ginkō Hō (Bank of Japan Law). Its legal status was changed from a joint-stock company to a special corporation, and its notes became entirely fiduciary (legally nonconvertible). A ceiling on note issue was to be decided by the finance minister, but under special circumstances he could also permit temporary issue beyond this limit. The Nippon Ginkō Hō was amended in June 1949. A policy board was established to determine monetary policy, including changes in the official discount rate.

The role played by the Bank of Japan during the 100 years since its establishment has been quite significant. Its chief contributions have been providing adequate bank reserves so commercial banks could fund industrial development and stabilizing funds markets during economic crises. A major responsibility of the Bank of Japan is to avoid inflation and thus maintain the value of the YEN. To do this, it uses such monetary policy measures as changes in lending rates, open market operations, and changes in reserve requirements. Direct credit expansion controls (known as *madoguchi shidō* or "window guidance") have supplemented these instruments. The Bank of Japan also acquired a new important role in the floating exchange rate system of the 1970s: it smoothed the foreign exchange market when currency value fluctuations were erratic.

📖——The Bank of Japan, *Nippon Ginkō—Sono kinō to soshiki* (1962). Yoshino Toshihiko, *Nippon Ginkō* (1963). *Rekidai Nippon Ginkō sōsai ron* (1971).

NAKAGAWA Kōji

Bank of Japan Building

Representative work of Meiji-period (1868–1912) Western-style architecture; located in Chūō Ward, Tōkyō. It was designed by TATSUNO KINGO, a Japanese student of Western architecture. Construction began in 1890 and was completed in 1896. The building presently occupies the southwest corner of the Bank of Japan's home office complex in Nihombashi. In a pattern repeated by later Japanese architects, Tatsuno traveled in Europe observing appropriate models prior to starting work on his design. The bank is an imposing, three-story brick construction faced with stone, with another floor below ground and with steel girders for beams and trusses. It is Renaissance in design but with massive columns recalling the Baroque. It demonstrated how quickly Japanese architects had mastered Western building styles and techniques.

WATANABE Hiroshi

Bank of Korea → Chōsen Ginkō

Bank of Taiwan → Taiwan Ginkō

Bank of Tōkyō, Ltd

(Tōkyō Ginkō). Japan's only specialized foreign exchange bank, so designated by the Foreign Exchange Bank Law of 1954. Established in 1946 as the successor to the YOKOHAMA SPECIE BANK (Yokohama Shōkin Ginkō). While the number of its domestic branches is limited by law, the size of its overseas network is comparable to that of the world's other leading international banks. The bank has 29 branches, 24 representative offices, and 26 affiliated banks in 39 foreign countries. Of the bank's total of 14,000 employees, 7,600 are non-Japanese working in overseas offices. As a result of the specialized nature of its activities, the bank has close business relations with many trading and manufacturing companies. Ever since the initial overseas economic expansion of Japanese enterprises in the 1950s, and particularly with the intensified internationalization of Japan's economy in recent years, the bank's activities have increased rapidly, in both domestic and overseas markets. In 1981 the bank's total assets were ¥16.4 trillion (US $74.4 billion) and deposits ¥10.6

trillion (US $48.1 billion), while the bank was capitalized at ¥80 billion (US $362.7 million). The head office is located in Tōkyō.

Bank of Yokohama, Ltd

(Yokohama Ginkō). A major regional bank, based in Kanagawa Prefecture, with its head office in the city of Yokohama. Among the 63 regional banks in Japan it has the largest deposits. Established in 1920, the bank has a total of 155 branches, which are located in the Tōkyō metropolitan area and other major cities. It has branches in London and New York as well as an office in Hong Kong. The bank's correspondence network covers 108 countries and 466 banks with 1,319 branches. In March 1982, the bank's total assets were ¥5.1 trillion (US $21.2 billion), deposits ¥4 trillion (US $16.6 billion), and capitalization stood at ¥30 billion (US $124.6 million).

Banko ware

(banko-yaki). Decorated pottery made principally in Mie Prefecture, in and around Yokkaichi. First made in the late 18th century by a local merchant, Nunami Rōzan (1718–77), who established kilns near Kuwana in Ise and later in Edo (now Tōkyō). This so-called Old Banko and Edo Banko included tea-ceremony wares, dishes, bowls, *sake* bottles, candlesticks, incense burners and containers and, most notably, tall Chinese Ming-style ewers with gracefully curved handles and spouts. Covered with a pale yellow, milky glaze, these products were popular for their exotic three-color designs mostly of red, green, and blue or purple, including some calico-print motifs. Rōzan's Kuwana kilns were revived by Mori Yūsetsu (1808–82) in the 1830s, mainly for production of *sencha* tea-ceremony wares. From the Meiji period (1868–1912), Banko-style pieces have been made at a number of other kilns in the Kuwana and Yokkaichi neighborhoods. *Frederick* BAEKELAND

bankruptcy

(hasan). In Japan, after a business enterprise has been declared bankrupt under the provisions of the BANKRUPTCY LAW (Hasan Hō) of 1922 (articles 126, 127, and 132), a number of alternatives are available. One of them is to apply for protection under the CORPORATE REORGANIZATION LAW (Kaisha Kōsei Hō). If protection is granted, which requires presenting a plan for reconstruction agreed on by management, the labor union, and the supporting financial institutions, the company is allowed to embark on a program of reconstruction. A number of companies in Japan have been successfully reconstructed after business failure. In some cases, this has involved major changes in management and the replacement of some managers with representatives from financial institutions or from outside management chosen by the financial institutions. In more serious cases of business failure, when no satisfactory plan for reconstruction can be worked out, the authorities may dispose of the company's assets. The proceeds from the sale of assets are distributed first to creditors based on seniority of debt. Any remaining amount is then distributed to shareholders. *C. Tait* RATCLIFFE

Bankruptcy Law

(Hasan Hō). Law of 1922 providing for judicial proceedings to liquidate the assets of an insolvent debtor and also for a composition proceeding for financial rehabilitation of the bankrupt. All kinds of debtors, including nonmerchants and corporations except public corporations like municipalities, are subject to the proceeding, which can be commenced voluntarily upon a debtor's own application or involuntarily upon an application by a creditor. When the court, located in the debtor's place of residence, finds a debtor insolvent, insolvency usually being inferred from his cessation of payment, it deems the debtor bankrupt and appoints an administrator, who takes over the assets of the debtor. The administrator has the power to void fraudulent or preferential transfers made by the debtor. Secured creditors are not affected but unsecured creditors must file their claims with the court in order to obtain dividends from the assets. Certain unsecured creditors enjoy priority over others. The bankrupt party can be discharged from the unpaid portion of claims if he obtains an order of discharge from the court. During the course of proceeding he can apply for a composition by submitting a plan. If such a plan is agreed upon by a majority of creditors, the bankruptcy proceeding is concluded without liquidation of assets. See also CORPORATE REORGANIZATION LAW. *TANIGUCHI Yasuhei*

Ban Nobutomo (1773–1846)

KOKUGAKU (National Learning) scholar. The fourth son of Yamagishi Koretomo, a *samurai* of the Obama domain in Wakasa Province (now part of Fukui Prefecture), he was adopted at age 13 by Ban Nobumasa, a samurai of the same domain. For several years Nobutomo served his domain in Kyōto and in Edo (now Tōkyō). In 1801 Nobutomo became an adherent of the philosophical school of MOTOORI NORINAGA, studying with MOTOORI ŌHIRA, Norinaga's adopted son. Around 1816 he took charge of the Obama *daimyō*'s library, resigning five years later because of illness and thereafter devoting himself entirely to study. Because of his scrupulous methodology he is considered one of the best of the Kokugaku scholars. A prolific author, he is particularly noted for his historical works and his philological studies of such classics as the NIHON SHOKI (720, Chronicle of Japan). *SUZUKI Eiichi*

Bansha no Goku

(Imprisonment of the Companions of Barbarian Studies). A campaign of repression by officials of the Tokugawa shogunate against WATANABE KAZAN, TAKANO CHŌEI, OZEKI SAN'EI, and other scholars of Rangaku (Dutch studies, or the study of Western science and culture through Dutch; see WESTERN LEARNING) in the late 1830s. Kazan, Chōei, and San'ei had organized an informal study group, the SHŌSHIKAI, to discuss Western ideas and their practical application. The group was also known as Bansha, an abbreviation of Bangaku Shachū, or the "Companions of Barbarian Studies." In 1837 Kazan and Chōei learned of the shogunate's determination to enforce its expulsion edict (GAIKOKUSEN UCHIHARAI REI) against the American ship Morrison, then attempting to repatriate Japanese castaways (see MORRISON INCIDENT). They wrote tracts advocating Western Learning and criticizing the NATIONAL SECLUSION policy as shortsighted. Chōei's pamphlet Bojutsu yume monogatari (1838, Tale of a Dream) was particularly widely read.

In 1839 the shogunate ordered a survey of the area around Edo Bay (now Tōkyō Bay) to strengthen its coastal defenses, and the inspector (metsuke) TORII YŌZŌ, a known xenophobe, was placed in charge. When the Western surveying methods applied by one of Chōei's students proved vastly superior to his own traditional methods, Yōzō launched a personal vendetta against Chōei and other Western Learning scholars. Twenty-six scholars, several of them associated with the Shōshikai, were arrested on charges that included criticism of shogunate policies, plotting to take over the Ogasawara Islands, conspiring with ŌSHIO HEIHACHIRŌ, leader of an urban insurrection in 1837, and luring shogunal vassals into "barbarian studies." Although the most serious accusations were proven false, Chōei and Kazan were convicted of criticizing the government. Kazan was sentenced to house arrest and Chōei to life imprisonment, but both men eventually committed suicide.

The shogunate's action severely curtailed the open pursuit of Western Learning and may have been responsible in part for the almost total concentration on science, technology, and other less politically controversial fields of study that ensued.

Bansho Shirabesho

(Institute for the Investigation of Barbarian Books). Japan's first central institution for the translation, study, and teaching of Western languages and scientific and technical subjects, and the precursor of Tōkyō University.

Starting in 1811, the Tokugawa shogunate (1603–1867) attached translators of Western books to its astronomical observatory, where interest spread initially from calendar making to geography, navigation, and general study of the West. After the visits of Commodore Matthew PERRY in 1853–54, the shogunate transferred its translators and Western library collection to a new and separate school designed specifically to train experts on Western subjects and handle diplomatic contacts and correspondence.

Opening as the Yōgakusho (Institute for Western Learning) in Edo (now Tōkyō) in 1855, it was renamed Bansho Shirabesho and moved to new quarters in 1856, with Koga Kin'ichirō (1816–84) as its first principal. Dutch, the original language of translation and research, was joined by English (in 1857), French (in 1860), and German (in 1860). (For the years these languages were first taught, see the section on language studies in WESTERN LEARNING.) The curriculum grew from early emphasis on military subjects such as metallurgy, surveying, and navigation to include mathematics, physics, chemistry, and mechanical engineering. A student dormitory was built in 1858 for some of the 200 shogunal and domainal retainers from all over Japan, and the staff of over 50 included such leading scholars of Western learning as KANDA TAKAHIRA, KATŌ HIROYUKI, NISHI AMANE, and TSUDA MAMICHI.

The institute was renamed Yōsho Shirabesho (Institute for the Investigation of Western Books) and moved again to new quarters in 1862. It was expanded as the Kaiseijo (Institute for Development, 1863–68), reopened by the Meiji government as the Daigaku Nankō in 1868, and joined to the Tōkyō Igakkō (Tōkyō Medical School) to form Tōkyō Imperial University (now Tōkyō University) in 1877.

■——R. P. Dore, *Education in Tokugawa Japan* (1965). Numata Jirō, *Bakumatsu yōgaku shi* (1951). Ōkubo Toshiaki, *Nihon no daigaku* (1943). *Ivan P. HALL*

banzai

The Japanese equivalent of the English "three cheers." Used at celebratory parties and welcoming or farewell banquets to express common congratulation, encouragement, or exhortation. The participants shout the word *banzai* (hurrah; literally, "ten thousand years") three times in unison, raising their hands in the air each time.

The word *banzai,* which is of Chinese origin, was in use in Japan from around the 9th century in the sense of "long life" to express respect for the emperor (it was then pronounced *banzei).* It went out of use for a long period, to be revived after the Meiji Restoration of 1868. It was only then that it became a triple cheer, an obvious imitation of the Western custom. An early instance of the *banzai sanshō* (triple *banzai*) came in 1883, when adherents of the FREEDOM AND PEOPLE'S RIGHTS MOVEMENT began shouting the slogan *jiyū banzai* (Long Live Freedom) three times in a row. Its firm establishment as a custom, however, dates from 11 February 1889, when university students, on the occasion of the signing of the Meiji CONSTITUTION, faced the emperor's carriage and shouted *banzai* three times. What was originally a prayer for the emperor's long life and the prosperity of the nation eventually became a vehicle for expressing group emotions on various occasions. The practice has more recently fallen into disuse, having largely been replaced by hand-clapping in unison three times. *TSUCHIDA Mitsufumi*

Baptist Church

The first American Baptist missionary, Jonathan Goble (1827–98), arrived in Japan in 1860 when Christianity was still proscribed under the Tokugawa shogunate. He succeeded in publishing the first Japanese translation of the Gospel according to Matthew in 1871. In 1872 Nathan Brown (1807–86) joined him and in 1876 the first Baptist church was built in Tōkyō. They established a theological school in Tōkyō in 1884 which expanded to become Kantō Gakuin University in 1949. The Southern Baptist Mission began its missionary activity in the western part of Japan in 1889. They built a school in Fukuoka in 1916 which became Seinan Gakuin University in 1949. The churches were united in 1918 but after World War II they separated again. The Nihon Baputesuto Remmei (Japan Baptist Convention), affiliated with the Southern Baptist Mission, is larger, claiming 25,159 members with 183 churches, whereas the Nihon Baputesuto Dōmei (Japan Baptist Union), affiliated with northern Baptist denominations in the United States, claimed 4,084 members with 53 churches (1980). Other Baptist denominations are still in an inchoate stage. *Kenneth J. DALE*

Bar Association → Japan Federation of Bar Associations

barley → wheat and barley

barrier stations → sekisho

baseball

Baseball is the most popular team sport in Japan, with high school, university, and professional games stirring the public and dominating the media during the spring and summer months.

Baseball was first played in Japan in 1873 at Kaisei Gakkō (now Tōkyō University) under the instruction of an American, Horace

Wilson. Around 1880 the first Japanese baseball team was organized at the Shimbashi Athletic Club, and several college teams were soon formed in Tōkyō. During the period 1890 to 1902, a team from the First Higher School in Tōkyō played and often defeated a team made up of American residents in Yokohama; the publicity from these games helped make baseball one of the most popular Western sports in Japan.

Amateur Baseball Organizations——Around 1900, baseball clubs were formed in middle schools throughout the country. Baseball became Japan's major school sport, with interscholastic competitions leading the way. The annual series between Waseda University and Keiō University (known as the Sōkeisen), the most popular intercollegiate rivalry, started in 1903. Three universities— Waseda, Keiō, and Meiji—formed a league in 1914, which by 1925 included three other universities, Hōsei, Rikkyō, and Tōkyō, creating the Tōkyō Big Six University Baseball League. Before 1945, the Big Six was Japan's most popular league, and it remains the favorite league in college baseball. By the late 1970s there were 253 college teams. Leading teams from each region of the country participate in the annual Japan Collegiate Baseball Championship.

High school baseball activity is dominated by the National Invitational High School Baseball Championship Tournament, held each year in March and April, and the All-Japan High School Baseball Championship Tournament, held in August. These events, which trace their origins back to 1924 and 1915 respectively, are held at Kōshien Stadium in Nishinomiya, Hyōgo Prefecture and are commonly known as the spring and summer Kōshien tournaments. Featuring schools that represent every Japanese prefecture, they receive extensive attention in the press, are broadcast live nationwide via radio and television, and consistently rival professional baseball in popularity.

Nonstudent amateur teams also compete in a number of regular leagues and tournaments, of which the Intercity Baseball Championship Tournament and the Japan Amateur Baseball Championship Tournament are the most important. All amateur activity, including school baseball, is supervised by the Japan Amateur Baseball Federation, which is composed of separate groups governing high school, college, and other amateur competition.

Development of Professional Baseball——When an American major league all-star team came to Japan in 1934, an All-Japan Team was selected from the best players of the nonprofessional teams. With these members as its core, the first professional team, the Dai Nihon Baseball Club, was organized at the end of 1934, and by 1936 seven professional teams had been formed. Though not as popular as amateur baseball before World War II, professional baseball rapidly grew into Japan's most popular spectator sport in the postwar years, with an annual attendance of over 14 million, and televised games became top-rated programs.

The present two-league system, consisting of the Central League and the Pacific League, was set up in 1950. Each league has six teams, all of which are owned and sponsored by large corporations. The home cities and names of the teams occasionally change when they are bought by new owners. In 1980 the Central League consisted of the Chūnichi Dragons, Hanshin Tigers, Hiroshima Tōyō Carp, Taiyō Whales, Yakult Swallows, and Yomiuri Giants. The Pacific League claimed the Hankyū Braves, Kintetsu Buffaloes, Lotte Orions, Nankai Hawks, Nippon-Ham Fighters, and Seibu Lions. Each team plays 130 games between early April and early October. The regular season is followed by the Japan Series, a seven-game match between the two league champions.

Invention and Spread of Rubber Ball Baseball——In 1919, a special form of the game using a hollow rubber ball was invented by Suzuka Sakae for young players. The ball is softer and less dangerous; the catcher needs no special protection other than a face mask; and the rest of the equipment is generally simpler and cheaper. The rubber ball was taken up by adult players as well and contributed greatly to the popularization of baseball in Japan. Rubber ball baseball is now played by more people than any other sport, and the number of teams registered with the Amateur Rubber Ball Baseball Association exceeded 70,000 in 1978. Including unregistered "sandlot" players, the number of people playing rubber ball is estimated to be over 10 million.

Japan–United States Baseball Games——The first Japanese baseball team to visit the United States was the Waseda University team in 1905. Two years later the first semiprofessional American team came to Japan from Hawaii, and, in the following years, several international matches were organized by colleges and clubs. Waseda University and the University of Chicago played 10 games be-

Baseball

		Japanese Professional Baseball Records (as of 1981)									
		Lifetime records							Season records		
		First		Second		Third					
Batters	Games	Nomura Katsuya	3,017	Ō Sadaharu	2,831	Harimoto Isao	2,336		—	—	—
	Runs	Ō Sadaharu	1,967	Harimoto Isao	1,523	Nomura Katsuya	1,509		Kozuru Makoto	1950	143
	Hits	Harimoto Isao	3,085	Nomura Katsuya	2,901	Ō Sadaharu	2,786		Fujimura Fumio	1950	191
	Doubles	Yamanouchi Kazuhiro	448	Ō Sadaharu	422	Harimoto Isao	420		Yamanouchi Kazuhiro	1956	47
	Triples	Busujima Shōichi	106	Kaneda Masayasu	103	Kawakami Tetsuharu	99		Kaneda Masayasu	1951	18
	Home runs	Ō Sadaharu	868	Nomura Katsuya	657	Harimoto Isao	504		Ō Sadaharu	1964	55
	Total bases	Ō Sadaharu	5,862	Nomura Katsuya	5,315	Harimoto Isao	5,161		Kozuru Makoto	1950	376
	Runs batted in	Ō Sadaharu	2,170	Nomura Katsuya	1,988	Harimoto Isao	1,676		Kozuru Makoto	1950	161
	Stolen bases	Fukumoto Yutaka	865	Hirose Yoshinori	596	Shibata Isao	499		Fukumoto Yutaka	1972	106
	Batting average	Wakamatsu Tsutomu	0.323	Harimoto Isao	0.319	Katō Hideji	0.314		Harimoto Isao	1970	0.383
Pitchers	Complete games	Kaneda Shōichi	365	Victor Starhin	350	Bessho Takehiko	335		Bessho Akira	1947	47
	Shutouts	Victor Starhin	83	Kaneda Shōichi	82	Koyama Masaaki	74		Noguchi Jirō	1942	19
									Fujimoto Hideo	1943	19
	Wins	Kaneda Shōichi	400	Yoneda Tetsuya	348	Koyama Masaaki	320		Victor Starhin	1939	42
									Inao Kazuhisa	1961	42
	Innings pitched	Kaneda Shōichi	$5,526\frac{2}{3}$	Yoneda Tetsuya	5,091	Koyama Masaaki	4,899		Hayashi Yasuo	1942	542
	Strikeouts	Kaneda Shōichi	4,490	Yoneda Tetsuya	3,351	Koyama Masaaki	3,159		Enatsu Yutaka	1968	401
	Earned run average	Fujimoto Hideo	1.90	Noguchi Jirō	1.97	Inao Kazuhisa	1.98		Fujimoto Hideo	1943	0.73

NOTE: Batting averages are for those who came to bat more than 4,000 times. Earned run averages are for those who pitched more than 2,000 times. Hits equal the sum of singles, doubles, triples, and home runs.
SOURCE: Asahi Shimbun Sha, *Asahi nenkan* (annual): 1981.

tween 1906 and 1936. Since 1972 a Japan–United States College Baseball Championship has been played annually between all-star teams selected from Japanese and American colleges, the match being held in either country in alternative years.

As for American major leaguers, a world tour team led by Charles Comiskey and John McGraw was the first to visit Japan in 1913. Major league all-star teams managed by Connie Mack that came to Japan in 1931 and 1934 with such notable players as Lefty Grove, Lou Gehrig, Babe Ruth, and Jimmie Foxx made a strong impression on the Japanese public and led to the formation of the first professional team in Japan.

After World War II, Japanese-American baseball interchanges became more frequent. In 1949 the San Francisco Seals of the Pacific Coast League visited Japan, followed by numerous major league teams. In recent years some Japanese professional teams have held spring training camp in America. Since 1936, over 200 Americans have played for Japanese professional teams. *WATANABE Tōru*

bashaku

(packhorsemen teams). Laborers who transported goods and foodstuffs from rural areas to the cities. They first appeared, under the name *shaba,* as early as the Heian period (794–1185) to meet the increasing dependence of Kyōto on rice and manufactures from outlying regions. By the late years of the Kamakura period (1185–1333) they had secured a virtual monopoly of overland shipment. Many of them were farmers who conducted trains of packhorses (roads in much of Japan were not suitable for carts) during the slack season. *Bashaku* were concentrated in the POST–STATION TOWNS—such as Ōtsu, Sakamoto, and Kusatsu in the province of Ōmi (now Shiga Prefecture) and Kizu in Yamashiro Province (now part of Kyōto Prefecture)—on the main approaches to important cities like Kyōto and Nara. These teamsters were generally employed by forwarding agents or horse breeders, although they were in some cases controlled by local warlords *(shugo daimyō)*. With the growth of cities in the medieval age, *bashaku* increased in numbers and importance and eventually gained control of their own enterprises. By the middle years of the Muromachi period (1333–1568) they had formed associations that played a central role in numerous popular uprisings of the 15th century (see BASHAKU IKKI). In the Edo period (1600–1868) the *bashaku* greatly broadened their commercial activities. They organized themselves into guilds (ZA), and many became rich wholesale merchants in the cities. *Philip BROWN*

bashaku ikki

(packhorsemen's uprisings). Uprisings of the 15th century led by the packhorsemen (BASHAKU) who monopolized the transport of goods from rural areas to the cities. They were particularly powerful in the provinces of Ōmi (now Shiga Prefecture) and Yamashiro (now part of Kyōto Prefecture), which supplied much of the food for the Kyōto-Ōsaka region. The *bashaku* staged uprisings at Ōtsu, Ōmi, in 1418 and at Sakamoto, Ōmi, in 1423 to protest a decline in the price of rice, the shipment of which was a mainstay of their business.

Because of their close contact with the villages along their routes, the *bashaku* soon made common cause with the farmers and led a major uprising in the Ōsaka area in 1428 to demand cancellation of cultivators' debts. They played a central role in other agrarian disturbances (TSUCHI IKKI) thereafter. *Philip BROWN*

Bashō (1644–1694)

Full name Matsuo Bashō. Poet, essayist, and writer of travel sketches in the early Edo period who helped perfect the art of HAIKU and HAIBUN in the formative years of these genres. The name Bashō ("banana tree") is a sobriquet he adopted around 1681 after moving into a hut with a banana tree alongside. He was called Kinsaku in childhood, Matsuo Munefusa after coming of age.

Early Years —— Bashō was born in 1644 at or near Ueno in Iga Province (now part of Mie Prefecture). His father seems to have been a low-ranking *samurai* who farmed in peacetime. Apparently intending to be a samurai, young Bashō entered the service of a local lord, Tōdō Yoshitada. Since Yoshitada (pseudonym Sengin) was fond of writing *haikai* (see HAIKU; RENGA AND HAIKAI) poems as a pastime, Bashō also began to write poetry, using the name Sōbō. His earliest surviving poems, dating back as early as 1662, are characterized by elegant humor and clever use of allusion to Heian-period (794–1185) classics and the Nō drama. When Yoshitada died prematurely in 1666, Bashō resigned his service and started roaming the Kyōto area, learning about fashionable ways of life in the capital. He continued to write *haikai* and in time gained a measure of local recognition. In 1672 he finished compiling a book of haiku matched in contest, *Kai ōi* (Covering Shells), himself posing as judge and commentator. The poems included are of little literary value, but the commentaries reveal his brilliant wit as well as his broad knowledge of the sophisticated city life of the day.

Settlement in Edo —— In 1672 Bashō moved to Edo (now Tōkyō), probably hoping to find good career opportunities in the fast-expanding city. At first he had to take on odd jobs, but gradually he established himself as a teacher of *haikai*. Under the new sobriquet Tōsei he wrote poems characterized by wordplay and earthy humor, frequently using colloquialisms of the time. When he alluded to classics, he often parodied or ridiculed them. This kind of style was popular in Edo and his students steadily increased in number. In 1680 he had enough good students to publish *Tōsei montei dokugin nijikkasen* (Best Poems of Tōsei's 20 Disciples). Later that year he settled in a small hut in the Fukagawa district of Edo and began calling himself Bashō shortly afterwards.

About this time Bashō began practicing Zen under the guidance of Master Butchō (d 1715), who happened to be staying nearby. Apparently Bashō was not at peace with himself, despite his increasing fame and material well-being. His poems in *Minashiguri* (Empty Chestnuts), an anthology of verse which he and his disciples published in 1683, suggest spiritual ambivalence and experimental disposition. Their strong Chinese tone and orthography create a masculine, heroic impression—a marked departure from his earlier styles. Also, many of the haiku contain one or more extra syllables. Obviously, Bashō felt an urge to break down convention and avoid staleness. The urge soon took on a more physical form, that of traveling, through which he hoped to enlarge the scope of his life, poetry, and vision of reality.

Westward Journey of 1684 —— In the fall of 1684 Bashō set out on his first significant journey, significant because it was for the sake of spiritual and poetic discipline. He traveled west along a main road near the Pacific coastline and arrived at his native town of Ueno about a month later. From there he visited Nagoya, where he led a team of poets in composing five excellent volumes of linked verse collectively known as *Fuyu no hi* (The Winter Sun). He also visited other nearby cities like Nara, Ōgaki, and Kyōto before returning to Edo the following summer. This journey resulted in Bashō's journal, *Nozarashi kikō* (1685; tr *The Records of a Weather-Exposed Skeleton*, 1966).

As a work of literature, *Nozarashi kikō* has weaknesses resulting from Bashō's inexperience in writing travel sketches. The prose is uneven and lacks the force that would characterize his later journals. The haiku that are scattered through the prose retain, in varying degrees, the traces of his earlier and more experimental poetry. The prose and poetry are not harmoniously interwoven, especially in the second half where the prose passages often seem more like short headnotes to the poems. Nevertheless, the journal has a serious theme that runs consistently beneath its surface: a search for liberation from tormenting self-doubts. To attain this aim Bashō was

Bashō

Detail of the first of two scrolls by the 18th-century poet-painter Buson containing the text of Bashō's *Oku no hosomichi* with illustrations. Bashō, left, is pictured setting out on his journey to the north with his disciple Kawai Sora. Ink and colors on paper. Height 28.2 cm. 1779. Itsuō Art Museum, Ōsaka Prefecture.

willing to risk his fragile constitution; the journal's title suggests his determination. He seems to have been successful in his search. Later sections of the journal show Bashō enjoying his life as an itinerant poet; self-doubts are no longer there. Through the journey he came to know exactly what he wanted.

For the next two years Bashō enjoyed a leisurely life in Edo, teaching poetry and composing poems. The celebrated haiku about the frog and the old pond dates from this time.

Furuike ya	The old pond!
Kawazu tobikomu	A frog jumps in—
Mizu no oto	Sound of the water.

In the fall of 1687 he made a trip to Kashima, a scenic town northeast of Edo, to see the harvest moon. The trip produced a short travel sketch, *Kashima kikō* (1687; tr *A Visit to Kashima Shrine*, 1966). The sketch unmistakably shows Bashō's awakening to the value of FŪRYŪ, an aesthetic ideal cherished by eremitic artists since medieval times. More than ever before he had become a seeker of beauty in nature.

Westward Journey of 1687 —— Shortly after his visit to Kashima, Bashō set out on another long journey westward. The route was roughly the same as before, until his arrival at Ueno. From there he traveled to Suma and Akashi on the Inland Sea, made his way up to Sarashina in the Japan Alps, and returned to Edo along a mountainous route. The trip, which altogether lasted 10 months, resulted in two more poetic diaries: *Oi no kobumi* (1688; tr *The Records of a Travel-Worn Satchel*, 1966) and *Sarashina kikō* (1688; tr *A Visit to Sarashina Village*, 1966).

Oi no kobumi covers the journey from its outset until Bashō's visit to Akashi. Its distinctive feature is an ideological tone. Bashō does not sermonize, but his esteem for eremitic poetry is so great that several early passages sound almost didactic. Later sections of the journal show him practicing what he has theorized. He emerges as a kind of aesthetic primitivist seeking out beauty in rustic surroundings and distilling his poetic response into 17 syllables.

Sarashina kikō, the shortest of Bashō's journals, sketches his moon-viewing trip to Sarashina. In its theme and structure it resembles *Kashima kikō*, except that the natural setting is far wilder here. In *Oi no kobumi* Bashō had advocated a "return to nature," but in *Sarashina kikō* he returned to nature in a truer sense.

Journey to the North —— Probably encouraged by the success of his trip to Sarashina, Bashō next undertook a long journey to the most underdeveloped part of Japan, the northern area of Honshū. Leaving Edo in the late spring of 1689, he traveled north to Nikkō, Shirakawa, Sendai, and Matsushima, which were all towns new to him. From Ishinomaki he turned west and cut across Honshū to Sakata on the Sea of Japan. After a visit to Kisagata he traveled down the coast to Niigata, Kanazawa, and Tsuruga, finally ending the journey at Ōgaki. Covering some 2,500 kilometers (1,500 mi) in 156 days, this longest journey of his life marked a climax in Bashō's literary career. He wrote some of his finest haiku during the journey. It was probably then, too, that he evolved his famous poetic principle known as SABI, a dialectic synthesis of gorgeous and lonely beauty. Above all, he transformed his experience into *Oku no hosomichi* (1694; tr *The Narrow Road to the Deep North,* 1966), one of the high points in the history of the Japanese poetic diary.

The merit of *Oku no hosomichi* is multiple. The haiku that are scattered throughout are of the highest quality, many of them showing the ultimate in *sabi.* The prose is at once smooth and stately, delicate and forceful, simple and expansive. Poetry and prose harmoniously complement one another. Subsections are strung together by the same subtle principle of unity used in linked verse. The main theme is a universal one: a quest for the ultimate beauty of nature and of man, which had been lost in the steadily decaying contemporary society. The journal's title is more metaphorical than literal, the author trod the narrow road far into the rugged north in search of a simple and sturdy culture remaining from olden days. In order to amplify this theme Bashō made a careful selection of material for inclusion in the journal, in some instances even departing from actual facts. He chose to be spiritually rather than factually true to his experience.

Sojourn in the Kyōto Area——Bashō spent the next two years visiting his old friends and disciples in and around Kyōto. Of the numerous places where he stayed during this period he especially enjoyed the sojourn at two small cottages, Genjūan and Rakushisha. The former, located in the woods near Lake Biwa, provided Bashō with ample time for meditation. Here he wrote an excellent *haibun, Genjūan no ki* (1690; tr *Prose Poem on the Unreal Dwelling,* 1955). This essay, together with the haiku and linked verse he wrote at this time, were later collected in *Sarumino* (1691; tr *Monkey's Raincoat,* 1973), an anthology best exemplifying his mature poetic style. In the spring of the next year he spent a few weeks at Rakushisha in Saga, a northwestern suburb of Kyōto. This experience resulted in his last major work, *Saga nikki* (1691; tr *The Saga Diary,* 1971–72).

Saga nikki, though not a travel sketch in the usual sense, shares some qualities with Bashō's other journals. For instance, haiku are scattered throughout it. The author is a traveler, though temporarily staying at one place. He does make a couple of short trips, and he also meets old and new friends, as a traveler does along his way. Above all, the diary is unified by the author's love for the peaceful life away from the bustle of the mundane world. Despite all these qualities, however, the diary lacks the density of texture and refinement of style characteristic of Bashō. This is probably because the surviving manuscript is not his final version.

Last Years——Bashō returned to Edo in the winter of 1691 and embarked on an extremely busy life. As a renowned poet, he was constantly surrounded by friends, disciples, and admirers. He also had a few people to take care of: a young invalid nephew, a middle-aged woman named Jutei with whom he had had a special relationship in his youth, and Jutei's children. Pressed by responsibilities, Bashō became increasingly depressed, and for a time in 1693 he even stopped seeing visitors altogether. Eventually he overcame the problem by striving for what he called *karumi* ("lightness"). This ideal, well reflected in an anthology called *Sumidawara* (A Sack of Charcoal), which his students published in 1694, envisioned a life of spiritual detachment while being physically bound to the world.

Bashō set out on his last westward journey in the summer of 1694. Apparently he wanted to travel as far as Kyūshū, but he fell far short of the aim. He contracted a stomach ailment in Ōsaka and died there in the autumn (28 November 1694 or Genroku 7.10.12). His last haiku indicates that he was still thinking of traveling and writing poetry as he lay dying:

Tabi ni yande	Fallen sick on a journey,
Yume wa kareno o	In dreams I run wildly
Kakemeguru	Over a withered moor.

Reputation and Influence——Bashō is said to have had more than 2,000 students at the time of his death. If this number is debatable, there is no doubt about his high reputation among contemporary and later poets. In the sense that he elevated haiku into a mature art form, he was the founder of the genre they all looked up to. Also, since his poetry went through various phases, he was able to appeal to poets of widely different temperaments. Urban poets were drawn to his early witty verses. Rural poets were more interested in his later verses written in a plainer style. BUSON (1716–84) adored Bashō the romantic, and ISSA (1763–1827) emulated Bashō the diarist. In the 20th century Bashō's influence has reached outside

haikai circles: some consider Bashō a Wordsworthian figure who sought a mystic union with nature; to others Bashō seems almost a precursor of French symbolism; to modern novelists like Akutagawa Ryūnosuke (1892–1927), Bashō appeared to be a humanist for whom the highest good was poetry. With the increasing interest in haiku outside Japan, his reputation is becoming international.

📖 ——*Kōhon Bashō zenshū,* 10 vols (Kadokawa Shoten, 1962–69). Harold G. Henderson, *An Introduction to Haiku* (1958). Imoto Nōichi et al, ed, *Bashō,* in *Kokugo kokubungaku kenkyūshi taisei,* vol 12 (1959). Donald Keene, *World Within Walls* (1976). Earl Miner, *Japanese Linked Poetry* (1979). Nippon Gakujutsu Shinkō-kai, ed, *Haikai and Haiku* (1958). Makoto Ueda, *Matsuo Bashō* (1970). Nobuyuki Yuasa, ed and tr, *Bashō: The Narrow Road to the Deep North and Other Travel Sketches* (1966). Makoto UEDA

Bassui Tokushō (1327–1387)

Also known as Battai Tokushō. Zen monk of the RINZAI SECT. Born in Nakamura, Sagami Province (now part of Kanagawa Prefecture). Tokushō decided to become a monk rather late in life (1357) and studied with the renowned master Kohō Kakumyō (1271–1361), JA-KUSHITSU GENKō (1290–1367), and others. Declining to reside at any well-established monastic institution, Tokushō stayed at various places in what are today Shizuoka and Kanagawa prefectures until 1380, when he settled at a hermitage in Enzan, Kai Province (now Yamanashi Prefecture). His rigorous and unpretentious spiritual discipline attracted many followers, religious and lay, and a collection of his instructions was published as *Wadei gassui shū* (1st ed, 1386). This, along with the later compilations *Enzan kana hōgo* and *Bassui Oshō goroku,* was written in Japanese (rather than Chinese; see GOROKU), unlike most writings by Zen monks of the time, and reached a wide audience especially during the Edo period (1600–1868).

📖 ——Furuta Shōkin, *Bassui* (1979). Ichikawa Hakugen et al, ed, *Chūsei zenka no shisō,* in *Nihon shisō taikei,* vol 16 (Iwanami Shoten, 1972). TSUCHIDA Tomoaki

Bataan

Mountainous, thickly jungled peninsula to the west of Manila Bay on Luzon Island in the Philippines, which gained notoriety during World War II as the site of a "death march." In May 1942 after a lengthy siege by Japanese forces, about 75,000 Allied captives, 12,000 of them Americans, were forced to march from Mariveles, at the tip of the peninsula, to Camp O'Donnell some 96 kilometers (about 60 mi) away. Although General Homma Masaharu (1887–1946), the commanding officer, had made arrangements for food and medical care, they were far from adequate, since there were twice as many prisoners as he had expected. Thousands died on the march and many more perished at the camp in the ensuing three months. The victims are remembered each year on Bataan Day, a national holiday in the Philippines.

Batchelor, John (1854–1944)

Anglican missionary; born in Sussex, England. Originally stationed in Hong Kong, but forced by reasons of health to live in a colder climate, he went to Hakodate in 1877 to preach among the Japanese on the northern island of Hokkaidō. However, he found it more urgent to work among the AINU, the native inhabitants of the island, and in 1879 was granted permission to do so. He lived among the Ainu people, built schools, and provided medical care, and thus spent more than 60 years in Hokkaidō until the beginning of World War II, which forced him to return to England. He also applied himself to the study of Ainu culture and language. Besides his best-known work, an *Ainu-English-Japanese Dictionary,* which was first published in 1889, he published the first Ainu translation of the New Testament (1897) and various papers on Ainu folklore.

Kirsten REFSING

bateren

Japanese approximation of the Western word "padre"; used to designate Christian priests, especially Jesuits, during the "Christian Century" (1549–1650) and Edo period (1600–1868). An analogous usage was *iruman* for the Portuguese *irmão,* Jesuit lay brother. Originally *bateren* was a standard neutral appellation, as is evident from its use in such sources as the *Shinchō Kō ki* (ca 1610, Chronicle of Nobunaga) and *Kirishitan ōrai* (ca 1568), an epistolary primer and the oldest extant Japanese text produced by the Jesuits themselves. Later the term assumed a distinctly sinister connotation in the popular literature of the KIRISHITAN MONOGATARI genre, which portrayed the grotesque Urugan Bateren (Padre Organtino), Furaten Bateren (the *fratres* or brothers of the mendicant orders under a collective anonym), and other *bateren* and *iruman* as evil magicians and agents of a Christian conspiracy intent on subverting and seizing Japan. The subcategory *korobi bateren* refers to apostate priests, such as the Jesuits Christovão Ferreira (Sawano Chūan) and Giuseppe Chiara (Okamoto San'emon), whom the Tokugawa shogunate (1603–1867) used in its anti-Christian inquisition.　　*George* ELISON

bath

(furo or *ofuro).* The typical Japanese bath consists of a tub deep enough for the bather to immerse the body up to the neck by sitting or squatting. Hot water is sometimes piped or transported to the tub, but more often it is heated in the tub by a fire underneath or at one end. There is a drain in the floor, and the bather washes and rinses the body completely before entering the tub to soak in the hot water. Although many Japanese have baths in their own homes, large numbers continue to take their daily bath in the public bathhouses, which have been a feature of popular Japanese culture since the Edo period (1600–1868). The main difference between public and home baths is one of scale.

Public Baths——As early as the Nara period (710–794), large temples such as TŌDAIJI and HŌRYŪJI provided a kind of public steam bath. Public baths were maintained by temples and by the wealthy for the poor and unfortunate until the Muromachi period (1333–1568). Bathing places for the general public became popular after the first commercial bath was constructed in Edo (now Tōkyō) in 1591. By the time of the Meiji Restoration (1868), there were 600 public baths *(sentō)* in Tōkyō, generally open from 6:00 AM to 8:00 PM. Not just for bathing, these became social haunts where bathers could spend leisurely hours playing games and eating. In the pleasure districts certain types of public bathing facilities for men provided female attendants called *yuna,* who not only washed the customers' backs while massaging with their fingertips, but also served tea and provided erotic pleasures on the second floor. Scenes in both these and the more innocent types of bathhouse were often depicted in the woodblock prints (UKIYO-E) of the period or in popular fiction, most notably in the *Ukiyoburo,* a comic work by SHIKITEI SAMBA.

Public baths (still called *sentō)* now have separate entrances, dressing rooms, and bathing rooms for men and women. Bathers carry their bath equipment in small basins. Just inside the entrance, they pay at an elevated desk, from which the attendant can see both male and female dressing rooms. Towels and clothes are left in large baskets, which are then placed on shelves or in lockers, and customers carry their equipment into the bathing room. Kneeling at small hot- and cold-water faucets lining the walls, they wash from their basins, filling them many times with water to rinse their bodies. Usually bathers wash before soaking in the large hot tubs and then get out and wash again, sometimes going back for a second or third leisurely soak in order to chat with friends and neighbors. The room might accommodate several dozen bathers, with one tub holding from 6 to 10 people. Etiquette still demands that bathers offer to wash the backs of their elders. *Sentō* are nowadays open from about 3:00 or 4:00 PM to 11:00 or 12:00 PM; because of inflation, the admission price rises yearly.

Because of the general improvement in the standard of living, people increasingly have baths in their own homes; many *sentō* are thus going out of business. To attract customers, *sentō* sometimes provide Muzak, electric or mineral baths, showers, jacuzzis, saunas, and cold tubs, as well as refreshments for sale, coin-operated hair dryers, and massage chairs in the dressing rooms.

Modern Family Bath——Modern-day baths in the home are in small rooms, always separate from the toilet. The room is tiled and equipped with a floor drain, so that the bather, sitting on a low stool, may wash outside the tub, filling a basin with hot water from it. Sometimes there is a shower in the room in addition to the tub for this purpose. After thoroughly rinsing off the soap, the bather gets into the tub, crouching and submerged up to the neck to soak. The bath water is kept as clean as possible so that later bathers can use it. Most household tubs hold only one person, although children might join their parents or bathe together. In traditional homes the father bathes first, and the others follow according to their rank in the

family. Although traditionally made of wood, tile, or more rarely metal, tubs are now often made of polypropylene reinforced with fiberglass. In some areas they are still heated with wood fires but more often by gas, and usually the bather can heat the water up again if it gets too cool or add cold water from a faucet if it is too hot. Some households pump the water into the washing machine afterwards in order to conserve water. On 5 May, CHILDREN'S DAY, sweet flag (SHŌBU) leaves are strewn into the bath; in midwinter *yuzu* (citron) are cut in half and tossed into the water for fragrance. Both these practices were originally for the purpose of exorcising evil spirits. In the past a variety of other herbs and leaves was tossed into the bathwater for medicinal purposes.

Other Customs——Mixed bathing *(kon'yoku)* can still be found in Japan, primarily at hot springs. Some large hotels at these resorts offer a dozen kind of baths, including waterfalls and swimming pools. Some restaurants provide bathing facilities for customers. Several customs of the *furo* have entered other aspects of Japanese life. The square cloth known as *furoshiki* ("bath spread"), used since the Edo period to carry toilet articles into the *sentō* and to stand on while dressing, is now a common article used to wrap gifts or to carry many other items.

bats

(kōmori). In Japanese, Kōmori is the general name for flying mammals of the order Chiroptera, which is divided into suborders Microchiroptera and Megachiroptera. The former, which includes the families Rhinolophidae and Vespertilionidae, is distributed throughout the four main islands of Japan; the latter is represented only by the *ōkōmori* (flying fox; genus *Pteropus),* which inhabits warm regions such as the OGASAWARA ISLANDS and the RYŪKYŪ ISLANDS. OKINOERABUJIMA, an island south of Kyūshū inhabited by the *ōkōmori,* is the northernmost limit of the world distribution of the family Pteropidae.

The most common bat throughout Japan is the *abura kōmori* (Japanese pipistrelle; *Pipistrellus abramus),* which lives near human dwellings and even in urban areas in large numbers. It roosts in houses or, rarely, in caves. The *kiku gashira kōmori (Rhinolophus ferrumequinum), usagi kōmori (Plecotus auritus),* and *yama kōmori (Nyctalus lasiopterus)* are often found in caves and dark crevices of forest trees. The number of individuals of all these species has been decreasing remarkably in recent years, probably because of the spraying of agricultural chemicals and deforestation, but no systematic investigation of the causes has been conducted.

IMAIZUMI Yoshiharu

The saying *tori naki sato no kōmori* ("bat in a birdless village"), denoting a fool who puts on airs in the absence of his superiors, appears in Japanese poetry. The shape of the common Japanese folding fan is said to have been suggested by the bat's wing, and the Japanese call Western-style umbrellas *kōmorigasa* ("bat umbrellas") by association with the shape.　　*SANEYOSHI Tatsuo*

batsu

A traditional type of clique or faction that is still found in modern Japan. Although factionalism in various forms has been evident in Japanese society for centuries, the word *batsu* became common only during and after the rapid Westernization in the Meiji period (1868–1912) as a convenient term for referring to factionalism based on surviving traditional social and political patterns.

A *batsu* consists of a group of persons with common ties based on institution, geographic region, family, or connection to the same person, who form an in-group, as, for example, in industry, government, a political party, or an educational institution. A *batsu* is basically hierarchical and paternalistic and frequently controls hiring, promoting, and the granting of political and business favors. Mere *batsu* affiliation without adequate training would not suffice to get oneself considered for a position, but on the other hand, qualified outsiders are also excluded from consideration. In extreme cases, once a *batsu* controls a resource, such as positions in a hospital or school, the resource is no longer open to outside competition. Members of a *batsu* carry an obligation *(giri;* see GIRI AND NINJŌ) to help each other and to repay their debt *(ON)* to their superiors, particularly to the group leader, who not only exercises paternalistic benevolence but also claims loyalty from subordinates.

Particular types of *batsu* may be distinguished by different prefixes, as in GAKUBATSU (school clique) or GUMBATSU (military clique). *Batsu* are usually found in professions requiring training, such as teaching, medicine, business management, civil service, and politics.

One of the oldest kinds of *batsu* is KEIBATSU, a clique formed through marriage alliances and having some political or economic power. While such "strategic marriages" occur at all levels of society, the term *keibatsu* is normally reserved for those at the highest level. The principle underlying *keibatsu* was in operation as early as the Heian period (794–1185), when the FUJIWARA FAMILY advanced its own interests by marrying its offspring to members of the imperial family; in the Kamakura period (1185–1333) the MINAMOTO FAMILY also used this system to great advantage. During the internecine wars of the 16th century, marriages among the families of warring *daimyō* were made for political and military expediency. In modern Japan leading politicians and industrialists are frequently related through a complex network of affinal ties.

Closely related to *keibatsu* is *mombatsu,* a clique based on family connection. In fact, *keibatsu* is often thought of as a subcategory of *mombatsu.* Though both terms refer to relationships created through marriage alliances, *mombatsu* also includes underlings or followers not related by blood. *Keibatsu* and *mombatsu* do not have clearly defined memberships, and in this respect differ from other *batsu.*

After the Meiji Restoration (1868), men from the former domains *(han)* of Satsuma, Chōshū, Tosa, and Hizen (now the prefectures of Kagoshima, Yamaguchi, Kōchi, and Saga, respectively) came to dominate the government and military through domain-based cliques called HAMBATSU. From about 1880, power became particularly concentrated in the hands of Satsuma and Chōshū men. Retiring from government, the *hambatsu* leaders became members of the Privy Council and, as elder statesmen (GENRŌ), maintained control from behind the scenes until the turn of the century. About this time also, Satsuma and Chōshū factions began their control of the army and navy.

Military men in government, after the end of the Meiji period, constituted their own *batsu (gumbatsu),* whose objectives were to influence civilian affairs or military policy. Within the military, the army and the navy constituted separate and competing *batsu. Gumbatsu* influence was strongest during World War II and was completely obliterated with Japan's defeat.

ZAIBATSU (financial cliques) are the financial-business-industrial conglomerates which emerged in the late 19th and early 20th centuries. At the top of the organizational hierarchy was a family like the Mitsui or the Iwasaki, who controlled a holding corporation, which in turn owned controlling stocks of companies in wide-ranging fields. *Zaibatsu* maintained an exclusivist policy, the controlling family jealously guarding its interest and reserving top appointments for its own members and close associates. After World War II, the *zaibatsu* became targets of a series of actions by Occupation authorities which resulted in a drastic reduction of the power of these families and the destruction of their holding companies (see ZAIBATSU DISSOLUTION). While the prewar corporate groupings which constituted the *zaibatsu* have largely survived, they lack the strong central control associated with *zaibatsu.* Their management staffs are composed almost entirely of college-trained professionals, recruited through corporate entrance examinations, although *batsu* based on educational, geographical, or other affiliations may play a part in hiring. The word *gurūpu* (group, see ENTERPRISE GROUPS) is now often used instead of *zaibatsu* to refer to the most powerful corporate groups in contemporary Japan.

Gakubatsu are cliques based on the college or university from which one has graduated. Schools with a long tradition and high standards—generally the former imperial universities—staff their faculty almost exclusively with their own graduates. In addition, they maintain certain affiliate schools of lesser prestige in which they place their graduates. This pattern of control is particularly prominent in medical schools, which, in addition to controlling teaching positions, also control hospital staffing. Other *gakubatsu* consist of the Tōkyō University graduates who dominate the central bureaucracy, such as the ministries of finance, home affairs, and foreign affairs. Since it is true that these graduates score the highest on the civil service examinations, the ministries cannot be charged with favoritism in hiring, but once hired, *batsu* members aid each other in career advancement.

A particularly modern incidence of *batsu* is found in political parties and trade unions divided by factionalism. These HABATSU (factions) are organized around prominent persons vying for leadership of the larger group. Other modern *batsu* include the regional cliques known as *chihōbatsu* or *kyōdobatsu.* Such *batsu,* composed of people from the same prefecture or locality who dominate a business or other organization, might well be called the modern *hambatsu.* Occasionally, small *batsu* or *ha* (factions) form within larger *batsu.* See also GROUPS.

——Fukui Haruhiro, *Party in Power* (1970). Robert A. Scalapino and Masumi Junnosuke, *Parties and Politics in Contemporary Japan* (1962). Harumi BEFU

be

Earlier called *tomo* or *tomo no o.* Hereditary occupational groups under the domination of the YAMATO COURT or of powerful chieftain families (UJI) prior to the TAIKA REFORM of 645; from approximately the 5th to the 7th century, these groups supplied labor, goods, and other economic services to the court, the imperial family, or other powerful families.

The prototype for the Japanese *be* is thought to have been social or administrative units in China and Korea. In Japan a group of low-ranking court officials called *tomo* or *tomo no o* had been in service to the Yamato ruler, but with the great influx of immigrants from Korea (see KIKAJIN) during the 5th and 6th centuries, the *tomo* were reorganized as the *momoamari yaso no tomo,* literally, 180 *tomo* or *be,* to allow for greater diversification of functions. At the head of each *be* was a leader called the TOMO NO MIYATSUKO, who supervised the *shinabe* (also known as *tomobe*) or workers.

The *be* can be roughly classified into three groups by the kind of work they performed. (1) *Be* composed of peasants and fishermen who delivered produce to the *tomo no miyatsuko* in the form of tribute: these included the *yamabe,* who gathered such mountain products as chestnuts, bamboo, and vines; the *imbe,* who were in charge of religious services; and the *hajibe,* who made *hajiki* (HAJI WARE) and HANIWA (clay images). (2) *Be* composed largely of *kikajin* who served as hereditary artisans in the offices and workshops of the imperial court: among these were the *kanuchibe,* who engaged in the production of iron weapons; the *nishigoribe,* who wove silken fabrics; the *kinunuibe,* who sewed clothes; the *umakaibe,* who raised horses or produced cattle feed; and the *kuratsukuribe,* who made saddles and other equipment. (3) *Be* which had been commended to the Yamato ruler or to his family by KUNI NO MIYATSUKO, local chieftains who had sworn allegiance to the Yamato court. These *kuni no miyatsuko* not only served the imperial family but also provided the imperial court with guards. Among the *be* in this group were the *toneribe,* who performed miscellaneous tasks and policing duties, the *kashiwadebe,* who worked in the imperial kitchens, and the *saekibe,* who performed military services.

In terms of ownership, *be* may be classified into *tomobe (shinabe),* owned by the imperial court as a whole; KOSHIRO AND NASHIRO, privately owned by the Yamato ruler; and *kakibe,* who were owned by powerful *uji* chieftain families. To the *koshiro* and *nashiro,* local *kuni no miyatsuko* dispatched as tribute young men and women to serve as TONERI (lower court officials) and UNEME (ladies-in-waiting) as well as *kashiwade* (stewards) and *yugei* (guards). *Kakibe* were given the names of the *uji* who owned them, e.g., the Sogabe, Kiibe, and Heguribe.

The *be* system can be considered to represent the basic sociopolitical structure of the primitive Japanese state: at the apex was the Yamato sovereign, who had secured the allegiance of powerful *uji* chieftains who were classified into *omi, muraji, tomo no miyatsuko,* and *kuni no miyatsuko.* Below them were the numerous *be* service groups, who provided labor and goods. At the bottom were the *yakko* and *menoyakko* (both later referred to as NUHI). Thus, the people of ancient Japan were organized in a hierarchy that was maintained by the ruling *uji* stratum. It was only after the Taika Reform, when the RITSURYŌ SYSTEM of government was adopted under the influence of Chinese civilization, that a more centralized form of state organization was established. See also UJI-KABANE SYSTEM. Hirano Kunio

beads, ancient

(tama). Beads were used in the prehistoric and protohistoric periods as body ornaments, decorations, and ritual objects; following the introduction of Buddhism in the 6th century, the practice of decorating the body ceased, and beads were used through the succeeding periods mainly in BUDDHIST ROSARIES. (Modern bead necklaces are commonly worn with Western clothing but never with *kimono.*)

The most significant Japanese bead is the *magatama* (curved jewel); a set of these was included as one of the three IMPERIAL

REGALIA as early as the 6th century. Developing from irregularly shaped, perforated jade pebbles as found in the Middle Jōmon period (ca 3500 BC–ca 2000 BC), the *magatama* became standardized as comma-shaped in the ensuing Yayoi period (ca 300 BC–ca AD 300); and in the Kofun period (ca 300–710), green *magatama* of jadite or chalcedony were important marks of status (see drawing at YAYOI PERIOD). *Magatama* are often discovered in the Kofun-period mounded tombs (KOFUN) or tunnel tombs (YOKOANA) such as the ŌZUKA TOMB or YOSHIMI "HUNDRED CAVE" TUNNEL TOMBS as part of necklaces strung with cylindrical jasper beads *(kudatama)*. From the 5th century onward, amber and crystal *magatama* became popular, and at the sources of these materials in Shimane and Yamanashi prefectures, *magatama* are still made today as pendants and other ornaments. The origin of the comma shape is unclear, although it possibly derives from bear-claw ornaments or a semicircular ornament of the Korean peninsula bronze-age cultures.

A variety of other beads were used in protohistoric ornamentation. Round types included stone beads, such as were found in Jōmon SHELL MOUNDS and the KAMEGAOKA SITE; shell and blue-glass beads, whose production techniques were developed in the Yayoi period; and silver, gilt-bronze, and multicolored glass beads of the Kofun period. In the Late Kofun period, shapes and materials proliferated; faceted beads *(kirikodama)*, jujube-shaped beads *(natsumedama)*, flat beads *(hiradama)*, and three-peaked beads *(miwadama)* are known in such materials as serpentine, rock crystal, amber, agate, jasper, jadite, lignite, and chalcedony.

Bead-making sites of the Jōmon, Yayoi, and Kofun periods are known from gemstone sources in Shiga, Ishikawa, Toyama, Kanagawa, Chiba, Ibaraki, and Shimane prefectures. The site in the town of Tamanoyu, Shimane, is especially noteworthy as having been integrated into the protohistoric BE system of production under the management of the IMBE FAMILY. The site is now a historical park, and a museum and reconstructed pit houses with special bead-making facilities illustrate the manufacturing process and products. Cylindrical beads made of jasper and *magatama* made of agate were special products of this site.

Bead-making sites also produced stone articles other than beads. In particular, the stone bracelets (made of green tuff or jasper; see BRACELETS, ANCIENT) and stone replicas of various objects (made of jasper, green tuff, or soapstone) of the Kofun period were produced at bead-making sites. The replicas range from finely made jasper vessels and replicas of sheathed knives found in tombs to coarse soapstone *magatama* and button-like biperforate discs *(yūkō emban)* discovered at ceremonial sites (see OKINOSHIMA SITE). Characteristic artifacts from bead-making sites include raw materials, unfinished articles, several kinds of polishing stones, and iron drill perforators.

📖 ——Harada Yoshito, *Gyokurui* (1968). *Gina Lee* BARNES

beanbag

(otedama). Japanese beanbags are made of colorful scraps of cloth and usually filled with red *azuki* beans or rice. They are round in shape and small enough to fit into the palm of a child's hand; some have bells attached. The game, traditionally for girls, uses a set of five, seven, or nine beanbags. There are various ways of playing. In the simplest, the player juggles the bags with one or both hands. In another, the player throws one bag up and, while it is in midair, tries to perform various manipulations with one or more of the other bags, the complexity and difficulty increasing as the game progresses. Sometimes two or more players compete against each other. This ancient game, which was originally played with pebbles, assumed its present form around the 17th century.

bean curd → tōfu

bean paste → miso

Beard, Charles Austin (1874–1948)

American historian and political scientist. Born in Indiana. He earned his doctorate at Columbia University, joining its faculty in 1904. Interested in city government, he became director of the New York City Training Center for Public Service. In 1922 he was invited by GOTŌ SHIMPEI, then mayor of Tōkyō, to conduct a study of Tōkyō's municipal government. As a result of his visit he published

The Administration and Politics of Tōkyō (1923). Just after the great TŌKYŌ EARTHQUAKE OF 1923, he returned to Japan, again at the request of Gotō, who was now home minister, and assisted in the work of reconstruction, serving as an adviser on administration.

bears

(kuma). In Japanese *kuma* is the general name for mammals of the family Ursidae. Two species are found in Japan, namely, the *higuma (Ursus arctos)* of Hokkaidō and the *tsukinowaguma (Selenarctos thibetanus)* of Honshū, Shikoku, and Kyūshū. The *higuma* is the largest carnivorous animal in Japan, with a head-and-body length of about 2 meters (79 in) and weighing about 400 kilograms (880 lb). Two types of color are known, yellowish black and burnt umber. It is comparatively common in woods near rivers or streams up to an elevation of 1,700 meters (5,600 ft) and occasionally inflicts damage on humans and domestic animals. About 200 *higuma* are taken annually, and their dried gallbladders are sold at a high price as a traditional stomach medicine.

The *tsukinowaguma* is of medium size, with a head-and-body length of about 1.4 meters (55 in) and weighing about 200 kilograms (440 lb). The body is black, with a white crescent mark on the chest. It closely resembles the black bear of the United States *(U. americanus)* in general appearance. It is fairly numerous in woods in central and northern Honshū. Although it is gentle and seldom injures humans or domestic animals, it is regarded as a nuisance from the standpoint of agriculture and forestry, and about 800 are killed annually, either for economic reasons or through hunting. As in the case of the *higuma*, the dried gallbladders are sold at extremely high prices. *IMAIZUMI Yoshiharu*

The image that most Japanese have regarding the *tsukinowaguma* is of an attractive or good-natured mountain creature; it appears only rarely as a dreadful beast in folk traditions and tales. Its pelt and *kumanoi* (dried gallbladder; like that of the *higuma* it is sold as a medicine) are its only important products in Japan. The *higuma* is extremely important in the legends and traditional lifestyle of the AINU people of Hokkaidō. *SANEYOSHI Tatsuo*

bedding

Japanese bedding *(futon)* consists of padded mattresses and quilts pliable enough to be folded and stored out of sight during the day. In traditional houses a room could thus serve multiple purposes. Although Western beds and bedding, as well as bedrooms, have gained in popularity, traditional bedding is still widely used. A *futon* consists of a *shikibuton* (quiltlike mattress) and a *kakebuton* (thick quilted bedcover), laid out on the floor at night for sleeping and put away in closets each morning. Other articles of bedding include pillows *(makura)*, sheetlike covers for quilts *(shikifu)*, robelike sleeved quilts *(kaimaki)* for winter use, and lightweight quilts and mosquito nets *(kaya)* for the summer.

The use of cotton quilting for bedding is said to have originated around the mid-16th century. Prior to that the ruling nobility and *samurai* slept on thick woven rush matting such as *tatami* or *goza*, and the common people used straw mats or simply loose straw. People covered themselves with *fusuma*, coverlets which had sleeves and neckbands like *kimono*. *Fusuma* for the ruling class were made from cotton fabric wadded with silk floss; commoners used *fusuma* made from hempen cloth that was quilted in thick layers or from hempen cloth wadded with hemp fibers or fibers from the heads of bulrushes or eulalia *(Miscanthus sinensis)*. Eventually *futon* stuffed with cotton came into use, but in general *futon* were used only to sleep on, *fusuma* being used as covers. *Shikibuton* and *kakebuton* covered with *shikifu* became popular as bedding from the Meiji period (1868–1912).

Standard measurements of *shikibuton* are 90 by 190 centimeters (35.4 by 74.5 in) or 102 by 210 centimeters (40 by 86 in). Cotton wadding is most widely used because of its resilience, retention of heat, and absorption of moisture. *Kakebuton* are 150 by 210 centimeters (61 by 86 in) or 170 by 210 centimeters (70 by 86 in). Synthetic fiber is now widely used inside *kakebuton* because it is warm and lightweight, but cotton, wool, and down are also used. The outside covers and linings of *futon* are made of cotton, synthetic fabrics, or silk and can be replaced when necessary. At night *futon* are wrapped in *shikifu,* a practice similar to Western sheeting, and during the day they are aired in the sun to maintain their resiliency.

Beautiful and luxurious *futon,* in a matched set of two *kakebuton* and two *shikibuton,* are often given to brides as part of their dowry. In the winter, *kaimaki*—kimonolike quilts with cotton wadding—are sometimes used in addition to *kakebuton,* since they completely wrap the shoulders.

Stone pillows, which have been discovered in ancient tombs, were probably the first pillows used in Japan. Later, wooden pillows *(komakura)* and pillows made from bundles of grass *(kusamakura)* came into general use. When a style of coiffure called *keppatsu* became popular in the Edo period (1600–1868), wooden pillows were replaced by raised pillows supported by a boxlike frame *(hako-makura).* Stuffed pillows *(kukurimakura),* made of cotton and filled with buckwheat chaff or tea grounds, replaced grass pillows. Nowadays, most pillows are stuffed with buckwheat chaff, kapok, or down.

There are a number of popular superstitions connected with pillows. In ancient times it was thought that during sleep the spirit left the body and dwelt in the pillow. As a result, many Japanese still have an aversion to stepping over pillows or throwing them. Another such belief is that going to sleep with a picture of a *takara-bune* (a ship laden with treasure and the SEVEN DEITIES OF GOOD FORTUNE) under the pillow would ensure good dreams. Because of the custom of laying out the dead with the head to the north, sleeping with the head in that direction is considered inauspicious.

Mosquito nets have been in use from ancient times. By the Heian period (794–1185) their use had already become fairly widespread, though the common people generally used smoke to repel mosquitoes or protected themselves with curtains made of sheets of paper pasted together. These were called *shichō.* Mosquito nets were widely used by all classes from the beginning of the Edo period. They were traditionally made of silk gauze or loosely woven cotton or linen and were light green, light blue, or white. In recent years, the use of synthetic fibers has become common. The nets are large enough to accommodate several sets of *futon* and are suspended by cords attached to hooks in the four corners of the room. With the increased use of window and door screens, *kaya* have almost disappeared from urban areas. *FUJINO Ichirō*

bees and wasps

(hachi). In Japanese *hachi* is the common name for members of the order Hymenoptera other than ants. More than 100,000 species are known worldwide, and several thousand species are presumed to live in Japan. The main species are *habachi* (sawflies), the larvae of which feed on leaves of plants; *kibachi* (horntails), which eat wood; *himebachi* (ichneumons), *komayubachi* (braconids), and *kobachi* (chalcids), which are parasites on other insects or small animals; *tamabachi* (gall wasps), which cause galls; *bekkōbachi* (spider wasps) and *jigabachi* (sand wasps), which prey on spiders and other insects; *hanabachi* (bees), which gather pollen and nectar; *suzumebachi* (hornets); and *mitsubachi* (honey bees), which live in colonies. The largest species in Japan is the *ōsuzumebachi (Vespa mandarinia latilineata). NAKANE Takehiko*

The first recorded appearance of bees in Japanese mythology is in the account in the KOJIKI (completed in 712) in which the deity ŌKUNINUSHI NO MIKOTO is put in a chamber full of bees as part of an initiation ceremony, suggesting that bees were dreaded by the early Japanese. A similar feeling of fear is expressed in the KON-JAKU MONOGATARI, written at the end of the Heian period (794–1185), but by the Edo period (1600–1868) it seems to have lost some of its intensity.

Based on evidence in the NIHON SHOKI (completed in 720), it is thought that the technique of beekeeping was introduced to Japan from Korea in the first half of the 7th century, and it can be conjectured from descriptions in the ENGI SHIKI (927) that beekeeping had spread throughout the country by the early years of the Heian period. However, at this time honey was rare and was consumed only by powerful and wealthy persons familiar with Chinese writings, in which it was considered a precious medicine and an elixir of life. Only in the Edo period did beekeeping become widespread among the common people, largely because of KAIBARA EKIKEN's book of natural history *Yamato honzō* (1708) and ŌKURA NAGATSUNE's book of agriculture *Kōeki kokusan kō* (1842–59), which taught the process of extracting honey. *SAITŌ Shōji*

Beheiren → **Peace for Vietnam Committee**

beigoma

A kind of small top *(koma)*; corruption of the word *baigoma* (shell top); originally made by filling a spiral seashell with sand and lead. It is also called *muchigoma,* or "whip top," from the fact that it has no shaft but is spun with a whipcord. Early in the 20th century *beigoma* made of cast metal were popular children's toys. The top is spun on a straw or cloth mat that is concave in the center; the player whose top spins the longest is the winner. See also TOPS. *SAITŌ Ryōsuke*

Benedict, Ruth Fulton (1887–1948)

American cultural anthropologist; author of *The Chrysanthemum and the Sword* (1946), a classic study of Japanese society. A graduate of Vassar College, she received her doctorate in anthropology in 1923 from Columbia University and taught there until her death. Benedict's work on Japan began during World War II in the Office of War Information in Washington, DC, where she helped to pioneer the study of national character and to develop techniques for cultural research at a distance by integrating published materials with interview data. Never having visited Japan or studied its language, Benedict used such English sources as Charles N. ELIOT's *Japanese Buddhism* (1935) and the pioneering work of the English anthropologist Geoffrey Gorer, especially his essay, "Japanese Character Structure and Propaganda: A Preliminary Survey" (1942). She also had access to contemporary Japanese films, including propaganda films, as well as the diaries of several captured Japanese soldiers. In addition, many Japanese residents of the United States were interviewed at length.

The immediate purpose of *The Chrysanthemum and the Sword* (tr into Japanese as *Kiku to katana,* 1949), the culmination of her studies, was to assist the American OCCUPATION authorities in their efforts to transform Japan into a peaceful and democratic state. Benedict stressed that Japanese social organization is hierarchical: it is important to know one's place or role (BUN) in the world, and proper placing of people allows for dignity of behavior even in the lower strata of society. She also wrote that the concepts of ON (gratitude) and *giri* (obligation; see GIRI AND NINJŌ), learned within the family, are crucial to understanding Japanese character and that the Japanese have little sense of guilt but a strong sense of shame. The book has been widely read in Japan as well as in the West. Although later scholars have criticized it on some points, there is general agreement that Benedict's research represents the first significant study of Japanese society by a non-Japanese cultural anthropologist.

——Margaret Mead, ed, *An Anthropologist at Work: Writings of Ruth Benedict* (1966). Margaret Mead, *Ruth Benedict* (1974). *Daniel A. METRAUX*

Benkei (?–1189)

Also called Musashibō Benkei. Legendary warrior-monk in the early part of the Kamakura period (1185–1333); loyal retainer of the tragic hero MINAMOTO NO YOSHITSUNE. Although a historical figure named Benkei is briefly mentioned in the AZUMA KAGAMI (ca 1266–1301; Mirror of Eastern Japan), the only detailed accounts of his life, from such late sources as the 15th-century romance GIKEIKI (tr *Yoshitsune,* 1966), are clearly apocryphal. According to these, Benkei was a man of extraordinary cunning, strength, and martial skill who so admired the young Yoshitsune that he became his retainer for life. Benkei accompanied Yoshitsune through all the campaigns of the TAIRA–MINAMOTO WAR (1180–85). After the war, the future shōgun MINAMOTO NO YORITOMO turned against his younger brother Yoshitsune, who fled with the faithful Benkei. When Yoshitsune was finally surrounded by his enemies, it was Benkei, fighting alone to the death, who bought the time that allowed Yoshitsune to commit an honorable suicide. Benkei's loyalty and courage are depicted in several Nō and *kabuki* plays, the most famous of which is the kabuki drama *Kanjinchō* (1840; tr *The Subscription List,* 1966). *Barbara L. ARNN*

Bentenjima

Island in the southern part of Lake Hamana, southwestern Shizuoka Prefecture, central Honshū. During the Edo period (1600–1868) a shrine was dedicated here to Benten (Benzaiten, goddess of good fortune). National roads and railways were introduced during the Meiji period (1868–1912). As the result of extensive land reclamation, Bentenjima is now composed of seven islands. A hot spring has been developed, and the area is popular for fishing, shellfish digging, and swimming.

Benzaiten → tembu

Beppu

City in central Ōita Prefecture, Kyūshū, on Beppu Bay. Beppu has long been famous for its hot springs—some 3,000—which together release 68,000 liters of water per minute. To accommodate its visitors (approximately 12 million annually), Beppu affords many hotels, Japanese-style inns, restaurants, and recreational facilities. Nearby are the scenic lake Shidakako and the Kijima Plateau, both easily accessible by the Yamanami Highway. There is an Institute of Balneotherapeutics, run by Kyūshū University, and a Geophysical Research Station, operated by Kyōto University. Beppu is also noted for its bamboo handicrafts. Pop: 136,488.

Beppu Bay

(Beppu Wan). Inlet of the southwestern part of the Inland Sea between the Kunisaki and Saganoseki peninsulas, central Ōita Prefecture, Kyūshū. Connected with the Pacific Ocean through the Bungo Channel. The port of Beppu is a major center of maritime transportation. Marine catches here include sardines and prawns. An industrial area is located on the southern coast of the bay. Also near the bay is Beppu Hot Spring. Area: approximately 230 sq km (88.8 sq mi).

Berry, John Cutting (1847–1936)

American medical missionary and educator in Japan from 1872 to 1893. Son of a Maine sea captain, Berry graduated from Jefferson Medical College in Philadelphia in 1871. In 1872 he accepted an appointment from the Protestant American Board of Commissioners for Foreign Missions as its first medical missionary to Kōbe and he became director of the Hyōgo Prefectural Hospital the following year. Moving to Okayama in 1879, he headed its new prefectural hospital until 1885, when he became first director of Dōshisha University's Medical School Hospital in Kyōto, adding later the first nurses' training school. Berry was also an advocate of prison reform; his influence on ŌKUBO TOSHIMICHI, the government leader, and on early penal reformers such as Tomeoka Kōsuke (1864–1934) led to major improvements in the legal and physical treatment of the imprisoned.

Upon returning to the United States, Berry became a private practitioner. Ōkubo's son Toshitake published a biography of Berry (Nihon ni okeru Berī Ō) in 1929. In 1940 Berry's daughter Katherine published A Pioneer Doctor in Old Japan, a personalized account of foreign life in early Meiji Japan. Dallas FINN

Bertin, Louis-Emile (1840–1924)

French naval engineer and architect who contributed to the development of the Japanese navy. Bertin was educated at the Paris École Polytechnique and quickly won international recognition as a naval architect. Hired by the Japanese government as a special adviser, he spent the years from 1886 to 1890 in Japan training engineers and naval architects, designing warships, and supervising the construction of warships and naval facilities. On his return to France, he served in a number of important posts in naval architecture and construction.

■ ——Takahashi Kunitarō, Gunji, vol 6 of Oyatoi gaikokujin (Kajima Shuppan Kai, 1968). Mark D. ERICSON

Besshi Copper Mine labor disputes

(Besshi Dōzan sōgi). Strikes in 1907 and 1925–26 at the Sumitomo Company's Besshi Copper Mine in Ehime Prefecture. The first strike took place in June 1907, when a miners' representative was fired after demanding higher wages and improved working conditions. When riots broke out, the army was called in to restore order. The company rehired all but 96 of the some 1,000 strikers, but 30 of the leaders were convicted on criminal charges. The second dispute lasted from December 1925 to February 1926. It began as a strike by the local branch of the SŌDŌMEI (Japan Federation of Labor), whose complaints about unjust firings and poor treatment of injured workers had been rejected. When the company fired 172 strikers, they sabotaged the mine's generating plant, and Sōdōmei members attacked the Sumitomo family residence in Ōsaka. The strike ended in failure when the prefectural governor stepped in as arbitrator and ordered the dismissal of the ringleaders with only token severance pay. TANAKA Akira

Betsugen Enshi (1294–1364)

One of a very few Sōtō Zen monks who are important figures in the history of GOZAN LITERATURE (Chinese learning as cultivated in the medieval Japanese Zen monasteries). Born in Echizen Province (now part of Fukui Prefecture), Betsugen studied in China from 1320 to 1329, returning in the same group as SESSON YŪBAI. His tastes in Chinese poetry were more "modern" than Sesson's, and his subject matter was predominantly secular. A pious monk, he also distinguished himself as a preacher. His poems are collected in two anthologies: those written in China, in the Nan'yūshū; and those written after his return, in the Tōkishū. Marian URY

Bibai

City in west central Hokkaidō, on the Ishikari Plain. Bibai began in 1891 as a government-sponsored settlement. At one time it was a flourishing coal-mining center, but now most of the mines are closed. Beds, plastic goods, briquettes, and chemicals are produced. It is also a rice market center. Pop: 38,554.

Bible, translations of

The Bible was introduced to the Japanese people in 1549 when Francis XAVIER arrived at Kagoshima. Xavier brought with him a manuscript of a Japanese version of the Gospel according to Matthew, which he had translated in Goa, India, with the help of a Japanese convert named Yajirō. During the ensuing years several attempts to translate the Bible were made by Jesuit missionaries like Juan Fernandez (1526–68) and Manoel Barreto (1562?–1620). There is also a reliable account that the entire New Testament was translated and published in Kyōto before 1612, when the Tokugawa shogunate issued the decree banning Christianity (see ANTI-CHRISTIAN EDICTS). However, no copy of any of these early translations is known to exist.

The oldest extant Japanese version of any portion of the Bible is the work of a Prussian missionary, Karl F. A. Gützlaff (1803–51). His translations of the Gospel according to John and the Epistles of John were published in Singapore in 1837, but not a single copy reached Japan until 1859. Bernard J. Bettelheim (1811–70), a British medical missionary to Okinawa from 1846 to 1854, translated several books of the New Testament (Luke, John, Acts, Romans), which were published in Hong Kong in 1855.

The first Protestant missionaries arrived in mainland Japan in 1859; between 1861 and 1872 translations of various portions of the Bible appeared as the result of individual efforts. The first partial translation by a Japanese appeared in 1872. Between 1874 and 1880, a committee representing six Protestant denominations, headed by Presbyterian missionary James Curtis HEPBURN, translated the entire New Testament. Hepburn also served as chairman of the Old Testament translation committee, which completed its work in 1888, thus making the whole Bible available in Japanese. Both committees included Japanese as well as Western translators.

This so-called Meiji version, though it was regarded as a masterpiece of translated literature and inspired many Japanese, Christian and non-Christian alike, became obsolete by the end of the Meiji period (1868–1912). This was particularly the case with the New Testament, because of the rapid development of biblical scholarship. Between 1910 and 1917 a committee produced a revised version of the New Testament which, with the 1888 edition of the Old Testament, became and remained the standard Bible for nearly half a century.

On the Roman Catholic side, translations of portions of the gospels were published in the 1890s by Michael Steichen and Noël Péri.

Emile Raguet (1852–1929) published his translation of the New Testament based on the Latin Vulgate in 1910. Done in collaboration with three Japanese, this translation was considered greatly refined and became the standard Catholic version. The Holy Orthodox church had published a translation of the New Testament in 1901. Meanwhile, a number of Japanese biblical scholars published individual translations. All were partial except for a translation of the New Testament by Nagai Naoji (1864–1945), the first edition of which was published in 1928.

After World War II, changes in the Japanese language led to an urgent need for a Bible in the colloquial language. (All previous versions had been in classical Japanese.) A new translation was produced by the Japan Bible Society in the four years between 1951 and 1955. It was entirely the work of a Japanese team of six led by Tsuru Senji and was based on the original language editions of the Bible. It is now used officially by most of the Protestant churches.

Catholic translators were no less keen on the need for new versions. In 1953 the first edition of Federico Barbaro's New Testament in colloquial Japanese appeared, and in 1964 he completed the entire translation, which was revised twice by 1975. Since 1958 Studium Biblicum Franciscanum in Tōkyō has been publishing a series of colloquial Bible translations which are unique among the Catholic versions in that they are based on critical editions of original texts rather than on the Latin Vulgate.

In 1966 a new era in Bible translation began when a joint Catholic-Protestant version was conceived. The Japanese Common Bible Translation project started officially in 1970 and after eight years of planning, organizing, translating, and editing, involving no fewer than 100 persons, the New Testament was published in September 1978. See also CHRISTIANITY.

■■——Ebisawa Arimichi, *Nihon no seisho—Seisho wayaku no rekishi* (1964). Nihon Seisho Kyōkai, ed, *Nihon seisho kyōkai hyakunen shi* (1975). United Bible Societies, ed, *The Book of a Thousand Tongues* (rev ed, 1972). Shimmi Hiroshi

bibliography

(shoshigaku). Modern academic discipline devoted to the scientific study of books. Although the word *shoshigaku* itself—a direct translation of the Greek-derived English word "bibliography"—is of comparatively recent origin, the foundations of modern bibliographic studies in Japan were laid around 1800. *Shoshigaku* defies exact definition; some regard its major concern to be the study of external characteristics of books, while others argue that it properly involves the study of books in all their aspects. The discipline as it has evolved and developed over the past two centuries has come to include a wide range of activities. In the past it has emphasized three major areas: historical bibliography, the study of manuscripts predating 1600 and printed books published before 1640; textual bibliography, the analysis of external and internal characteristics of extant works and a study of the transmission of their various texts; and descriptive bibliography, which applies the findings of the first two areas in the compilation of indices, annotated catalogs, and other reference guides. As a rule, the major concern of *shoshigaku* is works by Japanese authors from the inception of written literature, but foreign works, mainly Chinese, that were copied, published, and otherwise transmitted by the Japanese have occasionally been the object of study.

Origin and Transmission of Books—— Although it is impossible to pinpoint the date when books were first produced by the Japanese, it is almost certain they were being written in the 6th century. The earliest of these are no longer extant and are known only through their citation in later writings; they include the TEIKI, records of the imperial clan, and the KYŪJI, collections of myths, legends, and folk songs. Many of the earliest books were of a religious nature or content. Most famous is the *Hokekyō gisho,* an exegesis of the Lotus Sutra, one of three commentaries generally attributed to Prince SHŌTOKU (574–622) and recorded to have been composed during the years 611–615. A manuscript in the possession of the temple HŌRYŪJI in Nara is widely believed to be the autograph original, in Shōtoku's own hand. If this is true, it would be the oldest extant Japanese book. An awakening national consciousness in the 7th century also led to the compilation of a number of historical works, including the TENNŌKI AND KOKKI (Record of the Emperors and Record of the Nation) in 620. These were followed in the latter part of the century by several national legal codes: the ŌMI CODE (668), ASUKA KIYOMIHARA CODE (689), and TAIHŌ CODE (701).

It was not until the 8th century, however, that writing became widespread and several important literary and historical works were produced. The KOJIKI, compiled in 712, and the NIHON SHOKI, in 720, were followed in rapid succession by the various court-ordered provincial gazetteers known as FUDOKI; poetry anthologies, including the monumental MAN'YŌSHŪ; and a variety of other books, including the first devoted to poetic theory. During the same period, the copying of Buddhist scripture was undertaken on a vast, organized scale as a function of the state, centering about the Shakyōjo, a government agency devoted to that purpose, and was later taken over by the scriptoria of the major Nara temples. In addition to religious texts, the government also took charge of copying Chinese classical texts carried back to Japan by official missions and scholar-monks.

Literary activity further intensified in the 9th century with the spread of Chinese learning. Among the many works produced were some of truly monumental proportions: the SHINSEN SHŌJIROKU (815) in 30 books or scrolls, a genealogical record of clans residing in the provinces surrounding the capital; the *Tenrei banshō meigi* (830) in 30 books, the oldest extant dictionary produced by Japanese; the *Hifuryaku* (831), an encyclopedic compendium of ancient wisdom in 1,000 books; and the RUIJŪ KOKUSHI (892), a classified national history in 205 books.

During the first few centuries, all books were written entirely in Chinese characters, but various techniques were devised quite early to incorporate Japanese vocabulary and linguistic features into Chinese, and to adapt the Chinese script to record Japanese. Such experimentation finally led to the development of two systems of KANA, syllabic scripts derived from the abbreviation of Chinese characters which made possible a complete phonetic transcription of the Japanese language. The appearance of *kana* in the early 10th century set off a native literary outburst which increased in scope and variety with the years.

As books increased in numbers, attempts were made to preserve them. Under the RITSURYŌ SYSTEM of government, their collection and preservation was the responsibility of a government bureau called the ZUSHORYŌ (Bureau of Books), but the court and major temples were also independently involved. During the Heian period (794–1185), major clans maintained schools for their young men that doubled as library centers. Members of the nobility and leading scholars like SUGAWARA NO MICHIZANE (845–903) and ŌE NO MASAFUSA (1041–1111) were avid bibliophiles with rich collections.

Many temples constructed during the Kamakura period (1185–1333) contained libraries within their compounds, and even some members of the military aristocracy, the leading patrons of the newly risen Kamakura Buddhist sects, possessed their own libraries, the most famous being the KANAZAWA BUNKO (Kanazawa Library) founded by Hōjō (Kanazawa) Sanetoki (1224–76) in 1275. During the Muromachi period (1333–1568) it was largely scholarly members of the courtly class who collected Japanese books, while during the same period the ASHIKAGA GAKKŌ (Ashikaga School), an important center of Chinese learning, amassed a considerable collection of continental works.

First and foremost in collecting books during the Edo period (1600–1868) was the first shōgun, TOKUGAWA IEYASU (1543–1616), who in 1602 established a library, later known as the Momijiyama Bunko, within the precincts of Edo Castle. Following Ieyasu's lead, the three major Tokugawa branch families vied with each other in establishing libraries and promoting the collection of reliable manuscripts. Other *daimyō,* too, were enthusiastic collectors, the most famous being the Maeda family, whose SONKEIKAKU LIBRARY surpassed all others in quality as well as quantity. Many scholars also possessed collections of as many as 50,000 books.

Despite all these efforts, the vicissitudes of time and the ravages of man and nature took their toll, and many books were lost forever. Nevertheless, a survey of all important public and private libraries conducted in this century revealed the existence of the considerable figure of 500,000 books written or edited by Japanese prior to the year 1867. It is this mass of material which is the chief concern of *shoshigaku.*

Form and Characteristics of Japanese Books—— The books which predate 1867 may be broadly divided into two groups: manuscripts and printed editions. Printed books are further subdivided according to whether they were reproduced by block or movable type. Although printing began around the year 1000, for nearly five centuries it was largely restricted to Buddhist scripture and Chinese works, and the great majority of native works are known only through their laboriously copied manuscripts.

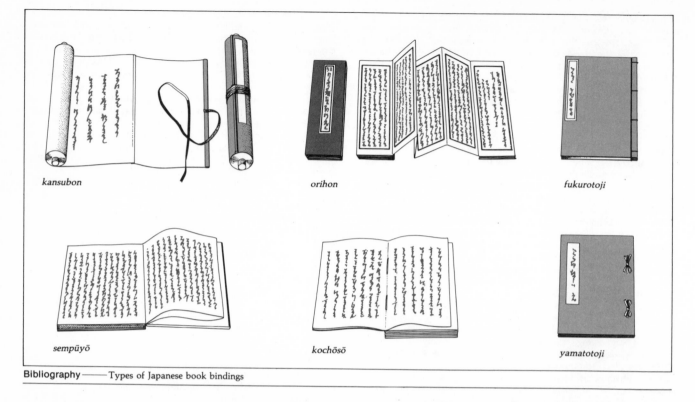

kansubon

orihon

fukurotoji

sempūyō

kochōsō

yamatotoji

Bibliography——Types of Japanese book bindings

Manuscripts. Manuscripts are of two types: autograph originals and copies. With the exception of various historical documents, diaries, and a few specimens of poetry, the great bulk of Japanese historical and literary writings is known only through often imperfect and untrustworthy copies, which may deviate greatly from the original. Of numerous manuscripts of the *Kojiki,* for example, the oldest was produced around 1371, while the earliest known manuscripts of many Heian-period works of literature date from the much later Muromachi period. All copies suffer to some degree in the process of transmission, and the further removed in time, the less accurate and trustworthy they are likely to be. The earlier manuscripts are naturally the most prized, though many of them are not without serious defects.

The early Japanese regarded certain books with special respect—scripture, legal codes, national histories, and imperial poetry anthologies, for example—and there was almost always a conscious effort exerted to reproduce faithfully the exemplar text. In some cases a copyist would go so far as to preserve the exact format of the earlier text, including the number of characters per line and the number of lines per page, or even to imitate its calligraphic style. However scrupulous a copyist might be, errors were unavoidable. In addition to simple slips and unconscious mistakes, there were numerous occasions when a copyist would create totally new passages because he could not recognize or read certain characters, or when damage to the exemplar rendered it illegible, leading the copyist to apply his own judgment and create lines which would lend context to obscure passages. In the case of other, ordinary books, including literary texts, much depended upon the copyist's attitude toward the work and his appraisal of its merits or value; the copyist might extract what he felt to be the most relevant or important passages, abbreviate or interpolate, or even rewrite certain portions.

The result is that numerous variants of a single title may exist, especially in the case of literary works. It is customary to distinguish the various texts of a work. They may be known by the name of the copyist or collator; by the geographical area, institution or reign in which the manuscript was transmitted or copied; by the style of language or script; or even by the type of paper or binding used.

Printed books. The oldest extant specimens of printed matter in Japan, and indeed, in the world, are the remains of the *Hyakumantō darani* (mantras of the million stupas), small pieces of paper printed with *dhāraṇī,* or Buddhist spells, which were placed in small stupas, or reliquaries, and distributed to major temples in or around Nara in 770. Buddhism has always regarded the copying of scripture as a meritorious act, and because it was one which provided an outlet for

the artistic as well as religious aspirations of the literate Heian nobility, copying took the place of printing when it stopped for more than two centuries. Buddhist scripture was not reproduced in print again until 1009, when a thousand copies of the Lotus Sutra were printed from wooden plates by imperial order, after which time the publications of scripture became an important undertaking of major temples.

Buddhist printing activity first took place at the major religious establishments of Kyōto, but a century later had spread to Nara, and from the 13th century major temples throughout the region centering about the capital became increasingly involved in the publication of religious texts. It is customary to distinguish various editions by the name of the temple or area in which they were printed. Foremost among the early editions were those printed by the KŌFUKUJI of Nara, a wealthy temple affiliated with the FUJIWARA FAMILY. Known as Kasuga editions *(kasugaban)* after the Fujiwara shrine (KASUGA SHRINE) of the same name, they boast a long tradition of superior printing quality. Following these are the Kōya editions, printed on Kōyasan, headquarters of the Shingon sect, and Eizan editions, printed at the center of the Tendai sect on Hieizan.

From the late 13th through the late 15th centuries, the great Zen monasteries of Kamakura and especially Kyōto were the most actively involved in the printing of books; their publications are known as GOZAN editions, Gozan being an old name for the most important Zen temples of the two cities. The earliest Gozan editions were Zen texts, in particular, collections of the aphorisms of the patriarchs, but later publications included poetry anthologies and Chinese classics, for the Zen clergy were the very conscientious educators of the military aristocracy.

The near monopoly of printing by the great Nara and Kyōto temples gradually weakened after the Ōnin War (1467–77), and *chihōban,* or "local editions," appeared in various areas of the country. *Chihōban* included for the first time Japanese works, among them texts for use at TERAKOYA, or temple schools, and dictionaries and primers for poetry composition.

Printing entered a new phase around 1590 when the techniques of movable type were introduced from two different sources almost simultaneously. Western techniques were brought by the Jesuit mission and those of the continent arrived via Korea. The influence of the Jesuits was short-lived and limited to the immediate vicinity of Nagasaki, producing a total of only about 30 titles before Christianity was proscribed by the government. Continental methods, however, greatly transformed the Japanese printing world: centered in Kyōto, movable type printing flourished until 1640. So important are the products of this early period that they are singled out for special study and are distinguished from later publications as *ko katsuji-bon*, or "old movable-type books." Besides the usual Buddhist works, Japanese books, including literary classics printed for the first time with *kana* script, number over 300 titles.

With the powerful encouragement and support of the shōgun Tokugawa Ieyasu, printing with movable type developed at a tremendous pace, and ordinary townsmen began to publish native works. The most outstanding productions of this period, and truly unrivaled in the entire history of Japanese printing, were classical literary editions published in the Saga area of Kyōto by HON'AMI KŌETSU (1558–1637) with the generous material support of the prosperous merchant Suminokura Soan (1571–1632). Not only did Kōetsu insist that binding and paper be as near perfection as possible, he chose for reproduction the most reliable texts available, and even copied in his own excellent hand the text to be transferred to type. Named variously after Kōetsu, his wealthy patron, or Saga, where they were produced, these magnificent editions are as much works of art as printed books. They created a heightened interest in native literature and indirectly stimulated the development of a new literature of the Edo period. Kōetsu also introduced *hiragana*, the cursive syllabic script, to the printed page, and a single piece of type might be carved with two, three, or four linked units to accommodate this more elegant style of calligraphy.

By the mid-17th century printing had become a recognized occupation, providing a livelihood to men who sought to meet the reading public's demand for the new literature of the city. The center of the publishing world remained Kyōto until around 1700, but then shifted to Ōsaka and Edo (now Tōkyō). Both the volume and scope of printed books increased through the end of the Edo period, but printing technology advanced very little until the introduction of metal movable type after the Meiji Restoration. Printers were unable to publish more than a very limited edition using the primitive wooden type known to them, and most popular books were printed with blocks.

External Characteristics of Extant Manuscripts and Printed Books——Many pre-Edo period books are not dated and do not provide the name of the original author or of the copyist; great variation may occur among different texts bearing the same title. The first stage in the examination of a given work is thus the analysis of its physical characteristics, including binding, paper, literary and calligraphic styles. Any of these may provide important clues toward an eventual dating of the work, for different styles and techniques appeared or were favored during different periods of history.

Bindings. The earliest Japanese books, including all written before the 9th century, were scrolls *(kansubon)*, created by pasting numerous sheets of paper edge to edge with a slight overlap to form a long strip. The weight of tradition, suitability for easy storage and preservation, and sometimes aesthetic considerations assured the continued survival of scrolls, but in many respects they were impractical and cumbersome, for a reader was obliged to unroll and roll simultaneously. The invention of *orihon* ("folding books") was the first attempt to provide greater convenience. A development from the scroll, instead of being rolled, it was folded accordion-style, and heavy paper was attached to the front and back surfaces to form covers. *Orihon* remained the preferred binding for particular works—Buddhist scripture, for example, because of certain conventions of recitation—yet actually they offered little improvement over scrolls. If not held carefully, the center portion had a tendency to fly out and the books soon fell apart.

It was discovered that some problems could be corrected by sealing one side of the "accordion," i.e., by applying a coat of paste to one edge of the closed *orihon*, and then covering front, back, and the newly created spine with another sheet of paper. This type of binding, called *sempuyō*, appeared in the 11th century. Although a decided improvement over earlier bindings, *sempuyō* could not hold up through numerous readings, and the paste which was used to create the spine was susceptible to the high humidity of the Japanese summer.

Scrolls, *orihon*, and *sempuyō* all were created by first joining the written or printed sheets of paper into a single length, but in the 12th century three new types of bindings appeared that more closely resembled the familiar codex of the West. For the first of these, each written or printed sheet was folded "butterfly-style" *(kochōsō)*, with text facing inward. These "butterflies" were then joined together in proper sequence by strips of paste applied to both sides of the fold to a depth of approximately five millimeters (about 0.2 in) inward.

Although much stronger and more durable than the earlier *sempuyō*, their greatest drawback was that two blank sheets followed each two pages of text. This problem was eliminated with another of the new bindings, made possible by heavier paper, which permitted writing or printing on both surfaces. Several sheets of paper were folded together in half to form a signature, and then several signatures were gathered together and bound at the folded edges with thread, similar to the type of binding most common for cloth books today. The third and simplest style of binding *(yamatotōji)* was probably devised by individuals who desired to keep their own poetry compositions or other jottings together for convenience. Each sheet of paper was folded in half, writing surface facing out. The folded sheets were stacked, four holes made in the right-hand margin, and the sheets tied together in two places with string, often fashioned from paper, to make a simple book with double leaves.

All of these bindings were largely supplanted by another, called *fukurotoji*, which was introduced from China and came into wide use during the 14th century. It was similar to the simple, tied bindings of the earlier two centuries, but much stronger, for four holes were made at equidistant lengths at the inner margin, and the sheets were bound together tightly with thread. Although the inner surfaces of the double leaves went unused, *fukurotoji* made possible the use of very thin paper.

Paper. Paper has always been the chief writing material of the Japanese. The varieties produced in the country are nearly countless, but three basic types, differentiated by the raw materials that go into their manufacture, have generally been used for books: *mashi*, *choshi*, and *hishi*. Which of the three was utilized was determined to some extent by the historical period, social class of the user, and purpose. *Mashi* was mainly used for religious and special books during the Nara period (710–794), but as more and more books came to be written, it was replaced by *choshi*. Although *choshi*, being quite coarsely textured, is inferior as a writing material, it is made from a common plant, so that raw material for its manufacture was always readily available. Most manuscripts of the Heian period through the Kamakura and Muromachi periods were written on *choshi*. *Hishi*, which replaced *mashi*, was widely regarded as the writing material par excellence by the Heian nobility, who used it for their tales and poetry collections. It was a finely textured paper, durable yet pliant, with a soft luster that appealed to their refined aesthetic sensibilities. Production of the raw material for *hishi* increased in the Kamakura period, and from that time it was widely used for manuscripts and printed books.

Scripts and writing styles. Manuscripts may be divided into three groups in terms of scripts employed: those written entirely in Chinese characters, those written largely or entirely in *kana*, and those which employed a mixed style of Chinese characters and *kana*. Because there are two systems of *kana*—*hiragana* and *katakana*—the second and third categories can be further subdivided.

Kana did not come into general use until the beginning of the 10th century, and all of the earliest books were written entirely in Chinese characters. Even with the development of *kana*, it remained customary up until the 17th century to write certain categories of books—those related to law or religion, for example—entirely in Chinese characters. The poetry anthologies, tales, and literary pieces of the cultivated aristocracy were generally written with *hiragana*, the more cursive and elegant of the two scripts. *Katakana*, on the other hand, was originally devised for textual glosses; books which contain a mixture of *katakana* and Chinese characters often reflect the origins of the script.

The Chinese characters used may be standard forms, nonstandard variants, or abbreviated forms. *Hiragana* was originally a much more prolix system than the simplified and standardized one known today, and it contained a variety of possible forms for writing a single syllable. Likewise, *katakana* varied according to the age in which a book was written.

Internal Characteristics of Manuscripts and Printed Books

It is standard practice to classify manuscripts according to their comparison with the ideal original: they range from mere fragments to, in a few cases, complete texts. To say a text is complete, however, does not imply that it is an altogether legitimate offspring of the original ancestor, for it may well be a contaminated text. Thus the bibliographer must ultimately undertake textual analysis and criticism of the various texts of a given work, historically order them, and define their relationships. Only then might it be possible to recover the shape and character of the original, determine its authorship, the age in which it was written, and the method of transmission.

The first groundwork in the area of modern textual bibliography was laid in the latter half of the 17th century by the Buddhist monk KEICHŪ (1640–1701), and continued through the middle of the 19th century at the hands of renowned scholars like KADA NO AZUMAMARO (1669–1736), KAMO NO MABUCHI (1697–1769), MOTOORI NORINAGA (1730–1801), HANAWA HOKIICHI (1746–1821), Kariya Ekisai (1775–1835), KONDŌ JŪZŌ (1771–1829), and YASHIRO HIROKATA (1758–1841). Enormous strides were taken during the first two centuries, but textual criticism suffered a slight setback following the Meiji Restoration when Western influences flooded into Japan, temporarily sweeping aside everything that seemed of the past. In the 1880s the Western, especially English, science of bibliography was introduced to the Japanese scholarly world, but, with its emphasis on printed books and incunabula, seemingly little was relevant to the Japanese situation, where manuscripts commanded an overwhelming numerical superiority, and its influence was felt only in the more practical area of library science.

Interest in the Japanese classics was revived in the early part of this century when a group of scholars at Tōkyō University came under the influence of the German science of philology and established a new discipline which they called *bunkengaku* (study of literary texts). In many respects *bunkengaku* was simply a revival of the textual-criticism approach of the late Tokugawa pioneers, systematized and fortified with theory and methodological discipline. Today *shoshigaku* and *bunkengaku* exist side by side; while there is some difference in emphasis and approach, their basic concern is much the same. The most important thing is that textual criticism has been most actively pursued by the followers of the newer discipline.

Thanks to the efforts of the Edo period and the continuing labors of leading scholars of this century, a number of important literary texts, including the *Tosa nikki* (see KI NO TSURAYUKI) and the SARASHINA NIKKI, have been restored. Collated editions of all of the masterpieces of Japanese literature—the *Man'yōshū* and the TALE OF GENJI *(Genji monogatari)*, to cite only two examples—are now available to the modern reader, and preparation of texts for numerous other less-known works progresses steadily. The greatest achievements of modern textual criticism have been in literature; much less has been accomplished in the area of history, where a traditional emphasis on primary sources has diverted most scholarly attention to diplomatics and similar historical records. One exception was the work of the modern historian KUROITA KATSUMI (1874–1946), who prepared collated texts of the most basic and important historical writings of the pre-Meiji period.

Descriptive Bibliography —— Although the emergence of modern, scientific bibliographic studies with emphasis on textual criticism was comparatively recent, enumerative and descriptive lists of books appeared as early as the Nara period. Unfortunately, most of the earliest of those have been lost, including the *Gunseki yōran*, an enormous annotated catalog compiled during the Heian period. Most valuable of the extant Heian catalogs is the *Nihonkoku genzaisho mokuroku* (ca 890), a complete listing of Chinese texts available in Japan at the time of its compilation.

Specialized catalogs appeared in the Kamakura period, including the *Honchō kokushi mokuroku*, a list of Japanese historical works, and the *Waka genzaisho mokuroku*, a list of Japanese poetical works. Most important of the enumerative lists of the period is the HONCHŌ SHOJAKU MOKUROKU, the oldest extant catalog of native Japanese books, which classifies 493 works according to genre.

Bibliographic cataloging increased during the Edo period, when lists appeared in rapid succession. In addition to general catalogs divided by subject or alphabetically, some were devoted to works dealing with a single title such as the *Man'yōshū* or *Nihon shoki*. Many of the Edo catalogs were annotated, beginning with the *Nihon shojaku kō* of HAYASHI GAHŌ (1618–80) of 1667, a listing of native works with a brief description of each. Some of the annotated catalogs were devoted to historical, geographical, or literary works, others to all books without distinction. One which deserves special mention is the *Gunsho ichiran*, a classified catalog of 1,729 major Japanese books compiled by Ozaki Masayoshi (1755–1827), which describes each selection in detail. First published in 1802, it was reprinted numerous times during the 19th century.

Early during the revival of bibliographic activity at the beginning of the 20th century, another important guide to Japanese books appeared, the *Kokusho kaidai* of Samura Hachirō (1865–1915). An annotated catalog of 15,000 titles selected from the collection of the Imperial Library in Ueno, Tōkyō, it was later supplemented in 1904 by an additional 10,000 titles. For many years following the publication of *Kokusho kaidai*, it and the earlier *Gunsho ichiran* were the most frequently consulted of the numerous existing catalogs, yet neither was altogether satisfactory. *Ichiran* contains only a limited number of entries, while *Kaidai* suffers from omissions and occasionally incomplete information.

In 1939 the publisher IWANAMI SHIGEO (1881–1946) initiated the project of editing and publishing a more accurate and inclusive catalog of Japanese books dating from earliest times to 1867. With the cooperation and assistance of the country's leading scholars, the project commenced with a nationwide "census" of books, an investigation which revealed the existence of more than a half million books and forced alteration of the original plans. It was decided to prepare an all-inclusive catalog, the *Kokusho sōmokuroku*, and provide only the most basic information about each entry. The project was published in 9 volumes, 1963–76. Now anyone investigating a certain title has the following information readily available: author or editor where known, length (number of *kan* or volumes), date of completion, and a list and brief description of the various manuscripts or printed editions and where they can be found.

Only a few years after the Iwanami project was completed, another enormous bibliography, the *Gunsho kaidai,* was published in 30 volumes, 1962–67. The *Gunsho kaidai* lists and describes in detail all of the more than 3,000 works contained in the monumental *Gunsho ruijū*, a classified collection of Japanese classics compiled during the late 18th and early 19th centuries by Hanawa Hokiichi and his son. In addition to the two giants of modern descriptive bibliography, specialized catalogs and indices have appeared, covering nearly all categories of books and all branches of learning. See also HISTORIOGRAPHY; LIBRARIES; PRINTING, PREMODERN; WASHI.
◼︎——David Chibbett, *The History of Japanese Printing and Book Illustration* (1977). Kawase Kazuma, *Ko katsujiban no kenkyū* (1937). Kawase Kazuma, *Nihon shoshigaku no kenkyū* (1971). Nagasawa Kikuya, *Shoshigaku josetsu* (1960). Uematsu Yasushi, *Hompō shoshigaku gaiyō* (1929). Wada Tsunashiro, *Hōsho yoroku* (1918). Wada Mankichi, *Nihon shoshigaku gaisetsu* (1944). Yamagishi Tokuhei, *Shoshigaku josetsu* (1977).   *Noburu* HIRAGA

Bigelow, William Sturgis (1850–1926)

American physician, devoted student of Japanese culture, and discerning early collector of Japanese art along with his friends Edward S. MORSE and Ernest F. FENOLLOSA. Born to a family of prominent Boston physicians, he graduated from Harvard College (1871) and Harvard Medical School (1874). He studied bacteriology in Vienna and Strassburg, and under Louis Pasteur in Paris. Already attracted to Japanese art, in Paris he began collecting Japanese prints. He later gave up medicine completely and in 1882 left Boston to accompany Morse on the latter's third trip to Japan.

Guided by the more experienced Morse and Fenollosa, Bigelow settled happily into a six–year residence in Tōkyō and Nikkō, traveling widely, collecting art, and studying Buddhism. Unlike those who applauded Japan's quick Westernization, Bigelow and his friends encouraged the Japanese to retain their spiritual and artistic traditions, contending that the West had much to learn from the East. While in Japan Bigelow gave financial help to OKAKURA KAKUZŌ in setting up the JAPAN FINE ARTS ACADEMY (Nihon Bijutsuin) and contributed articles on Japanese art to the magazine KOKKA.

After returning to Boston, his enthusiasm and respect for things Japanese was an influence in artistic circles and in his upper-class milieu. His devotion to Buddhism was set forth in his lecture "Buddhism and Immortality," delivered in 1908 at Harvard University. Bigelow served the Boston Museum of Fine Arts as trustee until his death and donated more than 40,000 paintings, prints, and other art objects which, with the addition of the Morse and Fenollosa-Weld collections, made the museum the finest early repository of Japanese art in America.

Faithful even in death to his Japan-acquired convictions, Bigelow was buried in Buddhist robes (a fact concealed by the closed coffin at his proper Bostonian funeral); he was cremated and half his ashes were buried beside those of his friend and fellow convert, Ernest Fenollosa, at Hōmyōin, a subtemple of Miidera above Lake Biwa near Kyōto.   *Dallas* FINN

Bigot, Georges (1860–1927)

French illustrator and topical cartoonist. Born in Paris, he studied painting at the Ecole des Beaux-Arts. In 1883 he went to Japan, where he studied Japanese art and taught painting for a while at the Army Academy. He also worked as an illustrator for the Japanese newspapers YŪBIN HŌCHI SHIMBUN and *Kaishin shimbun* and started his own cartoon magazine, *Tobae* (1887–90), for his satirical caricatures on current events and Japanese politics, customs, and everyday life. While in Japan, he also illustrated a number of books and worked as a foreign correspondent for French newspapers during the SINO-JAPANESE WAR OF 1894–1895. He returned to France in 1899.

bimbōgami

A type of deity said to bring poverty; one of many bearers of good or bad fortune, like the *fukunokami* (deity of good luck) and the YAKUBYŌGAMI (deity of illness), who are traditionally believed to reside in the home. Deities of misfortune such as *bimbōgami* are exorcised in a rite called *kamiokuri* ("sending off the gods"). Belief in the *bimbōgami*, first mentioned in the literature of the Edo period (1600–1868), is a phenomenon of city life, spawned by the privations brought on by the newly developing money economy of the age. The *bimbōgami* is commonly portrayed as a thin, pale figure with a tattered fan. Figuratively, the term refers to a person who is constantly indigent and unlucky.   INOKUCHI Shōji

bingata → Okinawan textiles

biography and biographical fiction

(*denki bungaku*). This article deals with biographies, autobiographies, and semiautobiographical works written since the late 19th century. The autobiography (*jiden* or *jijoden*) in Japan is generally lacking in individuality of style, and takes second place to a related genre, the *watakushi shōsetsu* (autobiographical fiction or the I-NOVEL), in literary quality. Biographical writing is often characterized by didacticism, or a tendency toward fictionalizing.

Autobiographical Works—— The earliest modern example of autobiography by a Japanese is educator UCHIMURA KANZŌ's *How I Became a Christian* (1895; published in the United States the same year as *Diary of a Japanese Convert*). *How I Became a Christian*, which was originally written in English, was translated into Japanese was *Yo wa ika ni shite kirisuto shinto to narishi ka* (1935). It tells of the spiritual process leading to his decision to embrace Christianity. The work was also translated into German and several other languages.

Uchimura's autobiography was closely followed by *Fukuō jiden* (1898–99; tr *The Autobiography of Yukichi Fukuzawa*, 1960). FUKUZAWA YUKICHI (1835–1901) was the leading figure of the Westernizing enlightenment movement of the early part of the Meiji period (1868–1912). In a clear, lively, almost conversational style, Fukuzawa recounts his life and his ideas, vividly describing his rebellion against the empty formalism of feudal society, his decision to take up Western studies, and his subsequent struggle to establish himself in the world. The reader is given an intimate view of how this ambitious spirit living in the midst of change and turmoil became the intellectual leader who exerted such a powerful influence on the minds of his countrymen. The autobiography is also valuable as a record of the intellectual and social climate in a crucial period of Japanese history, the Meiji enlightenment.

The writer TOKUTOMI ROKA, active in the late Meiji period, published such autobiographical works as *Omoide no ki* (1900–1901; tr *Footprints in the Snow*, 1970), *Shinshun* (1918), and *Fuji* (1925–28). The first of these, which recounts his youthful ambition to become famous and restore his family honor, his exposure to political novels and the FREEDOM AND PEOPLE'S RIGHTS MOVEMENT (Jiyū Minken Undō), his growing concern with freedom, and his quest for personal fulfillment, can be seen as a description of the development of the modern Japanese intellectual.

The writer and social activist KINOSHITA NAOE left his memoirs in *Zange* (1906). Especially rich in detail on his formative years, it describes his emergence as an early proponent of democracy. The autobiography of economist KAWAKAMI HAJIME (*Jijoden*, 1947–48) covers the period from his birth through his imprisonment as a self-proclaimed "casualty of the class struggle" to his release in 1937. He weaves his account of gradual self-awareness, evolving class consciousness, and intellectual growth with descriptions of social conditions and individuals. The autobiographies of ŌSUGI SAKAE (*Jijoden*, 1920–23) and ARAHATA KANSON (*Kanson jiden*, 1975) are

valuable as accounts of both their spiritual odysseys and of the leftist movement in the 1920s and 1930s.

MIYAMOTO YURIKO, a representative writer of proletarian fiction, produced a series of autobiographical novels: *Nobuko* (1924–26), *Futatsu no niwa* (1947), and *Dōhyō* (1949–50). Although lacking in objectivity, the novels may be seen as declarations of the author's own passionate conviction that she must live life as she sees fit. *Watakushi no aruita michi* (1955), the autobiography of HIRATSUKA RAICHŌ, an early Japanese feminist leader, is one of the most important documents of the women's movement in Japan.

In the first decades of the 20th century, the novelists of the Japanese naturalist school produced numerous autobiographies in fictionalized form. SHIMAZAKI TŌSON's tales of youth, *Oitachi no ki* (1912), *Sakura no mi no jukusuru koro* (1914–18), and *Haru* (1908), all have strongly autobiographical elements. TOKUDA SHŪSEI, in writing his autobiographical novel *Hikari o oute* (1938), did not even bother to change the names of his characters, apart from those of his relatives. Other naturalist writers such as TAYAMA KATAI and MASAMUNE HAKUCHŌ also left their memoirs.

Waga kokoro no henreki (1957–59) was a notable autobiography by NAGAYO YOSHIRŌ, a writer of the SHIRAKABA SCHOOL. Critic Kamei Katsuichirō's *Waga seishin no henreki* (1948), written as an attempt at self-renewal after Japan's defeat in World War II, is a compelling record of the frustrations and rebirth of a Japanese intellectual in a period of tumult. *Aru kokoro no jijiden* (1948–49) is the autobiography of the liberal journalist HASEGAWA NYOZEKAN. Setting his narrative against a vivid portrayal of Meiji society, he writes candidly of how his mind and spirit were molded by the realities of life.

Biographical Works—— Among the most notable Japanese biographies are MORI ŌGAI's series on little-known historical figures. *Shibue Chūsai* (1916), his study of a doctor-scholar of the Edo period (1600–1868), set a standard for the historical biography as a literary genre and has come to be regarded as one of his finest works. With much the same approach Ōgai also wrote *Izawa Ranken* (1916–17) and *Hōjō Katei* (1917–20).

Perhaps the best-known literary biography is KOMIYA TOYOTAKA's almost reverential account of his mentor, *Natsume Sōseki* (1938). Tokutomi Roka's disciple Maedakō Hiroichirō completed his important biography of Roka 10 years after his master's death (*Rokaden*, 1938). More recently Roka became the subject of a three-volume biography by NAKANO YOSHIO (*Roka Tokutomi Kenjirō*, 1972–74). Based on meticulous research, Nakano attempts to probe Roka's inner life—his efforts to reconcile the conflicting demands of flesh and spirit, his sense of inferiority and antagonism toward his brother Soho, and his inconsistency in championing both socialism and ardent nationalism. Nakano's work, which in a larger sense is a history of modern Japan's triumph and tragedy, must be counted as one of the masterpieces of modern Japanese biography.

ASAI Kiyoshi

biology

Biological study in Japan has progressed rapidly since 1877, when it was added to the curriculum of Tōkyō University, and today ranks among the world's best. Primate research, in particular, has been attracting widespread attention.

It is often said that modern science came to Japan from Europe during the Meiji period (1868–1912). However, the way had been paved long before this by medical and premodern descriptive pharmacognostic studies brought to Japan from China in ancient times and by the European-style biology that was first introduced to Japan by scholars of the so-called Dutch Learning (see WESTERN LEARNING) in the Edo period (1600–1868).

Around the 6th century, early forms of medical science and traditional descriptive pharmacognosy (*honzōgaku*) arrived in Japan from China. During the 8th and 9th centuries, Japanese scholars wrote several texts on these subjects. Japanese writing on Chinese pharmacognosy reached its highest level during the Edo period, as exemplified by ONO RANZAN's *Honzō kōmoku keimō*. During the same period, scholars of Dutch Learning were studying 18th-century European biology. This and Chinese-style descriptive pharmacognosy and medicine paved the way for modern plant taxonomy and European-style medicine in Japan (see MEDICINE: history of medicine).

After the Meiji Restoration of 1868, Japanese scholars began a systematic introduction of European biology. The first professors of biology at Tōkyō University were Edward S. MORSE, an American professor of zoology, and YATABE RYŌKICHI, a Japanese professor of botany who had studied biology in Europe and the United States.

In the beginning Japanese students of modern biological studies went to study in England and the United States, but later, just as in the field of medicine, the number of students going to Germany to study increased, making Germany the focal point for biological studies in Japan. ISHIKAWA CHIYOMATSU, Morse's assistant at Tōkyō University, went to Germany and studied under the biologist August Weismann (1834–1914), after which he returned to Japan to teach.

Toward the end of the Meiji period, Japanese biological studies advanced from the mere imitation of Western studies to more original research, as in the field of plant taxonomy by researchers such as MAKINO TOMITARŌ. Original research in genetics also began early. In the West the science of genetics had quickly developed after the rediscovery of Mendel's Law in 1900. TOYAMA KAMETARŌ independently carried out genetics research in Japan and was the first to confirm Mendel's Law as applied to insects. Genetics research expanded quickly in Japan. While chromosome-related research also made advances, it never developed into molecular genetics. In the field of chromosome research, KIHARA HITOSHI's genome-analysis of wheat is well known.

The fields of physiology and biochemistry came into their own in Japan during the Taishō period (1912–26) and especially during the early part of the Shōwa period (1926–). Medical researchers were the most active in these fields. The physiologist Hashida Kunihiko (1882–1945) and the biochemist Kakiuchi Saburō (1882–1967) published journals in European languages and tried to organize circles of people interested in their fields. The moving force in Tōkyō University's biology department was SHIBATA KEITA, who had studied in Germany. Here physiological and biochemical research was carried out, the most notable being an investigation of the relation of enzymes to respiration.

World War II brought a decline in biological research. After the war, with new information again flowing in from the West, research resumed, especially in the field of molecular biology. In addition to research based on information and methods from abroad, original work was also taking place, especially in the field of behavioral research on primates. A study of Japanese MONKEYS (nihonzaru), conducted under the leadership of IMANISHI KINJI of Kyōto University, demonstrated the kind of social structure that existed among them.

Research in Japan in the various fields of biology ranks among the best in the world, but in terms of research funding and staffing, Japan lags behind countries like the United States. There have been two Japanese nominees for the Nobel Prize in biology: KATŌ GEN'I-CHI, for his research in nerve physiology, and YAMAGIWA KATSUSA-BURŌ, who succeeded in artificially producing cancer cells.

In addition to the Botanical Society of Japan and the Zoological Society of Japan, there are societies devoted to physiology, biochemistry, genetics, embryology, and bionomics.

——Nihon Kagakushi Gakkai, ed, Seibutsu kagaku in Nihon kagakushi taikei, vol 15 (1965). Ueno Masuzō, Nihon hakubutsu-gaku shi (1973). Ueno Masuzō, Nihon seibutsugaku no rekishi (1939). *Suzuki Zenji*

bird-and-flower painting

(kachōga). One of three broad categories of East Asian art, the other two being jimbutsuga (figure painting) and SANSUIGA (landscape painting). Flowers and birds were first treated as an independent subject for painting in China but did not appear in Japanese art until the Muromachi period (1333–1568), when Japanese Zen priest-painters rendered ink monochromes of bamboo and plum or reeds and geese modeled after Chinese scholar paintings of the Song (Sung; 960–1279) and Yuan (Yüan; 1279–1368) dynasties. In the 15th century, professional artists in Japan began to paint delicate birds and elegant flowers in the naturalistic polychrome style that had matured in the 12th-century Chinese Imperial Painting Academy.

Japanese artists of the late 15th and 16th centuries established kachōga repertoires that set the style throughout the Edo period (1600–1868). SESSHŪ TŌYŌ magnified bird-and-flower motifs and merged them into landscape backgrounds progressing seasonally across large-scale screens, while KANŌ MOTONOBU suffused prevailing Chinese styles with lyrical YAMATO-E techniques that resulted in kachōga of captivating sensual appeal. The central figures of late 16th-century architectural interiors were the paintings of vividly col-

ored flowers and birds set against brilliant gold leaf created by Motonobu's grandson KANŌ EITOKU.

Edo-period artists could choose from a variety of kachōga styles and techniques: on a large scale they painted blossoming plum trees and strutting canes in ink monochrome, or spreading pine branches and swooping hawks in strong color and gold; on a small scale they depicted garden flowers and songbirds in chromatic hues, or lotus ponds and waterfowl in splashes of ink wash. RIMPA school artists following Tawaraya SŌTATSU were especially noted for lyrical interpretations of seasonal flowering grasses (shiki sōka) and splendidly decorative floral conceptions containing allusions to Japanese classical literature.

In addition to flower-and-bird conventional motifs and their ornamental combinations, some artists began to study their objective reality. Shaseiga, realistic sketches from nature, were made by Kanō-school artists such as KANŌ TAN'YŪ and Rimpa artists such as Ogata KŌRIN, but were most closely associated with the activity of MARUYAMA ŌKYO in his process of synthesizing established decorative traditions and fresh observation of nature.

The chief subjects of kachōga are birds and flowering trees (kaboku), flowering plants (kaki), or flowering grasses (soka). Subcategories include fruits and vegetables (sōka), grasses and insects (sōchū), and seaweed and fish (sōgyo). Animal paintings (sōjūga) of such subjects as dragons, tigers, monkeys, and horses form a distinctive group and are often but not always considered an independent category. *Carolyn WHEELWRIGHT*

Bird, Isabella Lucy (1831–1904)

British traveler and writer whose many books on exotic and remote areas won wide popularity in the English-speaking world during the late 19th century. In 1878 she undertook, with one attendant, a 1,200-mile horseback trip through northern Honshū and into Hokkaidō, which she described in Unbeaten Tracks in Japan (1881; tr Nihon okuchi kikō, 1973). Bird gave an honest, graphic picture of early Meiji Japan. She preferred the flea-infested countryside to Tōkyō, which she considered an ugly mixture of East and West. Impressed by free, open Hokkaidō, she found her stay with the AINU a refreshing change from the uniformity and order of the new Japan, and showed sharp insight into Japan's dilemma in embracing the material side of Westernization without regard for spiritual considerations. *Dallas FINN*

birds → animals

Birōjima

Island in Shibushi Bay, off the eastern coast of Ōsumi Peninsula, Kagoshima Prefecture, Kyūshū. A long narrow island lying north to south with a maximum width of about 80 m (260 ft) and a high point of 83 m (272 ft). The island is part of the Nichinan Coast Quasi-National Park; it is covered with subtropical plants which are protected as Special Natural Monuments by the government. Fountain palm trees (birō) are especially plentiful. Area: 0.2 sq km (0.08 sq mi).

Bisai

City in northwestern Aichi Prefecture, central Honshū, on the east bank of the river Kisogawa. Bisai developed as a POST-STATION TOWN on the highway Mino Kaidō. In the Edo period (1600–1868) it produced cotton textiles, but from the middle of the Meiji period (1868–1912), it shifted to woolen textiles. Pop: 55,088.

bitasen

1. Debased copper coins, privately minted and widely circulated from the 16th century; their lead content was sometimes as much as one-half. Also called bita kinsen. The rate of exchange between bitasen and coins of better quality varied according to locality. As a daimyō, TOKUGAWA IEYASU in 1570 established in the Kantō region an exchange rate of one EIRAKUSEN (an imported Chinese coin) to four bitasen. In 1604, a year after coming to power as shōgun, he imposed this exchange rate throughout Japan as part of his attempt to regulate the national currency. See also ERIZENI.

2. Iron and brass coins produced in the 18th century by the Tokugawa shogunate. The standard copper coinages, known by the

Lake Biwa

View from Katata on the western shore showing the Great Bridge of Lake Biwa.

generic term Kan'ei *tsūhō* (coins of the Kan'ei era), were supplemented by the minting of iron coins in 1739 and brass coins in 1768, which were called *bitasen* because of their lesser intrinsic value.

Bitō Nishū (1745–1813)

Confucian scholar of the Edo period (1600–1868), also known as Bitō Jishū. Born in Iyo Province (now Ehime Prefecture). As a student of Katayama Hokkai (1723–90), he was at first associated with the Ancient Learning (KOGAKU) school of Confucianism, but, coming under the influence of Rai Shunsui (1746–1816) and Nakai Chikuzan (1730–1804), he later became a champion of the Zhu Xi (Chu Hsi) school of Neo-Confucianism (SHUSHIGAKU). When in 1790 the shogunate issued its Kansei Prohibition of Heterodoxy (Kansei Igaku no Kin), one of the KANSEI REFORMS, Bitō was made a professor at the national academy, SHŌHEIKŌ. His works are representative of the official academicism of the time.

biwa

Short-necked plucked lute, of which various types are used for various kinds of music. The *biwa* is a distant relative of the European and of other Asian lutes, but derives immediately from the Chinese *piba* (p'i-pa). Both four- and five-stringed types were used already in Nara-period (710–794) court music, and several beautifully decorated instruments are preserved in the SHŌSŌIN at Nara (see photograph in that article). The 8th-century notation of 22 pieces for five-stringed *biwa* has also survived, but this instrument dropped out of use in Heian times (794–1185). The *biwa* was also used in Kyūshū from at least the 8th century for the so-called *mōsō biwa* (blind monks' lute) style of music; by the 9th century a version of it had reached Kyōto, and it came to be associated above all with the TENDAI SECT of Buddhism. Other lines developed in Chikuzen Province (now part of Fukuoka Prefecture) and, in the 12th century, in Satsuma Province (now part of Kagoshima Prefecture).

In court music the *biwa* plays simple figures to accompany the melody instruments of the GAGAKU ensemble; in *mōsō biwa* it accompanied chanting of the *Jishinkyō* (the Earth God Sutra); but in the 13th and 14th centuries a new kind of *biwa* music developed, to accompany episodes from secular military romances. This was HEIKYOKU, which in the 16th and 17th centuries had a tremendous influence on other styles of secular vocal music, especially those which were accompanied by the newly popular SHAMISEN.

In the 16th century a new type of *biwa* music grew out of an older style called Satsuma *mōsō*, through the efforts of Shimazu Nisshinsai (Tadayoshi; 1492–1568). Wishing to arouse the martial ardor of young men in his fief, he composed *biwa* songs on suitable themes, and his successors in turn added to the repertoire. This Satsuma *biwa* has remained the most popular of all *biwa* styles, and there are several subschools, notably the Kinshin *biwa*, founded by Nagata Kinshin (1885–1927), and the Nishiki *biwa*, founded by Suitō Kinjō (1911–73).

Between the late 1880s and early 1890s a further style of *biwa* developed in Kyūshū out of the old Chikuzen *mōsō* style. The founders of this Chikuzen *biwa* were Tachibana Kyokuō I

(1848–1919), Tsurusaki Kenjō (1864–1921), and Yoshida Takeko (1871–1923); they incorporated elements of *shamisen* song style, which made it attractive to lady amateurs. Again, various subschools developed, the Tachibana line being most prominent.

The *gaku biwa* of court music is a large instrument played with the neck held horizontally and with a comparatively small plectrum. In later styles a bigger plectrum was used, but the *biwa* was smaller, and was played in a more or less vertical position, following contemporary Chinese practice. *Biwa* of the various styles and schools differ in the number of their frets, which varies from four to six; the number of strings also ranges from three (in Satsuma *mōsō* music) to five (in certain types of Nishiki *biwa* and Kinshin *biwa* music). However, four is the usual number. A variety of tunings, finger techniques, and notation systems is also found. The instrument usually plays stereotyped melodic phrases in alternation with the chant; in contrast to China, no repertoire of instrumental lute solos ever developed in Japan. The chant texts are usually in a conventional 7–5 syllabic meter. See also BIWA HŌSHI.

Nakauchi Chōji and Tamura Nishio, ed, *Biwa zenshū*, vol 5 of *Nihon ongyoku zenshū* (Nihon Ongyoku Zenshū Kankō Kai, 1927). Hagiwara Akihiko, ed, *Satsuma biwa kashū* (1965). Yoshimura Gakujō, *Biwa tokuhon* (1933). Columbia, *Nihon biwagaku zenshū*, AL-4079/81 (3-record set). Polydor, *Biwagaku taikei*, SLJM-1031/37 (7-record set). David B. WATERHOUSE

biwa hōshi

("lute priest"). Itinerant performers, usually blind, who chanted works of vocal literature to the accompaniment of a BIWA (lute). *Biwa hōshi* shaved their heads and dressed as traveling priests but were not formally ordained. Their origins are obscure, but itinerant Buddhist lay-priest entertainers were also known in China and India, and the tradition possibly entered Japan from the Asian mainland with the spread of Buddhism. A 10th-century poem by Taira no Kanemori (d 990) is the first recorded use of the term *biwa hōshi*. Early *biwa hōshi* probably recited a variety of short tales, including accounts of the great battles of the TAIRA–MINAMOTO WAR (1180–85), but by far the most important work in the repertoire from the 13th century on was the HEIKE MONOGATARI (ca 1220; tr *The Tale of the Heike,* 1975). Akashi Kakuichi (d 1371), the most famous *biwa hōshi*, dictated a revised recitation version of *Heike monogatari* which has become the popular standard text. Kakuichi also founded a guild of *biwa hōshi* known as the Tōdōza ("proper path guild"), which was recognized by the Muromachi shogunate (1338–1573) as having control over all licensed *biwa hōshi*. This period marked the height of popularity of the performers among all social classes. Other types of popular performance outstripped the offerings of the *biwa hōshi* during the Edo period (1600–1868), and a very few performers today still maintain something of the musical traditions of the *biwa hōshi*. See also HEIKYOKU.

Kenneth D. Butler, "The Textual Evolution of the *Heike monogatari,*" *Harvard Journal of Asiatic Studies* (1966). Tomikura Tokujirō, "Biwa hōshira no yakuwari," *Kokubungaku kaishaku to kanshō* (November 1960). Susan MATISOFF

Biwako Canal

(Biwako Sosui). Canal in Shiga and Kyōto prefectures, central Honshū, extending from the city of Ōtsu on Lake Biwa to Kyōto, and joining the river Ujigawa at Fushimi. The water from Lake Biwa is used for drinking, irrigation, power generation, and industrial purposes. Work on the first part of the canal was initiated in 1885 and completed in 1890. The second part of the canal, from Ōtsu to Keage, was started in 1908 and completed in 1912. Length: 20 km (12 mi).

Biwa, Lake

(Biwako). In central Shiga Prefecture, central Honshū. Japan's largest freshwater lake. Divided into the North Lake and South Lake, the average depth of the former is more than 50 m (164 ft), while that of the latter is less than 5 m (16 ft). Known as the location of the eight scenic spots of Ōmi (see ŌMI HAKKEI) since ancient times, the lake has been designated a quasi-national park. Used as a main artery of transportation to provinces in the north since the Heian period (794–1185), when rice and other products of the Hokuriku region were transported over it to Ōtsu. Such activity also flourished in the Edo period (1600–1868). Overall development of the lake has been advocated since World War II, and a Lake Biwa Overall Development Special Measures Law was promulgated in 1972. The Great Bridge of Lake Biwa, a toll bridge connecting Ōtsu with Moriyama, was completed in 1964. Lake water is used for irrigation and for drinking. The lake is also used for power generation and for industrial purposes, providing industrial water to the Keihanshin (Kyōto-Ōsaka-Kōbe) Industrial Belt. Principal catches are sweetfish, trout, carp, crucian carp, and roach. Freshwater pearl culture is also carried out. Area: 673.8 sq km (260.1 sq mi); circumference: 188 km (117 mi); deepest point: 103.4 m (339.2 ft).

Bizen

City in southeastern Okayama Prefecture, on the Inland Sea. Bizen produces about 30 percent of Japan's refractory bricks. The Imbe district is the center for the production of BIZEN WARE, with more than 100 workshops. The Shizutani Gakkō, a school established by IKEDA MITSUMASA, the *daimyō* of Okayama, to educate the children in his domain, is now an educational center for young adults. Pop: 33,032.

Bizen ware

(bizen-yaki). Unglazed stoneware made in Okayama Prefecture (formerly Bizen Province) from at least the Kamakura period (1185–1333) to the present. Although several other kilns producing similar ware existed in medieval Japan, all but Bizen turned to glazes or terminated production. Typical wares have a vitrified body with surfaces of glossy gold, matt orange, iridescent blue-green, or rough, charcoal-like patches, all produced by sustained, high-temperature firings. These effects, originally produced accidentally through natural ash glazing from the wood fuel, are encouraged during 10-day firings. Fiery red glaze streaks are produced where straw wrapped around the pots has burned off. Bizen ware specialties include storage vessels, mortars, vases, and *sake* bottles. But production is diverse and has also included teabowls, sculpted figures, tiles, pipes, bricks, abstract sculptures, and even, during World War II, hand grenades.

It remains controversial whether early Bizen ware developed directly out of unglazed, high-fired SUE WARE or independently. Early Bizen ware consisted primarily of storage vessels and mortars made from coarse, gray, highly refractory mountain clay fired in subterranean through-draft kilns *(anagama)*. However, TEA CEREMONY ware began to be produced in the late 1400s and early 1500s. Dark, smooth, plastic, rice-paddy clay came to be mixed with mountain clay, and eventually was used alone in response to the tea masters' preference. Large kilns were fired communally by six families, Kimura, Mori, Kaneshige, Terami, Ōai, and Tongū, organized into three guilds.

The Azuchi-Momoyama period (1568–1600) was Bizen's golden age. Vigorously shaped ware with rich gold, red, brown, and black surfaces, crisscrossed with rhythmic slashes of a bamboo knife, were made to suit the taste of tea masters SEN NO RIKYŪ and FURUTA ORIBE. Records indicate that warlord TOYOTOMI HIDEYOSHI himself used a Bizen waste-water jar *(kensui)* in a 1587 Kyōto tea ceremony.

Edo period (1600–1868) wares had thinner walls and were shinier and more decorative, perhaps in response to the popularity of Kyūshū porcelains. Extremely thin-walled, white-glazed wares with gold trim and colorful slip-decorated bisque wares were made occasionally. The guilds served the Ikeda family, *daimyō* of Bizen. Their three kilns were gradually converted into linked-chamber climbing-kilns *(noborigama)*, at their largest 54 meters (177 ft) long by 5 meters (16.5 ft) wide, with firings requiring 30 to 50 days. However, smaller and more economical *noborigama* that could be fired in 10 days replaced these in the mid-1800s. In the Meiji period (1868–1912), tiles, pipes, and bricks became staple production items.

Approximately 200 potters work in Bizen today, in traditional as well as in innovative styles. The potter KANESHIGE TŌYŌ (1896–1967) was recognized as one of the LIVING NATIONAL TREASURES in 1956, as was Fujiwara Kei (b 1900) in 1970. Historical and contemporary Bizen ware are displayed in Imbe at the Bizen Pottery Traditional and Contemporary Art Museum (Bizen Tōgei Kaikan) and at the privately owned Bizen Ancient Ceramics Art Museum (Bizen Kotō Bijutsukan). The Fujiwara Kei Memorial Hall in nearby Katakami also contains an excellent collection.

▬——Katsura Matasaburō, *Bizen*, vol 8 of *Nihon no yakimono* (Kōdansha, 1975). *Jeanne* CARREAU

Black Dragon Society → Amur River Society

Black, John Reddie (1827–1880)

Newspaper editor and publisher active in Japan early in the Meiji period (1868–1912). Born in Scotland. Initially a British naval officer, he later became a merchant in Australia. Having failed in that venture, Black was en route to England when his ship made port in Yokohama. He was enchanted by the land and people and decided to remain in Japan. He found work as editor-in-chief of the English language newspaper the JAPAN HERALD run by A. W. Hansard and in 1867 commenced publication of his own English language paper, the *Japan Gazette,* which became noted for its comprehensive treatment of the Meiji Restoration. In 1872 he started the daily Japanese language newspaper *Nisshin shinjishi,* whose high quality and novel layout had considerable influence on contemporary newspapers. In 1873 he made public an internal government document criticizing the critical state of national finances. The government responded to this and other provocations by revising its press laws to permit tighter regulation and specifically to prohibit ownership of newspapers by foreigners. Claiming extraterritoriality, Black founded another newspaper, *Bankoku shimbun.* The Japanese government enlisted the aid of the British government, which in 1876 ruled against Black. Barred from newspaper work, he spent his last years writing *Young Japan* (1880), a useful source of information about early Meiji Japan. *KŌUCHI Saburō*

black ships → kurofune

Black Stream → Kuroshio

Bloch, Bernard (1907–1965)

American theoretical linguist whose work on Japanese in the 1940s resulted in a new and original analysis of the spoken language, based on the descriptive methodology of that period. His final article on Japanese, published in 1950, is unsurpassed as an example of the phonemic theory and practice of American structural linguistics.

Born in New York City and educated at the University of Kansas and Brown University, Bloch began his research on Japanese during World War II, first briefly at Brown University, and then at Yale, where he remained as professor of linguistics until his death. Recognized as a preeminent theoretician by his colleagues in the field, he served as editor of *Language* for 26 years. In his pioneer work on Japanese, he concentrated on the spoken language, using native speakers to provide the data. His interest in both the analysis and teaching of spoken Japanese marked a striking departure from traditional approaches, which tended to stress only the written language. He utilized the results of his research to produce textbooks for American students of Japanese, at the same time serving as coordinator and lecturer in Japanese language programs at Yale.

As a result of wartime conditions, his works on Japanese, viewed as landmarks in the field by scholars abroad, did not become immediately available within Japan. Even after resumption of normal scholarly exchanges, details of his work became familiar to relatively few Japanese.

His achievements in Japanese culminated in two works: *Bernard Bloch on Japanese* (1969), a reprint volume of previously published linguistic papers, and *Spoken Japanese* (1945), a two-volume textbook for Americans, coauthored with Eleanor Harz Jorden, using a format that was innovative at the time of its publication.

Eleanor H. JORDEN

"Blood Debt" Incident

A controversy that developed from the accidental discovery in February 1962 of mass graves of Chinese believed to have been massacred in Singapore and Malaya by Japanese soldiers during the occupation period (1942–45). The discovery of these concealed human bones became an important issue in the Singapore–Malaya merger controversy. Chinese connected with the Chinese Chamber of Commerce sponsored a movement to demand reparations from the Japanese and political parties opposing merger with Malaya seized the opportunity to turn the people against Prime Minister Lee Kuan Yew, who had been committed to the merger. Unable to ignore the highly charged atmosphere of anti-Japanese and antigovernment emotion and tension, Lee decided to support efforts to convince the Japanese that some indemnification was necessary. Lee's conciliatory stand was rooted in pragmatism, for he needed Japanese technical and industrial skills for the rapid industrialization of Singapore. He promised to settle the "blood debt" issue with Japan, arguing that the Japanese government was prepared to acknowledge its guilt by making reparations.

In October 1966 a settlement was reached with Singapore. The Japanese government agreed to a grant of ¥2.94 billion (US $8.2 million) and the loan of another ¥2.94 billion on liberal terms in lieu of further reparations. In May 1967 prime ministers SATŌ EISAKU of Japan and Tunku Abdul Rahman of Malaysia tried to settle the "blood debt" issue, agreeing that Japan would extend a grant of ¥2.94 billion in ships and other capital goods in lieu of further reparation. The Malaysian Parliament, however, balked at the signing of the agreement, complaining that the treaty would deprive Malaysia the right to demand further compensation. After more negotiations, the two governments reached an agreement to implement the settlement described above. This became effective on 7 May 1968 when Japan officially exchanged the agreement's protocol with Malaysia and Singapore.

📖——Yoji Akashi, "Japanese Policy Towards the Malayan Chinese, 1941–1945," *Journal of Southeast Asian Studies* (September 1970). *Akashi Yōji*

"blood tax" riots → ketsuzei ikki

Board of Audit

(Kaikei Kensa In). Independent department of the executive branch of the national government in charge of auditing government accounts. The board was established to comply with article 90 of the present constitution, which states, "Final accounts of the expenditures and revenues of the state shall be audited annually by a Board of Audit and submitted by the cabinet to the Diet, together with the statement of audit, during the fiscal year immediately following the period covered." The board's auditors regularly monitor the flow of incoming and outgoing money for government ministries, agencies, and public corporations. The auditors have the right to inform concerned authorities and request appropriate action if they discover any mismanagement or misuse of government funds. The board consists of the Audit Commission and the General Executive Bureau and is headed by three auditors appointed by the cabinet with the Diet's consent. *Daniel A. Metraux*

board of directors

(torishimariyaku kai). Corporate organ composed of individuals (the law stipulates a minimum of three) selected by the stockholders to determine company policies and supervise its operations, except for matters delegated by the COMMERCIAL CODE or the articles of incorporation to the authority of the STOCKHOLDERS' GENERAL MEETING.

Day-to-day management and representation of the company are left to the representative director (daihyō torishimariyaku), who is selected by the board of directors. Under express provisions of the Commercial Code, the board of directors has the authority to decide such matters as the convention of the stockholders' general meeting; the establishment, transfer, and abolition of branch operations; the selection and dismissal of managers; the selection of the representative director and determination of joint representation; the issuance of new stock; the approval of particular stock transfers (if restrictions on the transfer of stock are provided for in the company's articles of incorporation) or, in the case of disapproval of such transfers, designation of the person who has the right of first purchase of the stock; the capitalization of the legal reserve fund and determination of stock splits whereby new stock is issued without compensation; the issuance of company bonds; and so on.

In principle, each director has the right to call a meeting of the board. By decision of the board of directors, however, this right may be vested only in designated directors, such as the chairman of the board and the president. Notice of a board meeting may be given orally, but, since the OVERSEER (kansayaku) also has the right to attend, he too must be notified.

The attendance of a majority of the directors is required in order to constitute a quorum, and, to be accepted, resolutions must be approved by a majority of the directors in attendance. Only actual physical presence constitutes attendance for this purpose; neither attendance by the appointed agent (dairi) of a director nor voting by telephone or by document is permitted. Although there is no express provision in any law to this effect, parties affected by a decision of the board of directors may challenge it. Minutes of the board of directors' meetings must be kept and made available to the public. *Nagahama Yōichi*

boats, traditional → ships

Bōchō kaiten shi

History of the activities of the powerful Chōshū domain (now Yamaguchi Prefecture) during the critical last years of the Edo period (1600–1868) and the early years of the Meiji period (1868–1912); compiled by SUEMATSU KENCHŌ in 12 volumes in 1920. Written at the behest of the Mōri family, former daimyō of Chōshū, it emphasizes the role the domain played in the MEIJI RESTORATION. Drawing on a wide variety of documents, it remains an important source for the period.

bodhisattva

(J: bosatsu). In the Mahāyāna Buddhist tradition, which prevails in Japan, a being of great spiritual attainment who is destined for Buddhahood but who vows not to become a Buddha until all other beings have been helped to attain this state. The bodhisattva is ranked just below a Buddha and is a pivotal concept in the Mahāyāna tradition, which emphasizes the possibility of all beings attaining Buddhahood. In popular belief, the bodhisattva is viewed as a divine being with boundless compassion who intercedes on behalf of living creatures in distress. Bodhisattvas are invoked to provide relief from afflictions suffered in this world such as illness, poverty, natural disasters, and various forms of harassment and to comfort, rescue, or to help enlighten the souls of deceased relatives in the next world. The most popular bodhisattvas in Japan are KANNON (Skt: Avalokiteśvara), whose special attribute is compassion; JIZŌ (Skt: Kṣitigarbha), the protector of children; Fugen (Skt: Samantabhadra) and Monju (Skt: Mañjuśrī), both associated with wisdom; and MIROKU (Skt: Maitreya), who will be the next major Buddha to appear in the world. Great religious figures in history such as GYŌGI have also been called by this title. *Stanley Weinstein*

Bōeichō → Defense Agency

Bohai (Po-hai)

(J: Bokkai; Kor: Parhae). A kingdom in southeastern Manchuria and northeastern Korea, from 713 to 926, that maintained regular diplomatic and trading relations with Japan.

In 696 remnants of the defeated Korean state of KOGURYŌ joined with other, less-developed Tungusic tribesmen, fled the territory in which the Chinese Tang (T'ang) dynasty (618–907) had forced them to settle, and two years later declared themselves an independent nation. The Chinese eventually recognized the new kingdom, giving it the name Bohai in 713. Records are scanty, and little is known of Bohai's history beyond the names of its 15 kings.

Like Japan, Bohai during the 8th and 9th centuries enthusiastically embraced Chinese culture. Its administrative organization and the layout of its capital cities followed Chinese models. Its architecture was predominantly Chinese, although Korean influences were also present. Buddhism and Chinese literature were prevalent among the ruling class, and a few poems in Chinese written by ambassadors from Bohai have been preserved in Japanese anthologies.

In 727, when its relations with China were momentarily strained, Bohai sent its first official embassy to Japan, seeking a military alliance. No alliance was concluded, but friendly relations between the two countries continued for 200 years. Thirty-five missions from Bohai are recorded, some of them probably unofficial trading missions; in return, Japan sent 13 missions to Bohai. These missions were accompanied by extensive trade—usually Bohai furs for Japanese textiles—and cultural exchange; indeed, they were important for the introduction of Chinese culture to Japan. Bohai's ambassadors brought news of events in China and introduced a calendar that was used in Japan until the 17th century. Music from Bohai remains a part of the repertoire of GAGAKU, Japan's classical court music.

With the collapse of the Tang dynasty, Manchuria fell into chaos. In 926 the proto-Mongolian Khitan people conquered Bohai and incorporated it into their empire, which soon became the Liao dynasty (907–1125). Three years later, a group of Bohai officials appeared in Japan seeking aid in recapturing their homeland, but the Japanese declined to interfere. Despite occasional rebellions, the kingdom of Bohai was never reestablished, and its people were eventually absorbed by their conquerors.   *Robert BORGEN*

Boissonade de Fontarabie, Gustave Emile (1829–1910)

French legal scholar who was one of many foreign legal scholars employed by the Japanese government in the Meiji period (1868–1912). After receiving his doctorate in law from the University of Paris, he taught at the University of Grenoble. He went to Japan in 1873 at the invitation of the Ministry of Justice and remained until 1895. He served concurrently as an adviser to the Ministry of Foreign Affairs, the GENRŌIN (a short-lived protosenatorial body), and the Bureau of Imperial Rule (Dajōkan Hōseikyoku). As an instructor in the Ministry of Justice School of Law, he trained many legal scholars. He also made a major contribution to the compilation of legal codes such as the Penal Code and the CIVIL CODE, drawing up several drafts. Boissonade is also remembered for his successful petition to exclude torture in criminal cross-examination. His knowledge of international public law, as seen in both the disposition of the TAIWAN EXPEDITION OF 1874 and his opposition to any precipitous revision of the so-called Unequal Treaties (especially as proposed by Foreign Minister INOUE KAORU; see also UNEQUAL TREATIES, REVISION OF) had a great influence on Japan's foreign relations. He was the first foreigner to be awarded the First Class Order of the Sacred Treasure (1895).   *TANAKA Akira*

Bokkai → Bohai (Po-hai)

Bōkokurei Jiken → grain embargo controversy

bombori → lanterns

Bon dance → Bon odori

bonds, public

(kōsai). Fixed-interest securities issued by central or local governments. In Japan, the national and local governments in principle finance their expenditures with tax revenues under the FINANCE LAW (Zaisei Hō) and the Local Finance Law (Chihō Zaisei Hō). Both laws, however, contain special provisions which authorize the issuance of bonds to finance government construction or investment programs such as public works projects. The strict balanced-budget principle adopted by the two basic laws on public finance reflects the severe inflation during and after World War II, one cause of which was the huge volume of government bonds issued during the war.

Between 1947 and 1964 no bonds were issued for the general account of the central government. However, since 1965, when the Japanese economy was hit by a recession and the government was obliged to expand public-works projects, public bonds have been issued continuously. Local governments also finance public investment partly through the issuance of bonds, but they are less dependent on bonds than the central government.   *UDAGAWA Akihito*

bone articles

(kokkakuki). Tools and decorative items made from the bones, antlers, teeth, tusks, and claws of animals. These were most commonly used by the hunting and gathering societies of the Jōmon period (ca 10,000 BC–ca 300 BC) and the OKHOTSK CULTURE, although they are also found among Yayoi-period (ca 300 BC–ca AD 300) and Kofun-period (ca 300–710) remains (see the sections on prehistory and protohistory in HISTORY OF JAPAN).

Bone articles are found preserved in SHELL MOUNDS of the Earliest Jōmon phases; Middle Jōmon tools include barbed harpoon heads, fishhooks, and pronged fishing spears. Items of the Latest Jōmon phases in northeastern Japan include arrowheads made of wild boar tusk tips, deer antler reinforcements for the notched ends of arrow shafts and bows, antler and tusk ornaments, and revolving harpoon heads. Among the artifacts of the Okhotsk culture in Hokkaidō there are excellent examples of bonework. Hair and ear ornaments, needles, and sickle hafts are found with spear and arrow points, fishhooks, harpoons, axes, and hoes. The most common bone articles of the protohistoric period are knife hilts, some of them elaborately carved and painted with CHOKKOMON designs.

KITAMURA Bunji

Bon Festival

(Urabon'e). Buddhist observance honoring the spirits of ancestors; traditionally observed from 13–15 July (August in some areas). Also called Urabon or Obon. *Urabon* is said to be a Chinese-Japanese rendering of the Sanskrit *ullambana,* a memorial ceremony to rescue the souls of the dead from the tortures of hell. According to the sutra *Bussetsu urabonkyō* (Ch: *Foshuo Yülanpen jing* or *Fo-shuo Yü-lan-p'en ching*), *ullambana* began with the efforts of Mokuren (Skt: Maudgalyāyana), a disciple of Śākyamuni, to rescue his mother, who was suffering in purgatory. As instructed by his master, Mokuren devoted himself to ascetic practice from the 16th day of the fourth month to the 15th of the seventh month of the lunar year (the Buddhist practice known as *geango;* Skt: *vārṣika*). On the last day he made a lavish offering of food and drink to the assembled monks and priests; as a result, his mother was saved. The festival is known to have been observed in China by the early 6th century and in Japan since its first recorded occurrence in 657. During the Nara (710–794) and Heian (794–1185) periods, it was a rite at the court, but it subsequently became a popular custom observed by commoners as well. It would seem that the native tradition of welcoming back the souls of ancestors in late summer merged with the Buddhist concept of *ullambana* and with other elements from Japanese AGRICULTURAL RITES to become the Bon Festival as we know it today.

Typically at Bon, a "spirit altar" (shōryōdana) is set up in front of the BUTSUDAN (Buddhist family altar) to welcome the ancestors' souls; then a priest is requested to come and read a sutra (tanagyō) in front of the altar. Preparation for Bon may begin as early as the first day of July. The seventh day of July is known as Tanabata, or *nanoka bon* ("seventh-day Bon"); on this day in some areas the grave sites are cleaned and a path (called a *bommichi*) is prepared from the grave to the house, to ease the ancestors' return trip; lanterns or long strips of white cloth are displayed to serve as guides. To provide them symbolically with transportation, horses or oxen made of straw or vegetables may be offered on the altars or hung from the eaves. Flowers (called *bon-bana*) may be offered at the tomb or on the spirit altar. The welcoming fire (mukaebi), built on the 13th, and the send-off fire (okuribi), built on the 16th, are intended to illumine the path. Offerings on the spirit altar include vegetables, rice dumplings, noodles, and fruits. Pork is sometimes offered in Okinawa. In families where a death has occurred since the previous Bon, friends and relatives may offer lanterns. In some districts, *kusaichi* (grass markets) or *bon'ichi* (Bon markets) are set up to sell goods needed for celebrating Bon.

Bon and the NEW YEAR are the two high points of the Japanese festival calendar, and thematically they bear a close resemblance. On both occasions, custom strongly urges all members of a family, no matter how scattered, to gather together to honor their ancestors; public transportation systems are usually congested. In recent years certain observances associated with the Bon season—the TANABATA FESTIVAL, the BON ODORI, the NEBUTA FESTIVAL, DAIMONJI OKURIBI, and lantern floating (tōrō nagashi)—have become tourist attractions.   *KIMURA Kiyotaka*

Bonin Islands → Ogasawara Islands

bonito

(katsuo). A pelagic migratory fish of the class Osteichthyes, order Perciformes, family Scombridae. It reaches 1 meter (39 in) in length. Distributed in warm seas throughout the world, it is caught by pole fishing and round haul nets. In spring it comes to Japan from the south, swims north as far as the offing of the Tōhoku region and returns south in autumn. Bonito may be eaten as *sashimi* (sliced raw fish), *tataki* (briefly cooked, the inside remaining raw), *ni-*

Bonkei and bonseki

A *bonseki* of the Hosokawa school entitled *Taki* (Waterfall).

tsuke (boiled and seasoned), *katsuobushi* (dried), and *namaribushi* (steamed). It is also canned. The guts are made into *shiokara* (salted fish guts). ABE Tokiharu

In the Edo period (1600–1868), bonito became a favored fish of the common people. The season's first bonito *(hatsugatsuo)* was particularly prized; it is celebrated in a famous *haiku* by the poet Yamaguchi Sodō (1642–1716), "Green leaves to see, the cuckoo to hear, and the early bonito to taste." SAITŌ *Shōji*

bonkei and bonseki

Two types of miniature landscape arranged either on a flat tray *(bon)* or in a shallow bowl, and conveying strong seasonal associations. *Bonkei* recreate a world in miniature, using tiny grasses, trees, and moss, with stones and ceramic objects for added realism. *Bonseki* are miniature landscapes composed entirely of sand and stone. The practice of making landscapes in miniature seems to have first appeared in Japan in the Muromachi period (1333–1568). During the Edo period (1600–1868) a number of miniature-landscape schools, each with its own techniques and rules, appeared: Hosokawa, Sekishū, Chikuan, and Hino. See also BONSAI.

Bon odori

(Bon dances). Dances performed annually in either the middle of July or the middle of August, as part of the BON FESTIVAL celebrations to welcome the ancestor spirits on their annual return to the world of the living, and to bid them farewell at their departure. Evolving out of *odori nembutsu*, the popular Buddhist chants and folk dances of the late Heian (794–1185) and Kamakura (1185–1333) periods, the Bon *odori* was first mentioned in late 15th century literature. By the Edo period (1600–1868) it was a widespread national custom characterized by considerable local variation. While in many rural areas the Bon *odori* today retains some of its original religious significance, in the cities it has been greatly secularized, like the Bon Festival itself. The Bon *odori*, which varies from prefecture to prefecture, is usually performed by large groups of men, women, and children of all ages to the accompaniment of singing, hand clapping, drums, gongs, flutes, and occasionally the SHAMISEN. The costumes vary with locality, but loose, cotton summer *kimono (yukata)* and straw hats are popular attire. The dancers often move in circles around the musicians or around a temporary platform *(yagura)* set up in a broad open space. In some areas as part of the Bon *odori* the dancers visit homes where the family has experienced a death during the previous year. In the Bon *odori* of Nishimonai in Akita Prefecture, the dancers' faces are hidden by their straw hats, suggesting the ancient belief that the dead have returned to mingle with the living. Other famous Bon *odori* are the AWA DANCE of Tokushima and the Tsurusaki Odori of Ōita. In a few places, usually large urban areas or resorts, the Bon *odori* has become an entertainment spectacle staged for tourists. *Frank* HOFF

Bō no Tsu

Small fishing port in southwestern Kagoshima Prefecture. It was a flourishing seaport and religious center in the Nara period (710–794), when Japanese embassies to Tang (T'ang) China used it as their point of departure and return. During the Muromachi period (1333–1568), as the seat of the SHIMAZU FAMILY, Bō no Tsu became a major entrepôt of the trade with Ming China and the Ryūkyūs. With Hakata (see HAKATA MERCHANTS) and ANOTSU, it was one of the three principal ports of Japan. When the Tokugawa shogunate (1603–1867) adopted its NATIONAL SECLUSION policy and concentrated all foreign trade at Nagasaki early in the 17th century, the prosperity of Bō no Tsu abruptly declined.

bonsai

("tray planting"). The art of dwarfing trees or plants by growing and training them in containers according to prescribed techniques. The aim is to create a miniature tree that will replicate a large tree in nature. Bonsai can also refer to the miniature potted trees themselves.

Bonsai first appeared in China over one thousand years ago. In high mountains, or by the sea, conditions such as strong winds, heavy snow, and arid soil sometimes produce stunted trees; bonsai probably began when someone came upon a dwarfed tree and tried to transplant it or grow a similar one in a container. Although the early history of bonsai in China is unclear, we know that it was introduced to Japan in the Kamakura period (1185–1333) with the wave of cultural influence that accompanied the introduction of Zen Buddhism from China. The earliest reference to bonsai in Japan is in the *Kasuga gongen kenki,* a set of picture scrolls attributed to Takashina Takakane (fl 1309–30). From its introduction the Japanese have appreciated and refined the art of bonsai to an extent unapproached even in China.

Under certain conditions, trees growing in the wild that have been stunted by nature can be transplanted into containers, but a bonsai can also be developed from ordinary young trees or from seeds or cuttings. Bonsai can be grown indoors or out, although they do not thrive in centrally heated homes in winter, which tend to be too hot and dry, or outdoors in severe winter climates. Most bonsai range in height from 5 centimeters (approximately 2 in) to 1 meter (approximately 3 ft).

Bonsai are kept small by pruning branches and roots, and by repotting. Periodic repotting replaces nutrient-depleted soil and the size of the container partly determines the final size of the tree by dictating the amount of root growth. In addition, the grower controls size and shape by pinching off new growth and by wiring branches and trunk so that they will grow into the desired shape.

Bonsai grow in special trays or containers with drainage holes and often with small feet that elevate them slightly. While for much of the year a bonsai is kept out-of-doors in the temperate climate that characterizes most of Japan, on special occasions it is often placed in the *tokonoma*, the alcove in traditional Japanese-style rooms designed for the display of artistic objects. Bonsai generally have one main viewing side and must be positioned accordingly. Sometimes two bonsai are displayed together in the *tokonoma*: a major bonsai, usually larger and often elevated on a stand, and a companion bonsai.

An unglazed, dark-colored container is usually chosen for a classic bonsai, or to give a bonsai an aged look. A glazed container is more suitable for the companion bonsai; it is also sometimes used with flowering trees. There must always be a good proportion between the plant size, its height, and the container. As a rule, oval containers are used for deciduous trees and rectangular containers for evergreens. The choice of container also varies according to the style of the particular bonsai.

Major Styles —— *Upright style:* the trunk is straight; the depth of the container depends on the size of the trunk. *Slanting style:* the tree grows in a slant; if the tree leans left, it should be planted on the right-hand side of the container, and vice versa. *Cascading style:* the tree is trained to hang over the container in one direction, suggesting a waterfall; the slanting line of the tree is balanced by planting it near the opposite side of the container. The container, usually set on a tall stand, can be round, square, or hexagonal. *Weeping-cascade style:* the tree (a naturally "drooping" type) hangs over the container; the depth of the container depends on the height of the tree. Square, round, or rectangular containers are used. *Twisting-trunk style:* the tree is twisted or gnarled, and sometimes driftwood is incorporated into the arrangement to give the impression of great age, of a storm, or of dragons climbing into the sky with the upper foliage representing clouds. The tree is usually planted in a rectangular container. *Twin-trunk style:* the tree's trunk bifurcates near the soil line. The twin trunks, one larger than the other, often represent a couple: male and female, parent and child. The smaller trunk is placed closer to the side of the container. *Clumped style:* suckers are encouraged to grow from an original trunk and root system to create a stand of "separate" trees, representing a family or group. A rather shallow container is used. *Forest style:* trees of various sizes are planted in one shallow container. The largest is the "head of the family," with the other trees arranged around it. The trees are grouped not in a straight line but are balanced so that each one can be seen from the front. *Rock planting:* in the clasping style, a low rock, sometimes surrounded with gravel, is placed in a shallow oval or rectangular container; the plant grows so as to straddle the rock, with its roots exposed along both sides. In the clinging style, the tree grows out of a hollow crack in a tall rock set in a shallow container; the roots are covered by soil and moss.

Growing Bonsai——Bonsai are ordinary trees or plants, not special hybrid dwarfs. Some varieties of trees, however, are better suited for bonsai than others. Because leaf size is not greatly affected by the bonsai process, a small-leaf tree, whose leaves will be in proportion to the other parts of the dwarfed tree, is best. Popular types of bonsai include evergreens such as cedar, juniper, and pine; flowering and fruit trees such as azalea, cherry, and plum; and bamboo, maple, oak, and zelkova. In Japan, varieties of pine, bamboo, and Japanese plum *(ume)* are used most often.

Careful watering, often twice a day in summer, and periodic fertilizing are necessary to keep the trees healthy. Generally in the fall, from September to November, overgrown branches are trimmed to the desired length so that new growth will be even in the spring. In temperate climates the trees are placed in cold frames before the first frost to prevent damage to the tree or its container. Temperature in the cold frame should remain between 1.7°C (35°F) and 7.2°C (45°F). The cold frame is dug about 0.6 meters (2 ft) deep into the ground and extends 0.6 meters above the ground. A sash made of glass or heavy plastic sheet covers the frame and can be closed to protect the trees until spring.

It is sometimes necessary to neutralize the soil. This is done between November and February by sprinkling the soil lightly with garden lime. Two or three weeks after this application, diluted liquid garden fertilizer can be given to those bonsai that will not be transplanted or root-pruned in the spring. Trees that are root-pruned should be fertilized very gradually only after about two months have elapsed.

When buds begin to swell in late March to early May, it is time to transplant, root-prune, and replace the soil. Some trees are transplanted or repotted every year; some, every two years; others, only every three years. Spring is also the time for pinching off unwanted new growth. If insect pests are present, the plant should be sprayed as soon as warmer weather arrives.

Bonsai usually thrive in soil that is not too rich and that contains clay. The soil must be free from dust and coarse particles. A sieve or screen is used to strain the soil to the desired consistency. The soil mixture varies according to the variety of tree and personal preference but includes subsoil, sand, leaf mold, and peat moss. Two levels of soil are used to ensure proper drainage: the finer main soil and underneath a layer of coarse bottom soil. For optimum drainage, clean gravel is used at the bottom of the container.

The instruments necessary for maintaining bonsai include trimming shears to cut the branches or trunk, smaller trimming shears with long handles to trim small branches, wire cutters, concave cutters, tweezers to take off dry leaves, leaf-cutting shears, and nippers for shaping branches into the "struck-by-lightning" look.

Aesthetic and Philosophy——Bonsai can live hundreds of years if cared for properly. Prized specimens in Japan are passed on from generation to generation in the same family, admired not only for their age but also revered as a reminder of the people who have cared for them over the centuries. Old, venerable bonsai are often more respected and valued than young ones; however, age is not an essential quality of a good bonsai. It is more important that the tree produce the artistic effect desired, that it is placed in a proper container and is in correct proportion to it, and that it is in good health.

There are two basic styles of bonsai: the classic or dramatic (called *koten*), and the informal or comic (called *bunjin*, or "literati"). In the classic style, the trunk of the tree is wider at the base and tapers off as it reaches the top. It is just the opposite of the *bunjin*, a style more difficult to master.

Bonsai

A 60-year-old *ten no ume* (an evergreen shrub) in the weeping-cascade style. Spread of branches 35 cm. Kyūkaen, Ōmiya, Saitama Prefecture.

Bonsai

A 130-year-old juniper in the upright style. Tree height 85 cm. Kyūkaen, Ōmiya, Saitama Prefecture.

Bonsai often suggest scenes in nature. The artist never merely duplicates nature but rather expresses a personal aesthetic or sensibility by manipulating nature. The tree with a knotted and twisted trunk gives the appearance of old age. A forest scene may be created by planting several trees in a single tray. A pair of trees may represent a couple; three plantings, parents and child, and so on. The mood conveyed by a bonsai can suggest a dramatic scene from a NŌ play or a KABUKI dance, or a comic, foolish, or even grotesque character. But in all cases the bonsai must look natural and never show the intervention of human hands.

The bonsai with its own container and soil, physically independent of the earth since its roots are not planted in it, is a separate entity, complete in itself yet part of nature. This is what is meant by the expression "heaven and earth in one container." The principles of *bonsaidō*, or the "Way of bonsai," are rooted in SHINTŌ. Through the art of bonsai anyone can learn great love and respect for nature, and other universal, spiritual truths.

A bonsai tree should always be positioned off-center in the container. Not only is asymmetry important to the visual effect, but philosophically the center is where earth and heaven, or man and divinity, meet and communicate. Nothing should ever occupy this place. Another aesthetic principle in bonsai is the three-way rela-

Book illustration

One of the illustrations by Iwata Sentarō for the newspaper serialization of Yoshikawa Eiji's novel *Naruto hichō* in 1926–27.

tionship or triangle necessary for achieving visual balance and expressing the relation between a universal principle (life-giving energy or deity), the bonsai grower, and the tree itself. Tradition holds that three basic virtues are necessary when creating a bonsai: *shin-zen-bi* (truth, goodness, and beauty). It is also said that the successful bonsai grower must possess the qualities of benevolence, justice, courtesy, wisdom, and fidelity.

Bonsai Abroad —— Bonsai were introduced into the United States during the 1870s. In 1925, 32 Japanese bonsai were given to the Brooklyn Botanic Garden (New York), but it was not until after World War II that the art of bonsai aroused American interest. The two most comprehensive bonsai collections in the United States can be seen at the Brooklyn Botanic Garden and the National Arboretum (Washington, DC). Bonsai enthusiasts have also established clubs and collections in Canada, Europe, and many other parts of the world.

📖 —— Brooklyn Botanic Garden, *Bonsai for Indoors: A Handbook,* reprint from *Plants & Gardens* (1976). Brooklyn Botanic Garden, *Bonsai: Special Techniques,* reprint from *Plants & Gardens* (1966). Brooklyn Botanic Garden, *Handbook on Dwarfed Potted Trees: The Bonsai of Japan,* reprint from *Plants & Gardens* (1953). *Kokufū Bonsaiten,* an exhibition catalog available annually through membership in the Nippon Bonsai Assocation (3–42 Ueno Kōen, Taitō Ku, Tōkyō). Kyūzō Murata, *Bonsai, Miniature Potted Trees* (1964). Yūji Yoshimura and Giovanna M. Halford, *The Japanese Art of Miniature Trees and Landscapes* (1967). Frank Masao OKAMURA

bonus

(shōyo). A sum of money specially given an employee, ordinarily twice a year (June and December), in addition to regular monthly pay. Originally meant as an incentive, bonuses were given in appreciation for the employees' contribution to business performance. Over the years, however, this practice has become so widely established in Japan that it has become a part of the wage and, where the work force is organized, its amount is often negotiated through collective bargaining. Because the amount of the bonus varies largely according to business performance of individual corporations, it is an important factor giving flexibility to the level of wages in Japan in relation to business fluctuations. Bonuses are also paid to government employees and employees of public corporations in a sum based on the average bonus amount for private enterprise.

Bonuses are computed by multiplying the fixed monthly wage by a uniform multiple. In some cases (12 percent in 1976) bonuses are distributed according to evaluations made by management. In prin-

ciple, the bonus system applies only to regular, full-time employees and not to temporary workers, though they often receive small sums of bonus money. This is a major factor contributing to the difference in wages between regular and temporary workers. In 1977 the overall industrial average for the yearly bonus was equivalent to five months' worth of wages. For larger enterprises the bonus was higher.

As for how bonus money is spent as part of a worker's family budget, the figures for 1977 show that 17 percent of the summer bonus and 32 percent of the winter bonus went for consumptive expenditures; 64 percent of the summer bonus and 56 percent of the winter bonus went into savings. In general, the bonus money is primarily used to maintain living standards, going for such things as durable consumer goods, house payments, educational expenses, or retirement savings. KURITA Ken

book and magazine distributors

(shuppan toritsugigyō). Over 70 percent of all publications in Japan reach the reading public by way of bookstores and the distributors who supply them. Books and magazines are distributed in two ways: on consignment, which permits the return of unsold books, or by order, which does not. New publications are distributed largely on consignment. The high rate of returned books which this involves results in high labor and other costs for publishers, distributors, and bookstores. Nevertheless, consignment is still the method preferred by large publishing firms, which rely on mass production and mass distribution, since it makes it easier for bookstore owners to accept books which can be returned if not sold, and since it makes possible large in-store displays.

Publication distributors first appeared in Japan in the 1880s. Tōkyōdō was established in the 1890s as a distributor for HAKUBUN-KAN, an important Meiji-period (1868–1912) publishing house. Tōkyōdō expanded its business by handling other publishers' books and became the largest of the distributors. Under controls during World War II, all distributors in the country were integrated into one corporation, the Nihon Shuppan Haikyū Kabushiki Kaisha, which was disbanded in 1949 and reorganized into what are now the two largest distribution firms in Japan, the Tōkyō Shuppan Hambai Co, Ltd (Tōhan), and Nippon Shuppan Hambai Co, Ltd (Nippan), which control 70 percent of all publication distribution. After World War II the role of the distributor increased in importance as mass production and sales competition intensified. Generally the major distributors had more capital than many of the publishers, and sometimes gave the latter fiscal aid; thus they not only became involved in distribution but also gained a voice in the planning and production of mass publications. ISHIZAKA Etsuo

book illustration

(sashi-e). Book illustration has a long history in Japan, extending back to the 8th century, and has been graced by the work of many outstanding artists. Two of the earliest forms of book illustration in Japan were the illustrated Buddhist sutras of the Nara period (710–794), such as the *E inga kyō,* and the picture scrolls (EMAKI-MONO) of the latter part of the Heian period (794–1185) through the Kamakura period (1185–1333), such as the GENJI MONOGATARI EMAKI and the *Kitano tenjin engi.* In the Edo period (1600–1868), with the development of a townsman culture, especially during the Genroku era (1688–1704), illustrated reading material was published in large quantities. One well-known example is Ihara SAIKAKU's book, *Kōshoku ichidai otoko* (The Life of an Amorous Man), whose illustrations were done by Hishikawa MORONOBU, an early UKIYO-E artist. From the middle to the end of the Edo period, illustrated storybooks with a picture on each page—the genres known as *akahon, aohon, kurohon,* and *kibyōshi* (see KUSAZŌSHI)—became popular and led to the employment of many artists. Among the painters active in these genres were Suzuki HARUNOBU, TORII KIYONAGA, Kitagawa UTAMARO, UTAGAWA TOYOKUNI, UTAGAWA KUNISADA, Katsushika HOKUSAI, and Andō HIROSHIGE. Of these, Hokusai was especially skillful. He also illustrated 34 novels written by BAKIN.

Modern printing techniques were introduced into Japan in the Meiji period (1868–1912) and were used in the publication of a larger number of newspapers, magazines, and works of literature. The integration of word and picture in these publications attracted the attention of the public, and illustration gained ever wider use. When the KEN'YŪSHA group of authors was formed, centered on

OZAKI KŌYŌ, their works were illustrated by new artists like Tomi-oka Eisen (1864–1905) and Takeuchi Keishū (1863–1943) rather than by *ukiyo-e* painters. In particular, Keishū demonstrated an excellent technique in his illustrations for the nursery tales of Ozaki Kōyō and IWAYA SAZANAMI. Other artists active from the Meiji period to the beginning of the Taishō period (1912–26) include KABURAGI KIYO-KATA, Kajita Hanko (1870–1917), and TAKEHISA YUMEJI, who was known for his romantic, lyrical pictures.

From the Taishō period into the Shōwa period (1926–), Ishii Tsu-ruzō (1887–1973), the first artist to use conté crayon in illustration, won praise for his work in the novel *Daibosatsu Tōge* by NAKAZATO KAIZAN and in *Miyamoto Musashi* by YOSHIKAWA EIJI. Another artist active at this time was Kimura Sōhachi (1893–1959), who illus-trated *Muteki* by OSARAGI JIRŌ and *Bokutō kidan* by NAGAI KAFŪ. Although many considered illustrations to have less artistic value than paintings, Tsuruzō's and Sōhachi's illustrations demonstrated that illustration was in fact a respectable art form. The foremost illustrator of this age, however, was Iwata Sentarō (1901–74), who was well known for his work in *Naruto hichō* by Yoshikawa Eiji and *Akō rōshi* by Osaragi Jirō. Iwata particularly excelled in his por-trayal of women.

The first decade or so of the Shōwa period is known as the golden age of modern illustration. It was also the zenith of the popularity of reading material for teenagers. The detailed, graphic pen-and-ink illustrations of Kabashima Katsuichi (1888–1965) and the illustrations done by Itō Hikozō for *Kurama tengu* by Osaragi Jirō captured the imagination of the young of this time. Since World War II, well-known book illustrators have been Sugimoto Kenkichi (b 1903), who did the illustrations for *Shin Heike monogatari* by Yoshikawa Eiji; Miyata Shigeo (1900–1971), who illustrated *Jiyū gakkō* by SHISHI BUNROKU; and Ikusawa Rō (b 1906), who illus-trated *Hyōheki* by INOUE YASUSHI. More recently, the borrowed word *irasuto* (from the English "illustration") has been used in place of the Japanese word *sashi-e*. The number of graphic designers en-tering the field has increased significantly in recent years.

TASHIRO Hikaru

Booth, Eugene (1850–1931)

American missionary. Graduate of Rutgers College and Rutgers Theological Seminary. He went to Japan in 1879 as a missionary of the Reformed Church and founded a school for boys in Nagasaki the following year. Principal of Ferris Seminary in Yokohama from 1882 to 1923, he also participated in the planning of Tōkyō Wom-en's Christian University (Tōkyō Joshi Daigaku). Booth returned to the United States in 1922. His son Frank S. Booth (1880–1957), who was born in Nagasaki, spent most of his life in Japan and, as pres-ident of the Japan Engineering Company, helped develop the Japa-nese canning industry.

bosatsu → bodhisattva

Bose, Rash Behari (1886–1945)

Indian revolutionary committed to independence for his nation; he spent the years from 1915 to 1945 in Japan. The son of a minor Bengali bureaucrat, Bose at the age of 15 joined a group of young men determined to achieve India's freedom by violent methods. Subsequently, while in the employ of the Government of India For-est Research Institute, Bose masterminded both a bomb plot against the life of the viceroy of India, Lord Hardinge, in Delhi in December 1912, and an intended bombing in Lahore in May 1913. When the latter conspiracy was discovered prematurely by the British authori-ties, Bose went into hiding and finally fled from India aboard a Japa-nese ship on 12 May 1915, arriving in Japan on 5 June.

Bose's entry into Japan was facilitated by his use of the alias P. L. Thakur which, since the Japanese pronounced it "Takuru," led to the belief that Bose was a relative of Rabindranath TAGORE, a greatly respected figure in Japan. He subsequently used several aliases. It was the British embassy in Tōkyō that informed the Japanese gov-ernment that a dangerous Indian revolutionary was now at large in the country. Accordingly, Bose came under the surveillance of the Japanese police. In December 1915 British pressure resulted in a Japanese government extradition warrant for his deportation. How-ever, with the help of such radical Japanese pan-Asianists as TŌ-YAMA MITSURU and UCHIDA RYŌHEI, who had embraced Bose's cause as their own, Bose eluded the police and went into hiding. His

first refuge, one of 17 he was to utilize during the next nine years, was in the home of SŌMA KOKKŌ and her husband Aizō, owners of the famed Western-style bakery Nakamuraya in Shinjuku, Tōkyō. Bose married their daughter in 1918. The Japanese police gave up their search soon after Bose's disappearance, but for fear of being kidnapped or killed by the British or their agents, Bose remained in hiding until his naturalization as a Japanese citizen in 1923. His wife died in 1925.

After acquiring Japanese citizenship, Bose began to agitate openly for Indian independence. In 1924 he founded the Indian Independence League, which he said would cooperate with the In-dian National Congress movement for independence in India but seemed more to be a vehicle to promote himself personally and to solicit financial support from both the Indian community in Japan and sympathetic Japanese. Moreover, unlike the mainstream in-dependence leaders in India, at the time of the outbreak of the Sino-Japanese War in 1937 Bose supported Japan's cause, contending that it was in India's self-interest to do so.

After World War II began, Bose called upon Japan to eliminate British power from India and to solicit support to that end from overseas Indian communities throughout Asia. In turn, Bose urged Indians to assist the Japanese, whom he saw as the ultimate liber-ators of the subcontinent. After Premier TŌJŌ HIDEKI's 16 February 1942 speech, in which he encouraged the Indian populace to make use of the war in East Asia to secure their freedom, Bose was at last officially contacted by the Japanese government, which now sought to use his services. Bose responded eagerly and was named head of the new Indian Independence League, which was charged with the responsibility of leading a Japanese-sponsored Indian independence movement in all of Asia.

The arrival in Tōkyō of the charismatic Subhas Chandra BOSE in May 1943, however, removed Rash Behari from the leadership of the league. He died in January 1945, a figure on the periphery of the mainstream of India's fight for freedom. Moreover, because of his Japanese citizenship, wife, and son (who was in the Japanese army), he was not completely trusted by his fellow Indians. Bose, then, is perhaps more significant for what his life reveals about Japanese PAN-ASIANISM than as a symbol of the struggle for Indian indepen-dence.

■——Works by Bose: *Kakumei Ajia no tembō* (1930). *Shikkoku no Indo* (1933). *Kakumei no Indo* (1935). *Seinen Ajia no shōri* (1937). *Indo no yobi* (1940). *Dokuritsu Indo no reimei* (1942). *Do-kuritsu no tōsō* (1942). *Indo o kataru* (1942). *Indo shinryaku hishi* (1942). *Indojin no Indo* (1942). *Saigo no uta* (1943). *Bōsu wa yobu* (1944). Works about Bose: Ashizu Uzuhiko, *Dai Ajia shugi to Tō-yama Mitsuru* (1965). Nakayama Tadanao, *Bōsu to Rikarute* (1942). Sōma Kokkō and Sōma Yasuo, *Ajia no mezame* (1953).

Grant K. GOODMAN

Bose, Subhas Chandra (1897–1945)

Prominent Indian nationalist leader and organizer of an anti-British movement outside India during World War II. Born in Orissa, Bose studied at the University of Calcutta and at Cambridge. In 1921 he resigned from the Indian Civil Service and joined the Congress Party, of which he soon became a prominent leader in Bengal. He hoped to gain a majority within the Congress movement for his radical alternative to the nonviolent program of Mahatma Gandhi. In January 1938 he was elected president of the Indian National Congress, succeeding Jawaharlal Nehru, but resigned in April 1939 because of Gandhi's disapproval. He founded his own party, the Forward Bloc, but failed to make it the rallying platform for all leftist groups in India.

Bose welcomed the outbreak of World War II as an opportunity for India to free itself from British domination. In July 1940 he was arrested under the Defense of India Rules but released on bail in December on grounds of deteriorating health. Despite police sur-veillance he escaped in January 1941 and reached Berlin via Soviet Russia by the beginning of April. His major aim, which he never achieved, was to bring about a joint declaration by the Axis Powers on Free India. With the outbreak of the Pacific War in December 1941 Bose desired to go to the Far East, where thousands of Indian prisoners of war were being recruited by Mohan SINGH under Japa-nese military auspices for the anti-British INDIAN NATIONAL ARMY (INA), but it was not until February 1943 that a submarine was made available to take him to Japan.

In May 1943 Bose arrived in Tōkyō and was immediately ac-claimed the undisputed leader, the "revered leader" (*netaji* in Bengali) of Free India. This last brief period of his life was the peak of his political career. He became a virtual dictator of the movement, taking over command of the remnants of the INA and of the Indian Independence League from Rash Behari BOSE, another activist long exiled in Japan. On 21 October 1943 he proclaimed the Provisional Government of Free India, which was recognized by Japan and other Axis countries. In November of the same year Bose represented India at the Greater East Asia Conference in Tōkyō (see GREATER EAST ASIA COPROSPERITY SPHERE). The Japanese showed confidence in his ability to unify Indians outside India and direct their activities toward assisting Japanese military operations. Under Bose's leadership the INA was reorganized and during 1944 took part in the abortive Japanese attempt to penetrate India from Burma. Bose's expectation that the entire nation would rise in revolt against the British at the mere appearance of the INA on Indian territory proved illusionary. After the defeat at Imphal (see IMPHAL CAMPAIGN) the INA ceased to be an effective fighting force. Bose nevertheless refused to give up his faith in Japanese victory and the paralysis of British rule in India by internal revolt, neither of which appeared imminent after 1943.

Bose reportedly died on 18 August 1945 following an air crash near Taipei. Ironically, his standing in India was never so great as at the moment of his death. "If by some miracle he had returned to India," his biographer N. Jog says, "he would have carried everything before him as Napoleon did after his escape from Elba."

📖——Subhas Chandra Bose, *The Indian Struggle, 1920–1942* (1964). Milan Hauner, *India in Axis Strategy: Germany, Japan, and Indian Nationalists in the Second World War* (1982). Hugh Toye, *The Springing Tiger* (1959).   Milan HAUNER

Boshin Civil War

(Boshin Sensō). Series of battles that led to the overthrow of the Tokugawa shogunate and the restoration of the imperial rule; it began with the Battle of TOBA–FUSHIMI on 27 January 1868 (Keiō 4.1.3, a year designated *boshin* in the sexagenary cycle) and ended with the Battle of GORYŌKAKU on 27 June 1869 (Meiji 2.5.18).

By 1867 it was clear that the shogunate could no longer hold out against the proimperial (SONNŌ JŌI) forces led by the Chōshū and Satsuma domains. The shōgun TOKUGAWA YOSHINOBU was willing to relinquish a measure of his authority only on condition that the shogunate retained political primacy. In November 1867 he nevertheless agreed to accept a compromise solution (see KŌGI SEITAI RON), proposed by the Tosa domain, whereby he would return political authority to the emperor and head a council of *daimyō*. But by that time Satsuma and Chōshū had decided to overthrow the shogunate by force, and on 3 January 1868 their troops seized the imperial palace in Kyōto and proclaimed an "imperial restoration" (ŌSEI FUKKO).

Yoshinobu withdrew to Ōsaka Castle, but some of his vassals were unwilling to submit, and shogunate troops from the castle engaged in pitched battle with "imperial" forces at Toba and Fushimi, south of Kyōto. The better-organized imperial forces, though outnumbered, won easily, and Yoshinobu quietly left by ship for Edo (now Tōkyō). Imperial armies under the command of Prince ARISUGAWA NO MIYA TARUHITO then advanced toward Edo, but under an agreement reached by SAIGŌ TAKAMORI of Satsuma and the shogunal retainer KATSU KAISHŪ, the city surrendered peaceably. Yoshinobu was ordered into domiciliary confinement in Mito (now Ibaraki Prefecture), but there was still resistance from pro-Tokugawa forces. About 2,000 shogunate troops, who called themselves the SHŌGITAI, gathered at a temple in the Ueno district of Edo but were crushed by the troops of ŌMURA MASUJIRŌ. Domains in northern Honshū formed a league (ŌUETSU REPPAN DŌMEI) under the leadership of the collateral *(shimpan)* Aizu domain, but these too finally surrendered on 6 November after the Battle of Aizu, which had lasted since late summer (see also BYAKKOTAI). A final center of resistance was Ezo (now Hokkaidō), where ENOMOTO TAKEAKI had fled with eight shogunate warships and proclaimed a "republic." After heavy attack he surrendered in June 1869. With the conclusion of hostilities, the entire country came under the control of the new "imperial" government, although the problem of paying for the war, despite contributions from MITSUI and other merchant houses, was to plague its leaders for a number of years.

There is an ongoing debate within progressive schools of history in Japan regarding the class configuration that underlay the two sides in the civil war. Depending on which configuration is seen as basic, different characterizations are possible: that it was a confrontation between the bourgeoisie and an absolutist shogunate; that it was a military struggle between two kinds of absolutism (the shogunate and a constellation of forces that would ultimately form the Meiji government); or that it was a conflict between absolutist forces and those who advocated a sharing of political power among the emperor, the shōgun, and the daimyō *(kōgi seitai ron)*. A consensus on the effect of the Boshin Civil War on the formation of modern Japan will not soon be reached. See also MEIJI RESTORATION.   *TANAKA Akira*

Boshin Shōsho

Imperial rescript issued by Emperor Meiji on 13 October 1908; named for *boshin,* the designation in the sexagenary cycle for the year corresponding to 1908. Conservative elements in Japan had been alarmed by what they considered unhealthy intellectual and social trends in the years following the Russo–Japanese War (1904–05), namely, the growth of liberal thought emphasizing individualism and political freedom, the emergence of the socialist movement, and the popular predilection for luxury and extravagance. They were able to convince the second KATSURA TARŌ cabinet, which had replaced the liberal SAIONJI KIMMOCHI cabinet, to have a rescript issued exhorting the people to unite and correct these excesses. The edict, together with the IMPERIAL RESCRIPT ON EDUCATION issued in 1890, was endorsed by the government as the guideline for the nation's morals and ethics until the end of World War II.

Bōsō Peninsula

(Bōsō Hantō). Located in Chiba Prefecture, central Honshū, bounded on the east by the Pacific Ocean and on the west by Tōkyō and Sagami bays. It is hilly (highest peak: Atagoyama, 408 m; 1,338 ft) with many beaches to the south. The Bōsō Peninsula contains part of the rapidly growing Keiyō Industrial Region with petroleum, petrochemical, and shipbuilding industries. There is also extensive floriculture and truck and dairy farming, but the once prosperous fishing industry is declining. Southern Bōsō Quasi-National Park is situated along the southern coast and Suigō–Tsukuba Quasi-National Park is located in the north. The area of the peninsula is 2,600 sq km (1,004 sq mi).

botan → peonies

botanical gardens

(shokubutsuen). There are presently about 50 major botanical gardens in Japan. The KOISHIKAWA BOTANIC GARDEN, belonging to Tōkyō University, was the first to be established (1877). This had previously been a medicinal herb garden belonging to the Tokugawa shogunate (1603–1867). In 1878 a second botanical garden was established by the Faculty of Agriculture of Hokkaidō University in Sapporo.

Nonuniversity botanical gardens have been established by the Ministry of Health and Welfare (e.g., the Tsukuba Experimental Station of Medicinal Plants), pharmaceutical companies, local governments, and private concerns, each with different aims, such as research, education, and business. Among these are the Institute for Nature Study (part of the National Science Museum in Tōkyō) and the Kōbe Municipal Educational Botanic Garden (in the city of Kōbe). After World War II many leisure-resort botanical gardens were set up in which tropical plants were grown using heat from hot springs. One of the largest botanical gardens in Japan is the Kōbe Municipal Arboretum (0.42 sq mi or 1.09 sq km) followed by the Shinjuku Gyoen National Garden in Tōkyō (0.22 sq mi or 0.57 sq km). Both of these function more as parks than as botanical gardens.

Among specialty gardens there are: the Izu Cactus Park (Shizuoka Prefecture); the Fuji Bamboo Botanical Garden (Shizuoka Prefecture) where only bamboo and bamboo grass are grown; and a type of garden called a Man'yō botanical garden where only plants mentioned in the 8th-century anthology of poetry known as the MAN'YŌSHŪ are cultivated (one of these is in Nara Prefecture, another in Shizuoka Prefecture). Because of Japan's wide range of latitudes, it has plants adapted to the nearly subarctic zone in the north and the subtropical zone in the south. The former types are found in Hokkaidō University's Botanical Garden, and the latter are cultivated in the Miyazaki Prefectural Subtropical Botanic Garden. The Mt. Hakkōda Alpine Botanical Garden in Aomori Prefecture and the Nikkō Botanic Garden in Tochigi Prefecture are known for their alpine plants. *Suzuki Zenji*

Bousquet, Georges Hilaire (1845?–?)

French legal adviser to the Meiji government, one of the many FOR-EIGN EMPLOYEES OF THE MEIJI PERIOD. Bousquet was working as a lawyer for the Court of Appeals in Paris when the Meiji government in 1872 invited him to help with the translation and interpretation of the Napoleonic code. During his four years in Japan, together with Gustave Emile BOISSONADE DE FONTARABIE, he taught law at the Meihōryō (later the Law School of the Ministry of Justice) and assisted in the drafting of the CIVIL CODE and other legislation. He also served informally as a consultant to the Ministry of Justice. His book *Le Japon de Nos Jours* (1877) reveals a man of many interests and broad learning. (Bousquet is often confused with another Frenchman, the military adviser Albert Charles DU BOUSQUET, 1837–82.) *Tanaka Akira*

bows and arrows → arms and armor

Boxer Rebellion

(J: Giwadan no Ran or Hokushin Jihen). A xenophobic uprising by Chinese peasants in North China in 1900. It was quelled by a foreign expeditionary force, about half of whom were Japanese.

The "Boxers" (Ch: Yihe quan or I-ho ch'üan) were members of secret societies affiliated with a heterodox Buddhist sect known as the White Lotus. Loosely organized and led by men of lower-class social origins, they practiced boxing and magic arts and claimed to be invulnerable to weapons. Many were peasants who found themselves hard pressed by both natural disasters and the effects of foreign economic encroachment in China. These problems were especially severe in Shandong (Shantung) Province, where imported goods and foreign-built railways and ships had displaced native home industries, barges, and small businesses, leading to numerous antiforeign outbursts. Initially the Boxers' targets were Chinese Christians, foreign missionaries, and even the alien Manchu rulers of the Qing (Ch'ing) dynasty (1644–1912). However, by 1899 they had been persuaded by officials to become the Manchu court's instrument to eliminate foreigners. With the court's powerful backing their numbers increased, and the antiforeign movement spread to four or five provinces in North China. They destroyed bridges, railways, and telegraph lines, burned churches, and killed Christians because they considered these manifestations of foreign domination.

The climax came in June 1900, when the court allowed the Boxers to enter Beijing (Peking). Thousands of them swarmed into the capital, burning and pillaging. They killed a senior member of the Japanese legation and the German minister, von Ketteler. With the aid of Chinese regular troops, they laid siege to the British legation, where several thousand foreigners and Chinese Christians had taken refuge. Meanwhile, governors in South China condemned the Boxers and agreed with the foreign powers to confine the conflict to the north. Some 20,000 troops from eight nations—Japan, Russia, Great Britain, the United States, France, Austria, and Italy (in order of the number of troops committed)—were hastily assembled in Tianjin (Tientsin). On 14 August this allied force broke the siege and occupied Beijing. German troops arrived in October, and by winter approximately 45,000 foreign soldiers had entered North China and put down the Boxers.

The Manchu court then sued for peace and after nine months signed the Boxer Protocol on 7 September 1901. Responsible persons were severely punished (a number of high officials were executed), apology missions were sent to Japan and Germany, foreign legations acquired the right to self-protection by their own troops, and China agreed to pay an indemnity of $333 million.

The aftereffects of the Boxer Rebellion were far-reaching. Russia's refusal to withdraw its troops from Manchuria after the disturbance led to the RUSSO-JAPANESE WAR in 1904–05. The Manchu court, thoroughly discredited, would fall a decade later. Finally, the huge indemnity seriously impeded the Chinese government's efforts for reform and modernization. Most of the nations (following the example set by the United States in 1908) remitted the indemnity funds, either partially or entirely, to China for cultural activities. The Japanese Diet adopted such a measure in 1923. However, con-

Boxes

Writing box *(suzuribako)* by Kōrin. Lacquer and inlay on wood. Height 14.1 cm. 18th century. Tōkyō National Museum. National Treasure.

trol of this fund remained in Japanese hands, unlike that of the Americans, who established a foundation with wide Chinese participation.

━━━Ichiko Chūzō, *Kindai Chūgoku no seiji to shakai* (1971). Bertram Lenox Simpson, *Indiscreet Letters from Peking* (1907). Chester C. Tan, *The Boxer Catastrophe* (1955). *Madeleine Chi*

boxes

(hako). Japanese boxes are made from a variety of materials and have long been prized for their aesthetic as well as their utilitarian value, especially those decorated with lacquer. The general term applied to boxes in Japan is *hako* or, when combined with another character, *bako,* as in *bentōbako* (lunch box), *haribako* (sewing box), *hōjubako* (jewel box), and *suzuribako* (writing box). The size and design of these boxes vary greatly, from *kōgō,* just a few centimeters square, to large boxes as long as 50 centimeters (about 20 in) used for storing sutras or swords. Their shapes also vary greatly. While most are rectangular, square, or round, boxes in the shape of musical instruments, animals, and flowers are also found. The most typically Japanese box form is the INRŌ, a small container for medicine, drugs, or a seal, which consists of several sections held together by a cord.

Other important box types commonly used include: *bunko* (for manuscripts), *chabako* (for tea), *kagamibako* (for mirrors), *kutsubako* (for shoes), *fudebako* (for pencils and pens), *kōbako* (for incense), *kushibako* (for combs), *obibako* (for *obi*), *hashibako* (for chopsticks), *suebako* (for priestly robes), *tantōbako* (for swords), *tebako* (for toiletries), *jūbako* (stacked boxes for food), *sagejū* or *sagejūbako* (a set of tiered boxes with a frame handle for holding *sake* bottles and cups). The earliest boxes appeared during the Nara period (710–794) and may be found among the treasures of the SHŌSOIN art repository in Nara.

The most common material employed in making boxes is wood, usually decorated with lacquer (see LACQUER WARE). Depending upon the skill of the craftsman and the wealth and status of the person for whom it is intended, the design may be very simple or very elaborate, using many layers of lacquer and decorations in gold and silver powder, as well as mother-of-pearl and metal inlay. Another popular type of decoration consists of carved or engraved designs. Some of the finest of these boxes, especially the writing boxes designed by HON'AMI KŌETSU and KŌRIN, are considered outstanding works of art and today are listed as NATIONAL TREASURES.

Other materials used for boxes are bamboo, wood, bark, grass, and reeds. Ceramics, particularly plain and decorated porcelain, are also popular, especially for food containers. A smaller number of boxes are made with decoration or inlay of mother-of-pearl, coconut shell, tortoiseshell, horn, leather, cloth, and fungus. Boxes are also made of metal, notably copper, bronze, brass, silver, and gold. Many old boxes employ precious materials and today are regarded as priceless antiques, but even ordinary boxes made of common materials are often beautiful and are admired as fine examples of Japanese folk art. *Hugo* MÜNSTERBERG

Boy Scouts

Boy Scout activities in Japan began in Tōkyō in 1915. In 1922 the national organization known as the Boy Scouts of Nippon was formally established. It was disbanded during World War II but resumed activities again after the war. In 1956 the first all-Japan jamboree was held. In 1971 the Boy Scout world jamboree (the 13th) took place for the first time in Japan. During Boy Scout Week in May, many social service projects are conducted throughout Japan. In 1979 there were 3,403 Boy Scout troops with some 280,000 members in Japan. SHIBANUMA *Susumu*

Boys' Day → Children's Day

bracelets, ancient

(kushiro). Common body ornaments of the prehistoric and protohistoric periods. After the adoption of Buddhism in the 6th century, body ornamentation gradually ceased and bracelets were not worn again until the modern influx of Western culture.

Bracelets of the Early Jōmon period (ca 5000 BC–ca 3500 BC) were fashioned by opening a hole in the *akagai* or *sarubō* types of bivalve ark shells. In the Yayoi period (ca 300 BC–ca AD 300), bracelets began to be made of spiral shells. Scholarly opinions have it that South Pacific winged conch shells *(gohōra)* were cut vertically to make bracelets for men, and women wore ones made of *imogai* cone shells. Bronze bracelets imitating the shape of the spiked *suijigai* shell made their appearance together with bronze bells (DŌTAKU) and BRONZE WEAPONS during this period.

Shell and bronze bracelets continued into the Kofun period (ca 300–710)—some of the latter cast with attached bells (SUZU) but in addition, exquisitely fashioned stone bracelets made mainly of jasper or green tuff made their appearance. Hoe-shaped bracelets *(kuwagataishi)*—so called because their shape resembles that of a hoe blade—were actually stone imitations of the Yayoi-period conch shell bracelets. Wheel-shaped bracelets *(sharinseki)* were stone imitations of limpet shell *(kasagai)* bracelets. These retain the radiating pattern of ridges of the original shell around a central hole which was standardized at about 6 centimeters (2.4 in) in diameter regardless of the overall bracelet size. Larger, oval wheel bracelets are peculiar to the Kinai (Kyōto–Ōsaka–Nara) region, whereas round ones are found from Fukuoka to Chiba prefectures. Hoe bracelets are also centered in the Kinai but are distributed from Ishikawa and Aichi to Ōita prefectures. These stone bracelets—some decorated with CHOKKOMON designs—are thought to be treasures rather than everyday items, and they are often discovered together with BRONZE MIRRORS as funerary goods in the Kofun-period tomb mounds (see KOFUN) of western Japan. See also EAR ORNAMENTS, ANCIENT; BEADS, ANCIENT. KITAMURA *Bunji*

Brandt, Max August Scipio von (1835–1920)

German diplomat who went to Japan in 1862 as aide to Friedrich Albert EULENBURG, the Prussian delegate sent to conclude the Prusso-Japanese Treaty of 1861. He was appointed the first Prussian consul general in Japan in 1862 (at Yokohama) and wrote *Dreiunddreissig Jahre in Ost-Asien* (1901, Thirty-Three Years in East Asia).

Brazil and Japan

The relationship between Japan and Brazil may be said to be of a complementary nature. Japan has imported raw materials from Brazil, while Brazil has obtained capital and technology from Japan. Japanese emigration to Brazil, too, can be seen in this relationship. At the outset, emigration was for Japan a solution to the problem of overpopulation; for Brazil, immigrants supplied labor much needed on coffee plantations.

During the years preceding World War II, trade between the two nations grew rapidly. Japan wanted Brazil to take the place of the United States as a cotton supplier, and Japanese immigrants produced 50 percent of the Brazilian cotton exported to Japan. When, as a result of the war, Japan lost its overseas possessions and absorbed many repatriates, emigration to Brazil again increased. However, this rather massive agricultural emigration shifted into an industrial emigration from around the late 1950s, when Japan moved out of its immediate postwar period. Japan became a supplier of technicians whom Brazil needed for its industrialization, and Japanese industries began building factories in Brazil.

As Brazil entered a high-level economic growth period in the 1970s, the economic ties between the two nations evolved further with increasing trade and more Japanese industries moving to Brazil. In the late 1970s, Japan was a major partner of Brazil, providing capital and technology for the Brazilian government's resource development projects.

Early Relations——Diplomatic relations between Japan and Brazil were established on 5 November 1895, when a treaty of amity, commerce, and navigation was signed in Paris. In 1897 a Japanese legation was opened in Petropolis, in the state of Rio de Janeiro; Chinda Sutemi (1857–1929) was appointed the first minister there, and Enrique Carlos Ribeiro-Lisboa became Brazil's minister to Japan.

Both countries had started moving toward the treaty at the beginning of the 1890s. In 1892 the Brazilian government revoked its regulations prohibiting the immigration of Asians, and in 1894 the Prado Jordão Co of São Paulo inquired about Japanese immigration. On the Japanese side, an emigration office was set up in 1891 in the Ministry of Foreign Affairs, and in the same year the Kichisa Emigration Co was founded. In 1894 a set of rules for the protection of emigrants was enacted under Imperial Ordinance No. 42. In July of 1894 Nemoto Tadashi (1851–1933), an advocate of the cause of emigration and colonization, visited Brazil as an adviser to the Japanese Ministry of Agriculture and reported to the Colonists' Association headed by ENOMOTO TAKEAKI that the state of São Paulo was the most promising area for prospective Japanese settlement.

A 1902 Italian government ban on the passage of contract emigrants to Brazil, imposed because of poor conditions on coffee plantations, is supposed to have prompted the Japanese immigration. In 1906 Mizuno Ryō (1859–1951) visited Brazil looking for places suitable for Japanese settlement. When he returned to Brazil the following year, he negotiated and signed a contract with the minister of agriculture of São Paulo state to send 3,000 Japanese immigrants over the following three years. On 28 April 1908 Mizuno, as the president of the Imperial Colonization Co, and UETSUKA SHŪHEI, as its agent in Brazil, led the first 781 immigrants to Brazil on the steamer *Kasato maru* and landed at Santos on 18 June. Uetsuka's great efforts on behalf of the early immigrants won him the title of father of Japanese immigration to Brazil.

In 1908 Mizuno made a second immigration contract, which was followed by similar contracts concluded by the Takemura Colonization Co and Oriental Immigration, Inc. Immigration during this period totaled about 10,000, but it came to a halt in 1914, when the state government of São Paulo suspended its subsidies to Japanese immigrants for financial reasons. The total number of Japanese immigrants ultimately reached 190,000 in the period before World War II. See also BRAZIL, JAPANESE IMMIGRANTS IN.

Prewar Commerce——In 1906, two years before the arrival of the first Japanese immigrants, Fujisaki & Co sent a staff of four clerks to Brazil. They opened O Japão em São Paulo, a store selling Japanese goods, which was followed from 1909 on by the establishment of other stores in Rio de Janeiro, such as Japan Brazil Co, Hachiya & Co, Fujisaki & Co, Yamagata & Co, and Kyōto Products. The trade between Japan and Brazil through these merchants amounted in 1913 to £35,933 in imports from Japan, including such items as ceramics, celluloid, toys, toothbrushes, fans, and buttons, while Brazilian exports of rock crystal and coffee to Japan totaled £2,931. Japanese products accounted for two-tenths of 1 percent of the total value of Brazilian imports at that time.

Toward the end of World War I, when imports from Europe were disrupted, Brazil increased its imports from Japan, especially of metal products and sundry goods; they totaled £326,226 in 1918, £500,624 in 1919, and £591,806 in 1920, when they amounted to 0.7 percent of total Brazilian imports. In July 1919, the YOKOHAMA SPECIE BANK opened a branch in Rio de Janeiro. When European countries recovered from the war, however, and resumed trade with Brazil in 1922, Japanese steel products and machinery could not compete with European products, and trade between Japan and Brazil remained insignificant until 1936.

In the 1929 depression, Brazil learned a hard lesson from the oversupply of coffee and turned to the production of cotton. Thanks to development efforts by the Campinas Agricultural Experiment Station, São Paulo cotton began to gain a wider market from 1932, and 60 bales of sample cotton were sent to Japan in 1934. In 1935 Japan sent a trade mission to Brazil that led to a great expansion in trade between 1936 and 1941. This mission, led by Hirao Hachisaburō (1866–1946), consisted of representatives from TŌYŌBŌ CO, LTD; C. ITOH & CO, LTD; the Ōsaka Shōsen shipping line; MITSUI & CO, LTD; and the MITSUBISHI CORPORATION. Hirao's idea of replacing cotton from the United States with Brazilian cotton proved a success, for, apart from its one objective of helping Japanese immigrants in cotton production, Brazilian cotton was cheaper than the American product, and Japan was anxious to avoid dependence on the United States in view of the impending threat of war. Hirao himself established the Japan–Brazil Cotton Co in Ōsaka and opened a subsidiary in Brazil, Brazcot, with five cotton-processing factories at Japanese settlements in São Paulo state.

Following this expansion of trade, the government of Brazil relaxed its restrictions on foreign exchange and thus promoted imports from Japan. Japanese corporations such as TŌYŌ MENKA KAISHA, LTD, Konishi Shōten, Mitsui & Co, Bratac Trading, Kanematsu, and C. Itoh & Co opened branches in Brazil. Brazilian exports to Japan jumped from £158,098 in 1935 to £1,683,106 in 1936 and £2,122,106 in 1937, accounting for 5 percent of Brazil's total exports, and continued on this level until World War II.

After the Pacific War had started in 1941, Presidential Decree 4166 of February 1942 ordered the freezing of Japanese assets in Brazil. The Japanese in the Conde district of São Paulo and Santos were ordered to move out within 10 days, and in July Japanese diplomats in Brazil returned to Japan.

Postwar Relations and Japanese Investments —— In 1949 a Japanese trade mission visited Brazil and reached an agreement on foreign trade payments covering US $35 million (¥12.6 billion) worth of trade. Upon the arrival of five diplomatic officers in Rio de Janeiro in December 1950, diplomatic ties were restored between the two countries. The resumption of friendly relations was greatly promoted by the visit to Brazil of a Japanese sports delegation, including the then world-famous swimmers Furuhashi Hironoshin and Hashizume Shirō in the same year. Their visit gave great encouragement to the Japanese immigrants who had been distressed over Japan's defeat in the war.

In 1952 Brazil approved the entry of 9,000 Japanese families as immigrants, of which 5,000 families represented by Uetsuka Tsukasa were to be placed in the Amazon Basin and 4,000 families represented by Matsubara Yasutarō in the state of Mato Grosso. The first group of immigrants to the Amazon, consisting of 54 members, arrived in February 1953; the first group to Mato Grosso arrived at Santos in August 1953.

When President Juscelino Kubitschek de Oliveira (b 1902) took office in 1955, pledging that his presidency would achieve 50 years worth of development in 5 years, he introduced a free import licensing system for machinery and industrial facilities. Major corporations throughout the world responded favorably to this policy of attracting foreign capital, and Brazil thereupon entered a period of rapid industrial development.

Along with European and American corporations, Japanese companies, too, began small-scale capital investments in Brazil. In 1954 FUJI BANK, LTD, invested in Banco America do Sul, a bank run by Japanese immigrants. In 1955 the Tōyōbō Spinning Company became the first Japanese manufacturer to operate in Brazil, and soon Pilot Fountain Pen opened a branch. Their lead was followed by KANEBŌ, LTD, Hōwa Industries, Kurashiki Spinning, and AJINOMOTO CO, INC, in 1956; KUBOTA, LTD, YANMAR DIESEL ENGINE CO, LTD, Sadokin Lamp, San'yō Woolen, and Hakkoku Seiki in 1957; TOYOTA MOTOR CORPORATION, UNITIKA, LTD, and FUJI PHOTO FILM CO, LTD, in 1958; and Ishikawajima Shipbuilding and TAIYŌ FISHERY CO, LTD, in 1959. Usiminas Steel, a large-scale joint project of the governments of Japan and Brazil, was established in 1958 and opened in 1961. The first ship built by Ishikawajima in Brazil, the *Volta Redonda*, was launched in January 1961.

Brazil's political situation was thrown into chaos that year, however, as President Janio Quadros (b 1917) suddenly announced his resignation at a time of rampant inflation and Vice-President João Goulart (b 1918) assumed the presidency. Under Goulart's presidency, labor unions and left-wing parties gained strength and staged frequent walkouts, creating major problems for corporations such as Usiminas and Ishikawajima. Furthermore, as a result of inflation, the proportion of Japanese capital investment in Usiminas decreased from an initial 40 percent to 18 percent, leading to criticism of Japanese participation in the project from Japanese Brazilians. During the first stage of the entry of Japanese industries into Brazil, which spanned the period from the military coup in 1954 to the stabilization of the economy in 1967, a total of 79 Japanese corporations established branches in Brazil.

Postwar Trade —— In 1952 Japan and Brazil reached a bilateral agreement to adopt an open-account settlement. At the same time Brazil adopted a multiple exchange system, under which a limited amount of import exchange was auctioned by the Brazilian government. Since the Japanese yen was cheap compared with American or European currencies, trade expanded rapidly, from $10 million (unilateral) in 1952 to $70 million in 1954. The Japanese purchase of Brazilian cotton fell, however, because of bumper cotton crops in the United States, and Brazil's exchange with Japan was exhausted after September 1954. From February 1955 the authorized amount of Japanese import exchange was reduced, stabilizing around the $40 million level. In 1961 Brazilian exchange was decontrolled and the open-account system was replaced with a free-settlement system. This triggered massive imports of machinery by Japanese corporations in Brazil and pushed Brazilian imports from Japan up to $86 million. It was also a good year for Brazilian exports to Japan; because of the Cuban crisis, the Japanese turned to Brazil for sugar, and the amount of Brazil's exports to Japan reached $73 million. However, from 1962 to 1967, that is, until Brazil entered its period of higher economic growth, trade between Brazil and Japan remained on the average level of $40 million a year.

Brazil's economy grew at an annual rate of 9 percent from 1968 on and reached 11 percent from 1971 to 1973. Political and economic conditions, which had been unstable with a chronic inflationary trend up to the 1960s, improved in the 1970s, and inflation began to shrink. This period of high economic growth in Brazil coincided with an increasing reserve of foreign currency in Japan. Japan revalued the yen and relaxed its restrictions against currency outflow, thus motivating many more Japanese industries to branch out into Brazil. Two major Japanese trade missions visited Brazil in 1971 and 1972, and in the latter year a Japan Industrial Fair was held in São Paulo, sponsored by JETRO (Japan External Trade Organization). Brazil also sent its minister of planning and general coordination and minister of justice to Japan in 1972. A boom was created in Japan–Brazil relations, and over 150 Japanese corporations opened branches in Brazil between 1968 and 1973.

In view of this development, the government of Brazil adopted a policy of screening foreign investment instead of granting admittance to all as it had formerly done. As a result, Japanese industries producing goods for export to international markets and willing to operate jointly with Brazilian corporations expanded their role. In spite of the fact that Brazil's growth rate slowed down in 1974 due to oil price increases, Japanese industries went ahead with their plans for building factories in Brazil. According to annual reports of the Central Bank of Brazil, Japan's total direct investment and reinvestment in Brazil ranked sixth among all nations in June 1963, whereas in June 1976 it had risen to third after the United States and West Germany, and to second in direct investment, excluding reinvestment.

In the first half of the 1970s, bilateral trade between Japan and Brazil increased rapidly, from $380 million in 1970 to $640 million in 1972. The joint statement issued on Prime Minister TANAKA KAKUEI's visit to Brazil in 1974 expressed satisfaction with bilateral trade having surpassed the $1 billion mark. Trade in 1974 actually amounted to $2.06 billion, of which $1.39 billion was from Japan to Brazil and $670 million from Brazil to Japan.

Large-Scale Economic Cooperation —— In the latter half of the 1970s the focus of the economic relationship shifted to large-scale economic cooperative projects based on agreements between the two governments. In this connection, syndicate loans by private banks for large projects and the floating of yen-dominated bonds in Japan by the Brazilian government and Brazilian corporations were the main features on the trade scene.

In 1976 President Ernesto Geisel paid a visit to Japan to promote four large projects. These were the Cenibra project for producing 250,000 metric tons (275,575 short tons) of pulp a year and exporting half of it to Japan, the Albras aluminum refining project in the Amazonas, a project for developing 50,000 hectares (123,500 acres) of agricultural land in Cerrado, and the Tubarão steelworks project in which Kawasaki Steel was to take part. Each of these projects was too large for private enterprise to handle alone. However, these developments are only one element in the emerging cooperative relationship between Brazil and Japan. It is expected that the hundreds of Japanese firms in Brazil and the over 800,000 Brazilians of Japanese descent (1981) will play an increasingly vital role in Brazilian life in the years to come and make the link between the two countries stronger than ever.   *Saitō Hiroshi*

Brazil, Japanese immigrants in

It was on 18 June 1908 that the first Japanese immigrants, 781 in number, landed from the steamer *Kasato maru* at the port of Santos. Since then Japanese have continued to emigrate to Brazil, except for temporary interruptions during the two world wars. Naturally, there have been fluctuations in the number of emigrants, depending upon social and economic conditions in the two countries. Although the Japanese are relative latecomers to Brazil compared to European immigrant groups such as the Germans and Italians, whose roots go back to the 19th century, they have joined their predecessors in making substantial contributions to Brazilian society while at the same time raising their own status within that society. Their achievements in starting out as agricultural laborers and going on to play an important role in the growth and improvement of Brazilian agriculture have created the present positive image now enjoyed by Brazilians of Japanese descent in Brazilian society at large.

Emigration to Brazil —— The history of Japanese emigration to Brazil may be roughly divided into three periods. During the first, from 1908 to 1924, there were 40,000 Japanese emigrants. The government of the state of São Paulo provided half of their traveling expenses and received them as contract laborers (*colono*) on coffee plantations. The second period, from 1925 to 1941, was the peak period of Japanese emigration, promoted partly by the worldwide depression that started in 1929 and partly by the encouragement of the Japanese government. This period recorded 150,000 emigrants to Brazil. Most of them, like their predecessors, were contract laborers on coffee plantations, but some settled as independent farmers in the states of São Paulo, Paraná, and Pará. The third or postwar period began in 1953, when emigration was resumed, and by 1977 about 60,000 more Japanese had relocated in Brazil. Since Japan entered its period of high economic growth in the 1960s, however, the number of emigrants has decreased to less than 100 a year. Thus, total Japanese immigration over the 70 years since 1908 amount to approximately 250,000.

In the early 1980s the Japanese population in Brazil was estimated at over 800,000 of which about 20 percent were immigrants born in Japan. Although all the Brazilian states have some Japanese population, 75 percent of the total is concentrated in the state of São Paulo and 18 percent in Paraná. The city of São Paulo and its suburbs have the highest concentration of the Japanese population, with about 300,000 Japanese living in the greater São Paulo area. One factor contributing to this pattern is the large number of Japanese engaged in truck farming and horticulture. Another is that, as a result of the increasing diversity of occupations among Japanese, many now work in urban industries. In particular, many of the children born to first-generation immigrants on farms and sent to cities for higher education have tended to remain there. However, this concentration in large cities is partially countered by a simultaneous trend toward dispersion into newly developing inland areas.

Agricultural Areas —— The Japanese contribution to Brazil's agricultural development has been especially noteworthy, and agricultural activity also formed the basis for the later Japanese entry into commerce and industry. At the outset Japanese merchants dealing in farm tools and fertilizer found customers chiefly among Japanese farmers, while Japanese manufacturers in rural towns began by processing agricultural products or making farm equipment.

The contributions made by Japanese immigrants in agriculture took three main forms, of which the first was the introduction and improvement of foreign plants. Japanese immigrants brought with them numerous plants ranging from fruit trees to vegetables and ornamentals. Several, such as rape (*tsukena*), Japanese radish (*daikon*), shallot (*rakkyō*), shaddock (*ponkan*), kumquat (*kinkan*), persimmon (*kaki*), and loquat (*biwa*), have become popular among Brazilians. The second was the introduction of new agricultural techniques. The Japanese style of intensive farming on a small unit of land has proven innovative in Brazil. A good example of technology transfer, it has been further adapted to local conditions and gradually adopted by Brazilian farmers.

The third major contribution was the foundation of several large-scale cooperative associations, such as the Cotia Industrial Cooperative, the Sul Brasil Agricultural Cooperative, and the São Paulo Central Association, by Japanese immigrants. Although they were originally started to help Japanese to purchase production equipment and to merchandise their produce, they have grown remarkably, along with the economies of their regions, and today they rank among the leading agricultural organizations of Brazil. Special mention is due to the "Cotia Youth," 2,500 young Japanese immigrants accepted under an agreement between the Brazilian government and the Cotia Industrial Cooperative between 1955 and 1967, who are now making major contributions to Brazil's agricultural development.

Urban Areas —— From the 1950s on, a notable shift began among the Japanese population from agricultural to other industries. Although this was in keeping with the general demographic trend in Brazil, there were also particular circumstances that motivated Japanese immigrants toward cities. As they made up their minds to remain in Brazil instead of going back to Japan, many of them moved to cities for the education of their children. Also, an increasing number of the second- and third-generation Japanese in Brazil began to find careers in the professions, commerce, and industry.

Behind this transition lay what may be termed an identity crisis, which constituted a turning point in the history of Japanese immigration in Brazil. The news of Japan's defeat in World War II had left many Japanese immigrants, like the Japanese in Japan, in utter despair. Their identity as Japanese, which had always provided spiritual support for them in meeting the difficulties they encountered in a foreign country, was now lost. There were even hostilities between those who could not believe in the defeat of Japan and those who recognized the fact. When they finally emerged from this period of confusion, which continued for almost 10 years into the early 1950s, they regained a peace of mind based not on their identity as Japanese, as in the prewar period, but rather as Japanese Brazilians.

After having overcome this identity crisis they showed a marked difference in their attitudes. Many sold their farms and moved to São Paulo, running small businesses in order to give their children access to higher education. Thus, the number of Japanese youth who advanced to college increased in the late 1950s, and this trend continues today. Japanese Brazilians employed in tertiary industries (commerce, services, communications, public service, and so forth) now outnumber those in agriculture. According to a study undertaken at the University of São Paulo, the percentage of students of Japanese descent among those granted admission to the university in 1978 were: 17 percent in engineering and architecture; 15 percent in medicine, pharmacology, and biology; and an average of 12.8 percent in all other fields. Japanese Brazilians are now active in all areas of life in Brazil: politics, the academic world, finance, the arts, and Brazilian culture in general.

Another notable change is the increasing frequency of marriage with non-Japanese Brazilians. Until the 1950s ethnic purism prevailed among Japanese immigrants, and young Japanese who sought to marry Brazilians met strong objection from their parents. In the 1960s, however, parents grew more lenient, and today intermarriage has become so common that almost every Japanese family has Brazilians of non-Japanese ancestry among the spouses of their relatives.

New Patterns —— Immigration has taken different forms over the years. Japanese immigrants to Brazil until 1941 consisted mostly of workers on coffee plantations. In the first decade or so of the postwar period, too, most of the immigrants from Japan were laborers and independent farmers. Since Japan entered its period of high economic growth, however, the number of immigrants has decreased sharply and, instead, Japanese corporations have become major "immigrants," bringing capital, technology, and personnel. Although most Japanese employees of these corporations are only temporary residents in Brazil and therefore may not properly be called immigrants, the corporations themselves settle and operate in Brazil permanently. Moreover, some employees who go to Brazil for a temporary stay decide to remain there. See also BRAZIL AND JAPAN.   *Saitō Hiroshi*

brewing

(*jōzō*). Method of preparing beverages and other foods by fermenting, boiling, steeping, or infusing. The Japanese have traditionally brewed such products as SAKE, MISO, SOY SAUCE, and vinegar. The extensive use of *kōji* (rice, beans, or barley fermented with *Aspergillus* fungi) is characteristic of Japanese brewing. *Kōji* is used as the enzyme for breaking down starch in *sake* brewing (corresponding to malt in beer making); it also supplies the decomposition enzyme for protein in brewing *miso* and soy sauce.

Sake is a liquor made from nonglutinous rice. The rice is 70 to 75 percent polished and then steamed. The *kōji* is made by adding a fungus of the *Aspergillus oryzae-flavus* group to a portion of the steamed rice. Separately, a seed mash *(moto)* is made by leaving another quantity of steamed rice to ferment, producing a large amount of the *sake* yeast. A rapid-brewing seed mash, which requires 9 to 12 days to ferment, is now extensively employed. A mixture of steamed rice, *kōji*, and water, totaling 15 times the volume of the seed mash, is added in three stages over 4 days. The fermentation of the main mash *(moromi)* is complete in 20 to 22 days, during which time the alcoholic content reaches 18 to 19 percent. The brewing of *sake* is characterized by simultaneous saccharification and alcoholic fermentation, which is called parallel multiple fermentation. As a result, the main *sake* mash *(moromi)* has the highest alcoholic content among fermented liquors. In the triple-brewing method, which is utilized extensively now, a flavoring alcohol (a mixture of glucose, starch syrup, lactic acid, succinic acid, and sodium glutamate with high-quality alcohol) is added to the fermented mash. Dregs are removed by passing the fermented mash through a filter press, and the raw *sake*, clarified through further filtration, is heated to 60 to 63°C (140 to 145.5°F) for several minutes in order to pasteurize the *sake* and destroy the remaining ferment. It is then left to mature in a cool, dark storage area.

Miso is a traditional Japanese seasoning which is made by fermenting steamed soy beans mixed with rice *kōji* or malt *kōji* and salt. *Miso* has been made throughout the country since ancient times, in many varieties and often with specific local features.

Soy sauce is a liquid seasoning made by fermenting the *kōji* of soy beans and wheat with a solution of salt; it has a distinct aroma and flavor. Most *kōji* used in soy sauce is fermented with *Aspergillus sojae*, although *A. oryzae* is also used. A mixture of *kōji* and a solution of salt is placed in a wooden or concrete fermentation tank, where it matures with occasional churning at room temperature for up to one year. The mature mixture *(moromi)* contains about 18 percent salt and small amounts of salt-resistant lactic acid bacteria, *Pediscoccus sojae,* and salt-resistant yeast, *Sacchromyces rouxii.* The final product is made by pressing the fermented mash, heating the raw soy sauce to 80°C (176°F) to pasteurize it and solidify the integrated protein, and clarifying the liquid by removing the dregs. 📖——Nihon Shokuryō Shimbun Sha, ed, *Shokuhin sangyō jiten* (1972). AIDA Kō

bridges

(hashi). According to early chronicles, Japan's first bridge was built in Ikai no Tsu (in what is now Ōsaka Prefecture) in the 4th century. In 612 bridge-construction techniques were introduced from Paekche (Korea); bridges built at this time are thought to have featured handrails with round ornamental tops *(giboshi)* similar to those on Chinese bridges of the Tang (T'ang) period (618–907). Typical premodern Japanese bridges consisted of wooden foundation abutments and piers supporting walkways made of wooden planks. This kind of bridge continued to be built until the mid-19th century, and examples may be seen in the woodblock prints of HOKUSAI. However, there were several other bridges of various types built in the premodern period. Among these were the Kintaibashi, a series of wooden arches built in 1673 in Iwakuni (in what is now Yamaguchi Prefecture); the Saruhashi, a wooden bridge supported by a series of horizontal beams projecting out over a deep, narrow gorge in Ōtsuki (in what is now Yamanashi Prefecture); and the Kazurabashi, a suspension bridge made of vines in what is now Tokushima Prefecture. Over 40 stone arch bridges were built in the Kyūshū area. The oldest of these is the Meganebashi in Nagasaki, a double-arch stone bridge said to have been built by the Chinese monk Ruding (Ju-ting) in 1634. Most, however, were built in the 19th century.

After the Meiji Restoration (1868), European bridge-building techniques were introduced to Japan. In 1869 the first steel bridge was built in Nagasaki Prefecture. In the same year the first steel truss bridge, the Yoshidabashi, was completed in Yokohama. These were followed by the construction of the bridges Shinsaibashi in Ōsaka and Danjōbashi in Tōkyō. The oldest steel arch bridge in Japan is the Asakusabashi in Tōkyō, which was completed in 1898. The first reinforced concrete bridge was built in 1903 over a canal near Lake Biwa. By 1915, at least 167 steel bridges, 292 wooden bridges, and 3 drawbridges were built in Japan.

Bridges

			Span	Year
Type	Name	Prefecture	(meters)	completed
Steel				
Suspension	Kammon Bridge	Yamaguchi and Fukuoka	712	1973
Cable-braced	Suehiro Bridge	Tokushima	250	1975
Cantilever	Minato Bridge	Ōsaka	510	1974
Truss	Ōshima Bridge	Yamaguchi	325	1976
Arch	Ōmishima Bridge	Ehime	297	1979
Girder	Second Maya Bridge	Hyōgo	210	1975
Concrete				
Arch	Hokawazu Bridge	Saga	170	1974
Girder	Hamana Bridge	Shizuoka	240	1976

Japan's Longest Bridges, by Type

SOURCE: Nihon Dōro Kōdan (Japan Highway Public Corporation), *Nempō* (annual): 1981.

The technology of bridge construction made dramatic progress during the reconstruction period after the Tōkyō Earthquake of 1923. During this period three modern bridges—the Kiyosu, the Eitai, and the Kachidoki—were constructed over the Sumida River (Sumidagawa) in Tōkyō, marking the emergence of Japanese bridge-construction technology in its own right. Several major bridges were built after World War II, including the Saikai Bridge in 1955, the Wakato Bridge in 1962, the Amakusa Bridge in 1966, the Kammon Bridge in 1973, and the Minato Bridge in 1974. The technological experience gained in those projects was being used in the construction of a series of bridges connecting the islands of Honshū and Shikoku. The opening of the Ōmishima Bridge in 1979 was a major step toward that goal. KURANISHI Shigeru

Bridgestone Tire Co, Ltd

Major Japanese manufacturer of rubber products, including automotive tires and tubes, industrial products, chemical products, and golf balls. Founded in Kurume, Fukuoka Prefecture, in 1931 by ISHIBASHI SHŌJIRŌ, Bridgestone captured the dominant position of the Japanese tire industry, using only Japanese capital and technology. The firm is active in technological development and pioneered the development of rayon-cord tires, nylon-cord tires, and steel-cord tires in Japan. It has also introduced a great number of nontire products. Bridgestone also has four joint-venture manufacturing plants overseas, and is a major exporter of tires and industrial rubber products to over 150 countries. The company's future plans include acceleration of its international sales and manufacturing. It now has technical arrangements with Goodyear Tire and Rubber Co of the United States. Annual sales for 1981 totaled ¥514 billion (US $2.3 billion), of which tires and tubes accounted for 84 percent, and nontire products 16 percent; exports accounted for 33 percent. In the same year the company was capitalized at ¥23.76 billion (US $107.7 million). The head office is located in Tōkyō.

Brinkley, Frank (1841–1912)

Anglo-Irish journalist. Owner and editor of the Tōkyō English-language newspaper the *Japan Mail* from 1881 and a Tōkyō-based correspondent for the *Times* of London, notably during the RUSSO-JAPANESE WAR of 1904–05. Born in Ireland and schooled in Dublin, Brinkley arrived in Japan as a Royal Artillery officer of the British Legation in 1867, on the eve of the Meiji Restoration. In 1871 he resigned his commission in the army to become a military instructor for the new Meiji government. Later he taught mathematics at the national Engineering College (Kōbu Daigakkō), one of the predecessors of Tōkyō University, until he joined the *Japan Mail* in 1881. He was known for his broad, generally sympathetic interest in Japan's modernization and his opposition to the unequal treaties that imposed extraterritoriality on Japan. Brinkley did not favor the SINO-JAPANESE WAR OF 1894–1895, but criticized the TRIPARTITE INTERVENTION in its aftermath. His reporting was influential in Europe and America, and he has been credited with helping to mold the favorable public opinion of Japan in England that facilitated the ANGLO-JAPANESE ALLIANCE of 1902.

Broadcasting

Number of Households Subscribing to NHK

	Contracts for black and white TV reception	Contracts for color TV reception	Total	Diffusion rate[1] in percentages	
				all TVs	color TVs
1973	8,802,517	15,630,946	24,433,463	76.6	49.0
1974	6,589,370	18,335,615	24,924,985	76.4	56.2
1975	5,209,702	20,543,694	25,753,396	77.3	61.7
1976	4,282,310	22,262,448	26,544,758	82.6	69.3
1977	3,749,433	23,309,448	27,058,881	78.7	67.8
1978	3,345,790	24,427,429	27,773,219	79.7	70.1
1979	3,100,317	25,293,365	28,393,682	80.3	71.6
1980	2,920,295	26,011,397	28,931,692	80.7	72.6
1981	2,777,063	26,485,928	29,262,991	80.5	72.9

[1]Ratio of contracts to households based on the population census for 1976, 1978, 1981; Residents' Basic Registers (Jūmin Kihon Daichō) for all other years.
NOTE: Figures are for the end of March in each year.
SOURCE: Prime Minister's Office, Statistics Bureau, *Japan Statistical Yearbook* (annual): 1976, 1979, 1982.

Brinkley married the daughter of a former *samurai* family and was as much concerned with Japan's culture as with its politics. Fluent in Japanese, he translated several NŌ and KYŌGEN plays. His illustrated, multivolume *Japan: Its History, Arts, and Literature* (1901) was the first journalistic survey of Japanese history and culture in English. He also compiled a *Japanese-English Dictionary* (1896) that replaced that of James Curtis HEPBURN and a best-selling English grammar in Japanese. Brinkley is also remembered for donating his large collection of Japanese prints to the New York Public Library. His son John (1887–1964), a long-time journalist and teacher in Japan and a convert to Buddhism, was an official at the Tōkyō War Crimes Trial in 1946–48.   *Dallas* FINN

British Commonwealth Occupation Force

(BCOF). Air, sea, and land forces drawn from Great Britain, Australia, New Zealand, and India; stationed in Japan during the Allied OCCUPATION (1945–52). The BCOF was never large, numbering about 39,000 troops in mid-1946, and operated generally in the Chūgoku region and on the island of Shikoku. The Australian role in the BCOF was considerable, since the commander-in-chief was an Australian who had direct access to the Supreme Commander for the Allied Powers (SCAP) and was also responsible to an organization of British Commonwealth Joint Chiefs of Staff located in Melbourne. See also AUSTRALIA AND JAPAN.   *J. A. A.* STOCKWIN

Broadcast College

(Hōsō Daigaku). A planned public college, utilizing radio and television broadcasts, which was scheduled to go into operation in 1984. The proposed aim was to provide people with the opportunity to participate in and receive university-level course work, whatever their place of residence. The college was to be patterned after the British Open University. In 1975 a decision was made to allocate a nationwide network of UHF television and FM radio stations for use by the Broadcast College. In 1978 the Broadcast Education Development Center was established to begin drawing up concrete plans for operation of the college. The college and broadcasting network were slated to be operated by a special corporation to be known as the Hōsō Daigaku Gakuen through tuition fees and subsidies provided by the national treasury. Qualification for admission would require that a person be a high-school graduate. However, special consideration would also be given to qualified non-high-school graduates. Applicants would be selected by the drawing of lots. Credits would be acquired by listening to a minimum of two lectures a week and through schooling provided by local study centers. Upon successful completion of the study program the student would be awarded a Bachelor of Arts degree. The college would have three departments: domestic science, business-social science, and humanities-natural science.   NISHIMOTO *Yōichi*

broadcasting

Broadcasting is defined in Japan's BROADCASTING LAW (Hōsō Hō, 1950) and RADIO LAW (Dempa Hō, 1950) as "wireless communication intended for direct reception by the general public." Radio and television broadcasts transmitted by coaxial cable for direct public reception are sometimes included in the term "broadcasting," but legally they are differentiated from wireless broadcasting.

History of Broadcasting in Japan——The first radio broadcast in Japan was aired by Tōkyō Broadcasting Station, Inc, which began experimental broadcasts on 22 March 1925 and regular broadcasts on 12 July the same year. Ōsaka Broadcasting Station and Nagoya Broadcasting Station also began operations in 1925.

From the time of the Meiji Restoration in 1868 the government sought to control public communications. However, because of financial difficulties and radio's uncertain future, the Communications Ministry (Teishinshō; now the Ministry of Posts and Telecommunications) did not place radio broadcasting under its direct jurisdiction. Instead, under a Teishinshō ordinance of 20 December 1923, broadcasting stations were defined as nonprofit, private organizations that were to function as corporate juristic persons *(shadan hōjin)*. The Tōkyō, Ōsaka, and Nagoya stations were established under this definition; these were to be operated by fees collected from owners of radio sets.

Private management was such in name only, however, because the Teishinshō ordinance placed strict limitations on the ownership of private radio equipment for broadcast purposes. In actuality, the establishment of corporate juristic persons gave the government almost complete control of the three broadcasting stations. For example, the minister of communications was vested with the authority to exercise prior censorship of radio programs, similar to the authority granted by the Press Law and the Publication Law, which gave government officials the right to attend, express opinions, and countermand the decisions made at general meetings of corporate juristic persons. The minister could also dismiss officials of the broadcasting stations, and an authorization system was adopted for the appointment and dismissal of station officials. Soon after the establishment of the three broadcasting stations, the Communications Ministry, in an effort to disseminate radio broadcasts throughout the country, dissolved them and on 20 August 1926 established the Nippon Hōsō Kyōkai (NHK; Japan Broadcasting Corporation) to replace them. NHK opened affiliate radio stations in various regions of the country and monopolized the country's broadcasting industry until after World War II, when the current broadcasting system was established. As with its predecessors, NHK was placed under the strict supervision of the Communications Ministry.

With the rising popularity of news broadcasts, Western and Japanese music programs, radio dramas, and children's programs, the number of households with radio receivers increased dramatically. In 1932 there were more than 1 million radio sets in Japan. This number exceeded 2 million in 1935, and by 1944 it had climbed to 7.5 million, 50.4 percent of all households in Japan.

Meanwhile, with the outbreak of hostilities in China following the MANCHURIAN INCIDENT of 1931, NHK, which up to then had pursued a policy of "people first" broadcast programming, shifted to a policy of "nation first" broadcasts. Programs concerning political and military topics, feature commentaries and lectures on current events, and patriotic programs all increased. Numerous military leaders participated in these broadcasts, and the Broadcasting Council, a national organization created in 1932 to oversee broadcasting, included among its members the vice-ministers of the Communications Ministry, the Home Ministry, and the Ministry of Education. In 1934 the vice-ministers of the army, navy, and foreign ministries were also appointed as members of the council.

A major managerial reorganization of NHK was carried out in 1934, with Communications Ministry officials replacing civilian managers in the important posts of managing director and bureau chief of the central NHK station in Tōkyō. NHK's national network system became more centralized, and programming was wholly decided by the central Tōkyō station. NHK, which had been under the strict control of the Communications Ministry since its establishment, thus became a propaganda organ of the state earlier than did the print media. After the outbreak of the Sino-Japanese War in 1937, NHK was compelled to broadcast programs based on the policies of the Cabinet Information Department (later the Cabinet Information Bureau). It followed this program format until the end of World War II.

After the war the General Headquarters of the Allied OCCUPATION forces issued a memorandum regarding freedom of speech and freedom of the press; this set forth general occupational policy toward the broadcast and print media and established a radio code. Programs broadcast by NHK became subject to prior censorship for approximately a two-year period, beginning on 13 October 1945. This was modified to after-the-fact censorship, excluding material concerning the Allied countries and Occupation policy, from 1 August 1947, and was finally abolished altogether on 18 October 1949. The Occupation authorities issued other orders, including one for the separation of the press from the government, and abolished all legislation suppressing freedom of speech and the press in an effort to further Japan's democratization. NHK complied by eliminating all provisions in its articles of association granting authority to the government on 30 October 1945.

In the immediate postwar years, various attempts were made to establish private broadcasting stations. Occupation authorities refused these early requests, preferring to maintain NHK's monopolistic position during the early part of the Occupation period. The Allied Council for Japan was also in opposition, and these moves for private broadcasting stations proved unsuccessful.

A new broadcasting system was established in May 1950 with the enactment of the "Three Radio Laws," that is, the Broadcasting Law, the Radio Law, and the Law for the Establishment of the Radio Wave Management Commission. The last was aimed at establishing an independent commission, patterned after the US Federal Communications Commission, to oversee broadcasting and communication. The Radio Wave Management Commission conformed to specific guidelines laid down by the Occupation authorities. However, the Japanese government, which opposed delegating broadcasting and communication to an independent administrative commission, abolished the Radio Wave Management Commission shortly afterward, in July 1952. The Ministry of Posts and Telecommunications then took charge.

When the Broadcasting Law came into effect, NHK was reorganized; a new corporation was formed, taking over the facilities and staff of the former organization. This law also paved the way for private commercial broadcast stations. In April 1950 preliminary licenses were issued to a total of 16 private broadcast stations in 14 districts of the country. Actual broadcasting did not begin until September of the same year. Despite early pessimism about their commercial viability, these ventures soon showed large profits. Since then, numerous radio stations have been opened in various parts of the country; in August 1954 Japan's first and only shortwave broadcasting station, the Nihon Shortwave Broadcasting Co, Ltd, was started.

The way was opened to television broadcasting with the granting of a preliminary license to NIPPON TELEVISION NETWORK CORPORATION (NTV) on 31 July 1952; however, telecasting did not begin until the following year. The first actual telecast in Japan was made by NHK's Tōkyō station on 1 February 1953. Nippon Television, which started operating in August, was the first private company to telecast programs. Since there were only some 3,000 television sets in Japan when Nippon Television started telecasting, many advertisers doubted the effectiveness of television advertising. Their worries proved groundless when Nippon Television installed large-sized sets on busy street corners throughout Tōkyō and other large cities of the Kantō region to telecast world championship boxing and professional wrestling matches. Thousands gathered around these outdoor TV sets to view the matches, proof that television was a profitable advertising medium indeed. Nippon Television quickly began to show a profit.

In October 1957 licenses were granted to NHK and several additional private television stations. The number of television sets in Japan exceeded 1 million at the end of fiscal 1958 and four years later, at the end of fiscal 1962, numbered more than 10 million, covering 49.5 percent of all Japanese households. One factor contributing to the dissemination of television sets was the introduction of color broadcasting. Experimental color telecasts were initiated by NHK and Nippon Television in December 1957, with regular color broadcasts beginning in September 1960.

On 23 November 1963 (22 November in the United States), an experimental TV relay telecast via satellite was conducted between the United States and Japan. Received in Japan by NHK, Tōkyō Broadcasting System, and the Nippon Educational Television (now

ASAHI NATIONAL BROADCASTING CO, LTD), the relay happened to telecast details of the assassination of President John F. Kennedy. On 23 March 1964 experimental telecasts from Japan to the United States were conducted via satellite, and the Tōkyō Olympic Games, held that same year, were shown to a total of 21 countries via satellite hook-up to usher in the age of satellite broadcasting. Then in April 1978 the NATIONAL SPACE DEVELOPMENT AGENCY OF JAPAN had a medium-sized telecasting satellite launched by the United States National Aeronautic and Space Agency (NASA) at the Kennedy Space Center in Florida. This agency and the Ministry of Posts and Telecommunications, with the cooperation of NHK, conducted various experiments and equipment tests for three years.

NHK initiated nationwide FM radio broadcasts in March 1969. Aichi Music FM Broadcasting Company, a private commercial station (now called FM Aichi) commenced FM broadcasting in December of the same year; similar broadcasts in Tōkyō, Ōsaka, and Fukuoka followed.

Present-day Broadcasting in Japan——Japan's broadcasting system consists of two types of broadcast enterprise: NHK, which is a government-sponsored venture, and the various commercial companies. As already pointed out, NHK is a special corporation, neither a state-operated enterprise nor a public corporation like the Japanese National Railways. However, unlike the private companies, NHK's activities are subject to restrictions by the government and the Diet.

The Management Commission makes major decisions regarding NHK, including the content of programs, and is a governing organ with the authority to appoint the president and other high officials of NHK. The members of the Management Commission are appointed by the prime minister after obtaining the approval of the Diet. The prime minister is required to select persons from different regions and from a wide range of educational, cultural, scientific, and industrial fields. The budget, operating proposals, and fund-raising plans of NHK are all presented to the Diet for approval through the minister of posts and telecommunications.

The Broadcasting Law stipulates that individual owners make contractual arrangements with NHK in order to receive its broadcasts; through these contracts, NHK is assured of an independent revenue. Unlike the countries of Western Europe where the government collects radio reception fees from the public and then transfers the money to the broadcasting stations, in Japan NHK itself is responsible for collecting these reception fees. NHK is prohibited from broadcasting advertisements. Private stations are considered "general broadcasting entrepreneurs," and although the law has detailed provisions concerning NHK, it contains only three provisions governing programming by commercial stations. Although no specific provisions about the form of enterprise to be taken by private broadcasting stations or their management methods are mentioned, Japanese private broadcasting companies all take a corporate style and follow the commercial broadcasting pattern of the United States, operating with revenue from advertising.

Programming. The Broadcasting Law also stipulates the types of programs to be broadcast domestically. NHK is required (1) to broadcast high-quality programs that will both satisfy the demands of the public and elevate the country's cultural level; (2) to broadcast local as well as national programs; and (3) to contribute to the preservation of traditional culture and foster and publicize modern cultural events. Programs shown by both NHK and private commercial broadcasting firms are required by the Broadcasting Law (1) to guard against disturbing public peace and order and damaging morals; (2) to maintain political impartiality; (3) to include truthful news broadcasts; and (4) to present all sides of complex issues and to maintain a balance among educational, cultural, news, and entertainment programs.

The average daily length of television programming in fiscal 1979 for commercial broadcasters was 17 hours and 24 minutes; for NHK it was 17 hours and 50 minutes. Again in that year, radio broadcasting was longer than television broadcasting, with commercial radio stations averaging 22 hours per day and NHK 18 hours and 50 minutes.

Networks. NHK operates a nationwide broadcasting network. Private broadcasting stations licensed in their respective local regions also have their own networks. Competition among these networks is quite intense. Unlike the United States, where television networks were an outgrowth of radio networks, in Japan television networks developed earlier than radio networks because of the sudden proliferation of private television stations. At present commercial television broadcasting consists of four networks centered on the following key stations: TŌKYŌ BROADCASTING SYSTEM, INC (25 companies), Nippon Television Network Corporation (28 companies), FUJI TELECASTING CO, LTD (27 companies), and Asahi National Broadcasting Co, Ltd (18 companies). At the center of each of these networks is a news network: Japan News Network (JNN), Nippon News Network (NNN), Fuji News Network (FNN), and the Asahi News Network (ANN), respectively. General programming other than news is distributed through these networks.

Many television stations broadcast their own programs in addition to those supplied by the networks. Local stations in Japan are more independent than their US counterparts.

In commercial radio broadcasting, there are two major networks: the Japan Radio Network (JRN; an offshoot of Tōkyō Broadcasting System, Inc) and the Nippon Radio Network (NRN; an offshoot of Nippon Broadcasting System, Inc, and Nippon Cultural Broadcasting, Inc), both of which were established in 1965.

Financing. The ordinary operating revenues of NHK are obtained from viewer fees, government subsidies for NHK's international broadcasts, and miscellaneous revenues from other sources, with some 98 percent of the entire revenue represented by viewer fees. The distribution of television sets, excepting certain districts with poor reception, however, has reached the saturation point, so that it is difficult to foresee any large increase in revenue from future fees. (Radio fees were abolished in 1968.) On the other hand, NHK's expenses have increased with the rise in commodity prices and the expansion of NHK's operations. As a result, NHK has been deficit-ridden since fiscal 1972, and showed a profit only when viewer fees were raised in 1976. NHK again showed a deficit in 1979 and 1980, and fees were again raised. Another increase in fees in the future seems inevitable.

Private television broadcasting companies are showing large profits with the tremendous increase in revenue from television advertising. The revenue growth rate stagnated temporarily in the recession following the oil crisis of 1973, but advertisement expenditures paid to television firms exceeded those paid to newspapers in 1975, and television has been the top advertising medium ever since.

Television viewing. At the end of March 1980, 29 million households had television sets registered with NHK. Television sets are owned by practically all Japanese families, and according to a recent survey some 60 percent of them have more than two sets. The distribution rate of radio receivers is not certain, as NHK has abolished its fee system, but each family probably averages more than two sets counting transistor and car radios.

The average television viewing time of those over seven years of age in November 1978 was 3 hours and 37 minutes on weekdays. On Sunday this climbed to 4 hours and 21 minutes. Despite the popularity of sports, travel, and other recreational activities today, watching television, as indicated by these figures, is still a major way to spend leisure time in Japan. See also BROADCASTING, COMMERCIAL.

◾——Masami Itō, *Broadcasting in Japan* (1978). Nippon Hōsō Kyōkai, ed, *Fifty Years of Japanese Broadcasting* (1977). Nippon Hōsō Kyōkai, ed, *NHK nenkan* (annual). Nippon Hōsō Kyōkai Hōsōshi Henshūshitsu, ed, *Nihon hōsō shi*, 3 vols (1965). Nihon Minkan Hōsō Remmei, ed, *Minkan hōsō jūnen shi* (1961). Nihon Minkan Hōsō Remmei, ed, *Nihon hōsō nenkan* (annual). Uchikawa Yoshimi, *Nihon kōkoku hattatsu shi*, vol 2 (1980). Yūseishō, ed, *Tsūshin hakusho* (annual). TAKAGI Noritsune

broadcasting, commercial

(*shōgyō hōsō*). Japanese commercial broadcasting, as distinguished from public broadcasting (see NHK), dates from 1 September 1951 when the first privately owned radio stations went on the air in Ōsaka and Nagoya; commercial television followed on 28 August 1953. Beginning about 1960 radio fell on difficult times because of the rise in popularity of television. To win back their audience, radio stations changed their format, incorporating live programs that ran for several hours, celebrity shows, late-night broadcasts, and traffic reports, and began making a comeback in the late 1960s. Commercial FM broadcasts began in 1969.

Commercial television stations were allowed to open throughout Japan in 1957. Coverage of spectacular events such as the Crown Prince's wedding in 1959 and the Tōkyō Olympic Games in 1964 served to increase the number of television owners. Technological developments such as color programming and satellite-relay broadcasts paved the way for further growth of the television industry. By 1975 the amount of money spent on TV advertising had surpassed that for newspaper advertising, and television became the top advertising medium.

In the late 1970s there were 53 radio stations (48 AM, 4 FM, 1 shortwave) and 92 television stations (48 VHF and 44 UHF) licensed for commercial broadcasting. Advertising revenue for 1978 amounted to ¥90.8 billion (US $429.3 million) for radio and ¥651.8 billion (US $3.1 billion) for television. There were some 25,000 people employed in commercial broadcasting. NHK, by comparison, had 16,000 employees.

Commercial radio and television networks operate as cooperatives under the leadership of certain key stations. Among AM radio networks are the Japan Radio Network (JRN), led by TŌKYŌ BROADCASTING SYSTEM, INC (TBS); and the National Radio Network (NRN), with NIPPON CULTURAL BROADCASTING, INC and NIPPON BROADCASTING SYSTEM, INC, as key stations. Television networks include the Japan News Network (JNN) again led by TBS; the Nippon News Network (NNN) led by Nippon Television; the All Nippon News Network led by ASAHI NATIONAL BROADCASTING CO, LTD; and the Fuji News Network (FNN) led by FUJI TELECASTING CO, LTD.

Daily television viewing time for the average Japanese amounts to about four hours per day, demonstrating that television has indeed become an indispensable entertainment medium for the Japanese public. The prime viewing hours between 7:00 and 10:00 PM, when advertising is most effective, are referred to as the "golden hours," and during these hours there is fierce competition among stations for viewers. In 1978 Japan led the world in developing multiplex television sound broadcasts, which made possible stereo and dual language broadcasts. NOZAKI Shigeru

Broadcasting Law

(*Hōsō Hō*). Law defining the basic principles for regulation of broadcasting; passed in May 1950 together with a law regulating the use of radio waves (the Dempa Hō) and a law establishing a commission to supervise that use (the Dempa Kanri Iinkai Setchi Hō). These three measures, collectively known as the "Three Radio Wave Laws" (Dempa Sampō), all aimed to strengthen the autonomy of broadcasting and can be seen as part of the move away from government interference with the media that took place after World War II. The Broadcasting Law itself ensured independence and freedom for broadcasting while requiring that it maintain political neutrality. It also defined the purpose, management, and organization of the Japan Broadcasting Corporation, the public broadcasting network, better known as NHK. ISHIZAKA Etsuo

broadcasts, late-night

(*shin'ya hōsō*). Late-night radio broadcasts are an important part of the youth and automobile subcultures in Japan. Almost all commercial AM radio stations in Japan, particularly the large stations in cities like Tōkyō and Ōsaka, offer after-midnight broadcasts from 1:00 to 5:00 in the morning. Late-night programming started around 1960 as a response to the upsurge in television viewing and the ensuing drop in the popularity of radio. There are two main types of programs: the youth-oriented and the driver-oriented. Youth programming has had a strong influence on the youth subculture. The disc jockey acts as a sympathetic ear, responding to events in the daily lives of the young audience, who call in by telephone. Japanese and Western pop and rock favorites comprise most of the request numbers. Programs for late-night drivers, on the other hand, serve as promotion for the automobile industry. These programs are popular among long-distance truck drivers as well as students cramming for examinations. They tend to have women disc jockeys who act as radio companions for the drivers. Program format includes reading of fan mail, playing of request numbers (mostly Japanese popular music), and periodic reports on traffic conditions. Late-night television broadcasts, from one to two in the morning, are found mostly on commercial stations in large cities and tend to feature old movie favorites. NOZAKI Shigeru

brocade → nishiki

bronze age

(*seidōki jidai*). The Yayoi period (ca 300 BC–ca AD 300) is sometimes referred to as Japan's bronze age, although it has few of the features associated with Near Eastern or Chinese bronze-age civilizations. Both bronze and iron working, along with other Chinese and Korean ideas, entered Japan during the Yayoi period. This was also the time when wet-rice farming became firmly established in Japan. By the end of the period, western Japan was organized into small, preliterate states which were in active contact with other countries of East Asia. See also DŌTAKU; BRONZE WEAPONS; BRONZE MIRRORS; and the section on Yayoi culture in HISTORY OF JAPAN: prehistory.

Peter BLEED

bronze mirrors

(seidōkyō). Cast as round disks, the bronze mirrors of ancient China and Japan have one perfectly smooth side for reflection purposes; the back side is decorated and has a perforated knob in the center through which a cord can be passed. Bronze mirrors were first brought from China to Japan in the Yayoi period (ca 300 BC–ca AD 300). The technology for production was introduced soon after, and in the 3rd and 4th centuries the Japanese began producing bronze mirrors modeled on those of the Han dynasty (206 BC–AD 220). Although native mirrors differed in size, ranging from 5 to 45 centimeters (2–17.7 in) in diameter in comparison to Chinese mirrors, which measured between 15 and 20 centimeters (5.9–7.9 in), they imitated in exact detail such motifs as "flower petals" and "gods and beasts." Several hundred Late Han-dynasty Chinese mirrors have been excavated from tomb mounds (KOFUN) of the Kofun period (ca 300–710), and over 200 Chinese "god and beast" mirrors, judged to be of Three Kingdoms (220–265) manufacture, have also been unearthed. In time motifs peculiar to Japan, such as geometric CHOK-KOMON and FERN FROND DESIGN or village scenes came to be applied to native products of the 5th and 6th centuries. Mirrors with clusters of small bells (SUZU) cast into their rims were also produced. Mirrors continued to be imported from China during the Nara period (710–794); many of them are at the SHŌSŌIN repository in Nara.

By the Heian period (794–1185), the style of Japanese bronze mirrors *(wakyō)* had become quite distinct, with such native motifs as autumn grasses, flowing water, and flowers and birds being elegantly portrayed. Mirrors in this style were very thin and had small unadorned cord knobs. In the Kamakura period (1185–1333) the mirrors were more substantial and the motifs changed to realistic scenes. In the succeeding Muromachi period (1333–1568), auspicious motifs such as the pine, bamboo, and plum pattern or the crane and turtle pattern became very popular. Near the end of this period, under the influence of Song (Sung) dynasty (960–1279) China, handles were attached for convenience. Handled mirrors became extremely popular during the Edo period (1600–1868). During this period mirrors were made in various sizes and shapes and some were coated with mercury for better reflection. Mass production, however, contributed to a lowering of artistic quality. Bronze mirrors fell into disuse after the production of glass mirrors started in Japan in the late 19th century.

In ancient Japan, bronze mirrors were more treasures or ritual implements than utilitarian items. They were also important symbols of political authority, as attested by the inclusion of a bronze mirror (the Yata no Kagami) among the three IMPERIAL REGALIA. It would appear that powerful rulers obtained several mirrors from the same mold and distributed them to their subordinate chiefs as authority symbols.

One of the oldest native INSCRIPTIONS in Japan is preserved on a bronze mirror in the possession of the Suda Hachiman Shrine in the city of Hashimoto, Wakayama Prefecture. Written in KAMBUN script, it is an important documentary resource. But because the sexagenary cycle date (see JIKKAN JŪNISHI) mentioned in the text, namely *mizunoto hitsuji,* is variously applicable to any of several years, for example, 383, 443, and 503, it is difficult to ascertain the mirror's date of manufacture.

KATORI Tadahiko

bronze weapons

Weapons made of bronze *(seidō* or *dō),* an alloy of copper and tin, were in use in Japan mainly during the Yayoi period (ca 300 BC–ca AD 300). These included *dōken* (bronze swords), *dōhoko* (bronze spearheads), and *dōka* (bronze halberd heads). Bronze arrowheads *(dōzoku)* were in use from the Early Yayoi period (ca 300 BC–ca 100 BC) to the early part of the Kofun period (ca AD 300–710); however, this article is chiefly concerned with such weapons as bronze swords, spearheads, and halberd heads. The bronze weapons appearing at the end of the Early Yayoi period were imported, and these were not

Bronze mirrors

The back side of a 16th-century bronze mirror with a motif of paulownia and bamboo and a perforated knob in the shape of a turtle. The inscription at the bottom of the outer ring gives the maker's name, Ao Ietsugu, and the year of manufacture, 1588. Mercury-coated bronze. Diameter 22.1 cm. Tōkyō National Museum.

produced domestically until the latter part of the Middle Yayoi period (ca 100 BC–ca AD 100). From that time through the Late Yayoi period (ca 100–ca 300), bronze weapons were produced and used in western Japan, centering on northern Kyūshū.

Bronze weapons originated in China and were first introduced into northern Kyūshū from the Korean peninsula. The first metal-age product in Japan, these Korean-made bronze weapons were placed as auxiliary burial articles in burial jars, which succeeded pit burials and wooden coffins. Four narrow-blade swords and three narrow-blade spearheads have been found in Yayoi-period burial jars excavated at the Itazuke site in Fukuoka Prefecture, and narrow-blade bronze swords and sword points have been found in burial jars at the Uki Kunden site in Saga Prefecture. At the SUKU SITE in Fukuoka Prefecture, thought to be the location of the "country of Na" mentioned in the Chinese historical documents *Hou Han shu* (4th to 5th centuries) and WEI ZHI *(Wei chih;* late 3rd century), more than 10 bronze swords, spearheads, and halberd heads have been discovered in one burial jar of the Middle Yayoi period together with a total of more than 30 BRONZE MIRRORS of the Former Han dynasty (206 BC–AD 8). These bronze weapons and mirrors were symbols of the power of their possesser.

Bronze weapons do not appear to have been used for their original purpose in Japan. None show damage through use in battle, and in some cases only sword points were used as auxiliary burial articles. Further, only 13 bronze weapons have been discovered in the 119 burial jars excavated at the Uki Kunden site. Therefore, it can be surmised that bronze weapons in Japan were used, not for battle, but as symbols of power.

Bronze weapons came to be produced in Japan from the latter part of the Middle Yayoi period, diverging in shape from the narrow-blade weapons and taking on the form of medium-narrow, broad-blade, and flat-blade type weapons. At this time bronze weapons, hitherto auxiliary articles of burial in burial jars, came to be buried in pits dug on hills and other high places far away from villages. From several to as many as 48 bronze weapons per pit have been discovered deliberately buried in such pits. The fact that they have been excavated at places separated from individual graves provides evidence for their use as ritual implements to pray for a rich harvest or safety on the seas rather than as weapons.

At the time when bronze weapons were introduced to Japan, bronze swords and spearheads were concentrated in northern Kyūshū, but with the production of such weapons in Japan, the distribution area spread to the coasts of the Inland Sea. Eventually the Ōsaka Bay-type halberd head could be found in the Kinai (Kyōto–Ōsaka–Nara) region and the flat-blade sword along the coasts of the middle part of the Inland Sea. In some places the distribution of bronze weapons overlapped with that of DŌTAKU (bronze bells), indicating the existence of regional centers for religious services and festivals. From this, it may be supposed that the many minor states in Japan mentioned in the Chinese historical document *Han shu* (latter half of the 1st century) were moving toward consolidation centered about more powerful forces in northern Kyūshū and the Kinai region.

Swords—— The swords were piercing rather than cutting weapons. They are double-edged in form, with a center shaft protruding at the base and fitting into a hilt. Bronze swords can be classified into four types, according to shape. The narrow-blade sword (*hosogata dōken*), developing from the Liaoning-type bronze sword of the northeastern part of China and introduced into Japan from the Korean peninsula, is a narrow sword with sharp edges on both sides. The length of the body of the sword is less than 32 centimeters (12.6 in), and the standard length of the protruding shaft at the base is 2–3 centimeters (0.87–1.18 in). The cross section of the body of the sword is diamond-shaped. Some reports give the metallic content of this narrow-blade sword as roughly 75 percent copper, 15 percent tin, and 10 percent lead. The medium-narrow sword (*nakaboso dōken*), although similar in form to the narrow-blade sword, is longer, with some sword bodies measuring 40 centimeters (15.76 in) or longer. The blade has also become flatter. A mold for this type of sword has been discovered at Shikanoshima, Fukuoka Prefecture, in northern Kyūshū, indicating that it was made in Japan. The medium-breadth sword (*nakahiro dōken*), a longer and larger version of the medium-narrow sword, has a body more than 50 centimeters (19.7 in) long and a wider blade. It is characterized by a spoon-shaped widening of the blade toward the base. The flat-blade sword (*hiragata dōken*) has quite a wide body and almost straight edges, with the point tending to be rounded. The shaping of the blade toward the base has disappeared and instead, two thornlike protrusions are found roughly one-third the length of the blade from the base. Flat-blade swords with patterns on the blade have also been discovered.

Spearheads—— A piercing weapon; the lower part of the spearhead forms a tapered socket in which a handle was inserted, and a metal loop was attached to the side of this socket. Like bronze swords, bronze spearheads can also be classified into four types according to shape. The narrow-blade spearhead (*hosogata dōhoko*) is less than 50 centimeters (19.7 in) and generally 20–30 centimeters (7.8–11.82 in) in length. These spearheads narrow to a point in an elongated triangular shape. The medium-narrow spearhead (*nakaboso dōhoko*) is 50–70 centimeters (19.7–27.58 in) in length. This spearhead has straight-running edges and a rounded point. The medium-breadth spearhead (*nakahiro dōhoko*) is more than 70 centimeters (27.58 in) in length. These spearheads have a lengthened and flattened body, and in some cases no hole has been incised in the loop on the socket. The broad-blade spearhead (*hirogata dōhoko*) has a very flat body, and the loop on the socket is also flattened with the hole completely gone. Some reports give the metallic content of this spearhead as roughly 83 percent copper, 9 percent tin, and 8 percent lead, a ratio unsuitable for a weapon.

Halberd Heads—— Similar in form to spearheads but slanting to one side rather than rising straight from their base, halberd heads were attached to long shafts, forming an acute angle to them because of their tilted shape. At the base of the halberd heads are two holes for tightening it in its hilt. The bronze halberd heads also fall into four types according to shape, following a development from the narrow-blade type to the medium-narrow type, a medium-breadth type, and broad-blade type. There is also an Ōsaka Bay-type halberd head labeled according to its regional distribution.

The narrow-blade halberd head (*hosogata dōka*) is an imported weapon. Its usual length is 20–30 centimeters (7.8–11.82 in), and the body tapers as it proceeds toward the point. With the start of domestic production, the body became longer, and although at first the edges narrowed as they neared the point, they gradually came to run in a straight line to the point, with a rounding of that point in the medium-breadth type halberd head (*nakahiro dōka*). Ōsaka Bay-type halberd heads are sometimes decorated with saw-teeth or cross-latticework patterns. The more recent the bronze halberd heads, the smaller, flatter, and weaker they become. See also YAYOI CULTURE. *Saotome Masahiro*

Brooke, John Mercer (1826–1906)

American naval officer and scientist. Born in Florida; graduate of the United States Naval Academy (1847). The inventor of a deep-sea sounding apparatus, in 1858 he was commissioned to map the topography of the sea floor of the North Pacific. The following summer his schooner, the *Fenimore Cooper*, was wrecked in Japanese waters. In 1860 he and his men assisted the Japanese crew of the KANRIN MARU, the first Japanese ship to cross the Pacific (see also UNITED STATES, MISSION OF 1860 TO). Brooke's log of the trip is interesting for its keen observations of the Japanese sailors. He soon after resigned from the US Navy, joined the Confederate Navy during the American Civil War, and helped to reconstruct the ironclad warship *Merrimac*. From 1866 to 1899 he taught physics and astronomy at Virginia Military Institute.

Brother Industries, Ltd

Company engaged in the manufacture of various types of sewing machines, household electrical appliances, tooling machines, musical instruments, and office machines. Brother Industries was established in 1934 for the domestic production of sewing machines and, in the late 1970s, was the top maker in Japan of sewing machines, knitting machines, and typewriters. In 1954 it began diversifying its lines of business. It adopted its current name in 1962. Production and sales are administered separately. Domestic sales are carried out by Brother Machine Sales Co, while overseas sales are conducted chiefly by Brother International Co. The company's products are exported to more than 100 countries throughout the world. It is very active in introducing electronics innovations into sewing machines and other products. Sales for the 1981 fiscal year totaled ¥129.9 billion (US $580.6 million), of which sewing machines constituted 33 percent, office machines 26 percent, household electrical appliances 17 percent, tooling machines 18 percent, and knitting machines 6 percent. In the same year the export ratio was 42 percent and capitalization stood at ¥11.6 billion (US $51.8 million). The head office is located in Nagoya.

Brown, Samuel Robbins (1810–1880)

American educator and missionary. Born in East Windsor, Connecticut, Brown graduated from Yale University in 1832. He served as a teacher and missionary in China from 1839 to 1847, then returned to the United States to take up teaching and pastoral duties in upstate New York. In 1859 he was sent to Kanagawa by the Dutch Reformed Mission, becoming one of the first missionaries to enter Japan since the 17th century. For the next 20 years Brown served as an influential teacher and missionary in the village of Kanagawa (now part of Yokohama) and later in Yokohama. He was a founder and early president of the Asiatic Society of Japan, and he translated portions of the New Testament into Japanese. He also wrote *Colloquial Japanese* (1863) and *Prendergast's Mastery System Applied to English and Japanese* (1875).

▰——William Elliot Griffis, *A Maker of the New Orient: Samuel Robbins Brown* (1902). *Edward R. Beauchamp*

Brunton, Richard Henry (1841–1901)

Scottish engineer, employed in Japan from 1868 to 1875. At the insistence of British envoy Sir Harry PARKES that Japan fulfill its treaty obligations (see ANSEI COMMERCIAL TREATIES) by making its ports and waters safe and convenient for trade and navigation, the Japanese government engaged the Edinburgh firm of D. and T. Stevenson to chart Japan's waters for the first time and, in particular, to build lighthouses. Brunton headed this project, which was difficult and dangerous because of Japan's deeply indented and rocky coast. He greatly extended the work already begun by the French engineer François VERNY by erecting 34 lighthouses of brick, stone, iron, or wood along the length of the islands, as well as charting the Inland Sea and approaches to the major ports. His greatest and most expensive feat was the construction of the stone lighthouse at Mikomotojima, a rocky ledge off Shimoda. Returning home, Brunton continued his career as a civil engineer until his death in London. Portions of his Mikomoto lighthouse remain, and his lighthouse keeper's house from Sugashima, Ise Bay, has been preserved at MEIJI MURA near Nagoya. *Dallas Finn*

Brussels Conference

(Burasseru Kaigi). An international conference held from 3 to 15 November 1937 as a consequence of the China Incident, which occurred in July of that year (see SINO-JAPANESE WAR OF 1937–1945). After Japan rejected the Chinese government's attempt to bring the matter before the League of Nations, the United States attempted to force Japan into a settlement by pointing out that Japan's attack violated the Nine-Power Treaty, signed at the WASHINGTON CONFERENCE in 1922 by Great Britain, the United States, France, Italy, Belgium, the Netherlands, China, Japan, and Portugal. Thus, on

American initiative, the Brussels Conference was convened with eight of the original nine countries, along with the Soviet Union, taking part. Japan refused to attend. The conference achieved no concrete results; all the countries present agreed that the crisis should be settled on an international level, and the Chinese delegation called for firmer action against Japan, but in vain. The Japanese government's refusal to discuss the attack on China indicated its disregard of foreign opinion, an attitude that would continue right up to World War II.

Bryan note

A document communicated by American Secretary of State William Jennings Bryan (1860–1925) to the Japanese government on 13 March 1915, when negotiations on the TWENTY-ONE DEMANDS between China and Japan had reached a critical stage. In the note the American government reviewed its OPEN DOOR POLICY in China, affirmed American treaty rights, and acknowledged that Japan's "territorial contiguity" created "special relations" between Japan and the Chinese territories of Mongolia, Manchuria, and Shandong (Shantung). In conclusion, the note expressed Washington's deep concern over Japanese encroachment on Chinese sovereignty. Together with strongly anti-Japanese world opinion, the note helped to soften Japan's demands on China and to bring about a peaceful conclusion to their negotiations in May 1915. The text can be found in the *Papers Relating to the Foreign Relations of the United States, 1915.*   *Madeleine* CHI

B–29 bomber

A four-engine, long-range heavy bomber ("Superfortress") developed for the US Army Air Forces during World War II. B–29s were first used against Japan proper on 16 June 1944 (15 June in the Western Hemisphere), when they flew from Chinese bases to bomb steel mills in northern Kyūshū. On 25 November of that year, B–29s based in the Mariana Islands raided Tōkyō, and thereafter the flights covered all of Japan except Hokkaidō. These bombings spread terror throughout Japan, particularly after the predawn raid of 10 March 1945, in which more than 250 B–29s dropped some 2,000 tons of incendiary bombs over Tōkyō, destroying the heart of the city and killing or wounding 185,000 civilians. That they flew at an altitude of 10,000 meters (about 30,000 ft) and were almost invulnerable to antiaircraft fire greatly undermined Japanese morale in the last nine months of the war. On 6 August 1945 the B–29 *Enola Gay* dropped an ATOMIC BOMB over Hiroshima; three days later another B–29 dropped a second atomic bomb at Nagasaki. Japan initiated peace negotiations the next day.   HARADA *Katsumasa*

Buddha

(J: Hotoke; Butsu; Butsuda). In Buddhism an epithet applied to one who has attained enlightenment, i.e., perfect insight into the nature of the world and the beings that inhabit it. A Buddha is regarded as the embodiment of both wisdom and compassion. In the Theravāda Buddhism of Southeast Asia only one Buddha is recognized for the present world cycle, namely, Gautama, also known as Śākyamuni (J: Shaka), the historical founder of Buddhism, who lived in India in the 4th or 5th century BC.

According to the Mahāyāna tradition, which is the type of Buddhism practiced in Japan, China, and Korea, Śākyamuni is but one of countless Buddhas that are presently active throughout the cosmos. Although all Buddhas are equal in their wisdom and merit, they differ with respect to the specific vows they made before achieving Buddhahood. The most popular Buddhas in Japan are Shaka, who is particularly venerated in the TENDAI SECT, the NICHIREN SECT, and ZEN; AMIDA (Skt: Amitābha), who is the object of devotion in the Pure Land sects (the JŌDO SECT, JŌDO SHIN SECT, and JI SECT), and DAINICHI (Skt: Mahāvairocana), who is the central divinity in the SHINGON SECT as well as in the esoteric branch of the Tendai sect. See also BUDDHISM; BUDDHIST ART; BUDDHIST SCULPTURE.

Stanley WEINSTEIN

Buddha tiles

(sembutsu). Unglazed, baked clay tiles with mold-impressed Buddhist images such as the AMIDA trinity, bodhisattvas, and RAKAN; produced in Japan in the late 7th century under the influence of Chinese Tang (T'ang) dynasty (618–907) Buddhism. They were em-

bedded in the walls of temples and used as objects of worship. The Nara-period (710–794) tiles from the Tachibanadera and Okadera temples in the Asuka region of Nara Prefecture are noted for their lifelike realism. *Sembutsu* have also been found among the YAMADADERA REMAINS and the KUDARADERA REMAINS. See also BUDDHIST SCULPTURE.   KITAMURA *Bunji*

Buddhism

(J: Bukkyō). According to tradition, the founder of Buddhism, Siddhartha Gautama, was born about 446 BC as the first son of King Śuddhodana of the Śākya clan at the castle Kapilavastu, located in the center of the clan's domain in what is now Nepal. Some scholars, however, place the birthdate as much as a century earlier. Even though in his early years the prince was surrounded by luxury and comfort, he was not satisfied. He concerned himself with the whole problem of human existence, and at age 29 he left home to seek an answer through renunciation. After completing six years of asceticism, he experienced great enlightenment at Buddhagaya beneath the Bo tree, becoming the Buddha ("one who has awakened to the truth"). Thereafter, until his death at Kuśinagara at the age of 80, he traveled throughout central India sharing his wisdom. He became known by the honorary name Śākyamuni (the silent sage or holy one from the Śākya clan).

Early Buddhism —— Around the 6th century BC in the central Ganges River Basin and eastern India, several small nations came into being, each centered on a city of some size. Most of these were monarchies, but a few developed a confederate form of government and a monetary economy; commerce and industry flourished, and people became affluent. Brahmanism did not wield as much power as previously, and the traditional caste system fell into decay. Until then the priestly Brahmin class had occupied the highest stratum of an essentially agrarian society, but it was gradually replaced by the warrior (Kṣatriya) class. Numerous merchant and artisan guilds were formed, and the rich came to possess considerable social power. The general populace tended toward materialistic concerns, and a decline in public morality ensued.

Many iconoclastic thinkers appeared, denying the significance of Brahmanical ritualism and rejecting the authority of the Vedas. In defense, certain Brahmins compromised with popular folk beliefs; others clung tenaciously to their orthodox practice. Other thinkers, in addition, put forth doctrines stressing materialism, ethical relativism, determinism, and skepticism. One of the so-called Six Masters active at this time, Nigaṇṭha Nātaputta (also known as Mahāvīra), was the founder of Jainism, which, along with Buddhism, was to have a profound effect upon Indian thought and culture.

Philosophers became involved in endless arguments on metaphysical problems which had, ultimately, no solutions: Is the world finite or infinite? Are the body and soul one or separate? Do men continue to live after death or not? Gautama, well aware of the onesidedness and relative nature of these contradictory systems of thought, asserted that such metaphysical questions were meaningless. Instead of withdrawing from the world after attaining enlightenment, he sought to reach out to people and to teach them a truth transcending such mutually conflicting metaphysical arguments.

Buddhism, then, in its early state, did not expound any of the specific dogmas generally stressed by professional religionists. Buddhism attempted to point to and teach dharma, the "true eternal law" or "perennial norm" that would be valid for humanity for all ages. According to Buddhist teachings, the essence, or truth of religion (dharma), should not be limited to any particular set of religious doctrines and practices. Truth is universal, transcending conflicting beliefs and applicable to everyone. Thus, Buddhist doctrine is not specific, established dogma, but a practical wisdom or ethic that promises us the ideal state of humanity. Buddhism aims at transcending dogma peculiar to any school of thought.

In Gautama's view, life is suffering (Skt: duḥkha), in the face of which man is helpless. We experience suffering because everything is the result of ever-changing conditions and causes; human existence is always in flux and in transience (Skt: anitya; J: MUJŌ). Therefore, it is impossible to claim anything as belonging to oneself, or to assert that there is a self (Skt: ātman). By denying the existence of ātman, which was posited as the subject of knowing by the Upanishads and other philosophical schools, Buddhists also rejected the dichotomy between the subjective and objective world. According to them, actual existence is governed by various dharmas; in fact, all beings came into existence through the conditioning of innumerable causes. Our perplexing and painful existence stems from various causes, and if those causes are extinguished, the confusion and suffering would also dissolve. In Japanese this is called *engi* (dependent origination; Skt: *pratītyasamutpāda*). Buddhists do not believe in an almighty god or the "first principle"; instead, they think that the root of illusion and thus, suffering, is blind desire.

Those who wish to be free from suffering must come to a clear understanding (enlightenment) concerning suffering, impermanence, nonself *(anātman)*, and reality. To attain true knowledge *(prajñā)*, all lust and attachment—the root of illusion—must be extinguished. In order to achieve this, one must undergo spiritual discipline, abide by the precepts, and practice meditation. Only then will one be able to free oneself from myriad bindings and attain that freedom called *nirvāṇa* (J: *nehan*). The two extremes of hedonism and self-mortification are rejected; the Middle Way of no suffering and no pleasure is to be taken. Buddhism also emphasized compassion, teaching that it should be extended not only to other human beings but to all sentient beings.

Upon attaining enlightenment, the Buddha gathered around him a group of believers; this community adopted the organizational principles of the *saṃgha,* which generally referred to a confederate form of government or a guild. The religious *saṃgha* was composed of both mendicant monks and lay believers, male and female.

When a mendicant left home, he was expected to lead a life of celibacy, remain aloof from secular occupations, and refrain from economic transactions. Later, rules for the religious life were stipulated: 250 precepts for males *(bhikṣu),* and 500 for females *(bhikṣunī).* Lay believers were instructed to maintain a good household, engage in proper work, strive to help others, and secure honor and fortune through diligent effort so that, upon death, they would be reborn in heaven. Five precepts were particularly emphasized: (1) do not kill; (2) do not steal; (3) do not act immorally; (4) do not lie; (5) do not drink liquor. Sorcery, magic, and divination were strictly forbidden, and believers were told to reject the authority of the Vedas and to eschew ceremonies involving sacrifice.

In economic matters, one was exhorted to share what one gained, to repay one's debts, and to make every effort to resolve all economic problems not by relying on authoritarian power, but by appealing to the moral and ethical sense of the people involved. The mendicant was enjoined to advocate the equality of all people and to reject the socially discriminatory caste system. Within the religious community *(saṅgha),* which included outcastes as well as members of the educated castes, the monk's rank was determined according to the length of time of spiritual discipline since entering the order. The *saṅgha* received financial support from wealthy merchants, who also believed in abolishing the Brahmanical caste system.

The initial Buddhist view of the state was a form of social-contract theory, asserting that the king had attained his position by virtue of an agreement with the people. Early believers were generally averse to kings, whom they likened to thieves who exploited people. Later they offered a vision of an ideal kingship under which the state was governed according to the dharma. Gautama favored a confederate form of government.

The literature of early Buddhism exists in Pāli texts and in Chinese translations, as well as fragmentarily in Sanskrit. Pāli is thought to have been originally a branch of the ancient Magadha tongue, in which Gautama spoke, and to have evolved into a language of the scripture. Pāli scripture has survived in what is now Śrī Lanka, Burma, Thailand, Cambodia, Laos, among other places, and is composed of three main sections (the Tripitaka): *vinaya,* the rules and their explanations regarding discipline for monks and practitioners; *sūtra,* records of sermons by Gautama as well as his dialogues with his disciples; and *śāstra,* commentaries and treatises regarding the sutra section. As this literature was compiled after Gautama's death, it does not necessarily present a historically accurate rendition of his teachings.

Spread of Buddhism —— In the 3rd century BC, under King Aśoka, India was united as one country. In order to abolish the antiquated Brahmanical structure, Aśoka supported Buddhists, and Buddhism spread throughout the country. Around that time Buddhists split into two groups, the conservative elders (Theravādin), whose purpose was to maintain traditional rules, and others, who called for various changes within the religious order. These two groups further split into factions, so that by the 1st century BC there were as many as 20 factions, each supported by the military, merchant, or artisan class, acquiring large estates, and even lending large sums of money. Each faction compiled its own sacred texts according to its own viewpoint, engaged in the study of doctrinal issues, and produced massive treatises expounding its doctrines *(abhi-*

dharma). These groups tended to be self-righteous and aloof from the needs of the common people and in time came to be called the "lesser vehicle" (Hīnayāna) by their opponents. As for the common people, the Buddha was revered as a superhuman being, and veneration of the stupa (an edifice originally enshrining the Buddha's relics) became popular.

After the fall of the Maurya dynasty (ca 180 BC), foreign invaders poured in from the northwest, and northern India came under the rule of numerous invaders. During the Kuṣāṇa dynasty (ca AD 1st–ca AD 3rd century), cultural exchanges between various peoples were especially numerous.

Mahāyāna ("greater vehicle") Buddhism developed among the common people under the influence of such profuse cross-cultural activity and exchange. Mahāyānists believed in a series of Buddhas (apart from the historical Buddha)—Buddhas from the cosmic past and Buddhas-to-be, or bodhisattvas (J: *bosatsu),* who had deferred their own salvation until the salvation of all mankind. Many statues of Buddhas carved in Gandhara and Mathura reflect the spirit of this newly risen group. Although at the outset Mahāyāna Buddhists had no financial base such as large landholdings, their school spread rapidly among the common people, especially after it incorporated folk religious practices.

Several Mahāyāna texts were compiled. First to appear were the *Prajñāpāramitā* sutras (J: *Hannyakyō),* which taught that all things are empty (Skt: *śūnyatā;* J: *kū).* These were followed by the *Vimala-kīrti-nirdeśa-sūtra* (J: *Yuimakyō)* and the *Śrīmālādevī-siṃhanāda-sūtra* (J: *Shōmankyō),* which propagated lay Buddhism; the *Avataṃsaka-sūtra* (J: *Kegonkyō),* which taught the altruistic way of the bodhisattva and idealism; the Pure Land sutras, which advocated belief in Amitābha (J: AMIDA) Buddha; and the LOTUS SUTRA *(Saddharma-puṇḍarīka-sūtra;* J: *Hokkekyō* or *Hokekyō),* which taught that various Buddhist practices would lead practitioners to perfection and that ultimately there is one eternal Buddha.

Two major philosophical schools also arose in the Mahāyāna branch during this period. The Mādhyamika school, founded by Nāgārjuna (ca AD 150–ca AD 250), emphasized *śūnyatā* (emptiness), which was explained in terms of dependent origination and the middle path. The second school, Yogācāra, brought to doctrinal completion by Vasubandhu (AD 4th century), taught that the basis of our existence was a spiritual principle, *ālayavijñāna,* from which all things become manifest. The descendants in the latter school's lineage developed a logical philosophy of knowledge which culminated in the work of Dharmakīrti (fl AD 7th century).

In AD 320 the Gupta dynasty was established. With the development of an India-wide centralized feudalistic regime, Buddhism compromised with these feudalistic elements and with Brahmanism, which had witnessed a revival. This reemergence of Brahmanism has been linked to the decay of foreign trade, brought about by the collapse of the Western Roman Empire, and the reemphasis on the village economy, the main support of Brahmanism. In compromising with these elements, Buddhists developed esoteric teachings that incorporated elements of Brahmanism as well as some folk religious notions. Esoteric Buddhism, however, tended to be absorbed by Hinduism. At the beginning of the 12th century, when India was conquered by Muslims, many Buddhist monasteries were destroyed, and Buddhism all but disappeared from India.

The Diffusion of Buddhism in Asia —— King Aśoka had sent Buddhist missionaries not only to Asian countries but also to Grecian lands. What effect these efforts actually had upon the West is not clear, but a branch of Theravādin Buddhism was transferred to Ceylon (now Śrī Lanka) and then to Burma, Thailand, Cambodia, and other Southeast Asian lands. The Buddhist tradition in these areas is generally called "Southern Buddhism." It adheres to the earliest corpus of Buddhist scriptures, written in the Pāli vernacular and known as the Pāli Canon, and is considered the best contemporary representative of early Buddhism still practiced in the world.

In the Kashmir and Gandhara regions in northwest India, the Theravādin lineage, especially the Sarvāstivādin teachings, was popular. Later, Mahāyāna Buddhism became prevalent and from here spread throughout the western region. In Nepal as well, Mahāyāna Buddhism, especially the esoteric branch, was disseminated. This tradition has preserved Sanskrit Buddhist texts to this day. It permits priests to marry and the priestly position to be inherited.

From the 8th century, Mahāyāna Buddhism, predominantly esoteric Buddhism, was transmitted to Tibet, and upon fusion with indigenous folk beliefs, developed into what is popularly known as Lamaism. In Lamaism, or Tibetan Buddhism, some lamas ("superior ones") were worshiped as incarnations *(tulkus)* of their predecessors.

The Dalai Lama had command over both religious and governmental activities. Lamaism eventually spread even throughout Mongolia and the Jehol region of northeastern China.

Buddhism was introduced to China in the 1st and 2nd centuries AD. According to legend, it was introduced in AD 67 during the reign of Emperor Ming of the Later Han dynasty. Buddhist literature was subsequently translated into Chinese from Sanskrit (or its vernacular) originals. In fact, more translations were made into Chinese than into any other language. The earlier translations were not always faithful to the originals, however, for in order to comply with the Chinese view of human existence or with Confucian logic, Buddhist teachings were modified, and prolix sections were simplified. The Buddhism which came to flourish in China was chiefly Mahāyāna: among the so-called 13 major schools that developed in China, three were Hīnayāna sects, and the others were all Mahāyāna sects, including the Pure Land (Ch: Jingtu or Ching-t'u; J: Jōdo), Chan (Ch'an; J: Zen), Tiantai (T'ien-t'ai; J: Tendai), Huayan (Hua-yen; J: Kegon), Zhenyan (Chen-yen; J: Shingon), Faxiang (Fa-hsiang; J: Hossō), and Sanlun (J: Sanron). Each sect evaluated the various teachings of sutras in the canon and established its own doctrinal system. These were sometimes abstract philosophical arguments, but the tendency to toy with literary aspects of the scriptures was also common.

After the Song (Sung; 960–1279) dynasty, the Chan (Zen) sect (which is said to have existed in China from the 6th century or before) became especially prosperous and was divided into five lines and seven sects. Later Chinese Buddhism has been largely of the Chan school, incorporating tenets of Pure Land Buddhism and elements from popular Taoist beliefs.

Chinese Buddhism had been, at the beginning, a religion mostly of immigrants from India and Central Asia. But from the latter half of the 3rd century it spread among the Chinese common people. During the Tang (T'ang; 618–907) dynasty—generally considered the golden age of Buddhism in China—many people from the upper class renounced the world and joined Buddhist communities. From the time of the Song dynasty, when the gentry-intellectuals reformulated and upheld Confucian tradition (the so-called Neo-Confucianism), the number of Buddhists from this class dwindled. Membership eventually came to be limited to those from the lower classes. Buddhism was gradually modified to conform to the Chinese way of thinking: it became less speculative and more concrete; direct and intuitive expression came to be favored over abstract doctrine; and in keeping with Confucian ethics and the tendency to focus on man and life in the everyday world, stress was placed on one's relation to others, in the family and in hierarchical society.

Introduction of Buddhism into Japan—According to one of Japan's earliest chronicles, the NIHON SHOKI (720), Buddhism was introduced into Japan from Korea in AD 552, when the king of PAEKCHE sent a mission to the emperor of Japan bearing presents of "an image of Śākyamuni in gold and copper, several banners and umbrellas (both used in Buddhist ritual), and a number of sutras." According to current scholarship, however, the date of Buddhism's official introduction into Japan would more accurately be placed earlier at another traditional date, 538.

The reaction of the Japanese court was mixed. The emperor, we are told, leaped for joy; some of his ministers, notably the SOGA FAMILY, argued that Japan should follow the example of other civilized countries; others, particularly the MONONOBE FAMILY and the Nakatomi family, claimed that the native gods would be offended by the respect shown to a foreign deity. Buddhism was accepted after the Soga crushed the Mononobe in a battle.

Buddhism became prominent in the reign of the empress SUIKO. Her regent, the devout Prince SHŌTOKU (574–622), is considered the real founder of Japanese Buddhism. At the request of Empress Suiko, he lectured on three Mahāyāna sutras, and afterward wrote commentaries on them. He founded many monasteries, among them HŌRYŪJI, which contains the oldest wooden edifice extant in the world.

In the Nara period (710–794), under the aegis of Emperor SHŌMU, Buddhism became the state religion. Official provincial monasteries (KOKUBUNJI) were established in each province, and at TŌDAIJI, the head monastery, an enormous image of the Buddha (DAIBUTSU) was erected. Six schools were introduced from China during this period, and studies of Buddhist teachings began in earnest. The Risshū or RITSU SECT maintained as its most important principles the observation of strict monastic discipline and, above all, the correct transmission of holy orders. The monks of this sect strove to adhere to the discipline of a conservative line of early Buddhism, similar to that of the Theravādin in Southern Asia. The KUSHA SCHOOL, also of the conservative line, centered upon the treatise Kusharon (Skt: Abhidharmakośa), composed by Vasubandhu. The JŌJITSU SCHOOL was based on the Jōjitsuron (Skt: Satyasiddhi-śāstra) written by Harivarman (ca AD 250–ca AD 350). The SANRON SCHOOL was derived from the Mādhyamika school in India. A Mahāyāna school, it stressed the śūnyatā doctrine of emptiness. As implied by its name, Sanron ("The Three Treatises") was based on the Mādhyamaka-śāstra and the Dvādaśamukha-śāstra of Nāgārjuna and the Śata-śāstra of Āryadeva. The HOSSŌ SECT represented a kind of Buddhist idealism and was derived from the Yogācāra school in India. A Mahāyāna sect, it regarded everything as the manifestation of the fundamental mind-principle underlying all phenomena. The KEGON SECT was based on the Kegonkyō (Skt: Avataṃsaka-sūtra). The principal focus of worship in this Mahāyāna sect was the Buddha Vairocana. All these six sects were primarily scholastic, since their sphere of influence was limited to the monks and did not extend to the common people.

At the beginning of the Heian period (794–1185), the TENDAI SECT and SHINGON SECT were introduced to Japan. Even these two sects with highly developed philosophical systems were valued for their supposedly efficacious rituals. They received support principally from the ruling aristocratic class. At the beginning of the Kamakura period (1185–1333), Zen Buddhism was introduced from China and was especially favored by the dominant military class. The popular sects of NICHIREN and PURE LAND BUDDHISM were also organized around the same time. Thus, by the 13th century, all the major sects of Japanese Buddhism still active today had emerged: the Tendai sect, the Shingon sect, Zen, the Pure Land sects, and the Nichiren sect.

The Tendai sect. The Tendai sect was introduced into Japan by the priest SAICHŌ (767–822), also known as Dengyō Daishi. He had entered a monastery at an early age and been ordained at the age of 18 (785), but finding the ecclesiastical life of Nara uncongenial, he left the city and lived at first in solitude on Mt. Hiei (Hieizan) outside of Kyōto near his birthplace. He gradually attracted a group of companions and built a small monastery there.

In 804 he was sent by the emperor to China to search for the best form of Buddhism. He studied the school of Tiantai (J: Tendai) at its headquarters, as well as the Zhenyan (Shingon) and Chan (Zen) schools. He returned the next year, bearing books and knowledge. Eventually, the humble monastery he had founded grew into a religious community, ENRYAKUJI, of some 3,000 temples.

The Tendai sect, based on the Lotus Sutra (J: Hokkekyō), teaches that every person can become a Buddha and urges each one to endeavor toward that end. The most remarkable characteristic of Tendai, however, is its comprehensive and systematic character; it finds a place for all scriptures, regarding them as stages of a revelation progressively disclosed by the Buddha according to the growing understanding of his listeners.

Our common sense tells us that parts depend on one another and all depend on the whole. But the so-called complete or perfect teaching (J: engyō) of the Tendai school goes beyond this notion and sees the whole and the parts as one. The whole cosmos and all the Buddhas are present in a grain of sand or on the tip of a hair. According to a celebrated maxim, one thought is the 3,000 spheres (that is, the whole universe), and the 3,000 spheres are but one thought. In other words, the relationships involved in the simplest thought are so numerous that they imply the whole universe, our perceptions and thoughts being identical with absolute reality. This leads to the Tendai doctrine concerning ontology. There are three levels to existence: the void (Skt: śūnya), the temporary, and the middle. All things that exist depend on mutual relations. If we try to isolate anything and to conceive of it as existing without any relationships, it is impossible to think of such a state, and in fact such a state of being is nonexistent. As temporary formative parts of the whole, however, things do exist; the whole would not realize its true nature if it did not manifest itself in particulars. So in this sense, all things have phenomenal existence. Things exist or do not exist depending on our view of their relatedness, but the middle exists absolutely. Phenomena and the one absolute truth are, if rightly regarded, synonymous. When the significance of each of the three is properly understood, this is the enlightenment obtained by the Buddha himself.

The Shingon sect. Shingon Buddhism was introduced to Japan by KŪKAI (774–835), or Kōbō Daishi. He went to China, where he spent two years (804–806) studying Shingon under Huiguo (Huikuo), the celebrated abbot of the Qinglong (Ch'ing-lung) temple at

Chang'an (Ch'ang-an). He is also said to have applied himself to Sanskrit studies under the guidance of an Indian monk called Prājña, and is believed to have introduced into Japan the slightly altered form of the Sanskrit script called *siddham* (J: *shittan*), which is written in vertical columns and extensively used in Shingon books. Prājña is believed to have cooperated with Nestorian priests in making translations, and, through him, Kūkai may have come into contact with Christians.

Kūkai returned to Japan in 806. In 816 he was given land on Mt. Kōya (KŌYASAN) in Kii Province (now Wakayama Prefecture) to found a monastery. He died at the temple KONGŌBUJI on Kōyasan in 835. According to Shingon tradition, however, he did not die but merely entered a state of meditation to await the time of the descent of Maitreya (J: MIROKU), the future Buddha. In the annals and legends of Japanese Buddhism, there is no more celebrated name than his, and whether as saint, scholar, poet, calligrapher, painter, or sculptor, he is familiar to all Japanese.

Shingon means "true word," that is, a sacred spell (or mantra). Mystical rituals, gestures, and syllables (Skt: *dhāraṇī*), as well as sacred drawings (mandalas), were used extensively. These features appealed to the common people of Japan, who wanted a religion that they believed would ward off evil, and the Shingon sect was welcomed.

In Shingon there are definite esoteric doctrines that can be communicated only orally from master to disciple. He who has not yet been initiated cannot claim to understand the explanations. In the initiation ceremony called *kanjō (or kanchō; Skt: abhiṣeka)*, the initiate is sprinkled with holy water. Because of its similarity to Christian baptism, *kanjō* is sometimes rendered, misleadingly, "baptism" in English. This aspersion is not performed when people first become members of the sect; rather it is a form of initiation into the higher mysteries, and regarded as an exceptional privilege.

Pure Land Buddhism. Pure Land Buddhism arose in the 1st or 2nd century AD in India. It was based on the longer and shorter versions of the *Sukhāvatī-vyūha* sutras and on the *Amitāyurdhāna-sūtra*. These sutras speak of the Western Paradise of the Pure Land (Skt: Sukhāvatī; J: Gokuraku), where believers were supposed to be born after death as a reward for their faith and good works.

The savior of this school is Amida (Skt: Amitābha), or the Buddha of Unlimited Light, who presides over the Pure Land. In the past, when he was still a bodhisattva, Amida made 48 vows, the 18th of which read: "If, upon my obtaining Buddhahood, all beings in the ten quarters should desire in sincere faith to be born into my country (i.e., the Pure Land), and if they should not be born by thinking of me as little as ten times, I will not attain the highest enlightenment" (i.e., become Buddha). Now that Amida has become a Buddha, according to believers, he fulfills his vows, helping anyone to achieve salvation who invokes his name with sincerity and faith.

Pure Land Buddhism was transmitted to Japan in the 6th century; from the 10th to the 13th centuries it saw the formation of many schools: RYŌNIN (1073–1132) founded the YŪZŪ NEMBUTSU SECT; HŌNEN (1133–1212), the JŌDO SECT; SHINRAN (1173–1263), the JŌDO SHIN SECT; and IPPEN (1239–1289), the JI SECT.

The Nichiren sect. The indigenous Nichiren sect was founded by NICHIREN (1222–82), the son of a low-level estate overseer. He had become a monk at an early age, first studying the Shingon school and then the Tendai school. There, he came to the conclusion that only one scripture was needed, namely, the Lotus of the Good Law (*Saddharmapuṇḍarīka-sūtra*) or Lotus Sutra, and that the deliverance of the country from its sufferings could best be achieved by proper worship of the Lotus Sutra and the Śākyamuni Buddha.

Nichiren was a born religious prophet; he wandered all over the country, literally beating his drum to awaken people to the truth of the Lotus Sutra. Because of his harsh criticisms of other sects and the government, he was soon in trouble with the authorities and suffered a long chain of persecutions, but he miraculously escaped each time. His fervor brought him many disciples; to this day, religious zeal is a characteristic of the followers of this sect.

After World War II, many religious groups, the so-called Shinkō Shūkyō (NEW RELIGIONS), were organized. Several of the largest of these groups (SŌKA GAKKAI, RISSHŌ KŌSEIKAI, REIYŪKAI, Myōchikai, etc) draw upon Nichiren's teachings and the Lotus Sutra, and adopt the chanting of the *daimoku*, i.e., "Namu Myōhō rengekyō" ("I place my faith in the Lotus Sutra of the Good Law").

Zen Buddhism. As a specific form of Buddhism, Zen first arose in China, and was a peculiarly Chinese version of the kind of Buddhism brought from India by the sage Bodhidharma (J: Daruma) about AD 527. Bodhidharma's Buddhism was a form of Mahāyāna

centered on *dhyāna* (Ch: *chan*; J: *zen*). The nearest English equivalent of *dhyāna* is "contemplation" or "meditation," but these English words may carry a static connotation quite foreign to *dhyāna*. *Dhyāna* means immediate insight into the nature of reality or life. In China, Dhyāna Buddhism was strongly influenced by Taoism and Confucianism and emerged in the 7th century as the body of religious practices that we know today.

The Tendai monk EISAI (1141–1215) first brought back Dhyāna or Chan Buddhism from China in 1191. The Zen Buddhism he introduced is called the RINZAI SECT. The form introduced by DŌGEN (1200–1253), who also studied in China, is known as the SŌTŌ SECT.

The Rinzai Zen sect, centered in five major temples in Kyōto and five in Kamakura (see GOZAN), obtained support among the ruling class, including warriors *(samurai)* as well as court nobles. The Sōtō sect, on the other hand, found followers first among powerful provincial families, but after Keizan Jōkin (1268–1325), the founder of SŌJIJI, adopted rituals from the esoteric Shingon sect, the Sōtō sect quickly spread among the common people.

In the Edo period (1600–1868), the Chinese monk INGEN (Ch: Yinyuan or Yin-yüan; 1592–1673) introduced Zen anew from China and established the ŌBAKU SECT. This sect's practices were almost identical with those of the Rinzai sect, but it also incorporated practices from Pure Land Buddhism, since the Chan school during the Ming dynasty (1368–1644) had assimilated faith in Amida Buddha.

Under the TOKUGAWA SHOGUNATE, Buddhism and its network of temples was used to eradicate Christianity (see SHŪMON ARATAME). But it also came under the strict regulatory power of the shogunate. Sectarian divisions which had been established in previous times continued, and the organization of various religious groups became firmly fixed. The doctrines of the various schools were also formalized. Any reform movement aimed at the Tokugawa political system and/or the system of ideas it espoused gained almost no support within Buddhism, although there were signs of modernizing thought, such as SUZUKI SHŌSAN's occupational ethics. One should also mention the popularization of Zen by Shidō Bunan (1603–76), BANKEI YŌTAKU (1622–93), and HAKUIN (1685–1769), and the movement to return to the true meaning of Buddhism as revealed in the original Sanskrit texts, led by Fujaku (1707–81), Kaijō (1750–1805), and JIUN ONKŌ (1718–1804). After the Meiji Restoration (1868), the government sought to establish SHINTŌ as the national religion, and many Buddhist temples were disestablished (see HAIBUTSU KISHAKU). Since then, Buddhist organizations have had to struggle for survival and to adjust to the developments of the modern age, and it has become common for priests to eat meat and to marry.

Characteristics of Japanese Buddhism —— Several characteristics of Buddhism that are distinctly Japanese can be observed. First, Japanese Buddhism has a tendency to emphasize the importance of human institutions. While Indian and, in some measure, Chinese Buddhism tended to be reclusive, Japanese Buddhism has emphasized practical morality and its accompanying work ethic. Buddhism in Japan has been involved at every level of the complex, hierarchical society, stressing the importance of human relations, family morals, and reverence for ancestors. It has also tended to compromise with nationalistic tendencies in the name of *chingo kokka*—national peace through religious discipline. In keeping with the inclination among Japanese to revere a charismatic person, worship of the founders of various sects is widespread. Each sect or school has a tendency toward exclusivity, putting an undue emphasis on the master-disciple lineage.

Japanese Buddhism tends to be nonrationalistic in character. The Japanese generally do not favor rationalistic speculation, and in religion, too, they have failed to develop a grand doctrinal system. They are inclined to respond more intuitively and emotionally to the salvific message of Buddhism. Preferring simple symbolic representation, they have been drawn to such invocations as *Namu Amida Butsu* ("I place my faith in Amida Buddha") or *Namu Myōhō rengekyō* ("I place my faith in the Lotus Sutra of the Good Law").

Another characteristic is the tendency to accept things as they are. Japanese Buddhists seek to understand the absolute (Buddha) through adherence to the phenomenal world. The result is an inclination to equate the world or the individual self with the ultimate. Consequently, the Japanese have generally shown religious tolerance, but at the same time lack a willingness to confront issues. Again, religious discipline and monastic rules tended not to be reinforced but allowed to lapse and deteriorate.

Finally, there has been a remarkable openness toward accommodation with ancient shamanistic practices, and more notably, with the native cult of Shintō. Buddhism very early arrived at an understanding and coexistence with Shintoism. Even today, the Japanese see no contradiction in being a Buddhist and Shintoist at the same time. Although Buddhist temples *(tera)* and Shintō shrines *(jinja)*, as well as their respective priests, are strictly differentiated, few devotees pronounce themselves adherents of one religion to the exclusion of the other. Indeed, it is not unusual for one to have a Shintō wedding and a Buddhist funeral.

Japanese Buddhism Today——Statistically, Japan is a country of Buddhists. More than six-sevenths of the population profess the Buddhist faith. Buddhism in Japan, divided into 13 principal sects, maintains 80,000 temples with 150,000 priests. Several colleges and institutes in Kyōto and Tōkyō are chiefly dedicated to the study of Buddhist theology.

The following criticisms, however, may be made of present-day Buddhism: Buddhist influence on Japanese intellectuals has been rather insignificant; its dogmas have become unintelligible to the public; and few people show active interest in the religion. Priests chant sutras and other holy scriptures with due solemnity in rituals, but these are regarded as empty formulas. The Buddhist ideals of human life have been forgotten, and the religion is thought to possess little spiritual or moral value. Although publications concerning religion are increasing in number, students of religious studies are diminishing.

The future outlook of Buddhism in Japan is hard to predict, because it depends largely upon the efforts of Japanese Buddhists themselves, both priests and laymen, and the efforts of scholars. The scientific study of Buddhist philosophy, which in recent years has made remarkable progress in Japan, is still far beyond the understanding of the public because of the tendency of some scholars to focus on the technicalities of dogma.

Hopeful signs for revival, however, have developed. New organizations for the practice and spread of the Path of the Buddha have been formed at various places. Sermons and lectures, Buddhist books, and even kindergartens and nurseries run by Buddhist priests are increasing in number. Many of the new religions which have arisen since World War II show Buddhist influences. International activities by Japanese Buddhists also are steadily increasing. Missionaries are being sent abroad, especially to North America. Many books and articles are being published in Western languages, and Japanese scholars are collaborating with foreign scholars in compiling Buddhist encyclopedias in Western languages. The entire body of the Tibetan scriptures has been published by a Japanese institute, and a complete bibliography of Buddhistic articles published in various countries has now been published in Japanese. Scholars and students from North and South America, Europe, and Asian countries, such as India, China, and Śri Lanka, come to Japan for Buddhist studies. Several groups have set up relief organizations for refugees and projects for helping developing Asian countries to improve their standards of living, and Buddhists have been active in striving to bring peace to the world.

▄▄——Masaharu Anesaki, *History of Japanese Religion* (1930, repr 1963). Charles Eliot, *Japanese Buddhism* (1935, repr 1959). Yoshito Hakeda, *Kūkai: Major Works, Translated, with an Account of His Life and a Study of His Thought* (1972). Joseph M. Kitagawa, *Religion in Japanese History* (1966). W. Kohler, *Die Lotus-Lehre und die modernen Religionen in Japan* (1963). Laurel Rasplica Rodd, *Nichiren: Selected Writings* (1980). Junjirō Takakusu, *The Essentials of Buddhist Philosophy*, ed Wing-Tsit Chan and Charles A. Moore (1947). NAKAMURA Hajime

Buddhism and Japanese literature

The relationship between Buddhism and the literary arts has been a long and deep one in Japan. The initial rise of literacy and development of a written literature took place in Japan at a time when Buddhism was held in especially high esteem by the literati of China and Korea. Since at this formative stage of their own literature the Japanese were deeply influenced by continental tastes also in religion and philosophy, an early engagement in Japan between Buddhism and literature resulted. Over the subsequent centuries it involved at least the following four things: first, the presence of Buddhist terms, themes, and concepts as symbols within this literature; second, the direct use of literary modes for Buddhist didactic purposes; third, extensive efforts to resolve either real or potential conflict between the practice of Buddhism and the pursuit of literary vocations; and fourth, a distinctly Buddhist contribution to the Japanese literary aesthetic. Although the following account is historical, the discussion deals with all four of these.

The first collection of verse by Japanese poets was the KAIFŪSŌ (751). Written in Chinese and clearly patterned after T'ang models, it includes references to the concept of karma, the practice of meditation, and a monk's need to separate from secular society. The MAN'YŌSHŪ (ca 759), however, is more important not only because it is in Japanese but because in it can be seen the process whereby the Japanese received, resisted, and transformed continental Buddhism. For instance, in the following drinking song by Ōtomo no Tabito (665–731) there is an undisguised ambivalence about karma and transmigration, concepts at this point regarded more modish than compelling:

Ima no yo ni shi	Getting my pleasures
Tanoshiku araba	This way in my present life
Komu yo ni wa	May make me turn
Mushi ni tori ni mo	Into an insect or a bird
Ware wa narinan	In the life to come.

Certain poems of the *Man'yōshū* express the Buddhist emphasis upon the inescapable impermanence of all things (MUJŌ). Some scholars note, however, that, whereas continental Buddhism had stressed a detached and objective contemplation of impermanence, the Japanese in their earliest literature preferred to experience the impermanence of things with an emotional engagement, something of a sweet melancholy. This trend toward the aestheticizing of *mujō* continued in the subsequent Heian period (794–1185); whereas Buddhists in India had once gone to cemeteries to observe the impermanence of rotting corpses, the courtier poets of the Heian period much preferred its more gentle and exquisite forms—most notably in cherry blossoms and falling maple leaves.

Prose literature, however, was from the beginning much more easily harnessed to direct didactic ends. Beginning with the NIHON RYŌIKI around 822, the genre of *setsuwa* gave a long series of authors opportunities to tell stories which, for instance, concretely illustrated the workings of karma or demonstrated the sometimes miraculous powers that resulted from great devotion to Buddhism (see SETSUWA BUNGAKU). In the monumental KONJAKU MONOGATARI of the early 12th century the art of storytelling achieved consummate skill. Whether or not its purpose is other than that of telling good stories, it is at least certain that the structure of the work, by presenting a sequence of tales that take place in India, then China, and finally Japan, in its own way implies the classic Buddhist concept of the succession of the dharma through each culture. Examples of didactic Buddhist *setsuwa* are too numerous to mention, but it is important to note that these continued for many centuries. In fact, in many ways the *Myōkōnin den* with its stories of pious but simple people in the Edo period (1600–1868) is a late example of this genre; its tales tell of the benefits that resulted from uncompromised faith in Amida's power and rebirth in the Pure Land.

In contrast to the fairly overt moralizing in much of the narrative literature, the poetry of the Heian period was suffused with a much more subtle presence of Buddhism. The court poets were literati, people generally expected to have some familiarity with the major Buddhist scriptures. This was especially so in the case of the *Hokkekyō* (LOTUS SUTRA) revered in the TENDAI SECT. A result of this was a type of poetry often rich with subtle allusions to events, themes, and images in the Buddhist texts. For example, the following anonymous poem in the *Go shūishū* (1086) is prefaced by a note which says that three ladies-in-waiting were on the way to a lecture in separate carriages but, having got caught in the rain, all climbed into one carriage and reached the lecture hall successfully:

Morotomo ni	Our party rode out
Mitsu no kuruma ni	In three vehicles
Norishikado	But all of us
Ware wa ichimi no	Together got dampened
Ame ni nureniki	By the impartial rain.

The art in this poem lies in its recourse to symbols; its author has concealed within it two references to separate portions of the *Hokkekyō* and fused these into a single experience. The *Hokkekyō* is a sutra which was originally designed to unify a fracturing Buddhist community in India by insisting upon a single, common vehicle for enlightenment in spite of what appeared to many to be three differing, and competing, types of teaching. Elsewhere in this sutra an extended metaphor illustrates the point about a single teaching adjusted for different mentalities in terms of one cloud which showered an equally beneficial rain upon plants and trees of greatly differing heights. All this rich allusion is present in what otherwise would appear to be the *Go shūishū*'s simple and direct poem about three ladies of the court caught in a downpour. In this context their arrival at the lecture hall serves as a symbol for a common attainment of nirvana after it becomes clear that "three vehicles" must be replaced by "one vehicle."

For much of the Heian period Buddhist monks and nuns in Japan had entered to a considerable degree into the literate life of the Heian court and had written even "secular" poetry without great hesitation. Criticism of this practice, however, eventually surfaced and became quite strong in the Kamakura period (1185–1333). Discussion of this point often centered around the fact that Bo Juyi (Po Chü-i; 772–846), the T'ang poet called Haku Rakuten by the Japanese and often revered by them as the paragon of Buddhist poets, had twice given his poetry away to monasteries in China and dismissed it as so much "worldly writings" and as "floating phrases and fictive utterances" (*kyōgen kigo* in Japanese). This was sufficient precedent in Japan for YOSHISHIGE NO YASUTANE (ca 931–1002), an important poet, to refuse to write poetry in his later years. But at the end of the Heian period, a time of crisis for the culture of the court, the criticism of Buddhist monk-poets became stronger and carried over into the next period; the priest Mujū (1226–1312), for instance, in his *Shasekishū* cited Bo Juyi's phrase and himself called poetry something superficial to which foolish persons easily get attached.

On the other side of this ongoing argument was FUJIWARA NO TOSHINARI (Shunzei; 1114–1204), whose *Korai futei shō* was, at least in part, a defense of poetry from within a Buddhist perspective. Shunzei appealed to Tendai philosophy in order to criticize those who drew a sharp line between the secular and the sacred and subordinated the former to the latter. In addition, Shunzei appealed to the more general Mahāyāna Buddhist principle that "there is no nirvana apart from *saṃsāra*" or no enlightenment apart from the world of suffering. On the basis of this he even boldly claimed that the succession of imperial collections of poetry in Japan was the Japanese equivalent to the long line of Buddhist patriarchs in Indian and Chinese history.

Shunzei's arguments were part of a deep change that was taking place at the time in the thinking about the relationship of Buddhism to literature. It was to have a lasting effect upon Japanese literary aesthetics. Buddhist poets such as Shunzei were no longer satisfied with poetry that seemed to be "Buddhist" by virtue of specific allusions and direct allegory, verse in which the natural phenomena of the world were used to "point beyond" themselves to specific holier entities elsewhere. What Shunzei and others were coming to insist upon has been called "tenorless symbolism" by the scholar Konishi Jin'ichi; it is connected with the growing appreciation of the term YŪGEN and involves the recognition of a religious profundity within natural phenomena and experiences themselves, without the need for specific symbol and allegory. Shunzei, for instance, recognized it in the following verse by his son Teika (FUJIWARA NO SADAIE; 1162–1241):

Miwataseba	Gaze out far enough
Hana mo momiji mo	Beyond all cherry blossoms
Nakarikeri	And scarlet maples,
Ura no tomaya no	To those huts by the harbor
Aki no yūgure	Fading in the autumn dusk.

This is a type of verse which embodies depth and tranquility without having to be religious or symbolic in the customary way.

SAIGYŌ (1118–1190) was a monk who struggled with the problem of the relationship between Buddhism and poetry throughout most of his life. Intellectually his solution to the problem was akin to Shunzei's. Saigyō, however, made quite extensive pilgrimages, and these enabled him to write verse that combined Shintō's traditional affirmation of the natural world with concurrent Buddhist discussions of the Buddha-nature of plants and trees (*sōmoku jōbutsu*). It is evidenced, for instance, in the following:

Ko no moto ni	Tired from travel,
Tabine o sureba	I'm falling asleep under
Yoshinoyama	A tree in Yoshino
Hana no fusuma o	While a spring breeze gathers
Kisuru harukaze	And pulls over me a quilt of petals.

Saigyō became, however, the paradigmatic Buddhist poet for the Japanese when his contemporaries discovered after his death that some time earlier he had accurately predicted that death as one which would fall on the anniversary of the Buddha's final nirvana

and would, at the same time, correspond with certain natural events treasured by the Japanese. He had written:

Negawaku wa	Let it be this way:
Hana no shita nite	Under the cherry blossoms,
Haru shinan	A spring death,
Sono kisaragi no	At that second month's midpoint
Mochizuki no koro	When the moon is full.

The translation of this and the preceding poem © 1978 by William LaFleur. Reprinted by permission of New Directions Publishing Corp.

Saigyō repeatedly noted that the compensation for having left the "householder's life" and entered into an eremitic one was an unparalleled proximity to nature. In this way he brought together values held in Buddhism with others in the Shintō tradition.

In prose the most eloquent argument for the reclusive life came from the pen of KAMO NO CHŌMEI (1156?–1216); his *Hōjōki*, written in 1212 and based upon a 10th-century work in Chinese, depicts a *mujō* from which nothing can escape, an impermanence that touches all things and every level of society. Yet the *Hōjōki* is saved from gloom by prose that is skillfully cadenced and descriptions that are memorably vivid. It rightly became a classic.

With the development of *renga* (see RENGA AND HAIKAI) or linked verse, a form that flourished between the 13th and 19th centuries, there arose an opportunity for Buddhists to note an especially close tie between a specific literary form and a cardinal teaching of their religion. Whether or not the origins of *renga* are in Buddhism, it is at least clear that many *renga* poets detected a connection between this form's multiple authorship and the classic Mahāyāna contention that there are no independently existent "selves" or, in positive terms, that all things are deeply interrelated. NIJŌ YOSHIMOTO (1320–88), for instance, had stated categorically: "In linked verse it is interdependence that is primary. Its poetry consists of interdependence." Many of the finest *renga* poets were Zen monks; for them there was a continuity between the experience of the meditation hall and the need in *renga* composition for a mental unity among a party of individuals striving to create a single poem.

In their theoretical thinking about linked verse many of these poets drew directly upon the resources of Mahāyāna Buddhism. A priest who was perhaps also the best of *renga* poets, SHINKEI (1406–75) in his *Sasamegoto* defined literary experience in classical Buddhist terms: "The beginner enters from the shallow to the deep; and once he has attained the depths, he emerges again into the shallow; this is the essential rule of all disciplines. Cause produces effect; effect in turn leads to cause." This is an appeal to the concept of karma in order to recognize that, in any final analysis, the shallow is as necessary and important as the deep; this is a conclusion logically arrived at on the basis of the principle of dependent co-origination in Buddhism. At the same time it gives express articulation to a significant development in the literary aesthetic of medieval Japan, namely, the equalizing of all phenomena within the world of poetry. This is, of course, especially evident in *haikai*, a form of verse that insists upon lifting up the otherwise lowly and ignored for observation and appreciation. A celebrated verse by Yosa BUSON (1716–84) does it very well:

Harusame ya	Spring rain:
Monogatariyuku	Straw raincoat and fine umbrella
Mino to kasa	Go on talking together

A comparison with the *Go shūishū* poem about court ladies caught in the rain and climbing into a single carriage to go to a lecture can be instructive here. Both poems treat a unification process thematically, yet the earlier poem had done so by means of complex allusions and an allegorical set of referents. Buson's *haikai*, by contrast, seems to have become freed from the lode of the Buddhist tradition. Nevertheless, it has followed the philosophical trajectory of the Mahāyāna precisely through the way it rejects the allegorical mode as something which forced the "lowly" (the symbol) into the service of the "high" or the "deep" (the symbolized). As such it is a development which, while superficially involving a "secularization" of verse, also pursues a process whereby Buddhist ideas were being translated into specific literary modes and expectations in Japan.

Matsuo BASHŌ (1644–94), the most famous of Japanese poets, referred to himself as "half-layman, half-priest" and typified the manner in which many Japanese poets conceived of their art as at least a semireligious vocation. His superb *haikai* very often suggest the interdependence of opposites in nature and in human experience—as, for instance, that of silence and sound in the following:

Shizukasa ya	The quietness:
Iwa ni shimiiru	Shrill cicada cries
Semi no koe	Soaked into boulders.

Kobayashi ISSA (1763–1827) was a priest of the JŌDO SHIN SECT (True Pure Land sect). His best work is semiautobiographical, a combination of prose and verse entitled *Oraga haru*. Issa's writing demonstrates both his unusual compassion for suffering creatures and his refusal to benumb his own suffering in life through religious explanations that seemed to him sometimes too facile. There is both candor and piety in his expressions of his pain.

Probably the most conspicuously Buddhist poet of modern times has been MIYAZAWA KENJI (1896–1933), a science teacher whose verses were written in a free form. His poems use modern scientific terminology to celebrate the myriad phenomena of nature but at the same time tell of the poet's deep devotion to something as ancient as the *Hokkekyō*.

——Bukkyō Bungaku Kenkyūkai, ed, *Bukkyō bungaku kenkyū* (1963–73; 1974–76). Konishi Jin'ichi, *Image and Ambiguity: The Impact of Zen Buddhism on Japanese Literature* (1973). William R. LaFleur, *Mirror for the Moon: A Selection of Poems by Saigyō (1118–1190)* (1978). William R. LaFleur, *The Karma of Words: Buddhism and the Literary Arts in Medieval Japan* (forthcoming). Manako Fujiko, *Kokubungaku ni sesshu sareta bukkyō* (1972). Herbert E. Plutschow, "Is Poetry a Sin? Honjisuijaku and Buddhism versus Poetry," *Oriens Extremus* 25:2 (1978).   William R. LaFleur

Buddhist architecture

A major style of religious architecture in Japan which originated in Chinese and Korean structural forms; a general term used to describe systems of buildings within Japanese Buddhist monasteries or temple compounds that, taken together, comprise great architectural ensembles of BUDDHIST ART. A temple was a place dedicated to worship of the Buddha. It functioned as a place of residence for monks and nuns, for it was here that they engaged in study of the Buddhist scriptures (sutras) and received training in ascetic practices. Special buildings existed for each of these purposes. It was also a place where lay worshipers gathered, and facilities and space for this function were also important.

Pagoda and Principal Temple Halls —— An ensemble of temple buildings was called a *garan* and by the 8th century typically consisted of seven basic structures (*shichidō garan*; for this and other technical terms, see glossary at end of article). The most important of these structures were the pagoda (*tō*; see PAGODA), a multistoried tower where sacred relics believed to be the remains of the Buddha were enshrined; the main hall (*kondō*, or "golden hall"; later replaced by the term *hondō*), where the principal images of the Buddhist deities to be worshiped and other statues were installed; and the lecture hall (*kōdō*), where monks assembled to listen to sermons on the teachings of Buddha and to perform rituals.

When Buddhism was first introduced into Japan, the sacred relics of the Buddha were the central feature of the faith. Therefore, the pagoda became the center of the monastery. Excavations of the original site of ASUKADERA, the oldest true Buddhist temple in Japan whose construction was begun in 588, reveal that a pagoda was at the center of the ground plan and main halls stood on both sides and to the rear of it. At SHITENNŌJI (ca 593) the main hall is located behind the pagoda. Both of these arrangements, which are two of the earliest Buddhist temple plans, indicate that the pagoda was considered the most important building. By the time Kawaradera was built (ca mid-7th century; see KAWARADERA REMAINS), the arrangement had become asymmetrical, as if one of the main halls at Asukadera had been eliminated; at HŌRYŪJI (7th century) the main hall and pagoda were built side by side and were thus accorded equal treatment. When YAKUSHIJI, completed in the late 7th century, was built in the ancient imperial capital of FUJIWARAKYŌ, however, the main hall had become the central element of the monastery compound and the pair of pagodas a decorative feature. Both TŌDAIJI (798) and DAIANJI (744) had two pagodas, but these were considerably removed from the center of the temple complex. Finally, at KŌFUKUJI (completed 8th century) there was only one pagoda standing in a corner of the compound. The same was true of TŌSHŌDAIJI (759) and also of early temples of esoteric Buddhism built on level sites. The pagodas referred to above were three-, five-, or seven-storied towers. The SHINGON SECT and TENDAI SECT, the two main schools of esoteric Buddhism, increasingly built mountain monasteries, and their pagodas were more freely sited. Changes in the siting of pagodas reveal a gradual transformation in temple ground plans over the centuries accompanying the evolvement of Buddhist faith in Japan and the development of new architectural styles.

In the Asuka (latter part of the 6th century to 710) and Nara periods (710–794), the main hall, in which the primary object of worship (*honzon*) was enshrined, was called the *kondō*. At first, as in the temple plan of Asukadera, two or three main halls surrounded a pagoda in a temple complex, but gradually there came to be just one main hall located in the center of the monastery compound, an arrangement which subsequently remained unchanged. The next most important building after the main hall was the lecture hall (*kōdō*), which was located behind the main hall. In early times the lecture hall was separated from the main hall, but the two were gradually brought closer together and were finally connected by a covered corridor (*kairō*). Ordinarily the lecture hall was a more spacious building than the main hall as it had to accommodate the large numbers of priests and monks who gathered there to study and recite the Buddhist scriptures. Tendai and Shingon sect temples such as ENRYAKUJI and Kyōō Gokokuji (see TŌJI) had lecture halls, but temples of esoteric Buddhism generally did away with the terms *kondō* and *kōdō* after the latter part of the Heian period (794–1185); the term *hondō* was used for the main hall instead. At the same time, there were changes in the monastery ground plan, such as the expansion of the outer sanctuary (*gejin*).

The monastery site plan regained axial symmetry with ZEN sect temples. The central structures of the Zen monastery were the Buddha hall (*butsuden*), which corresponded to the old *kondō*, and the doctrine hall (*hattō*), which corresponded to the old *kōdō*. Both were one-storied structures with an additional roofed structure (*mokoshi*) attached. Among the Buddhist sects popular in the middle ages (13th–16th centuries), the NICHIREN SECT had a main hall not greatly different from that of esoteric Buddhist sect temples, but its founder's hall (*soshidō*) became a large-scale building. The outer sanctuary of the main hall was particularly spacious in the temples of the JŌDO SECT and the JŌDO SHIN SECT, two Pure Land schools of Buddhism. In ordinary Pure Land temples the main hall stood alone, but in temples of the head temple (*honzan*) class, the *nyoraidō*, which corresponded to the *hondō*, was joined by the *mieidō* (portrait chapel), a hall dedicated to the founder of the sect and surpassing the *nyoraidō* in size. In addition to the above-mentioned types of halls, which were the primary buildings in a Japanese Buddhist temple plan, each of the various sects erected other buildings within the monastery compound to serve their particular needs. These were generally smaller than the main halls.

Gates and Corridor —— In temples of the Asuka and Nara periods, there was an inner gate (*chūmon*) in the middle of the front of the rectangular inner court or precinct containing the main hall and pagoda. A roofed-over corridor (*kairō*) extended from the left and right sides of the inner gate and enclosed the main hall and pagoda. In early monasteries, the corridor completely closed off the precinct, and the lecture hall was located outside and behind the corridor. Asukadera and Hōryūji originally had this arrangement. As styles changed, however, the corridor was connected to the lecture hall as at Shitennōji and Yakushiji. The corridor at Kōfukuji terminated to the right and left of the main hall. This style subsequently became very common. The precinct defined by the inner gate and corridor was, as the place where Buddhist ceremonies were observed, the most sacred part of the monastery. In the earliest temples, the corridor was a single bay wide, but in the Nara period a double-bay corridor became common. The double-bay corridor eventually fell into decline, and no temples with double-bay corridors have survived.

In the Asuka and Nara periods, the temple precinct grounds were enclosed by earthen walls (*tsuijibei*) with gates on each side. The names of the gates derived from the direction in which they faced, as in the "great south gate" (*nandaimon*) and "great east gate" (*tōdaimon*). Among these, the great south gate was the front or main gate of the temple and the most important. In early times it was located very close to the inner gate (*chūmon*) and was smaller than the *chūmon* in size. It came to rival the inner gate in size in the Nara period. The other gates, though called "great gates" (*daimon*), were not particularly large.

In Tendai and Shingon sect temples, too, the inner gate and covered corridor existed in early temples built on level sites such as

Kyōō Gokokuji and DAIGOJI. An earthen wall with gates is also to be found at Kyōō Gokokuji. In general, however, esoteric Buddhist temples were built on mountainous sites and only had gates arranged according to the contour of the mountain slope. Nevertheless, the gate was regarded as next in importance to the main hall and pagoda, even in esoteric Buddhist temples. The most common type of gate was the two-storied gate (rōmon). In Zen sect temples there was a gate called the sammon that corresponded to the inner gate; from this a corridor extended to the Buddha hall. No examples of such corridors survive. In front of the sammon was a pond (hanchi), and in front of the pond was a small gate called the sōmon.

The various sects of Buddhism which flourished from the medieval period did not build covered corridors. They only had a gate at the entrance to the temple precinct, and this gate had no special character. Instead, feudal period temples of all sects put importance on other gates with special functions, such as the chokushimon (imperial messenger gate) and onarimon (a gate to receive an imperial or shogunal visit). Such gates also exist at Zen temples (e.g., DAITOKUJI) and at Jōdo Shin temples (e.g., NISHI HONGANJI). Several of these gates are numbered among the best examples of Azuchi-Momoyama-period (1568–1600) architecture.

Bell Tower, Sutra Repository, and Storehouse —— Among the seven main building types of Nara-period temples were two types of two-storied, towerlike (rō-zukuri) buildings: the drum or bell tower (korō or shurō), from which a drum or bell was sounded marking the times of daily observances, and the sutra repository (kyōzō or kyōrō), where collections of canonical texts were stored. These were built behind the covered corridor to the left and right. At Zen sect temples the bell tower and sutra repository originally stood to either side of the sammon. No actual examples, however, have survived. Bell towers continued to be built, but after the middle ages they were generally of the hakamagoshi style in which the first floor walls slant outward; a one-storied structure of just four columns also became more popular.

For the storehouse (azekura), struts were first erected and then horizontal members of a triangular section piled up with interlocking corners, as in a log cabin. Many of these were built in temple compounds in the ancient period as sutra repositories or treasuries. Those at Tōdaiji and Tōshōdaiji survive.

Buildings for Monks —— In Nara-period temples the refectory or dining hall (jikidō) was constructed behind or to the side of the monastery. The dormitories (sōbō) stood behind the monastery. In Zen temples the kuin, or kitchen, was attached to the corridor on the east and the sōdō, a hall used for meditation (zazen), to the corridor on the west. The meditation hall at TŌFUKUJI still exists. In Zen temples the bathing area was located to the southeast of the sammon and the latrine (tōsu) to the southwest. Since daily activities such as bathing and elimination were also viewed as an integral part of Zen training, these buildings were considered important and were included among the seven main building types.

Although in principle monks lived in groups, priests from aristocratic backgrounds at Tendai and Shingon temples often established separate quarters called shiin. In Zen the practice arose of followers attending the grave of a renowned priest and establishing separate quarters, similar to the shiin, called tatchū. Eventually, many shiin and tatchū came to be clustered around the main monasteries of all sects.

Styles of Buddhist Architecture —— The Asuka style of temple architecture was derived from 5th and 6th century Chinese architecture. No original examples of Asuka-style architecture have survived in Japan, but the present Hōryūji provides valuable information on the architectural forms of that period. Next to be introduced into Japan was the Tang (T'ang) style, which became the predominant style of the Tempyō era (729–749; see TEMPYŌ CULTURE); from the Kamakura period (1185–1333) this became known as wayō, or Japanese style. In the wayō style horizontal members (nageshi) were used to connect columns, and bracket complexes were restricted to above the columns; the standard complex was the three-armed bracket complex (mitesaki), and the intermediate support between bracket complexes was either a block-on-strut (kentozuka) or a frog-leg-strut (kaerumata). The eaves had paralleled rafters. The doors were flush and windows mullioned; there was originally no nosing (kibana)—a projecting or carved end of a member—and no sculpture. The wayō style had generally broad proportions and little decoration; thus it was a simple, clear style.

The daibutsuyō, or "great Buddha style," and the Zen style were introduced in the Kamakura period. In the great Buddha style, penetrating ties (nuki) connected large columns; sashi hijiki, a type of bracket arm, was used and the bracket complexes employed ranged up to six-armed complexes; between columns a free rafter (yūri odaruki) was used. Fan raftering (ōgi-daruki) was employed at corners, and the front of the eaves was covered by a fascia. A paneled door (sankarado) was used, and in the interior, the structure consisted of a thick beam called a rainbow beam (kōryō) and a strut with a round section. A distinctive nosing was employed. In the Zen style, columns stood on footing stones (soban), penetrating ties connected columns, and the bracket complex was of a type called close bracketing (tsumegumi) in which the complex was placed both on top of the columns and in between as an intermediate support; basically it was a three-armed bracket complex, but the style was distinctive. Fan raftering was used and curved prominently upward. The effect was lively, with paneled doors, arched windows (katō mado), and many nosings and sculptures. Rainbow beams and vase-shaped struts (taiheizuka) were employed.

Eventually an eclectic style (setchūyō) developed, which mingled features of the wayō style with the great Buddha and Zen styles. Even aside from this, afterward there was a marked intermingling of the wayō with the Zen style, and pure wayō became increasingly rare during the Muromachi period (1333–1568). See also BUDDHIST ART.

● **Glossary**

Buddha hall　See main hall.

butsuden　See main hall.

chūmon　See gates.

daibutsuyō　See great Buddha style.

dharma hall　See lecture hall.

dormitories (sōbō)　Temple dormitories were long, narrow buildings, divided into cells for one or more monks. The buildings were often arranged to form a U, but sometimes they were placed in parallel rows. They were usually located near the lecture hall, either to its north or to each side of it. An important example preserving Nara-period features is the Higashi Muro (East Dormitory) of Hōryūji's Eastern Precinct (Tōin).

eclectic style (setchūyō)　A hybrid style of architecture which developed after the Kamakura period. It is considered to be a blend of two other hybrid styles, one of which is itself a blend of the great Buddha style (daibutsuyō) and the Japanese style (wayō) and the other a blend of the Zen style (zenshūyō) and the Japanese style. Examples of the eclectic style are the main halls of Kanshinji and Kakurinji.

garan　Variously translated as "monastery," "monastic compound," and "temple," this term is derived from the Sanskrit word samghārāma (communal dwelling). It is used in reference to large-scale temples with numerous halls. See also shichidō garan.

gates　There were two types of gates in temples of the Asuka and Nara periods: the outer gates to the temple grounds proper and the inner gate that opened on the main precinct of the temple. Among the outer gates (daimon), which were named after the cardinal points, the "great south gate" (nandaimon) was the front or main gate. The inner or middle gate (chūmon) opened on the main precinct containing the pagoda and main hall, being integrated with the covered corridor (kairō) that enclosed this precinct; the inner gate of the Western Precinct (Saiin) at Hōryūji is a surviving example of this type. In Zen temples, the massive sammon (triple gate), which was located in front of the Buddha hall (butsuden), corresponded to the inner gate of Asuka- and Nara-period temples; the sammon at Tōfukuji is the oldest example of this type.

gejin　See outer sanctuary.

great Buddha style (daibutsuyō)　Also called "Indian style" (tenjikuyō). A southern Chinese style of architecture that was introduced during the early Kamakura period by the priest Chōgen at the time of the reconstruction of Tōdaiji. That temple's nandaimon (great south gate) exemplifies this style.

hattō　See lecture hall.

hondō　See main hall.

inner sanctuary (naijin)　　The area within a hall where the altar and object of worship were located and priests performed rituals.

Japanese style (wayō)　　Until the Kamakura period, this was the established mode in Buddhist architecture. Derived from the prevailing Nara-period style (itself a version of Tang-dynasty forms), it involved broad proportioning and little decoration. Among the few extant examples is the main hall at Saimyōji.

kōdō　　See lecture hall.

kondō　　See main hall.

lecture hall　　In most temples of the Asuka, Nara, and later periods, the lecture hall was called *kōdō*. Usually the largest structure in early temples, it was the building where monks assembled for instruction, study, or ritual. Surviving examples are the Dempōdō of Hōryūji's Eastern Precinct (Tōin) and the lecture hall at Tōshōdaiji. At Zen temples the lecture hall was called the dharma hall or doctrine hall (*hattō*; also called *hōdō*); important examples include the doctrine halls at Shōkokuji and Daitokuji.

main hall　　In temples of the Asuka and Nara periods, the main hall, which housed the principal object of worship, was called *kondō* (literally, "golden hall"). Most temples contained only one main hall, although Asukadera had three grouped around a pagoda. Surviving examples of Asuka- and Nara-period *kondō* include the main hall of Hōryūji's Western Precinct (Saiin) and that at Tōshōdaiji. In Heian-period temples of the Tendai and Shingon sects, the main hall was called *hondō* (literally, "main hall"); eventually other sects adopted the term as well, and *hondō* became the common word for "main hall." However, at Pure Land temples the term *nyoraidō* (Nyorai hall, *nyorai* being an epithet for the Buddha) was used for the main hall. In Zen temples the main hall was called Buddha hall (*butsuden*).

mokoshi (literally, "skirt layer")　　A roofed area built below the eaves of a main roof and similar to a lean-to in construction. The *mokoshi* was used to give the impression (from the outside) of an extra story in pagodas and other halls. The oldest surviving examples of *mokoshi* are those of the East Pagoda at Yakushiji and those of the pagoda and main hall in the Western Precinct (Saiin) of Hōryūji.

naijin　　See inner sanctuary.

nandaimon　　See gates.

nyoraidō　　See main hall.

outer sanctuary (gejin)　　Within a hall, the area that was used for worship by laymen, as opposed to the inner sanctuary (*naijin*).

pagoda (tō)　　A multistoried, towerlike structure originating in the ancient Indian stupa and housing sacred relics of the Buddha, the pagoda was the focal point of the early temple compound. Most pagodas were either three-storied or five-storied, although a two-storied type was built for Tendai and Shingon temples. Surviving examples of early pagodas include the five-storied pagoda of Hōryūji's Western Precinct (Saiin), the three-storied East Pagoda at Yakushiji, and the five-storied pagoda at Daigoji.

sammon　　See gates.

setchūyō　　See eclectic style.

shichidō garan (seven-halled temple)　　A term used to designate the standard layout of the early temple compound, which typically consisted of at least seven basic structures: (1) the pagoda (*tō*); (2) the main hall (*kondō*); (3) the lecture hall (*kōdō*); (4) the drum or bell tower (*korō*; also called *shurō*); (5) the sutra repository (*kyōzō*; also called *kyōrō*); (6) dormitories (*sōbō*) for monks or nuns; and (7) the *jikidō* (dining hall). In early temples the pagoda and main hall, which served as the ceremonial core of the temple, were often situated in a nuclear compound that was enclosed by a covered corridor (*kairō*) which separated them from other structures.

Five main types of seven-halled temple are recognized for the Asuka and Nara periods: (1) the Asukadera type, in which three main halls are grouped around the pagoda; (2) the Tennōji or Shitennōji type, in which the main hall is located behind the pagoda; (3) the Hōryūji type, in which the pagoda and main hall are built side by side; (4) the Yakushiji type, in which a pair of pagodas flanks the main hall; and (5) the Tōdaiji or Kōfukuji type, in which the pagoda is located some distance from the main hall.

sōbō　　See dormitories.

tō　　See pagoda.

wayō　　See Japanese style.

zenshūyō　　See Zen style.

Zen style (zenshūyō)　　Also called Chinese style (*karayō*). A Song- (Sung-) dynasty architectural style introduced from China along with Zen Buddhism during the Kamakura period. With structures much smaller than those of the Japanese style and much more complex in structural detail, it represented a significant change from earlier patterns. The relic hall (*shariden*) at Engakuji is a major example of this style.

——William Alex, *Japanese Architecture* (1963). Werner Blaser, *Japanese Temples and Tea Houses* (1956). Toshio Fukuyama, *Heian Temples: Byodo-in and Chuson-ji* (1976). Yukio Futagawa, *The Roots of Japanese Architecture* (1963). J. Edward Kidder, Jr., *Japanese Temples: Sculpture, Paintings, Gardens, and Architecture* (n.d.). Minoru Ooka, *Temples of Nara and Their Art* (1973). Hirotaro Ota, ed, *Japanese Architecture and Gardens* (1966). Hirotaro Ota, ed, *Traditional Japanese Architecture and Gardens* (1972). A. L. Sadler, *A Short History of Japanese Architecture* (1941, repr 1963). Alexander C. Soper, *The Evolution of Buddhist Architecture in Japan* (1942, repr 1978).　　　　　　　　　　*Itō Nobuo*

Buddhist art

Like Japanese BUDDHISM itself, Japanese Buddhist art was a national variant of an international tradition. Its primary iconic symbols originated in India; the basic structural systems of temple building and styles of sculpture, painting, and calligraphy were imported from China and Korea. In Japan, these art forms were altered by aesthetic attitudes and craft traditions unique to the Japanese people and responsive to their spiritual needs. The result was one of the world's richest and most eloquent traditions of religious art and architecture, one that virtually dominated the visual arts in Japan until the establishment of neo-Confucianism as an official state creed in the 17th century.

This essay reviews the major ideological aspects of Buddhist art in Japan, explicates its relationship to architectural settings, traces its evolution in broad historical stages, and defines basic aesthetic principles and the components of artistic styles. See also BUDDHIST SCULPTURE; PAINTING; BUDDHIST ARCHITECTURE; TEMPLES; SHINTŌ ART; and articles on individual Japanese Buddhist temples and their patrons.

Mahāyāna Mainstream——When it was formally transmitted to Japan from China and Korea in the 6th century, the Buddhist faith exerted a powerful appeal among the ruling classes and became virtually a state creed. For the next 200 years, almost all major Japanese Buddhist monuments and art forms were made at government expense or with the patronage of families of the highest rank. The climax of the early history of Buddhist art in Japan was the building of a single monument, the TŌDAIJI monastery in Nara. Founded by the emperor SHŌMU (701–756; r 724–749), Tōdaiji was conceived as the headquarters of a system of official state monasteries (KOKUBUNJI) that would extend to each provincial capital. Student-monks from all over Japan came to Tōdaiji to be certified as having completed their training and to be ordained as monks. The emperor and members of his family were themselves ordained there, and upon Shōmu's death, his widow donated to Tōdaiji his luxurious personal possessions, which now make up much of the treasure in the SHŌSŌIN art repository.

In scale and cost, Tōdaiji was colossal; the ceremonial *honzon* (main object of devotion) of the temple was a giant statue 16.1 meters (52.8 ft) high made of bronze and coated with gold. Called the Nara Daibutsu, the image symbolized a newly evolved figure in the Buddhist pantheon: DAINICHI ("Great Illumination"; Skt: Mahāvairocana), the supreme spiritual principle of the Buddhist cosmos, the source of all being and also a holy analogue to the Buddhist monarch from whom all political authority stemmed. Similar colossal images of the same deity were constructed in China and Korea. However, in Japan, a reaction against the cost of Tōdaiji and religious interference in governmental affairs led to the removal of the seat of government from Nara to Nagaokakyō and eventually to Kyōto.

Buddhist art——Western Precinct of Hōryūji

View from the south of the Western Precinct of Hōryūji in Nara Prefecture. The path leads north from the south gate *(nandaimon)* to the central gate *(chūmon)* and corridor *(kairō)* enclosing the nuclear compound. The latter contains the pagoda and main hall, both late 7th century, with the lecture hall directly to their north.

Buddhist art——The Kichijōten at Yakushiji

8th-century painting of the goddess Kichijōten. Colors and gold on hemp. 53.3 × 32.0 cm. Yakushiji, Nara Prefecture. National Treasure.

The forms of Buddhism and Buddhist art that first arrived in Japan were chiefly those of the "Greater Vehicle" (Skt: Mahāyāna; J: Daijō Bukkyō), which stressed salvation through the worship of a pantheon of deities who protected the Buddhist nations and their rulers and provided them with material blessings as well as spiritual ones. The doctrines and styles of art were chiefly those that had flourished around the metropolitan Chinese centers of the faith, Chang'an (Ch'ang-an), Luoyang (Loyang), and Nanjing (Nanking), as well as the Korean capitals at Puyŏ and Kyŏngju. In the Japanese capital at Nara, Mahayanism was divided into six doctrinal schools, which were relatively consistent in doctrine: the JŌJITSU SCHOOL, KUSHA SCHOOL, SANRON SCHOOL, KEGON SECT, HOSSŌ SECT, and RITSU SECT. In later centuries, these schools lost much of their influence; some were amalgamated with the SHINGON SECT and the TENDAI SECT, others simply died out. Nevertheless, this initial stage of Japanese Buddhism, called here the "Mahāyāna Mainstream," had an indelible impact; its basic religious values, closely linked with its major offshoots—ESOTERIC BUDDHISM, PURE LAND BUDDHISM, and

ZEN—have continued within the fabric of Japanese religious life until the present. Similarly, the Mahāyāna Mainstream forms of temple architecture, sculpture, and painting provided the stylistic matrix from which all later religious art in Japan evolved.

Architectural setting. Even though Mahāyāna Buddhism offered to laymen a path to salvation, it nonetheless continued to emphasize the practice of monasticism. Consequently, the primary Japanese Buddhist sanctuary, though generally called a "temple" in English (J: *tera, dera,* or *ji*), was in fact a place of withdrawal from secular life for communities of monks or nuns and should more precisely be called a monastic compound, or *garan* (from Skt: *saṃghārāma,* communal dwelling). This monastic compound, whether rural or urban, was isolated from its surroundings by a series of enclosure walls within which, in an atmosphere of quiet, ordered beauty, monks and nuns followed an austere routine: long hours of seated meditations, dining on a meager vegetarian fare, studying and reciting the canonical texts, and chanting at rituals for the sake of the dead or to mark the holy days of the calendar. The first wave of Buddhist building in Japan produced over 26 such compounds in what is now the Kyōto-Ōsaka region, most notably ASUKADERA (founded by SOGA NO UMAKO in 588) and SHITENNŌJI in Ōsaka and HŌRYŪJI in the countryside south of Nara (both founded by Prince SHŌTOKU in 593 and 607 respectively); only Hōryūji has preserved something of its original layout and imagery.

The monastic compound normally consisted of at least seven typical structures *(shichidō garan):* (1) the *tō,* a pagoda or multistory tower housing in the foundation a holy relic; (2) the *kondō* (literally, "golden hall"), a building housing images of the primary deities worshiped at the temple (this hall and the pagoda formed the symbolic and ceremonial core of the compound and were often set apart from the rest of the temple by an enclosure wall or covered corridor *[kairō]);* (3) the *korō,* a drum or bell tower where the times of daily routine would be sounded from wake up in the morning to sleep at night; (4) the *kyōzō,* a sutra storage hall for the collection of canonical texts; (5) the *kōdō,* a lecture hall where monks gathered to hear sermons, recite holy texts, or perform collective rituals such as repentance or celebration of the Buddha's birth; (6) the *sōbō,* dormitories housing the tiny cells where monks or nuns slept at night and stored their meager possessions; and (7) the *jikidō,* a dining hall where vegetarian meals were served in a solemn, ceremonial fashion. Also part of the basic compound were the gates that linked the community to the secular world, storage structures for temple treasures and food supplies, bathhouses, latrines, offices or scriptoria, and kitchen gardens. As time went on and the faith evolved, many new types of building were required: baptismal halls *(kanjōdō)* in esoteric Buddhist temples; meditation halls *(zendō);* halls devoted to the cult of a specific deity *(amidadō* and *go dai myōō dō).* However, these additions did not affect the traditional, basic layout.

The early monastery compounds were built according to the principles of Chinese geomancy on a flat plot of land strictly oriented to the four cardinal points of the compass, with the main entrance facing south. This symmetry and orientation have remained a fundamental trait of Japanese Buddhist architecture and art to the present day. The structural system also originated in China, where wooden construction techniques used in palaces and administrative halls had been adapted for Buddhist buildings. From an engineering standpoint, this meant that a simple trabeate (post and lintel) system employing large wooden timbers was used to form the basic skeletal framework of these buildings; walls were not load-bearing but were made of plaster on a lathing of bamboo. Roofs were sheathed with heavy gray tiles, and roof supports were an intricate arrangement of rafters, trusses, and internal beams that distributed the great weight of the tiles down through a system of bracket arms onto the main pillars.

Following Chinese and Korean precedent, early Japanese temple buildings rested on heavy masonry platforms, but in one important respect the Japanese did not follow mainland practice. Instead of building large temple structures of stone or brick, they manifested a strong national preference, seen also in the choice of materials for sculpture, to use wood as a primary building material. The Japanese did, however, reflect Chinese practice by painting pillars, beams, and doors of temple buildings in cinnabar *(shu,* a red sulphide of mercury) and adding gilt bronze beam endings and other ornaments; in contrast, traditional Shintō buildings, notably at the ISE SHRINE, were often left unpainted and little adorned.

Painting and sculpture. Throughout the monastery were found a great variety of religious art forms—in the main hall, in the lecture hall, even in the dining hall and bath. In fact, so great was the artistic demand that large Nara temples like Tōdaiji and KŌFUKUJI operated sculpture and painting workshops (BUSSHO) that served other establishments as well. The most symbolically significant of the art forms were the statues in the main hall of the deities to whom a temple was primarily dedicated. In sanctuaries of the Shingon and Tendai sects, these were often closed from view and treated as secret images (hibutsu), but in most other temples, the cult statues were displayed upon an altar platform and were seen from a position of worship in front of and well below the eye level of the image. Interior walls were often painted with images of deities and paradise scenes. Buddhist temples also made extensive use of paintings on hanging scrolls (KAKEMONO), which could be unrolled and hung as the devotional object in a specific ceremony. A work of sculpture or painting employed in this way is often designated as sonzō (votive image).

Early Buddhist traditions held that the everyday world was profane and that the path to enlightenment led to spiritual realms of unearthly beauty. Thus East Asian worship halls and their imagery were endowed with rich ornamentation, reflecting the sense of joy and delight that is expressed in basic Mahāyāna texts such as the LOTUS SUTRA (J: Myōhō renge kyō), the Mahāprajñāpāramitā-sūtra (J: Dai hannya haramitta kyō), and the Sukhāvati-vyūha (J: Amida kyō). The prevailing tone of East Asian Buddhist votive imagery can be denoted by the Japanese term shōgon (Skt: alaṃkāra; adornment or majestic manifestation).

Paintings and sculptures representing the main Buddhist deities were made according to a system of idealization of the human form that was developed in India during the Gupta period (320–600) and adapted to East Asian canons of taste. All deities were depicted with harmonic, mathematical proportions. In particular, the bodhisattvas (J: bosatsu; see BODHISATTVA) were usually shown as youthful and svelte, even to the point of weightlessness, their faces given introspective, compassionate expressions with no traces of mortality, egoism, or other imperfections of ordinary human beings. They were bejewelled, their scarves and draperies flowing in rhythmic patterns; they were brightly colored, even gilded. Dressed more soberly in monastic robes, without ornaments, were the fully enlightened Buddhas (J: NYORAI; Skt: tathāgata), such as Shaka (Skt: Śākyamuni, the historic founder of the faith), Yakushi (Skt: Bhaiṣayaguru, the healing Buddha), or Amida (Skt: Amitābha, the lord of the Western Paradise). Their high stature was often denoted by greater weight and bulk, but they were never portrayed as ordinary mortals.

In Japan, the best preserved and most fully resplendent images in this Mahāyāna Mainstream tradition are the early 8th-century bronze statues in YAKUSHIJI, Nara, depicting Yakushi and two flanking bodhisattvas; in the same temple and slightly later in date is the painting on hemp of Kichijōten (Skt: Śrīmahādevi), goddess of beauty and learning, shown as an opulent Chinese-style court woman with flowing, transparent robes. The level of urbane aestheticism seen in these works, fully up-to-date with mainland styles, was the result of little more than a century of development of Japanese Buddhist art. The initial stages of the tradition, dating from the early 7th century, are represented by the great bronze Yakushi and Shaka Trinity statues in the Hōryūji main hall. Made by KURATSUKURI NO TORI, these statues reflected the artistic norms of Chinese stone sculptors of the early 6th century.

Although most Mahāyāna Buddhist painting and sculpture were created in the spirit of opulence and idealism, some works employed a much different aesthetic tenor, that of realism, for figures of low degrees of sanctity. Guardian figures, for example, were shown with scowling faces and muscular bodies, as in the dry clay statues of the Benevolent Kings (Niō) in the chūmon (central gate) of Hōryūji, circa 710; quasi-historical figures were depicted in a portrait-like manner, as in the hollow dry-lacquer statues of the Ten Great Disciples of Śākyamuni (Jū Dai Deshi) in the Hokuendō (North Octagonal Hall) of Kōfukuji, Nara, about 733–739. China and Japan also developed a remarkable tradition of realistic portraiture of living Buddhist monks of great distinction, the oldest surviving example of which is the hollow dry-lacquer portrait of the blind Chinese missionary GANJIN (Jianzhen or Chien-chen; 688–763) made at the time of his death and preserved at the temple he founded, TŌSHŌDAIJI, Nara.

Realism in Buddhist sculpture and painting flourished throughout East Asia during the 7th and 8th centuries—at the peak of Tang (T'ang, 618–907) China's prosperity. In the 12th and 13th centuries, realism again came into vogue; in Japan the revival coincided with the rebuilding of Tōdaiji and Kōfukuji after their destruction in the TAIRA–MINAMOTO WAR. Prominent in the reconstruction campaign was the monk Shunjōbō Chōgen (1122–1206), chief solicitor of Tō-

Buddhist art —— Niō at Hōryūji

One of the two Niō (Benevolent Kings) in the central gate of the Western Precinct of Hōryūji, Nara Prefecture. Clay. Height 378 cm. Ca 710.

Buddhist art —— Statue of Asanga by Unkei

Imaginary portrait of the Indian philosopher Asanga (J: Muchaku). Wood. Height 193 cm. 1208. Hokuendō, Kōfukuji, Nara. National Treasure.

daiji, who employed members of the KEI SCHOOL of sculpture. From this movement came some of the most moving and eloquent examples of Buddhist realism: the giant statues of the Indian philosophers Asanga (J: Muchaku) and Vasubandhu (J: Seshin), portraits carved from imagination in 1208 by UNKEI and assistants for Kōfukuji, and the posthumous portrait statue of Chōgen himself at Tōdaiji.

Realism played a major role in another genre of East Asian Buddhist art, namely narrative painting (monogatari-e) done chiefly in the format of a horizontal handscroll (EMAKIMONO). Although this art form came to great prominence in Japan, it had first arisen in Chinese court circles, where it was employed to depict events of interest to the ruling class: visits of ambassadors bearing gifts, tales of court romance, events of heroism or filial piety or treachery. The handscroll format was readily adaptable to Buddhist themes, such as the pictorial biographies of celebrated monks, holy miracles, and the histories of temples. The oldest of the Japanese emakimono are versions of a biography of Śākyamuni called the Illustrated Sutra of Cause and Effect (E inga kyō) of the late 8th century. Closely modeled on early Tang prototypes, the most complete example belongs to DAIGOJI, Kyōto. In Japan, emakimono continued as an art form it employed a director *(azukari)*, a master scribe, scribes of lesser ranks, paper mounters, and other assistants. Moreover, individual monks would copy short texts, particularly the Heart Sutra (J: *Hannya shingyō;* Skt: *Prajñāpāramitā-hṛdaya-sūtra*) as a mode of daily personal devotion. Certain monks became celebrated calligraphers owing both to their strength of character, which was revealed in the quality of their handwriting, and to their devotion to this art form. Perhaps the most notable of these early Japanese Buddhist calligraphers were SAICHŌ (767–822) and KŪKAI (774–835).

The official Buddhist canon of texts in East Asia, called the *issaikyō* or *daizōkyō* in Japan, consisted of 5,048 volumes in the 8th century and ultimately grew to 11,970. As an act of piety, a complete or partial set of texts would be ordered by an aristocratic patron and donated to a temple; the empress KŌMYŌ (701–760), wife of Shōmu, for example, commissioned three complete sets, one of them to commemorate the death anniversary of her mother. Efforts were made to procure the finest quality papers and inks; important texts, such as the Lotus Sutra, were copied in gold and silver inks upon indigo-dyed paper or silk. In the Heian period (794–1185), individual scrolls were provided with illustrated frontispieces. In the 12th century, the custom of commissioning ornate copies of texts reached an apogee, the most celebrated example being a set of 33 scrolls dedicated in 1164 by TAIRA NO KIYOMORI (1118–81) to the ITSUKUSHIMA SHRINE. Given in thanks for the rise of the TAIRA FAMILY to the pinnacle of military and political authority, this set of scrolls, the *Heike nōkyō*, was written on papers ornamented with random decoration of gold and silver leaf; the frontispiece illustrations were made by Kyōto court painters in a variety of narrative painting styles.

Esoteric Buddhism——The construction of Tōdaiji in Nara was inspired by a combination of political interests with the esoteric *(mikkyō)* system of Buddhist thought that was introduced into Japan in the 8th century. The gradual assimilation of this religious system is reflected by certain prominent works of art such as the wall painting of the Eleven-Headed KANNON in the *kondō* of Hōryūji, done about 711, and the giant hollow dry-lacquer statue of Kannon with eight arms in the lotus hall *(hokkedō;* also known as the Sangatsudō or Third Month Hall) of Tōdaiji, completed around 732. The latter is the oldest surviving image of this particular form of Kannon, known as Fukūkenjaku (Skt: Amoghapāśa, literally, "he whose noose [of salvation] is never empty").

Japanese esoteric Buddhism of the 8th century is frequently designated by the terms *zōmitsu* or *zatsumitsu* ("miscellaneous esoterism," indicating the random or partial aspects of its acceptance), in contrast to "fully developed esoterism" *(mammitsu)*, which, in the early 9th century, came rapidly to dominate the religious and artistic life of the nation. The persons most responsible for the remarkable leap in intellectual content of Japanese *mikkyō* were the celebrated monks Saichō and Kūkai, founders of the Japanese Tendai and Shingon sects, respectively. The emergence of these sects also coincided roughly with the movement of the seat of government from Nara to Nagaokakyō and then, in 794, to Heiankyō (now Kyōto), where it remained until the modern era.

Dainichi was the most prominent deity in the religious philosophy of esoteric Buddhism. Perhaps equally prominent was its characteristic emblem, the Indian *vajra* (J: *kongō*), an implement with "the hardness of a diamond and the energy of a thunderbolt," symbolizing the power of Buddhist illumination to penetrate the darkness of ignorance. In fact, esoterism itself was called the Vajrayāna (the Diamond, or Thunderbolt, Vehicle) to distinguish it from the earlier stages of Buddhism, from which it was markedly different. In its art forms, esoterism was filled with a strong current of Indian symbolic and aesthetic concepts similar to those in the resurgent Hindu faith: deities were endowed with multiple heads and arms or shown as frightful and demonic in their power to destroy evil through violence. Female deities were emphasized, reflecting the revival in India of long dormant cults of the mother goddess.

Another distinctive trait of esoterism was its capacity to absorb elements from non-Buddhist religious systems. Indian Buddhism had traditionally been tolerant of folk deities and allowed them to be worshiped so long as this did not interfere with its own practices. This religious principle is called henotheism, and in Japan it made possible a close rapprochement with Shintō. Shrines of the Shintō gods or *kami* were erected as guardians of Buddhist monastic compounds, and conversely, Buddhist sanctuaries were built adjacent to Shintō shrines. The syncretic combination of the two creeds, called RYŌBU SHINTŌ, was greatly stimulated by esoterism in the 9th and 10th centuries, and encouraged the creation of hybrid religious prac-

Buddhist art——The Fukūkenjaku Kannon at Tōdaiji

Fukūkenjaku Kannon flanked by attendants. Dry-lacquer, gilt. Height 362 cm. Ca 732. Sangatsudō, Tōdaiji, Nara. National Treasure.

Buddhist art——The Renge Kokūzō at Jingoji

Renge Kokūzō, one of five Bodhisattvas of the Void at Jingoji, Kyōto. Wood, painted. Height 94.2 cm. 9th century. National Treasure.

devoted both to courtly and Buddhist purposes, and reached an extraordinary degree of sophistication in the 12th and 13th centuries, as in the depictions of the legends of the temple atop Mt. Shigi (SHIGISAN ENGI EMAKI) and of the history of the Kegon sect *(Kegon engi emaki)*.

Calligraphy and printing. Buddhism, throughout its history, placed heavy emphasis upon the written word and strongly promoted CALLIGRAPHY (the art of elegant writing) and also printing. In Japan, certain large monasteries contained scriptoria *(shakyōsho;* literally, "sutra-copying offices"), rooms devoted to the copying of holy texts. The largest was at Tōdaiji, Nara, during the 8th century;

tices such as the mountain asceticism of SHUGENDŌ and of hybrid deities such as Zaō Gongen, the Shintō *genius loci* of Mt. Yoshino who became the wrathful protector of the Buddhist sanctuary there.

In esoterism, the numbers of Buddhist deities increased enormously, staggering the imagination of the layman with their sheer complexity; at the same time, the huge pantheon was systematically organized into classes and groups. This principle of organization is implicit in the Sanskrit term *tantra* (loom, framework, system, model) that had long been used to denote Indian esoteric literature, both Buddhist and Hindu. This principle also promoted the popularity of the MANDALA, one of the most characteristic art forms of esoterism. The mandala is a depiction of deities or their symbols in a schematic, geometric fashion; it can be made in two dimensions, as in a painting, or in three, as in the placement of statues. Most often, painted mandalas are composed in an entirely symmetrical manner, with the most sacred element shown in the center. In their symmetry and centrality, they suggest spiritual equipoise and a sense of wholeness; they depict a sphere of being beyond the everyday world, one that is timeless and sublime. Mandalas were prominently displayed in Shingon and Tendai temples; most important were the paired mandalas of the Thunderbolt and Matrix realms (KONGŌKAI and TAIZŌKAI). Several important early pairs of Shingon mandalas have survived, the oldest being the badly worn Takao Mandala of JINGOJI, Kyōto, done in the early 9th century in gold and silver paint on indigo-dyed silk; a better preserved example of the same type is the 11th-century pair of mandalas at Kojimadera, Nara Prefecture. A pair of polychrome mandalas dating around 900 are preserved in Tōji, Kyōto.

Esoteric Buddhism also gave great prominence to elaborate rituals such as the *goma* ceremony, a burning of wooden sticks inscribed with prayers. Performed with elaborate bronze implements and accompanied by the ringing of bells and chimes, this ceremony was directly descended from ancient Indo-Iranian fire rituals. Dramatic *goma* ceremonies are still performed today, for example, in the Main Hall (Kompon Chūdō) of ENRYAKUJI atop Mt. Hiei (Hieizan), Kyōto Prefecture.

Architecture. The East Asian esoteric Buddhist sects built sanctuaries in dramatic and remote mountain settings. There, the monks practiced religious asceticism far from the distractions of urban life and in an atmosphere reinforced by the presence of awesome natural forces: towering peaks and waterfalls, deep forests, intense winter cold—a context that strengthened the spiritual linkage between Buddhism and the quasi-animistic traditions of Chinese Taoism or Japanese Shintō.

In Japan, the headquarters of the Shingon sect was built on Mt. Kōya (Kōyasan) at an elevation of approximately 1,000 meters (3,281 ft) amid forbidding mountains. The Tendai headquarters, Enryakuji, was built atop the more accessible Mt. Hiei, not far from Kyōto but at an altitude of about 850 meters (2,789 ft). At both sites, the terrain is so rough that the buildings were distributed in an irregular fashion, in contrast to the rational checkerboard arrangement of the city monasteries. Nonetheless, the individual buildings were usually oriented to the four cardinal points of the compass.

New building types appeared in the esoteric sanctuaries. Most notable was the *tahōtō* (literally, "many-jewelled pagoda"), which, reflecting the strengthened Indian component of esoterism in general, contained beneath its primary roof a large domical element reminiscent of the hemispheric shape of the oldest of the Indian stupas. Usually these pagodas enshrined statues of the Five Wisdom Buddhas (Go Chi Nyorai), emblems of the five-part division of primordial intelligence. Kūkai built in 816 a giant stupa (Kompon Daitō) of this type, 46 meters tall (150.9 ft), as the symbolic core of KONGŌBUJI on Mt. Kōya; standing on the site today is a steel and concrete replica completed in 1932.

A smaller type of esoteric stupa, usually solid and monolithic, was the GORINTŌ (literally, "five-wheel pagoda"), used as a funerary monument. Its five structural parts symbolized the five elements that made up the material world: square base (earth), spherical body (water), pyramidal roof (fire), topped by an inverted hemisphere (wind), and a jewel-shaped finial (the air, or the void). By the thousands, stone *gorintō* were erected, for example, in the *okunoin*, the mortuary precinct of the Kongōbuji near the funeral shrine of Kūkai. Other building types developed by esoteric Buddhism included a *kanjōdō* (for a baptismal ceremony), a *mieidō* (hall enshrining a patriarch's portrait), special votive halls like the *godaidō* (for the Five Wisdom Kings; J: Go Dai Myōō). These new type buildings did not, as a rule, involve major structural innovations.

Buddhist art——The Nyoirin Kannon at Kanshinji

An esoteric form of Kannon. Wood, painted. Height of body 108.8 cm. 9th century. Kanshinji, Ōsaka Prefecture. National Treasure.

Buddhist art——The Yakushi at Jingoji

Image of the healing Buddha Yakushi, carved from a solid block of wood. Height 169.7 cm. Ca 783. Jingoji, Kyōto. National Treasure.

Painting and sculpture. Stylistically, esoteric devotional imagery was based on Mainstream Mahāyāna forms, but the new ideology fostered several distinct nuances of aesthetic expression in both sculpture and painting. Most obvious was the heightened sense of demonism as shown by the oldest surviving esoteric paintings of this kind, a set of hanging scrolls on silk each depicting one of the Five Forceful Ones (Go Dai Rikiku) in the KŌYASAN TREASURE HOUSE on Mt. Kōya. Dating from the early 10th century, each of the five male deities emit swirling tongues of bright red flame, their faces contorted with rage; the standing figures are dramatically posed, as

Buddhist art——Interior of the Sanjūsangendō

Some of the hall's 1,001 images of the Thousand-Armed Kannon. Wood, lacquered and gilt. 12th–13th centuries. Sanjūsangendō, Kyōto.

though lunging at their enemies. In sculpture, similarly demonic forms may be seen in the set of Five Wisdom Kings on the altar platform of the lecture hall of Tōji, Kyōto. Part of a large set of 21 statues commissioned by Kūkai around 839, these statues give forth a powerful sense of wrathful fury and force.

A different aesthetic tenor in esoteric imagery was that of static mystery and introspection that is clearly apparent in the set of five statues of the Bodhisattvas of the Void (Go Dai Kokūzō Bosatsu) in the *tahōtō* of Jingoji, Kyōto, also dating from the first half of the 9th century. Made of polychrome wood, each about 95 centimeters high (37.4 in), the statues are posed in virtually identical seated positions; in their rigidity and precisely wrought metal crowns and symbolic implements, they express a sense of profound mystery and purposiveness. Of the same date and materials is the wooden image of Nyoirin Kannon at the Kanshinji, Ōsaka Prefecture; this figure, miraculously well preserved because for centuries it has been treated as a secret image, has a strongly androgynous character; the face is rounded and feminized, as are the body forms. Even though it otherwise lacks obvious secondary female characteristics, it clearly reflects the importance of the female principle in esoteric theology.

Coinciding with the rise of esoterism in Japan was a tendency to carve votive statues in solid blocks of wood and to leave their surfaces unpainted. Many of these plain wood statues were heavy and massive, their robes displaying strong surface patterns and their faces imbued with a sober, brooding expression, a striking reversal of the elegance and grace of much Mahāyāna Mainstream imagery. The most celebrated examples are the statues of the healing Buddha Yakushi at Jingoji, Kyōto, and GANGŌJI, Nara, the former said to have been carved around 783. Some of the early plain wood sculptures do retain the elegance of the Mahāyāna Mainstream style, notably the Eleven-Headed Kannon statues at the Hokkeji, Nara, and the Kōgenji, Shiga Prefecture; but the heavy, anticlassic mode predominates in this distinct tradition of early Heian-period sculpture, particularly during the Kōnin (810–824) and Jōgan (859–877) eras, after which this mode is sometimes named. The preference for making plain wood statues is a distinctive trait of Japanese Buddhist art, derived in part from the Japanese feeling for the inherent sanctity of noble trees *(shimboku)*. It is related to the ready availability of fine timbers, especially cypress *(hinoki)* and camphor *(kusunoki)*, but it was also reinforced by a tradition within Buddhism itself for the use of aromatic sandalwood *(byakudan)* in the carving of statues of special sanctity.

Pure Land Buddhism——Although esoterism has remained to the present day a major element in Japanese religious life, its preeminence began to wane by the end of the 10th century. Japanese Buddhist thinkers, especially around the Heian capital, became increasingly preoccupied with Pure Land doctrines, an ancient, well-established religious tradition centered on AMIDA (Skt: Amitābha), the Buddha dwelling in the Western Paradise where the pious devotee seeks to be reborn in the next life.

Amidism had been a prominent part of the first wave of Mahāyāna Mainstream Buddhism in Japan as demonstrated, for example, by a wall painting in the *kondō* of Hōryūji (ca 711) depicting Amida preaching in paradise and flanked by his two attendant bodhisattvas,

Kannon (Skt: Avalokiteśvara) and Seishi (Skt: Mahāsthāma-prāpta). The monastery of TAIMADERA in Nara Prefecture contained a huge tapestry depicting Amida's paradise and said to have been woven in 763; also at the Taimadera was performed an annual ceremony, the Neri Kuyō, in which monks and devotees wearing splendid robes and masks enacted Amida's approach to earth to receive a devotee on the point of death and to convey him or her to the Western Paradise.

Aesthetically, Pure Land Buddhist art and ritual differed strongly from those of esoterism. Greatest emphasis was placed on depictions of paradise as a place of palatial luxury and perfection where the devotee, in an ideal setting and freed from the imperfections of this world, would hear the teaching of Amida and his attendants and attain SATORI (Skt: *nirvāna*).

Architecture. The Heian-period revival of Amidism was greatly stimulated by the writings of the Tendai monk GENSHIN (Eshin Sōzu; 942–1017), which gained great currency among the Kyōto aristocracy obsessed with the gloomy portents of the age of the "end of the Buddhist law" *(mappō;* see ESCHATOLOGY). FUJIWARA NO MICHINAGA (966–1028), for example, constructed a hall of the nine Amidas *(kutaidō)* within the grounds of his family temple, the Hōjōji, at the eastern edge of the capital; the nine statues of Amida reflected the doctrine of the nine levels of paradise *(kuhon jōdo)* where the devotee is reborn according to the degree of sanctity in the previous life. The Hōjōji burned in 1058. Although there were more than two dozen *kutaidō* erected in the Kansai area, today the only surviving example is one that was begun in the 1040s in the JŌRURIJI monastery in the mountains northeast of Nara.

Other surviving monuments of the revived Pure Land beliefs among the Heian-period aristocracy are the *amidadō* (Amida hall) of the Byōdōin in the Kyōto suburb of Uji, built by Michinaga's son FUJIWARA NO YORIMICHI (990–1074) in 1053, and the nearby *amidadō* of the Hōkaiji built by the HINO FAMILY. In the CHŪSONJI monastery at Hiraizumi in Iwate Prefecture in the far north is a remarkable if tiny mortuary chapel of the ŌSHŪ FUJIWARA FAMILY called the Konjikidō (Golden-colored Hall). Although a great wave of Amidist temple building swept through the nation in the 11th and 12th centuries, the scale of these buildings tended to be small, reflecting an emphasis upon the salvation of individual patrons and their families rather than upon religion as a state institution.

Rarely were the *amidadō* erected in isolation; they were usually added to an already existing compound of the traditional kind. Furthermore, for the first time some of the large monasteries of the 11th and 12th centuries were provided with man-made ponds with irregular contours, not unlike those made for aristocratic villas built in the SHINDEN-ZUKURI mode. The pond at the Byōdōin was excavated in roughly the shape of the Sanskrit character for *A,* as in Amida. In the center of Michinaga's Hōjōji was a large pond with an island in the middle. A pond built during this period in front of the Jōruriji *amidadō* has recently been drained and the rock arrangement restored to its original configuration.

Painting and sculpture. The rapid tempo of Pure Land building in the 11th and 12th centuries was accompanied by a great increase in the production of Buddhist images. In fact, Japan, like other Buddhist countries, came under the influence of a certain "principle of large numbers": the concept that the donation of worthy objects to a temple improved the spiritual merits of the donor—the greater the number of objects, the greater the merits. These merits, moreover, could be employed to assist others (such as a deceased kinsman in the hope of an auspicious rebirth). By the thousands, therefore, beautifully ornamented sutra texts were copied; the complete Issai-kyō was donated to Jingoji, Kyōto, by the retired emperor GO-SHIRAKAWA (1127–92) and three major sets of texts were given by the Ōshū Fujiwara family to the Chūsonji in the 12th century.

In addition to the many *amidadō* being erected, all of which required Buddhist statuary, there were also numerous *sentaidō* (thousand-image halls) housing statues of Kannon or JIZŌ (Skt: Kṣitigarbha). The best known surviving example is the SANJŪSANGENDŌ (Hall of the 33 Bays) in Kyōto, enshrining 1,001 large statues of the Thousand-Armed Kannon and over 30 attendant figures; the ensemble was completed in 1254 after the original hall of 1164 had been burned.

To meet such a demand, sculpture workshops developed techniques of mass production of wooden statues using prefabricated parts that were pegged and glued together in the technique called *yosegi-zukuri* (assembled woodblock construction). Employing as many as 50 pieces of wood, carefully cured and dried, craftsmen

Buddhist art——Raigō triptych at Mt. Kōya (Kōyasan)

Colors and gold on silk. Mid-12th century. Yūshi Hachimankō Jūhakkain, Kōyasan, Wakayama Prefecture. National Treasure.

assembled very large statues that were both light in weight and free from the danger of cracking and splitting that had afflicted statues carved from solid blocks of wood. The man credited with perfecting the *yosegi* techniques was JŌCHŌ (d 1057). Together with his father, Jōchō had worked on numerous projects for the imperial family and the Fujiwara clan, but today the only surviving work by Jōchō is the wooden Amida of 1053 in the Phoenix Hall of the Byōdōin. Seated in the meditative position upon a delicately carved pedestal, the image is imbued with great clarity and coolness of expression; the drapery folds of the garment are mathematically perfected and abstract; and aesthetically this statue is considered to be a distinctly Japanese achievement within the framework of international Buddhist symbolism. Also in the Phoenix Hall and carved by Jōchō and his assistants are 52 attendant figures placed on the interior walls—extraordinarily delicate and lyrical in expression—as well as the wooden canopies suspended over the Amida figure, carved in delicate floral patterns from thin planks of cypress.

Until the end of the 12th century, Jōchō's workshop, the Shichijō Bussho, was the most active in the capital, and the Jōchō style remained the prime expression of metropolitan Buddhist sculpture. Variants on that style may be seen as far north as Hiraizumi. There, in the Konjikidō of Chūsonji, and beautifully preserved in a setting that retains much of its ornamental splendor, are three altar platforms erected over the mummified bodies of three generations of leaders of the Ōshū Fujiwara family who died in 1124, 1157, and 1187, respectively. On each altar is a similar set of statues consisting of an Amida Trinity, six standing images of Jizō (for the six realms in which living beings can be reborn), and the Four Heavenly Kings (Shitennō).

In painting, the late-Heian-period revival of Pure Land ideology was most clearly manifested in the so-called RAIGŌZU, scenes depicting Amida coming to welcome a dying person and conveying him or her to Paradise. Although Amida *raigō* are most common, *raigō* of other deities, such as Kannon or Jizō, were also popular. On the backside of doors and interior walls of the Phoenix Hall of the Byōdōin are eight scenes of people of different social levels and degrees of sanctity in the process of dying and being received by Amida and his heavenly host. These paintings bear an unconfirmed attribution to TAKUMA TAMENARI (fl mid-11th century), a prominent court painter and member of a long-lived family dynasty of Buddhist artists believed to be the forerunners of the TAKUMA SCHOOL. These paintings employ a traditional Buddhist style (in depictions of Amida and his host) and a native Japanese landscape style (in background scenes of the local countryside in different seasons).

The most spectacular of the early *raigō* paintings is a triptych of silk (the three panels together measuring about 210 by 410 cm or 6.9 by 13.4 ft), now preserved on Mt. Kōya but originally kept on Mt.

Hiei, where it was attributed to none other than Genshin himself. The triptych was done, however, in the mid-12th century, a century and a half after Genshin's death, and depicts Amida seated in a stiff, frontal pose flanked by his two attendant bodhisattvas, Seishi and Kannon, the latter holding a lotus pedestal upon which to convey to paradise the person to be reborn. The surrounding entourage of bodhisattvas, music-making angels, and monks is painted with such a developed sense of visionary beauty that this triptych is one of the finest and most characteristic expressions of the Buddhist conception of *shōgon* (majestic manifestation).

As the ideas of the Pure Land evangelists such as HŌNEN (1133–1212) and SHINRAN (1173–1263) gained in currency, the need for devotional paintings increased dramatically. *Raigō* paintings were often used as visual solace for those about to die; many of them were simplified to show just the Amida Trinity or even Amida alone, painted on a dark indigo blue background. Others, however, remained crowded with figures; the most eloquent of the late 13th-century examples is the *Hayaraigō* of the CHION'IN, in Kyōto, which shows the descent of Amida and his entourage in profile, placed in pulsating cloud trails in a complex landscape. Also coming to great popularity in the 13th and 14th centuries were paintings of the Western Paradise that were used as accompaniment for sermons and prayers. In particular, a veritable cult grew up around the giant 8th-century mandala at the Taimadera, which was meticulously copied in countless versions.

The elegance and abstraction of the art forms commissioned by the Heian aristocracy began to give way to greater realism and a greater willingness to depict death and human suffering with an almost sadistic attention to gruesome detail. This new element in the emotional tenor of Japanese art was perhaps a reflection of the collapse in the 1150s of the social order dominated by the FUJIWARA FAMILY and the bloody struggles for supremacy among military clans in the Taira–Minamoto War. Characteristic of this changed atmosphere were the large numbers of scrolls depicting the unhappy fate awaiting men and women who were not pious Buddhists, or whose descendants had not worked for their salvation. Most characteristic were the *Gaki-zōshi* (Scrolls of Hungry Ghosts) depicting men and women reborn as grotesque, subhuman creatures feeding on excrement or dead bodies. Other narrative scrolls, such as the JIGOKU-ZŌSHI showed in excruciating detail the sufferings of men and women consigned to hell or reborn as a lower form of being. Buddhist texts, particularly in the Tendai tradition, had long featured descriptions of such matters. An imagery of hell and karmic retribution had developed as a counter-current to the strongly idealistic depictions of paradise and the savior deities, but it was not before the late 12th century that the visual arts began to feature them prominently.

Buddhist art——Scroll of Hungry Ghosts

Detail of a narrative handscroll. Colors on paper. Height 27.2 cm.
12th century. Kyōto National Museum. National Treasure.

Buddhist art——Relic hall (shariden) at Engakuji

This 15th-century hall was moved to Engakuji in the late 16th century.
Kamakura, Kanagawa Prefecture. National Treasure.

Another major outlet for this horrific trend was the imagery of
the Ten Kings of Hell (Jūōzu), 10 seated magistrates judging the
degree of punishment to be enforced by a host of gnarled and dis-
torted demonic jailers. This imagery had been imported from China
after the reopening of formal contacts in the 1160s; there it had
developed in the Tang period in a syncretic combination of Buddhist
and Taoist elements. Two of the most prominent of the kings were
Yama, the ancient Vedic god of death (J: Emma Ō), and the person-
ification of Taishan (T'ai-shan; J: Taizan Ō), the mountain abode of
the dead in Shandong (Shantung) Province. In front of paintings and
sculptures of the Ten Kings, services in honor of a dead person
would be offered on 10 occasions in order to ensure that person's
escape from punishment.

Symptomatic of the great prominence to which Pure Land Buddhism and the cult of Amida had risen were the founding of the
New Doctrine (Shingi) sect of Shingon and the building of the Kamakura Daibutsu during the period 1242–52. The New Doctrine
sect had originally been founded on Mt. Kōya by the monk KAKU-
BAN (1095–1143) but was regularly persecuted as heresy; in 1288 his
successors fled from Mt. Kōya and established their headquarters at
the Negoroji (Daidempōin) in Wakayama Prefecture. Their heresy
was the conviction that Amida, not Dainichi, served as the primary
demiurge in the Buddhist pantheon, that it was he who occupied the
center of the Shingon mandala. The Kamakura Daibutsu, erected in
the newly established seat of the shogunate, was an emblem of religious and political authority rivaling (but slightly smaller than) the
Nara Daibutsu. However, instead of depicting the esoteric deity
Dainichi, as did the Nara statue, it represented Amida in his distinctive seated position and hand gesture, the Mida jōin, and was a work
of considerable aesthetic sophistication (see DAIBUTSU).

Zen Buddhism——The rise of the ZEN (Ch: Chan or Ch'an) sect in

the 13th century brought radical changes in Japanese religious art
and in the culture of the ruling classes. Zen had been formally
introduced into Japan by the Tendai monk EISAI, who, on his second
trip to China, had received instruction in Linji (Lin-chi; see RINZAI
SECT) Chan Buddhism. One of the so-called Five Sects of the Southern Chan tradition in China, Linji was unusually receptive to the
visual arts and to poetry and was flourishing in monasteries around
the Southern Song (Sung; 1127–1279) capital of Hangzhou (Hangchow) at the time when contacts between Japan and Song China
were most lively. Eisai was soon followed by other Japanese monks,
such as ENNI (1202–80), who studied in Hangzhou for six years and,
after returning to Japan, helped establish Tōfukuji in Kyōto. From
Linji temples around Hangzhou came well-schooled Chinese missionaries: Lanqi Daolong (Lan-ch'i Tao-lung; J: RANKEI DŌRYŪ;
1213–78), who helped found KENCHŌJI in Kamakura; Wuan Puning
(Wu-an P'u-ning; J: Gottan Funei; 1197–1276), a most learned and
senior figure; and Yishan Yining (I-shan I-ning; J: ISSAN ICHINEI;
1244–1317), who had particular influence in literary and artistic matters. Through men such as these, the Linji sect found a welcome
audience among the Kyōto aristocracy and the leading military families of Kamakura. Also influential was the brilliant Japanese cleric
DŌGEN (1200–1253), who introduced to Japan the doctrines of the
Chinese Caodong (Ts'ao-tung; see SŌTŌ SECT). Those doctrines
were less syncretic in character than those of the Linji sect and were
focused more on the disciplines of meditation; Sōtō Zen did not play
so prominent a role in the flowering of Japanese art forms.

Even though numerous legends tell of Chinese Chan monks denouncing Buddhist texts and images and even destroying them, the
Linji sect absorbed much of the ecumenical spirit of Song Neo-
Confucianism and allowed its monks to pursue cultural activities
that were strongly secular in character—literary studies, poetry,
painting, and calligraphy. Devotional painting, however, also continued to play an important role in Chan ritual; monastic compounds
were provided with gardens that gave an idyllic background to austerities and meditation, and poetry gatherings among monks and
laymen were seen as spiritual exercises, as was the ritual of drinking
tea.

Architecture. In Japan, Zen Buddhist monasteries were constructed in large numbers, beginning in the 1190s with Eisai's temple, Shōfukuji, in what is now Fukuoka Prefecture. Some were
huge, metropolitan compounds, such as Tōfukuji in Kyōto (founded
1236) and Kenchōji in Kamakura (founded 1253); others were tiny,
isolated hermitages or small village temples. The ravages of time
have taken an unusually heavy toll of early Japanese Zen monastery
buildings, and perhaps only Tōfukuji has preserved its original architectural character to a marked degree; but even there important
early buildings have been lost and many alterations have been made.

The Zen sect introduced to Japanese Buddhist architecture major
changes in layout, nomenclature, furnishings, and structural details—all derived from Buddhist architecture of south central China.
Most prominent of the innovations was the massive ceremonial
gateway called, after its three-bay entry, the triple gate (sammon).
Supplanting the traditional central gate (chūmon), the sammon usually contained inside its second story an array of statues of the 16
arhats (J: RAKAN) flanking an image of the White-Robed Kannon.
Other changes included the renaming of the main hall (kondō or
hondō) as the Buddha hall (butsuden), where public ceremonies
were held (e.g., the day-long commemoration of the death of Śākyamuni, or the rites marking the death anniversary of the temple
founder); and renaming the lecture hall (kōdō) as the dharma hall
(hattō), where monks held their regular assemblies, heard lectures
on texts, and underwent formal interrogations (mondō) by their
teachers. A prominent position on the central axis of the temple was
given to the abbot's quarters, called the hōjō (literally, "the 10-foot-
square," after the fabled tiny house of Vimalakīrti, the all-wise Indian layman), which became the monastery headquarters and the
most lavishly decorated and equipped of the temple dwelling structures.

The mode of building imported into Japan for use in Zen monasteries was given the simple generic name karayō (Chinese mode). In
total effect, karayō structures were smaller and daintier than the
established Japanese mode (wayō) of temple buildings, and much
more complex in detail. The exterior walls contained delicate tran-
som windows. The roof supports were extremely complicated, with
tiny bracket clusters emerging from the columns themselves, and
between the columns the clusters rested on horizontal beams.
Moreover, brackets were used in the interiors to support the ceilings
as well. Karayō employed masonry floors (ishidatami) instead of the

conventional Japanese raised wooden flooring, and it introduced a whole new vocabulary of altar platforms, offering tables, and ritual implements such as gongs and clappers. The most historically significant of the surviving examples of *karayō* is the present relic hall *(shariden)* of ENGAKUJI in Kamakura, which dates from the early 15th century, but has been given an inappropriate thatched roof instead of its original Chinese-style tile roof.

From the 13th century onward, Japanese Zen monasteries also developed the *tatchū*, or subtemple, a semiautonomous cluster of residential and service buildings housing a small community of monks within an enclosure wall and set apart from the ceremonial center of the compound. In the 16th century, MYŌSHINJI, in Kyōto, was said to have contained over 80 *tatchū*; today DAITOKUJI, in Kyōto, has 18. Supported by their own patrons, the *tatchū* usually consisted of an abbot's hall *(hōjō)*, monks' residence *(sōbō)*, founder's memorial stupa and worship hall, storehouses, and servants' quarters. Even though they covered very modest amounts of land, the *tatchū* had room for small gardens that were carefully composed and maintained in order to enhance the aura of quiet beauty. But in keeping with the austerity of Zen taste, many small gardens were constructed without ponds or streams, although, by means of "dry landscapes" *(karesansui)*, they evoked the presence of water through smooth sand and gravel raked to suggest a brook or the open sea. Despite the limitations on space and the size of plants and rocks, the medieval Zen garden became a major expression of the Zen vision of the unity of religious and natural values.

Painting and sculpture. The rather clear-cut division of Zen monastery compounds into two sectors, public-ceremonial and private-meditative, is reflected by a division of its visual imagery. For public-ceremonial halls, sculpture and painting in the hieratic Mahāyāna tradition generally continued in use: large-scale pictures of the death of Śākyamuni, for example, such as the one dated 1408 and painted by MINCHŌ (1352–1431) for Tōfukuji, Kyōto; votive sculptures of Shaka or Amida; and quasi-realistic statues of the careworn mortal seekers of salvation such as the 16 arhats in the *hattō* of Mampukuji, Kyōto.

For use in the *tatchū*, the private sectors, more informal imagery was employed. Painted portraits of patriarchs, from Bodhidharma to the sixth Chinese Chan patriarch, Huineng, were kept as testimony of the correct transmission of the DHARMA. Moreover, the painted portrait *(chinsō)* of a teacher, given to a disciple when he left the master's tutelage, would be honored in the disciple's own subtemple as proof of his intellectual and spiritual lineage. Among the Zen *chinsō*, both Chinese and Japanese, are some of the most subtle and expressive explorations of human character in the entire history of art: most notably the painting dated 1238 of Wuzhun Shifan (Wuchun Shih-fan; 1177–1249), the preeminent Southern Song cleric, brought back from China by Enni, and the glowering image of IKKYŪ Sōjun (1394–1481) sketched by his disciple Bokusai and kept in Ikkyū's subtemple, the Shinjuan of Daitokuji, Kyōto. Similarly, portrait statues of the founders of a monastery or *tatchū* were frequently enshrined and honored on death anniversaries: for example, the wooden statue of Wuxue Zuyuan (Wu-hsüeh Tsu-yüan; 1226–86) in Engakuji, Kamakura; or the hauntingly austere portrait of Dongming Huiri (Tung-ming Hui-jih; 1272–1340) in the Hakuun'an, Kamakura. See PORTRAIT PAINTING.

Another type of painting that flourished in Zen circles was the so-called *dōshakuga*, pictures of Taoist and Buddhist subjects, a large class of imagery that included numerous subdivisions. Altogether, the *dōshakuga* were characterized by radical deviations from the norms of traditional Mahāyāna art through the use of secular modes of painting, with a great deal of innovation in the handling of brush and ink, simplification of pictorial motifs, and development of individualistic styles of painting. Most prominent of the *dōshakuga* subjects was the White-Robed Kannon (Byakue Kannon), a largely Chinese invention showing the bodhisattva of compassion in an informal guise, seated on a rocky pedestal in a grotto facing a turbulent sea. The most celebrated example of this theme is the hanging scroll by the Southern Song Chan monk MOKKEI (Ch: Muqi or Much'i; d 1239), now in Daitokuji, Kyōto; painted on silk in pale washes of black ink, it shows the deity in a realistic manner enveloped in a misty atmosphere. This is a classic example of what the Japanese called *suibokuga* (INK PAINTING), for it was done in ink alone on silk without the reinforcement of bright colors or gold and silver pigment—a severe limitation of artistic materials that was in harmony with the spirit of austerity and restraint cultivated in the Zen community.

Included in the *dōshakuga* imagery were the so-called *zenkizu*

Buddhist art———Zen portrait by Minchō

The Zen patriarch Enni (Shōichi Kokushi). Hanging scroll. Colors on paper. 267.4 × 139.7 cm. Early 15th century. Tōfukuji, Kyōto.

(scenes of Zen activities), depictions of quasi-legendary figures, chiefly of the Tang dynasty, as exemplars of Chan ideals: the eccentric monk Pudai (P'u-tai; J: Hotei), who, claiming to be an incarnation of MIROKU (Skt: Maitreya), wandered from village to village with his large bag, picking up and giving away worthless items; the two poets, Hanshan and Shide (Han-shan and Shih-te; see KANZAN AND JITTOKU), whose innocent, childlike acceptance of the world was a reflection of Chan's nondualistic vision; of the monk Danxia (Tan-hsia; J: Tanka) in the act of burning a statue of the Buddha. Prominent among the Japanese *dōshakuga* was the celebrated painting by SESSHŪ TŌYŌ (1420–1506) depicting the second Chan patriarch Huike (Hui-k'o; J: Eka) proffering his severed right arm to Bodhidharma, painted in 1496 and now in the Sainenji, Aichi Prefecture. Also important was a set of paintings on sliding doors in the Daisen'in of Daitokuji, attributed to KANŌ MOTONOBU (1476–1559); included among them was a painting of the sixth patriarch Huineng (638–713) fleeing for his life and the monk Xianyan (Hsien-yen; active 9th century) attaining enlightenment at the sound of a rock striking a bamboo stalk.

Closely linked with *zenkizu* as direct expressions of Zen ideas were the calligraphic exercises in which a distinguished monk would write a phrase or evocative saying for the edification of a disciple or visitor. Designated as *bokuseki* ("ink traces"), these would often be written in a bold, assertive style based on Tang Chinese exemplars and far different from the delicate, flowing scripts cherished by the Japanese court aristocracy. *Bokuseki* were highly valued and were frequently mounted in fine brocade and cherished both for their artistic value and their historical associations.

In addition to painting and calligraphy themes with overt Zen content, monks in the Linji tradition employed motifs that arose from Chinese nature imagery. Here again, for painting, the works that served as the most prominent exemplars for later generations of Japanese were done by the Southern Song artists, and especially the monk painter Mokkei. Preserved in Daitokuji are two of his paintings on silk, one of a gibbon mother and her offspring seated in a pine tree, and the other of a crane striding boldly before a bamboo grove; these two large hanging scrolls together with the White-Robed Kannon described above form a triptych whose combination of ecclesiastic and secular themes is an apt reflection of the Linji outlook. Also by Mokkei are sections of a long handscroll preserved in Japanese private collections and depicting the Eight Views of the Xiao (Hsiao) and Xiang (Hsiang) rivers in central China (see SHŌSHŌ HAKKEI). These works heralded the acceptance in Japan of pure landscape as a painting theme that gave scope for the expression of Rinzai spiritual values.

Buddhist art——Zen painting (zenga) by Hakuin

The first Zen patriarch Bodhidharma (J: Daruma). Detail of hanging scroll. Ink on paper. 222.8 × 36.5 cm. 1751. Jōjūji, Aichi Prefecture.

In Japanese Rinzai monasteries by the late 14th century, monk-painters were producing *shigajiku,* long, narrow hanging scrolls of landscapes or birds and flowers whose upper portions were reserved for poetic inscriptions by fellow monks. Such paintings were apparently produced for literary gatherings of men from the monasteries, and the direct combination of poetic and artistic values in a single art form demonstrated the universality of Zen aesthetics. Moreover, as Japanese monk-painters became more skilled, they developed virtually a professional artist's approach to the craft and became adept at more than one style of painting. Sesshū, for example, executed meticulous landscapes in the manner of Chinese court painting; he copied fan paintings by Southern Song masters; he perfected the difficult technique of "broken ink" (HABOKU) landscape painting; and he did rigidly iconic figure paintings. By the late 15th century, this flexibility in taste and universality of outlook had permeated deeply into the life of the Japanese intelligentsia and provided the matrix for a remarkable synthesis of taste: a love of the NŌ theater, ink painting and calligraphy, Chinese-style poetry, landscape gardening, and—perhaps central to all others—the TEA CEREMONY.

Latter-day Buddhism——The Japanese Buddhist establishment suffered grievously in the civil wars of the Sengoku period (1467–1568). Most of the major Kyōto Zen monasteries were burned or damaged, and the lavish support they had received from the Ashikaga shogunate or from the court aristocracy was greatly reduced. In 1567 much of Tōdaiji, including the *daibutsuden,* was burned in military action; Tōdaiji's bronze *daibutsu* and the *daibutsuden* were rebuilt, but not until 1688. In 1571 Enryakuji was almost completely destroyed at the order of warlord ODA NOBUNAGA.

There was a gradual restoration of public order and prosperity from the end of the 16th century under the national unifier TOYOTOMI HIDEYOSHI and subsequently under the Tokugawa shōguns. Hideyoshi undertook large-scale repairs of many of the Nara temples. He also erected a huge temple compound overlooking Kyōto, Hōkōji, as well as a giant wooden statue, the Kyōto Daibutsu, that served as an emblem of political authority as did the *daibutsu* of Nara and Kamakura in the past. Hōkōji, a major landmark of the capital, was joined with the Toyokuni Shrine, built in Hideyoshi's honor, but unfortunately earthquakes and fires have reduced both to a shadow of their original grandeur. After Hideyoshi's death, TOKUGAWA IEYASU built for him a memorial temple, Kōdaiji in Kyōto, whose mortuary chamber *(tamaya)* was lavishly ornamented in black and gold lacquer.

Ieyasu planned his own funeral monument, a vast Shintō–Buddhist sanctuary at NIKKŌ, in what is now Tochigi Prefecture, which was constructed by his son Hidetada (1579–1632) and grandson Iemitsu (1604–51). The chief Buddhist component at Nikkō is Rinnōji, the Shintō ones being the TŌSHŌGŪ and the Taiyūin; all the buildings there employ a highly ornate system of architectural decor based in large measure on the florid styles of late Ming (1368–1644) Chinese palatial building and decorative arts. Branch shrines of the Tōshōgū were built by the Tokugawa and their vassals, and thereby the supremely ornate style of building found at Nikkō spread throughout the nation. The best preserved examples are the Tōshōgū in Ueno Park, Tōkyō; the Tōshōgū attached to the Konchiin of NANZENJI, Kyōto; and the Tokugawa Family Shrine atop Mt. Kōya.

The Tokugawa shogunate, endeavoring to bring all facets of the social and cultural life of the nation under its control, sought to dominate the Buddhist establishment as well. In 1602, for example, Ieyasu required that the powerful and wealthy JŌDO SHIN SECT and its Kyōto headquarters, HONGANJI, be divided (and thereby weakened); the two parts became the NISHI HONGANJI and HIGASHI HONGANJI divisions of the sect, each with its own Kyōto headquarters and network of branch temples. The shogunate also interfered with the imperial administration's role of assigning honorary ranks to the clergy, which led to the Purple Robe or SHIE INCIDENT of 1627. The income and organization of the various sects were brought under uniform regulation, and considerable patronage was provided by the shogunate and leading *daimyō.*

Despite lavish patronage, the Buddhist community lost the central position in national polity and cultural life that it had previously enjoyed. The upsurge of neo-Confucian orthodoxy throughout all of East Asia also affected Japan, where the unifying ideology of the Tokugawa regime and its widespread educational system constituted an official state Confucianism with an emphasis upon rationalism and ethics (see SHUSHIGAKU). With certain exceptions, the leading artists of the Edo period refrained from major religious commissions. The KANŌ SCHOOL and TOSA SCHOOL, who were patronized by the shogunal regime and the imperial family, did continue to paint traditional Buddhist subjects: KANŌ TAN'YŪ (1602–74) produced handscrolls illustrating the history of the Tōshōgū, and in 1661 the Tosa school produced lavishly decorated copies of the Lotus Sutra for the retired emperor GO-MIZUNOO in honor of the memory of Ieyasu.

By the end of the 17th century, Japanese high culture had ceased to find its main artistic outlets in conventional Buddhist imagery. Even a sincerely pious follower of the NICHIREN SECT like HON'AMI KŌETSU (1558–1637), a man who lived for over 20 years in a colony of artisans bound together by religious ideals at Takagamine near Kyōto, poured virtually all of his creative talents into secular-style art forms. The BUNJINGA ("literati painting") master IKE NO TAIGA (1723–76), also a man deeply moved by Zen and Pure Land Buddhism, channeled his religious instincts into largely secular forms of expression. Nonetheless, Buddhist values continued to exert a profound influence upon Japanese art and taste, especially through the tea ceremony, the *shoin-zukuri* style of building, and garden design—all of which had long been integrated into the life of Zen Buddhist monasteries.

Painting. One distinctive mode of Buddhist painting, however, managed to survive. In the early 17th century, Rinzai monk-painters began to work in a starkly simple manner. Employing a self-consciously primitive style, they abstained from the complex, sophisticated painting techniques that had been perfected by monk-artists in the Muromachi period (1333–1568). This process of stylistic inversion, or willful retrogression, was most clearly seen in the work of the Kyōto monk Isshi Monshu (1608–46), a short-lived but highly influential painter and tea master. Isshi had mastered the ink-painting manner of the Kanō school and that of MIYAMOTO MUSASHI (1584–1645), a flamboyant *samurai* swordsman and painter, but Isshi turned willfully to making highly simplified paintings of Bodhidharma (done often with a single line) or of bird and flower themes. Equally simple, almost childlike in their direct mode of execution, were the paintings of TAKUAN SŌHŌ (1573–1645), abbot of Daitokuji and leader of the Purple Robe Incident. His calligraphies, on the other hand, continued to convey the deep subtlety of Zen modes of thought.

While not organized into a formal school, the tradition of the Zen monk-amateur painter flourished to the end of the Edo period and has recently been given the name ZENGA to distinguish it from its predecessors. The tradition was considerably reinforced by the arrival in Kyōto of Chinese monks of the Ōbaku (Ch: Huangbo or Huang-po) sect of Fujian (Fukien) Province, a latter-day branch of the Linji school. A number of these monks sought refuge in Japan during the Manchu conquest of China, and the founder of the

Ōbaku school in Japan, the monk Yinyuan (Yin-yüan; J: INGEN; 1592–1673), was an accomplished calligrapher; his followers Muan (J: Mokuan, 1611–84) and Jifei (Chi-fei; J: Sokuhi; 1616–71) were painters as well as calligraphers, and the Ōbaku monks brought a sense of renewed contact with Chinese traditions to the Zen community. The Ōbaku temple of Mampukuji at Uji, founded in 1663, became a major source of religious and cultural instruction.

The towering figure in Japanese *zenga* was the monk HAKUIN Ekaku (1686–1768), who is often credited with having revitalized the Rinzai tradition. Even though he spent much of his career in the somewhat isolated village temple of Shōinji at Hara in Suruga Province (now Shizuoka Prefecture), he exerted enormous influence as a preacher and as one who restored to prominence the study of the Zen mental exercises called KŌAN. As a painter, he produced literally hundreds of ink paintings and calligraphies to promulgate his ideas, working in a highly expressionistic, individual style. His work also had a strong populist flavor, for he was devoted to the salvation of villagers and country folk. Another prominent master of the *zenga* idiom was SENGAI GIBON (1750–1837), who, in his later years, was abbot of Shōfukuji in Kyūshū. The principles of *zenga* and Zen calligraphy were not limited, however, to the Rinzai monks. They were practiced by the aristocracy—by the emperor Go-Yōzei (1572–1617; r 1586–1611), for example, and the courtier KONOE NOBUTADA (1565–1614)—and by monks of other sects: the Shingon figure JIUN ONKŌ (1718–1804) and the Sōtō monk-poet RYŌKAN (1758–1831).

Sculpture. Great quantities of conventional Buddhist sculpture were produced in the Edo period but have not been the object of much scholarly research. Art critics have felt that this sculpture was derivative in quality and lacked the presence of powerful, creative personalities. The influence of late Ming or early Qing (Ch'ing) dynasty (1644–1912) Chinese styles, themselves comparatively routine or florid in character, can be widely seen in Japan: in the giant wooden Four Heavenly Kings (Shitennō) figures in the *daibutsuden* of Tōdaiji, for example, or the set of the 500 arhats in Gohyaku Rakanji, Tōkyō, or the statues of the 16 arhats in the *hattō* of Mampukuji, Kyōto, which were carved by a Chinese sculptor. Otherwise, the majority of Edo-period sculptors tended to draw inspiration from great figures of the past, from Jōchō, for example, or the KEI SCHOOL.

However, the primitivist tendencies seen in *zenga* also appeared in the work of a handful of "eccentric" Buddhist sculptors. The Zen monk ENKŪ (1632–95) made a youthful vow to carve 120,000 Buddhist images during his lifetime and must have come close to that number, working in rough planks of wood and even large wood shavings, often making only slight alterations, such as the suggestion of an eye or nose and mouth, to give the form a recognizable shape. Another example was MOKUJIKI Gogyō (1718–1810), an itinerant monk of Shingon and Pure Land persuasion, who produced large numbers of roughly carved, highly personal interpretations of Buddhist iconography.

◼️ ——Stephen Addiss, *Ōbaku: Zen Painting and Calligraphy* (1978). Yasuichi Awakawa, *Zen Painting* (1970). Kurt Brasch, *Zenga* (1961). H. H. Coates and R. Ishizuka, *Hōnen, The Buddhist Saint: His Life and Teaching* (1925). Serge Elisséeff and Matsushita Takaaki, *Japan: Ancient Buddhist Paintings* (1959). Jan Fontein and Money L. Hickman, *Zen: Painting and Calligraphy* (1970). Jan Fontein and Pratapaditya Pal, *Museum of Fine Arts, Boston: Oriental Art* (1969). Toshio Fukuyama, *Heian Temples: Byōdō-in and Chūson-ji* (1976). Ryōichi Hayashi, *The Silk Road and the Shōsō-in* (1975). Shin'ichi Hisamatsu, *Zen and the Fine Arts*, tr Gishin Tokiwa (1971). Haruki Kageyama, *The Arts of Shintō* (1973). Takeshi Kobayashi, *Nara Buddhist Art: Tōdai-ji* (1975). Takaaki Matsushita, *Ink Painting* (1974). Isshū Miura and Ruth Fuller Sasaki, *Zen Dust* (1960). Hisashi Mōri, *Japanese Portrait Sculpture* (1977). Hisashi Mōri, *Japanese Sculpture of the Kamakura Period* (1974). Tōichirō Naitō, *The Wall Paintings of Hōryū-ji*, ed and tr W. R. B. Acker and Benjamin Rowland, Jr. (1943). Jōji Okazaki, *Pure Land Buddhist Painting* (1977). Hideo Okudaira, *Narrative Picture Scrolls* (1973). Minoru Ōoka, *Temples of Nara and their Art* (1973). Robert Treat Paine and Alexander Soper, *The Art and Architecture of Japan*, rev ed (1975). John M. Rosenfield, *Japanese Arts of the Heian Period* (1967). John M. Rosenfield and Elizabeth ten Grotenhuis, *Journey of the Three Jewels* (1979). Barbara Ruch, "Medieval Jongleurs and the Making of a National Literature," in John Hall and Toyoda Takeshi, ed, *Japan in the Muromachi Age* (1977). E. Dale Saunders, *Mudrā: A Study of Symbolic Gestures in Japanese Buddhist Sculpture* (1960). Takaaki Sawa, *Art in Japanese Esoteric Buddhism*, tr R. L. Gage (1972). Dietrich Seckel, *The Art of Buddhism* (1964). Yoshiaki Shimizu and Carolyn Wheelwright, ed, *Japanese Ink Paintings from American Collections: The Muromachi Period* (1976). Alexander Soper, *The Evolution of Buddhist Architecture in Japan* (1942). D. T. Suzuki, *Zen Buddhism and Its Influence on Japanese Culture* (1938). Ryūjun Tajima, *Les deux grands mandalas et la doctrine de l'esotérisme shingon* (1959). Ichimatsu Tanaka, *Japanese Ink Painting: Shūbun to Sesshū*, tr Bruce Darling (1972). Kenji Toda, *Japanese Scroll Painting* (1935).

John M. ROSENFIELD

Buddhist rites

Many Buddhist sects in Japan possess their own distinctive rites. The rites can be divided into two main categories: those which religious practitioners perform among themselves and those conducted on behalf of the laity.

The first category may be subdivided into rites conducted with the aim of developing and deepening personal religious faith, such as offerings and daily recitation of sutras or mantras, and rites centering on devotion toward Buddhas, patriarchs, and sect founders. The latter include the services for Shaka Kōtan'e (Buddha's birthday) on 8 April and Nehan'e (Feast of the Buddha's Entry into Nirvana) on 15 February, as well as the various memorial services conducted for the founders of particular sects, such as Daishikō on 23 November (for the founders of the SHINGON SECT and the TENDAI SECT) and Hōonkō (for SHINRAN, the founder of the JŌDO SHIN SECT), celebrated on 28 November in the temple of Higashi Honganji and 16 January in Nishi Honganji.

Rites conducted for the laity may also be subdivided into rites beseeching the protection of Buddhas, bodhisattvas, and heavenly beings for the sake of national security or the good fortune of groups or individuals and rites for the deceased (see ANCESTOR WORSHIP). All categories of rites are carried out at temples and monasteries with no sense of contradiction between those intended for monastic and those intended for lay purposes. There are, however, differences among temples as to which type of rite is given more emphasis. One temple may emphasize services for the monks' spiritual exercise, and another may stress rites of supplication for the laity. Since the Edo period (1600–1868) the majority of temples in Japan have emphasized funeral and memorial services, a tendency which derived from the way in which Buddhism was established in Japan.

Officially introduced to Japan in the middle of the 6th century, it was not until the Muromachi period (1333–1568) that Buddhism became established among the common people. In order to achieve this end, Buddhism had to answer the immediate needs of the people, and one of the ways it did so was by assuming responsibility for funeral rites. The indigenous religious tradition of Shintō tended to look with loathing upon death, which was regarded as a source of ritual impurity (KEGARE). Buddhism responded to the needs of the people by easing their fear of death, purifying death's defilement, and performing rites to comfort the restless departed spirit. Buddhist temples increasingly emphasized funeral rites and memorial services. The policies of the Tokugawa shogunate mandating universal registration at Buddhist temples also served to institutionalize this specialty of funerals and memorial services, and these remain the major social functions of temples today. However, in adapting to Japanese culture, Buddhism was considerably affected by native ancestor worship and AGRICULTURAL RITES, resulting in the religious syncretism evident in almost all Japanese rites and festivals today.

Annual rites include the following. Shushōe: rites carried out at the New Year, including supplications for peace for the nation, and prosperity for the people. Nehan'e: rites performed on 15 February in commemoration of the Buddha's death and entry into parinirvana or complete extinction. Higan'e: rites conducted on the three days before and after the spring and autumn equinoxes, amounting to approximately one week each. The original purpose was attaining the Way of the Buddha; the word *higan* means the other shore or the Pure Land, and the recitation of the NEMBUTSU and PILGRIMAGES were major features. Activities on Higan today, however, tend to center on visits to the graves of departed family members to conduct memorial services. Shushōe and Higan'e are Buddhist rites unique to Japan. Shaka Kōtan'e or Busshōe (Buddha's birthday), also known as Kambutsue (rite of bathing the Buddha) and popularly as Hana Matsuri (Flower Festival): the main practice of this occasion (8 April) consists in sprinkling a figure of the infant Buddha with sweet tea. Urabon'e (Skt: Ullambana), conducted 13–16 July (15–16 Au-

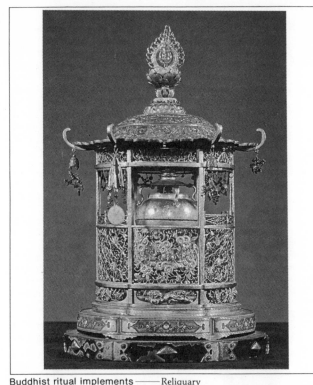

Buddhist ritual implements——Reliquary

This lantern-shaped openwork reliquary encloses a central relic urn surmounted by a miniature image of the Buddha Dainichi beneath a four-legged canopy. The reliquary is capped by a flame-ringed Sacred Jewel *(hōju;* Skt: *cintāmaṇi)* on a lotus mount. Gilt bronze. Height 37 cm. 1249. Saidaiji, Nara. National Treasure.

gust in some localities): the souls of deceased family members are believed to return to the home during this period, and family members perform rites to greet them (see BON FESTIVAL). Jōdōe (feast commemorating the attainment of Buddhahood): ceremonies take place on 8 December, the day when Śākyamuni is said to have attained perfect enlightenment.

Occasional rites include the following. Tokudoshiki: the word *tokudo* originally had the religious meaning of "crossing to the other shore," or attaining enlightenment. In actual practice it refers to the ordination ceremony in which a lay person has his or her head shaved, receives the Buddhist habit and precepts, and becomes a monk or nun. Goma (burning; Skt: Homa): a ceremony practiced in ESOTERIC BUDDHISM. Fire, as a symbol of the Buddha's wisdom, burns away illusion and defilement, thereby effecting a symbolic union between the Buddha and the practitioner. Kanjō (Skt: Abhi-ṣeka): one of the most important esoteric rites of the Shingon sect, representing the transmission of the secret truth and conferral of status. Water, representing Buddha's wisdom, is poured on the head of the monk to symbolize the transmission of Buddhahood.

HOSHINO Eiki

Buddhist ritual implements

(butsugu). Buddhist implements and instruments provide the material means for a wide variety of religious activities, from the most casual and everyday matters to the most sacred and elaborate ceremonies. The array of Buddhist objects reflects the ancient Indian origins of many Buddhist articles, their long historical development, and the diversity of usage among traditions, such as esoteric Buddhism, Pure Land, and Zen.

Common to Buddhist traditions are basic items such as the monk's robes *(kesa),* originally patched together from discarded material, and the almsbowl *(hachi).* These characterize the simplicity and self-imposed poverty of the mendicant life. The religious wanderer's water jug *(byō* or *suibyō;* Skt: *kuṇḍikā)* of Indian origin traveled across Asia to Japan. An oval bottle with a stubby protrusion on the shoulder through which it could be filled and a long slender neck with a stopper from which one could drink, this jug came to be used for the ceremonial sprinkling of water for symbolic purification—of an altar area, for example. Later, by the 12th century, a ewer with a graceful s-shaped spout and lotus decoration came to be used. Together with a basin and towel stand, it made up a lustration set *(fusatsu yōgu)* for a monthly rite of repentance and purification that was descended from the Indian Buddhist *uposatha* ceremony.

Simple ceremonies of reverence employ three elements (incense, light, and flowers), whether celebrated by Mahāyāna or Theravāda Buddhists. In Japan, this practice is reflected in the simplest altar set *(mitsugusoku),* which consists of three parts: a censer for burning incense *(kōro),* a candlestick *(shokudai),* and a flower vase *(kabin).* This would be the minimum furnishing for every family altar (BU-TSUDAN), while more public gatherings would use a pair of candlestands and two vases around the central censer (forming a set of five, *gogusoku).* Mahāyāna monks traveled with a censer derived from Indian prototypes. The oldest examples found in Japan are from about the 6th or 7th centuries and are metal with a long, curving "magpie tail" handle *(jakubigata ekōro).* Common altar censers also include tripod or five-legged forms derived from or based on Chinese models.

Remembrance of the Buddha has been marked by reliquaries *(shari yōgu),* which vary from simple rectangular boxes to elaborate gilt-metal stupas decorated with openwork floral motifs and which serve to house a bone (Skt: *śarīra)* or relic symbolic of the historical Buddha. Stupa-shaped reliquaries, small images, and even sutras are commonly placed in miniature shrines *(zushi).* The most common form of Buddhist shrine is four-sided, roofed, and with a large, solid base. Double doors opening outward provide access to the shrine interior. Simple, pocket-sized shrines are also made for individual use.

This common Buddhist heritage has been elaborated variously by different strands of tradition. Although the categories necessarily overlap, items may be divided into those most common in exoteric traditions (such as NARA BUDDHISM and exoteric Tendai), those characteristic of esoteric Buddhism, and those associated with Pure Land and Zen.

Exoteric Buddhism——A large bell *(bonshō)* made of cast iron or bronze is struck to announce the time of the ceremony. Monks then enter the main hall of the temple, where a *shumidan,* a square platform with low railings mounted on a multistepped base (often decorated with Buddhist motifs) occupies the central area. The shape, as the name implies, symbolizes Mt. Sumeru (J: Shumisen), the Cosmic Mountain of ancient Indian tradition. Also deriving from this pre-Buddhist cosmology are the canopy *(tengai)* and multicolored banners *(ban* or *hata)* that mark the cosmic significance of a charismatic figure. Brought from the ancient Korean kingdom of PAEKCHE in 538, these fittings have taken various forms in Japan. The Konjikidō of the temple CHŪSONJI in Hiraizumi, Iwate Prefecture, has an elaborately carved canopy-like wooden structure that is supported by four large pillars. More common is a stylized lotus flower of wood or metal suspended over altars or images. Banners may be of silk brocade or openwork metal. Hung before the image or images may be a stylized basket of flowers *(kego)* or floral wreath *(keman),* made of leather, wood, or openwork metal.

Before an image are placed two small altar tables *(wakizukue)* which hold offerings and ritual implements and flank the celebrant's low, square seat *(raiban).* This frontal arrangement became standard from the mid-8th century, replacing such variations as tables at the four directional points around the image. Various other tables hold offerings, and a low desk *(kyōzukue)* serves as a sutra-lectern.

Reverence for sutras is expressed by their proper handling. Exquisitely crafted boxes *(kyōbako)* of lacquered wood or metal are used for their storage. Usually rectangular in shape, these containers often accommodate several scrolls. Individual sutra scrolls may be protected by ornamental covers *(kyōchitsu)* made of cloth or bamboo strips and finished with brocade and metal fittings.

The monk celebrant may carry a staff of office. The staff in longest use is the *shakujō,* a walking stick with clanking metal rings to alert small living things that might be accidentally crushed underfoot. Also of Indian origin is the *shubi,* an oblong, fan-shaped brush which symbolized the preaching of holy words. An Indian backscratcher was adapted into a short staff *(nyoi)* with a stylized cloud-shape on one end, used by Buddhists as the emblem of transmitting the dharma.

There are various musical instruments, most probably of Chinese origin, for marking hours for monastic discipline or punctuating ceremonies. Several of them are gongs; for example, the *kei,* a cast-bronze chevron-shaped gong suspended from a wooden frame; the *waniguchi* (literally, "crocodile's mouth"), which is hollow and open at the lower rim to form a double gong; and the *dora,* a large and thick round gong, struck with a stubby beater. Other types may be represented by the *nyō,* a castanet-like rattle on a handle.

Nara Buddhism made use of the Indian *kuṇḍikā* water jug in a metal form (examples are preserved in the SHŌSŌIN of Tōdaiji and at HŌRYŪJI), as well as a container resembling a vase with an egg-shaped body and long slender neck flaring at the rim, a descendant of the Indian vessel (Skt: *kalaśa*) for the nectar of immortality. This water holder was associated with various bodhisattvas, especially with KANNON (Skt: Avalokiteśvara). A dragon-spouted pitcher was used for recreating the Buddha's first bath at his birthday celebration.

Esoteric Buddhism——Shingon and Tendai esotericism continued to use exoteric Buddhist implements, with enlarged or specifically esoteric interpretations, and added complex elaborations of their own. The elaboration of ritual objects dates most notably from the importation of Chinese and Indian teachings and usage by KŪKAI and SAICHŌ. A central theme of both Shingon and Tendai Buddhism is the interpenetration of two conceptually distinguishable aspects of reality, the Womb or Matrix Realm (TAIZŌKAI) and the Diamond or Thunderbolt Realm (KONGŌKAI). The esoteric altar is a MANDALA, a circular or square diagram that symbolically represents the Buddhist universe. Implements embodying the twin aspects of Taizōkai and Kongōkai are arranged on the altar in symbolic patterns for use in secret ceremonies. The adamantine wisdom of the Diamond or Thunderbolt Realm is symbolized by the *vajra* (J: *kongōsho*), an ancient Indo-Aryan thunderbolt weapon, now much stylized as a short bronze baton with prong(s) arranged symmetrically, the same number at each end. The Buddhist vajra embodies the incisive power of wisdom to disarm hindrances to enlightenment. A five-pronged vajra, employed only by the chief officiant, is associated with the five kinds of wisdom of the Five Great Dhyāni Buddhas (Go Chi Nyorai), as well as with the five elements (J: *gorin*), the five senses, and many other sets of five. A three-pronged vajra is linked with karma and its manifestations in body, speech, and mind. Two three-pronged vajras, when crossed, form a twelve-pointed symbol for the twelve units of cause and effect in the phenomenal world. A single-pronged vajra symbolizes the Buddha or the dharma and reflects the unity of the universe. There are also vajras with jewel tips (J: *hōjusho*), and those with stupas at each end (J: *tōsho*) to represent Mahāvairocana Buddha (J: Dainichi Nyorai), the figure central to and uniting the Diamond and the Womb mandalas.

The Womb or Matrix Realm is symbolized by a bell with vajra handles (J: *kongōrei*). The vajras and the bells together represent the unity of the two aspects of the universe as embodied in Mahāvairocana. Separately considered, the bells may be engraved with Sanskrit characters for the figures they represent in the mandala, especially the Dhyāni Buddhas and Fudō Myōō (Skt: Acala), together with the other Five Bright or Wisdom Kings (J: Go Dai Myōō) and the Four Heavenly Kings (J: Shitennō). Kūkai and Saichō each brought from China a set consisting of a five-pronged bell and a five-pronged vajra.

Mahāvairocana is also represented by the *cakra* (J: *rimpō*), an ancient Indian wheel-symbol for royalty that was later associated with the teaching of the dharma. The esoteric Buddhist cakra, linking very ancient solar symbolism for kingship with the solar Buddha Mahāvairocana, has eight vajra-shaped spokes.

The complex esoteric rituals involve various other articles, placed in significant order with vajras, bells, and cakra on the altar. The Shingon sect uses a lotus flower altar *(kegyōdan),* consisting of a square platform with a double row of lotus petals around the base as its great altar and an altar with legs curved like an elephant's tusks for incense rituals. Esoteric Tendai tradition uses a plain box-like table altar for both purposes. The great altar is marked off as an area of special meaning and power by four posts *(shiketsu),* linked with five-colored braided silk cords. This altar is set in various ways by the different schools, but one basic pattern might include standing lamps at the four corners and two sides, flower vases on the platform at the four corners and the center, and a censer in the middle of each side with containers for food and water offerings beside it. Vajra-handled bells are placed on each side (a set of single, triple, and five-pronged, together with a jeweled one) while the corresponding vajras are immediately before the celebrant. In the center with one vase is the cakra, the stupa-vajra and the stupa-bell, representing Mahāvairocana, and in the four inner corners are the crossed karma-vajras.

Pure Land Buddhism——Objects especially characteristic of

Buddhist ritual implements——Floral wreath (keman)

One of a group of three from the canopy of the altar in the Konjikidō at the temple Chūsonji. Two mythical bird-like beings *(karyōbinga;* Skt: *kalavinka)* are depicted in low relief against a background of peony-like flowers *(hōsōge).* Gilt bronze. 29.3 × 32.7 cm. 1124. Chūsonji, Iwate Prefecture. National Treasure.

Buddhist ritual implements——Esoteric implements

Single-pronged *vajra* (right), three-pronged *vajra* (center), and five-pronged *vajra* bell (left). During rituals these objects are placed in a specified order on a special altar. Gilt bronze. 25.0 cm (right), 24.5 cm (center), 24.0 cm (left). Early Heian period. Kongōbuji, Wakayama Prefecture.

Pure Land Buddhism include the *nenju* (rosary) for marking off recitations of the mantra (in this case the NEMBUTSU) and various rhythm instruments. The *shōko,* a small round gong, suspended from above, or the *fusegane,* a similar gong placed horizontally on short legs on the floor, may be beaten in time with the chant. Another percussion instrument important to this tradition is the *mokugyo,* a fish- or dragon-shaped drum of hollow wood.

Zen——Zen usage has favored other instruments, such as the *umban,* a suspended gong in the shape of a stylized cloud; the *gyoku,* a wooden split-drum in the form of a fish; and the *kinsu,* a bowl-shaped inverted bell, placed on the floor and struck to regulate chanting rhythm. The censer, used only in Zen Buddhism, is remarkable for its eight legs. The Zen monk's staff may vary from the *shujō,* a long walking staff, to the *hossu,* a short staff with a tail-like brush that is descended from the Indian yak-tail fly-whisk. A staff used to awaken the drowsy meditator or to communicate a nonverbal experience of enlightenment is the short *kyōsaku.*

■——Ishida Mosaku, *Mikkyō hōgu* (1965). Kurata Bunsaku, *Nihon bukkyō bijutsu no genryū* (1978). Kurata Osamu, *Butsugu,* no.

Buddhist sculpture———The Shaka Triad at Hōryūji

Gilt bronze triad of Shaka with attendants. Height of Shaka 86.4 cm. 623. Main hall *(kondō)*, Hōryūji, Nara Prefecture. National Treasure.

Buddhist sculpture———The Miroku at Kōryūji

7th-century Korean image of the bodhisattva Miroku. Red pine. Height of body 84.2 cm. Kōryūji, Kyōto. National Treasure.

16 of *Nihon no bijutsu* (August 1967). E. Dale Saunders, *Mudrā* (1960). ———— Jane T. GRIFFIN

Buddhist rosary

(*juzu* or *nenju*). A circular string of small beads used to keep count in reciting the name of Buddha (see NEMBUTSU). Held in the hand or worn around the neck, the *juzu* is a symbol of the Buddhist believer, especially the adherent of the JŌDO SECT (Pure Land sect). There are usually 108 beads symbolizing the 108 evil passions of humankind that must be subdued. The beads are commonly made of nuts from the bo (pipal) tree, quartz crystals, or sandalwood. ———— *ŌUCHI Eishin*

Buddhist sculpture

Before the transmission of BUDDHISM to Japan in the 6th century, the only sculpture native to Japan was clay figures. These were of two types. One, called *dogū*, was made in the Jōmon period (ca 10,000 BC–ca 300 BC; see JŌMON FIGURINES). The other, made of low-fired clay, was known as HANIWA and created to be placed in and around tombs during the Kofun period (ca 300–710).

Buddhist sculpture was introduced to Japan from China and Korea, and from the 6th through the 8th centuries, Japanese Buddhist sculpture closely followed continental prototypes. A more native style of sculpture did not evolve fully until the 9th century, when wooden sculpture began to flourish; from the 15th century, the Buddhist sculpture tradition waned (see BUDDHIST ART). SHINTŌ images were first produced under the influence of Buddhist images from the early 9th century on (see SHINTŌ ART).

In addition to the predominant sculptures of human figures, MASKS became a significant art form for GIGAKU dance in the 8th century, then for *bugaku* dance and *gyōdō* (Buddhist sutra recital procession) in the Heian period (794–1185). In the 14th century, NŌ masks and decorative wood carving of architectural features, including exterior and interior bracketing and interior transoms *(ramma)*, attained prominence. Below is a brief historical survey of Japanese figure sculpture, followed by more technical sections on Buddhist sculptors, sculptural techniques, and image types and their significance within the Buddhist tradition.

Historical Survey———*Pre-Buddhist clay figures.* Jōmon culture, which covers a period of over 10,000 years, is best known for its unique earthenware figurines, or *dogū*, which were modeled from clay that was later baked. *Dogū*, which appeared late in the Jōmon period, are strange and mysterious-looking human representations often having supernaturally large eyes that resemble a pair of gog-

gles. *Dogū* were apparently used by shamans in the religious practices of the time and, with a power of expression that is commonly found among primitive sculpture the world over, many of them are outstanding works of art (see JŌMON CULTURE).

In the Kofun period arose a new ceramic tradition of unglazed, low-fired ceramic vessels called *haniwa*. *Haniwa* were placed on and around the mound-shaped tombs of important persons. These vessels are classified into two types: cylindrical *haniwa* and figural *haniwa*. The cylindrical *haniwa* are older and were followed by *haniwa* in the shape of buildings, containers, birds, animals, and, finally, human figures. *Haniwa* in the shape of animals and humans are simple and direct in their modeling, and convey both vitality and optimism. After Buddhist art was introduced from Korea and China, the production of *haniwa* ceased.

Asuka and Nara periods (latter part of the 6th century–794). Buddhist images were imported to Japan from Korea for the first time in the middle of the 6th century, and the Japanese began sculpting their own Buddhist images very soon thereafter, in the late 6th and early 7th centuries, with the encouragement of the empress SUIKO (r 593–628) and her nephew Prince SHŌTOKU (574–622). The style of the earliest Japanese Buddhist images initially followed their Chinese and Korean models. During the 7th century, a sculpture influenced by Chinese Six Dynasties (222–589) and Northern Wei (386–535) sculptural styles (as reinterpreted by Korean Buddhist sculptors) was predominant in Japan. The Korean style of the Three Kingdoms (57–668), especially representations of seated bodhisattvas in meditation, were extremely popular in Japan. Yet Japanese sculptors did not merely imitate Chinese and Korean styles. Rather there was a tendency, already visible in the Asuka and the early Nara periods, to change continental styles to suit the taste of the Japanese people.

The oldest temples in Japan, built mainly in the vicinity of ASUKA and Nara, include HŌRYŪJI (607) in Nara, SHITENNŌJI (593) in Ōsaka, and KŌRYŪJI (603) in Kyōto. Some of the images made for these temples have survived and provide examples of the styles then predominant. The bronze Shaka Triad (Śākyamuni flanked by two bodhisattvas) in the main hall *(kondō)* of Hōryūji bears inscriptions that date the casting of the image to 623 and that name the sculptor, Tori Busshi (KURATSUKURI NO TORI). Other early surviving masterpieces in Hōryūji are the wooden figures of Guze Kannon (a variant of Avalokiteśvara; see KANNON) in the octagonal-shaped Dream Hall (Yumedono) and the Four Heavenly Kings (Shitennō) in the main hall. These both date from the middle of the 7th century and may have been made in Tori's workshop. In Kōryūji there is a statue of the bodhisattva MIROKU (Maitreya), an imported image

Buddhist sculpture——The Gakkō at Tōdaiji

This image of the bodhisattva Gakkō and a companion image of the bodhisattva Nikkō are part of a group of attendant figures for Fukūkenjaku Kannon, the main icon of the lotus hall *(hokkedō)* at Tōdaiji in Nara Prefecture. Clay, originally painted. Height of full standing figure 207 cm. 8th century. National Treasure.

Buddhist sculpture——The Shikkongōshin at Tōdaiji

The guardian deity Shikkongōshin, one of the "angry" gods who protect Buddhism, wielding a thunderbolt. The work shown is a secret image *(hibutsu)* long stored in a cabinet in the lotus hall *(hokkedō)* at Tōdaiji in Nara; rarely open to view, it retains much of its original condition. Clay, painted. Height 173.9 cm. 8th century. National Treasure.

made of Korean red pine. Other examples of early Buddhist sculpture in Japan include a surprisingly large number of small bronze statuettes, such as the "48 Buddhas" (SHIJŪHATTAI BUTSU) once owned by Hōryūji.

The Nara period (710–794) marked the golden age of Japanese Buddhist art. Early in the 8th century, temples began to be built throughout the country, starting with the Nara temple TŌDAIJI founded by the emperor SHŌMU (r 724–749). This resulted in an increased demand for Buddhist images. The materials for Buddhist statuary at this time were the same as those used in China and Korea: bronze, clay, hollow and wood-core dry-lacquer, low-fired clay plaques, repoussé bronze plaques, stone, and wood. The Japanese experimented with all these materials and mastered their use; however, bronze and lacquer were the preferred materials.

Many monumental bronze images were cast during this period, the most impressive being the great Buddha of Tōdaiji, known as the Nara Daibutsu (see DAIBUTSU). Over 16.1 meters (53 ft) high, it was burned and recast twice, so that all that remains of its original form is the lower part of the body and the lotus pedestal decorated with beautiful engraving. In the lotus hall *(hokkedō)* at Tōdaiji is a group of well-preserved Buddhist images from the 8th century. Baked clay tiles *(sembutsu;* see BUDDHA TILES) and repoussé bronze plaques (OSHIDASHIBUTSU) of this period are still being excavated at early temple sites all over the country. Even clay figures, which are especially fragile, have survived, such as the Miroku at the TAIMADERA in Nara.

YAKUSHIJI and TŌSHŌDAIJI in Nara are two other important Nara-period temples. Yakushiji still possesses the masterpieces Yakushi Triad (Bhaiṣajyaguru flanked by two bodhisattvas) and Shō Kannon (Skt: Āryāvalokiteśvara). Tōshōdaiji is known for its main image of hollow dry-lacquer, a large statue of Rushana (Skt: Vairocana), and for the oldest portrait statue in Japan, a hollow dry-lacquer statue of GANJIN (Ch: Jianzhen or Chien-chen), the Chinese monk who founded the temple. The images at Tōshōdaiji clearly reflect the influence of Tang (T'ang; 618–907) sculpture. The Chinese sculptors who came to Japan with Ganjin succeeded in imitating in wood and lacquer the techniques used for carving stone in the Tang dynasty; their studio flourished at the end of the 8th century and established the foundation for the flowering of wooden sculpture in Japan during the Heian period.

Heian period (794–1185). At the very end of the 8th century, the capital was moved from Nara to HEIANKYŌ (present-day Kyōto). Many high-ranking Japanese monks, including KŪKAI and SAICHŌ,

went to study in China during the 9th century and brought back the teachings of ESOTERIC BUDDHISM together with the new iconography of the esoteric sects. With the introduction of the kings of wisdom or light (MYŌŌ; Skt: *vidyārāja*) and other multiarmed and multiheaded deities into the Buddhist pantheon, the range of sculpted images became wider. But perhaps the most significant change that occurred was the shift of Japanese Buddhist sculpture from bronze and wood-core dry-lacquer to wood. The Japanese preference for wooden sculpture may be considered a natural development in a country where wood was so abundant.

At TŌJI (Kyōō Gokokuji) in Kyōto, the temple of the founder of the SHINGON SECT, Kūkai, there are 21 wooden images, of which 15 are original and essentially undamaged. This group is arranged in the form of a sculptural MANDALA and contains a set of Five Wisdom Kings (Go Dai Myōō), the earliest example of this iconographic type in Japan and the models for later images of wisdom kings.

The more baroque style of late Tang sculpture, which was introduced to Japan together with the new esoteric sects, featured more natural representation of human forms. Buddhist images became more massive and magnificent, more three-dimensional in facial features and bodies. The technique of representing drapery developed and increased in complexity, utilizing sharply carved lines.

During this period the sculpting of Buddhist images spread to the provinces, and there as well as in the cities, private workshops (BUS-SHO) were established by Buddhist sculptors, in contrast to the earlier government workshops. It is noteworthy that even in the Tōhoku district, which was considered a barren area for art, a seated figure of Yakushi dated 862 was sculpted for Kuroishidera (Iwate Prefecture).

At the beginning of the 9th century, the preferred technique for wood was single woodblock construction *(ichiboku-zukuri)*. The hollowing of single woodblock sculptures developed as a way to prevent cracks from appearing. Before long, this technique was developed into a rudimentary form of *yosegi-zukuri*, or joined woodblock construction, where a log was split and the whole core removed. This was further developed to a technique in which more than two pieces of wood were joined together to form an image, and each section of the wood was carved to almost the same thickness.

The joined woodblock technique was refined by the great Buddhist sculptor JŌCHŌ during the 11th century. The seated image of AMIDA (Skt: Amitābha) in the Phoenix Hall of the temple BYŌDŌIN (1053) is the only surviving example of his work, although it is recorded that he created several hundred works. The elegant and

Buddhist sculpture —— The Yakushi Triad at Yakushiji

The healing Buddha Yakushi with attendants. Bronze. Early 8th century. Main hall *(kondō)*, Yakushiji, Nara Prefecture. National Treasure.

Buddhist sculpture —— The Rushana at Tōshōdaiji

Representation in hollow dry-lacquer of Rushana. Height 339.4 cm. 8th century. Tōshōdaiji, Nara Prefecture. National Treasure.

peaceful face of this statue and the carefully arranged and graceful lines of the draperies reflect the taste of the courtly culture flourishing at that time and reveal a Japanese style that had freed itself from the influence of China and Korea. Jōchō's skill was so outstanding that this style dominated Japanese sculpture through the late 11th and 12th centuries, when idealized and graceful images of Amida, the lord of the Western Paradise, became increasingly popular.

Kamakura period (1185–1333) and later. In 1180, Tōdaiji and KŌFUKUJI, the biggest temples in Nara, were burnt during the Taira–Minamoto war. Fortunately, the *hokkedō* and some other halls at Tōdaiji survived, but at Kōfukuji, most of the buildings and the temple treasure were lost. When the restoration and replacement of the images in these temples was begun at the beginning of the 13th century with the aid and support of the Kamakura shogunate, sculptors such as KŌKEI, his son UNKEI, and his disciple KAIKEI, all of whom lived in Nara and had until that time been generally ignored in favor of sculptors of the IN SCHOOL and the EN SCHOOL in Kyōto, gained a unique opportunity and were challenged to make monumental images and complicated sculptural projects (see KEI SCHOOL). The practice of using inlaid crystal eyes on images had begun at the end of the 12th century, so the images produced thereafter looked much more lively and realistic than those of the late

Heian period. Furthermore, the joined woodblock technique was refined to allow sculptors to produce more complicated and monumental representations, which suited the tastes of the ruling warrior class and at the same time were based on a close study of classical 8th- and 9th-century sculpture.

Unkei and Kaikei were the outstanding sculptors of the Kamakura period. Unkei was known for his powerful, dignified style; Kaikei's sculpture, more decorative and idealized, was deeply influenced by Chinese Song (Sung; 960–1279) sculpture. The styles of these two masters spread all over the country and later exerted an influence on the Buddhist sculptors of the Edo period (1600–1868).

During the Kamakura period many ZEN temples were built throughout the country. As new sects of Buddhism were founded, such as the NICHIREN SECT, JI SECT, and JŌDO SHIN SECT, the demand for Buddhist images increased and more local sculptors appeared; most were more or less imitators of the styles of Jōchō and the Kei school.

The single woodblock sculpture popular in the 9th century was thus revived in the late 13th to 14th centuries. Artists sculpting in this revived style preferred thick wood. Accordingly, the carving was quite deep and sharp, but still maintained an overall sense of unity; these images exhibited a style unique to the period. From the 15th century onward, Buddhist sculptors tended to be town artisans of little distinction. This situation lasted until the Edo period, when a more amateur style of sculpture by Buddhist monks appeared. The single woodblock sculptures by nonprofessionals such as Mokujiki Gogyō (see MOKUJIKI) or ENKŪ, roughly carved as devotional acts, remain unique and charming.

Buddhist Sculptors —— Many of the greatest works of Japanese Buddhist sculpture can be identified as the works of individual artists. Tori Busshi was the most important sculptor of the 7th century. In addition to creating the Shaka Triad, he is also known prior to this project to have made a cast-bronze *jōroku* image of the Buddha Shaka for the ASUKADERA, which, though heavily repaired, is still extant. Judging from the number of small bronze images in the Tori style that exist today, it appears that his workshop was a center of sculptural activity in Japan in the first half of the 7th century.

In the earliest days of Japanese Buddhist sculpture, statues were made at the order or request of the court aristocracy. During the Nara period it was the government that was primarily responsible for temple building and the commissioning of images. The most typical example from the 8th century was the building of Tōdaiji, a major project with obvious political overtones. For each temple-building project, an office for the construction of that particular temple was established, and Buddhist sculptors were employed as government officials for the office. Therefore, a sculptor such as KUNINAKA NO MURAJI KIMIMARO, who was in charge of the project to cast the great Buddha at Tōdaiji, the most important single sculpture of the 8th century, enjoyed relatively high social standing as a government official. Although we know much about the great Buddha project, the statue is heavily restored, and detailed information on the other works of Kimimaro is lacking. At Tōshōdaiji, as already mentioned, a temple founded by Ganjin, records indicate that Chinese sculptors of the 8th century had accompanied the monk to Japan and made wooden statues, using the temple as their workshop. Judging from the number of extant images, quite a large number of Buddhist sculptures must have been made during this century. Unfortunately, the names of only a few individual sculptors, such as Nuribe no Otomaro and Mononobe no Hirotari, are known today.

In the Heian period, historical documents and inscriptions on images record for us rather clearly the biography and background of individual Buddhist sculptors. We know very little of the sculptors of the 9th century, but after the 10th century, from the time of a sculptor named Kōshō (fl 990–1020), the father and teacher of Jōchō, we can tell in quite a bit of detail the achievements of the heads of the *bussho*, private sculptural workshops, which were no longer related to government offices. Jōchō is the best known of these sculptors, who were patronized by the wealthy aristocrats of the Heian capital. Documents tell us that he was chosen to sculpt many of the Buddhist statues commissioned during his lifetime. His works found great favor with the FUJIWARA FAMILY, the most influential aristocrats and patrons of the arts. Jōchō profited from his relationship with them; not only he but all the sculptors of his studio developed great reputations. His fame permitted him to set up a private workshop that became one of the major centers of sculpturing in Kyōto. To Jōchō's school belonged many good sculptors such as Kakujo, CHŌSEI, Inkaku, INSON, Ken'en, and Myōen. These sculptors and their school were the leaders in Buddhist image making until the end of the 12th century. Each school set up independent studios, such as the Shichijō Bussho led by Kakujo, the Shichijō Ōmiya Bussho, and the Sanjō Bussho, each of which had a unique style and helped make Kyōto the center of Buddhist image making until the start of the Kamakura period.

At the end of the 12th century, after Tōdaiji and Kōfukuji were burned, large-scale restoration was required, and the center of Buddhist image making moved from Kyōto to Nara. The Nara sculptor Kōkei, his son Unkei, his disciple Kaikei, and Unkei's sons and successors, including TANKEI, Kōun, Kōben, and Kōshō, achieved great reputations. Large numbers of works with inscriptions made in the provinces by artists who followed the styles of these so-called Kei-school sculptors, are also extant.

Materials and Techniques —— All the materials and techniques for sculpting Buddhist images in China and Korea had been introduced to Japan by the end of the Nara period. Not only were there variations in commissions for particular images and styles, but artists and patrons preferred different materials in succeeding periods as well. Gilt-bronze Buddhist images (KONDŌ BUTSU) predominated from the time of the first introduction of Buddhist sculpture to Japan to the end of the Nara period. A great number of these images, both large and small, were made by the lost-wax technique.

In this technique the artist first formed a clay core for the image. A layer of yellow wax or beeswax equal to the intended thickness of the bronze was applied over the clay core and modeled into the final form. The wax layer was then covered with an outer mold, which was heated so that the layer of wax would melt out through channels in the mold. In the resulting space between the two molds, the sculptor poured melted bronze, casting the image. Often iron bars were placed in the clay core to prevent the statue from warping during the casting or cooling stage. Between the core and the outer mold small bronze struts were inserted where necessary to keep the space between the core and the mold uniform, and iron or copper nails were inserted in the molds to keep them from moving or sliding during the casting process. After cooling, the image would be smoothed and the surface polished. Occasionally an engraver would add designs. Finally, the statue was plated in gold with a mercury amalgam. About 95 percent of the material used for gilt-bronze images cast before the 9th century was copper with small amounts of tin and other metals. Later the composition of the bronze changed. The great Buddha at Kamakura, cast in the 13th century, is about 25 percent lead. Hence an analysis of the composition of the bronze is a good test of the age of an image.

For clay figures (sozō), a wooden core was first carved into the general shape of the image. Straw ropes were tied around parts of the wooden core to prevent the clay from falling off when it was built up on the surface. The first layer of clay was coarse and mixed with finely chopped straw. Then several layers of fine finishing clay were applied and modeled by the artist to form the final image. Once the shape of the image was completed and dry, the entire statue was painted.

The large statues of guardian deities in the chūmon (central gate) at Hōryūji (ca 710) are typical of large-scale works in clay, although they have been heavily restored. To make clay images of this size, a central wooden pillar was first erected, and around it something resembling a basket was woven from pieces of wood. The statues remained hollow and the clay was placed on top of the armature. However, this technique was rare for the time and only became more common for clay statues during the 13th and 14th centuries.

There are two types of dry-lacquer images (kanshitsuzō): dry-lacquer statues, with the core of the image left hollow, and wood-core dry-lacquer statues, with the image built on a wooden armature. In the hollow dry-lacquer technique, a clay core that more or less followed the intended form of the statue was modeled. On the surface of this core several layers of linen cloth soaked with lacquer were applied. The features of the face and details of the drapery were modeled with a lacquer paste. When the lacquer dried, the clay center was removed through the base (for a seated image) or from small cuts in the back or arms (for a standing image). A wooden frame was placed inside the image to reinforce it and prevent warping. Finally, the statue was painted brightly.

Wood-core dry-lacquer images can be seen as the prototypes for wooden sculpture. That is, when the layers of lacquer paste became thinner, more of the form of the underlying wooden core was expressed, and the image came to resemble wooden sculpture. Two sections of wood, representing the front and back of the body, were sometimes placed together to form the wooden core for a seated

Buddhist sculpture ——The Five Wisdom Kings at Tōji

Interior of the lecture hall (kōdō) at Tōji in Kyōto, showing the mandala-like arrangement of the Five Wisdom Kings. Grouped around a large image of Fudō (center) are Gōzanze (right front), Kongō Yasha (right back), Gundari (left front; not shown), and Daiitoku (left back). Wood, painted. Height of Fudō 173.2 cm. 9th century. National Treasure.

image. When a single piece of wood was used for the entire image, a hollow was made in the back, both above and below the waist, in order to prevent the core from cracking inside its lacquer covering. Wood-core dry-lacquer imagery was easier to make and less costly than hollow dry-lacquer imagery, since the wooden core did not have to be removed and less of the costly lacquer was needed. In both techniques, the hands were often made by applying dry-lacquer over iron or copper wire. Both types of image were finished with gilding or with bright paint.

It is generally assumed that images on baked clay plaques or tiles with relief sculpture of a deity or trinity were originally made from a model. Such a model, used as a negative mold, would be filled with clay, which was left to dry, removed, and fired. Tiles made in this fashion were finished by applying gold foil or by painting. Judging from the complete or broken tiles excavated in great quantities from the sites of old temples in the Asuka region, many people believe that a large number of Buddhist plaques decorated the inner walls of temple halls to reproduce the world of the "thousand Buddhas" (see SENTAI BUTSU). Since many tiles would be needed for such a project, and the technique easily lent itself to mass production, this seems to explain the existence of a large number of tile plaques with the same design. It is probable that Buddhist tile plaques were made mainly in the early Nara period, when such simple theological representations would have been popular.

Repoussé copper plaques (oshidashibutsu) resemble tile plaques in the arrangement and appearance of the images. This type of sculpture was made by hammering a copper plate that had been placed on the surface of a cast-copper prototype. Some of the prototypes have been preserved in the 8th-century SHŌSŌIN art repository and in Nara temples. One of the advantages of repoussé plaques was that it was possible to make more than one image from a single prototype, so that different combinations (independent images, trinities, or pentads) could be easily created. A magnificent atmosphere could be created by placing these images on canopies within a hall, and extant examples of plaques thus used are not exceptional. However, unlike with the fired tiles, this technique was more exacting and time-consuming, and it is not probable that images of this type were made in great numbers. In most cases, gold foil was applied to finish the work. Even today a few examples with original gilt surfaces remain.

Stone sculpture was not popular in Japan, unlike in China or Korea, where it was one of the most popular forms of Buddhist imagery. The number of stone sculptures made in Japan in the early period is very small. This is partly because the amount of marble available in Japan was limited and its quality poor, but possibly also because stone did not suit the taste of the Japanese. There are a few isolated examples of Japanese stone sculpture from the 8th century, and from the Heian period the only major group of stone sculpture is a group of about 60 Buddhist images carved on the face of a cliff in the living stone at Usuki in Ōita Prefecture, Kyūshū. Some stone sculpture does exist in Japan, particularly in the form of popular

Buddhist sculpture——The Amida at Byōdōin

Gilt wood image of Amida by Jōchō, 1053. Height 283.9 cm. Phoenix Hall (Hōōdō), Byōdōin, Kyōto Prefecture. National Treasure.

Buddhist sculpture——The Jizō from Tōdaiji

Early-13th-century image of the bodhisattva Jizō by Kaikei. Wood, painted. Height 89.8 cm. On exhibit at Nara National Museum.

tutelary deities such as JIZŌ, but the mainstream of Buddhist sculpture is without doubt the tradition of sculpting in wood.

The development of techniques of wood sculpture, from single woodblock construction *(ichiboku-zukuri)* to joined woodblock construction *(yosegi-zukuri),* was of major significance in Japan. The types of wood employed by sculptors varied according to period and to the area where the statue was being made. The main material during the Asuka period was the camphor tree *(kusunoki),* because it was elegant and fragrant and quite similar to the wood used for wooden images in China. The katsura tree was one of the main woods used for sculpture from central Japan to the Tōhoku region, while Japanese torreya *(kaya)* was frequently used in Shikoku and

Kyūshū. Some sculptors had their own preferences for particular types of wood. Unkei, for example, chose *katsura* for his important masterpieces. In general, the most popular woods used widely for Buddhist sculpture were *hinoki* (cypress) and *kaya.* After these, *katsura, kusunoki, keyaki* (zelkova), *sugi* (cryptomeria), and *nire* (elm) were often used. Chinaberry *(sendan),* paulownia *(kiri),* and pines *(matsu)* were also sometimes used. In addition to these domestic woods, hard, aromatic sandalwood *(byakudan)* was specially imported for a small type of image known as *danzō,* or "sandalwood image."

Although sculptors began hollowing and removing the core of wood-core dry-lacquer images in the 8th century, it was only after the second half of the 9th century that wooden sculpture was almost exclusively hollowed. For large seated images, two separate pieces of wood were used, forming either the front and back or left and right sides of the body. At first the sculptor simply split the trunk of a tree down the center, hollowed out the inside, and fitted the two pieces back together to make his image. The hands and decorative carving of the drapery were added with separate pieces of wood. From the 11th century on, a perfected joined woodblock technique, using many blocks of wood assembled and then hollowed, became the most popular technique for making Buddhist images. Statues made in this way could be sculpted at the artist's workshop in the city and then transported in pieces to the temple where it could be reassembled. Moreover, such statues were lightweight and advantageous in that the artist did not have to go to the trouble of locating a single piece of wood big enough to accommodate large-scale sculptural projects.

An adze, a chisel, and a spear-like plane were the tools most often used by the Japanese Buddhist sculptors. Until the 11th century the tools used by the sculptors were quite limited, and the blade of the chisel, the primary tool, was wide and not very curved. From the end of the 12th century, a chisel with a narrower blade was used. Kaikei seems to have been the first to start using a narrower chisel better suited to the detailed carving that distinguishes his works. In the case of images made by the joined woodblock technique, the joints of the wood sections were fixed together with iron nails or iron clamps; no examples have been found where lacquer was used as a binding agent. From the end of the Heian period, cloth was sometimes applied over the joints on the outer surfaces of an image to fix two wood sections together, and at times the entire surface was covered with cloth soaked in lacquer to create a uniform hard surface for the statue.

When statues were made in the single woodblock technique, they were generally carved so that the core of the tree would not be used, and this prevented the images from cracking. On large statues where the core of the tree had to be included, the artist carved the image with the core running up the back so that the section of the tree that cracked most easily could be partially removed by hollowing. Often accessories made of copper, gilt bronze, or metal openwork were used for the canopies, mandorlas, or halos, and bases of images in order to provide them with an appropriate setting and to impart a solemn atmosphere. Kaikei and his followers, in particular, used very elaborate and beautifully designed metal open-work accessories for their images.

The halo or mandorla *(kōhai)* and the pedestal *(daiza)* were the two most important additions to wooden images. The base was usually carved of wood with inset lotus petals. Mandorlas were often carved, though some were simply flat boards with painted decorations. Sometimes the mandorlas were of metal; the most splendid gold-plated or silver examples are considered masterpieces of metalworking.

Image Types——Buddhist deities can be roughly divided into four groups. The first and most important in the Buddhist hierarchy are the NYORAI (Skt: *tathāgata),* or Buddhas who have attained enlightenment. *Nyorai* are depicted wearing monks' robes with no decoration. Their different hand gestures, known as *mudrā,* reflect the differences in their religious orientation or purpose. Dainichi (Skt: Mahāvairocana); Amida (Skt: Amitābha); Yakushi (Skt: Bhaiṣajyaguru); and the historical Buddha, Shaka (Skt: Śākyamuni), all have different *mudrā* symbolizing their particular functions.

Second in importance in the Buddhist hierarchy are the *bosatsu* or BODHISATTVAS, deities who are one step before the final stage of attaining enlightenment and becoming Buddhas. Some bodhisattvas are represented in the shape of the historical Buddha when he was still a prince and had not yet renounced the world. The hair of a bodhisattva is often tied into a topknot, then crowned with an ornament. The upper part of the body is usually bare and draped with

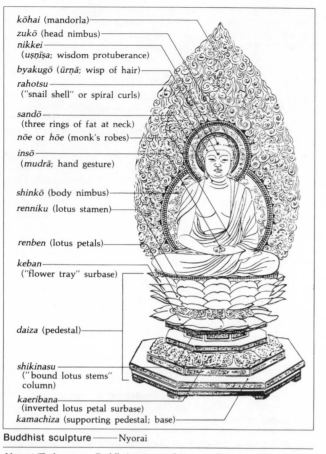

kōhai (mandorla)
zukō (head nimbus)
nikkei
(uṣṇīṣa; wisdom protuberance)
byakugō (ūrṇā; wisp of hair)
rahotsu
("snail shell" or spiral curls)
sandō
(three rings of fat at neck)
nōe or hōe (monk's robes)
insō
(mudrā; hand gesture)
shinkō (body nimbus)
renniku (lotus stamen)
renben (lotus petals)
keban
("flower tray" surbase)
daiza (pedestal)
shikinasu
("bound lotus stems"
column)
kaeribana
(inverted lotus petal surbase)
kamachiza (supporting pedestal; base)

Buddhist sculpture ——— Nyorai

Nyorai (Tathagata or Buddha) iconographic type. Representation of Amida. Other major images included in this category are Shaka, Yakushi, Dainichi, and Rushana.

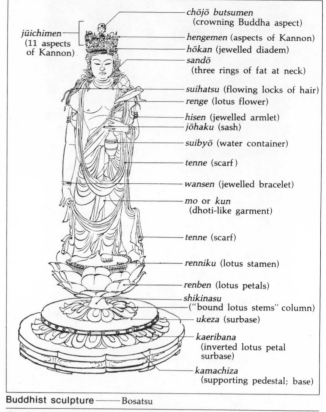

jūichimen
(11 aspects
of Kannon)
chōjō butsumen
(crowning Buddha aspect)
hengemen (aspects of Kannon)
hōkan (jewelled diadem)
sandō
(three rings of fat at neck)
suihatsu (flowing locks of hair)
renge (lotus flower)
hisen (jewelled armlet)
jōhaku (sash)
suibyō (water container)
tenne (scarf)
wansen (jewelled bracelet)
mo or kun
(dhoti-like garment)
tenne (scarf)
renniku (lotus stamen)
renben (lotus petals)
shikinasu
("bound lotus stems" column)
ukeza (surbase)
kaeribana
(inverted lotus petal
surbase)
kamachiza
(supporting pedestal; base)

Buddhist sculpture ——— Bosatsu

Bosatsu (bodhisattva) iconographic type. Representation of Jūichimen (11-Headed) Kannon, one of the many forms of the bodhisattva Kannon; other popular forms include the ones called Shō Kannon, Senju Kannon, and Nyoirin Kannon. The lotus flower and water container are attributes (*jibutsu*) of Kannon. Other major images in the *bosatsu* category are Miroku, Fugen, Monju, and Jizō.

necklaces and bracelets. A sash called a *jōhaku* runs from the shoulder to the side of the trunk across the chest and a scarf hangs from the shoulder, while a sort of skirt or dhoti (*mo*) covers the lower half of the body.

Each bodhisattva has a particular function in the Buddhist hierarchy: Kannon (Skt: Avalokiteśvara) is the incarnation of Buddhist compassion; Monju (Skt: Mañjuśrī), Buddhist wisdom; Fugen (Skt: Samantabhadra), Buddhist practice; and Miroku (Skt: Maitreya), the Buddha of the future. Each type of Buddha is flanked by two attendant bodhisattvas. Shaka, the historical Buddha, is flanked by Fugen and Monju; Yakushi, the healing Buddha, is flanked by Nikkō (Skt: Sūryaprabha) and Gakkō (Skt: Candraprabha); and Amida, lord of the Western Paradise, is flanked by Kannon and Seishi (Skt: Mahāsthāma-prāpta). DAINICHI, the cosmic Buddha and chief Buddha of the esoteric sects, is the only Buddha represented in jewelled garb that could be mistaken as that of a bodhisattva.

The third group in the Buddhist hierarchy comprises the *deva* (*tembu*), originally Indian gods who were not included in the Buddhist pantheon and not native to Buddhism but incorporated for particular purposes. Most are guardians represented as ferocious warlike figures with weapons in their hands, while others have the appearance of ordinary beings. Guardian generals (*shinshō*), the Two Kings (Niō or Kongō Rikishi), and the Four Heavenly Kings (Shitennō) are the most often sculpted among this iconographic class. As with bodhisattvas, particular groups of devas are affiliated with particular Buddhas and bodhisattvas to form distinct iconographic groups.

The fourth iconographic class in the Buddhist hierarchy includes the kings of wisdom or light (*myōō*), who were introduced into Japan with esoteric Buddhism at the start of the 9th century. The *myōō* are represented as ferocious images full of anger. The best sculptural examples of this type are the Five Wisdom Kings (Go Dai Myōō), consisting of Fudō (Skt: Acala) surrounded by Gōzanze (Skt: Trailokyavijaya), Gundari (Skt: Kuṇḍalī), Daiitoku (Skt: Yamāntaka), and Kongō Yasha (Skt: Vajrayakṣa) in the lecture hall at Tōji in Kyōto. This is the smallest group of deities. In the Buddhist hierarchical scheme the *myōō* are more important than the devas

and less important than the bodhisattvas. In the esoteric sects they are considered to be especially important and powerful.

In addition to these four major groups of Buddhist images, there is one other group of images, which was developed in Japan from the fusion of the Buddhist and the native Shintō traditions. One example of this type of deity is Zaō Gongen, said to have revealed himself to a SHUGENDŌ ascetic secluded on Mt. Kimpu (Kimpusen) in the Yoshino district south of Nara. Deities of this syncretic nature are often associated with a particular locale.

Iconography and Sizes ——— The iconographic traits of each of the four classes of Buddhist deities are determined by their "original vow," which symbolizes a particular part of the Buddhist doctrine. The Buddhas, for example, have 32 major and 80 minor iconographic traits, many of which cannot be represented in sculpture, while other characteristics, such as the extracranial protrusion, tuft of hair between the eyes, webs between the fingers, and elongated earlobes, are present in almost all sculptures of Buddhas. Each iconographic variation of a given deity is determined by a combination of the different iconographic traits and *mudrā*, so that, for example, different types of Kannon, Dainichi, or Miroku may be depicted.

Śākyamuni is often represented in sculpture at different points in his life: at birth, during his ascetic practices, descending from the mountains, preaching his first sermon, dying, and ascending from his coffin. Amida is represented in nine different ranks, each with different *mudrā*, iconographical appearance, and attributes. Because many variations of the same Buddha or Buddhist deity occur, especially with deities of the esoteric sects, special knowledge is required to identify each variation accurately. Exhaustive iconographic reference works explaining the purpose and the meaning associated with each deity and the variations of each individual deity were compiled as early as the 10th century by esoteric Buddhist monks and were relied upon to elucidate Buddhist theology. KAKUZENSHŌ (1176–1218) is one such compendium. Buddhist sculpture also includes portraits of Indian, Chinese, and Japanese patriarchs, distinguished priests, and eminent figures connected with the Buddhist religion. Prince Shōtoku, the earliest and most famous patron and supporter

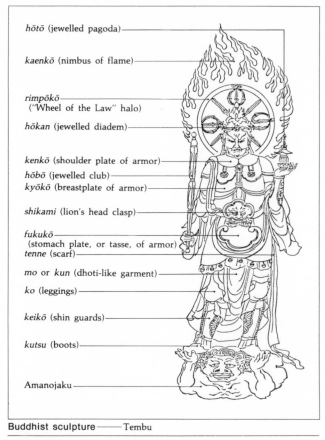

hōtō (jewelled pagoda)

kaenkō (nimbus of flame)

rimpōkō
("Wheel of the Law" halo)

hōkan (jewelled diadem)

kenkō (shoulder plate of armor)
hōbō (jewelled club)
kyōkō (breastplate of armor)

shikami (lion's head clasp)

fukukō
(stomach plate, or tasse, of armor)
tenne (scarf)

mo or *kun* (dhoti-like garment)

ko (leggings)

keikō (shin guards)

kutsu (boots)

Amanojaku

Buddhist sculpture —— Tembu

Tembu (*devas* or heavenly beings) iconographic type. Representation of Bishamonten, also classified as one of the Shitennō; attributes of this icon are the jewelled pagoda and jewelled club. Others of this type include Taishakuten, Benzaiten, Kichijōten, the Shitennō, and the Hachibushu.

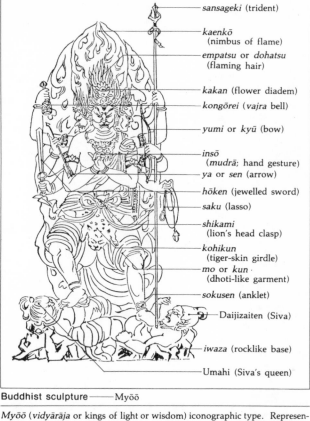

sansageki (trident)

kaenkō
(nimbus of flame)

empatsu or *dohatsu*
(flaming hair)

kakan (flower diadem)

kongōrei (*vajra* bell)

yumi or *kyū* (bow)

insō
(*mudrā*; hand gesture)
ya or *sen* (arrow)

hōken (jewelled sword)

saku (lasso)

shikami
(lion's head clasp)

kohikun
(tiger-skin girdle)
mo or *kun*
(dhoti-like garment)

sokusen (anklet)

Daijizaiten (Siva)

iwaza (rocklike base)

Umahi (Siva's queen)

Buddhist sculpture —— Myōō

Myōō (*vidyārāja* or kings of light or wisdom) iconographic type. Representation of Gōzanze, with trident, *vajra* bell, bow, arrow, jewelled sword, and lasso as attributes. Other major images of this type include Fudō, Daiitoku, Gundari, and Kongō Yasha (with Gōzanze these form the Go Dai Myōō).

of Buddhism in Japan, is often represented in sculpture at various stages of his life, in the same way as the historical Buddha; thus there are many representations of Prince Shōtoku at the ages of 2, 7, 16, and as an adult. Other Japanese Buddhist patriarchs are represented not as transhistorical figures but as individuals.

The most common position for Buddhist images is either standing or sitting with legs crossed. In addition to these two positions, there are other positions: seated on a chair with both legs pendant; seated with one leg pendant and the other bent to the side; seated like the Nyoirin (Skt: Cintāmaṇicakra) Kannon, with one leg bent to the side and the knee of the other raised. When Shaka is represented in *nirvāna*, he is always lying on his right side with his head to the north and his face to the west. There are as well variations of standing postures.

There are many standard sizes for Buddhist images. Bronze images in the Asuka and early Nara periods as well as in the late Nara period are often referred to in historical documents by their size. The standard unit of measure was the *itchakushu-han* (one *shakushu* and a half). *Itchakushu* is generally thought to refer to the span between the Buddha's thumb and middle finger; however, since this is a mythical measurement, there are many different opinions concerning its actual length. In fact, the term *itchakushu-han* is used to refer to the early small bronze images about 30 centimeters (1 ft) in height, and was probably not used as a strict measure. There are also three-*shaku* (1 m or 3 ft) images; larger than life-size *han-jōroku* images (1.2 m or 4 ft for seated and 2.4 m or 8 ft for standing ones); and the most popular *jōroku* images (2.4 m for seated and 4.9 m or 16 ft for standing ones). There were some colossal statues as well, such as the bronze *daibutsu* at Tōdaiji that was originally 53 *shaku* (16 m or 53 ft) high. Because it has been burned and recast twice, it is now only 14.9 meters (49 ft) high. In the early periods, however, the Japanese also sometimes referred to the Tang Chinese *shaku* and the Koguryŏ Korean *shaku*. Consequently, it is difficult to provide equivalents for the measurements mentioned in historical records.

Objects inside Buddhist Images —— As has been discussed previously, the practice of hollowing Buddhist images began in the late 8th century. In conjunction with this practice there began in the 9th century the custom of inscribing the interior of a sculpture with dedicatory passages describing how and why an image was made and of placing objects connected to the patron or his family and relatives—relics of the Buddha, sutras, or Buddhist incantations—inside. The earliest known inscription is the one dated 862 inside the seated Buddha Yakushi at Kuroishidera in Iwate Prefecture. There are innumerable later examples, among which one of the most unusual is the standing Buddha Shaka, the main image of Seiryōji in Kyōto, a statue made in 985 in China and brought to Japan in 987. In this image were found relics of the Buddha, documents, other Buddhist objects, as well as replicas of the five most important internal organs fabricated of silk and brocade. Other objects found inside images sometimes include typical examples of painting contemporary with the sculpture, miniature sculptures, historical documents, metalwork, and so forth. In some cases the historical value of these small objects is greater than that of the larger image itself.

Preservation Programs —— In 1897 the first law was passed in Japan to protect important temples and shrines and individual objects. The present law designates certain works of art as either Important Cultural Properties (Jūyō Bunkazai) or NATIONAL TREASURES (Kokuhō), and the administration of this law is the responsibility of the Agency for Cultural Affairs. Through the investigation and reexamination of temple treasures to determine which meet the criteria and should be given one of the two designations, many excellent works of Buddhist sculpture previously not well known have been rediscovered all over the country. Also, since governmentally financed restoration work began in conjunction with this system of designating art objects, many details of structure, technique, and construction have also come to light. This has made a great contribution to research on Japanese sculpture. In 1979, the number of sculptures designated Important Cultural Properties was 2,435, among which 115 masterpieces were designated National Treasures.

National budget —— Table 1

General Account Budget, 1982
(in millions of US dollars)

Revenues	Amount	Percentage
Tax and stamp receipts	152,143.5	73.7
Monopoly profit	3,164.6	1.5
Receipts from government enterprises and properties	58.5	0.03
Receipts from the sale of government properties	279.5	0.1
Miscellaneous receipts	7,196.3	3.5
Public bonds	43,369.8	21.0
Carried-over surplus	171.5	0.08
Total	206,384.1	100.0

Expenditures	Amount	Percentage
Social security		
Public assistance (aid to needy)	4,343.8	
Social welfare (aid to those incapable of self-support)	7,145.0	
Social insurance (including unemployment insurance)	22,918.3	
Public health service	1,767.3	
Measures for the unemployed (retraining programs; unemployment relief work projects)	1,565.7	
Total	37,740.2	18.3
Education and science		
National government's share of expenses for compulsory education	9,212.3	
Transfer to the National School Special Account	4,307.5	
Promotion of science and technology	1,630.0	
Public school facilities	2,192.6	
School education assistance (subsidies for school lunches, textbooks, etc)	2,484.7	
Scholarships on loan basis	377.4	
Total	20,204.8	9.8
National debt	32,527.1	15.8
Pensions and other		
Pensions for civil servants	562.6	
Pensions for veterans and war-bereaved families of soldiers	6,605.6	
Administrative expenses	43.2	
Aid to war-bereaved families of the unrepatriated	647.6	
Total	7,858.9	3.8

Expenditures	Amount	Percentage
Local finance		
Local Allocation Tax	38,347.1	
Temporary special grants to local governments	0.0	
Interest support	1,684.9	
Total	40,032.0	19.4
National defense	10,743.3	5.2
Public works		
Erosion and flood control	4,598.5	
Road improvement	7,863.4	
Harbors, fishing ports, and airports	2,175.9	
Housing	3,195.0	
Public service facilities	4,100.8	
Improvement of conditions for agricultural production	3,737.4	
Forest roads and water for industrial use	741.1	
Reserve for adjustment	48.8	
Disaster reconstruction	1,186.7	
Total	27,648.0	13.4
Economic cooperation (promotion of foreign trade and economic aid to developing countries)	1,957.2	0.9
Measures for small businesses	1,037.7	0.5
Measures for energy	2,339.6	1.1
Foodstuff control	4,113.9	2.0
Miscellaneous	18,726.9	9.1
Reserves	1,453.9	0.7
Reserves for public works expenditures	—	—
Grand total	206,384.3	100.0

NOTE: Initial budget estimates for fiscal year 1982 (1 April 1982–31 March 1983). Converted into US dollars for the convenience of the reader at the rate of $1.00 = ¥240.72. Figures may not add to totals because of rounding.

SOURCE: Ministry of Finance, Budget Bureau, *The Budget in Brief, Japan 1982* (annual): 1982.

Sometimes a single designation may be given to a group of 1,000 images. Over 90 percent of the images registered by the government are Buddhist, confirming that most Japanese sculptural works do indeed stem from that religion.

Among the great number of Buddhist images referred to in the historical documents from the Asuka period on, many have been lost because of fires, natural disasters, and wars. Although many masterpieces of Buddhist sculpture have disappeared, if we include the numerous small bronze images, works from the time of the introduction of Buddhism to Japan are not rare, and even today early sculptures are still being discovered all over the country.

It is fortunate that there are some datable works from the very early period, for these can be used as standards of comparison for newly discovered works. Of all of the different genres of early Japanese art, Buddhist sculpture is the richest in surviving examples. Of those dating before the 9th century, most come from the Nara area with its temples such as Hōryūji, Tōdaiji, Tōshōdaiji, and others. Other early masterpieces are found in Kyōto, Ōsaka, and Shiga prefectures. The investigation and research of cultural properties is an ongoing process, and about 20 Buddhist images are designated Important Cultural Properties each year.

📖 ——Bunkachō, *Jūyō bunkazai: Chōkoku hen,* vol 5 (Mainichi Shimbunsha, 1977–78). *Butsuzō jiten* (Yoshikawa Kōbunkan, 1962). *Genshoku Nihon no bijutsu,* 30 vols (Shōgakukan, 1966–72). Sherman E. Lee, *Japanese Decorative Style* (1972). *Nara rokudaiji taikan,* 14 vols (Iwanami Shoten, 1966–76). *Nihon chōkoku shi kiso shiryō shūsei: Heian jidai zōzō meiki hen* (Chūō Kōron Bijutsu Shuppan Sha, 1966–77). *Nihon chōkoku shi kiso shiryō shūsei: Heian jidai, jūyō sakuhin hen* (Chūō Kōron Bijutsu Shuppan Sha, 1966–77). *Nihon no bijutsu* (Shibundō, 1966–). Robert Treat Paine and Alexander C. Soper, *The Art and Architecture of Japan* (1975). Dietrich Seckel, *The Art of Buddhism* (1964). Tōkyō Kokuritsu Hakubutsukan, *Heian jidai no chōkoku* (1972). Tōkyō Kokuritsu Hakubutsukan, *Kamakura jidai no chōkoku* (1976). *Yamato koji taikan,* 7 vols (Iwanami Shoten, 1976–78). KURATA Bunsaku

budget, national

The general account of the national government is usually regarded as the most important of all government budgets. Table 1 shows revenues and expenditures in the initial general account budget for fiscal year 1982 (1 April 1982–31 March 1983); Table 2 gives the budgets for the 38 special accounts operative in 1982.

Social security. Various outlays for public assistance programs, social welfare programs, social insurance programs, public health services, and unemployment measures are included in this category.

Public assistance provides support to individuals who are unable to meet the cost of living. This assistance includes livelihood aid, educational aid, medical aid, housing aid, vocational aid, maternity aid, and funeral aid. The national government provides 80 percent

National budget———Table 2

Special Account Budgets, Fiscal 1982
(in millions of US dollars)

Special accounts for government enterprises		**Special accounts for insurance** *contd*	
Mint Bureau	86.8	Fishing boat reinsurance and fishery mutual aid reinsurance	199.2
Printing Bureau	283.9	Export insurance	863.0
National Forest Service	2,735.4	Machinery installment credit insurance	44.7
Specific land improvement	648.5	Reinsurance of compensation for motorcar accidents	7,014.1
Alcohol monopoly	164.5	Post office life insurance and postal annuity	20,450.7
Postal services	17,976.8	Laborers' accident insurance	22,674.0
Postal saving	22,367.3		
Harbor improvement	1,369.6	**Special accounts for public investment and loans**	
Airport improvement	1,019.8	Trust Fund Bureau	36,509.9
Road improvement	9,025.0	Industrial investment	95.3
Flood control	4,637.4	Finance for urban development	196.4
National property special consolidation fund	461.1	**Special accounts to consolidate funds**	
Special accounts for management		Promotion of electric power resources development	765.3
Foreign exchange fund	4,968.1	Allotment of Local Allocation Tax and transferred tax	75,608.5
National schools	6,123.8	National debt consolidation fund	101,512.1
National hospitals	2,454.6	Coal and petroleum and alternative energy sources programs	2,258.0
Opium control	7.2	Total	471,279.6
Foodstuff control	43,803.6		
Special measures for establishment of farms	143.2		
Motorcar inspection and registration	142.6		
Special accounts for insurance			
Earthquake reinsurance	69.5		
Welfare insurance	61,025.6		
Seamen's insurance	1,095.9		
National pensions	21,931.1		
Agricultural mutual aid reinsurance	501.1		
Forest insurance	46.0		

NOTE: Converted into US dollars for the convenience of the reader at the rate of $1.00 = ¥240.72
SOURCE: Ōkurashō (Ministry of Finance), *Zaisei kin'yū tōkei geppō* (monthly): April 1982.

of this assistance and local governments 20 percent. Social welfare programs are intended to support those people who find it difficult to support themselves and for whom care is necessary—such as children, the aged, and the physically and mentally disabled.

Social insurance can be classified into health insurance, pensions, and unemployment insurance. The health insurance system consists of employee insurance and national health insurance. Employee insurance covers persons employed by firms, while national health insurance covers the self-employed and those without employment. The pension system, similarly, has two classes. Employee pension insurance covers persons employed by firms, while national pension insurance covers other persons. Pensions are paid on the basis of old age, disability, and the death of the insured. See PENSIONS; MEDICAL AND HEALTH INSURANCE.

Part of the health insurance and pension systems are administered by the national government, while other programs are administered by local governments. While these programs depend mainly on contributions made by employers and employees, subsidies from the general account are also substantial.

Measures to combat tuberculosis, poliomyelitis, and other communicable diseases, cancer, and mental illness are the main programs carried out by the public health service (see MEDICINE: public health). To cope with unemployment, there are unemployment insurance, unemployment relief works, and special measures to promote employment. See also SOCIAL SECURITY PROGRAMS.

Public works. One of the features of Japanese public expenditure is a relatively high level of government investment. The main emphasis since the late 1960s has been on public works aimed at increasing social overhead capital, the development of which had been neglected in comparison with private capital stocks during the rapid growth of the private economy. Social capital includes erosion and flood control projects, road construction, port, harbor and airport facilities, housing, public service facilities, improvement of conditions for agricultural production, forest roads, and water supply for industrial use. Of these, the heaviest investment is in road construction projects, which are managed primarily through the Road Improvement Special Account. The expenditures in this special account consist of expenses for projects under the direct control of the

national government, subsidies to local governments, and investments in public expressway corporations. The main sources of revenue for these expenditures are transfers from the general account. The gasoline tax revenue is earmarked for road construction and transferred to the special account. In 1966 a new tax was imposed on liquefied petroleum gas consumption for automobiles, the revenue of which is also used for road construction. See also ROADS; EXPRESSWAYS.

Education. Schools for compulsory education (elementary schools, middle schools, and schools for the blind and the deaf) are operated by local authorities; the national government is required by law to provide one-half of the teachers' salaries in these schools as well as one-half of the expenses for teaching materials. This outlay occupies almost one-half of the education expenditure. Other outlays are expenses for public school facilities, school education assistance, transfers to the National Schools Special Account, loans to students, and the promotion of science and technology.

The revenue and expenditures of national universities and hospitals attached to national schools are managed through the National Schools Special Account. The expenditures are financed by transfers from the general account and other revenue sources such as tuition fees and hospital revenue. See also EDUCATION.

Transfers to the Foodstuff Control Special Account. The FOODSTUFF CONTROL SPECIAL ACCOUNT was originally created to stabilize the prices of agricultural products by controlling the purchase and sale of rice, wheat, barley, and other commodities. However, sale prices of domestic rice and some other crops are not high enough to cover the government's purchase price and overhead expenses. As a result, a large deficit has developed in this special account, and funds are transferred from the general account each year to cover the deficit. In fiscal 1982, ¥498 billion (US $2.06 billion) was appropriated for this purpose.

Economic cooperation. In fiscal 1982, the government expenditure for economic cooperation was estimated at ¥471 billion ($1.95 billion), an increase of 10.8 percent over fiscal 1981. Government economic assistance to developing countries has increased rapidly.

Local Allocation Tax. This expenditure, which equals 32 percent of the income tax, corporation, and liquor taxes, is distributed by the national government through a special account for allotment of the

Local Allocation Tax and transferred tax in order to assist local finance. Local governments can use these grants at their discretion. The national government allocates these grants according to the financial needs of each local government in order to adjust inequality in their revenues. See also FINANCE, LOCAL GOVERNMENT.

Noguchi Yukio

bugaku → gagaku

bugei jūhappan

(the eighteen martial arts). A list of military techniques considered essential in the training of SAMURAI in the Edo period (1600–1868). Archery (KYŪDŌ), spear and sword fighting (*yari* and KENDŌ), and HORSEMANSHIP (*bajutsu*) were the principal skills. In most versions of the list, the other 14 skills were: *yawara* (present-day JŪDŌ); swimming *(suieijutsu); sword drawing (IAI); dagger throwing (shuriken); needle-spitting (fukumibari); spying (NINJUTSU); gunnery (hōjutsu);* use of the short sword *(tantō),* the NAGINATA (halberd), the KUSARIGAMA (chained sickle), and the staff *(bōjutsu);* and restraining techniques with the JITTE (truncheon), the *mojiri* (a staff with numerous barbs on one end), and rope *(torite).* *Inagaki Shisei*

bugyō

(commissioners). Administrative officials of premodern Japan. The term originally meant to carry out orders received from a superior. During the Heian period (794–1185) *bugyō* were appointed on a temporary basis to perform ceremonies at the imperial court. MINAMOTO NO YORITOMO, the founder of the Kamakura shogunate (1192–1333), appointed *bugyō* more formally to oversee such administrative functions as the judiciary, shogunal household affairs, temples and shrines, and civil engineering projects. Under the Muromachi shogunate (1338–1573) *bugyō* continued to supervise administrative and judicial affairs. During the Sengoku period (1467–1568) many *daimyō* who had established themselves as territorial hegemons set up boards of three to five *bugyō* as general supervisors of civil administration in their domains. The national unifier TOYOTOMI HIDEYOSHI had a board of five commissioners (Gobugyō) to assist him in implementing policies and appointed lesser-ranking *bugyō* to carry out special projects such as land surveys and road construction. When civil and judicial administration was rationalized under the Tokugawa shogunate (1603–1867), *bugyō* became middle-ranking administrators with well-defined duties. Some continued to supervise construction projects and land surveys; others served as governors of cities and territories under direct shogunate control (Ōsaka, Nagasaki, Sado, Nikkō, etc). Most famous were the "three commissioners" (SAMBUGYŌ): the commissioners of temples and shrines (JISHA BUGYŌ), the Edo city commissioners (EDO MACHI BUGYŌ), and the commissioners of finance (KANJŌ BUGYŌ). Toward the end of the Edo period, when contact with the West increased, commissioners of foreign affairs (GAIKOKU BUGYŌ) were appointed to oversee diplomatic matters and the training of a Western-style army and navy. After the Meiji Restoration of 1868 the title was no longer used. *Patricia Sippel*

bukan

Registers containing information on *daimyō* and *hatamoto* (direct shogunate vassals) published by commercial publishers during the Edo period (1600–1868). A *daimyō* was listed with his domain *(han)* and assessed land value *(kokudaka),* office, castle, genealogy, term of attendance in Edo (now Tōkyō), and other pertinent information. A *hatamoto* was listed with his fief *(chigyō)* and official rank. The first of these registers, the *Chitai fukenki,* appeared in the Kan'ei era (1624–44). The *Shōtoku bukan* put out by Suharaya Mohei in Edo in 1716 (Shōtoku 6) was revised and published annually until the end of the Edo period. In Kyōto, Izumoji Izumi no Jō's *Taisei bukan* first appeared during the Gembun era (1736–41) and continued to be published annually until the end of the Edo period. Invaluable as a source of information on the changing status of daimyō and *hatamoto,* various *bukan* were assembled in 1935–36 in the 13-volume *Daibukan* by Hashimoto Hiroshi.

buke densō

(court liaison officers). Imperial court officers who transmitted messages between high court officials and the shogunate in the Muro-machi (1333–1568) and Edo (1600–1868) periods. The post was first established at the time of the Kemmu Restoration (1333) and was subsequently regularized by the Muromachi shogunate. During the Edo period the title was normally held by two court nobles whose appointment was subject to shogunal approval. They carried ceremonial messages back and forth, received shogunal officials at court, and at times exercised considerable influence as political mediators and negotiators. In 1868, when the Meiji Restoration was proclaimed, the office was abolished. *Conrad Totman*

bukehō

(warrior house law). General term for regulations and laws *(hō)* applied to the warrior class *(buke)* from the late 12th to the mid-19th century. Unlike the laws for court nobles *(kugehō)* and the laws governing land rights *(honjohō)*—both of which developed from the Chinese-inspired codes of the RITSURYŌ SYSTEM instituted in the 7th and 8th centuries—*bukehō* was originally a body of customary law based on the family system and feudalistic hierarchy of the military class. It initially coexisted with the earlier laws, but with the consolidation of WARRIOR GOVERNMENT after the 12th century, it gradually absorbed their functions and became the paramount law of the land. *Bukehō* was first codified by the Kamakura shogunate (1192–1333) in the GOSEIBAI SHIKIMOKU (1232). This code was inherited, with some modifications (see KEMMU SHIKIMOKU), by the Muromachi shogunate (1338–1573), and during the Sengoku period (1467–1568) served as the basis for the domainal codes (BUNKOKUHŌ) of many warrior houses. By the 15th century *bukehō* had begun to include regulations binding not only the warriors but the common people as well. Under the Tokugawa shogunate (1603–1867) extensive regulations for farmers and townspeople appeared in such shogunal codes as the BUKE SHOHATTO (1615, Laws for the Military Houses). Although Tokugawa rule was highly centralized, domainal codes *(hampō)* remained in force. *Bukehō* disappeared at the time of the Meiji Restoration (1868), when the warrior class was legally abolished.

buke seiji → warrior government

Buke Shohatto

(Laws for the Military Houses). Codes of conduct issued by the TOKUGAWA SHOGUNATE (1603–1867) to control the *daimyō* (domainal lords). During the 16th century, regional warlords (SENGOKU DAIMYŌ) had issued sets of rules (BUNKOKUHŌ) to guide their followers. After establishing hegemony over his rivals in 1600, TOKUGAWA IEYASU sought to strengthen his control by issuing a large number of regulations for military houses *(buke),* the imperial court and Kyōto aristocrats *(kuge),* and Buddhist temples and Shintō shrines.

During 1613 and 1614 in particular, Ieyasu ordered a group of scholars to prepare sets of integrated codes. The project was headed by the Zen monk SŪDEN and the Confucian scholar HAYASHI RAZAN, who directed scholars recruited from the major Zen temples (GOZAN) of Kyōto in exhaustive study of past codes, compilations, and treatises, both Japanese and Chinese, and extensive interrogation of learned monks, court nobles, and other scholars. By the summer of 1614 their task was nearly complete. Ieyasu's plans were temporarily delayed by his confrontation with TOYOTOMI HIDEYORI (see ŌSAKA CASTLE, SIEGES OF), but after Hideyori's defeat in 1615, Ieyasu's successor, TOKUGAWA HIDETADA, issued the completed 13-article code for military houses. Shortly afterward he issued a code for the court and aristocrats (KINCHŪ NARABI NI KUGE SHOHATTO) and a number of regulations for specific sects, temples, and shrines.

The 13 articles of Ieyasu's Buke Shohatto are as follows: (1) Civil learning *(bun)* and the military arts *(bu)* must both be cultivated. (2) Carousing and licentious conduct must be controlled. (3) Those who break the laws must not be sheltered in any domain. (4) Daimyō, lesser fief-holders, and stipended officials must promptly expel any soldier in their employ who is accused of treason or murder. (5) Henceforth men of a given domain must not fraternize with those of other domains. (6) Even modest repairs of castles must be reported without fail. New construction is absolutely forbidden. (7) If there be in neighboring domains any who organize factions and make plots, they must be reported at once. (8) Marriages must not be arranged without proper authorization. (9) Daimyō must abide by pertinent regulations when calling on the shōgun. (10) Articles of dress must not be inappropriate to one's status. (11) People not of high rank may ride in palanquins only with proper authorization. (12) *Samurai* of all domains must live frugally. (13) Domainal lords must choose officials talented in affairs of state.

In the comments that accompanied each article, the authors explained the reason for the regulation or cited precedents. A precedent frequently invoked was the SEVENTEEN-ARTICLE CONSTITUTION (604) attributed to Prince SHŌTOKU.

Both Ieyasu's emphasis on formulating codes and the specific contents of each code reflected his belief, shared by Sūden and Razan, that it was important to define relationships clearly, to assure all honest people a proper social place, and, once the great pattern of society had been properly arranged, to prevent any disruption of that order.

In 1631 and 1635 the third shōgun, TOKUGAWA IEMITSU, revised and expanded the Buke Shohatto to 19 articles. Later, in 1683 and 1710, minor changes were made, but the basically hortatory and prohibitory nature of the guidelines remained unaltered.

The importance of these codes was more symbolic than administrative. During the first half of the Edo period (1600–1868), when a new shōgun took office, daimyō were assembled in Edo Castle to hear a reading of the Buke Shohatto. In the latter half of the period even this ritualized invocation of the code was abandoned. By then, however, its basic prohibitions had long since been internalized by the daimyō and even incorporated into their own domainal codes. Moreover, the actual administration of justice rested not on these guidelines but on an extensive corpus of specific laws and precedents (*osadamegaki* and OFUREGAKI) that were compiled and updated periodically throughout the period.

━━━━ Ishii Ryōsuke, *Tokugawa kinrei kō* (1959). Nakamura Kōya, *Tokugawa Ieyasu Kō den* (1965). George Sansom, *A History of Japan, 1615–1867* (1963). Conrad TOTMAN

Bukōsan

Also known as Bukōzan. Mountain south of Chichibu, western Saitama Prefecture, central Honshū. It is formed almost entirely of limestone; excessive quarrying has destroyed its shape. Height: 1,336 m (4,382 ft).

Bullet Train → Shinkansen

bullfighting

(*tōgyū*; also known as *ushizumō* and *tsukiai*). A rural sport at least 300 years old and still popular in several traditional bullfighting towns scattered over the Japanese archipelago. Unlike the bullfight in Spain, *tōgyū* pits bull against bull, men assist as handlers, bloodshed is rare, and losers live to fight another day. In Japan, bulls are not specially bred for fighting but are bought as promising youngsters by entrepreneurs and sold to fanciers. A fighting bull becomes an important and pampered member of his owner's family and is remarkably docile when not in the ring. Training includes roadwork up mountain paths to increase stamina and agility and, before tournaments, a diet of raw eggs and *mamushizake* ("snake wine") for increased energy and fighting spirit. In action, handlers called *seko* stand by the bulls and hold their heads down in optimum attack position while delivering a steady and lively stream of directive encouragements. A match ends when one bull is driven to its knees or turns and runs. *Tōgyū* has a great, bucolic charm, which stems in part from the obvious camaraderie between man and beast. Also, to those familiar with Japanese wrestling (see SUMŌ), it is amusing to find the ancient pageantry, organization, and language of the human sport transferred almost intact to the bullring. For there is, after all, a more than passing similarity between a *sumō* wrestler over six feet tall weighing 417 full-fleshed pounds and a one-ton fighting bull. The short story "Tōgyū" (1949) by INOUE YASUSHI gave bullfighting a moment of national fame when it won the Akutagawa Prize in 1950. John E. THAYER III

Bumbuku chagama

(The Miraculous Teakettle). A folktale of an animal repaying human kindness. A poor man saves a badger (or a fox) which, in gratitude, changes itself into a teakettle so that the man can sell it to a temple. Hurt by the fire, or polished too hard, the kettle returns to its original form and runs back to the man. The badger then trans-

forms itself into a girl and is sold as a prostitute, or in another version, into a horse that is sold to a rich man, and so on, each time fleeing back to the man and making him richer. The story is found throughout Japan in many variations, often retold as the history of a particular teakettle treasured by a temple or family. The most famous one is associated with the temple Morinji in the city of Tatebayashi, Gumma Prefecture. *Bumbuku* is an onomatopoeia for the sputtering of a teakettle. SUCHI Tokuhei

Bummei ittōki

(On the Unity of Learning and Culture). A handbook on statecraft written by the classical scholar ICHIJŌ KANEYOSHI in the middle of the Bummei era (1469–87). Written at the request of the shōgun Ashikaga Yoshihisa (1465–89; r 1474–89) for his own guidance, it admonished the ruler to pray to the war god Hachiman, to observe filial piety, to be upright and compassionate, to pursue the arts, and to devote himself to government. The mildness and moral idealism of these precepts reflect the merely ceremonial position to which the Ashikaga shōguns had been reduced in a period of civil wars.

bummei kaika → Meiji Enlightenment

Bummeiron no gairyaku

(Outline of a Theory of Civilization). A work of political philosophy published in 1875 by the educator, thinker, and journalist FUKUZAWA YUKICHI. It was a product of the period of Japanese intellectual development when it was still hotly debated whether Japan should modernize on the Western model. Fukuzawa, who believed that history consisted of the progress of civilization, argued that the Western nations had reached the highest level of civilization and urged that Japan emulate both their spirit and their external forms—especially the former—in order to modernize and be truly independent. The book was Fukuzawa's most sustained philosophical contribution to the encouragement of Westernization, overshadowing his best-sellers GAKUMON NO SUSUME and SEIYŌ JIJŌ.

━━━━ Fukuzawa Yukichi, *Bummeiron no gairyaku* (1875), tr David Dilworth and G. Cameron Hurst as *An Outline of a Theory of Civilization* (1973). G. Cameron HURST III

bun

A position and set of duties assigned to each member of society in relation to other members thereof. The closest English equivalent is "status" or "role." The term is used either as an independent noun, as in *bun o wakimaeru* ("know one's place"), or as part of a compound noun like *mibun* ("one's social standing").

The concept of *bun* has been important in Japanese society especially since the Edo period (1600–1868), when each person was assigned to a well-defined position in the feudal hierarchy. During the Muromachi period (1333–1568), upward social mobility had been possible, but the Tokugawa rulers froze the social hierarchy, and movement between social classes became virtually impossible. This Tokugawa practice seems to have been responsible for making the Japanese highly status conscious concerning family background and occupation. Even today, when most Japanese consider themselves part of a homogeneous middle class, such terms as *mibun* are still commonly used. While social mobility is common, a person's status will in the end be determined by his family background as well as the education he has received and the occupation he has chosen.

Age and sex are also criteria for *bun* differentiation, stemming from Confucian notions of family hierarchy. Idealized family roles are then projected onto society as a whole, manifested in a variety of patterns of superior-inferior relationship. One example of this is the pattern known as OYABUN-KOBUN (literally, "parent-child" relationship).

In each case, the inferior owes respect to his superior in both language and actions but in return can expect to be taken care of in certain regards. The superior receives deference but in turn has certain responsibilities toward the inferiors who have a close relationship with him. In almost any sort of social group today, the Japanese feel at ease when each knows where he stands, how he is expected to behave toward each of the others, and how the others are expected to behave. Takie Sugiyama LEBRA

bunchi seigen rei

(laws restricting the partitioning of farmlands). Enacted by the Tokugawa shogunate during the Edo period (1600–1868). Along with the TAHATA EITAI BAIBAI KINSHI REI (Prohibition Against Permanent Alienation of Farmlands) of 1643, these were the most fundamental land laws of the shogunate. *Bunchi* is the practice whereby farmers divided their landholdings among their heirs. Since unrestricted *bunchi* would result in a continual subdivision of farm lands, making it difficult for farmers, who were then Japan's principal taxpayers, to make a living, and for the government to collect taxes, the shogunate periodically issued *bunchi seigen rei* from 1673 on. In the beginning, only village heads owning lands with yield of more than 20 *koku* (1 *koku* = about 180 liters or 5 US bushels) of rice and other farmers owning lands with yields of more than 10 *koku* were allowed to partition their holdings. In 1713, however, the law was revised and partitioning was permitted to both village heads and other farmers having lands with yields of more than 10 *koku* or of one *chō* (1 *chō* = about 2.5 acres or 1 hectare) or more in area. Although there were some minor changes afterward, this remained the general standard. Following the shogunate's policy, the *daimyō* also enacted similar laws in their domains. Both the shogunate and domainal lords seem to have taken special care to enforce them, but they were not always strictly obeyed. With the annulment of the Tahata Eitai Baibai Kinshi Rei in 1872, this law was also apparently abolished. *UEDA Nobuhiro*

Bunchō → Tani Bunchō

bundan

In modern Japanese literature, the term refers both to a literary elite and the literary establishment. In the narrow sense of the word it denotes a small, exclusive community of professional writers, living in isolation from society, characterized by special mores and lifestyle, and dedicated to the ideal of pure literature.

The beginnings of the *bundan* in Japan are usually ascribed to the KEN'YŪSHA (Friends of the Inkstone)—the first literary society, founded in 1885 by the novelist OZAKI KŌYŌ (1867–1903). The proliferation of newspapers, magazines, and publishing houses in the 1880s created a propitious environment for the professionalization of writing. Under the impact of Western culture, a reconsideration of the value of literature and its social role occurred, and this gave writers an increased aura of respectability. The Ken'yūsha, through its contacts with the worlds of journalism and publishing, became the first professional association of writers to extend patronage to its members. The incipient professional self-awareness—indicated by the publication of their own coterie magazine, *Garakuta bunko* (1885–89), the first in Japan—combined with their belief in literature as an independent discipline among the arts, created the foundations of the modern *bundan*. Their view of literature as a source of sentimental entertainment, however, had a traditional character, as did the internal social structure of the group in which the hierarchical order of master-pupil relationships among its members was preserved.

The next generation of naturalist writers, who started their activities around 1906, shaped the modern character of the *bundan*. They combined 19th-century European romantic notions of self-expression with a naturalistic, pessimistic view of human nature and society. Educated on Western ideas of individualism and freedom, these writers rebelled against the restrictive social order of imperial Japan and its ideology of a family state by abandoning their family roles, leaving the universities, and refusing to enter on career-oriented paths of employment. Mostly of lower middle-class country origin, they sought an independent life in Tōkyō where they formed a small community of individualists, relying for their subsistence on the profusion of magazines and publishing houses. The level of that subsistence, with very few exceptions, remained near the poverty line throughout the Meiji (1868–1912) and Taishō (1912–26) periods. It meant life in cheap rented accommodations, generally small literary output, illicit affairs, and failing health. A feeling of shame and guilt pervaded the lives of these writers, but they also had a strong sense of self-righteousness and purity because of their uncompromising moral stand, which was based on their belief in the redeeming quality of art. They formed an inward-looking community of nonconformists, who, often at considerable psychological cost, managed to ignore the ideology of the surrounding state and aimed at a unity of life and art—a quality best reflected in the emergence of the new literary genre of the I-NOVEL *(watakushi shōsetsu)*, which recorded the vicissitudes of the author's personal life. As the authors competed among themselves in the truthfulness of their confessions, the need for a fictional narrative did not develop, and the I-novel remained the dominant literary form in the *bundan* for nearly 50 years. The spirit of the I-novel, with its constant focus on crisis or drama in the author's private life, contributed toward the development of the characteristically *bundan* type of self-destructive personality *(hametsu-gata)*. A line of writers from CHIKAMATSU SHŪKŌ (1876–1944) and KASAI ZENZŌ (1887–1928) to DAZAI OSAMU (1909–48) moved from crisis to crisis in their lives through a process of steady disintegration that often ended in suicide. The harmonious personality *(chōwa-gata)* remained a distinct minority in the *bundan*. It is represented by writers from SHIGA NAOYA (1883–1971) and TAKII KŌSAKU (b 1894) to OZAKI KAZUO (b 1899), whose upper-class upbringing imbued them with idealism and optimism and encouraged them to seek reconciliation with the world through a close identification with the natural workings of the universe. Social consciousness remained weak among the *bundan* writers. The *bundan* way of life reached the peak of its development in the Taishō period, and the great Tōkyō Earthquake of 1923 symbolically marked the beginning of its decline. The Marxist literary movement (see PROLETARIAN LITERATURE MOVEMENT) of the early 1920s attacked the whole ethos of the *bundan*, criticizing its lack of political and social involvement. Although the proletarian movement was short-lived, it succeeded in shaking the *bundan's* belief in the righteousness of its moral stand, and this uncertainty was most keenly revealed by the suicides of the two famous *bundan* personalities ARISHIMA TAKEO (1878–1923) and AKUTAGAWA RYŪNOSUKE (1892–1927).

On the other hand, the state was becoming increasingly less likely to tolerate small enclaves of liberty like the *bundan*. With the approach of the war, measures taken against the *bundan* included CENSORSHIP, banning, closure of literary magazines, restrictions on printing paper, and the forming of organizations to solicit writers' support for the war effort. In addition, the rise of a mass society and the development of mass media that followed the Tōkyō Earthquake obscured the borderline between pure and popular literature (see POPULAR FICTION). It gave the writers new market opportunities that increased their standard of living, and as the demand for their work grew there began a gradual process of reintegration into the fabric of society which has continued and greatly intensified during the postwar era of affluence.

The postwar *bundan* generally includes the established, famous, and popular writers. It operates through a number of literary organizations that formally represent writers' interests. The traditional pattern of patronage by an established writer exists simultaneously with a system of literary prizes designed to help new talents emerging in the pages of literary magazines. The elitist image of the *bundan* is still reinforced by some exclusively *bundan* activities (like the *bunshigeki*, the yearly drama performance performed every year by *bundan* members); but in reality, an established writer lives as a fully integrated and respected member of society, and not merely as a member of a circumscribed literary group. See also NATURALISM.

📖 ——Hirano Ken, *Geijutsu to jisseikatsu* (1964). Nakamura Mitsuo, *Meiji, taishō, shōwa* (1972). Senuma Shigeki, "Bundan," in *Nihon kindai bungaku daijiten*, vol 4 (Kōdansha, 1977). *Irena POWELL*

Bungakukai

(The Literary World). 1. A small coterie monthly of vast literary influence considered to have founded the turn-of-the-century romantic literary movement; published in 58 issues from January 1893 to January 1898. Members included Hoshino Tenchi (1862–1950), KITAMURA TŌKOKU, SHIMAZAKI TŌSON, UEDA BIN, and later HIGUCHI ICHIYŌ, TAYAMA KATAI, and YANAGITA KUNIO. Originally affiliated with JOGAKU ZASSHI, a women's magazine which published the first four issues, *Bungakukai* broke away when Tōkoku and others became dissatisfied with *Jogaku* editor IWAMOTO YOSHIHARU's strict brand of Christian idealism; *Bungakukai* turned toward high quality literature and art. Tōkoku's poetry and criticism were the journal's central feature until his premature death in 1894; Ichiyō's stories followed by Tōson's poems are considered to represent *Bungakukai's* subsequent evolution. Though this journal's youthful members were of differing views and literary styles, their interest in the cultural traditions of East and West, especially European romanticism, established them as founders of the Japanese romantic tradition.

2. Coterie journal. Japan's leading coterie journal for its first 10 years, it developed into a major commercial literary monthly after World War II. Publication began in October 1933, and except for the periods 1933–36 and 1947–49 (and a period of suspension during World War II), it has been published by BUNGEI SHUNJŪ, LTD. Original members were KOBAYASHI HIDEO, KAWABATA YASUNARI, UNO KŌJI, HIROTSU KAZUO, HAYASHI FUSAO, TAKEDA RINTARŌ, and Fukada Kyūya (1903–71); later members included YOKOMITSU RIICHI, IBUSE MASUJI, KAWAKAMI TETSUTARŌ, HORI TATSUO, ŌOKA SHŌHEI, ABE TOMOJI, SHIMAKI KENSAKU, and FUNAHASHI SEIICHI. Kobayashi and Kawakami did much of the editing. It became a dominant power in the literary world. *Bungakukai* brought together writers from various literary schools in a conscious attempt to protect literature from the growing fascist movement. It paid close attention to contemporary European culture, and published special issues on topics like "politics and literature" and "women writers." Yet *Bungakukai* actively supported the war effort. It ceased publication in 1944 because of measures imposed by the military authorities on the publishing media. After a brief revival as a coterie monthly (1947–49; new members included NIWA FUMIO, ISHIKAWA TATSUZŌ, DAZAI OSAMU, and SAKAGUCHI ANGO), it became one of the more widely read commercial literary journals of the postwar era. It has published such popular contemporary novelists as YOSHIYUKI JUNNOSUKE, KOJIMA NOBUO, KURAHASHI YUMIKO, ENDŌ SHŪSAKU, KAIKŌ KEN, ŌE KENZABURŌ, ISHIHARA SHINTARŌ, and MARUYAMA KENJI. *Theodore W.* GOOSSEN

Bungei

(The Literary Arts). 1. A popular literary monthly magazine established at the beginning of the so-called period of literary revival that followed the suppression of the PROLETARIAN LITERATURE MOVEMENT. First published by Kaizōsha from November 1933 to July 1944, the magazine was later moved to Kawade Shobō and was still in existence in the early 1980s (see 2 below). Aimed at attracting a broad spectrum of readers, *Bungei*'s editorial policy of including popular literature while also introducing new writers and foreign literary trends made it the most commercially successful literary journal of its time. Important contributors included ISHIZAKA YŌJIRŌ, DAZAI OSAMU, OKAMOTO KANOKO, HAYASHI FUMIKO, TAKAMI JUN, NAKANO SHIGEHARU, and ODA SAKUNOSUKE. Besides fiction, *Bungei* published plays and numerous works in translation from Europe, Russia, and especially China. It also featured criticism by such noted critics and writers as KUBOKAWA TSURUJIRŌ, KAMEI KATSUICHIRŌ, HAYASHI FUSAO, UNO KŌJI, and MIYAMOTO YURIKO. During World War II, it was forced to devote considerable space to articles supporting the war effort. When Kaizōsha was closed by the authorities in 1944, *Bungei*'s name and paper ration were transferred to Kawade Shobō by the Japan Publishers' Association.

2. A leading literary magazine of the postwar era published since November 1944 by Kawade Shobō. Undergoing frequent changes of editorship, this *Bungei* adopted a more popular approach in its editorial policy than did its predecessor. Among its early contributors were SATŌ HARUO, KAWABATA YASUNARI, DAZAI OSAMU, IBUSE MASUJI, and MISHIMA YUKIO. From about 1950 *Bungei* began to devote more space to works by new writers and critics and introduced such men of letters as NOMA HIROSHI, NAKAMURA SHIN'ICHIRŌ, and NAKAMURA MITSUO. It helped cultivate the talents of the first crop of postwar writers (see POSTWAR LITERATURE). Publication ceased in 1957 because of company financial difficulties. It was revived in 1962 when Kawade Shobō was newly reorganized. Since then it has continued to publish original works and criticism of wide-ranging interest in the field of contemporary literature. *Theodore W.* GOOSSEN

Bungei jidai

(Literary Age). Literary magazine published from October 1924 to May 1927. Members of this small coterie monthly included YOKOMITSU RIICHI, KAWABATA YASUNARI, KON TŌKŌ, and KATAOKA TEPPEI. Opposed to the so-called Japanese NATURALISM, its young members disclaimed any thought of starting a literary movement, yet were credited with having created the neo-impressionist or SHINKANKAKU SCHOOL. With the exception of some short stories by Yokomitsu and Kawabata, *Bungei jidai* published little of lasting

literary value, but it was highly significant because it offered the only fresh alternative to the snowballing PROLETARIAN LITERATURE MOVEMENT. *Theodore W.* GOOSSEN

Bungei kurabu

(Literary Club). The first large-scale literary magazine in Japan aimed at a mass audience; published by HAKUBUNKAN, a leading Tōkyō publishing house, from January 1895 to January 1933. An amalgamation of various other Hakubunkan publications, *Bungei kurabu* showed the strong influence of the KEN'YŪSHA coterie of writers. Initially the magazine adhered to serious literature and shunned commercialism. Among its numerous early contributors were such noted writers as KAWAKAMI BIZAN, HIROTSU RYŪRŌ, KOSUGI TENGAI, IZUMI KYŌKA, and HIGUCHI ICHIYŌ. In an effort to maintain a large readership it also welcomed contributions of poetry and prose from readers, which appeared in a special section. It was, together with SHINSHŌSETSU, the leading fiction magazine of the period. Later it put out special editions on popular oral storytelling traditions such as KŌDAN and RAKUGO and by 1907 had become transformed into a popular entertainment magazine, which was further popularized in the Taishō period (1912–26). By the beginning of the Shōwa period (1926–) *Bungei kurabu* was headed into decline as Hakubunkan's influence in the publishing world was weakened by rival firms. After an attempt to repeat earlier successes by capitalizing on the growing popularity of mystery and detective stories by writers like EDOGAWA RAMPO, it eventually ceased publication. *Theodore W.* GOOSSEN

Bungei sensen

(Literary Battlefront). Important leftist literary monthly published from June 1924 to July 1932, first by Bungei Sensen Sha and later by the Labor-Farmer Artists League (Rōnō Geijutsuka Remmei). *Bungei sensen* became a prime force in the PROLETARIAN LITERATURE MOVEMENT and functioned as a literary organ for several leftist writers' alliances. Succeeding TANE MAKU HITO, the *Bungei sensen* group included Komaki Ōmi (b 1894), AONO SUEKICHI, MAEDAKŌ HIROICHIRŌ, and HIRABAYASHI HATSUNOSUKE among its original collaborators. They were later joined by HAYAMA YOSHIKI, HAYASHI FUSAO, KUROSHIMA DENJI, KURAHARA KOREHITO, HIRABAYASHI TAIKO, and others. An on-going series of factional disputes among adherents of the Japanese left wing over the application of Marxist theory prevented the proletarian movement from coalescing into a united front as can be seen in the shifting of *Bungei sensen* members. After a bitter dispute that arose in June 1927 over the so-called Fukumotoism (see FUKUMOTO KAZUO), 16 *Bungei sensen* adherents were dismissed from the Nihon Puroretaria Geijutsu Remmei (Japan Proletarian Arts League). Aono, Hayama, Hayashi, Maedakō, Kurahara, and others whose names were removed immediately formed the Labor-Farmer Artists League and made *Bungei sensen* its organ. Later that same year this group split when leader YAMAKAWA HITOSHI was criticized by the Comintern, and Kurahara, Hayashi, and others withdrew from the league and organized the Zen'ei Geijutsuka Dōmei (Avant-garde Artists Union). Meanwhile, Aono, Hayama, Maedakō, and the other remaining members used *Bungei sensen* to voice their criticism of the Zen Nihon Musansha Geijutsu Remmei (All Japan Proletarian Art League), better known by the acronym NAPF from its Esperanto name Nippona Artista Proleta Federacio (see LITERARY GROUPS), and its organ SENKI. By 1931, when it shortened its name to *Bunsen*, its influence had largely been usurped by *Senki* and the powerful NAPF organization it had opposed. During its existence, however, *Bungei sensen* played a crucial role in the history of proletarian literature and introduced many new writers; its peak circulation was 20,000. *Theodore W.* GOOSSEN

Bungei shunjū

Major general-interest monthly magazine. Founded by KIKUCHI KAN in 1923 as a literary journal, it was virtually dominated by Kikuchi in its early years. At first it carried only essays and criticism, but in time it began to publish short fiction and serialized novels, drawing attention to itself as a forum for young talent. Members of its managing coterie included YOKOMITSU RIICHI and AKUTAGAWA RYŪNOSUKE. In 1926 *Bungei shunjū* shifted to a general-interest format, though it still retained a strong literary flavor. Since 1935 it has announced the winners of the prestigious Akutagawa Prize (see LITERARY PRIZES). It was also the first magazine to publish transcriptions of informal discussions *(zadankai)* on wide-ranging topics by writers and critics. It suspended publication in 1945, then started up again the following year. In the late 1960s and early 1970s it pioneered in investigative journalism, especially at the time of the bribery scandal involving former Prime Minister TANAKA KAKUEI. It has launched the careers of many reporters since the initiation of the prize for nonfiction writing named for ŌYA SŌICHI. Circulation was 720,000 in 1979.   *Arase Yutaka*

Bungei Shunjū, Ltd

(Kabushiki Kaisha Bungei Shunjū). Publishing house begun by the writer KIKUCHI KAN in January 1923 with the publication of BUNGEI SHUNJŪ, a primarily literary magazine. By sponsoring public lectures by famous authors, the company succeeded in establishing rapport with readers in outlying areas and built up a respectable following. In 1931, Kikuchi, who had proved himself an able entrepreneur, put out another monthly, the *Ōru yomimono,* which carried popular novels on social themes. In 1935 he set up the Akutagawa and Naoki prizes in honor of the writers AKUTAGAWA RYŪNOSUKE and NAOKI SANJŪGO, awards which still carry the highest prestige (see LITERARY PRIZES). Since World War II the company has expanded its publishing activities; besides *Bungei shunjū* it also publishes a weekly, the *Shūkan bunshun,* and the *Bunshun bunko* series of literary works.   *Arase Yutaka*

Bungo Channel

(Bungo Suidō). Between western Shikoku and eastern Kyūshū, connecting the Inland Sea with the Pacific Ocean. The northern and narrowest section is known as the Hōyo Strait. Because of the effects of the Kuroshio Current, the climate is hot and humid; subtropical plants grow on the islands in the channel. Fish are plentiful. Length: 50 km (31 mi); width: 35 km (22 mi); deepest point: 418 m (1,371 ft).

Bungo Takada

City in northern Ōita Prefecture, Kyūshū, on the Kunisaki Peninsula. Formerly a castle town, it is now the political and economic center of the peninsular area. Principal products are rice, mandarin oranges, vegetables, and traditional bamboo handicrafts. The temples Fukiji and Maki no Ōdō each house Buddhist images that date to the Heian period (794–1185). Pop: 21,041.

bunjinga

(literati painting; Ch: *wenrenhua* or *wen-jen-hua*). Also known as *nanga* or "Southern painting." A school of Japanese painting of the 18th and 19th centuries based in theory on the Chinese tradition of the scholar–amateur artist *(wenren* or *wen-jen).* The artists' work displayed a remarkable individuality but they had in common a mutual admiration for Chinese culture, particularly the literati painting of the Yuan (Yüan), Ming, and Qing (Ch'ing) dynasties (13th–19th centuries), which they knew largely through Chinese woodblock-print manuals of painting and a smattering of paintings of uneven quality.

In China, the literati style referred to landscape painting by scholar-gentlemen proficient in the skills of calligraphy, poetry, and painting. Any display of virtuosity in brushwork was disdained, while deliberate blandness and awkwardness were seen as an appropriate lack of affectation. Attempting to express the inner rhythm of nature rather than merely its external appearance, they cultivated individual expression as opposed to the purely technical proficiency that they saw as characterizing the tradition of academic painting.

Japanese *bunjin* (literati) artists had only a limited understanding of the ideals and long and complex tradition of the Chinese scholar-artists, since during the Edo period (1600–1868) contact with the outside world, including China, was restricted by the shogunate. Nevertheless, by the 18th century Chinese studies had gained considerable prestige, in part because of official Tokugawa endorsement of Confucian philosophy, the moral bulwark of shogunal authority. Limited foreign trade was permitted through the port of Nagasaki and some Chinese paintings came to Japan this way. (Such foreign influences gave rise to the so-called NAGASAKI SCHOOL.)

In addition to imported paintings, some Chinese emigré artists produced work in Nagasaki, including the ŌBAKU SECT Zen monks. Two of the most influential painting manuals that were brought in and translated were the *Eight Albums of Painting (Bazong huapu* or

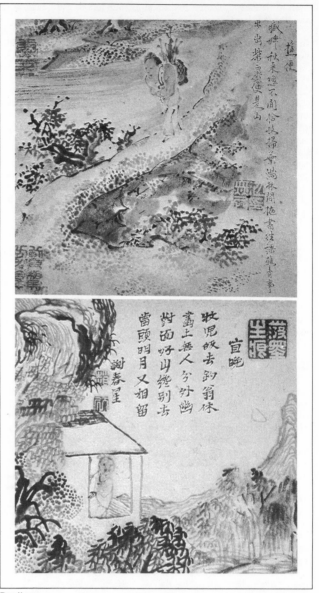

Bunjinga

Convenience of Cut Wood by Ike no Taiga (top) and *Pleasure of Evening* by Yosa Buson (bottom). From *Jūben jūgi* (The Ten Conveniences and Ten Pleasures), a jointly painted picture album based on a Chinese literati poem. Color and ink on paper. Each 17.9 × 17.9 cm. 1771. Kawabata Yasunari Kinen Kai, Kanagawa Prefecture. National Treasure.

Pa-chung hua-p'u; J: *Hasshu gafu),* published in the 1620s in China and first printed in Japan in 1672, and the *Mustard Seed Garden Manual (Jieziyuan huazhuan* or *Chieh-tzu-yüan hua-chuan;* J: *Kaishien gaden),* published in China in 1679 and introduced to Japan in the early 1700s. But the woodblock print reproductions could not convey the subtleties of Chinese brushwork, which was instead rendered in crisp outlines. Thus, although they painted predominantly Chinese subjects in what they considered the Chinese manner, the work of the Japanese *bunjin* from the start had a remarkably eclectic and distinctively Japanese character.

Furthermore, unlike their Chinese counterparts, the Japanese *bunjin* were not necessarily scholars or amateur artists, nor did they come from a wealthy, homogeneous, bureaucratic class. But for these very reasons, they were free from the restrictions of an established orthodoxy. It was enough for them to understand the literati tradition as a rejection of academic styles, and to them academic style meant specifically the officially recognized styles of the KANŌ SCHOOL and TOSA SCHOOL. With these exceptions, any style was deemed a legitimate model. Japanese *bunjin* emulated not only Chinese literati painting but Chinese academic painting as well as a variety of indigenous art trends, especially that of the RIMPA decorative tradition of the 17th to 19th centuries.

The Japanese *bunjin* generally concentrated on traditional Chinese themes: landscapes, birds-and-flowers, the "four gentlemen" (SHIKUNSHI: plum, orchid, chrysanthemum, and bamboo), and other standard motifs rendered in ink and light color. Compositions were created with layers of brush strokes, and ink tones applied in a wide variety of combinations and patterns. Inscriptions, frequently containing a poem, were an important element of many works and were often added by friends of the artist rather than by the artist himself.

The first generation of Japanese *bunjin* consisted of GION NANKAI, a Confucian scholar of the *samurai* class; SAKAKI HYAKUSEN, a professional artist of merchant background proficient in the Kanō and Tosa styles; and YANAGISAWA KIEN, like Nankai, a Confucian-trained scholar of the samurai class, who shared with Hyakusen an early training in the Kanō tradition. Their common bond was their mutual desire to escape from established methods of artistic expression and to emulate Chinese taste.

The second generation of *bunjin* painters included IKE NO TAIGA, whose style and originality ultimately became a standard of *bunjinga* quality. In addition to his wife, IKE NO GYOKURAN, his more notable disciples included TOTOKI BAIGAI, Kimura Kenkadō (1736–1802), Kuwayama Gyokushū (1743–99), and Noro Kaiseki (1747–1828).

Taiga's close contemporary was Yosa BUSON, admired as the most lyric of all *bunjin* painters and as one of Japan's leading HAIKU poets. Buson's followers were not as numerous as those of Taiga, but two especially, KI BAITEI and the MARUYAMA–SHIJŌ SCHOOL artist MATSUMURA GOSHUN, became well-known figures. Their works might be considered typical of the *bunjinga* movement as a whole in that they illustrate a synthesis of the Buson style of lyricism and the more forceful, spontaneous manner associated with Taiga. YOKOI KINKOKU also demonstrated in his dramatic style a special appreciation of Buson.

Succeeding generations of *bunjinga* artists were more diverse. In Kyōto circles of like-minded literati, artists assembled around such notable figures as URAGAMI GYOKUDŌ and AOKI MOKUBEI. Gyokudō was a true exemplar in both his life and his art of the eccentric "free spirit" inherent in the concept of *bunjinga*. The only later artist to approximate Gyokudō's bold style of painting was Mokubei. Like Gyokudō and many other *bunjin,* Mokubei had other major talents; he made his living and established his fame as a distinguished potter. Other members of the Kyōto *bunjinga* group included OKADA BEISANJIN and his son OKADA HANKŌ, and slightly later, URAGAMI SHUNKIN, YAMAMOTO BAIITSU, TANOMURA CHIKUDEN, NAKABAYASHI CHIKUTŌ, and the literary luminary RAI SAN'YŌ.

Relaxed laws governing foreign imports afforded *bunjinga* artists of the later 18th and 19th centuries greater opportunities to view examples of Chinese painting, and works by such artists as Chikuden reflect a more informed understanding of Chinese styles and aesthetics.

In Edo (now Tōkyō) the influence of art from Europe was strongly felt. Works by the two leading *bunjinga* artists there, TANI BUNCHŌ and WATANABE KAZAN, display a dynamic eclecticism, with influences evident from Western styles, Japanese styles, and the Chinese BIRD-AND-FLOWER PAINTING manner of SHEN NANPIN (Shen Nan-p'in).

The Kyōto artist TOMIOKA TESSAI, who also admired Western painting, is sometimes hailed as the last member of the *bunjinga* school. In the Meiji period (1868–1912), Japanese literati painting was severely criticized by Ernest F. FENOLLOSA, OKAKURA KAKUZŌ (Tenshin), and others as derivative and trivial, and it has only recently been the subject of scholarly study and appreciation.

——James Cahill, *Scholar Painters of Japan: The Nanga School* (1972). Cal French, *The Poet-Painters: Buson and His Followers* (1974). Tōkyō Kokuritsu Hakubutsukan, *Nihon no bunjinga* (1966). Yoshiho Yonezawa and Chū Yoshizawa, *Japanese Painting in the Literati Style,* tr Betty Monroe (1974). Yoshizawa Chū, Yamakawa Takeshi, et al, *Nanga to shasei* in vol 18 of *Genshoku Nihon no bijutsu* (1969).   Cal FRENCH

Bunka and Bunsei eras

Strictly, the years 1804–18 (Bunka era) and 1818–30 (Bunsei era); more broadly, the long rule (1787–1837) of the shōgun TOKUGAWA IENARI—of which they were the central portion—as well as the years when Ienari ruled as retired shōgun (ŌGOSHO) until his death in 1841. The Bunka and Bunsei eras were a time of political stability and economic prosperity, but signs of the catastrophe that was to overtake the Tokugawa shogunate from the 1830s onward were already apparent. Shogunal mismanagement of the economy hastened the breakdown of the entire BAKUHAN SYSTEM on which the shogunate was founded. In the rural villages, agricultural production foundered, and population decreased as the trend toward raising cash crops became more pronounced. The intrusion of foreign ships into Japanese waters threatened the policy of NATIONAL SECLUSION. At the same time, the arts flourished as never before among townsmen and the wealthier farmers.

The Shogunate and the Economy —— The first six years of Ienari's rule, the period of the chief senior councillor (*rōjū shuseki*) MATSUDAIRA SADANOBU and the KANSEI REFORMS (1787–93), were marked by great austerity and political probity. Thereafter Ienari surrounded himself with such men as Mizuno Tadaakira (1762–1834; *rōjū* from 1818) and Tanuma Okimasa (the fourth son of TANUMA OKITSUGU), who conducted a regime of unparalleled corruption and encouraged Ienari in an extravagance that threatened to bankrupt the shogunate. To replenish the treasury, the gold and silver coinage was debased on eight separate occasions between 1818 and 1832, resulting in extreme inflation.

During this period, far-reaching changes took place on the farms. In the Ōsaka region and throughout western Japan there was a rapid increase in the production of cash crops like cotton and rapeseed and of manufactured goods, and farmers sought to bypass the wholesale merchant monopolies (KABUNAKAMA) in Ōsaka by selling directly to merchants in other provinces. The resulting commercialization of the agricultural economy destroyed the self-sufficiency of the rural areas and severely disrupted their traditional society. While many farmers prospered, many more were reduced to tenantry or forced to migrate to the cities. Although there were no significant crop failures during this period, and rural prosperity remained generally high, peasant uprisings (HYAKUSHŌ IKKI) and urban riots (UCHIKOWASHI) became more frequent.

In view of these signs of social dislocation, which threatened the very structure of the *bakuhan* system, in 1805 the shogunate established the Kantō Law Enforcement Division (Kantō Torishimari Deyaku) to strengthen public security. In 1827 it instituted a system of local law enforcement, known as *yoseba kumiai mura,* in the Kantō region.

Arrival of Foreign Ships —— From about 1800 foreign ships appeared with alarming frequency in Japanese waters. The arrival of A. E. LAXMAN and N. P. REZANOV may be seen as part of Russian plans to develop Siberia and to increase trade in the North Pacific. In the PHAETON INCIDENT of 1808, the British directly challenged the Dutch monopoly of the NAGASAKI TRADE. The shogunate tightened maritime defenses and promoted exploration of EZO (now Hokkaidō), annexing that entire region between 1807 and 1821. Determined to adhere to its seclusion policy, in 1825 the shogunate issued an order to expel foreign ships (GAIKOKUSEN UCHIHARAI REI). It also suppressed those who advocated opening the country, imprisoning several in the BANSHA NO GOKU incident of 1839.

Culture and Learning —— This period is perhaps best remembered as one of cultural brilliance. The culture of the townsmen (*chōnin bunka*), led by the merchant class, had been centered in the Kyōto–Ōsaka region since the GENROKU ERA (1688–1704); now it was focused in Edo (now Tōkyō) and matured aesthetically. The novels of Takizawa BAKIN, RYŪTEI TANEHIKO, and JIPPENSHA IKKU, the plays of TSURUYA NAMBOKU, the *ukiyo-e* prints of Andō HIROSHIGE and Katsushika HOKUSAI, and the *haiku* of Kobayashi ISSA are all examples of a great flourishing of the arts.

The coming of foreign ships brought about a renewed interest and advance in WESTERN LEARNING, particularly in natural history, economics, and medicine. Knowledge of the outside world inevitably resulted in criticism of the shogunate's isolationist policies. As the weaknesses of the Tokugawa shogunate were laid bare, there was also an upsurge in classical Japanese learning (KOKUGAKU, or National Learning). The scholar HIRATA ATSUTANE argued that the imperial institution should be restored to its former position of primacy in the state, an idea that was to inspire the anti-Tokugawa movement in the final years of the shogunate.

                                                KAWAUCHI Hachirō

Bunka Hōsō → Nippon Cultural Broadcasting, Inc

Bunka shūreishū

Early-Heian-period imperial anthology of classical Chinese poetry (*kanshi*); compiled in 818 by FUJIWARA NO FUYUTSUGU and others at the behest of Emperor Saga. It contains some 140 poems in the

Chinese *shi (shih)* form arranged topically according to the classification scheme found in the *Wen xuan (Wen hsüan;* J: *Monzen),* a 6th-century Chinese anthology of poetry and prose which greatly influenced Japanese writing in classical Chinese at the time. See CHINESE LITERATURE AND JAPANESE LITERATURE.

bunke → honke and bunke

bunko → paperback books

bunkokuhō

(domainal codes). The laws *(hō)* by which the SENGOKU DAIMYŌ or regional hegemons of the Sengoku period (1467–1568) controlled their territories *(bunkoku).* Also known as Sengoku *kahō* (Sengoku house laws). With the breakdown of the authority of the MURO-MACHI SHOGUNATE, the Sengoku daimyō consolidated their holdings as virtually independent political and economic entities and drew up their own domainal laws. These were often extensions of old family laws (KAKUN) but were also strongly influenced by the laws of the shogunate, particularly the GOSEIBAI SHIKIMOKU (1232) drawn up by the Kamakura shogunate (1192–1333).

In general, *bunkokuhō* reflected the twin roles of the Sengoku daimyō as proprietary lord of his domain and as master of his vassals. The most important regulations concerned the control of vassals. The lord reserved the right to interfere with a vassal's succession to an estate or family name and also to approve his marriage or decision to take holy orders. There were also restrictions on travel and prohibitions concerning the transmission of messages to other domains or the hiring of merchants from other domains as servants. Regulations concerning commoners were equally stringent; they were forbidden from cultivating lands in secret or from moving or running away. Under *bunkokuhō,* offenders were severely punished, kinsmen or close associates frequently being punished as well *(renza).* The practice of punishing both parties in a feud (KENKA RYŌSEIBAI) also came to be widely applied.

Some representative domainal codes are the ŌUCHIKE KABEGAKI (1459–95) of the Ōuchi family, the Imagawa Kana Mokuroku (1526) drawn up by Imagawa Ujichika, the SHINGEN KAHŌ (1547; 1554) of Takeda Shingen, the YOSHIHARU SHIKIMOKU (1567), and the YŪ-KIKE HATTO (1556) of Yūki Masakatsu. Many of these were incorporated by the Tokugawa shogunate in the early 1600s when it drew up its own laws for governing the country.

The ties between lord and retainer in this period were far weaker than they were to be in the Edo period (1600–1868). Retainers frequently defied their own lord and joined the service of another one. The relatively powerful status enjoyed by retainers is reflected in some *bunkokuhō,* which were designed to curb despotic tendencies or arbitrary actions on the part of the lord. The Yoshiharu Shikimoku is a typical example of this type of law. MOMOSE Kesao

Bunkyō Ward

(Bunkyō Ku). One of the 23 wards of Tōkyō. On the eastern edge of the Musashino Plateau. A residential area with many schools and universities and printing and publishing firms. Popular sights include the Kōrakuen Garden, Rikugien Garden, Koishikawa Botanic Garden, the temple Gokokuji, and Yushima Seidō, a Confucian shrine. Pop: 202,239.

Bunkyū Sannen Hachigatsu Jūhachinichi no Seihen → Coup d'Etat of 30 September 1863

bunraku

The professional puppet theater of Japan. From an embryonic beginning in the early 17th century, it developed rapidly to attain its ultimate phase of artistic perfection and maturity during the 18th century and, since that time, has been perpetuated by performers who have striven to maintain the high standards of artistry and the many traditions associated with the theater. It is one of the three major surviving forms of art—the others being HAIKU poetry and the KABUKI theater—that the Japanese developed during the Edo period (1600–1868), when their country was a world unto itself, virtually isolated from nations that lay beyond her protective waters.

Bunraku——Performance

Principal operator with puppets in the final scene of Chikamatsu Monzaemon's play *Sonezaki shinjū.* The lovers Tokubei and Ohatsu have paused on a bridge as they make their way toward Sonezaki, the site of their double suicide. Unlike the principal operator, assistant puppeteers (right) remain hooded during the performance.

Bunraku——Performance

Scene from the popular sixth act of *Kanadehon chūshingura.* Suspected of disloyalty by his comrades, who have pledged to avenge the murder of their lord, retainer Hayano Kampei (left) performs *harakiri.* While he is dying his innocence is proved, and Senzaki Yagorō (right) rescinds an earlier decision and adds Kampei's name to the list of loyal retainers.

The name *bunraku* is of relatively recent origin. Originally it designated a troupe organized in the early 19th century by Uemura Bunrakuken (d 1810), an entrepreneur who had come to the city of Ōsaka from the nearby island of Awaji (Awajishima). Because this troupe is the only one to have endured commercially in modern Japan, its name has become synonymous with the professional puppet theater. The more precise Japanese term for "puppet theater," *ayatsuri jōruri,* appropriately denotes the component elements of the theater: *ayatsuri* means "puppetry" and JŌRURI refers to the dramatic text and the art of chanting it. Historically, it was the fortuitous joining of two independent art forms, puppetry and *jōruri,* that gave birth to the Japanese puppet theater, which is now called bunraku.

Conventions of the Theater——The bunraku theater presents dramas both serious and entertaining, as well as beautifully choreographed dances, for an audience primarily of adults with cultivated sensibilities. Parts of a performance may be as profound and moving as any Western tragedy, while other parts may be as sprightly and amusing as a musical comedy. The performance is a composite of four elements: the puppets, which are approximately one-half to two-thirds life size; the movement given to the puppets by their operators; the chanter, who transforms the words of the text into a dramatic performance; and the rhythmical musical accompaniment provided by the player of the three-stringed SHAMISEN (or *samisen).* To add further to the complexity of the performance, each puppet portraying a major character is operated jointly by three men.

Bunraku———Stage

Performance in progress at the National Theater of Japan, Tōkyō. The chanter and the *shamisen* accompanist are seated on a revolving dais to the audience's right. The puppet stage is equipped with partitions that both partially conceal puppeteers and provide the floor level for puppets.

Bunraku———Puppet operators

View from the wings. A chief operator on elevated clogs manipulates a puppet in the passage formed by the partitions of the *bunraku* stage.

Bunraku puppets, unlike European marionettes, are not operated by strings. The principal operator with his left arm and hand supports the puppet and manipulates the mechanisms controlling the movable eyelids, eyeballs, eyebrows, and mouth; with his right hand he operates the puppet's right arm. The first assistant functions solely to operate the puppet's left arm, and the second assistant operates the puppet's legs. Most female puppets do not have legs, for Japanese women of premodern times generally wore flowing robes of ankle length or longer which concealed the lower body. The movements of a female puppet's legs are represented through the appropriate manipulating and shaping of the lower part of the *kimono*. The play *Sonezaki shinjū* (1703; tr *The Love Suicides at Sonezaki,* 1961) contains an unusual turn in the plot that hinges on the hero caressing the heroine's foot. Because the heroine's foot in this instance must be seen by the audience, a replica of a foot is held so as to protrude below the hem of the kimono and then dropped to the floor, out of the view of the audience, at the conclusion of the episode.

The puppeteers are usually dressed inconspicuously in black robes of coarse weave; the assistant operators wear black hoods over their heads and are "invisible" insofar as the audience is concerned. Though the principal operator may also be similarly hooded—usually in scenes that require the utmost delicacy in the expression of emotion by the puppets—he is most often seen full face by the audience. Like the distinguished chanters and *shamisen* players, he is a celebrated figure in the theater. At times bedecked in ceremonial dress of lustrous black silk, or even luminous white silk and a ceremonial vest of brilliant hue, he becomes a part of the total visual spectacle. The first assistant may perform unhooded and colorfully attired, but only in special dance pieces.

The chanter typically speaks on behalf of all puppets on the stage—men, women, and children—and so his vocal range must extend from a raspy bass to a silky falsetto. Occasionally, when the scene is one of pageantry, several chanters may perform together, each assigned to speak on behalf of one of several puppets on stage, as in the grand opening scene and the famous teahouse scene in the best known of all bunraku plays, *Kanadehon chūshingura* (1748; tr *Chūshingura: The Treasury of Loyal Retainers,* 1971). Pageantry is, in the main, a borrowing from the kabuki theater.

A distinguishing aural feature of bunraku is the melodious, deep-toned strumming of the solo *shamisen,* which contrasts with the lively high-pitched tanging of the tenor *shamisen* of the kabuki theater. In kabuki, an ensemble of 10 or more *shamisen* may perform in unison or heterophonically in such colorful plays as those known collectively as the KABUKI JŪHACHIBAN (repertory of 18 spectacular kabuki plays). In bunraku, the exceptional use of a *shamisen* ensemble occurs usually when a kabuki extravaganza is adapted for performance in the puppet theater.

The performance of bunraku requires a coordination of effort by the various performers so that the synchronization of puppets, voice, and *shamisen* seems always to be perfect. The coordination seems almost magical because there is no visual contact between the puppeteers on stage and the chanter and *shamisen* player, who face the audience from their elevated position slightly removed from the stage. The *shamisen* player assumes the role of conductor; the pace of the narrative and the timing of the action are dictated by his strumming. There are exceptions, however, as in the fourth act of *Kanadehon chūshingura* when En'ya Hangan, condemned to death by HARAKIRI, slowly takes up his dagger and then pauses briefly before plunging the blade into his side. Because the strumming and chanting must be resumed simultaneously with the sudden movement of the puppet, all eyes must then be focused on the puppeteers, who will give the cue.

The audience of bunraku is entertained in many ways. Spectators may glance occasionally at the source of the melodious song or impassioned chanting, for the connoisseur is said to attend performances primarily to listen. Many will watch the *shamisen* player as he demonstrates his virtuosity in strumming an interlude while the set is being changed. Others might shift their gaze momentarily to the doll operators in admiration of their expressive interpretation. The puppet, however, is the ultimate object of attention, and the audience may laugh and weep with the dolls, which on stage seem to be infused with life.

Early History——The earliest extant written reference to puppetry in Japan dates from the 11th century. Doubtless even earlier, itinerant hunters and their women earned money by entertaining in the cities, the men presenting episodic plays with small puppets, which they operated with their hands, and the women working as prostitutes. Their outlandish attire and nomadic ways, quite uncommon in the primarily agricultural society of Japan, led the Japanese of those times to believe that those people had come from the Asian mainland. Eventually, it is said, they settled in untaxed lands throughout Japan, with an unusually large number becoming domiciled in the area of Nishinomiya, near the present city of Kōbe, and in Sanjō on the island of Awaji, which even today is known as the birthplace of professional puppetry.

The traditional accounts of the origin of puppetry on Awajishima lend considerable dignity to both the art and its performers. According to one such account, a Shintō priest by the name of Dōkumbō from Nishinomiya kept the sea calm by praying to Ebisu, the patron god of fishermen. When Dōkumbō died and the sea again became tempestuous, another priest, named Hyakudayū, had a doll made in the image of Dōkumbō and spoke prayers to the god Ebisu through the mouth of the doll, impersonating the voice of the dead priest. The fame of Hyakudayū's skill at puppetry spread widely, and he was summoned to the capital for a command performance at the imperial palace. Such was his success that he was assigned the task of pacifying deities in many provinces. His travels eventually brought him to Sanjō village on Awajishima, where he was stricken with illness and died, and his disciples transmitted the art of puppetry to the villagers. Be that as it may, in western Japan in the 16th century, it was not uncommon to see a puppeteer operating a pair of dolls on a stage made of a wooden box carried chest high, enacting episodes from the lives of famous warriors of the past.

Also during the 16th century and earlier, blind bards garbed in Buddhist robes were chanting historic episodes described in the HEIKE MONOGATARI (The Tale of the Heike), a medieval narrative that depicts the epic war between the Taira and Minamoto families which took place in the 12th century. These bards accompanied themselves on the lute, an instrument that originated in Persia and was transmitted in ancient times through China to Japan. During the tumultuous closing decades of the 16th century, a form of melodic narrative called KŌWAKA or *kowaka-mai* came to be highly favored among the warring feudal barons, some of whom preferred the pathos it evoked to the subdued elegance of the NŌ drama. The performers of the *kowaka-mai* chanted tales describing the heroic feats and tragedies of medieval warriors—in particular, the Genji general MINAMOTO NO YOSHITSUNE (1159–89), who is the best liked of all heroes in Japanese history, and the famed Soga brothers, who devoted their short lives to a vendetta that culminated in 1193 in their slaying of the man who had murdered their father. See SOGA MONOGATARI.

The chanting of medieval narratives changed remarkably with the evolution of a style of chanting called *jōruri*. The name *jōruri* was derived from one of the first works to be chanted in this style, *Jōruri Hime monogatari* (Tale of the Lady Jōruri) or *Jūnidan sōshi* (Story in Twelve Parts), a story about the young Yoshitsune courting and winning the love of the beautiful Lady Jōruri, and of Jōruri, after Yoshitsune is dead, invoking Shintō and Buddhist deities to restore him to life. It was also about that time, in the late 16th century, that the *shamisen* was imported into Japan from Okinawa; that three-stringed instrument with its exotic sound came to be preferred over the lute as an instrumental accompaniment for the chanters of *jōruri*. *Shamisen* players developed great virtuosity on the instrument and composed many new melodies which, in turn, influenced the style of *jōruri* chanters.

According to the earliest accounts of such collaboration, a Buddhist miracle play titled *Amida no munewari* (Amida's Riven Breast) was performed in 1614 before the retired emperor Go-Yōzei (1571–1617), and the puppeteer may well have been Hikida Awaji no Jō, who is said to have founded the first professional puppet troupe on Awajishima. The true origin, however, is shrouded in obscurity. Bunraku caught the fancy of the townspeople—commoners who were low on the social ladder but who came gradually to dominate the economy, art, and material culture of the new era. With little access to the Nō drama, by then largely restricted to the aristocracy, including the *samurai*, the townspeople welcomed the colorful, quick-paced, lively spectacle of the new popular theater—first kabuki, and then bunraku.

Stages of Development—— Although puppetry thrived initially in the new city of Edo (now Tōkyō) largely on the strength of plays depicting the exploits of an imaginary hero named Kimpira and his three stalwart companions, by the mid-17th century it was flourishing principally in Ōsaka and Kyōto, where puppeteers and chanters of *jōruri* were achieving new heights of artistry. The popularity of bunraku rose in spectacular fashion in 1686, when the chanter Takemoto Gidayū (1651–1714) of Ōsaka emerged from relative obscurity to garner accolades for the virile strength and beauty of his chanting style. It was his collaboration, however, with the greatest playwright of the Edo period, CHIKAMATSU MONZAEMON (1653–1724), that led to the transformation of bunraku from popular entertainment into artistic theater. Until then, plays had been based mostly on *kōwaka-mai* texts and other stories written in the two or three centuries preceding the Edo period, as well as such primitive *jōruri* pieces as *Lady Jōruri* and those about the legendary Kimpira.

Chikamatsu employed the imagery, diction, and literary techniques of classical prose, drama, and poetry in writing plays that focused on both historical and contemporary subjects and that emphasized prevalent codes of morality and ethics as thematic material. The success of his *Love Suicides at Sonezaki*, first produced in 1703, started a vogue for dramas treating love affairs between merchants and prostitutes. In most of these the tragedy results from the inability of a pair of lovers to resolve the conflict between accepted social codes and their own emotions. (See GIRI AND NINJŌ.)

In the early stages of the development of bunraku, only the puppets were fully visible to the audience; the doll operators, chanter,

fukeoyama (mature woman character type)

musume (unmarried young woman character type)

Bunshichi (mature warrior character type)

Danshichi (forceful warrior character type)

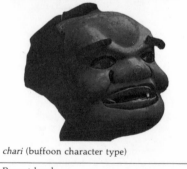
chari (buffoon character type)

Bunraku——Puppet heads

Puppet heads *(kashira)* are divided into types based on age, sex, and temperament. Some types like Bunshichi and Danshichi are named after the role for which they were originally used; however, all heads are used for a variety of roles, modified by costume and wig changes.

and *shamisen* player performed behind a curtain stretched across the stage. The puppets were held aloft and operated by hands thrust up through the skirt. When *Love Suicides at Sonezaki* was presented, the celebrated puppeteer Tatsumatsu Hachirobei attempted a daring innovation by operating the heroine doll in full view of the audience; his unusual good looks doubtless contributed to the success of this experiment. Thus began the tradition of including the doll operators in the visual presentation of bunraku. In 1705, Takemoto Gidayū chanted one act of a new play in full view of the audience, and this marked the beginning of the tradition of adding the chanter and shamisen player as well to the total visual spectacle of the theater.

Takemoto Gidayū died in 1714, and his successor, Gidayū II, could not duplicate his chanting style. With the specific intent of creating a play that would give advantage to the idiosyncratic chanting style of Gidayū II, Chikamatsu wrote *Kokusen'ya kassen* (tr *The Battles of Coxinga*, 1951), which opened in 1715 and enjoyed a record run of 17 months. The play, with its setting in China, focused on the theme of sacrificing beloved ones for the cause of moral righteousness. Another successful Chikamatsu play performed in 1721 by Gidayū II was *Onna-goroshi abura no jigoku* (tr *The Woman Killer and the Hell of Oil*, 1961), in which an ineffectual hero follows an obviously inevitable path toward self-destruction because of his inherent moral weaknesses.

Many of the techniques used in bunraku today were developed after Chikamatsu's death. In 1727, puppets acquired movable eyelids and mouths and prehensile hands. In the year following, the location of the chanter and *shamisen* player was shifted away from a lowered position in front of stage center to the right of the stage, as seen from the audience. The three-man puppet was introduced in 1734, and by 1736 puppets could roll their eyes and move their eyebrows. Set designs and stage mechanisms became much more elaborate.

At this time, the kabuki theater with its host of talented actors and a repertory of crowd-pleasing plays (many of them borrowed from bunraku) began seriously to challenge the commercial supremacy of bunraku. In the course of the preceding century, doll operators had so refined their technique as to achieve the maximum effect of stylized realism in character portrayal. Kabuki actors adopted many of the puppets' gestures in order to enhance their own performance. They were influenced also by the singing and chanting style of bunraku. When a bunraku play was adapted for the kabuki stage, the actors often imitated the puppets whose roles they were acting.

The heads of bunraku puppets represent character types rather than unique individuals—for example, the same *musume* (maiden) head is used to represent all young, beautiful, good-hearted heroines, and the head called Bunshichi (the name of a male character) is used for puppets of righteous middle-aged males tormented by a deep-felt grief. The characterizations, therefore, tend to be two-dimensional rather than rounded. A portrayal by an uncomely or clumsy actor would naturally be inferior to that by a handsome puppet speaking with the marvelous voice of a professional chanter. Still, an actor's individuality inevitably emerges in performance, despite the stylized costume and makeup, and gifted actors often add new dimensions of interpretation to the roles they perform on the kabuki stage. Bunraku performers, therefore, borrowed in turn from the kabuki theater. In the teahouse scene in *Kanadehon chūshingura*, for instance, the puppet's portrayal of the hero Yuranosuke is modeled on the interpretation given the role by the great kabuki actor of Edo, SAWAMURA SŌJŪRŌ (1685–1756). In a kabuki version of the same play presented in 1772, a villainous character named Sadakurō was transformed by the actor Nakamura Nakazō (1736–80) from a shabby, rustic highwayman into a tawdry big-city rogue. The same Sadakurō in bunraku has far greater audience appeal when he is groomed and dressed like his kabuki counterpart.

The Final Stage —— Bunraku attained its full flowering in the mid-18th century, particularly during the period of its artistic rivalry with kabuki, by which it tended more and more to be overshadowed. With the passing of the better playwrights, bunraku declined gradually, even though its performers attained new heights of artistry and skill. Innovations have been attempted in an effort to attract a larger audience, but modernity does not seem to blend well into the traditional fabric of the puppet theater. The production of *Hamlet* deserves mention in the history of bunraku as an experiment, not as a mark of artistic achievement. Even when modern Japanese characters are presented—Emperor Meiji (1852–1912) and General Nogi Maresuke (1849–1912) of Russo-Japanese War fame,

for instance—the awkwardness of puppets wearing Western trousers shatters the illusion of reality so completely that the effect seems ludicrous.

Bunraku has had its vicissitudes, especially after Japan's defeat in 1945. Bunraku, along with many other arts, languished as more and more Japanese looked askance at the older, traditional aspects of their own culture. Dissension within the bunraku theater itself, over whether or not to become unionized, led to a breach that in 1949 divided the theater into two smaller, rival troupes, neither of which had the resources or assemblage of illustrious performers needed to stage the kinds of captivating productions that would continually attract theatergoers. By the time the troupes were reunited in 1963, bunraku was tottering on the verge of commercial extinction.

Members of the bunraku theater have been devoting much effort to cultivating an appreciation of their art among school-age Japanese. Their productions have been viewed enthusiastically by audiences in the United States and Europe. The Japanese government has lent them support, bestowing recognition on the most distinguished performers by designating them LIVING NATIONAL TREASURES. The most recent to be so honored are the superb puppeteer Kiritake Monjūrō II (1900–1970), the *shamisen* player Tsuruzawa Kanji VI (1887–1975), known for his full sound and delicate melodies, and the magnificent chanter Takemoto Tsudayū IV (b 1917).

Thanks to a new appreciation of things traditional among younger Japanese, bunraku may enjoy a mild revival. The question remains, however, will the performers remain adequate in both quality and number to sustain the theater? Traditionally, a puppeteer must spend 10 years operating only the legs, and another 10 years operating the left arm, before he may become a principal operator. The training of chanters and *shamisen* players is equally rigorous. The aspirant must selflessly dedicate himself to the theater, for his is a profession that places great demands on him while providing few rewards. Nevertheless, he may derive great satisfaction from looking back into the past in order to transmit traditional Japanese artistic and human values to the future.

—— Barbara Adachi, *The Voices and Hands of Bunraku* (1978). Bunrakuza, ed, *Bunraku* (1959). C. J. Dunn, *The Early Japanese Puppet Drama* (1966). Donald Keene, *The Battles of Coxinga* (1951). Donald Keene, *Bunraku* (1965). Donald Keene, *World within Walls* (1976). Donald Keene, tr, *Major Plays of Chikamatsu* (1961). Donald Keene, tr, *Chūshingura: The Treasury of Loyal Retainers* (1971). Donald H. Shively, *The Love Suicide at Amijima* (1953). Wakatsuki Yasuji, *Ningyō jōruri shi kenkyū* (1943). James T. ARAKI

Bunroku Keichō no Eki → invasions of Korea in 1592 and 1597

Bunten

Abbreviation of Mombushō Bijutsu Tenrankai (Ministry of Education Fine Arts Exhibition). Annual exhibitions begun in 1907 under official government sponsorship. With the rising interest in art during the Meiji period (1868–1912), the Ministry of Education appointed a group of established artists to the Bijutsu Shinsa Iinkai (Fine Arts Screening Committee) to select works of art for its official exhibitions. The Bunten was thereafter held each year until 1918. In 1919 the committee was disbanded because of growing discord between artists of traditional and Western styles. The Imperial Fine Arts Academy (Teikoku Bijutsuin) was next formed to take responsibility for an annual exhibition, to be named Teiten (Teikoku Bijutsu Tenrankai; Imperial Fine Arts Exhibition). Despite the reorganization, in-fighting continued, prompting Minister of Education Matsuda Genji (1875–1936) to reorganize the academy in 1935. This move only led to more heated disputes and to the 1937 dissolution of the Imperial Fine Arts Academy and the subsequent creation that same year of a new body, the Imperial Art Academy (Teikoku Geijutsuin) whose purview included literature and music, as well as the visual arts. The Ministry of Education then took direct supervision of the exhibitions, which were renamed Shin Bunten (New Bunten), and continued them until 1944. The Shin Bunten resumed activities after World War II, in 1946, under the name Nihon Bijutsu Tenrankai (Nitten; Japan Art Exhibition). Under the Allied Occupation the Nitten was placed under the management of JAPAN ART ACADEMY (Nihon Geijutsuin). However, the Japan Art Academy itself remained under the Ministry of Education, and the Nitten thus came under severe attack for its strongly establishment character. Since 1958 it has been run by a corporation formed for the purpose, Nitten, Inc.

burakumin

Japan's largest minority group, the *burakumin,* have the same racial, cultural, and national origins as the rest of their fellow Japanese. As a people physically not distinguishable from any other Japanese, they intermingle with the rest of the populace, but when identified as *burakumin,* they are subject to prejudice and discrimination. Oppression against the ancestors of this group began hundreds of years ago when the group in power adopted a social stratification system to protect its own status and class. Indignities persist because the *burakumin* continue to be labeled and regarded as somehow hereditarily different from the majority.

It is not clearly known when and why this group became differentiated from the rest of Japanese society. The word *burakumin* itself dates from the late 19th century. When the coexistence of Buddhism and indigenous Shintō came about in the early part of the Heian period (794–1185), the Shintō association of pollution with death was linked with the Buddhist teaching against the killing of animals. Those who were engaged in work dealing with the dead and slaughtering of animals were considered polluted, and this defilement was thought to be contagious. Thus, not only was contact with people engaged in such occupations shunned, but there also emerged a pattern of residential segregation. Early references to the *eta* ("pollution abundant") as "butchers" *(toji)* and "river-bank dwellers" *(kawaramono)* are found in written sources published in the Kamakura period (1185–1333). It was during the Edo period (1600–1868) that discrimination was formalized and legalized through the warrior-farmer-artisan-merchant-*eta-hinin (shi-nō-kō-shō-eta-hinin)* hierarchical status system.

The label HININ (nonhuman) was first used in the Nara period (710–794) to refer to a person taking part in a treasonous plot against the emperor. Later, people who tried to escape from corvée labor and other services to the imperial family were included in the nonhuman category. Persons who became beggars and vagrants were also called *hinin.* During the early feudal period actors *(maimai),* SARUGAKU performers, and fabric dyers *(aoya)* were designated as *eta-hinin,* although the two outcaste groups remained separate endogamous groups. In the Edo period the *hinin* made a living mainly in entertainment, the guarding of criminals, and begging, while the *eta* had a virtual monopoly in occupations associated with animal processing and the production of leather goods. Sometimes people were put into the *hinin* category as punishment for certain crimes, such as adultery or attempted double suicide. Such individuals could in certain circumstances be reinstated through a specified act of contrition or securement of a respected sponsor and payment of a fee.

The central and local governments of the Edo period had numerous regulations that rigidly controlled the occupation, residence, marriage, style of dress, and social behavior of the outcastes. They were permitted to work in only those occupations thought to be polluting, demanding, or undesirable. They disposed of the dead, tended graves, guarded tombs, swept streets, and collected garbage. They also worked as butchers, tanners, and leather craftsmen. They also were allowed to engage in the making of bamboo goods, straw sandals, and lamp wicks. Their residence was limited to designated hamlets *(buraku;* hence the term *burakumin).* During the Edo period, when class distinction, prejudice, and discrimination were most marked, a *burakumin* youth was beaten to death by a gang. The case was brought before the Edo magistrate, and the decision handed down was that an *eta* was worth only one-seventh of a commoner.

In 1871 the new Meiji government issued an edict legally abolishing the derogatory names of *eta* and *hinin* and stipulating that they be treated as "new common people." No follow-through measures were provided to implement their emancipation, however, and they continued to be relegated to "unclean" work while at the same time losing their monopoly on the more lucrative leather-crafts industry. The emancipation edict had little effect on the Japanese people in general and only worsened economic conditions for the *burakumin.* The *koseki* (household register) system, as well as the existence of special hamlets, made the *burakumin,* now officially known as *shin heimin* (new commoners), liable to ready identification.

One response to continued discrimination was the organization in 1902 of the Bisaku Heiminkai (Bisaku Common People's Association) by young men from a town in Okayama Prefecture. Similar associations were established in many other localities where oppression against the *burakumin* prevailed. Their main objective was to urge *burakumin* to better themselves socially, economically, and educationally so that they would be accepted into the mainstream society. However, such organizations had little effect in altering the deeply embedded discriminatory attitude of the majority of the people toward the *burakumin.*

In 1922 the Suiheisha (Levelers or Equalizers) movement was founded. The tactic changed from self-improvement to thorough denunciation *(tetteiteki kyūdan):* those who discriminated were to be forced to apologize. Following a hiatus during World War II, the fight against discrimination was reactivated when former leaders of the Suiheisha established the Buraku Kaihō Zenkoku Iinkai (All-Japan Committee for Buraku Liberation). At its Tenth Annual Convention in 1955, the hundreds of national delegates endorsed changing its name to Buraku Kaihō Dōmei (Buraku Liberation League). The group, now reorganized, worked toward the goal of equality made explicit in the new postwar constitution. It continued to challenge discrimination on the individual level and increased activities on the societal level, with a focus on ending discriminatory practices in the structure of Japan's family, government, economic, and educational systems.

In response to the movement, the national government established a Special Integration Policy Deliberation Committee in 1965. After several years of investigation and deliberation, the first specific policy for improving the lot of the *burakumin* was implemented by the government; the enabling law took effect in 1969, with funding to cover a 10-year period. The main objectives of the integration law were to improve living conditions in the ghettos *(dōwa chiku)* and to promote programs to eradicate discrimination. While substantial improvements have been made in a number of ghettos, many have received almost no benefits from the special integration policy. The integration law was extended for a period of 3 years to 1982 with a stipulation that a more realistic appraisal be made of conditions relating to *buraku* issues.

There is considerable statistical variation as to the precise number of *buraku* ghettos and population. A government census of 1935 shows that there were 5,365 *dōwa chiku* and a population of just under a million *burakumin* living in the "special" hamlets located throughout Japan, with concentrations in the Kinki, Chūgoku, Kyūshū, and Shikoku regions. The census taken in 1975 reports that there are 1,841,958 people (of whom 1,119,278 are *burakumin*) living in 4,374 ghettos. Thousands of non-*burakumin* have moved into *dōwa chiku* for economic reasons, though the 1975 census shows a reduction of almost a thousand *dōwa chiku.* Those who have firsthand knowledge claim that there is a significant undercount of the *buraku* population and ghettos and that discrimination is more widespread than is believed.

For example, in Kagoshima Prefecture, the government census reports that there are 32 *dōwa chiku* and no discrimination, but in reality there are over a hundred *dōwa chiku* and considerable discrimination. Tōkyō prefectural officials admit that discrimination against the *burakumin* still exists, but they state that there are no *dōwa chiku* in the metropolitan area; yet a number of *dōwa chiku* are known to exist. Nagasaki Prefecture reports that there are no *dōwa chiku* and no discrimination, but in reality, there are some 52 ghettos and much discrimination against *burakumin* in employment.

Close to half of eligible *burakumin* workers were unemployed several years ago when the unemployment rate for the general population was very low. It is estimated that today there are from 2 to 3 million *burakumin,* or over 2 percent of the Japanese people, over 5,000 *dōwa chiku,* and continued discrimination, especially in marriage and employment. Thousands of "passing" *burakumin* live outside the ghettos, and while their identities remain unknown, there is always the fear that they will become "visible" through the private investigations into one's personal background that are routinely carried out in Japanese society on such occasions as marriage and employment.

The effect of past and current discrimination is still apparent in the *burakumin*'s lower educational attainment and economic and social status when compared with the mainstream population. Occasionally, when shattered marriage plans or hopeless job applications lead to tragedies such as suicide, the public is sympathetic, but until recently there has been very little information about the *burakumin* in the mass media. Even during the 1971 centennial of the emancipation edict, there was virtually no mention of the nation's largest minority by the major communications network.

In the late 1970s, however, leading newspapers did begin reporting on a long-standing conflict between the Burakumin Liberation League and the Japan Communist Party. The Communists insisted that the integration policy of the government should be aimed at all working-class people, rather than focusing on the *burakumin* per se. League members pointed out that, while a disproportionate number of *burakumin* share a marginal existence with members of the lowest socioeconomic class, they are particularly affected by discrimination. The conflict became a major issue in the election and administration of Tōkyō governor MINOBE RYŌKICHI and prompted thousands of league members to demonstrate against the government.

Another mobilizing incident for the league was the Sayama case, which involved a *burakumin* convicted of murder in 1974. Supported by a record number of over 4 million persons who signed a petition attesting to the *burakumin*'s innocence, the league requested the Appeal Court, and subsequently the Supreme Court, to reexamine the murder verdict. In 1977 the Supreme Court, while admitting the evidence was circumstantial, let the lower court decision stand, and refused to examine new evidence of the defense. The trial and decision have become a symbol of discrimination against all *burakumin*. Several political parties, including the Communists, have used incidents such as this to garner votes.

The investigations that are routinely carried out before marriage or employment are often specifically to ascertain whether a person is of *burakumin* background. Over 150 companies in Japan are reported to have purchased a book entitled *Buraku chimei sōkan* (Buraku Locations Register) and several other similar publications. The main purpose of these publications is to make identification of a *burakumin* more readily possible, since the *koseki* (household register) is no longer available to the public except with the permission of the family being investigated.

At present many educators and concerned people are involved in efforts to eliminate discrimination through education. One movement, *dōwa kyōiku* (integration education), began when several teachers became concerned about their *buraku* students' high absence rate and made home visits. In 1978, at the 30th annual conference of the Zenkoku Dōwa Kyōiku Kenkyū Kyōgikai (All-Japan Integration Education and Research Council) some 12,000 people convened in Tōkyō. Currently, *dōwa kyōiku* is a part of education from the nursery to the university level, especially in areas where there are high concentrations of *burakumin*. In the last decade, over 40 institutions of higher learning have begun to offer courses on or related to integration education. There is hope that such educational efforts will minimize discrimination against *burakumin* in the near future; still, deeply embedded prejudices will not easily be eradicated from the Japanese.

I. Roger YOSHINO and Sueo MURAKOSHI

bureaucracy

The organizational machinery and the body of officials charged with administering a nation's public policies. All highly industrialized societies are characterized by both public and private bureaucracies, that is, complex institutions organized into bureaus composed of functional experts. The Japanese public bureaucracy is composed of a single national government bureaucracy, various local governmental bureaucracies, and the bureaucracies of a number of public and semipublic corporations.

History and Development——*Premodern.* Virtually all scholars agree that earlier civilizations such as the Song (Sung) dynasty (960–1279) in China, the New Empire in Egypt, and the Roman Empire had governmental institutions that, for their time, were highly bureaucratized. Yet, Max Weber has convincingly argued that such institutions lacked a number of features typically associated with modern forms of bureaucratic organization and that government bureaucracy, as it is known today, is a comparatively recent development congruent with the emergence of a money economy and the rise of the modern state. Only in 17th-century Europe did governmental organizations begin to manifest the central traits of modern bureaucracy, namely, a fixed and regularized distribution of jurisdictions ordered and delimited by rules, a fixed system of superordination and subordination of offices, the clear separation of public and private spheres of activity, the development of functional expertise, a cadre of officials working more or less full time in their official capacities, and the establishment of relatively stable written rules of behavior.

Bureaucratic precursors can be found in Japan as early as the Nara period (710–794) and possibly even earlier (see RITSURYŌ SYSTEM). Bureaucratic strands wind through all of Japan's subsequent history, and bureaucratic patterns of organization can be found with greater or lesser frequency in different geographical areas and time periods. It was really with the establishment and institutionalization of the Tokugawa shogunate in the early 17th century, however, that the level of national consolidation became sufficiently high to talk meaningfully of a *national* bureaucracy (see BAKUHAN SYSTEM). Even then, the "national" government represented by the shogunate directly controlled only about a quarter of the nation's land area, while the rest was under the relatively autonomous and widely differentiated administration of some 250 different domainal *(han)* governments. In both shogunal and domainal administrations, vassalage, birth, and chance were far more frequent determinants of administrative rank, official duties, and opportunities for promotion than proven technical competence or written regulations. Simultaneously, the development of a civilian bureaucracy was hampered by the ideological and social predominance of the military. Yet during the 250 years of the Tokugawa peace, civilian administration increased in areas such as justice, finance, tax collection, and religious supervision, and the shōgun's administrative office *(goyōbeya)* took on increased significance. Merit was never totally ignored as the basis for appointment during Japan's early history, but as governing became more complex, proven competence became increasingly important as a basis for appointment and promotion. This was particularly so during the later years of the Tokugawa regime, both in the central government and in many of the individual domains, particularly in Satsuma, Chōshū, Mito, and Hizen.

These long-standing trends toward the development of a professional civilian bureaucracy were catalyzed by Commodore PERRY's armed visits (1853 and 1854) and the perceived Western threat to Japanese sovereignty. A premium was placed on competence in areas such as military science, finance, foreign languages, and technology. By the waning years of the Tokugawa regime, vast governmental reorganization had begun, and individuals came increasingly to be recruited for their proven abilities.

Meiji period (1868–1912). A series of steps taken during the early years of the Meiji government provided the basis for the creation of a truly modern national bureaucracy. The abolition of feudal domains and the establishment of the PREFECTURAL SYSTEM in 1871, the LAND TAX REFORM OF 1873–1881, the creation of a standing conscript army (see CONSCRIPTION ORDINANCE OF 1873), and the ending of all *samurai* privileges by 1876 (see SHIZOKU) worked collectively to consolidate the power of the national executive. With the creation of a cabinet system in 1885, the promulgation of Imperial Ordinance No. 37 (Kanri Fukumu Kiritsu) in July 1887, and the introduction of the Meiji CONSTITUTION in 1889, the main outlines of the national bureaucratic system, modeled on that of Prussia, were established. Recruitment was by demonstrated qualifications, typically tested through open and competitive examinations. A strong legalistic basis for bureaucratic activity was established. Tōkyō University was founded with the primary purpose of training technically skilled civil officials. Civilian and military bureaucracies were separated and put on a par, both having direct relations to the emperor. Service was to the emperor and the nation, rather than to region or class. Certain minimal guarantees of security were granted to governmental administrators. Public administration became a permanent career. Written rules assigned differentiated responsibilities among various offices. Four ranks and 14 grades of office differentiated among levels of administrative responsibility.

The architects of the Meiji regime viewed a powerful parliament, local autonomy, elections, and party government as major threats to the strong state, urban-based industrialization, and national coherence that were deemed essential to protect Japanese sovereignty and advance the "national interest." Thus they made efforts to ensure the autonomy and power of the state bureaucracy and to protect efficient administration from the perceived dangers of localism and politics. Personal and organizational relations between government and bureaucracy were intimate; 36 percent of pre–World War II cabinet ministers, for example, were former bureaucrats. Party patronage and the spoils system were correspondingly rather minimal. Although the first party cabinet of ŌKUMA SHIGENOBU and ITAGAKI TAISUKE in 1898 saw an early flirtation with patronage as a means of ensuring political control over the bureaucracy, in 1899 YAMAGATA ARITOMO in conjunction with the PRIVY COUNCIL pushed through an amendment to the 1893 Civil Service Appointment Ordinance (Bunkan Nin'yō Rei) that severely restricted the scope of the appointments that elected politicians could make within the bureaucracy. As the parties and the Diet increased their influence, links between the bureaucracy and parties improved. Top positions in various ministries came to be reallocated following changes in the party in power. But for the most part this meant replacement of one career civil servant by another deemed more favorable to the ruling party. Rarely did a career politician skilled only in matters of practical politics find himself holding a second-, third-, or lower-tier position within the central administration.

A favorable educational background was virtually essential to a high-level bureaucratic career. Tōkyō University had been established in 1877 as a training ground for government administrators, and its Law Faculty became the breeding ground for an elite class of legally and administratively trained civil servants. One study of Japan's Who's Who in 1937 shows that 74 percent of the senior civil servants had graduated from Tōkyō University, a full 47 percent from its Law Faculty. An additional 9 percent came from Kyōto University. Only 17 percent of these top officials lacked a degree from one of these two institutions. In addition, 85 percent of the prefectural governors serving between 1900 and 1945 were graduates of Tōkyō University.

An interesting facet of this educational requirement, however, was that it spurred the creation of a truly meritocratic civil service. Unlike most of the European civil services at the time, Japan's had a disproportionately low percentage boasting noble birth. The same survey mentioned above, for example, shows that 72 percent of these top civil servants came from a commoner background.

Under the Meiji regime, each minister was appointed by, and was directly responsible to, the emperor. Collective cabinet responsibility and the responsibility of the prime minister as head of government were diminished. Particularly significant in this regard was the so-called right of supreme command (tōsuiken), which provided that the emperor had supreme command over the armed forces. Individual military ministers appointed by the emperor were thus responsible directly to him and not to the prime minister, the cabinet, or any other civilian authority. The result was that Meiji Japan had two clearly separate national bureaucracies, one civilian, the other military. The military element was able to manipulate its powers under this right to gain control over the composition of various cabinets and over certain facets of government policy making, particularly during the 1930s.

Both civilian and military bureaucracies exerted extensive power over the formulation of most facets of national policy. Although article 37 of the constitution of 1889 provided that every law required the consent of the Diet, few laws actually originated there. Most were drafted within the various agencies of the national bureaucracy and then presented by the government for ratification. Also important to bureaucratic influence were the so-called IMPERIAL ORDINANCES. Technically issued by the emperor, these ordinances in fact provided an important extralegislative channel for direct bureaucratic control over wide areas of public policy making, a control that carried the important legitimation provided by the imperial seal.

Occupation period. Widespread changes were effected in Japanese society, economics, and politics during the seven years of US military OCCUPATION (1945–52). Many impinged on the government bureaucracy, including the elimination of the military bureaucracy, the dissolution of the HOME MINISTRY, the reduced constitutional status of the emperor, the increased power given to the Diet and local governments, and the constitutional guarantees of civil rights. Moreover, bureaucrats were made responsible to the prime minister and the cabinet, rather than to the emperor. At the same time, no concerted effort was made to alter the socioeconomic composition of the national civil service or to provide structural changes designed to increase the political responsiveness of the bureaucracy, either to elected parliamentary officials or to the general public.

The most noteworthy influence on the civil service was that of the US Personnel Advisory Mission to Japan. Its recommendations (April 1947) were almost exclusively technical, oriented toward the creation of a more efficient civil service. The report called for the introduction of "specialization and scientific management," including detailed standards for recruitment, training, position classification, compensation, employee evaluation, health, safety, welfare, recreation, employee relations, retirement, employment statistics, and the like. Most of these measures were effected through the National Civil Service Law (21 October 1947), which, with the National Government Organization Law (10 July 1948), continues to provide the main legal outline of the national bureaucratic service.

The most politically significant step taken in regard to the national bureaucracy during the Occupation involved placing an explicit ban on the right of public employees to strike and, in most cases, to engage in collective bargaining. This measure, which weakened the power of public sector unions and the political left, has been the cause of continuous controversy in Japanese politics.

The national bureaucracy today. The National Government Organization Law provides for four types of administrative organs: ministries, offices on the ministerial level, agencies, and commissions. The first two compose the primary administrative organs of the national government, with the PRIME MINISTER'S OFFICE (Sōrifu) being the only actual "office on the ministerial level." Agencies and commissions, collectively referred to as external organs (gaikyoku), are outside the direct lines of ministerial organization and oversee various special areas of administration either substantially different from the main work of a ministry or else those that might overlap, or involve conflict with, one or more of the ministries. In that they cannot submit proposed legislation or cabinet orders directly to the Diet, nor issue ministerial orders, they hold slightly less formal power than the ministries or the Prime Minister's Office, but in most other respects they are similar. Examples of agencies are the IMPERIAL HOUSEHOLD AGENCY, the ECONOMIC PLANNING AGENCY, and the DEFENSE AGENCY. Among Japan's commissions are the Fair Trade Commission, the CENTRAL LABOR RELATIONS COMMISSION, the NATIONAL PERSONNEL AUTHORITY, and the NATIONAL DEFENSE COUNCIL.

In 1979 there were 12 main ministries (shō) in the Japanese government (Justice; Foreign Affairs; Finance; Education; Health and Welfare; Agriculture, Forestry, and Fisheries; International Trade and Industry; Transport; Posts and Telecommunications; Labor; Construction; and Home Affairs). Each is headed by a minister (daijin), who is almost invariably an elected member of parliament. The heads of these ministries serve also as members of the cabinet (naikaku). Each minister is assisted politically by one or, in a few instances, two parliamentary vice-ministers (seimu jikan), who are also usually parliamentarians and whose primary responsibilities involve liaison between the ministry and parliament. The minister and the parliamentary vice-minister are typically the only politically responsible officials serving in a ministry; the remainder of the ministry is composed of members of the appointed civil service.

At the top of each ministry's appointed civil service is an administrative vice-minister (jimu jikan), who oversees all administrative matters within the ministry's jurisdiction. Each ministry is typically divided into 6 to 12 functional bureaus (kyoku), headed by bureau chiefs (kyokuchō), plus a secretariat (kambō) responsible for ministerial records, statistics, personnel, public relations, financial accounts, and the like. The bureaus may be subdivided either into several departments (bu), each with a department head (buchō), or directly into anywhere from 4 or 5 to 10 or 12 sections (ka). The section is the basic working unit of a ministry and is headed by a section chief (kachō) and an assistant (fukukachō), who oversee the 20 to 30 people normally assigned to a typical section. Most ministries also include auxiliary organs such as research institutions, hospitals, museums, and libraries. Many also oversee one or more of the detached agencies or commissions mentioned above (e.g., the Tax Administration Agency under the Ministry of Finance or the Social Insurance Agency under the Ministry of Health and Welfare). Finally, each ministry has from one to several dozen advisory committees (shingikai) composed of representatives of private interest groups, and individual experts designed to provide ongoing or temporary advice on matters under the jurisdiction of the ministry.

In addition to their headquarters in the Kasumigaseki area of Tōkyō, most ministries and agencies maintain a number of local offices designed to gather information and to provide services essential to the fulfillment of the agency's mission. Such offices are staffed by members of the national bureaucracy and are responsible to the national headquarters. They are separate from the various local government bureaucracies set up at the prefectural or municipal levels, which are under local control and are staffed by civil servants recruited by and responsible to the various local governments.

In contrast to the 12 main ministries, the Prime Minister's Office has a dual character. The main office (hombu) employs approximately 3,500 individuals and deals with various specialized responsibilities. It is divided into the Prime Minister's Secretariat and divisions dealing with personnel, national prizes and decorations, government pensions, and statistics. In addition, it has several attached institutions such as the SCIENCE COUNCIL OF JAPAN, the NATIONAL ARCHIVES, and the Statistical Training Institute. The main office also oversees some 55 to 60 advisory committees.

In addition, the Prime Minister's Office has a second set of responsibilities, involving oversight of 3 commissions (Fair Trade Commission, NATIONAL PUBLIC SAFETY COMMISSION, and Environmental Disputes Coordination Commission), plus some 10 detached agencies (Imperial Household Agency, ADMINISTRATIVE MANAGEMENT AGENCY, HOKKAIDŌ DEVELOPMENT AGENCY, Defense Agency, Economic Planning Agency, SCIENCE AND TECHNOLOGY AGENCY, ENVIRONMENT AGENCY, OKINAWA DEVELOPMENT AGENCY, NATIONAL LAND AGENCY, and Defense Facilities Administration Agency). Most of these are of slightly lower prestige than the 12 main ministries, but all have an autonomous organizational structure. They are typically organized in roughly the same manner as the main ministries and are headed by ministers of state, several of whom serve in the cabinet.

There are some 1.2 million full-time personnel in the Japanese national government. Of these, some 297,000 (25 percent) are members of the SELF DEFENSE FORCES (269,000) and Defense Agency personnel (28,000). An additional 357,000 (30 percent) work in one of the five government enterprises (POSTAL SERVICE, national forestry service, government printing, government mint, and alcohol monopoly). Slightly over 125,000 more (10 percent) are part of the national school system. The remaining 421,000 or so make up the general administrative staff of the national government. Most of this last group are assigned to one of the 12 main ministries or one of the dozen or so bodies in the Prime Minister's Office. Finally, the national government employs 800,000 so-called temporary employees, most of whom work for a governmental agency on nearly a full-time basis but lack the additional stature and benefits provided by a technically full-time appointment.

Local government bureaucracy. Japan has a two-tiered system of local government. The 47 larger units (*to, dō, fu,* and *ken*) are known collectively as prefectures. Within these prefectures are some 3,300 cities (*shi*), towns (*chō*), and villages (*son* or *mura*) known collectively as municipalities. The municipality is the lowest level of government. There are no county governments or unincorporated areas in Japan. Thus, all Japanese citizens are simultaneously residents of both a municipality and a prefecture.

Each local government is organized to take on a variety of administrative functions that differ somewhat with its size, geography, and socioeconomic characteristics. Almost all personnel who work for a local governmental body have the status of local civil service personnel. These nearly 3 million local public officials are appointed and paid by local public bodies.

In principle, local governmental entities are autonomously governed and staffed and are administratively independent of the central or national government. In fact, a good deal of national governmental work is delegated to local government agencies or officials. Such delegated tasks and those performing them are often directly overseen by a central government agency. Moreover, local government agencies rely heavily on central government financing. The national government collects about two-thirds of all tax receipts while local governmental bodies collect the remaining one-third. Yet, the spending pattern is just the reverse, with local governments accounting for about two-thirds of total government spending. General and bloc grants from the central government provide for the difference, but these are seen by many as bringing with them various constraints on local bureaucratic autonomy.

Public corporation bureaucracies. There are slightly more than 100 so-called PUBLIC CORPORATIONS in Japan. Each has its own independent legal existence but is supervised by one of the national government agencies and its budget is overseen by the Diet. The functions performed by these corporations are wide-ranging, including fields as diverse as transportation, education, land development, cultural exchange, public broadcasting, telecommunications, horse racing, energy development, livestock promotion, finance, small and medium industry protection, and a host of other areas. Some 920,000 individuals work in these corporations. Approximately half of their top officials are former senior civil servants who take these positions following retirement from main-line agencies.

These three components, national government, local government, and public corporation, employ over 5 million full-time public employees (*kōmuin*). Although this represents nearly a tenfold increase in the size of Japan's bureaucracy since the 1940s and although Japan is often thought of as a bureaucratized country, this figure is still significantly lower than that for most other major industrialized countries. Differences in administrative structure, institutional variation, and methods of calculation make accurate comparisons difficult, but government employees represent approximately 8, 9, 6, and 7 percent, respectively, of the total populations of the United States, Britain, West Germany, and France. In Japan, the figure is about 4.5 percent. Of the employed portion of the population, Japan's 9 percent in government service is well below the 18, 20, 14, and 16 percent for the United States, Britain, West Germany, and France. Although exclusion of the military component in all countries brings the Japanese figures somewhat more into line, even then only West Germany is in any real sense parallel to Japan in the comparatively small size of its government bureaucracy.

National Civil Service System——Primary responsibility for political and administrative oversight of the national civil service rests with the cabinet and the individual ministers. In addition, the National Personnel Authority (NPA), a semiautonomous agency composed of three commissioners appointed by the cabinet with the consent of both houses of the Diet is responsible for enforcement of the National Civil Service Law concerning recruitment, promotion, compensation, and adjudication of disputes involving public employees. The ADMINISTRATIVE MANAGEMENT AGENCY (AMA) is in charge of overseeing the organizational needs and managerial efficiency of all agencies. It shares certain of these responsibilities with the Personnel Bureau of the Prime Minister's Office.

The national civil service is divided into 8 normal and 2 special "grades," plus some 16 "services." One's service designation is based on the general category of work performed (e.g., administrative, educational, taxation, public security, research, medical, etc), while the grades reflect the presumed level of difficulty and responsibility of one's job.

Entrance and career patterns. There is little horizontal entry into the top or middle ranks of the national bureaucracy. Entrance and promotion are based primarily on written and oral examinations administered by the NPA. The most significant examination is the Principal Senior A-Class Entrance Examination (Kokka Kōmuin Shiken Jōkyū Kō). Competition there is intense and has become increasingly so with time. In 1960 there were 12 applicants for each success; in 1972 the figure was up to 20; in 1976 it was nearly 40. Those who pass this examination usually enter the civil service at grade six and can expect rapid advancement to top positions. Most can anticipate ultimately achieving a position in the top three grades, which represent approximately 15,000 positions, of which about half are truly important.

Although in principle any Japanese citizen is eligible to compete for any public office for which he or she is otherwise qualified, in fact, a rather narrow and homogeneous group dominates the ranks of the successful applicants. Educational background plays the largest part in this success, and the oral examination serves as an additional check on homogeneity. In 1976, for example, 53,935 applicants took the senior civil service examination, of whom only 1,336 passed. Of those who were successful, 461 (35 percent) were graduates of Tōkyō University and 193 (14 percent) were from Kyōto University. The next highest numbers were achieved by Tōhoku (51), Nagoya (42), and Kyūshū (41), all national universities. Only 12 other universities out of Japan's more than 400 placed 10 or more graduates on the passing list. Despite slight variations from year to year, the general pattern has been the same throughout the 1970s. Although contemporary dominance by Tōkyō and Kyōto universities is less than it was during the Meiji period, it remains exceptionally high.

Such educational homogeneity becomes even more pronounced in the senior ranks of the national civil service. In the early 1970s over 60 percent of those holding the rank of section chief or above were graduates of Tōkyō University. The bulk of the top civil servants also have backgrounds in legal studies. In 1972–73, 77 percent of the bureau chiefs and 91 percent of the administrative vice-ministers were graduates of law faculties.

Once an individual is appointed to a post, he typically remains with the same agency for the duration of his career. In a survey of civil servants holding top positions during the years 1949–59, one scholar found that approximately one-third had been with a single agency, one-third had served with one additional agency for a brief period and then returned to the agency of initial appointment, and only one-third had served in three or more ministries. More recent data shows that fully two-thirds of those holding top posts in the early 1970s had served in only one ministry, while less than 9 percent had served in three or more ministries.

Advancement within the civil service tends to be primarily a function of seniority. Transfers occur once every two years or so, and members of an entering group tend to move up as a cluster through a variety of positions in the agency. The most successful individuals can expect to achieve the position of section chief after approximately 15 years of service, assistant bureau chief after 22–25 years and bureau chief after 25–28 years. The position of administrative vice-minister, available only to a select few, is usually achieved after 28–30 years. Typically, this position is held for two or three years, after which the vice-minister and any remaining members of the group that entered the ministry with him will retire. Their age at this time is most often 51–55.

Postbureaucratic careers. Early retirement serves to rejuvenate the bureaucracy continuously as channels of promotion open up for talented individuals in lower ranks. At the same time, it creates the problem of finding subsequent employment for those of proven competence in the prime of their working lives. With government pensions low and financial responsibilities high, most retired bureaucrats find second careers, very often in private industries or public corporations overseen by the agencies with which they worked (see AMAKUDARI).

Compared to the total number of bureaucrats retiring every year, the proportion who go on to careers in politics is relatively small. Yet those who do are an influential group in national and local party politics. Almost without exception, politically oriented former bureaucrats join the ruling LIBERAL DEMOCRATIC PARTY (LDP). Slightly more than a quarter of the LDP's freshman candidates in the 1976 election for the House of Representatives were former career officials. Approximately 20 percent of Japan's postwar cabinet ministers have been former bureaucrats. Eighteen prefectural governors serving in the mid-1970s were former high-ranking national government officials, while an additional seven had been career officials in local governments. Even more significantly, in the 25 years following the formation of the LDP in 1955, the office of prime minister was held for only 5 years by men who could be described as professional politicians. During the remaining 20 years, former bureaucrats occupied the office.

The National Bureaucracy in Politics —— *Competition and coordination.* It is difficult to speak meaningfully of the national bureaucracy as though it were a unified entity. It is, in fact, composed of a number of highly diverse organizations with overlapping and not infrequently contradictory organizational purposes. Nor are all agencies of equal prestige or influence. Ministries such as Finance, International Trade and Industry, Construction, and Agriculture, Forestry, and Fisheries are traditionally seen as politically powerful, while Labor, Education, and Posts and Telecommunications are usually viewed as much weaker. The reasons for these comparatively wide variations relate to many factors, including differences in historical mission, control over resources, quality of personnel, and alliance with private organizations.

Because career patterns are dominated by service in a single ministry and because lateral entry is rare, loyalty to one's agency (or section within an agency) tends to be extremely high. This produces positive effects in terms of loyalty, work satisfaction, and the like, but it also exaggerates natural bureaucratic tendencies toward tunnel vision and compartmentalization. Sectionalism tends to be high, and agencies or even sections within the same agency frequently resist cooperation and coordination, each seeking to maximize a particular sphere of influence. Certain ministerial rivalries have achieved a degree of notoriety in Japanese politics, such as those between Finance and International Trade and Industry, for example, or between the so-called economic ministries and the so-called service ministries. Yet some coordination of otherwise competing ministries is achieved through the informal but nonetheless powerful conference of administrative vice-ministers that meets weekly, just before cabinet meetings. Its primary function is to iron out organizational disputes and to resolve differences in the goals and programs of different government agencies. In addition, various interministry teams are often established to analyze and make policy recommendations on specific problems such as the reversion of Okinawa or the energy crisis.

Public policy formation. Despite such cleavages and variations in power, certain broad generalizations about the role of bureaucratic agencies in policy formation can be isolated. One thing is certain: Japan's top-level bureaucrats have a high degree of self-confidence in their ability to solve the country's problems, and they are highly skeptical of the ability of elected officials to deal with such matters. One survey showed that nearly 90 percent of the top officials surveyed felt it was bad for elected officials to intervene in public administration, and a slightly higher percent held that the administrative vice-ministers and senior bureau chiefs should not change when the cabinet changes. A different survey showed 80 percent of the surveyed bureaucrats holding that it was they, rather than the elected politicians of the country, who were solving Japan's general policy problems. This figure compared to only 21 percent of the British and 16 percent of the West German bureaucrats surveyed.

The tasks of government in a modern industrial society are highly complex and often depend on extremely detailed and technical information. In this regard, bureaucratic expertise is invaluable, providing agencies and individual bureaucrats with a high degree of influence. Matters such as interest rates, airport sitings, control of toxic substances and effluents, pensions, international trade, tariffs, agricultural prices, public construction, and a host of other matters are simultaneously highly technical and politically sensitive.

The result is that bureaucratic powers in public policy formation are substantial in Japan. Approximately 90 percent of all legislation passed by the Diet since 1955 was drafted within a bureaucratic agency, and top-level bureaucrats often become behind-the-scenes managers of these bills once they are in the Diet. In addition, individual agencies have the power to issue ministerial ordinances (*shōrei*), and the cabinet can issue CABINET ORDERS (*seirei*), both of which provide powerful extralegislative instruments that can supplement and occasionally bypass the legislative process and the political difficulties and predispositions toward compromise that it involves.

Bureaucratic agencies also have significant power to shape the conceptualization and discussion of political issues. The policy program of the LDP is typically composed of proposals advocated by the various government agencies. Most agencies also oversee a number of advisory commissions designed in theory to provide outside expertise on political problems. A high proportion of the members of such commissions are former civil servants; the ministry defines the guidelines for the problem being investigated; ministerial staff oversee the actual investigations and generally write up the final reports. Agencies also utilize the so-called power of ADMINISTRATIVE GUIDANCE vis-à-vis the organizations of socioeconomic sectors whose actions they oversee. Finally, the fact that most agencies frequently send their "retired" personnel on to second careers in important posts in society, as noted above, further fosters bureaucratic influence. Rarely if ever are the links back to the former home agency totally severed; instead there is close coordination in many areas between a government agency, private-sector groups, and, where relevant, functional committees of the LDP. The overall result is to provide most national bureaucratic agencies with tools by which to influence and shape public and private socioeconomic activities within the country. At the same time, bureaucratic power is not unchecked; political parties, interest groups, single-issue movements, parliament, and public opinion provide important counterweights to the policy-making powers of bureaucratic agencies.

Public unionization and strikes. The relative closeness between the top levels of the bureaucracy and the political and economic establishment of Japan is directly counter to relations at lower levels. Employees of national and local government agencies, as well as within the public corporations, have been highly unionized since the early years of the US Occupation. Most of these are allied with SŌHYŌ and the JAPAN SOCIALIST PARTY. Union radicalism in the period 1945–47 led the American Occupation authorities to deny to most Japanese government employees the right to strike or to bargain collectively. In a few organizations, such as the national railways, the tobacco monopoly, the postal service, and the telephone and telegraph corporation, where strikes are prohibited, collective bargaining is allowed. Nevertheless, government employees stage strikes and work actions with considerable frequency. Often the key goal is to gain the right to strike. To date, such rights have not been granted, and the federation of unions of public employees (KŌRŌKYŌ) remains one of the main organizational opponents of the present government. See PUBLIC EMPLOYEES.

Bureaucratic Reform —— All modern industrialized countries have evidenced dissatisfaction with one or another aspect of their national bureaucracies. In some, particularly the Nordic countries, major efforts have been directed toward making these agencies more responsive to citizens. In others, especially in Britain, the chief concern has been with changing the class composition of top civil servants. Particularly in the United States and West Germany, strong efforts have been made to ensure that bureaucratic agencies are responsive to elected political executives. In still others, including Japan, the prime concern has been with improving administrative efficiency. This has been the trend throughout the postwar period, but a major step in this direction came as a result of the 1964 report of the Provisional Council on Administrative Reform (Rinji Gyōsei

Chōsakai). This massive 16-volume report called for a variety of simplifications in bureaucratic procedure, increased coordination by the cabinet, clarification of responsibility among various agencies, a rationalization of budgeting and accounting, and the overall modernization of the civil service system.

Following this report, numerous measures have been taken to reduce the size and complexity of the national bureaucracy. In November the elimination of one bureau in each ministry and the consolidation of several public corporations were ordered. The following year saw adoption of a plan to cut the civil service by 5 percent in four years. Similar plans with slightly different cuts and target dates were adopted in 1972, 1975, and 1977. The consequence has been that Japan, alone of all the major industrialized countries of the world, has had a relatively stable size for its national civil service over the past decade. In addition, the growth in the number of public corporations and adivsory committees has been stabilized.

One of the more significant parallels, however, has been the rapid increase in the size of the nation's local bureaucracies. From approximately 2.25 million in the mid-1960s, local civil servants had increased to nearly 3 million by the mid-1970s. Many formerly national government functions are clearly being decentralized to local levels. See also LOCAL GOVERNMENT.

Administrative Management Agency, Prime Minister's Office, ed, *Organization of the Government of Japan* (annual). Ari Bakuji et al, *Gendai gyōsei to kanryōsei* (1974). Gyōsei Kanri Chō, ed, *Gyōsei kanri nempō* (annual). Gyōsei Kanri Chō, ed, *Gyōsei kikōzu* (annual). Gyōsei Kanri Iinkai, ed, *Gyōsei kaikaku no genjō to kadai* (annual since 1966). *Gyōsei kikō shirīzu* (1974). Honda Yasuharu, *Nihon neokanryō ron* (1974). Inoki Masamichi, "The Civil Bureaucracy: Japan," in Robert E. Ward, ed, *Political Modernization in Japan and Turkey* (1964). Isomura Eiichi and Kuronuma Minoru, *Gendai Nihon no gyōsei* (1974). Chalmers Johnson, "The Reemployment of Retired Government Bureaucrats in Japanese Business," *Asian Survey* 14 (1974). Chalmers Johnson, "Japan: Who Governs?: An Essay on Official Bureaucracy," *Journal of Japanese Studies* 2.1 (1975). Chalmers Johnson, *Japan's Public Policy Companies* (1978). Kubota Akira, *Higher Civil Servants in Postwar Japan* (1969). Kubota Akira and Tomita Nobuo, "Nihon seifu kōkan no ishiki kōzo," *Chūō kōron* 1079 (February 1977). Kusayanagi Daizō, *Kanryō ōkokuron* (1975). Ōta Kaoru, *Yakunin o kiru* (1973). T. J. Pempel, "The Bureaucratization of Policymaking in Postwar Japan," *American Journal of Political Science* 18.4 (1974). Rinji Gyōsei Chōsakai, ed, *Hōkokusho* (1964). Rinji Gyōsei Chōsakai, ed, *Gyōsei no kaikaku* (1968). Bernard Silberman, "The Bureaucratic Role in Japan, 1900–1945: The Bureaucrat as Politician," in Bernard Silberman and Harry D. Harootunian, ed, *Japan in Crisis* (1974). Tsuji Kiyoaki, *Nihon kanryōsei no kenkyū* (1952). T. J. PEMPEL

buri → yellowtail

Burma and Japan

Before World War II, relations between Japan and Burma barely existed, as Burma was politically and economically under British control. Actual relations between the two countries began with the Pacific War, when Japan sought to expel the European powers from Southeast Asia. Late in 1940, two Burmese nationalists smuggled themselves out of Burma by ship and reached Amoy, China. There they were discovered by Japanese military police authorities and flown to Tōkyō, where Colonel Suzuki Keiji (1897–1967) gave them full support. Suzuki and several other officers of the Imperial Army and Navy established the MINAMI KIKAN, a military intelligence bureau for operations in Burma. Eight voyages were undertaken between Japan and Burma in 1941, and young Burmese were smuggled out of Burma to Japan for military training. These so-called Thirty Comrades were trained on Hainan Island in China for several months, and the Burma Independence Army (BIA) was organized in Bangkok under the command of Colonel Suzuki. Early in 1942 the BIA marched into Burma together with the Japanese Imperial Army. By May almost the entire country had come under Japanese occupation, and a Japanese military administration was established. The BIA, which had grown to a strength of 100,000, was disbanded and reformed as the Burma Defence Army with three battalions. On 1 August 1942, General Iida Shōjirō (1888–1980), the commander of the Imperial Army in Burma, inaugurated a new government with BA MAW as its head. The following year Prime Minister TŌJŌ HI-

DEKI of Japan promised to recognize Burma as an independent state, and on 1 August 1943 Burmese independence was declared.

This move, however, had little meaning, as Burma continued under Japanese occupation, and the Japanese were not sympathetic toward Burmese sentiments. Anti-Japanese feelings mounted. By the beginning of 1944, young officers of the Burma National Army (formerly BIA) started to organize a resistance movement. In August, AUNG SAN and other officers of the BNA met with prominent leaders of the Burma Communist Party and the Burma Revolutionary Party and discussed means of resisting the Japanese. This meeting is regarded as the beginning of the Anti-Fascist People's Freedom League, which was later to become Burma's ruling party. Resistance began all over the country on 27 March 1945 and continued against the British after the war. Burma achieved full independence from Britain in 1948.

Burma's declaration of war against Japan was withdrawn in 1952, and a Peace Treaty and Reparations Agreement were concluded in November 1954. Japan's reparations payments to Burma, which began in 1955, totaled $200 million, and an additional reparations program totaling over $140 million was started in 1965. The main achievements of the reparations and economic cooperation programs have been the Balugyaung hydroelectric power plant and the so-called Four Projects consisting of the production of buses, trucks, agricultural machinery, and electrical equipment. Japan's exports to Burma always exceed its imports from Burma.

J. F. Cady, *A History of Modern Burma* (1958). Maurice Collis, *Last and First in Burma* (1956). W. H. Elsbree, *Japan's Role in Southeast Asia Nationalist Movements, 1940 to 1945* (1953). F. C. Jones, *Japan's New Order in East Asia: Its Rise and Fall, 1937–1945* (1954). Thakin Nu, *Burma Under the Japanese* (1954). ŌNO TŌRU

bushi → samurai

bushidan

Independent warrior bands or leagues, primarily based on kinship, from around the 10th to the 16th century. They arose from the more militant of the local landholders (MYŌSHU) or from branches of the nobility that had been sent to the provinces, like the TAIRA FAMILY and the MINAMOTO FAMILY. As the authority of the central Heian government declined, these local leaders largely took control of provincial government *(kokuga)* and private estates (SHŌEN), and formed military groups from related and dependent families. Kinship bonds were especially important because each family's inheritance was divided among all sons and even daughters until at least the mid-14th century (see SŌRYŌ SYSTEM). But there was a clear hierarchy within each league: those who were related by blood to the head of the band were called *ienoko* or *kenin*, and those who were not were called *rōtō*, although in time these distinctions became blurred and kinship ties became more fictive than real. The head of an alliance of warrior leagues was called *tōryō*.

Bushidan appeared in all sizes and areas, but they became largest and most powerful in the Kantō region, especially those of the MIURA FAMILY, the HATAKEYAMA FAMILY, and the Chiba family. Most *bushidan* became officially subordinate to the Kamakura shogunate (1192–1333) and then the Muromachi shogunate (1338–1573), but they often maintained considerable independence when shogunate power weakened. However, the internal nature of the *bushidan* began to change, with less emphasis on true kinship ties. Leagues based more on locale than on kinship came to be called *tō* (see MATSURATŌ and MUSASHI SHICHITŌ). The system of feudal DAIMYŌ domains evolved slowly from the former leagues, finally replacing them entirely in the 1500s. See also SAMURAI.

bushidō

(literally, "the Way [*dō*] of the warrior [*bushi*]"). A term that came into common use during the Edo period (1600–1868) to designate the ethical code of the ruling *samurai* class. *Bushidō* involved not only martial spirit and skill with weapons, but also absolute loyalty to one's lord, a strong sense of personal honor, devotion to duty, and the courage, if required, to sacrifice one's life in battle or in ritual.

Although *bushidō* assumed its mature form as a deliberately articulated ethical system and martial cult only in the 17th and 18th centuries, the warrior class had dominated the political life of Japan from the time of the establishment of the Kamakura shogunate by MINAMOTO NO YORITOMO in the late 12th century. Earlier, warrior bands held together by kinship bonds, regional ties, and fierce personal loyalty to their leaders had become active in the provinces from about the 10th century with the erosion of central imperial authority. To understand the development of *bushidō*, therefore, it is essential to grasp the character of the nascent warrior ethic in these centuries, especially the nature of the relationship between warrior retainers and their feudal overlords.

Early Warrior Society and Bushidō ——— In medieval military chronicles and tales (*gunkimono*) such as HŌGEN MONOGATARI, AZUMA KAGAMI, and TAIHEIKI, which glorify the exploits of medieval warriors, we find the expressions "the customs of those who bear bows and arrows" (*yumiya toru mi no narai*) and "the customs of the eastern warriors" (*Bandō musha no narai*). These expressions clearly distinguished the customs and virtues of the emerging warrior bands, especially those of the Kantō region of eastern Japan, from the "customs of the court nobility" (*kuge no narai*) and from the "western" warrior bands, like the Taira, who had become enmeshed in the web of the cultivated society of Kyōto, to the detriment of their martial spirit. Medieval warrior house codes (KAKUN) laid down distinctive ethical standards for samurai, stressing absolute loyalty and willingness to fight to the death for one's lord on the battlefield. There is some danger, however, in accepting these accounts as literal descriptions of the actual behavior or ethics of the mass of medieval warriors. By their very nature *gunkimono* tended toward the idealization of heroism and villainy. *Kakun* were frequently written by aging warrior leaders for the express purpose of guiding their chosen successors in maintaining authority and getting the best out of their followers.

Clearly, the key to understanding the Japanese warrior ethic prior to the Edo period lies in an understanding of the medieval lord–retainer nexus involving favor from the lord and service from the retainer. There are several different interpretations of this relationship. The historian WATSUJI TETSURŌ has argued that the core of the medieval lord-vassal relationship was a "total, unconditional self-renunciation on the part of the follower to his lord." Against this idealistic view, Ienaga Saburō (b 1913) has argued that the relationship was basically economic and contractual: the follower's loyalty could be held only as long as the lord was able to bestow favors. Between these extremes, Kawai Masaharu (b 1914) has suggested that such idealistic or materialistic interpretations are too general to explain the complexities of nearly 500 years of warrior history. His more flexible interpretation is that some warriors were bound almost unconditionally to their lords while others enjoyed a more nearly contractual relationship, the strength of the bond varying with the prevailing personal, local, and historical circumstances. According to this view, dependent warriors offered their service and loyalty in accord with a strict warrior ethic and with little consideration of material returns, while more independent warriors traded their loyalty to the highest bidder or arbitrarily changed sides to further their fortunes. With regard to *bushidō* before the Edo period, therefore, we can suggest that although a distinct *bushi* ethic based on absolute loyalty was taking shape, many warriors gave only qualified allegiance to their nominal overlords, saw the relationship in quasi-contractual terms, and vigorously pursued their own self-interest. The volatility of *bushi* loyalty patterns was both cause and effect of the phenomenon of "the lower overturning the upper" (GEKOKUJŌ), which was such a prominent feature of medieval Japan.

Transition to Tokugawa Bushidō ——— Perhaps the most revealing literary expression of the warrior spirit in the transitional period of war and unification under Toyotomi Hideyoshi and Tokugawa Ieyasu in the late 16th century is provided by the master-swordsman, *rōnin* (masterless samurai), Zen devotee, and painter MIYAMOTO MUSASHI in his *Gorin no sho* (ca 1643; tr *The Book of Five Rings*, 1974). This is a treatise on strategy and the art of war, a survival manual for warriors in a troubled age. The work opens with a clear statement of Musashi's conception of the raison d'être of the *bushi*: "The way of the warrior is frequently said to lie in the resolute acceptance of death. Warriors, however, have no monopoly on this virtue: monks, women, and peasants, too, can confront death bravely out of a sense of duty or shame. The true distinction of the *bushi* lies in applying military strategy to overcome other men, whether in single combat or mass encounters, thus gaining glory for his lord and himself."

Even during Miyamoto Musashi's lifetime, however, independence and military adventuring were being sharply curtailed as Hideyoshi, Ieyasu, and their satellite *daimyō* and domainal governments pressed forward the policies of disarming the peasantry, separating warriors from the soil, and bringing them into castle towns where the majority were put on rice stipends. Cut off from direct

control of land and peasants, reduced to fixed stipends in an age of rising costs, and with opportunities for advancement through warfare restricted under the NATIONAL SECLUSION policy and Tokugawa Peace, samurai became increasingly dependent on the shogunate or their domainal governments for survival. They were consequently much more susceptible to pressures for expressions of unilateral loyalty than they had been in the preceding age of wars. During the long Tokugawa Peace, the samurai, as the topmost tier in the status hierarchy, were gradually converted from fighting men into a ruling elite, most of whose time was taken up in the administration of their domains, or in the ceremonial requirements of alternate-year attendance (SANKIN KŌTAI) at the shogunal capital of Edo (now Tōkyō). While the supremacy of the samurai was symbolized by the two swords they wore at their waists, their new role as warrior-administrators was buttressed and defined by conscious comparison to the Chinese administrative elite, the *shi* (shih), the adoption by the Tokugawa regime of Neo-Confucian teaching, and the identification of feudal with Confucian virtues.

It was in the relatively stable social and intellectual climate of Tokugawa Japan rather than in the cut and thrust of an age of wars that *bushidō*, as the ethical system and martial cult of a "tamed" samurai class, came to fruition. It is hardly surprising that, in keeping with the twofold character of the Edo-period samurai, *bushidō* should also have manifested a twofold character. The idealized medieval tradition of absolute loyalty and willingness to die for one's lord survived, but was now overlaid with Confucian ethics. The underlying native tradition found its most eloquent expression in the *bushidō* classic HAGAKURE (1716), the reflections of Yamamoto Tsunetomo, a samurai of the Saga domain (now Saga Prefecture). Tsunetomo always regretted the fact that his desire to commit *seppuku* (HARAKIRI) upon the death of his lord—a practice known as JUNSHI—was frustrated by the Tokugawa, who had outlawed the practice in their quest for social order. The major theme of *Hagakure* is summed up in the sentence, "*Bushidō* is a way of dying." This beautification of sacrificial death—whether a death-in-life of selfless service to one's lord or the physical ordeal of *seppuku*—as the ultimate expression of manliness is a far cry from the urge for self-assertion and conquest expressed in Musashi's *Gorin no sho*. According to the *Hagakure*, the samurai ideal and essence of *bushidō* are expressed in self-effacing service: "Whenever one is taken into service to the lord, he should serve the lord without any consideration of his own self. Even if he is dismissed or is ordered to commit *seppuku*, he should accept the action as one of the services to the lord and should be sincerely concerned with the destiny of the lord's house wherever he may be. Such should be the fundamental spirit of the Nabeshima [Saga domain] samurai. As far as I am concerned, I have never thought of attaining Buddhahood, which would not suit me at all, but I am completely prepared to be born seven times as a Nabeshima samurai in order to work for the cause of the domain."

The Confucianized *bushidō* tradition has been referred to as *shidō* (the Way of the *shi*) by the historians Naramoto Tatsuya (b 1913) and Sagara Tōru (b 1921). It first found detailed expression in the writings of the samurai scholar and military strategist YAMAGA SOKŌ, who stressed that samurai, to justify their existence in Tokugawa society where they had neither to fight nor to contribute to production, had a duty to devote themselves to moral and political leadership of society. They were to be exponents of civilian as well as military arts who would embody both Confucian and feudal virtues and realize in practice the Way of moral virtue in the exercise of government: "The business of the samurai consists in reflecting on his own station in life, in discharging loyal service to his master if he has one, in deepening his fidelity in associations with friends, and, with due consideration of his own position, in devoting himself to duty above all. However, in one's own life, one becomes unavoidably involved in obligations between father and child, older and younger brother, and husband and wife. Though these are also the fundamental moral obligations of everyone in the land, the farmers, artisans, and merchants have no leisure from their occupations, and so they cannot constantly act in accordance with them and fully exemplify the Way. The samurai dispenses with the business of the farmer, artisan, and merchant and confines himself to practicing this Way." [Translation from Ryusaku Tsunoda, Wm. Theodore de Bary, and Donald Keene, ed, *Sources of the Japanese Tradition* (New York: Columbia University Press, 1958), vol 1, p. 390. Used by permission.]

This composite indigenous and Confucianized *bushidō* regulated much of the ethical behavior and intellectual inquiry of the samurai class in the Edo period. Ideas of *bushidō* were spread in the domainal schools and fencing academies as well as in many of the

Bush warbler

writings of the age. *Bushidō* motivated the 47 former retainers of Asano Naganori to avenge their dead, disgraced lord (see FORTY-SEVEN RŌNIN INCIDENT). It also shaped the debate on feudal authority versus loyalty that followed the incident and influenced the shogunate's decision to order the *rōnin* to commit *seppuku*. In the mid-19th century *bushidō* served as a yeast for the activism of young samurai from the domains of Satsuma (now Kagoshima Prefecture) and Chōshū (now Yamaguchi Prefecture) who, under the slogan "Revere the Emperor, Expel the Barbarians" (see SONNŌ JŌI) set in motion the challenge to Tokugawa authority that was to culminate in the MEIJI RESTORATION (1868). The emphasis on action, purity of motivation, loyal service, and political and intellectual leadership inherent in *bushidō* helps to explain why the samurai class could serve as the moving force of the Restoration movement, then go on to destroy the feudal system of which they had been the apex, and ultimately play an influential role in the modernization of Japan.

The Legacy of Bushidō——Although the Meiji Restoration and the dismantling of the Tokugawa feudal structure involved the abolition of the samurai class, it did not mean the end of *bushidō* as a compelling emotive force. *Bushidō* was temporarily submerged in the early Meiji surge of modernization and Westernization. From the mid 1880s, however, and especially after the Sino-Japanese War (1894–95), as the cultural pendulum began to swing in a more overtly nationalist direction, *bushidō* found new expressions. The philosopher INOUE TETSUJIRŌ, for instance, sought to harness *bushidō* to the service of the Meiji state by equating it with patriotism and devotion to the emperor. The ardent Christian UCHIMURA KANZŌ identified *bushidō* with loyalty to Christ: "I am one of the least among the children of the samurai stock, and one of the least among the disciples of Jesus Christ our Lord. But one of the least as I am in both those capacities, the samurai that dwells in my present self will not suffer itself to be either overlooked or made little of. Just what benefits me as a samurai's son is self-respect and independence. It becomes me as a samurai's son to be a hater of all trickery, fraud, and dishonesty. The code of Bushidō is no less than the law of Christianity that tells us: 'Love of money is the root of all evil.'" [Translation from Furukawa Tesshi, "The Individual in Japanese Ethics," in Charles A. Moore, ed, *The Japanese Mind* (Honolulu: University of Hawaii Press, 1967), p. 237. Used by permission.]

In *Bushido: The Soul of Japan*, published first in English in 1900, the scholar and educator NITOBE INAZŌ, also a Christian, presented *bushidō*, stripped of the most extreme of its militaristic, antimodern, and anti-Christian aspects, as a vehicle to define for Western readers all that was most admirable in the Japanese tradition, including such virtues as politeness, generosity, honor, loyalty, and self-control. Nitobe argued that the influence of *bushidō*, which, he claimed, had spread from the warrior class to permeate all of Japanese society, was still alive in the physical endurance, fortitude, and bravery of the Japanese. It was perhaps partly under the influence of the subsequent *bushidō* revival that General NOGI MARESUKE, a hero of the Russo-Japanese War (1904–05), in an extreme expression of loyalty committed *seppuku* on hearing of the death of the Meiji emperor in 1912.

Nitobe's *Bushido* was influential. The book was widely read after the Russo-Japanese War by foreigners who wondered how tiny Japan had brought the tsarist empire to its knees. The more martial aspects of *bushidō* came into vogue again in the militarist 1930s, and many young Japanese conscripts read the *Hagakure* or Nitobe's *Bushido* on their way to the front. In her attempt to explain Japanese psychology to Westerners, Ruth BENEDICT, in *The Chrysanthemum and the Sword* (1946), drew heavily upon Nitobe's theme.

In the aftermath of World War II, *bushidō* again fell into disfavor. Foreign critics like Lord Russell of Liverpool in *The Knights of Bushidō* (1958) pointed to *bushidō* as representing all that was most despicable in Japanese wartime behavior. Most Japanese disowned *bushidō* as part of the ideological equipment of the prewar militarists who had led Japan to defeat and humiliation and as incompatible with their postwar democratic society.

One Japanese who sought to reinstate *bushidō* in postwar Japanese society was the novelist MISHIMA YUKIO. For Mishima, *bushidō* encapsulated much of what was most uniquely Japanese. It was to be the means of assuring a return to national pride and cleansing the corruption of modern Japanese society through an "imperial reconstruction of Japan" (*hōkoku* Nippon). Mishima was attracted by the *Hagakure* and fascinated by the sword and the cult of death in *bushidō*. He wrote *Hagakure nyūmon* (1967; tr *On Hagakure*, 1977). In the short story "Yūkoku" (1961; tr "Patriotism," 1966) and later works he glorified *seppuku*. Mishima also directed and acted in the film version of "Yūkoku," playing the part of the hero, an army lieutenant who disembowels himself after an abortive coup d'etat. These were rehearsals for Mishima's own death. On 25 November 1970, Mishima and four members of his private militia, the Tate no Kai, burst into the office of the commander of the Self Defense Forces in Tōkyō. After taking the general hostage, Mishima appealed to members of the Self Defense Forces to follow him in a military coup. When, as he had expected, his appeal was ignored, Mishima and his lieutenant Morita Masakatsu (1945–70) took their lives in the *bushidō* manner. No feudal warrior could have dispatched himself more painfully than Mishima, or with a more punctilious regard for the traditional prescriptions of the etiquette of death.

Bushidō has thus had a long and checkered history. The clamor over Mishima's death, together with the ongoing vogue for samurai films and samurai novels, suggests that however anachronistic, abhorrent, or absurd the *bushidō* tradition may seem at the conscious level to most contemporary Japanese, it still exerts considerable fascination.

━━━Furukawa Tesshi, "The Individual in Japanese Ethics," in Charles A. Moore, ed, *The Japanese Mind* (1967). Ienaga Saburō, "Shujū dōtoku no ichikōsatsu," *Shigaku zasshi* 62.3 (1953). Kawai Masaharu, *Chūsei buke shakai no kenkyū* (1973). Ivan Morris, *The Nobility of Failure* (1975). Naramoto Tatsuya, *Bushidō no keifu* (1971). Inazō Nitobe, *Bushido: The Soul of Japan* (1905). Josiah Royce, *The Philosophy of Loyalty* (1930). Sagara Tōru, *Bushidō* (1968). Daisetz T. Suzuki, *Zen and Japanese Culture* (1959). Watsuji Tetsurō, *Nippon rinri shisō*, 2 vols (1952). Yamamoto Tsunetomo, *Hagakure* (1716), tr William Scott Wilson as *Hagakure: The Book of the Samurai* (1979). *Martin C. COLLCUTT*

bush warbler

(*uguisu*). *Cettia diphone*. Member of the family of small birds called Muscicapidae; known for its beautiful song. Both the male and female are an olive-brown color, with a white eye ring and fairly long tail; total length is about 15 centimeters (6 in). Feeding on insects, it breeds throughout Japan in mountainous areas where dwarf bamboo (*sasa*) grows. Between April and August it builds ball-shaped nests made of dried leaves in dwarf bamboo thickets, where the female lays four to six reddish brown eggs; the *hototogisu* (little cuckoo; *Cuculus poliocephalus*) often lays its eggs in the bush warbler's nest. In autumn and winter, bush warblers move down to the plains, often dwelling in garden hedges or groves in parks. Their range includes, besides Japan, northeastern China, Korea, Sakhalin, and the Philippines. See also REED WARBLERS. *TAKANO Shinji*

The Japanese people have long loved the plaintive, whistling song of the *uguisu*, which they pronounce as *hōhokekyo*; to them it signifies good luck and rejoicing. Other names for the *uguisu*, such as "spring bird" (*harudori*), "spring-announcing bird" (*harutsugedori*), "first song" (*hatsune*), and "flower-viewing bird" (*hanamidori*) indicate its seasonal significance when it begins to sing in fields and towns around February or March (a time roughly corresponding to the first month of the old lunar calendar). In particular, Japanese literati and artists have prized the combination of "warblers and plum blossoms," an aesthetic theme apparently borrowed from China. The bird appears frequently in Japanese poetry and art as a motif paired with bamboo, willows, cherry trees, or pine.

Unlike most other small birds, which stop singing around July, the *uguisu* continues to sing until early September. In her 11th-century work *Makura no sōshi*, the court lady SEI SHŌNAGON criticized this bird for "crying in an aging voice until the end of summer," but in the poetry of the Edo period (1600–1868), the "out-of-season" song of the *uguisu* after August was considered quite elegant. These birds have been raised as pets since at least the 16th century.

Saitō Shōji

business concentration

A situation in which a relatively small number of large corporations account for a significant share of the gross assets, sales volume, capital, value added, and number of employees in an industry or in the national economy. In terms of gross assets Japan's top 100 corporations (excluding banks) accounted for 22.6 percent of the gross assets of the nation's 1,350,000 business firms in fiscal 1977. This concentration ratio is lower than the 1967 figure (27.3 percent), but there were only 580,000 incorporated firms in 1967. If the 1977 ratio of the top 100 companies to the total numbers of firms (0.007 percent) is used for fiscal 1967, the number of top bracket corporations drops to about 20 companies accounting for 19 percent of corporate assets at the time. This represents an increase of 3.6 points from the 1967 figure. The overall concentration index of the top three corporations in individual commodity markets likewise grew to 104 in 1976 (1967 = 100). Thus, it is clear that business concentration in the Japanese economy has been steadily accelerating.

Masuda Yūji

business cycles

(*keiki hendō*). While achieving rapid economic growth, the post–World War II Japanese economy has experienced the type of business fluctuation common to the market economies of the world. The Economic Planning Agency's chronology of postwar business cycles records the following periods of prosperity: the Korean War boom (peak in June 1951); the post–Korean War boom (peak in June 1954); the "Jimmu boom" (peak in June 1957); the "Iwato boom" (peak in December 1961); the Olympic boom (peak in October 1964); the "Izanagi boom" (peak in July 1970); and the postrevaluation boom (peak in November 1973). (The names Jimmu, Iwato, and Izanagi refer to the mythological accounts of the origin of the Japanese and suggest the popular belief that the nation was enjoying unprecedented heights of prosperity. These booms were punctuated by cyclical recessions with troughs in October 1951, November 1954, June 1958 (the *nabezoko* or pan-bottom recession), October 1962, October 1965 (the *tenkeiki* or turning point recession), December 1971, and March 1975.

Production, employment, and profits grew more rapidly during periods of prosperity and less rapidly during recessions. In terms of gross national product in constant prices, which is the standard measure of the level of economic activities, these business fluctuations took the form of variations in annual growth rates. Through the mid-1970s the growth rates were always positive, with GNP never declining from one year to the next, the only exception being 1974. This reflects Japan's extremely vigorous postwar economic growth.

Japan's business cycles manifest themselves as interactions among overseas economic developments, the government's anticyclical policies, and the behavior of the private sector of the economy. Each business cycle development has been associated with its own immediate causes. In the years immediately after World War II, business fluctuations were closely related to government policies. During the Allied Occupation of 1945–52, the PRIORITY PRODUCTION PROGRAM of inflationary financing of reconstruction through the Reconstruction Finance Bank and price differential subsidies was associated with the economic recovery, while the deflationary DODGE LINE was held responsible for the recession which followed. In the early 1950s the expansion of exports and other factors, including large expenditures by American military forces in Japan and Korea, led to the Korean War and post–Korean War booms. The increase in private plant and equipment investment was the leading factor contributing to the Jimmu boom and Iwato boom of the late 1950s and early 1960s. The Olympic boom was another such boom, though short-lived. The end of each of these booms during the period of rapid growth was brought about by tight monetary and fiscal policies introduced by the government to deal with the unfa-

vorable developments generated in the country's balance of international payments. The recession of 1965 was the severest to that point in the postwar period.

Although American military expenditures related to the Vietnam War served as a stimulus, the expansion of private plant and equipment investment was again the leading force behind the long Izanagi boom, which ended when the government adopted restrictive policies to combat wholesale price inflation in an increasingly inflationary international situation. Government policies to counteract the deflationary impact of the yen revaluation were associated with the postrevaluation boom, while the recession which followed, the deepest of all the postwar recessions, was related to higher oil prices, which applied a deflationary shock to the economy and forced the realignment of domestic industries based on new cost conditions.

The monetary instruments of the government's anticyclical policy include the discount rate and the "window guidance" (a kind of informal control known as *madoguchi shidō*) of the BANK OF JAPAN, which influences the lending activities of the major banks, while the fiscal instruments include public works' expenditures and budgetary deficits. Income transfer mechanisms, such as unemployment insurance and progressive income taxes, serve as "automatic stabilizers" to moderate business fluctuations. The development of techniques and institutions of economic management to control the vagaries of prosperity and depression is responsible for preventing the more violent business fluctuations of the type experienced in the prewar period.

The dating of prewar business cycles is more difficult, but some periods of prosperity and depression can be identified. These include the prosperity of the late 1870s, the depression of the early 1880s (see MATSUKATA FISCAL POLICY), the prosperity of the second half of the 1880s (a business formation boom), the depression of 1890, the prosperity of the mid-1890s during the Sino-Japanese War, the depression after the middle 1890s in reaction to the Sino-Japanese War boom, the depression of the early 1900s (due to contraction of export and domestic demand), the prosperity during the first half of the 1900s during the Russo-Japanese War, the depression of 1907–08 in reaction to the Russo-Japanese War boom, the prosperity around 1910 (a business formation boom), the depression of 1914, the prosperity during the second half of the 1910s due to World War I, the depression of the early 1920s (in reaction to the World War I boom), the prosperity during the mid-1920s (a miniboom after the TŌKYŌ EARTHQUAKE OF 1923), the crisis of 1927, the depression of the late 1920s, and the prosperity of the 1930s due to recovery and armament. See also ECONOMIC HISTORY.

Kogiku Kiichirō

business, wholesale and retail

Throughout the 1970s the number of Japanese wholesale and retail businesses increased steadily. In 1979 there were 1.6 million retail stores, grossing over ¥74 trillion (US $256 billion). Most retail stores are small and run by the owner's family; for example, in 1979 some 61 percent of retail stores had two employees or fewer, while only 0.3 percent had over 50 employees. Supermarkets and department stores, less than 1 percent of the total number of retail stores, accounted for 20 percent of the total sales, and their share has been increasing yearly. In 1979 also there were 370,000 wholesale firms with combined sales of ¥275 trillion (US $1.26 trillion), nearly four times that of retail stores. This indicated the prominence of wholesale businesses in the Japanese economy as well as the existence of a complicated and inefficient DISTRIBUTION SYSTEM in Japan.

Okada Yasushi

Buson (1716–1784)

Also known as Yosa Buson or Taniguchi Buson. Leading *haikai* (see HAIKU) poet of the late 18th century and, along with BASHŌ (1644–94) and ISSA (1763–1827), one of the great names in all of *haiku*. A distinguished BUNJINGA painter, he perfected the *haiga* ("haiku sketch") as a branch of Japanese pictorial art. His best-known painting disciple, MATSUMURA GOSHUN (1752–1811), also known as Gekkei, founded the Shijō school.

Early career. Son of a wealthy landowner, Buson was born near Ōsaka. However, he inherited none of the family's riches. As a youth he went to seek his fortune in Edo (now Tōkyō). For five years (1737–42) he belonged to a *haikai* linked verse circle (see RENGA AND HAIKAI) over which Hayano Hajin (1666–1742) presided. Here he learned the rudiments of linking verses and the traditions of the Bashō school *haikai* as transmitted by Ransetsu (1654–1707) and TAKARAI KIKAKU (1661–1707). After Hajin's death Buson spent much time around Yūki, north of Edo, where he painted, practiced *haikai,* and wrote *Hokuju Rōsen o itamu* (1745, Elegy to Hokuju Rōsen), the first of his innovative poems that foreshadow modern free verse. At this time, Buson also visited places in northeastern Japan famed in Bashō's poetic diary, *Oku no hosomichi* (1689; tr *The Narrow Road to the Deep North,* 1966). About a dozen or so paintings from this period also have been handed down, some unsigned and others with signatures such as Shikan (Child of China) and Naniwa Shimei, the latter of which points to his origins near Ōsaka.

Establishment in Kyōto. After a period of moving from place to place, Buson settled in Kyōto in the late 1750s. He was active in Mochizuki Sōoku's (1688–1766) poetry circle, and was also actively painting in the Chinese-inspired *bunjinga* style. By practicing both poetry and painting, he aspired to the ideals of the *bunjin* (Ch: *wenren* or *wen-jen;* literati) of China. Many noted paintings by Buson date from the 1760s, when he achieved technical mastery of his style. One of Buson's commissions involved collaborating with IKE NO TAIGA on a landscape series based on Chinese poems, *Jūben jūgi* (1771, Ten Pleasures and Ten Conveniences), now a National Treasure.

After Sōoku's death in 1766, Buson gradually spent more time on poetry. He was acclaimed Hajin's successor and in 1770 took the name Yahantei (Midnight Hermitage) for his studio. In painting his best-known name is probably Shunsei (Spring Star).

Master of the Midnight Hermitage. Buson found his distinct voice partly from association with two dissimilar poets, TAN TAIGI (1709–71) and Kuroyanagi Shōha (d 1772), both of whom helped him to develop his style, known for its spontaneousness and sensuality. Following their passing, Buson emerged as the central figure of a *haikai* revival known as the "Return to Bashō" movement.

In 1775 his own poetry group built a clubhouse, the Bashōan (Bashō Hut) for their regular *haikai* and linked-verse gatherings. At about the same time, Buson prepared several illustrated scrolls and screens, including the text of *Oku no hosomichi.* These helped canonize Bashō as a grand saint of poetry. Although Buson sought to emulate Bashō, his own poetry is much more subjective in its pursuit of romantic lyricism, delicate sensitivity, and mood.

Meanwhile, Buson's reputation as a painter continued to grow. Many outstanding works date from these last years. As if aware that Buson did not have long to live, the poet KATŌ KYŌTAI (1732–92) organized a great poetry festival in 1783 in honor of the Bashō centenary, though only 90 years had passed since Bashō's death. Buson himself died on 17 January 1784.

One recent edition of Buson's work gives almost 3,000 *haiku,* roughly three times the number by Bashō. For lyrical mastery of language Buson stands equal to Bashō, but Bashō surpasses him in skill as a *haikai* prose writer and in number of disciples. No one in Japan, however, compares with Buson in mastery of the twin arts of poetry and painting.

— Cal French, *The Poet-Painters: Buson and His Followers* (1974). Ōtani Tokuzō, Okada Rihei, and Shimasue Kiyoshi, ed, *Busonshū* (1972). Sasaki Jōhei, *Yosa Buson* (1975). Shimizu Takayuki and Kuriyama Riichi, ed, *Buson, Issa* (1976).   Leon M. ZOLBROD

bussangaku

The study of local products, whether natural, processed, or manufactured. *Bussangaku* was encouraged in the 18th and 19th centuries as part of official programs established in domains throughout Japan to increase production of cash crops and to develop markets for their specialized products as a means of augmenting domainal revenues (see KOKUSAN KAISHO). *Bussangaku* initially focused on the collection and classification of specimens but eventually led to scientific experiments and technological innovations. An exposition held in Edo (now Tōkyō) in 1757 by HIRAGA GENNAI and TAMURA RANSUI greatly stimulated interest in this practical science.

bussho

Workshop where Buddhist sculptures were carved, or by extension, a group of sculptors of the same school working in the workshop. During the Nara period (710–794), *bussho* were institutions for the carving of Buddhist sculptures that were established on temple construction sites or other convenient places. As the carving of Buddhist sculptures became widespread, leaders of each school had their own workshops at their homes, where they and their fellow sculptors worked under the patronage of nobles. The earliest example of such a *bussho* can be found in the middle part of the Heian period (794–1185). In the Kamakura period (1185–1333) *bussho* developed into guild-like organizations (see ZA). The Shichijō *bussho* of the KEI SCHOOL, the Sanjō *bussho* of the EN SCHOOL, and the Shichijō-Ōmiya *bussho* of the IN SCHOOL (all named after the founders' residences in Kyōto) are well known. A large number of such *bussho* existed during the Muromachi period (1333–1568), not only in Kyōto but also in Nara and Kamakura. However, most of these *bussho* had disappeared by the beginning of the Edo period (1600–1868).

bussokuseki

("stone footprints of the Buddha"). Representations of the Buddha's footprints carved in stone, showing the "wheel of a thousand spokes" *(sempukurin)* that symbolizes the *dharma,* or Buddha law, believed to have been miraculously imprinted on the soles of the Buddha's feet as one of the 32 mystic signs attesting to his Buddhahood. These representations of the Buddha's footsteps on stone were, along with the *bodhi* tree, the *stupa,* and other symbols, among the first Buddhist icons. The oldest extant *bussokuseki* in Japan is preserved in the temple YAKUSHIJI in Nara. The footprints are incised on the flat top of a breccia pillar roughly hexagonal in shape (height: 75.7 cm or 29.8 in; width: 109 cm or 42.9 in). The history of the pillar as inscribed on its sides states that the carvings were made in 753. The model for the carving was a tracing made in Tang (T'ang) dynasty China (618–907) by a Japanese envoy to the Chinese court; the tracing in turn was made from a rubbing brought back to China by the monk Xuanzang (Hsüan-tsang) from his historic visit to the Deer Park in Sarnath. Next to the *bussokuseki* pillar is a slate stele (height: 193.9 cm or 76.3 in; width: 48.5 cm or 19.1 in) of a similar date on which are inscribed 21 ancient Japanese Buddhist poems attributed to the empress KŌMYŌ. These poems of 38 syllables have come to be called *bussokuseki no uta;* they resemble WAKA but have an extra 7-syllable line at the end.
Aya Louisa McDonald

butsudan

A small cabinet or niche containing an image of Buddha flanked by the family ancestral mortuary tablets *(ihai).* Along with the *kamidana* (SHINTŌ FAMILY ALTAR), the *butsudan* is the sacred place in every household. Originally, the term meant a platform in a Buddhist hall where images were placed. In ancient times, it was made of earth or stone but since the medieval period it has commonly been made of wood. Only the rich could have their own small temple at home in the early days, but the small cabinet-form *butsudan* became common in almost every family when the Tokugawa shogunate (1603–1867) required each household to register with a temple of a certain Buddhist sect (see SHŪMON ARATAME). Also Buddhism by then had a firm place in domestic life and had the principal role in the traditional ANCESTOR WORSHIP of each household. The image placed inside the *butsudan* may be a statue or a picture of Buddha, and the cabinet may be placed in a special room. The shape of the *butsudan* varies somewhat among sects. Offerings of food, flowers and incense are made regularly upon the *butsudan* and Buddhist scriptures are read in front of it.   *Ōuchi Eishin*

Butsurui shōko

A dictionary of Japanese dialects of the latter part of the Edo period (1600–1868). It was written by the *haiku* poet Koshigaya Gozan (also known as Aida Gozan; 1717–87) and published in 1775 in five volumes. The work contains approximately 550 entries with 4,000 annotated dialectal words. The entries are divided into seven categories such as heaven-and-earth, humankind, animals, and so forth. One of the few works on dialects of this time, it is a valuable source on the Japanese language in the Edo period.   *Uwano Zendō*

butterbur → fuki

butterflies

(*chō*). Diurnal insects belonging to the order Lepidoptera. About 20,000 species are known worldwide, of which 265 species of nine families are recorded in Japan.

Family Papilionidae: 19 species including the *gifuchō (Luehdorfia japonica)* and *jakō ageha (Byasa alcinous)*, which are endemic to Japan; the *hime gifuchō* (L. puziloi); the *usuba shiro chō (Parnassius glacialis)*; seven species of the genus *Papilio*, the larvae of which attach themselves to citrus fruit trees; two species (*G. doson* and *G. sarpedon*) of the genus *Graphium* found abundantly in southern Asia; the *benimon ageha (Pachliopta aristolochiae)* and others, found in the southern part of Japan.

Family Pieridae: 29 species including species of the genera *Anthocharis, Leptidea, Aporia* and *Gonepteryx*, distributed in East Asia and the Palaearctic region; genera *Hebomoia, Eurema,* and *Catopsilia,* distributed widely in the tropics; four species of the genus *Pieris*; two species (*C. erate* and *C. palaeno*) of the genus *Colias*.

Family Nymphalidae: 61 species, a little less than one-third of which is the so-called fritillary, including the genera *Argynnis, Argyronome* and *Melitaea*. This family includes the Asama *ichimonji (Ladoga glorifica)*, the only endemic species; the *ichimonji chō* (L. camilla); the *ōmurasaki (Sasakia charonda)*, the best-known Japanese species; the *komurasaki (Apatura ilia)*, the *kujaku chō (Inachis io)*, the *kiberi tateha (Nymphalis antiopa)* and the *hiodoshi chō (N. xanthomelas)*, which are distributed widely in Europe; the *ishigake chō (Cyrestis thyodamas)*, the *ruri tateha (Kaniska canace)*, the *futao chō (Polyura eudamippus)*, the *tateha modoki (Precis almana)*, and Yaeyama *murasaki (Hypolimnas antilope)*, which are also distributed in southern Asia; the *sakahachi chō (Araschnia burejana)* and *gomadara chō (Hestina japonica)*, which are also found in East Asia; and six species of the genus *Neptis*.

Family Satyridae: 27 species including the *takane hikage (Oeneis asamana)*, the Daisetsu *takane hikage (O. daisetsuzana)*, the *satoki madara hikage (Neope goschkevitschii)*, and three species of the genus *Ypthima*, which are endemic to Okinawa; genera *Erebia, Coenonympha,* and *Lasiommata*, which are found largely in northern Japan; two species of genus *Melanitis*, which are plentiful in the tropical zone; and four species of the genus *Lethe*.

Family Danaidae: 19 species including the *asagi madara (Parantica sita)*. Species other than this can be found in the islands in southern Japan, including six species of genus *Euproea*, the *ōgo madara (Idea leuconoe)*, and the *komon asagi madara (Tirumala hamata)*.

Families Libytheidae and Curetidae: only one species each.

Family Lycaenidae: 73 species including about 20 species of the group once called the *zephyrus*, which is distributed throughout East Asia; the *urakin shijimi (Ussuriana stygiana)*, the Fuji *midori shijimi (Quercusia fujisana)* and *benimon karasu shijimi (Strymonidia iyonis)*, which are endemic; the genera *Panchala, Spindasis, Niphanda, Celastrina, Taraka, Pithecops,* and *Shijimia*.

Family Hesperiidae: 35 species with thick bodies including the Ogasawara *seseri (Parnara ogasawarensis)* and *asahina kimadara seseri (Ochlodes asahinai)*, which are endemic to the Ogasawara and Ishigaki Islands respectively; the *kochabane seseri (Thoressa varia)*, which is found only in the main islands; the large *aoba seseri (Choaspes benjaminii)*; the genera *Pyrgus, Erynnis, Daimio, Carterocephalus, Parnara,* and *Pelopidas*; and the *Erionota torus*, a recent introduction to Okinawa which is harmful to the banana.

NAKANE Takehiko

Although numerous plants and animals are mentioned in the 8th-century poetry anthology *Man'yōshū*, there is not a single reference to the butterfly. In an attempt to explain this some writers point out that in 644, according to the chronicle *Nihon shoki* (720), the government proscribed a popular variant of Taoism that venerated the larva of the swallowtail butterfly as a god. By the middle of the Heian period (794–1185) the butterfly had come to be regarded as "something loveable" as SEI SHŌNAGON fondly describes it in her *Makura no sōshi* (ca 996). Her contemporary MURASAKI SHIKIBU, in the *Tale of Genji*, wrote of butterflies adorning Genji's palace, Rokujōin. The TSUTSUMI CHŪNAGON MONOGATARI, which appeared about a century later, contains a story about a young lady of noble birth who loved insects, among them butterflies. From the Muromachi period (1333–1568), the butterfly became a popular motif in decorating furniture and armor.

▬——Shirōzu Takashi, *Genshoku Nihon chōrui zukan* (1976). *Nihonsan chōrui daizukan* (Kōdansha, 1975). SAITŌ Shōji

buyaku

General term for corvée labor. Under the RITSURYŌ SYSTEM of administration established in the 7th century, labor services required

Byōdōin

The Phoenix Hall (Hōōdō) at Byōdōin. Dedicated to the Buddha Amida, the hall was completed in 1053. National Treasure.

by the authorities were called YŌEKI. The term *fueki* (or *bueki*) referred to both corvée labor and other miscellaneous taxes to be paid with various goods. With the decline of central government power, these terms fell into disuse toward the end of the Heian period (794–1185) and were replaced by *buyaku*.

Under the SHŌEN (estate) system of land tenure, which prevailed from the 9th to the 15th century, tax requirements were classified into rice tax (called *shotō* and later NENGU) and KUJI, which included both labor and miscellaneous products. At first *buyaku* meant mainly agricultural labor, but soon the term was applied to such work as reclamation and irrigation projects, repair of roads and the buildings of the *shōen* proprietors (RYŌSHU), the transportation of tax rice, and military duties (GUN'YAKU). These services were requisitioned not only by estate proprietors but also by the JITŌ (shogunate-appointed land stewards) and later by the SHUGO (military governors) as well, thus becoming an enormous burden on the peasantry. Late in the 16th century the national unifiers ODA NOBUNAGA and TOYOTOMI HIDEYOSHI restrained their vassals from exacting long periods of *buyaku*. During the Edo period (1600–1868), cash payments came to replace most labor requirements (see KUNIYAKU), although some services were retained, such as the maintenance of post stations (SUKEGŌ).

Buzen

City in eastern Fukuoka Prefecture, Kyūshū, on the Suō Sea. Buzen produces rice, vegetables, and lumber. Electric power plants and metalwork factories are located in the coastal industrial area. Many of its residents commute to the city of Kita Kyūshū. It is the gateway to Yaba–Hita–Hikosan Quasi-National Park. Pop: 31,701.

Byakkotai

(White Tiger Brigade). A corps of a few hundred youths, the sons of *samurai*, organized in March 1868 by the pro-Tokugawa Aizu domain (now part of Fukushima Prefecture) to resist the forces of the imperial restoration in the BOSHIN CIVIL WAR. After several months of fighting, the Byakkotai was decimated by an imperial army in the Battle of Tonokuchihara (part of a longer conflict known as the Battle of Aizu, which had begun in the late summer) on 8 October 1868. Twenty survivors made their way back to Wakamatsu Castle, the Aizu stronghold, but seeing it in flames and believing their cause to be lost, they repaired to a nearby mountain, Iimoriyama, and committed suicide. The group subsequently became a popular symbol of loyalty, determination, and courage. The Aizu domain surrendered on 6 November.

byōbu → screen and wall painting

Byōbugaura

Coastal area south of the city of Chōshi, northeastern Chiba Prefecture, central Honshū. The Shimōsa Plateau juts out into the Pacific Ocean with cliffs approximately 60 m (196 ft) high for a distance of 10 km (6.2 mi) in the form of a folding screen (*byōbu*, hence the name Byōbugaura, literally, "folding-screen coast"). It forms part of the Suigō–Tsukuba Quasi-National Park.

Byōdōin

A temple founded in the 11th century at Uji, southeast of Kyōto. Originally a large compound of buildings, its chief antique relic today is the *amidadō,* popularly known as the Hōōdō (Phoenix Hall). A hall dedicated to the Buddha AMIDA (Skt: Amitābha), this is one of the finest examples of the aristocratic art and architecture of the latter part of the Heian period (794–1185). It was originally built as a model of Amida's heavenly palace in the Pure Land (see PURE LAND BUDDHISM), and it resembles depictions of that palace in East Asian paintings from as early as the 8th century.

The site of the temple along the cool banks of the Uji River had long been favored by the aristocracy as a refuge from the summer heat of Kyōto. In 998 FUJIWARA NO MICHINAGA, minister of the left and the most powerful political figure of his time, restored a rural villa there, where in his latter years he retired to practice Buddhist meditation and austerities. This villa was converted into a temple in 1052 by his son, FUJIWARA NO YORIMICHI, and in 1053 the *amidadō* was completed; the installation of this hall's main image, a statue of Amida, was celebrated with a lavish vegetarian feast.

Yorimichi was subject to severe criticism for the great expense of these projects; nonetheless, during his lifetime a *hokkedō* (lotus hall) was built and also a large *tahō* ("many-jeweled") pagoda housing a gilded image of the Go Chi Nyorai (Five Wisdom Buddhas). In 1066 a *go dai myōō dō* (hall dedicated to the Five Wisdom Kings; Go Dai Myōō) and bell tower were added—the bell is now a NATIONAL TREASURE—along with a two-story monks' dwelling and a hall in honor of Yuima (Skt: Vimalakīrti). A hall enshrining a statue of Fudō Myōō (Skt: Acala; see MYŌŌ) was built in 1073.

In the Kamakura period (1185–1333), a *kannondō* (Kannon hall) was built to enshrine a Heian-period 11-headed statue of the bodhisattva KANNON (Skt: Avalokiteśvara). Both hall and image are still extant. To the rear of the *amidadō* are monks' dwelling quarters in the SHOIN-ZUKURI style. One of these, the Yōrin'an, is said to have been brought from the castle of the late 16th-century hegemon TOYOTOMI HIDEYOSHI at nearby Fushimi.

From the Edo period (1600–1868), the *amidadō* has been popularly called the Phoenix Hall (Hōōdō) because of the bronze birds that ornament its roof and the bird-like shape of the ground plan. The two side wings and the end pavilions are small in scale and serve no practical purpose other than to create the illusion of the heavenly palace. The lake in front was originally larger than its present size and was given the shape of the Sanskrit letter *A.* Water completely encircled the hall by means of a small canal, which still runs under the rear corridor, enhancing the symbolic role of the building as a place of purity removed from the mundane world. It is thought that originally the aristocracy viewed the temple from a small pavilion, now lost, which looked on the front of the building from across the lake. The intricate splendors of the interior were usually sealed from view.

The Phoenix Hall still retains its aesthetic coherence even though it has often been damaged and restored, especially in the roof and canopies. The dais for the main image was once inlaid with lacquer, mother-of-pearl, and silver; traces of the design are still visible. The ornamental canopies over the head of the image are intricately carved with open-work floral motifs. Attached high on the inner wall around the image are 52 small wooden images of bodhisattvas praying, dancing, and playing musical instruments on clouds. The majority of these are as old as the hall itself.

On the inside of the doors and walls of the hall were painted scenes depicting various aspects of Amida's powers of salvation. Eight of them were based on the *Kan muryōju kyō* (Skt: *Amitāyurdhyāna-sūtra*) and show Amida coming to receive a dying person destined for rebirth in one of the nine levels of paradise; behind the seated Amida statue was a depiction of that paradise. These paintings have been attributed to TAKUMA TAMENARI, head of a well-known painting workshop active at the time. The paintings are too poorly preserved to confirm or deny this attribution, but the extant fragments of landscape scenes are done in the native Japanese YAMATO-E style, which is thought to have flourished in court circles at this time.

Dominating the interior of the hall is the large statue of Amida, one of the masterpieces of its age and now designated a National Treasure. It is the only extant work known to have been carved by JŌCHŌ. Its great size (278.7 cm or 110 in high) was made possible by the use of the so-called *yosegi-zukuri* (assembled wood-block) technique; but despite its scale, the statue has an abstracted, refined, even withdrawn quality. Its seven-level lotus pedestal is also from the workshop of Jōchō, as is the halo with 12 small celestial beings carved in a delicate tracery of clouds and drapery. In the halo over the head of Amida is a small image of Dainichi Nyorai, which is technically the principal deity *(honzon)* of the temple. The original statue of Dainichi in the main hall was lost in the fire of 1336, which destroyed all but the Phoenix Hall and the Kannon hall. When the Amida statue was repaired in the Meiji period (1868–1912), in its hollow stomach was found a small, brightly painted lotus pedestal on which a *dhāraṇī* formula (a mystical spell used in esoteric Buddhism) was written in Sanskrit. This object is thought to date from the time of the image's dedication.

The temple's original affiliation was with the Jimon branch of the TENDAI SECT. The first resident monk was Myōson (971–1063), the head of MIIDERA temple in Ōtsu. The Byōdōin has been affiliated with both the Tendai sect and the JŌDO SECT from the 14th century, but it no longer serves in the performance of regular Buddhist ceremonies.

▰——Toshio Fukuyama, *Heian Temples: Byōdō-in and Chūson-ji* (1976).

John M. ROSENFIELD

C

cabinet → **prime minister and cabinet**

Cabinet Library

(Naikaku Bunko). Part of the NATIONAL ARCHIVES, located in Kitanomaru Park, Chiyoda Ward, Tōkyō. With about 500,000 old and rare volumes, the library is one of the largest branches of the NATIONAL DIET LIBRARY. Some of the collections of distinguished provenance are the Momijiyama Bunko of TOKUGAWA IEYASU, the collection of the SHŌHEIKŌ, the Confucian college of the Tokugawa shogunate, and books assembled by the Wagaku Kōdansho, the research bureau founded by HANAWA HOKIICHI. Collections of *daimyō* and provincial scholars are also included.

Theodore F. WELCH

cabinet order

(seirei). Within the class of laws promulgated by administrative agencies and called orders *(meirei)*, those promulgated by the cabinet are called cabinet orders. Cabinet orders rank above ministerial orders *(shōrei)*, which are promulgated by individual ministers.

Under the 1889 Meiji Constitution, the cabinet could deviate from the will of the IMPERIAL DIET and issue independent orders necessary to preserve public order or to advance the welfare of the people, as well as emergency orders having the same effect as statutes (HŌRITSU) to respond to a crisis. Under the present CONSTITUTION, however, the Diet is the sole legislative body, and these types of orders are no longer permitted. The cabinet or a minister may only issue executive orders *(shikkō meirei)*, establishing regulations for the implementation of statutes, and delegated orders *(inin meirei)*, determining matters delegated by statute. Delegated orders, moreover, may not involve as sweeping a delegation as was found in the NATIONAL MOBILIZATION LAW of 1938. No penalties may be established without a specific statutory delegation. Although the scope of cabinet orders is limited in these ways, as the role of administrative organs grows in Japan, more and more often laws only establish general outlines, and cabinet and ministerial orders are used to give the outlines substantive content.

ITŌ Masami

cable television

Also known as CATV (Community Antenna Television). CATV was originally designed to serve areas in large cities where television reception is hampered by tall buildings as well as other areas which have difficulty picking up regular television signals. The first CATV system in Japan was put into operation in 1954 in Ikaho, Gumma Prefecture. Since then cable television has experienced considerable growth. The most remarkable development of CATV has been in the area of independent television broadcasting. However, because of the high cost of equipment and labor, the success of these independent cable-broadcast ventures has been uneven. In 1973 a law was passed which set strict regulations on licensing and reporting, further hindering the free development of independent broadcasting. The development of reciprocal cable transmission through the use of optical fiber is in the experimental stage. As of 1978 there were over 19,000 CATV facilities nationwide. *HAYASHI Shigeju*

Cabral, Francisco (?-1609)

Portuguese Jesuit priest who served as the Superior of the Christian Mission in Japan from 1570 until 1581. Born in the Azores, he left for India in 1550 and entered the Society of Jesus there. Arriving in Japan in 1570, he worked indefatigably as Mission Superior, but his insistence that Japanese Christians should adapt themselves to the language and culture of European missionaries rather than the reverse as well as his insistence on tight restrictions on the admission of Japanese into the Society of Jesus clashed with the more liberal views of the visitor, Alessandro VALIGNANO. Cabral left Japan in 1583 and died in Goa. See also CHRISTIANITY. *Michael COOPER*

Cachon, Mermet de (1828-1870)

French Catholic priest and missionary in Japan who played an important role in politics and diplomacy in the last years of the Tokugawa shogunate (1603-1867). A member of the French Société des Missions Etrangères (Society for Foreign Missions), Cachon came to Okinawa in 1855 and began his study of Japanese. After serving as interpreter for the first French embassy to Japan in 1858, he went to Hakodate, where he spent several years in missionary and teaching activities. He left Japan in 1863 but returned the following year as interpreter for Léon ROCHES, then the French minister to Japan. He developed close ties with Tokugawa officials and came to enjoy an unusual degree of access to, and the confidence of, the shogunate. As Roches's interpreter, adviser, and representative, Cachon had a crucial role in the development of a special relationship between France and the Tokugawa regime, which produced reforms aimed at strengthening the shogunate. He left Japan in 1866 for reasons of poor health; on his return to Paris he published a French-English-Japanese dictionary and served as adviser and interpreter for the Ministry of Foreign Affairs.

■ ——Meron Medzini, *French Policy in Japan during the Closing Years of the Tokugawa Regime* (1971). *Mark D. ERICSON*

Cai E (Ts'ai O) (1882-1912)

(J: Sai Gaku). A brilliant military and political figure in early Republican China. Born in Hunan, Cai E participated in the radical reform movement that flourished in that province briefly in the late 1890s. After the collapse of the movement, he followed LIANG QICHAO (Liang Ch'i-ch'ao) to Japan where he studied at the Army Academy in Tōkyō. Returning to China, he played a prominent role in overthrowing Qing (Ch'ing) authority in Yunnan and subsequently, together with Liang, led the Yunnan-based movement to rescue the Chinese republic from the imperial pretensions of YUAN SHIKAI (Yüan Shih-k'ai). *Ernest P. YOUNG*

Cairo Conference

(Kairo Kaigi). A meeting of the leaders of the Allied forces fighting Japan in World War II; held in Cairo in November 1943. Following the conference, US President Franklin D. Roosevelt, British Prime Minister Winston Churchill, and Chinese Generalissimo Chiang Kai-shek issued the Cairo Declaration, which contained the first public outline of their postwar plans for the territory occupied by Japan. Disclaiming any interest in territorial expansion themselves, the Allies agreed that Japan should be stripped of all conquests made since 1914. These included Korea, whose independence the Allies agreed upon, and parts of China, such as Taiwan, Manchuria, and the Pescadores. They also demanded the unconditional surrender of Japan. These points were later reiterated, with additional conditions relating to the USSR, at the YALTA CONFERENCE and then at the Potsdam Conference (see POTSDAM DECLARATION).

calendar, dates, and time

Since 1 January 1873 the Japanese have used the Gregorian calendar. Except for the practice of numbering years serially from the year in

Calendar, dates, and time

The 24 Points (sekki and chūki) of the Old Solar Calendar

Season	Name of sekki or chūki		Meaning	Associations	Gregorian date
Spring	Risshun	立春	Beginning of spring	Old Solar New Year	4 or 5 February
	Usui	雨水	"Rainwater"	Snow turns to rain	19 or 20 February
	Keichitsu	啓蟄	"End of insect hibernation"	Warmer weather; insects emerge	5 or 6 March
	Shumbun	春分	Vernal equinox		21 or 22 March
	Seimei	清明	"Pure and clear"	Southeasterly winds bring pleasant weather	5 or 6 April
	Kokuu	穀雨	"Grain rains"	Grains germinate in spring rains	20 or 21 April
Summer	Rikka	立夏	Beginning of summer		5 or 6 May
	Shōman	小満	"The lesser ripening"	All things growing	21 or 22 May
	Bōshu	芒種	"Grain beards and seeds"	Rice transplanting	6 or 7 June
	Geshi	夏至	Summer solstice		21 or 22 June
	Shōsho	小暑	"The lesser heat"	Summer heat increases	7 or 8 July
	Taisho	大暑	"The greater heat"	Maximum summer heat	23 or 24 July
Autumn	Risshū	立秋	Beginning of autumn		7 or 8 August
	Shosho	処暑	"Manageable heat"	Autumn winds bring a lessening of heat	23 or 24 August
	Hakuro	白露	"White dew"	Autumn weather; birds migrate	8 or 9 September
	Shūbun	秋分	Autumnal equinox		23 or 24 September
	Kanro	寒露	"Cold dew"	Leaves turn color; the height of autumn	8 or 9 October
	Sōkō	霜降	"Frost falls"	First frost; the end of autumn	23 or 24 October
Winter	Rittō	立冬	Beginning of winter		7 or 8 November
	Shōsetsu	小雪	"The lesser snow"	Light snowfall	22 or 23 November
	Taisetsu	大雪	"The greater snow"	Heavy snowfall; winter weather	7 or 8 December
	Tōji	冬至	Winter solstice		21 or 22 December
	Shōkan	小寒	"The lesser cold"	Cold weather increases	5 or 6 January
	Daikan	大寒	"The greater cold"	Maximum winter cold	20 or 21 January

which a reigning emperor ascended the throne, the Japanese method for designating dates does not differ from the Western. Hence, 12 October 1980 was identical with the Japanese date, the 12th day of the 10th month of the 55th year of Shōwa (1926–). Before 1873, however, the official Japanese calendar was a lunar calendar. That is to say, it was based on completely different principles from those of the solar calendars that the Western world has used for civil purposes since Roman times.

Solar and Lunar Calendars——Both solar and lunar calendars take as their basic counting unit the year, corresponding with greater or less exactitude to the period of the earth's revolution around the sun, and the month, approximating the period of the moon's revolution around the earth. Astronomers describe the motions of these heavenly bodies with mathematical accuracy, and thereby define units of time which one may call the natural year and the natural month, or lunation. These units do not contain a whole number of days or months. Civil calendars, both solar and lunar, remedy this problem in a variety of ways.

A solar calendar is one that takes as its main basis for measuring time the natural year, modifying it for civil purposes only to the extent of reckoning calendar years as whole numbers of days (either 365 or 366). If the leap years in such a calendar are carefully apportioned, it will never deviate far from the year of nature. The vernal equinox will fall on or about 21 March in our own solar calendar until the end of time. Inasmuch as the number of natural months in a natural year is an unwieldy fraction somewhere between 12 and 13, societies with solar calendars customarily ignore the lunation as a practical unit for measuring time. The "month" used for civil purposes in these calendars is merely one of 12 more or less equal divisions of a civil year.

In lunar calendars the basic unit of measurement is a civil month, which differs from the lunation only to the degree necessary to ensure that each contains a whole number of days (29 or 30). A lunar calendar, properly constructed, is a close reflection of the phases of the moon. A full moon occurs on or about the same day of every civil month. In the Chinese and Japanese civil calendar, a new moon occurred on the first day of the month. In order for each civil year to contain a whole number of months, the lunar calendar year deviated considerably from the natural year. Twelve months totaled about 353 days (nearly two weeks short of a natural year), while 13 months (about 383 days) was even wider of the mark. The Chinese and Japanese civil year normally contained 12 months, but in order to

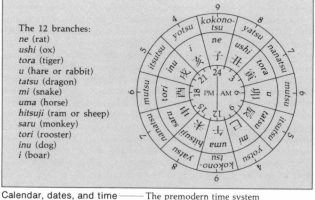

The 12 branches:
ne (rat)
ushi (ox)
tora (tiger)
u (hare or rabbit)
tatsu (dragon)
mi (snake)
uma (horse)
hitsuji (ram or sheep)
saru (monkey)
tori (rooster)
inu (dog)
i (boar)

Calendar, dates, and time——The premodern time system

The 12 parts of the day and the two ways of naming them, using either the 12 branches of the sexagenary system or numbers.

assure that there would be a rough correspondence between a certain month of the civil year and a certain season of the natural year, a 13th month was added, or intercalated, in some years. This combination of features—close correspondence between civil and natural months plus inexact correspondence between civil and natural years—marks the essential difference between the old Japanese lunar calendar and the solar calendar of the Western world.

The Old Solar Calendar——Although the Japanese civil calendar was a lunar calendar, farmers needed a calendar that would tell them the best times for planting and harvests, activities that followed the seasons of the natural year. In short, they needed a solar calendar. Ancient Chinese astronomers provided one that was both simple and accurate, and which became an unofficial calendar for Japanese farmers. The nomenclature of this old solar calendar is still in common use among Japanese, and its workings must be understood for the bearing they had on the operation of the official lunar calendar.

The natural year was measured by reference to the period between two successive occurrences of the winter solstice. In fact the winter solstice was not taken as the *beginning* of the solar year; it was the midpoint of the first of 12 divisions (called *setsu*) of the year.

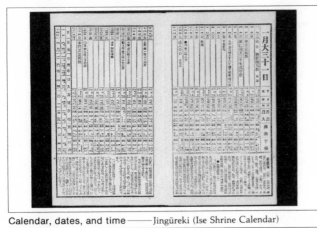

Calendar, dates, and time —— Jingūreki (Ise Shrine Calendar)

Calendar for January 1983. From 1873 (when the solar calendar was adopted) to 1945 all official Japanese calendars were calculated by the Tōkyō Astronomical Observatory and published by the Ise Shrine. The shrine lost its connection with the government observatory after World War II, but it continues to issue its own calendar-almanac.

Each *setsu* was of absolutely equal duration, that is, each contained a fractional number of days—about 30.44. The beginning of a *setsu* was known as *sekki*, and the midpoint of a *setsu* was known as *chūki*. As the winter solstice marked the first *chūki* of the solar year, the first *sekki*, which began the year, occurred about 15 days earlier, approximately 6 December in the Gregorian calendar.

Each *sekki* and *chūki* had its own name, often highly expressive of weather or agricultural phenomena. These 24 points (Nijūshi-sekki) in the old solar calendar correspond very closely to dates of the Gregorian calendar; any deviation is a result of the fact that a point in the Gregorian system itself sometimes differs by as much as a whole day from the corresponding point in the natural solar year.

The Old Civil Calendar —— In order to make the lunar civil calendar of Japan correspond at least roughly to the seasons of the natural year, calendar makers made use of certain devices relating to the old solar calendar just described. Civil months in the Japanese calendar were numbered from 1 to 12, and the numbers were derived according to the following formula. The lunar month containing the first *chūki* (which was of course the winter solstice, a point in the solar year) was always numbered the 11th of the civil year. Similarly, the civil month including the second *chūki* was the 12th, and that containing the third *chūki*, which fell on about 19 February in the Gregorian calendar, was considered the first month (Shōgatsu). Hence the rule for determining the beginning of the Japanese civil year: it fell on the first new moon preceding the third *chūki* of the solar year. The Gregorian date corresponding to the Japanese New Year varied, but it was always between 21 January and 19 February. For example, although the year Meiji 2 (second year of the Meiji period) is commonly referred to as 1869, in fact it began on 11 February 1869 and ended on 31 January 1870.

Intercalation of additional months was determined in the following way. Some civil months contained no *chūki*, for the period between successive *chūki* was about one day longer than the lunation that determined a civil month. If a *chūki* fell within a few hours immediately preceding a new moon, the next *chūki* fell just after the next new moon. In such a case, the whole intervening civil month was called intercalary (*jun* or *uruu*) and took its number from the preceding civil month. Thus, a month designated as intercalary third (Uruu Sangatsu) fell between the third and the fourth months of the civil calendar. An intercalation occurred regularly about one month out of every 30.

The Japanese did not invent the system, but adopted it from China in AD 604. Chinese and Japanese normally applied long-established formulas, rather than relying on direct astronomical observations, for intercalation and for determining when to start a new month. If the formulas were slightly inaccurate, a month might be intercalated too soon or too late, or the first day of a civil month might fall a day before or after the appearance of a new moon. Invariably the Chinese devised the necessary corrections first, the Japanese following suit some years or centuries later. As a consequence, the Chinese and Japanese civil calendars occasionally differed in the designation for a day or a month.

Excellent records have been kept of the exact duration of every civil month and year, and these supply the basis for conversion to Gregorian equivalents which modern scholars require. There are three calendrical conversion tables for Japanese dates. The earliest, that of William Bramsen (1880, *Japanese Chronological Tables),* contains inaccuracies and has been superseded by the other two: *Sansei sōran* (Naimushō Chirikyoku, 1932), an official publication, and *Japanese Chronological Tables* by Paul Tsuchihashi, issued in 1952. Both of these give the Western date corresponding to the first day of every Japanese civil month. The instructions below for the conversion of dates may be used for any of these three tables. (A table of correspondences for each day of the Chinese and Japanese lunar calendars and its Gregorian equivalent has been compiled by Gaimushō Bunshoka for the years 1700–1911: *Nihon gaikō bunsho: Kindai in'yōreki taishō hyō,* prefaced 1951).

The Japanese calendrical tables cited above differ as to which of the two Western calendars, the Old Style (OS) Julian calendar, or the New Style (NS) Gregorian calendar, they use in converting Japanese dates of a given period. Dates through 15 October 1582, NS (4 October, OS) normally convert to the Julian calendar. Only in very special cases is a Gregorian date justified. For example, data on solar or seasonal phenomena might be more meaningful if expressed in Gregorian terms, which correspond more closely to the natural year than do those of the Old Style. For dates between 1582 and 1752, it may be convenient to use whichever calendar was current in the country or society with which you are dealing.

A date in the Japanese lunar calendar conveys three pieces of information: the year, the month, and the day of the month. There are four different methods for specifying a year of the old civil calendar. (1) The name of a calendrical era, or NENGŌ, and the number of a year within the era. Take for example the fifth year of Keichō, in which the Battle of Sekigahara occurred. Keichō was an era that began in 1596. (2) Using the sexagenary cycle, the fifth year of Keichō might also be called *kōshi no toshi*, or *kanoe-ne no toshi*, a designation indicating the 37th year of the cycle, in this case the cycle that began in 1564. (3) For dates in early Japanese history, a year was identified by its number in the reign of an emperor. (4) The fifth year of Keichō might also be designated as the year 2260 of the continuing era dated from 660 BC, the legendary date of the founding of the Japanese imperial dynasty.

Nengō —— The use of relatively brief calendrical eras known as *nengō* was an imitation of Chinese practice, adopted in Japan in AD 645. The first Japanese era name, commemorating the revolutionary political changes of that year, was Taika, or Great Reform. Except for a brief lapse in the latter part of the 7th century, *nengō* have been in continuous use ever since.

Customarily a new era was declared by the imperial court within a year or two after the accession of a new emperor. In addition, at two points in each sexagenary cycle, the first year and the 58th, which were thought to be auspicious, a new era was usually proclaimed. Moreover, the era might be changed for a variety of other reasons—for example, after some felicitous or unlucky event.

The name of an era might indicate the reason for its adoption, as in the case of the Wadō (literally, "refined copper") era (708–715), proclaimed because of the first minting of copper coins (WADŌ KAIHŌ) in Japan. More often, however, the literal significance of a *nengō* is neither obvious from its appearance nor realized generally by Japanese people. For the most part, the characters are of pleasant connotation and allude to tags from the classics of Chinese Confucianism. The characters of a *nengō* are invariably pronounced according to one or another of their Sino-Japanese ON READINGS.

Premodern *nengō* are not reign names. Only after 1868 did the Japanese adopt the practice of including the entire reign of an emperor in one era. Meiji, the era proclaimed in that year, continued until the death of the reigning sovereign in 1912. His son's reign, coterminous with the Taishō era, lasted until 25 December 1926. The Shōwa calendrical era began on 25 December, thus Shōwa 1 lasted for only a week. Meiji and later *nengō* differ from all previous ones in that they have been or will be designated as official posthumous names of the emperors whose reigns they commemorate.

The proclamation of a new era could occur at any time in the civil year. It is customary among scholars, however, to refer to the entire year in which a new era began, including the portion before the change, as the first year of the new era, though of course one encounters dating by the preceding *nengō* in contemporary documents. The years 1912 and 1926 are called the 45th year of Meiji and 15th year of Taishō, respectively, before the emperors' deaths.

To find the Western equivalent for a Japanese year, take the Western year in which the *first* year of the *nengō* era began, subtract one (to obtain the hypothetical "zero" year), and add the number of the Japanese year. For example, to convert the year Shōwa 43, we learn from a *nengō* table (see the table in NENGŌ) that the first year of Shōwa began in 1926, subtract one (1926 − 1 = 1925), and add 43; the Western year is revealed as 1968.

Because premodern Japanese years were not exactly coterminous with Western ones, as explained above, special caution is required when dating events that occurred in the last two months of a Japanese year. For example, the shōgun Ashikaga Yoshimitsu is usually said (even in Japanese reference works) to have ruled from 1368 (Ōan 1) to 1394 (Ōei 1). A careful historian will notice, however, that he took office on the 30th day of the 12th month of Ōan 1 (7 February 1369) and abdicated on the 17th day of the 12th month of Ōei 1 (8 January 1395), so that Yoshimitsu ruled in fact from 1369 to 1395.

Occasionally in premodern works one comes upon era designations that were never officially adopted by the Japanese court. These are known as *shi nengō*, private or unofficial *nengō*. Students of Japanese art history often see references to the *shi nengō* Hakuhō, denoting the period from 673 to 686, when no official *nengō* was in use.

During the period of the NORTHERN AND SOUTHERN COURTS from 1336 to 1392 both the Northern (Kyōto) Court and the rival Southern (Yoshino) Court reckoned dates according to their own *nengō*. The Southern Court is widely regarded as the legitimate one (see NAMBOKUCHŌ SEIJUN RON). The year Ōan 1 mentioned above is Shōhei 23 in the Southern Court's calendar.

The Sexagenary Cycle —— In addition to cardinal numerals, the Chinese and Japanese employ two sets of terms for purposes of enumeration (see JIKKAN JŪNISHI). One set contains 10 terms known as *jikkan*, the 10 stems. The other contains 12 terms called *jūnishi*, the 12 branches.

Since ancient times, East Asian peoples have used these two sets of terms to enumerate years (and other units) of their civil calendar. When both series are used together they form a greater cycle of 60 combinations, as 60 is the least common multiple of 10 and 12. The first combination in the sexagenary cycle is formed of the first stem and the first branch, followed by the second stem and the second branch, and so on. The 11th combination consists of the first stem and the 11th branch, the 12th the second stem and 12th branch, and the 13th the third stem and first branch.

The year 604, in which the Japanese officially adopted the Chinese calendar, was the first of a sexagenary cycle. A cycle began in 1924, and another will begin in 1984. Each of the 10 stems corresponds to a certain final digit in the number of a year in the Christian era. *Kō*, or *kinoe*, the first stem, always appears in the sexagenary designation for a year of the Western calendar ending in the digit four (1944, 1954, 1964, etc).

The Japanese "National Era" —— The method of counting years from the legendary founding of Japan was begun in the early Meiji period (1868–1912) and commonly used until the end of World War II, when it was abandoned. To find the Western equivalent for a year, simply subtract 660 from the number. The word *kigen* (the beginning of the dynasty) or *kōki* (imperial era) is sometimes prefixed to such dates to differentiate them from years of the Christian era.

Reign Years —— For dates of the 7th century and earlier, when official *nengō* did not exist, years may be designated by number within the reign of an emperor. In this case the official posthumous name of the emperor is used, and it is usually followed by the word *tennō* (sovereign) to distinguish the designation from a true *nengō*. For example, the seventh year of the reign of Emperor Jomei (Jomei Tennō *shichinen*) is equivalent to 635/636. This system appears similar to that for assigning *nengō* today. However, it differs in one important respect. The "first year" of a reign is taken, for calendrical purposes, to be the first full calendar year after the emperor's accession, rather than the year in which the accession took place, as with *nengō* today. To calculate the Western equivalent of a Japanese year identified in this way, one must first find the year of the emperor's accession, then add the number of the Japanese year.

Months —— All civil months (except the first, which was usually known as Shōgatsu) were designated by number, or, if intercalary, by the character *jun* or *uruu* plus the name of the preceding month. Terms of the sexagenary cycle could theoretically be applied to months, but almost never were in practice.

In addition to their formal Sino-Japanese names (Shōgatsu or Ichigatsu, Nigatsu, Sangatsu, etc), the months had informal or poetic ones of native Japanese origin, as follows:

1. Mutsuki
2. Kisaragi
3. Yayoi
4. Uzuki
5. Satsuki
6. Minazuki
7. Fuzuki
8. Hazuki
9. Nagatsuki
10. Kannazuki
11. Shimotsuki
12. Shiwasu

These names are rarely used as parts of full dates.

Formal histories of premodern Japan sometimes included as part of a date the word for the season of the year. Spring was considered to contain the first three civil months, summer the next three, and so on. An intercalary month was always considered to belong to the same season as the month preceding it.

Times of Day —— Japan lies in a standard time zone which mariners call "plus nine." That is, standard time in that zone is always nine hours later than it is at the Greenwich meridian, and hence 14 hours later than in New York, which is zone "minus five." The difference in hour usually makes for a difference in date. For example, the Pearl Harbor attack that began the Pacific War occurred on 7 December 1941, Hawaii time, but 8 December Japanese time.

Until the Meiji period, when the Western system for telling time came into general use, the Japanese described times of day in two different ways. One of these made use of the same 12 branches of the sexagenary system. The period from sunset to sunrise was divided into six equal parts, and the period from sunrise to sunset also in six equal parts, but not necessarily of the same duration as the other six. The first branch, *ne* (rat) corresponded to the fourth period after sunset, roughly 11:00 PM to 1:00 AM. Sometimes a cyclical sign might be used for the beginning of a period, rather than its whole duration. Hence, the derivation of the modern Japanese words for AM and PM are *gozen* and *gogo*, which mean before and after the hour of the horse, respectively. The character for horse, *go* or *uma*, is the seventh of the 12 branches.

The other system divided the day into the same 12 parts, but assigned numbers to them. The "hour of the rat" might also be called the ninth hour (*kokonotsu-doki*). The next period was the eighth hour, the next the seventh, and so on, counting backward until the last period of the forenoon, which was the fourth hour. For times of day from (roughly) noon to midnight, the same six numbers were used over again, beginning with nine and running back to four. See also PERIODIZATION; SHIBUKAWA SHUNKAI; TAKAHASHI YOSHITOKI.

Herschel WEBB

calligraphy

(*shodō*; the Way of writing). In Japan, as in other East Asian countries in the Chinese cultural sphere, calligraphy is considered one of the fine arts. It implies not merely the skillful writing of characters, in the usual meaning of the English word "calligraphy," but also the entire culture associated with it as a discipline. It is a sister art to poetry and painting.

In China, the birthplace of East Asian calligraphy, these three disciplines—poetry, calligraphy, and painting—were maintained as essential learning and appropriate subjects for every aspiring cultured man and woman, young and old, throughout the ages. Excellence in writing was believed to be a revelation of superior inner character. The respect accorded to calligraphy in Japan was essentially an extension of its status in China.

Along with mastery of the fundamentals of writing with *fude* (brush) and *sumi* (Chinese ink), the aim of *shodō* is to develop the practitioner's moral stature. In Japan as well as in China, the attainment of excellence in calligraphy signified an accomplishment of character on the part of the practitioner. Virtually all men of letters through the history of Japan have been accomplished calligraphers; sons of warriors were regularly trained in calligraphy as well as in the martial arts, and all parents saw to it that their children acquired a good writing style. Something of this respect for *shodō* has survived in the modern elementary and middle-school curriculum in the form of *shūji*, the Japanese equivalent of penmanship.

To understand the history of Japanese calligraphy, however, one must turn back over a thousand years, to its origin. In the beginning Japan had no written language, and began to adopt Chinese writing only around the 5th century AD, relatively late in comparison to

Calligraphy —— A calligrapher at work

A calligrapher writing with a slender brush *(hosofude)*, his implements placed to his right. A round weight aids in securing the paper.

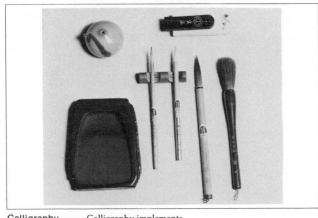

Calligraphy —— Calligraphy implements

Shown (in clockwise order from top left) are a ceramic water-dropper *(suiteki)*, a stick of *sumi*, two thick brushes *(futofude)*, two slender brushes *(hosofude)* on a brushrest, and an inkstone *(suzuri)*.

vored to various degrees in later periods (see POETRY AND PROSE IN CHINESE). In addition to writings in Chinese, however, all the major works of Japanese literature became subjects for calligraphy, both poetry and prose. Although printing existed in Japan from the 8th century, it was not until the end of the 16th century that it took over as the major mode of reproducing literary texts, and even then calligraphy played an important role in woodblock-printed books.

Various types of Chinese-character scripts, or SHOTAI, are practiced. The different types of scripts are actually a reflection of the historical development of writing in China. *Tensho,* or archaic script, is traditionally used for carving official stamps or SEALS and originated during the Qin (Ch'in) dynasty (221 BC–206 BC). *Reisho,* or clerical script, was used for official documents. These are very ancient Chinese scripts and did not come into extensive use in Japan until the Edo period (1600–1868), when Chinese historical studies received much attention. More common is *kaisho,* or block-style script, perhaps the most popular style since the characters are easily recognizable; it is used in modern movable types as well. *Gyōsho,* or "running-style" script, is created by a faster movement of the brush and some consequent abbreviation of the character, as well as a running together of certain of the strokes that make up the character. This script is frequently used for informal writing. *Sōsho,* or "grass writing," is a true cursive style that abbreviates and links parts of a character, resulting in fluid and curvilinear writing. In *sōsho* writing, variations in the size of different characters may occur in a column, and some characters may be joined to the next, creating rhythmic and artistic forms.

These five types of script can be mastered through copying the style of a particular master calligrapher. Students study all types of script and begin by copying the style of the master they admire. The first goal of an aspiring calligrapher is therefore emulation. However, the greatest masters are said to have gone beyond emulation and to have established their own styles of writing.

Compared to writing styles, calligraphy implements have changed very little since the early days of this art in Japan. There are two basic kinds of brush: *futofude* (thick brush) and *hosofude* (slender brush); the former is generally used for the main body of writing, and the latter usually for writing inscriptions and the signature at the end of a work or for small-character calligraphy or fine cursive writing. *Sumi,* or Chinese ink, is usually made of soot from burned wood or oil mixed with hide or fishbone glue and dried into a stick. To make liquid ink the stick is rubbed on an inkstone, or *suzuri,* that has an indentation at one end to hold a small pool of water. The *suiteki,* or small water-dropper, either ceramic or metal, completes the paraphernalia. When not in use, this writing equipment is kept in a *suzuribako,* or writing-equipment box, which is often made of lacquer and quite elaborate.

Any comprehensive survey of the art of calligraphy in Japan must mention connoisseurship and collection activities, which developed significantly in the Edo period. Indeed, successive Tokugawa shōguns employed the Kohitsu ("old brush") family—a professional name given to several generations of a single family—to specialize in authentication of ancient calligraphies and manuscripts. Some very ancient calligraphic works known as *kohitsugire* ("old brush fragments"), many of them fragmentary pieces from the 8th to the 14th centuries, are probably the most expensive items in the art market today. The extent to which these *kohitsugire* are jealously guarded by collectors and the stunning monetary price attached to them explains in part why so few examples of early Japanese calligraphy are in foreign museums.

Calligraphy and scholarship have long gone hand in hand in Japan. Historical studies of calligraphy have contributed much to the development of Japanese textual studies in general, especially those which deal with ancient manuscripts and documents (see DIPLOMATICS).

Early History —— The earliest Japanese writing in Chinese is found in INSCRIPTIONS in stone or metal, and among the oldest of these are the cast or incised inscriptions on a bronze mirror excavated in Wakayama Prefecture and a bronze sword recently unearthed at the INARIYAMA TOMB in Saitama Prefecture. The writing found on these archaeological objects, however, is artless in comparison with contemporary examples from the mainland and the Korean states.

With the introduction of Buddhism and Confucianism to Japan around the 6th century, numerous examples of Chinese writings entered Japan, mostly sutras and Buddhist commentaries written in brush and ink on paper in varied script styles. The earliest record of writings being brought to Japan appears in the history NIHON SHOKI (720) regarding the presentation of sutra commentaries by the king

neighboring states on the Korean peninsula. At first the Japanese copied Chinese texts and studied and wrote in Chinese, but very soon they began using Chinese characters, or KANJI, in new ways to suit the requirements of the Japanese language. With no other way to represent the inflections and grammatical particles of Japanese, some characters were employed to represent sounds regardless of meaning. The poetry anthology MAN'YŌSHŪ (ca 759), for example, was written almost exclusively using Chinese characters to convey Japanese syllables, a method of writing now known as *man'yōgana* (see the section on the Manyō writing system in MAN'YŌSHŪ). Ultimately, this practice led to the abbreviation of certain characters and the creation in the 9th century of Japanese syllabaries, or KANA, that could be used either alone or, later in the development of Japanese writing, in combination with Chinese characters. The Japanese *kana* script was in wide use by the 10th century and emerged as a unique and major calligraphic form after the 11th century.

Nevertheless, for a long time the Chinese language retained its status in Japan as the literary language of the elite, and it was faof Paekche in 552. The earliest extant handwritten text by a Japanese is thought to be the *Commentary on the Lotus Sutra* (see SANGYŌ GISHO), which is purported to have been written by Prince SHŌTOKU (574–622). It is written in a typical clerical-cursive style that was current in China from the late 4th century to the late 6th century. This style was widely practiced by scribes and literati alike even after the Tang-dynasty (T'ang; 618–907) style was introduced in the 7th century. As in painting and sculpture, the Japanese were following a style that was already over 100 years old in China.

From the late 7th century through the 8th century, early Tang dynasty calligraphic styles were rapidly mastered in Japan, notably through increased sutra copying activities that began in earnest with the establishment of the official sutra copying bureau (Shakyōjo) in the capital city of Nara. Surviving examples of ancient sutra copies (*koshakyō*) show Japanese mastery of the mixed styles of Chinese calligraphy masters of the Tang dynasty and earlier such as Wang Xizhi (Wang Hsi-chih; ca 307–365?) and Ouyang Xun (Ou-yang Hsün; 557–638).

The calligraphic examples of the Nara period (710–794) are best preserved in the SHŌSŌIN imperial art repository in Nara, where both dated and undated Buddhist sutras and commentaries as well as official documents and letters have been well preserved. Known as Shōsōin *monjo* (Shōsōin documents), some of these Buddhist sutras are accompanied by frontispiece designs, the best-known being the scroll of *Bommōkyō* (*Brahmajāla-sūtra; The Net of Indra*), a seminal work of early Japanese painting. Two of the most important calligraphic examples from the Shōsōin collection are a transcript of Wang Xizhi's *Gakkiron* (Ch: *Leyilun* or *Lo-i-lun*), dated 744 and written by Empress KŌMYŌ (701–760), and the inventory of items offered to the temple TŌDAIJI, dated 756 and 758, also written by Empress Kōmyō.

The Shōsōin documents evidence not only the transmission to Japan of the major styles of Chinese calligraphy but also reveal how the Japanese transformed the writing habits of the Chinese. In some of these documents, both official and private, the stroke order, that is, the sequential order of writing a character, has been abbreviated in a uniquely Japanese way. Documents in the block style almost always follow the Chinese models, but clearly by the 8th century the Japanese had begun to develop a unique way of abbreviating stroke order in the cursive style, anticipating the cursive *kana* syllabaries.

Heian Period (794–1185) —— The 9th century saw Japanese calligraphy emerging as a major art form. The pioneer and early shaper of Japanese calligraphy was the monk KŪKAI (774–835), who lived in China between 804 and 806 and not only brought back to Japan the calligraphic style of Yan Zhenqing (Yen Chen-ch'ing; 709–785), then popular in metropolitan Tang China, but also established an awareness of the theoretical aspects of calligraphy as an aesthetic form. Because of his extraordinary career as the founder of the esoteric Shingon Buddhist tradition and a calligrapher par excellence, many calligraphic works have been attributed to Kūkai, though a large number are of doubtful authenticity. The most unquestionably accepted work is *Fūshinjō*, a collection of his letters to SAICHŌ, the founder of the Tendai sect of Buddhism and an eminent calligrapher in his own right who had also sojourned in China.

Kūkai and his contemporaries Emperor SAGA (786–842) and courtier TACHIBANA NO HAYANARI (d 842) are known as the Sampitsu (the Three Brushes), a term of respect given to them in the 17th century as the three outstanding early Heian-period masters of Japanese calligraphy. The calligraphy of the Sampitsu consisted of various Tang styles: the revived mode of Wang Xizhi and the expressive "crazy cursive style" of Huai Si (Huai Ssu; 725–785?), Yan Zhenqing, and Ouyang Xun. However, at the end of the 9th century Japan officially terminated its embassies to China and entered a period of "Japanization" of its arts. From the middle of the Heian period, developing what they had learned from China, the Japanese proved to be both interpretative and innovative. This was a period that saw great developments in literature as well; the KOKINSHŪ anthology of WAKA poetry, compiled by the court poet KI NO TSURAYUKI and others, appeared in 905, and the TALE OF GENJI by MURASAKI SHIKIBU around the year 1000. Both of these works became models for the use of *kana* rather than Chinese characters for writing Japanese literature.

The major transformation in calligraphy from a rigid emulation of Chinese styles to creative assimilation occurred in the mid-Heian period, the 10th and 11th centuries. This was the time of the Sanseki (Three [Brush] Traces): ONO NO TŌFŪ (also known as Ono no Michikaze; 894–966), FUJIWARA NO SUKEMASA (also known as Fujiwara no Sari; 944–998), and FUJIWARA NO YUKINARI (also known as Fujiwara no Kōzei; 972–1027). Known for his transcription of Bo

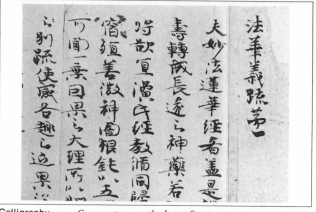

Calligraphy —— Commentary on the Lotus Sutra

Detail from the first of the four scrolls of *Hokke gisho* (Commentary on the Lotus Sutra), showing its opening lines. Attributed to Prince Shōtoku, it is dated between 609 and 615. The characters on the far right, which identify the work, were added in the 8th century. Each scroll 25.5 × 1,330.2 to 1,528.0 cm. Imperial Household Agency.

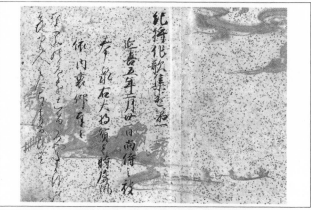

Calligraphy —— Anthologies of the Thirty-Six Poetic Geniuses

First page of the collection of poems by Ki no Tsurayuki. After the volume title (right) and introduction (middle three lines), the first poem appears in two lines of fine writing on the left. Ink on colored paper with gold leaf. Each page 17.9 × 15.8 cm. 1111. Nishi Honganji, Kyōto. National Treasure.

Juyi's (Po Chü-i) poems, Kōzei also perfected the *kana* style of writing. In describing this break from the direct influence of Chinese styles, which occurred in both painting and calligraphy, the term *wayō* (Japanese mode) is often used.

No *kana* writing actually by the hand of Kōzei is known to exist, but the 11th-century transcripts of the *Kokinshū* poems, known as *kōyagire* (Mt. Kōya fragments), are generally regarded as classic Kōzei-style *kana* calligraphy. The Kōzei style became the model to be followed by courtier-calligraphers during the rest of the Heian period and the Kamakura period (1185–1333), when it became known as the Sesonji-school style, after the name of the temple associated with Kōzei, and into the Muromachi period (1333–1568).

A noteworthy diversity of calligraphic styles in this line is observable in extant manuscripts dating from the early 12th century, one important example being the *Anthologies of Thirty-Six Poetic Geniuses* (*Sanjūrokunin kashū*), a set of sumptuously illuminated codices dated to around 1111 and preserved at the temple Nishi Honganji in Kyōto. The Nishi Honganji codices contain calligraphy by no fewer than 20 different hands, and the poems in Chinese characters, as well as those in *kana*, reveal the typical *wayō* aesthetic of the late Heian period.

The *wayō* trend in calligraphy was transmitted from generation to generation of Kōzei's descendants. The grandson of Kōzei, Korefusa (1030–95), Korefusa's grandson Sadanobu (1088–1156?), and Sadanobu's son Koreyuki (fl ca 1160) were some of the notable cal-

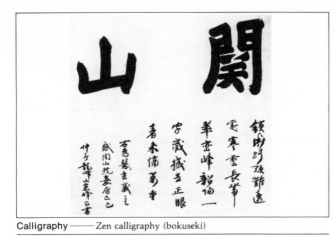

Calligraphy——Zen calligraphy (bokuseki)

Written in 1329 by Sōhō Myōchō, this *bokuseki* consists of a *jigō* (religious name presented by a Zen master to his disciple) and the particulars of its bestowal. The two large characters read "Kanzan," the name presented; the work itself is entitled *Kanzan jigō*. Hanging scroll. Ink on paper. 66.7 × 61.8 cm. Myōshinji, Kyōto. National Treasure.

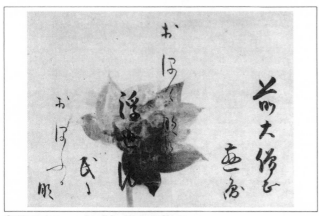

Calligraphy——Scroll by Hon'ami Kōetsu

Detail of a fragment of a poem-scroll of the collection *Hyakunin isshu*. Shown are the title and name of the priest-poet Jien (two lines on far right) and part of a poem by him. Written over lotus flower decoration. Ink over silver and gold wash on paper. Entire fragment 33.3 × 69.0 cm. 17th century. Tōkyō National Museum.

ligraphers who with great care transmitted Kōzei's style. Koreyuki authored the calligraphy manual *Yakaku teikinshō* for use within the family. The tradition continued through the Muromachi period, with some 17 generations of distinguished calligraphers in the same family line. In the meantime, a new school arose from among the high Fujiwara aristocrats: Fujiwara no Moromichi (1062–99) and his grandson Tadamichi (1097–1164) established the Hosshōji school of calligraphy (named after Tadamichi's retirement residence), which was continued well into the Kamakura period by Go-Kyōgoku Yoshitsune (FUJIWARA NO YOSHITSUNE; 1169–1206), Tadamichi's grandson, and came to be known as the Go-Kyōgoku school.

In addition, a handful of imperial family members excelled in calligraphy from the late Heian into the Kamakura period. Retired Emperor GO-TOBA (1180–1239), known through his *waka* poems written on thin paper *(kaishi)* at poetry contests held during his visits to the Kumano Shrines, was an outstanding imperial calligrapher. Another excellent calligrapher was Emperor FUSHIMI (1265–1317), who enthusiastically followed the style of Kōzei.

The *wayō* direction of calligraphy established in the late Heian period was not confined to transcripts of poetry in *kana*. It can be seen in contemporary devotional sets of Buddhist sutras as well. The sets of the Lotus Sutra, such as the *Kunōji kyō* (1141) and the sumptuously illuminated *Heike nōkyō*, offered to the Itsukushima Shrine by TAIRA NO KIYOMORI (1118–81) in 1164, are the finest examples of sutra manuscripts. The intimacy and elegance of the writing are matched only by the sophistication and refinement of the accompanying pictorial designs.

Kamakura (1185–1333) and Muromachi (1333–1568) Periods

The perfection of *wayō* calligraphy in the Heian period was followed by individuation of styles and modes in the hands of the calligraphers of the Kamakura period. Two main developments that continued through the Muromachi period should be noted: first, the continuous transmission of the orthodoxy of the Sesonji school through a hereditary family lineage, resulting in a growing mannerism within that school; second, the appearance of strong personalized styles of calligraphy, most notably by the poet-calligraphers FUJIWARA NO TOSHINARI (also known as Fujiwara no Shunzei; 1114–1204) and his son FUJIWARA NO SADAIE (also known as Fujiwara no Teika; 1162–1241). The antiorthodox trend within the *wayō* tradition should be seen in the context of the entirely new Chinese Song-dynasty (Sung; 960–1279) styles that were transmitted to Japan with ZEN Buddhism during this period.

The long-stagnant, orthodox Sesonji school was revitalized by the gifted imperial prince Son'en (1298–1356), the sixth son of Emperor Fushimi, and his followers, who came to be known as the Shōren'in school. Son'en's aesthetic predilection was nowhere better stated than in the calligraphy treatise *Jubokushō* (1352), which he wrote for his grandnephew Emperor Go-Kōgon (r 1351–71), in which he mentioned four master calligraphers of the Heian period, SUGAWARA NO MICHIZANE, Ono no Tōfū, Fujiwara no Sukemasa, and Kōzei, as the models to be followed. Son'en noted the polarity of styles represented by that of the orthodox Tang and the eccentric Song, the traditional and the deviant, and he observed the continuity and rupture in the transmission of styles from China to Japan. He stressed the superiority of Japan's adherence to the tradition of Chinese calligraphy from Wang Xizhi to the Tang masters, in contrast to Song China, where changes had been rampant.

Nevertheless, Chinese Song calligraphy had a great impact on Japanese calligraphers, especially through Zen monks. Pilgrims went to and from China throughout the 13th and 14th centuries, bringing back with them a significant number and variety of books, as evidenced from the library inventory of the Fumon'in subtemple of Tōfukuji taken in the early 14th century. Among the objects the monks brought back from China were calligraphic works of contemporary as well as past masters. EISAI and DŌGEN returned from their pilgrimages to China during the late 12th and early 13th century, respectively. Their surviving calligraphic works reflect the Southern Song revival of Northern Song calligraphy, a new trend in China as seen in the works of Su Shi (Su Shih) and Huang Tingjian (Huang T'ing-chien). Shunjō (1166–1227), a priest of the Ritsu sect, also wrote in their styles. Huang Tingjian was eagerly emulated by the monks at the GOZAN temples, too, including the monk KOKAN SHIREN (1278–1346), who mastered both the semicursive *gyōsho* and cursive *sōsho* modes of writing. But no calligrapher was more artistically aware of the expressive potential of Song calligraphy than SŌHŌ MYŌCHŌ (1282–1337). His powerful calligraphy follows Song styles, particularly that of Huang Tingjian, without being overly imitative.

But not only did Japanese monks travel to China, Chinese monks journeyed to Japan as well. The monk Lanqi Daolong (Lan-ch'i Taolung; J: RANKEI DŌRYŪ; 1213–78) was one of the early arrivals from China, and he brought with him the style of the Song calligrapher Zhang Jizhi (Chang Chi-chih), best known for his regular script. Zhang's calligraphic style had a strong impact on subsequent Japanese calligraphy, particularly during the early 17th century, perhaps most notably in the style of artist-craftsman HON'AMI KŌETSU (1558–1637).

In the meantime, traditional Sesonji and Shōren'in *wayō* calligraphy had developed along family lines, reaching a point of stagnation in the 16th century, but their influence spread to various strata of society. This diffusion into society resulted in the application of calligraphic writing styles to all kinds of written formats: official documents, letters, inventories by merchants, and signs. Behind this phenomenon was an economic factor—the skilled and the gifted members of the formerly privileged educated class now had to barter their talents to survive. Thus, from the Kamakura and Muromachi periods through the Edo period emerged a plethora of schools of calligraphy, such as the Go-Kyōgoku, Fushimi In, Asukai, Jiraku, and Sōgi schools. The Shōren'in school became popularly known as *oieryū*, or "honorable family school."

Bokuseki

Calligraphy done by Zen monks is known as *bokuseki* ("traces of ink"), to distinguish it from works by non-Zen clerics. With the development of the aesthetics of the TEA CEREMONY, *bokuseki* became collectors' items. *Bokuseki* was part of a major Zen literary and artistic movement in the Muromachi period (see GOZAN). If a young monk aspired to a high position in the Zen monastic community, it was essential that he excel in the arts of poetry and calligraphy. Thus, the leading Zen monks were noted calligraphers as well as literary figures: MUSŌ SOSEKI (1275–1351), Kokan Shiren, SESSON YŪBAI (1290–1346), TESSHŪ TOKUSAI (fl 1342–1366), and ZEKKAI CHŪSHIN (1336–1405), to name a few, left excellent works of calligraphy. Such works in time became prized possessions of the monastic communities, attaining the status of icons and symbols of transmissions within the Zen monasteries.

In the Edo period the Daitokuji monk Kōgetsu Sōgan (1574–1643), himself an accomplished calligrapher, emerged as the connoisseur of Zen calligraphy par excellence. His *Bokuseki no utsushi*, a voluminous notebook on Zen calligraphy and certain paintings, included sketches and copies of the calligraphy of many Chinese monks. But the most comprehensive biographical lineage of Zen calligraphers was the two-volume *Bokuseki soshi den*, published in 1805, with texts from 119 Chinese and 104 Japanese Zen monk-calligraphers.

Azuchi-Momoyama (1568–1600) and Edo (1600–1868) Periods

Wayō calligraphy was from time to time revitalized by a few creative individual calligraphers. Three such talents during the late 16th century through the first half of the 17th century were the aristocrat KONOE NOBUTADA (1565–1614), the craftsman-artist Hon'ami Kōetsu, and a monk of esoteric Shingon Buddhism, SHŌKADŌ SHŌJŌ (1584–1659). These three are called Kan'ei no Sampitsu, or the Three Brushes of the Kan'ei Era (1624–44), although the era designation applies only to the last two. Konoe Nobutada's writing, although he is said to have learned the Shōren'in style, was highly individualized, bold, and vigorous. His inscriptions of traditional Japanese poems and Zen phrases adorn many scrolls and screens. Kōetsu was also tutored in the Shōren'in style at the outset, but later he incorporated a Chinese cursive style, particularly that of Zhang Jizhi, in his *kana* calligraphy. The eclectic Shōkadō Shōjō likewise began with the Shōren'in style, but his mature *kana* style was later shaped by the study of the fluid Chinese scripts of Kūkai and the *kana* of Kōzei. Shōkadō established his own school of calligraphy, known as the Takimoto school after the site south of Kyōto where he spent his retirement years.

New Chinese Influences

The establishment of the ŌBAKU SECT of Zen Buddhism in Uji, south of Kyōto, in 1661 encouraged close contacts between the Japanese and the Chinese Ōbaku monk-calligraphers. The Mampukuji monks INGEN (1592–1673), Mokuan (1611–84), and Sokuhi (Ch: Jifei or Chi-fei; 1616–71) were known as the Ōbaku Sampitsu, the Three Brushes of Ōbaku. All had emigrated from China and worked in the calligraphic styles then current there. But of the Chinese Ōbaku monks, Dokuryū (Ch: Dili or Ti-li; 1596–1672) had the most influence on Japanese calligraphy. It was his style that inspired calligraphers such as Kō Ten'i (also known as Fukami Gentai; 1649–1722), who became an official scholar for the Tokugawa shogunate and thus transmitted Dokuryū's style to Edo (now Tōkyō).

The new waves of Ming-dynasty (1368–1644) styles of calligraphy were received enthusiastically by Japanese men of letters, who, following their sinophile intellectual and artistic persuasion, took them as models and established a new orthodoxy called *karayō* (Chinese mode), in contrast with *wayō*. HOSOI KŌTAKU (1658–1735), RAI SAN'YŌ (1781–1832), and SAKUMA SHŌZAN (1811–64) are among the more famous calligraphers of this Chinese mode, which was greatly favored by literati (*bunjin*) scholars and artists throughout the Edo period. These late Chinese stylistic influences on Japanese calligraphy were extremely durable and formed a major current in the Japanese calligraphic tradition. The *wayō* tradition in time was overshadowed by the *karayō* tradition, as is reflected in the numerous calligraphy manuals and instruction texts that flooded the literate world of Japan from late Edo into the Meiji period (1868–1912).

In the modern era calligraphy as an art has continued to thrive. Calligraphy is represented, along with painting and sculpture, at the annual government-sponsored Nitten exhibitions. In postwar Japan, avant-garde calligraphy (*zen'ei shodō*) was born—a genre in itself. This recent trend in calligraphy asserts new artistic forms of pure abstraction, coming close to some aspects of Western 20th-century pictorial art and deviating sharply from the traditional script styles and emulative aspects of the art.

🔖——*Shodō zenshū*, 28 vols (Heibonsha, 1965–68). Ch'en Chih-mai, *Chinese Calligraphers and Their Art* (1966). Lucy Driscoll and Kenji Toda, *Chinese Calligraphy* (2nd ed, 1964). Shen C. Y. Fu,

Traces of the Brush: Studies in Chinese Calligraphy (1977). Nakata Yūjirō, ed, *Shodō geijutsu*, 24 vols (1971–73). Yujiro Nakata, *The Art of Japanese Calligraphy* (1973). Nishikawa Yasushi, ed, *Shodō* (1969). Hisao Sugahara, *Japanese Ink Painting and Calligraphy* (1967). Ueda Sōkyū, *Shodō kanshō nyūmon* (1963). Wan-go Weng, *Chinese Painting and Calligraphy: A Pictorial Survey* (1978). William Willetts, *Chinese Art* (1958). Chiang Yee, *Chinese Calligraphy* (3rd ed, 1973).   Yoshiaki SHIMIZU

Calpis Food Industry Co, Ltd

(Karupisu Shokuhin Kōgyō). Manufacturer and wholesaler of soft drinks and milk products. Established in 1948. The company is known for its main product, Calpis (Calpico in the US market), a soft drink made from lactic bacteria (*Lactobacillus acidophilus*) which was invented around 1919 by Mishima Kaiun, the company's founder. The company's rate of self-invested capital is high (77 percent in 1981); sales for 1981 totaled ¥47.9 billion (US $218.8 million), and the company was capitalized at ¥3.2 billion (US $14.6 million) in the same year. Corporate headquarters are located in Tōkyō.

Cambodia and Japan

The first known contact between Cambodia and Japan was during the 16th and 17th centuries, when trade was begun and residential quarters for Japanese merchants (NIHOMMACHI) were established in Phnom Penh and Pinhalu.

However, Cambodia and Japan did not have much in the way of contact until 1940. When the Thai–Indochinese border dispute culminated in war in December 1940–January 1941, Japan intervened and forced the French to accept Thai claims on the western provinces of Cambodia and Laos. (The Thai government returned these conceded territories after the end of World War II.) In July 1941 Japan and France reached an agreement on the joint defense of Cambodia, and Japanese troops were stationed in Cambodian territory. In March 1945 the Japanese army overthrew the French administration throughout Indochina and had Norodom Sihanouk (at the time reigning king) declare Cambodia's independence. Japanese patronage of Cambodia ended in August 1945 with Japan's defeat.

After the SAN FRANCISCO PEACE TREATY was signed in 1951, diplomatic relations were resumed. When both countries opened legations in 1954, Cambodia released Japan from paying war reparations; Japan, in turn, promised to give economic and technical aid to Cambodia in the following year. Both legations became embassies in 1955, and in the same year Norodom Sihanouk visited Japan and signed a friendship treaty. In 1970 General Lon Nol deposed Sihanouk, and Japan officially recognized the new government. Economic relations between Japan and Lon Nol's Cambodia did not develop smoothly, however, since Cambodia was engaged in an intense civil war. Japanese aid tended to be limited to small-scale humanitarian and technical support. As soon as the forces of Pol Pot captured Phnom Penh in April 1975, the Japanese government recognized the new regime, although the establishment of ambassadorial relations was delayed until August 1976.

When open conflict broke out between Cambodia and Vietnam and between China and Vietnam in the first months of 1979, Japan sided with China and the ASEAN countries to support the Pol Pot forces. Japan also began providing substantial amounts of aid to Cambodian refugees who fled over the Cambodian border to Thailand.

🔖——Iwao Seiichi, *Nan'yō nihommachi no kenkyū* (1940). Kajima Heiwa Kenkyūjo, ed, *Nihon gaikōshi*, vols 22, 24, 27, 29 through 32 (1971–73). Kokusai Seiji Gakkai, ed, *Taiheiyō sensō e no michi*, vols 6 and 7 (1963).   SHIRAISHI Masaya

camellias

(*tsubaki*). Evergreen trees of the tea family (Theaceae), genus *Camellia*, indigenous throughout Japan except Hokkaidō. They are also widely grown as ornamental flowering trees. Two species of camellia are native to Japan: the *yabutsubaki* (*Camellia japonica*) and the *yukitsubaki* (*C. rusticana* or *C. japonica* var. *decumbens*). From these two many horticultural varieties have been developed.

The *yabutsubaki*, also known as *yamatsubaki*, grows on hills and in thickets along the coasts of Honshū, Shikoku, and Kyūshū. It reaches more than 10 meters (33 ft) in height. The bark is grayish white; its thick, glossy alternate leaves are oval in shape and pointed at both ends. The *yabutsubaki* starts to blossom in November in warm areas and in early spring in colder areas. The single, usually red, flowers have five petals which merge together at the base and take on a cylindrical shape. The flower produces abundant nectar at its base which attracts small birds for pollination. After flowering, it yields round fruits which are pressed to produce camellia oil.

The *yukitsubaki* is a shrub which grows in regions of deep snow along the coast of the Sea of Japan in northern Honshū. It is one to two meters (3–7 ft) in height. After the snow thaws in late spring, the *yukitsubaki* produces mostly red flowers with deep yellow stamen filaments. In regions where the *yukitsubaki* is indigenous, a double-flowered variety is cultivated.

Approximately 200 horticultural varieties of camellia were already recorded in a Japanese publication of 1695. The flowers of horticultural varieties range in color from white to pink, dark red, and streaked types. There are also many variations in the shapes of the flowers and the leaves. The *kingyotsubaki* has leaves divided into two to five (but usually 3) lobes at the tip, so that their shape resembles the tail of a goldfish. The *otometsubaki* is a rather large tree with pink flowers whose petals grow very densely and conceal the stamen. The *chiritsubaki* has narrow leaves and red and white striped double flowers. The petals are separated and, unlike those of other varieties, fall one at a time. The *wabisuke* has small, single, half-open white flowers and generally blooms in cold weather. The *hatsukari* blooms from November to April with white or reddish purple flowers that do not open fully.

The *kantsubaki* (*C. hiemalis*) originated in China but is grown in Japan today. It is 1 to 1.5 meters (3–5 ft) in height and has many branches. The thick, dark green leaves are oval in shape and curled at the tip. It produces pink or deep red double flowers in early winter. The *tōtsubaki* (*C. reticulata*) is another Chinese import, widely planted as an ornamental. The surface of the leaf has recessed veins which look like grooves on the leaf. In spring, its red, pink, white, or particolored flowers bloom at the tips of the branches.

The camellia has been known among the Japanese since ancient times, when its stems and leaves were burned to produce *murasaki-zome*, a type of purple dye. Camellia wood is hard and has long been used for making various implements. At the same time, the oil pressed from the seeds of the camellia was prized for cooking and as hair oil. It was in the Edo period (1600–1868) that the camellia was first cultivated as a garden plant, and many new varieties were developed in this period. Today, it is planted in gardens as an ornamental tree, particularly in semi-shady areas, and also used as a windbreak. Varieties with small leaves are used in BONSAI, and some types are popular in early spring flower arrangements. The plant is also used for practical purposes: leaves dried in the shade are burned as a mosquito repellent, and leaves soaked in salt water are used in confections.

The camellia was first described in Europe in a book by Engelbert KAEMPFER in 1712. It is said that the first camellia tree was brought to Europe in 1739 and the first double-flowered variety in 1787. Since then many other varieties have been introduced around the world, particularly after World War II, and new varieties have been developed in Europe and North America. See also SAZANKA.

MATSUDA Osamu

camphor tree

(*kusunoki*). *Cinnamomum camphora*. Also known as *kusu*. An evergreen tree of the laurel family (Lauraceae) which grows wild in warm regions of Honshū westward from the Kantō region, as well as in Shikoku and Kyūshū. It is also widely cultivated. The trunk sometimes grows over 20 meters (66 ft) in height and reaches a diameter of 2 meters (7 ft). The tree has a long lifespan; gigantic trees as old as 800 to 1,000 years are found in Japan. It is distinguished by fine cracks in the bark and slender twigs. The leaves are alternate, ovate, leathery, and glossy. In late spring it produces panicles of small white flowers which later turn yellowish. The fruit is globular and turns black when ripe. The tree has an attractive scent.

The wood is hard and glossy, and is used for ornamental woodwork in buildings. It has long been prized for use in carvings, musical instruments, and furniture. It has also been used in shipbuilding.

The *kusunoki* is well known as a source of camphor and camphor oil and was formerly cultivated for this purpose, but its importance as a source of these products has declined.

MATSUDA Osamu

Canada and Japan

Relations between Japan and Canada can be divided into two periods separated by World War II: until 1945 they were merely minor trading partners; thereafter, the two nations began to interact on a friendly basis as equals. Although relations have been generally friendly, there does exist a certain basic difference in that Japanese foreign policy is marked by a strong orientation toward the major powers, whereas Canada has tried to play an independent role as a middle-size power.

Prewar Relations——The first contact between Japan and Canada took place in 1873, when two Canadian Methodist missionaries, George Cochran (1835–1901) and Davidson McDonald (1836–1905), landed at Yokohama. Cochran was instrumental in the conversion of such Meiji leaders as NAKAMURA MASANAO, Yokoi Tokio (1857–1928) and Hiraiwa Yoshiyasu (1856–1933); McDonald, a doctor, not only established the first Methodist church in Japan but also contributed to the development of modern medicine in Japan. By the turn of the century, dozens of Methodist missionaries had come to Japan from Canada and converted thousands of Japanese. The Canadian Methodist mission put special emphasis on local evangelism and education, founding several universities and women's colleges. In introducing Western Christian values, Canadian Methodism has played a major role in Japan's modernization.

Nagano Manzō (1855–1924) became the first Japanese "immigrant" to Canada when he jumped ship there in 1877. Many Japanese thereafter immigrated to Canada; they thought of North America as the promised land, and Canada in turn needed cheap labor to develop its west coast. By 1908 there were about 7,600 Japanese in British Columbia. As the Japanese and Chinese population increased, however, anti-Asian sentiment grew, culminating in the Vancouver Riot of 1907, in which, after a huge anti-Asian demonstration at Vancouver city hall, a crowd of some 5,000 attacked Japanese and Chinese settlements and destroyed much property. With the intervention of the national government, the problem was settled with a promise of compensation for damages suffered in the riot. After this incident, the Japanese government regulated the number of immigrants to Canada in accordance with the Lemieux Agreement (1908); eventually the total number of Japanese immigrants to Canada per year, including wives and children, was limited to 150. Nevertheless, immigration continued to be a sore point in Japan–Canada relations, and after the signing of the ANGLO-JAPANESE ALLIANCE of 1902, the issue became even more complicated. In order to avoid being caught between Japan and Britain in regard to the immigration problem, Canada took the initiative in bringing about the abrogation of the alliance at the WASHINGTON CONFERENCE of 1921–22.

In 1929 Canada, which had attained autonomy in its foreign policy, established a legation in Tōkyō, marking its entry into the so-called Pacific basin community. Trade with Japan was the major reason for this Canadian move. Canada was eager to sell its natural resources, especially lumber and minerals, to Japan, and by the 1930s Japan had become the fourth most important export market for Canada. A Japanese legation had been established in Canada in 1928, and even after Japanese aggression in Chinese territory in the MANCHURIAN INCIDENT of 1931, Canada tried to keep its relations with Japan as friendly as possible. Prime Minister W. L. Mackenzie King believed that it was in Canada's interest to avoid entanglement in big power policies. Japan's attack on Pearl Harbor in 1941, however, led to a rupture in diplomatic relations between the two countries. Canadians of Japanese descent as well as Japanese nationals were forced to evacuate from a defense zone in Canada extending for a hundred miles from the Pacific coast. They were housed in camps and in ghost towns in mining areas, and their property was sold at auction.

Postwar Relations——Canadian policy toward Japan after the war had three major aims: to ensure that Japan would never again threaten Canada's security or world peace, to democratize Japan, and to help Japan's economic rehabilitation with an eye to future trade with Japan. In line with these principles, Canada played the role of mediator among the Allied Powers during the Allied Occupation of Japan (1945–52). For example, when the member nations of the FAR EASTERN COMMISSION could not agree on the basic principles for a new constitution of Japan (the United States emphasized the importance of the separation of powers, the Soviet Union called for a socialist constitution, the United Kingdom insisted on a parliamentary cabinet system, and Australia hoped to abolish the emperor system), it was Canada that harmonized these conflicting demands into the general principles of Japan's new CONSTITUTION. E. Herbert NORMAN, a Canadian diplomat and prominent historian of Japan, also played a significant role as adviser to the Supreme Commander of the Allied Forces (SCAP); his book, *Japan's Emergence as a Modern State* (1940), was read widely by SCAP staff members. In comparison with the other powers, Canada could afford to be generous, partly because it had not been directly attacked by Japanese forces.

With the signing of the SAN FRANCISCO PEACE TREATY in 1951, Japan and Canada resumed diplomatic relations; in the following year their legations were raised to the status of embassies. Japan's primary goal after the defeat was to recover full membership in the community of nations. Canada supported Japan by taking the initiative for Japanese membership in GATT (General Agreement on Tariffs and Trade) in 1955, the United Nations in 1956, and the OECD (Organization for Economic Cooperation and Development) in 1963. Japan, on the other hand, looked to Canada primarily for its abundant natural resources, and postwar Japan–Canada trade increased rapidly. In the decade from 1964 to 1974, Canada's exports to Japan increased 6.7 times and its imports from Japan 8.2 times; by 1972 Japan had passed England to become the second most important nation (after the United States) for Canada's exports. During this same decade the trading pattern between the two nations changed: in the early phase most Japanese exports to Canada were textiles, sundries, and consumer goods. By 1974 mechanical and electrical products such as automobiles, television sets, and radios constituted 65 percent, and steel materials 20 percent, of Japan's total exports to Canada. This trading pattern of Japan exporting industrial goods to Canada in exchange for raw materials has remained unchanged.

Although trade has been the most vital concern for both countries, the bilateral relationship has been strengthened in other areas as well. The joint communiqué of 1974, for example, proclaims that Japan and Canada will make constant efforts to cultivate, expand, and enrich their cooperative relationship in political, economic, cultural, scientific, technological, and other diverse fields, thereby placing the relationship on an ever broader and deeper basis. A whole range of questions are reviewed at the periodic meetings of the Japan–Canada Ministerial Committee inaugurated in 1961. An academic exchange program has also been established, with Japanese students and scholars receiving scholarships to study and conduct research in Canada, and their Canadian counterparts coming to Japan under the sponsorship of the Japanese government. In 1976 a Cultural Agreement was signed between the two nations together with a "Framework Agreement for Economic Cooperation between Japan and Canada." The Japanese Association for Canadian Studies was founded the following year. Japanese immigrants are now welcomed by Canada. In 1966 the Canadian government opened a special visa office in Tōkyō in order to invite more qualified Japanese to Canada, and in recent years Japanese immigrants to Canada have numbered approximately 1,000 per year.

Relations Today —— Canada, in search of its own identity independent from the United States, has always considered Japan an ally in fulfilling its diplomatic goals. In the first Ikeda–Diefenbaker communiqué of June 1961, for example, Canada emphasized that both countries would work together to increase aid to developing nations in Asia and to strengthen the functions of the United Nations. The second communiqué of October 1961 stressed the need for mutual cooperation in protesting nuclear tests by the big powers. Canada also sought Japan's support for world disarmament and the promotion of détente. In the Tanaka–Trudeau communiqué of 1974 Canada urged Japan to join it in working for peace and the welfare of mankind. All these assertions emanated from Canada's hopes of playing a significant role as a middle-size power. Trudeau's Third Option of 1972, which emphasized Canada's autonomous diplomacy vis-à-vis the United States and its closer ties with Japan and the European community, should also be understood in this context. In contrast to this, Japan's fundamental goal since 1945 has been the attainment of economic success in close cooperation with the United States; it has not yet found its own distinct role. In fact, in negotiations leading to the 1974 joint communiqué, Prime Minister TANAKA KAKUEI is said to have called Canada's approach "too philosophical." Thus, beneath the friendly relations between Japan and Canada there exists a potential for disagreement.

◼ ——Nobuya Bamba, *Japanese Diplomacy in a Dilemma* (1980). Bamba Nobuya, "Nihon Kanada kankei no tenkai," *Kokusai mondai*, no. 203 (February 1977). J. B. Brebner, *North Atlantic Triangle* (1966). A. R. M. Lower, *Canada and the Far East, 1940* (1973).

BAMBA Nobuya and KATŌ Hiroaki

Canada, Japanese immigrants in

The history of Japanese and Japanese Canadians in Canada may be conveniently divided as follows: the period up to 7 December 1941, the Pacific War and its constraints up to 1 April 1949, and the period since 1949.

From 1877 to 1941 —— The first Japanese settler in Canada is believed to have come in 1877. There was sparse but steady migration after that with a heavy, yet transitory, migration in the last years of the 1890s, when perhaps 12,000 immigrants came. The 1901 census found fewer than 5,000 Japanese in Canada, most of them in British Columbia. Between that census and 1941, the immigration data, admittedly sketchy in the early years of the century, showed an additional 25,000 Japanese arriving, with a peak of more than 10,000 in the years 1905–08. Yet the 1941 census showed only 23,000, of whom 13,687 (about 59 percent) were native-born Canadians. Some 96 percent of all Japanese Canadians lived in British Columbia, a concentration similar to, but greater than that existing on the Pacific Coast of the United States, where 74 percent of a considerably larger population resided in 1940. The settlement of Japanese along the Pacific Coast of North America can be regarded as one general migration: some who entered via Vancouver eventually settled in the United States, while some who entered at Seattle and other American ports settled in Canada.

During this period the Japanese Canadian experience in British Columbia was one of relative success in the economic sphere and relative failure in social and political spheres. The Japanese immigrants accounted for only 2 to 3 percent of British Columbia's population. They were particularly important in fishing and in agriculture, specializing in pomiculture and market gardening. Although few Japanese were rich or even well-to-do by 1941, most of them were at least of lower middle class status as petty entrepreneurs and small proprietors. These economic successes, however, were accompanied by political and social animosity, and probably even contributed to that animosity, although it was clearly inspired by racial prejudice. As was the case in the United States, Japanese immigrants in Canada followed a substantial immigration of Chinese, and, by the 1890s, western Canada had a full-blown anti-Oriental tradition with its own indigenous version of the "YELLOW PERIL" phobia. Canada, however, as a part of the British Empire, was inhibited by imperial concerns: the existence of the ANGLO-JAPANESE ALLIANCE (1902–23) meant that it was impossible for Canada to pass the same kind of discriminatory legislation against Japanese immigrants that it had against Chinese, who were all but excluded by a prohibitively high head tax. Executive agreements between Canada and Japan kept immigration at a trickle after 1919; until the Pacific War immigration averaged only 255 per annum, which was less than repatriation in many years. Canadian law allowed Japanese immigrants to become naturalized citizens on much the same terms as other aliens and, by 1941, 64 percent of the Japanese-born aliens in Canada had become Canadian citizens. But in British Columbia, where almost all of the Canadian Japanese lived, the most important right of a citizen, the right to vote, was denied them. Persons of Asian birth or descent could not vote even if they were citizens, naturalized or native-born. This restriction is in sharp contrast to regulations in the United States, where Japanese and other Asians were not eligible for naturalization, but where all native-born citizens over 21 years of age could vote. These disparities can be explained by institutional differences between Canada and the United States. Canadian provinces could set up racially discriminatory suffrage requirements, while American states were obliged by a written national constitution to treat all citizens with at least formal equality.

World War II and the Immediate Postwar Period (1941–1949)

The Japanese attacks across the Pacific placed all Canadian Japanese, regardless of citizenship, nativity, or loyalty, in peril. Most Canadians were convinced that "once a Jap always a Jap," and as the Pacific War news worsened in the winter of 1941–42, there were rising demands for some kind of drastic action against Canadian Japanese. Although the Canadian military leadership was aware that the Japanese navy and army posed no real threat to British Columbia, and not a single act of sabotage or espionage by a resident Japanese was ever discovered, civilian fears approached panic proportions. Little evidence of a joint Canadian-American policy toward Japanese residents has been uncovered, but Prime Minister William Lyon Mackenzie King and other Canadian officials were willing to follow the American lead in many matters. Only five days after President Franklin D. Roosevelt signed Executive Order 9066 which enabled the United States Army to evacuate West Coast Japanese Americans, Mackenzie King's government issued Order in Council PC 1486 (24 February 1942) which gave the government control over the movements of all persons of Japanese origin in certain "protected areas" including the hundred-mile-wide strip along the Pacific Coast where almost all Japanese Canadians lived. To accomplish what became an evacuation of some 20,000 men, women, and children, the government depended upon its national police force, the Royal Canadian Mounted Police, and a newly established federal body, the British Columbia Security Commission, which was empowered to require "any person of the Japanese race, in any protected area in British Columbia, to remain at his place of residence . . . or to proceed to any place within or without the protected area at such time and in such manner as the Commission may prescribe." Provisions were also made for an Alien Property Custodian to confiscate all property that Japanese were forced to abandon, including some 1,100 fishing boats which had been seized in early December. No adequate compensation was made for these confiscations. Those few Japanese who did not live in "protected areas," or who had been able to leave coastal British Columbia before the order, were not subjected to special federal restraint, but many local governments had anti-Japanese provisions of their own. In Calgary, Alberta, to cite one example, Canadian Japanese had to have special permits to reside within the city limits.

The Canadian government, unlike the American, did not spend large sums to incarcerate its Japanese residents. Rather than using troops and barbed wire, it utilized climate, geography, and a few policemen in forcing adults to stay in isolated "road camps"—some of them thousands of miles to the east in northern Ontario—and keeping women and children in remote rural villages called "interior housing centres." Some Japanese families were allowed into other provinces, chiefly southern Alberta, where, often under execrable conditions, they harvested sugar beets and other crops.

The end of the war, in August 1945, did not bring an end to the exclusion of Japanese Canadians from their former homes. The King government decided that "it would be unwise and undesirable . . . to allow the Japanese population to be concentrated in [British Columbia] after the war." Many of the restrictions on Japanese Canadians were simply kept in force; many of them were not allowed to return to coastal British Columbia until after 1 April 1949. In addition, both the government and private pressure groups encouraged persons of Japanese origin to remigrate or emigrate to Japan. As a result, the Japanese Canadian population actually declined between 1941 and 1951—from 23,149 to 21,663—and, more significantly, the center of Japanese population shifted away from British Columbia where, by 1951, only one Japanese in three still lived.

Post-1949—— The postwar years have seen great changes in the lives of Japanese Canadians and in the ways in which they are regarded by their fellow citizens. In a country which now embraces multiculturalism as an official policy, Japanese Canadian citizens enjoy full rights, even in British Columbia. In 1964, Prime Minister Lester B. Pearson, Mackenzie King's political heir, stated publicly that the treatment meted out to Japanese Canadians had been "a black mark against Canada's traditional fairness and devotion to the principles of human rights." The Japanese Canadian population has resumed its slow growth—the 1971 census found over 37,000—but Ontario rather than British Columbia is now the major locus of the Japanese Canadian population. That population has become progressively more urbanized, and second and third generation Japanese Canadians have on the whole assimilated middle class patterns of education and employment. Despite a small amount of resumed immigration from Japan and a steady population growth, some Japanese Canadian leaders have posited the possible disappearance of the ethnic group due to the quite high rate of exogamous marriage among the third generation. At the same time, however, a heightened ethnic consciousness was becoming apparent in the late 1970s, in which organizations like the National Japanese Canadians Citizens Association sponsored research and publication about the Japanese Canadian past and celebrated it with conferences and exhibitions. In addition, problems arising in the 1970s from Canada's traditional French-English rivalry have made most Canadians, regardless of ethnicity, more sensitive to ethnic and racial questions than ever before.

■ ——Ken Adachi, *The Enemy That Never Was: A History of the Japanese Canadians* (1976). Barry Broadfoot, *Years of Sorrow, Years of Shame* (1977). Roger Daniels, *Concentration Camps: North America: Japanese in the United States and Canada during World War II* (1981). Roger Daniels, "The Japanese Experience in North America: An Essay in Comparative Racism," *Canadian Ethnic Stud-*

ies 9.2 (1977). Robert A. Huttenback, *Racism and Empire: White Settlers and Colored Immigrants in the British Self-Governing Colonies, 1830–1910* (1976). Forrest La Violette, *The Canadian Japanese in World War II* (1948). Howard Palmer, *Immigration and the Rise of Multiculturalism* (1975). Charles A. Price, *The Great White Walls Are Built: Restrictive Immigration in North America and Australia, 1836–1888* (1974). Ann G. Sunahara, *The Politics of Racism: The Uprooting of Japanese Canadians during the Second World War* (1981). W. Peter Ward, *White Canada Forever: Popular Attitudes and Public Policy toward Orientals in British Columbia* (1978). Charles H. Young et al, *The Japanese Canadians* (1938).

Roger DANIELS

candles → lighting equipment

Canon, Inc

World's largest manufacturer of 35-mm single-lens reflex cameras since 1976, when the Canon AE-1 was introduced. Manufacturer of cameras and accessories, copiers, calculators, and other optical and electronic products. Canon was incorporated in 1937 to carry out the commercial production of Japan's first 35-mm still camera with a focal-plane shutter. This camera had been developed by Precision Optics Research Laboratories, the predecessor of Canon, organized in 1933. The founder of the present company was Mitarai Takeshi, a medical doctor. Over the years Canon has developed innovative products incorporating numerous technological advances. It introduced the first electronic calculator to use the 10-key system (1964), the first plain-paper copier alternative to the xerographic process (1968), the first plain-paper copier using liquid toner (1972), and the first single-lens reflex 35-mm camera with a built-in microcomputer (1976). The combination of electrophotography with electronics and optics technology resulted in the development of Canon's laser beam printer. In 1981 total sales were ¥282.1 billion (US $1.3 billion), of which camera sales accounted for 51 percent, electronic calculators 11 percent, copiers 30 percent, and other products 8 percent. Approximately 74 percent of net sales in 1981 were outside Japan, with 34.5 percent in the United States and Canada, and 28.5 percent in Europe. In the same year the company was capitalized at ¥15.6 billion (US $71.3 million). Corporate headquarters are located in Tōkyō.

cant → ingo

Cao Rulin (Ts'ao Ju-lin) (1876–1966)

(J: Sō Jorin). Japanese-educated Chinese politician; leader of pro-Japanese politicians in early Republican China. Cao is best known as an important target of the May 1919 student demonstrations (see MAY FOURTH MOVEMENT). He acquired admiration for Japan as a student at Chūō University in Tōkyō. Upon returning to China, he enjoyed the confidence of important Chinese officials and rose rapidly in the bureaucracy. In 1915, as vice minister of foreign affairs, he negotiated with the Japanese over the TWENTY-ONE DEMANDS. From 1916 to 1919 he associated himself with the government of DUAN QIRUI (Tuan Ch'i-jui), which was maintained through dubious dealings with the Japanese, notably the NISHIHARA LOANS. Cao and his two friends, Lu Zongyu (Lu Tsung-yu; 1875–1941), a Waseda graduate, and Zhang Zongxiang (Chang Tsung-hsiang; 1877–1940s), who had studied at Meiji University, were key figures in these transactions. For his services Cao gained control of the ministries of finance and communications but at the same time incurred the indignation of patriotic Chinese. When it became known that he had been involved in the agreements confirming Japanese succession to German rights in Shandong (Shantung), student demonstrators burned his house in Beijing (Peking) on 4 May 1919. He resigned a month later. Cao continued to work for the Japanese, unsuccessfully, for the repayment of the Nishihara Loans. He remained on the fringe of politics until the early 1940s and may have been considered by Japanese militarists for a significant post in a Japanese-sponsored government during World War II. Cao left Mainland China in 1949 and lived in Japan for seven years, after which he moved to the United States.

Madeleine CHI

capacity to act

(kōi nōryoku). Legal term. The capacity to perform valid juristic acts autonomously. Japanese judicial decisions and legal theory pro-

Capital formation —— Table 1

	Total GDCF	Total GFCF	Private			Government				Changes in stocks	GNP growth rate
			Total	Dwellings	Plant and equipment	Total	Dwellings	Plant and equipment	General government		
1952–54	25.2	21.4	14.7	2.9	11.8	6.7	0.3	2.1	4.2	3.8	6.0
1955–59	28.8	24.4	17.7	3.3	14.4	6.8	0.5	2.6	3.8	4.4	7.6
1960–64	36.5	32.4	23.9	4.5	19.4	8.5	0.4	3.4	4.8	4.1	11.6
1965–69	33.1	30.5	22.0	6.0	16.0	8.5	0.4	3.6	4.5	2.6	10.9
1970–74	37.1	35.0	26.0	7.1	18.9	9.0	0.5	3.3	5.2	2.1	7.2
1975–77	31.5	30.9	22.1	7.1	15.0	8.8	0.5	3.1	5.2	0.6	4.4

Composition of GDCF as Percentage of GNP

NOTE: GNP: Gross national product at market prices. GDCF: Gross domestic capital formation. GFCF: Gross fixed capital formation.
SOURCE: For 1952–64, figures are based on the old System of National Accounts (SNA) as reported in Economic Planning Agency, *Annual Report on National Income Statistics* (annual): 1977. For 1965–77, figures are based on the new SNA as reported in Economic Planning Agency, *Annual Report on National Accounts* (annual): 1979.

Capital formation —— Table 2

Composition of GFCF as Percentage of GNP

	Total GFCF	Private			Government			GNP growth rate
		Total	Dwellings	Plant, equipment, and animals	Total	Nonmilitary	Military	
1890–99	16.3	12.5	3.6	8.9	3.8	2.2	1.6	1.2
1900–09	15.4	10.2	2.7	7.5	5.3	3.4	1.9	1.6
1910–19	18.5	13.2	2.3	10.9	5.3	3.7	1.6	4.6
1920–29	18.3	11.1	2.2	8.9	7.3	5.6	1.7	1.9
1930–39	20.2	11.1	1.5	9.6	9.2	4.8	4.4	4.8
Average	17.7	11.6	2.5	9.2	6.2	3.9	2.3	2.8

NOTE: GNP: Gross national product at market prices. GFCF: Gross fixed capital formation.
SOURCE: Kazushi Ohkawa et al, *National Income* (1974).

tect infants, mentally ill persons, alcoholics, and others who do not have the mental capacity to comprehend the consequences of their acts, i.e., persons without the capacity to form intent *(ishi nōryoku)*, by deeming their juristic acts invalid. The concept of capacity to bear responsibility *(sekinin nōryoku)*, seen in the case of torts *(fuhō kōi)*, corresponds to this capacity to form intent. The presence or absence of capacity to form intent and of capacity to bear responsibility is judged on an individual basis.

The reason for this system is that it is very difficult to prove in fact, that the capacity to form intent did not exist at the time the act was performed. Furthermore, when such lack of capacity is proved, the result is that the other party to the transaction suffers an unforeseen loss. Therefore the CIVIL CODE provides that, as a matter of law, certain persons have insufficient capacity to form intent and deems their acts voidable without inquiring into their actual capacity to form intent in each case. *OKA Takashi*

capacity to enjoy rights

(kenri nōryoku). Legal term. Under the CIVIL CODE, both natural persons *(shizenjin)* and juristic persons *(HŌJIN)* have the capacity to enjoy legal rights and duties. Foreigners are an exception in some instances (see FOREIGNERS, LEGAL STATUS OF). All natural persons possess the capacity equally. A fetus does not, as a rule, have the capacity to enjoy such rights, but in order to protect the unborn, the Civil Code does recognize, retroactively upon its live birth, a fetus's capacity to enjoy rights in certain instances. See also CAPACITY TO ACT. *OKA Takashi*

capital formation

A component of gross national product (GNP) consisting of fixed capital goods and changes in inventories. Fixed capital goods are tangible, reproducible assets durable for more than a year, while inventories consist of raw materials, goods in process, and finished products. The role of capital formation in the economy is to increase the net capital stock and to help introduce new technology embodied in capital goods.

Capital formation is the critical variable in a country's economic growth. To make output grow at all, a country must increase its capital stock and improve its technology, as well as use more labor and natural resources. But to make output grow faster, a country must allocate a larger proportion of GNP to expanding the capital stock, i.e., to capital formation.

When World War II ended, Japan's capital stock was ravaged and obsolete. It took several years for the country to recover and regain its prewar productivity level. After this process was completed in the mid-1950s, Japan's economic growth began to accelerate. Its GNP growth rate was a little over 7 percent per annum in the 1950s, but rose to over 10 percent per annum in the 1960s (see Table 1). Correspondingly, the proportion of GNP occupied by gross fixed capital formation increased from a little above 20 percent to over 30 percent.

As the labor force was only growing a little more than 1 percent per annum, significant capital deepening (increase in the capital-labor ratio) took place during the decades after World War II. Continued deepening could not have been sustained without technological change. If the technology remained unchanged, capital deepening would have pushed the profitability of new capital downward, and the inducement to invest would have quickly disappeared. There was very rapid technological change through the 1950s and, in particular, the 1960s, which counteracted the tendency toward diminishing returns on new capital. Innovations were based on technology imports from the United States and Western Europe (see TECHNOLOGY TRANSFER). Thanks to these innovations, Japan closed

Capital formation——Table 3

GDCF as Percentage of GNP[1], 1960-1969 Average							
	GDCF	GFCF	Residential construction	Other construction	Machinery and equipment	Changes in stocks	Capital consumption allowances	GNP growth rate, 1960-70
United States	17.6	16.7	3.9	3.5	9.3	0.9	9.8	4.0
United Kingdom	18.5	17.5	3.4	——14.1——		1.0	7.8	2.7
EEC[2]	25.2	23.5	6.0	7.5	10.0	1.7	9.6	5.3
West Germany	26.6	25.1	5.9	——19.2——		1.5	9.8	4.8
France	25.7	23.4	6.7	7.1	9.6	2.3	10.1	5.8
Japan	34.8	31.5	5.7	——25.8——		3.4	12.5	11.2

[1] Gross national product at market prices, for EEC, France, and Japan; gross domestic product in purchasers' values, for United States, United Kingdom, and West Germany.
[2] Consisting of Belgium, Luxembourg, France, West Germany, Italy, and the Netherlands.
NOTE: GDCF: Gross domestic capital formation. GFCF: Gross fixed capital formation.
SOURCE: Organization for Economic Cooperation and Development, *National Accounts of OECD Countries, 1960-1970* (1972). For source of figures for Japan, see Tables 1 and 4.

Capital formation——Table 4

Domestic Saving by Source as Percentage of GNP				
	Government saving	Capital consumption allowance	Corporate saving	Household saving	Total[1]
1952-54	5.9	7.9	3.1	6.6	24.7
1955-59	5.5	9.5	3.6	10.7	28.9
1960-64	7.5	11.2	4.8	12.1	35.8
1965-69	5.5	13.8	4.8	11.5	36.0
1970-74	6.5	13.6	3.8	13.3	38.1
1975-77	2.5	12.9	-1.0	16.2	32.3

[1] Includes statistical discrepancy.
SOURCE: For 1952-64, figures are based on the old System of National Accounts (SNA) as reported in Economic Planning Agency, *Annual Report on National Income Statistics* (annual): 1977. For 1965-77, figures are based on the new SNA as reported in Economic Planning Agency, *Annual Report on National Accounts* (annual): 1979. (For 1965-69, the breakdown of net domestic saving is not available. Government saving is extrapolated by the old SNA data; corporate saving is taken as is from the old SNA; household saving is derived as a residual.)

the technology gap with the advanced Western countries. By 1970 the productivity level in Japanese industry was comparable to that in American industry. Thus technological progress and capital formation went hand in hand. Innovations maintained the prospective profitability of capital accumulation, and the strong inducement to invest kept capital formation high, making rapid economic growth possible.

Historical and International Comparisons——Although Japan's modern economic growth before World War II has been much discussed, it was much less rapid than postwar growth. Table 2 shows an average GNP growth of less than 3 percent per annum and a fixed capital formation of about 15 percent of GNP, after excluding unproductive military investment.

An international comparison of Japan and several advanced economies in the 1960s, as given in Table 3, reveals that Japan grew about twice as fast as the Western European countries and the United States. The proportion of net fixed capital formation (after deducting depreciation) was also about twice as high in Japan as elsewhere. This means that Japan's capital stock came to be much newer than that of other countries. Since better technologies are

embodied in new capital goods, Japanese productivity improved rapidly. (In addition, we note that inventory investment was very much higher in Japan, again because of its more rapid growth.)

Production and Welfare——Japan's capital formation has been very much biased toward expanding the capacity of the economy to produce tangible goods. Japan spent a much larger proportion of business investment funds on plant and equipment than other advanced nations did. Still the aggregate level of housing investment increased in the late 1960s and the 1970s to a level comparable to that in Western Europe. However, the stock of dwellings remains inadequate in Japan, with limited space per dwelling and high population density in metropolitan areas. The price of urban land has soared and even small houses are exorbitantly expensive. In 1970, the value of the housing stock as a percentage of GNP was 0.6 percent (in gross terms) and 0.2 percent (in net terms) in Japan, in contrast to the American percentages of 1.3 and 0.8 respectively.

Public capital formation has been heavily oriented toward creating industry-related capital stock such as highways and superexpress train lines. This emphasis has been to the detriment of social overhead capital related to the living environment, though great improvements have been made over the prewar period. Japan is still much poorer than other advanced nations in public housing, waste disposal and sewerage systems, public parks, libraries, and other cultural facilities, even though these shortcomings are being gradually rectified.

Relation to Saving——Capital formation must be financed through saving. An economy cannot realize a high growth potential if its people are unwilling to sacrifice consumption and save instead. Japan's rapid growth in the 1960s was possible because its people were willing to save more, both individually and collectively (see CONSUMPTION AND SAVING BEHAVIOR).

In a national accounting sense, investment always equals savings. By comparing Tables 1 and 4, we can see that both the government and the business sectors saved less than they invested. (Business saving is the sum of capital consumption allowances, i.e., depreciation, and retained corporate profits.) This means that the household sector has been the net lender in the economy.

Banks and other financial institutions have channeled excess funds from the household sector to the business sector through their deposit and loan operations. Large firms' heavy dependence on bank loans (instead of equity or corporate debentures) for financing investments has been a well-known feature of postwar economic growth in Japan (see CAPITAL STRUCTURE). Government borrowing has also been indirect. The main method has been the issue of government bonds, which are purchased mostly by financial institutions.

The costs of all this borrowing have usually been controlled. The government has maintained deposit and loan rates at artificially low levels, so the Bank of Japan has had a powerful influence upon regulating the flow of funds in the economy. The government has also exercised a strong influence upon the allocation of funds among firms and industries. This has been an important lever in the execution of its industrial policy.

Developments in the 1970s —— As Japan closed the technology gap with the West, new technology became less abundant, and the inducement to invest weakened considerably. Japan's GNP grew more slowly in the 1970s. The international economic climate became less secure with the demise of fixed exchange rates (see MONETARY POLICY), and the OIL CRISIS OF 1973 brought worldwide inflation and stagnation. However, capital formation did not decline immediately. The capital accumulation in the early 1970s led to excess capacity after the oil crisis; capital formation, particularly business investment in plant and equipment, fell in the late 1970s.

If the level of savings had not been reduced at the same time, the economy would have entered a more severe recession. Fortunately, savings did decrease. The brunt of adjustment was assumed by significant decreases in retained corporate profits and by large deficits (negative savings) by government. Consequently, Japan's growth rate was maintained at a little less than 6 percent per annum from 1975 to 1978. However, household saving continued to rise in the 1970s, partially because inflation and other uncertainties prompted households to save more for the future.

In addition, Japan's exports have remained strong despite substantial revaluations of the YEN since 1971, and large trade surpluses have developed (see BALANCE OF PAYMENTS). Japan has also been increasing direct investment abroad as demand for capital formation at home has weakened.

■ —— Emi Kōichi, *Shihon keisei* (1971). Ōkawa Kazushi et al, *Shihon sutokku* (1966). Ōkawa Kazushi et al, *Kokumin shotoku* (1974). Kazushi Ohkawa and Henry Rosovsky, *Japanese Economic Growth* (1973). Henry Rosovsky, *Capital Formation in Japan, 1868–1949* (1961). Kazuo SATŌ

capital markets

A mechanism for investment of savings and a source of long-term financing for economic development. The primary functions of capital markets are to provide a wide range of possible investments for corporations, individuals, or other entities with funds to invest, and at the same time to give borrowers a source of funds to finance investment and long-term working capital. Normally, a market where lending and borrowing take place for a period of less than a year is referred to as a money market. Where agreements extend over a year, the market is referred to as a capital market.

Capital Markets in Japan —— Early in the post–World War II period, Japan began to structure a financial system which emphasized the use of banks rather than financial markets as intermediaries in channeling the flow of savings from households and other entities into the industrial sector. This is essentially a "nonmarket" type of financial organization. The choices available to savers are generally determined by neither negotiation nor a market mechanism, but by the fiat of the BANKING SYSTEM authorities. At the same time, the uses of savings and the rates which are charged can generally be controlled more readily than in markets, where both borrowers and lenders may reject offers to invest or borrow.

Japan chose this nonmarket type of financial system because it appeared to be more easily controlled and therefore the better system for channeling household savings into industrial development. During the period of rapid economic expansion lasting approximately from the mid-1950s to the early 1970s, this system performed well in meeting the financial requirements of economic development. Some commentators have expressed the view that Japan probably could not have achieved such consistent and rapid economic development without the smoothly functioning system that transferred savings through the banking system to appropriate industries. The behavior of capital markets overseas tends to bear out this observation to some extent. Prices of stocks and bonds, two types of capital market instruments, may be influenced by factors other than industrial development priorities, sometimes making it difficult for corporations to have the range of choices which such markets should theoretically provide.

Despite Japan's heavy reliance on bank intermediaries, the two principal types of capital markets have grown along with the rest of the financial system—a stock or equity market and a bond market. As a result of the sheer size of Japan's economy, even though these markets have grown up as secondary sources of capital, they rank among the largest of their kind in the world when measured in numbers of transactions. Nevertheless, until recently their development relative to the size of the economy and their interrelationships with the international financial system have been severely restricted.

Banks and the Bond Market —— The principal providers of investment and working capital are Japan's three specialized long-term credit banks and the trust banks. These institutions are permitted to issue savings certificates of maturities ranging from one to five years, depending on the type of institution. Long-term funds from this source have generally been insufficient to meet the needs of the corporate sector, thus presenting other types of banks with the opportunity to lend on a semipermanent basis to corporations. This is particularly true of the leading commercial banks or "city banks," which in principle specialize in short-term lending. Commercial banks "roll over," or renew, their loans to corporations after a specified interval of less than a year. For this reason, the percentage of short-term financing utilized by Japanese corporations, as indicated on their balance sheets, is higher than for corporations in the United States and Europe (see CORPORATE FINANCE).

An additional source of long-term capital is the bond market, one of the world's largest in value of issues listed and total transactions. Although it provides only a minor part of corporate financing, this market in recent years has become one of the primary sources for financing central and local government deficits. Prior to the deep recession following the OIL CRISIS OF 1973, the Japanese government depended very little on deficit financing. Tax revenues generally grew more rapidly than expenditures, thereby eliminating the need to raise additional funds from the bond market, as the United States and other nations have done. But because of the seriousness of the recession, the Japanese government was obliged to provide additional stimuli to bring about economic recovery in 1975 and subsequently. Because of the decline in revenues relative to planned expenditures, the government embarked on a program of issuing government debt. In effect, the government was borrowing the surplus of savings in the private sector and spending it to fill in the gap between the actual and potential levels of production. This led to a rapid increase in the importance of government issues in the Japanese bond market and to a greater significance for the market itself.

Because of the importance of financial intermediaries in Japan, however, the bond market differs from the theoretical model, where large numbers of investors "bargain" together to arrive at interest rates. Interest rates for new issues are in effect negotiated between the government and large financial institutions and securities houses. Securities companies and leading banks (so-called commissioned banks) organize a group of other financial institutions to underwrite issues in what is referred to as the "issue market."

Along with the issue market, there is a secondary market where the financial institutions which originally purchased the bonds may sell them or purchase additional issues at their discretion. Price determination in this market is much closer to the bidding process of bond markets in the United States and Europe. To an increasing degree, trends in the secondary market influence rates in the issue market. For example, in 1978 the government wanted to issue a predetermined amount of debt at a fixed rate. Although this could have been accomplished in the issue market, the secondary market would have been more difficult to control. Because of the volume of government issues, prices in the secondary market declined in the latter part of the year, thereby raising the rate on government bonds. This ensured that the underwriters of the bonds in the issue market would be forced to sell them at a lower price in the secondary market. Pressures mounted on the government until it increased the issue rate in early 1979 to make the bonds more attractive. See also GOVERNMENT BONDS, NATIONAL.

The Equity Market —— The equity market in Japan is also one of the largest of its kind in the world in the value of listed issues and of shares traded. The process of issuing new shares has some features in common with the process for bonds since, depending on the issuing company, major banks and securities companies may take an active role, with banks absorbing a significant portion of the issue. This process, however, is not totally unlike the process in the United States and Europe, where issues are generally sold to a group of investors, who in turn often sell them to a large shareholder group. The concentration of the institutional investor group is higher in Japan than elsewhere, and the degree of institutional involvement depends on the popularity of the stock issue.

At one extreme, large industrial companies with relatively little general appeal to shareholders may rely heavily on their banks to absorb new issues in a process similar to the issuance of bonds. Legally, banks are forbidden to underwrite securities, but in practice their role in the underwriting process for such companies is indispensable.

At the other extreme, where a company is rapidly growing and appeals to a broad shareholder group, the majority of the new issue is absorbed by the securities companies, which in turn sell a large portion to the general public and some portion to such institutional investors as insurance companies, trust banks (which manage pension funds), and others.

The concentration of institutional investors is high: for example, the management of pension funds is almost entirely carried out by 23 insurance companies, seven trust banks, and one city bank with trust bank operations. This compares to more than 1,000 significant institutional investors in the United States. This high concentration makes it very important for the securities company underwriting the issue to obtain the cooperation of the rest of the underwriting group, since a significant sale of the new issue into the equity market with the incorrect timing could adversely affect the share price. Where institutional investors are larger in number, the underwriter can generally exercise a stabilizing influence when necessary.

Internationalization of the Market—— One of the most pressing tasks for Japan in the late 1970s and early 1980s is the integration of its domestic capital market with the international financial system. A primary role of an international capital market is to permit countries having trade surpluses to coexist with those having trade deficits. The country accumulating a surplus can lend to the country experiencing a deficit. This offsets pressures for disruptive currency changes and provides more time for adjustment in the industrial structure of surplus and deficit countries.

The opening of Japan's capital market to international lending and borrowing would make a substantial contribution toward increasing the stability of international financial and monetary systems. It would also reduce criticism of Japan for pursuing high goals for economic growth, reduce pressures for immediate and rapid increases in imports which can prove highly disruptive to domestic industry, and in the longer term provide Japan with another source of income similar to that accruing to such international financial centers as London and New York. The opening of the capital market would also permit Japan to make a substantial contribution to financing development in other nations through the export of its excess monetary liquidity.

A number of movements have been made in this direction, and Japan appears likely to continue to make progress toward opening its capital markets. The number of yen-denominated bonds issued by foreign governments, government agencies, and entities other than private corporations in Japan has risen substantially in recent years. Although only a limited number of foreign corporations are listed on the Tōkyō Stock Exchange, changes in certain legal requirements could bring increased interest overseas in tapping the Japanese equity market, just as Japanese corporations have increasingly begun to utilize American and European equity markets. It appears that private corporations will also increasingly be permitted to issue yen-denominated bonds in Tōkyō, since legal regulations requiring collateral for all bond issues of private companies have been revised. In a broader sense of the word "market," syndications are another aspect of the Japanese capital market; these too have increased substantially in volume in recent years.

Although a number of important changes still have to be made to permit Japan to participate fully in the international financial system, it is clear that the role Japan could play as an international lender is a large one indeed. One simple measure is the size of Japan's gross national product (GNP) in dollar terms, which in early 1979 was in excess of US $1 trillion, roughly half the size of the US GNP and virtually on a par with the United States on a per capita basis. See also ECONOMIC HISTORY: contemporary economy; CAPITAL FORMATION; CONSUMPTION AND SAVING BEHAVIOR; FOREIGN EXCHANGE CONTROL; STOCK EXCHANGES.   C. Tait RATCLIFFE

capital punishment

(shikei). Public debate in Japan concerning the retention or abolition of capital punishment has continued since the Meiji period (1868–1912), but as of 1982 no legislative action had been taken by the Diet to abolish the death penalty. In the courts the number of cases in which the death penalty is handed down has declined steadily. Only a few such cases come up each year. In addition, in most cases where persons have received the death sentence, the execution of the sentence is usually greatly delayed by repeated appeals for a retrial or reduction in sentence.

Under the present criminal code, crimes for which capital punishment may be prescribed include sedition, foreign insurrection, arson, high explosive bombing, murder, and homicide associated with such crimes as derailment of trains, poisoning of water supplies, armed robbery, and rape. Among these the only crime which carries a mandatory death sentence is participation in armed foreign intervention in Japan (gaikan yūchizai) under the category of foreign insurrection. For all other crimes listed above, penal servitude for life or specific prison terms can also be handed out.

The Deliberative Council on the Legal System (Hōsei Shingikai), which in 1974 was assigned the task of wholesale revision of the criminal code, also deliberated the question of the abolition of the death penalty. As a result of its deliberations the council concluded that it was still premature to abolish capital punishment and decided to retain it. However, the council deemed it desirable that the death penalty be restricted as much as possible and reduced the list of crimes for which the death penalty could be prescribed to sedition, foreign insurrection, murder, and homicide committed during robbery or rape. It stressed that "application of capital punishment be made with particular care" and also recommended that crimes for which capital punishment was mandatory be eliminated. At the end of 1982, the council's recommendations had not yet been implemented.

The present constitution prohibits "cruel punishments" in article 36, and the question of whether or not capital punishment violates this prohibition has been argued in the courts. On this question, the Supreme Court has decided that capital punishment is recognized by the due process provisions of article 31 of the constitution and that the present method of execution by hanging cannot be considered cruel. The Supreme Court at the same time concluded that capital punishment is definitely not a desirable form of punishment and recommended that efforts be made toward its reduced use and eventual abolition.   SAWANOBORI Toshio

capital structure

The ratio of a company's capital (or shareholders' equity) to liabilities; also called capital-liability ratio. Generally, the higher the ratio of capital to liabilities, the greater the flexibility available to a company in its financial payments and the greater the financial stability. Because of a combination of circumstances, including high rates of economic growth, the typical Japanese company has a significantly lower ratio of capital to total liabilities than companies in the United States. This was not the case prior to World War II, when capital-liability ratios were between 50 and 60 percent. But early in the postwar period, Japan chose to finance much of its growth through financial intermediaries, primarily commercial and long-term credit banks. This provided for ease of allocation and control from a policy point of view. From the firm's point of view, financing through borrowings was less costly than through the sale of equity because tax provisions permitted the deduction of interest as an expense, while dividends had to be paid from after-tax income. The financial decision making of companies was also influenced by the fact that equity shares had to be issued at a fixed or par value, generally well below the market value. Equity, therefore, became a relatively expensive source of funds. As a result of these and other factors, Japanese companies have tended to favor borrowing, leading to high ratios of liabilities to equity. Operating with apparently more risky financial ratios is commonplace in Japan, and credit analysis is therefore frequently more demanding than in the United States or Europe. See also CORPORATE FINANCE.   C. Tait RATCLIFFE

Capron, Horace (1804–1885)

US commissioner of agriculture (1867–71) and agricultural adviser to the Japanese government (1871–75). Born in Attleboro, Massachusetts, Capron had a diverse career that included cotton manufacturing, a job as a Bureau of Indian Affairs agent in Texas, military service during the American Civil War, and progressive farming. He went to Japan in 1871 to work as a highly paid adviser to the Hokkaidō Colonization Office (KAITAKUSHI), which was in charge of the development and settlement of Hokkaidō. During his tenure there he introduced large-scale farming with American agricultural methods, implements, seeds, and livestock.

—— John A. Harrison, "The Capron Mission and the Colonization of Hokkaidō, 1868–75," Agricultural History (1951).

                    Edward R. BEAUCHAMP

Caraway, Paul Wyatt (1905–   )

American lieutenant general who was from 1961 to 1964 high commissioner of the RYŪKYŪ ISLANDS and commander of the US Army

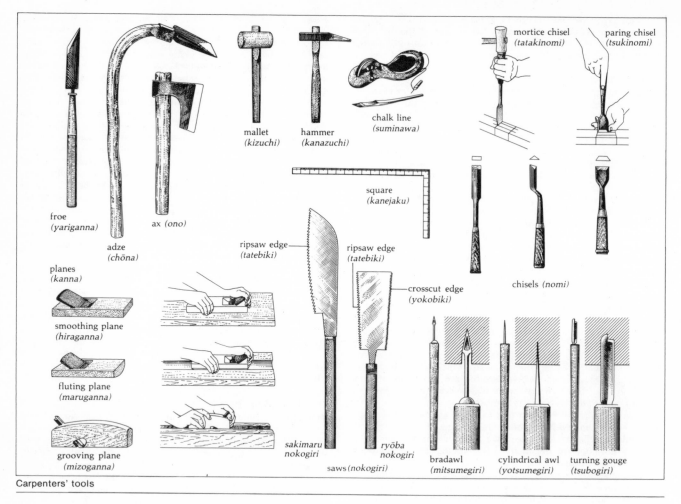

froe
(yariganna)

adze
(chōna)

ax (ono)

planes
(kanna)

smoothing plane
(hiraganna)

fluting plane
(maruganna)

grooving plane
(mizoganna)

mallet
(kizuchi)

hammer
(kanazuchi)

chalk line
(suminawa)

mortice chisel
(tatakinomi)

paring chisel
(tsukinomi)

square
(kanejaku)

ripsaw edge
(tatebiki)

ripsaw edge
(tatebiki)

crosscut edge
(yokobiki)

chisels (nomi)

sakimaru
nokogiri

ryōba
nokogiri

saws (nokogiri)

bradawl
(mitsumegiri)

cylindrical awl
(yotsumegiri)

turning gouge
(tsubogiri)

Carpenters' tools

forces there. A career officer, he had also served in Europe, Korea, and Japan. In Okinawa he was a vigorous administrator who carefully preserved United States rights and resisted steps toward autonomy for the Ryūkyū Islands at a time when President John F. Kennedy and Prime Minister IKEDA HAYATO had agreed on further joint efforts to improve the well-being of the Ryukyuan people. See also OKINAWA.   Richard B. FINN

carp

(koi). *Cyprinus carpio*. Freshwater fish of the class Osteichthyes, order Cypriniformes, family Cyprinidae. It is distributed in the temperate and subtropical zones in Asia and Europe and lives in lakes, marshes, ponds, and rivers. It grows to over 1 meter (39 in) in length. It is an important food fish in Japan; in addition to the edible carp, there are specially bred ornamental varieties. One of these, the *nishikigoi* (also known as *irogoi* and *hanagoi*), originally bred in Niigata Prefecture, is world famous. There are over 20 types of *nishikigoi,* and expensive specimens are displayed at annual fairs.
                                            ABE Tokiharu

The Japanese have long praised the *koi* as the "king of river fish" in contrast with the *tai* (sea bream), the "king of sea fish." With the "king of birds," the crane, these are said to constitute the "three ultimates in food." This threesome has been prominent in literature and fine arts, and is considered highly auspicious. On CHILDREN'S DAY, most families with boys set up carp streamers as symbols of strength and perseverance; this practice originated from a Chinese legend of a carp that was transformed into a dragon after it had jumped up a waterfall in the upper reaches of the Yellow River.
                                            SAITŌ Shōji

carpenters' tools

(*daiku dōgu*). Prototypes of many of the basic tools used by Japanese carpenters came from the Asian continent between the latter

part of the Yayoi period (CA 300 BC–CA AD 300), when iron implements were first introduced into Japan, and the Nara period (710–794). Indigenous refinement of these primary hand tools and the development of related tools with highly specialized functions kept pace with the evolution of traditional Japanese architecture.

In cutting, framing, and joining timbers, usually from the soft, straight-grained wood of conifers such as cedar and cypress, the Japanese carpenter employs a large variety of tools, among which are saws (*nokogiri*), planes (*kanna*), chisels (*nomi*), awls (*kiri*), hammers (*kanazuchi* or *gennō*), knives, gauges, an ax (*ono*), adzes (*chōna*), squares (*kanejaku*), and chalk lines (*suminawa*). As in other parts of Asia, the effective stroke in sawing or planing is toward the body and not away from it, as in the West.

There are two types of hand saw: ripsaws (*tatebiki*) for cutting with the grain and crosscut saws (*yokobiki*) for cutting against the grain. Crosscut saws have been found in tombs of the Kofun period (ca 300–710). The teeth have three edges, are beveled, and are set to avoid binding. Ripsaws were not employed until the 15th century. Until then wedges were used to split wood along the grain. The teeth of ripsaws have two edges and are set but not beveled. Today, the most widely used variety of saw has teeth for cutting with and across the grain, notched on opposite sides of a single steel sheet. Blades are broader at the tip than at the base. The length of the handle, a straight wooden shaft, is equal to the length of the blade. The basic complement of saws is four; the number of teeth per centimeter increases as blade length is reduced.

The standard plane, a rectangular block of oak wood with a blade inserted in an angled slot, was not introduced until the Muromachi period (1333–1568). Previously, wood surfaces were first dressed with an adze. Ridges were then smoothed with a *yariganna,* a long-hafted tool with a blade shaped much like that of a spear, and a finish was given by rubbing with the dried stems of the scouring rush (*tokusa*). In addition to a set of four planes for increasingly fine stages of flat surface finishing, a large number of planes for particular tasks were developed: for smoothing the sides of channels, planes with blades either on the left or right to avoid working against the wood grain, curved planes of varying degrees of concavity or convexity, miniature planes, and planes for tonguing and grooving, running moldings, and for routing.

Chisels are of two varieties: *tatakinomi,* used with a hammer to cut mortises, and *tsukinomi,* manipulated with the hands to smooth sides of mortises or to dress the ends of channels inaccessible to planes. Primitive chisels have been found in Kofun-period burial mounds. The basic set of *tatakinomi* consists of nine chisels with cutting edges increasing in width in 3 millimeter (0.12 in) increments. Because the square timbers used in Japanese buildings are fitted together using mortise and tenon, chisels are used at every stage of construction.

The square and chalk line are the basic tools for calculating and laying out the dimensions of timbers. Measurements determined by the square are inscribed on rough-hewn timbers with the chalk line and the timbers then cut. The chalk line, in use from the Nara period, preceded the appearance of the square, the first record of which dates from the early 10th century. In the traditional Japanese system of architecture, angles are not figured with compass and protractor, but expressed, using the square, as functions of tangents. Incised on the steel or bronze square are three sets of scale marks: the front side is graduated in standard units of linear measure; on the inside edge of the reverse side are graduations equivalent to approximately 1.57 standard units; and on the outside edge are graduations equivalent to approximately 1.414 standard units. The circumference of a circle can be graphically determined by transposing the length of the diameter in standard units to equivalent units on the inside edge of the reverse side and multiplying by two. The length of a diagonal line drawn between opposing corners of a square can be determined by transposing the length in standard units of one side of the square to equivalent units on the outside edge of the reverse side. Among various calculations, the square can be used to determine the size and number of timbers that can be cut from a log, length of timbers for differing degrees of roof slope, and measurements for polygonal timbers and structures.

A survey conducted in 1943, before the general proliferation of hand-operated power tools, found that the customary complement of tools used by Japanese carpenters consisted of 179 items. This comparatively large number may be attributed to at least two factors: first, all pieces of a Japanese structure are fashioned to interlock precisely, an intricate system of construction employing few nails but requiring a wide variety of specialized tools; second, the Japanese preference for plain, unpainted wood surfaces necessitated the development of numerous tools which perform the same or similar functions but differ in quality of finish or precision of cut.

MURAMATSU Teijirō

carrying poles → tembimbō

cartels

Agreements among a number of corporations in competitive lines of business for controlling competition and markets, or associations to enforce such control.

In Japan, cartels and associations of entrepreneurs are in principle forbidden by the ANTIMONOPOLY LAW (1947). In severe business slumps, however, exceptions are permitted, and entrepreneurs and associations of entrepreneurs can form, as an emergency measure, antirecession cartels (subject to rigorous approval conditions). By March 1978 a total of 53 such cartels had been approved under this law. The number of antirecession cartels approved was 6 for 1958, 2 for 1962, 18 for 1965, 13 for 1971, and 14 for 1974.

The relationship between cartels and the movements of the Japanese economy in the 1970s can be summarized thus: cartels tended to be concentrated in industries with highly competitive market structures, cartels appeared frequently in the early 1970s when the economic growth rate slowed down, and the profit ratios of the industries which formed cartels in the first half of the 1970s proved to be lower than their counterparts in noncartelized industries. Slowdowns in the economic growth rate tend to prompt industries with noncompetitive structures to form tacit agreements for cooperation and those with competitive structures to create cartels, and in the course of the 1970s competitive business behavior showed a marked decline.

MASUDA Yūji

Cary, Otis (1851–1932)

American Congregational missionary, professor of homiletics and practical sociology at the Dōshisha Theological Seminary from 1892

to 1918, and the first of three generations to serve in Japan. Born in Foxboro, Massachusetts, he attended Amherst College (where he became acquainted with NIIJIMA JŌ, who was later to found Dōshisha; see DŌSHISHA UNIVERSITY), and Andover Theological Seminary. After his ordination in 1877, he was immediately assigned to mission work in Japan, initially to Okayama, where the governor invited Cary, his wife, and three other missionaries to be the first Western residents. Besides teaching and making evangelical tours into the country (socialist KATAYAMA SEN was one of those who heard him), he wrote and, with collaboration, translated Christian manuals and tracts into Japanese. He went to Dōshisha in Kyōto after protracted negotiations with the Ministry of Education for permission to teach the new field of sociology. His book *Japan and Its Regeneration* (1899), a survey of Japan at the turn of the century, went through many editions. In 1907 Cary was invited by Andover Seminary to give the Hyde Lectures, which formed the basis for his *A History of Christianity in Japan* (1909). The work is in two volumes, the first covering the Roman Catholic and Greek Orthodox record, the second the Protestant. Amherst College honored him with a DD in 1904. After retirement the Carys served for several years as independent missionaries among the Japanese immigrants in Utah. Writing *A History of Children in New England* occupied his declining years; he died in Bradford, Massachusetts. He was a meticulous and scholarly man, of New England wit and wisdom. Two of his four children (Frank and Alice) succeeded him in missionary careers in Japan.

Otis CARY

Casio Computer Co, Ltd

(Kashio Keisanki). Manufacturer and distributor of electronic instruments. It is one of the largest makers of high-grade electronic calculators in the world, with a monthly production of 1.5 million units. It is also a leader in the production of digital watches, and has entered the field of electronic musical instruments and office computers. Established in 1957, the company stresses product development and has been successful in introducing several radically new items to the market. It has three sales companies overseas as well as one foreign production plant. Sales for the fiscal year ending March 1982 totaled ¥150.8 billion (US $626.5 million). Pocket calculators accounted for 51 percent of this total, while digital watches accounted for 35 percent and office computers and other products 14 percent; exports made up 64 percent of all sales. In 1982 the company's capitalization stood at ¥6.1 billion (US $25.3 million). Corporate headquarters are located in Tōkyō.

castles

(shiro). Military fortifications originally designed to provide protection against enemy attack but which, with the rise of FEUDALISM, became distinctive architectural forms serving the dual function of palatial residence and seat of military and political power of feudal barons.

Japan being an island nation, wars with foreign lands were rare from the early history of the country. Military strongholds built to guard against attack from without by foreign forces were largely limited to the coastal areas of Kyūshū. Internal wars, however, occurred from time to time, and over the centuries various types of field and permanent fortifications were built by territorial rulers throughout the country. From the 16th century permanent fortifications came to center on the Japanese feudal castle, and the heyday of the feudal castle as an architectural form was the Azuchi-Momoyama period (1568–1600), a time of especially active castle construction. Fortifications varied considerably in design and character from period to period, but with the rapid development of the feudal castle the similarities in construction became more marked than the differences.

Ancient Fortifications —— Three types of fortification have been identified as existing in ancient Japan: the grid-pattern city *(tojō),* the mountain fortress *(yamajiro),* and the palisade *(ki).* Interestingly, remains or traces of the three are found in widely separated areas of Japan, and they differ, too, in their function and character.

The grid-pattern city. This was a Chinese city-type, of which Chang'an (Ch'ang-an) and Luoyang (Loyang) were representative examples. In Japan, the Chinese model furnished the inspiration for the building of similar grid-pattern cities, beginning with the ancient imperial capitals of FUJIWARAKYŌ and NANIWAKYŌ (the site and layout of the latter have been archaeologically verified) and culminating in HEIJŌKYŌ (now Nara) and HEIANKYŌ (now Kyōto). The

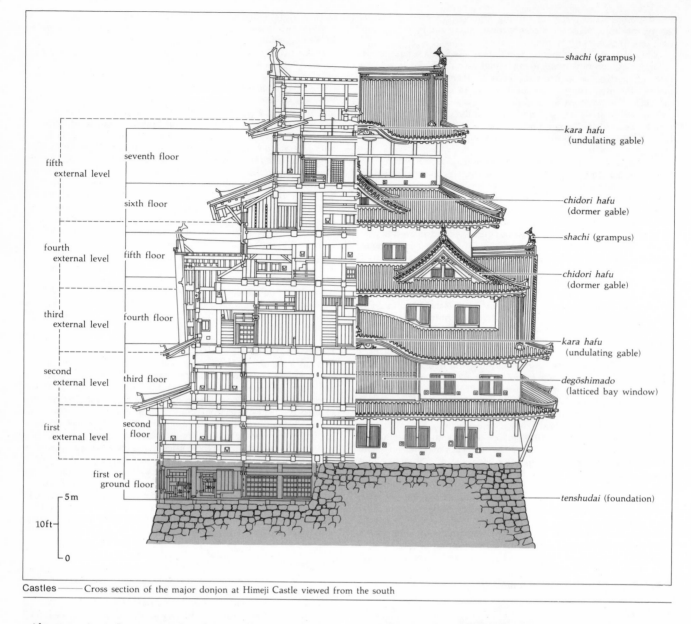

fifth external level — seventh floor

fourth external level — sixth floor — fifth floor

third external level — fourth floor

second external level — third floor

first external level — second floor

first or ground floor

5 m

10 ft

0

shachi (grampus)

kara hafu (undulating gable)

chidori hafu (dormer gable)

shachi (grampus)

chidori hafu (dormer gable)

kara hafu (undulating gable)

degōshimado (latticed bay window)

tenshudai (foundation)

Castles —— Cross section of the major donjon at Himeji Castle viewed from the south

grid-pattern city in Japan was more of a government and political center than a truly defensive facility. In China, however, the grid-pattern city did function as a fortification in that the city had heavy reinforced walls, gates, and battlemented towers at intervals along the wall to protect it from attack by outside enemies. The Japanese attempted to copy this system, but in actual construction the Japanese grid-pattern city wall was a slight earthen embankment less than 3 meters (9.8 ft) in height and affording little real protection; the wall eventually disappeared altogether in Japan.

The mountain fortress. Ruins of ancient mountain fortresses *(yamajiro)* have been found distributed in an area centered in northern Kyūshū. The site of Ōno Castle in present-day Fukuoka Prefecture, originally constructed in 665 during the reign of Emperor TENJI to protect Dazaifu (the ancient seat of the administrative capital of Kyūshū and headquarters of the western defense commissioner) against foreign forces, is suggestive of the character and dimensions of the mountain fortress. Remnants of its earthen and stone walls remain standing even today at the rugged mountain site, and excavations of the site have revealed numerous traces of buildings. Similar ruins of *yamajiro* can be found throughout western Japan. Rows of stones known as *kōgoishi*, once thought to be connected to some sort of ancient religious ritual, have also been identified as remains of ancient mountain fortresses. They apparently functioned to buttress the earthwork walls. The remains known as MIZUKI, part of the outworks of Dazaifu, also reveal an ancient defense facility, whose long earthworks and moat were constructed at a point where mountains come together and close off a plain.

The palisade. Unlike mountain fortresses, palisades *(ki)* were semi-permanent fortifications built for the purpose of advancing racial borders against the people known as the Emishi in northern Japan. Historical records show that palisades had already been built at Nutari (see NUTARI NO KI) and Iwafune (see IWAFUNE NO KI)— both in what is now Niigata Prefecture—by 647 and 648, respectively, and many more such fortifications were constructed between then and the beginning of the Heian period (794–1185). These ancient field fortifications have all long since disappeared, and only recently have large-scale excavations of these palisade sites begun to be conducted.

The *yamajiro* were built on mountains, but palisades were built on plains or plateaus. Along the periphery of the palisade ran an outer corridor which was rectangular or irregular in shape depending on the contour of the land, and inside there was an inner corridor. The *yamajiro* were defensive facilities, but the palisades were more regional government outposts than fortifications.

Medieval Castles —— The only time Japan was called on to defend itself against foreign aggression was during the MONGOL INVASIONS OF JAPAN, the first in 1274 and the second in 1281. After the first invasion was repelled, the need for improved coastal defenses was recognized, and a long stone wall was erected along much of the shore of Hakata Bay. Parts of this wall still survive. Though by no means a castle, it was noteworthy as a large-scale military facility built for foreign defense purposes.

The mountain fort. Internal wars were frequent in Japan during the middle ages. From the Nambokuchō period (1336–1392) to the Sengoku period (1467–1568), territorial warlords repeatedly engaged

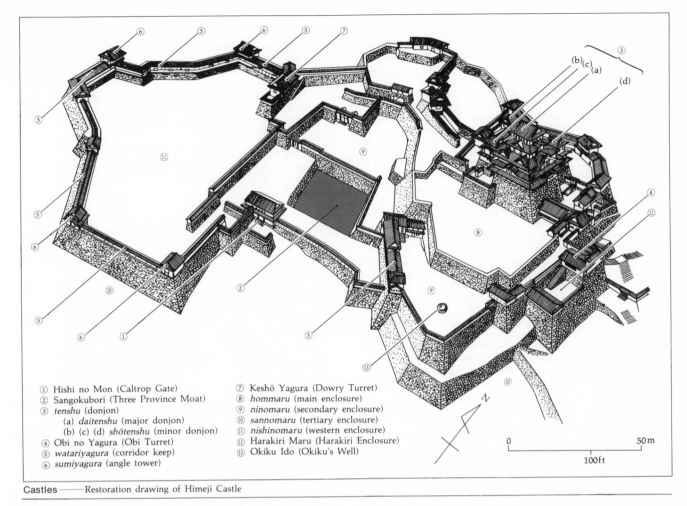

① Hishi no Mon (Caltrop Gate)
② Sangokubori (Three Province Moat)
③ *tenshu* (donjon)
    (a) *daitenshu* (major donjon)
    (b) (c) (d) *shōtenshu* (minor donjon)
④ Obi no Yagura (Obi Turret)
⑤ *watariyagura* (corridor keep)
⑥ *sumiyagura* (angle tower)
⑦ Keshō Yagura (Dowry Turret)
⑧ *hommaru* (main enclosure)
⑨ *ninomaru* (secondary enclosure)
⑩ *sannomaru* (tertiary enclosure)
⑪ *nishinomaru* (western enclosure)
⑫ Harakiri Maru (Harakiri Enclosure)
⑬ Okiku Ido (Okiku's Well)

Castles ——— Restoration drawing of Himeji Castle

Castles ——— Himeji Castle

A partial view of the castle from the south. Behind the main donjon, two of the minor donjons can be seen. National Treasure.

in fighting, and castles were constructed throughout the country. A typical castle of the time was a place where a warrior chieftain dwelt only when necessary. These castles utilized the existing topography of the land and their forms varied, but many were small semipermanent fortifications built at the tip of steep mountain ridges. To prevent enemy approach, two or three lines of advance fortifications were built. Along the ridge line a trench was dug, the peak and mountainside were terraced, and palisades were erected around the perimeter. Because these castles utilized the natural features of the mountain sites they occupied, stone walls were uncommon, and since these facilities were used only in times of war, they were not built to last.

By the Sengoku period, however, there was constant warfare so that it became necessary to build more permanent structures. Mili-

tary chieftains built fortifications similar to their own residences, with the addition of raised watchtowers on the roof. This was the beginning of castle, especially donjon (*tenshu* or *tenshukaku;* see glossary for this and other technical terms), architecture in Japan. Although recent studies have disproved the theory that the existing donjon of Inuyama Castle was moved there from the Sengoku-period Kanayama Castle in what is now Gifu Prefecture (it is now assumed that its construction does not antedate the year 1599), it nevertheless demonstrates the features of the earliest type of donjon. The structure rests on a stone foundation wall but is fundamentally a two-storied building with an *irimoyazukuri* (semigabled) roof which is surmounted by a watchtower encircled with a balcony and balustrade. The donjon of Inuyama Castle is suggestive of what the towers of these mountain forts must have been like.

The plain castle. Most castles of the middle ages were of the mountain castle type and were used only in times of war. Ordinarily the warrior chieftain lived in a fortified residence located on a plain or low plateau. This was the origin of the plain castle (*hirajiro*) and the so-called hill-on-the-plain castle (*hirayamajiro*). An example of the *hirajiro* is EDO CASTLE in Tōkyō. The *hirayamajiro* was generally sited on a low-lying plateau set in a plain. It is architecturally representative of the feudal castle (see next section). Based on careful site planning (*nawabari*) and constructed of thick stone walls (*ishigaki*), donjon, gates, and outer earthen walls, the *hirayamajiro* was not only a skillfully devised defense facility but also an aesthetic achievement and a symbol of its lord's power and wealth. The majority of surviving castles are *hirayamajiro*.

Azuchi-Momoyama and Edo Period Castles ——— There was a great development in castle building during the Azuchi-Momoyama period (1568–1600), and the castle became a complex of many structures. Castles became representative of the architecture of the period. With the reorganization of the feudal system by the Tokugawa shogunate (1603–1867), the *daimyō* abandoned their inconvenient mountain fortresses and built castles in the center of their domains. Many of these castles were located on a low plateau in the middle of a plain, and the *hirayamajiro* thus became the standard type. By skillful siting, the main and minor compounds were arranged in a complex manner, and an ensemble of buildings was constructed centered on the donjon. The castle was not composed solely of defensive facilities but included the residences of the castle lord and his chief retainers. Located as it was, near a plain, the feudal castle now required additional fortifications. Stone walls developed, moats (hori) were dug, and earthworks added. Around these castles developed CASTLE TOWNS (jōka machi). The castle became not just a defensive facility but the administrative and economic center of its region. The architecture and lavish interior decorations of the castle symbolized the castle lord's authority.

The rise of the castle. The military hegemons ODA NOBUNAGA and TOYOTOMI HIDEYOSHI were responsible for major developments in castle architecture. Between 1576 and 1579, Nobunaga constructed the central part of an enormous castle project at Azuchi in what is now Shiga Prefecture. According to a recent study, AZUCHI CASTLE had a seven-storied tower which rose to a height of 32.5 meters (105 ft) above the top of the stone foundation walls and 46 meters (151 ft) including the stone foundation walls. The first or ground floor was approximately 19 meters (63 ft) square and set in the middle of an area defined by the interior walls of the stone foundation. This floor was in effect a cellar (J: anakura or ishikura). A Buddhist stupa stood in the center of an open space that extended upward some 19 meters from the ground floor to the level of the fifth floor. The second floor formed an irregular octagonal pattern; the third floor was rectangular in plan and contained reception areas decorated with paintings, with a stage thrusting out into the empty space in the middle; on the rectangular fourth floor, a bridge crossed the multistoried open space, which was surrounded by private rooms; the fifth floor was loft space; the octagonal-shaped sixth floor contained paintings on Buddhist themes depicted in vivid colors; and the seventh, square-shaped floor had panels depicting Chinese emperors and men of virtue.

Azuchi Castle was destroyed after the death of Oda Nobunaga. The tradition of the large-scale, sumptuous castle begun by Azuchi Castle was continued in Fushimi Castle (1594) and ŌSAKA CASTLE (1583), both built by Hideyoshi and no longer extant. After the Battle of Sekigahara (1600) through the Keichō era (1596–1615), there was a surge of castle construction by daimyō throughout the country. Many of these survive today or did until World War II.

The decline of the castle. By 1615 the Tokugawa shogunate, seeking to secure complete control over the country, ordered that there could be only one castle to each domain. Each daimyō was permitted to maintain only his main castle; all others had to be destroyed and even the one permitted to remain could not be repaired without permission. The art of castle architecture went into a gradual decline during the Edo period (1600–1868). Toward the end of shogunal rule Western-style fortifications were introduced. The Goryōkaku (pentagonal fortress) built between 1857 and 1864 by the Tokugawa shogunate at Hakodate in Hokkaidō is an example.

Castle-Building Techniques and Design——The most important step in building a castle was the site planning (nawabari). Ideally, a castle was composed of a main compound or ward (hommaru) centered around the donjon, surrounded by or connected with minor compounds or enclosures. There were several entrances to the castle, but the important ones were called the ōte and karamete. The former was the main entrance and the latter the rear entrance. In case the castle was overrun, the karamete could be used as an avenue of escape. A moat surrounded the castle, and natural features of the land were also employed in its fortifications. In order to reach the donjon it was necessary to traverse a maze-like route.

The donjons of some of the major castles of the Edo period, such as those of Himeji (1609), Nagoya (1612), and Edo (1638), were even larger in size than that of Azuchi Castle. There were different architectural types of donjon: the single type; the compound type, where a minor keep projected from a side of the main donjon; the linked type, where the main tower and a minor keep were connected by a passageway; and the group type, where the major donjon was joined by passageways to several "minor donjons" (shōtenshu). The donjon had originated from the watchtower built atop a warrior's residence; this was reflected in the form of some of the donjons built during the heyday of castle construction in the particularly large roof at the middle level, above which the donjon suddenly became smaller. A noteworthy aspect of donjon design was the roof, which was typically decorated with dormer gables (chidori hafu) and undulating gables (kara hafu). Built into the tower walls and the connecting galleries (corridor keeps; watari yagura) were machicolations (overhanging chutes for dropping stones on attackers; J: ishiotoshi),

which were originally conceived for defensive purposes but became simply decorative.

The principal construction material of a castle was wood. The early donjon had exposed wood members such as columns, horizontal members, and eaves, but at the height of the castle-building era most surfaces came to be plastered for the sake of increased protection against firearms. The walls were loopholed with apertures (sama or hazama) from which arrows could be shot and muskets fired. Both the inner ward and the outer enclosures were reinforced with small towers (yagura) which had a structure and design similar to the donjon's. The entrances to various parts of the castle were sometimes fortified with masugata (bastions laid out so as to form a rectangular courtyard), from which flanking fire could be directed upon assailants and in which defenders could group for a sudden sally. So-called mounted exits (umadashi) were earthworks constructed in front of the main gateways (koguchi) to mask the egress of mounted soldiers from the castle. Two gates peculiar to castle architecture were the kōraimon and the yaguramon. The kōraimon was one bay wide, with support posts on either side; it had a main roof over the two supporting pillars and auxiliary roofs projecting from them. The yaguramon was a two-storied gatehouse whose first level served as an entranceway while the second, from which it took its name, was a magazine (yagura; literally, "store for arrows;" the same word is used for the small towers of the castle).

Foundation walls were built of stone. Most curtain walls were earthen, but there were also wooden walls. Due to their vulnerability to fire arrows, however, the latter were mainly provisional or temporary in nature. Many loopholes punctuated these walls, and they were decorated in various ways, giving them interest as a design.

Remains. The oldest surviving donjon, possibly dated as early as 1576, may be that of Maruoka Castle in Fukui Prefecture. Donjons from the period of greatest castle construction activity are those at Matsumoto Castle in Nagano Prefecture (with a "minor donjon" on its northwest side; ca 1597), Inuyama Castle, Hikone Castle in Shiga Prefecture (1606), HIMEJI CASTLE (with east, west, and northwest "minor donjons"), and Matsue Castle in Shimane Prefecture (1611). The donjons at the castles of Uwajima in Ehime Prefecture (1665), Marugame in Kagawa Prefecture (ca 1642–ca 1672), Bitchū Matsuyama (now the city of Takahashi) in Okayama Prefecture (ca 1683), Kōchi in Kōchi Prefecture (1747), Hirosaki in Aomori Prefecture (1810), and Iyo Matsuyama in Ehime Prefecture (1854) date from the latter part of the Edo period. Some donjons survived the Edo period only to be lost to military action in the disturbances accompanying the Meiji Restoration (namely, the donjons of Aizu Wakamatsu in 1868 and Kumamoto in 1877), while several others were demolished as a result of the early Meiji government's policy (e.g., those of Hagi Castle in Yamaguchi Prefecture and Kokura in Fukuoka Prefecture). Famous donjons lost during World War II were those of NAGOYA CASTLE, Okayama Castle, and Hiroshima Castle. There have been numerous "reconstructions" of castles in recent years, but the viewer should not expect an accurate picture from them.

● **Glossary**

apertures or loopholes (sama or hazama)   Small openings in walls or castles used to observe the outside and for shooting arrows and bullets. Rectangular openings were for shooting arrows, but those for firearms were round, triangular, or square, their variety perhaps for decorative purposes.

compound or ward (kuruwa)   A division of the entire castle area defined by earthwork, stone walls, or moat. The central or main compound (hommaru) contained the donjon and towers, the second compound (niinomaru) usually contained the lord's residence, and the third compound (sannomaru) contained the residences of retainers.

donjon (tenshu or tenshukaku; "main tower")   The most important building in castle architecture from the latter part of the Muromachi period (1333–1568) through the Edo period. The donjon originated in the watchtower built atop a warrior's residence. The feudal castle donjon began with that of Azuchi Castle, built in 1576.

moats (hori)   Refers to manmade ponds, waterways, or simply trenches. In castles they were built for defensive purposes in several rings. Inner moat (uchibori) and outer moat (sotobori) are the most commonly found names.

site planning (nawabari)   The Japanese term usually refers to the practice of fixing a building's outline on the prospective site by stretching *(hari)* ropes *(nawa)*. In the case of castles the word refers to the site planning of the entire castle.

stone walls (ishigaki)   These were used as moat embankments or as foundation walls. Walls were built vertically in older times on sites with foundation soil, but where the ground was not stable, walls with a concave profile came to be used both for structural and decorative reasons.

towers (yagura)   Probably derives from *ya kura*, literally meaning "arrow storage," and refers to a two-storied structure from which arrows were shot. In feudal castles, the name *yagura* is given to one- to three-storied structures other than the donjon. Depending on its location or form, it had such names as angle tower *(sumiyagura)* and level tower *(hirayagura)*. A tower with a passageway beneath it was called a gatehouse *(yaguramon)*.

——Fujioka Michio, *Nihon no shiro* (1966). Inoue Munekazu, *Nihon no shiro no kiso chishiki* (1978). Naitō Akira, Mizuno Tōji, and Yuasa Kōzo, *Shiro no nihonshi* (1979). Morton Schmorleitz, *Castles in Japan* (1974).   *Itō Nobuo*

castle towns

(*jōka machi;* literally, and in fact, "city under a castle"). The administrative center of a *daimyō* domain. From the mid-16th century until the Meiji Restoration of 1868, the *jōka machi* was the characteristic form of Japanese urbanism. The rate of expansion of urban centers during the 17th century and their 18-percent share of the national population in the 18th century have seldom if ever been equaled in any other premodern society. Concentrating with extraordinary intensity a domain's diverse activities in one urban location, the castle towns perhaps best typify the nature of Edo-period (1600–1868) society.

The antecedents of *jōka machi* can be traced back to the turbulent 14th and 15th centuries, when local magnates built wooden fortresses, often situated on bluffs and protected by walls or moats, to secure control over surrounding territories. Full-fledged urban communities emerged in the 16th century with the enforced resettlement of *samurai* around their lord's castle and the joining of markets (see MARKET TOWNS) and castles in a single location.

Initially, castle towns were small, consisting of the castle complex and separate nuclei such as the dwellings of powerful vassals. Increasingly, however, they mirrored in their central locations and their imposing city plans the growing authority of the daimyō. The relatively few daimyō who survived the internecine warfare of the 16th century converted their cities from defensive outposts to administrative and commercial headquarters for mobilizing the area's resources. Even in the early Edo period cities continued to be relocated, in part to place them in the most advantageous transportation centers. With the consolidation of diverse activities in these cities, population growth accelerated and urban land use acquired a regular form, more or less corresponding to a national model, one example of which could be found in Edo (now Tōkyō). After the advent of Tokugawa rule in 1600, separate branch-castle settlements were abolished under the rule "one domain, one castle." The number of *jōka machi* stabilized at between 200 and 250.

The centrality of the castle symbolized the ruler's extensive regulation of urban life. Segregation of elite residences and the strict correspondence of a lot's size and proximity to the castle with its samurai resident's rank revealed the authorities' preoccupation with the differentiation of social strata, as did the initial, though often ineffective, designation of urban commoners' (CHŌNIN) wards. These highly ordered features of the castle town, which had appeared rather suddenly, began to disappear even more abruptly after the abolition of the feudal domains in 1871 (see PREFECTURAL SYSTEM, ESTABLISHMENT OF). Yet long before the mass exodus of former samurai following the Meiji Restoration, the basic urban plan had accommodated a growing amount of diversity, including a scarcely controlled urban sprawl and an often chaotic mix of samurai and commoner residential areas. See diagram on following page.

With the exception of the shogunal capital of Edo, which is often not classified as a *jōka machi,* the castle towns dominated the urban hierarchy of Japan. They monopolized local and regional military and administrative functions and prevailed as well in commerce, crafts, and diverse specialized services. Apart from the imperial capital at Kyōto and the few cities (such as Edo and Ōsaka) under

direct shogunate administration, almost all of the large population concentrations occurred in *jōka machi*. As a rule of thumb, one-tenth of a domain's population lived in its castle town. Indeed, its residents usually included all the samurai of the domain, except for those obliged to be in temporary attendance at Edo (see SANKIN KŌTAI). In short, a castle town's actual population reflected the domain's overall population and compactness, the number of its samurai, their degree of dispersal, and the importance of varied urban activities, especially commerce. At one extreme, the *jōka machi* of a tiny domain might have had fewer than 1,000 residents and been unable to support even a periodic market. In contrast, prosperous castle cities boasted tens of thousands of inhabitants and a bustling commercial life.

By the early 18th century most large *jōka machi* had reached their peak populations; their population losses over the next 150 years contrast with the continued gains realized by some smaller, local centers less encumbered by restrictive monopolies and duties. Despite their declining populations in the latter half of the Edo period, however, the larger *jōka machi* continued to embody the distinctive Edo pattern of urban concentration and planning.

——John W. Hall, "The Castle Town and Japan's Modern Urbanization," in John W. Hall and Marius B. Jansen, ed, *Studies in the Institutional History of Early Modern Japan* (1968). Nakabe Yoshiko, *Jōka machi* (1978). Gilbert Rozman, *Urban Networks in Ch'ing China and Tokugawa Japan* (1973). Takeo Yazaki, *Social Change and the City in Japan* (1968).   *Gilbert Rozman*

catfishes

(*namazu*). Freshwater fish of the class Osteichthyes, order Siluriformes, family Siluridae. The name *namazu* is used to denote the three catfish species found in Japan, or more specifically *Parasilurus asotus*, the most common species. Two other species are indigenous to Lake Biwa. The larger of these, the Biwako ōnamazu (*P. biwaensis*) grows to 70 centimeters (28 in) in total length. The common *namazu*, found in Japan and the east coastal regions of the Asian continent, grows to 50 to 60 centimeters (20–24 in) in length. It lives on the muddy bottoms of streams and swamps, especially where water weeds flourish. The fry have six barbels, like the European catfish, but the Japanese species loses two barbels later. *Kabayaki* (charcoal broiling and flavoring with soy sauce) and *tempura* (deep frying) are the customary ways to prepare *namazu*.   *Abe Tokiharu*

Many Japanese legends impute a mysterious power to the *namazu*'s strange shape. One of these tales has it that earthquakes are caused by the shaking of a giant *namazu* living under the ground. In the latter half of the Edo period (1600–1868) the *namazu* came to be thought capable of predicting earthquakes and at the time of the great Edo earthquake of 1855, *namazu* appeared extensively in caricatures and woodblock prints.   *Saitō Shōji*

Catholic Church → Christianity

Catholic missionaries

Catholic missionaries first came to Japan in 1549, when Francis XAVIER arrived in southern Kyūshū. Converts are said to have reached 300,000 by the end of the century, but under a series of edicts issued by the Tokugawa shogunate in the early 17th century, Christianity was proscribed, foreigners were forbidden to enter the country, and the church was all but extinguished. See CHRISTIANITY.

Catholic missionary activity was resumed in 1859, a year after the signing of a French-Japanese commercial treaty, when Prudent Girard of the Foreign Mission Society of Paris (MEP) arrived for the pastoral care of foreigners. Bernard Petitjean, MEP, discovered in 1865 the so-called KAKURE KIRISHITAN ("hidden Christians"), who had secretly been practicing their religion, in Nagasaki. The anti-Christian edicts were formally abolished in 1873 by the new Meiji government, making it possible for missionary work to begin on a freer basis. In 1876 the one vicariate apostolic of Japan was divided into the two vicariates apostolic of Yokohama and Nagasaki. Pope Leo XIII established residential bishops in 1891, with Tōkyō as the first archdiocese with suffragan sees in Hakodate, Ōsaka, and Nagasaki. The Dominicans arrived in 1904, and the Jesuits in 1907. By 1941, 16 different men's and 13 women's missionary groups were at work. In 1940 all non-Japanese bishops were replaced by Japanese.

Today the foreign missionary personnel amounts to 998 priests, 143 brothers and 748 sisters, representing 49 men's and 110 women's religious groups (1981).

In southwestern Japan missionaries had to adjust their activities to the sensibilities of the descendants of the formerly persecuted "hidden Christians," who had a fairly conservative mentality. The other parts of the country allowed for more creativity. A remarkable pastoral worker was Sauveur Candau, MEP (1897–1955), who insisted on taking into consideration the intuitive and aesthetic Japanese character and rejected purely Western logical methods in approaching the Japanese.

Educational institutions and schools were founded by sisters, brothers, and priests from the early part of the Meiji period (1868–1912) on. The Sisters of St. Maur were the first, arriving in 1872. They were followed by the Sisters of St. Paul de Chartres in 1878, the Sisters of Chauffailles in 1889, and the Society of the Sacred Heart of Jesus in 1908. The last now operates Sacred Heart University in Tōkyō (Seishin Joshi Daigaku). Sister Hermanna Mayer (1877–1955) was outstanding in the educational activities of the Society of the Sacred Heart of Jesus. The Marianist Brothers started schools for boys as early as 1888. At the request of Pope Pius X, the Jesuits Joseph Dahlmann (1861–1930), Hermann Hoffner (1864–1937), and Hermann Heuvers (1890–1977) laid the foundations of Sophia University (Jōchi Daigaku) in 1913. It received its university charter in 1928. Its president in 1982 was Yanase Mutsuo, SJ (b 1922). An outstanding Jesuit is Pedro Arrupe, a former missionary in Japan and the present superior general of the Society of Jesus. The Fathers of the Divine Word Society (SVD) opened a middle school in Nagoya in 1932 that developed into the Catholic University of Nagoya (Nanzan Daigaku) in 1949. Its president in 1982 was Johannes Hirschmeier, SVD (b 1921).

A number of missionaries have distinguished themselves through their scholarship. Famous linguists were Emile Raguet, MEP (1854–1929), who compiled a French-Japanese dictionary, and Eusebius Breitung, OFM, who compiled a German-Japanese dictionary. Willem Grootaers, CICM (b 1911), is a specialist in Japanese dialectology who collaborated in the writing of the *Nihon gengo chizu* (Linguistic Atlas of Japan). Beatus Theunissen, OFM, and Angelus Aschoff, OFM (b 1910), were active in the Franciscan Institute of Language Studies in Tōkyō.

Professors who taught at Japanese universities included Pierre Aurientis, MEP, who was professor of French language and French literature at Kyōto University, and Marianist Brothers who taught French at Tōkyō University. Joseph Dahlmann, SJ, taught German literature, and Pierre Humbertclaude, SM (b 1899), taught French literature at the same university. Canadian Dominicans, who arrived in Sendai in 1928, took charge of the French courses at Tōhoku University. Vincent Pouliot, OP (b 1903), brought the university milieus of Kyōto into contact with Thomistic philosophy from 1945. Philip Deslauriers, OP, taught medieval philosophy at Kyūshū University in Fukuoka and was succeeded by Louis Deliveau, OP.

Historical studies on Japan's so-called Christian century (1549–1650) have been carried out by Joseph Laures, SJ (1891–1959), Hubert Cieslik, SJ (b 1914), and Joseph Jennes, CICM (b 1902). The Jesuits started in 1938 the scholarly journal *Monumenta Nipponica.* Its editor in 1982 was Michael Cooper, SJ (b 1930).

Active in the field of East Asian religions and philosophies were Aimé Villion, MEP (1843–1932), a specialist in Buddhism, and Jean Marie Martin, MEP, a specialist in Shintō. A specialist in the NEW RELIGIONS is Henry van Straelen, SVD; Joseph Spae, CICM (b 1913) is the author of works on Japanese religion. Edward Papinot, MEP (1860–1942) published in 1909 a *Historical and Geographical Dictionary of Japan.* Heinrich Dumoulin, SJ (b 1905), and H. M. Enomiya Lasalle, SJ (b 1898), are known for their comparative studies of Buddhism and Christianity. Maurus Heinrichs, OFM (b 1904), is the author of a dogmatic theology written from the Chinese and Japanese background. Wilhelm Creemers, OFM, is an authority on SHRINE SHINTŌ, and Matthias Eder, SVD (b 1902), is a specialist in Japanese folklore.

Translations of the New Testament have been made by Emile Raguet, MEP, and of the Old Testament by Eusebius Breitung, OFM, both in classical Japanese. The Old and New Testaments were translated into the colloquial language by Frederic Barbaro, SDB (b 1913). Bernardin Schneider, OFM (b 1917), is a member of an ecumenical group working on a modern new Bible translation. Hildebrand Yaiser, OSB (b 1901), is noted for his efforts to adapt the Catholic liturgy to Japan.

residences of high-ranking samurai

residences of middle-ranking samurai and upper-class commoners

residences of foot soldiers and ordinary commoners

Castle towns —— Hikone

Plan showing the layout of the castle town Hikone during the 17th century. Traces of the hierarchical arrangement of quarters remain today.

Herman Heuvers, SJ, was active in the field of arts and authored several Nō and *kabuki* plays; Thomas Immoos, SMB (b 1918), is a specialist in the history of Japanese theater and Shintō. Well-known painters are Albert Carpentier, OP (b 1918), and Gaston Petit, OP (b 1930).

A Catholic encyclopedia in five volumes *(Katorikku daijiten)* was published through the efforts of Johann Baptist Kraus, SJ, and Titus Ziegler, OFM, from 1940–60.

Charitable and social welfare institutions were also an important part of missionary work. Germain Testevuide, MEP (1849–91), established the first leper asylum in 1887, 20 years before the government took similar initiatives. A second one was founded in 1898 by the Franciscan Missionaries of Mary. Joseph Flaujac, MEP (1886–1959), organized from 1927 a vast network of institutions for tuberculosis patients.

Maxmilian Kolbe, the founder of the Franciscan Conventual Mission, was a propagator of Marian devotion. A martyr in a German concentration camp, he was canonized as a saint in 1982.

Jean Murgue, MEP (b 1908), began social action for young workers in 1949. Leopold Tibesar, MM, was the leader of the Catholic Rehabilitation Committee for repatriates after World War II. Robert Vallade, MEP (b 1914), is known for his activity among the ragpickers of Ōsaka and Kōbe, and Brother Zeno, OFM Conv., is known throughout Japan for his work among the destitute.

With regard to the contemplative life, the first Trappist (Cistercians) monastery was started in 1887; a second monastery was founded in 1927. The Trappist Sisters founded a convent in 1898, and three more followed in 1933 and 1954. Other contemplative orders in Japan are the Carmelite Sisters, the contemplative Domini-

Cats

Colored fan print by Utagawa Kuniyoshi with a punning allusion to six famous classical poets. 19th century. Tōkyō National Museum.

can Sisters, the Poor Clares, the Sisters of the Precious Blood, the Sisters of the Most Holy Redeemer, and the Passionist Sisters.

—— Richard H. Drummond, *A History of Christianity in Japan* (1971). Joseph Jennes, CICM, *History of the Catholic Church in Japan, from Its Beginnings to the Early Meiji Period, 1549–1873* (rev ed 1973). Joseph J. Spae, CICM, *Catholicism in Japan* (1964). Joseph L. Van Hecken, CICM, *The Catholic Church in Japan since 1859,* tr and rev John Van Hoydonck, OMI (1963).   *Ernest D. PIRYNS*

cats

(neko). The domestic cat *(Felis catus)* was introduced to Japan from Korea and China in ancient times, although there are no reliable records as to the precise date or route. Judging from historical records which note that a black cat was presented to Emperor Kōkō (830–887; r 884–887) from China and that one was presented to Emperor Ichijō (980–1011; r 986–1011) from Korea, it may be gathered that the cat was still a rare and highly prized animal in the 9th and 10th centuries. It is believed to have become fairly common by the close of the Heian period (794–1185). As a rule systematic breeding has not been practiced in Japan, but the variety known as the Japanese cat has since ancient times been described as a white short-haired cat with black and brown spots. Cats with long tails were once favored, but from the latter half of the Edo period (1600–1868) those with stubby tails became popular.

According to a survey in 1976, 3 to 5 percent of the 34 million households in Japan had cats. In contrast to this, 12 to 15 percent of households had dogs. Today Siamese and Persian cats seem to be particularly popular.   *IMAIZUMI Yoshiharu*

There are many stories in Japanese literature relating to cats, such as the one in the KONJAKU MONOGATARI about a man who had a phobia of cats. An observant, if cynical, cat was made the central character and narrator in *Wagahai wa neko de aru* (1905, *I Am a Cat*) by NATSUME SŌSEKI. As in many other countries there is a folk belief that cats when killed will avenge themselves, and a whole subgenre of stories about "monster cats" *(bakeneko)* has sprung up. In folk art, the MANEKINEKO, a cat figurine with one of its forepaws raised as if to beckon, is believed to draw customers to a shop and bring riches to the owner.   *SANEYOSHI Tatsuo*

—— Imaizumi Yoshinori and Imaizumi Yoshiharu, *Neko no sekai* (1975). Kamo Giichi, *Kachiku bunka shi* (1973). Kimura Kikuya, *Neko* (1973).

cattle

(ushi). Japanese cattle are believed to have been bred from cattle introduced from Korea to Japan in the Yayoi period (ca 300 BC–ca AD 300). Until the end of the 19th century they were used mainly for draft purposes, since eating animal flesh was prohibited by Buddhism. Most of the cattle now being bred in Japan, known as black Japanese cattle *(kokushoku wagyū),* are of native stock crossed with such European breeds as Shorthorn and Brown Swiss. Dairy cattle

are primarily Holstein and Jersey, and beef cattle are Shorthorn. The Tajima *ushi,* raised in the Tajima district of Hyōgo Prefecture and especially famous as beef cattle, has an average shoulder height of 130 centimeters (51 in) and weight of 600 kilograms (1,300 lb). Its meat is marbled generously (this is called *shimofuri*) and is particularly favored by the Japanese. Efforts have been made to preserve the Mishima *ushi,* the only pure Japanese cattle, which are indigenous to the Mishima district of the city of Hagi, Yamaguchi Prefecture, by prohibiting interbreeding. A small number of water buffaloes are raised in Okinawa Prefecture. See also AGRICULTURE: livestock.   *IMAIZUMI Yoshiharu*

As an important draft animal, the cow or bull figures in many folk legends and customs in agricultural areas, particularly in southern Honshū and in Kyūshū. The bullfights at Tokunoshima in Kagoshima Prefecture and Uwajima in Ehime Prefecture are well known. In Japanese BULLFIGHTING *(tōgyū),* the contest, however, is not between bull and matador, but between two bulls, the loser being the animal that flees.   *SANEYOSHI Tatsuo*

—— Kamo Giichi, *Kachiku bunka shi* (1973). Saeki Arikiyo, *Ushi to kodaijin no seikatsu* (1967). Saitō Shōji, *Nihonjin to shokubutsu, dōbutsu* (1975).

cedar, Japanese → sugi

cement industry

Japan is one of the world's major producers of cement, ranking second after the USSR. In 1978, 84.4 million tons were produced, of which about 10 percent was exported. Some 23 companies were in business in the late 1970s, with 5 of them accounting for 60 percent of all production. However, since it is a capital-intensive industry with a uniform product, price competition is severe. The industry is concentrated in coastal areas, with clusters of large factories utilizing kilns with annual capacities of over 1 million tons each. In the 10 years preceding the 1973 oil crisis, production grew at an annual rate of about 10 percent because of the lively investment in plant and equipment by Japanese industry, but since 1973 the annual rate of increase has dwindled to about 2 percent. Cement production is now a typical mature industry with little room for technological innovation, and increased competition among Japan's cement producers is expected in the future.   *MURAKAMI Yumi*

censorship

(ken'etsu). Government censorship in Japan from the beginning of the Edo period (1600–1868) until the end of World War II was aimed at the suppression of antigovernment and antiimperial ideas and activities, as well as Christian thought in the Edo period and socialism in the 20th century. Explicit sexual material was also censored. Since World War II laws against obscenity have constituted the only official censorship.

Edo Period—— Censorship during the Edo period was primarily directed at four areas: Christianity, writings critical of the shōgun TOKUGAWA IEYASU and the Tokugawa family, criticism of the shogunal government and of the official ideology (Neo-Confucianism; see SHUSHIGAKU), and explicit sexual materials.

Christian writings were first censored after the religion was banned in Japan in 1613. In 1630 the importation and distribution of 34 Christian books published in Chinese was strictly forbidden. Some of these were scientific texts, but they were banned along with anything that contained the words "God," "Jesus," or "the West." A book censor was installed at the NAGASAKI KAISHO, the monopolistic association of Nagasaki merchants that controlled foreign trade. This ban on all Western books, mitigated somewhat in 1720 to allow import of scientific works, was in large part responsible for the lag in development of natural science in modern Japan.

The first Tokugawa shōgun, Ieyasu, was declared a deity *(kami)* following his death in 1616 and the same distinction was subsequently extended to all later shōguns and their families; thereafter it became a crime to criticize or desecrate the ruler, his family, or the government. The first such crime recorded was in 1648 when Nishimura Dembei, the owner of an Ōsaka bookstore, published a lampoon of the shōgun's ancestors. He was sentenced to death. Subsequently the shogunate also severely suppressed criticism of its official ideology, Neo-Confucianism, as well as all works on any other philosophy. YAMAGA SOKŌ was arrested in 1666 for promoting the KOGAKU ("Ancient Learning") school of Confucianism, and KUMAZAWA BANZAN was placed under house arrest in 1687 for promoting the thought of the Ming Confucian Wang Yangming.

The first official prohibitions of such publications were established in 1723 by ŌOKA TADASUKE, the Edo (now Tōkyō) town magistrate (EDO MACHI BUGYŌ). He issued two decrees, the Yomiuri Kinrei (Prohibition of Broadsides) and the Shuppan Rei (Publication Decree). The latter decree, which became the model for all such regulations until the Meiji period (1868–1912), prohibited the following publications: all new interpretations of Confucianism, Buddhism, Shintō, medicine, and poetry; erotic books; genealogies; and books about the Tokugawa family. Authors and publishers were also required to identify themselves in all publications. The censorship of publications was delegated to a committee of eight officials selected from the Shomotsuya Nakama, an officially recognized association of book dealers, who served on a rotating basis with rather broad authority. Aside from the decade from 1841 to 1851, when such merchants' associations were banned, this group exercised self-censorship of publishing until 1868.

During the KANSEI REFORMS (1787–93), restrictions on political writing and obscenity were tightened, and in 1790 a new edict regarding publishing was issued. It became necessary to obtain prepublication permission for books and KUSAZŌSHI (light novels). HAYASHI SHIHEI was censored for his writings on national defense, and SANTŌ KYŌDEN was sentenced to 50 days of house arrest in handcuffs for obscenity. The painter Kitagawa UTAMARO was imprisoned for 50 days on charges of including sexual innuendos in a triptych of the shōgun Tokugawa Ienari.

In 1841 censorship authority for religious texts and poetry was turned over to the Yushima Seidō, the shogunal institute for Confucian studies established in 1691, while municipal authorities took control of popular history and popular literature. In that year RYŪTEI TANEHIKO was forbidden from any further writing after his alleged spoof of shogunal court life. TAMENAGA SHUNSUI was convicted of obscenity, as was TERAKADO SEIKEN, who was stripped of his *samurai* rank and banished from Edo. Censorship authority was returned to the publishers' association in 1851.

Meiji Period——The emphasis of government censorship shifted after the Meiji Restoration of 1868. The emperor, his sanctity, and the imperial system replaced the shōgun as the focus of protection. Socialism and communism, rather than Christianity and anti-Confucian scholasticism, came to be seen as subversive ideologies. Control of erotic literature continued unchanged.

During the early years of the Meiji government, censorship laws and decrees, as well as the responsible government agencies, were continually changing. In 1869 the first ordinance concerning publishing control was promulgated: the PUBLICATION ORDINANCE OF 1869 (Shuppan Jōrei). The ordinance listed as objects of censorship works of Christian proselytism (this ban was lifted in 1872), criticism of the government, libel, and obscenity. It required prepublication submission of the author's name and address and a summary of the proposed content, as well as the submission of five copies of each book after publication. A government office to examine publications was established, and the publishers' association, left largely without a role, dissolved around 1875.

In 1870 the publishing control office was incorporated into the DAJŌKAN government system, with various bureaus taking responsibility for subjects within their purview. Then in 1875 all censorship and publication control was moved into the Naimushō (HOME MINISTRY).

Newspapers fell under a separate system of censorship, which began shortly after the first modern newspapers appeared in the 1860s. Small newspapers reported the events of the BOSHIN CIVIL WAR accompanying the restoration of imperial rule, but once the Meiji government was in place, newspapers were required to obtain official permission, and criticism of the government was suppressed. The Shimbunshi Inkō Jōmoku (Ordinance regarding Newspaper Publication) of 1869 was the first modern newspaper law, and it contained provisions similar to the publication ordinance, except that newspapers were subject only to postpublication censorship.

In response to the upsurge of political activity in the 1870s (see FREEDOM AND PEOPLE'S RIGHTS MOVEMENT), the government promulgated a succession of new laws limiting freedom of speech: the LIBEL LAW OF 1875 (Zamboritsu), the PRESS ORDINANCE OF 1875 (Shimbunshi Jōrei), a revised Publication Ordinance, and Publication Ordinance Penalties (Shuppan Jōrei Bassoku). The Libel Law (incorporated into the Penal Code in 1882) ordered up to three years imprisonment for authors and artists whose work abused a person or

damaged his or her reputation, regardless of whether or not the content was true. The intent of the law was to inhibit criticism of the emperor and his family, the government, and all bureaucrats.

The Shimbunshi Jōrei was so severe that it was referred to as the "newspaper abolition law." All criticism of the government was completely forbidden under a maximum penalty of three years in prison. Many advocates of freedom of speech were fined and imprisoned under this ordinance. In 1876 the government authorized the prohibition or suspension of newspapers violating the ordinance, and in 1883 a large security deposit was required for newspapers to publish. In the first month, the new requirements forced 47 newspapers to stop publishing, and by the end of the year, the nation's 355 newspapers had been reduced to 199. Between 1875 and 1880, over 200 cases of fines or imprisonment were recorded.

The Shuppan Jōrei was revised in 1887 to include the provisions of the Libel Law and the Shimbunshi Jōrei; the revision also added the crime of obscenity and placed penalties for this on the author, in contrast to the newspaper laws, which held the publishing company liable. Prepublication censorship of some manuscripts was reinstated and provisions became more intricate and severe. At the same time the translation of information about the antitsarist Narodniki Movement in Russia was prohibited. Out of some 600 magazines launched between 1877 and 1880, hardly any could publish more than three issues due to government repression. The Shimbunshi Jōrei was amended in 1887 to prohibit the sale of foreign-language newspapers that carried objectionable material. Controls were then relaxed for a period, and all publications were subject only to postpublication censorship. Other measures were taken to solidify the power of the Meiji government, including the passage of the PEACE PRESERVATION LAW OF 1887 (Hoan Jōrei) and the issuance of the IMPERIAL RESCRIPT ON EDUCATION in 1890.

The government utilized prepublication censorship under imperial authorization during periods of crisis, such as the Sino-Japanese War of 1894–95 and the Russo-Japanese War of 1904–05, and a censorship department was installed in the ARMY MINISTRY (Rikugunshō). The Shuppan Jōrei, which had been revised and amended countless times, was replaced by the PUBLICATION LAW OF 1893 (Shuppan Hō), establishing the system of publication control that was maintained until the end of World War II. During this period, an average of 100 publications per month were banned. These included allegedly licentious works by Ihara SAIKAKU, SHIMAZAKI TŌSON, MORI ŌGAI, and NAGAI KAFŪ. In 1904 the socialist HEIMIN SHIMBUN (People's Newspaper) was ordered to suspend publication after printing an abridged version of the Communist Manifesto. The Shimbunshi Jōrei was replaced by the PRESS LAW OF 1909 (Shimbunshi Hō); it was made to conform with the Publication Law and detailed punitive provisions were added. This law remained in effect until 1949.

After 1910 the government intensified the repression of the socialist movement, and all socialist-related material was banned retroactively to 1899. The Mombushō (Education Ministry) removed all previously unsuppressed materials from public schools and libraries. Many publications were censored for allegedly threatening public morality, including Boccacio's *Decameron* in 1910, and Zola's *Nana* and Flaubert's *Madame Bovary* in 1913. In 1913 alone 1,096 books were banned.

Taishō Period (1912–1926)——Immediately after Japan entered World War I in 1914, the military ministries announced the implementation of prior censorship and issued standards for newspaper articles. The Home Ministry also suppressed any article concerning the national treasury as threatening to create a financial disturbance. Sale of Tōkyō's six newspapers and 50 local papers was suspended after Japanese troops were dispatched to Siberia in 1918 (see SIBERIAN INTERVENTION). During the nationwide protests over the price of rice in the same year, sale of the *Ōsaka asahi shimbun* and 138 other newspapers was also suspended, but the ban was lifted after one day in response to strong objections from publishers.

This was a period of great social ferment, and the government was heavy handed in its attempts to prevent the spread of democratic and socialist opposition. Issues of such magazines as CHŪŌ KŌRON were banned on occasion, as were the works of ideologues ŌSUGI SAKAE, KINOSHITA NAOE, ABE ISOO, novelists MORITA SŌHEI, TANIZAKI JUN'ICHIRŌ, SHIGA NAOYA, and the poet HAGIWARA SAKUTARŌ. The works of Tolstoy and Dante's *Divine Comedy* were banned because of their illustrations. In 1920 the bulletin of the Research Institute for the Japanese Economy at Tōkyō University was confiscated after it published MORITO TATSUO's introductory paper on Kropotkin, and both Morito and the editor ŌUCHI HYŌE were prosecuted (see MORITO INCIDENT).

The government increasingly promoted belief in the divinity of the imperial line and in 1919 the sale of the portrait of any member of the imperial family by street vendors was prohibited, as was the use for wrapping purposes of newsprint carrying the emperor's photo. Sale of some 50 newspapers was suspended in 1921 during a behind-the-scenes dispute over a candidate for crown princess (KYŪCHŪ BŌ JŪDAI JIKEN). Because magazines were being banned with such regularity, KAIZŌ waived its right to freedom of publication in 1919 and voluntarily submitted its manuscripts to the Tōkyō Metropolitan Police Department for prior censorship. After the 1920 Morito Incident, most other magazines and publishing houses followed suit. The ASAHI SHIMBUN was the first newspaper to establish a department to screen articles, creating its own system of self-censorship. Films were included under censorship laws in 1925.

The PEACE PRESERVATION LAW OF 1925 (Chian Iji Hō) systematized the repression of both socialism and the movement for Korean independence. It was later expanded to include religious groups and intellectuals; in 1928 the death penalty was added for certain violations of the law. An ideological prosecution system (shisō kenji) was established, and a SPECIAL HIGHER POLICE force (Tokubetsu Kōtō Keisatsu) began to deal with ideological offenses throughout Japan. Censorship continued, extending from literary and academic magazines to such popular women's magazines as FUJIN KŌRON and the girls' magazine Shōjo no tomo; political censorship was applied to KITA IKKI, SAKAI TOSHIHIKO, YOSHINO SAKUZŌ, YAMAKAWA HITOSHI, ARAHATA KANSON, and KOIZUMI SHINZŌ, among others. The literature of KIKUCHI KAN was banned, as were the works of Lenin, Bukharin, Kropotkin, and Sinclair Lewis, and the Kama Sutra. In 1923 there were 893 cases involving political ideology and 1,442 cases involving public morality; in 1925 the figures were 225 and 772, respectively.

The Early Shōwa Years (1926–1936) —— The first decade of the Shōwa period (1926–) was a time of developing Japanese imperialism, accompanied by the suppression of political and social movements. In 1924 the Publication Department (Toshoka) of the Home Ministry had been divided into three sections: censorship, general affairs, and investigation. Systematic censorship was thus created and a policy of thorough control was enacted. The Home Ministry had ended its cooperation with voluntary prior censorship of publications in 1919 and continued to refuse reinstatement of the practice, despite repeated requests from editors, publishers, and theater directors. Leftist writers and filmmakers formed the Ken'etsu Seido Kaisei Kisei Dōmei (Organization for the Revision of the Censorship System), but their efforts were fruitless.

In 1933 the government sent officials to Italy and Germany to study the censorship systems in those countries; from these models new repressive legislation was prepared. With the increase in publications advocating war after 1934, the army, navy, foreign, and home ministries required publishing companies to attend regular advisory sessions. The Publication Law was revised to include harsher penalties and incorporate recordings under its provisions. All censorship came under the jurisdiction of the Home Ministry, including that of foreign newspapers, which were subject to banning if their distribution was suspended more than twice in one year. In 1936 an information and propaganda committee was formed within the cabinet.

During this period newspapers were suspended in June 1932 for reporting the assassination attempt on the visiting head of the LYTTON COMMISSION; magazines were for a time subject to prior censorship, so the number of suspended editions dropped, but numerous magazines were seized for profaning the emperor and the imperial household. The political works banned included books by TACHIBANA KŌZABURŌ, HANI GORŌ, MIKI KIYOSHI, MINOBE TATSUKICHI, KAWAKAMI HAJIME, HASEGAWA NYOZEKAN and SANO MANABU. Many of the literary works of KOBAYASHI TAKIJI were banned, along with those of FUNAHASHI SEIICHI and KUROSHIMA DENJI. The popular song "Wasurecha iya yo" (Please don't forget) and a book of lectures on Esperanto were also prohibited. Foreign writers added to the list of those whose works were proscribed included many Russians, H. G. Wells, and James Joyce. Between 1927 and the end of 1932, a total of 12,213 works were banned for political reasons, with a peak of 5,037 in 1932. During the same years, 3,526 works were prohibited for their effect on public morality, with a peak of 1,035 in 1927. After 1932 figures are not available.

Since many of these materials were destroyed, it is difficult to determine the precise criteria used to censor books. The following appear to have been grounds for censoring political thought: desecrating the imperial family, espousing the formation of revolutionary groups, emphasizing the class bias of the courts and legal system,

agitating for direct action or terrorism, advocating the independence of Japan's colonies, criticizing the Diet system or the military, agitating for war, inciting or covering up crimes, and lending support to those accused of crimes. Criticism of foreign heads of state or their representatives in Japan and the printing of secrets were also prohibited because such acts could create obstacles in diplomatic relations. Censorship to protect public morality covered the following areas, among others: SHUNGA and other erotic books; descriptions of sex; postcards, paintings, and photographs exposing the pubic region; depictions of men and women embracing and kissing; items counter to general morality; descriptions of abortion methods; discussion of atrocities; and items stimulating interest in brothels and red-light districts.

The War Period (1937–1945) —— Between 1937 and 1945 the Japanese war effort dominated domestic politics, and censorship formed one part of an extensive thought control system. The Publication Law was greatly expanded in 1937, and several records were banned that year, including "Kissa musume" (Coffeehouse Girl). The same year a group called the Shuppan Konwakai (Publishing Gathering) was formed by editors of publishing companies and censors from the Home Ministry to consult on censorship. In 1938 the Home Ministry notified publishers of authors whose work should not be published. Police stations were also ordered to report the pen names of all individuals under surveillance for ideological reasons. The country was divided into 13 sections and the Publications Control Committee (Shuppambutsu Tōsei Iinkai) was created to regulate publications. In 1939 prior censorship was ordered for all librettos and scripts, and the automatic extension of permission to reprint previously approved works was revoked.

Penalties were stiffened and extended to publishers as well as authors. Those companies convicted of violating the Peace Preservation Law were thereafter completely forbidden from publishing. In 1940 the cabinet's Information Department (Jōhōbu) was elevated to an Information Bureau (Jōhōkyoku), which consolidated the functions of the information departments of the military ministries and the Foreign Ministry, and the Criminal Affairs Bureau of the Home Ministry. The bureau had direct control over all news, advertising, and culture.

The 1941 revision of the NATIONAL MOBILIZATION LAW (Kokka Sōdōin Hō), passed in preparation for World War II, totally eliminated publishing freedom. A second list of banned writers was sent to publishers, and prepublication censorship was imposed on all periodicals through the Information Bureau. All periodicals except general-interest magazines were ordered to merge; 572 literary, women's, music, art, and photography magazines were consolidated in 174. A Temporary Mail Control Ordinance (Rinji Yūbimbutsu Torishimari Rei) was also issued, giving censors the authority to open and censor mail leaving and entering Japan. Senders were required to print their addresses clearly on all mail.

In 1942, after the war began, newspapers were ordered to merge or cease publication and their number was reduced to 54, or about one-sixteenth of their previous number. In 1943 the Information Bureau prohibited as many as 1,000 performances of foreign music and banned the sale of jazz records. As government repression grew ever harsher, the Nihon Shuppankai (Japan Publishers Association) cooperated by conducting investigations within the industry. Books were first submitted in outline, then the manuscript and printer's proofs were handed over to the association for censorship. The government took over the distribution of paper, releasing supplies only for the publication of matters relating to so-called national policy.

In 1944 the publishers association also took over the censorship of periodicals and the merger of magazines. Only 34 magazines were left in operation: three general magazines (Kōron, Gendai, and Chūō kōron), seven current events magazines (such as Kaizō, Shūkan asahi, and Shūkan mainichi), nine graphic news, five entertainment, two popular, three women's, and five juvenile magazines. The association formed a qualifications council to conduct investigations and mergers. Approval was given to 156 companies; the Chūō Kōron Sha and Kaizōsha houses were subsequently ordered to disband. In 1945 newspapers were limited to one per prefecture. Under orders from the Information Bureau, the publishers association formed a Publishing Emergency Measures Network (Shuppan Hijō Sochi Yōkō), tightened censorship, and further restricted the allocation of paper supplies.

Numerous works of social thought and history were banned during the war years, including books by YANAIHARA TADAO and Yoshino Sakuzō and articles by OZAKI HOTSUMI, KURATA HYAKUZŌ, and ISHIWARA JUN. Banned works of literature included SHIMAKI KENSAKU's novel Saiken (1937), NIWA FUMIO's short story

Aiyoku no ichi (1937), TOKUDA SHŪSEI's collection of stories *Nishi no tabi*, (1941), and ODA SAKUNOSUKE's novel *Seishun no gyakusetsu* (1941). The writings of HAYASHI FUMIKO, SHIMOZAWA KAN, KATAOKA TEPPEI, ISHIKAWA JUN, AKUTAGAWA RYŪNOSUKE, TAKAMURA KŌTARŌ, SATOMI TON, KISHIDA KUNIO, and MUSHANOKŌJI SANEATSU were also either censored or banned. The Nō play "Ohara gokō" was considered irreverent and banned from the stage. Foreign writers banned during this period include Anatole France, Charles Baudelaire, André Gide, Somerset Maugham, and Pearl Buck. Some 2,120 foreign books and periodicals were banned (628 books and 1,492 periodicals); many of these reported on the Chinese resistance to the Japanese.

Occupation Period (1945–1952) —— During the post–World War II Allied OCCUPATION, the instruments for suppressing the freedom of speech—the publication and newspaper laws—were abolished, but new controls were exercised under the Occupation Press Code, while the control of obscenity remained under the Japanese police. The first act of censorship by the Occupation forces was aimed at the DŌMEI TSŪSHINSHA, a wire service whose operations were suspended in 1945 after it published reports about assaults on Japanese women by American military personnel. The company was then prohibited from overseas transmission and its domestic dispatches subjected to prior censorship; on 31 October the news service was dissolved by order of the Supreme Commander for the Allied Powers (SCAP). In addition, all mail, telephone, and telegraph communications were censored, and the nation's five major daily newspapers were reviewed before publication. The Japanese government decided that photographs of the emperor's visit to SCAP commander Douglas MACARTHUR were irreverent and banned that day's editions of the *Asahi shimbun*, MAINICHI SHIMBUN, and YOMIURI SHIMBUN.

The Press Code was officially announced on 21 September 1945. Its preface proclaimed that, rather than restricting freedom of speech in Japan, the code would establish that freedom by fostering an understanding of both its meaning and the responsibilities of those involved in publishing. The code was applied to all publications but was especially aimed at newspapers. It proscribed articles that threatened to disrupt public peace, contained untrue or unconstructive criticism of the Occupation, reported distrust or animosity toward the Occupation troops, or described movements of the Occupation forces. The code also prohibited news articles that were colored by the opinions of the reporter. Thus a thorough censorship system was instituted. Announcement of the code was followed by detailed enforcement measures that required the prepublication censorship of most items, including fiction.

Under these regulations, editors were typically called in and shown printer's proofs with the deleted portions marked in red ink; the reasons for deletion were not explained. It was prohibited to make any reference to the censorship operation, to indicate censored passages in any way, or to use ellipsis points, circles, or x's, regardless of their purpose. Thus SHIGA NAOYA was required to change "town of xx" to "town of Hirakawa" before his *An'ya kōro* (1922, 1937; tr *A Dark Night's Passing*, 1976) could be reprinted. Certain wartime vocabulary was also censored, such as the terms *hakkō ichiu* (universal brotherhood) and *eirei* (spirits of fallen heroes). One of Hans Christian Andersen's fairy tales was censored because it contained the word *gunkan* (military ship), and a scholar of classical Japanese named Chūgi (literally, "loyalty") had difficulties with the authorities. SCAP also drew up a blacklist of correspondents for foreign newspapers and news services, forbidding the publication in Japanese newspapers of translations of their dispatches.

In 1946 the Home Ministry eliminated all censorship procedures and thus formally put an end to the Japanese system of publication control. The last indictment for the crime of lese majesty was in response to a placard used during the SHOKURYŌ MĒDĒ (Food May Day) demonstrations on 19 May 1946; the placard used the imperial first-person pronoun (*Chin*, "We") and read, "We are eating plenty; you people can starve to death" (*"Chin wa tarafuku kutteru zo; nanji jimmin uete shine"*).

In 1947 the Home Ministry, the police, and the public prosecutor's office issued a deluge of antiobscenity measures, but the Home Ministry was dissolved by SCAP in the same year. The following year the American Copyright Federation entered a protest with MacArthur over the banning of Edgar Snow's *Red Star Over China*. MacArthur denied that the works had been banned and claimed that reports of censorship in Japan were malicious lies; despite the denial, prepublication censorship of 13 daily newspapers and three news services was changed to postpublication censorship soon after the protest, and this too was lifted four months later.

Despite the relaxation of Occupation censorship, restrictions were placed on Japanese publications about China and the Soviet Union after cold war hostilities intensified in 1949. The CIVIL INFORMATION AND EDUCATION SECTION OF SCAP acquired the power to ban translations by requiring that all works that fell under international copyright law be granted permission prior to publication. In 1950 MacArthur put an indefinite ban on Communist Party publications such as the newspaper AKAHATA; during the subsequent RED PURGE, 47 media companies were disbanded and 694 people purged from newspapers, news services, and broadcasting companies. In 1951 intensified control of obscene materials prompted the Japan Publishers Association (Nihon Shuppan Kyōkai, established 1946) and representatives of distributors and retailers to ask for moderation. In 1952 the Occupation came to an end and the Press Code was lifted; the same year, the SUBVERSIVE ACTIVITIES PREVENTION LAW (Hakai Katsudō Bōshi Hō) was passed, and the PUBLIC SECURITY INVESTIGATION AGENCY (Kōan Chōsa Chō) began its operations.

During the Occupation, the magazine *Ryōki* was banned as obscene, and *Shinchō* was investigated for printing ISHIZAKA YŌJIRŌ's *Ishinaka sensei gyōjōki* (1948, An Account of the Deportment of Professor Ishinaka). The literary work *Yojōhan fusuma no shitabari* (The Paper Lining of the Sliding Doors in the Four-and-a-Half-Mat Room), represented as the work of Nagai Kafū and later the subject of an obscenity trial (see YOJŌHAN FUSUMA NO SHITABARI TRIAL), first appeared at this time, as did the Japanese translation of D. H. Lawrence's *Lady Chatterley's Lover*. The translator and publisher of the latter were indicted and later convicted under the obscenity statutes (see LADY CHATTERLEY'S LOVER CASE). The magazine *Sekai gahō* was also banned for using photographs of Titian and Tintoretto paintings for its frontispiece.

Post-Occupation Period (1952–) —— With the end of the Occupation in 1952, official censorship of political ideas ceased. Article 21 of the 1947 CONSTITUTION guarantees FREEDOM OF SPEECH as follows: "Freedom of assembly and association as well as speech, press, and all other forms of expression are guaranteed. No censorship shall be maintained, nor shall the secrecy of any means of communication be violated." Since that time, obscenity has been the primary target of publication controls. Article 175 of the Penal Code carries the following provision: "A person who distributes or sells an obscene writing, picture, or other object or who publicly displays the same, shall be punished . . ." Imported publications, films, pictures, and photographs are covered by customs laws, and customs authorities are given the power to delete or confiscate obscene materials.

The Supreme Court ruled in 1957 that the constitutional protection of free expression does not preclude the banning of obscenity. In 1969 the court ruled that guarantees of academic freedom cover items with artistic or intellectual value that would otherwise be prohibited by obscenity statutes. The court stated the standard for judging obscenity in 1957 as "that which wantonly stimulates or arouses sexual desire or offends the ordinary sense of sexual modesty of ordinary persons, and is contrary to proper ideas of sexual morality." In 1969 and again in 1971 the court ruled that obscenity be judged in reference to the entire publication and that the intent of the author, publisher, and readers should not be considered. However, with regard to publications in a foreign language, the court ruled in 1970 that consideration be given to the nature of the potential readership. Such inconsistencies and the extremely vague definition of obscenity are central to the issue of freedom of expression in contemporary Japan. In general, it appears that the government follows standards that differ little from those of the prewar period discussed above. Furthermore, the various media, with an eye toward avoiding prosecution have developed systems of self-censorship that enforce the vague government standards; serious questions can be raised as to whether this is an effective way to defend freedom of expression.

Self-censorship codes have been established for the film, publishing, and newspaper industries. The 1949 Motion Picture Code of Ethics (Eiga Rinri Kitei) was revised in 1959 by the MOTION PICTURE CODE COMMITTEE (established in 1949 as the Eiga Rinri Kitei Kanri Iinkai; name changed to Eirin Kanri Iinkai in 1957; commonly known as Eirin). The Principles of Publishing Ethics (Shuppan Rinri Kōryō) were set forth in 1957 by the JAPAN MAGAZINE PUBLISHERS ASSOCIATION (Nihon Zasshi Kyōkai) and the Nihon Shoseki Shuppan Kyōkai (JAPAN BOOK PUBLISHERS ASSOCIATION). Enforcing the principles is now the responsibility of the Council on Publishing Ethics (Shuppan Rinri Kyōgikai, est 1963), an association of magazine and book publishers, distributors, and booksellers. The Principles of Newspaper Ethics (Shimbun Rinri Kōryō) were adopted by the industry in 1946. In addition, media organizations formed a number of self-policing organizations in 1955 in response to campaigns for enacting legislation to protect the morality of youth. These include the Mass Communication Ethics Group (Masukomi Rinri Konwakai) and the Special Committee for the Purification of Publishing (Shuppan Jōka Tokubetsu Iinkai).

Organizations of concerned citizens also developed at this time. These included the Society to Protect the Children (Kodomo o Mamoru Kai), the Central Council on Youth Problems (Chūo Seishōnen Mondai Kyōgikai), Ban Harmful Books (Akusho Tsuihō), and the Society to Promote Self-Discipline in Publishing (Shuppan no Jishuku o Motomeru Kai). In response to this developing trend, the Japan Artists Association (Nihon Bungeika Kyōkai, est 1945) formed a Society for the Protection of Freedom of Speech and Expression (Genron Hyōgen no Jiyū o Mamoru Kai). The artists' association also issued a statement protesting the suppression of works of classical literature after the 1960 indictment of Marquis de Sade's *Juliette* (its conviction on obscenity charges was upheld by the Supreme Court in 1969; see DE SADE CASE).

Other obscenity cases after the Occupation include those of the film *Kuroi yuki*, directed by Takechi Tetsuji, which was acquitted in 1969; NIKKATSU CORPORATION's films *Koi no karyūdo* and *Meneko no nioi*, which were acquitted by the Tōkyō District Court in 1978, in large part because the films had been approved by Eirin; a volume of photos and the script of ŌSHIMA NAGISA's film *Ai no korīda* (The Realm of the Senses), which was acquitted in 1979; and Nakagawa Gorō's story "Futari no rabu jūsu," which had been ruled obscene and was on appeal to the Supreme Court in 1981. Pornographic video films produced by Nikkatsu for use in motels have been found obscene, as has the genre of magazines called *binīrubon* (literally, "vinyl book," a name derived from the plastic wrapping on such magazines while they are in the bookshop). Other magazines found to be obscene include *Fūfu zasshi, Jitsuwa zasshi, Kitan kurabu, Riberaru, Dekameron, B & B, Eros, Pang, SM furontia, SM fan, SM serekuto, SM kitan, Shūkan manga Q, Shūkan tokuhō, Shūkan gendai, Shūkan sankei,* and *Shūkan shinchō*. Some 57 books have been banned from sale, including the revised and pirated versions of *Lady Chatterley's Lover*, Takeda Shigetarō's *Ashiya fujin*, and translations of Henry Miller's *Sexus* and John Cleland's *Fanny Hill*.

In addition to official censorship of obscenity, the government has engaged in prosecutions over the invasion of privacy, most notably the AFTER THE BANQUET CASE, in which MISHIMA YUKIO was convicted in 1964 for his novel *Utage no ato* (1960, tr *After the Banquet*, 1963). Legal action under the privacy and libel laws has been considered by the Imperial Household Agency to discourage publications that show disrespect for the imperial family. Another form of publication control has been the government system of authorizing textbooks for use in public schools (see IENAGA TEXTBOOK REVIEW CASE).

There have also been a number of incidents of political pressure applied to prevent or disrupt publication. In 1961, after the publication of FUKAZAWA SHICHIRŌ's "Fūryū mutan" in *Chūo kōron*, a right-wing youth who considered the piece irreverent toward the imperial family attacked and seriously injured the wife of the Chūo Kōron Sha president; this prompted a public apology from the company. In the same year, right-wing activists claimed that two novels by ŌE KENZABURŌ—*Sebuntīn* and *Seiji shōnen shisu*—were insulting to the youth who had assassinated the socialist leader ASANUMA INEJIRŌ, and persistent threats to the author were made. In the latter case the work was not reprinted, a situation which meant that political pressure had the effect of censorship. In 1961, in response to such incidents, the Japan Artists Association issued a public statement on the elimination of violence ("Bōryoku haijo"), and the Japan Publishers Association issued a position paper on the freedoms and responsibilities of publishing ("Shuppan no jiyū to sekinin").

TAMAI Kensuke

census

(*kokusei chōsa*). In Japan, the first census was conducted in 1920. Although a law concerning a national census had been enacted in 1902, for political and financial reasons it was not immediately instituted; since 1920 a census has been conducted every 5 years. A formal national census is carried out every 10 years, while midway through the period a simplified census is taken. (However, because of the confusion that prevailed at the close of World War II, there was no census in 1945, though in 1947 a provisional census was

conducted.) Figures for territories presently held by Japan (roughly corresponding to its four main islands) can be obtained for any time, excluding certain omissions related to the 1947 census. However, for the interval during which Okinawa was a trust territory of the United States it is necessary to integrate results of the censuses taken by the Ryūkyū government. On various occasions censuses were also conducted in the pre–World War II Japanese colonial possessions (Taiwan, Korea, Sakhalin, various Pacific island groups, and the southern tip of the Liaodong [Liaotung] Peninsula).

At present the national censuses are conducted in accord with the Statistics Law, issued and instituted in 1947. The agency for their execution is the Statistics Bureau of the Prime Minister's Office which, with the assistance of prefectural governors, conducts censuses through reliance on city, ward, town, and village mayors. The main purpose of the census is to determine the permanent population as of midnight on 30 September. Specific items in the census include the number of family members, sex, age group, nationality, and employment or schooling. There are also additional items which are deemed to be of importance at the time of the census, and at each census there is some variation in the definitions of certain items.

Results of the census are indispensable for the maintenance of population statistics. Figures announced each year projecting population growth are later revised by working back from the latest census to the previous one. Life expectancy tables are formulated according to results obtained from the national census, and information concerning the family contained in the census is used as a statistical basis for sample surveys related to the family. For example, the Employment Status Survey and the Family Income and Expenditure Survey use as their basis information contained in the national census. Results of the census are of great importance to the fulfillment of every function of government. For example, the number of Diet members is determined by reference to the most recent national census.

MIZOGUCHI Toshiyuki

Central Council for Education

(Chūo Kyōiku Shingikai; or Chūkyōshin). One of the advisory councils for the minister of education; established in 1952. The council studies, reviews, and makes recommendations about fundamental policies related to education, culture, and the arts and sciences. It is composed of a maximum of 20 persons who are appointed by the minister of education with the approval of the cabinet for two-year terms.

The council resulted from a reorganization of the EDUCATION REFORM COUNCIL, which was created in 1946 to study and review educational reform. Since the 1950s the council has provided the basic framework for educational policy. Until 1955 it focused on compulsory education, the maintenance of the political neutrality of teachers, and improvements in the textbook compilation system. Also, to help realize the goal of equal opportunity in education, it gave advice on matters such as the salaries of teachers in secondary schools, the promotion of special education and of education in isolated areas, and the encouragement of private school education.

During the period of high economic growth up to 1965, the council made reports related to improving the junior college system, promoting science and technical education, and encouraging the expansion of scholarships and aid. Most of the policies based on these recommendations have been enacted. On the other hand, opinions are divided about the 1966 report on "The Expansion and Maintenance of Upper Secondary Education" and the 1971 report on "Basic Policies of Overall Expansion and Maintenance of Future School Education," and discussions continue as to whether these two proposals ought to be pursued.

NAKAJIMA Naotada

Central Glass Co, Ltd

Chemical company engaged in the production and sale of glass, chemical products, and fertilizer. It is the third largest producer of glass in Japan. Its forerunner was the Ube Soda Industrial Co, Ltd, a chemical company established in 1936 in Yamaguchi Prefecture. In 1953 it started production of ammonium chloride for fertilizer, and in 1958 it began to manufacture sheet glass. It took its current name in 1963 and since then has expanded its operations in the fields of glass and chemical products. Using advanced technology obtained from the United States and Europe, in 1969 it began mass production of plate glass by the float process. It established a joint venture manufacturing subsidiary in 1973 and a sales firm in 1975, both in

Thailand. Annual sales for the fiscal year ending March 1982 totaled ¥158.1 billion (US $656.8 million), of which glass products made up 48 percent, chemical products 33 percent, and fertilizer 19 percent. In the same year the export ratio was 11 percent and the firm was capitalized at ¥8.7 billion (US $36 million). Corporate headquarters are located in Tōkyō.

Central Labor Relations Commission

(Chūō Rōdō Iinkai; abbreviated as Chūrōi). A labor relations commission comprised of eight members, each appointed by the minister of labor from the labor, management, and public sectors. The commission's chairman is chosen from the public sector. It is an external ministerial bureau of the Ministry of Labor. The main duties and powers of the commission are as follows. First, during times of labor strikes and other forms of dispute, it provides conciliation, mediation, arbitration, and emergency adjustment services. It has superior jurisdiction over matters that involve important problems for two or more prefectures or the whole country. Second, it screens the qualifications of labor unions, approves the expanded application of labor agreements, and adjudicates unfair labor practices. In adjudicating unfair labor practices, the commission has the power to review and overrule orders of the local labor relations commissions. Third, the commission establishes its own regulations, such as the details of the investigation procedures for unfair labor practices, the qualifications of labor unions, and the jurisdiction of labor relations commissions. In addition, the commission has the power to provide general guidance regarding interpretation of the laws and basic policies relating to the duties and administration of local labor commissions. See also MINISTRY OF LABOR.   KATŌ Shunpei

ceramics

history of ceramics
ash-glazed wares
lead-glazed wares
medieval ceramics
Edo-period wares
production techniques in Japanese ceramics

HISTORY OF CERAMICS

The history of ceramics in Japan stretches over twelve thousand years. The Japanese archipelago, abundantly supplied with the raw material for ceramics, clay in all its forms, was one of the places where neolithic man first began to manipulate the material into usable forms. Appreciation for clay and its multitude of possible uses has been a steady force in Japanese culture, and there are probably more potters per capita in Japan today than anywhere else in the world.

Until recently the history of Japanese ceramics has been written in terms of tidy, compartmentalized units defined by historical periods, individual pottery-making centers, or particular wares, and connoisseurship of extant objects has been the primary aim. Today, however, Japanese ceramic history is in the hands of the archaeologists, and the results of their intensive widespread excavations in the decades following World War II have attracted scholars from a broad range of other disciplines. These scholars recognize the importance of ceramics (excavated or not) as a source of information for many fields, including social and economic history. Led by archaeology, present scholarship is tending to look away from the fixed definitions and theories and focus instead on the transitions between the traditionally designated periods and the interactions between kilns and types of wares or between pottery and other materials, across space and time. The vast amount of new information has yet to be fully assimilated.

The Japanese islands contain all the major types of materials that fall into the classification of clay, ranging from veins of primary clay lying deep in the mountains, close to the parent igneous rock from which they were formed by chemical and physical weathering, to broad beds of secondary clay mixed with sand and organic material deposited by running water along riverbanks and valley floors. Some secondary, or transported, clays are easily accessible and re-

quire only bonfire temperatures (600–900°C or 1112–1652°F) to harden into the soft, porous, red ceramic substance called earthenware. Primary clay must be mined, processed, and fired within a kiln in order to reach a temperature high enough (1000°C or 1832°F or more) to turn it into a hard, nonporous, beige, gray, or white material termed pottery, stoneware, or porcelain depending upon hardness and purity. The pure white clay called kaolin is the material for porcelain, turning glass-like and translucent when fired; the related feldspars are required for making glassy coatings, or glazes, on high-fired wares. The terms are imprecise, and the distinctions lie along a continuum. According to the Japanese rule of thumb, low-fired pottery, when struck, thuds; high-fired ware rings.

When considered within the context of East Asian ceramics as a whole, dominated by the great technological achievements of China, it is remarkable that Japanese use of high-firing clays did not begin until the 5th century BC, and then only after the necessary technology was introduced from the Korean peninsula. For most technical advances or stylistic changes in the centuries that followed, Japan was dependent upon the stimulus of continental imports, including huge quantities of ceramic objects as well as technicians and information. Porcelain clay was not utilized in Japan until the beginning of the 17th century, and once again the efforts of immigrant Korean potters were responsible. In the development of ceramic materials, China was the great innovator, and all of Japan's advanced technology came directly or indirectly from that source; more often than not, China also set the style. Yet, also typical of Japan's attitude toward ceramics was the fact that, while the newer wares representing advanced technology might be accorded the position of highest status, they by no means obliterated existing wares and techniques, which for the most part continued unaffected. As a result, Japanese ceramics became steadily richer in variety, and the ceramics produced in Japan today cover the full range from earthenware directly descended from neolithic precedents to the most demanding Chinese-style glazed wares.

This Japanese predilection for accumulating rather than editing ceramic techniques is related to the disposition to single out individual pieces for appreciation, an attitude that was crystallized in the aesthetic of the TEA CEREMONY as early as the 16th century but whose roots go back much further. It is noteworthy that the form of tea-drinking initially introduced to Japan from China emphasized categories of ceramics and types of wares appropriate to certain uses, rather than outstanding individual pieces. It was the Japanese form of tea drinking that measured individual connoisseurship through the ability to appreciate particular pieces and that, through the custom of giving such pieces names culled from classical poetry, linked them to the highest cultural tradition. In few other cultures have ceramics been accorded such affection or respect. Because of the special nature of the tea ceremony, moreover, this appreciation encompassed both the purely formal attributes of the ceramic object and its suitability to its practical role in the ritualized preparation and serving of tea. Both these concerns overrode any concern with technical perfection, and indeed tea-ceremony connoisseurship, while cultivating a high level of lay awareness of technology regarding qualities of clay and glaze, may be said to favor the flaws and imperfections resulting from an incomplete mastery of technology. Contemporary Japanese potters, heir to this attitude, insist that it gives them a respect for the clay itself not to be found in other, more detachedly masterful ceramic-producing cultures.

Earthenware——The earliest appearance of pottery in Japan corresponds both to a warming trend in the climate and to changes in vegetation that encouraged a more settled life. It seems to have been almost twelve thousand years ago that people in Japan began to use sedimentary clay—gathered in the immediate vicinity of small, temporary settlements—to form vessels. JŌMON POTTERY imprinted with "cord-impressed" patterns dates from as early as 10,000 BC, evidence of the earlier existence of twisted vine or plant fibers probably used for forming baskets whose use preceded pottery. Jōmon ceramics in its earliest form resembles a deep, cylindrical basket with a pointed bottom.

The primary use of clay, especially earthenware, has always been for forming containers intimately connected with collecting, preparing, serving, and storing food; and pottery vessels were of major significance in supporting the developing Jōmon mode of life. Early vessels served all storing, soaking, and boiling purposes, but by the middle of the Jōmon period (ca 10,000 BC–ca 300 BC), potters in the central mountainous area of Honshū had developed the full range of basic pottery shapes, as determined by both the properties and limi-

Ceramics —— Sue ware

Tall-necked jar with natural ash glaze produced by ash deposits formed during firing. The neck and shoulder are decorated with simple combed lines. Unearthed in Toba, Mie Prefecture. Gray stoneware. Height 55 cm. 7th–8th century. Tōkyō National Museum.

Ceramics —— Seto ware

Jar with translucent green glaze over an incised arabesque motif. The rounded shoulder and incised floral decoration are typical of early Seto wares. Glazed stoneware. Unearthed in Shizuoka Prefecture. Height 35.3 cm. 14th century. Tōkyō National Museum.

tations of clay and the requirements of use. These basic shapes have changed little throughout Japan's long ceramic history, despite alterations in type of clay, glaze, and ornamentation. The jar *(tsubo)* with a small neck opening easily sealed by a lid of leaf, fabric, wood, or clay has been used for storage of seeds and grains or prepared foodstuffs (often in liquid or brine to prevent spoilage), for carrying and keeping water, and in small sizes for serving liquids. The vat *(kame)* with a mouth almost as wide as the body was used in small or medium sizes for stewing and boiling and in the largest sizes for storing water, liquids, and pickled or fermented foods. The flat-bottomed basin *(hachi)* was used for preparation of foodstuffs, by grinding, kneading, or mixing; it was also inverted over jar or vat openings as a lid.

The development of this range of shapes in the area corresponding to modern Nagano Prefecture may be related to the fact that the largest concentration of Jōmon sites occurs there, in the interface between the broad-leaf deciduous vegetation of eastern Japan and glossy-leaf vegetation of the west, yielding the greatest variety and abundance of food. But it is significant that this area also created the most dramatically ornamented Jōmon pottery, with heavy rims convoluted, asymmetrical, and embellished with added coils, animal forms, and faces. Such pots—as well as the small clay figurines called *dogū*—raise the question of the relationship of pottery, especially earthenware, to ritual. Food preparation, with its life-giving aspect, has never been far removed from religious propitiation, and the lifespan of the fragile earthenware pot is associated complexly with the human life cycle; even the earliest Jōmon pots show intentional markings that cannot be interpreted strictly on technical grounds. Long after more durable materials—high-fired ceramics, metals—had replaced earthenware for practical use, it survived in ritual usage within the Imperial Palace, temples, and shrines (beginning with ISE SHRINE).

A principal cause of change in ceramics—technical variation, additions to the repertory of shapes—is change in dietary pattern, and the introduction of rice cultivation to Japan is reflected in the transition from the elaborate, heavy Jōmon style to the smooth, thin, symmetrical, minimally ornamented style of the succeeding Yayoi period (ca 300 BC–ca AD 300). The change also reflects the shift of habitation centers from highlands to river deltas: whereas Jōmon clay is usually stiff, requiring considerable temper and too coarse to take a fine finish, pots of the Yayoi period are formed from plastic,

fine-grained clay found in the deltas where the rice was grown. Moreover, whereas ceramics in the Jōmon period had been not only the major utensils for all domestic purposes but also the primary form of artistic expression, Yayoi culture had access to other materials introduced from the continent, especially bronze. In the Yayoi period another frequent use of clay is first encountered: making replicas of objects originating in more costly and higher-status materials, in this case the clay miniatures of the bronze gong-shaped objects called DŌTAKU that seem to have been a focal point of community worship. Even certain design elements of Yayoi pots—such as raised horizontal ridges—suggest the aesthetic influence of cast metal. Some of the simplest pot styles prevailed in central Honshū, which was also the center for metal casting, yet the importance of clay molds for casting cannot be overlooked. There is clear evidence that pottery continued to have an important ritual role, especially in relationship to burial: in Kyūshū, large burial urns were specially made; in eastern Japan, jars with haunting human faces on the shoulder or neck were used for reburial of bones (after corpse had been buried once and allowed to decompose). See also PREHISTORIC BURIALS.

On the basis of ethnographic data, it is usually assumed that Jōmon potters were women, supplying intermittently the ceramic requirements of their own households. Beginning in the Yayoi period, some archaeologists have distinguished between smaller pots made by women and the larger Kyūshū burial pots (as tall as 80 cm, 31.5 in) presumably made by men who worked as community specialists. The stamped decor on late Yayoi pottery suggests simplified production in large quantities, and there are marks that have been interpreted as a means of identifying the maker. See also YAYOI POTTERY.

Specialized pottery production may have been related to the development of a class structure—based on control of wealth and manifest by the use of special artifacts, including the so-called palace-style pottery ornamented with red cinnabar-bearing earth, in certain graves—that eventually led to the appearance of conspicuous above-ground tombs after which the KOFUN PERIOD (ca 300–710) was named. Clay cylinders, or HANIWA, circling the raised mounds served as offering stands when the tombs were focal points of community ritual; tomb mounds were later reduced to a more ornamental function, topped with elaborate figurines representing shamans, mounted warriors, and animals that are traditionally held to be clay substitutes for human sacrifice. Within the tombs, elaborate offerings of metal weapons and armor were replaced by the 6th century with pottery replicas. Pottery grave goods also included miniature sets of the portable clay stove, tall flanged pot, and steamer that were introduced from the continent.

During the Kofun period influences from the Korean peninsula wrought radical changes in Japanese culture, beginning with the introduction of Buddhism and including a multitude of special technologies for various materials. Following the arrival, by the mid-5th century, of the method of making high-fired ceramics (called SUE WARE), pottery use divided. *Sue* ware was superior for storing liquids and was also important for Buddhist ceremony, but earthenware (now known as HAJI WARE) was indispensable for cooking purposes and also for animistic rites that survived from the older culture. At first earthenware technology was improved through contact with the continental skills: clay was more carefully selected, a fast wheel was employed for shaping small plates and cups, and the craftsmen worked in special regional groups, their organization similar to that of the *sue* makers. Although the characteristic *haji*-ware shape was a small, round-bottomed *kame* with a separate clay stand, some vessels imitated shapes originating in *sue* ware, also metal and wood, and a great variety of tableware shapes appeared. Eventually earthenware objects were phased out by high-fired glazed ceramics, either native or imported, and by lacquered wooden vessels for table use and by iron pots for cooking. Nevertheless, archaeological sites dating as recently as the Edo period (1600–1868) yield huge quantities of earthenware saucers, apparently used mainly as oil lamps.

High-fired Pottery—— Unlike the makers of earthenware, who found clay easily at hand, makers of high-fired pottery have more specialized requirements. The locations of deposits of suitable high-firing clay were gradually discovered by the groups of potters making *sue* ware, and for the most part those areas became the established centers for all high-fired ceramic production that followed, in many cases operating into the present day. Recent archaeology has done much to establish the continuity of such centers, formerly obscured by the transformation from *sue* to stoneware or high-fired glazed ware and sometimes eventually to porcelain.

Historical records show that the introduction of high-firing ceramic technology to Japan was accomplished by the actual immigration of Korean craftsmen, and the settlements of potters, beginning with the first major site at Suemura, south of modern Ōsaka, were closely linked to the YAMATO COURT or to noble families and temples. As the new high-status ware, *sue* ware at first borrowed ritual shapes formerly made in earthenware (such as miniature pots attached to the shoulder of a full-sized vessel), the complex shapes being assembled like the Korean prototypes from coiled and wheel-thrown elements. New shapes arriving from Tang (T'ang; 618–907) China, however, made predominant use of the wheel. As a tool for rapid replication of standard shapes, the wheel was essential for increased production.

Glazed Ceramics—— Early *sue* ware was blackened by smoking at the end of firing to make it waterproof, and the same technique was used in the related ceramic technology of tile making. But contact with Tang China not only changed *sue* shapes but also lowered the status of that ware by introducing intentionally glazed ceramics in two forms: polychrome lead-based glaze on refined earthenware and feldspar-based glaze on high-fired pottery. The new wares were superior both functionally and ornamentally.

Lead-glazed ware was the first of the two to be produced in Japan (see section on lead-glazed wares, below). Plain green-glazed pieces were being made by the latter half of the 7th century, and polychrome glazes were added by the early 8th century, but from the 9th century until the demise of the ware at the end of the 12th century the glaze reverted to plain green. This was the result not of technical decline, as was formerly believed, but of a conscious attempt to replicate the imported Chinese ceramics glazed in various shades of the iron-tinted greenish ash glaze known as celadon in the West. The later green lead-glazed wares reproduced celadon shapes, but they were not true facsimiles, and their disappearance reflected the success of the actual technological duplication of the feldspathic glaze applied to a high-fired gray or white body that was achieved at the SANAGE kilns, in the vicinity of modern Nagoya. Sanage had begun as a *sue*-ware center, but the fortuitous availability of white clay made it the natural locale for the development of ash-glaze techniques, encouraged by direct support of the Heian court, its most eager customer.

Whereas western Japan had direct access to imported Chinese goods that replaced *sue* ware in that area, eastern Japan found a

Ceramics——Raku ware

Attributed to the 16th-century potter Chōjirō, this teabowl is prized for its simplicity and asymmetry. Hand-shaped rather than turned on the wheel, with a reddish body resulting from low firing of an iron-bearing clay with a transparent lead glaze, its thick walls and soft contours are characteristic features. Height 8.5 cm. Egawa Museum of Art, Hyōgo Prefecture.

Ceramics——Oribe ware

A Mino ware, Oribe is noted for its painted decoration in underglaze iron oxide and for its distinctive green copper glaze. This 16th-century square bowl is a typical example, with stripes and flowers in underglaze and an irregular area of green glaze covering its right third. Glazed stoneware. Width 22.7 cm. Nezu Art Museum, Tōkyō.

ready substitute in ash-glazed Sanage wares imitating the appearance of Chinese wares (see section on ash-glazed wares, below). Production increased as paths of distribution widened, but by the end of the 10th century Sanage wares were no longer strictly luxury goods. The majority of pieces were roughly made and crudely fired in stacks without saggers to protect the glaze, and glazing was in any case confined to the rims. By the 12th century, most central Sanage kilns were making only the unglazed, popular tablewares called YAMACHAWAN.

The disappearance of ash glaze at Sanage, once interpreted simply as a decline in technique resulting from diminished patronage from the old central government following its own decline, is now seen, in a larger context, as the result of a division of labor among kilns. A movement from eastern Sanage toward better sources of white, kaolin-like clay led to the establishment of a new center for glazed ware in Seto (see SETO WARE). Under the patronage of the Kamakura shogunate (1192–1333) and Zen temples, Seto began copying newly introduced Southern Song (Sung; 1127–1279) forms—four-eared jars, flasks, and vases for religious use as well as water droppers, ewers, and covered jars for warriors' mansions. Amber or green ash glaze was applied over carved, stamped, or sprigged ornament. By the 14th century, Seto had also perfected use of the iron-brown *temmoku* glaze inspired by brown-glazed teabowls brought back from China and important for the new fashion of tea-drinking. The great bulk of Seto pieces are excavated from

Ceramics ——Shino ware

Irregular application of feldspathic white glaze over iron-oxide painted decoration identify this noted teabowl as an example of Shino ware (a type of Mino ware). Its asymmetry of shape and decoration is well suited to the tea ceremony. Glazed stoneware. Height 8.9 to 9.5 cm. Late 16th century. Private collection. National Treasure.

Ceramics ——Bizen ware

This large 16th-century jar displays the glossy reddish brown surface typical of Bizen ware. Surface decoration includes both incised designs and the characteristic firemarks produced where straw wrapped around the pot burned away during firing. Unglazed stoneware. Height 40.6 cm. 16th century. Tōkyō National Museum.

dence that the change was facilitated by imported technology if not by actual immigrant potters from Korea. There was new inspiration from objects as well in the wares imported from Ming (1368–1644) China. Many new tableware shapes were introduced, and it is now being suggested that the effort to imitate Ming porcelain with its underglaze cobalt decoration led to the development of the opaque, white feldspathic glaze with underglaze iron decoration that became popular, late in the century (on new shapes) as Shino ware. The copper-green glaze familiar from 1600 onward on Oribe tea wares has also been shown by kiln excavations to have been developed by the early 16th century and is thought to have been influenced by the green-and-yellow polychrome ware from southern China known in Japan as Kōchi *sansai* ("three color").

Stoneware —— In the 12th century, when some Sanage potters moved toward Seto and others made *yamachawan,* still others moved southward onto the Chita Peninsula toward a source of high-firing, nonplastic clay suitable for making large, hard, unglazed vessels of the type known as stoneware in the West and *yakishime* or *sekki* in Japan. The utilitarian shapes (jars, vats, and basins, the latter a mortar incised with combed ridges known as *suribachi*) were required for use in relation to improved farming methods (double-cropping and fertilizing in particular) on regional landed estates (SHŌEN), and the movement of potters in response to this need was made possible in part by the gradual dissolution of centralized government control over ceramic production and its replacement by the unit of the *shōen.* The so-called Owari kiln group consisting of Seto, Sanage, and Tokoname provided the full range of required ceramics in that area; elsewhere, glazed tablewares were brought in, but the large stonewares, difficult to transport, were made locally. Their makers were not professional potters but farmers who made pots once or twice a year as the farming cycle permitted, using the clay without alteration and employing simple coiling and scraping construction methods that show remarkably little improvement in skill over time. The only exceptions to this pattern were the few kilns with direct access to an ocean harbor. Tokoname *kame,* some exceeding 90 centimeters (35.4 in) in height, are distributed all along the Pacific coast, and Tokoname seems to have been the most important source of technical guidance to medieval stoneware kilns starting operation elsewhere (see TOKONAME WARE). Tokoname potters probably also spread the typical medieval kiln (a variation of the tunnel kiln but at a steeper angle and with a flame-diverting pillar behind the firebox) and encouraged the shift from reduction to oxidation firing for the sake of more economical use of fuel and a greater rate of success (see section on production techniques in Japanese ceramics, below).

The archaeologist Narasaki Shōichi discerns altogether six types of high-firing ceramic production during the medieval period: (1) Seto and Mino, where production of glazed wares carried on a Heian-period ash-glazed ware tradition; (2) the kilns in the former ash-glazed ware center of Sanage, which fired only unglazed tablewares; (3) the kilns of Sanage lineage that turned to production of large stoneware jars, vats, and mortars (Tokoname ware, Atsumi ware, Kosai ware, Kaneyama ware, Nakatsugawa ware, and others); (4) the kilns that had produced *sue* ware in the Heian period but which, under the influence of Tokoname, turned to production of medieval stonewares (ECHIZEN WARE, Kaga ware, Sasagami ware, and various wares produced in what is now Miyagi Prefecture); (5) the kilns that employed *sue* firing techniques at first but changed, by the early 13th century, from reduction to oxidation firing (including SHIGARAKI WARE, IGA WARE, TAMBA WARE, and BIZEN WARE); (6) the *sue*-derived kilns that continued to produce reduced black ware (Suzu ware, Kameyama ware, Iizaka ware, Kamei ware, and Kanai ware).

Archaeologists have shown that during the early medieval period kiln sites were typically moved away from the *sue* or ash-glazed ware sites deeper into the mountains toward sources of appropriate clay. With the growing commercial significance of ceramics in the Muromachi period (1333–1568), however, kiln sites once again moved closer to settlements. Types of wares changed: with the development of coopers' skills, wooden tubs replaced large stoneware vats, but new small jars and buckets appeared for use in association with special products such as flax and oil. With increased output, potters became more professional: pieces became lighter and more uniform. Jars in particular were influenced by identification as storage and transportation vessels for tea leaves. Beginning with tea jars, everyday wares began to be glazed, resulting in further improvements in kiln structure. Mino potters dispersed glazing technology to stoneware kilns.

eastern Japan, with Kamakura as the focus, in a continuation of the distribution pattern of Sanage glazed wares. Chinese ceramics predominate in western sites.

Seto kilns reached their peak in the mid 15th century, but their development was cut short by the outbreak of the ŌNIN WAR (1467–77). The center for glazed wares shifted subsequently across provincial boundaries into Mino (now part of Gifu Prefecture), which had also produced first *sue,* then Sanage-type, and finally Seto-type glazed wares (see MINO WARE). But the kilns were controlled no longer by distant institutions but by numerous local warriors eager to develop products for cash income. Mino wares were distributed widely to cities and castle towns. At the beginning of the 16th century a change occurred in the kiln, as the through-draft or tunnel kiln *(anagama)* introduced with *sue* ware was replaced by the larger, more reliable *ōgama* ("great kiln"), and there is growing evi-

Nevertheless, the same kilns that were striving to develop glazes were also influenced by the interest of the tea ceremony in unglazed pieces (particularly in ceramics imported from Southeast Asia, known as *namban* wares) to make unglazed tea-ceremony vessels. Bizen produced the outstanding early pieces in this mode, but around 1600 the conscious manipulation, at the Iga kilns, of the features of unglazed medieval stonewares, including "natural" ash glaze, represented the epitome of the artifical naturalism espoused by many adherents of the tea ceremony. Kiln excavations and extant pieces indicate widespread copying of popular types: Iga-style pieces were made in Mino, while Mino-style wares were fired at Karatsu (see KARATSU WARE), and there is every indication that potters from kilns making popular wares went elsewhere to sell their skills (as in the excavation of Bizen-type wares from Kaga-ware kiln sites in what is now part of Ishikawa Prefecture). Finally, potters from various locales were attracted to work at the new kilns within the commercial center of Kyōto, beginning a long period when KYŌTO CERAMICS set the standard in quality for the nation.

Edo-Period Ceramics —— Japan's INVASIONS OF KOREA IN 1592 AND 1597 gave military leaders the opportunity to bring Korean potters, with their superior skills of throwing and glazing, to Japan to work in their domains. There is growing evidence that the reputation of Korean pottery may have rested not only on esteemed imported tea wares but on the work of Korean potters who had reached certain pottery centers in Japan—Tamba, for instance, where they introduced the kiln type known as *jagama*—prior to the invasions of Korea. Kilns established or improved by Korean potters formed the basis of pottery production during the Edo period (1600–1868), which took place for the most part within the unit of the domain. The domain kilns *(han'yō)* as commercial ventures, strictly controlled, were important elements of the domain economy, producing both ordinary market wares and special pieces for presentation. Many domainal leaders also maintained kilns for firing the amateur pottery (*oniwa-yaki* or "garden ware") that was a popular pastime, although such kilns were frequently operated by a professional brought from Kyōto. The enormous commercial market for pottery in all its forms also gave rise to corresponding classes of merchants, ranging from the tea-ware dealers who also supplied tea and imported antiques to the wholesalers in the major cities.

Porcelain —— Korean potters in the Arita area of northern Kyūshū discovered porcelain clay in the early 17th century (see RI SAMPEI; ARITA WARE). Domainal sponsorship guided the development of porcelain as the most important commercial and high-status ceramic. The desire to make porcelain had been stirred by imported Ming porcelains, and Chinese ware had provided the earliest models, but by the mid-17th century a second crucial influence was added in the form of the European market. Recent documentary research has shown that the Dutch East India Company not only placed enormous orders but also provided explicit models and directions for what was wanted in Europe. Special preference was accorded the ware decorated with polychrome enamels and underglaze cobalt on a milk-white porcelain body that was formerly attributed to generations of potters named Kakiemon, (see KAKIEMON WARE) but has recently been renamed "Kakiemon-style Arita ware" in view of the huge scale of production, beyond the capacity of any individual.

Porcelain of coarser varieties was widely distributed and had a far-reaching impact on other ceramic centers. Kilns that did not succeed in finding their own supplies of porcelain clay were moved to develop substitutes such as white slip to cover a dark clay body. By the early 19th century many Kyōto kilns were firing porcelain exclusively, and later in the century, after the Meiji Restoration (1868) and the disbanding of the domain system, countless short-lived porcelain kilns sprang up in rural localities as farmers sought to enter the open commercial market.

The opening of the country to the West brought new opportunities for exporting porcelain from centers at Kyōto and Yokohama. Japanese ceramics also felt the impact of Western ceramic technology and taste through the work of the German technician Gottfried WAGENER in Arita, Kyōto, and Tōkyō, and through participation in the international expositions in Europe and the United States. Major ceramic centers opened training laboratories and began the process of transforming the workshop into the factory.

Modern Ceramics —— Contemporary Japanese ceramics may be said to have begun shortly after 1900 with the emergence of the "studio potter" with an individual name and style. Although the precedents for the artist-potter reach back in Kyōto as far as the Raku family (see RAKU WARE), NONOMURA NINSEI, or Ogata KEN-

Ceramics —— Karatsu ware

Strong Korean influence is evident in this water jar for use in the tea ceremony. A typical example of decorated Karatsu *(ekaratsu)*, it bears a simple design of reeds in iron-oxide underglaze over which has been applied a feldspathic glaze with greenish tones. Glazed stoneware. Height 16.1 cm. 16th or 17th century. Idemitsu Art Gallery, Tōkyō.

Ceramics —— Imari ware

This white porcelain jar with representational decoration in underglaze cobalt blue is an early example of Imari, one of the Arita wares. The Chinese- or Korean-inspired design of human figure, pine, and blossoming plum is characteristic of this ware. Height 23 cm. 17th century. Umezawa Memorial Gallery, Tōkyō.

ZAN, most traditional potters were anonymous artisans following their families' precedents. The studio potter of the 20th century came to ceramics by choice rather than by birth, and the typical eclectic style represents a strong knowledge of Japanese ceramic history. ITAYA HAZAN (1872–1963), for example, was trained as a sculptor and KITAŌJI ROSANJIN (1883–1959) began making pottery to supply his own gourmet restaurant.

The first BUNTEN government exhibition to include ceramics alongside painting and sculpture was held in 1927, and the postwar creation of the government designation of LIVING NATIONAL TREASURES influenced the emergence of individual potters at traditional ceramic centers and fostered public awareness of characteristic local clays and techniques. The potters awarded the title of Living National Treasure have been: ARAKAWA TOYOZŌ (b 1894) for Shino and Black Seto wares; Fujiwara Kei (b 1899) for Bizen ware; HAMADA SHŌJI (1894–1978) for trailed glazes; ISHIGURO MUNEMARO

Ceramics——Kutani ware

Plate with tortoiseshell-pattern border and boldly rendered peonies and butterflies. The rich colors and vigorous brushwork are typical of the early examples of Kutani ware known as Old Kutani. Porcelain with white glaze and overglaze enamels in blue, green, purple, yellow, and red. Diameter 40.5 cm. 17th century. Umezawa Memorial Gallery, Tōkyō.

Ceramics——Kakiemon ware

Attributed to Sakaida Kakiemon, this jar with lid bears the milk-white porcelain body and polychrome representational decoration for which this ware is noted. Overglaze enamels in orange red, azure blue, green, and yellow. One of the Arita wares. Height 60.9 cm. Late 17th century. Idemitsu Art Gallery, Tōkyō.

(1893–1968) for iron glaze; KANESHIGE TŌYŌ (1896–1967) for Bizen ware; KATŌ HAJIME (1900–1968) for overglaze-enamel porcelain; Kondō Yūzō (b 1902) for underglaze cobalt; MIWA KYŪWA (or Kyū-setsu; 1895–1981) for HAGI WARE; Nakazato Muan (b 1895) for Karatsu ware; TOMIMOTO KENKICHI (1886–1963) for overglaze-enamel porcelain. The more recent designation of Traditional Handcraft Products (Dentōteki Kōgeihin) has provided government support for the continuation of traditional skills at ceramic centers.

The contemporary Japanese potter is heir to the full range of Japanese ceramic tradition. He or she works in the context of an exceptionally high level of public interest and support, stimulated by frequent exhibitions, in museums, galleries, and department stores, of historical pieces and a strong activity in the publishing industry. There are even private museums for the work of living potters. Pot-ters develop and present their work at annual group exhibitions of the major craftsmen's associations as well as in annual or biennial one-person shows at department stores and private galleries. Growth of car-ownership has also fostered direct visits to the pot-ter's workplace and has turned once-remote pottery-making towns into lively tourist centers.

The problems faced by the modern Japanese potter include not only those that stem from the gradual disappearance of Japanese traditions such as the institution of apprenticeship but also those that are shared by potters worldwide, especially the scarcity or high cost of raw materials.

▬▬——In English: Richard Cleveland, *200 Years of Japanese Porcelain* (1970). *Famous Ceramics of Japan* (Kōdansha International, 1981–), translations of Koyama Fujio, ed, *Nihon no yakimono*, 26 vols (Kōdansha, 1975–77). Soame Jenyns, *Japanese Porcelain* (1965). Soame Jenyns, *Japanese Pottery* (1971). Fujio Koyama, *The Heritage of Japanese Ceramics* (1973). Fujio Koyama, ed, *Japanese Ceramics from Ancient to Modern Times* (1961). Fujio Koyama and John A. Pope, supervisors, *Oriental Ceramics: The World's Great Collections*, 12 vols (1976–78; repr 1981–). Tsugio Mikami, *The Art of Japanese Ceramics* (1972). Roy Andrew Miller, *Japanese Ceramics* (1962). Edward S. Morse, *Catalogue of the Morse Collection of Japanese Pottery* (1979). Herbert H. Sanders with Kenkichi Tomimoto, *The World of Japanese Ceramics* (1967). Seattle Art Museum, *Ceramic Art of Japan: One Hundred Masterpieces from Japanese Collections* (1972). Seattle Art Museum, *International Symposium on Japanese Ceramics* (1973). Penny Simpson, Lucy Kitto, and Kanji Sodeoka, *The Japanese Pottery Handbook* (1979).

In Japanese: Zauhō Kankōkai, ed, *Sekai tōji zenshū (Catalogue of World's Ceramics)*, 16 vols (Kawade Shobō, 1955–56), contents and summaries in English. *Karā Nihon no yakimono*, 15 vols (Tankōsha, 1974–75). Zauhō Kankōkai, ed, *Sekai tōji zenshū (Ceramic Art of the World)*, 22 vols (Shōgakukan, 1975–), title page, contents, and list of plates in English. Narasaki Shōichi, *Tōgei (I)*, vol 22 of *Genshoku Nihon no bijutsu* (Shōgakukan, 1980). *Nihon no yakimono*, 11 vols (Tankō Shinsha, 1970). Nihon Tōji Kyōkai, ed, *Tōsetsu* (April 1953–), monthly periodical, title and contents in English. Tanaka Sakutarō and Nakagawa Sensaku, *Tōgei*, vol 19 of *Genshoku Nihon no bijutsu* (Shōgakukan, 1966). Tanikawa Tetsuzō and Kawabata Yasunari, ed, *Nihon no tōji*, 30 vols (Chūō Kōron Sha, 1974–76). Tanikawa Tetsuzō, ed, *Nihon tōji zenshū*, 30 vols (Chūō Kōron Sha, 1975–77). *Tōki kōza*, 13 vols (Yūzankaku, 1971–76). *Tōki zenshū*, 30 vols (Heibonsha, 1957–63). Tōki Zenshū Kankōkai, ed, *Tōki daijiten*, 6 vols (Gogatsu Shobō, 1980; repr of 1934 ed). Tōyō Tōji Gakkai, ed, *Tōyō tōji* (1974–), annual reports published irregularly, contents, title page, summaries in English.

Louise Allison CORT

ASH-GLAZED WARES

Japanese pottery with an intentionally applied ash glaze, more recently called *shirashi,* was first made during the latter half of the 8th century at the SANAGE kilns east of the present-day city of Nagoya. Sanage was the major center of production throughout the Heian period (794–1185).

The earlier ash glazing on the upper surface of SUE WARE, a widely produced gray stoneware, was the result of wood ash accidentally settling on the pot during firing and fusing with the body. It is usually uneven and dark olive green in color, with rivulets down the sides. Although the first intentionally ash-glazed ceramics at Sanage also have a translucent dark olive green glaze, its application is fairly even. This glaze was probably made by sprinkling dry wood ash thinly over the shoulder of jars or the interior of bowls prior to firing.

Sue ware with and without a naturally occurring ash glaze was also produced at Sanage, often fired in the same kiln with the intentionally ash-glazed wares. However, the intentionally glazed pieces are almost all harder than the *sue* pieces, the result of their having been placed nearest to the firebox where the kiln reached its highest temperature. In addition, the clay body of the intentionally glazed pieces is whiter and noticeably finer than the body of the *sue* pieces.

The shapes produced at the earliest ash-glaze kilns include tall-necked jars, water vases, various kinds of bowls and dishes, vases with two handles, and horizontal jars. Most are a continuation of shapes seen in *sue* wares, with some variations. Everyday dining utensils and storage jars were generally made in *sue* ware, while objects for use in religious ceremonies or other rituals were made as ash-glazed wares.

The early ash-glaze kilns were a variety of the through-draft or tunnel-kiln *(anagama),* made by digging a trench, approximately 8 meters (26.2 ft) long, about 1 meter (3.3 ft) deep, and 1.5 meters (5 ft) wide, up the side of a hill whose angle of incline was about 25 degrees, then covering the top with a mud roof. During the late 8th century neither a true oxidizing nor a true reducing atmosphere was achieved within the kiln, but because of the small size of the mouth of the kiln and the presence of wood burning there, a more or less consistent reduction atmosphere existed within. By the early 9th century, however, the kiln structure was improved so that the atmosphere in the kiln could be better controlled. This was made possible by the introduction of a removable pillar (bun'embō) placed in the mouth of the kiln to help direct the flame and control the amounts of air entering the chamber. Also, the angle of incline was increased from 25 to 35 degrees to raise the temperature in the kiln. These changes in the kiln structure, as well as the addition of several minerals to the wood ash, resulted in a distinctive, lighter green glaze that was to be the mainstay at Sanage.

Also at this time the first distinctly new, foreign-influenced shape appeared, a teabowl with a rather high footrim with a sharp edge. This bowl was patterned after Chinese Yue (Yüeh) celadons then being imported from Zhejiang (Chekiang) Province. More Chinese-inspired shapes appeared at Sanage during the following decades of the 9th century, including jars with two ear-like handles on their shoulders. Temples, government offices, and members of the upper-class were eager to acquire imported wares, but because of insufficient supplies, turned to Sanage, where production expanded rapidly. In the 10th century, another wave of imported wares from China resulted in more new shapes at Sanage. These shapes included small pitchers with handles, ewers, spittoons, and more. New decorative techniques were also adapted, such as incising the surface with floral patterns, using underglaze iron paint, and reticulating.

A vigorous trade with China in the 11th century provided ample supplies for upper-class customers and resulted in a slump of production at Sanage. The potters, who had sacrificed much of the former quality in the name of mass production, began making an even less attractive and poorly glazed and fired ash ware. A handful of kilns continued making this kind of ware and also the useful small bowls called YAMACHAWAN. At the end of the Heian period, ash-glaze technology spread to several areas in central Japan, but Seto was to become the major production center of glazed wares through the 16th century (see SETO WARE).

📖 ——Narasaki Shōichi, Aichi Ken Sanageyama seinanroku koyō-shi gun, 4 vols (1956–59). Narasaki Shōichi, Shirashi, vol 6 of Nihon tōji zenshū (Chūō Kōron Sha, 1976).   Richard L. MELLOTT

LEAD-GLAZED WARES

The first type of color-glazed ceramics to be made in Japan. Production of lead-glazed wares began around the late 7th or early 8th century at kilns in or around the present-day city of Nara and gradually spread to other areas of central Honshū and to outlying areas, where it continued until about the end of the 12th century.

All these lead-glazed wares seem to have been fired twice; first the body was fired, then after receiving a coat of lead glaze the piece was fired again. Depending upon the temperature, the atmosphere in the kiln, and the iron content of the clay, the body can vary widely in color and hardness. The wares produced during the Nara period (710–794) usually have a soft, buff, or slightly reddish earthenware body, since they were fired at a low temperature (less than 800°C or 1472°F) under oxidizing conditions; but after the 9th century most lead-glazed wares have a hard, gray, or reddish body. The body of the gray wares was fired in a reducing atmosphere. The glaze is thin, often uneven, and made of a 50 to 65 percent lead flux, the colors—green or yellowish brown—being the result of the addition of small amounts of copper or iron oxide. Since the glaze matures at a low temperature, about 750° to 800°C (1382°–1472°F), it is not very durable and tends to chip or rub off easily.

The origin of the lead-glazing technique in Japan is a matter of heated debate among archaeologists. All agree that the ultimate source was the lead-glazed wares of China, but at issue is whether the technique was a direct importation or came by way of the Korean peninsula. Examples of lead-glazed wares from both countries have been excavated in Japan.

The early glazed wares of Nara, produced under direct government control, include three-color wares, usually green, white, and yellowish brown, called sansai tōki; two-color wares, usually green and white, called nisai tōki; and green-glazed wares called ryokuyū tōki. The 57 pieces of color-glazed pottery preserved in the 8th-century SHŌSŌIN art repository in Nara form the largest, most repre-

Ceramics —— Kyōto ware

Square plate made by Kenzan and decorated by his brother Kōrin. The design of a blossoming plum tree, by Kōrin, and the inscription, by Kenzan, are executed in iron oxide on a ground of white slip. Glazed stoneware. Width 21.0 cm. Early 18th century. Nezu Art Museum, Tōkyō.

Ceramics —— Modern wares

This polychrome porcelain jar with lid, produced by Katō Hajime in 1968, shows the ornate decoration typical of much of his work. The design of birds and flowers is executed in gold on a vermilion red ground in a technique derived from late Ming-dynasty (1368–1644) Chinese porcelain styles. Height 21.5 cm. Tōkyō University of Fine Arts and Music.

sentative collection of these early wares. Formerly thought to be of Chinese origin, the Shōsōin pieces are now known to have been made in Japan, although the kilns where they were made have not been found. Most of the Shōsōin pieces were used as dining utensils or for religious ceremonies. They consist of bowls and dishes, one drum body, one pagoda, and one bottle. The shapes were modeled after Chinese three-color wares and Korean green-glaze wares.

In the 9th century, production seems to have shifted to the area of the new capital, Kyōto, where three-color wares were quickly eliminated in favor of green-glazed wares. Two kilns, one in Kami-Gamo and the other in Iwakura, both now part of the city of Kyōto, have been excavated and have yielded green-glazed wares with a dark gray body covered by a dark green glaze. In addition, a great many fragments of green-glazed wares, and a few of two-color wares, have been found at various other archaeological sites in

Kyōto Prefecture. These include both gray and dark-red bodied wares. The glaze color varies from light green to a dark green, and vases, bowls, dishes, and jars for religious use were the most common shapes.

From the mid-10th century until the end of the 12th century, several kilns at SANAGE, the center for production of ash-glazed stoneware near the present-day city of Nagoya, also produced green-glazed wares. Other outlying areas produced green-glazed wares, such as Mino (now part of Gifu Prefecture) during the 11th century and probably some kilns in northern Kyūshū, but these sites are not yet well studied.

📖——Miyazaki Kazuo, ed, *Nihon no sansai to ryokuyū* (Gotō Bijutsukan, 1974). Narasaki Shōichi, *Sansai, ryokuyū*, vol 5 of *Nihon tōji zenshū* (Chūō Kōron Sha, 1977). *Richard L. MELLOTT*

MEDIEVAL CERAMICS

From the 12th century through the 16th century, the most characteristic Japanese ceramic products were sturdy, unglazed stonewares made in a limited set of shapes, primarily for utilitarian storage: the wide-mouthed vat, the narrow-necked jar, and the mortar. Also produced were red earthenware (HAJI WARE) cooking vessels; tablewares made of earthenware, gray tileware *(gaki)*, and glazed as well as unglazed high-fired ceramics; and glazed vessels associated with religious and ceremonial use, gift-giving, and tea-drinking. Throughout the medieval period, glazed ceramics were also imported from China and Korea, and these set the standard of luxury.

Medieval ceramics first attracted wide interest in the 1950s, following the coining of the term "Six Old Kilns" to designate the only medieval kiln sites well known at the time, those that had produced SETO WARE, TOKONAME WARE, ECHIZEN WARE, SHIGARAKI WARE, TAMBA WARE, and BIZEN WARE. Archaeologists now dismiss the concept as obsolete, having uncovered evidence of more than 30 centers making unglazed stonewares, including Tōkita, Takōda, and Shinanoura (Miyagi Prefecture); Iizaka (Fukushima Prefecture); Sasagami (Niigata Prefecture); Kanai (Gumma Prefecture); Kamei (Saitama Prefecture); Suzu and Kaga (Ishikawa Prefecture); Kosai (Shizuoka Prefecture); Atsumi (Aichi Prefecture); Kaneyama, Nakatsugawa, and Mino Sue (Gifu Prefecture); Kameyama (Okayama Prefecture); Sue (Kagawa Prefecture); and one site in Kyūshū (Kumamoto Prefecture). Other kiln centers, such as those producing MINO WARE and IGA WARE, known for their late 16th-century tea wares, have been shown to have medieval antecedents. Mino, however, like Seto belongs to the special category of kilns that produced high-quality glazed wares.

Expansion and improvement of farming on medieval manors (SHŌEN) was the major impetus to the production of medieval stonewares, but archaeology has shown that the versatile jars also served as sutra burial containers, cinerary urns, and cash jars. During the Kamakura period (1185–1333), when most stonewares were used primarily within the manor, the only large unglazed wares to be distributed widely were those from kilns with direct access to sea transport: Tokoname, Atsumi, Bizen, and Suzu. Stoneware technology was introduced from these kilns to other areas that had formerly produced the gray stoneware known as SUE WARE. The large Tokoname vat was widely imitated, and Tokoname also led the change from the reduction firing typical of both earlier wares to the more economical oxidation firing.

In the Muromachi period (1333–1568), however, as control of manors shifted to local warriors, unglazed stonewares became valuable sources of cash income, and they were distributed through an expanding merchandising system to a network of markets centering around Kyōto. What had formerly been all-purpose vessels tended to be used for specific cash crops, especially tea. The popularity of imported Chinese jars spurred changes in tea-jar design to conform with foreign models and served particularly as an incentive for the use of glaze by kilns that had formerly produced only unglazed wares. Mino was the most important source of technical guidance.

Throughout the 16th century, followers of the rustic *wabi* style of TEA CEREMONY cultivated a preference for unglazed ceramics. At first, they favored "found wares" from local kilns, chiefly Bizen and Shigaraki, but from around 1550 they patronized potters who intentionally made tea wares in the style of the unglazed *namban* wares imported by Portuguese traders from Southeast Asia. For such tea wares, Bizen set the standard.

📖——Louise Allison Cort, "Medieval Japanese Ceramics and the Tea Ceremony," *Keramos* 85 (July 1979). Narasaki Shōichi, *Seto, Bizen, Suzu*, vol 43 of *Bukku obu bukkusu: Nihon no bijutsu* (1976). *Louise Allison CORT*

EDO-PERIOD WARES

The Edo period (1600–1868) saw the continuation of the innovative use of stylized design motifs on stoneware and technological advances in kiln construction that had begun in the late 16th century. Older ceramic centers turned to production of wares for the TEA CEREMONY as well as for utilitarian use; the newer kilns in the Mino area (now part of Gifu Prefecture; see MINO WARE) and at the Korean-influenced kilns in Hizen Province (now Nagasaki and Saga prefectures) in Kyūshū did likewise. Early-Edo-period ceramics displayed a vitality that reflected the spirit of the regime, and more particularly, the taste of the tea masters. The most significant and noticeable changes in the early Edo period involved the decorated wares, particularly Shino ware, Oribe ware, and KARATSU WARE. The more austere wares, such as RAKU WARE, IGA WARE, and BIZEN WARE, underwent more subtle changes in form and design.

The introduction from Korea of the *noborigama* or climbing kiln in the late 16th century revolutionized the firing of stonewares and made possible the successful firing of porcelain after suitable porcelain clays were discovered in Kyūshū by immigrant Korean potters (see RI SAMPEI) in the early 17th century. The production of high-fired wares was perhaps the most important technological advance in the Edo period, or for that matter, in the subsequent history of Japanese ceramics. The earliest porcelains produced were celadons, plain white wares, and underglaze blue decorated wares. These early porcelains, often called early *(shoki)* Imari or early Hizen ware, were modeled and decorated in the contemporary Korean manner. As greater facility with the medium was achieved, the forms and designs began to reflect the more highly valued wares of Ming-dynasty (1368–1644) China. Shortly after the middle of the 17th century, porcelains for export were being made to order for the Dutch East India Company trade. These were generally blue-and-white porcelains modeled either on Ming prototypes or on specific designs selected by the Europeans.

By this time the peace and political stability imposed by the Tokugawa regime had done much to increase the wealth of the nation. Demand for ceramics increased at all levels of society, and the industry thrived. The wide general demand for utilitarian wares and tea-ceremony stonewares and the increasing demand for export porcelains resulted in a general expansion of production centers and the development of new kiln sites. The use of overglaze polychrome enamels on both pottery and porcelain—the knowledge of which was probably first gained from the Chinese in the 1640s—was a pivotal point in the history of ceramics in Japan, and in Europe as well.

The second half of the 17th century saw the full flowering of decorated wares, a trend that had begun in the Azuchi–Momoyama period (1568–1600). In Kyūshū, colorful Imari ware (see ARITA WARE) and KAKIEMON WARE were shipped to Europe in great quantities; the finer quality Kakiemon and NABESHIMA WARE porcelains were reserved for the local rulers. Attaining great popularity with the upper classes in and around Kyōto, decorated earthenware or stoneware known as *kyō-yaki* (see KYŌTO CERAMICS) was created by great potter-decorators such as NONOMURA NINSEI (active mid-17th century) and Ogata KENZAN (1666–1743). Of the many new kilns that opened in the latter half of the 17th century, most produced traditional utilitarian wares and specialized wares for the tea ceremony. Only isolated ventures, such as Himetani ware and KUTANI WARE, attempted the costly and difficult production of porcelain in competition with the dominant kilns in the Arita area of Kyūshū. While highly decorative and colorful pottery and porcelain were extremely popular with the *daimyō* and the increasingly affluent middle classes of the urban centers, the taste for the more subdued and rustic stonewares favored by the devotees of tea never abated. Likewise, homely stonewares for everyday use continued to be produced as they had been for centuries, but in ever greater numbers for a growing population that could afford more amenities.

The vitality and growth of the Japanese ceramic industry continued into the 18th century, but by around 1725 there began a decline in the quality and the inventiveness that had reached an apex in the wares of the Genroku era (1688–1704). During the second half of the 18th century, new kilns and expanded older centers produced greater quantities of rather uninspired wares for a larger and more affluent, but less discriminating, populace. The export center at Arita in Kyūshū also showed a decline in quality, partly due to the competition from the Chinese, who were once again active in the porcelain trade. This is not to say that nothing of merit was produced in the second half of the century, but with the exception of a few bright spots, such as the inspired BANKO WARE of Ise Province (now part of Mie Prefecture) and the continuing production of time-proven utilitarian wares, ceramics of this period tended to be uninventive and repetitive.

The 18th century was plagued by natural disasters and severe economic and political woes that sapped the spirit of the people. However, that same climate spurred the cultural development of literature, philosophy, and religion. In painting, dramatic new trends were set in motion. But this cultural renaissance would not influence Japanese ceramics until slightly later, when the ceramic industry itself was on a stronger economic base. As the 18th century drew to a close, there was a veritable explosion of new sites throughout the country and a resurgence of activity in and around the old kiln centers. Just as Ogata KŌRIN (1658–1716), his brother Kenzan, and Nonomura Ninsei had been the great arbiters of ceramic taste a century before, so OKUDA EISEN (1753–1811), NIN'AMI DŌHACHI (1783–1855), and AOKI MOKUBEI (1767–1833), among others, led the way in the early 19th century to a new aesthetic in the Japanese ceramic art. Although these men and other potters of the period were heavily influenced by Chinese Ming and Qing (Ch'ing; 1644–1912) ceramics and by the painters and potters of the RIMPA style, their pots show a very personal artistic improvement. By and large, the work is quite colorful with its use of overglaze enamel decoration. In addition to the work of the major Kyōto potters, artistic trends developed in the Seto area by such artists as Hirosawa Kurō (1772–1844) and Katō Shuntai (1802–77). The early part of the 19th century was marked by a pronounced revival of interest in the past; potters responded by producing amazingly faithful copies and interpretations of earlier wares, to the great confusion of later scholars and collectors.

The spread of kilns throughout the country added not only to the quantity of wares but also to their diversity and liveliness. As potters moved about more freely and as quality improved in the newer production areas, provincial styles of high quality began to appear. The high point of the early 19th century is considered to be around the time of the Bunka (1804–18) and Bunsei (1818–30) eras. The great increase in production throughout the country around 1800 was not restricted to pottery and stoneware; as early as the last quarter of the 18th century, porcelain was being fired in Shikoku, and by the turn of the century porcelain-producing kilns were springing up all over the country. Kyūshū no longer had the monopoly on the making of porcelain. This meant that porcelain eventually came to be used as everyday household ware.

One of the major factors in the flowering of ceramic production in 19th-century Japan was the great improvement made in transportation and, hence, in distribution; in addition, for the first time it was feasible to transport clay to kilns. Prior to this development kilns had to be located close to firewood and water sources and where there were natural deposits of good clay. Technological improvements in the handling of clay and kiln design contributed greatly to the success of the industry.

Toward the end of the Edo period the very factors that so enriched its last phase also worked to seriously undermine the art. The highly decorative aesthetic style of the early 19th century was tempered by the personal restraint of the great masters. Technical virtuosity was all-important. But a decorative style combined with great technical knowledge and a high production rate proved difficult to control with taste, and the wares of the late Edo period and the Meiji period (1868–1912) tended to be rich and florid.

Richard S. CLEVELAND

PRODUCTION TECHNIQUES IN JAPANESE CERAMICS

Pottery can be made either by hand-forming or wheel-forming methods. Handmade pieces can be coil-made, hand-formed, or slab-built. In the coil method (*himo-zukuri*), the clay is rolled into long coils, and perhaps with the aid of a small hand-turned wheel, the coil is used to build up pots of a variety of shapes and sizes. The hand-forming method (*tebineri*) is often used to make RAKU WARE tea bowls. A thick, circular slab is formed into a bowl by raising the outer part, and then the shape is articulated by both tools and the hands. The slab method (*tatara-zukuri*), in which slabs of the same thickness are joined, is used for flat or square pieces. There are also rarer techniques, such as forming bowls by pressing a ball of clay against the elbow until the proper thickness is attained.

Another technique is mold casting, used to make pots that are angular or decorated on the surface. Plaster molds for the inside and outside of the piece are cast, and clay is then pressed against both

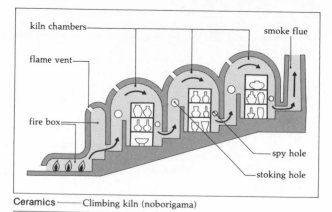

Ceramics —— Climbing kiln (noborigama)

Cross-section of a large Edo-period three-chambered climbing kiln. Built on an incline, as on a hillside, this type of through-draft kiln fired as high as 1300° to 1400°C. When heat within the chambers successively reached the flash point, the stoking holes were unplugged and fuel added. The arrows indicate the direction of heat flow.

molds. Another casting technique is pouring slip, or liquid clay, into a cast that has the negative shape of the pot, and then pouring the slip out when the plaster has absorbed enough water to produce a wall with the proper thickness.

Tools —— The wheel (ROKURO) is commonly used in Japan, and the Japanese potter is trained to make pieces of the same dimensions quickly. Both clockwise- and counterclockwise-turning wheels are used, according to the tradition of the area or the potter's personal preference. There are different wheels: handwheel (*terokuro*), kickwheel (*kerokuro*), and electric wheel (*denki rokuro*). The handwheel is favored by many individual potters and has a large, heavy head strutted to a wooden base, both made from ZELKOVA, and is powered by a stick held in the hand. When the wheel is spinning sufficiently fast, the potter puts down the stick and brings his hands to the clay. Because of its weight, the handwheel continues to rotate for a considerable time.

The kickwheel may have come to Japan in the late 16th century with the influx of Korean potters at that time. It has a small wheel-head and is powered by the foot. This wheel needs almost constant kicking but the hands are free for throwing. Many contemporary wheels are powered by electricity but are the same height as traditional wheels, with the potters working them while sitting cross-legged at a bench.

Japanese potters may use a variety of tools and usually make their own. In throwing work, interior or exterior shapes may be molded by wooden ribs or, for taller or small-mouthed pieces, by throwing sticks. Dimensions are often still measured by a traditional bamboo tool called a "dragonfly" (*tombo*), which it resembles in shape, although today calipers are just as common. There are many simple bamboo tools for cutting, marking, or scraping, including combs for incising patterns. Rims are trimmed with a "bow" (*yumi*) and finished with a piece of chamois leather or the fingers. Traditionally, work is either thrown off the lump or, for larger pieces, the clay is weighed for each item. Pots are cut from the lump or wheel-head by a twilled cutting cord or a piece of wire, and the shell-like marks are sometimes left. Trimming is done with metal or wooden trimming tools (*kanna*). A special technique called tobiganna (literally, "jumping trimming tool"), in which the tool is used to make chatter marks on the pot, is exploited at Onta (see ONTA WARE).

Kilns —— Currently used kilns can be divided into through-draft, down-draft, and up-draft kilns, although simple pit firing was done in the Jōmon (ca 10,000 BC–ca 300 BC) and Yayoi (ca 300 BC–ca AD 300) periods. The through-draft kilns are structured to allow the heat to flow to the back of the kiln with the help of the chimney, located in the rear. These kilns (*anagama*) usually have one chamber and are capable of reaching temperatures of 1200° to 1300°C (about 2200° to 2400°F). There are longer kilns using the same principle (called rifle kilns, *teppōgama*, or snake kilns, *jagama* or *hebigama*) which have several chambers. These kilns are semisubterranean and are usually built up hillsides like roofed-over ditches. Most wares in the medieval period were produced in single-chamber-through-draft kilns.

The most sophisticated through-draft kiln is the climbing kiln (*noborigama*), which can reach temperatures of 1300° to 1400°C

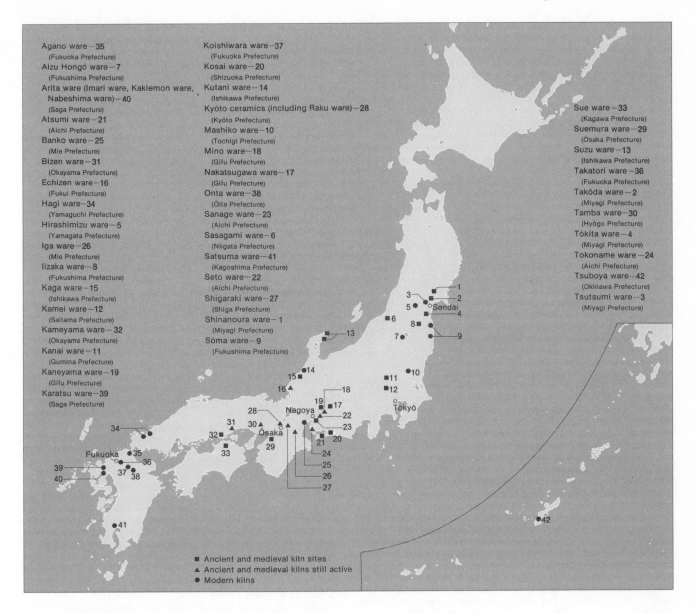

Agano ware—35
(Fukuoka Prefecture)
Aizu Hongō ware—7
(Fukushima Prefecture)
Arita ware (Imari ware, Kakiemon ware,
Nabeshima ware)—40
(Saga Prefecture)
Atsumi ware—21
(Aichi Prefecture)
Banko ware—25
(Mie Prefecture)
Bizen ware—31
(Okayama Prefecture)
Echizen ware—16
(Fukui Prefecture)
Hagi ware—34
(Yamaguchi Prefecture)
Hirashimizu ware—5
(Yamagata Prefecture)
Iga ware—26
(Mie Prefecture)
Iizaka ware—8
(Fukushima Prefecture)
Kaga ware—15
(Ishikawa Prefecture)
Kamei ware—12
(Saitama Prefecture)
Kameyama ware—32
(Okayama Prefecture)
Kanai ware—11
(Gumma Prefecture)
Kaneyama ware—19
(Gifu Prefecture)
Karatsu ware—39
(Saga Prefecture)

Koishiwara ware—37
(Fukuoka Prefecture)
Kosai ware—20
(Shizuoka Prefecture)
Kutani ware—14
(Ishikawa Prefecture)
Kyōto ceramics (including Raku ware)—28
(Kyōto Prefecture)
Mashiko ware—10
(Tochigi Prefecture)
Mino ware—18
(Gifu Prefecture)
Nakatsugawa ware—17
(Gifu Prefecture)
Onta ware—38
(Ōita Prefecture)
Sanage ware—23
(Aichi Prefecture)
Sasagami ware—6
(Niigata Prefecture)
Satsuma ware—41
(Kagoshima Prefecture)
Seto ware—22
(Aichi Prefecture)
Shigaraki ware—27
(Shiga Prefecture)
Shinanoura ware—1
(Miyagi Prefecture)
Sōma ware—9
(Fukushima Prefecture)

Sue ware—33
(Kagawa Prefecture)
Suemura ware—29
(Ōsaka Prefecture)
Suzu ware—13
(Ishikawa Prefecture)
Takatori ware—36
(Fukuoka Prefecture)
Takōda ware—2
(Miyagi Prefecture)
Tamba ware—30
(Hyōgo Prefecture)
Tōkita ware—4
(Miyagi Prefecture)
Tokoname ware—24
(Aichi Prefecture)
Tsuboya ware—42
(Okinawa Prefecture)
Tsutsumi ware—3
(Miyagi Prefecture)

■ Ancient and medieval kiln sites
▲ Ancient and medieval kilns still active
● Modern kilns

(about 2400° to 2600°F), sufficient for firing porcelain and which was introduced into Japan from Korea in the early 17th century. The climbing kiln has multiple chambers, the maximum number being around 20, although modern kilns number only three to five chambers. A modern four-chambered climbing kiln can reach 1200°C (2200°F) easily in 36 hours, but larger kilns in the past took many days to fire.

Up-draft kilns simply pull the heat up by means of a chimney located at the top, and down-draft kilns allow the heat to rise and then flow down to where the chimney opening is located. In the late 19th century, European-style kilns were introduced, including coal-fire kilns and oil or gas kilns. The electric kiln has recently become very common where there is enamel production or strict pollution control. Much of the ceramic production of modern Japan is fired in climbing kilns or single-chamber down-draft kilns, with oil or gas. These kilns are easy to control, labor-intensive, and their performance is guaranteed.

Glazes—— Before the glaze is applied, whether it be chemical or natural, the piece is almost always biscuit-fired *(suyaki)* at a low temperature to transform the still water-soluble clay to a substance hard enough to carry the thick, wet glaze without crumbling. Most biscuit-fired pieces are pink, or red if the clay has a high iron content. Glaze is applied, and the ware is ready for the final firing or firings.

The earliest glazing was unintentional and came from the ash of the wood used in firing. This was a natural glaze and was only possible with the advent of the through-draft kilns. Deliberate glazing was done somewhat later and was primarily lead glazing on low-

temperature wares. Some effort was made to try to reproduce Chinese celadon using green ash glaze, as with SANAGE ware and SETO WARE (see the section on lead-glazed wares, above). After the influx of the Korean potters in the 17th century, there was a burst of activity, and the use of underglaze cobalt blue was introduced. Each ceramic site has its own methods of production. Depending on the effects desired, there may be several glaze firings; in some places, the fuel used to fire the kiln is crucial to the outcome of the glazed surface.

Glaze application is done using several methods. Dunking is prevalent if the entire piece is to be glazed in one color. Painting with a brush before a transparent glaze is applied allows the design to show through. If a negative design is sought, a wax resist is used, or sometimes the glaze is carved away with a tool. Designs or characters can be dripped on with an applicator for a fluid and loose effect. Natural ash-glazing is still done in several places, as in the production of BIZEN WARE.

■ ——David Hale, *Tōhoku no yakimono* (1974). Koyama Fujio, *Nihon tōji sōran* (1969). Herbert H. Sanders with Kenkichi Tomimoto, *The World of Japanese Ceramics* (1967). Penny Simpson, Lucy Kitto, and Kanji Sodeoka, *The Japanese Pottery Handbook* (1979). Tamura Kōichi, *Tōgei no gihō* (1970).   *David* HALE

Cerqueira, Luis de (1552–1614)

Second and last Catholic bishop to work in Japan during the early period of CHRISTIANITY. Born in Vila de Alvito, Portugal, he entered the Society of Jesus in 1566 and taught theology at the University of Evora until he was consecrated bishop in 1593. He arrived in Nagasaki in 1598 to succeed the expelled Bishop Pedro Martins (1542–98). Cerqueira ordained the first Japanese priests in 1601 and established a diocesan clergy. He was received in audience by the retired shōgun TOKUGAWA IEYASU at Fushimi in 1606. His term of office was marked by the controversy between the JESUITS and friars and by the increasing anti-Christian hostility of the Japanese authorities. He died in Nagasaki, just as the Tokugawa government ordered all foreign missionaries to leave Japan.   Michael COOPER

certified public accountant

(kōnin kaikeishi). Responsibilities of certified public accountants in Japan include the audit and certification of financial reports, preparation of financial reports, investigation and design of accounting systems, and consultation on financial matters. All functions are performed at another's request and for due compensation. In order to become a certified public accountant, one has to pass a government-sponsored, three-stage examination and have one's name registered. The first-stage examination is in general skills, the second in accounting theories, and the third in accounting practices. Those who have passed the first- and second-stage examinations are called junior accountants and are allowed to practice all accounting functions except audits and certifications. Of an accountant's business, by far the most important is the auditing of financial statements. This particular business includes expression of the auditors' opinions on the fairness of the financial statements made public by corporations. By disclosing a corporation's window dressing or other malpractices, certified public accountants uphold the truthfulness of financial statements, thereby protecting all interested parties, including stockholders and creditors. Auditors are allowed to establish their own corporations with the aim of strengthening their position vis-à-vis corporations. Certified public accountants have established the Japan Association of Certified Public Accountants.

WAKASUGI Akira

cha → tea

chadō → tea ceremony

Chaguchagu Umakko

Horse festival held on 15 June (formerly the 5th day of the 5th month of the lunar calendar); the one at the Komagata Shrine (formerly Sōzen Shrine) in the town of Mizusawa in Iwate Prefecture attracts many tourists. The surrounding area, a part of the former Nambu domain, has long been known for its fine horses, called nambu-goma. Boys and girls in festive attire mount decorated horses, which are led to the shrine, where respects are paid to the tutelary god of horses. Votive plaques called EMA with pictures of horses as well as prayers for health and safekeeping are offered. The bells on the horses are said to make the sound "chagu chagu."

INOKUCHI Shōji

chambara

SAMURAI sword fights, especially in films and plays. The term originates in the onomatopoeia "chan-chan-bara-bara," an approximation of the dramatic, staccato rhythm of the background music played for silent films. Chambara films first flourished during the silent era and continued to be popular after talking pictures were introduced.

SAITŌ Ryōsuke

Chamberlain, Basil Hall (1850–1935)

One of the foremost Western interpreters of things Japanese. Born of a distinguished family in Southampton, England, on 18 October 1850. Following his mother's untimely death, Chamberlain was brought up by his grandmother between the ages of 8 and 16. During this time he lived in continental Europe and was educated at a French lycée; he also studied under an English tutor. His father intended him for the world of banking, but at age 18 he was stricken with maladies of the eyes and throat. As a result, his physician

recommended travel, and Chamberlain landed in Japan on 29 May 1873.

He taught at the imperial naval school in Tōkyō from 1874 to 1882. His most important position, however, was as professor of Japanese at Tōkyō University beginning in 1886. It was here that he gained his fame as a student of Japanese language and literature. His works include the first translation of the KOJIKI into English (1906), The Language, Mythology, and Geographical Nomenclature of Japan Viewed in the Light of Aino Studies (1887), A Practical Guide to the Study of Japanese Writing (1905), Things Japanese (1890), A Handbook of Colloquial Japanese (1888), Aino Fairy Tales (1887), The Classical Poetry of the Japanese (1880), and, with W. B. Mason, A Handbook for Travelers in Japan (1891), which went through numerous editions.

Plagued by poor health during most of his time in Japan, Chamberlain retired to Geneva, Switzerland, in 1911. There he studied classical Greek and Latin and published several volumes of poetry and other works in French.

📖 ——Kazuo Koizumi, comp, Letters from Basil Chamberlain to Lafcadio Hearn (1936). Kazuo Koizumi, comp, More Letters from Basil Hall Chamberlain (1937).   Edward R. BEAUCHAMP

Changgufeng (Ch'ang-ku-feng) Incident

(J: Chōkohō Jiken). A clash between Russian and Japanese armies in July 1938 on the boundary of the Japanese puppet state of MANCHUKUO (Manchuria) and Russian Siberia. The incident was a result of the long-standing Russo-Japanese rivalry in the area which had been exacerbated by the ANTI-COMINTERN PACT formed between Japan and Germany in November 1936. A hill in the Jiandao (Chien-tao) area north of the Tumen River, Changgufeng strategically faced the frontiers of Manchuria, Korea, and the maritime provinces of Siberia. In the summer of 1938 Russian troops fortified the peak of the hill, the jurisdiction of which was in dispute. The Japanese military in Manchuria attempted to push them back but failed. In August 1938, overriding the desires of the military in Manchuria for a full-scale attack, the Japanese General Staff and War Ministry negotiated a settlement giving the Russians Changgufeng. Japan's experience of the Russians' superior technology in the Changgufeng Incident and the more serious NOMONHAN INCIDENT of 1939 was a factor in its strategic shift from Northeast Asia to Southeast Asia (see SOUTHERN EXPANSION DOCTRINE) after 1941.

Chang Hsüeh-liang → Zhang Xueliang (Chang Hsüeh-liang)

Chang Po-go (?–841 or 846)

(J: Chō Hōkō). Adventurer of the ancient Korean kingdom of SILLA who briefly controlled maritime traffic between Silla, China, and Japan in the early 9th century. Chang traveled to China as a youth and joined the Tang (T'ang) Chinese army. After witnessing Koreans being sold into slavery by Chinese pirates, he returned to Silla in 828 and informed the Silla king of the situation. The king sought to end the slave trade by appointing Chang to police sea trade from a base on Wando, an island strategically located on the Sino-Korean and Japanese sea lanes. Exploiting his position, Chang developed a considerable amount of power and disrupted the exchange of goods and ideas between China and Japan; this was to be a significant factor in the attenuation of Japan's sinification in the Heian period (794–1185). Chang provided transportation and aid for the monk ENNIN on the latter's trip to China in 838. He amassed great wealth and influence in Silla politics before being assassinated as a result of court intrigue in 841 or 846.   C. Kenneth QUINONES

Chang Tso-lin → Zhang Zuolin (Chang Tso-lin)

Chang Tzu-p'ing → Zhang Ziping (Chang Tzu-p'ing)

Chanoine, Charles Sulpice Jules (1835–1915)

French army officer and military adviser to Japan. A graduate of the St. Cyr Military Academy, Chanoine served for two years as chief of the French forces in China and was selected to head the 15-man mission of instructors requested by the Tokugawa shogunate through Léon ROCHES, the French minister in Japan. Arriving in Japan in 1867, Chanoine began training Japanese troops and presented a comprehensive program to reorganize and modernize the shogunate army to the shōgun TOKUGAWA YOSHINOBU. His plans for a new French-style army became a key element in the reforms promoted by Roches and shogunal officials such as OGURI TADAMASA for strengthening and preserving the Tokugawa regime. The mission's efforts met with only limited success before the MEIJI RESTORATION in 1868, although French-trained shogunal troops proved their mettle in battle. Chanoine and his men were obliged to return to France in early 1869, since the new Japanese government lacked funds to keep them and doubted their loyalties.

■ ——Jean-Pierre Lehmann, "The French Military Mission to Japan, 1866–1868, and Bakumatsu Politics," *Proceedings of the British Association for Japanese Studies,* vol 1, part 1 (1976).

Mark D. ERICSON

cha no yu → tea ceremony

characters → kanji

charcoal making

(sumiyaki). Charcoal has been used in Japan since the ancient past in the smelting and casting of metals. In the Edo period (1600–1868), the demand for charcoal increased rapidly with the spread of HIBACHI braziers and *kotatsu* heaters. With the switch to modern heating, the use of the *hibachi* has declined and charcoal making has greatly diminished. In many places in western Japan it is believed that the method for making charcoal was first taught by the priest KŪKAI (774–835). There are several superstitions and taboos about charcoal making. For example, charcoal makers were often required to lead an ascetic life, and women were forbidden at the charcoal huts. Corpses and dead animals were also considered contaminating and were kept away from the kiln and hut.

Charter Oath

A statement of national policy pledged by Emperor MEIJI to his imperial ancestors; also called the Imperial Oath of Five Articles (Gokajō no Goseimon). It was read aloud on 6 April 1868 (Keiō 4.3.14) by the deputy chief executive *(fukusōsai)* SANJŌ SANETOMI in the presence of the emperor and more than 400 officials in the Shishinden (Enthronement Hall) in Kyōto. Much of the language is abstruse or ambiguous; misleading translations abound. The oath reads: "(1) An assembly shall be widely convoked, and all measures shall be decided by open discussion. (2) High and low shall be of one mind, and the national economy and finances shall be greatly strengthened. (3) Civil and military officials together, and the common people as well, shall all achieve their aspirations, and thus the people's minds shall not be made weary. (4) Evil practices of the past shall be abandoned, and actions shall be based on international usage. (5) Knowledge shall be sought all over the world, and the foundations of imperial rule shall be strengthened."

In later years, the oath was idealized as a farsighted statement of changeless imperial policy, including support for a parliament. After World War II, it was even interpreted as supporting democracy, and was reissued verbatim on 1 January 1946 in the name of Emperor Hirohito.

But the oath was designed for short-term purposes in 1868, when the new Meiji government was unstable, divided over objectives, deeply in debt, facing the uncertainties of a civil war, and embarrassed by violence against foreigners (see MEIJI RESTORATION). Article 1 was intended not as a promise of a parliament, but as a pledge that leaders from the Satsuma and Chōshū domains (now Kagoshima and Yamaguchi prefectures) would share power with other anti-Tokugawa *daimyō* and *samurai.* The Confucian rhetoric of articles 2 and 3 was meant to rally political and especially financial support from wealthy and influential men outside the ruling coalition. Articles 4 and 5 were designed to curb attacks on foreigners and to give imperial sanction to a policy of Westernization that had many opponents within the government.

Furthermore, only two of the foremost leaders of the Restoration, KIDO TAKAYOSHI and IWAKURA TOMOMI, had much to do with the oath. The five articles in the oath's first draft were conceived of and composed by a junior councillor *(san'yo),* YURI KIMIMASA, in January 1868 and revised by another junior councillor, FUKUOKA TAKACHIKA, probably in early February. But it was only when this version of the oath attracted the notice of Kido in late March that the project was accelerated or perhaps revived. Kido deleted one article, added article 4, and saw the oath through minor changes, possibly made by Iwakura. Yet even Kido, the ideologue of the Restoration, saw the oath as a short-term tactical device, and the practical-minded ŌKUBO TOSHIMICHI did not even bother to attend the oath ceremony.

■ ——Ōkubo Toshiaki, *Meiji kempō no dekiru made* (1956). Osatake Takeki, *Nihon kensei shi taikō* (1938). Osatake Takeki, *Ishin zengo ni okeru rikken shisō* (4th ed, 1946). Robert M. Spaulding, Jr, "The Intent of the Charter Oath," in Richard K. Beardsley, ed, *Studies in Japanese History and Politics* (1967).

Robert M. SPAULDING

Chaya Shirojirō

The name of successive heads of the Chaya family, a wealthy merchant house of the Azuchi–Momoyama period (1568–1600) and Edo period (1600–1868); with the Gotō and Suminokura families, one of the "three millionaires" *(sanchōja)* of Kyōto. The Chaya were prominent in Kyōto townsmen's affairs from late in the Muromachi period (1333–1568), being mentioned among the leaders of the MACHISHŪ in the so-called Lotus Confederation (1532–36; see TEMMON HOKKE REBELLION). The family's enduring prosperity, however, is attributable to the close ties that Shirojirō I (Kiyonobu; 1545?–96) established by the 1560s with the future shōgun TOKUGAWA IEYASU, whom he served as a trading and intelligence agent in the Kyōto-Ōsaka area and as a supplier of military equipment. Shirojirō I played a vital role in conducting Ieyasu to safety from the Kyōto area after the HONNŌJI INCIDENT of 1582; during the ensuing hegemony of TOYOTOMI HIDEYOSHI, he maintained confidential contacts with the imperial court on Ieyasu's behalf and was the intendant (DAIKAN) of Tokugawa holdings in Ōmi Province (now Shiga Prefecture). He acted as Ieyasu's quartermaster in the ODAWARA CAMPAIGN of 1590 and later that year, upon Ieyasu's transfer to the Kantō region, was assigned important responsibilities in the city planning of Edo (now Tōkyō), Ieyasu's new capital. Shirojirō II (Kiyotada; 1582–1603) was at Ieyasu's side at the Battle of SEKIGAHARA (1600); after the victory, Ieyasu appointed him head townsman *(sō machigashira)* in Kyōto and put him in a supervisory position over the commerce of the Kyōto–Ōsaka region. Shirojirō III (Kiyotsugu; 1585–1626) was from 1607 active in Nagasaki as Ieyasu's agent in the regulated silk trade (ITOWAPPU) with the Portuguese; from 1612 he became involved in the Japanese overseas trade with Southeast Asia, and by 1635, when the Tokugawa shogunate terminated this trade, the Chaya had sent at least 11 "vermilion seal ships" *(shuinsen;* see VERMILION SEAL SHIP TRADE) abroad, principally to Cochin China (now part of Vietnam). Apart from his trading activities, which included provisioning the Tokugawa armies with Dutch munitions in the Ōsaka Campaigns of 1614–15 (see ŌSAKA CASTLE, SIEGES OF), Shirojirō III acted as an adviser to Ieyasu, nominally in retirement at Sumpu (now the city of Shizuoka), counseling him on foreign and commercial affairs. These services to the Tokugawa earned the Chaya a privileged position as purveyors of textile goods *(gofuku goyō shōnin)* to the shogunate, one that they retained, with a brief interruption in the early 19th century (the time of Shirojirō X Nobukuni), throughout the Edo period.

George ELISON

chemical industry

The Japanese chemical industry was created in the 1870s when the government imported technologies for the production of glass, inorganic chemicals, cement, and other products from Europe and the United States. During the early years of the 1900s, the electrochemical industry was developed, utilizing the surplus power generated by hydroelectric plants. In the 1930s the coal chemical industry was created as a result of the rising cost of electricity and the government policy of fostering coal mining. Thus, just prior to the outbreak of World War II, production in the chemical fertilizer, rayon, and soda industries had reached international levels. However, during World War II the superannuation of production facilities, a dramatic decline in imported raw materials, and damage caused by air raids reduced production capacity to one-fifth of the prewar level. After the war, the first industry to recover was chemical fertilizers, because of the urgent need to increase food production.

In the second half of the 1950s, the Japanese PETROCHEMICAL INDUSTRY made its debut, spurred by two major factors: first, the conversion of energy production from hydroelectric power and coal to oil resulted in a surplus of naphtha (a product of oil refining and an important material for petrochemical production), and, second, the enactment of the Foreign Investment Law facilitated the introduction of foreign technology. The petrochemical industry witnessed rapid growth, with the reduction of manufacturing costs through expansion in the scale of production. The industry constructed a total of 17 huge, modern production complexes in such places as Kashima (Ibaraki Prefecture), Chiba (Chiba Prefecture), Kawasaki (Kanagawa Prefecture), Yokkaichi (Mie Prefecture), Sakai (Ōsaka Prefecture), Mizushima (Okayama Prefecture), Iwakuni (Yamaguchi Prefecture), Ōtake (Hiroshima Prefecture), Tokuyama (Yamaguchi Prefecture), Niihama (Ehime Prefecture), and Tsurusaki (Ōita Prefecture).

According to government statistics, 409,000 workers were employed by the chemical industry in 1979 (4.0 percent of the entire industrial work force). Value added by the industry amounted to ¥6.2 trillion (US $28.2 billion). Value added per worker was ¥15 million (US $69,000), considerably more than the ¥6.56 million (US $30,350) average for manufacturing industries. In 1977 the Japanese petrochemical industry had an ethylene production capacity of 5.3 million metric tons (5.8 million short tons) a year, second only to that of the United States. Both petrochemicals and basic chemicals are dominated by general chemical companies belonging to the former *zaibatsu* groups, but fine chemicals (pharmaceuticals, cosmetics, paints, photographic sensitive material, printing ink, and synthetic detergents) are dominated by large independent enterprises. Since the early 1970s, development of the basic chemical industry has been hampered by such factors as the dramatic rise in oil prices and the problem of pollution in the districts where the industrial complexes are situated. As a result, basic chemical enterprises are increasingly attempting to enter the fine chemical field.

Suzuki Hiroaki

chemistry

Modern chemical research in Japan began with foreign professors who were invited to teach in Japan by the Meiji government (see FOREIGN EMPLOYEES OF THE MEIJI PERIOD) and with young Japanese scholars selected for study in Europe and the United States from the ranks of teachers and students at the Kaisei Gakkō (forerunner of Tōkyō University).

A number of these scholars who had studied abroad made the first important contributions to chemical research in Japan. NAGAI NAGAYOSHI, who studied at the University of Berlin, went on to discover ephedrine upon his return home. It was he who established the science of organic chemistry in Japan. ASAHINA YASUHIKO was chief among Nagai's several students in this field. Sakurai Jōji, a graduate of the University of London, was the first to introduce physical chemistry into Japan; his students included such outstanding physical chemists as IKEDA KIKUNAE and Katayama Masao. The world of chemistry in Japan commemorated Sakurai Jōji's achievements by establishing the Sakurai Prize (first awarded in 1910), which later became the Chemical Society of Japan Award. TAKAMINE JŌKICHI, a graduate of the Kōbu Daigakkō (later the engineering department of Tōkyō University) who later studied in England and Scotland, made notable contributions to Japan's chemical industry. He succeeded in the production of the enzyme preparation known as Taka-Diastase and the crystallization of adrenaline.

Development of facilities for chemical research included the founding in 1917 of the INSTITUTE OF PHYSICAL AND CHEMICAL RESEARCH, which was followed by several other such facilities. The Tōkyō Chemical Society, founded in 1878, became the Chemical Society of Japan in 1921; this merged in 1948 with the Society of the Chemical Industry, Japan (established 1898). The journals issued by the Chemical Society of Japan include *Chemistry and the Chemical Industry* (from 1948) and *Nippon kagakukai shi* (Journal of the Chemical Society of Japan; from 1972). The total membership of the Chemical Society of Japan and the Society of the Chemical Industry, Japan for the year 1910 came to several thousand. Membership in 1979 was about 32,000.

About 8,000 of those engaged in chemical research are university employees. The chemical industry employs about 3,200 researchers. If those employed in research laboratories are added to these numbers there are a total of some 50,000 chemical researchers in Japan.

Japanese Achievements in Chemistry —— Some of the most outstanding achievements in Japanese chemical research date from the period before World War II. In the field of complex chemistry, there is Shibata Yūji's research on the absorption spectrum and structure of cobaltammine complex salts in 1915. Tsuchida Ryūtarō's studies on the absorption spectrum of complex salts (ligands) in 1938 were an expansion of Shibata's earlier research. These studies, together with SHIBATA KEITA's studies on metal complex catalysis, became the basis of study of the chemical complexes in Japan, a field which in both accomplishment and number of researchers stands near the top by world research standards.

Research in the field of geochemistry developed from the mineral studies done in 1920 by Shibata Yūji and Kimura Kenjirō on rare-earth elements originating in East Asia. Research has been done on hot springs and mineral springs as well as on the radiochemistry of radioactive dusts. Sugawara Ken carried out chemical research in 1939 on the metabolic processes occurring in Japanese lakes.

In the area of analytical chemistry, Shikata Masuzō invented the polarograph; Komatsu Matsusuke carried out research on the amalgam method; and Kiba Toshiyasu studied methods for decomposing strong phosphoric acid.

Achievements in physical chemistry include Katayama Masao's publication of "Katayama's Formula" on surface tension in 1915, and the work carried out by his pupil MIZUSHIMA SAN'ICHIRŌ in 1925 toward proving molecular polarization by means of the dispersion of electromagnetic waves. Students of Mizushima carried out cooperative research on the rotational isomer and went on to study the electron configuration of molecules and the interaction of molecules through intermolecular forces from the vantage point of quantum chemistry. There was also structural analysis research using X-rays done by NITTA ISAMU and his students, studies on reaction velocity performed by Horiba Shinkichi and Horiuchi Hisao, and research on rheology in colloids by Samejima Jitsusaburō.

In the field of organic chemistry, there have been numerous studies, including the 1916 research of Tsujimoto Mitsumaru on shark liver oil, MAJIMA TOSHIYUKI's studies in 1918 concerning Japanese lacquer, the work of Asahina Yasuhiko on Chinese herbal medicines in 1912, toad poison research by Kotake Munio in 1927, and studies on hinokitiol in 1936 by NOZOE TETSUO. There are also the studies done by Kita Gen'itsu and SAKURADA ICHIRŌ concerning synthetic rubber, plastics, and chemical fibers such as rayon and Vinylon. The successful extraction of the substance later known as vitamin B₁ in 1910 by SUZUKI UMETARŌ was the first of many accomplishments in the biochemistry field.

Since the late 1950s, when a strong petrochemical industry was firmly established in Japan, there have been significant advances in plastics, synthetic rubber, fine chemicals, and other chemical products by both university and chemical industry researchers. By the late 1970s, Japanese firms were exporting chemical technology through patent transfers, sales of patent rights, and reciprocal agreements. See also CHEMICAL INDUSTRY; PETROCHEMICAL INDUSTRY.

Sakanoue Masanobu

Chemulp'o, Treaty of

(Saimoppo Jōyaku). An agreement between Korea and Japan, signed on 30 August 1882, that resolved tensions resulting from the IMO MUTINY of the previous month. Both China and Japan had dispatched troops to Korea when the military uprising occurred but the question of responsibility for the mutiny and reparations for the loss of Japanese lives and property remained unresolved. Japan sent an expeditionary force to Seoul to settle the issue. After negotiations among the Koreans, Japanese, and Chinese at Chemulp'o (present-day Inch'ŏn), the Koreans agreed to punish those responsible for the mutiny, pay Japan a ¥550,000 indemnity and the costs of stationing and maintaining a Japanese legation guard in Seoul, submit formal apologies, and extend travel and trade rights for the Japanese in Korea. The treaty was soon after undermined by the KAPSIN POLITICAL COUP in 1884. See also KOREA AND JAPAN: early modern relations.

C. Kenneth Quinones

Cheng Ch'eng-kung → Zheng Chenggog (Cheng Ch'eng-kung)

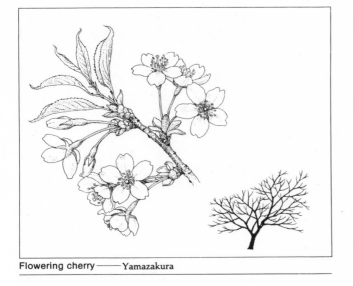

Flowering cherry —— Yamazakura

Cheng Hsiao-hsü → Zheng Xiaoxu (Cheng Hsiao-hsü)

Chen Tianhua (Ch'en T'ien-hua) (1875–1905)

(J: Chin Tenka). Chinese revolutionary. A native of Hunan Province, Chen went to Japan on a government scholarship in 1902 or 1903 and soon joined the rapidly growing contingent of young Chinese revolutionary activists in Tōkyō. Returning to China in 1904, he participated with HUANG XING (Huang Hsing) and others in an abortive revolutionary plot. Meanwhile, he wrote stirring pamphlets in the vernacular, calling for the overthrow of the Qing (Ch'ing) dynasty by a united front of all classes, for Westernizing reforms, and for militant antiimperialism.

Escaping arrest after the uprising, Chen again went to Japan. He briefly abandoned his revolutionary strategy and tried to organize Chinese students in Japan in presenting a patriotic and reformist petition to the Qing rulers. In July and August of 1905 he played a leading role in establishing the Tongmeng Hui (T'ung-meng Hui; United League), China's first national republican revolutionary society, which joined SUN YAT-SEN and radical Chinese students in Japan in a common revolutionary cause.

In December 1905, while the Chinese student community in Tōkyō was in an uproar over regulations issued the previous month by the Japanese Ministry of Education to "control" Chinese and Korean students, Chen committed suicide. In a last testament, he wrote that his act was intended to shock Chinese students in Japan into a disciplined devotion to their country's salvation. He also warned against an alliance of unequals between China and Japan, saying that Japanese ambitions regarding China were all too evident and that China would merely be absorbed like Korea. ———— Ernest P. YOUNG

Ch'en T'ien-hua → Chen Tianhua (Ch'en T'ien-hua)

cherry blossom viewing → hanami

cherry, flowering

(sakura). Prunus spp. Any of a number of deciduous trees of the family Rosaceae which grow wild in mountainous areas throughout Japan and are also widely cultivated. The name sakura is generally used for those species of cherry appreciated for the beauty of their blossoms rather than those grown for their fruit. The sakura is foremost among plants mentioned in Japanese literature. The wood is excellent and is used for building, carving, and block printing.

The traditional Japanese values of purity and simplicity are thought to be reflected in the form and color of the blossoms. The Japanese preference for the delicate cherry blossom is often contrasted to the Chinese emphasis upon the flashier peony. Since the trasted to the Chinese emphasis upon the flashier peony. Since the cherry flowers bloom very briefly and then scatter, they have also become a convenient symbol of the Japanese aesthetic sense, an ephemeral beauty.

The cherry is one of the oldest flowers known in Japan. The word appears in the KOJIKI, a book of history completed in 712, and the MAN'YŌSHŪ, an anthology of poems compiled in the late 8th century, contains about 40 poems which mention the tree and praise its blossoms. At that time, however, Japanese culture was heavily influenced by China and the Man'yōshū followed the traditions of Chinese poetry, mentioning the ume (plum) more often than the sakura. During the Heian period (794–1185), popular enthusiasm for cherry blossoms was such that the word hana (flower) was simply taken as a synonym for sakura. By the time of the Kokinshū, a 10th-century poetry collection, the sakura had become the more significant subject in poetry.

The cherry blossom has become intimately identified with Japanese culture. In a poem expressing an appreciation that is both horticultural and chauvinistic, Motoori Norinaga wrote, "If someone wishes to know the essence of the Japanese spirit, it is the fragrant cherry blossom in the early morning."

Excellent specimens of cherry blossoms can be produced from seedlings, and the ease with which the plants are reproduced has helped in establishing their intimate connection with everyday life in Japan. They were planted abundantly in gardens and along main thoroughfares in Kyōto. Cherry blossom viewing parties had already been established as annual events in the days of Emperor Saga (r 809–823). In the Edo period (1600–1868), cherry trees were planted in great numbers in Edo (now Tōkyō), and outings for cherry blossom viewing flourished. Numerous horticultural species were developed at this time, some of which have remained popular to the present day.

The following are representative varieties of flowering cherry admired in Japan:

The yamazakura (P. donarium var. spontanea) grows wild in mountainous areas south from central Honshū and has long been cultivated. It reaches a height of about 7 meters (23 ft). The bark splits crosswise. The leaves are oblong, with toothed edges. The flowers are of medium size, pink or nearly white. This variety is distinguished from the similar somei yoshino by the lack of hairs on the leaves and flower parts.

The ōshimazakura (P. donarium var. spontanea subvar. speciosa) grows wild mainly in the Izu Islands but is widely planted elsewhere. It ranges from 3 to 10 meters (10–33 ft) in height. The flowers are single-petaled, large and white. The leaves are used for wrapping a confection called sakuramochi. Since it is a sturdy variety with large flowers, it is frequently used in the development of new ornamental strains.

The shidarezakura (P. itosakura), also known as itozakura, is an ornamental variety which sometimes reaches 20 meters (66 ft) in height. The thicker branches spread crosswise, and long slender branches hang down vertically. It has long been planted in temple gardens. The flowers are usually single and pinkish white; some are red or double.

The somei yoshino (P. yedoensis) is planted in parks and along river banks, reaching a height of about 7 meters (23 ft). It is thought to be a hybrid of the ōshimazakura and ubahigan-zakura (P. itosakura var. ascendens). It matures in about 20 years and bears large, pink, single-petaled flowers but is relatively short-lived and susceptible to disease.

The ōyamazakura (P. donarium var. sachalinensis) grows wild in mountain areas, north from central Honshū; its branches are thicker and darker and its flowers deeper in color than the yamazakura. The kasumizakura (P. verecunda) has branches, leaves, and flowers slightly smaller than those of the ōshimazakura. The higanzakura (P. subhirtella), growing mainly westward from central Honshū, is the earliest blooming of all varieties. The jūgatsuzakura is usually a small tree. It blooms slowly from around October through the winter, with most flowers opening in April. The mamezakura (P. incisa), also known as fujizakura, is found mainly in the mountains of central Honshū, especially around Mt. Fuji (Fujisan). It is valued for bonsai cultivation. The minezakura (P. nipponica) grows in high mountain regions northward from central Honshū.

The above are mainly natural species; the horticultural varieties developed from them number about 300.

The first foreign description of Japanese flowering cherries was in 1712 by the German naturalist E. KAEMPFER (1651–1716). Sap-

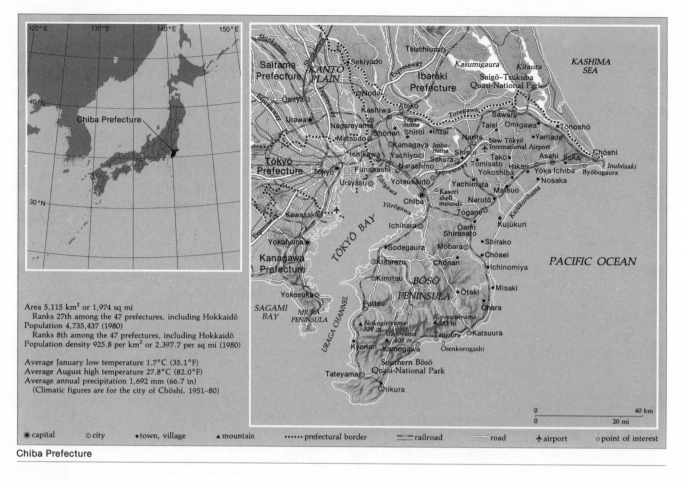

Area 5,115 km² or 1,974 sq mi
  Ranks 27th among the 47 prefectures, including Hokkaidō
Population 4,735,437 (1980)
  Ranks 8th among the 47 prefectures, including Hokkaidō
Population density 925.8 per km² or 2,397.7 per sq mi (1980)

Average January low temperature 1.7°C (35.1°F)
Average August high temperature 27.8°C (82.0°F)
Average annual precipitation 1,692 mm (66.7 in)
  (Climatic figures are for the city of Chōshi, 1951–80)

◉ capital   ○ city   • town, village   ▲ mountain   ••••• prefectural border   ══ railroad   ═══ road   ✈ airport   ○ point of interest

Chiba Prefecture

lings are said to have been imported to Europe in 1822 by the Swedish botanist C. P. Thunberg (1743–1828). The first Japanese cherries in the United States are said to have been double-flowered trees imported in 1862. Thereafter many more were taken to the United States, the most famous being the more than 1,000 trees of 11 varieties given to the city of Washington as a goodwill present by Tōkyō mayor Ozaki Yukio in 1909. Many of the flowering cherries growing in different parts of the world were introduced from Japan.

——Uehara Keiji, *Jumoku daizusetsu* (1961).

MATSUDA Osamu

chestnut

(kuri). *Castanea crenata*. The Japanese chestnut tree is distributed from Hokkaidō to Kyūshū, but few chestnuts are harvested for eating in Hokkaidō or northern Honshū. The large fruits are suitable for cooking and are made into candied chestnuts, sweet jelly *(yōkan)*, and sweet caramelized chestnuts. As it is hard to remove the pellicle of the Japanese chestnut, Chinese chestnuts are imported in large quantities. The rot-resistant wood is used for house foundations and for furniture. Chestnuts other than *C. crenata* are not grown in Japan because of the large amount of rainfall.

NAGASAWA Katsuo

Chiang Kai-shek (1887–1975)

(J: Shō Kaiseki). Chinese head of state, military commander, and party leader. A native of Zhejiang (Chekiang) Province, Chiang entered the Baoding (Paoting) Military Academy in 1907. From 1908 to 1910 he attended the Shimbu Gakkō, a military school in Tōkyō, after which he served in a Japanese field artillery regiment for training. Japanese military ideals greatly shaped Chiang's attitudes.

Chiang joined the revolutionary United League (Tongmeng Hui or T'ung-meng Hui) in Japan and returned to China during the revolution of 1911. After YUAN SHIKAI (Yüan Shih-k'ai) took power in 1912, Chiang returned to Japan. In 1913 he was briefly in China for the abortive revolution against Yuan. In late 1915 he returned to China and spent the next two years in Shanghai, where he was associated with the Green Gang, a secret society.

In 1918 Chiang joined with SUN YAT-SEN in Guangzhou (Canton) and joined Sun's Nationalist Party, the Guomindang (Kuomintang; KMT). He went to Moscow for four months in 1923 to study the Red Army. After his return he founded the Huangpu (Whampoa) Military Academy and created a KMT party army. Chinese communists and Soviet advisers were then active and influential in the KMT. Chiang himself was influenced by the Leninist theory of imperialism and Soviet organizational techniques while hostile to the communist goal of social revolution.

Sun died in 1925, and Chiang gradually became the most powerful KMT leader. In 1926 he launched the so-called Northern Expedition against the warlords and in 1927 carried out a violent purge against the communists. By 1928 the KMT had brought political unity to the country, and a national government was established in Nanjing (Nanking) with Chiang at its head.

Chiang's government faced two major challenges: Japan seized Manchuria in 1931 and was encroaching on North China, and the communists established a base in Jiangxi (Kiangsi) Province. Since Chiang regarded the communists as the greater threat, he resolved to crush them before resisting Japan. This policy was unpopular, and late in 1936 he was compelled to abandon it in favor of resistance against Japan (see XI'AN [SIAN] INCIDENT). Full-scale fighting broke out in 1937 (see SINO-JAPANESE WAR OF 1937–1945; WORLD WAR II), forcing Chiang's government inland to Chongqing (Chungking) for the duration of World War II.

Although among the victors, China had deteriorated politically and economically during the war. The civil war between the KMT and the communists started in 1946, and in 1949 Chiang and his government fled to TAIWAN. Chiang continued to lead the KMT government on Taiwan until his death in 1975.

——Howard Boorman and Richard Howard, ed, *Biographical Dictionary of Republican China*, vol 1 (1967). Pichon Loh, *The Early Chiang Kai-shek: A Study of His Personality and Politics, 1887–1924* (1971).

Robert ENTENMANN

Chian Iji Hō → Peace Preservation Law of 1925

Chian Keisatsu Hō → Public Order and Police Law of 1900

Chiaochou concession → Jiaozhou (Kiaochow) concession

Chiba

City in northwestern Chiba Prefecture; capital of Chiba Prefecture; about 34 km (21 mi) southeast of Tōkyō on Tōkyō Bay. Under the control of the Chiba family from the 12th to the 15th century, it developed as a prosperous castle town, and during the Edo period (1600–1868) was a POST-STATION TOWN serving several highways. With the opening of a railway line between Chiba and Tōkyō in the middle of the Meiji period (1868–1912), it became the prefecture's political, economic, and cultural center. During World War II Chiba was a military base and since then it has developed rapidly into an industrial center, with large steel mills and electric power plants. The port of Chiba handles one of the largest import-export volumes in Japan. Chiba University, a cultural hall, and a prefectural art museum are here. The KASORI SHELL MOUNDS, an extensive Jōmon-period (ca 10,000 BC–ca 300 BC) archaeological site, are located 5 km (3 mi) east of Chiba Station. Pop: 746,428.

Chiba Prefecture

(Chiba Ken). Located in central Honshū and bordered by Ibaraki Prefecture to the north, the Pacific Ocean to the east and south, and Tōkyō Bay, Tōkyō, and Saitama Prefecture to the west. Composed of an extension of the KANTŌ PLAIN in the north and hilly BŌSŌ PENINSULA to the south. The rivers TONEGAWA and EDOGAWA form Chiba's northern and western borders, respectively. Its population is mainly concentrated in the northwestern part, which has become a residential and industrial satellite of the Tōkyō-Yokohama urban belt.

Under the ancient provincial system (KOKUGUN SYSTEM), it was divided into the three provinces of Shimōsa, Kazusa, and Awa. It was incorporated into the modern prefectural system in 1875.

Its mild climate and relatively level terrain are suited for truck farming, rice production, and dairy farming. Commercial fishing in Tōkyō Bay, once important, has become impossible because of industrial pollution. Traditional industries such as soy-sauce manufacture and weaving were prominent before World War II. Petrochemical, electrical, steel, shipbuilding, and other companies are located in the northwestern section. The NEW TŌKYŌ INTERNATIONAL AIRPORT in Narita is Japan's major center for international air transport.

Chiba is an important recreation area, with numerous beaches providing fine ocean bathing, especially the KUJŪKURIHAMA area on the Pacific Coast. The temple Shinshōji at Narita attracts over a million pilgrims and visitors to the prefecture annually. There are also four quasi-national parks, Suigō-Tsukuba in the north and Southern Bōsō, a seacoast area, in the south. Area: 5,115 sq km (1,974 sq mi); pop: 4,735,437; capital: Chiba. Other major cities include FUNABASHI, ICHIKAWA, MATSUDO, and CHŌSHI.

Chiba University

(Chiba Daigaku). National coeducational university located in the city of Chiba, Chiba Prefecture. It was founded in 1874 as Kyōritsu Hospital. It became Chiba College of Medicine (Chiba Igaku Semmon Gakkō) in 1901 and took its present name in 1949. It has departments of science, humanities, education, medicine, pharmacology, nursing, engineering, and horticulture, and is known for its strength in the natural sciences and its Research Institute for chemobiodynamics. Enrollment in 1980 was 9,018.

Chichibu

City in western Saitama Prefecture, central Honshū. A commercial and silk-producing center since the Edo period (1600–1868), Chichibu has a thriving cement industry that utilizes limestone from the mountain Bukōsan. An all-night festival held at the Chichibu Shrine in early December attracts many visitors. Pop: 61,284.

Chichibu Basin

(Chichibu Bonchi). In the Chichibu Mountains, western Saitama Prefecture, central Honshū. This rectangular fault basin, consisting of the flood plain of the river Arakawa's upper reaches, has ravines with exposed crystalline schists. Limestone is quarried at the mountain Bukōsan, and the numerous mulberry fields contribute to the area's flourishing sericulture. Chichibu is the major city. The gorge known as Nagatoro is located at the basin's edge. Area: approximately 100 sq km (38.6 sq mi).

Chichibu Cement Co, Ltd

Producer of cement; established in 1923 and ranked sixth in the industry in 1981. It has jointly developed the SF-type (suspension preheater and flash furnace) cement calcination process with ISHIKAWAJIMA-HARIMA HEAVY INDUSTRIES CO, LTD, and is a leader in cement equipment and technology. The company provides technical advice concerning cement manufacture to numerous countries, including Taiwan, Greece, Peru, and Saudi Arabia. Future plans call for the construction of cement plants in coastal areas. Sales for the fiscal year ending May 1982 totaled ¥83.3 billion (US $352 million), and the company was capitalized at ¥2.1 billion (US $8.9 million) in the same year. Corporate headquarters are located in Tōkyō.

Chichibu Incident

(Chichibu Jiken). A peasant uprising in the Chichibu region of Saitama Prefecture in November 1884. One of the so-called gekka (gekika) jiken, "incidents of intensified violence," of the second decade of the Meiji period (1868–1912) in which peasants of the Kantō region, led by members of the FREEDOM AND PEOPLE'S RIGHTS MOVEMENT, rebelled against the government. In Chichibu the rebels were mostly peasants impoverished by deflationary policies implemented in the early 1880s by Finance Minister MATSUKATA MASAYOSHI. In the late 1870s and earlier, Chichibu peasants, artisans, and merchants had prospered from a growing domestic and foreign market for silk, silkworms, and mulberry. Rising economic expectations had persuaded many peasants to mortgage their lands and homes to finance increased sericulture production. Matsukata's policies, however, withdrew cheap money from circulation, thereby drastically cutting domestic consumer demand for silk. Forced now to sell approximately 40 percent more products in order to pay old and new taxes, peasants in ever increasing numbers defaulted on their loans.

The Chichibu rebellion, however, was triggered more by creditors' refusal to allow a moratorium on repayment of loans than by the economic depression and impoverishment. Led by many of the men who later took charge of the rebellion, for several years the peasants attempted to negotiate new loan terms and petitioned for government intercession. Only after appeals to both government and creditors had been denied did the peasants revolt.

During the first 10 days of November 1884, peasant rebels from Chichibu marched into battle carrying signs and banners that read, "Popular Rights; Itagaki Taisuke, the Divine Rectifier; World Renewal" (Jiyū minken; Itagaki Taisuke Daimyōjin; Yonaoshi). Well over 6,000 peasants, many from the neighboring prefectures of Nagano and Gumma, joined the rebellion. The peasants associated their movement with millennial ideas of "world renewal" (yonaoshi) and with the JIYŪTŌ (Liberal Party), sometimes calling themselves "soldiers of the Liberal Party" (Jiyūtō no tsuwamono) and thus identifying themselves with its president ITAGAKI TAISUKE. The rebels claimed that they fought "in order to equalize wealth, to aid the poor," and to help those who either directly or indirectly claimed association with the Liberal Party or the Indigents' Party (KOMMINTŌ). They established the Headquarters of the Revolution (Kakumei Hombu) in the town of Ogano on 1 November. Their immediate objective was to destroy all public and private documents concerning loans, mortgages, or debts of any kind. Consequently, they attacked government offices and loan sharks' shops and occupied villages and towns, engaging in armed resistance against police and army troops. Some claimed they ultimately intended to invade Tōkyō, drive out the government, and establish a new era of a free citizenry, with peace and prosperity for all. By 10 November, however, the rebellion had been suppressed by regiments from the Tō-kyō military garrison, and some 3,000 peasants had been arrested. While most of these escaped with fines averaging about ¥1.5, some received sentences of five to eight years. The eight leaders (three in absentia) were tried and sentenced to death. In February 1885, less than three months after they were arrested, five were hanged.

Only two rebel leaders had direct ties to the Liberal Party, and Itagaki denounced the rebellion. Some leaders, like the rebel army's supreme commander, Tashiro Eisuke, were attracted by the Liberal Party's program, and Kikuchi Kambei, his chief of staff, had joined the Indigents' Party, itself greatly influenced by the party movement and liberal ideology. For the most part, the leaders of the uprising were local patrons, or self-styled "Robin Hoods" (*kyōkaku*), who acted as negotiators, advisers, and protectors for their "clients in time of trouble." Nonetheless, many of them as well as their followers borrowed language from, and claimed moral allegiance to, Itagaki's people's rights movement, because they associated it with their belief in the need to change the world and "level (the people in) the world" (*yonarashi*).

📖 ——Roger W. Bowen, *Rebellion and Democracy in Meiji Japan* (1980). Ide Magoroku, *Chichibu kommintō gunzō* (1973). Nobutaka Ike, *The Beginnings of Political Democracy in Japan* (1950). Inoue Kōji, *Chichibu jiken* (1968). Irokawa Daikichi, *Meiji no bunka* (1970). Irwin Scheiner, "The Mindful Peasant: Sketches for a Study of Rebellion," *Journal of Asian Studies* 32.4 (1973).

Irwin SCHEINER

Chichibu, Prince (1902–1953)

(Chichibu no Miya Yasuhito). Imperial prince and military officer. Second son of Emperor TAISHŌ and brother of Emperor HIROHITO. After a period of study at Oxford University, he attended the Army Staff College. Upon graduation he was assigned to various regimental posts and to General Staff Headquarters. During the 1930s it was rumored that he was generally sympathetic to the KŌDŌHA, the extremist faction in the army eager for national reform. He became ill, however, and was obliged to curtail his official activities. After World War II he served as head of several athletic organizations.

Chichibu–Tama National Park

(Chichibu-Tama Kokuritsu Kōen). Situated in the KANTŌ MOUNTAINS, it is the national park closest to Tōkyō, stretching west from the boundary of Tōkyō Prefecture into Saitama, Nagano, and Yamanashi prefectures. The eastern region of the park, known as OKU TAMA, is dominated by the peaks Kumotoriyama (2,108 m or 6,619 ft) and Mitakesan (940 m or 3,083 ft). The western region of the park, known as OKU CHICHIBU, is dominated by the three peaks of KIMPUSAN (2,595 m or 8,512 ft), Kokushigatake (2,592 m or 8,502 ft), and KOBUSHIGADAKE (2,483 m or 8,144 ft). From these mountains flow two major rivers, TAMAGAWA and ARAKAWA, which are dammed to the east at Lake Oku Tama and to the north at Lake Chichibu, respectively. These artificial lakes supply water and electricity to the Tōkyō area.

Two famous mountain shrines here are Mitake Shrine at the summit of Mitakesan in the east and Mitsumine Shrine on top of MITSUMINESAN (1,100 m or 3,608 ft) in the north. They house training centers for the mountain ascetic sect (SHUGENDŌ). The gorge called SHŌSENKYŌ, at the southwestern edge of the park, is celebrated for the beauty of its scenery. Among other tourist attractions are cherry blossoms in the Lake Oku Tama region, abundant wildlife, forests of Japanese hemlock (*kometsuga*), Maries fir (*aomori todomatsu*), and the stalactites in a cave at Nippara, north of Lake Oku Tama, which is over 500 m or 1,640 ft deep (see NIPPARA SHŌNYŪDŌ). Area: 1,216 sq km (469 sq mi).

Chichijima

Also known as Peel Island. Island in the Pacific Ocean, 1,000 km (621 mi) south of Tōkyō. It is the largest island in and the political and economic center of the OGASAWARA ISLANDS and is administered by the Tōkyō prefectural government. It is composed largely of hilly land and valleys with tropical plants. It possesses the only good port in these islands at Futami Bay. The first inhabitants were 5 Europeans and 20 Hawaiians from a whaling boat who settled there in 1830, but Japanese emigrants to the island increased after 1876. An important base of the Japanese navy during World War II,

Japanese chicken —— Shōkoku

Chichijima was occupied by the United States after the war but reverted to Japan in 1968. It is part of Ogasawara National Park. Area: 24.5 sq km (9.46 sq mi).

chicken, Japanese

(*nipponkei* or *nihonkei*). *Gallus gallus domesticus* Brisson. Breeds of native domesticated chicken, either indigenous or developed in Japan in historical times. The term "Japanese chicken" does not refer to one pure native breed but covers various strains. It does not include commercial breeds developed after the Meiji period (1868–1912) through crossing with modern foreign breeds. Presently, there are approximately 30 breeds, of which 16 are designated by the government as protected animals under the Law for the Protection of Notable Natural Objects (Tennen Kinembutsu Hogo Hō).

Breeds and Varieties —— Jidori (or jitori). The indigenous Japanese fowl is divided into two types: ordinary size (*futsū jidori*) and small size (*ko jidori*), both of which are relatively small. In general, they are a typical primitive breed, closely resembling the red jungle fowl (*Gallus gallus*, L.) in color and conformation. Coloration is predominantly black breast, red with black tail, yellow or gray legs, and usually red earlobes, though these may sometimes be white. They have single combs. The cock's crow is sonorous but brief. The eggs are usually brown to light brown, and the hens lay an average of about 100–150 eggs a year, a relatively high productivity rate for such a primitive breed. The meat is considered to be of very good quality. Presently, several purebred varieties still exist as distinct types in different localities, such as the Gifu *jidori*, Tosa *jidori*, and Ise *jidori*, among which the Tosa *jidori* is presumed to be the closest to the original type. These three varieties were designated as government-protected animals in 1941. Varieties of Japanese indigenous chicken include short-legged "creeper" types and also a rumpless variety originated from mutation of a local small type *jidori*. The latter, developed in the Kōchi (Tosa) area, is called *uzura-o* ("quail-like tail") and was given government protection in 1937.

Shōkoku. Widely believed to have been introduced to Japan by a government envoy from Tang (T'ang) China during the Heian period (794–1185), the breed may have existed in Japan from an earlier period. It has an elegant posture, trailing its considerably long tail on the ground. It makes a prolonged crow at the same time every morning and so has been kept as a time announcer since ancient times. The breed was also used in the annual cockfights (*tori-awase*) of the Heian court, and they were kept in shrines as sacred birds. Chickens assumed to be of this breed are often depicted in scrolls of the period. The *shōkoku* is larger than the indigenous fowl (*jidori*). Feather coloring is silver-duckwings, golden-duckwings, or white. A single comb, red earlobes, and yellow legs are considered optimum. They are hardy and easy to raise, producing about 100–150 eggs annually. Egg color ranges from light brown to near white. The *shōkoku* breed was subsequently used in improving or establishing other Japanese breeds. Its long tail has been transmitted to the *onagadori* (long-tailed Japanese fowl); its prolonged crow has been inherited by several "crowing" breeds, such as the *tōtenkō, koeyoshi,* and *tōmaru*. Thus, along with the *jidori*, it is considered one of the major basic strains that have contributed to the formation of the many breeds of Japanese native fowl. The breed was recognized as a government-protected animal in 1941.

Onagadori. Also called *chōbikei,* the long-tailed Japanese fowl. The tail feathers of the cock of this breed grow longer every year without molting, sometimes reaching 7–8 meters (23–26 ft) or more. This remarkable breed was developed during the Edo period (1600–1868) in the Tosa area (Kōchi Prefecture) from a mutation that probably occurred in the local *shōkoku* strain. The breed was protected by the local feudal government, and their long tail-feathers were used to decorate spears carried in the vanguard of the processions of the *daimyō.* Coloring is silver-duckwings, white, or brown; and yellow legs are most desirable. They have single combs and usually white earlobes. In order to protect their tails, the cocks are confined in specially designed cages placed in an elevated position, with the tail hanging down outside the cage. In exercising the cock, one must follow him everywhere, carrying his tail to prevent it from touching the ground and being damaged. The government designated this breed as a special protected animal in 1923. It has been known in the West as the Yokohama (in Germany as the Phoenix) since the end of the 19th century. However, the quality of the breed abroad has never been as fine as in Japan.

Chabo. The Japanese bantam. Generally believed to have been imported from the Champa region (Indochina) through foreign trade during the Edo period and to have been named after its place of origin. It is an extremely small bantam, with short legs, usually yellow, a proportionately large head with a well-developed single comb, and descended wing-carriage. There are many varieties, mainly classified by feather coloration, the most famous of which is the *katsura chabo* (black-tailed white). Though hardy and easy to raise, it is difficult to obtain show-quality individuals. This attractive bantam has gained steady popularity in the West under the name of Japanese bantam ever since its importation in the mid-19th century.

Shamo. The Japanese game fowl. Originated from a game breed imported from Southeast Asia (possibly Siam) in the Edo period and later improved in Japan. The breed was used in cockfighting. There are three varieties, classified according to size. General appearance is similar to the Indian game breed, sturdy and muscular, with upright posture, giving an impression of power. Feather color may vary. It has a small walnut or pea comb, piercing eyes, strong thick legs, and sometimes a bald chest. The meat is of excellent quality, considered by many to be the best among chickens. It was designated a government-protected animal in 1941.

Ukokkei. The Japanese silky fowl. Generally thought to be a mutant type brought into Japan during the Edo period and developed as a breed after some improvement. Thus, at present it is considered to be one of the native Japanese chickens. Peculiarities of this breed include their plumage, which resembles silky hair more than feathers, and their skin and flesh, which are darkly-pigmented, extending to the bones. They have a feather-crowned head, sometimes bearded, turquoise-blue earlobes, hairy legs, and five-toed feet. There are two varieties: white and black. In traditional medical science, the meat and eggs were believed to have curative powers for some diseases.

History and Folklore —— The red jungle fowl is thought to be the chief ancestor of domesticated chickens, which accompanied the agricultural complex based on rice cultivation as it spread through much of Asia. In Japan, the chicken may have been introduced in the Late Jōmon period (ca 10,000 BC–ca 300 BC), although almost all authentic examples were found later, in the Yayoi period (ca 300 BC–ca AD 300). It is most likely that the domestic fowl of that time was a primitive type much like the present day *jidori.*

There are many HANIWA pottery figures from the Kofun (Tomb) period (ca 300–710) which represent chickens, their incidence second only to that of horse figures among the animal *haniwa.* Figures in the shape of hens are more common than those of cocks. Chickens are also mentioned in Japanese mythology, implying that they had some important cultural significance in Japan from early times. The current Japanese word for chicken is *niwatori;* a much older term is *kake.* In many ancient texts, the word *kake* is preceded by an epithet such as *niwatsudori* or *ietsudori,* and it is likely that the former gradually gained independent usage, without the noun *kake.* There are two explanations of the meaning of *niwatori:* "courtyard bird" and "bird with cinnabar plumage." By the beginning of the historical era, certainly by the Nara period (710–794), we know that there was a clan charged with the care of birds *(torikaibe),* although it is not certain that these were chickens. However it is clear that, soon afterward, this clan did definitely keep chickens, probably for eggs,

meat, or ceremonial purposes. In the Heian period, because cocks had the important function of proclaiming the time with their crowing, there was a government office called Tori no Tsukasa, charged with announcing the time. In the Heian court, a great cockfighting event *(tori-awase)* took place every year on the third day of the third month. This had probably originated in association with Shintō ritual or divination. Throughout subsequent periods, there have been certain shrines that featured similar festival events or kept chickens in their precincts as sacred birds. Cockfighting was also a popular sport for commoners, even though the government often issued ordinances forbidding the practice. As can be seen in paintings from the Heian and Kamakura (1185–1333) periods, such fighting cocks were bigger than the indigenous *jidori* and more like the *shōkoku* breed.

Chickens also figured in folk beliefs in ancient times, being used for divination or sacrificial purposes. Since the crowing of cocks signifies the rising sun, that is, the end of darkness, this probably led to the belief that chickens could drive away evil spirits or misfortune. They have consequently had a relationship with funerals, and this may also be related to their prominence in early *haniwa* pottery figures. In Japanese mythology, the tale called "Ama no iwato" relates how the sun goddess, Amaterasu, was coaxed out of a cave where she had hidden by the antics of other gods and goddesses and the voices of crowing cocks.

In contrast to these auspicious associations of chickens, there have been some areas in Japan where the keeping of chickens and the eating of chicken flesh or eggs were prohibited. On the whole, however, the use of chickens for food has been recorded in Japan since ancient times. A famous ordinance of 676, based on the Buddhist prohibition of eating flesh, includes chicken meat with the flesh of cattle, horses, monkeys, and dogs. It seems, however, that eating birds was never considered as serious an offense as eating quadrupeds. The ancient ENGI SHIKI (905–927, Procedures of the Engi Era) even lists various recipes for the preparation of bird meat and eggs. Chicken meat and eggs were also used as remedies in traditional medicine.

Much can be learned about the size, shape, and coloration of chickens from ancient times through the medieval period by observing art objects such as picture scrolls or illustrated books. After the Azuchi–Momoyama period (1568–1600) and continuing into the Edo period, we find chickens painted by many famous artists and represented in woodblock prints. The *jidori,* and the *shōkoku,* comprised most of the native domestic stock, but after foreign trade began to flourish, many new types of chicken were imported, helping to form various new native breeds. When Japan was opened to the West in the 19th century, European and American fanciers began to take notice of Japanese fowls, especially the *chabo* (Japanese bantam) and the *onagadori* (long-tailed Japanese fowl). As foreign breeds were imported, however, farmers who kept chickens for practical purposes abandoned native breeds for the more productive Western chickens. Several crossbred commercial breeds, such as the Nagoya (for eggs and meat), the Mikawa (for eggs), and the Tosa *kukin* (for meat), were developed in the Meiji and Taishō (1912–26) periods and were once quite popular among farmers. After World War II, highly improved new commercial breeds became widespread, and at the present time, the native breeds are mostly kept as pets by a few fanciers intent on preserving them.

◼—Ikata Sadaaki, *Nihon kodai kachiku shi* (1945). Katō Songo, *Japanese Breeds of Fowl* (1949). Koana Hyō, *Nihonkei no rekishi* (1951). Naora Nobuo, *Nihon kodai nōgyō hattatsu shi* (1956). Saitō Akira, *Nihonkei* (1977). Shibata Seigo, *Nihon kodai kachiku shi no kenkyū* (1969).   Hiroshi SAKAMOTO

chidori → plovers

Chifuren

(abbreviation of Zenkoku Chiiki Fujin Dantai Renraku Kyōgi Kai; National Federation of Regional Women's Organizations). Chifuren was founded by YAMATAKA SHIGERI in 1952 with the aim of elevating the status of women, reforming home and social life, and promoting social welfare. With a membership of around six million, the organization is especially active in consumer protection issues such as campaigning against the practice of pricing some products more cheaply for export and boycotting commodities protected by resale price maintenance contracts. See also CONSUMER MOVEMENT.

Chigasaki

City in southern Kanagawa Prefecture, central Honshū, at the mouth of the river Sagamigawa. Since the opening of the Tōkaidō Main Line of the Japanese National Railways in 1889, Chigasaki has become a residential area with numerous villas and beach resorts. It is rapidly becoming a suburb of the Tōkyō–Yokohama district, with emergent industries. Pop: 171,013.

chigo

Children attendants in temples, and warrior and noble households. Nowadays the word *chigo* refers to parish children, often age three, five, or seven, who dress in traditional attire and parade at shrine and temple festivals. *Chigo* are often chosen to offer sacred wine, perform dances, and be archers at ceremonies that accompany Shintō observances. In the past children were considered uncontaminated by the world, and young boys performed special functions at Shintō and Buddhist ceremonies. They were also regarded as being capable of divine possession; gods were called down to enter the child, in the hope that the deity would perform some function, such as exorcising a sick person. At some festivals, a young boy was chosen as a representative *(tōya)* of the parishioners to ride on a horse and was expected to fall asleep when the gods entered him. It was a bad omen if he did not fall asleep. (Although the young boys who served as *chigo* at Buddhist temples in premodern Japan were ostensibly servants or attendants, in reality they were often the "female" partners for male homosexual monks. In the Meiji period [1868–1912] *chigo* referred to a male student who was the object of an older male student's affection. See also HOMOSEXUALITY.)

Ōtō Tokihiko

chigyō

(usufruct, proprietorship). The enjoyment or exercise of certain rights to land. Originally meaning "to carry out the functions of office," the term differed in usage according to period. As the RITSURYŌ SYSTEM of centralized administration instituted by the TAIKA REFORM (645) gradually broke down in the 10th century, it was replaced by the *bunkoku* or CHIGYŌKOKU system whereby the imperial house, the court nobility, and certain religious institutions were granted special administrative rights and powers of taxation in designated provinces. Since the proprietors remained in the capital, delegating their functions to tax managers (ZURYŌ), the term *chigyō* bore a fiscal rather than a political connotation.

At about the same time, under the growing private estate (SHŌEN) system of proprietorship, in which vast tracts of rice land were concentrated in private hands—typically on several levels of tenure—*chigyō* came to mean the actual exercise or enjoyment of rights to the land, as opposed to *shiki*, the possession of those rights. For example, *shitaji chigyō* referred to control over the land itself, *shotō chigyō* referred to control over land rents and labor, and so forth. When one person came to hold and exercise all of these rights, he was said to hold ICHIEN CHIGYŌ (sole proprietorship). A distinction was also made between rights formally held but not exercised *(fuchigyō)* and those exercised without formal entitlement *(tōchigyō* or de facto rights). During the Kamakura period (1185–1333) legitimate rights that had not been exercised for 20 years were forfeited, while the shogunate gave official recognition (ANDO) to *tōchigyō* that had been exercised for 20 years. By the middle of the Muromachi period (1333–1568), when *shōen* had become virtually the private domains of the military governors (SHUGO) appointed by the shogunate, *chigyō* meant simply overlordship of territory. The territorial lords, now called SHUGO DAIMYŌ, allotted land to their retainers *(chigyōnin),* who reciprocated with military service *(chigyōyaku).*

In the Edo period (1600–1868) *chigyō* retained generally the meaning of "fief," land allotted to retainers by the shogunate or daimyō within their domains. More strictly, it referred to the retainer's right to tax and administer his fief and, by extension, to the rice stipends (also called KURAMAI) issued to those retainers without land.

Philip BROWN

chigyōkoku

(proprietary province). A province *(koku)* whose usufruct (CHIGYŌ) was assigned to an individual or a temple. From the late 10th century retired emperors and imperial kinsmen received allotment provinces *(bunkoku)* to supplement their incomes; later such provinces, called *chigyōkoku,* were assigned to courtiers and religious institutions as well. Proprietorship was a great source of income and patronage, especially during the period of rule by retired emperors (INSEI); in his retirement, Emperor GO-TOBA (1180–1239; r 1183–98) held three provinces himself and had power of assignment over 37 more. The proprietor remained in the capital and appointed relatives or clients as tax managers (ZURYŌ) of their holdings, which were administered in much the same way as private estates (SHŌEN). Originally assigned for fixed terms of four years, these proprietorships became hereditary and virtually indistinguishable from *shōen*. At the beginning of the Kamakura period (1185–1333), the shōguns and their vassals became proprietors, and by the 13th century two-thirds of the provinces were hereditary *chigyōkoku*. Chigyōkoku disappeared in the 15th century, when the provinces came under the control of regional lords (SENGOKU DAIMYŌ).

G. Cameron HURST III

Chihōkan Kaigi → Assembly of Prefectural Governors

chijimi

General name for crepe fabrics. The first large-scale production of silk crepe was at Akashi (in what is now Hyōgo Prefecture) during the early part of the Edo period (1600–1868). Echigo Province (now Niigata Prefecture) and Awa Province (now Tokushima Prefecture) also became noted in the Edo period for their crepe fabrics. Traditional production methods are virtually the same as for Western crepe de chine and georgette. Crepe fabric may be made from cotton, linen, silk, or synthetic fibers, but the word *chijimi* used alone generally refers only to cotton crepe; silk crepe is called CHIRIMEN. Cotton and linen crepe are very absorbent and cool to wear and are still often used for traditional Japanese summer clothing and for undergarments.

Yasuko YABE

Chijiwa Miguel (ca 1570–?)

One of the four young envoys sent by the CHRISTIAN DAIMYŌ of Kyūshū on the MISSION TO EUROPE OF 1582. Born Chijiwa Seizaemon and baptized Miguel, he was a kinsman of the *daimyō* ARIMA HARUNOBU and ŌMURA SUMITADA, both sponsors of the mission. The mission visited Spain, Portugal, and Italy, had a papal audience in 1585, and returned to Japan in 1590. Chijiwa entered the Society of Jesus in 1591 but later left. His subsequent career is unknown.

Adriana BOSCARO

Chikamatsu Hanji (1725–1783)

Generally regarded as the last major playwright of the BUNRAKU puppet theater. Born in Ōsaka. His father, Hozumi Ikan (1692–1769), a Confucian scholar, was a close acquaintance and admirer of the playwright CHIKAMATSU MONZAEMON. In the early 1750s, following in the line of this great dramatist whose name he took, Hanji began writing for the Takemotoza theater.

After long years as an apprentice staff writer under the tutelage of Takeda Izumo III (see TAKEDA IZUMO), he became head playwright. As chief dramatist of the Takemotoza, Hanji was destined to wage a desperate struggle against the rising popularity of the KABUKI theater. His plays suggest a compromise with the change in public taste: the reduced length of the narrative passages (traditionally delivered by the chanters) and the greater emphasis on spoken dialogue in his works appear to bring them closer to the basic form of the kabuki play. Hanji also tried to emulate kabuki in scale and grandeur by employing elaborate and colorful stage settings. The most outstanding example is found in Act I of *Imoseyama onna teikin* (1771, An Example of Noble Womanhood), where two *hanamichi* (an elevated ramp through the audience to the stage) are placed at opposite ends of the stage front so that the puppets and their operators, representing the retinues of two feuding families could travel simultaneously through the audience.

While critics have argued that he had abetted the rapid erosion of the puppet theater by adopting the style and technique of kabuki, the public acceptance of his brilliant plays and their successful adaptations on the kabuki stage may have actually forestalled its ultimate decline. In addition to *Imoseyama onna teikin*, his major plays, written in collaboration with others include: *Ōshū adachigahara* (1762, Sodehagi's Petition to the Gods), *Ōmi Genji senjin yakata* (1769,

Chikamatsu Monzaemon

Chikamatsu in the latter part of his life. Detail of a contemporary copy of an 18th-century hanging scroll. Tsubouchi Memorial Theater Museum, Waseda University, Tōkyō.

Moritsuna's Camp), and *Igagoe dōchū sugoroku* (1783, The Vendetta at Iga). In all, he wrote about 50 plays.

▰——Donald Keene, *World within Walls* (1976). Kitani Hōgen, *Jōruri kenkyū sho* (1941). Sonoda Tamio, *Jōruri sakusha no kenkyū* (1944).　　　　　　　　　　　　　　*Ted T. Takaya*

Chikamatsu Monzaemon (1653–1724)

Edo period (1600–1868) playwright, especially for the puppet theater called BUNRAKU or *ningyō jōruri*, and also for the KABUKI theater. Generally considered Japan's greatest dramatist. His pen name was Chikamatsu Monzaemon, or simply Chikamatsu, and his family name was Sugimori, boyhood name Jirōkichi, and adult given name Nobumori. He belonged to a *samurai* family from the province of Echizen (now part of Fukui Prefecture). However, the family left the Echizen area for Kyōto some time between 1664 and 1670, his father having apparently abandoned his feudal service. In Kyōto Chikamatsu served various members of the court aristocracy in an unknown capacity and seems to have seized the opportunity to build upon the early cultural training that he would have received as the son of a samurai, since considerable knowledge of Buddhism, Confucianism, and Japanese literature is apparent in his plays.

There is a good deal of legend and surmise about how his connection with the theater started. The first puppet drama definitely attributable to him is *Yotsugi Soga* (1683, The Soga Heir). Two years later he started to write for the JŌRURI chanter Takemoto Gidayū. The year 1684 saw his first kabuki play, and by 1693 he had turned almost entirely to writing for this live theater, particularly for the Kyōto actor SAKATA TŌJŪRŌ I. In 1703 the interrupted connection with Gidayū was resumed, and in 1705 he moved his residence from Kyōto to Ōsaka and maintained his position as writer for the Takemotoza, Gidayū's puppet theater, until his death. Gidayū died in 1714. Chikamatsu's wife, about whom the only information that seems to remain is in funeral records, died in 1734. He had two sons, Tamon and Matsuya Tabei; the former was an artist working in the city of Sakai, and the latter was involved in theater management in the city of Ōsaka.

Puppet Plays——The puppet theater for which Chikamatsu wrote was on a fairly small physical scale. Puppets had not yet developed into the present complicated three-man type but were manipulated by one man who inserted his hands from below. The public stages were extremely simple, and performances could be given in large rooms in residences of warriors or aristocrats. The words of the play were delivered by a chanter, accompanied by a SHAMISEN player. Chikamatsu's function was to supply the material for the chanter. This material amounted to far more than mere dialogues and formed a complete narrative with scene settings and comments all incorporated into the text, which could be read like a novel. Nearly 100 such puppet plays were certainly written by him, and he probably collaborated in the writing of several more in his early days.

These early plays contain many elements of the war chronicles from which they were derived, including the *michiyuki* or poetic journey, in which a trip undertaken under emotional stress is recounted with a great deal of allusion linked to the places traversed. His first certain play, *Yotsugi Soga,* includes such a scene, along with other elements from old forms such as the Kimpira plays (see JŌ-RURI), but it also shows some innovations. The plot involves the efforts of two brothers to avenge a slight upon their masters, the Soga brothers, after the deaths of the latter in connection with the famous Soga vendetta (see SOGA MONOGATARI). They eventually do this with the help of the mighty warrior Asahina, with the two brothers farcically quarreling over who should strike the first blow. The new elements include the parts played by the two courtesan mistresses of the Soga brothers, who perform the play's *michiyuki* when they travel to tell the dead heroes' mother of her sons' fate. The *michiyuki* theme concerns the pitiful destiny of prostitutes and the impossibility of lasting relationships with those they love.

This is the first appearance of a theme that runs through much of Chikamatsu's work: the high-principled mistress. It is continued in his next important play, *Shusse Kagekiyo* (1686, Kagekiyo Victorious), his first for Gidayū, in which Akoya, the mistress of the general Taira no Kagekiyo, betrays him to his enemies out of jealousy, but later seeks his forgiveness. He bitterly rejects her as well as their children and is unmoved when she kills them and herself. In the end he is beheaded, but the bodhisattva Kannon's head is found substituted for his own, and Kagekiyo lives to make peace with Minamoto no Yoritomo, his conqueror. The treatment shows a realistic conflict of emotions, and thus this play is generally classified as "new *jōruri*," although such elements as the hero's colossal strength and his miraculous survival clearly link it with "old *jōruri*."

The next two decades saw little development in *jōruri*, and during this period Chikamatsu devoted most of his attention to the live kabuki theater. He nevertheless wrote about 20 puppet plays, typical historical pieces *(jidai-mono)*; only in 1703, when he once again concentrated on writing for Gidayū, did he discover a new vein which was to make the "new *jōruri*" a reality, the *sewa-mono*, or drama of contemporary life. The first decade of the 18th century saw a vogue for double suicides by lovers hoping to be together eternally in the next world. Following a precedent of the novelist Ihara SAIKAKU (1642–93) of basing stories on actual incidents, Chikamatsu turned the suicides of Tokubei, a shop clerk, and Ohatsu, a prostitute, into the play *Sonezaki shinjū* (1703; tr *The Love Suicides at Sonezaki*, 1961) in a mere three weeks. The play was a great success, and Chikamatsu went on to write over 20 such love suicide dramas during his career. Most were based on the brothel system, whereby a father received money for selling his daughter into service for a specified number of years, it being possible to buy out the woman's term of service if one wanted to take her into one's household. The tragedy often arose from the efforts of the lover to acquire the necessary sum, as he had often used up his resources in becoming her favorite client. In *Sonezaki shinjū*, Tokubei manages to retrieve a payment made in connection with his proposed marriage to another girl, only to be tricked out of it. In *Shinjū ten no Amijima* (1712; tr *The Love Suicides at Amijima*, 1953) the paper-merchant hero uses up his business capital and is only prevented by his father-in-law from allowing his devoted wife to sell her clothes to help buy the release of his mistress. Chikamatsu's successful portrayals caused such an increase in the frequency of these suicides that the authorities made them a crime, with a surviving partner decreed guilty of murder, and the corpses of the lovers exposed like those of common criminals.

One or two domestic pieces *(sewa-mono)* do not involve prostitutes but instead feature "respectable" women caught in the snares of fate and passion. All are marked by realistic dialogue, a characterization which sometimes manages to avoid stereotypes, and occasional poignant passages such as the journey to the suicide in the grove at Sonezaki.

Chikamatsu never completely abandoned writing historical dramas. From 1703 until his death he composed some 50 or more of them for the puppet theater, but all except one have passed into near oblivion. The single exception is *Kokusen'ya kassen* (1715; tr *The Battles of Coxinga*, 1951), which in some ways can be thought of as Chikamatsu's most successful work. It ran for 17 months, an unprecedented phenomenon, since most theater programs were changed monthly, or even within the month if attendance was down. In the play the hero, a fantastic treatment of the historical figure who drove the Dutch from Formosa, is a half-Chinese, half-Japanese fisherman who goes off to China to restore the Ming dynasty after its overthrow by the Manchus. It is a play of violent contrasts, with rough humor, comic comparisons between Chinese and Japanese, a famous fight with a tiger, scenes of bloodshed and eye-gouging, and a ripped-open womb in a puppet Caesarian that would do credit to the goriest Elizabethan drama. It is an indication of Chikamatsu's genius as a playwright that he was able to write plays that made such full use of the puppets' limited capabilities. The effect of this and of other historical plays, when performed with the puppetry that reached its full development after his death, is very striking even today. It compares unfavorably, however, with the sober but subtle realism of his domestic pieces, in which the tragedies of ordinary people of the merchant class elevate them at least to the level of the superhuman characters in the historic plays. The conflicts of duty and human affection (GIRI AND NINJŌ) that beset them moved audiences to tears and were to form the most characteristic theme of the puppet theater.

Kabuki Works —— Chikamatsu served as staff writer with the kabuki theater of Sakata Tōjūrō, a famous player of lovers' roles, in Kyōto for about 10 years up to 1705. Inferior to that of the actor, his function consisted of suggesting a plot and then supplying appropriate dialogue in sessions where all could join in with their ideas. Inevitably this led to much improvisation and to an emphasis upon the effect produced on the stage. Complete texts from the period have rarely survived. It seems likely that the main result for Chikamatsu was an improvement in his ability to write dialogue, in which, as his later puppet *sewa-mono* demonstrate, he excelled. He was involved in about 30 kabuki plays.

There has been much speculation about why he switched from *jōruri* to kabuki and back. An early dissatisfaction with puppets and a belief that live actors were more effective may have been replaced by discontent at the inferior position of the kabuki writer. He left kabuki when its star, Tōjūrō, was about to retire and when the success of *Sonezaki shinjū* had rescued Gidayū from financial difficulties.

With Matsuo BASHŌ (1644–94) and Ihara Saikaku, Chikamatsu forms the trio of outstanding authors of the brilliant period at the end of the 17th century. His puppet plays were works of outstanding genius, and established the tradition upon which *bunraku* was to develop into the world's most advanced puppet theater. He created characters of realistic complexity, and showed the tragedy and pathos of their entrapment by circumstance. He used fully the resources of word play in the Japanese language to obtain an allusive depth which generally resulted in the heightening of whatever emotion was being portrayed, whether tragic or comic. Nowadays not often given in their original form, Chikamatsu's plays have been skillfully adapted by such writers as CHIKAMATSU HANJI (1725–83) to suit the improved puppetry, simplify the language which later audiences were finding difficult to appreciate fully, and make the texts less of an integrated chanting performance and more like conversation. Later developments and refinement in the puppet theater have led to the virtual disappearance of lesser authors like KI NO KAION (1663–1742), but Chikamatsu's ability to make his portrayals of humans overcome all the difficulties of the form for which he was writing has meant that his reputation has been enhanced rather than lessened.

●—— C. J. Dunn and Bunzō Torigoe, tr, *The Actors' Analects* (1969). Donald Keene, *The Battles of Coxinga* (1951). Donald Keene, *Major Plays of Chikamatsu* (1961). Donald Keene, *World within Walls* (1976). Asatarō Miyamori, *The Masterpieces of Chikamatsu Monzaemon, the Shakespeare of Japan* (1926). Mori Osamu, *Chikamatsu Monzaemon* (1959). Mori Osamu, Torigoe Bunzō, and Nagatomi Chiyo, ed, *Chikamatsu Monzaemon shū I*, vol 43 of *Nihon koten bungaku zenshū* (Shōgakukan, 1972). Mori Osamu and Torigoe Bunzō, *Chikamatsu Monzaemon shū II*, vol 44 of *Nihon koten bungaku zenshū* (Shōgakukan, 1975).   Charles DUNN

Chikamatsu Shūkō (1876–1944)

Novelist. Real name Tokuda Hiroshi. Born in Okayama Prefecture. Graduate of Tōkyō Semmon Gakkō (now Waseda University). His first wife, despairing over the poverty and misery of their life together, left him; Chikamatsu recounted the loneliness and pain he experienced at her leaving in *Wakaretaru tsuma ni okuru tegami* (1910). Other autobiographical novels (see I-NOVEL) of this period are *Giwaku* (1913) and *Kurokami* (1922), which established him as a prominent writer of the so-called Japanese naturalist school. After his remarriage in 1922, his novels, such as *Ko no ai no tame ni* (1924), continued to be colored by his personal life but in a calmer, more subdued mode, often reflecting his profound love for his children.

Chikubashō

(literally, Bamboo Stilts). Muromachi-period (1333–1568) book of moral instruction for *samurai*. Completed in 1383 by Shiba Yoshimasa (1350–1410), a deputy shōgun (*kanrei*) of the Ashikaga shogunate, it details samurai rules of behavior and stresses the importance of cultivating both the martial and the classical arts.

Chikubushima

Island approximately 5 km (3 mi) off the north shore of Lake Biwa, Shiga Prefecture, central Honshū. Composed of granite but completely covered with green foliage, this island forms one of the so-called Eight Views of Lake Biwa (Biwa Hakkei). It is the site of the Tsukubusuma Shrine and of the temple Hōgonji. Area: 0.14 sq km (0.05 sq mi).

Chikugo

City in southern Fukuoka Prefecture, Kyūshū. Formerly a POST-STATION TOWN and market town, it is now the center of the milling, machinery, and forestry industries. The cultivation of rice, grapes, pears, and rush for making *tatami* mats are other principal activities. Together with the neighboring city of KURUME, the area is known for its ikat dyed cloth, called *kurume-gasuri*. The Kyūshū Agricultural Experiment Station of the Ministry of Agriculture, Forestry, and Fisheries is located here. The Funagoya Hot Spring nearby is noted for its large wood of camphor trees. Pop: 41,698.

Chikugogawa

The longest river in Kyūshū; in Ōita, Kumamoto, Fukuoka, and Saga prefectures. The Kusugawa, which originates in the mountains of Kujūsan, and the Oyamagawa, which originates in the mountains of Asosan, converge in the Hita Basin to become the Mikumigawa. It flows into the Chikushi Plain to become the Chikugogawa and empties into the Ariake Bay. Forestry thrives on its upper reaches, and fertile grain fields are located along the middle and lower reaches. A total of 20 electric power plants are located on the river. There are plans to use the water for drinking and for industry in the cities of Kita Kyūshū and Fukuoka. The water is already utilized for irrigation. The industrial city of Kurume is situated on the river. Precipitation on the upper reaches averages 2,000 mm (78.8 in) annually. Length: 123 km (76 mi); area of drainage basin: 2,860 sq km (1,104 sq mi).

Chikuhō Coalfield

(Chikuhō Tanden). Located in northeastern Fukuoka Prefecture, northern Kyūshū. Situated on the river Ongagawa. The coal produced here provided the fuel base for development of heavy industries in northern Kyūshū early in the 20th century. One of the largest coalfields in Japan, almost all of the mines have been abandoned since the late 1950s. Length: approximately 50 km (31 mi); width: approximately 20 km (12 mi); area: approximately 800 sq km (309 sq mi); volume of deposits: approximately 2.4 billion metric tons (2.64 billion short tons).

Chikumagawa

River in northeastern Nagano Prefecture, central Honshū, originating at the mountain Kobushigatake in the Kantō Mountains. After flowing through the basins of Saku, Ueda, Nagano, and Iiyama, it enters Niigata Prefecture to become the SHINANOGAWA. Forty electric power generating plants are located along the river. Length: 223 km (138 mi).

Chikuma Shobō Publishing Co, Ltd

Publishing house, founded in 1940 by Furuta Akira, in cooperation with the writer USUI YOSHIMI. In 1946 it first published the intellectual monthly *Tembō* (Views). In 1953 Usui planned and edited the first publication of *Gendai Nihon bungaku zenshū* (Collected Works of Modern Japanese Literature). This successful undertaking comprised 56 volumes and was later increased to 99 volumes, providing a model for later collections of literature by Japanese authors. In 1978 the company went bankrupt, but soon reentered the publishing business.   KOBAYASHI Kazuhiro

Chikura

Town in southern Chiba Prefecture, central Honshū, on the southeastern tip of the Bōsō Peninsula. Chief industries are fishing and greenhouse cultivation of flowers and vegetables. The town is part of the Southern Bōsō Quasi-National Park. Tourist attractions include swimming beaches and hot springs. Pop: 15,772.

Chikushino

City in west central Fukuoka Prefecture, Kyūshū. Formerly a POST-STATION TOWN and market town on the road leading to DAZAIFU, the government outpost in Kyūshū in ancient times, it is now a satellite city of Fukuoka. It is known for its locally produced rice, mandarin oranges, tea, and vegetables. The Goróyama tomb and the remains of the Kii palisade nearby are the principal tourist attractions. Pop: 57,968.

childhood and child rearing

In Japan affection for children is nearly universal. As the old expression *kodakara* ("child-treasure") indicates, the Japanese have long cherished their offspring as heaven-sent treasures. Children are generally well-protected (or even overprotected), often remaining passive recipients of maternal nurturance and indulgence. Discipline is lenient and children's needs are respected. In contemporary Japan, however, carefree childhood ends early, as the importance of scholastic excellence becomes emphasized and the pressures of highly competitive ENTRANCE EXAMINATIONS for institutions of higher education begin to make themselves felt. Nevertheless, physical and emotional closeness to parents, particularly to the mother, continues to characterize Japanese childhood, and it remains a period that a person looks back upon with nostalgia.

Legal Definition of Childhood——In every society, customs and laws divide an individual's life span into various phases and periods. The age at which a Japanese person legally leaves childhood and enters adulthood is 20. An individual below the age of 20 is classified as a juvenile *(shōnen)*, and as such has no voting rights, is forbidden to smoke or drink, and requires parental consent to marry another juvenile. However, minors acquire certain rights at the age of 18, including the right to marry (for men), to apply for a firearms permit, and to receive a teacher's diploma. Women are allowed to marry at the age of 16. Minors above the age of 15 are allowed to work, with certain restrictions (see JUVENILE WORKERS, PROTECTIVE LEGISLATION FOR).

Children in Folk Culture——In Japanese folk culture of the past, people believed that the birth of a baby had to take place in the presence of a supernatural being called *ubugami* (birth deity). It was also believed that when a baby was born an ancestral spirit entered into it, with the midwife playing the role of "implanting the ancestral spirit." At birth, when the spirit entered, the baby cried for the first time and became "human." Such a spirit, however, was believed to be "unstable" while the child was small, and was liable to leave the baby, causing its death. A series of rituals after birth (the naming ceremony between the 3rd and the 14th day, the visit to a tutelary shrine on the 31st or 32nd day, the first eating ceremony on the 100th day, and visits to a shrine at the ages 3, 5, and 7, SHICHIGO-SAN) were therefore performed to "secure" the anchorage of the spirit. These ceremonies also functioned to introduce the baby and child to the community.

Age seven was considered the end of childhood. Children below that age were thought to be closer to the supernatural world, and certain behavior which would be considered sacrilegious on the part of adults was permitted them. However, it was also thought that the spirits within children easily left their bodies to join other spirits. When a child suffered from an illness whose cause was unclear, it was believed that the spirit within the child wanted to leave the body.

Traditionally, the Japanese believed that for the successful growth of a child, rearing by its natural parents alone was not enough. The child needed the nurturance and protection of many other people, who played the role of "ritual parents." In many locales, when boys and girls came of age at puberty (13 to 15 for boys, 13 to 17 or at the time of first menstruation for girls), they entered a new ritual relationship with an adult couple who became their ritual parents. The latter served as the mentors, guarantors, and often the employers of the youths. Trust and reliance were also often extended to supernatural beings.

Childhood in Contemporary Culture——The custom of establishing ritual parent-child relationships has all but disappeared, but ceremonies after birth and visits to shrines are still in common practice. The Shichigosan visits to shrines remain memorable occasions for children, who are specially dressed up for the day and photographed by their parents. Such festivities are abundant in Japanese childhood. Special dolls are displayed annually on the DOLL FESTIVAL on the third of March (a celebration for girls), and on CHILDREN'S DAY on the fifth of May (basically a celebration for boys). The latter is also celebrated with long carp pennants fluttering in the wind.

Married couples rarely go out together for pleasure except when accompanied by their children. Baby-sitters are virtually unknown. Parents take their children on picnics, to films, to plays, exhibitions, athletic events, Shintō shrines, Buddhist temples, and amusement parks. Kindergartens and grade schools hold an annual field day *(undōkai)* which is attended by pupils and their parents, grandparents, and teachers.

The mother looks to her offspring for joy and entertainment. As the children mature, her prestige and virtue are judged according to their achievements, and personal sacrifices to this end are considered ennobling. When a family has a child preparing for an important school entrance examination, especially a son, all the other family members make a variety of "self-sacrifices" (no television after 8 PM, no Christmas or New Year celebration, etc) to help the child succeed; this in turn puts a heavy burden on the child. For children in such a situation not much time is left for typical childhood amusements such as watching television.

The father's relationship to his children is very much dependent upon his occupation. White-collar workers in large urban centers may seldom be home during the young child's waking hours. The children mostly see him on weekends. Care is provided exclusively by the mother. Other fathers generally have more extensive contact with their children.

Despite their high degree of dependence upon their parents and other family members, friends are very important to Japanese children, and friendships formed during childhood often remain firm throughout their lives. Annual reunions of grade-school classes (to say nothing of those of high schools) are faithfully attended.

Physical and Emotional Closeness——Mother-child relationships and relationships among family members in general are characterized by physical and psychological closeness. While kissing, hugging, and other such overt demonstrations of affection for infants are rarely seen, Japanese mothers often hold and rock their babies. They tend to view their babies as extensions of themselves, and psychologically the boundaries between the mother and the infant tend to be blurred. They are also likely to feel that they know what is best for their babies and that there is no need for the babies to tell them what they want, for they are virtually one. As a result, Japanese children become quite dependent, tied to home and mother. They are more likely to cling fast to their mother and to run and catch up with her in public rather than go off exploring new surroundings. Little boys who behave like fierce warriors at home often become the soul of timidity in public. In general, people are not socialized to be independent and individualistic, and dependency (AMAE) is encouraged well into adulthood.

There is also a strong tendency for family members to sleep in the same room or adjacent rooms, even when others are available. An individual can expect to sleep in a two-generation group, first as a child and then as a parent—over approximately half of his life.

These trends toward "group" life assure that the child grows up in an atmosphere of interdependence; thus there develops a subsequent struggle for a separate identity which, in the course of life, is never completely fulfilled.

Shitsuke——The word for training, disciplining, and educating children is *shitsukeru* (verb) or *shitsuke* (noun). The term in its current usage means to teach standardized behavior in daily life or to educate them in manners and etiquette. Its original meaning, however, was to correct inappropriate behavior and develop an adequately trained member of the community. The term was not limited to technical training but also pertained to the teaching of values, beliefs, and manners commonly accepted and approved by the community. Essentially the method was to let children and youths learn by imitating their teachers, who would then correct the pupils' mistakes. This teaching mode still survives in such traditional fields as flower arrangement, the tea ceremony, and the martial arts.

The goal of *shitsuke* in traditional culture was to produce an individual who was hardworking, kindhearted, and reticent. It was considered both unforgivable and antisocial either to disturb the peace and harmony within the community, or to defy those of higher status. The best and most commendable way of life was to act in and through the group. Each person was to adopt the way of thinking and manner most appropriate for his or her status in life.

At present, interpersonal relationships are still considered important. Early lessons include playing harmoniously, offering toys and sweets to others, and respecting others' property. Children are told not to want something that belongs to others, make other children cry, say spiteful things, have vicious thoughts, trouble others, or engage in mischief to a stranger. It is also thought important to have one's thought processes, emotions, and expressions under control. The demands of propriety are still rather restrictive—the formal sitting position, appropriate facial expressions, the avoidance of verbal animosity, and so forth. Children are typically quiet in the presence of strangers. The Japanese parent extends to the child the kind of respect that in the United States is normally reserved for adults. Physical compulsion is not used. Conversation, although geared to the lesser age level of a child, shows respect. Adults rarely chastise children or express disapproval.

Positive methods of obtaining compliance are extensively used and praise is frequent. The mother provides a continuous stream of explanations for the young child as to what behavior is appropriate and proper. Parents tend to feel that the best instruction is provided through setting an example.

The negative mechanisms for ensuring compliance among young children show considerable variety. The predominant form is a slap administered to the buttocks, but it can be applied to a different part of the body. Apparently the objective is an acknowledged break of rapport rather than the infliction of physical pain. Other methods include shaming the child by pointing out the effect his behavior would have upon himself and his family; threats of sanctions by a religious deity; depriving the child of privileges or objects; and threats that the child will be abandoned, given away, or taken away by a beggar, idiot, monster, or ghost.

At an older age, punishment is dependent upon the extent to which the child knows that what he is doing is wrong, rather than upon the seriousness of the offense. The concept "spare the rod and spoil the child" is meaningless in the light of Japanese attitudes.

Father and Mother as Disciplinarians——As the child matures the father tends to play a more important role as disciplinarian, but he joins the wife in doing this rather than taking over her role. In general mothers act as disciplinarians, often completely replacing their husbands as the authority figure. The traditional images of the stern father and the protective mother (*gempu jibo*) are apparently no longer the acknowledged reality in many homes: the Japanese father seems to have become "insignificant," as many writers have recently pointed out. This tendency is particularly evident in urban homes. In the rural community, the father is frequently still the disciplinarian. If it is correct to assume that traditions are usually retained in rural communities longer than in urban areas, this phenomenon should suggest that the father was formerly more important as an authority figure than he is at present. This traditional tendency is also stronger among those with lower educational levels and lower income.

Moral Masochism and Feelings of Guilt——When a child is disobedient to her, a mother may resort to what Freud termed "moral masochism"—hurting oneself to generate guilt in another person with the eventual result of being able to control that person through guilt. The Japanese mother may not verbalize her suffering for her children, but she lives it out before their eyes. She will not criticize her children so much as herself if they behave badly. Her quiet suffering is extremely effective in inducing guilt, and expiation of guilt feelings is a primary motivation behind Japanese achievement. Antisocial behavior, failure, and laziness are all seen as "injuring" the parents and thus produce feelings of guilt. Success becomes a way of paying back one's parents, not only for the burden of raising their children but also for suffering incurred in the process by the mother and, to a lesser extent, the father.

Age and Sex Differences——Parents generally expect different behavior from their sons and their daughters and from older and younger children as well. Boys are expected to be physically strong, to be achievement-oriented, and to take the initiative. Girls, on the other hand, should be less self-assertive, more obedient to their parents, and emotionally sensitive and sympathetic to others. Older children are expected to look after their younger brothers and sisters, who in turn are urged to depend upon and follow their elders. In the event of a dispute over a toy, the elder must give in to the younger. The latter reciprocates with the accord of prestige and obedience due an older sibling. These expectations sometimes cause resentment on the part of one or both. Occasionally an elder brother takes advantage of his opportunities to restrict and punish. The terms of address used by siblings indicate rank differences among them; older children may address their younger sibs simply by their first name, but young children usually address their elders by the terms "elder brother" and "elder sister," without using the first name. Heavy responsibility still tends to fall upon the shoulders of the eldest child, particularly the eldest son, the heir of the family.

Japanese parents tend to be especially permissive and indulgent toward young children. The request of a young child is met whenever reasonable and possible. Some adults comment that people don't understand the importance to a child of his wishes. Occasionally youngsters take advantage of the mother's kindness, stooping down in front of a store and refusing to leave until a desired article is purchased. The mother, unable to talk the child out of the request, may pacify with sweets, stoop down alongside and sit it out, or make a promise that both know will not be kept.

In extreme cases, the according of every wish, sometimes every demand, produces a rather obstreperous child. Whatever the case, the process is gradually reversed from the age of four, as expected responsibilities for maintaining "face," and meeting the appropriate demands of propriety and etiquette become important. By age 11, behavioral traits have undergone a radical change. The child is now a humble and studious pupil, sensitive to the needs of others, and appreciative of the kindnesses received.

Recent Developments——Psychologists and teachers have recently been voicing concern over the increasing lack of autonomy and self-reliance among contemporary Japanese children. They argue that, as a consequence of maternal overprotection, children are becoming increasingly compliant and capable under directed guidance but surprisingly incapable of making their own judgments and decisions when left alone. Mothers, who are much less bound by household chores than before (thanks to electric appliances, and frozen and "instant" foods), overly expend their energies in child care, so that their offspring do not learn to act independently. Some scholars observe that children now are less openly rebellious against their parents. This particularly pertains to the father, who appears to be moving toward what has formerly been conceived of as maternal behavior, i.e., toward more responsibility for child care and involvement in play activities. Today, he functions less often in a disciplinary role. An increase in the number of working mothers, in one respect at least, would appear to have a negative effect, in that guilt over limited contact leads to excessive indulgence. Some critics have advocated the reintroduction of spartan training in the schools. Only with the passage of time will it be possible to assess the impact of current changes upon future adults. See also EDUCATION; FILIAL PIETY; HAJI; IKIGAI; JAPANESE PEOPLE, PSYCHOLOGY OF.

■──Aoki Kazuo et al, "Comparative Study of Home Discipline: Rural and Urban, Sex and Age Differences," in R. Hill and R. Koenig, ed, *Families in East and West* (1970). Doi Takeo, "Amae: A Key Concept for Understanding Japanese Personality Structure," in R. J. Smith and R. K. Beardsley, ed, *Japanese Culture: Its Development and Characteristics* (1962). Doi Takeo, *Amae no kōzō* (1971), tr John Bester as *The Anatomy of Dependence* (1973). Betty B. Lanham, "Aspects of Child Care in Japan: Preliminary Report," in D. G. Haring, ed, *Personal Character and Cultural Milieu* (1956). Betty B. Lanham, "The Psychological Orientation of the Mother-Child Relationship in Japan," *Monumentica Nipponica* 26.3/4 (1966). Betty B. Lanham, "Relation of History to Expectations of the Future: Japan's Youth of the Past and the Present," *Asian Profile* 2.5/6 (1974). Ezra Vogel, "Entrance Examination and Emotional Disturbances in Japan's New Middle Class," in R. J. Smith and R. K. Beardsley, ed, *Japanese Culture: Its Development and Characteristics* (1962). Hiroshi Wagatsuma, "Some Aspects of Changing Family in Contemporary Japan—Once Confucian, Now Fatherless?" *Daedalus* 106 (Spring 1977).   *Hiroshi* WAGATSUMA and *Betty B.* LANHAM

children and television

Japanese children between the ages of 3 and 6 watch television approximately three hours a day; those between 10 and 12 watch about two hours a day during the week and on Saturday and three and a half hours on Sunday. In the Tōkyō metropolitan area about 50

Children's Day —— Koinobori

Throughout Japan families with male children mark Children's Day by displaying *koinobori* (carp "banners"; actually a sort of wind sock), as does this rural household near Mt. Fuji. The number of *koinobori* does not necessarily correspond to the number of sons in the family.

percent of all households watch television during the evening meal, and this average rises to about 66 percent in farm villages.

Animated films about monsters and space dramas are popular with young children as are stories of everyday life and famous people. Musical programs and programs with adult themes are popular with older children. There are presently no standards for advertising on children's shows, and programming has become a focus of concern. Groups involved with problems of programming and advertising include the National Congress of the Parents and Teachers Association of Japan, the National Assembly for Youth Development, and the Forum for Children's Television, a citizen's group. In addition to improvement in program content, they are working for self-policing by television stations of early morning animated movies, restrictions on the showing of adult programs in time periods when children watch television, and the setting of standards for television advertising aimed at children.   *Gotō Kazuhiko*

Children's Day

(Kodomo no Hi). Festival held on 5 May; one of five traditional celebrations (see SEKKU). Known as the Tango Festival (Tango no Sekku) or Iris Festival (Shōbu no Sekku), the fifth day of the fifth month has been observed since ancient times. This became a festival for boys corresponding to the DOLL FESTIVAL for girls on the third day of the third month. In 1948, 5 May was designated a national holiday and renamed Children's Day; however, it is still observed in most families in the traditional way as a festival for boys. It is customary on this day for families with male children to fly carp streamers *(koinobori)* outside the house, display warrior dolls inside, and eat *chimaki* (rice cakes wrapped in cogon grass or bamboo leaves) and *kashiwamochi* (rice cakes filled with sweet bean paste and wrapped in oak leaves).

In China, from ancient times it was customary on this day to gather medicinal herbs and hang mugwort (J: *yomogi*) from the eaves of the roof in order to repel disease. When the custom was imported to Japan, it became associated with the taboos and purification rituals surrounding rice planting (see AGRICULTURAL RITES). The first reference to the Tango Festival in historical documents dates back to the fifth day of the fifth month of 839. Since irises (*shōbu;* correctly, sweet flag) were also believed to repel evil spirits, in the Nara period (710–794) people wore iris garlands on their heads on this day. In the Heian period (794–1185), both the court

nobility and the common people suspended iris and mugwort from the eaves of their roofs in order to repel evil influences. Even today, the practice of hanging a combination of iris and mugwort or iris and cogon grass from eaves is widespread. Allied customs include drinking rice wine with iris petals in it and taking baths with irises floating in the water *(shōbuyu).*

With the rise of the warrior class in the 12th century, the term *shōbu* became associated with a homonym meaning "reverence for the martial arts," and the practice of giving little boys kites with pictures of warriors on them became widespread. In the Edo period (1600–1868), streamers with pictures of carp were also presented to boys. The carp was traditionally thought to be a fish of success, because of an ancient Chinese legend about a carp that swam upstream and turned into a dragon. This notion combined with the practice of setting up poles of cedar in the rice fields at the time of the rice planting in order to receive the god of the rice field *(ta no kami)* to produce the practice of displaying carp streamers outside. The display of warrior dolls and armor is in imitation of the girls' Doll Festival on 3 March.   *INOKUCHI Shōji*

children's literature

(jidō bungaku). Before the Meiji period (1868–1912), there was no literature written specifically for children, and children's literature consisted of folktales, legends, and myths from the past. OTOGI-ZŌSHI, which were illustrated books, originally intended for adults, based on, for example, folktales of the 8th-century anthology FU-DOKI and the legends collected in the 12th-century anthology KON-JAKU MONOGATARI, were the main sources of literary entertainment for children.

The publication in 1891 of IWAYA SAZANAMI's *Koganemaru,* the story of a dog's vendetta against a tiger and a fox, is generally considered to be the beginning of modern children's literature in Japan. *Koganemaru* was the first of 32 books for children published by HAKUBUNKAN, each written by a different well-known author. Iwaya Sazanami became the first editor of the children's magazine *Shōnen sekai,* which Hakubunkan began publishing in 1895. Although Iwaya Sazanami was a pioneer in the field, the didacticism of his tales was objected to by such writers as OGAWA MIMEI and SUZUKI MIEKICHI, who wanted to make children's literature more creative and artistically refined. As an alternative to *Shōnen sekai,* Suzuki Miekichi began publishing in 1918 the magazine AKAI TORI, which was particularly popular among the children of middle-class families. It was around this time that the word *dōwa* (children's tales) came to replace the older words *shōnen bungaku* (juvenile literature) and *otogibanashi* (fables). Among the contributors to *Akai tori* were the novelists AKUTAGAWA RYŪNOSUKE, TSUBOTA JŌJI, Niimi Nankichi (1913–43), and ARISHIMA TAKEO and the poets KITAHARA HAKUSHŪ and SAIJŌ YASO.

Around 1920 Japan's children's literature entered its golden age, and the magazines *Ryōyū* and *Dōwa* were published by Hamada Hirosuke (1893–1973) and Chiba Shōzō (1892–1975), respectively. These magazines, however, sacrificed plot for artistry and were gradually overshadowed by more commercially oriented magazines such as SHŌNEN KURABU, whose motto was *omoshirokute tame ni naru* (entertaining and educational). *Shōnen kurabu* carried historical romances, adventure and detective stories, tales of explorations and warfare, and humorous stories; its contributors included novelists of POPULAR FICTION such as YOSHIKAWA EIJI, OSARAGI JIRŌ, and EDOGAWA RAMPO. The magazine was immensely popular and in the 1920s and 1930s attained an unprecedented level of circulation.

The rise of the PROLETARIAN LITERATURE MOVEMENT in the late 1920s led to the formation of the Shinkō Dōwa Sakka Remmei (League of New Writers of Children's Literature), which advocated the ideological education of children through literature. The league published the magazine *Dōwa undō,* but the magazine was discontinued after three issues because of internal dissension. The league split up into communist and anarchist factions, each of which subsequently published the magazines *Shōnen senki* and *Dōwa no sekai.* This proletarian movement ceased to exist by the late 1930s, but it contributed to the establishment of the concept of children as full members of society and exercised great influence on the postwar social realism school of children's literature.

Soon after World War II ended, a number of magazines with a humanistic orientation, such as *Akatombo, Ginga,* and *Kodomo no hiroba,* appeared. This humanistic approach can also be seen in such novels as Takeyama Michio's (b 1903) *Biruma no tategoto*

(1947–48, tr *The Harp of Burma*, 1966) and Ishii Momoko's (b 1907) *Non chan kumo ni noru* (1947). With Japan's economic recovery in the 1950s, many publishers came to place greater emphasis on profit, and numerous comics appeared. This trend, compounded by a lack of creativity among authors of children's literature, resulted in the decline of the above magazines and a temporary lull in the creative children's literature movement. As the commercial market was closed to most writers of children's literature, young writers turned to the small literary coterie magazines to publish their works. In the 1960s, publishers again became interested in creative children's literature and began to publish the works of such authors.

In 1981 a total of 2,598 children's titles were published in Japan by 145 publishing companies, and children's literature has come to be an accepted field of study in universities. There are associations of writers of children's literature, such as the Jidō Bungakusha Kyōkai and the Nihon Jidō Bungeika Kyōkai; academic organizations devoted to the study of children's literature, such as the Nihon Jidō Bungaku Gakkai; and prizes for children's literature, such as the Nihon Jidō Bungakusha Kyōkai Shō, the Nihon Jidō Bungeika Kyōkai Shō, the Noma Jidō Bungei Shō, and the Akai Tori Shō.

📖——Kan Tadamichi, *Nihon no jidō bungaku* (1966). Nihon Jidō Bungaku Gakkai, *Jidō bungaku kenkyū hikkei* (1976). Nihon Jidō Bungaku Gakkai, *Nihon jidō bungaku gairon* (1976). Torigoe Makoto, *Nihon jidō bungaku shi nempyō* (1975). Yokotani Teru, *Yokotani Teru jidō bungaku zenshū* (1974).　　　HAMANO Takuya

children's songs

Children's songs in Japan fall roughly into three categories: *warabe uta*, traditional songs children sing at play; *dōyō*, songs written for children by poets and musicians; and *shōka*, songs composed for classroom use.

Warabe uta may be considered children's folk songs that have been transmitted through the generations. They are an integral part of children's play, and while some are about nature or annual events, most of them are sung to such activities as drawing pictures, bouncing balls, skipping rope, and playing pat-a-cake and tag. *Warabe uta* include counting songs, teasing songs, parodies, tongue-twisters, and the like. These songs are creatively changed by the children themselves, new songs sometimes replacing old ones. Most Japanese children know at least 20 different *warabe uta*. *Warabe uta* have also been found to be eminently suited to the musical education of the very young, being of familiar tonality and narrow vocal range.

Dōyō were first written in the Taishō period (1912–26), when there was a conscious movement to compose songs of high artistic quality for children. Poets like KITAHARA HAKUSHŪ, SAIJŌ YASO, and Noguchi Ujō collaborated with YAMADA KŌSAKU, NAKAYAMA SHIMPEI, Hirota Kōtarō, Motoori Nagayo, and other composers who had studied Western music. These songs, which were published in children's magazines such as *Akai tori* and *Kodomo no kuni*, were recorded and became a permanent part of the repertoire. The movement, which lost momentum during the late 1930s and on through the war years, has since been revived.

With the establishment of universal education in 1872, *shōka* became part of the primary school curriculum. In 1911, the Ministry of Education put out songbooks for use in elementary schools and laid down guidelines for music in the classroom. The music reflected Western influence, some of the melodies being directly borrowed. Set usually in 2/4 time and with simple melodic lines, many of them used the so-called *yonanuki* scale ("minus 4 and 7" scale, i.e., do-re-mi-sol-la). The words to these songs tended to be serious and didactic, stressing loyalty to the emperor and respect for parents, commemorating the deeds of great men, or praising the beauties of nature and the Japanese spirit. Couched in *bungo* (classical Japanese) or in stiff and formal *kōgo* (spoken Japanese), the songs have little, if any, meaning for children of today. They are, nevertheless, still fondly cherished by many adults as part of their childhood.　　　KOSHIBA Harumi

Child Welfare Law

(Jidō Fukushi Hō). Law requiring national and local government bodies to ensure the proper health care of all children. The law was enacted in 1947 as a substitute for the Youth Education Law (1933) and the Child Abuse Prevention Law (1933), which were directed at the protection and education of problem children. It specifically guarantees the right of existence (SEIZONKEN) of all children (constitution, art. 28).

The law's main provisions are as follows. The national government, prefectures, cities, towns, and villages each are required to establish child welfare councils, which investigate and survey matters regarding the mentally infirm, nursing and expectant mothers, and children and report their opinions to the appropriate institutions. The prefectures are required to establish child consultation centers staffed by qualified child welfare officials. Children's committees must be maintained in the wards of the cities, towns, and villages. In addition, welfare offices must carry out activities necessary for the health and welfare of children. This law also established minimum standards for the national government to follow when it sets up and manages homes for orphans, educational facilities for delinquent children, nursing clinics, maternity hospitals, homes for widows and their children, facilities and educational institutions for handicapped children, and child health facilities.

The law also provides education for institutionalized children corresponding to compulsory education, and for consultation, examination, and admission of handicapped children to welfare institutions. The prefectural governors are required to take special measures for children without guardians. These include providing them with necessary guidance, appointing foster parents or guardians, arranging for their admission to welfare institutions or their commitment to family court. The expenses necessary for child welfare are borne by the national or local government, but expenses for child-rearing and such are collected from the child or the party with the duty of support.

The law forbids public viewing of deformed children and employment of children as beggars, in circuses, acrobatics, and light amusements, as well as in eating and drinking establishments.

KATŌ Shunpei

chin → Japanese spaniel

China and Japan

CHINA AND JAPAN TO 1911

For more than two millennia, until the weakness of the Qing (Ch'ing; 1644–1912) dynasty was exposed during the Opium War of 1840–42 and its painful aftermath, China had been for Japan, as for other nearby countries, a bountiful source of advanced civilization and institutional and technical progress. The Japanese developed their own distinct civilization within the Japanese archipelago— Japan was never merely a miniature replica of China. Still, it is valid to stress that until the 19th century Japanese civilization was continually deepened and reshaped by the vigorous introduction and transformation of elements of Chinese civilization through official and unofficial contacts, either directly or via the Korean peninsula. Without the powerful illumination of the lamp of Chinese civilization, the Japanese might well have remained deprived of a written language, legal codes and effective political institutions, art and agricultural technology, and advanced religion, philosophy, and ethics.

The long relationship between Japan and China, however, was not necessarily constant, uniform, equal, or reciprocal. Compared with Korea, where geographical proximity laid the country open to virtually incessant Chinese influence, Japan was far enough from the continent to regulate the degree and rate of influence, at least in official relations. There were long periods when the Japanese regarded conditions in China as too chaotic to maintain official relations or when, for reasons of political stability within Japan, monks, scholars, and merchants were forbidden to sail to China. Throughout these two millennia—during periods of barbarian conquest and dynastic decline as well as in periods of imperial grandeur—the Chinese remained secure in the conviction of the superiority and centrality of their civilization. For Chinese rulers and thinkers their realm was the "central country" whose emperor held a heavenly mandate to rule "all under heaven." It was therefore both an obligation and an advantage for the barbarians on the periphery to render tribute and homage, and to partake of China's civilization. On the whole, the Chinese elite were indifferent or condescending to the Japanese. China always loomed very much larger in the minds of Japanese rulers and thinkers than did Japan in Chinese official circles.

The Japanese, for their part, were not passive recipients. From an early stage in their relationship with China, Japanese rulers sought to qualify or reject Chinese claims of political and cultural superiority. In their diplomatic dealings with China they asserted the equality of the Japanese sovereign (TENNŌ) with the Chinese emperor and resisted the Chinese diplomatic principle that diplomatic relations implied Japan's tributary status. The Japanese were also prepared, on occasion, to challenge Chinese dynasties for control of the Korean peninsula. They produced paintings and books in which Japanese bested Chinese masters in their own skills or, like the scholars of National Learning (KOKUGAKU) in the 18th century, argued that Japanese cultural traditions were superior to those of China. One major element in Japanese development has been the tension between the awareness of a heavy cultural debt to China and the assertion of a vital, self-conscious Japanese cultural tradition.

In spite of the interruptions, tensions, and onesidedness inherent in the relationship, the Japanese elite continued throughout their pre-19th-century history to draw heavily on China in all areas of civilization. The common people in Japan, however, had no direct contact with China, except perhaps for an occasional commercial or piratical venture, and only a very diluted understanding of Chinese learning and institutions. And it was not until the late 19th century, when Japan was rapidly transforming itself, under Western pressure, into a modern nation-state, that some Chinese began to recognize the possibility of learning from Japan or to perceive a serious threat to China in Japanese economic and military development.

Prehistory—— The Chinese contribution to the earliest phases of Japanese prehistory is far from clear. The wandering tribes whose stock eventually mingled to form the Japanese people came to Japan in trickles and waves over tens of thousands of years. If the Japanese language is a reliable indicator, the dominant ethnic strains came from northern Asia. Japanese, like Korean and the North Asian Altaic languages, is agglutinative. Linguistically, it is quite distinct from the largely monosyllabic, isolating Sino-Tibetan languages. This linguistic difference, accentuated by Japan's relative isolation from the Asian mainland, has been a major factor contributing to and preserving the identity of Japanese culture in its relations with its powerful neighbor, China. Studies by linguists, archaeologists, and mythologists, however, have shown the presence of elements from Southeast Asia, Polynesia, and China in the early stages of Japanese cultural development. From China, or via China, the inhabitants of the Japanese archipelago derived their knowledge of wet-rice agriculture, bronze, and iron. Probably introduced by way of the Korean peninsula, these novel technologies spread through much of Japan during the Yayoi period (ca 300 BC–ca AD 300; see YAYOI CULTURE). The widespread adoption of rice agriculture transformed a loosely organized hunting and gathering society into a sedentary, agrarian village society with developing social and political hierarchies. Bronze contributed to the religious and ceremonial aura of local chieftains; iron was used for the blades of agricultural tools and for weapons. Together, these three advanced technologies gave powerful impetus to the development of early Japanese social and political organization. See also HISTORY OF JAPAN: prehistory.

The Ancient Period—— The earliest documentary references to contacts between the inhabitants of the islands of Japan and China are found in dynastic chronicles of China dating from the 1st century AD. (The earliest Japanese chronicles, the KOJIKI and NIHON SHOKI, were compiled only in the 8th century AD, although they purport to relate the history of the ruling dynasty from the age of the gods.) The Chinese chronicles refer to the people of the eastern seas as WA, using a character signifying "dwarf," or as "eastern barbarians" (wa is the Japanese pronunciation; Ch: wo). The earliest accounts refer to 100, that is, very many, "countries" or tribal units in Wa. An entry relating to Wa in the Chinese history Hou Han shu (History of the Later Han Dynasty) for the 2nd century AD describes disorder in Wa and the reimposition of authority by a shaman-queen, HIMIKO, who ruled over 30 countries from her own country of YAMATAI and maintained relations with the Chinese imperial court. The Hou Han shu and WEI ZHI (Wei chih) accounts of the Wa also record that other tribal chieftains were eager to enter into diplomatic relations with China on Chinese terms. According to the Hou Han shu, in AD 57 the king (wang; J: ō—a title given to a recognized tributary ruler in the Chinese international order) of the country of Nu (J: Na) in Wa sent an embassy bearing tribute to China. The embassy was received by Emperor Guangwu (Kuang-wu; r 25–57), who presented it with a golden seal enfeoffing the ruler of Na with the title "king of the state of Na of Wa [Japan], [vassal] of Han." A gold seal identical to the description of the one mentioned in the Han history was found more than 17 centuries later in a field in Kyūshū (see KAN NO WA NO NA NO KOKUŌ NO IN). Scholars now generally accept its authenticity as the one presented by Guangwu. If it is the seal in question, it confirms the accuracy of the Chinese record and indi-cates the extent of Chinese cultural and political influence over Japanese chieftains in the middle Yayoi period.

By the mid-4th century, political unification of tribal units was being pushed forward by a dynasty (see YAMATO COURT) centered in the Yamato region (now Nara Prefecture) at the eastern end of the Inland Sea for whose chieftains huge tomb mounds, or tumuli (KO-FUN) were constructed. Japanese had also secured a foothold on the Korean peninsula (see KAYA) and were actively involved in the struggles among the Korean kingdoms of PAEKCHE, SILLA, and KOGURYŌ for control of the peninsula.

To consolidate their position, Japanese chieftains clearly considered it helpful to have some form of recognition from China. The Chinese history Song shu (Sung shu, History of the Liu–Song Dynasty) mentions FIVE KINGS OF WA who brought tribute and petitioned the Liu–Song court to be confirmed in their rulership of Wa and in their interests on the peninsula. Several of these rulers were granted such titles as "king of Wa" or "great general pacifying the East." Whether these "kings" were rulers of Yamato or merely petty chieftains from northern Kyūshū is still conjectural. The first of them, San, has been identified by some modern scholars with Emperor NINTOKU and by others with Emperor ŌJIN. The reigns of Ōjin and Nintoku, the legendary 15th and 16th sovereigns, are described in detail in the Nihon shoki. Huge keyhole-shaped tumuli on the Yamato Plain bear the names of these early Yamato rulers (see ŌJIN MAUSOLEUM; NINTOKU MAUSOLEUM), but there is no surviving evidence to link them positively to the chieftains who were enfeoffed as kings of Wa, and the relationship is likely to remain a mystery. It is clear, however, that during the 5th century western Japan, perhaps Yamato, was in constant and direct contact with southern China and that the Japanese were operating within the Chinese tribute system and absorbing advanced continental civilization as well as seeking Chinese acquiescence in Japanese activities on the Korean peninsula.

Chinese and Koreans were active in this diffusion of culture into Japan. Unsettled conditions on the Korean peninsula brought to Japan displaced groups of Koreans and Chinese (KIKAJIN). These groups included scribes, potters, weavers, and metalworkers. Many of them were devoted to BUDDHISM and had some knowledge of CONFUCIANISM. Accorded privileges by rulers and great families who were eager to draw on their skills, these immigrants not only introduced new technological expertise in a wide range of skills, they also opened the way for the Japanese adoption of the Chinese writing system, Chinese social and political ideas, and Indian and Chinese religious values.

In 589, after more than four centuries of disunity, China was reunified under the Sui (589–618) and Tang (T'ang; 618–907) dynasties. Under these powerful empires China offered a renewed stimulus to similar efforts at unification, centralization, and cultural development in Korea and Japan.

For Japan, the 6th century was a painful one. Internally, the Yamato court was bitterly divided between rival kin-groups (UJI, here called families for convenience). This struggle was most sharply exposed in the clash between the MONONOBE FAMILY and Nakatomi family on the one hand and the SOGA FAMILY on the other over the question of whether the court should give formal acceptance to Buddhism. The ramifications of the dispute transcended the personal religious beliefs of the Yamato rulers. To traditional-minded families like the Mononobe and Nakatomi, Buddhism was an alien religious system, an advance guard for even greater intrusion of Chinese culture and institutions into the fabric of Japanese society, and a threat to the indigenous SHINTŌ religion.

The victory of the pro-Buddhist, procontinental, and reform-minded Soga family in 587 marked not only the beginning of state patronage and promotion of Buddhism in Japan but also the inauguration of a several-hundred-year period during which Japanese society was reshaped on the model of the Sui and Tang imperial systems. The new reform policies were pressed ahead by Prince SHŌTOKU (574–622), regent for Empress SUIKO (r 593–628), and SOGA NO UMAKO (d 626). The Chinese calendar (see CALENDAR, DATES, AND TIME) was adopted and a revised system of Chinese COURT RANKS instituted. Shōtoku has also been given credit for the promulgation of the SEVENTEEN-ARTICLE CONSTITUTION, a code of conduct for government officials based on Confucian and Legalist principles, and for the compilation of the earliest national histories (TENNŌKI AND KOKKI), although the latter do not survive. With Soga no Umako, Shōtoku worked to consolidate the position of Buddhism as spiritual protector of the state. Temples were built, Buddhism was given a prominent position in the Seventeen-Article

Constitution, and commentaries on the sutras, some of them attributed to Prince Shōtoku himself, were issued. The drive behind these reforms involved more than shallow imitation of Sui institutions. Shōtoku has been revered for giving added dignity to the Yamato rulers by setting them at the apex of a centralized, sinified, and more impressive court hierarchy. He may also have been seeking to restore Japanese pride and compensate for recent Japanese reverses on the Korean peninsula by strengthening the country and establishing close diplomatic and cultural relations with Sui China.

To sustain the reforms, five embassies were dispatched to Sui between 600 and 614 (see SUI AND TANG [T'ANG] CHINA, EMBASSIES TO). The embassies included monks and scholars, some of whom returned immediately to Japan and reported on institutions and conditions in China while others remained in China, some for as long as 20 years. Shōtoku has always been given credit for asserting Japan's national dignity in his diplomatic relations with China. ONO NO IMOKO, the leader of the 607 embassy, bore a letter addressed by "the Son of Heaven in the land where the sun rises" to "the Son of Heaven in the land where the sun sets." According to Chinese records, the Sui emperor was angered by this impertinent form of address on the part of a barbarian tributary. The fact that missions from Japan continued to be received by the Sui, and later the Tang, court and that Shōtoku does not seem to have pressed the issue in subsequent correspondence suggests that Japanese assertiveness may have been the unintended result of diplomatic inexperience. Whether by accident or design, however, Shōtoku had inscribed in the documentary record and in the historical consciousness of the Japanese people a declaration of independence of, and equality with, imperial China.

Monks and scholars who had been on one or another of the missions to Sui China played important roles as informants in the early years of a second surge of Tang-inspired innovation initiated with the TAIKA REFORM of 645. During the ensuing century Japan was transformed. Chinese administrative and penal institutions (the RITSURYŌ SYSTEM) were adopted, the country divided into provinces governed by officials (KOKUSHI) dispatched from the court, a census carried out, and a land allotment system (HANDEN SHŪJU SYSTEM) and tax system (SO, YŌ, AND CHŌ) instituted. In 710 a new capital, HEIJŌKYŌ (now the city of Nara), was established, a smaller version of the Chinese capital. The Japanese ruler, now referred to as tennō (heavenly sovereign), was invested with all the trappings of Chinese imperial dignity and provided with an elaborate bureaucracy staffed by court nobles. Chinese influence was also strongly felt in religious, intellectual, and cultural life. Buddhist monasteries proliferated, and new teachings and texts were introduced. Major provincial monasteries (KOKUBUNJI) were linked in a nationwide network under the leadership of TŌDAIJI in Heijōkyō and their spiritual energies harnessed to the spiritual protection of the state and the imperial family. Chinese styles of architecture, sculpture, painting, and music were adopted, and the Japanese courtly elite devoted themselves to study of the Chinese classics, poetry, and history. Remains of grid-shaped field patterns (see JŌRI SYSTEM) in western and central Japan, the surviving treasures of temples like HŌRYŪJI and Tōdaiji, the objects from China and the SILK ROAD belonging to the SHŌSŌIN collection, Japan's earliest official histories (see RIKKOKU-SHI), and the poetry of the KAIFŪSŌ all provide eloquent testimony to the powerful influence of Tang China on 7th- and 8th-century Japan.

As with Shōtoku's reforms, the post-Taika reforms were based on direct observation of Chinese institutions. Between 630 and 838 the Japanese court sent at least 15 embassies to China. The largest of these included 4 vessels and as many as 600 men. Among the voyagers were the scholar KIBI NO MAKIBI and the monks SAICHŌ, KŪKAI, and ENNIN. Kibi, a court official, made two visits to China, on the first of which he stayed for nearly 20 years. He brought back with him to Japan Chinese views and texts on Confucianism, Buddhism, astronomy, divination, civil administration, and military organization. A brilliantly painted scroll dating from early in the Kamakura period (1185–1333), the Kibi Daijin nittō ekotoba, illustrates his legendary exploits as a heroic representative of Japan triumphantly overcoming, with the aid of Japanese divinities (kami), the attempts of Chinese scholars and officials to humiliate him in tests of Chinese cultural expertise. Although painted at a time when the full flood of borrowing from China had subsided, the Kibi scroll can still be taken as an expression of the mixed feelings of inferiority and assertiveness that were inherent in Japan's cultural dependence on China.

In 784 Emperor KAMMU, to free the imperial house from the influence of overweening courtiers and politically ambitious Bud-

dhist prelates, ordered that a new capital should be established. Ten years later the move to HEIANKYŌ (now the city of Kyōto) was completed. Larger than Heijōkyō, Heiankyō too was built on the model of the Chinese capital. Although the great Nara monasteries were forbidden to move to Heiankyō, Saichō was permitted to establish the monastery ENRYAKUJI on Mt. Hiei (HIEIZAN) to the northeast of the new capital. There he introduced the TENDAI SECT (Ch: Tiantai or T'ien-t'ai) teachings and monastic practices he had learned in China. With its emphasis on the supreme efficacy of the LOTUS SUTRA and a vigorous, regulated monastic life, Tendai quickly became the most powerful school of Japanese Heian Buddhism. Although its influence was confined mainly to the clerical world and the narrow circle of the Heian aristocracy, Tendai was later to provide the womb for ZEN and popular devotional Buddhism. Under the patronage of Emperor SAGA, Kūkai introduced esoteric SHINGON SECT teachings via the monasteries Kyōō Gokokuji (TŌJI) in Kyōto and KONGŌBUJI on Mt. Kōya (KŌYASAN) in what is now Wakayama Prefecture. Kūkai's esoteric doctrine and the tantric symbolism accompanying it were so attractive to monks and laymen that they rapidly infiltrated Tendai monasteries and won many adherents at court. At least some of the esotericization of Tendai Buddhism can be attributed to Ennin, a disciple of Saichō who traveled widely in China before assuming the leadership of Enryakuji. Ennin has left for posterity a detailed diary of his pilgrimages in China. Entitled Nittō guhō junrei kōki (Records of a Pilgrimage to China in Search of the Law), it conveys the grandeur and cosmopolitan quality of Tang civilization while revealing the Chinese Buddhist institution both at its apogee and in persecution. Although most of the knowledge of China transmitted during these centuries was conveyed by Japanese scholars and monks, there were Chinese who accompanied missions returning to Japan. The monk GANJIN, for instance, after several shipwrecks and the loss of his sight eventually reached Japan to establish the RITSU SECT (Ch: Lü) and the monastery TŌSHŌDAIJI.

The reform effort that ran through the Nara (710–794) and early Heian (794–1185) periods reshaped Japanese society and brought an immeasurable increase in the level of sophistication of administrative practice and cultural activity. Japan was not, however, turned into a mere small-scale replica of China. Some of the deepest recesses of Japanese social and spiritual life proved remarkably resistant to sinification. The acceptance of Buddhism and Confucianism did not lead, as the Mononobe family leaders had feared, to the eradication of the indigenous devotion to the ancestral or natural kami. Shintō was able to coexist with Buddhism as the Japanese deities were made into local manifestations of Buddhas and bodhisattvas. Shintō ceremonies remained a vital part of court and aristocratic family observances, and a ministry of Shintō ritual retained a prominent place within the Chinese-style government structure. In another area, the Japanese did not create a bureaucracy based on merit as defined by performance in a nationwide examination system. The officials who staffed the ritsuryō government continued to be drawn from the hereditary court nobility. Higher education in the classics was provided for the children of the nobility, but birth rather than scholastic attainment determined their social and political role. There was in ancient Japan, therefore, no self-sustaining bureaucracy capable of defusing family rivalries around the imperial throne or checking the accumulation of power by the FUJIWARA FAMILY. Further, the nationalization of all agricultural lands and the taxation of all peasants were never enforced as thoroughly as the legal codes would suggest. Much of the old aristocracy of powerful kin-groups remained firmly entrenched in the provinces, retaining its local authority under the veneer of Chinese institutions. Finally, as the poetic anthology MAN'YŌSHŪ indicates, Japanese poets of many different social levels were capable of fashioning the unwieldy Chinese characters into expressions of Japanese sentiments, styles, and themes (see POETRY AND PROSE IN CHINESE).

By the close of the 9th century, society and economy in Japan were obviously departing from the Chinese model of centralized political control in the direction of private and personalized relationships of the kind that had characterized Japan in the earlier period. As the Chinese-style land and tax systems, provincial administration, and military organization were eroded or modified, and as Buddhism, Confucianism, and Chinese learning and culture took on their own pattern of development in Japan, new borrowing from the continent seemed less urgent to the Japanese. Institutions that a century before had smacked strongly of Chinese influence were now regarded by the elite as thoroughly Japanese. The court nobility felt freer to depart from Chinese models and to respond to problems in a more eclectic manner. The shift of interest from China was encouraged by reports of dynastic decline and social disorder. The obvious weakening of the Tang empire convinced Japanese officials that the hazards of the voyages were no longer worth the benefits that might accrue from them. SUGAWARA NO MICHIZANE's refusal to lead an embassy to China in 894 was based on reports of turmoil there. This action ended official contacts between Japan and China for several centuries.

Although official missions to China had been halted, Chinese influences on Japan had not been entirely eliminated. An occasional Chinese vessel came to Kyūshū to trade, and Japanese monks went privately to China. While court ladies like MURASAKI SHIKIBU and SEI SHŌNAGON were using the newly developed KANA syllabaries to create a brilliant vernacular literature, the court nobility continued to conduct official business in Chinese, to delight in study of the Chinese classics, and to prize Chinese art objects (karamono).

The Medieval Period (13th–16th Centuries)——The warriors (bushi), who asserted increasing military and political control from the 12th century, displayed considerable interest in the cultural and commercial benefits of contact with China. TAIRA NO KIYO-MORI, realizing that there were profits to be made from trade with the Southern Song (Sung) dynasty (1127–1279), built port facilities in Hyōgo Bay (Ōwada no Tomari) and cleared the Inland Sea of pirates. Swords, sulfur, and alluvial gold dust provided export items for which Chinese merchants traded textiles, incense, art objects, and copper cash.

The HŌJŌ FAMILY, who controlled the warrior government of the KAMAKURA SHOGUNATE (1192–1333) as regents, were also eager to maintain at least private contacts with Song China. Commerce was centered in Hakata (now Fukuoka) and regulated by a shogunate official, the commissioner for Kyūshū (Chinzei bugyō). The Hōjō and their leading warrior retainers developed a passion for Chinese art objects, the acquisition of which, they believed, gave them a measure of cultural éclat. Although the Nara court, in imitation of Tang China, had minted coins (WADŌ KAIHŌ), these had never circulated widely or contributed to the development of a coinage-based economy. The Song copper cash (SŌSEN) imported to Japan during the 13th century, however, circulated in sufficient quantities to help stimulate the growth of limited commercial and market activity. This development was not entirely welcome to the Hōjō regents as feudal overlords, since it had a destabilizing impact on provincial warriors, many of whom went into debt, mortgaged or sold their lands, and were consequently unable to meet their feudal military and service obligations.

The Hōjō became much more enthusiastic about another import from Song China: Zen Buddhism. Song-style RINZAI SECT and SŌTŌ SECT Zen teachings were introduced to Japan by EISAI, DŌGEN, and other Japanese Zen pioneers and, from the mid-13th century, by a score of émigré Zen masters led by Lanqi Daolong (Lan-ch'i Taolung; J: RANKEI DŌRYŪ). A few nobles and provincial warriors displayed an early interest in the novel Chinese meditative teachings, but it was due largely to Hōjō patronage and example that Rinzai Zen was able to establish an independent sectarian identity and become one of the most influential branches of Japanese Buddhism. Meditation, or zazen, was at the core of Zen monastic and lay practice, but the newly built Zen monasteries, especially the Rinzai GO-ZAN (Five Mountains or Five Temples) group in Kamakura and Kyōto, were also outposts of Chinese culture. They served as channels through which Chinese and Japanese Zen masters introduced to medieval Japan the whole range of Song literati cultural interests, including CALLIGRAPHY, INK PAINTING and PORTRAIT PAINTING, Neo-Confucian ideas of social and political order, and new styles in monastic and domestic architecture, as well as Zen vegetarian cuisine and the monastic TEA CEREMONY (see also GOZAN LITERATURE). This influx of Chinese culture in the 13th century widened the intellectual horizons of Japanese warriors and nobles and enriched Japanese culture, especially elite culture.

The destruction of the Song empire and the conquest of South China by the Mongols in the late 13th century brought Japan face-to-face for probably the first time in its history with the imminent threat of foreign invasion and conquest. Having secured control over China and Korea, Khubilai Khan bent his energies on the subjugation of Japan. From 1268, envoys were sent to Japan demanding tributary submission to Mongol hegemony. The natural disinclination of Japan's warrior rulers to yield to foreign threats was stiffened by Chinese Zen monks in Japan, some of whom were ardent Song loyalists. Japanese rejection of Mongol diplomatic pressures brought the ill-fated invasion attempts in 1274 and 1281 (see MONGOL INVASIONS OF JAPAN). Large fleets carrying Mongol and conscripted Korean and Chinese forces were repelled by Japanese warriors and destroyed in timely storms, or, as the Japanese thought

of them, "divine winds" (kamikaze). While the invasion fever was at its peak, although Japanese attention was focused on the continent, direct contact was severely curtailed. By the end of the 13th century, however, although a third invasion attempt was still rumored, monks and merchants had resumed their interrupted contacts with China.

The MUROMACHI SHOGUNATE (1338–1573), whose founder, ASHIKAGA TAKAUJI, had toppled the Kamakura shogunate in 1333 and then ousted his erstwhile ally Emperor GO-DAIGO to establish a warrior regime, adopted a generally positive policy toward diplomatic, cultural, and commercial relations with China. This interest was partly reciprocated by the early emperors of the Ming dynasty (1368–1644). In 1341 ASHIKAGA TADAYOSHI, the powerful younger brother of Takauji, encouraged the dispatch of a trading mission to raise funds for the building of the Zen monastery Tenryūji (see TENRYŪJI-BUNE). Relations with China, however, were taken to an extreme by the powerful third shōgun, ASHIKAGA YOSHIMITSU.

Yoshimitsu won the favor of the Ming emperors by curbing the activities of the freebooters, or "Japanese pirates" (WAKŌ), who infested the coastal waters of East Asia. Knowing that tribute sent to China was always reciprocated with even more lavish gifts by the Chinese emperors and believing that the Chinese imperial aura would add to the prestige of the shogunal office, Yoshimitsu in 1401 sent the monk Soa and a Hakata merchant named Koizumi to request diplomatic and commercial relations with Ming China. Yoshimitsu was properly deferential in his approach, and the Chinese emperor responded favorably. The shōgun was recognized by the Ming court as "king of Japan" (Nihon kokuō) and used this tributary designation in his diplomatic correspondence with the Chinese court. Vessels bearing tribute were permitted to enter Chinese ports for trade and, to distinguish these official Japanese missions from the marauding ventures of the wakō, the shogunate was given a set of tallies by the Chinese authorities. Only vessels bearing tallies matching those retained by the Chinese authorities were permitted to trade (see TALLY TRADE).

Yoshimitsu dispatched the first embassy under these terms in 1404; five more were sent by 1410. After an examination of their credentials at the port of Ningbo (Ningpo), the missions proceeded north to Beijing (Peking) for the exchange of tribute gifts, diplomatic courtesies, and trade goods. Since the missions were regarded by the Chinese as tribute-bearing embassies, all costs in China were defrayed by the imperial treasury. In return for Japanese copper, sulfur, gold, swords, fans, screens, and lacquer ware, the missions yielded copper coins, silk and cotton yarn, high-quality silk fabrics, and fine porcelains. Initially the traffic was controlled by the shogunate, which invited the great Zen temples and favored merchants to participate. Zen monks handled the diplomatic correspondence, acted as translators and consultants on conditions in China, and led the expeditions. Kyōto Zen monasteries, especially Tenryūji and SHŌKOKUJI, as well as the shogunate, derived considerable income from the early missions.

This unusually close relationship with China was very much Yoshimitsu's doing. His motivation was complex. There was certainly a streak of sinophilia in his makeup. He was a generous patron of Zen monasteries and well versed in Song thought. The so-called Golden Pavilion (KINKAKUJI), which he built as a private retreat in the northern hills of Kyōto, was a brilliant blending of Chinese with indigenous aesthetic elements. Yoshimitsu was an avid collector of Chinese works of art. He liked to wear Chinese dress and hold lavish Chinese banquets. On occasion, he stated, the Chinese emperor visited him in his dreams. But there was much more to Yoshimitsu's interest than mere adulation of things Chinese. He skillfully used the panoply of ceremonial pomp accompanying the dispatch and reception of missions to enhance shogunal dignity in his dealings with the imperial court and powerful daimyō. Moreover, the commercial benefits of the relationship were particularly important to the Ashikaga shōguns, whose landed resources were meager. The luxury goods coming from China could be sold at a good profit or used to secure political support. Ming coins (KŌBU-SEN; EIRAKUSEN) went into circulation, further contributing to commercial development, which the shōguns tried, not always very successfully, to tax. Yoshimitsu was also reflecting a growing eagerness for foreign trade and cultural contact with China on the part of Japanese merchants, western daimyō, and Zen temples.

Yoshimitsu's pragmatic acceptance of the title "king of Japan" earned him censure in his own day and since. Critics from the imperial court claimed that by using the appellation Nihon kokuō Yoshimitsu was both infringing on imperial prerogatives and placing

Japan in a subordinate relationship to China. Ashikaga Yoshimochi (1386–1428; r 1395–1423), the fourth shōgun, broke off the relationship with the Ming on the grounds that it was demeaning to Japan's national honor. The missions were reinstated by ASHIKAGA YOSHINORI in an effort to bring some relief to increasingly straitened shogunal finances. Between 1433 and 1547, 11 embassies were dispatched in a combined total of some 50 vessels. After Yoshinori's assassination in 1441, however, the authority of the shogunate waned, and with it central control over the tally trade, which came to be dominated in the late 15th century by the ŌUCHI and HOSOKAWA daimyō families of western Japan and the HAKATA MERCHANTS and SAKAI MERCHANTS whom they patronized. In an armed incident in Ningbo in 1523, Ōuchi forces bested their rivals, the Hosokawa, and secured monopoly control of the trade, which continued until their destruction in 1551. In its later phases the relationship became unsatisfactory to the Ming court. Although the Japanese warrior families presented the proper tallies, they were clearly not rulers with whom the Chinese emperors could maintain a tributary relationship. They came seeking only trade, and their visits brought disorder in their wake. Moreover, from the mid-15th century, early Ming interest in maritime activity had given way to growing concern about Mongol pressures on the northern land frontier along the Great Wall. With the exception of those Chinese merchants who had profited from the relationship, few can have expressed regret when vessels bearing tallies ceased to come from Japan in the 16th century.

The ending of the tally trade marked the end of an era in Japanese cultural development. Muromachi-period culture had fed on the China trade and the Zen monks who were so actively involved in it. Chinese models in architecture, interior and garden design, aesthetics, painting, and calligraphy—as transmitted through Zen monasteries—had stimulated the creative talents of men like the dramatist ZEAMI and the painter SESSHŪ TŌYŌ (see also HIGASHIYAMA CULTURE). By the beginning of the 16th century these cultural interests had spread from Zen monasteries into secular society in the provinces. Merchants in Hakata and Sakai competed with daimyō in collecting Chinese books and objects of art and in entertaining Zen monks and men of culture. Yamaguchi, the Ōuchi stronghold in western Japan, prospered commercially and culturally from the China trade and became one of several "little Kyōtos" that developed during this period. As the Chinese cultural surge spread beyond the cloisters of Zen monasteries, its Chinese tone was modulated with Japanese strains as it blended into the rich wave of Muromachi culture.

But even as the last tally mission was setting out for China, new political and cultural horizons were opening in Japan. In 1543 the first Europeans, some Portuguese seamen, came ashore on the island of Tanegashima. Their arrival ushered in nearly a century of Western trading and religious and cultural interaction with Japan, diverting at least some attention from China and drawing Japan into a wider international context. One year earlier ODA NOBUNAGA, the warrior who would overthrow the failing Muromachi shogunate, reimpose some measure of unity and order on a country afflicted by provincial warfare, and promote Christianity as a counter to the influence of institutional Buddhism, had held his coming-of-age ceremony. Ceaseless campaigning in Japan, coupled with an active involvement with Western technology and culture, left Nobunaga little opportunity for furthering relations with China.

Under Nobunaga's successor, TOYOTOMI HIDEYOSHI, diplomatic relations between Japan and China reached their lowest point in premodern times. In 1592 Hideyoshi, frustrated by Korean refusal to offer tribute to Japan and allow passage for Japanese troops and vessels to attack Ming China, dispatched an army of 150,000 warriors to the continent (see INVASIONS OF KOREA IN 1592 AND 1597). His aim was to make himself master of East Asia by subjugating Korea and destroying the Ming. The invasion plan reflected Hideyoshi's megalomania, but it was more than a fantastic dream. By extending his conquests to the continent, he hoped to divert warrior energies from opposition to his policies in Japan, to provide spoils for his retainers, and to create trading opportunities for merchants, whom he sponsored and taxed heavily for their privileges.

In the face of stiff opposition by Korean forces and Ming armies sent to the aid of a beleaguered tributary, Hideyoshi's generals were forced to engage in peace negotiations in 1596. Hideyoshi laid seven demands before the Ming negotiators, including cession to Japan of Korea's four southern circuits, revival of the tally trade with the Ming, the sending of a Ming princess as a consort for the emperor of Japan, and the sending of Korean princes and ministers as hostages. The Ming government dismissed Hideyoshi's demands and re-

sponded by reasserting the traditional tributary relationship. A Ming envoy brought a document enfeoffing Hideyoshi as "king of Japan" but ignoring his seven demands. Furious, Hideyoshi ordered his armies to resume fighting in Korea. They had little hope of overthrowing the Ming but fought for territory in the peninsula to be used as spoils for Japanese warriors, who so far had nothing to show for their efforts.

Hideyoshi's death in 1598 ended the bitter and fruitless continental wars. All three parties had suffered. Much of Korea had been laid waste, whole villages wiped out, and thousands sent as captives to Japan. In the sense that the Japanese invaders had been forced eventually to withdraw, the Korean people were able to claim a victory. But it was a victory that had been bought at a terrible cost, and their rulers had been mere spectators to the negotiations between Japan and China. For the Ming government, too, the cost in men and money had been heavy. While a serious invasion threat had been repulsed and dynastic honor demonstrated in the defense of a close tributary, the defense effort further weakened a dynasty already beset with problems on other frontiers. For the Japanese, the expedition had been a military disaster. Far from strengthening his domestic position, the inconclusive Korean wars fed dissatisfaction with Hideyoshi's regime in Japan. Behind them, the returning Japanese armies left a legacy of suspicion and enmity. For Japan the only gains from the ill-fated expeditions were cultural by-products of attempted conquest. Among the prisoners of war brought to Japan were Korean scholars and craftsmen. As a result of the invasions, new techniques in movable-type printing, ceramics, and agriculture were introduced to Japan. The famous kilns of Arita, Karatsu, Imari, Satsuma, and Hagi, for instance, were all by-products of Hideyoshi's challenge to Ming supremacy.

The Edo Period (1600–1868) —— TOKUGAWA IEYASU, who rapidly asserted his military supremacy after Hideyoshi's death and established the Tokugawa shogunate (1603–1867), sought to ease the strained relationship with China and Korea. He was particularly eager to reopen official trading relations with Ming China. The Ming emperors and later their successors, the Manchu emperors of the Qing (Ch'ing) dynasty (1644–1912), however, enforced a maritime embargo and refused to enter into official relations with the Tokugawa shogunate. What he could not obtain officially Ieyasu was quite willing to secure privately. Throughout most of the 16th century Chinese merchants had been willing to flout their government's embargo and trade in Japanese ports, especially for silver, a commodity that was becoming plentiful in 16th-century Japan and was much in demand in China. In 1611 Ieyasu encouraged Chinese merchants to trade in Nagasaki. By 1630 there were several thousand Chinese residents in that city, a Chinese community with its own temples and markets had taken shape, and Chinese junks regularly entered the harbor. Moreover, a vigorous entrepôt trade between Japanese and Chinese merchants was being carried on in the Ryūkyū Islands, Taiwan, Luzon, and as far afield as Siam (see VERMILION SEAL SHIP TRADE).

While Ieyasu and his immediate successors were tolerant of the commercial activities of the Chinese community, they were growing increasingly hostile to the Iberian missionary effort in Japan and disposed to sacrifice trade with Western countries in order to eradicate what they perceived as a Christian threat to social and political order. In 1639 Portuguese vessels were prohibited from visiting Japan, and Japanese were forbidden to build ocean-going vessels or to travel abroad. For the ensuing two centuries Japan's cultural and commercial contacts with the outside world were restricted to those via the Dutch and Chinese communities in Nagasaki and the periodic embassies from Korea. It should be noted that the so-called NATIONAL SECLUSION (Sakoku, or "closed country") policy was directed most firmly at Western countries, especially the Catholic West. During this period Japan was less tightly sealed off from contact with, and influence from, China and Korea; but, in contrast with earlier periods, Japanese officials, monks, merchants, and scholars were no longer free to visit the continent to seek learning or profit. Those interested in the outside world were limited to the trickle of goods and information that seeped into Japan through Nagasaki.

In 1644 the Ming dynasty, after bitter resistance, was overthrown by the Manchus. The Ming emperors had called upon the Tokugawa for support but the shogunate, although sympathetic, declined, and it also ignored pleas from the Ming loyalist ZHENG CHENGGONG (Cheng Ch'eng-kung, or "Koxinga"), who held out on Taiwan. Dynastic change in China did not impede private trade with Japan. After 1635, Chinese merchants were restricted to Nagasaki. For most of the 17th century, in contrast to the dozen or so Dutch trading vessels that might visit Japan in a good year, between 30 and 115 Chinese merchant junks might sail into Nagasaki Bay (see NAGASAKI TRADE). The Chinese ships brought silks, cotton goods, spices, medicines, hides, and books. These were traded for lacquer and iron goods, marine products, copper, gold, and silver. Before the end of the century the trade had reached such proportions that the shogunate felt obliged to regulate it and to limit the outflow of silver. In 1685, imports by Chinese vessels were limited to a total annual value of 6,000 kan (1 kan=3.75 kg or 8.27 lb) of silver. In 1688 the shogunate ordered that no more than 70 Chinese vessels might enter Nagasaki each year and that the Chinese residents of the city, who had thitherto lived where they pleased, should be confined to a designated Chinese quarter. Further restrictions were imposed on the Nagasaki trade in 1715 by the shogunal adviser ARAI HAKUSEKI in an effort to reduce the continuing drain of precious metals. Although the number of Chinese ships visiting Nagasaki dwindled to fewer than 25 a year by the mid-18th century, private commercial contact with China was maintained throughout the Edo period.

During the Edo period, it was in the intellectual realm that Chinese influence upon Japan was exerted most powerfully. Although Japanese samurai scholars were denied the opportunity to visit China and depended for their knowledge on the flow of Chinese books into Nagasaki, their reverence for, and application of, Chinese learning was a major element in a secular intellectual flowering unmatched in any previous period of Japanese history.

A harmonious political order based on Song-dynasty Neo-Confucian ideas of family and social hierarchy, as expounded by HAYASHI RAZAN and his followers, appealed strongly to the Tokugawa shōguns as an ideological buttress for their political control system. The function of the samurai elite in Tokugawa society was enhanced by association with the Chinese Confucian scholar-official, the shi (shih). YAMAGA SOKŌ, a student of Hayashi Razan's, blended Chinese Confucian moral virtues with traditional Japanese warrior values to formulate BUSHIDŌ, a more systematized and Confucianized version of the warrior code in which samurai, who were being steadily transformed from fighting men into administrators and functionaries, were encouraged to give selfless loyalty to their overlords. The strong agrarian emphasis in Neo-Confucian thought found expression in the Tokugawa status hierarchy, in which the peasantry, as producers of rice and taxes, ranked second to samurai in importance while the merchants were given the lowest status, one that bore little relationship to their growing influence within Tokugawa society.

Song Neo-Confucian teachings of the Zhu Xi (Chu Hsi; 1130–1200) tradition (SHUSHIGAKU) were not the only variety of Confucianism to stimulate Edo-period thinkers. On occasion the shogunate issued bans against heterodox teachings, i.e., Confucian schools critical of the Zhu Xi synthesis. Orthodoxy was impossible to enforce, however, since, unlike China, Japan did not have a nationwide civil-service examination system, and the daimyō were often willing to patronize "heterodox" Confucian scholars who could not find employment with the shogunate. In Japan, as in China, Zhu Xi's philosophy was repudiated by scholars who insisted on the authenticity of pre-Song classical sources. Yamaga Sokō, mentioned above, rejected Neo-Confucian metaphysics toward the end of his life. ITŌ JINSAI and his followers went back to the Confucian Analects for inspiration, while OGYŪ SORAI, one of Japan's most accomplished sinologues, found in the earlier Six Classics the purest repository of the Confucian Way. The ideas of Wang Yangming (1472–1528), who had criticized Zhu Xi for failing to pay due attention to man's intuitive understanding of his own moral nature and the need to carry this intuitive understanding through into the activities and relationships of everyday life, were expounded in Japan by NAKAE TŌJU and other scholars (see YŌMEIGAKU).

Chinese Confucian studies thus provided the bedrock for the bulk of samurai philosophical speculation, scholarship, and political thought in the Edo period. They also contributed to a more critical interest in Japan's own past and its unique political structure of ruling shōgun and reigning emperor. Eventually, as Western pressure on Japan mounted in the early 19th century, this interest would undercut both Chinese intellectual supremacy and shogunal political authority. Hayashi Razan began work on a history of Japan that was completed by his son under the title Honchō tsugan (1670, Mirror of the Japanese Dynasty) and accepted as an official history by the shogunate. It was written in Chinese, based on Chinese models, and reflected a Confucian rationalist attitude to the past. The statesman and scholar Arai Hakuseki was also devoted to historical inquiry and

is noted for his concern for evidence and his skepticism toward traditional beliefs.

Ultimately more subversive of the position of the shogunate was the DAI NIHON SHI (History of Great Japan), which was begun in the 17th century under the sponsorship of TOKUGAWA MITSUKUNI, lord of the Mito domain (now part of Ibaraki Prefecture). The Dai Nihon shi incorporated many of the attitudes of the Chinese émigré scholar and Ming loyalist Zhu Shunshui (Chu Shun-shui; J: SHU SHUNSUI, 1600–1682). Confucian moral values and loyalism to the Japanese imperial house permeated the writing. As long as the Tokugawa shogunate retained unchallenged political supremacy as the loyal interpreter and executor of the imperial will, Mito historiography was merely a reinforcement of the prevailing political order in Japan. When, however, the shogunate stumbled during the foreign crisis of the 1850s and its right to rule was challenged, the Dai Nihon shi provided an obvious means of legitimation for emperor-centered nationalism and a source of antishogunal polemic in the movement that culminated in the MEIJI RESTORATION of 1868.

Chinese influence on Tokugawa society was not restricted to the realms of philosophical and historical enquiry. Medical texts, agricultural manuals, herbals, and treatises on astronomy and technology were imported and disseminated. Motifs from Ming- and Qing-dynasty stories found their way into Tokugawa literature, while themes from Chinese art and mythology emerged in the Japanese prints of the floating world (UKIYO-E). Ming-dynasty Zen Buddhism was introduced to Japan in 1654 by the monk Yinyuan (Yin-yüan; J: INGEN), who enjoyed shogunal patronage and established the temple MAMPUKUJI at Uji. Modeled on his home temple, Mampukuji became the center of the flourishing ŌBAKU SECT of Zen. Ōbaku Zen served as both a positive and a negative stimulus to Japanese Buddhists. Many monks and laymen were attracted by the syncretic Ming Zen, which incorporated the practices of PURE LAND BUDDHISM within the traditional Zen monastic framework. Those monks of the older Zen schools in Japan who rejected Ōbaku syncretism were challenged to restore some vitality to Rinzai and Sōtō practice. Culturally, Ōbaku monasteries served as centers for the diffusion of Ming and Qing styles in calligraphy, portraiture, painting, sculpture, and architecture.

Thus, while the Edo period is generally thought of as a time of vernacular and popular cultural development, the influence of Chinese learning and culture has to be reckoned with in almost every sphere of activity. And, while much of this Chinese influence was felt most strongly in the elite sector of society, some did reach a wider audience. The popular SHINGAKU ("Heart Learning") doctrine, for instance, taught that one could know heaven by knowing one's own true nature and that this nature, or heart, could only be known by the elimination of selfishness through the stern practice of such Confucian virtues as loyalty, filial piety, diligence, and thrift. The Chinese classics were incorporated into the curriculum of samurai education in the proliferating domain schools and even into the more rudimentary education given to commoners in the village schools, or TERAKOYA. In a more practical sphere, improvements in husbandry and agricultural technology made during the Edo period owed much to information derived from Chinese manuals. See EDUCATION: Edo-period education.

Not surprisingly, dependence on Chinese learning created tensions in Japanese intellectual circles. Scholars became increasingly aware of the anomaly of using Chinese ideas, often from classical texts, to explain Japanese phenomena. Some also recognized that extreme sinophilia could involve a conflict of loyalties with Japanese traditions. The devoted Neo-Confucian scholar YAMAZAKI ANSAI was one of the first to express this tension. When asked what he would do if Confucius and Mencius were to lead a Chinese invasion of Japan, he replied that he would capture them and put them to the service of his own land. Ansai went on to develop an eclectic blend of Confucian and Shintō thought.

During the 18th century, Japanese questioning of Chinese intellectual leadership went further. Interest in Japan's past, much of it stimulated by Chinese example, led to a new appreciation of Japanese culture and the Shintō tradition. MOTOORI NORINAGA, and scholars of the National Learning (KOKUGAKU) school, argued that the pure emotional perceptions mirrored in ancient Japanese myths and literature were truer guides to human understanding and behavior than Chinese Confucian moralizing and rationalization. Other scholars, a small but growing group, looked not to ancient China or Japan for learning but to the West, as represented by the Dutch in Nagasaki. Dedicated scholars laboriously translated Dutch books on geography, medicine, astronomy, and other sciences (see WESTERN

LEARNING). As the threat from the West mounted in the late 18th and early 19th centuries, some of these scholars, at great personal risk, turned their attention to military and strategic studies, a course that quickly led them afoul of the shogunate's seclusion policy.

By the 1860s, with China's military weakness exposed by defeat in the Opium War and Japan itself threatened with subjugation by the treaty demands of the United States and the Western powers, Chinese learning and example seemed to many Japanese scholars and officials to be increasingly irrelevant. Most of the slogans of the day stressed reliance on the Japanese spirit and traditions, stiffened with Western technological expertise.

The Meiji Period (1868–1912) —— Relations between the new Meiji government and the Qing empire in the late 19th and early 20th centuries began well but deteriorated rapidly through minor clashes over Okinawa and Taiwan to all-out war over Korea. While the Manchu government struggled to cope in traditional ways with foreign intrusion and domestic uprisings, the Meiji oligarchs set Japan on a modernizing course that brought national unification and burgeoning industrial and military strength. The Meiji leaders aimed at securing Japan's release from the Unequal Treaties (see UNEQUAL TREATIES, REVISION OF) by showing that the country was an equal of the Western powers. Internally this meant the adoption of Western institutions and the pursuit of a policy of FUKOKU KYŌ-HEI ("Enriching the Country and Strengthening the Military," an ancient Chinese phrase). In the international arena this drive developed into a policy of imperialism that could succeed only at the expense of traditional Chinese claims to supremacy in East Asia.

Relations between the Meiji government and the Qing dynasty began on a friendly footing. Among the first actions of the Restoration leaders in 1868 was the dispatch of an envoy to China to announce the inauguration of the new imperial government and request treaty relations. Some Chinese officials, including the influential minister LI HONGZHANG (Li Hung-chang), argued that efforts should be made to befriend Japan to keep it out of the orbit of the Western powers and, if possible, to harness its energies in joint resistance to Western intrusion in East Asia. A treaty of friendship signed between the two governments in 1871 instituted diplomatic representation, low tariff rates, and extraterritorial privileges for citizens of both countries. Unlike treaties made with the Western powers, the treaty of friendship did not contain a "most favored nation clause" demanding that rights granted to other nations be automatically accorded to the other signatories. It was, therefore, an equal treaty which, for the first time in history, set Sino-Japanese relations on a mutually recognized even footing. The treaty of 1871 remained in force until the SINO-JAPANESE WAR OF 1894–1895. But it had hardly been signed when tensions developed in the relationship between the two countries.

The first crisis sprang from Japanese designs on the Ryūkyū Islands, of which OKINAWA was the largest, and on TAIWAN. Throughout the Edo period the Satsuma domain had exercised effective control over Okinawa, which the Ming and Qing governments had continued to regard as a tributary kingdom. The Meiji leaders sought to extend Japanese control over the Ryūkyūs in 1871 by declaring them to be a domain (han) under direct control of Japan, with their king as a satellite chieftain (see RYŪKYŪ KIZOKU MONDAI). Qing and Ryukyuan protests were ignored.

Having laid claim to sovereignty over Okinawa, the Japanese government used this as a lever to force its claims on Taiwan. In adopting a forward policy on Taiwan those in control of the new government were trying to mollify critics who were pressing for a large-scale Korean expedition. A military campaign against Korea would, the leaders argued, antagonize the Western powers as well as China and jeopardize Japan's domestic reform policies. Probing the strength of Chinese control over Taiwan seemed a safer outlet for samurai energies. A pretext for the expedition was not hard to find. In 1871 Okinawan fishermen had been killed by aborigines on Taiwan, and in 1873 some fishermen from Okayama Prefecture suffered a similar fate. Protesting these affronts to "subjects of Japan," the Meiji goverment launched the punitive TAIWAN EXPEDITION OF 1874, demanding that the Qing government pay compensation for the lost lives and bear the costs of the expedition. With British intervention a settlement was eventually reached whereby the Japanese force withdrew and the Qing government agreed to pay a large indemnity and recognize Japanese claims over the Ryūkyūs. For the Chinese, the Taiwan Expedition brought the first of a series of forced indemnities and territorial alienations, and with it the sharp awareness that Japan's growth now represented a serious threat to China's interests. To the Meiji leaders the expedition brought a first diplo-

matic victory and confirmed China's vulnerability. Far from satisfying samurai belligerents, it fed their appetite for expansion. Thus, although the oligarchs continued to urge the priority of domestic reform and nation building, they were to find it impossible to curb the appetite for empire whetted by the successes in Okinawa and Taiwan. Indeed, they shared the vision of adding to Japan's international stature by asserting its leadership in East Asia but were more cautious with regard to the timing of its implementation.

Differences between Japan and China over Korea were to have even graver consequences for Sino-Japanese relations than the Taiwan conflict. To the Qing government Korea was a particularly close tributary over which China had for many centuries exerted unquestioned influence. In Japan, even before the end of the Edo period some thinkers had begun to view Korea, as Hideyoshi had done, as a natural area for Japanese influence and a staging area for continental expansion. Among the Meiji leaders was a group who felt very strongly that control over Korea was vital to Japan's security and international recognition. Samurai bellicosity was fueled by Korean refusal to enter into treaty relations with the new government in Japan. During the SEIKANRON, or "invade Korea debates," of 1873, advocates of expansion within the oligarchy, led by SAIGŌ TAKAMORI, ETŌ SHIMPEI, and ITAGAKI TAISUKE, argued vigorously for a punitive expedition that would force Korea to abandon its seclusion policy and come to terms with Japan. Feelings ran so high over the issue that the leadership suffered its first major split. The idea of a Korean expedition was rejected as premature and dangerously disturbing to the Western powers by ŌKUBO TOSHIMICHI, IWAKURA TOMOMI, and KIDO TAKAYOSHI, who managed to divert samurai energies into the Taiwan adventure, but in doing so drove Saigō, Etō, Itagaki, and their followers into opposition.

The Taiwan expedition reduced, but did not end, Japanese pressure on Korea. In 1876, in the unequal Treaty of KANGHWA, the Yi dynasty was forced to establish diplomatic relations with Japan, open several ports for trade, and grant extraterritorial privileges to Japanese in Korea. The treaty also contained a declaration of Korean "independence." This was intended as a denial of Qing control, but, since China still regarded Korea as a tributary state, it merely increased Sino-Japanese tensions. During the following two decades both China and Japan worked to strengthen their positions on the peninsula: the Chinese by propping up the SUGUP'A party and other conservative elements in the Yi regime, training government troops, and linking Korea commercially to China; the Japanese by encouraging those Koreans who were demanding reform and independence and by engaging in political subversion. War broke out in 1894 when Japanese troops that had purportedly been sent to help quell the TONGHAK REBELLION clashed with similar Chinese forces. See KOREA AND JAPAN: early modern relations.

To most international observers the outcome was a foregone conclusion: China would rout Japan. All parties except the Japanese were stunned, therefore, when Japanese forces defeated the Qing armies on land and sea in less than a year. The Japanese armies, it was clear, were better led, better armed, better organized, and more united than their Chinese opponents. In the Treaty of SHIMONOSEKI (1895) the Qing government was forced to pay a heavy price for defeat. It was obliged to recognize the independence of Korea, to cede to Japan the Liaodong (Liaotung) Peninsula, Taiwan, and the Pescadores, to pay an indemnity of 200 million taels, to open more ports for trade, and to grant to the Japanese the legal and taxation privileges enjoyed by the Western powers under the Unequal Treaties. Some of the fruits of victory were snatched from the Japanese by the TRIPARTITE INTERVENTION of Russia, France, and Germany, who, for the sake of "peace in Asia" and the "integrity of Korea," forced the Japanese to return the Liaodong Peninsula to China in exchange for an additional indemnity.

The effects of the Sino-Japanese War were far-reaching. China's weakness, clearly exposed, would be further exploited by the powers in a scramble for concessions. There had been an unprecedented shift in the East Asian balance of power from China to Japan, one that would persist until Japan's defeat in 1945. The Japanese had demonstrated military and naval strength based on a slight, but growing, industrial sector. By force of arms, Japan had joined the ranks of the imperialist nations but still found itself suspect among them and confronted by imperial Russia. Among the Japanese people the startling victories and colonial acquisitions fostered imperialist sentiment, increased national determination to emulate the great powers, and encouraged feelings of disdain for China as a once-great empire on the verge of dissolution.

Following the Sino-Japanese War Qing officials tried, ineffectually, to institute limited administrative reform of the imperial system and to cope with the spreading encroachment of Western merchants, missionaries, and soldiers. These intrusive forces sparked nativist reactions, of which the most violent was the BOXER REBELLION of 1900. The Manchu government was held accountable for Boxer excesses by the foreign powers and forced to pay a heavy indemnity. Japanese troops were urged by the same foreign powers to help raise the siege of the beleaguered legations in Beijing and did so with exemplary moderation, hoping thereby to win the respect of the West without ruining relations with the Qing government. Discouraged Chinese intellectuals looked either to the West or to Japan for the means to restore dignity to China. By 1906 there were at least 8,000 Chinese students in Japan studying the Meiji parliamentary, legal, and educational systems as well as those Western writings most admired by the Japanese. They were also able to observe Japan's victory over Russia in 1905 (see RUSSO-JAPANESE WAR) and the country's continuing industrial growth. Many of these students shifted quickly from dreaming of reforming the Qing imperial system to plotting its destruction. Among these students were LU XUN (Lu Hsün), ZHOU ZUOREN (Chou Tso-jen), CHEN TIANHUA (Ch'en T'ien-hua), and HUANG XING (Huang Hsing). Another sojourner in Japan was SUN YAT-SEN, who in 1905 formed a revolutionary alliance in Tōkyō and later briefly tasted power in the short-lived Chinese Revolution of 1911, which brought down the Manchu regime and ended imperial rule in China.

Japan can, therefore, be placed among the forces of change in late Qing China. In the late 19th and early 20th centuries the Chinese could variously view Japan as an imperialist threat, even more dangerous than the Western powers because of its proximity, obvious designs on Korea and Manchuria, and growing industrial and military strength, or as a source of inspiration for traditional-minded or revolutionary reformers eager to reassert China's integrity, independence, and leadership in East Asia. Japanese troops marching to the aid of Westerners held hostage by the Boxers represented Japan as an imperialist and a collaborator with the foreign powers despoiling China. But at the same time Manchu reformers and republican nationalists could, and did, from their very different standpoints, learn much from the experience of Meiji Japan. Any hopes for cooperation between the two countries that may have existed were dashed, however, by the rapid demise of the Chinese Republic after 1911, by the eclipse of Sun Yat-sen, and by China's humiliation under Japan's imposition of the TWENTY-ONE DEMANDS in 1915. The image of Japan as possible mentor or model faded. The image of Japan as aggressor loomed larger.

■———W. G. Beasley and E. G. Pulleyblank, ed, *Historians of China and Japan* (1961). Martin Collcutt, *Five Mountains: The Rinzai Zen Monastic Institution in Medieval Japan* (1980). Francis Hilary Conroy, *The Japanese Seizure of Korea, 1868–1910* (1960). Wm. Theodore de Bary, ed, *The Buddhist Tradition in India, China, and Japan* (1969). Heinrich Dumoulin, *A History of Zen Buddhism* (1963). Jan Fontein and Money L. Hickman, *Zen Painting and Calligraphy* (1970). Yoshito S. Hakeda, *Kūkai: Major Works* (1972). Kyotsu Hori, "The Mongol Invasions and the Kamakura Bakufu," PhD dissertation, Columbia University (1967). Inoue Mitsusada, "The Ritsuryō System in Japan," *Acta Asiatica* 31 (1977). Akira Iriye, "Imperialism in East Asia," in James Crowley, ed, *Modern East Asia: Essays in Interpretation* (1970). Marius B. Jansen, *The Japanese and Sun Yat-sen* (1954). Marius B. Jansen, *Japan and China: From War to Peace, 1894–1972* (1975). Joseph M. Kitagawa, *Religion in Japanese History* (1966). Maruyama Masao, *Studies in the Intellectual History of Tokugawa Japan*, tr Mikiso Hane (1974). Marlene M. Mayo, ed, *The Emergence of Imperial Japan: Self-Defense or Calculated Aggression?* (1970). Richard H. Minear, "Ogyū Sorai's *Instructions to Students*: A Translation and Commentary," *Harvard Journal of Asiatic Studies* 36 (1976). James W. Morley, ed, *Japan's Foreign Policy, 1868–1941: A Research Guide* (1974). *Nihon shoki* (720), tr W. G. Aston as *Nihongi: Chronicles of Japan from the Earliest Times to A. D. 697* (1896, repr 1956). David S. Nivison and Arthur F. Wright, ed, *Confucianism in Action* (1959). Robert Treat Paine and Alexander Soper, *The Art and Architecture of Japan* (1974). Richard Pearson, "The Contribution of Archaeology to Japanese Studies," *Journal of Japanese Studies* 2.2 (1976). Edwin O. Reischauer, *Ennin's Diary: The Record of a Pilgrimage to China in Search of the Law* (1955). Edwin O. Reischauer, *Ennin's Travels in T'ang China* (1955). Gilbert Rozman, *Urban Networks in Ch'ing China and Tokugawa Japan* (1973). Sugimoto Masayoshi and David L. Swain, *Science and Culture in Traditional Japan, A.D. 600–1854* (1978). Tanaka Takeo, "Japan's Relations with Overseas Countries," in John Whitney Hall and Toyoda Takeshi, ed, *Japan in the Muromachi Age* (1973). Ronald Toby, "Reopening the Question of Sakoku: Diplomacy in the Legitimation of the Tokugawa Bakufu," *Journal of Japanese Studies* 3.2 (1977). Ryusaku Tsunoda, Wm. Theodore de Bary, and Donald Keene, ed, *Sources of Japanese Tradition* (1958). Ryusaku Tsunoda and L. Carrington Goodrich, ed, *Japan in the Chinese Dynastic Histories* (1951). Y. T. Wang, *Official Relations between China and Japan, 1368–1549* (1953). Burton Watson, *Japanese Literature in Chinese* (1975). Arthur F. Wright, ed, *The Confucian Persuasion* (1960). Arthur F. Wright and Denis Twitchett, ed, *Confucian Personalities* (1962).   Martin C. COLLCUTT

CHINA AND JAPAN AFTER 1912

The Chinese Revolution of 1911 and the Twenty-One Demands

In October 1911 a revolution broke out in China, triggered by the 10 October military uprising in Wuchang (Wu-Ch'ang), Hubei (Hupeh) Province. The Qing (Ch'ing; 1644–1912) dynasty, beset by a financial crisis, was on the brink of collapse. Sympathetic to the survival of a sister monarchy, Japan supplied the Qing with weapons on the condition that they respect Japanese interests in Manchuria. Japan suggested that the Manchus continue to rule, but only nominally; actual political authority would be placed in the hands of the Han Chinese. Japan asked Britain for its cooperation, but to no avail. The Yangzi (Yangtze) Valley area, which had been a sphere of British influence, had fallen to revolutionary forces who advocated the establishment of a republic. Britain sided with the republicans and supported the establishment of a republic headed by YUAN SHIKAI (Yüan Shih-k'ai), a leader of the northern provinces of China. In January 1912 SUN YAT-SEN became the provisional president of the revolutionary government in Nanjing (Nanking). Emperor Xuantong (Hsüan-t'ung; see PUYI [P'u-i]) stepped down from his throne in February, thus marking the end of the Qing dynasty. At the same time, Yuan succeeded Sun as provisional president of the revolutionary government. Taking advantage of the confusion created by the revolution, Japan strove to expand its influence south of the Yangzi River, but these efforts largely failed.

In April 1913 Yuan Shikai managed to stabilize his government with a 25-million-pound REORGANIZATION LOAN from Japan, Britain, France, Russia, and Germany. At the same time Yuan put added pressure on the disgruntled revolutionary factions of his government, especially the Nationalist Party (Guomindang or Kuomintang). In July these revolutionaries attempted a second revolution, but it failed. Sun Yat-sen, HUANG XING (Huang Hsing), Li Liejun (Li Liehchün), and other leaders were forced to flee to Japan. In July of the following year, a China Revolutionary Party was established in Tōkyō with Sun as its head. Japan thus became a base of anti-Yuan movements by revolutionary factions.

With the outbreak of WORLD WAR I in July 1914, European involvement in China weakened, providing Japan with a golden opportunity to expand its interests there. After declaring war against Germany, Japan seized the JIAOZHOU (KIAOCHOW) CONCESSION, the Shandong (Shantung) Railway, and all other German interests in Shandong Province. In January 1915 Foreign Minister KATŌ TAKAAKI ordered Minister Hioki Eki (1861–1926), stationed in China, to present Yuan Shikai with the TWENTY-ONE DEMANDS. The principal demands included China's acceptance of Japan's succession to the former German concessions in Shandong Province, an extension to Japan's lease of the territories of Port Arthur (Ch: Lüshun) and Dalian (Ta-lien; J: Dairen), and joint Japan–China management of the Hanyeping (Han Yeh P'ing) Company, the huge coal and iron complex in central China. Most infamous perhaps was item 5, which stipulated that China employ Japanese political, financial, and military advisers, allow joint Sino-Japanese policing of certain districts, and purchase Japanese weapons and munitions. China secretly informed Britain, the United States, and other Western powers of Japan's demands in the hope that they would intervene. The government also fomented anti-Japanese sentiment among its people and initiated a boycott on Japanese goods. Eventually, on 7 May, Japan withdrew item 5 but delivered an ultimatum, forcing China to agree to all the other demands on 9 May.

The May Fourth Movement and the Washington Conference

Dissatisfied with Yuan's resistance to the Twenty-One Demands and his attempt to have China side with the Allied powers in World

War I through secret negotiations, Japan started to plan his downfall. It strongly opposed Yuan's effort to assume the title of emperor and instigated disturbances in Shandong and Manchuria. A trouble-weary Yuan died in June 1916.

To fill this political vacuum, competition arose among the Anhui (Anhwei) clique of DUAN QIRUI (Tuan Ch'i-jui), the Zhili (Chihli) clique of Feng Guozhang (Feng Kuo-chang), the Fengtian clique of ZHANG ZUOLIN (Chang Tso-lin) and other northern warlords, the Guangdong (Kwangtung) Military Government of Sun Yat-sen, and the warlords of Guangxi (Kwanghsi) and Yunnan provinces. The TERAUCHI MASATAKE cabinet gave strong financial support to the Duan Qirui clique in the form of the NISHIHARA LOANS. In August 1917 the Duan cabinet, with backing from Japan, entered World War I and in May 1918 signed a Sino-Japanese military pact pledging Chinese support for the dispatching of Japanese troops through Manchuria to Siberia. In August 1918, in consort with the Allies, the Terauchi cabinet launched its anti-Bolshevik SIBERIAN INTERVENTION, but it was soon forced to resign because of widespread rice riots at home (see RICE RIOTS OF 1918).

The succeeding HARA TAKASHI cabinet was formed in September 1918. World War I ended in November 1918, and two months later a peace conference opened in Paris. The Chinese representative demanded that Japan return to China the German Jiaozhou Concession in Shandong, since China had fought for the Allied cause. However, because during the war Britain, France, and Russia had promised Japan their support at the forthcoming peace conference, Japan's claim to the Shandong concessions was recognized.

In Beijing (Peking) on 4 May 1919 some 4,000 university students protested this decision and raided the residence of the pro-Japanese Transportation Minister CAO RULIN (Ts'ao Ju-lin; see MAY FOURTH MOVEMENT). After some of these students were arrested by military police, demonstrations broke out in cities throughout the country, including Shanghai and Nanjing. In June Beijing was placed under martial law, and Shanghai was the site of a general strike that lasted until the government dismissed Cao and other pro-Japanese officials. In the end China did not sign the Treaty of VERSAILLES with Germany. Then in July 1920 the military power of the Anhui clique, which had been nurtured by Japan, was destroyed in battle by the Zhili clique.

In November 1921 the United States opened the WASHINGTON CONFERENCE to discuss disarmament and the China problem. The discussions on China sought to restore the cooperation among Western powers that had existed in China before being disrupted by Japan during World War I. However, the rise of nationalism in China after the May Fourth Movement made it necessary for all the powers to reexamine the nature of their interests in China and to reformulate their policies there. The NINE-POWER TREATY and a treaty concerning Chinese customs duties, both concluded at the Washington Conference, stipulated their cooperation in fostering a stable and unified government in China. Also at this conference Japan concluded a separate treaty with China returning the Shandong concessions (see SHANDONG [SHANTUNG] QUESTION).

The Antiwarlord and Antiimperialist Movements —— In 1923 China demanded Japan's return of Port Arthur and Dalian, stating that their original lease to Russia (made in 1897 for 25 years) had expired. Japan's rejection of the demand resulted in a Chinese boycott of Japanese goods. In January 1924 the Chinese Nationalist Party's First National Congress was opened in Guangzhou (Canton) by Sun Yat-sen. It adopted procommunist and pro-Soviet policies and called for the abrogation of all of China's unequal treaties with foreign countries. The new Duan Qirui government, which represented a coalition of military cliques, asked Sun to come to Beijing. On his way to Beijing, Sun stopped at Kōbe to give a speech calling on Japan to support China's effort to end the unequal treaties. In December Sun arrived in Beijing only to learn that the Duan government, in order to win recognition from the powers, had already pledged to respect the unequal treaties. Sun died in Beijing in March 1925.

In the spring of 1925 Chinese workers at Japanese spinning mills in Shanghai and Qingdao (Tsingtao) initiated a series of strikes. The Qingdao strikes were suppressed by the Fengtian clique; in Shanghai one worker was killed. During the resulting demonstrations many workers were killed or injured by policemen of the Shanghai International Settlement acting under the command of the British (see MAY 30TH INCIDENT). Anti-Japanese and anti-British general strikes then virtually brought the activities of the international settlement to a halt. The Chinese directed the strikes principally against Britain in hope of driving a wedge between Japan and Britain, but Foreign Minister SHIDEHARA KIJŪRŌ sought cooperation among all

the powers in order to counter the antiimperialist movement in China. The Shanghai strikes were finally suppressed by the Fengtian clique in September. This incident made many Chinese realize that the overthrow of the warlords was a necessary prerequisite to the removal of the imperialists.

The Unification of China by the Nationalist Government

The Northern Expedition was initiated by CHIANG KAI-SHEK, commander of the National Revolutionary Army, in July 1926. It was the Nationalist government's aim to destroy or subjugate Wu Peifu (Wu P'ei-fu), Sun Chuanfang (Sun Ch'uan-fang), Zhang Zuolin, and other warlords in order to unify China and defeat the imperialists. The northward advance of Chiang's army from Guangdong proceeded smoothly, and by November it occupied Wuhan, Jiujiang (Chiuchiang), Nanchang (Nan-ch'ang), and several other cities in central China. The British settlement in Hankou (Hankow) was also seized in January 1927. The British, viewing the situation with grave concern, decided to dispatch troops to defend the Shanghai International Settlement. They proposed that Japan do likewise, but Foreign Minister Shidehara rejected this offer. When the National Revolutionary Army arrived in Nanjing and attacked the offices of the Japanese and British consulates-general on 24 March, Japan did not join in the bombardment of Nanjing by British and American warships (see NANJING [NANKING] INCIDENT). However, public opinion in Japan was dissatisfied with such moderation, and in April the WAKATSUKI REIJIRŌ cabinet was succeeded by the TANAKA GIICHI cabinet.

Meanwhile the confrontation between the left- and right-wing factions in the Chinese Nationalist Party intensified, and on 12 April Chiang Kai-shek led an anticommunist coup d'etat in Shanghai. In June the Tanaka cabinet dispatched Japanese troops to Shandong Province on the pretext of protecting Japanese nationals residing there. At the same time it ordered YOSHIZAWA KENKICHI, the Japanese minister in Beijing; YOSHIDA SHIGERU, the Japanese consul-general in Fengtian (Mukden; now Shenyang); and Mutō Nobuyoshi (1868–1933), the commander of the GUANDONG (KWANTUNG) ARMY, the Japanese field army in Manchuria, to attend the Far Eastern Conference (TŌHŌ KAIGI) in Tōkyō. At the conference it was decided that Japan would support the moderate Chiang government, eliminate "communist elements" in China, and secure the safety and security of Manchuria.

The failure that year of the Northern Expedition led to the withdrawal of Japanese troops from Shandong. However, when the Northern Expedition was relaunched in April 1928, the Tanaka cabinet immediately sent Japanese troops to Shandong, where at Jinan (Tsinan) they clashed with Chinese troops on 3 May. The Japanese troops shelled and occupied Jinan, killing many Chinese soldiers and civilians. The Revolutionary Army bypassed Jinan and occupied Beijing in July. Zhang Zuolin, who had withdrawn his troops from Beijing to Manchuria under pressure from Japan, was killed in a train explosion in a plot masterminded by staff officer Kōmoto Daisaku of the Japanese Guandong Army. Zhang's successor, ZHANG XUELIANG (Chang Hsüeh-liang), made a compromise with the Chiang government, allowing the Nationalist flag to be flown over Manchuria. The Nationalist government had now finally achieved the unification of the entire Chinese mainland.

The principal foreign policy goal of the Nationalist government was the revision of the unequal treaties. In 1928 Britain, the United States, and several other powers recognized China's right to tariff autonomy and established official diplomatic relations with the Nationalist government. Japan concluded a customs agreement in May 1930, but only on the condition that China impose Japanese-specified rates of customs duty on important Japanese export goods for three years. By 1933, however, Manchuria had already been made a puppet state of Japan (see MANCHUKUO), and China had become too weak to enforce its own customs duties in the northeastern provinces.

The Manchurian Incident —— In Manchuria Japan's principal interest was the SOUTH MANCHURIA RAILWAY (SMR), to which it acquired rights under the Treaty of PORTSMOUTH (1905). However, the development and improvement of Chinese railway systems were viewed as a threat by many Japanese who lived in Manchuria, and, further, in order to defend Japan from the Soviet Union, the Guandong Army in Manchuria began to plan for the military occupation of Manchuria and Inner Mongolia. It was with this in mind that several officers in the Guandong Army blew up a length of the SMR on the night of 18 September 1931 (see LIUTIAOGOU [LIU-T'IAO-KOU] INCIDENT). Japanese troops quickly occupied Mukden, Changchun, Andong (Antung), and other cities. Units of the Japanese Korean Army, at the request of the Guandong Army, crossed the Yalu River and invaded Chinese territory. The leader of the Fengtian clique, Zhang Xueliang, in Beijing at the time of the Liutiaogou Incident, ordered his troops in Manchuria not to resist the Japanese forces. The Nationalist government immediately protested Japan's invasion of Manchuria to the League of Nations. The League Council passed a resolution demanding that the Guandong Army return to its former position. The Guandong Army leaders then decided to set up Manchuria and Mongolia as independent countries and stepped up military operations. By November Japanese troops had taken over Qiqihaer (Tsitsihar), the central city in Heilongjiang (Heilungkiang) Province, and by January 1932 they occupied Jinzhou (Chinchow), Zhang Xueliang's seat of government after his retreat from Mukden. On 7 January the United States, which had viewed these events with great concern, informed the governments of Japan and China that it would not recognize the results of Japan's violation of China's territorial integrity or its infringement of international treaties (see NONRECOGNITION POLICY). The Chiang government ordered a nationwide boycott of Japanese goods, and the sale of Japanese goods in China came to a virtual standstill.

The SHANGHAI INCIDENT broke out on 28 January 1932, triggered by the killing a few days earlier of a Japanese priest, and Japan seized the opportunity to dispatch troops to Shanghai. The Chinese troops put up strong resistance but were forced to retreat after a general offensive by Japanese troops in March. After the signing of a cease-fire agreement in May, Japanese troops withdrew from Shanghai. The puppet state of Manchukuo was established in March 1932 with Puyi as head; on 15 September Japan signed the Japan–Manchukuo Protocol and took over the new state's diplomacy and defense.

In February 1932 a League of Nations commission headed by Victor A. G. R. Lytton had been dispatched to Japan, China, and Manchuria. The LYTTON COMMISSION's report, presented to the league in October, refuted the Japanese claim that the Manchurian Incident had been in self-defense and that Manchukuo had been voluntarily established by Chinese living in Manchuria.

Japan opposed the commission's recommendation that Manchuria be placed under international control, and, when the league was about to approve this recommendation, Japan informed the body in March 1933 that it would resign (see LEAGUE OF NATIONS AND JAPAN). In May the Japanese army invaded Hebei (Hopeh) Province. On 31 May the Chinese army concluded the TANGGU (TANGKU) TRUCE with the Japanese army then advancing toward Beijing and Tianjin (Tientsin). The Chinese agreed to set up a neutral zone in northeastern Hebei, south of the Great Wall, and the Japanese agreed to withdraw their troops north of the wall.

The North China Problem——The Nationalist government felt it could not mount an all-out resistance to Japan in the Manchurian and Shanghai incidents since it feared an attack by Chinese communist forces who held power in Jiangxi (Kiangsi) Province and other large areas of the country. Chiang Kai-shek intended to eliminate the communist army first and then concentrate on fighting the Japanese. But as Japanese aggression became more blatant, the recovery of lost territory became the battle cry of Chinese nationalism.

Japan, under the pretext of self-rule, began operations to separate the five northern provinces from the rest of China in 1935. The HE-UMEZU (HO-UMEZU) AGREEMENT and the DOIHARA-QIN (DOIHARA-CH'IN) AGREEMENT, signed in June 1935, led to the weakening of Nationalist government influence in Hebei and Chahar provinces. Under strong pressure from the Japanese army, a puppet government, the EAST HEBEI (HOPEH) ANTICOMMUNIST AUTONOMOUS GOVERNMENT, was set up in East Hebei. At the same time widescale smuggling, encouraged by the Japanese army, led to a precipitous decline in the Nationalist government's custom revenues. Outraged Chinese students and intellectuals held a large anti-Japanese demonstration in Beijing on 9 December (see DECEMBER NINTH MOVEMENT).

Meanwhile, as a result of campaigns by the Nationalist army, the communist Red Army forces were compelled to retreat from their Jiangxi soviet district in October 1934. Led by MAO ZEDONG (Mao Tse-tung) on the Long March, they succeeded in joining forces in October 1935 at the communist army base in Yan'an (Yenan) in Shanxi (Shansi) Province. On 1 August 1935 the Communist Party issued its AUGUST FIRST DECLARATION and called for the establishment of a United Front against Japan.

In 1936 the HIROTA KŌKI cabinet demanded from the Nationalist government the conclusion of a Sino-Japanese military alliance and the hiring of Japanese political and military advisers. However, negotiations between the two governments soon broke down.

On 12 December Chiang Kai-shek, in Xi'an to lead a punitive expedition against the communist army, was captured by Zhang Xueliang in the XI'AN (SIAN) INCIDENT. Zhang and others had been in secret contact with the Chinese communist forces and now demanded a reorganization of the Nationalist government, the suspension of civil war, and the release of anti-Japanese leaders. The Nationalist government decided to send a punitive expedition against Zhang, but since it portended a large-scale civil war, ZHOU ENLAI (Chou En-lai) and others in the Chinese Communist Party mediated to gain Chiang's release. As a result, Chiang returned safely to Nanjing.

The consequences of the Xian Incident gradually became clear in 1937. The Nationalist government demanded that Japan retract past acts, such as the creation of the East Hebei Anticommunist Autonomous Government, and that Sino-Japanese diplomatic relations be established on an equal footing. The Nationalist government also decided to cooperate with the communists to resist Japan. It was against this background of rising anti-Japanese feeling and heightened tension between the two countries that the MARCO POLO BRIDGE INCIDENT occurred on 7 July 1937.

The Sino-Japanese War of 1937–1945——In itself the Marco Polo Bridge Incident, an exchange of fire between Japanese and Chinese soldiers near Beijing, was a minor incident. But many Japanese saw it as a pretext for launching an all-out war against the Nationalist government. Consequently, when a Japanese naval officer was shot in Shanghai the following month, general war became nearly inevitable (see also SINO-JAPANESE WAR OF 1937–1945). The Japanese army in North China steadily advanced southward until the Chinese forces put up strong resistance at Shanghai. A Japanese contingent landed at Hangzhou (Hangchow) Bay in early November, routed the Chinese forces, and occupied the capital Nanjing on 13 December. Peace negotiations, carried out before and after the occupation of Nanjing with Germany as mediator, collapsed, and on 16 January 1938 the KONOE FUMIMARO cabinet declared that Japan no longer considered the Nationalist government as a party to its negotiations and that it intended to set up its own regimes in occupied China.

Moving its capital from Nanjing to Hankou, the Nationalist government continued its resistance. Japan meanwhile mobilized a force of 300,000 which advanced toward the upper reaches of the Yangzi River and occupied the strategic city of Wuhan in October 1938. Guangzhou, the largest city in southeastern China, was taken in the same month. The Nationalist government again shifted its capital, this time to Chongqing (Chungking) in Sichuan (Szechwan) Province. The Konoe cabinet announced on 3 November 1938 that the ultimate purpose of Japan's war in China was the establishment of a new political order in East Asia (TŌA SHINCHITSUJO), but it was clear from the Japan-China New Relations Policy, drawn up at an imperial conference that same month, that Japan was intent on dominating China both politically and economically.

One of the leaders of the Nationalist Party, WANG JINGWEI (Wang Ching-wei), was troubled over the growing power of the Chinese Communist Party since the outbreak of the war, and, hoping to counter this by making peace with Japan, he escaped from Chongqing in December 1938 and went to Hanoi. The Japanese quickly contacted Wang and persuaded him to set up a new regime in Japanese-occupied territory. Thus the REORGANIZED NATIONAL GOVERNMENT OF THE REPUBLIC OF CHINA was established in Nanjing in March 1940. The Wang regime, however, failed to win even the slightest support from the Chinese people, and, although the Japanese army had succeeded in occupying the principal cities and districts along important railroads, its management of occupied areas was always threatened from the rear by Nationalist and Chinese communist armies.

The Outbreak of World War II and Japan's Defeat——With the outbreak of WORLD WAR II in Europe in September 1939, the influence of Britain, France, and the other European countries in China waned and the United States came to be the most active Western opponent of Japan's invasion of China. In July 1939 the United States abrogated its trade and navigation treaty with Japan. In September 1940 Japan concluded a military alliance with Germany and Italy (TRIPARTITE PACT). As tensions mounted between Japan and the United States, the two countries initiated negotiations in the spring of 1941, with China as the principal issue. Negotiations broke down in November, when the United States demanded that Japan withdraw all its armies from China, including Manchuria. On 8 December Japan declared war on the United States, Britain, and other allied countries, and on the following day China declared war on Japan.

During World War II China became one of the principal fronts for the Allied forces. The fact that a million Japanese soldiers were engaged on the Chinese mainland proved to be of great aid to the Allies. In November 1943 the CAIRO CONFERENCE, attended by Chiang Kai-shek of China, Franklin D. ROOSEVELT of the United States, and Winston Churchill of Britain, called for the postwar reversion of Manchuria and Taiwan to China. As Japan's situation deteriorated in the face of the Allied counteroffensive in the Pacific, Japanese troops in continental China began to be deployed on the southern fronts. In the Supreme War Council meeting of September 1944, Japan decided to push for a peace plan with Chiang that would allow for his return to Nanjing, the establishment of a unified Chinese government, and the retention of Manchuria under Japanese rule. However, Japan had no opportunity to propose these peace terms, and its position in China deteriorated markedly. In 1945 command of the air over China was completely in the hands of the US Air Force, and the Nationalist army, fortified with American equipment and weapons, began to take the offensive on the ground. The Japanese Army was forced to withdraw its troops to the outskirts of Beijing, Nanjing, Wuhan, Jinan, and other cities.

With Japan's defeat in sight, the Nationalist government began to place more emphasis on its confrontation with the communists. In fact, it was criticized in some quarters for not using against Japan all of the weapons, munitions, and other war matériel supplied by the Allies. (In 1937, at the start of the Sino-Japanese War, the communist army had numbered only 30,000 to 40,000 men; by 1945 it had increased to 910,000 regular troops and 2,200,000 civil militiamen. As Mao Zedong claimed, the communist forces constituted the main force in the war against Japan.)

On 8 August 1945 the Soviet Union declared war on Japan and its troops poured into Manchuria. With Japan's acceptance of the peace terms of the POTSDAM DECLARATION and its surrender to the Allied forces on 14 August, the Nationalist government instructed the Japanese army in China to defend Beijing, Tianjin, Shanghai, Nanjing, Wuhan, and three other large cities from communist forces and to return them to the Nationalist government. The Japanese army complied.

On 9 September the supreme commander of the Japanese expeditionary forces in China, General Okamura Yasuji, surrendered in Nanjing to HE YINGQIN (Ho Ying-ch'in), the supreme commander of the Chinese Nationalist Army. In the following month the 230,000 Japanese soldiers stationed in Taiwan were disarmed by the Chinese army. The repatriation of Japanese soldiers and civilians from China began in November, and by May 1946, 1,660,000 Japanese had returned home. In its eight-year war with China, Japan had suffered 410,000 dead and 900,000 injured. The toll of dead and wounded on the Chinese side was 3,100,000, not including countless civilian casualties.

Postwar Japan-China Relations —— After Japan's defeat, a full-scale civil war broke out between the Nationalist and communist armies in July 1947. The communists occupied Beijing at the end of 1948, took over Nanjing in April 1949, and Shanghai in May. On 1 October the People's Republic of China (PRC) was established in Beijing. The Nationalist government fled to Taiwan, where it maintained itself as an independent government. With the establishment of the People's Republic of China, a new chapter in Sino-Japanese relations began.

On 14 February 1950 the PRC concluded with the Soviet Union a 30-year Treaty of Friendship, Alliance, and Mutual Assistance. They pledged mutual assistance, military and otherwise, if either party was attacked by Japan or countries allied with Japan. This military alliance was to have great significance for subsequent Japan–China relations.

Four months later, on 25 June, the KOREAN WAR broke out. American forces entered the war immediately and continued to play a major role even after the organization of the United Nations force. American and South Korean troops were initially driven back by North Korean regiments but later took the offensive and crossed the 38th parallel to occupy P'yŏngyang on 20 October. At this stage Chinese forces crossed the Yalu River and fought under the banner Resist America and Aid Korea. China was declared an aggressor by the United Nations and, together with Taiwan, was not invited to join Japan and 48 other countries in signing the SAN FRANCISCO PEACE TREATY on 8 September 1951. The same day Japan concluded a security treaty with the United States (see UNITED STATES–JAPAN SECURITY TREATIES), thereby recognizing the continued stationing of American forces in Japan. On 24 December Prime Minister Yoshida Shigeru sent a letter to John Foster DULLES, adviser to the US State Department, promising that Japan would establish diplomatic relations not with the PRC but with the Nationalist government on Taiwan. At the time of the implementation of the San Francisco Peace Treaty on 28 April 1952, Japan signed a separate peace treaty with the Taiwan government. Thus, Japan and the Chinese mainland once again came into direct confrontation.

The Kishi Cabinet and Japan-China Relations —— Although diplomatic relations between Japan and China were in a state of complete rupture, a private Sino-Japanese trade agreement was concluded in June 1952. The agreement was signed by Nan Hanchen (Nan Han-ch'en) and Kōra Tomi, who had arrived in Beijing via Moscow. It was a barter transaction calling for an exchange of goods valued at £30 million. A second agreement was concluded in October 1953 and a third in May 1955 with virtually the same terms. The third agreement, made at the time of the second HATOYAMA ICHIRŌ cabinet, stipulated the opening of sample fairs, the establishment of commercial missions, and the granting of diplomatic privileges to the representatives of these missions.

However, after the establishment of the KISHI NOBUSUKE cabinet in February 1957, Japan–China relations began to cool. Prime Minister Kishi's approval during a visit to Taiwan of the Nationalist government's announced intention to reconquer mainland China greatly angered the Chinese government. Zhou Enlai declared in July 1957 that Kishi viewed the 600 million people of China as enemies.

The fourth private trade agreement between the two countries was concluded on 5 March 1958. But in April Chief Cabinet Secretary Aichi Kiichi said that he would neither permit the granting of diplomatic privileges to members of the Chinese trade mission nor the raising of China's national flag in Japan, and China's attitude stiffened. Nan Hanchen, the president of the China Council for Promotion of International Trade, informed Japan that the agreement would be implemented only if the obstacles created by the Japanese government were removed. Then on 2 May, a Japanese youth hauled down the national flag of China at a Chinese postal stamp fair held in Nagasaki (see NAGASAKI FLAG INCIDENT). Angered at the mild reaction of the Kishi cabinet, China informed the Japanese government in July that thenceforth it would cut off all negotiations with Japan, including those on the repatriation of Japanese nationals.

Trade with China and the Nationalist Government Opposition

In July 1960 the IKEDA HAYATO cabinet succeeded the Kishi cabinet in the wake of widespread disapproval of the latter's handling of the renewal of the United States–Japan Security Treaty. The following year Japan supported the American resolution at the 1961 UN General Assembly to treat the issue of Chinese representation as a "serious matter," and China criticized the Ikeda cabinet. In Japan public opinion strongly favored the establishment of diplomatic relations with China, particularly to expand trade. Also, as its relations with the Soviet Union worsened, China began to explore ways of improving its relations with Japan. In October 1962 Takasaki Tatsunosuke, a member of the ruling Liberal Democratic Party, visited Beijing; the following month he signed a memorandum with LIAO CHENGZHI (Liao Ch'eng-chih) calling for mutual trade worth an average of £36 million a year for five years. The Japanese side pledged to defer Chinese payment for Japanese goods and accept installment payments on its purchase of industrial plants. Trade based on this agreement came to be known as LT Trade (for Liao–Takasaki), and in 1964 the establishment of the Takasaki Office in China and the Liao Office in Japan was approved.

Japan's moves to improve relations with Mainland China met with the disapproval of the Nationalist government on Taiwan. In August 1963 the Nationalist government recalled its ambassador to Japan in protest against the EXPORT–IMPORT BANK OF JAPAN's loans to finance a plan by KURARAY CO, LTD, to establish a synthetic fiber plant in China. Relations worsened when in October Zhou Hongqing (Chou Hung-ch'ing), an interpreter with the Chinese oil pressure machinery inspection group then visiting Japan, asked for asylum at the Soviet Embassy in Tōkyō. Angered at the return of Zhou to China, the Nationalist government closed its embassy in Tōkyō (see ZHOU HONGQING [CHOU HUNG-CH'ING] INCIDENT). The Ikeda government dispatched former Prime Minister Yoshida Shigeru to Taiwan in February 1964, and in May Yoshida sent a letter to the Nationalist government stating that the Export-Import Bank of Japan would not finance Kuraray's plans for a plant in China. Appeased, the Nationalist government named a new envoy to its embassy in Tōkyō. The Japanese government sought to improve its relations with the Nationalist government by providing it with yen loans worth $150 million in April 1965.

The Great Proletarian Cultural Revolution, which broke out in China during the autumn of 1965, greatly reduced Chinese diplomatic activities. In March 1966, talks between the leaders of the Chinese Communist Party and a JAPAN COMMUNIST PARTY delegation headed by MIYAMOTO KENJI broke down over their different policies toward the Soviet Union. Thereafter, members of the Japan–China Friendship Association and other pro-China groups in Japan were divided, one faction supporting the Japan Communist Party's neutral stand and the other the Chinese Communist Party's anti-Soviet line.

In September 1967 Prime Minister SATŌ EISAKU visited Taiwan. His meeting with Chiang Kai-shek as well as his cabinet's strong support of the Nationalist government at the United Nations incurred the anger of the PRC. Nonetheless, on 6 March 1968 China and Japan signed a one-year "memorandum trade" agreement to replace the expired LT trade treaty. Negotiations for the memorandum trade were influenced by political considerations, and the volume of trade fell far below the LT level. In November 1969 the SATŌ–NIXON COMMUNIQUÉ, concerned with the reversion of Okinawa, declared that Japan placed great importance on the maintenance of security in the Taiwan area and the Republic of Korea; China regarded this as the rebirth of Japanese imperialism.

The Establishment of Japan-China Diplomatic Relations

In October 1970 Canada recognized China, and later that year a majority of the United Nations General Assembly members voted for China's membership. In 1971 China was formally admitted into the United Nations. In July Henry A. Kissinger, national security adviser to President Nixon, visited China, paving the way for President Nixon's visit to Beijing the following February. These dramatic changes had a strong impact on Japan's hitherto passive stance.

The TANAKA KAKUEI cabinet, formed in July 1972, proclaimed as one of its basic goals the normalization of diplomatic relations between Japan and China. On 29 September, during a visit to Beijing, Tanaka issued a joint communiqué with Chinese Premier Zhou Enlai. It stated that Japan recognized the People's Republic of China as the legal government of China and the island of Taiwan as an integral part of China's territory. It also declared that China had withdrawn its war reparations claim against Japan and that the two countries would henceforth peacefully resolve all differences, not seek hegemony in Asia and the Pacific, and oppose any other nation's attempt to gain hegemony there. Later, Foreign Minister ŌHIRA MASAYOSHI announced that as a result of this new policy, the 1952 peace treaty concluded with the Nationalist Chinese government was nullified. The Nationalist government on Taiwan severed diplomatic relations with Japan, and the two countries recalled their ambassadors. Relations between Japan and Taiwan have since then been on a private, unofficial level, through such organizations as the Japan–Taiwan Interchange Association and the Association of East Asian Relations.

In March 1973 the first Japanese ambassador to Beijing, Ogawa Heishirō, and the first Chinese ambassador to Tōkyō, Chen Chu (Ch'en Ch'u), arrived at their respective posts. Subsequently agreements on trade, air, navigation, fishery, and other matters were concluded between the two countries. Formal negotiations on a peace treaty were initiated in January 1975 between Vice Foreign Minister Tōgō Fumihiko and Ambassador Chen. However, negotiations proved difficult: the Chinese insisted that the term "antihegemony" be inserted in the text of the peace treaty, while the Japanese, worried lest any negative reference to the Soviet Union harm its relations with that country, opposed its inclusion. Foreign Minister Miyazawa Kiichi, while attending the UN General Assembly in September that year, informed Chinese Foreign Minister Qiao Guanhua (Ch'iao Kuan-hua) that to the Japanese the term "antihegemony" did not signify any specific third country, implied no joint Japan–China action, and was applicable to any area of the world. However, the Chinese once again disagreed, and negotiations were suspended. In 1976 the political scene in China changed drastically. In January Prime Minister Zhou Enlai died, in September Mao Zedong died, and in October the so-called Gang of Four were arrested. Deng Xiaoping (Teng Hsiao-p'ing) was reinstated and, as deputy chairman, he told a visiting New Liberal Club delegation from Japan in September 1977 that China's Treaty of Friendship, Alliance, and Mutual Assistance with the Soviet Union would not be renewed when it expired in February 1980.

The CHINA–JAPAN PEACE AND FRIENDSHIP TREATY was finally signed between Foreign Minister Sonoda Sunao of the FUKUDA TAKEO cabinet and Chinese Foreign Minister Huang Hua on 12 August 1978. Article 2 of the treaty states that neither country will seek hegemony in the Asia-Pacific region or in any other region, and that each is opposed to efforts by any other country or group of countries to establish such hegemony. Article 4 states that the treaty does not affect the position of either party regarding its relations with third countries, thus indicating that the treaty and the US–Japan Security Treaty could exist together. Deputy Prime Minister Deng Xiaoping arrived in Tōkyō in October, and documents of ratification were exchanged.

Since the normalization of relations in 1972, the volume of China–Japan trade has expanded steadily. Japan's exports to China in 1978 amounted to $3.05 billion (3.1 percent of Japan's total exports for that year) while imports totaled $2.03 billion (2.5 percent of total imports). Thus, trade between the two countries exceeded the $5 billion mark, and China has become one of Japan's most important export markets.

▬▬——John Hunter Boyle, *China and Japan at War, 1937–1945: The Politics of Collaboration* (1972). Robert Butow, *Tojo and the Coming of War* (1961). Alvin D. Coox and Hilary Conroy, ed, *China and Japan: Search for Balance Since World War I* (1978). James B. Crowley, *Japan's Quest for Autonomy: National Security and Foreign Policy, 1930–1938* (1966). Frank Dorn, *The Sino-Japanese War, 1937–1941* (1976). Fujii Shōzō, *Sombun no kenkyū* (1966). Gaimushō, ed, *Nihon gaikōshi nempyō narabini shuyō bunsho*, 2 vols (1965–66). Gaimushō Ajiakyoku Chūgokuka, ed, *Nitchū kankei kihon shiryō shū: 1949–1969 nen* (1970). Hata Ikuhito, *Nitchū sensō shi* (1972). Akira Iriye, *After Imperialism: The Search for a New Order in the Far East, 1921–1931* (1965). Akira Iriye, *The Chinese and the Japanese: Essays in Political and Cultural Interaction* (1980). Marius B. Jansen, *The Japanese and Sun Yat-sen* (1954). Marius B. Jansen, *Japan and China: From War to Peace 1894–1972* (1975). Shuichi Kato, *The Japan-China Phenomenon: Conflict or Compatibility?* (1974). Kawahara Hiroshi and Fujii Shōzō, ed, *Nitchū kankei no kiso chishiki* (1974). Chae-jin Lee, *Japan Faces China: Political and Economic Relations in the Postwar Era* (1976). Lincoln Li, *The Japanese Army in North China 1937–1941: Problems of Political and Economic Control* (1975). Yale Maxon, *Control of Japanese Foreign Policy: A Study of Civil Military Rivalry, 1930–1945* (1957). Wolf Mendl, *Issues in Japan's China Policy* (1978). James W. Morley, ed, *Japan's Foreign Policy, 1868–1941: A Research Guide* (1974). Sadako Ogata, *Defiance in Manchuria: The Making of Japanese Foreign Policy, 1931–1932* (1964). Okabe Tatsumi, *Chūgoku no tainichi seisaku* (1976). Masamichi Rōyama, *Foreign Policy of Japan, 1914–1939* (1941).   Usui Katsumi

chinaberry

(*sendan*). *Melia azedarach* var. *japonica*. A deciduous tree of the family Meliaceae which grows wild on hills and coastal areas of Shikoku and Kyūshū and is also planted in house gardens. It reaches a height of more than 7 meters (23 ft). Its bipinnate-tripinnate compound leaves grow on alternate sides near the tips of the branches. The leaflets are pointed and oval in shape. In May and June flower stalks appear on the twigs and produce clusters (panicles) of attractive flowers, light purple or occasionally white. With the end of the flowering season elliptical fruits develop. Fruits (drupes) ripen yellowish and nearly round, and remain on the tree after the leaves have fallen off. Known as *kurenshi*, they were used for medicinal purposes.

In ancient times this tree was called *afuchi*, while the word *sendan* referred, especially in Buddhist contexts, to the sandalwood (*Santalum album*), which is now called *byakudan*. In the Heian period (794–1185) branches of the chinaberry were customarily bound together with leaves of the SHŌBU plant and used to decorate the eaves of houses on 5 May (see CHILDREN'S DAY). On the other hand, the heads of executed criminals were customarily hung from this tree, and by the Edo period (1600–1868) it had become an object of aversion. Today these associations have been forgotten, and the *sendan*'s flower is widely admired in season.   MATSUDA Osamu

China Incident of 1937 → Sino-Japanese War of 1937–1945

China-Japan Peace and Friendship Treaty

(*Nitchū Heiwa Yūkō Jōyaku*). When the government of Japan and the government of the People's Republic of China normalized relations by a joint communiqué of 29 September 1972, the two governments agreed to enter into negotiations for the purpose of concluding a treaty of peace and friendship (Joint Communiqué para. 8). Negotiations started in November 1974, but the conclusion of the treaty had to wait until 12 August 1978, when it was finally signed in Beijing (Peking). The treaty is not a treaty of peace in the technical sense, which puts an end to the legal state of war, but a treaty for the consolidation and development of relations of peace and friendship. Thus it does not deal with the settlement of problems relating to the termination of the legal state of war. It provides, as the basic guiding principles governing the relationship between the two countries, that "the two countries shall develop durable relations of peace and friendship between them on the basis of the principles of mutual respect for sovereignty and territorial integrity, mutual nonaggression, noninterference in each other's internal affairs, equality and mutual benefit, and peaceful coexistence" (art. 1). One problem which became the source of great controversy in the course of the negotiations was the question of the antihegemony principle. The Chinese side insisted on its inclusion in the treaty, but the Japanese side could not agree on its inclusion unless the precise legal character was sufficiently clear to the extent that the principle did not restrict the foreign policy of Japan with respect to any other country. Agreement was reached in the form of two provisions. In article 2 of the treaty, the two countries declare that neither of them should seek hegemony in the Asia-Pacific region or in any other region and that each is opposed to efforts by any other country or group of countries to establish such hegemony. At the same time, it is stipulated in article 4 that the treaty shall not affect the position of either country regarding its relations with third countries.

The treaty does not contain anything beyond what had already been stated in the Joint Communiqué of 29 September 1972, but its successful conclusion can be regarded as signifying the completion of the political process of normalization and the consolidation of the basis for peaceful and friendly relations between Japan and the People's Republic of China. OWADA Hisashi

chindai

(army camps). Temporary organs for military administration established in February 1868, immediately after the Meiji Restoration. Set up in provinces formerly under direct shogunal control and in other vital areas, they were abolished later in the same year. *Chindai* also refers to headquarters for local army commands established in 1871. Initially established in Tōkyō, Ōsaka, Kumamoto, and Sendai, these were responsible for recruiting former domainal troops. Later, with the division of the country into six military districts, two more were added, in Nagoya and Hiroshima. In 1888 the *chindai* were reorganized and renamed *shidan* (divisions). See also IMPERIAL JAPANESE ARMY.

Chinese characters → kanji

Chinese Eastern Railway

(known in Japan by such names as: Tōshin Tetsudō, Tōshi Tetsudō, and Hokuman Tetsudō). In 1896 Russia gained permission from China to extend the Trans-Siberian Railroad through China directly across northern Manchuria to Vladivostok. That rail line, the Chinese Eastern Railway (CER), shortened the distance to Vladivostok by about 560 km (350 mi) compared to the all-Russian route north of the Amur River and also provided opportunities for the Russians to exploit northern Manchuria economically, to interfere in Chinese politics, and to bring military power swiftly to bear in the Far East. In 1898 Russia exacted Chinese consent to build another line, from Dairen (Ch: Dalian or Ta-lien; now part of Lüda) and PORT ARTHUR north to the CER; this later became known as the SOUTH MANCHURIA RAILWAY (SMR). These railways formed a framework over which Russian influence spread rapidly through Manchuria. After the Japanese victory in the RUSSO-JAPANESE WAR of 1904–05, Russia ceded the SMR to Japan, and Manchuria was thereafter effectively divided into a Russian sphere of influence in the north, centered on the CER, and a Japanese sphere in the south, based on the SMR.

In a flush of idealism at the time of the Bolshevik Revolution, the new Soviet government announced its intention to return the CER to China without compensation. The Russians quickly changed their minds, however, and in 1924 concluded agreements with Chinese authorities that specified joint Sino-Soviet management of the CER

as a commercial enterprise. The Japanese conquest of Manchuria (see MANCHURIAN INCIDENT) in 1931 created a crisis in Japanese-Russian relations. It brought Japanese power to the very border of the Soviet Union at just the time when some Japanese military leaders were calling for a preemptive war against the Russians, and it changed the CER from a potent agent of Russian influence in a weakened China to a narrow thread of Russian interest surrounded by hostile Japanese power. In case of war, the Japanese could seize the railway without difficulty, and the Japanese GUANDONG (KWANTUNG) ARMY stationed in Manchuria could easily use the Russian railway presence to manufacture a pretext for war if it wished. Under those circumstances, the Russians sought to sell the CER to Japan. Negotiations dragged on for almost two years, but were concluded in March 1935 with an agreement whereby Russia sold the CER to the Japanese puppet state of Manchukuo for ¥140 million. Soon afterward it was placed under the control of the South Manchuria Railway Company. *James E. SHERIDAN*

Chinese literature and Japanese literature

The traditional literature of Japan—that is, Japanese literature prior to the emergence of a modern literature in the 1880s—was profoundly influenced by the literature of China in many respects. Chinese literature was one of the sources from which Japanese literature was created. The oldest anthology of poetry in the Japanese language is the MAN'YŌSHŪ (Collection for Ten Thousand Generations or Collection of Ten Thousand Leaves), which was compiled in the late 8th century. Even before the *Man'yōshū*, however, Japanese writers had created the KAIFŪSŌ, an anthology of poems in KAMBUN (classical Chinese) modeled in form after Chinese *shi (shih)*. It was only after they had first learned to read and appreciate Chinese literature, while themselves composing poems and belletristic prose in Chinese, that the Japanese of ancient times created a literature of their own.

Originally Japan had no written language. Archaeological evidence suggests that Chinese characters initially came into use in the first half of the 5th century. Chinese civilization came into Japan either directly or via the Korean peninsula through immigrants. Immigrants who came from China first moved to Korea and, after settling there, later crossed over to Japan. A numerically small class, they had a monopoly on the art of writing. The Chinese and Japanese languages belong to separate families; basic vocabulary and word order also differ. For the Japanese of those early days the study of Chinese was extremely difficult, and the Japanese must have puzzled over how to record Japanese words with Chinese characters. In fact Chinese characters had first come to Japan in the middle of the 1st century, but it was only after four centuries that the Japanese found a way of using them to write Japanese words, by having them represent only the sounds of the Chinese words that they symbolized.

Yamato Period (ca 300–710) —— By sometime in the 4th century the YAMATO COURT was beginning to be established in central Japan. The first half of the 6th century saw the formal introduction of Buddhism, via Korea, and with it the importation of Chinese secular learning. At the end of the 6th century, Prince SHŌTOKU, the imperial regent, adopted the Chinese system of government offices and the Buddhist religion. The changes he inaugurated revolutionized the world view of the ruling court aristocracy, whose power was based on the clan system. In 604 he promulgated the SEVENTEEN-ARTICLE CONSTITUTION. Two of the 17 articles promote Buddhism and prescribe Buddhist ethics, but the other 15 are Confucian prescriptions. They use phrases from such Confucian works as the Five Classics (see FOUR BOOKS AND FIVE CLASSICS), the *Lunyu (Lun-yü; The Analects)*, and the *Xiaojing (Hsiao-ching; The Classic of Filial Piety)*, either paraphrased or quoted verbatim. This shows that Japan at that time, or at least Prince Shōtoku and his circle, possessed a high degree of familiarity with the Chinese classics, especially those of Confucianism. In the year 600, Shōtoku sent an embassy to the Chinese court, at that time under the rule of the Sui Dynasty (581–618), and in 607 he sent ONO NO IMOKO to China; these missions were the beginning of direct official cultural intercourse. The sending of official embassies was also carried out during the Tang (T'ang) Dynasty (618–907), continuing until 894. In addition to inviting Chinese monks to visit Japan and founding Buddhist temples, Prince Shōtoku personally lectured on the sutras, in particular the LOTUS SUTRA, and wrote commentaries on them in Chinese. These are the oldest extant writings by a Japanese in the Chinese language. Shōtoku seems to have stood alone as a religious and political leader, but what he accomplished in the spheres of social thought and culture formed the foundation for the full-scale acceptance of Chinese civilization.

With the TAIKA REFORM of 645, the Yamato government, under the imperial house, was reorganized along the lines of the Chinese bureaucratic system. Legal compilations were made in the Chinese language; these were modeled after the criminal and civil codes of the Tang court.

Nara Period (710–794) —— Both Nara, the capital during this period, and HEIANKYŌ (now the city of Kyōto), the capital during the following period, were formed on the plan of Chang'an (Ch'ang-an), the Chinese capital, an indication of how extensively Chinese civilization had permeated Japan. Buddhist culture flourished. Music from China and Korea was performed at court, and nobles composed Chinese poems at banquets. Social intercourse with envoys from Silla was conducted through the exchange of poems. Persons who had studied in China were active in the fields of government and literature, and the ability of noblemen to write both prose and poetry in Chinese reached a high level. In 712 Ō NO YASUMARO completed the KOJIKI (Record of Ancient Matters). He wrote the preface to it in splendid classical Chinese, in a style called *pianwen* (*p'ien-wen;* parallel prose), which was popular in the Six Dynasties period (221–589). Many of the poems in the *Kaifūsō* were composed by court nobles on social occasions. Their literary value is not high, but it is worth noting that they were greatly influenced by the poetic taste of Six Dynasties China. The Japanese read, in particular, the *Wen xuan* (*Wen hsüan;* J: *Monzen*), an anthology of poetry and prose compiled by Xiao Tong (Hsiao T'ung; 501–531), and made this work their model.

The *Kojiki,* chiefly a chronicle of traditional lore concerning the emperors of past ages, contains myths, legends, folk songs, and anecdotes. It was written in Chinese, for the most part, but there are also passages in which Japanese words are recorded phonetically in Chinese and the rules of Japanese grammar are followed. Such passages are in an altered *kambun* form, very different from the standard Chinese of the preface; it might, in fact, be appropriate to call these passages the first written literature in the Japanese language. According to Kojima Noriyuki, the *kambun* style of the *Kojiki* was influenced by the style of the Chinese translations of Buddhist scriptures that were originally in Sanskrit. The *Kojiki*'s content shows the influence of Indian mythology and other elements which had been introduced to Japan through Chinese books on history, myth, and legend and through Buddhist texts translated into Chinese. In contrast to the *Kojiki* and the FUDOKI (provincial gazetteers), which are written in a Japanized literary Chinese, Japan's first official history, the NIHON SHOKI, is written in genuine Chinese. This work takes as a model the narrative portions of the histories of China, as do some individual passages in the former two works.

As has been stated before, the *Man'yōshū* is the oldest extant anthology of Japanese poems; included in it are poems in the Japanese language by authors whose Chinese poems appear in the *Kaifūsō*. This anthology freely utilizes the method of recording Japanese words with Chinese characters used solely for their sound, without regard to their meaning. These "borrowed characters" are called *man'yōgana*. The poets whose work is preserved in the *Man'yōshū* were of many different social classes, including courtiers and officials. They were all influenced to some extent by Chinese poetry and prose. In the poems of ŌTOMO NO TABITO and YAMANOUE NO OKURA, Chinese elements are especially conspicuous. Okura had been sent to China as an ambassador; he was well read in Chinese literature, from the Confucian classics and Buddhist scriptures to popular stories. His writings express humanistic ideas founded on Confucian teaching. Among the poems of the *Man'yōshū* are a number which take their subject matter from myths and legends of China; in addition, some of the aesthetic sense in poems celebrating the beauties of nature was developed through an appreciation of Chinese literature.

The *Kakyō hyōshiki* (772) of Fujiwara no Hamanari, a work on Japanese poetics, bases its treatment of the rhetoric of WAKA poetry on Chinese poetic theory. In the history of literary criticism it is a pioneering work. It, too, was written in *kambun*.

Heian Period (794–1185) —— During the first century of the Heian period, national histories and law codes written in *kambun* were compiled, and the composition of poetry and prose in *kambun* flourished (see POETRY AND PROSE IN CHINESE). Anthologies of Chinese poems (*kanshi*) include the *Ryōunshū*, BUNKA SHŪREISHŪ, and *Honchō reisō*; anthologies of prose and poetry together include the KEIKOKUSHŪ and HONCHŌ MONZUI, compiled by FUJIWARA NO

AKIHIRA. Literary composition in Chinese was practiced by the nobles in the court of Emperor SAGA. He himself was an outstanding poet and one of the very few in Japanese history who composed *ci (tz'u)*, a complex Chinese poetic form in which the meter follows irregular musical rhythms.

The learned monk KŪKAI was well versed in Chinese poetry and prose; his *Bunkyō hifuron*, written in *kambun*, was intended to serve as a reference book in the study of Chinese literature. The work is a critical review of *pianwen* literature from the Six Dynasties to mid-Tang, and its value as a source for the history of literary criticism is high. SUGAWARA NO MICHIZANE wrote poems that are simple and easy to understand. In his hands the *kanshi* became a form in which the individual could express his thoughts and emotions; it was no longer just a foreign literary form.

Kyōkai, a priest of the temple YAKUSHIJI in Nara, completed the NIHON RYŌIKI about 822. This is the first collection of Buddhist anecdotes (see SETSUWA BUNGAKU), often of a homiletic nature, based on a variety of legendary material. It was inspired by Chinese collections of Buddhist anecdotes, and it is written in *kambun*. Its *kambun*, like that of the *Kojiki*, is a hybrid form, known as HENTAI KAMBUN, in which Japanese and Chinese are mixed—as Chinese it is rather strange.

As literary activity in *kambun* flourished and then declined, *man'yōgana* continued to be used. A phonetic syllabary called KANA (literally, "borrowed names") then came into being. In the Heian period, *kana* was first used only by women when they wrote privately. However, *kana* script was used in the KOKINSHŪ, the first imperial anthology of classical poetry, compiled by KI NO TSURA-YUKI. This gave the script a social recognition which led to the birth of a literature in the spoken language written in *kana*. Many of the writers of this literature were women of the nobility.

The *Kokinshū* contains a preface in Japanese, which was written in *kana*, and also a *kambun* preface; these were influenced in part by the views expressed in Chinese works on the theory of poetry such as Zixia's (Tzu-hsia) preface to the *Shijing* (*Shih-ching;* tr *The Book of Songs,* 1937) and the *Shipin* (*Shih-p'in;* Classification of Poetry) by Zhong Hong (Chung Hung).

TAKETORI MONOGATARI (tr *The Tale of the Bamboo Cutter,* 1956), the earliest example of MONOGATARI BUNGAKU (narrative literature), takes its material from Chinese legend. The story of the heroine Kaguyahime was obviously suggested by that of Chang E (Ch'ang O) or Huan E (Huan O), who fled to the palace of the moon. The episodes in which Kaguyahime must choose from among five noble suitors reflects the period when, after the cessation of the embassies to Tang (T'ang) China (see SUI AND TANG [T'ANG] CHINA, EMBASSIES TO), trade with the mainland continued through the agency of Song (Sung) merchant ships, and Buddhist priests continued to go to China for study.

In the Heian period Japanese literature was repeatedly stimulated afresh by new movements within Chinese literature. Japanese literature of this time was influenced especially by the work of the Tang poet Bo Juyi (Po Chü-i; 772–846; known in Japan as Haku Rakuten from an alternate Chinese name, Bo Letian or Po Le-t'ien). The anthology of his poems and prose, titled *Boshi wenji* (*Po-shih wen-chi;* J: *Hakushi monjū*), was the favorite reading of Japanese nobles, scholars, and poets. Although in China his poems on political and social topics were popular, in Japan it was his poems of sorrow and of leisure and contentment which were most widely read. The WA-KAN RŌEISHŪ, compiled by FUJIWARA NO KINTŌ, is an anthology of outstanding couplets from Chinese poems by both Japanese and Chinese authors and of *waka*; one-quarter of its content consists of the poems of Bo Juyi. This book was read by many; its influence can be seen even in the verses of *imayō* (see MUSIC, TRADITIONAL), popular songs of the 11th and 12th centuries.

MURASAKI SHIKIBU, author of the great masterpiece of the Heian period the TALE OF GENJI *(Genji monogatari),* had in her youth studied Sima Qian's (Ssu-ma Ch'ien) *Shiji* (*Shih-chi;* tr *Records of the Grand Historian of China,* 1961) with her father. The opening of her story takes its idea from Bo Juyi's narrative poem "Changhen ge" (Ch'ang-hen ko; Everlasting Remorse). Murasaki's literary rival SEI SHŌNAGON was the author of superb prose in which many Chinese literary elements were also present, as she herself proudly acknowledged. Her masterpiece, *Makura no sōshi* (The Pillow Book) is said to be modeled in form after the miscellany *Yishan zazuan* (I-shan tsa-tsuan) by the Tang author Li Yishan (Li I-shan).

For the literary men who lived in the Heian capital, China was a distant, exotic country. The long romance UTSUBO MONOGATARI (Tale of the Hollow Tree) begins with an episode in which the hero's grandfather, sent as an ambassador to China, falls victim to a storm en route and is washed up on the shores of Bosi (Po-ssū), in what is now part of Malaysia; both China and Bosi are described as exotic lands. SUGAWARA NO TAKASUE NO MUSUME, author of SARASHINA NIKKI (Sarashina Diary; tr As I Crossed a Bridge of Dreams, 1971), is said to have written a number of prose tales. One of them, HAMA-MATSU CHŪNAGON MONOGATARI (The Tale of the Hamamatsu Middle Counselor), used Tang China for its background. However, the Tang court and its customs as depicted in this book are simply a projection of Heiankyō and its customs: an abstract, imaginary geography unrelated to the real China.

In the late Heian period, a time of social and political change, one of the religious works that held a special charm was the ŌJŌYOSHŪ (The Essentials of Pure Land Rebirth), written in kambun by the monk GENSHIN. This book, which aroused admiration among pious Buddhists in Song China as well, exerted a vast influence on artistic and literary works of every sort, beginning with the EIGA MONOGA-TARI (Tales of Glory). One important result of this work was that much Chinese vocabulary from the Buddhist scriptures was assimilated into colloquial Japanese, and the use of wakan konkōbun (Japanese with a heavy admixture of Chinese loanwords) became general.

KONJAKU MONOGATARI (tr as Tales of Times Now Past, 1979) came into existence toward the end of this period. This book consists of three parts: Tenjiku (India), Shintan (China), and Honchō (Japan), and it contains anecdotes from the Buddhist scriptures in Chinese as well as Chinese traditions and legends. Such collections of anecdotes contributed to the increasing spread of Chinese traditional lore. Another book thought to have been composed in this final part of the Heian period is Kara monogatari, a collection of brief tales and anecdotes adapted from Chinese sources and retold in Japanese. The sources of its contents are such works as Han Wu nei zhuan (Han Wu nei chuan), Xijing zaji (Hsi-ching tsa-chi), You xian ku (Yu hsien k'u), and Bo Juyi's narrative poem "Changhen ge," as well as historical works.

Kamakura and Muromachi Periods (1185–1568)

During this period a feudal system developed, and warriors became the ruling class in place of the court nobility. A number of GUNKI MONOGATARI, long tales about warriors which tell of battles and revenge, were composed at this time. Such works are well suited to the age that produced them. The masterpieces of the genre are the HEIKE MONOGATARI (tr The Tale of the Heike, 1975), written at the beginning of the Kamakura period, and a later work, the TAIHEIKI (Chronicle of Great Peace; tr Taiheiki, 1959). Gunki monogatari are written in wakan konkōbun, and they have a powerful effect. They narrate the spectacles of warfare in an episodic fashion, and their prevailing tone is one of Buddhist pessimism. These characteristics are most pronounced in the Heike monogatari, which was widely disseminated as oral literature. Chinese historical anecdotes were inserted into the text in many places without any regard for the development of the plot. This technique was also used extensively in other works of the genre, such as the GEMPEI SEISUIKI (The Rise and Fall of the Genji and the Heike), Taiheiki, and SOGA MONOGA-TARI, no doubt because readers of the time welcomed it. Because of the popularity of the gunki monogatari, the Chinese traditions and legends that they incorporated deeply influenced the libretti of the NŌ theater and other literary genres as well.

TRAVEL DIARIES made their appearance during this period. These diaries, of which one example is the KAIDŌKI, were written in wakan konkōbun. However, the most important example of belletristic writing in wakan konkōbun is the Hōjōki of KAMO NO CHŌ-MEI. Its style is terse, a skillful adaptation of the techniques of kambun prose composition; the Buddhist conviction of universal transience, expressed so forcefully in the Ōjō yoshū, permeates the work. From the end of the 12th century through the 13th century, Buddhism freed itself of the predominantly magical and ritualistic character which it had previously borne and took root in the hearts of the people.

The monk EISAI returned from China in 1191 and introduced the RINZAI SECT of ZEN Buddhism (Ch: Chan or Ch'an) to Japan; thereafter Zen came to have numerous adherents, becoming one of the major currents of the new Buddhism. Many of the warriors who constituted the newly risen ruling class became enthusiastic converts. In China this was the time of the Southern Song Dynasty (1127–1279); Zen borrowed the Song bureaucratic system for the organization and administration of its monasteries and became a religion of the aristocracy. In Japan the warriors, as a new aristocracy, favored Zen, promoting and protecting it. Zen monks con-

ducted ceremonies and devotions for the warrior class; they also took on the responsibility of drafting foreign diplomatic documents and furnished counsel in government. Some went to China on diplomatic missions and even undertook commercial duties. Though they strictly adhered to the monastic system of Zen, they also brought to Japan the forms of social intercourse used by the Chinese scholar gentry, forms founded on education in Confucianism and belles lettres.

The AZUMA KAGAMI (Mirror of Eastern Japan), a history of the Kamakura period (1185–1333), is written in kambun which is heavily Japanized, an indication of how the ability to write in classical Chinese had declined among the educated classes as a whole. Among Zen monks, however, study and appreciation of Chinese learning and fine arts continued, even though within restricted spheres. After the end of the Southern Song court, eminent Chinese Zen monks came to Japan, some through voluntary exile, some for missionary work, and they brought with them Song Neo-Confucianism, in particular, the new interpretations of the Chinese classics taught by Zhu Xi (Chu Hsi; 1130–1200), which the Zen monks studied. The Zen monasteries, which from the final years of the Kamakura period through the Muromachi period (1333–1568) were protected and regulated by the central government, were as a group called the GOZAN, and the literature produced by Zen monks was called GOZAN LITERATURE. Poetry in Chinese composed by Japanese reached its high point in Gozan literature. Kambun literature of the Edo period (1600–1868) is often tinged with Confucian feudalistic morality, but Gozan literature is free of this influence.

One of the founders of Gozan literature, KOKAN SHIREN, was an outstanding scholar and poet. He was a disciple of ISSAN ICHINEI (Yishan Yining or I-shan I-ning), a learned monk who had come to Japan in 1299 as an emissary of the Chinese government. Kokan wrote the GENKŌ SHAKUSHO, a history of Japanese Buddhism in biographical form, in classical Chinese and also tried his hand at critical writing on Chinese poetry, in which he espoused the work of Tang poets who were not well known in Japan at that time: Li Bo (Li Po), Du Fu (Tu Fu), and Han Yu (Han Yü). He was an ardent admirer also of Han Yu's prose. In 1307, SESSON YŪBAI went to China, which was at that time under the sway of the Mongols. There he encountered much hardship; his experiences are described in his poems. CHŪGAN ENGETSU was an outstanding poet and a student of Du Fu's poetry. MUSŌ SOSEKI, who was an outstanding religious figure and played the part of adviser in practical affairs to the Ashikaga shogunate, had two disciples who were accomplished poets, GIDŌ SHŪSHIN and ZEKKAI CHŪSHIN. Thanks to these two poet-monks, Gozan literature experienced its golden age.

Two Chinese anthologies which were much read by Zen monks of this period were the Santi shi (San-t'i shih), a collection of shi poems in the three most popular forms, and Guwen zhenbao (Ku-wen chen-pao), an anthology of belletristic prose. Both books were widely read in later ages as well.

The Gozan, centers of scholarly studies and the arts, gradually took on a largely secular orientation, until in many of the monasteries the monks completely lost sight of the fundamental religious nature of Zen. Those who reacted against this tendency left the Gozan and went into the provinces to practice religion. This was known as rinka (literally, "under the trees"), a metaphor for seeking refuge from public office in a life of seclusion. Rinka monks recruited followers from powerful provincial families and merchants, as well as renga (linked verse; see RENGA AND HAIKAI) masters, waka poets, doctors, and traveling artists. The most famous example of a rinka monk is IKKYŪ Sōjun, author of Kyōunshū, an anthology of Chinese poems. The Nō playwright ZEAMI wrote dramatic masterpieces which use many expressions from the sermons of the Zen masters; these sermons were usually written in kambun.

During the last part of the Muromachi period, the monk Sakugen Shūryō (1501–79) twice went to the Ming court to conduct trade negotiations. He left behind a diary of his travels. Together with the renga poet SATOMURA JŌHA, he wrote kanwa renku. These poems are composites in which the mood is created by the linking of Chinese couplets with waka hemistichs. Sakugen's travels to China became so well known that they are mentioned even in the works of the great 17th-century novelist SAIKAKU, an example of how the legacy of Gozan literature entered popular culture.

The Edo Period (1600–1868)

From the second half of the 15th century onwards, a series of civil wars took place. The ŌNIN WAR (1467–77) inflicted great damage on Kyōto and its environs, but with that one exception, commercial life in Japan developed unaffected by these disturbances, and the spread of learning and the arts to the provinces continued unabated. In the Edo period the feudal system of rule by military houses matured fully. The *bushi* (warrior class) held the dominant position in society, but the common people, especially the CHŌNIN (townsmen), became prominent as a class and made progress in the field of learning and the fine arts. The ruling warrior class promoted Neo-Confucianism (SHUSHIGAKU), using this ideology to support its system of government; as a result, education in the Chinese classics spread to the common people.

In China the Ming dynasty (1368–1644) lost power, and in 1644 the country came under Manchu rule with the founding of the Qing (Ch'ing) dynasty (1644–1912). Zhu Shunshui (Chu Shun-shui; J: SHU SHUNSUI) was one of a number of Chinese who fled to Japan at that time and brought fresh inspiration for scholarship and technology.

In the sphere of Confucian learning the schools of ITŌ JINSAI and OGYŪ SORAI were active, the former in Kyōto and Ōsaka, the latter in Edo (present-day Tōkyō). These teachers opposed the doctrines of Zhu Xi and his followers and stressed the importance of philological techniques in the study of Confucian texts; in this way they influenced the study of Japanese literature as well.

A large number of superior poets who wrote in Chinese appeared. The composition of Chinese prose and poetry became, in fact, an important current in literature and remained so until the early 1890s.

The following were some notable poets of the period: ISHIKAWA JŌZAN, ARAI HAKUSEKI, HATTORI NANKAKU, KAN SAZAN, TANOMURA CHIKUDEN, RAI SAN'YŌ, YANAGAWA SEIGAN, and ŌNUMA CHINZAN. Tanomura Chikuden was also an outstanding painter in the Chinese style, and he wrote Chinese poems not only in the *shi* form but in the *ci* form, otherwise generally neglected by Japanese poets. Rai San'yō is known also as an author of prose. San'yō wrote a popular history of Japan in *kambun* entitled *Nihon gaishi*.

The Edo period in Japan coincides with the Qing dynasty in China. However, it was not the literature of the Qing but rather that of the Ming which appealed to the Japanese. During the middle years of the Edo period, the Japanese inclined especially to the critical ideas of the Ming poet Li Panlong (Li P'an-lung; 1514–70) and his group, exalting the verse of the poets who preceded Du Fu and the prose written during the Former Han dynasty (206 BC–AD 8). Hattori Nankaku introduced the *Tangshi xuan (T'ang-shih hsüan)*, an anthology of Tang poems by an anonymous compiler, which replaced the *Santi shi* in popularity. In the mid-Edo period, the poet Yamamoto Hokuzan (1752–1812), espousing the theories of the Ming poet Yuan Hongdao (Yüan Hung-tao; 1568–1610), which emphasized the importance of individual expression, criticized the tastes then prevailing among *kanshi* poets. As a result, the poetry of the Tang lost popularity as the model for imitation, and that of the Song came to be preferred. The style in poetry thus became simpler, while in prose the work of Han Yu and Su Shi was admired and imitated. It was not until the end of the Edo period that the work of early Qing poets received attention.

During the Edo period, the shogunate put into effect the policy of Sakoku (NATIONAL SECLUSION). However, foreign relations were maintained with Korea, and trade with China continued at Nagasaki in Kyūshū. The Chinese who took part in the trade resided in that city, in segregated quarters. Not only Nagasaki but the temples of the ŌBAKU SECT of Zen, which were built by monks newly arrived from China, had a foreign aura that offered literary men some fresh impressions. The interest of the Japanese in Chinese colloquial literature developed from these beginnings. The imports that passed through Nagasaki included books from ports in China located in Jiangsu (Kiangsu) and Zhejiang (Chekiang), where publishing thrived. The Tokugawa shogunate strictly regulated the importation of books, censoring those thought to be seditious, but it did sponsor the translation of scientific works and allow translation of literary works from China.

The pioneer in the study of Chinese colloquial literature was Okajima Kanzan (1674–1728), famous as the translator of the romance *Shuihu zhuan (Shui-hu chuan;* English tr *All Men Are Brothers,* 1933). This translation, published 30 years after Kanzan's death, left a deep impression on authors of works in the popular fictional genre of the late Edo period known as YOMIHON, including BAKIN. Kanzan's linguistic ability was such that he was able to translate the *Taiheiki* into Chinese, producing a romance in the manner of a Chinese colloquial novel. It was through Kanzan that Ogyū Sorai and his school became interested in Chinese colloquial literature and aware of the importance of Chinese philology. Subsequently, Okada Hakku (1692–1767) and Sawada Issai (1701–82) translated and introduced the colloquial short fiction of the Ming dynasty.

During the Edo period, *Jiandeng xin hua (Chien-teng hsin hua;* New Tales by the Trimmed Lamp), a collection of stories written in classical Chinese by the Ming writer Qu You (Ch'ü Yu; 1347–1433), was extremely popular. This collection also greatly influenced Korean literature. In the 16th century, copies printed in Korea were brought to Japan, and thereafter came many adaptations. The Confucian HAYASHI RAZAN included stories adapted from it in his *Kaidan zensho,* and another writer, ASAI RYŌI, used its stories in his *Otogi bōko.* Printed copies of *Tangyin bishi (T'ang-yin pi-shih;* tr *Parallel Cases from under the Pear Tree,* 1956), detective stories by the 13th-century writer Gui Wanrong (Kuei Wan-jung), were brought from Korea. This work appeared in Japanese translation in 1651, and it was widely read during the Edo period, becoming a source for Edo detective stories. SAIKAKU utilized elements from *Jiandeng xin hua* and *Tangyin bishi* in his stories. CHIKAMATSU MONZAEMON composed his drama *Kokusen'ya kassen* (tr *The Battles of Coxinga,* 1951) with the fall of the Ming court as its theme; however, the manners of the characters are not those of China but rather reflect the lives of the Kyōto and Ōsaka townspeople of Chikamatsu's day. This was the unfortunate result of Japan's seclusion. At the same time, however, the play is full of allusions to the Chinese classics and Buddhist scriptures, showing that the legacy of Chinese literature had been incorporated into Japanese literature and was now essentially inseparable from it.

The 17th-century HAIKU poet BASHŌ had a profound understanding not only of such Tang poets as Li Bo and Du Fu but also of such Song poets as Su Shi and Huang Tingjian (Huang T'ing-chien), a knowledge that aided him in creating his own poetic world. One of his disciples, MORIKAWA KYOROKU, in 1706 published an anthology of HAIBUN (a mixture of haiku poetry and prose) entitled *Fūzoku monzen,* adopting for its arrangement the method used in *Wen xuan* and *Guwen zhenbao.* Haiku has close connections with Chinese literature.

BUSON was both a haiku poet and a painter. As a painter he discovered fresh meaning in the aesthetic taste of the Yuan and Ming, while his haiku poems, products of a painter's vision, have Chinese literary elements at the source of their creation. Their atmosphere is in many ways that of the world of the Chinese literati.

The fiction writer UEDA AKINARI took the materials for his collection of dreamlike tales of the supernatural, *Ugetsu monogatari* (Tales of Moonlight and Rain), from Ming and Qing colloquial short fiction such as *Gujin xiaoshuo (Ku-chin hsiao-shuo;* Tales Ancient and Modern), *Jingshi tongyan (Ching-shih t'ung-yen;* Penetrating Tales to Startle the World), and *Xihu jiahua (Hsi-hu chia-hua;* Superior Tales of the West Lake). He evidently also consulted Asai Ryōi's *Otogi bōko.*

Bakin, the most prolific of Edo period *yomihon* writers, got the ideas for many of his novels from Chinese colloquial literature. His *Chinsetsu yumiharizuki* is the story of the adventures of MINAMOTO NO TAMETOMO, a historical personage, but the plot of the story after Tametomo crossed the sea to the Ryūkyū Islands is derived from the *Shuihu hou zhuan (Shui-hu hou chuan),* a sequel to *Shuihu zhuan.* The most famous of his long novels is NANSŌ SATOMI HAKKENDEN (Satomi and the Eight "Dogs"). The ideas for its plot come principally from *Shuihu zhuan;* in writing it, Bakin also consulted other works of Chinese colloquial fiction, including the *Sanguo zhi yanyi (San-kuo chih yen-i;* tr *Romance of the Three Kingdoms,* 1925).

In the middle part of the Edo period, light verse in Japanized Chinese *(kyōshi)* and prose compositions in Japanized Chinese enjoyed great popularity. Among the works of this genre are many parodies. The genre's origin lies in the *kanwa renku* of Gozan literature and the poems of Ikkyū Sōjun. The outstanding practitioners of *kyōshi* were Hatanaka Dōmyaku (d 1801) in Kyōto and ŌTA NAMPO in Edo. NARUSHIMA RYŪHOKU wrote *kyōshi* and prose in *kyōshi*-style during the final years of the Edo period and the beginning of the Meiji period (1868–1912).

The Modern Period ——— After the MEIJI RESTORATION in 1868, a change took place from a feudal system of government to a monarchic system. What is called "modern literature" in Japan begins in the late 1880s, some 30 years before the establishment of a similar movement in China. With the SINO-JAPANESE WAR OF 1894–1895, the Japanese ceased to consider Chinese literature the source of Japanese literature. Nevertheless, in the daily life of society, the inherited tradition of Chinese literature continued to be an important element in the cultural background of novelists. For example, among writers active in the Meiji period, MORI ŌGAI and NATSUME SŌSEKI had a profound understanding of Chinese literature. Even FUTABATEI SHIMEI, who was the first to make translations into colloquial Japanese and whose theoretical and practical literary activity built the foundation of modern literature, wrote *kanshi* and was fond of reading Qing-dynasty belles lettres. In like manner the lyric poet SHIMAZAKI TŌSON included in *Wakanashū*, his first anthology, several Chinese poems by his friend Nakano Shōyō (1867–94). KŌDA ROHAN was a student of both Japanese and Chinese literary classics. The afterglow of the glory of Chinese literature in Japan can be seen in the work of other prominent writers like NAGAI KAFŪ and SATŌ HARUO. Among the latter's work is an anthology of the works of Chinese women poets translated into beautiful Japanese.

In China in the early part of the 20th century there had been a movement for the study of European and Russian literature which came via modern Japanese literature. A proletarian literary movement arose in China in the early 1930s, and Chinese and Japanese literature began to show reciprocal influence, but this was destroyed by the war. Some Japanese authors did seek their material in China, but with the progress of the war, this sort of literature degenerated into an instrument of the national war policy and lost its artistic independence. An author whose stories based on the Chinese classics retained their integrity as literature was NAKAJIMA ATSUSHI. Another writer, TAKEDA TAIJUN, in 1942 wrote the biographical essay *Shiba Sen* (Ch: Sima Qian or S'su-ma Ch'ien), which discusses the structure of the world of the *Shiji*. Through a study of Chinese classical and modern literature and a personal experience of the war, he created a special way of looking at the world, distinctively Japanese, which served as the foundation for his literary activity. His friend, the critic Takeuchi Yoshimi (1910–77), in 1944 wrote a literary portrait of the modern Chinese writer LU XUN (Lu Hsün). His research on Lu Xun and modern Chinese literature led him to discuss this novelist as a radical intellectual whose pen was a weapon of war in the society of developing China. Takeuchi was active in discussing a variety of ideological questions that appeared in postwar, modernized Japan, in particular those related to modern literature. There are other Japanese writers who continue to utilize wartime experiences in China as subject matter. However, the structure of the cold war, following upon the great wars of the 20th century, has given rise to distortions in the literary intercourse between China and Japan. Whether or not Japanese and Chinese literature will influence each other as equals will be the question from now on.

◼ Asō Isoji, *Edo bungaku to Chūgoku bungaku* (4th ed, 1972). Fujikawa Hideo, *Edo kōki no shijin tachi* (1966). Ishizaki Matazō, *Kinsei Nihon ni okeru Shina zokugo bungaku shi* (1940). Kanda Kiichirō, *Nihon ni okeru Chūgoku bungaku,* 2 vols (1905–07). Kawaguchi Hisao, *Heianchō Nihon kambungaku shi no kenkyū,* 2 vols (1959–61), includes an English summary and detailed bibliography. Kojima Noriyuki, *Jōdai Nihon bungaku to Chūgoku bungaku,* 3 vols (1962–65). Okada Masayuki, *Nihon kambungaku shi* (rev ed, 1954). Burton Watson, *Japanese Literature in Chinese,* 2 vols (1975–76).

IMAMURA Yoshio

Chinjufu

(Headquarters for Pacification and Defense). Military headquarters established during the Nara period (710–794) in northern Honshū to subjugate the EZO tribes who inhabited that area. The Chinjufu was commanded by a *seii tai shōgun* ("barbarian-subduing generalissimo") appointed by the central government. First located at TAGAJŌ (now in Miyagi Prefecture), the base was moved further north to IZAWAJŌ (now in Iwate Prefecture) after the major conquest of the Ezo by SAKANOUE NO TAMURAMARO in 801. By the middle of the 11th century the power of the imperial court had waned, and local warrior families, such as the Kiyohara family and the ŌSHŪ FUJIWARA FAMILY, took over the base. It was temporarily revived during the KEMMU RESTORATION (1333–36) but soon fell into disuse. In the Meiji period (1868–1912) the term *chinjufu* was applied by the government to naval bases, a usage that lasted until the end of World War II. The naval bases were located at Yokosuka (Kanagawa Prefecture), Kure (Hiroshima Prefecture), Sasebo (Nagasaki Prefecture), and Maizuru (Kyōto Prefecture).

chinju no kami

(literally, "pacifying guardian god"). The tutelary deity of a given locale. While the *chinju no kami* is technically distinct from the UJIGAMI (clan deity) and UBUSUNAGAMI (deity of one's birthplace), in popular practice these categories of deities are now often indistin-

guishable; where such a distinction was observed, the *chinju no kami* generally presided over a larger geographic territory than did the *ujigami* or *ubusunagami*, encompassing several villages or an entire province. The *chinju no kami* was often officially recognized as a regional deity by local lords and landholders, who contributed to the support of its shrine.

The term *chinju no kami* has also been applied, in its specific sense of "guardian deity," to the gods who protect the grounds of a temple, a castle, or a private residence. *Ōtō Tokihiko*

Chino

City in eastern Nagano Prefecture, central Honshū, on the slopes of the mountain YATSUGATAKE. Chino's cold and dry winters make it ideal for processing agar-agar *(kanten),* a vegetable protein made from seaweed. Since World War II, there has been an emerging electronics and precision instrument industry. Tourist attractions include the highland called TATESHINA KŌGEN and the lake Shirakabako. Pop: 43,942.

Chinsetsu yumiharizuki → Bakin

Chion'in

Head temple of the JŌDO SECT of Buddhism, located in Higashiyama Ward, Kyōto. The precincts of the Chion'in include the site where HŌNEN, the founder of the Jōdo sect, settled after leaving the mountain HIEIZAN in 1175 to proclaim his new Pure Land teachings and the site where he later died after returning from exile. The original temple, honoring Hōnen, was built in 1234 by his disciple Genchi (1183–1238). The temple suffered destruction several times, including during the ŌNIN WAR (1467–77), which ravished Kyōto, but was restored each time. In 1523 the temple became the head temple of the Jōdo sect. The Chion'in was richly patronized by the Tokugawa family. Ieyasu (1543–1616), the founder of the Tokugawa shogunate, donated land and built several buildings, including the main hall, in memory of his mother. His son Hidetada (1579–1632), the second shōgun, built the colossal gateway *(sammon)* and scripture repository. After the temple was destroyed by fire in 1633, it was rebuilt by the third shōgun Iemitsu (1604–51); this is the building which stands today. In 1607 Chion'in was designated a *monzekidera,* or temple whose abbot must be chosen from the imperial family or the aristocracy. A son of Emperor Go-Yōzei (r 1586–1611) was appointed its first imperial abbot.

The colossal two-story ceremonial gate at the entrance to the temple complex is the largest surviving structure of its kind in Japan and representative of the massive Zen-style temple gateways erected during the early part of the Edo period (1600–1868). Its walls and ceilings are richly decorated with paintings. The interior of the main hall is known for its ornate carvings, paintings, and mandalas. In the larger of two abbot's living quarters the sliding doors which partition off the rooms are painted with landscapes attributed to Kanō Naonobu (1519–92), an early KANŌ SCHOOL artist. Among the temple's many art treasures are an early 14th-century scroll depicting Hōnen's life and a RAIGŌZU depicting AMIDA Buddha and accompanying bodhisattvas descending to receive the faithful. Although the Meiji government confiscated some of its land in 1871, the temple has retained control over much of its original, extensive land holdings. *Stanley WEINSTEIN*

Chiossone, Edoardo (1832–1898)

Italian artist and copperplate engraver employed by the Japanese government from 1875 to 1891; responsible for designing Japan's first modern paper money and training Japanese to perform all phases of this operation. His work reinforced the image of the Meiji government and set a high aesthetic standard for Japanese money.

Outstanding examples of Chiossone's work were the first and second government issues made in Japan (1878 and 1881) and the first and second Bank of Japan notes (1884 and 1888). His designs blended Eastern and Western motifs. They showed Japanese ideographs and numbering predominantly, but increasingly added arabic numerals and English translations of important words. His copper-engraved portraits of Emperor Meiji and Empress Shōken can be seen today in the Treasure House of Meiji Shrine in Tōkyō.

Dallas FINN

Chiran

Town in southwestern Kagoshima Prefecture, Kyūshū. Chiran is noted for its tea and tobacco. *Samurai* homes and gardens dating from the Edo period (1600–1868) can still be seen. An air base constructed here during World War II served as the base for KAMIKAZE suicide missions; a memorial has been built in their honor. Pop: 14,846.

chirimen

(silk crepe). It is believed that the technique for making silk crepe was transmitted in the late 16th century by a Chinese artisan who came to the city of Sakai. Some varieties of *chirimen* are known by the way the crimping in the fabric is produced: *hitokoshi chirimen, uzura chirimen, shibori chirimen, ro chirimen,* and *kinsha chirimen.* Other varieties are known according to production area, such as Tango *chirimen* (Kyōto Prefecture), Kiryū *chirimen* (Gumma Prefecture) and Gifu *chirimen* (Gifu Prefecture). *Chirimen* is still widely used for high-quality traditional clothing (KIMONO, *haori,* and OBI) and accessories. See also CHIJIMI. *Yasuko* YABE

Chiryū

City in central Aichi Prefecture, central Honshū. A POST-STATION TOWN on the Tōkaidō, a major highway during the Edo period (1600–1868), today it is a satellite city of Nagoya. Textile mills and sewing machine plants are located here. Pop: 49,432.

Chishakuin

Head temple of the Chizan branch of the SHINGON SECT of Buddhism, located in Higashiyama Ward, Kyōto. It was originally built in the 14th century as part of the Dai Dembōin temple complex in Negoro, Wakayama Prefecture, where it emerged as a major seat of Shingon learning. After Toyotomi Hideyoshi (1537–98), in a campaign to gain control over the country, burned down the temples at Negoro in 1585, Gen'yū (1529–1605), who was then abbot, fled to Kyōto, where he propagated the Shingi (New) Shingon doctrines. Tokugawa Ieyasu (1543–1616), the founder of the Tokugawa shogunate, became a patron of Gen'yū and donated the land in Kyōto on which the present temple stands. Reestablished in 1600, Chishakuin is widely respected for its scholarly traditions. In 1872 the government designated it and HASEDERA as the two head temples of the Shingi branch of the Shingon sect. In 1900 Chishakuin established itself as the head temple of the Chizan branch, which had 2,825 affiliated temples in 1977. The temple is famous for its garden and paintings, which date from the late 16th century.
Stanley WEINSTEIN

Chishima Islands → Kuril Islands

Chishimakan Incident

(Chishimakan Jiken). International incident arising from the collision in November 1892 of the new Japanese torpedo gunboat *Chishima* and the steamship *Ravenna* of the British Peninsular and Oriental Navigation Company off Ehime Prefecture. The *Chishima* sank, and the Japanese government sought damages of ¥850,000, first from the British consul at Yokohama and then from the British Court at Shanghai. When the court ruled in favor of the P&O, Japan appealed to the Privy Council in London. Another hearing took place in Yokohama, and in 1895 the P&O agreed to a settlement of £10,000 (about ¥91,000). The outcome heightened Japanese public demand for revision of the Unequal Treaties imposed by the Western nations (see UNEQUAL TREATIES, REVISION OF).

Chishima Volcanic Zone

(Chishima Kazantai). Volcanic zone extending about 1,400 km (869 mi) from central Hokkaidō to the Kamchatka Peninsula. It includes the Kuril Islands (Chishima Islands). There are numerous active volcanoes, some of which have heights exceeding 1,000 m (3,280 ft). Major peaks include Oakandake, Meakandake, Tokachidake, and Asahidake (2,290 m; 7,511 ft) which is Hokkaidō's highest. There are many calderas and caldera lakes. The zone contains the three national parks of Shiretoko, Akan, and Daisetsuzan.

Chiso Kaisei → Land Tax Reform of 1873–1881

Chisso Corporation

(Chisso). Manufacturer of industrial chemicals, synthetic resins, chemical fertilizers, and fiber. The company is the successor of the Nippon Nitrogen Fertilizer Co (Nippon Chisso Hiryō), the corporate nucleus of the Nitchitsu industrial combine, which Noguchi Shitagau (1873–1944) directed and which controlled over 50 chemical firms in Japan and Korea before World War II. The serious mercury poisoning of hundreds of residents of the city of Minamata in Kumamoto Prefecture was caused by effluents from the Chisso fertilizer factory in that city. The poisoning first appeared in the mid-1950s, but the company refused to take responsibility for the pollution and continued to discharge waste into the ocean. The company was sued by victims of the poisoning and found guilty of negligence by the Kumamoto District Court in 1973 (see POLLUTION-RELATED DISEASES). Compensation paid to victims between 1973 and 1981 totaled ¥51.6 billion (US $202.2 million), a portion of which was borne by the national government. Sales for the fiscal year ending March 1982 totaled ¥118.2 billion (US $491 million); it was capitalized at ¥7.8 billion (US $32.4 million) in the same year. The company's head office is in Tōkyō. Chisso was removed from the Tōkyō Stock Exchange in March 1978.

Chita

City in Aichi Prefecture, central Honshū, on the west coast of the Chita Peninsula. The city has long been famous for its Chita cotton. Seaweed (*nori*) is cultivated on the coast. More recently, thermoelectric plants and shipyards have been constructed on reclaimed land. Pop: 64,832.

Chita Peninsula

(Chita Hantō). Located in western Aichi Prefecture, central Honshū. It divides the bays of Ise and Mikawa. The peninsula was formerly the site of large tracts of paddy fields. Gardening and dairy farming have flourished since the construction of the Aichi Canal. The northern part, near the city of Nagoya, is rapidly being both industrialized and transformed into a residential area. The southern part of the peninsula is part of Mikawa Bay Quasi-National Park. Tourism, farming, and fishing are the principal industries. Area: 355 sq km (137 sq mi).

Chitose

City in southwestern Hokkaidō on the river Chitosegawa. It was first settled in 1869; one of East Asia's largest salmon and trout hatcheries is located here. A naval airfield built before World War II was taken over by the US Occupation Forces in 1945. It is now the largest airport in Hokkaidō. Principal industries are food processing, nonferrous metals, furniture, and dairy farming. It is part of Shikotsu-Tōya National Park. Pop: 66,788.

chitsuroku shobun

A series of measures (*shobun*) adopted by the government after the MEIJI RESTORATION (1868) to abolish the hereditary stipends (*chitsuroku*) previously granted to the nobility and members of the *samurai* class, as well as the government allowances (*shōtenroku*) paid to those who had assisted in overthrowing the Tokugawa shogunate (1603–1867).

As a part of the Restoration reforms, in June 1869 the court aristocracy and former *daimyō* were classified as *kazoku* (see PEERAGE), while all other samurai were designated SHIZOKU. The following year the new government announced a reform of the domain (HAN) system, primarily as a way of reorganizing the payment of stipends to daimyō. In 1871, however, when the domains were abolished and replaced by prefectures (see PREFECTURAL SYSTEM, ESTABLISHMENT OF), the reform was halted, and in its stead a move was initiated to change the stipend system. The cost of rice stipends alone constituted 30 percent of government expenses; the passage of the CONSCRIPTION ORDINANCE OF 1873 and the need to raise funds for the new army and navy made the matter all the more urgent. The LAND TAX REFORM OF 1873–1881 provided that land taxes would thenceforward be paid in fixed sums of money and allowed the government to operate on a modern budget system.

In December 1873 the government instituted a graduated tax on stipends and a law giving former samurai with stipends of less than 100 *koku* (1 *koku*=about 180 liters or 5 US bushels; see KOKUDAKA) the option of receiving a lump-sum payment, half in cash, half in government bonds called *chitsuroku kōsai*, equaling a six-year stipend. The law was later changed to include those with more than 100 *koku*. Beginning in September 1875, it was decided that stipends would be paid in cash. Then, in August 1876, the government decreed that all stipends would be commuted to government bonds on a sliding scale: former daimyō would receive 5 to 7½ times their annual income in government bonds called KINROKU KŌSAI bearing 5 percent interest; former samurai with stipends between 20 and 200 *koku* would receive 7¾ to 11½ times their annual income in bonds bearing 6 percent interest; and those with stipends of 20 *koku* or less would receive 11⅖ to 14 times their income in bonds bearing 7 percent interest. The bonds would not be redeemable for a five-year period, but thereafter a lottery would be held each year for 30 years and selected bonds would be redeemed. Thus, bonds amounting to the enormous sum of ¥174,630,000 were issued to some 310,000 individuals. (The annual budget at the time amounted to about ¥59,000,000.) Statistics indicate that of this sum 18 percent went to former daimyō (0.2 percent of those paid off) and 62 percent went to 260,000 lower-ranking samurai (84 percent of those paid off).

These measures were a blow to the samurai and together with the loss of other feudal privileges were to lead to uprisings such as the AKIZUKI REBELLION OF 1876, the JIMPŪREN REBELLION, the HAGI REBELLION, and the SATSUMA REBELLION. It was found that by 1880 more than half of the poorer samurai had sold off their bonds. In contrast, the daimyō, who had received relatively generous settlements, were able to live comfortably and, as stockholders in the newly formed NATIONAL BANK system, became wealthy capitalists.

📖——Fukaya Hiroji, *Shintei kashizoku chitsuroku shobun no kenkyū* (1974). Niwa Kunio, *Meiji ishin no tochi henkaku* (1962).

KATŌ Kōzaburō

Chiyoda Chemical Engineering & Construction Co, Ltd

(Chiyoda Kakō Kensetsu). Japan's largest plant engineering firm. Builder of oil and natural gas plants and chemical plants. Established in 1948 by former employees of the Mitsubishi Oil Co, Ltd. A pioneer in the field of plant engineering, the company expanded swiftly in the late 1950s during the boom in construction of seaport oil refineries and petrochemical plants. Overseas business was initiated in 1959 with the export of a chemical plant to the Usiminas Iron and Steel Works in Brazil, and continued with the export of oil refineries as well as synthetic resin and chemical fertilizer plants to Korea, Southeast Asia, the Middle East, and Eastern Europe. Eighty percent of the firm's earnings are accrued overseas; since the mid-1970s an increasingly large part has come from contracts with oil-producing countries. Company exports also include plants for water treatment and desulfurization of exhaust gases which were developed in the 1960s. Subsidiary firms have been established in the United States, Singapore, Iran, and Saudi Arabia. Although the company's principal stockholders are firms affiliated with the Mitsubishi group, its management is independent. Sales for the fiscal year ending September 1981 totaled ¥269.8 billion (US $1.2 billion), of which 88.6 percent came from construction of oil and natural gas plants, 8.4 percent from petrochemical plants, and 3 percent from other projects. In the same year the company was capitalized at ¥6.4 billion (US $27.8 million). Corporate headquarters are in Tōkyō.

Chiyoda Ward

(Chiyoda Ku). One of the 23 wards of Tōkyō. The city's, and Japan's, economic and political center. Site of the Imperial Palace, the Diet building, various ministries, and judicial organs. During the Edo period (1600–1868), many *samurai* homes were located here. Chiyoda Ward's population is the smallest among the 23 wards. Government offices are located in the Nagatachō and Kasumigaseki districts, while business offices are concentrated in the Marunouchi and Ōtemachi districts. A number of universities are located in the Kanda district, while the Akihabara district is noted for its numerous wholesale and discount stores. Pop: 54,801.

chiyogami

A type of Japanese paper decorated with brightly colored, woodblock-printed patterns. Used today for a variety of handicrafts, such as covering small boxes and making *kimono* for paper dolls, *chiyogami* was first produced by UKIYO-E artists in the late 18th century. The word is a combination of *chiyo*, literally "a thousand generations," and *kami (gami)*, or paper, and has auspicious connotations similar to those evoked by the pine, bamboo, and plum blossom motifs with which it is often printed. See also WASHI.

SAITŌ Ryōsuke

chlorella

Chlorella spp. General term for species of green algae of the division *Chlorophyta*, family *Chlorellaceae*, genus *Chlorella*. Chlorella are very common in freshwater areas and often turn the water green. Since chlorella are hardy and prolific, they are easily produced in pure cultures and have long been used in research on photosynthesis. Chlorella have also been promoted as a food supplement since 1948 because they are particularly rich in protein and vitamins. Large-scale culture has already been attempted successfully in Japan. Species suitable for consumption are cultivated indoors by being shifted into consecutively larger containers and are finally placed outdoors in a large round culture reservoir under natural light until their full nutritive value is reached. Because the most suitable temperature for the growth of chlorella is approximately 25-30°C (77-86°F), outdoor culture reservoirs are best located in subtropical areas. Chlorella is currently sold in pill form, as problems of digestion and taste keep it from becoming a staple foodstuff rather than a food supplement. However, it is already used as food in space travel and in many other ways.

KAZAKI Hideo

Chōdensu → Minchō

Chōfu

City in Tōkyō Prefecture, 20 km (12 mi) west of central Tōkyō. A POST-STATION TOWN on the Kōshū Kaidō, a major highway in the Edo period (1600–1868), it is now a residential suburb, with electrical equipment and food-processing factories, and an important transportation center. The Chōfu Airfield for small aircraft is northwest of the city. Well-known tourist spots are the Jindai Botanical Gardens and the temple Jindaiji. Pop: 180,535.

Chōfu

District in the eastern part of the city of Shimonoseki, Yamaguchi Prefecture, western Honshū, on the Kammon Strait. Once the capital of Nagato Province (now part of Yamaguchi Prefecture), in the Edo period (1600–1868) it became a castle town of the Mōri family. It is now a residential area undergoing rapid industrialization. Chōfu is part of the Kita Kyūshū Industrial Zone.

Chōheirei → Conscription Ordinance of 1873

Chōjirō (1516–1592)

Kyōto potter and generally acknowledged originator of RAKU WARE. His father was a tilemaker, probably from Korea, and Chōjirō also began his career as a tilemaker. He soon attracted the attention of the tea master SEN NO RIKYŪ (1522–91) and under his guidance began making Raku ware for the tea ceremony. Chōjirō's bowls are soft bodied, low-fired, and shaped by hand. They often have warm red or rich black lead glazes such as those used in Ming-dynasty wares. Many of his teabowls, either black, red, or white Raku, have survived, and several are designated as Important Cultural Properties (see NATIONAL TREASURES). These bowls, which may actually include some by his assistants, are simple and unpretentious in design and shape, possessing a raw yet inviting tactile quality.

Ellen F. CARY

Chōjū giga

Also called *Chōjū jimbutsu giga* (Scrolls of Frolicking Animals and Humans). A group of ink paintings on scrolls (EMAKIMONO) and a few detached segments mainly depicting various animals, some behaving as if they were human. Dating from the Heian (794–1185) and Kamakura (1185–1333) periods, two sequences depict human priests and laymen playing various competitive games and contests. The principal surviving scrolls of the *Chōjū giga* are the four in the KŌZANJI, a temple in the northeastern section of Kyōto. In addition, there are several important detached segments that must once have been attached to the Kōzanji scrolls: one in the Tōkyō National Museum, one formerly in the Masuda Collection, one in the R. B. Martin Collection (on loan to the Brooklyn Museum), and one recently discovered in a private collection.

Among the Kōzanji scrolls, scroll A, measuring 30.6 by 1,148 centimeters (12 by 452 in), is the most famous, consisting entirely of caricatures of animals behaving as monks and laymen. The monkeys, hares, and frogs participate in sports such as swimming, archery, and wrestling, and entertainment such as dancing. At the very end of the scroll, a monkey in the guise of a Buddhist priest recites before a frog enthroned as a Buddha. Scroll B, measuring 30.7 by 1,189 centimeters (12.1 by 436.2 in), consists entirely of depictions of various animals, both real and mythical, all in a more or less continuous landscape setting. Scroll C, measuring 31.3 by 1,133 centimeters (12.3 by 446 in) begins with a sequence of games among human monks and laymen. Included in this sequence are games such as *go* and backgammon, as well as contests such as tug-of-war employing strings tied around ears, necks, or waists; a staring contest; a cockfight; and a dogfight. The second part of scroll C depicts games and contests among monkeys, hares, and frogs, including a magic competition among monkeys and frogs. Scroll D, measuring 31.2 by 933 centimeters (12.3 by 367.3 in), depicts human clerics and laymen engaged in such activities as a miracle competition among priests and itinerant monks known as *yamabushi,* various rituals, games, and amusements.

Study of the *Chōjū giga* scrolls has been complicated by their somewhat disordered and incomplete condition. Their very early history is unknown, but a document of the late 16th century in the Kōzanji mentions five scrolls in the temple at that time. By the latter part of the Edo period (1600–1868), however, only the present four scrolls remained.

Although obviously related in subject matter and general style of depiction, the scrolls incorporate the work of more than one artist and do not all belong to a single period. At present, scrolls A and B are considered to be works of the late Heian period, while scrolls C and D are likely to have been produced in the 13th century, during the Kamakura period. Scroll C has an inscription at the end, dated 1253.

Traditionally, the paintings of the *Chōjū giga* were attributed to TOBA SŌJŌ (1053–1140). Recent studies have suggested, however, that even within Kōzanji scroll A, more than one artist might have been involved. The high quality of draftsmanship, using ink exclusively, in scrolls A and B especially suggests that the artists were experienced in depicting Buddhist subjects.

Unlike other surviving scroll paintings from the Heian and Kamakura periods, the *Chōjū giga* scrolls contain no text. The meaning of the contests and games within the scrolls has been the subject of much discussion. There is strong evidence of a satirical intent in the depictions of the activities of monks and priests, and in the mimicry of human activities by animals. It has also been suggested that there is a relationship to Chinese or Indian legends, or to other Buddhist or secular subjects prevalent in the late Heian period.

The *Chōjū giga* scrolls treat a subject unique among extant paintings of the late Heian to Kamakura periods, and they do not seem to correspond to any known literary text. Their lively manner of depiction using only ink prefigures the rise of ink monochrome painting as a major mode of Buddhist painting during the Kamakura and Muromachi (1333–1568) periods (see INK PAINTING). See also HAKUBYŌGA.

📖——Tani Shin'ichi, ed, *Chōjū giga,* vol 4 of *Shinshū Nihon emakimono zenshū* (Kadokawa Shoten, 1976).　　*Ann* YONEMURA

chōka

("long poem"). Also called *nagauta.* A form in Japanese classical verse (WAKA) consisting of any number of alternating 5- and 7-syllable lines ending with an extra 7-syllable line. Distinguished from the 31-syllable TANKA ("short poem"). The *chōka* was often followed by one or more 31-syllable envoys in *tanka* form, called *hanka* or *kaeshiuta,* that summarized or elaborated on its theme.

The form flourished in the late 7th and early 8th centuries and was perfected by KAKINOMOTO NO HITOMARO. The MAN'YŌSHŪ (ca 759), the oldest extant anthology of Japanese poetry, contains 265 *chōka,* the longest of which is 149 lines, the shortest only 7. By the Heian period (794–1185) the form had nearly died out.

Susan Downing VIDEEN

Chōkaisan

Composite volcano in the Chōkai Volcanic Zone. Also known as Chōkai Fuji, Dewa Fuji, or Akita Fuji. It is on the border between Akita and Yamagata prefectures, northern Honshū. On the crater rim are peaks such as Shōgatake, Gassammori, Sensumori, Nabemori, and Shichikōsan, as well as the lake called Torinoumi. The central peak of Chōkai Quasi-National Park, it erupted in 1974 for the first time in 153 years. Ōmonoimi Shrine is on Chōkaisan's summit. Height: 2,230 m (7,314 ft).

Chōkai Volcanic Zone

(Chōkai Kazantai). Volcanic zone extending along the Sea of Japan coast from southern Hokkaidō to Niigata Prefecture. The zone centers on the highest peak, CHŌKAISAN (2,230 m; 7,314 ft), and is dominated by the Dewa Mountains. Other important peaks include IWAKISAN and GASSAN. Most of the volcanoes are conical. There are numerous hot springs. Parts of the Chōkai Volcanic Zone are included in Oga and Chōkai quasi-national parks and Bandai–Asahi National Park.

Chōkei, Emperor (1343–1394)

The 98th sovereign *(tennō)* in the traditional count (which includes several nonhistorical emperors); reigned 1368–83. He was the eldest son and successor of Go-Murakami (1328–68; r 1339–68), second emperor of the short-lived Southern Court (1336–92; see NORTHERN AND SOUTHERN COURTS). His enthronement ceremony is thought to have taken place at Sumiyoshi. Because the Southern Court was hard pressed by the superior forces of the Northern Court and the Muromachi shogunate, Chōkei was forced to change his residence frequently during his 14-year reign, staying in temples designated as "temporary palaces." In 1383 he abdicated in favor of his brother GO-KAMEYAMA. An amateur of classical literature, he wrote *Sengenshō,* a commentary on the TALE OF GENJI. Documentation for Chōkei's life and reign is extremely scanty and uncertain, and it was not until 1926 that he was placed on the official list of emperors.

G. Cameron HURST III

chokkomon

("straight-curved pattern"). A form of decoration of obscure origin and uncertain meaning found on Kofun-period (ca 300–710) objects of the 4th to the 6th centuries. The pattern is generally composed of crossing diagonal lines imposed over fragmented concentric circles; it is found painted, incised, or cast on shell bracelets, bone sword guards, stone headrests, BRONZE MIRRORS, and HANIWA funerary sculptures. On a larger scale, it may be carved on stone coffins, walls, or other parts of the ORNAMENTED TOMBS found in western Japan. The *chokkomon* design has been variously explained as a skeuomorph, a plaited rope, a device to bind the spirit to the tomb chamber, a pattern to placate the spirit of the dead, or as simple cosmic symbolism. See also HISTORY OF JAPAN: protohistory.

📖——Saitō Kazuo and Usa Shin'ichi, "Chokkomon no kenkyū," *Kodaigaku kenkyū,* vol 6 (1952), vol 7 (1952), vol 11 (1955).

J. Edward KIDDER, JR.

Chōkōdō ryō

(domains of the Chōkōdō). The Chōkōdō was a chapel built in 1185 by the powerful retired emperor GO-SHIRAKAWA in his Rokujō palace in Kyōto. To this chapel he commended numerous estates *(shōen);* its holdings eventually amounted to more than 180 separate proprietorships, in 42 provinces, which yielded an enormous income. In 1192 Go-Shirakawa bequeathed the Chōkōdō *ryō* to his daughter Princess Sen'yō Mon'in (1181–1252). In 1267 the estates passed to Emperor GO-FUKAKUSA, and after the division of the imperial house into two branches, they became the principal economic asset of the Jimyōin line. During the period of the NORTHERN AND

SOUTHERN COURTS (1336–92), these domains were largely appropriated by provincial warriors, and they were completely dispersed during the ŌNIN WAR (1467–77).   *G. Cameron HURST III*

Chōkokuji → Hasedera

chokurei → imperial ordinance

Chōkyōsai Eiri (fl late 18th century)

UKIYO-E artist. Also known as Hosoda Eiri. Specialized in portraits of contemporary beauties *(bijinga)*; influenced by the style of Kitagawa UTAMARO. Eiri, along with Hosoda Eishō, is one of the best-known disciples of HOSODA EISHI. There is some question concerning the identity of Chōkyōsai Eiri; he is considered by some to be the same person as Rekisentei Eiri or Shikyūsai Eiri, but others maintain that these are all different people. Eiri's portrait prints of his contemporaries, the novelist SANTŌ KYŌDEN and the JŌRURI performer Tomimoto Buzen, are unusual among *ukiyo-e* portraits of the time, which usually depict *kabuki* actors and *sumō* wrestlers.

Chōmonkyō

Gorge on the middle reaches of the river ABUGAWA, Yamaguchi Prefecture, western Honshū. A quartz porphyry gorge abounding in sheer cliffs, deep ravines, gigantic rocks, and waterfalls. Designated a Place of Scenic Beauty in 1923, it is part of the Chōmonkyō Prefectural Natural Park. It attracts numerous tourists in the *ayu* (sweetfish) fishing season and in autumn when the leaves turn crimson. Yunose Hot Spring is located here. Length: 12 km (7.5 mi).

chōnaikai

(neighborhood associations). Also called *chōkai* or *jichikai.* Quasigovernmental organizations that have limited responsibility for local administration and coordinate numerous local activities in urban neighborhoods of up to several hundred households. In the past, *chōnaikai* exercised considerable control over many facets of residents' lives, in the manner of rural *burakukai* (hamlet associations), with which they are historically linked. Since World War II, however, *chōnaikai* have generally become moribund, thriving only in relatively traditional urban districts such as SHITAMACHI.

Modern *chōnaikai* descend from local administrative systems, highly developed during the Edo period (1600–1868), that held local residents communally responsible for collecting taxes, maintaining order, and enforcing orthodox behavior. After the Meiji Restoration (1868) these local groups lost legal standing, but in the 1920s they reappeared in many urban neighborhoods. In Tōkyō, particularly, *chōnaikai* were revived in the chaotic aftermath of the Tōkyō Earthquake of 1923.

In 1940 *chōnaikai* as well as subgroups called *tonarigumi* or *rimpohan* (consisting of about 10 neighboring households) became legally mandatory in all cities. Under strict government supervision throughout the war, they were responsible for rationing, civil defense, and stifling dissent. Because they were closely linked to the war effort, and presumably antidemocratic, Occupation authorities abolished *chōnaikai* and *tonarigumi* after the war.

Partially resurrected in the early 1950s, *chōnaikai* are now nominally independent voluntary associations, but most still maintain close ties with local governments, and in most membership is still virtually ascribed for all households. Typically dominated by *yūryokusha* (bosses)—usually influential local shopowners and small-scale industrialists—*chōnaikai* are generally conservative and subservient to local governments, acting as their agents and taking responsibility for many municipal services, such as street lighting, local sanitation, and traffic safety.

Chōnaikai also play an important role in social life. They organize numerous other local groups (e.g., children's, youth, women's, and old people's clubs; crime and fire prevention committees; and shopkeepers associations) and recreational activities and trips, as well as providing a vehicle for informal social ties among neighbors. One of their most important symbolic activities is organizing local festivals *(matsuri),* which, though now largely devoid of religious meaning, are conducted with much ceremonious display and *sake*, and are a great source of local pride and identification, especially in older *shitamachi* neighborhoods. See also GONINGUMI; LOCAL GOVERNMENT; NEIGHBORHOOD ASSOCIATIONS.   *Theodore C. BESTOR*

Chōnin

Detail from *Night Stalls in Junkeichō,* a woodblock print by Hiroshige showing *chōnin* life in Ōsaka. Ca 1834. Private collection.

Chongqing (Chungking) government

(Jūkei *seifu*). The Guomindang (Kuomintang; KMT; Nationalist Party) government of China during the period of the SINO-JAPANESE WAR OF 1937–1945 after its move from Nanjing (Nanking) to Chongqing in the southwestern province of Sichuan (Szechwan). In December 1937 the Chinese capital at Nanjing fell to the Japanese. The Guomindang government fled west to Hankou (Hankow), Hubei (Hupeh) Province. When the Japanese took the latter city in October 1938, the Guomindang moved further west to Chongqing, where it remained until 1946, continuing its resistance to the Japanese in an uneasy alliance with the Chinese Communist Party. Deprived of its financial base, the Guomindang government was forced to print money, contributing to a staggering inflation. In addition, it had to contend with local provincial authorities, swollen military and administrative establishments, illicit trade with areas held by Japanese troops, and Japanese bombing. Under these circumstances its authoritarianism and corruption grew unchecked. The Guomindang government returned to Nanjing in the spring of 1946.

chōnin

(townsmen). The inhabitants—other than nobles, *samurai,* and priests—of urban administrative districts or *chō (machi)* in premodern times, especially in the Edo period (1600–1868). In a more restricted sense it is sometimes used to describe commoners owning real property in, and participating in the administration of, such urban districts. Much of the literature on *chōnin* concentrates on the upper echelons, that is to say, the wealthy financiers and wholesale merchants who formed the hub of national economic life under the Tokugawa shogunate (1603–1867). This concentration is due both to their economic importance and to the fact that the records of these large establishments survive in great quantities. It should be noted, however, that the vast majority of *chōnin* were poor artisans, peddlers, and day laborers. Under the Tokugawa system of social classes—*shi* (samurai), *nō* (farmers), *kō* (artisans), and *shō* (merchants)—*chōnin* were either artisans or merchants, but the term is basically a classification of townsmen for administrative purposes rather than on simply geographical or occupational lines (see SHI-NŌ-KŌ-SHŌ).

Although there were urban communities much earlier, *chōnin* first became important as an object of urban administration around 1600. They were always subordinate to the samurai authorities, and autonomous city communities of the kind that appeared in medieval Europe did not develop in Japan. The ubiquitous guilds, groups, and other associations of townsmen were for control purposes rather than for self-government. Typically the premodern Japanese city grew up around a castle, which formed the center of feudal administration, and the function of *chōnin* was to serve the needs of that administration and of the samurai who staffed it. Official policy was that they should be confined to that role, but once a city reached a certain size, further growth was largely to serve the needs of the *chōnin* themselves. Under the Tokugawa political system, cities thus became something of an anomaly, and the authorities, who had originally worked to attract townsmen to their cities, thenceforward discouraged urbanization. At the same time the shogunate and those daimyō whose CASTLE TOWNS were large enough used the urban economic organizations to control the economic life of the territories under their administration, although with decreasing success as rural economic life developed.

Although despised by the samurai authorities of premodern Japan and by their successors, the governing classes of the Meiji period (1868–1912), chōnin were an essential part of the economic system and contributed much to Japanese culture. After the MEIJI RESTORATION of 1868 chōnin disappeared as an administrative class, but they continued to play an important economic role and stubbornly maintained their culture and way of life against official efforts to impose samurai norms.

Early History —— The term chōnin (machibito, machiudo) originated in Kyōto, where the smallest geographic unit or block was known as a chō. Kyōto was for most of the Heian period (794–1185) occupied mainly by the nobility, temples, and their retainers, centered on the imperial court. Their households were largely self-sufficient and, although the city plan provided for two marketplaces, were supplied by farmers from neighboring villages. Toward the end of the period, however, shops and resident merchants appeared in various parts of the city. Their proprietors were the first chōnin. A similar group emerged in Kamakura, the headquarters of the Kamakura shogunate (1192–1333), and in the 15th and early 16th centuries a few medium-sized towns and a hundred or so smaller ones grew up around ports, communications centers, large temples, and the seats of local barons. They did not, however, develop further as autonomous city communities.

It was with the unification of the country under ODA NOBUNAGA and TOYOTOMI HIDEYOSHI in the late 16th century and the urbanization of the samurai class that large cities first emerged to serve the needs of the military leaders. The building of castles at Ōsaka, Fushimi, Nagoya, and later Edo (now Tōkyō) brought large numbers of people to the sites to serve the needs of the military establishments, and many settled there in areas (machi) designated for the purpose.

Chōnin as an administrative class first became established under the social and political system set up by the Tokugawa shogunate in the early 17th century. The discussion that follows is concerned mainly with the major cities, that is to say, Kyōto, Ōsaka, and Edo. The larger daimyō domains had castle towns such as Nagoya, Sendai, Kanazawa, Hikone, or Kumamoto with several thousand inhabitants, and regulation of their chōnin was modeled on that of Edo, although on a much smaller scale. Some major ports like Nagasaki, Shimonoseki, Shimizu, and Chōshi also had substantial communities.

Emergence of the Chōnin Class —— At the beginning of the 17th century each of the three major cities had a distinctive character. Kyōto, the seat of the imperial court, was already an established financial and handicraft center. With the decline of the nobility and their estates (SHŌEN) Kyōto had ceased to be the national center to which the economic surplus of Japan flowed to support the aristocracy in the style to which they had been accustomed in the Heian period. During the Muromachi period (1333–1568) the townsmen of Kyōto found a new function in catering to the needs of the military leaders who settled in the city, and the wealthiest of them mixed freely with the military and aristocracy and participated fully in the cultural life of the city. With the end of the wars of the 16th century and the unification of the country under the Tokugawa shogunate, demand for Kyōto's financial services and handicraft products increased, and the removal of the center of national administration to Edo in 1603 did not have an immediate adverse effect on the life of the city. The leaders of the Kyōto chōnin community were still those who had served the leading military figures through the wars of the late 16th century as financial agents, quartermasters, and confidants and who had on occasion accompanied their patrons on their campaigns. In the course of their services some, like SUMINOKURA RYŌI, GOTŌ MITSUTSUGU, and CHAYA SHIROJIRŌ, had acquired licenses, tax privileges, and patents that gave them a preeminent position in interregional trade within Japan as well as in foreign trade. In social background and culture they were not sharply differentiated from the military leaders themselves. This culture was shared by the doctors, artists, and practitioners of the various traditional arts who lived in the city. Most of the townsmen, however, were small shopkeepers or artisans who worked for masters in the textile trades and other handicraft industries.

Development of the two other major cities dates from the unification of the country and was actively promoted by the unifiers themselves. Ōsaka originally grew up around the fortified ISHIYAMA HONGANJI temple, founded in 1496, and lacked the aristo-

cratic traditions of Kyōto. With the occupation of the city first by Nobunaga and then Hideyoshi and the building of ŌSAKA CASTLE, begun in 1583, the city entered a new era. The building of this castle required the deployment of large numbers of workmen and vast quantities of materials, and leading merchants who had been associated with Hideyoshi were appointed to organize them. After the Tokugawa shogunate destroyed the remnants of the Toyotomi faction in 1615 (see ŌSAKA CASTLE, SIEGES OF), the city was reorganized and merchant communities were brought from Sakai, Fushimi, Hirano, and other neighboring areas. Leading merchants like the Yodoya were put in charge of the town community. From this time on, Ōsaka was the principal center into which the revenues of western Japan flowed, mainly in the form of rice. It was also the chief entrepôt and processing center for products such as oil, cotton, sake, miso, soy sauce, and charcoal. Under the Tokugawa shogunate there was only a small garrison stationed in the city, and Ōsaka became the city of chōnin par excellence. By the late 17th century its DŌJIMA RICE MARKET, warehousing facilities (see KURAYASHIKI), and financial services were well developed and were essential to the working of the BAKUHAN SYSTEM of shogunate and domains. Organized in guilds (KABUNAKAMA), the merchants and financiers of Ōsaka were the channel through which the shogunate sought to control the national economy as a whole.

Edo, as the seat of the shogunate and the place where all daimyō maintained establishments under the SANKIN KŌTAI (alternate attendance) system, was by contrast the city of samurai. The chōnin community began with the recruitment of large numbers of construction workers for the building of EDO CASTLE and the residences of the daimyō. Building contractors, artisans, and merchants were encouraged to settle in Edo to supply the needs of the shogunate and the large numbers of samurai who were posted there. Within 50 years, however, the chōnin population, mainly construction workers, small shopkeepers, and peddlers, had grown to such a size that its own consumption needs provided the basis for further growth and diversification.

The provincial castle towns arose from the removal of samurai and commerce from the countryside and their concentration in the administrative center. Although frequent fires maintained the construction industry in Edo, in the provincial towns it tended to lose its preeminence once the castle building was completed. Few of these towns grew to any great size, and their chōnin largely remained in the role of suppliers to the samurai establishment and providers under official supervision of commercial services in the domain. In ports and communication centers life seems to have been somewhat freer. Nagasaki, as the only official port for overseas trade, had a special administration in which licensed participants in the trade played an important part.

The chōnin of Japanese cities and towns thus had a variety of beginnings and included all sorts and conditions of people. With the development of the Tokugawa system in the second quarter of the 17th century, however, they became standardized as an administrative category. Kyōto, perhaps because it had the longest experience of chōnin, provided the model. The codes issued by ITAKURA KATSUSHIGE, the Kyōto deputy (Kyōto shoshidai) from 1603 to 1619, in city administration as in other fields formed the basis for much of Tokugawa legislation. Similar ordinances defining the status of chōnin were issued for Edo in 1650 and for Ōsaka in 1660. These and the many that followed gave the chōnin an identity defined by sumptuary regulations and special systems of administrative control. These controls were administered in detail both by geographic units (chō) and, perhaps more importantly, through occupational groups (see also MACHI YAKUNIN; MACHIBURE).

Further Development of Chōnin —— As the Japanese economy and interregional trade developed, urban communities became not simply providers for the needs of the ruling class but also a major source of demand on their own account. This change took place in Edo and Ōsaka around the end of the 17th century. As commercial services developed, the official merchants appointed at the beginning of the century found their functions increasingly taken over by a new group of entrepreneurs who organized and often financed production and distribution over quite wide areas of Japan and especially the collection of goods in Ōsaka and their supply to Edo. Much of this trade was among chōnin themselves and was not confined to supplying the shogunate and its retainers. Official attempts to control this trade in the interests of shogunal policy took the form of encouraging or even requiring associations of merchants (nakama, kabunakama), which received some privileges in return for being amenable to official direction. The ton'ya nakama (wholesale merchant guilds; see TOIYA) of Ōsaka founded in the 1660s to 1680s and the TOKUMI-DOIYA (Ten Groups of Wholesalers) of Edo founded in 1694 were typical of this trend. Artisans too, who now worked mainly for masters or as day laborers rather than for the government, were controlled through associations of master craftsmen.

In Edo the population doubled in the second half of the 17th century and reached one million (including samurai and their dependents) by 1720. About half of these were chōnin who came to the city from other parts of Japan. The new merchants typically came from Ise, Ōmi, or Ōsaka and brought their staff and apprentices with them. Their Edo branches formed small paternalistic communities that retained strong links with their home bases. Artisans, however, soon lost contact with their origins and developed a way of life that became typical of Edo. Much of the growth of the Edo chōnin community took the form of an influx of unskilled laborers from villages in the Kantō and Tōhoku regions, and supervision of these large numbers of urban poor posed a continuing problem for the authorities. Outside of Edo few towns reached the stage where the demands of the chōnin community itself provided a basis for continued growth. Manufacturing towns were rare, as industry tended to develop in rural areas.

Strata of Chōnin —— Although the great financiers and wholesale merchants of Ōsaka and Edo were the leaders of the chōnin community, they were by no means representative of the class as a whole, which in fact included a wide range. At the other end of the scale was a much larger number of poor peddlers and laborers who barely made ends meet. In between were smaller wholesalers, retailers and stallholders, building contractors, master craftsmen, independent tradesmen, and their employees and apprentices, as well as contract and casual workers. The entertainment industry—the "gay quarters" and their unofficial competitors, eating and drinking establishments of all kinds—and inns, then as now, employed relatively large numbers of people.

In Edo only a small minority of chōnin owned land. The remainder rented premises mostly in small back-street tenements, and many had no fixed address at all. In 1832 over half the chōnin of Edo were classed as poor, which meant that they led a hand-to-mouth existence. These 200,000 or so urban poor were a potential source of unrest, and in times of famine or high prices, such as in 1733 (Kyōhō 18), 1787 (Temmei 7), and the 1830s (Tempō era), rioting became a serious problem. From time to time the shogunate ordered all Edo residents who were unable to prove any official affiliation or sponsorship to return to their villages (see HITOGAESHI). This was done, for example, as part of the KANSEI REFORMS (1787–93) and again in the TEMPŌ REFORMS (1841–43). These orders were combined with stricter controls over chōnin and some urban relief measures. Although these measures failed to produce any lasting reduction in the urban population, they were reasonably effective in maintaining law and order within the city.

Daily Life —— The wealthy chōnin of Kyōto, Edo, Ōsaka, and Nagasaki lived, at least on the surface, a strictly regulated life devoted to business and the maintenance of their credit and reputations. Most of the larger establishments codified rules of both business and private conduct for themselves and their employees. Despite the economic power that their wealth gave them, they were always strictly subject to the samurai authorities, and their codes of conduct always stressed this. Regulations, tradition, and etiquette were punctiliously observed. Although their style of life was regulated by sumptuary laws and conspicuous extravagance was liable to bring summary punishment, rich chōnin lived in a style unthinkable for the average Japanese and beyond the reach of most samurai. Their houses were usually plain on the outside but richly furnished, and their storehouses contained many art treasures. Clothing, in theory limited to cotton or plain silk, could nevertheless be very expensive and lined with sumptuous materials. Chōnin such as KINOKUNIYA BUNZAEMON and NARAYA MOZAEMON, who made huge fortunes in the boom conditions of Edo in the Genroku era (1688–1704), indulged in extravagances that made them a byword for free spending. The Edo FUDASASHI (financiers of the direct retainers of the shogunate) lived in a style that brought continual rebukes from the authorities and furnished the model for kabuki heroes like Sukeroku.

Edo was always a samurai city. Although chōnin made up at least half of the population, they were allotted only 16 percent of the city area. For most of them, therefore, life was very cramped, and the living space occupied by the average family of three or four was about 9 square meters (10.8 sq yd). Because most of the Edo chōnin came as single immigrants, males outnumbered females by almost two to one, and this influenced their style of life in many ways. For most Edo chōnin, life was a constant struggle and involved working from dawn until after dark. Wives and children usually had to contribute to the family income by engaging in various by-employments. Nevertheless, city life was in many ways preferable to life in the poorer villages. Most importantly, chōnin were virtually free of tax obligations. There was usually some work available, and although wages were low, by working hard enough even poor chōnin could usually eat rice every day. Moreover, life in the city was socially much freer than in the village. While established merchants paid great attention to their social obligations, most chōnin, especially in Edo, were free of the social ties accumulated over centuries in the village. Only one in three Edo chōnin was born in the city, and most moved frequently because of fires or fluctuating economic fortunes and so often hardly knew their neighbors. Socially, too, urban society was much more mobile than village society. By talent, hard work, or good fortune chōnin could rise in the world and make a name for themselves in ways unthinkable in a village. Of course only a small minority actually made good, but the possibility of success continued to attract people to the cities. Life was also more varied and interesting than on the farm. For those who could afford it, entertainment was always available in many forms. The house rules of many substantial merchants forbade visiting the pleasure quarters and other such frivolous entertainments, but they were nevertheless well patronized. Festivals and street entertainers provided amusement even for the poor, and literary and musical hobbies were popular and well catered to. In such circles even chōnin of modest means could associate with intellectuals, artists, and samurai in a way that was impossible for commoners outside of the cities. Thus, although city life lacked the security of life in the villages, chōnin, perhaps making a virtue of necessity, were proud of their independence and self-reliance. This pride still survives among some independent artisans, but it was the restricted and dependent status of the villager and the paternalistic practices of the large commercial establishments that formed the model for the lifestyle of most Japanese workers today.

Chōnin Culture —— Much of the art, literature, music, and drama of the Edo period is associated particularly with chōnin. Practitioners of these arts were indeed almost all chōnin, but their clientele was by no means limited to their own class. Samurai patronized the KABUKI theater, and many of its themes were designed to appeal to them. Samurai themselves tended to practice more classical arts like Chinese calligraphy and painting, Chinese and Japanese classical poetry, and NŌ drama, but their wives and daughters often studied the music of the SHAMISEN. Theatrical groups visited villages all over Japan once or twice a year, and in some villages farmers even performed plays themselves. Thus the distinction between chōnin culture and the culture of other classes was, at least by the 19th century, perhaps not quite as sharp as commentators of the Meiji period (1868-1912) would have us believe. Nevertheless, it was distinctive enough to be broadly rejected by the political and intellectual leaders of the Meiji period. In the course of the "samuraization" of Japanese culture in the Meiji period and since, the contribution of chōnin to the economic and cultural development of modern Japan has been minimized. In fact, however, they played an essential role in the expansion of traditional economic activity and, when the time was ripe, participated fully in the development of modern industry and commerce. In the cultural field too, they contributed much to the life of modern Japan and tenaciously maintained their SHITAMACHI culture against the samurai-type official ethic until in the postwar period both became so attenuated as to be scarcely recognizable.

📖 ——Chihōshi Kenkyū Kyōgikai, ed, Nihon no machi (1958). Harada Tomohiko, Chūsei ni okeru toshi no kenkyū (1942). Ishida Ichirō, Chōnin bunka (1961). Kōda Shigetomo, Edo to Ōsaka (1934). Mitamura Engyo, Edo no seikatsu (1941). Miyamoto Mataji, Ōsaka chōnin ron (1959). Nakabe Yoshiko, Kinsei toshi no seiritsu to kōzō (1967). Nishiyama Matsunosuke, ed, Edo chōnin no kenkyū, 3 vols (1973). Sakata Yoshio, Chōnin (1939).   Sydney CRAWCOUR

chōnindō

("Way of the merchant," as distinguished from BUSHIDŌ, "Way of the warrior"). A term which came into use in the Meiji period (1868-1912) to designate the behavioral and ethical code of the townsmen (CHŌNIN) or merchant class during the Edo period (1600-1868). It affirmed the pursuit of profit through the exercise of business acumen and frugality and advocated respect for propriety and fulfillment of social and familial obligations as the prerequisites

Chōsei

One of the Twelve Divine Generals by Chōsei, 1064. Wood, lacquered and painted. Height 121.5 cm. Kōryūji, Kyōto. National Treasure.

of financial success. In the 18th century, when the townsmen began to question and redefine their role in Tokugawa feudal society, quasi-religious schools of popular philosophy such as Sekimon Shingaku (see SHINGAKU), founded by ISHIDA BAIGAN, and others led by such scholars as NISHIKAWA JOKEN appeared and fostered a sense of pride and collective identity in the merchant class. See also CHŌNIN KŌKEN ROKU.   *IMAI Jun*

Chōnin kōken roku

Set of instructions completed by Mitsui Takafusa (1684–1748) in 1728 to explain the MITSUI house laws to his descendants and to ensure the family's continued prosperity. Takafusa, a third-generation Mitsui, set down his father Takahira's oral account of the vicissitudes of over 40 Kyōto merchant houses in his lifetime. He intersperses the narrative with appropriate morals and lessons on the behavior befitting a merchant, especially vis-à-vis members of the ruling *samurai* class, and points out the dangers of extravagance, lending to *daimyō*, and purveying goods to the shogunate. It is an invaluable source of information on the life of merchants during the late 17th and early 18th centuries.

Chōri Co, Ltd

Trading firm specializing in textiles which also handles chemical products, machinery, and other commodities. The majority of its products are made by TŌRAY INDUSTRIES, INC; ASAHI CHEMICAL INDUSTRY CO, LTD; and TEIJIN, LTD. Established in 1861, it is the largest handler among Japanese trading firms of synthetic yarns and textiles, and it has become a market leader and systems organizer in the domestic textile industry. It has a total of 22 overseas branches and is involved in 14 joint ventures overseas engaged in the import and export of synthetic fibers and chemical products. Sales for the fiscal year ending March 1982 totaled ¥589.8 billion (US $2.5 billion), of which 71 percent consisted of textiles. In the same year foreign trade accounted for 25 percent of the company's activity and the firm was capitalized at ¥7.8 billion (US $32.4 million). Corporate headquarters are located in Ōsaka.

chōsan

(literally, "flight"). Abandonment of land by tenant farmers in order to avoid payment of annual taxes (NENGU) and compulsory labor service (BUYAKU). The term came into use late in the Heian period (794–1185), replacing the earlier term *chōbō*, to describe the ab-

sconding of peasants under the pressures of the HANDEN SHŪJU SYSTEM of land allocation. Peasants unable to meet their obligations usually fled to neighboring estates (SHŌEN) or simply became vagrants. In the Kamakura period (1185–1333) tenants often defected en masse to demand the lightening of tax and labor burdens or to protest the corrupt practices of *shōen* officials; they would hide in the mountains while negotiations took place and afterward return to the land. Early in the Muromachi period (1333–1568) these protests developed into shows of force (GŌSO) and even violent uprisings (IKKI); and from the Sengoku period (1467–1568) onward, growing numbers of peasants abandoned their land permanently and moved to the cities. During the Edo period (1600–1868), in spite of shogunate interdictions, peasants continued to abscond; indeed it was not uncommon for entire villages to flee to neighboring domains, which would then help negotiate conditions for their return. As late as 1850, for example, several thousand peasants of the Morioka domain (now part of Iwate Prefecture) ran away to avoid their obligations.

Chōsei (1010–1091)

Heian-period (794–1185) Buddhist sculptor; leading disciple of the well-known sculptor JŌCHŌ. Founder of the Sanjō BUSSHO (workshop), which came to be known as the EN SCHOOL of Buddhist sculpture. In 1065 he was awarded the Buddhist rank of *hokkyō* in appreciation of the statues he made for the Kyōto temple Hōjōji. He attained the rank of *hōgen* in 1070 and *hōin*, the highest Buddhist rank, in 1077. Among his surviving works are the Nikkō Bosatsu (Suryaprabha), the Gakkō Bosatsu (Candraprabha), and the Twelve Divine Generals at the temple Kōryūji in Kyōto.

chōsen

Official documents regarding local affairs; issued from around the middle of the Heian period (794–1185) through the 14th century. Many of these were sent to local subordinates by provincial governors (KOKUSHI) or by the top officials of the government headquarters in Kyūshū (DAZAIFU), who often stayed in Kyōto and administered their provinces without moving to their assignments. The documents took their name from the two characters *chō* (provincial governor) and *sen* (decree) with which they usually began. In format they followed the style of KUDASHIBUMI and up to the 12th century bore a provincial seal *(kokuin)*. See also DIPLOMATICS.

Chōsen Ginkō

(Bank of Korea). The central bank of Korea during the period of Japanese colonial control (1910–45). Established by the Japanese in 1909 as the Kankoku Ginkō, the bank took the place of the Japanese Daiichi Kokuritsu Ginkō (First National Bank), which had established a Korean branch in 1878 and had operated as the central bank of Korea after the conclusion of the Russo-Japanese War of 1904–05. The bank was reorganized in 1911 after the annexation of Korea by Japan, and the name was changed to Chōsen Ginkō to reflect the Japanese colonial name for Korea. It was managed by the Government-General of Korea until 1924, when the Japanese Ministry of Finance assumed supervision. The Japanese government appointed the board of governors, but the bank's stock was owned by private Japanese banks and corporations. The bank issued the Korean currency, controlled domestic prices, and serviced international trade through branches in Manchuria, the major ports of China and Japan, London, and New York. The bank was dissolved by order of the Allied forces at the end of World War II.   *C. Kenneth QUINONES*

Chōsen Kaikyō → Korea Strait

Chōsen tsūshinshi

Delegations from the Korean YI DYNASTY to the TOKUGAWA SHOGUNATE during the Edo period (1600–1868). Relations between Japan and Korea had been broken off with the INVASIONS OF KOREA IN 1592 AND 1597. However, after the establishment of the Tokugawa shogunate the strong desire of the SŌ FAMILY of Tsushima, an island in the Korean Strait, for the restoration of trade with Korea led to the resumption of friendly relations between the two countries.

Chōsen tsūshinshi ——Korean delegation of 1811

Sketch of the Korean delegation in Japan, with the Korean envoy in a palanquin carried by Japanese bearers and accompanied by Korean attendants. Detail of one print from *Sketches of the Procession of the Korean Tributary Mission.* Ca 1811. Tōkyō Metropolitan Central Library.

The first envoy, accompanied by 467 attendants, came to Edo (now Tōkyō) in 1607 to offer congratulations to Tokugawa Hidetada, who had become shōgun two years earlier. There was a total of 12 delegations, usually for auspicious occasions such as the succession of a new shōgun; the last visit took place in 1811. Each envoy was accompanied by hundreds of attendants, necessitating large expenditures on the Japanese side as well. The shogunal adviser ARAI HAKUSEKI simplified the receptions for these envoys, but the Korean visits continued to have a special significance for Japan during this period when the policy of NATIONAL SECLUSION was in effect.

Chōshi

City in northeastern Chiba Prefecture, central Honshū, at the mouth of the river Tonegawa. A major fishing port, with the largest catch of sardines, bonito, and tuna in the prefecture, Chōshi has numerous marine product processing plants. Soy sauce is another important industry. On the nearby cape INUBŌZAKI there is a lighthouse built by the English engineer Richard Henry Brunton. Pop: 89,415.

Chōshū Expeditions

Two punitive expeditions, in 1864 and 1866, by the Tokugawa shogunate against the Chōshū domain (now Yamaguchi Prefecture). By the 1860s the imperial court in Kyōto had gained substantial influence in national politics, and the great domains, notably Satsuma (now Kagoshima Prefecture) and Chōshū, vied for influence in Kyōto and, by extension, in national policy making. In 1863 antiforeign, antishogunate forces from Chōshū managed to gain control of the Kyōto court, but were driven out by a superior Satsuma force in the COUP D'ETAT OF 30 SEPTEMBER 1863. In the summer of 1864, Chōshū activists attempted to regain control of Kyōto, but failed (see HAMAGURI GOMON INCIDENT). They were labeled "enemies of the court," and the shogunate was given a mandate to punish them, thus precipitating the first Chōshū expedition.

By the fall of 1864 Chōshū was surrounded by a shogunal army, but the order to attack was never issued. An attack on Chōshū land batteries by Western forces (see SHIMONOSEKI BOMBARDMENT) had already weakened the domain, and a conservative clique had managed to oust the antiforeign radicals from power. Chōshū accepted mild terms of surrender, and the shogunate withdrew its forces, assured that Chōshū posed no further threat to its national policies. By the spring of 1865, however, difficulties with the shogunate arose once more. The radicals, led by TAKASUGI SHINSAKU, staged a successful coup against the conservative clique, and immediately began to defy the shogunate and criticize its ineffective and self-serving policies; they also reinforced their irregular units of riflemen (KIHEITAI). Although strapped for funds and hard-pressed by other domestic and international problems, the shogunate after some delay mounted a second expedition in the summer of 1866 with the shōgun TOKUGAWA IEMOCHI at its head. This time, however, not only did several important domains refuse to supply troops, but Chōshū had managed to win the support of Satsuma (see SATSUMA–CHŌSHŪ ALLIANCE). The campaign went badly for the shogunal army, and Iemochi's death in the fall of 1866 was used as a pretext to withdraw forces. The failure of the second Chōshū campaign severely dam-

aged the shogunate's national prestige and contributed greatly to its downfall in November 1867.

📖 ——Albert M. Craig, *Chōshū in the Meiji Restoration* (1961).

Chōsokabe family

Warlords in Tosa Province (now Kōchi Prefecture), Shikoku, and later *daimyō* there in the Sengoku period (1467–1568). Said to be descended from the HATA FAMILY or the SOGA FAMILY, the Chōsokabe fought for the Minamoto in the TAIRA–MINAMOTO WAR leading to the founding of the Kamakura shogunate in the late 12th century. During the dynastic wars of the period of the Northern and Southern Courts (1333–92), the Chōsokabe fought under the neighboring HOSOKAWA FAMILY, military governors (SHUGO) for the Muromachi shogunate, and became one of the leading families of Tosa. After a brief interruption of the male line at the beginning of the 16th century, the family rose again under the leadership of Chōsokabe Kunichika (1502–60). His son CHŌSOKABE MOTOCHIKA brought all of Shikoku under his sway, but after his defeat by the forces of TOYOTOMI HIDEYOSHI in 1585, his domain was reduced to Tosa alone. His domainal legal code (see CHŌSOKABE MOTOCHIKA, 100-ARTICLE CODE OF), is a model of its kind. His son Morichika (1575–1615) sided with the losing Toyotomi faction in the Battle of SEKIGAHARA (1600), and his domain was confiscated. When Morichika was executed by the Tokugawa after the final assault on the Toyotomi at Ōsaka Castle in 1615 (see ŌSAKA CASTLE, SIEGES OF), the Chōsokabe were completely destroyed.

Chōsokabe Motochika (1539–1599)

Military leader and *daimyō* of Tosa Province (now Kōchi Prefecture) in Shikoku during the Azuchi-Momoyama period (1568–1600). The warrior CHŌSOKABE FAMILY had been based for several generations in Tosa. After Motochika became head of the family in 1560, he gradually eliminated his rivals in the area, expelled the provincial governor Ichijō Kanesada (1543–85), and took full control of Tosa in 1575. By 1583 he had conquered the whole of Shikoku. In 1585, however, he was defeated by the forces sent by the national unifier TOYOTOMI HIDEYOSHI and was left with Tosa Province alone. Motochika then retired to Tosa for the rest of his days except for temporary service under Hideyoshi in Kyūshū in 1597 and in the INVASIONS OF KOREA IN 1592 AND 1597. He is also remembered for his cadastral survey of Tosa in 1587 (the registers are preserved in the Kōchi Prefectural Library) and for his domainal legal code of 1597 (see CHŌSOKABE MOTOCHIKA, 100-ARTICLE CODE OF).

Chōsokabe Motochika, 100-Article Code of

(Chōsokabe Motochika Hyakkajō or Chōsokabe Okitegaki). Domainal laws (BUNKOKUHŌ) issued by CHŌSOKABE MOTOCHIKA, *daimyō* of Tosa (now Kōchi Prefecture), and his son Morichika (1575–1615) in 1597. Applicable to both his retainers and the general population of his domain, they include regulations governing litigation procedures, tax payments, and inheritance of property, as well as relations between the *samurai* and other classes. The code supplies valuable information on political, economic, and social conditions at the end of the 16th century.

chōtei → conciliation

Chou En-lai → Zhou Enlai (Chou En-lai)

Chou Hung-ch'ing Incident → Zhou Hongqing (Chou Hung-ch'ing) Incident

Chou Tso-jen → Zhou Zuoren (Chou Tso-jen)

Chōya gunsai

A collection of official and unofficial writings of the Heian period (794–1185) compiled by the scholar-official Miyoshi Tameyasu (1049–1139), this anthology was intended mainly as a reference for officials charged with drafting state documents. It was modeled on earlier literary collections, and its first 3 fascicles were devoted to poetic works. The remaining 27 fascicles, 9 of which are now lost, presented a meticulously classified collection of official documents, together with occasional comments on proper bureaucratic procedure and documentary style. Although the 548 datable items in the extant version range in date from 737 to 1132, over 80 percent date from 1067 to 1132, the period when the compiler was active as an official in the capital bureaucracy. Tameyasu usually avoided duplicating items found in earlier collections and attempted to provide samples of all forms of document used in the central government of his day; his work is now the principal source of information on the documentary procedure of the early period of rule by retired emperors (INSEI). Consistent with the purpose of the work, it contains little information on village or estate (shōen) administration, although it presents a wealth of material on administration at the provincial level. The author sometimes included documents solely on the grounds of their historical value, and thus preserved valuable information on relations between Japan and Song (Sung) dynasty (960–1279) China, as well as such incidents as the epidemic of 737, the incursion of Jurchen pirates (TOI) into northern Kyūshū (1019), and the activities of MINAMOTO NO YOSHIIE in the EARLIER NINE YEARS' WAR (1051–62). *Cornelius J. KILEY*

chōzen naikaku → "transcendental" cabinets

Christian art, 16th and 17th centuries → namban art

Christian Churches, Japan Association of

(Nihon Kirisutokyō Rengōkai). An association of all Japanese Christian church bodies. Thirty-two Christian denominations and 39 independent church bodies constitute the association. It was established in 1946 for the purpose of maintaining communication among churches and guarding freedom of religion in Japan. It is affiliated with the JAPAN FEDERATION OF RELIGIONS. Major Protestant denominations and organizations participate in the subordinate committee, the National Christian Council of Japan (NCC; Nihon Kirisutokyō Kyōgikai). A member of the international body of the World Council of Churches, it is actively committed to the work of the ecumenical movement. *Kenneth J. DALE*

Christian daimyō

(kirishitan daimyō). Regional rulers of the latter part of the Sengoku period (1467–1568) and the Azuchi-Momoyama period (1568–1600) who were baptized Christians. Under this loosely applied term are included some of the epoch's greatest names, such as ŌTOMO SŌRIN (Dom Francisco; 1530–87), as well as a number of petty barons, such as Amakusa Hisatane (Dom João; dates unknown), who scarcely deserve to be called daimyō but are celebrated as noble lords and Christian heroes in the reports of contemporary Jesuit missionaries. The daimyō were viewed as indispensable buttresses of the Christian mission by the Jesuits, who sought methodically to capture first the elite and then, through them, the populace. They justified their Jesuit mentors' expectations by actively assisting in the conversion of their territories, sometimes through force, intimidation, and the destruction of native religious symbols and institutions. They were not, however, proof against pressure: severely tested when the na-

tional unifier TOYOTOMI HIDEYOSHI restricted the practice of Christianity in 1587, the "Christian daimyō" disappeared when the Tokugawa regime in 1612 began persecuting the religion. Few of them suffered for their faith.

Their motives for conversion varied, as did the measure of their devotion and constancy. The first of the "Christian daimyō," ŌMURA SUMITADA (Dom Bartolomeu; 1533–87), lord of the Sonogi region of Hizen Province (now part of Nagasaki Prefecture), was attracted to baptism in 1563 by the Jesuits' promise to ensure that Portuguese trading ships would call at harbors in his domain; he not only proved a zealous propagator of Christianity but even ceded the area of Nagasaki to the Jesuit order in 1580. His son and successor Yoshisaki (Dom Sancho; 1568–1615), however, in 1606 expelled the Jesuits from the Ōmura domain, suspecting them of an intrigue against him in the transfer of some tracts of land. Arima Yoshisada (Dom André; 1521–77), lord of the Takaku region of Hizen, became a Christian in 1576 in the hope of Portuguese trade and the expectation of military assistance against his powerful neighbor Ryūzōji Takanobu (1529–84) of the Saga region of Hizen (now part of Saga Prefecture). Military supplies from a Portuguese ship were in fact delivered by the Jesuits to his son ARIMA HARUNOBU (Dom Protasio; 1567–1612), who was baptized in 1580 and cooperated energetically in making the Arima domain solidly Christian. Dom Protasio's son Naozumi (Dom Miguel; 1586–1641), however, connived at his father's disgrace and death in 1612, ingratiated himself with the Tokugawa regime by apostatizing, and persecuted the Christians of Arima upon being installed as daimyō. (The Arima are the sole example of three generations of "Christian daimyō" in the same family, although Naozumi's apostasy makes that example imperfect.) Ōtomo Sōrin of Bungo Province (now part of Ōita Prefecture) was the leading power of Kyūshū when he was baptized in 1578 after 27 years of sympathetic intercourse with Jesuit missionaries, whose enterprise he admired and protected; he remained faithful throughout the nine years of defeat and calamity that followed, but his son Yoshimune (Dom Constantinho; 1559–1605), baptized in 1587 and secured in his Bungo domain by Toyotomi Hideyoshi's invasion of Kyūshū, apostatized when Hideyoshi issued his anti-Christian edicts later that year.

Some daimyō were drawn to Christianity by the model of a valued friend, and their example in turn influenced others. For instance, TAKAYAMA UKON (Dom Justo; 1552?–1615; baptized in 1564 upon his father Dario's conversion), certainly the best known and perhaps the ideal "Christian daimyō," influenced GAMŌ UJISATO (Dom Leão; 1556–95) to become a Christian, and Ujisato helped Ukon to persuade KURODA YOSHITAKA (Dom Simeão; 1546–1604). Gamō seems to have lost his zeal in 1587, two years after his baptism, when Hideyoshi turned against Christianity; by 1591 he had become one of Japan's five greatest daimyō, but there is no evidence of his fostering the religion in his 919,000-koku (see KOKUDAKA) domain in northern Honshū. In contrast, Kuroda kept his faith under the persecution; Hideyoshi's death in 1598 and being part of the victorious Tokugawa side in the great conflict which led up to the Battle of SEKIGAHARA (1600) gave him and his family the opportunity again to demonstrate their commitment to Christianity. Yoshitaka himself (although formally retired from affairs since 1589) helped the missionaries diplomatically after Sekigahara, interceding for them with the future shōgun TOKUGAWA IEYASU (1543–1616); his son KURODA NAGAMASA (Dom Damião; 1568–1623) encouraged mission activities in his 523,000-koku fief centered at Fukuoka; Yoshitaka's brother Sōemon (Dom Miguel Luís; d 1610) and the latter's son Dom Paulo (d 1612), who administered Akizuki (now part of Fukuoka Prefecture), a part of the great Kuroda domain, assisted in the mass baptism of practically the town's entire population. Among those influenced to turn Christian by Yoshitaka was Mōri Hidekane (Dom Simão; 1566–1601), the daimyō of a 130,000-koku domain at Kurume (now part of Fukuoka Prefecture) in Kyūshū, whose wife was Ōtomo Sōrin's daughter Maxentia; he not only furthered the mission in his own castle town but was also influential in obtaining the missionaries' preference in other domains of the great MŌRI FAMILY, and in 1600 a Jesuit residence was established through his efforts at Hiroshima. Mōri Hidekane was on the losing side in the war of 1600, but he and his samurai were given refuge by Kuroda Nagamasa. Dom Damião, however, in the end did not remain loyal to Christianity but bent before the Tokugawa regime's fiat and expelled the missionaries from his domain in 1613.

For all their mutual friendships, family relationships, and occasional gestures of solidarity, the "Christian daimyō" never formed a united front. Although Hideyoshi in one of his anti-Christian edicts of 1587 drew attention to the Christians' potential for "conjurations" and demanded that lords above a certain level of income obtain his permission before joining the foreign religion, there were no conjurations or cabals among the Christian lords as such. When their interests demanded, or when their overlord ordered, they fought other Christians. The best example is the revolt of the "Five Amakusa Barons" (Amakusa Goninshū) against KONISHI YUKINAGA (Dom Agostinho; 1556?–1600) when he was installed by Hideyoshi as the daimyō of Uto in Higo Province (now Kumamoto Prefecture) in 1589; the Amakusa Islands, included in Konishi's fief, had been contended over and parceled out between the families of the Goninshū for a century. At least three of the five (Amakusa Hisatane João, Ōyano Shigemoto Jacobe, and Sumoto Shigemichi Bartolomeu) and their families were Christians; so was Konishi's captain Ijichi Bundayū Paulo, whom they defeated and killed, destroying his force of three thousand. If not for the Christian religion of the participants, which gives the affair an exotic flavor, this would qualify as a typical rebellion of members of the KOKUJIN class of provincial gentry against the imposition of authority from the outside. The forces mustered by Hideyoshi's regime to quell it included the "Christian daimyō" Konishi, Arima Harunobu, and Ōmura Yoshiaki, as well as the notorious anti-Christians KATŌ KIYOMASA (1562–1611) of Kumamoto and Matsuura Takanobu (1529–99) of Hirado. The rebellion ended on New Year's Day 1590 (Tenshō 17.11.25) with a great slaughter of the Christian garrison and refugees in Hondo fortress—an atrocity, the Jesuit reports allege, perpetrated solely by Katō Kiyomasa's troops, while Konishi did his best to alleviate the savagery. Konishi and Katō subsequently served as the two principal field generals of Hideyoshi's INVASIONS OF KOREA in 1592 AND 1597. After Hideyoshi's death, Konishi became a leader of the anti-Tokugawa coalition which in 1600 met disaster at Sekigahara. The Konishi in that coalition were, however, counterbalanced by the Kuroda: a daimyō's Christian beliefs had nothing to do with his taking the one or the other side.

Among the "Christian daimyō" who lost and were dispossessed in 1600 was the hegemon ODA NOBUNAGA's (1534–82) grandson, Oda Hidenobu (Sambōshi; Christian name Paulo?; 1580–1605), the lord of a 135,000-koku domain at Gifu. The Jesuit Organtino had in 1595 baptized him secretly, lest Hideyoshi be aroused. In view of the Jesuits' method of working from the top down, it is interesting to note that Hidenobu had in 1582 been declared his assassinated grandfather's heir at the council Nobunaga's generals held in Kiyosu to decide the succession; if realizable, such a designation offered dazzling prospects. To be sure, it was empty from the start, and historical developments had long since rendered illusory any prospect of Hidenobu's rise to power; but the Jesuits' faith in the "Christian daimyō" was misplaced in any event. By and large, they pursued their own interests before those of their church. They were daimyō first, and Christians second.

The notable exception was Takayama Ukon. While Ukon's early career was that of a typical Sengoku daimyō, the second half of his life was marked by an extraordinary devotion to his Christian faith. Ukon exerted himself to convert the populations of his fiefs—Takatsuki in Settsu (now part Ōsaka Prefecture) until 1585, and then Akashi in Harima (now part Hyōgo Prefecture)—to Christianity. For his uncommon zeal, he was castigated by Hideyoshi but refused to recant and was dispossessed in 1587; at the outset of the general persecution of Christianity in 1614, he was expelled from Japan by the Tokugawa regime, and died the next year in exile in Manila. See also CHRISTIANITY.

■——Charles Boxer, *The Christian Century in Japan, 1549–1650* (1951). George Elison, *Deus Destroyed: The Image of Christianity in Early Modern Japan* (1973). Luis Frois, S.J., *Historia de Iapam*, tr Matsuda Kiichi and Kawasaki Momota as *Furoisu nihonshi*, 12 vols (1977–80).   George ELISON

Christianity

Christianity was introduced into Japan in the middle of the 16th century; claims that Nestorian missionaries had reached the country in earlier centuries have yet to be substantiated, although Japanese travelers may well have come into contact with Nestorians in China. Christianity was generally tolerated in Japan until the beginning of the 17th century, but the Tokugawa shogunate eventually proscribed the religion and persecuted its adherents. When relations with Western countries were restored in the middle of the 19th century, Christianity was once more introduced into Japan and has continued to exist there, with varying fortunes.

Introduction to Japan——The expansion of Portuguese colonial and mercantile power in Asia during the first half of the 16th century was accompanied by a surge of Catholic missionary zeal to preach Christianity to the peoples of the newly discovered countries. Portuguese traders first reached Japan in 1543, and in the following year a man from Kagoshima named Yajirō (often called Anjiro in contemporary European accounts) fled the country in a Portuguese ship to avoid arrest for manslaughter. Yajirō was baptized in Goa in 1548 and aroused the interest of the Jesuit missionary Francis XAVIER (1506–52) by recounting to him the possibilities of evangelizing Japan. As a result Xavier, accompanied by Yajirō and two Spanish JESUITS, Cosme de Torres (1510?–70) and Juan Fernández (1526–67), set out for Japan and arrived in Kagoshima on 15 August 1549.

Xavier preached in Kagoshima, Hirado, and Yamaguchi with some success, but his efforts were hampered by the inadequate services of Yajirō as interpreter; owing to this deficiency and to Xavier's employing Buddhist terms in his sermons, the missionaries were sometimes regarded in the first few years as propagators of a foreign Buddhist sect. To avoid this misunderstanding the Jesuits soon began using European religious terms (such as *kirishitan*, Christian; *sakaramento*, sacrament; *paraiso*, heaven, and so forth); although this usage distinguished Christian teaching from Buddhism, it served to stress the "foreign" element in the newly introduced religion.

Wishing to obtain permission to evangelize throughout Japan, Xavier journeyed to Kyōto in the hope of obtaining an audience with the emperor; on the failure of this mission he returned to Yamaguchi in the spring of 1551. Seeing the respect shown by the Japanese for China, he decided to visit the Middle Kingdom and begin proselytizing there. Leaving behind his two Jesuit companions, he sailed from Japan in November 1551 and died in December of the following year on a small island near the Canton estuary.

Xavier's work in Japan was continued by Torres and Fernández, and in the course of time reinforcements arrived; but their number remained small, and by 1579 there were still only 55 missionaries in the country. The fact that Japan was in the midst of military strife and did not enjoy unified rule helped their work to some extent, for there was no central government which could forbid their entering the country (as was the case later in China); and if missionaries were not made welcome in one particular domain, they could always transfer elsewhere. In general the early missionaries were well received by local rulers, or *daimyō*, who often associated them with the lucrative Portuguese trade in Chinese silk. Although this association proved helpful in the early stages of missionary endeavor, it was later to become a disadvantage when Portuguese commerce in Japan declined and the initial Japanese enthusiasm for the West began to wane.

Expansion——Missionary activity was concentrated in Kyūshū, although a Christian community was also established in the Kyōto region in the 1560s. In 1570 missionaries took soundings in the bay of Nagasaki and helped establish the place as the official port for Portuguese shipping; the Jesuits in fact had virtual control of the city for 10 years. In 1563 the first Christian daimyō, ŌMURA SUMITADA, received baptism, and by 1579 no fewer than six daimyō had been converted, thus adding considerable impetus to the work of evangelization. Some of these Christian rulers, such as Ōtomo Yoshishige (1530–87), KONISHI YUKINAGA, and TAKAYAMA UKON, suffered considerably on account of their adopted faith but remained steadfast to the end of their lives. By 1579 the number of Japanese Christians was reckoned to be about 100,000, but this figure includes converts who embraced the faith at the behest of their Christian lords and whose religious faith had yet to be fully developed. Missionary work was aided by the social instability caused by the military upheavals of the period and by the generally weakened state of Buddhism at that time. Many missionaries were educated and zealous men, and Christian works of charity, such as public hospitals, aroused widespread admiration.

Within 30 years of its introduction Christianity had become a significant movement in Japan and had begun to attract the attention of leaders striving to reunite the country. Contemporary letters of Jesuits, especially the Portuguese Luis FROIS (1532–97), describe in fascinating detail visits to castles and conversations with some of the prominent personalities of the time. One such ruler was ODA NOBUNAGA, who particularly favored the missionaries and granted them generous concessions, although his largesse was at least partly motivated by his wish to play off the Christians against the Buddhist sects that were opposing his quest for power.

In 1579 the Italian Jesuit Alessandro VALIGNANO (1539–1606) arrived to conduct the first of three inspection tours of the mission.

He insisted on missionary adaptation to traditional Japanese ways and set out detailed rules concerning language, housing, and etiquette. Despite his insistence on conforming to Japanese customs in everyday life, the European religious outlook of the 16th century precluded any fundamental adaptation of the Christian message. Valignano was also eager to recruit more Japanese into the Jesuit order, and he founded a college and two schools; in 1580 he appointed Gaspar Coelho (1527?–90) as superior of the mission to succeed the inflexible Francisco CABRAL (d 1609), who opposed the establishment of an indigenous clergy. Valignano visited Nobunaga several times in Kyōto and Azuchi, and on his leaving Japan in early 1582 he was accompanied by four boys forming the embassy (called Tenshō Ken'ō Shisetsu; see MISSION TO EUROPE OF 1582) to Rome on behalf of the Christian daimyō of Kyūshū.

Nobunaga met a violent death in 1582, but his successor, TOYOTOMI HIDEYOSHI, continued to favor the missionaries and amicably showed Coelho around Ōsaka Castle in 1585. In the following year the ruler went to Kyūshū on a military campaign. Probably as a result of seeing for himself the extent of Christian influence in Kyūshū and of Coelho's rash offer to enroll the support of Christian daimyō, Hideyoshi abruptly issued a decree in July 1587 expelling all missionaries from Japan. The edict was neither obeyed nor enforced, but it marked the end of the initial favorable period of Christian mission work. In 1591 Hideyoshi received Valignano, then on his second tour of inspection, with every sign of cordiality, and five years later he met Pedro Martins (1542–98), the first bishop to arrive in Japan.

It was during this period that the Jesuits were joined by Spanish Franciscan friars from the Philippines, with Dominican and Augustinian friars arriving in 1602. This influx of new missionaries added impetus to the work of evangelization, but national rivalries between the Jesuits and the friars gave rise to petty, unseemly quarrels among the religious orders concerning the right to preach in Japan and appropriate methods of evangelization.

Martyrdoms —— In October 1596 the Spanish ship *San Felipe* foundered off Shikoku, and its rich cargo was seized by the Japanese authorities. An acrimonious controversy between Japanese, Jesuits, and friars resulted from the confiscation, and Hideyoshi once more turned against the Christian church, condemning to death the Franciscans and their parishioners in Kyōto. On 5 February 1597, 26 Christians—6 Franciscans, 3 Jesuits, and 17 laymen—were crucified at Nagasaki (see TWENTY-SIX MARTYRS). No further hostile action was taken, and missionary work continued unobtrusively; Hideyoshi even invited the Portuguese Jesuit João RODRIGUES (1561?–1633) to visit him only a week or so before the ruler's death in September 1598. By this time the church had reached its greatest expansion, the number of Christians being estimated at about 300,000; their ranks included not only various daimyō but also influential courtiers, soldiers, and officials.

The political vacuum created by Hideyoshi's death was filled by TOKUGAWA IEYASU, who after his victory at the Battle of SEKIGAHARA in 1600 became the de facto ruler of Japan. Although not so favorably disposed toward the missionaries as Nobunaga and Hideyoshi apparently had been, Ieyasu was willing to tolerate their presence in order not to jeopardize the profitable Portuguese trade. To this end he employed Rodrigues as his commercial agent in Nagasaki and received Bishop Luis de CERQUEIRA (1552–1614) in audience in 1606. However, the arrival of the Dutch in 1609 and the English in 1613 complicated the situation for the Christian community, and contemporary European Catholic-Protestant religious controversy was introduced to Japan. The establishment of Dutch and English trade broke the Portuguese commercial monopoly, allowing Ieyasu to act more freely against the missionaries.

As the final showdown between Ieyasu and Hideyori, son of the late Hideyoshi, approached, Ieyasu turned against the church, knowing that his rival commanded considerable sympathy and support in western Japan, where Christian influence was strongest. In February 1614 the Tokugawa government proscribed Christianity and ordered missionaries to leave the country. In November of that year most of the 141 missionary personnel, accompanied by Takayama Ukon, sailed for exile in Manila and Macao. Some 40 missionaries managed to remain and continue their work under cover; among their number were a few Japanese priests, the first ordination of Japanese having taken place in 1601.

Persecution and Suppression —— For a few years no concerted action was taken against the Christians, and they were able to practice their religion unobtrusively; fresh contingents of missionaries were smuggled into the country in Portuguese vessels. But the government eventually brought pressure on the regional daimyō to

eradicate Christianity in their domains, and organized persecution commenced. In September 1622, 51 Christians were executed at Nagasaki in the "Great Martyrdom," witnessed by 30,000 spectators. On TOKUGAWA IEMITSU's succeeding his father Hidetada as the third shōgun in 1623, the anti-Christian campaign was intensified; in December of that year 50 Christians were burned alive in Edo (now Tōkyō). Rewards were posted for information leading to the arrest of missionaries, and from around 1629 the practice of *efumi,* the rite of publicly trampling on a Christian medallion (see FUMIE), was introduced to detect secret Christians. Scenes of martyrdom, however, often served to increase the fervor of the faithful, and the authorities eventually had recourse to torture, such as suspension in a pit (*anatsurushi*) or in the Unzen sulfur springs, in order to encourage apostasy.

It has been estimated that about 3,000 believers were put to death for their religion; this figure does not include the many Christians who died as a result of their extended sufferings in prison or in exile. Some Christians took refuge in remote regions, while others recanted, at least outwardly, their religion. In view of the hideous tortures threatening both them and their families, Christians had every inducement to make a formal retraction of faith, and the suffering of the *anatsurushi* made even some dedicated missionaries break down and publicly apostasize.

The fact that missionaries and laity were able to continue for so long without detection in various parts of the country indicates that there was a good deal of sympathy for them on the local level and that officials were often willing to turn a blind eye to their presence. Hasegawa Gonroku, governor of Nagasaki from 1615 to 1625, several times showed his sympathy for the hunted missionaries and finally resigned his post in order not to be involved in bloodshed.

In 1633 some 30 missionaries were put to death, and by 1637 only five were left at liberty. In this latter year an insurrection took place that was to mark the final stage of the mission and bring about the end of Japan's relations with the West. Although a social rather than a religious uprising in its initial stage, the SHIMABARA UPRISING of 1637–38 rapidly took on the character of a Christian uprising; the revolt was put down only with unexpected difficulty, and the insurgents and their families, numbering about 40,000, were massacred. In 1639 the government banned further trade with the Portuguese in Macao, and it put to death 60 members of the embassy and crew who arrived in Nagasaki in the following year to plead for a resumption of commerce. Contact with the West was completely severed, except for merchants of the Dutch East India Company, who were confined on the man-made islet of DEJIMA in Nagasaki harbor.

In a futile attempt to aid the persecuted Christians, two groups of missionaries (called the Rubino Groups after their organizer, Antonio Rubino) tried to enter Japan from the Philippines in 1642 and 1643, but they were immediately rounded up and arrested. The members of the first group were executed, but those of the second group succumbed under torture and apostasized, some spending the rest of their lives in the KIRISHITAN YASHIKI, or Christian prison, in Edo. One final attempt to enter the country was made in 1708 by the Italian missionary Giovanni Battista SIDOTTI (1667–1714). He was immediately arrested, questioned by the Confucian scholar ARAI HAKUSEKI, and confined in the Kirishitan Yashiki, where he died (his death date is often erroneously given as 1715).

No information is available about subsequent Christian activity until the final years of the Tokugawa regime. Signboards offering rewards for information about hidden missionaries continued to be displayed, and Dutch ships entering Nagasaki were rigorously searched for disguised missionaries trying to slip into the country. A number of anti-Christian tracts were in circulation, the best-known work being *Ha Daiusu* (Against Deus), written by Fucan FABIAN (1565?–after 1620), an apostate Japanese Jesuit, in 1620.

The Japanese are noted for their religious tolerance, and the anti-Christian campaign was occasioned by social and political rather than purely religious factors. Christian exclusivism, with its unwillingness to tolerate Shintō and Buddhism, naturally aroused resentment in some circles, and the foreign administration of the mission was a drawback at a time when the Japanese were becoming increasingly disillusioned with the West. Missionaries were sometimes alleged to be a potential "fifth column" preparing the way for Iberian colonialism. More significantly, the Tokugawa shogunate was always on the alert for any possible coalition of disaffected elements which might threaten its hegemony, and a union of Christians was regarded as a potential danger in this respect. Finally, the Christian insistence on the primacy of the individual's conscience as the ultimate norm of moral behavior and action was viewed as subversive in a society which attached such overwhelming importance to unquestioning and absolute obedience to the commands of superiors.

Reintroduction —— With the arrival of Commodore Perry in 1853 and again in 1854, Japan's period of isolation came to an end, and Westerners were again allowed to enter the country. The Treaty of Amity and Commerce of 1858 (see HARRIS TREATY) permitted American residents in Japan free exercise of their religion, and similar agreements were signed with other Western powers.

In anticipation of the opening of Japan, a Catholic priest had gone to Okinawa as early as 1844, and in 1859 the priest Prudence Girard (1821–67) took up his appointment as interpreter for the French consul general in Edo, while another Catholic priest settled in Hakodate. In the same year, representatives of three Protestant churches reached Japan, including James C. HEPBURN (Presbyterian, 1815–1911), still known for the system of romanizing the Japanese language that bears his name, and Guido Herman F. VERBECK (Dutch Reformed, 1830–98). Ostensibly these pastors came to Japan to serve foreign residents, but their true aim was to begin direct work among the Japanese. Language difficulties and the anti-Christian regulations still in force prevented much progress during the first few years.

Kakure Kirishitan —— In March 1865 Bernard Petitjean (1829–84), who had arrived in 1862, was contacted by a group of Japanese at Nagasaki who identified themselves as Christians. Within a short time various communities of KAKURE KIRISHITAN, or "hidden Christians," had been discovered in the Nagasaki region. Living in remote areas where government surveillance was at its weakest and where the early Christian faith had had time to send down deep roots, these communities had preserved their religion in secret for more than two centuries. Inevitably the unlettered peasants' understanding of doctrine had been corrupted in the course of time, and many of the original Latin hymns and prayers had become garbled beyond recognition. The Kakure Kirishitan biblical account called *Tenchi hajimari no koto* is a remarkable document incorporating both Shintō and Buddhist elements, yet in many places it paraphrases sections from the Bible—for example, the account of the Crucifixion—with considerable accuracy.

Of the approximately 60,000 Kakure Kirishitan discovered at that time, only about half chose to return to the newly introduced church; for various reasons the rest preferred to remain with their centuries-old traditions and garbled prayers. More than 90 percent of the inhabitants of the island of Ikitsuki, near Hirado, are said to be Kakure Kirishitan even today.

The anti-Christian laws were still in effect, and the newly discovered Christians were jailed or exiled to other parts of the country (see PERSECUTIONS AT URAKAMI). The establishment of the Meiji government in 1868 did not bring them immediate relief, and it was only in 1873, largely as a result of the intercession of foreign diplomats and popular indignation abroad, that the authorities withdrew religious sanctions and allowed the uprooted peasants to return to their homes.

In theory the abrogation of the anti-Christian laws permitted the different churches to begin their work among the Japanese populace, although freedom of religion was not specifically granted in Japan until the promulgation of the Meiji Constitution in 1889; even then only qualified religious freedom was guaranteed, "within limits not prejudicial to peace and not antagonistic to their duties as citizens." This qualification was later to be invoked against Christians in times of extreme nationalism.

Catholic —— Catholic activity was entrusted to the Paris Foreign Mission Society until the beginning of the 20th century, when other missionary orders began entering the country; the French influence on the developing Catholic church in Japan in the last century was therefore particularly strong. A steady if unspectacular expansion took place, and by 1937 the Catholic population was reported as 118,000, with a preponderance of the faithful living in the Nagasaki region. In 1891 an episcopal hierarchy was set up, with an archbishop appointed for Tōkyō. Efforts were made to build up a Japanese clergy, and Nagasaki was entrusted to the first Japanese bishop in 1927. Emphasis was also laid on education, and a network of schools, mostly administered by members of religious orders, was established throughout the country. In 1913 SOPHIA UNIVERSITY (Jōchi Daigaku) was founded in Tōkyō; the Sacred Heart College, founded as a small school for women in 1915, was reorganized as a women's university (Seishin Joshi Daigaku) in 1948; and Nanzan University was founded in Nagoya in the following year.

Orthodox —— In 1861 Ivan Kasatkin (1836–1912), better known as Father NIKOLAI, reached Hakodate to serve as chaplain for the Russian consulate there. In 1872 he transferred to Tōkyō, where he established a branch of the Russian Orthodox Church (see HOLY ORTHODOX CHURCH). Nikolai encouraged the formation of a local clergy, and the first Japanese Orthodox priests were ordained as early as 1875. Appointed bishop in 1880, Nikolai consecrated the Orthodox cathedral in Kanda, Tōkyō, in 1891; damaged in the TŌKYŌ EARTHQUAKE OF 1923, the cathedral was repaired in 1929 and still remains a landmark in the capital. The Orthodox church was placed in a difficult position during the Russo-Japanese War of 1904–05 and received no further funds from its mother church after the Russian revolution. A zealous and dedicated churchman, Nikolai died in 1912, at which time there were about 30,000 Orthodox believers in Japan. By 1931 this number had grown to 40,000, but in recent years the church's influence has declined, and in 1980 membership was 10,689.

Protestant —— In the first 10 years of activity in Japan, the Protestant church was represented by four denominations (Anglican-Episcopal Church, Presbyterian Church, Dutch Reformed Church, and the American Baptist Free Mission Society), and progress was slow; up to 1872 only five Japanese are said to have accepted baptism. But the following 20 years witnessed great, and sometimes spectacular, expansion in both numbers and influence as representatives of other churches arrived, mostly from the United States. From the beginning great importance was attached to education as a means of spreading the Christian message, and the churches were fortunate in acquiring the services of some outstanding teachers. The educational impact was further increased by the founding of Dōshisha English School (now DŌSHISHA UNIVERSITY) in Kyōto in 1875, by NIIJIMA JŌ (or Joseph Hardy Neesima) on his return to Japan from studying in the United States. Both Aoyama Gakuin (now AOYAMA GAKUIN UNIVERSITY) and St. Paul's School (now RIKKYŌ UNIVERSITY) were established in Tōkyō in 1874. The Christian contribution to the development of women's education in the Meiji period is also noteworthy. The expansion of Protestant higher education has continued in modern times, and in 1953 International Christian University (Kokusai Kirisutokyō Daigaku) was founded in Tōkyō.

One of the most influential missionary teachers in Meiji times was Guido Verbeck, who numbered among his pupils the future statesmen ŌKUMA SHIGENOBU and SOEJIMA TANEOMI. The educational apostolate was also aided by the contribution of *yatoi*, or foreign advisers recruited by the Meiji government, for many of these men were dedicated Christians and spared no effort to spread Christianity in the course of their official work (see FOREIGN EMPLOYEES OF THE MEIJI PERIOD). Willaim E. GRIFFIS, who taught in Fukui and then in Tokyo, is a good example of this type of worker. William S. CLARK lectured for a brief period at the Sapporo Agricultural College in 1876 and made a deep impression on his students; his hearty exhortation, "Boys, be ambitious!" is still quoted today. Captain L. L. JANES taught at Kumamoto, and under his influence 35 students, the "Kumamoto Band," pledged their Christian faith in January 1876.

The converts to the Protestant churches in that period were mostly from the former *samurai* class, and the Christian teaching presented to them was characterized by a nontheological, ethical, and biblical approach. Missionary teachers were often regarded as the representatives of a new and superior civilization, and Christianity was popularly identified with the West. Enthusiasm for things Western continued for a time, with TSUDA MAMICHI even advocating in the journal *Meiroku zasshi* (1874–75) that Japan should officially adopt Christianity, the religion of the successful and prosperous Western nations (see MEIROKUSHA). The inevitable reaction to this excessive enthusiasm eventually set in, intensified by widespread indignation at the Western powers' reluctance to abrogate the "Unequal Treaties" (see UNEQUAL TREATIES, REVISION OF). The promulgation of the Meiji Constitution in 1889 and of the IMPERIAL RESCRIPT ON EDUCATION in the following year marked the end of the period of uncritical admiration for the West. In addition, the introduction of new theological teachings and of historical criticism of the Bible during the last decade of the century caused dissension and bewilderment among the members of some of the churches.

Uchimura Kanzō —— The drawbacks of associating Christianity too closely with the West are well illustrated in the case of UCHIMURA KANZŌ, the founder of the MUKYŌKAI, or Non-Church Movement, and his views are not without relevance in any discussion of present-day Christianity in Japan. As a young student at Sapporo, Uchimura fell under the indirect influence of Clark (who had already left Sapporo) and became a Christian. But his acceptance of his new faith was conditioned by his admiration for his teachers. On 1 December 1878 he wrote in his diary, "The Rev. Mr. H. our beloved Missionary was again in the town, and we joined his church without scrutinizing *pro* or *con* of his or any other denomination. We only know that he was a good man, and thought that his church must be good too."

In 1884 Uchimura went to the United States for theological studies, somewhat naively expecting to find a Christian utopia there, only to be thoroughly disillusioned by "the unchristian features of Christendom." In later years Uchimura refused to be identified with any particular church, declaring that "the odium of Christianity is in its churches." His Christian fervor was matched only by his love for his country, giving rise to his most quoted statement, "I love two J's and no third; one is Jesus, and the other is Japan. I do not know which I love more, Jesus or Japan." He insisted on the need for a "Japanese Christianity" untainted by Western influence. Although expressed in extreme terms, some of the issues raised by Uchimura have yet to be satisfactorily resolved by the Christian churches in Japan.

Social Activity —— The beginning of the 20th century found Christianity firmly established in Japan, even if some of the popular esteem in which it had formerly been held had waned. The nationalist spirit fostered by the Russo-Japanese War militated against the churches, and the patriotic loyalty of Christians was sometimes held suspect in view of their exposure to a "foreign" religion. But it was in this period that Christians made a notable contribution to the foundation and development of the socialist and trade union movements in an effort to solve the grave social problems caused by Japan's rapid industrialization. The Social Democratic Party (Shakai Minshutō) was formed in 1901, and many of its founding members, such as KATAYAMA SEN and ABE ISOO, were active Christians. Another Christian, SUZUKI BUNJI, founded the YŪAIKAI, or Friendship Association, at the Unitarian church in Mita, Tōkyō, in 1912. This organization developed into the Nihon Rōdō Sōdōmei, or Japan Federation of Labor. Suzuki was its president from 1912 to 1930; he was eventually succeeded in that post by another Christian, MATSUOKA KOMAKICHI. The Nihon Nōmin Kumiai, or Japan Farmers' Union, was founded in Kōbe in 1922 by two Christian socialists, KAGAWA TOYOHIKO and Sugiyama Motojirō (1885–1964), the efforts of the former on behalf of the poverty-stricken workers being particularly outstanding. Despite this contribution at the time of their foundation, many of the social movements were later split by political and ideological disputes, and much of the initial Christian influence was weakened or lost.

In addition to the Christian participation in these national organizations, the churches have sponsored a wide variety of social and medical projects, such as hospitals, sanatoria, leprosaria, orphanages, old-people's homes, and institutions for mentally retarded children; and the image of Christianity is often associated with such work in popular estimation. In recent times most of the care of Vietnamese refugees reaching Japan has been undertaken by the churches.

Nationalism —— The steadily increasing spirit of nationalism during the 1930s raised difficult problems of conscience for Christians. In May 1932 the "Yasukuni Incident" occurred when two or three Christian university students refused on religious grounds to bow at the YASUKUNI SHRINE in Tōkyō, thus giving rise to accusations of Christian lack of loyalty and patriotism. After prolonged negotiations a compromise was reached with the government authorities, and in 1936 Catholics were informed by Rome that such ceremonies constituted "a civil manifestation of loyalty" and "reverence toward the imperial family" and were therefore permissible. The National Christian Council of Protestant Churches concurred with this interpretation. Despite these declarations, attendance at shrines during the ultrapatriotic 1930s and the subsequent Pacific War was to cause a dilemma of conscience for many Christians. In recent years the government has proposed that the Yasukuni Shrine be once more turned into a national monument for the war dead and that it should be supported by state funds. Attempts to pass the necessary legislation through the Diet have been abandoned on several occasions owing to the determined opposition to the plan, many of the opponents being Christians who still recall the prewar Yasukuni Shrine as a symbol of ultranationalism.

With the approach of the Pacific War foreign Catholic bishops tendered their resignations, and since that time members of the hierarchy have been Japanese. Foreign missionaries of all churches were interned or repatriated during the war or at best allowed very limited freedom to continue their work. Government pressure led to the formation in 1941 of the Nihon Kirisuto Kyōdan, or the UNITED CHURCH OF CHRIST IN JAPAN, a union of some 30 Protestant

churches entirely administered by Japanese. When religious freedom was granted after the war, a number of churches, including some of the Anglican churches and the Lutheran church, withdrew from the union, but the Kyōdan is still regarded as the most influential Protestant body in Japan today. The war produced widespread dislocation in the Christian community; many members were killed in action or in air raids (especially at Nagasaki with the dropping of the ATOMIC BOMB), and a large proportion of churches were destroyed.

The immediate postwar period witnessed a marked revival in Christian activity, and this resurgence had the clear support of General Douglas MACARTHUR and the OCCUPATION authorities. In response to pleas for help, churches abroad sent personnel and material to the Japanese Christians. The social upheaval and disillusionment caused by the nation's exhaustion from war and military defeat prompted many Japanese to turn to Christianity in search of meaning in their lives. This period, coinciding approximately with the Occupation, 1945–51, was of limited duration, and the disorganization of the churches in the postwar years prevented their taking full advantage of the favorable opportunity.

The present situation of Christianity in Japan is characterized in general by unobtrusive activity, with emphasis still placed on education as a means of spreading the gospel message. A development in recent years has been the growing ecumenical spirit between the Protestant and Catholic churches. *The Japan Christian Yearbook* and *Kirisutokyō nenkan* (Christian Yearbook) as well as the *Shūkyō nenkan* (the government yearbook on Japanese religions) now include information on all churches, both Protestant and Catholic, and a joint Christian Pavilion was sponsored at the Expo Fair at Ōsaka in 1970; a work of immense significance is the joint translation of the Scriptures published in 1978. Nevertheless, contacts between the different churches at the grassroots level are still often tenuous or nonexistent. Discussions have been held between Christian and Buddhist scholars in an effort to reach a better understanding between the two religions. A "Catholic Zen" retreat house has been established on the outskirts of Tōkyō, and regular sessions of *zazen* (Zen Buddhist meditation) are held to help Christians acquire a deeper spiritual appreciation of their own religion.

Statistics —— In 1980, according to the *Shūkyō nenkan*, Christians numbered 973,340 or about 1 percent of the total Japanese population. The Catholic church was divided into 16 dioceses and numbered 360,203 members with 814 churches. The Holy Orthodox Church claimed 10,689 members with 43 churches. Membership of the Protestant churches stood at 602,458. A partial breakdown of Protestant churches and groups follows: Nihon Kirisuto Kyōdan numbered 133,812 members with 1,391 churches; Iesu no Mitama Kyōkai Kyōdan (SPIRIT OF JESUS CHURCH), 109,222 members with 140 churches; Nihon SEIKŌKAI (Anglican-Episcopal Church of Japan), 55,567 members with 277 churches; Nihon Baputesuto Remmei (Japan Baptist Convention; see BAPTIST CHURCH), 25,159 members with 183 churches; Nihon Fukuin Rūteru Kyōkai (Japan Evangelical Lutheran Church), 19,341 members with 141 churches; Kyūseigun (the SALVATION ARMY), 9,793 members with 92 headquarters; Matsujitsu Seito Iesu Kirisuto Kyōkai (Church of Jesus Christ of Latter-Day Saints), 41,103 members with 202 churches.

Conclusion —— Although the number of professed Japanese Christians is small and makes up a little less than 1 percent of the total population, Christian influence is more widespread than this low figure might suggest. A survey conducted in 1977 revealed that "latent Christians" may number two or three times the official figure of church membership. The proportion of Christians among novelists and artists is particularly notable.

There are various problems which the Christian churches must resolve before the religion can enter the mainstream of Japanese life. In popular estimation Christianity is still regarded as a "foreign" creed, preaching admirable ideals but still not suitable for ordinary Japanese people. Because of its "foreign" nature, Christianity has been persecuted when demands for national identity have been strong. It will be noticed that Christianity has been widely accepted in Japan during periods of upheaval when the normal social structure was unstable (the 16th century, the early Meiji period, and the immediate postwar period), but once the social equilibrium was restored interest rapidly waned. Christianity has yet to establish itself within the cultural setting of Japan, and the Christian movement remains on the periphery of Japanese society. Apart from the Nagasaki region, it has yet to make any appreciable impact on rural communities, and draws its strength from the urban, professional class.

Much of Christian teaching differs radically from the more traditional patterns of Japanese thought and outlook: Christian monotheism versus traditional polytheism; the concept of a transcendent God versus the immanent deities of Japan; an individual ethic versus a group-oriented ethic; absolute moral values versus a more flexible situational ethic, and so forth. Buddhism, also an imported religion, has adapted its teachings over the centuries to be more in accord with the traditional Japanese outlook and temperament, and has thus succeeded in integrating itself into Japanese society. It is doubtful whether organized Christianity can accommodate itself to the same extent, but there still remains much scope for preaching and expressing Christian doctrine in a more Japanese form. The fact that so many different churches are represented in Japan may not be an insurmountable barrier, as the Japanese are accustomed to the diversity of Buddhist sects, but a united Christian front would certainly present a more suasive appeal.

——C. R. Boxer, *The Christian Century in Japan* (1951). Otis Cary, *A History of Christianity in Japan* (rev ed, 1975). Dohi Akio, *Nihon purotesutanto kyōkai no seiritsu to tenkai* (1975). Richard H. Drummond, *A History of Christianity in Japan* (1971). Ebisawa Arimichi and Ōuchi Saburō, *Nihon kirisutokyō shi* (1970). Fukuda Kiyoto, *Uchimura Kanzō* (1954). Charles H. Germany, *Protestant Theologies in Modern Japan* (1965). Hiyane Antei, *Nihon kirisutokyō shi* (1949). Charles W. Iglehart, *A Century of Protestant Christianity in Japan* (1959). Agency for Cultural Affairs, ed, *Japanese Religion: A Survey by the Agency for Cultural Affairs* (1972). Joseph Jennes, *A History of the Catholic Church in Japan* (1959). Carl Michalson, *Japanese Contributions to Christian Theology* (1960). Natori Jun'ichi, *Historical Studies of Christianity in Japan* (1957). Diego Pacheco, "The Europeans in Japan, 1543–1640," in Michael Cooper, ed, *The Southern Barbarians* (1971). Irwin Scheiner, *Christian Converts and Social Protest in Meiji Japan* (1970). Joseph J. Spae, *Catholicism in Japan* (1964). Suzuki Norihisa and Joseph J. Spae, *Nihonjin no mita kirisutokyō* (1968). Yokoyama Shun'ichi, *Kagawa Toyohiko* (1952).　　　　Michael COOPER

Christmas

Christmas was first celebrated in Japan as a religious observance in the middle of the 16th century by the converts of Spanish and Portuguese missionaries (see CHRISTIANITY). It was only in the early part of the Meiji period (1868–1912) that it was observed on a larger scale, but even then it was mainly confined to churches and schools sponsored by foreign missionaries. Christmas decorations and cards were also introduced, and from the early 20th century the custom of exchanging presents started to take hold among the Japanese. From the early 1930s, department stores began holding Christmas sales, which conveniently coincided with the year-end bonus and the custom of presenting SEIBO (year-end presents). Christmas Day is not a holiday in Japan, although many people go to Western-style parties on Christmas Eve, and parents sometimes give their children "decoration cakes" sold in bakeries and department stores.

TSUCHIDA Mitsufumi

Chrysanthemum and the Sword → Benedict, Ruth Fulton

Chrysanthemum Festival

(Kiku no Sekku or Chōyō no Sekku). Festival held on 9 September; now the least celebrated of the five SEKKU or seasonal celebrations. In China this day was called chongyang (ch'ong-yang; J: chōyō) and was known for the custom of drinking chrysanthemum wine (kikuzake). In Japan it was adopted as an official event in the Heian period (794–1185). Because the ninth month of the lunar calendar fell at the time of the rice harvest, the festival was closely associated with harvest rites in rural villages. The custom of holding elaborate chrysanthemum exhibits to compare gardeners' skills dates from the Edo period (1600-1868).　　　　INOKUCHI Shōji

chrysanthemums

(kiku). *Chrysanthemum morifolium*. The chrysanthemum, a perennial flowering herb of the family Compositae, has been cultivated in Japan since ancient times and is celebrated as one of the representative plants of autumn. Its woody stem reaches a height of about 1

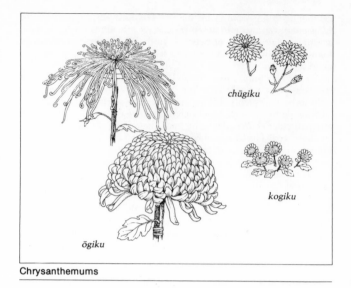

chūgiku

kogiku

ōgiku

Chrysanthemums

meter (39 in); the leaves are alternate and petioled. In autumn the stem tip branches out and each branchlet grows a flower head. It has been said to be a hybrid which arose in China from a natural or artificial cross of the *chōsen nogiku* (*C. zawadskii* var. *latilobum),* which is found in northern China and has white or red flowers, and the *shima kangiku* (*C. indicum),* a yellow-flowered species found in southern China. See also RYŪNŌGIKU.

There are records to indicate that chrysanthemums were introduced to Japan in the 5th century from China for medicinal purposes, but not a single poem about them is found in the *Man'yōshū,* a poetry anthology completed in the late 8th century. The introduction of ornamental varieties is presumed to have occurred late in the Nara period (710–794) or early in the Heian period (794–1185). Their cultivation in the gardens of the imperial court and by the aristocrats of the capital is described in literary works of the mid-Heian period. Also during this period a Chrysanthemum Festival (Chōyō no Sekku) was celebrated on 9 September of the lunar calendar, during which chrysanthemum wine was drunk and cotton which had been placed on a chrysanthemum flower the previous evening to absorb the flower's dew and scent was used to wipe the body in order to achieve a long life. These practices all derived from the Chinese view of the chrysanthemum as a magical plant.

Chrysanthemums became widely popular in the middle of the Edo period (1600–1868), when many unique varieties were developed and techniques for growing the plants in flower beds, as cascades, and in pots were perfected. At the beginning of the Meiji period (1868–1912), chrysanthemum cultivation fell into a temporary decline, but in the middle of the same period the revival of the Chrysanthemum Festival at the imperial court restored general enthusiasm for the plant. In the Taishō period (1912–26), several chrysanthemum fanciers' groups were formed which have continued to the present day. Many new varieties are still being introduced.

Autumn chrysanthemums are roughly classified horticulturally by the size of the flower head into three categories: *ōgiku* (large), *chūgiku* (medium), and *kogiku* (small). There are also many types with particular regional associations such as the *sagagiku* of Kyōto, the *isegiku* of Mie Prefecture, the *higogiku* of Kumamoto Prefecture, and the *minogiku* of Gifu Prefecture.

Varieties that bloom in spring *(harugiku),* summer *(natsugiku),* winter *(kangiku),* and throughout the year *(shikizaki)* have been developed in Japan. There is also a variety known as the *ryōrigiku* which is cultivated as food. In addition to these native species, numerous European chrysanthemums are cultivated in Japan. Chrysanthemums with large flowers, imported to France from China, are said to be the progenitors of European chrysanthemums; they were later crossed with chrysanthemums imported from Japan in the Edo period. They have generally developed along lines different from the traditional Japanese forms, with an emphasis on large size, spherical flower shapes, and brilliant colors.

In recent years the growing demand for cut flowers in Japan has prompted the Japanese to import large quantities of European chrysanthemums and to grow the large- and medium-flowered types for cut flowers through most of the summer, autumn, and winter months by adjusting their flowering times with special cultivation techniques. These European chrysanthemums, however, are botanically of the same species as the Japanese.

The chrysanthemum has long been considered one of the noblest of all flowers by the Japanese, and the crest of the imperial household is a design based on the chrysanthemum flower.

MATSUDA Osamu

Chūbu Electric Power Co, Inc

(Chūbu Denryoku). Power company providing electricity to the five central Japanese prefectures of Shizuoka, Aichi, Gifu, Mie, and Nagano. Established in 1951 with capital provided by the Chūbu Power Distribution Co and the Japan Electric Generation & Transmission Co as part of the reorganization of the electric power industry after World War II, it ranks third in size among Japan's nine electric power companies, after TŌKYŌ ELECTRIC POWER CO, INC, and KANSAI ELECTRIC POWER CO, INC. Since the company serves a number of large industrial and commercial cities such as Nagoya and Yokkaichi, it has witnessed rapid growth; the volume of power consumed in the five prefectures has risen annually by 5 to 6 percent. The company has 13 thermal electric plants, 168 hydroelectric plants, and one atomic power plant, generating 75.5 percent, 15.4 percent, and 9.1 percent, respectively, of its total power supply. Five of the thermal plants have capacities of over 1 million kilowatts; the largest, the Chita plant, has a capacity of 3.4 million kilowatts. The atomic power plant was constructed in Hamaoka in Shizuoka Prefecture and began operations in 1976. The total volume of electricity sold during the 1981 fiscal year was 65.5 billion kilowatt-hours. Sales for the fiscal year ending March 1982 totaled ¥1.6 trillion (US $6.6 billion) and capitalization stood at ¥293.8 billion (US $1.2 billion). Corporate headquarters are located in Nagoya.

Chūbu-Nippon Broadcasting Co, Ltd (CBC)

(Chūbu-Nippon Hōsō). A commercial radio and television broadcasting station based in the city of Nagoya serving the three surrounding prefectures of Aichi, Gifu, and Mie. It was established in 1950, at the same time as the MAINICHI BROADCASTING SYSTEM, INC, in Ōsaka, as one of the first commercial radio stations in Japan. Original backing came from the Chūnichi shimbun, a local daily newspaper, and financial interests in the greater Nagoya area. It began operating a television station in 1956 and went on to become an influential Chūbu (central Honshū) region broadcasting enterprise. As one of the key affiliate stations of the Japan News Network (JNN), a group of 25 commercial stations centered on TŌKYŌ BROADCASTING SYSTEM, INC (TBS), it also televises a wide variety of drama and educational programs to a national viewing audience.

NAKASA Hideo

Chūbu region

(Chūbu chihō). Encompassing Niigata, Toyama, Ishikawa, Fukui, Yamanashi, Nagano, Gifu, Shizuoka, and Aichi prefectures. Geographically divided into three districts: the Hokuriku district on the Sea of Japan side, the Central Highlands (or Tōsan), and the Tōkai district on the Pacific seaboard. The principal city of the region is NAGOYA.

The Chūbu region is largely a mountainous region dominated by the JAPANESE ALPS (the Hida, Kiso, and Akaishi mountains), lying in a generally north to south alignment. It contains numerous volcanoes including Mt. Fuji (Fujisan; 3,776 m or 12,385 ft), the highest peak in Japan, and some of Japan's longest rivers: the Shinanogawa, Kisogawa, and Tenryūgawa. The Niigata Plain on the Sea of Japan coast is one of the largest rice-producing areas in Japan, and the Nōbi Plain on the Pacific coast is the most densely populated and highly industrialized area in this region. Numerous inland basins, including the Nagano, Matsumoto, and Takayama basins, have very cold winters. The Pacific side is generally mild, and the Sea of Japan side has long snowy winters.

The Chūbu region includes three large industrial zones. The Chūkyō Industrial Zone around Nagoya dominates the area's economy and is the third ranking industrial region in Japan. The Tōkai Industrial Region consists of numerous industrial centers, such as Shimizu, Hamamatsu, and Toyohashi, located between the Chūkyō and Keihin industrial zones. The Hokuriku Industrial Region includes chemical fiber and fertilizer plants, natural gas, aluminum and petroleum refineries, and metal industries.

The Nōbi Plain and the other plains of the Hokuriku region are important rice-producing areas. Shizuoka Prefecture is Japan's major tea-producing area and produces a large crop of mandarin oranges each year as well as strawberries in early spring. Grapes and peaches in Yamanashi Prefecture and apples in Nagano Prefecture are also important products. Fishing is important along all coastal areas.

In 1966 the Chūbu sphere (Chūbuken) was designated as a wide-area economic bloc (encompassing the greater part of the Chūbu region and part of the Kinki region) in order to establish stronger economic ties between the Hokuriku and Tōkai regions. Seven national parks (Bandai–Asahi, Jōshin'etsu Kōgen, Chichibu–Tama, Fuji–Hakone–Izu, Chūbu Sangaku, Southern Alps, and Hakusan) are in the region as well as 11 quasi-national parks. Area: 66,743 sq km (25,763 sq mi); pop: 19,985,213.

Chūbu Sangaku National Park

(Chūbu Sangaku Kokuritsu Kōen). Situated in central Honshū, in Nagano, Niigata, Toyama, and Gifu prefectures, this rugged region is dominated by the HIDA MOUNTAINS, also known as the Northern Alps, with peaks averaging 3,000 m (9,840 ft), towering escarpments, ravines, and gorges, which have made this the foremost hiking and climbing area in Japan. In the center of the park rises the group of mountains known as TATEYAMA, the highest peak of which is 3,015 meters (9,889 ft). Together the group is considered one of Japan's three sacred mountains (the other two are FUJISAN and HAKUSAN). To its north lie SHIROUMADAKE (2,933 m; 9,620 ft), its broad plateau covered with alpine flowers in summer, and KASHIMA YARIGATAKE (2,890 m; 9,479 ft). South of Tateyama are YAKUSHIDAKE (2,926 m; 9,597 ft), YARIGATAKE (3,180 m; 10,430 ft), HOTAKADAKE (3,190 m; 10,463 ft), the third highest mountain in Japan, famed for its steep escarpments, and NORIKURADAKE (3,026 m; 9,925 ft). The forests in the area consist mainly of Japanese beech (buna), Japanese oak (nara), and evergreen conifers. The rivers AZUSAGAWA and KUROBEGAWA cut deep canyons through the forests. The gorge KUROBE KYŌKOKU (60 km; 37 mi long), which terminates at the KUROBE DAM, is spectacular in the fall foliage season. Among the numerous hot spring resorts are Babadani, beside the river Kurobegawa, and Shirahone and Hirayu, both on the slopes of Norikuradake. Area: 1,698 sq km (655.4 sq mi).

Chūchō jijitsu

(True Facts of the Central Realm). Historical work in two volumes by the Confucian scholar YAMAGA SOKŌ. Written in 1669 in Akō, where he had been banished for criticizing the shogunate-supported Zhu Xi (Chu Hsi) school of Neo-Confucianism (SHUSHIGAKU). Sokō condemned the sycophantic attitude of Confucian scholars to Chinese culture and claimed that in its history and natural features Japan was in no way inferior to China. Drawing on his reading of the accounts of Japan's mythic past in the 8th-century chronicle NIHON SHOKI, he stated that the teachings of Shintō were equal to those of the Chinese sages and that under Japan's earliest rulers an ideal government had already been realized. Thus Sokō asserted that it was Japan, not China, that was the true Middle Kingdom or central realm.

Chūgan Engetsu (1300–1375)

Zen monk of the Rinzai sect. One of the finest of the poets whose names are associated with GOZAN LITERATURE (Chinese learning in medieval Japanese Zen monasteries). His verse combines exceptional technical facility with the impress of his personal suffering. Born in Kamakura, son of a low-ranking samurai who was exiled soon after his birth, he was placed in a Kamakura temple at the age of seven. A man of unswerving devotion to principle and a strong emotional need for friendship, Chūgan found his mature years embittered by the need to choose sides in factional quarrels and the resulting estrangement from old friends. He caused a scandal by writing the Nihonsho, a history of Japan which argued that the imperial house was descended from that of the Chinese Duke of Zhou (Chou); the history was suppressed by imperial order. Chūgan studied in China from 1325 to 1332. His poems are collected in the anthology Tōkai ichiō shū.

Marian URY

chūgen

A type of low-ranking retainer in the service of a warrior; popularly known as orisuke. The term, which was in use from the 13th century through the Edo period (1600–1868), literally means "middle space," indicating that such men were ranked between the lowliest *samurai* or footsoldiers (ASHIGARU) and the menials (*komono* or *kobito*), who were assigned only the most minor duties. *Chūgen* were trained to fight in groups during battle, and in peacetime they served their masters in various other ways, such as guard duty. *Chūgen* were regularized as part of the Tokugawa bureaucracy during the Edo period. About 600 of them were divided into three groups and placed under the charge of the junior councillors (WAKADOSHIYORI); they guarded gates or served as standard-bearers. The *daimyō* had similar low-ranking retainers in their own domainal governments.

chūgen

The custom of giving gifts at midsummer, particularly at the time of the Buddhist BON FESTIVAL (all souls' day festival) and the gifts themselves. Traditionally, offerings to the souls of deceased family members made during Bon, in the 7th month of the lunar calendar, were distributed to relatives and others so as to share symbolically divine qualities among mortals. This custom (now carried out in July except in those areas where Bon is observed in August) has become secularized in recent years, so that even though gifts are given in coincidence with the Bon Festival, they are no longer offerings to the souls of the deceased but are purchased at a store and delivered directly to a family. Stores have capitalized on the Japanese penchant for gift-giving and have helped make Bon into a major calendrically determined gift-giving occasion, next only to the year-end gift giving (SEIBO). The large midyear bonus, amounting to one to three months' salary, has also encouraged spending on *chūgen*. Traditionally, noodles and staples, clothes, and footgear were preferred *chūgen* items. Also, businesses distributed towels and fans to customers as *chūgen* gifts. Nowadays, while foodstuffs are still most popular, many other kinds of articles are given. *Chūgen* gifts are never given within a family but are customarily presented to one's social superior, such as a teacher of traditional arts, and not to those below one's own status. See also GIFT GIVING.

Harumi BEFU

Chūgoku Electric Power Co, Inc

(Chūgoku Denryoku). Company supplying electricity to the prefectures of Hiroshima, Okayama, Tottori, Shimane, and Yamaguchi in western Honshū. It was established in 1951 by taking over the assets and operations of the Chūgoku Electric Supply Co, Ltd, and the Japan Electric Generation & Transmission Co. The CHŪGOKU REGION has few sites suitable for hydroelectric generation. Consequently the company has relied mainly on thermoelectric generation, and its volume of thermoelectric generation is now the greatest among Japan's nine electric power companies. Since 1974 the company has been expanding its Shimane nuclear power plant and building a new nuclear power plant in Yamaguchi Prefecture to meet the high demand for electricity in the industrialized Inland Sea region. It has also been pushing a 10-year plan to switch from oil to coal as a source of energy. Its total generating capacity in 1981 was 7.8 million kilowatts, of which 72 percent was furnished by thermoelectric plants, 21 percent by hydroelectric plants, and 7 percent by nuclear power plants. In the fiscal year ending in March 1982 annual revenue totaled ¥815.6 billion (US $3.4 billion) and the company was capitalized at ¥174.3 billion (US $724 million). Corporate headquarters are located in Hiroshima.

Chūgoku Mountains

(Chūgoku Sanchi). Mountain range extending east to west through the entire Chūgoku region, western Honshū. It forms the watershed between the north and south portions of western Honshū, i.e., the San'in and San'yō regions. There are numerous peaks in the 1,000 m (3,280 ft) range including SAMBESAN (1,126 m; 3,693 ft), DŌGOYAMA (1,269 m; 4,162 ft), and KAMMURIYAMA (1,339 m; 4,392 ft). Forming a plateau, it has prosperous cattle-raising and forestry industries. The mountains are composed primarily of granite, and the production of iron sand has long been carried out. It has numerous hot springs; mountain climbing and skiing are available.

Chūgoku region

(Chūgoku chihō). Encompasses the entire western tip of Honshū, comprising Hiroshima, Okayama, Shimane, Tottori, and Yamaguchi

prefectures. With the Chūgoku Mountains as the dividing line, the Inland Sea side is called the San'yō region and the Sea of Japan side is called the San'in region. The principal city of the region is HIROSHIMA.

It is a mountainous region dominated by the Chūgoku Mountains and the highland Kibi Kōgen. There are numerous coastal plains, including the Okayama and Izumo plains, as well as many small basins in the mountains. The San'yō region has wider plains than the San'in region and its population is also greater. The most heavily populated areas are along the Inland Sea coast around the cities of Hiroshima, Kurashiki, and Okayama.

The Inland Sea coast is a major area of industry and commerce, with numerous oil refineries, steel mills, automobile plants, shipyards, and chemical, petrochemical, and cement factories. In recent years industrial complexes of interrelated factories have been constructed along the Inland Sea. The Okayama Plain and the coastal plains along the Sea of Japan are important areas for the production of rice. The warm dry climate of the Inland Sea coast is also ideal for citrus fruits and grapes. The waters off the coast were once among Japan's richest fishing grounds, but catches have been on the decline in recent years because of industrial pollution. Three national parks are in the region, as well as five quasi-national parks. Area: 31,748 sq km (12,255 sq mi); pop: 7,586,254.

chūgū

(empress, consort). In the Heian period (794–1185), a title for a principal wife of an emperor; similar to the title KŌGŌ. Fujiwara no Onshi (885–954), daughter of Fujiwara no Mototsune (836–891) and wife of Emperor DAIGO, was the first of several empresses to be designated *chūgū* instead of the customary *kōgō*. When Emperor ICHIJŌ was forced in 1000 to take FUJIWARA NO MICHINAGA's daughter Shōshi (JŌTŌ MON'IN) as his second empress (the first was FUJIWARA NO TEISHI), she was designated *chūgū*, the senior lady retaining the title *kōgō*. The same practice was followed later whenever an emperor had two empresses. Although at first the *chūgū* was ranked somewhat lower than the *kōgō*, the titles came to be used interchangeably, and at times only a *chūgū* was appointed.

G. Cameron HURST III

Chūgūji

A convent-temple affiliated first with the HOSSŌ SECT, later with the SHINGON SECT, and since World War II, with the Shōtoku sect of Buddhism. Also known as Ikaruga convent, Chūgūji, located east of HŌRYŪJI was moved 300 meters west of its original site during the Muromachi period (1333–1568) when it became part of Hōryūji. Tradition has it that Chūgūji was once a palace built in 595 by Prince SHŌTOKU for his mother. After her death it was converted into a temple where the prince worshiped his mother as the founder. In her honor he had an image made of Nyoirin KANNON as the main icon of the temple. The image extant is seated in the half-lotus meditation position. Designated a National Treasure, it has been identified as MIROKU *bosatsu* (see BODHISATTVA) and was made during the Asuka period (latter part of the 6th century–710). Another National Treasure of Chūgūji consists of two embroideries known as the *Tenjukoku mandara* (Tenjukoku Mandalas). They were made at the time of Shōtoku's death in 622 and depicted the prince in a paradise known as Tenjukoku. Now only fragments partly rewoven in the 13th century survive. *Lucie R. WEINSTEIN*

Chu Hsi school → Shushigaku

chūkan shōsetsu

("midway" or "middlebrow fiction"). A term referring to a type of novel or short story standing midway between "serious" and "popular" literature and incorporating some of the qualities of both. It has been said that the term itself was first used in the early post-World War II period by HAYASHI FUSAO to describe the kind of fiction which was beginning to appear in popular magazines at the time.

After World War II the new age of democracy brought a rapid increase in the output of popular journalism catering to an ever widening range of readership. This was especially true of middlebrow literature as seen in successive publication of new magazines such as *Bessatsu bungei shunjū* (1946), *Nihon shōsetsu* (1947), and

Shōsetsu shinchō (1947). The emphasis there was on immediate interest, and the catchy yet ill-defined expression *chūkan shōsetsu,* first used then, was perhaps well suited to the type of fiction that predominated in such publications.

As time went on, it tended more and more to mean the application of some of the techniques of the serious novel to material that was increasingly common and sensational. But, from the late 1950s, with the new affluence of society as a whole, literature followed the general trend toward mass production and mass consumption. Although such writers as ISHIZAKA YŌJIRŌ, INOUE YASUSHI, FUNAHASHI SEIICHI, and TAMURA TAIJIRŌ sought to maintain a level of artistry in their works, the emphasis on the story element was stepped up, and the level of literary interest went steadily down. Under such conditions, the old distinction between pure fiction which had centered around the I-NOVEL *(watakushi shōsetsu)* since the 1910s and popular, or sensational, fiction became even more vague. In fact, what would once have been referred to as *chūkan shōsetsu* seemed almost to have become, in an essentially middlebrow culture, a kind of "high class" popular literature. See also FŪZOKU SHŌSETSU; POPULAR FICTION. *John* BESTER

Chūkyō Industrial Zone

(Chūkyō Kōgyō Chitai). Centered on the city of Nagoya. Japan's third largest industrial zone, it extends east to Toyohashi in Aichi Prefecture, north to southern Gifu Prefecture, and west to northern Mie Prefecture. Traditionally the center of Japan's textile and ceramic industries, numerous heavy and chemical industries have developed here recently. They include chemical fibers in Gifu and Okazaki, automobiles in Toyota, petroleum refining and petrochemical industries in Yokkaichi, and steel, machinery, and vehicle industries in Nagoya.

chūma

(packhorse service). During the Edo period (1600–1868) most commodities were transported by boat. In mountainous Shinano Province (now Nagano Prefecture), however, that was not possible, and both agricultural and manufactured goods were moved to market by packhorse. Early in the 17th century this service, known as *chūma* ("in-between horses"), was supplied by farmers who hired out their workhorses as pack animals in competition with those of the licensed forwarding agents (TOIYA) at the post stations on the major routes. Disputes were ended for a time when the Tokugawa shogunate officially recognized the *chūma* in 1673. With the growth of industrial and commercial activity in the 18th century, however, the *chūma* carrying trade expanded greatly and became organized. In response to lawsuits brought by the forwarding agents, the shogunate in 1764 limited and regulated the *chūma* service but did not abolish it. Disputes continued until the Meiji period (1868–1912), when better communications (roads and railways) in central Japan made *chūma* and *toiya* alike obsolete. *Conrad* TOTMAN

Chungking government → Chongqing (Chungking) government

Chūnichi shimbun

A leading daily newspaper of central Japan published in the city of Nagoya. The paper was launched in 1942 when two prominent Nagoya dailies, the *Shin Aichi* and the *Nagoya shimbun,* merged to form the *Chūbu Nippon shimbun.* In 1965 its name was changed to *Chūnichi shimbun.* The *Chūnichi* wields considerable influence in central Japan and boasts the largest circulation for a regional news publication. The paper is managed by the Chūnichi Shimbunsha which publishes two other papers, the *Hokuriku shimbun* (in Kanazawa) and the *Tōkyō shimbun.* Circulation was 1.8 million in 1979.

Chūō kōron

(The Central Review). An important monthly general-interest magazine. It was originally launched in 1887 as the *Hanseikai zasshi,* a small coterie magazine of a Kyōto student group known as the Hanseikai which was devoted to character building and abstinence from alcohol. The magazine moved to Tōkyō in 1896, and in 1899 the name was changed to *Chūō kōron.* It became more of a literary journal as time went by. TAKITA CHOIN joined the magazine as editor and expanded it into a general-interest magazine that included articles on politics, literature, education, religion, and economics. In

the early decades of the 20th century it provided writers like TANIZAKI JUN'ICHIRŌ, SHIGA NAOYA, and AKUTAGAWA RYŪNOSUKE with a forum for their writing and helped launch their careers. YOSHINO SAKUZŌ and ŌYAMA IKUO, two champions of TAISHŌ DEMOCRACY, exerted considerable influence on political opinion through their contributions to the magazine. Toward the end of World War II it was suppressed by the Japanese military authorities. Publication resumed in 1946, and *Chūō kōron* continues to wield a strong influence on Japanese public opinion. Circulation is 180,000 (1979).

Chūō Kōron Sha, Inc

Publishing house. Started by a study group at the Buddhist temple Nishi Honganji in Kyōtō in 1887 in order to publish the magazine *Hanseikai zasshi.* The focus of the magazine moved from religion to criticism, and the magazine was renamed *Hansei zasshi* in 1892. The publishing house moved to Tōkyō in 1896, and in 1899 the title of the magazine was changed once again to CHŪŌ KŌRON (The Central Review). Under the vigorous management of Asada Komanosuke and the editorial guidance of TAKITA CHOIN, it eventually became recognized as the best magazine of its kind in Japan. The writings of the well-known political scientist YOSHINO SAKUZŌ and fiction by various authors helped to establish the reputation of *Chūō kōron.* In 1916, Shimanaka Yūsaku started *Fujin kōron,* a magazine for women, and as president, in 1929, decided to publish books as well. During World War II the firm was suppressed by the government because of its liberal stance, and was finally ordered to close down in 1944. After the war, besides reviving the two journals, the company started two new magazines, one on science, *Shizen* (1946), and one on the literary arts, *Umi* (1969). *ARASE Yutaka*

Chūō Kyōiku Shingikai → Central Council for Education

Chūō University

(Chūō Daigaku). A private coeducational university located in the city of Hachiōji, Tōkyō Prefecture. Its predecessor was the Igirisu Hōritsu Gakkō (the English Law School), founded in 1885. The school developed with an emphasis on the study of British and American jurisprudence. In 1903 it became Tōkyō Hōgakuin Daigaku (Tōkyō College of Law) and in 1905 took its present name. The university has produced the nation's largest number of graduates entering the LEGAL TRAINING AND RESEARCH INSTITUTE. It maintains faculties of law, economics, commerce, letters, science, and engineering, and is known for its Institute of Economic Research, Institute of Accounting Research, Institute of Business Research, Institute of Comparative Law in Japan, Institute of Cultural Science, Institute of Health and Physical Science, and the Institute of Social Science. Night courses are offered in all departments. Enrollment in 1980 was 23,468.

Chūō Ward

(Chūō Ku). One of the 23 wards of Tōkyō. On the mouth of the river Sumida (Sumidagawa). Commercial and economic center with many textile and paper wholesale dealers. The Nihombashi district is a banking and shopping area. The Kyōbashi and Ginza districts are thriving shopping and amusement centers. A central wholesale market is located in the Tsukiji district. The Kabutochō district where the Tōkyō Stock Exchange is located is called the Wall Street of Japan. A large part of the ward's old well-developed canal network has been filled in to make land for roads and buildings. Pop: 82,643.

Chūritsu Rōren

(abbreviation of Chūritsu Rōdō Kumiai Renraku Kaigi; Federation of Independent Unions). Federation of independent labor unions formed in 1956 by 13 unions, with 750,000 members, not affiliated with any national labor organization. Since 1959, the federation has taken part in the annual spring wage offensive (SHUNTŌ) along with SŌHYŌ (General Council of Trade Unions of Japan). Although the federation has always been a loose one, regular meetings have been held since 1974 to strengthen ties within the organization. Since many of its unions are in growth industries, it has great influence on nationwide wage bargaining patterns. Chūritsu Rōren takes a moderate political stance and advocates the unification of a labor front based on private sector workers, a position which resembles that of DŌMEI (Japanese Confederation of Labor). In 1978, with 10 affiliated organizations comprising 1,320,000 individual members, it was the third largest of Japan's labor federations. See also LABOR.

KURITA Ken

Chūseikai

(Upright Party). Political party formed in December 1913 by 21 members of the Ekirakukai, a small Diet group, and 16 members of the Seiyū Kurabu, a breakaway faction of the RIKKEN SEI-YŪKAI. Founded by OZAKI YUKIO, HANAI TAKUZŌ, Hayami Seiji (1868–1926), and several other inveterate critics of the oligarchs (genrō), with the aid of the Kokumintō (National Party) and the RIKKEN DŌSHIKAI (Constitutional Association of Friends), it opposed the YAMAMOTO GONNOHYŌE cabinet, which was supported by the oligarchs and the Seiyūkai. After the Chūseikai won 33 seats in the election of March 1915, Ozaki was named minister of justice in the second ŌKUMA SHIGENOBU cabinet. In October 1916, with the establishment of the TERAUCHI MASATAKE cabinet, almost all of the members of the Chūseikai were absorbed into the KENSEIKAI, successor to the Rikken Dōshikai, and the party was formally disbanded.

Chūsonji

Head temple of the TENDAI SECT of Buddhism in the Tōhoku (northern Honshū) area of Japan; located in the town of HIRAIZUMI in Iwate Prefecture. There is a tradition that the Buddhist priest ENNIN (794–864) founded the temple during a trip to the Tōhoku area. According to temple inscriptions, however, Chūsonji was founded by Fujiwara no Kiyohira (d 1128), who had undertaken the project in honor of the emperors Horikawa and TOBA. It is thought that Kiyohira built the temple in order to console the souls of the warriors who had been killed during the EARLIER NINE YEARS' WAR (1051–62) and the LATER THREE YEARS' WAR (1083–87). Although Kiyohira has been connected by some scholars with the powerful Fujiwara family in Kyōto, his family, known as the ŌSHŪ FUJIWARA, had long been settled in the area and as Tōhoku people were considered culturally inferior to the Kyōto Fujiwara. Chūsonji was the chief product of Kiyohira's desire to build a city that would rival Kyōto. Construction was begun in 1105, and the temple was dedicated in 1126 at a lavish ceremony to which the emperor sent his representatives.

The original complex contained an esoteric pagoda (tahōtō) as well as several Amida halls (amidadō)—notably the Daichōjuin (Great Hall of Longevity) and the Konjikidō (Golden-Colored Hall)—a sutra repository (kyōzō), a bell tower, a great gate, and other buildings. Kiyohira's son, Motohira (d 1157?), and grandson, Hidehira (d 1187), added further halls and other facilities. The finished complex had over 40 temples and shrines, as well as over 300 cells for priests; it was indeed a magnificent accomplishment and was said at the time to have exceeded the glory of the temple BYŌ-DŌIN in Kyōto.

During these three generations the Ōshū Fujiwara was at the peak of its cultural prosperity. In 1189, however, Kiyohira's great-grandson, Yasuhira (1155–89), was killed by MINAMOTO NO YORI-TOMO. The prestige of Chūsonji thereafter declined progressively. A fire in 1337 destroyed many of the buildings; some of these were rebuilt by the DATE FAMILY in the 17th century. Today only two buildings in the temple precincts remain from the Fujiwara era: the Golden-Colored Hall and the sutra repository.

Although the Golden-Colored Hall is not the main hall of the temple, it is Chūsonji's best-known structure, preserving a number of national treasures and important cultural properties. Its interior decorations are lacquered and covered with gold leaf. There are three daises on which there are images of AMIDA, Avalokiteśvara (J: KANNON), and Mahāsthāma-prāpta (J: Seishi), as well as images of the bodhisattva Kṣitigarbha (J: Rokujizō; see JIZŌ) and the Two Deva Kings (J: Niten). There is some controversy as to whether the Golden-Colored Hall was originally built as an Amida hall representing the Pure Land or a burial hall, since the full mummies of Kiyohira, Motohira, and Hidehira, as well as the head of Yasuhira (who had been beheaded) were placed inside the daises.

The upper section of the sutra repository was burned down during the fire of 1337, and it is now a single-storied structure housing several national treasures. Inside is a platform on which the image of Muñjuśrī (J: Monju), the bodhisattva of wisdom and intellect,

Chūsonji

Interior of the Konjikidō. The central dais, with an image of the Buddha Amida flanked by attendant figures, contains the mummy of Kiyohira, the founder of Chūsonji. Gold leaf covers the ceiling and floor, with inlaid decoration in mother-of-pearl and other semiprecious materials. 12th century. Hiraizumi, Iwate Prefecture. National Treasure.

stands. On the walls are shelves on which lacquered sutra cases have been placed. The sutra repository is well known for its scriptures written in alternate lines in gold or silver ink. Most of the scriptures, however, were transferred to Kōyasan (one of the headquarters of the Shingon sect; see also KONGŌBUJI) at the time of TOYOTOMI HIDEYOSHI (1537–98), and there are now only 15 left at Chūsonji. In addition to the aforementioned scriptures, the sutra repository also keeps a complete set of the Song (Sung) dynasty edition of the Tripitaka. In the newly constructed treasure house, many other important objects, including a statue of Mahāvairocana (J: Dainichi Nyorai) in the form of Ekākṣara-uṣṇīṣa-cakra (J: Ichiji Kinrin) is preserved.

Hoyu ISHIDA

Chūuki → Chūyūki

Chūyūki

Also called Chuuki, Nakauki, Munetada Kō ki, or Gurin. Diary of the Heian-period (794–1185) courtier Fujiwara no Munetada (1062–1141). The diary runs to 109 books covering the years 1087–1138. It contains a wealth of information on political, economic, social, and religious affairs in the early years of rule by retired emperors (INSEI). Munetada was also known by his branch of the Fujiwara family and his official rank, as Nakamikado Udaijin (the Nakamikado minister of the right); the Chūyū of the title is an abbreviation based on alternate readings of two of the Chinese characters in that name.

G. Cameron HURST III

Chūzan'ō

(King of Chūzan). Title of kings who ruled in the Ryūkyū Islands from the 14th century until the establishment of Okinawa Prefecture in 1879. After a long period of political fragmentation, in the mid-14th century three kingdoms (Hokuzan, Chūzan, and Nanzan) emerged on the island of Okinawa. Their rulers entered into tributary relations with the Ming dynasty (1368–1644) of China and received the titles Hokuzan'ō, Chūzan'ō, and Nanzan'ō respectively. In 1422 King Shō Hashi (1372–1439) of Chūzan united the three kingdoms. He and his successors in later royal dynasties continued to be invested by the Chinese court as king of Chūzan even after the unification of the archipelago, and the title became synonymous with that of king of the Ryūkyūs. Many literary works on Okinawa refer to it as Chūzan. See also OKINAWA.

Chūzenji, Lake

(Chūzenjiko). Also called Lake Chūgūji and Lake Sachinoumi. Lake in the city of Nikkō, northwestern Tochigi Prefecture, central Honshū, located under the southern slope of the mountain NANTAISAN. The waters of the lake flow eastward to become the KEGON FALLS. Futarasan Shrine, Chūzenji Hot Spring, and numerous inns, souvenir shops, and summer villas are located on the banks of the lake. It is part of Nikkō National Park. Area: 11.5 sq km (4.4 sq mi); circumference: 21 km (13 mi); depth: 163 m (535 ft); altitude: 1,269 m (4,162 ft).

cicadas

(semi). In Japanese, semi is the common name for insects of the order Hemiptera, family Cicadidae. About 1,500 species of these insects are known in the world, of which 20–30 live in Japan. Japanese cicadas range from 1 to 5 centimeters (0.4–2 in) in length; the largest in size is the kumazemi (Cryptotympana facialis). The larva period is from two to six years. The adults feed on sap from the branches and trunks of trees, with some species, like the aburazemi (Graptopsaltria nigrofuscata), sucking juice from fruits, and others, like the iwasaki kusazemi (Mogannia iwasakii), sucking sap from grass. NAKANE Takehiko

In the Japanese poetry of the Nara (710–794) and Heian (794–1185) periods, the cicada appears as an insect of autumn and a symbol of solitude and melancholy. However, this is no doubt due to the influence of Chinese literature. In the HAIKU of the Edo period (1600–1868), it has become a symbol of the thriving life of full summer, and it is as a summer insect, which appears early in the season and stays until the very end, that most Japanese now think of the cicada. SAITŌ Shōji

citizens' movements

(shimin undō). A term that originally referred to nationwide campaigns of the 1950s and early 1960s in which ordinary citizens (shimin) temporarily joined left-wing student, labor, and socialist organizers to oppose the ruling conservative party's decisions on specific social and political issues. The most notable instances were the movements to ban atomic weapons (see ATOMIC WEAPONS, MOVEMENT TO BAN), terminate the UNITED STATES–JAPAN SECURITY TREATIES, and end the Vietnam War (see PEACE MOVEMENT). From the mid-1960s shimin undō came to refer to local protests by groups of ordinary citizens against industrial pollution and environmental destruction caused by economic development. These movements and protests built on a tradition of citizen activism that dated back to the ASHIO COPPER MINE INCIDENT of the 1890s.

Early postwar citizens' movements. The terms "citizens' movement" and "citizens' faction" (shiminha) were coined in 1960 to recognize and encourage the involvement of ordinary citizens in demonstrations against the renewal of the United States-Japan Security Treaty. A "citizens' faction" was formed by a small but highly visible group of progressive intellectuals anxious to spread opposition to the treaty beyond the confines of the left-wing establishment. After the treaty was renewed, activists strove for a time to form local citizens' movements against government social and political policies, but with little success.

Environmental movements. In the mid-1960s the term shimin undō came to be used interchangeably with jūmin undō (residents' movements) to describe local opposition to industrial pollution and development. The spectacular growth of the economy after 1955 had intensified urban congestion, disrupted the rural economy, introduced a variety of new and toxic industrial chemicals into the environment, and generally polluted air and water supplies. A public that in the 1950s had been willing to overlook these side effects of industrial development turned in the 1960s to protest against this intolerable array of "public hazards" (kōgai). Rural protest against environmental disruption had long been regarded as insignificant, reactionary opposition to economic modernization. But with the participation of middle-class urban elements, it gradually acquired the integrity and status of a progressive citizens' movement.

Victims' movements. The genesis of rural, and later much urban, opposition to "public hazards" lay in the so-called "victims' movements" (higaisha undō). Although many participants in antipollution citizens' movements formed in the late 1960s and early 1970s called themselves "victims" of environmental hazards, the term strictly refers to several groups of farmers, fishermen, and their families who suffered physical harm from POLLUTION-RELATED DISEASES. They included victims of Minamata disease, or physical deformity and disability caused by mercury poisoning; victims of the itai-itai disease, a degenerative bone condition attributed to cadmium poisoning; and victims of Yokkaichi asthma, a particularly debilitating lung disorder.

Major pollution suits. These farmers and fishermen possessed few of the material, organizational, and ideological resources needed to win recognition and compensation, but they soon attracted the attention and interest of doctors, lawyers, scientists, professors, students, high school teachers, journalists, and others with the resources and willingness to aid them through political action. Gradually, as more traditional avenues of redress proved ineffective, these previously apolitical victims allowed themselves to be represented in court by the activists. Medical and environmental scientists provided the evidence for a strong legal case against several companies said to be responsible for the pollution that caused the diseases. Activist lawyers, many of them affiliated with left-wing labor and political organizations, provided the legal expertise needed to file suit for damages. The rest provided various kinds of practical support and by their very presence imbued the cases with the features of a social movement. By 1973 all of these suits had ended with landmark judgments in the plaintiffs' favor.

Preventive environmental movements. Constant media coverage of the victims' suits between 1967 and 1973 won them considerable public sympathy. More important, it stimulated intense concern about all types of pollution and aroused citizens to organize local movements to prevent pollution hazards from reaching lethal proportions elsewhere. Residents of several coastal communities targeted for industrial development, horrified by the fate of residents of Yokkaichi and other sites of concentrated heavy industry, organized citizens' movements to block plans for oil, chemical, and power plant construction. The building of roads, railways, airports, power plants, sewage treatment plants, and other public facilities, once opposed only by those whose land was taken for the projects, now faced opposition from a broad social coalition concerned about "environmental impact." Housewives, already organized to protest prices, product quality, and other CONSUMER MOVEMENT issues, formed special groups to attack urban problems like traffic, smog, and refuse disposal.

Finally, an informal network of environmental activists, made up largely of advocates and theoreticians of citizens' movements, took shape in the 1970s. Active supporters of the victims' movements were joined by free-lance pollution critics in organizations like Ui Jun's Independent Forum (Jishu Kōza) at Tōkyō University. This loosely organized group held weekly public lectures by leaders of antipollution citizens' groups and came to function as a national clearinghouse for the sharing and dissemination of ideas about pollution control and citizen's movements.

Organization of citizens' movements. By the early 1970s antipollution and antidevelopment protest had achieved the force and character of a general social movement; 3,000 groups might be active at any given time. Each local movement took pride in its independence and grass roots character. But much of their activity, although localized in spirit and purpose, had assumed a standard form. The typical citizens' movement styled itself as a nonpartisan, nonideological neighborhood coalition organized to protest a specific pollution problem or development project. It tended to rely on existing organizations to arouse local interest in its goals, but usually it created a council designed to transcend established political and cultural divisions within the community. Participants were wary of involvement by the opposition parties, particularly the Japan Communist Party, but would accept help from individuals with relevant skills. In fact, experts were often the organizers of citizens' movements in their own local areas.

With the successful legal resolution of the major pollution suits in 1973, citizens' movements became less visible. Few had built permanent organizations, and other issues supplanted pollution on the domestic political agenda. But the burst of activity between 1967 and 1973 seems to have established citizens' movements as the preferred method for future handling of pollution and development problems. At the very least, decisions on economic development will henceforth require consideration of environmental impact and citizen participation.

■—— "Chiiki kaihatsu to shakaiteki kinchō," Chiiki kaihatsu 154 (1977), a special edition containing several excellent articles on citizens' movements. Margaret A. McKean, "Citizens' Movements in Urban and Rural Japan," in James White, ed, Social Change and

Community Politics in Urban Japan (1976). Matsushita Keiichi, "The Politics of Citizen Participation," *Japan Interpreter* 9.4 (1975). "Peasant Uprisings and Citizens' Revolts," *Japan Interpreter* 8.3 (1973). Shinseikatsu Undō Kyōkai, ed, *Chiiki kaihatsu to jūmin undō* (1965). Bradford L. Simcock, "Developmental Aspects of Anti-Pollution Protest in Japan," in Louis Kriesberg, ed, *Research in Social Movements, Conflicts, and Change* (1979). Frank G. Upham, "Litigation and Moral Consciousness in Japan: An Interpretive Analysis of Four Japanese Pollution Suits," *Law and Society Review* 10.4 (1976). "Zenkoku no shimin undō," *Shimin* 1 (1971), results of a mail survey of about 100 citizens' movements.

Bradford L. SIMCOCK

Citizen Watch Co, Ltd

(Shichizun Tokei). Japan's second largest wristwatch maker after K. HATTORI & CO, LTD, Citizen Watch was established in 1930 to manufacture wristwatches domestically; it now also produces lens shutters, adding machines, and machine tools. During World War II the company produced weapon components such as fuses, but it returned to the manufacture of wristwatches after the war. It concluded a business tie-up with Bulova Watch Co of the United States in 1960, thus entering the overseas market. Citizen has sales companies in the United States and West Germany, as well as watch manufacturing companies in South Korea, Taiwan, Hong Kong, and Mexico. It plans to produce watches for China on a consignment basis. Total sales for the fiscal year ending March 1982 were ¥132.5 billion (US $550.4 million), with an export ratio of 62 percent. The company was capitalized at ¥10.3 billion (US $42.8 million) in the same year. Corporate headquarters are located in Tōkyō.

C. Itoh & Co, Ltd

(Itōchū Shōji). One of Japan's major GENERAL TRADING COMPANIES. It is the third largest trading firm in the country, after the MITSUBISHI CORPORATION and MITSUI & CO, LTD, and has been traditionally strong in the fields of textiles and fuel. The company traces its origins to 1858, when Itō Chūbei started selling hemp cloth in provincial districts. He began to engage in foreign trade in 1884, and with the growth of Japan's cotton textile industry, the company developed into a trading firm importing cotton and exporting cotton yarn. It expanded its operations to China, Manchuria, Korea, and Southeast Asia; by the early 1940s it had become Japan's third largest trading company. After World War II, it was divided into C. Itoh & Co and the MARUBENI CORPORATION. Transactions centered chiefly on textiles in the early postwar years, but with the rapid growth of the Japanese economy and the development of heavy and chemical industries, C. Itoh expanded its operations to include machinery, metals, chemicals, fuel, and foodstuffs and became a comprehensive trading company. It was successful in developing undersea oil fields in Indonesia in 1970, thereby increasing investments in overseas resources development projects. Its purchases of DD (direct deal) oil from Middle Eastern countries have increased greatly in recent years, indicating the company's eagerness to develop energy resources. In 1976 it absorbed the Ataka Corporation, thus strengthening its iron and steel and chemical products divisions. C. Itoh has a total of 70 overseas branches and offices, as well as 43 overseas affiliates. Sales for the fiscal year ending March 1982 totaled ¥12.7 trillion (US $52.8 billion), of which oil and chemical products constituted 30 percent, metals 16 percent, machinery and construction 21 percent, textiles 13 percent, foodstuffs 15 percent, and other products 5 percent; the volume of foreign transactions was 58 percent and domestic transactions 42 percent. The company was capitalized at ¥43.2 billion (US $179.5 million) in the same year. Head offices are located in Tōkyō and Ōsaka.

civic education

(*shimin kyōiku*; formerly called *kōmin kyōiku*). In Japan civic education (education about the rights and obligations of a citizen) is an obligatory part of school education. In the years before World War II, under the name of *kōmin kyōiku*, it was used to inculcate a nationalistic ideology based on such concepts as respect for the emperor and filial piety. Since the war it has aimed at educating responsible members of a democratic and peaceful nation. It is essentially a part of school education, mainly given in social studies classes; however, it is also available in adult education classes and in public lectures at universities.

TAKAMURA Hisao

Civil Code

(Mimpō; Mimpōten). The first project to construct a civil code in Japan was headed by G. E. BOISSONADE DE FONTARABIE, who drafted the code, using the French civil code as a model; the code was enacted in 1890 and is referred to as the "old civil code." This version faced strong opposition, however, and did not go into effect in 1893 as the legislation required. The opposition was based on the concern that the Japanese people's traditional concepts of obligations and responsibilities would be damaged by the civil code. A new committee to examine legal codes was established, with HOZUMI NOBUSHIGE, TOMII MASAAKI, and UME KENJIRŌ as members. They also were influenced by the French Civil Code, but took as their model the first draft of the German Civil Code that had just been made public.

The first three chapters of a new Civil Code (General Provisions, Real Rights, and Obligations) were promulgated in 1896, and the next two (Domestic Relations Law and Inheritance Law) in 1898. These five chapters compose the Civil Code that is in effect to this day. The law of real rights and the law of obligations are called property law, while the domestic relations law and the inheritance law are called family law. Property law follows different principles from family law; the former can be said to be based on rationality, while the latter is basically nonrational. Property rights are often based on legal fictions that derive from a system of stable transactions and other similar systems, while family law is based on actual situations. Although the general provisions cover the entire code, it is said that they are for the most part provisions for property law.

The code, being a product of modern liberalism, is founded on the principles of freedom and equality. Based on a private property system, it has as its main supports the principles of absolute property rights and freedom of contract. However, the continuing development of Japanese capitalism brought about increasing inequalities, while issues emerged that could not be resolved under the principles of the code. After World War I, for example, housing problems developed to the point that the provisions in the code for rental relations could no longer provide adequate solutions; large enterprises also developed to the point that they were employing large numbers of workers and the code's coverage of labor-management relations and employment conditions could not respond to all of the issues raised. In response to these economic requirements that emerged from developments within capitalism and in order to ensure actual equality, legislation such as the Leased Land Law, the Leased House Law, and the Labor Standards Law (see LABOR LAWS) was enacted. In the area of mortgages, the code was again insufficient, and the Law for the Hypothecization of Factory Property (1905), the Trust Law (1922), and the Enterprise Security Law (1958) were thus enacted. (See also LEASED LAND RIGHTS and LEASED HOUSE RIGHTS.)

The fundamentals of freedom and equality were limited to the property law sphere, while family law was formed around the household system of premodern times. However, the post–World War II constitution took the concepts of respect for the individual and the basic equality of the sexes as basic tenets, and major amendments to the inheritance and domestic relations chapters thus became necessary. These were enacted, and the old household system was abolished. Two new influential provisions were also added to the code: one established that private rights defer to the public good, and the other recognized the equality of men and women. During the 1970s, a reexamination of the property system for married couples and the inheritance law system was conducted by the Ministry of Justice, and the inheritance system was amended effective at the beginning of 1981. See also INHERITANCE LAW; OBLIGATION; RIGHTS IN THINGS.

ENDŌ Hiroshi

Civil Code controversy

(Mimpōten ronsō). Dispute among legal specialists from 1889 to 1892 over the nation's first modern code of private law. Promulgated in 1890, the "old civil code" (kyū mimpō) had not been implemented because of strong criticism from some legal experts, and in 1898 it was replaced by the "new civil code" (shin mimpō). The controversy ostensibly centered on the charge that the code would disseminate the values of egalitarian Western civilization and thereby undermine the traditional Japanese family system. But the real issue was the French style and inspiration of the code, most of its critics having been trained in English law and most of its supporters in French law.

In the first two decades of the Meiji period (1868–1912) the Japanese government drafted six Western-inspired codes of law. It initiated these changes partly to further centralization of the political system and partly to "modernize," that is, Westernize, Japanese law and so gain the foreign powers' agreement to revise the Unequal Treaties of 1858–60 and relinquish the extraterritorial privilege of exemption from Japanese law (see UNEQUAL TREATIES, REVISION OF). The first of the six codes to be started, the CIVIL CODE was nonetheless the last to be completed, since it sought to put within the scope of written national law matters previously regulated by regional custom.

From 1870 on, various agencies worked on drafts of a civil code, but made little progress until a French legal adviser, G. E. BOISSONADE DE FONTARABIE, was put in charge in 1880. By 1886 Boissonade had completed most of a five-book code patterned after the French civil code. The remaining sections, dealing with inheritance and family law, were thought to require specialized knowledge of Japanese customs and were therefore drafted in 1887 by two Japanese, Isobe Shirō (1851–1923) and Kumano Toshizō (1854–99). However, both Isobe and Kumano had law degrees from French universities, and their draft showed strong French egalitarian influence. In 1888 the code review committee of the Ministry of Justice completely revised the Isobe–Kumano draft to give legal support to the samurai family tradition of an authoritarian headship and undivided inheritance of property by the heir.

Meanwhile, the German legal adviser K. F. Hermann ROESLER had drafted the COMMERCIAL CODE. The civil and commercial codes were undergoing final review in the GENRŌIN and the PRIVY COUNCIL when the first public sign of controversy appeared in May 1889. The Hōgakushi Kai, a society of law graduates of Tōkyō University, demanded that the government postpone promulgation of the two codes and open them to public examination and debate, because both regulated matters previously governed by local custom, and because it was believed that the two were internally inconsistent, with French legal principles in the Civil Code and German in the Commercial Code.

This demand was ignored because the government, having spent nearly 20 years in drafting the codes, was intent on promulgating them before the first Diet came into being in November 1890. Further delay would impede renegotiation of the unequal treaties and would subject the codes to the uncertainties of Diet politics. Consequently, both codes were promulgated in 1890, the Commercial Code to take effect on 1 January 1891 and the Civil Code on 1 January 1893. But as soon as the first Diet convened, a two-year postponement of the Commercial Code was voted by large majorities in both houses of the Diet, over strenuous objections from the government.

Encouraged by this success, critics of the government began demanding both a postponement of the Civil Code and a thorough revision of both codes. The inflammatory title of an August 1891 article by HOZUMI YATSUKA became the battlecry of the "postponement faction" (enkiha): "If the Civil Code comes in, loyalty and filial piety will be destroyed" (Mimpō idete, chūkō horobu). That dire prediction might have been warranted by the 1887 Isobe–Kumano draft of the sections on family and inheritance, but it grossly misrepresented the revised sections that had actually been promulgated in 1890.

The chief difference between the "postponement faction" and the "quick enforcement faction" (dankōha) was that most "postponers" were trained in English law and most "enforcers" were trained in French law. Since the Penal Code, in force since 1882, was closely patterned after French law, enforcement of a French-style civil code would give men trained in French law an enormous advantage not only in the bar examinations but more importantly in the new civil service examinations, which were based chiefly on law. Hozumi's 1891 article first appeared in the journal of the Tōkyō Hōgakuin, a private law school (predecessor of Chūō University) that then taught only English law and became the headquarters of the "postponement faction." A rival private law school, Meiji Hōritsu Gakkō (predecessor of Meiji University), which taught French law, was the stronghold of the "quick enforcement faction." At both schools, the faculty consisted almost entirely of part-time lecturers who were judges, government officials, or law professors at Tōkyō University. Thus the controversy quickly involved many of Japan's most influential law graduates, as well as the law students whose employment prospects would be materially affected by the outcome of the dispute. Critics therefore argued not only that the family sections of the code would subvert tradition, but that the entire code

was flawed by substantive omissions, internal inconsistencies, and stylistic defects.

The "postponement faction" won a crucial victory in 1892, when both houses of the Diet, by large majorities, passed a law postponing the Civil Code (and a large part of the Commercial Code) until the end of 1896, to allow time for reconsideration. The government reluctantly appointed a Codes Investigating Committee (Hōten Chōsakai). Although the committee included prominent enforcers as well as postponers, the latter were in the ascendant, and wholesale revision of the Civil Code became inescapable. The "New Civil Code," completed in 1898 after a second postponement, was closer to German law than to French, both in structure and in content. Yet the sections on family and inheritance law in the old and new codes were more similar than those on other subjects, and some provisions on family and inheritance had been closer to Japanese tradition in the old code than they were in the new one. See also LEGAL SYSTEM: history of Japanese law.

📖 ——Hoshino Tōru, Meiji mimpō hensan shi no kenkyū (1943). Hoshino Tōru, Mimpōten ronsō shi (1944). Hozumi Nobushige, The New Japanese Civil Code (1912). Ishii Ryōsuke, Meiji bunka shi: Hōseihen (1954), tr and adapted by William J. Chambliss, Japanese Legislation in the Meiji Era (1958). Nakamura Kikuo, Kindai Nihon no hōteki keisei (1956).   Robert M. SPAULDING

civilian control of the military

Because of Japan's bitter experience with militarism in the past, the framers of the 1947 CONSTITUTION stipulated in article 66 that the prime minister and cabinet ministers had to be civilians. In creating the SELF DEFENSE FORCES too, a provision was made that its head, the director-general of the Defense Agency, would be responsible to the prime minister. The existence of the NATIONAL DEFENSE COUNCIL, an advisory body to the prime minister, plays an important role in ensuring civilian control over the military.   IWASHIMA Hisao

Civil Information and Education Section of SCAP

(Minkan Jōhō Kyōiku Kyoku). Abbreviated as CIE; an organization under SCAP (Supreme Commander for the Allied Powers) in charge of overseeing education in occupied Japan from September 1945 until April 1952. The main purpose of the CIE was to eliminate the militaristic and ultranationalistic elements in the pre–World War II educational system and to build a new system based on democratic principles. Since the Occupation was carried out under the principle of "indirect rule," in which actual governance was done by the Japanese government under the supervision of the Allied Powers, the activities of the CIE were chiefly to instruct and advise the Ministry of Education and to see that it carried out the educational policies of SCAP. The planning and execution of educational policies were the main functions of an operations committee made up of the CIE, the Ministry of Education, and the EDUCATION REFORM COUNCIL. The CIE was the driving force in this committee. See also EDUCATIONAL REFORMS OF 1947.   TAKAKURA Shō

civil liberties, protection of

(jinken yōgo). Rights and protections based on human rights, freedom, equality, and the dignity of man include FREEDOM OF SPEECH, FREEDOM OF ASSEMBLY, FREEDOM OF ASSOCIATION, FREEDOM OF RELIGIOUS FAITH, and FREEDOM OF THE PRESS, as well as EQUALITY OF THE SEXES UNDER THE LAW, EQUALITY UNDER THE LAW, ACADEMIC FREEDOM, and many other kinds of political, procedural, cultural, medical, and socioeconomic protection.

Civil liberties protections are embodied in the 1947 CONSTITUTION, which transferred sovereign power from the emperor to the people (art. 1) and enacted a code of human rights (art. 10–40). Whereas the 1889 constitution had defined the emperor as the sole repository of state power, since 1947 the power to make laws has resided solely in the Diet (art. 41), executive power in the cabinet (art. 65), and judicial power in the judiciary (art. 76). Separation of powers is strictly observed. The RENUNCIATION OF WAR clause (art. 9) discourages the disregard for civil liberties that often accompanies militarism.

To reinforce civil liberties, a Civil Liberties Bureau (Jinken Yōgo Kyoku) was established within the MINISTRY OF JUSTICE under the Civil Liberties Commissioners Law of 1949. This law provided for as many as 20,000 commissioners, drawn from all walks of life and appointed in a nonpolitical fashion, to promote civil liberties ideals and practice. As of 1 January 1978, 10,626 commissioners had been appointed. The commissioners receive no salary and are employed by no government ministry. Moreover, committees of inquest or of prosecution, composed of ordinary citizens chosen by lot, provide lay surveillance of public prosecutors' failure to prosecute. The educational system accords great importance to the teaching of civil liberties.

Women, guaranteed equality with men by the constitution, have shown increasing awareness of their rights and have formed many organizations to promote their liberties. The government has formulated a National Plan of Action to improve the status of women and subscribes to the goals of the United Nations Women's Decade (1976–85).

The Lawyers' Law (Bengoshi Hō) of 1949 makes it the duty of every lawyer to protect human rights. Subcommittees of the JAPAN FEDERATION OF BAR ASSOCIATIONS concentrate on special problems such as prisoners' rights, police investigation, and religious freedom.

The impact on civil liberties of modern technology in cases involving behavior manipulation, cybernetics, genetic engineering, eugenic surgery, recombinant DNA experimentation, and environmental rights is the subject of active concern.

Problem areas in civil liberties include BURAKUMIN (outcasts), KOREANS IN JAPAN, FOREIGNERS IN JAPAN, mixed-blood children (KONKETSUJI), refugees, and atomic-bomb victims *(hibakusha)*. See also MINORITIES.

◼——Dan Fenno Henderson, ed, *The Constitution of Japan: Its First Twenty Years, 1947–67* (1969). Hiroshi Itoh and Lawrence W. Beer, *The Constitutional Case Law of Japan: Selected Supreme Court Cases, 1961–70* (1978). Hideo Tanaka, assisted by M.D.H. Smith, *The Japanese Legal System: Introductory Cases and Materials* (1976).
C. G. Weeramantry

Civil Procedure, Code of

(Minji Soshō Hō). A body of law by which disputes between private individuals are received and processed through the Japanese courts. The resulting final judgment embodies the parties' substantive rights and duties, which may then be enforced by state powers of execution. There are thus two distinct phases: the procedures for trial resulting in a judgment and the procedures for enforcement of the judgment. The prejudgment and judgment procedures are contained in the Code of Civil Procedure, but the procedures for enforcement of judgments were taken out of the code and, after extensive revision, were enacted in the new Civil Execution Law (Minji Shikkō Hō, Law No. 4, 1979), effective 1980.

Definitions —— The term civil was derived in modern Europe from the Latin *civitas* meaning citizen, and the Japanese translated "civil" as *minji* when the modern Japanese Code of Civil Procedure was drafted in the late 19th century. Civil procedure applies only to adjudication of disputes between private individuals or entities. Civil procedure is thus distinguished from CRIMINAL PROCEDURE whereby violations of the criminal law charged against a suspect may be adjudicated. In a criminal proceeding the state itself is the party moving against the suspect, the defendant. In other governmental suits, civil procedure is supplemented by special rules for administrative suits applicable to noncriminal, public law disputes typically between the state, its officials, and agencies as one party and a private citizen alleging misuse of authority as the other. Procedure is sometimes also called "adjective" law, and is thus distinguished from substantive law, which defines the rights and duties of private citizens in their ordinary relationships with each other.

Function —— In a theoretical sense, it is necessary to remember that the distinction between procedural law and substantive law may be deceptively facile, just as is the interplay between means and ends or form and substance in other fields of discourse. At this level, Sir Henry Maine reminds us of the importance of procedure in the growth of the common law: "substantive law has at first the look of being gradually secreted in the interstices of procedure." Thus, in justiciable law, all lawyers learn early that "there is no right without a remedy" administered by the courts.

With the above qualifications in mind, we may say that procedure, in Japan as elsewhere, exists for the sake of enforcing substantive law. Procedures for trial and procedures for enforcement of judgments supply but another inducement, besides social pressures, for individuals to comply with the prescriptions of the substantive law. To that end it provides a mechanism by which the compulsion of the state can be invoked to examine carefully and decide a dispute so as to secure compliance with the substantive law, should other inducements to the defendant fail. Procedural law is thus aptly called the "handmaiden of justice."

In addition, procedural law embodies its own values (concurrent with substantive values) related to fairness, impartiality, and truth in fact-finding. These values are state-enforced policies concerning the way in which a dispute should be handled. In addition, civil procedure aims at timeliness, economy, and efficiency, which sometimes may be balanced against other procedural or substantive policies.

Historical Background —— The mature system of Japanese civil procedure centers on the Code of Civil Procedure (hereafter CCP), first enacted in 1891. It was at that time a Western importation, highly innovative in the Japanese context, as was justiciable law (or lawyers' law) in general. The CCP was the culmination of over 20 years of study. During this time, many experiments with Western-style procedures were undertaken. The goal was to replace the decentralized administration of justice found in the Tokugawa administrative and conciliatory system up to 1868. Perhaps because of the Tokugawa legacy of settling civil disputes at the local level with little intervention from centralized agencies of the shogunate, the balance in Japan even today between civil litigation and alternative social methods for dispute resolution leaves a major role for amicable adjustment by mediation, consultation, conciliation, and compromise. Some of these methods are entirely consensual and informal, but others, still in large part consensual, are implemented by legal procedures embodied in separate procedural statutes such as the Civil Conciliation Law (1951) and the Domestic Relations Adjustment Law (1948). See DISPUTE RESOLUTION SYSTEMS OTHER THAN LITIGATION.

Leading up to the enforcement of the CCP in 1891, the Japanese government appointed a French jurist, Emile Gustave BOISSONADE DE FONTARABIE to study the French code of 1806. The draft CCP that he produced in 1883 was, however, not adopted. Instead the government shifted its attention to the German CCP of 1877, which was the newest procedural law in Europe at the time. A Prussian adviser, Herman Techow, was then appointed to compile a new draft CCP. He completed his draft in 1886 chiefly following the German model, but drawing also from the Prussian, Austrian, and French codes for occasional provisions and concepts. For example, the French code influenced the procedures for execution of judgments in old Book VI, which remain in revised form in the new Civil Execution Law (1979). With only minor changes the new Diet under the Meiji Constitution (1889) enacted the Techow CCP in 1890, and it was enforced in 1891. After more than three decades of experience, the CCP's first five books (I General Provisions; II First Instance; III Appeals; IV Retrial; and V Summary Procedure) were thoroughly revised, and the new version was enacted and enforced in 1926. The final three books (VI Compulsory Execution [KYŌSEI SHIKKŌ], VII Public Preemptory Notice [*kōji saikoku*], and VIII Arbitration [*chūsai*]) were left untouched. (See the section below on the format of the Code of Civil Procedure.)

Just after World War II the Code of Civil Procedure was again amended, but in contrast to the Code of Criminal Procedure (entirely rewritten, mainly to safeguard rights of the accused; see CRIMINAL LAW), the amendments to the CCP were limited to the following important points suggesting some American influence: responsibility for examining witnesses and producing other evidence was shifted from the court to the parties; and new Rules of Civil Procedure were issued under the new rule-making powers of the Supreme Court to implement the changes in the procedure for examining witnesses.

In the 1960s two important revisions were made. Book V-II was added to the CCP in 1964 to implement summary proceedings to collect bills and checks. In 1966 the Marshals' Law (Shikkōkan Hō) was passed as a separate statute to strengthen and rationalize the position and functioning of the court's enforcement officers (see MARSHAL).

Finally, beginning in earnest in 1968, the Ministry of Justice began drafting a substantial revision of CCP Book VI on compulsory execution. These procedures had been recognized as outmoded soon after their enforcement in 1891, but they remained essentially unchanged when the first five books were amended in 1926. After a decade of work, the revision was enacted in 1979 in the form of a consolidation of Book VI and the separate Auction Law (1898). The revision became an extensive new and separate law—the Civil Execution Law, in 198 articles (plus four supplemental articles). From the old Book VI only Chapter 4 ("Provisional Attachments and Provisional Dispositions") was retained in the CCP (arts. 737–747 and 755–763), and a new CCP Book V-III entitled "Confirmation of Judgments and Suspension of Execution" (old arts. 498–501 and 511–513) was added. Technical though this subject is, the new Civil Execution Law is a substantial advance in the Japanese procedures for enforcing judgments. Major controversial issues, such as the "equality principle" enabling other creditors to participate in distribution, were not reformed to the satisfaction of their advocates, but still the new law should lend a new efficiency to Japanese justiciable law.

Relation of the CCP to Other Laws——The CCP, supplemented by the new Civil Execution Law, provides the basic rules for dealing with civil lawsuits and the enforcement of judgments in the Japanese courts. But these rules operate in a much broader legal context of underlying, collateral, or subsidiary laws. They begin with the 1947 CONSTITUTION, which provides specifically (art. 32) that "No person [*nanibito mo,* including aliens] shall be denied the right of access to the courts." Article 82 then provides that "Trials shall be conducted and judgment declared publicly." Also, article 76 provides that "the whole judicial power is vested in a SUPREME COURT and in such inferior courts as are established by law." Extraordinary courts are prohibited (art. 76.2), and the independence of judges is specifically guaranteed (art. 76.3). Article 77 also grants, for the first time in Japan, important rule-making power to the Supreme Court, empowering it to regulate certain activities of the courts, bar, bench, procuracy (prosecution), and other court officials. Significantly, article 81 provides for a new power of judicial review in Japan: "The Supreme Court is the court of last resort with power to determine the constitutionality of any law, regulation or official act." After some early scholarly debate, article 81 was found by the Supreme Court in the SUZUKI DECISION (1952) to embody a litigious condition to JUDICIAL REVIEW of statutes (somewhat analogous to our "case or controversy" doctrine). Thus the courts will not review acts of government for constitutionality in the abstract, as is sometimes done in European countries. Also, the Supreme Court has on occasion indicated that its powers do not cover that indistinct group of important issues called "political questions." These, the court has held, are to be resolved, except in extreme cases, only by the political branches of government, the legislature or the executive (see SUNAGAWA CASE).

A court system in four tiers was established by the Court Law (1947) as follows: 1 Supreme Court (14 justices and the chief justice); 8 high courts; 50 district courts and 50 family courts; 575 summary courts. The summary courts and district courts are both courts of first instance, with the summary courts limited to claims of ￥300,000 or less as of 1980. The system for appealing civil judgments to higher courts differs from the American system in that the first Japanese appeal (e.g., from summary to district court, or district to high court) is called a *kōso* appeal and allows the appellant to attack the judgment on both the law and the facts. By comparison, facts found by a jury at first instance in the American system cannot normally be challenged or appealed, but in Japan, where a jury is not used, the first appellate court may review the lower court findings of fact as well as law. The second appeal, *jōkoku,* in Japan may raise only questions of law or of constitutional right; unlike the American writ of *certiorari,* the Japanese *jōkoku* appeal on any legal issue may be taken, not as a matter of discretion, but as a matter of right. A *jōkoku* appeal to a high court from a district court's *kōso* review of a judgment first decided in a summary court is final, unless a constitutional question is raised. On constitutional issues decided in the high court, a second *jōkoku* appeal to the Supreme Court is allowed. Thus whenever a constitutional issue is raised and the statute is found unconstitutional, the Supreme Court always has the last word (by at least 8 of the 15 justices). Dissenting opinions are not infrequent. Note also that purely legal questions raised by orders (*meirei*) or rulings (*kettei*) in the lower courts may be challenged by a separate system of appeals, called *kōkoku* appeals.

Besides the Court Law, there are other laws basic to the civil litigation system, including, for example, the Lawyers' Law (see LAWYERS), the Marshals' Law, and the Law concerning Civil Procedure Costs. These among others regulate the roles of professionals in lawsuits.

The overall legal context of the civil procedure system also involves two kinds of auxiliary procedure. The first is the important Noncontentious Cases Procedure Law (1898) and the related statute for domestic affairs, the Domestic Relations Adjustment Law (1948). The concept here is that the broad judicial powers (*shihōken*) are divided overall into two kinds: trial power over contentious cases (*soshō jiken*) and a kind of administrative power over noncontentious cases (*hishō jiken*). Typical examples of noncontentious cases in Japan are: certain matters concerning personal status; public auctions of property in which a creditor has a security interest (now included in the new Civil Execution Law); permission to sell leaseholds; certain corporate liquidations; and others. This is important judicial work, and the courts handle well over 200,000 such cases annually. They are brought by a single party (or parties in agree-

ment) and do not normally involve disputes over rights, but it is deemed important that the parties' declarations affecting their status or rights be confirmed by a court. One major facet of the judicial handling of noncontentious cases is in domestic affairs (e.g., presumptive death; incompetency; permission to adopt a minor; forfeiture of parental rights; selection of a guardian; distribution in succession; and probate of wills).

While the conceptual division of contentious from noncontentious cases is clear enough, controversies have arisen in practice as to whether certain arguably contentious issues may be involved in concluding a noncontentious case. In several contested instances in recent years the Supreme Court has held by a divided court that such disputed issues, as for example the spouses' duty to cohabit (Civil Code 752), may be subsumed in the solution of a noncontentious case. The courts' reasoning is that, if the loser chooses, he can still get his day in court (Constitution, arts. 32 and 82) later by attacking, in a contentious case (i.e., formal lawsuit), the noncontentious holding.

Besides noncontentious procedures, much Japanese civil litigation involves subject matter for which special procedures have been provided either in the CCP or in separate statutes. The leading examples of special procedure in the CCP are the informal procedures (CCP Book II, Chapter 4) for cases in the summary courts (claim value ￥300,000 or less), or debt collection procedure (*tokusoku tetsuzuki,* CCP Book V); and for suits on bills and checks in either the summary or district courts (CCP Book V-II). Also, CCP Book VI still provides special procedures for provisional remedies supplemented by the new Civil Execution Law, Chapter 3.

Some of the other important separate statutes are: the Personal Affairs Procedure Law for matrimonial matters, adoption, paternity, parent and child, and the like; the BANKRUPTCY LAW for debtors and creditors; the Composition Law for agreeable solutions worked out between a debtor and his creditors; the CORPORATE REORGANIZATION LAW for relieving enterprises from financial difficulty; and the Administrative Cases Procedure Law for disputes between the government and private parties. In all of these suits, the rules provided by the special statutes govern where applicable, but the CCP applies where the special statute has no special rule. In addition, the special statute for CONCILIATION (*chōtei*) and the special provisions in the CCP Book VIII for arbitration (*chūsai*) and compromise (WAKAI; CCP arts. 136 and 356) provide aids for these alternative methods of dispute resolution.

Format of the Code of Civil Procedure——While the foregoing is an overall view of the legal context for civil litigation in Japan, what sort of problems are treated within the CCP itself? As "adjective" law, the CCP exists to enforce rights accorded by the substantive law in the CIVIL CODE, the COMMERCIAL CODE, and a host of other statutes. As we have seen, civil litigation may be seen in its social context as an added inducement to litigants to do right as provided in the substantive law. The inducement flows from the added disadvantage incurred from lawyers' fees, court costs, lost time, and adrenalin spent in litigating, plus perhaps the social stigma attached to litigiousness and being forced to comply; provided, of course, that the defendant knows, as is sometimes the case, that he ought to lose. In addition, the CCP embodies independently important Japanese policies in favor of fairness, notice, orality, immediacy, timeliness, probity, economy, and the like in handling disputes.

The overall framework of the code is Germanic; it is divided into eight major books (*hen*). Book I is entitled *General Provisions (Sōsoku).* It provides rules for relations between courts laterally and within the court hierarchy; capacity and joinder of parties; representatives, including lawyers; court costs (e.g., filing and witnesses' fees); and general rules for oral argument, dates, services of documents, and decision making by the courts. All such basic rules apply throughout in other, more specific matters treated in the other seven books. Book I lends a systematic aspect to Japanese procedural law; it is applicable throughout the whole litigation process, unless overridden in specific provisions.

Book II is entitled *Proceedings at First Instance (Dai isshin no soshō tetsuzuki).* It deals with various aspects of the "trial" in separate chapters, including the rules of evidence. Also more informal procedures for the summary courts are provided in Chapter 4.

Book III is entitled *Appeals (Jōso).* In separate chapters it covers the first appeal (*kōso*) on both law and facts; the final appeal (*jōkoku*) on the law only; and the special appeals (*kōkoku*) mostly for intermediate rulings (*kettei*) and orders (*meirei*).

Book IV is entitled *Retrial (Saishin).* It provides for extraordinary retrial of suits even after the final judgment, but for very special listed reasons only.

Book V is entitled *Dunning Procedure* (*Tokusoku tetsuzuki;* sometimes translated as summary procedure). These rules provide for an abbreviated trial in summary courts on certain legal instruments or fungible or money claims.

Book V-II, added in 1964, is entitled *Special Provisions concerning Litigation of Bills and Checks* (*Tegata soshō oyobi kogitte soshō ni kansuru tokusoku*). It provides for suits on bills and checks in the summary court, or district court if the amount sought comes to the jurisdictional amount of ¥300,000.

New Book V-III (1979) is entitled *Confirmation of Judgments and Suspension of Execution* (*Hanketsu no kakutei oyobi shikkō teishi*). As explained above, Book VI was extensively amended in 1979 to delete compulsory execution provisions, so that it now provides only for provisional attachment (*kari sashiosae*) and PROVISIONAL DISPOSITION (*kari shobun*) in aid of enforcement of an eventual judgment in pending suits.

Book VII is entitled *Public Peremptory Notice* (*Kōji saikoku;* alternative translation, *General Pressing Notice*) and deals with certain instances specifically covered by substantive laws. An example is nullification of a check that has been stolen or lost and may be misused in the hands of third parties if allowed to remain valid. It is one of the few actions analogous to the *in rem* action of common law.

Finally, Book VIII, entitled *Arbitration* (*Chūsai*), covers rules by which the courts enforce in certain instances the consensual regime provided in arbitral contracts and awards.

The Japanese and American Systems Compared——— This whole area of procedural law, including the enforcement of judgments covered in the new Civil Execution Law, is "lawyers' law" of the most technical sort. The above outline of the matters treated in detail by more than 800 articles of the CCP, and in turn augmented by numerous special statutes, affords only an abstract glimpse of the problems covered. Perhaps a better understanding may be obtained by explaining several major ways in which Japanese procedures differ from the procedural features of American litigation.

1. The Japanese have a unitary litigation system. It is, therefore, the purpose of the CCP, with the other statutes described above, to create a single judicial and procedural system for handling civil lawsuits. Its singular simplicity contrasts with the American dual national system of federal and state courts and procedures. In particular it does not need the recondite body of constitutional and subsidiary rules necessary to regulate federal-state judicial relations, especially in the areas of jurisdiction and enforcement of judgments from one court in another.

2. The Japanese courts do not use a jury, and there is no need, therefore, to distinguish sharply in the rules, as Americans must, between findings of fact (for the jury) and law (for the judge). In Japan, judges always decide both. Several other major differences in Japanese procedure can be traced to the lack of a jury (see below).

3. "Trial," without a jury in Japan, is not a continuous, concentrated, and dramatic event as it is in the American system; rather it is a series of short sessions, normally beginning within a few weeks of filing the complaint and spaced a few weeks apart thereafter. At each session usually a single issue or witness is examined as designated in advance by the judge, until the case is finally ripe for decision. An average case may have six to a dozen such short hearings, extending over a year or more in complex controversies. Thus each judge is, of course, handling a number of cases over the same period of time.

For each hearing a party must prepare and serve on the other party a preparatory brief (*jumbi shomen*), and after each session the court clerk (*shokikan*) must prepare a summary (or protocol; *chōsho*) of all that transpired so that the judges can consult it to recall the progress of the case at each successive session. If deemed necessary, a stenographic transcript can be made, but verbatim transcripts are not as common as in the US system. Paperwork for the parties, in the form of "briefs" for each session, is heavy in such a system, despite the principle of orality (*kōtō benron*); for the judges it would seem to be an even heavier burden to review the same files each time a hearing comes up. Actually oral presentation is often abbreviated because the lawyers simply refer the judge to the required briefs on file.

This episodic mode of trial is another Japanese feature that would not be possible with a jury system. A jury trial, of course, requires that the entire evidence of both sides be presented to the assembled jury for a verdict at a concentrated and continuous trial. Since World War II, Japanese courts have also tried to get the bar to prepare cases in advance and to concentrate trials, in the interest of judicial efficiency, but with indifferent success. One merit of epi-

sodic trial is that an astute judge can identify the key issues and get them aired within a few weeks, and in many cases, the parties can thus see the strengths and weaknesses of their positions early. This often persuades reasonable parties to settle; whereas American litigants often must wait a year for a trial date before they or their lawyers "settle on the courthouse steps," as the saying goes.

4. Compromise (*wakai*) settlements agreeable to the parties may be encouraged by the Japanese judge at any stage of a trial, and the judge may summon the parties to appear for the purpose of discussing a compromise. In American trials, the judge has no such powers and his role is to decide the case, not actively to promote a settlement. This Japanese practice giving the judge power to facilitate a compromise is both congenial to Japanese traditional practices and compatible with the German sources of the modern Japanese CCP. Compromise powers are also effective. Roughly one quarter of all regular suits filed are concluded by such a compromise.

5. The Japanese bar is very small (about 12,000), so that Japanese courts, especially the summary courts, hear many more cases than American courts do in which one or both parties plead their own cases without the aid of lawyers. Thus the parties must depend more or less on the judge for legal advice. This puts a heavier burden on the judge and requires him to take firm control of the proceedings, which is in part responsible for the next difference between the Japanese and American systems.

6. The district courts and high courts have a system of "career judges." Normally, new judges are young professionals, who go on the bench immediately after they finish their legal education at the LEGAL TRAINING AND RESEARCH INSTITUTE; usually they have a university law degree before they enter the institute (see LEGAL EDUCATION). They serve an initial period as assistant judges (*hanjiho*); then, on becoming full-fledged judges, they normally spend the remainder of their lifetime careers as judges (see JUDGES). Whatever its merits and demerits, such a system of career experts does avoid the vagaries of the elective political bench and the irrationality that some experts feel a lay jury brings to the civil litigation process.

7. The Japanese LAW OF EVIDENCE is quite simple compared with the complex American rules against opinion, hearsay, and the like, which are thought to be necessary to avoid misleading the US lay juries. Japan's career judges, with their experience and strong control over the proceedings, can reject (or discount the probity of) dubious evidence. Thus there is little need for a complex and artificial screen of rules to filter evidence. On this score the Japanese system is refreshingly simple and effective. The same is true of the court's handling of expert witnesses. Experts in Japan are appointed by the judge, though he normally consults the parties about acceptable appointments. This practice can avoid the more unseemly aspects of an adversary system where an "expert" for the plaintiff too often opines that something is black, and just as dutifully the "expert" for the defendant opines that it is white—or so it may seem to the inexpert jury.

8. Japanese practice has virtually no discovery procedures; only the procedure for preserving evidence of ill or departing witnesses is available, and only in very limited circumstances. Whereas, the American lawyer can take early recorded depositions of parties and witnesses and get a clearer picture of the evidence in the case before trial. But since "trials" in Japan start soon after filing, actually the successive short sessions have a function like the American method of discovery of clarifying issues early for the lawyers as they go along, instead of discovering evidence while waiting for a trial date as necessary in the American jury system. The Japanese courts also have very limited powers, by American standards, to order the production of documents in the hands of the opponent or witnesses, even though their relevance to the truth in the case is apparent.

9. Pleadings, too, have quite a different role in Japan because amendment is liberally allowed at any session up to the very closing of oral hearings. In the American jury system, pleading coupled with discovery must enable the parties to prepare for a single concentrated trial before the jury, and so amendments must be limited at some point. Yet the American theory of an "action" has become quite broad and promotes liberal pleadings compared to the pleading pitfalls of Japan's rigid definition of an "action" or "claim," which combines with the next point to make the effect of a Japanese judgment quite narrow.

10. There is no collateral estoppel effect for Japanese judgments. Coupled with a narrow definition of an "action," this narrow judgment in a contract claim, for example, can be disadvantageous to a party who may wish to assert the judgment as a defense to a second suit, in say, tort, arising out of the same transaction. Collateral estoppel effect means that facts necessary to the judgment (and also

necessary to a different collateral claim) may not be retried between the same parties in a second suit on a different cause of action. Japan does not recognize this rule, and without it Japanese pleading assumes great importance in some cases.

11. The Japanese appellate system, as mentioned above, is two-tiered. The distinctive part, in comparison with the American system, is the first appeal *kōso;* it may open up the whole case again on both facts and law. Again, in the United States such a practice is foreclosed in appeals by jury fact-finding at first instance, which must stand on appeal; there is, therefore, no way to reexamine jury findings on appeal except on the narrowest of grounds. Whether the added expense, burden, and delay of Japanese dual levels of fact finding yield enough in certainty and justice is arguable, if lawyers are as competent and attentive as they should be at first instance. But in Japan many suits are brought without lawyers, and this may be one reason for Japanese reexamination of facts at the first appeal.

12. Among remedies available in the Japanese courts the power of contempt, so useful to American judges, is notably lacking. Consequently, enforcement of injunctions and other orders of the court is rather toothless compared to the American system, because the Japanese judge, rather than acting directly, must rely on the prosecutor via the criminal law process. The effect of this limitation is felt both at trial and in compulsory executions.

13. In compulsory execution, the judgment creditor who finds the debtor's property and moves against it does not have priority over all other unsecured creditors, but must divide with other creditors of equal rank when there is not enough to go around. In American practice the diligent judgment creditor is rewarded; his claim on the defendant property, which he finds and brings to execution, is usually superior to that of other unsecured creditors. The relative toothlessness of the Japanese plaintiff's hard-earned judgment is said to be derived from the "principle of equality" found in French execution law at the time the code was adopted.

14. Finally, jurisdictional theory in Japan rejects the traditional American idea that personal jurisdiction over the defendant is both necessary and sufficient in personal actions. Japan requires notice to the defendant, but it is a procedural requirement, not jurisdictional. Rather, Japanese jurisdiction *(saibanken)* is based on the theory that the court's power to decide a case depends on certain contacts that the parties, the transaction, or the dispute have with the territory over which the court presides. Recent trends in American "long-arm" practices, which find jurisdiction based on "minimal contact" with the court, are bringing Americans closer to the Japanese concepts of jurisdiction. Still, the differences are important. Also, Japanese practice has little that corresponds to the basic American concepts of *in rem* or *quasi-in rem* jurisdiction. The Japanese courts almost exclusively act against the person—what Americans call *in personam* jurisdiction. Without calling it *"in rem,"* the public peremptory notice proceeding and certain suits in the field of personal or family relations do, however, resemble the American *in rem* practice.

Only the major differences between Japanese and American civil procedure have been mentioned. A multitude of other detailed differences could be enumerated. Among the salient differences, however, it will be noted that many are grounded in the American system of jury trial. See also JUDICIAL SYSTEM; LEGAL SYSTEM.

📖 ——Code translation: Eibun Hōreishū, tr, *Code of Civil Procedure* (1975). Four Japanese treatises: Kaneko Hajime, *Minji soshō hō taikei* (rev ed, 1975). Mikazuki Akira, *Minji soshō hō*, vol 35 of *Hōritsugaku zenshū* (Yūhikaku, 1959). Mikazuki Akira, *Minji soshō hō* (1979). Shindō Kōji, *Minji soshō hō*, vol 30 of *Gendai hōritsugaku zenshū* (Chikuma Shobō, 1974). Commentaries: Kikui Tsunahiro and Muramatsu Toshio, *Zentei minji soshō hō* (1978). Saitō Hideo et al, ed, *Chūkai minji soshō hō* (1968–). Urano Yūkō, *Chikujō kaisetsu minji shikkō hō* (1979). Case commentary: Muramatsu Toshio et al, *Hanrei kommentāru: Minji soshō hō* (1976). Western-language materials, general: Baumgärtel, ed, *Grundprobleme des Zivilprozessrechts: Japanische Veröffentlichung·in Deutscher und Englischer Sprache* (1976). Takaaki Hattori and Dan Fenno Henderson, *Civil Procedure in Japan* (1982). Tanabe Kōji, "The Process of Litigation: An Experiment with the Adversary System," in Arthur von Mehren, ed, *Law in Japan* (1963). Special topics: Fujita Yasuhiro, "Japanese Rules of Jurisdiction," *Law in Japan* 4 (1970). Taniguchi Yasuhei, "Constitutional Guarantees in the Civil Procedure of Japan," in Mauro Capalletti and Denis Tallons, ed, *Fundamental Guarantees of the Parties in Civil Litigation* (1973). Supreme Court decisions: John M. Maki, *Court and Constitution in Japan* (1964). Hiroshi Itoh and Lawrence Beer, *The Constitutional Case Law of Japan* (1978). Dan Fenno HENDERSON

Clark, Edward Warren (1849–1907)

American educator and Episcopalian minister. Clark attended Rutgers College in New Jersey where, with his friend William Elliot GRIFFIS, he befriended several Japanese students. In 1871 he became the first foreign teacher at the Denshūjo, a leading center of Western studies in Shizuoka. He taught science, English, and, unofficially, the Bible there until 1873, when he was invited to Tōkyō to teach chemistry at the Kaisei Gakkō, a predecessor of Tōkyō University. After returning to the United States in March 1875, Clark became an Episcopalian pastor in upstate New York. He also wrote two books on Japan and remained active in promoting US–Japanese understanding.

📖 ——Edward Warren Clark, *Life and Adventures in Japan* (1878). A. Hamish Ion, "Edward Warren Clark and Early Meiji Japan: A Case Study of Cultural Conflict," *Modern Asian Studies* (1977).
Edward R. BEAUCHAMP

Clark, William Smith (1826–1886)

American educator, scientist, and entrepreneur who became one of the more famous advisers to the Japanese government during the 1870s phase of modernization. Born on 31 July 1826 in Ashfield, Massachusetts. He was graduated from Amherst College in 1848 with high academic honors. His interest in science resulted in his going to Germany to study at Georgia Augusta University in Göttingen. In 1852 he received a PhD degree, having written a dissertation on the chemistry of meteorites. He then joined the Amherst College faculty and during the following 15 years earned a reputation as a fine teacher, an educational innovator, and a fund raiser for the college. When the Civil War broke out in 1861, he joined the 21st Regiment of Massachusetts Volunteers with the rank of major. He served with distinction and rose to be colonel, but resigned his commission and returned to Amherst College in 1863.

Clark became a leader in the successful campaign to obtain for the town of Amherst a new state agricultural college, one of the first land-grant colleges. In 1867 he resigned from Amherst to become the first active president of Massachusetts Agricultural College (MAC) on the eve of its opening. He soon won a national reputation for both himself and his college because of his enormous energy and innovative leadership.

In 1876 he was engaged for one year (on leave from MAC) by the Japanese government to serve as the first president of a projected agricultural college in Sapporo, Hokkaidō. He arrived there on 31 July 1876, his 50th birthday. Two weeks later he presided over the opening of Sapporo Agricultural College (SAC; now part of HOKKAIDŌ UNIVERSITY), which was modeled after MAC. For the next eight months he planned and developed the curriculum, directed a building program, and taught four hours daily. He also served as technical adviser on agricultural matters to the·agency responsible for the development of Hokkaidō, introducing new crops, implements, machinery, and techniques and writing many technical reports. In his spare time he persuaded his students to sign a "Covenant of Believers in Jesus," an event which led to their formal conversion shortly after his departure in April 1877. According to one of them, he turned in his saddle as he rode away from his students and shouted in farewell, "Boys, be ambitious!" a phrase still familiar to almost all Japanese.

Clark resigned from MAC in 1879 in order to accept the presidency of a floating college, an ambitious project which was canceled shortly before departure. Clark then entered into a partnership to form a mining company on Wall Street. The business initially brought him a considerable fortune but failed, apparently as a result of shady business dealing by his partner who disappeared. Clark's fortune vanished as did the investments of a large number of his fellow Amherst residents and many others. His health steadily declined, and after four years of inactivity he died on 9 March 1886.

📖 ——John M. Maki, "William Smith Clark: A Yankee in Hokkaidō," unpublished manuscript translated into Japanese by Takaku Shin'ichi and published under the title *Kurāku: Sono eikō to zasetsu* (1978). *John M.* MAKI

classical Japanese

The literary language of premodern Japan, especially that used in the poetry and prose of the Heian period (794–1185), which served as a model for the literature of later periods. Referred to in Japanese by a number of terms such as *wabun, kobun,* and *bungo.* Although the literary language originally corresponded closely to the spoken, by the Edo period (1600–1868) the two were widely divergent. Early in the Meiji period (1868–1912) there arose a movement to develop a literary form of the modern spoken language (see GEMBUN ITCHI). Now little used except in the composition of classical poetic forms such as TANKA, classical Japanese is nevertheless taught in high schools and universities for the study of classical literature and other premodern writings.

The definition above identifies classical Japanese with the style primarily of the belles lettres of the 9th, 10th, and 11th centuries, including such works of fiction as the *Genji monogatari* (TALE OF GENJI), such poetic anthologies as the KOKINSHŪ, such diaries as the *Tosa nikki* of KI NO TSURAYUKI, and such collections of essays as the *Makura no sōshi* (tr *The Pillow Book*) of SEI SHŌNAGON. The language of these works is referred to as *wabun* (Japanese writing) to distinguish them from other writings of the period written in Chinese (KAMBUN). The original texts of the *wabun* works were written almost exclusively in the *hiragana* phonetic script (see KANA), and Chinese characters (KANJI) were used rarely if at all. Their vocabulary consists mainly of native Japanese words *(wago),* and the use of words of Chinese origin *(kango)* is quite limited. It is assumed that there were no significant differences between the spoken and written languages of this period because narrative and dialogue passages within the works do not show any notable differences.

Many scholars classify works of later periods such as the *Tsurezuregusa* (tr *Essays in Idleness*) of YOSHIDA KENKŌ and the TOWAZUGATARI (tr *Confessions of Lady Nijō*) as examples of classical Japanese because these were written intentionally following the grammatical and stylistic features of Heian period *wabun.* While their language is in that sense classical, it must be noted that they make more extensive use of vocabulary of Chinese origin than do true works of the Heian period. There are also not a few scholars who consider the style called *wakan konkō bun* (literally, "writing in which Japanese and Chinese are mixed") a kind of classical Japanese. As early as the Nara period (710–794) the Japanese had invented a peculiar method of reading Chinese. That is, they read a Chinese sentence as if it were a Japanese sentence by reading the Chinese characters as Japanese words; by rearranging words according to Japanese word order (which differed markedly from that of Chinese); and by supplying Japanese grammatical particles and inflectional endings (see KAMBUN). Eventually fixed patterns and rules developed for the hybrid sentences produced from this reading practice, and there emerged a corresponding style of written "Japanese" that had the same characteristics. This style of written "Japanese" is called the *kambun kundoku* style (i.e., style resembling Chinese read as Japanese). In the Kamakura period there occurred a mixing of the *wabun* tradition and the *kambun kundoku* style, and this finally developed into a refined literary style of Japanese called *wakan konkō bun.* Writing in this style uses words and expressions of both Japanese and Chinese origin, sometimes including Japanese colloquial or idiomatic expressions. Many texts are characterized by seven-and-five syllable meter. War tales such as the HEIKE MONOGATARI (tr *Tale of the Heike*), essays such as the *Hōjōki* (tr *The Ten Foot Square Hut*) of KAMO NO CHŌMEI, and travel writings such as *Kaidōki* (A Journey along the Tōkaidō) are written in this style.

The characteristics of classical Japanese compared with modern Japanese may be summarized as follows.

Orthography —— *Rekishiteki kanazukai,* "historical *kana* spelling," is the convention that was in common use until the spelling reform initiated by the Japanese government shortly after the end of World War II. This system represents in general the pronunciation of Japanese of the early Heian period. All words written in *kana* in classical Japanese texts are spelled according to this older convention, although some deviations are found in certain texts.

The most important rules for reading words spelled according to the old system (where it differs from the modern one) are as follows. (1) The *kana* sequences that represent *au, ahu, ou, ohu, oho,* and *owo* should be pronounced as /ō/, e.g., *kohori* ("ice") pronounced as /kōri/. (2) The sequences that represent *iyau, iyou, eu,* and *ehu* should be pronounced as /yō/, e.g., *kehu* ("today") pronounced as /kyō/. (3) The sequences that represent *iu* and *ihu* should be pronounced as /yū/, e.g., *kihushiyo* ("fatal spot") pronounced as /kyūsho/. (4) Noninitial *h*'s followed by *a* should be pronounced as /w/, and noninitial *h*'s in other positions are silent, e.g., *kaha* pronounced as /kawa/; *kaheru* "to change" pronounced as /kaeru/.

The standardization of the forms of *hiragana* was carried out by the Japanese government in 1900. Until then several different *hiragana* could be used to represent the same syllable, even within a single work. The variant nonstandard forms of *kana* are called *hentaigana.* The use of *hentaigana* is seen in all works of classical Japanese not in standardized editions.

Grammar —— While modern Japanese has only five conjugation classes of verbs (in the traditional classification, namely, the *kamiichidan, shimoichidan, yodan, kahen,* and *sahen* classes), classical Japanese has nine (the *kaminidan, shimonidan, rahen,* and *nahen* classes in addition to the five classes above). In modern Japanese, there is a large number of verbs that belong to the *shimoichidan* class; however, in classical Japanese only a single verb, *keru* ("to kick"), conjugates in this pattern, and *shimoichidan* is in effect an irregular conjugation class. For an explanation of these terms, see JAPANESE LANGUAGE.

In modern Japanese, the same form, e.g., *taberu* "to eat" is used both at the end of a sentence, as in *watashi wa sakana o taberu* ("I eat fish"), and before a noun as a modifier, as in *sakana o taberu hito ga ōi* ("many are the people who eat fish"). In classical Japanese, however, different forms are used in these positions; that is to say, under normal circumstances, the *shūshikei,* "the conclusive form," must be used in sentence final position, while the *rentaikei,* "the attributive form," is required before nouns. In classical Japanese the *shūshikei* and *rentaikei* of many verbs differ, as *ware sakana wo tabu* ("I eat fish"), and *sakana wo taburu hito ohoshi* ("many are the people who eat fish").

In classical Japanese there is a larger variety of *jodōshi* (inflecting suffixes) than in modern Japanese, especially those indicating "conjecture" (*mu, ji, beshi, maji, ramu, rashi, meri, kemu,* and *mashi*).

In classical Japanese, mode and aspect are more often indicated by morphological elements, while in modern Japanese they are more often specified by syntactic devices.

Unlike their use in modern Japanese, in classical Japanese the attributive forms of verbs and adjectives sometimes stand alone (i.e., without an explicit word modified), thus functioning as noun phrases with such meanings as "person who does . . . ," "thing that does . . . ," "doing . . . ," "person who is . . . ," "thing that is . . . ," and "being . . . ;" e.g., *shinuru wa yasushi* ("it is easy to die").

In modern Japanese, when a noun within an underlying sentence becomes a noun-phrase-head (modified by the rest of its original sentence) within a complex sentence, that noun is transposed in the modifying sentence, e.g., *onna ga oni ni natta* ("a woman became a demon") as compared to *oni ni natta onna ga iru* ("there is a woman who became a demon"). In classical Japanese, however, the noun may stay in its original position; e.g., *onna oni ni naritari* ("a woman became a demon") as compared to *onna no oni ni naritaru ari* ("there is a woman who became a demon").

In classical Japanese, there is a group of emphatic particles called *kakari joshi,* the presence of which, depending on the type of particle, demands that the sentence be concluded in either the *rentaikei* (attributive form) or the *izenkei* (perfective form) that would normally be expected in the sentence final position. There are no such particles in modern Japanese.

Subjects and other referent phrases in classical Japanese are more frequently omitted than they are in modern written Japanese. Also frequent is the omission of the case particles *ga, wa,* and *wo* as also often seen in modern spoken Japanese. *Akira* KOMAI

class structure

Changed circumstances of life in Japan since the beginning of the Meiji period (1868–1912) and, in particular, the occupational and associated social changes characterizing modern times, have presented serious problems of classification to scholars of Japanese social stratification. Most scholars have thought that a range of definable social classes exists. In particular, much reference has been made to the "middle class" and the "new middle class." An analysis of the population for 1960 by the Japanese sociologist Odaka Kunio distinguished five classes, consisting of an uppermost class (3 percent), upper-middle class (18 percent), lower-middle class (19 percent), intermediate stratum (32 percent), and lower class (28 percent). An analysis made today using the same basis of judgment as that employed for the population of 1960 would doubtless yield quite different proportions and it would certainly fail to agree with popular native opinion concerning social classes. Moreover, much disagreement exists today over the traits or criteria used to distinguish classes and which segments of the national population might appropriately be regarded as having these traits. Some current opinion labels as the "affluent proletariat" much of the population that is intermediate in its standard of living and has generally been called middle class.

For many years debate has revolved about the validity of defining class boundaries on the basis of occupations, incomes, and educational attainments. For example, although white-collar workers have in the past generally been regarded as members of the middle class, a growing trend of opinion merges many of them with blue-collar workers, thus giving them an assignment lower than middle class. The classification of farmers has long been a problem. Prior to the postwar land reform, the classification "farmers" was, at one extreme in income, standard of living, and education, comprised of wealthy owners of great landholdings who were absentee landlords. In between were owner-operators of holdings that varied in size but were generally small. At the other extreme were many impoverished tenant farmers. As a result of the postwar land reform, both extremes have disappeared and farming is practiced by owner-operators of small farms, but general assignment of farmers to a social class is still a problem because many of the male farmers of today are also commuting employees of urban industries in one capacity or another.

The problem of classification has been beset by progressive changes that have obscured many of the former markers of social status as well as by other changes. Differences in such once obvious indicators of social class as distinctive speech, demeanor, etiquette, clothing, hairstyle, and dwellings have become blurred. In pre-Meiji times many of these markers of status were enforced by sumptuary laws, which limited certain goods and privileges to certain social classes. The waning of these customs was a more or less gradual process after the abolition of the restraining laws. Attitudes and values that once characterized the distinctive social classes of former times have become similarly obscured, a circumstance that might be expected in a democratic society with unusually well-developed media of mass communication that operate to foster uniformity of thought and where standards of living of most citizens have tended to become increasingly similar. The assignment of social status to the hundreds of new occupations that have arisen with the industrialization of Japan is not always immediately clear, although it is linked with incomes and is subject to change.

The value or validity of self-appraisals of social status versus those presumably based upon objective criteria is another issue, since the two opinions do not coincide. Most citizens of Japan today appear to regard themselves as being "middle class," or at least characteristically so declare themselves, although the range of their incomes and other potentially distinguishing traits is fairly substantial. As reported in Japanese newspapers in 1977 (covering 1976) a survey of the condition of people's livelihoods published by the Economic Planning Agency of the national government reported, on the basis of opinion surveys, that nearly 9 of every 10 Japanese regard themselves as having a medium standard of living. The white paper also declared that a "middle-class consciousness" is prevalent among Japanese people. Differences were small in the proportions of people of varying occupational backgrounds who declared themselves to be members of the middle class, although their occupations varied considerably and included types of employment that have traditionally held low social status. Among people in professional and managerial positions, 83.2 percent identified themselves as middle class. The proportion of those engaged in farming and fishing so identifying themselves was 75 percent, and of manual laborers, 73 percent. Other opinion surveys in the 1970s have reported similar results.

These circumstances are congruent with the strong postwar trend toward a leveling of incomes and other forms of wealth in the nation, and are linked with demographic changes that represent changes in the occupational structure brought by increasing industrialization. The urban industrial population has grown dramatically in the past century and the rural population has correspondingly declined. In 1975, 48.7 percent of the labor force consisted of white-collar workers in various occupations ranging from professional and managerial to clerical positions, whereas only about 41 percent were industrial and manual laborers and 12 percent were farmers. In popular Japanese opinion, employment as a white-collar worker, an occupational category that did not exist before Meiji times, has for several decades denoted middle-class social affiliation. Continuity in occupations from generation to generation is, of course, obviously impossible in any industrial or industrializing nation and the many new occupations required for successful industrialization have varying statuses of prestige relating to the amount of formal education they require and the incomes they provide. The population of modern Japan shows no indication of crystallizing in the near future into a stable set of occupations or, accordingly, into a stable hierarchy of classes. In view of the circumstances of continuing change, it is not surprising that the formulation of any scheme of class structure is difficult.

Classes in the Meiji Era—— As compared with conditions applying at the end of the Meiji era, however, certain generalizations may be made with assurance about the class structure of modern Japan, and trends of change are evident. Before 1868 Japan was one of the most rigidly stratified societies known to the world. Class affiliation came by birth and was only rarely raised by personal effort. The imperial family and the nobility stood at the top, followed by a much larger group of *samurai*, the retainers of the nobles. Far below them stood the commoners, who composed the bulk of the population. Far lower than the commoners were a much smaller group of people whose position resembled that of the outcastes of India.

Modern Classes—— A trend toward increasing opportunities for upward social movement by the ordinary citizen and thus also toward placing greater value upon personal achievement has been evident for a full century. With notable exceptions that will later be discussed, the pre-Meiji structure of social classes resting upon hereditary ascription has vanished, and associated attitudinal as well as legal barriers to upward movement in social status have weakened or disappeared. Although the entire nation may generally be described as being in a state of flux with respect to a hierarchy of classes, some retention of the past remains and, here and there, the retention is marked. Continuity of social assignment is evident in the category that composes the utmost elite and, still more plainly, among those who in former times were assigned the very lowest social positions.

Although no clear classification with precise and fine gradations may be made, the social strata of modern Japan may be described impressionistically in a way that appears to represent the ideas of most scholars if not those of many of the nation's citizens. Japanese society consists today of a small class of the highly elite; a large and growing but poorly defined class of middle range in which much intraclass movement occurs and which, within its ill-defined upper and lower borders, represents a fairly wide gradation of statuses; a lower class that is also poorly defined and from which movement upward to middle status is common; and, far removed in prestige from all others, a class of Japanese nationals which, as in the past, continues to hold the status of a pariah caste, essentially constituting a minority group.

Minority group members of non-Japanese ethic affiliation or background consist only of about 600,000 Koreans, whose status is low but anomalous, and about 15,000 persons, genetically much mixed with Japanese, who are identified as Ainu and who, because of their small number, have no importance in the national social order. Nationals other than Koreans whose ethnic backgrounds are "foreign" are few and consist principally of Chinese, a few occidentals, and people of mixed occidental-Asiatic parentage. Their social positions appear to be anomalous and variable and they are not regarded as minority groups. All of these minority groups appear to be regarded by the Japanese as outside the scheme of the general social order and they will be omitted from further discussion.

The highly elite group is composed of members of the imperial family, members and descendants of the former peerage or nobility, which was abolished after World War II, who have retained wealth, and members of families with long-established wealth and power. Old wealth has a highly enhancing patina in Japan, and the position of the *narikin*, or "newly rich," is uncertain. Below the elite and at the topmost level of the middle range is a much larger population composed of industrialists, professional men of many kinds, and administrators, followed by a large and growing group within which several substrata may be distinguished. These are principally urban workers called SARARĪMAN, "salary man," (that is, white-collar workers who are paid monthly salaries) in various administrative, technical, and clerical occupations. Lower class status is generally attributed to industrial workers in skilled or unskilled occupations and, increasingly in modern scholarly opinion, to people holding simple clerical positions, such as in department stores and shops. Modern farmers are generally assigned to lower middle or lower class.

Modern Debate over Class—— But let us note carefully that this description of class hierarchy does not accurately represent popular views or even full scholarly consensus, which presently does not seem to exist. The question of whether or not modern Japan indeed has a class system has arisen as a recent scholarly if not a popular issue. The hierarchical social ranking of individuals, based upon a host of traits, unquestionably exists. However, such social classes, based on a given set of traits as the classifier, do not constitute a system of stratification embracing the whole society that closely resembles the systems of Western societies. A notable difference is the lack of conflict or feelings of conflict between the Japanese classes, as exemplified, for example, in the Western idea of conflict between capitalists and proletariats or between other classes of haves and have-nots. It is perhaps this trait of the Japanese social order that has led to the questioning of the existence of social classes. A very recent expression of scholarly opinion asks whether or not the concept of a huge middle class that prevails in both scholarly and popular opinion in Japan is not an illusion based solely upon the subjective feeling among most people that their own standards of living approximate the average for the nation.

But the criteria of classes need not, of course, include the existence of interclass conflict. Moreover, since the Japanese language includes a large number of well-established, nonscholarly terms referring to social classes, it is certain that the ordinary citizen of Japan as well as the majority of its scholars concerned with this matter do indeed conceive of their society as being stratified. The essential problem has been to gain a clear picture of the native view and to present it in ways that make it comprehensible to non-Japanese. Japanese popular conceptions of social classes that we translate as upper, middle, and lower doubtless differ from the meanings of the English terms, and we have already presented information that strongly suggests this. For example, the United States, and also European nations, have no precise counterpart of the very special, exalted status of the emperor and other members of the imperial family, and these nations have no truly close counterpart of Japan's class or caste of pariahs. It is probably true, however, that scholarly and popular views of social classes do not agree in any large industrial society and that concepts of class attributes vary in many subtle ways from society to society. Nevertheless, the Japanese concepts of upper, middle, and lower class are at least similar to those of the United States and the prestige accorded to specific occupations in Japan conforms fairly well with attitudes in the United States.

Continuities from the Past—— Changes in the social hierarchy of Japan occuring in the past century have never involved disruptive social upheaval, although a comparison of the conditions in 1868 and today makes the change that has taken place seem revolutionary. Various trends of continuity are evident, of which the continued high status of the Japanese imperial line is an example. The so-called BURAKUMIN class retains the lowest status and is reported to have grown, relatively as well as absolutely. A publication of 1966 by DeVos and Wagatsuma reports that in approximately one century this group increased in size seven times faster than the general population. This statement is based upon estimates of the modern population, since no census of *burakumin* is taken, and it may be exaggerated. Estimates of the present number vary between one and three million as against an official count of 383,500 in 1871, at the time of their legal emancipation from pariah status. Growth appears to have come from various sources: natural increase, the drawing of members from the larger society, and, in some measure, from a redefinition of outcastes to include another category of lowly people formerly called HININ ("nonhumans").

Mention may also be made of small, local groups of near-pariah status whose existence and identity have not been known nationally to the public. The largest of these groups appears to have been the *ebune*, "houseboat(ers)," formerly landless people living on boats who were distributed principally on the coast of the Inland Sea and Kyūshū. Although not *burakumin*, the local status of these people was far below that of ordinary citizens and little higher than that of *burakumin*. Information on the present status of the *ebune* and other similar small groups is not available, but it seems certain that their position in local society continues to be low.

It is certain also that, despite having legal equality, the *burakumin* remain outcastes, socially inferior to other people and the subjects of discrimination. Living principally in central Japan in and near the cities of Ōsaka, Kōbe, and Kyōto, most of the *burakumin* continue to live in segregated communities. Constituting essentially a minority group, but lacking ethnic distinction from other Japanese, they are characterized by low incomes and standards of living, low levels of attainment in education and professional skills, relatively poor health, and, as with depressed ethnic minorities in other nations, high rates of crime and juvenile delinquency and relatively great dependency upon agencies of social welfare.

Evidence of continuity and of the weight of past tradition is also evident in other ways in connection with social classes and social mobility. Japan has long been regarded as an achieving nation among whose people an analogue of the Protestant ethic is well established. Modern times have seen no diminution of this set of values, which is intimately connected with social mobility. In the

20th century, the key to achievement, and thereby to rising in social status, has been advanced education. Ideally, it is democratically available to all. Yet evidence is abundantly available that many factors beyond native intelligence bear upon the selection of those who receive advanced education and those who do not. In 1976, 39 percent of Japan's high school graduates were admitted to institutions of higher education, a figure exceeded only by that in the United States. The future professional careers of many of these students imply a rise in social status. Such upward movement has been common for people with backgrounds of affiliation with the middle class, but much less common for those coming from lower class backgrounds—and seemingly by far the least common for members of the outcaste group.

As in many other nations that have experienced social upheavals, peaceful or violent, the descendants of the former elite of Japan appear to have retained their old familial statuses of prestige fairly well. Thus, as noted earlier, perpetuation of position through the generations is the most highly marked at both extremes of social status. The rate of occupational mobility among manual laborers has long been noted as low, although intergenerational mobility in occupation has been predictably high for a great many years. Although the ratio of farmers in the national labor force has dropped greatly in the past century, a change from farming to other occupations has not always brought elevation in social status.

A study by Mannari Hiroshi of the social and educational backgrounds of nearly 1,000 men who were judged to be the nation's most outstanding persons in industry and commerce in the years 1960 and 1970 appears to show that opportunities for upward social movement are not equally available to everyone. Nearly all of these men, who might reasonably be classified as being of upper class, had college educations and the vast majority, nearly 90 percent, came from the upper class (about 60 percent) or the middle class (about 30 percent). Among the men from farming families, the great majority were descendants of landlords or owner-operators of farms. Although the number of men from farm backgrounds was large, the rate of movement upward from the category of farmers was only about one-half of that expected on the basis of the proportion of farmers in the national labor force (nearly one-half) at the time the business executives became mature.

Parental occupations of the business elite, in descending order of frequency, were farm landlord or owner-operator of farm, owner and executive of large business concern, owner of small business concern, government official and professional man, white-collar worker, laborer, and others. Less than 10 percent of the business elite came from occupational backgrounds judged as lower class, that is, poor farmers and common laborers.

Nearly one-third of the business leaders identified themselves as being of samurai backgrounds, an identification that is meaningful since their average age was 62 years, implying that they were reared with the idea that they had and should have high status. The tendency of the descendants of samurai to retain high social status was earlier noted in analyses of random samples of persons listed in the Japanese *Who's Who* for the year 1903, when 37 percent were identified as coming from the samurai class, and the year 1925, when 29 percent were so identified.

The retention of elitism in Japan is also evident in other ways, such as the hierarchic rating of universities, a matter that relates to social mobility. The largest and, as employers, the most desirable industrial concerns have tended to employ only graduates of what are regarded as the finest universities. This trend toward favoring the elite is tempered by the fact that admission to these universities is based upon examinations and is uncompromisingly democratic. Movement upward by means of education is nevertheless difficult for people of the lowest social backgrounds because of a complex of psychological factors as well as the cost of the preliminary education fitting them for admission to fine universities and the cost of the advanced education.

These statements about perpetuation of socially prestigious status through the generations do not, of course, imply rigidity at the topmost and bottommost levels but point only to trends, which appear to be weakening. Japan has indeed become democratic as compared with the past, but great elevation in the social status of any family line does not often appear to be accomplished quickly. Instead, movement to high status often appears to be a matter of generational steps onward, of which the most difficult is movement from the lower class.

■——Asō Makoto, "Kindai Nihon ni okeru erīto kōsei no hensen," *Kyōiku shakaigaku kenkyū* 15 (1960). Harumi Befu, *Japan, An Anthropological Introduction* (1971). Robert E. Cole, *Japanese Blue*

Collar: The Changing Tradition (1971). George DeVos and Hiroshi Wagatsuma, ed, Japan's Invisible Race: Caste in Culture and Personality (1966). Fujishima Taisuke, Nihon no jōryū shakai (1965). Fukutake Tadashi, Japanese Society Today (1974). Hayashi Chikio, Susato Shigeru, and Suzuki Tatsuzō, Nihon no howaito karā (1964). Mannari Hiroshi, The Japanese Business Leaders (1974). Nihon Shakai Gakkai Chōsa Iinkai, Nihon shakai no kaisōteki kōzō (1958). Nishihira Shigeki, "Shokugyō no shakaiteki hyōka," Tōkei sūri kenkyūjo sūken kenkyū, report 12 (1964). Kunio Odaka, "The Middle Classes in Japan," Contemporary Japan 28 (1964). Tominaga Kenichi, "Studies of Social Stratification and Social Mobility in Japan," in Edward Norbeck and Susan Parman, ed, The Study of Japan in the Behavioral Sciences (1970). Ezra F. Vogel, Japan's New Middle Class (1963). Yasuda Saburō, Shakai idō no kenkyū (1971).

Edward NORBECK

Claudel, Paul Louis Charles (1868–1955)

French diplomat, poet, and playwright who, as French ambassador to Japan, contributed much to deepening Franco-Japanese relations. Regarded by the French as one of their greatest modern poets and religious playwrights, Claudel began his diplomatic career in 1890 by taking first place in the examinations for the Foreign Ministry. After a distinguished 30-year career in the French diplomatic corps, with posts in the United States, China, Europe, and South America, he served as ambassador in Tōkyō from December 1921 to February 1927. During his stay in Japan, Claudel sought to strengthen cultural relations between the two nations and worked to establish the Maison Franco-Japonais. He won the good will of the Japanese through his aid efforts following the disastrous TŌKYŌ EARTHQUAKE OF 1923. Claudel developed an understanding of and love for the Japanese spirit and culture; his lectures and writings on Japan were collected in L'Oiseau noir dans le soleil levant (1928, Black Bird in the Rising Sun). One of his greatest plays, Le Soulier de satin (1927, The Satin Slipper), was completed during his stay in Tōkyō. In 1927 he was assigned to Washington, where he played a key role in negotiating the KELLOGG–BRIAND PACT. He ended his diplomatic career in Brussels in 1935. Claudel continued to write numerous plays, poems, and essays and was elected to the Academie Française in 1946.

Mark D. ERICSON

Clean Government Party → Kōmeitō

climate

As a nation straddling a number of climatic zones from north to south and subject to the atmospheric influence of both the Eurasian continent to the west and the Pacific Ocean to the east, Japan is characterized by a wide diversity of climates, dramatic changes in weather, and clearly differentiated seasons.

Although the total land area of the nation is only some 377,000 square kilometers (145,500 sq mi), the islands stretch from about latitude 20° N at the southernmost point of Japan, the island of OKINOTORISHIMA, 700 kilometers southwest of the IŌ ISLANDS, to about latitude 45°30' N at the northernmost point of HOKKAIDŌ. This distance is roughly equivalent to that between the southern tip of the Florida peninsula in the United States and the Canadian border. Hence, the difference between the climate of Japan's southern and northern extremes is great. The northernmost island, Hokkaidō, lies in the subarctic zone; central Japan (Honshū, Shikoku, and Kyūshū), in the temperate zone; and the southern islands, in the subtropical zone. This dispersion through various climatic zones is reflected in differences in flora and fauna and in the length of the growing season.

A second major influence on the climate of Japan is the archipelago's location in the temperate monsoon zone of East Asia. The monsoons of this region are seasonal winds that flow eastward off the continent in winter and northward from the South Pacific in the summer. Japan's seasons are largely determined by these winds and the shifts in weather caused by the transition between the winter and summer wind patterns. Japan is also part of the Circum-Pacific orogenic zone and has mountainous terrain running through the center of its main islands. Land to the leeward of these mountain ranges is shielded from the full impact of the monsoon winds: heavy snows, brought by the winter winds, fall on the Sea of Japan coast, which faces northwest, but not on the Pacific coast; conversely, summer typhoons often strike the southeast coast but not the Sea of Japan coast.

Complex local variations in Japan's climate are introduced by radical variations in geomorphology which appear as soaring moun-

tains, small basins, deep valleys, and narrow plains areas. This factor is reflected in marked variations in the propensity of plants to root and grow in various regions. Japan's weather is also moderated by a warm ocean current, the KUROSHIO, which flows along the Pacific coast. The above factors combine to create the widely varied seasons, dramatic changes in weather, and climate that have affected the lives and lifestyles of the Japanese people.

Seasons in Japan——Winter (fuyu). The monsoon that brings winter to Japan develops as a series of anticyclones over Siberia in late November. It continues through the end of February, when the Siberian high recedes. During this period, the force of the winds is determined by fluctuations in the strength of the Siberian high. When the Siberian high develops and a large pressure gradient is created between it and the Aleutian low, strong northwest winds blow for several days at a time. As the wind moves south in a gradual curve, it finally becomes a northeastern gale and approaches the southwestern islands. When the Siberian high weakens, reducing the above-mentioned pressure gradient, the strength of the wind decreases. This phenomenon is continually repeated throughout the winter.

The air which breaks out as the winter monsoon is part of the Siberian air mass, a continental polar air mass which originates within the Siberian high area. This air mass begins dry and highly stable in its source region, but as it approaches the Sea of Japan area, it accumulates heat from the lower strata of the atmosphere and becomes increasingly unstable. At the same time it also picks up water vapor from the ocean and becomes increasingly moist. As clearly documented in satellite photographs, a characteristic cloud layer develops by the time the air mass reaches the central and eastern sections of the Sea of Japan. When this air mass reaches the northern slopes of the Japanese archipelago, it ascends sharply, develops a thick layer of clouds, and drops a heavy snowfall. This mountainous region is called the "snow country," or yukiguni. Accumulations of snow surpass 4 meters (approximately 13 ft) on occasion, and overnight snowstorms that leave more than 1 meter (3.3 ft) of additional snow are not unusual. As this air mass continues southward, the amount of snowfall decreases. In Kyūshū, snow is rare and remains on the ground for only a day or two; snow never falls on the Ryūkyūs.

Having dropped heavy snows on the windward side of Japan, the air mass is extremely dry by the time it passes over the mountain range of central Japan to the leeward side. Clouds disappear and the sky remains clear for most of the winter. This dramatic contrast in climate is reflected on maps which record the distribution of such meteorological phenomena as the amount of precipitation, the depth of snow, the number of clear days, the insolation ratio, and the amount of clouds. Snow and rain do fall on the Pacific Ocean side of Japan occasionally during the winter, but this precipitation is due to extratropical cyclones originating in the East China Sea. Such storms occur only occasionally.

Spring (haru). As the temperature on the Asian mainland rises, the strength of both the Siberian high and the associated monsoons weakens, signaling the end of winter and the beginning of spring. A series of fast-traveling anticyclones which pass over Japan within a period of several days and frontal zones alternate. The temperature in all regions rises. Spring is blossom time, and flower viewing (HANAMI) is a popular pastime. Cherry blossoms first appear in the southern islands in mid-March, in the Tōkyō area in late March, in northeastern Honshū in middle and late April, and finally in Hokkaidō in mid-May. In northern districts of Japan where spring comes late, the plum, cherry, and peach all bloom at virtually the same time and are awaited with great anticipation. In snowy regions, spring sometimes brings flooding streams and rivers caused by melting ice and snow.

Early summer (shoka). Together with the weakening of the Siberian high, the domain of the continental frigid air mass shrinks back toward the mainland gradually and is replaced by a continental tropical air mass which advances toward the Japan archipelago from the Yangzi (Yangtze) River basin. The atmosphere becomes very dry and an extended period of ideal springtime weather called satsukibare, or clear May weather, begins. The temperature rises sharply and there may even be days as hot as those of late summer in early June. However, early summer does not pass directly into a hot summer season, but is rather followed by the baiu season (rainy season, also called tsuyu), which affects all regions of Japan, especially its western parts.

The baiu season. Beginning generally after the first week of June, the Okhotsk Sea maritime air mass, a blocking anticyclone which forms in the Okhotsk Sea, makes its way toward Japan from

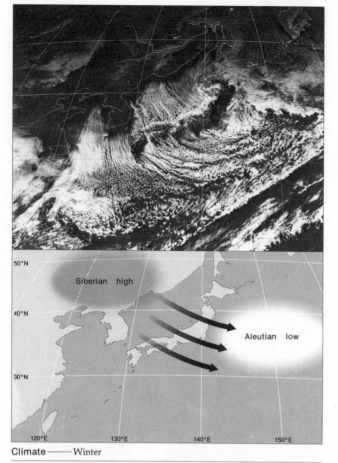

Climate——Winter

Cloud patterns produced by monsoon winds from the Siberian high.
Photo from weather satellite Himawari, 29 January 1982.

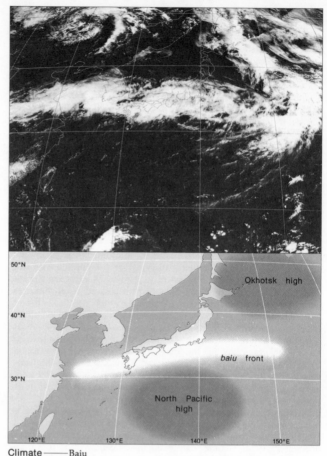

Climate——Baiu

Thick rain clouds produced by the *baiu* front cover a large part of the
Japanese archipelago. Himawari photo, 3 July 1982.

the northeast. At the same time, in the southern seas off Japan, the
North Pacific high gradually increases in strength and creates the
tropical Bonin air mass, which also blows toward the Japan archipelago. These two air masses meet when they reach Japan, resulting
in a polar front, the *baiu* front, which stretches east to west across
the islands. The two air masses reach an equilibrium, which is perpetuated by the general circulation pattern of the air, and the *baiu*
front moves slowly over Japan. A thick layer of clouds and heavy
rains develops along this front, and the stormy weather is aggravated
by the frequent emergence of extratropical cyclones. The combination of these conditions gives rise to a rainy season of considerable
length.

Each small movement of the slowly changing *baiu* front brings
complex and continual changes in the weather as well as high humidity, all of which contribute to a dreary physical and psychological oppressiveness characteristic of rainy season weather. The *baiu*
front gradually progresses northward: the rainy season arrives in the
Ryūkyūs in the beginning of June, in central Japan in mid-June, and
finally in northeastern Honshū in late June. The rainy season continues for about one month in each of these regions. Rains during the
baiu season are not generally heavy, although localized torrential
rainfalls are at times caused by the movement of extratropical cyclones, the intensification of the *baiu* front, or the local terrain,
which creates rising air currents. Heavy rainstorms are most common toward the end of the rainy season, which comes with the
dissipation of the Okhotsk high-pressure area.

Midsummer (manatsu). Midsummer commences as the Bonin
air mass originating in the North Pacific high begins to dominate the
entire archipelago. Throughout summer, air pressure continues to
be high in the south and low in the north. However, since the difference between these two atmospheric areas is relatively small, the
summer monsoon winds blow much more weakly than those of the
winter. Furthermore, the Bonin air mass is much more stable than
the Siberian air mass of winter. For these reasons, the Pacific slope,
which is on the windward side of the summer monsoons, is not
subject to long periods of bad weather like those found on the Sea of

Japan coast in the winter. Although thunderstorms sometimes develop, mainly in interior basins and mountains, summer is typically
a period of uninterrupted clear, hot weather, much like in the tropics. Midsummer possesses the features of a short, dry season, which
comes to an end with the approach of TYPHOONS in late summer.

Fall (aki). When August ends, as the North Pacific high recedes
gradually to the south, the force of the Bonin air mass begins to
weaken, and a new season develops with continental frigid air
masses becoming dominant. During the change of seasons, however, one air mass is frequently replaced by another, precipitating an
ever-changing weather pattern in the region of Japan. The cold air
front, which remains north of Japan through spring and summer,
begins moving southward in September. This results in another
rainy period, the *shūrin* season, which arrives in Hokkaidō at the
end of August and reaches the southern islands in the beginning of
October. Rainfall is generally heaviest in northern Japan during the
shūrin season. In mid-October, Japan is often traversed by migratory anticyclones and by oblong high-pressure zones extending from
east to west. This season is characterized by refreshing and relaxing
clear autumnal weather with comparatively light and pleasant winds.
Fall foliage and the first frost appear very early in this period in
northern Japan and spread slowly southward as the season progresses. At the end of November, fall ends and winter begins with
the appearance of the monsoons.

Weather and Japanese Life——Among the literary traditions of
the Japanese is the poetic form known as the HAIKU. Limited to a
mere 17 syllables, these poems deftly capture natural scenes or aspects of life related to particular seasons. Such poetry is a reflection
of the close relationship that exists between Japanese life and the
climate. References to weather and the seasons in introductory
greetings in everyday correspondence and standard expressions concerning the seasons customarily used to open formal letters also
indicate an awareness of seasons and climate. Annual events and
festivals observed in various localities over the year are also intimately connected with the seasons, although some of these have lost
their original meaning and function.

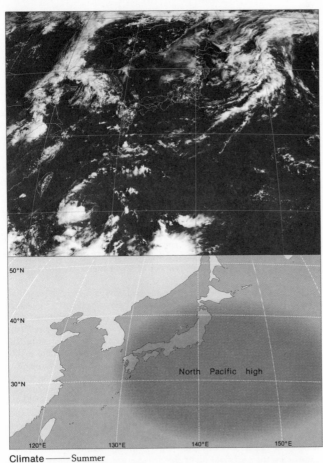

Climate —— Summer

Generally clear sky resulting from the North Pacific high. Himawari photo, 5 August 1982.

Climate —— Typhoon

Typhoon Number 18, 1982, its center just south of Honshū. Himawari photo, 12 September 1982.

Life in the snow country. The region situated along the Sea of Japan, particularly its northern section, is subject to the heaviest snowfalls. In midwinter, almost daily storms drop layer after layer of deep snow, completely cutting off each village from the outside world. Houses in this region are specially designed to withstand the severity of such winter weather. Sturdy, steep roofs with a unique underlying framework are constructed to withstand the heavy accumulation of snow. Shutters are fitted with glass panes, and special windows placed high in the wall serve as a kind of skylight to admit light when the snow piles up along the outside walls. In a number of larger cities in this region, special passageways *(gangi)* were built between the eaves of adjacent houses in central sections to allow free movement of visitors and townspeople even during periods when the snow was very deep. In farming villages that were totally snowbound in the winter months, large quantities of pickled vegetables and wood or charcoal fuel necessary for survival until the spring thaw were prepared and stored during the busy harvest season in late autumn. Since it was impossible to do any outside work in the winter, many of the able-bodied men left their homes to work in warmer regions or urban centers as factory workers or traveling salesmen. In recent years, advancing industrialization and urbanization have had a great impact on the people of the snow country, causing radical changes in their traditional lifestyle. The number of villagers commuting to the cities has increased sharply, the flow of money in the economy has spread to outlying parts, and an urban style of living has become predominant.

The effect of the monsoons. The winter monsoon winds blow so fiercely that they seem to cut through the body like a cold steel knife. The ordinary Japanese home, designed to allow for the passage of cool breezes to ease the oppressive heat of summer, offers little protection from strong winter gales. The winter monsoon winds are especially severe in the region facing the Sea of Japan where the gales blow directly through wind gaps in the mountains. Some relief against the force of these winds is provided by planted rows of trees in populated areas. In the typhoon-prone Ryūkyūs, high stone walls are built around each home. Lines of trees are also planted along railroad tracks in northern Japan to impede snowdrifts and blowing snow.

Heating and changes in lifestyle. The winter in Japan is characterized by comparatively low temperatures for its latitude, so that, with the exception of the balmy southern districts, some form of heating is essential during the winter season. Particularly in Hokkaidō, where the winters are most severe, indoor central heating has been in use from the time when the area was first settled. However, in other regions, especially in rural villages, most houses were not centrally heated. Instead, thick layers of clothing were worn, and such traditional heating devices as the HIBACHI, a coal brazier, the *kotatsu,* a low-standing table with a charcoal heating element sunk into the floor, and the *irori,* a centrally located open hearth found predominantly in large farmhouses, were commonly used to ward off the winter cold. Full use of all rooms in the home was thus impossible, and movement was strictly limited to quiet activities in small sections of rooms nearest the source of heat. However, with the gradual spread of more effective forms of heating such as the kerosene stove, the traditional heating devices have fallen out of use, and major changes have come in the traditional winter living patterns of the people. Just as the spread of propane gas for cooking accelerated the urbanization of rural lifestyles, changes in methods of heating have also greatly contributed to the convergence of life in the country with that in the city.

Summer lifestyles and air conditioning. With the exception of northern Japan, the climate in midsummer is uncomfortably hot and humid. This is especially true in densely populated urban areas, where houses stand very close together. Recently, however, air conditioning has become common in public facilities, office buildings, and private homes. In Tōkyō some trains and platforms of a few subway stations are now equipped with air conditioning. The widespread use of air conditioning is reflected in the fact that consumption of electric power reaches its peak in the summer.

Land Utilization and the Climate —— *Cultivation of rice.* Annual cultivation of rice takes place in almost all parts of the country. The size of rice paddies varies from those in the Niigata Plain that stretch farther than the eye can see to tiny, terraced plots in mountainous and hilly regions. In northeastern Japan, where the winter is very cold and snowy, rice crops are planted only once a year, while in southwestern Japan two crops can be planted. A variety of techniques is now employed in rice cultivation. For instance, there is a growing tendency to harvest crops increasingly early in the year, finishing reaping operations by late August to avoid possible damage to crops by the typhoons which arrive at the end of the summer. In districts where farmers must deal with the danger of low temperatures in the summer or extremely cold water in irrigation reservoirs, improved hybrid rice seed, new agricultural techniques, and a wealth of farming methods and strategies are now employed.

Agriculture in warm districts. Since intensive cultivation of arable land has long been widespread in Japan, dry-field farming, which takes advantage of climatic conditions, developed quite early, with major cities providing a ready market. The Pacific coast region, which experiences warm winter temperatures, provides a typical example of the forced raising of vegetables, flowers, fruits, and other crops out of season. Together with improvements in the means of transportation, artificial cultivation has spread gradually from the Kantō district to Kyūshū. The increased availability of hothouses has resulted in the rapid spread of raising crops out of season to districts subject to cold winter temperatures. This trend has accelerated with the increasing difficulty of surviving economically on the income from rice crops alone. However, in the case of tea and American varieties of oranges and other citrus fruits, whose producers are engaged in keen competition, cultivation is limited to warmer regions.

Agriculture in highland areas. The volcanic slopes, high-mountain plateaus, and other sections in the high altitudes of central Japan have become major locations for dry-field farming in recent years. Since harvesttime comes earlier here than in the lowlands, the early shipping of off-season vegetable produce, especially cabbage, Chinese cabbage, and lettuce, guarantees advantageous selling prices on the city markets.

Crop damage due to weather. In years when the strength of the Okhotsk maritime air mass persists over an unusually long period and causes an abnormally long *baiu* season, midsummer fails to appear at all, and instead a period of continual low temperatures and the absence of sunshine, known as a "cool summer" (*kyōrei*), ensues. Such cool summers cause crop failures and food shortages. Northern Japan, especially along the Pacific slopes, is most vulnerable to the intrusion of the Okhotsk air mass and has often experienced food shortages due to cool summers. Prior to the establishment of a government-run emergency relief system, substantial numbers of farmers were forced into bankruptcy and had to disband their households after their crops failed.

Drought. Midsummer is typically a time of uninterrupted dry and clear weather. Therefore, the annual *baiu* season is essential to ensure an ample supply of water in public reservoirs and irrigation reservoirs for crops. However, in years when the *baiu* season is short because the front is weak, fails to develop, or passes unusually quickly over Japan, there is a serious danger of drought. This danger is greatest in western Japan, especially the Inland Sea area, and in years of severe drought conditions, all places in this region, from the smallest farming village to the largest city, suffer critical water shortages throughout the summer. Relief from such water shortages is long in coming unless a typhoon appears. When such typhoons do occur, although they replenish the water supply, they can also precipitate floods.

Floods. With the exception of the winter snows on the Sea of Japan coast, all precipitation is brought by such phenomena as typhoons, extratropical cyclones, or storm fronts. Heavy rainfalls occur frequently, but extremely heavy downpours of more than 100 millimeters (approximately 4 in) in a day are confined to certain especially rainy regions. Rivers and streams in Japan are generally small and narrow, with riverbeds that drop steeply as they move toward the sea, so that in districts subject to heavy rainfalls, rivers soon fill with rainwater and quickly overrun their banks. In areas with hilly or mountainous terrain, there is the added danger of landslides and large-scale rock slides along the rising slopes of small valleys. Such slides are not new to Japan, but the extensive land development of modern times has created further slide conditions and increased the occurrence of land damage. With the spread of urbanization, even areas vulnerable to floods and landslides are being used to build new housing developments.

The foehn phenomenon. In the early spring when the cyclones develop rapidly over the Sea of Japan, the foehn phenomenon (in which a warm, dry, erratic wind is deflected down the side of a mountain) frequently occurs in the region facing the Sea of Japan. As a result of the strong effects of the foehn in this region, large fires are a serious danger. The cities of Tottori, Noshiro, and Akita are among the numerous places that have suffered from such fires.

■ —— Eiichirō Fukui, *Climate of Japan* (1977). Japan Meteorological Agency, *Climatic Atlas of Japan* (1971, 1972). Wadachi Kiyoo, *Nihon no kikō* (1958). Yazawa Taiji, *Monsoons and Japanese Life* (1979). YAZAWA *Taiji*

cliques → batsu

cloisonné

(*shippō*; literally, "seven precious stones"). A type of enameling in which artistic designs are created by applying enamel glass to metal. Thin metal strips or wires are attached to a metal base, producing cells into which enamels of different colors are poured. Then this is fired and the resulting surface smoothed by grinding and polishing. Alternatively, cells can be carved out of solid metal in a technique known as *champlevé*, hammered out of sheet metal in *repoussé*, or cast.

The earliest example of enameling in Japan is a small hexagonal plaque with amber and white enamels in a floral pattern. Excavated from the Kengoshi tomb mound at Asuka, Nara Prefecture, it is attributed to the Asuka period (latter part of the 6th century to 710). The Kengoshi plaque seems to have been made in Japan using the Korean enameling technique of pouring molten glass onto the metal form. This is indicated by the convex surface of the enamel, the irregular protrusions, and the incomplete filling of the interstices.

Another early example is a mirror in the SHŌSŌIN treasury at Nara, whose objects are traditionally dated prior to 756. The silver mirror is decorated with opaque brown and translucent dark and light green enamels forming a lotus blossom delineated with silver gilt wires and gold cloisons. The enamels are left unpolished and lie in concave pools between the wires. Although some scholars have questioned the early dating of the Shōsōin mirror, it is clear that the basic technology for enameling was known to the Japanese in the 8th century.

An example from the Heian period (794–1185) can be found in the Hōōdō (Phoenix Hall) of the temple BYŌDŌIN at Uji. This hall, which was dedicated in 1053, has door fittings with *champlevé*-enameled designs. The *Taiki bekki*, a diary compiled in the mid-12th century, mentions "glass painted silver"; but after the Heian period there are no documentary references to cloisonné until the second half of the 15th century when a Chinese cloisonné *hu* (a type of vessel) is mentioned as having been imported for the pleasure of the shōgun Ashikaga Yoshimasa (1436–90). The renowned artist SŌAMI (ca 1455–1525) liked cloisonné and used it extensively in his arrangement of the reception hall of Yoshimasa's Higashiyama palace at what is now the temple Jishōji (popularly known as GINKAKUJI). The *Kundaikan sō chōki*, an annotated inventory of the time, records *hibachi*, coal tongs, and wine cups and stands of cloisonné, and even illustrates the cup and stand.

It was not until the 17th century that cloisonné become widely used in Japan. Many pieces from the early part of the Edo period (1600–1868) are architectural embellishments—doorpulls for sliding screens and nail covers on rafters. Other examples are cloisonné fittings for swords and for chests, or accoutrements for a scholar's desk such as brush holders and water droppers for making ink. Although enameled pieces have been attributed to the Azuchi-Momoyama period (1568–1600), it is possible that some of these may have originated in China during the Wanli reign (1573–1619). The year 1634 is the first recorded date for early Edo-period objects of unquestioned Japanese manufacture. This is when the Jōrakuden of Nagoya Castle was refurbished with white and green enamels applied to nail covers and to red copper doorpulls. Other dated enameled works are the 1634 fittings at the TŌSHŌGŪ mausoleum at Nikkō, traditionally credited to Hirata Dōnin (1591–1646; also known as Hirata Hikoshirō), who was the maker of the Jōrakuden doorpulls. Japanese literary sources credit him and his numerous descendents with introducing major developments in the enameler's art. Another early master is Kachō (dates unknown), who is credited with the exquisite doorpulls at the KATSURA DETACHED PALACE in Kyōto. In contrast to the ornate manner of the Tōshōgū, the Kyōto style is simpler, and the enamels are less colorful and more subdued. Enameled works were in high vogue during the Edo period and sophisticated tea masters such as KOBORI ENSHŪ (1579–1647) commissioned leading enamelers like Kachō to create suitable objects for their buildings.

Japanese *shippō* of the first half of the 17th century tended to have the enamels applied over the entire metal surface. About the middle of the century the enamels were applied selectively in spots only as colorful accents. It was a more artistic use of both enamel and metal, utilizing each where it could be most effective in the design. The nail covers at the SHUGAKUIN DETACHED PALACE, created in 1659, exemplify this refined artistry. The period from the mid-17th century through the 18th century was a golden age for the artistic creation of enameled objects. This era, with its apogee in the early 18th century, is characterized by a complete technical mastery and a balanced use of the medium toward artistic ends. A passage in *Sōken kishō,* a 1781 manual on sword ornaments, lauds Hirata Narikado (1684–1757) as the best of the Hirata line of *shippō* craftsmen and considers his work superior to anything imported from China. His large atelier trained an extraordinarily talented group of apprentices. One of the finest creations in the early 18th century was the residence built for the *daimyō* Maeda Tsunanori (1643–1724; popularly known as Shōun Kō) in Edo. The nail covers created for this palace harmoniously match the bird-and-flower screens painted by masters of the KANŌ SCHOOL and exemplify the artistic excellence of cloisonné created during this period.

After the heights attained in the early 18th century, there is a gradual decline in artistic quality, with heavy and less sensitive lines and a glassy porcelain look. This was not reversed till the 1830s when Kaji Tsunekichi (1803–83) developed new techniques for making enamels based on a study of "Dutch" (i.e., European) enameled wares. By the mid-19th century Tsunekichi and his followers stimulated a modern revival in the enameler's art. Around 1875, the German Gottfried WAGENER introduced the methods of modern European enameling, which eventually led to the mass export production of cloisonné objects in factories in Tōkyō, Kyōto, and Nagoya. In the 1880s Namikawa Sōsuke (1847–1910) of Tōkyō succeeded in developing a technique called *musen shippō* (lineless *shippō*), in which the enamels are not separated by metal lines. This permitted tonal gradations of great subtlety, and Sōsuke created pictorial works with refined delicacy. At the same time Namikawa Yasuyuki (1845–1927) of Kyōto distinguished himself in the traditional *yūsen shippō* (*shippō* with lines) in which the enamels are separated by cloisons, reproducing classic Japanese paintings in a naturalistic style.

Although modern Japanese cloisonné production is largely aimed at the commercial market, we look forward to a vigorous revival of this ancient and colorful art.

——Dorothy Blair, *A History of Glass in Japan* (1973). James L. Bowes, *Japanese Enamels* (1886). James L. Bowes, *Notes on Shippō* (1895). Sir Harry Garner, *Chinese and Japanese Cloisonné Enamels* (1962). Yoshimura Motoo, *Shippō* (1966).　　　George KUWAYAMA

cloister government → insei

clothing

A commonly used word for clothing in Japanese is KIMONO; however, this word usually refers to Japanese traditional clothing (also called *wafuku*) as opposed to Western-style clothes (*yōfuku*). The floor-length garment with rectangular sleeves and front panels crossed over the chest and bound at the waist with a broad sash (*obi*) is more accurately termed a *kosode*. The history of Japanese clothing is in large part the history of the evolution of the *kosode*, a process which in turn was connected with the Japanization of imported styles and TEXTILES.

Most Japanese clothing styles derived from Chinese, Korean, or Mongolian fashions. The loose shirt and baggy trousers in vogue in 5th-century China were imported, then slowly adapted to the Japanese climate and lifestyle. Two major styles of clothing emerged, one retaining the simple shirt and trousers and the other evolving more and more layers of long, flowing garments. The lower classes favored the first for its ease of movement; the aristocracy perfected the second, refining the elegant lines and color combinations to suit the varying tastes of successive periods. In the 13th century, when the military aristocracy came into power, the two styles mingled. By the 16th century the *kosode,* which had been an undergarment, emerged from beneath layers of discarded outer robes to be transformed into the gaily decorated kimono characteristic of the Edo period (1600–1868). The material, design, and decoration of the *kosode* developed along with new weaving and dyeing techniques.

Prehistoric Clothing (to AD 300) —— No clue to the type of clothes worn during the Jōmon period (ca 10,000 BC–ca 300 BC) has as yet been unearthed, though various kinds of bracelets, necklaces, and ear ornaments as well as clay figurines have been found, particularly in what is now the Kantō district. It seems likely, however, that people used fur and bark to cover their bodies.

By the Yayoi period (ca 300 BC–ca AD 300), the picture becomes clearer. With the rise of SERICULTURE came the knowledge of weaving techniques. Contact with the continent through trade with China's expanding Han dynasty, the Three Kingdoms of Korea, and the Mongolian nomads spurred these developments. Engravings of human figures appearing on Yayoi period DŌTAKU (bronze bell-shaped ritual objects) excavated in what is now Kagawa Prefecture depict men wearing a sort of poncho. The earliest written account of Japan, contained in the Chinese chronicle WEI ZHI *(Wei chih),* describes the clothing of the early Japanese people as follows:

Every man has a tattoo on his face or arms. He wears his hair in a loop at each side and wraps his head with cloth bombax. His garment is a sheet of cloth tied here and there. It is hardly stitched at all. The women bind their hair above the ears and use a sheet of cloth for a dress which they don by slipping their heads through a single hole at the center. The people cultivate rice and flax. They spin silk and weave both flax and silk into cloth of good quality.

Yamato and Nara Periods (300–794) —— Objects unearthed from the tombs of the 4th and 5th centuries include many HANIWA clay figurines, which supply important clues to the clothing of the time. Men wore an upper garment called *kinu,* a long garment with straight sleeves tied with cords at the wrists and elbows and secured at the waist with a broad belt. As a lower garment the men wore *hakama* or loose trousers, which tied just below the knees. Women wore a combination of *kinu,* similar to the men's shirt, and in place of trousers a pleated wrap-skirt called *mo.* The material was generally vegetable fiber such as asa (bast fiber), though aristocrats wore silk at times. The textiles were either dyed or had woven patterns. Similar clothing appears on figures in wall paintings in Korean tombs of the Koguryŏ dynasty (37 BC–AD 668) and on stone paintings of the Northern Wei (386–ca 535). Direct borrowing by the Japanese seems possible since other artifacts unearthed from the tombs indicate trade between Japan and the continent.

The 6th century saw revolutionary changes in Japan owing to the importation of Buddhism and the Chinese government system. Following the practice of the Sui court (589–618), Prince SHŌTOKU (574–622) established uniforms or rules of dress for aristocrats and court officials, and these remained the basic garments through the early 8th century. Paintings such as the *Shōtoku taishi gazō* (1069) in the Imperial Household Agency show figures in loosely draped gowns with oval neck openings and sleeves long enough to cover the hands. Fragments of the 7th–century *Tenjukoku shūchō* (two embroidered Buddhist hangings illustrating paradise) in the Nara temple Chūgūji show a man in loose shirt and trousers. Here, the *kinu* shirt is looser than its predecessor and has an extra decoration at the hem, and the *hakama* trousers are no longer tied at the knee. Appearing from under the hem of the shirt and over the *hakama* is an added pleated petticoat (*hirami*). In another fragment of the same embroidery, a woman is shown wearing a loose *kinu* shirt and a flowing *mo* pleated skirt. The statue of Lady Maya at the Tōkyō National Museum also shows a typical upper-class dress of wide-sleeved *kinu* shirt and trailing *mo* skirt. All suggest the strong influence of Han-dynasty fashion.

The latter half of the 7th century saw several reforms of the official clothing styles. The most dynamic resulted from the TAIHŌ CODE of Emperor Mommu, enacted in 701. This was one of a long series of reform codes whose content can only be deduced from the subsequent YŌRŌ CODE, enacted in 718 (effective 757). Following the system used in Tang (T'ang) China (618–907), garments were divided into three categories: ceremonial dress, court dress, and working clothes. Styles imitated those of the Tang court. Men wore an outer garment (*hō*) with long, loose, straight sleeves over loose trousers (*uenohakama*), a pleated, skirtlike garment (*hirami*) being visible under the outer garment. Women wore long, loose, flowing gowns (*i*) with broad, long sleeves over their pleated, trailing skirt (*mo*). These garments remained the standard dress of the court aristocracy for several centuries.

Heian Period (794–1185) —— As Japan drew away from conti-

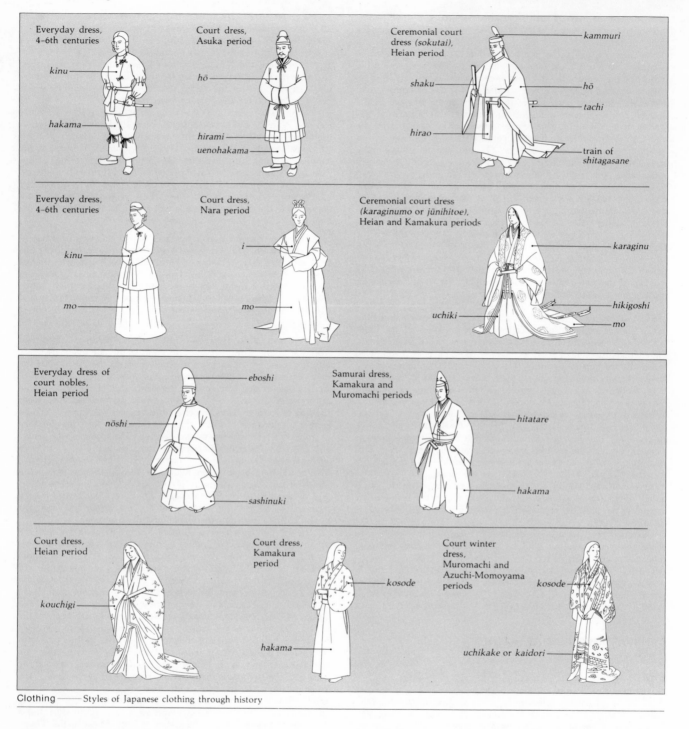

Everyday dress, 4-6th centuries
kinu
hakama

Court dress, Asuka period
hō
hirami
uenohakama

Ceremonial court dress (sokutai), Heian period
kammuri
shaku
hō
tachi
hirao
train of shitagasane

Everyday dress, 4-6th centuries
kinu
mo

Court dress, Nara period
i
mo

Ceremonial court dress (karaginumo or jūnihitoe), Heian and Kamakura periods
karaginu
hikigoshi
uchiki
mo

Everyday dress of court nobles, Heian period
eboshi
nōshi
sashinuki

Samurai dress, Kamakura and Muromachi periods
hitatare
hakama

Court dress, Heian period
kouchigi

Court dress, Kamakura period
kosode
hakama

Court winter dress, Muromachi and Azuchi-Momoyama periods
kosode
uchikake or kaidori

Clothing —— Styles of Japanese clothing through history

nental influence, clothing began to develop along uniquely Japanese lines. Clothing became simpler in cut, more elaborate in its layers, more voluminous. In the early years of the period, clothing was in a transitional stage from Chinese to Japanese styles. By the 11th century, a gradual adaptation of Nara clothing to the climate and lifeways of Japan brought about the loosely layered outfits known as *sokutai* for men and *uchiki* for women.

Heian men's clothing. The Heian aristocrat wore different types of clothes according to the formality of the occasion and the type of activity. For the most formal occasions he wore the *sokutai*, which is still donned today at court ceremonies at the Imperial Palace. Despite many added details and alterations, the basic form remained the loose trousers with overshirt. However, the trousers were given body by stiff, broad-hemmed, divided skirts *(ōguchi)* worn underneath. All the upper garments *(hō)* were longer and looser than their Nara equivalents and included many additional layers. The sleeves of the outermost mantle were made of two widths of material stitched together and hanging down, covering the hands. Being

wider, they were also larger vertically and draped in large squares to the sides of the arms. The arm opening was left unsewn. Under the mantle, the courtier wore a sleeveless vest. Under this was a sleeved garment called a *shitagasane* with a long train that trailed on the floor. Beneath this was the middle garment, *akome*, and still closer to the skin was the unlined *hitoe*. All these were held in place by belting the mantle with a stiff leather strap decorated with stones called an *ishi no obi*, and with a flat band called *hirao*. For headgear there was a stiff, black, lacquered crown *(kammuri)*. Finally, there were socks *(shitōzu)* and lacquered, wooden shoes. A long sword *(tachi)*, a rounded flat tablet *(shaku)* carried on ceremonial occasions, and a bag or, later, an oblong box with fish-shaped metallic decorations *(gyotai)* completed the costume. For less formal court wear and in leisure time the men wore the same upper garments over laced pantaloons secured at the ankle *(sashinuki)*. These were given a puffy look by the stiff *ōguchi* underneath. Courtiers who were in attendance at the palace overnight wore *tonoi shōzoku*, a combination of *hō* mantle, *sashinuki* laced pantaloons, and a special belt.

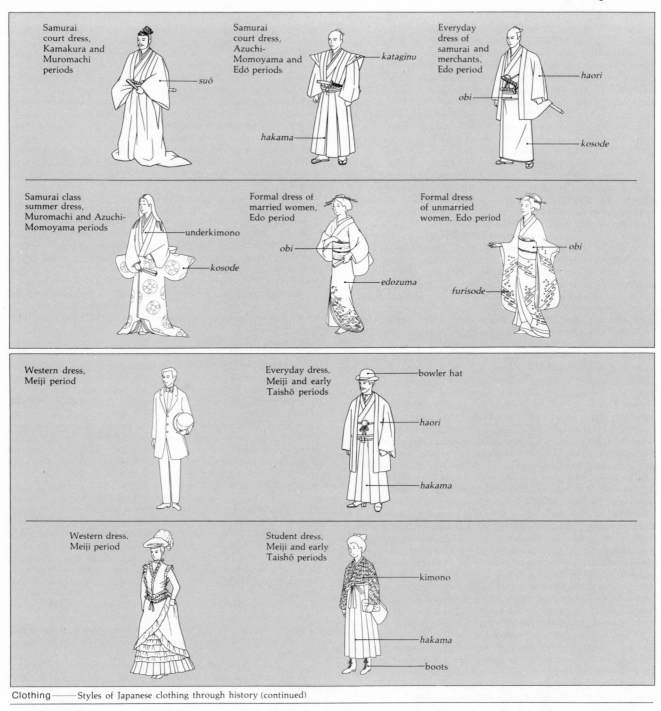

Clothing —— Styles of Japanese clothing through history (continued)

For everyday wear, the courtiers replaced the *hō* with the shorter, more manageable *nōshi* mantle, which differed also in having two side strips joining the front and back panels at the bottom. When hunting, courtiers wore a bast-fiber mantle with loose sleeves that could be laced tight at the wrist (*kariginu*). This was to become the formal dress of the warrior leaders in the next period. In all the less formal outfits, the laced *sashinuki* pantaloons replaced the *uenohakama* trousers and a tall black lacquer hat (*eboshi*) substituted for the *kammuri* crown.

Heian women's clothing. Freed earlier from the influence of Chinese styles, women's clothing developed more quickly into typically Japanese styles. Heian dress includes three classifications of women's clothing: formal wear, everyday wear, and traveling clothes.

The formal counterpart of the men's *sokutai* was the *karaginumo*, the costume of the ladies-in-waiting. After the 16th century this costume was often referred to as the 12–layered garment (*jūnihitoe*) because of the many layers of kimono worn one over the other. The complete outfit was composed of the following parts: an unlined robe (*hitoe*) and loose red trousers (*hakama*); numerous layers of lined robes (*uchiki*); a lustrous silk robe (*uchiginu*); and on top of these an outer garment called *uwagi*. All of these kimono had essentially the same shape: straight panels with rectangular sleeves. Over these layers a pleated rectangular cloth, a vestige of the *mo* skirt, was secured so that it trailed behind, lying on top of the other skirts as an embellishment. A number of narrow, flat strips of cloth (*hikigoshi*) were allowed to trail along the *mo*. Finally, a short jacket with half-sleeves called a "Chinese coat" (*karaginu*) was slipped over the shoulders. All the layers were secured loosely at the waist with a sash, allowing the edges of the undergarments to show along the front of the body and at the sleeves.

The most important element of this formal dress is the *uchiki*, the layers of lined robes also called *kasane-uchiki* or *kasane* (layers). Each was a soft, silk garment a little longer than floor length with broad sleeves. The number of *uchiki* worn at one time averaged between five and ten, though there could be more. At the close of the 11th century the usual number of *uchiki* settled at five.

The individual garments that made up the formal costume were generally dyed in solid colors, the appropriateness of which was decided by status and season. Only purple and crimson were prohibited, as they were reserved for the outer robes of the imperial family and the highest-ranking nobles. In combining the layers of *uchiki*, great consideration was given to the combination of colors. They had either gradually lightening shades of the same color with the innermost layer being pure white (*usuyō*), or they had contrasting colors whose juxtaposition suggested some natural beauty and seasonal change. Since each layer of the *uchiki* was longer than the one over it, the edge of each color showed, making a striking effect when draped along the front of the body.

For everyday occasions, women wore a more simplified version, called *kouchigi*, leaving off the outer *karaginu* cloak and *mo* decorative panel. At other times they wore a loose upper garment with trousers, not dissimilar to the Nara period costume. In summer an unlined upper garment (*hitoe*) was often worn with trousers. When traveling, women would hide behind a veil made of strips of cloth (*mushitare-ginu*) hung from a straw hat (*ichimegasa*), or they would cover their heads with an unlined garment (*kinukazuki*). To ease mobility, women folded up their *kinu* robe, tucking it under the belt so the hem fell to about the knees. Young girls wore a *kazami*, originally an undergarment, or an *akome*, also worn by servants at the court. Ordinary women wore much simpler clothes, including short, sleeveless robes called *tenashi*.

Kamakura (1185–1333) and Muromachi (1333–1568) Periods

With the establishment of the Kamakura shogunate and the decline of the prestige and power of the imperial court, a new style of life emerged. The elegant sensitivity of the courtier gave way to the simple, dynamic life of the military man, serious, strong, ready for battle. Changes in clothing reflect the shift in leadership. The soft, luxurious silk characteristic of the Heian court was replaced by the stiffened garments of the military aristocracy. Both lacquer and vegetable starch were used to give body to the materials.

Men's clothing. Only the highest officials, including the shōgun, wore the formal *sokutai* left over from the Heian period. The informal hunting jacket (*kariginu*) became the standard uniform of the samurai, along with a similar cloak, the *suikan*, made of stiffened silk, gauze, or bast fiber.

For everyday wear, matched cloth combinations were the norm. The upper garment, called a *hitatare*, had a broad collar which was crossed in front of the body, a style that became the basic form in later centuries. Its broad sleeves, made by sewing two widths of cloth together, had, like the *kariginu*, cords at the cuffs for tightening. Originally the *hitatare* was worn by the working classes, but in the Kamakura period it was adopted by the warriors in service of the shogunate, and by the Muromachi period it had become the formal dress. Later it rose to the role of ceremonial dress when worn in combination with trailing, pleated trousers (*nagabakama*). One distinguishing characteristic of the *hitatare* style is that the upper garment is worn tucked into the trousers rather than belted over them.

Two variations of the *hitatare* were common: the *daimon*, or *hitatare* with large crests dyed on the sleeves and center back, and the *suō*, a broad-sleeved upper garment generally made of bast fibers. When this was worn with long pleated trousers of the same material and pattern, the combination was called *kamishimo*. Another variation on the *hitatare* that became fashionable in the Muromachi period was the *chōken*, made a little longer and woven out of silk gauze.

Women's clothing. At the beginning of the Kamakura period, a combination of the *uchiki* robes and *hakama* skirt-trousers was worn as the formal outfit. Later these were replaced by the small-sleeved undergarment, the *kosode*, worn with *hakama*. The *kosode* sleeves differed from the *uchiki* in being only wristlength and in being sewn up at the outer edge to form a pocket. In the Muromachi period an extra jacket called *uchikake* or *kaidori* with very small sleeves was worn on top of the *kosode* to complete the formal dress of upper-class women. After the 17th century, this *uchikake* gained popularity as formal wear among commoners as well, and today it is worn as part of the bridal outfit.

Among the various ways of draping the *kosode*, the style known as *koshimaki*—slipping the upper portion off the shoulders and wrapping it around the waist, leaving the underkimono showing—became the most common summer style for the ladies of the samurai class after the middle of the Muromachi period. Another style involved wearing a *hakuginu* mantle over the *kosode* and leaving off the pleated skirt-trousers.

Azuchi-Momoyama Period (1568–1600)

In the latter part of the 16th century, the powerful generals Oda Nobunaga and Toyotomi Hideyoshi, great patrons of the arts, encouraged a wave of bold, decorative brilliance. This found echoes in clothing, which grew more sumptuous. New contact with the West through the Portuguese and trade with China influenced styles and techniques.

The samurai continued to wear a combination of matched upper and lower garments. The upper garment, however, was without sleeves and resembled a broad-shouldered vest (*kataginu*). Like its forerunner, the *suō* combination with long *hakama*, this is called *kamishimo*. Gradually the material was made stiffer and the flare of the shoulders was increased through the use of whalebone. This combination of top with trailing pleated trousers (*nagabakama*) continued as formal wear for samurai throughout the following Edo period.

In addition the samurai sometimes wore robes called *dōbuku*. These had been worn since the Muromachi period by warriors-turned-priests and by others at funerals and Buddhist ceremonies. Later the *dōbuku* was widely adopted by both samurai and commoners for daily wear, usually over a *kosode* or *hitatare*. Similarly, the *jittoku* traveling jacket could be worn by men of all classes, though in the Edo period it became the standard outfit for doctors and Confucian scholars.

Women continued to wear *kosode* with an *uchikake* cloak for warmth in the winter, and in the summer they folded down the upper part of the *kosode*, wrapping it around their waists for coolness.

Edo Period (1600–1868)

The 250 years of Tokugawa government was a period of peace and growing prosperity. The wealthy and growing merchant community (CHŌNIN) supported new forms of artistic expression. The KABUKI theater and the entertainment quarters led the fashions in clothing and hairstyles.

During this period the *kosode* was the basic garment for both men and women and was worn by the military as well as the merchant class. With Azuchi-Momoyama-period advances in dyeing techniques, the *kosode* had become more brilliantly decorated. This tendency accelerated during the Edo period, particularly with the development of YŪZEN dyeing and TIE-DYEING patterns. The vertical length of the sleeves was increased, though the horizontal length remained the same, ending at the wrists and never covering the hands. The overall decorative patterns were replaced by designs that accentuated the shoulders and hem or divided the garment into sections with contrasting patterns. In the 18th century *kosode* were often decorated around the hips or hem or obliquely from shoulder to opposite hem, a style called *edozuma*. In the latter half of the period, however, the lavishness of the bourgeoisie was curtailed by frequent government regulations restricting the types, colors, and materials of clothing worn by commoners. Under these circumstances, the people turned to more subtle avenues of expression and to cultivating a new sense of beauty (see IKI AND SUI). Plain overall patterns such as stripes, checks, and dots (KOMON) executed in quiet colors became popular. These were balanced by a growing elaborateness in HAIRSTYLES and generous use of exquisitely worked accessories.

The development of the OBI, the sash tied around the waist to hold the *kosode* in place, was closely connected with styles in textile design. During the Edo period the *obi* changed from a narrow band to a stiff belt approximately 30 centimeters (1 ft) wide and 4 meters (13 ft) long. Decorated with rich embroidery or woven, raised designs, it was tied in a variety of decorative ways either in front or back of the body.

Over the *kosode* the Edo man often wore a *haori* jacket. Its straight collar folded to the outside and two short strings tied to the front panels could be knotted at the chest. A short jacket variation on this was the *kawahoribaori*. The *jimbaori* was a sleeveless coat worn by generals in camp. Firemen wore a *kajibaori* or fire-coat made of leather or wool (see FIREMEN'S UNIFORMS, TRADITIONAL). The *hifu* coat, generally worn by old men and doctors, was very similar to the *haori*, except that it had a stand-up collar. Other coats included the short *hanten* and the *happi*, worn by workmen and decorated with the name of a shop or a crest. It was not until the Meiji period (1868–1912) that women began to wear *haori*.

In an attempt at simplification, the Tokugawa shogunate reformed clothing regulations for the military class toward the close of the period. Eliminating the cumbersome trailing *nagabakama*, the standard uniform became a combination of *kosode*, ankle-length *hakama*, and *haori*. The *daimyō* of some domains went further and adopted a combination of narrow-sleeved upper shirt and narrow-legged pants called *momohiki* as their military uniform, because they felt it would facilitate training in Western-style fighting.

These were not the only garments inspired by the West. A number of early Edo-period fashions appeared in response to contact with the Portuguese. In imitation of 16th-century European fashion, the *karusan,* a type of *hakama* that was puffed at the hips and tight over the lower leg, enjoyed brief popularity. From the Portuguese large cape came the Japanese *kappa* raincoat. The *juban* kimono worn under the *kosode* derived its name from the Portuguese word for underwear: *gibão.* This undergarment was later employed as an outer garment worn for work or for festivals.

Modern Developments —— After the Meiji Restoration of 1868 the Japanese slowly changed over to Western clothing, a more revolutionary development than the adoption of Chinese styles in the 6th century. The process began with the government decree that civil servants like soldiers, police, and postmen should wear Western dress. The styles were modeled on European uniforms and special wool factories were established to provide the appropriate material. Soon students were also wearing Western uniforms. By World War I almost all men dressed in trousers, shirt, and jacket.

Women were slower in adopting Western styles, partly because they did not participate extensively in the modernization of the society. The aristocracy, however, sported imported Western gowns and accessories at the European-style balls held at the ROKUMEIKAN from 1883 to 1889. For most women, the influence of the West began with accessories: ribbons, ankle-boots, parasols, shawls. Only after World War I did professional and educated women with progressive attitudes begin to adapt Western clothing as their daily wear. Schools for Western-style sewing appeared, yet it was not until after World War II that the habit of wearing Western clothing became the norm for all classes. Today most Japanese women wear their traditional kimono only on special occasions, such as festivals and weddings. Men wear traditional clothing even more rarely. The cotton summer kimono or *yukata* is worn by both men and women at resorts and for summer festivals.

▰ —— Ema Tsutomu, *A Historical Sketch of Japanese Custom and Costumes* (1936). Hinonishi Sukenori, *Zusetsu Nihon fukushoku shi* (1953). Kawabata Sanehide, *Nihon fukushoku shi jiten* (1969). Kawakatsu Ken'ichi, *Kimono* (1956). Kitamura Tetsurō, *Nihon fukushoku shi* (1976). Helen Benton Minich, *Japanese Costume and the Makers of Its Elegant Tradition* (1963). Yamanobe Tomoyuki, *Nihon no fukushoku bijutsu* (1962).   ISHIYAMA Akira

coal

(sekitan). The coal industry was slow to develop in Japan and had its real beginning after the Meiji Restoration (1868). It grew rapidly with the introduction of Western mining techniques and prospered during the period before and after World War I. As the major source of energy for Japan, coal was highly exploited during World War II and the postwar reconstruction period. During the 1960s, coal was replaced by petroleum, and production was reduced. In recent years large amounts of coal have been imported.

Coal is said to have been first discovered in Japan in Miike, Kyūshū, in 1469, but it was not commonly used as fuel until the 19th century. (Coal was not a popular fuel at first because of its offensive odor. It was, however, used to boil seawater in the salt farm areas bordering the Inland Sea.)

With the Meiji Restoration, coal was used as fuel for steamships and locomotives. Small coal mines were opened one after another in various places. The Meiji government took over the operation of the TAKASHIMA COAL MINE and the MIIKE COAL MINES and introduced Western mining techniques. Inclined shafts replaced random mining as the first step toward modernization, but mining was still done with chisels and picks.

From 1880 to 1900, concentration of capital and the merger of smaller mines were carried out. The Takashima and Miike mines were sold to MITSUBISHI and MITSUI, respectively. The production of coal reached 1 million metric tons (1.1 million short tons) per year in 1883, 3 million (3.3 million short tons) in 1891, and 5 million (5.5 million short tons) in 1896. In 1888 about 1 million metric tons, or half the annual production, were exported to China and Southeast Asian countries and, of the remaining 1 million metric tons, 36 percent was used for steamships, 20 percent for factories, and 35 percent for salt production. In 1896, 2.2 million metric tons (2.4 million short tons) were exported and, of the remaining 2.8 million metric tons (3 million short tons), 20 percent was used for steamships, 55 percent for factories, and 16 percent for salt production.

During the first quarter of the 20th century, the coal industry entered the period of greatest activity, with the concentration of capital leading to large enterprises. Mining was modernized by the introduction of electric machinery to replace steam-driven machines and the improvement of conveyance systems.

The production of coal, which reached 10 million metric tons (11 million short tons) in 1903, rose to 20 million metric tons (22 million short tons) in 1913 and 30 million metric tons (33 million short tons) in 1919. Only about 3 million metric tons were exported, and 60 percent of the total production was consumed by domestic industries.

In 1926 a worldwide economic depression began, and there was a rush to rationalize the coal mining industry. Coal production was at a level of 20–30 million metric tons a year, and maintenance of price was sought by the introduction of production cartels. Improvements in productivity were also made, and the per capita efficiency of coal production, which had been about 10 metric tons (11 short tons) per month throughout the Meiji and Taishō (1912–26) periods, doubled to about 19 metric tons (21 short tons) per month in 1933.

Enlarged munitions production after 1931 raised the demand for coal. Production, which had been 40 million metric tons (44 million short tons) per year in 1936, reached 50 million metric tons (55 million short tons) in 1939. A Coal Mining Department was established in the same year within the Fuel Bureau of the Ministry of Commerce and Industry to administer and control coal production. The production level of more than 50 million metric tons per year was maintained until 1944.

After World War II, new mining methods were developed and increased coal production was adopted as a high priority policy, together with iron, steel, and fertilizers (see PRIORITY PRODUCTION PROGRAM). Annual production, which dipped once to 20 million metric tons, recovered to a level of 40 million metric tons, reaching 50 million in 1957. Per capita production returned to the prewar level of about 18 metric tons (20 short tons) per month in 1960.

Before 1900 coal had been produced mainly in northern Kyūshū, but thereafter coal mines were developed in Hokkaidō, the JŌBAN COALFIELD, and the UBE district. Postwar priority production was promoted mainly in these areas and coal mining was placed under state control for a short period.

The postwar reliance on imported oil forced the coal mining industry to rationalize after 1955. It became impossible to absorb the soaring costs caused by increased mining depth, and a policy of reducing production scale by closing down unprofitable mines was carried out (see MIIKE STRIKE). In recent years annual production has averaged 20 million metric tons.

Coal mine workers numbered 460,000 in the period directly following World War II, but had dropped to 20,000 in the late 1970s. Per capita efficiency has increased to 75 metric tons (83 short tons) per month, more than three times the prewar level. The number of coal mines has shrunk from a postwar high of 853 in 1951 to 26. Japanese coal reserves include 1 billion metric tons (1.1 billion short tons) as proved reserve and 8.4 billion metric tons (9.3 billion short tons) as estimated deposits.

The general decline of coal usage in Japan, however, was reversed after the OIL CRISIS OF 1973. Coal was reconsidered as a major source of energy, and the Japanese government has since then been increasing coal imports. In 1978, 60 million metric tons (66 million short tons) or about three times the annual domestic production were imported. About 50 million metric tons were used for iron and steel manufacture.

The leading coal-mining companies in the late 1970s included the Hokkaidō Colliery & Steamship Co, the Matsushima Kōsan Co, the MITSUI MINING CO, LTD, the NITTETSU MINING CO, LTD, and the SUMITOMO METAL MINING CO, LTD. See also ENERGY SOURCES.
▰ —— Asahi Shimbun Seibu Honsha, ed, *Sekitan shiwa* (1970). Kuboyama Yūzō, *Sekitan kōgyō hattatsushi* (1942).   HAGA Namio

cockfighting

(tōkei). Also known as *tori-awase.* Popular in ancient times in India, Persia, China, and Southeast Asia, cockfighting was introduced to Japan from China early in the 8th century. In the Nara (710–794) and Heian (794–1185) periods it became an amusement popular among the nobility. By the Kamakura period (1185–1333) cockfighting matches were held annually each March. Cockfighting became an occasion for gambling, and in the Edo period (1600–1868) the large fighting cock, or *shamo,* came to be used exclusively. Officially

banned in 1873, cockfighting continues sporadically in local areas. The cockpit is a dirt ring surrounded by a barrier of straw matting. The fighting cocks are led to the ring, their feathers moistened, and bets are placed. When one bird refuses to fight or is ejected from the ring three times, he is declared the loser.　INOKUCHI Shōji

Cocks, Richard (1566–1624)

Manager of the English East India Company's trading post in Japan during its 10-year existence from 1613 to 1623. He was born in late 1565 at Seighford, Staffordshire, the third son of Robert Cocks, a yeoman farmer. The East India Company sent half-a-dozen merchants to Japan and set up a trading post, or "factory," in the port town of Hirado (now part of Nagasaki Prefecture, Kyūshū) under the supervision of Cocks. The manager made two visits to Edo (now Tōkyō), during the first of which, in 1616, he was received in a brief audience by the shōgun TOKUGAWA HIDETADA.

The English enterprise in Japan was a commercial disaster. The remote port of Hirado was not so accessible as Nagasaki, the Portuguese center of operations, and the arrival of English shipping with fresh supplies was irregular. Unlike the Portuguese, the English were unable to import Chinese silk, and much of their stock consisted of woolen goods for which there was little demand. Commercial rivalry was intense, and the more businesslike Dutch often undercut the prices of their English competitors. Misled by incompetent interpreters and prone to worry and doubt, Cocks was unable to exercise the firm leadership that the situation required. His problems were aggravated by the unruly conduct of his English staff and of visiting ships' crews.

As the Japanese government increasingly curtailed English trading privileges following the death of TOKUGAWA IEYASU in 1616, the fortunes of the trading post further declined. In 1623 the post was closed down by the East India Company, and Cocks and his staff were recalled in disgrace, leaving behind considerable debts owing to the company. Worn out by worry about the court proceedings awaiting him in London, Cocks died at sea on 27 March 1624 while returning to England. Although undeniably an ineffective and muddled administrator, Cocks cannot be held solely responsible for the commercial failure.

Cocks's chief claim to fame rests on his incomplete diary, which runs from June 1615 to January 1619, and again from December 1620 to March 1622; this account is supplemented by a score of lengthy letters. The diary is a rich source of information about daily life in Hirado, business transactions, and visits to temples and monuments. Cocks's quaint style and erratic spelling tend to obscure the fact that he was a keen and sometimes shrewd observer. Of particular interest are the entries describing EDO CASTLE, the great Buddha (DAIBUTSU) in Kamakura, the temple known as SAN-JŪSANGENDŌ in Kyōto, religious festivals, popular entertainment, earthquakes, suicides of retainers on the death of their lord, and the severe penalties for crime. His accounts of vague and inconsistent rumors (concerning, for example, the death of Ieyasu) strikingly illustrate the way in which the common people were kept in ignorance of contemporary political events.

━━━━ *Diary Kept by the Head of the English Factory in Japan: Diary of Richard Cocks, 1615–1622*, 3 vols (1978–80). Michael Cooper, "The Second Englishman in Japan: The Trials and Travails of Richard Cocks, 1613–1624," *The Transactions of the Asiatic Society of Japan*, Third Series, vol 17 (1982). N. Murakami, ed, *Diary of Richard Cocks, Cape-Merchant in the English Factory in Japan, 1615–1622*, 2 vols (1899).　Michael COOPER

coeducation

In Japan, Confucian morality long advocated educating male and female students separately, especially during the premodern period. In the Meiji period (1868–1912), when a modern school system was developed, compulsory primary education was made coeducational under the EDUCATION ORDER OF 1872. After World War II coeducation was instituted throughout the entire school system in the EDUCATIONAL REFORMS OF 1947. In practice, however, many private schools continued to be for boys or girls only. Furthermore, within the educational curriculum some courses are given separately for boy or girl students.　OKUDA Shinjō

coffee houses

(*kissaten*). Shops chiefly intended for enjoying nonalcoholic beverages and snacks, though many such shops serve alcoholic beverages as well. The early part of the Meiji period (1868–1912) saw the opening of "milk halls," but it was not until 1889 that Japan opened its first modern coffee shop, the Kahii Sakan, in Tōkyō's Ueno district. A two-story Western-style building, it provided newspapers, magazines, playing cards, and games like GO and SHŌGI to encourage customers to spend time in the shop. Thereafter, coffee shops began to proliferate in the Ginza area. During the Taishō period (1912–26), some of these shops expanded into bar-restaurant operations with hostesses serving Western cuisine and alcoholic beverages. However, *kissaten*, which specialized in coffee, continued to flourish except for a decline during World War II. Following the war, specialty coffee shops became popular, offering customers the opportunity to listen to particular kinds of recorded music, like jazz or rock, or to dance. At one time all-night coffee shops were popular with young people as a refuge for those who had missed the last train home. Problems ensued, however, and strict regulations were established in 1956 governing their operation. Given the lack of privacy in Japanese homes, coffee shops fill a special need in Japanese society, providing a place for relaxation, business discussions, personal writing, and meeting friends.　TSUCHIDA Mitsufumi

collective bargaining right

(*dantai kōshōken*). One of the three FUNDAMENTAL LABOR RIGHTS guaranteed by article 28 of the 1947 constitution. The Labor Union Law (Rōdō Kumiai Hō) also provides that an employer's refusal to bargain without a justifiable reason is an UNFAIR LABOR PRACTICE, and a LABOR RELATIONS COMMISSION may order the employer to bargain. Japanese law thus guarantees the right to engage in collective bargaining as a right separate and independent from the RIGHT TO ORGANIZE LABOR UNIONS and the RIGHT TO STRIKE and also creates a mechanism whereby the employer is legally compelled to sit down with the workers' representatives and bargain in good faith. This setup is taken from the Wagner Act (1935) of the United States. In contrast, in England, West Germany, and France there is no legal mechanism to compel a recalcitrant employer to engage in collective bargaining, and the only way to do so is for the employees to engage in a strike against the company.

The manner in which the right to bargain collectively is protected, however, differs greatly between the United States and Japan. First, the United States had adopted an exclusive representation system, but in Japan a number of labor unions may coexist within a single enterprise, where each possesses an equal right to bargain. Second, American employers and unions have an obligation to bargain, but a Japanese labor union does not have such an obligation. Third, in the United States the obligation to bargain can be enforced only through an order of the National Labor Relations Board. In Japan, since the right to engage in collective bargaining is also protected by the constitution, it has been argued—though the matter is far from being settled—that courts also have the power to order collective bargaining. At the very least, it is universally recognized that an employer's unjustified refusal to engage in collective bargaining constitutes a tort, and a court may order the employer to compensate the labor union for damages. See also LABOR LAWS.

SUGENO Kazuo

collective labor agreements

(*rōdō kyōyaku*). Labor agreements reached by collective bargaining, as contrasted with those arrived at by individual bargaining (see EMPLOYMENT CONTRACTS). In Japan the overwhelming majority of collective agreements are concluded between company unions and their individual companies. The Trade Union Law of 1949 gives binding legal force to collective agreements that stipulate better working conditions than those in individual employment contracts (see LABOR LAWS). The law also extends to all workers in an establishment any collective agreement that already applies to three-fourths or more of its workers. The labor minister or a prefectural governor may declare that an agreement accepted by a majority of the workers in a particular occupation in a locality holds for all other workers there in that occupation, when either party to such an agreement requests such an extension. Also, procedural terms or obligatory provisions of a collective agreement, that is, terms of an agreement governing areas outside working conditions, are also deemed by the courts to establish certain legal obligations and rights between the parties to the agreement. However, there is disagreement whether the legal enforcement of such provisions of collective agreements is practical or desirable.

━━━━ Tadashi Hanami, *Labour Law and Industrial Relations in Japan* (1979).　HANAMI Tadashi

Colonialism —— Table 1

	Korea	Taiwan	Sakhalin (Karafuto)	Guandong Territory	Pacific Islands
Japan's Colonies					
Date of annexation	1910	1895	1905	1905	1914
Size (sq km)	220,792	35,961	36,090	3,462	2,149
Total population in 1939 (thousands)	22,800	5,896	355	1,274	129
Japanese population in 1939 (thousands)	650	323	346	190	75
Japanese as percentage of total population in 1939	2.9	5.5	97.5	14.9	58.1

SOURCE: Takumushō (Department of Overseas Affairs), *Takumu tōkei, 1939* (1941).

Colonialism —— Table 2

	Export to Japan	Import from Japan
Trade between Colonies and Japan (percentage of colony's total trade, 1939)		
Korea	73.2	88.5
Taiwan	86.0	87.5
Sakhalin (Karafuto)	99.9	99.8
Guandong Territory	58.7	78.6
Pacific Islands	93.2	96.0

SOURCE: Takumushō (Department of Overseas Affairs), *Takumu tōkei, 1939* (1941).

colonialism

Japan was the only non-Western colonial power in the world until it was stripped of all its colonial possessions in 1945 as a result of defeat in World War II. At the time its colonies included Korea, TAIWAN, the southern half of Karafuto (the Japanese name for the island of SAKHALIN), the GUANDONG (KWANTUNG) TERRITORY (Japan's territory on the Liaodong [Liaotung] Peninsula in southern Manchuria), and the Pacific Islands, totaling some 298,454 square kilometers (115,203 sq mi), or more than three-quarters the area of Japan.

A colony, called *gaichi* in Japanese as opposed to *naichi* or metropolitan Japan, may be defined as a territory where the constitution and the Diet-enacted laws were not, as a rule, enforced and whose inhabitants, with customs and traditions different from those of the Japanese, were regulated by special ordinances of the colonial governor. Accordingly, such territories as Hokkaidō, the Bonin Islands, and Okinawa, all of which had been made parts of Japan proper before the promulgation of the constitution in 1889, were not colonies. Nor should Manchuria or other Chinese territories under Japanese occupation during World War II be considered colonies, as they were never officially annexed. Table 1 summarizes data on the size, population, and date of annexation of Japan's five colonies.

Korea was the most important colony in size, geographic proximity, and historical ties. Its colonial experience was unique in two ways. First, it was annexed in 1910 as a result not of military conquest but of a treaty agreement (see KOREA, ANNEXATION OF). The Japanese government pledged, however half-heartedly, to provide "equal treatment" for Koreans. Accordingly, an unusually large number of Koreans were employed in the colonial government at all levels, even including the police force. Second, the Koreans possessed a strong cultural identity fostered by more than 2,000 years of history as an independent nation. Once the country was annexed, this cultural identity manifested itself in a strong nationalist movement with open demands for restoration of independence. The only other colony in which a nationalist movement appeared was Taiwan. There, however, the nature of the movement was reformist, de-manding only a greater degree of home rule under Japanese sovereignty.

Taiwan, Japan's first colony, acquired in 1895 following the Sino-Japanese War (see SHIMONOSEKI, TREATY OF), served as a training ground for numerous colonial officials whose experience later proved valuable in the administration of other colonies. Programs successfully implemented in Taiwan, such as land survey, population census, and government monopolies, set precedents for other colonies. More important, the island was the most profitable colony within the Japanese empire. Like Korea, it shipped half its annual rice harvest to Japan. Taiwan's sugar industry enabled Japan to become the fourth largest cane sugar producer in the world, and it attracted an enormous amount of private Japanese investment capital. Within 10 years of annexation the colonial administration of Taiwan achieved financial self-sufficiency. It took Karafuto 28 years, the Guandong Territory 30 years, and the much smaller Pacific Islands 10 years to accomplish the same goal. The Korean administration required subsidies from Tōkyō throughout the 35 years of Japanese rule.

Karafuto was acquired in 1905 following the Russo-Japanese War (see PORTSMOUTH, TREATY OF). Unlike Korea and Taiwan, it was a settlement colony, virtually all of whose inhabitants were Japanese. In 1941 the native population (mostly AINU) numbered only 1,697 and was declining (there were also more than 21,000 Koreans). As a settlement colony, Karafuto was in many respects more integrated with Japan than were other colonies. After 1907 the colonial judiciary became a part of the Japanese judiciary, directly supervised by the Ministry of Justice in Tōkyō. Colonial education was restricted to Japanese children and was heavily subsidized by the central government. Military rule was terminated in 1907 in Karafuto, well ahead of other colonies, and in 1943 the colony was made part of Japan proper.

The Guandong Territory was first ceded to Japan in 1895, along with Taiwan, but was retroceded to China as the result of intervention by Russia, Germany, and France (see TRIPARTITE INTERVENTION). Later it was leased to Russia. When Japan defeated Russia in 1905, the lease was transferred to Japan together with the right to control the SOUTH MANCHURIA RAILWAY and a narrow stretch of land on both sides of the line. The territory, therefore, was unique in two ways. First, it was a leased territory over which Japan did not have real sovereignty. Second, its colonial government was entrusted with the administration of the railway, paving the way for the penetration of the Japanese GUANDONG (KWANTUNG) ARMY deep into the heartland of Manchuria. After the creation of MANCHUKUO following the MANCHURIAN INCIDENT, Japan initiated in 1934 a system of appointing its ambassador to the puppet state concurrently as governor-general of Guandong. He governed the peninsula from his embassy in Mukden (now Shenyang).

The Pacific Islands consisted of most of what is known as Micronesia and comprised more than 1,400 tiny volcanic islands scattered in the Pacific Ocean north of the equator and south of the Tropic of Cancer, east of the Philippines and west of the international date line (Guam and Wake Island excluded). Long controlled by Spain, which had acquired them in the early 16th century, the islands were purchased by Germany in 1899 following the Spanish-American War. Shortly after the outbreak of World War I in 1914, they were seized by the Japanese navy. At the Versailles Peace Conference, the Pacific Islands were declared a class-C territory of the League of Nations, which in turn awarded Japan the mandate to rule them as a part of its empire. Japan retained control of the islands even after its withdrawal from the League in 1933. Technically, therefore, the Pacific Islands were a mandated territory over which, like the Guandong Territory, Japan held no real sovereignty. The native population was small, maintaining a steady level of about 50,000 throughout the 30 years of Japanese rule; they were rapidly outnumbered by Japanese settlers, most of them from Okinawa, who numbered 84,000 in 1942.

Administratively the islands were divided into six districts: Saipan (the Mariana Islands); Jaluit (the Marshall Islands); Ponape and Truk (the eastern Caroline Islands); and Yap and Palau (the western Caroline Islands). The Nan'yōchō, the government that oversaw the six district governments, was located on the island of Koror in the Palau district. The district governor was often a police lieutenant. The natives were ruled indirectly through their tribal chiefs, and the Japanese settlers enjoyed a degree of democracy similar to that practiced in Japan. See also SOUTHEAST ASIA, THE PACIFIC ISLANDS, AND JAPAN; SOUTHERN EXPANSION DOCTRINE.

Colonial Institutions —— The colonial government in each colony was headed by a governor. Entrusted with a broad range of political, legislative, and judicial powers, he ruled his colony as a virtual sovereign. He formulated and implemented colonial policies, with the exception of defense and foreign affairs, which were under the jurisdiction of the central government. The colonial governor was authorized to issue special ordinances that had the binding force of Japanese law (governors of the Guandong Territory and the Pacific Islands did not have this power). Furthermore, in Korea and Taiwan he could appoint and dismiss judges at will and through his special ordinances regulate the functions and organization of colonial law courts at all levels. To implement his orders at the grassroots level the governor relied on a large number of trained local officials, who in turn were supported by an efficient police force. He received his ultimate support from the colonial garrison, of which he was concurrently the commander-in-chief before 1919.

Reflecting the greater importance of Korea, Taiwan, and the Guandong Territory, the governors of the three colonies were called *sōtoku* or governors-general; as officials of *shinnin* rank, they belonged to the highest rank of the Japanese bureaucracy, being invested by the emperor in person. In contrast, the chief colonial officers of Karafuto and the Pacific Islands were known merely as *chōkan* or chief administrators; they were ranked at the *chokunin* level, the second-highest in the bureaucratic hierarchy. The governor-general of Korea was the most powerful of the colonial governors, his prominence in the government second only to that of the prime minister of Japan. He alone enjoyed the privilege of reporting directly to the emperor (until 1919) and to the prime minister (until 1942); all other colonial governors were under the supervision of relevant cabinet-level colonial officers (e.g., ministers of colonial affairs, home affairs, or foreign affairs). See KOREA AND JAPAN: Japanese colonial control of Korea.

Before 1919 all colonial governors were military officers in active service and were ex officio commanders of the colonial garrisons. Here, too, variation existed. In Korea, only generals or admirals were appointed to the post of governor-general. In Taiwan, lieutenant generals and vice admirals were also eligible. In the Guandong Territory, only army officers were eligible, whereas in the Pacific Islands, only navy officers were considered. In Karafuto, where security was never a problem, the garrison commander was not automatically named to serve concurrently as the chief administrator. In 1919, in line with the trends of the so-called TAISHŌ DEMOCRACY, civilian rule was introduced to all five colonies, establishing the system of separation between civil and military authorities. The civilian governor, however, was authorized to "request" the use of military force from the garrison commander. In Korea, where the celebrated March First Movement (SAMIL INDEPENDENCE MOVEMENT), the first major anti-Japanese rebellion since the annexation, had just been suppressed, military officers (in civilian clothes) continued to hold the post of governor-general, reform notwithstanding.

At the national level, the colonial institution underwent three stages of evolution. From 1895 to 1929 there was no independent, cabinet-level colonial institution. All colonial affairs were handled by a bureau attached to the office of the prime minister or to the Home Ministry. Its functions were limited to coordination and data compilation. In June 1929 the Ministry of Colonial Affairs (Takumushō) was created, marking the beginning of the second stage. Although it was created for the purpose of exercising uniform supervision over all five colonies, the power to formulate colonial policies remained in the hands of colonial governors, and the ministry never interfered in the administration of individual colonies. In December 1934, upon the creation of Manchukuo, the Bureau of Manchurian Affairs (Taiman Jimukyoku) was established within the office of the prime minister, and the Guandong Territory was placed under its control. It was on this occasion that the practice of appointing the ambassador to Manchukuo as governor-general of the Guandong Territory was introduced.

The third stage began in November 1942, at the peak of Japan's military expansion in Asia. The Greater East Asia Ministry (Dai Tōa Shō) was created to replace the Bureau of Manchurian Affairs and the Ministry of Colonial Affairs. This new superministry was charged with supervising the Guandong Territory and the Pacific Islands, together with Manchukuo and other areas under Japanese occupation, whereas the Home Ministry was made the central institution for Korea, Taiwan, and Karafuto. In addition, all ministries in the central government were authorized to direct (rather than just to supervise) the governments of the latter three colonies in areas related to their respective functions (e.g., colonial education by the Ministry of Education). The move apparently was designed to hasten the political integration of the three colonies so as to meet the wartime need for matériel and for psychological unity of the colonies and the homeland.

Goals and Outcome —— Japan's intention was to convert the colonies into defense outposts of the empire as well as springboards for expansion. This goal was achieved in both China and the Pacific. Earlier, Japan had aspired to become a world power equal in prestige with the Western nations. Now, as a colonial power, Japan had achieved that goal as well.

There was an effort to make the colonies absorb some of Japan's excess population, but the results were mixed. Colonization was successful in Karafuto and to a lesser degree in the Pacific Islands; in Korea, Taiwan, and the Guandong Territory, which were already heavily populated, it failed. Japanese residents in the latter colonies were mostly officials, business employees, and their families, whose presence frequently caused friction with the native population. Despite repeated efforts and generous subsidies, the three colonies did not attract a significant number of agricultural settlers. There were more Korean laborers who migrated to Japan than Japanese who settled in Korea.

Japan hoped to develop an integrated economy in which it would provide the colonies with capital and technology in return for supplies of foodstuffs, raw materials, and lucrative opportunities for investment. All available economic data clearly indicate that Japan succeeded in interlocking the economies of the five colonies with its own. Table 2 reveals but a glimpse of the degree of economic interdependence achieved.

It must be emphasized that economic development was carried out with the welfare of Japan, not of the colonies, in mind and that it was often achieved at great expense to the native population.

Japan envisioned an empire in which the colonial people would learn to speak Japanese and accept the Japanese way of life and in which the constitution and laws of Japan would be applied equally to all. These goals were to be achieved through education and acculturation. In this respect Japan could claim success only in Karafuto, where the size of the native population was insignificant. In Korea integration efforts failed. In 1943, for example, even after more than 30 years of colonial rule, only 20 percent of Koreans could comprehend the Japanese language. Nothing the Japanese did in Korea, including education and the introduction of home rule more generous than in other colonies, seemed to lessen the Koreans' desire for independence.

In Taiwan, the policy of integration produced different results. The 1943 record shows that 62 percent of Taiwanese could speak Japanese and that the percentage was rising rapidly. More than half the laws enforced on the islands originated in Japan, and the governor-general could not issue legislative ordinances unless no applicable Japanese law existed. Above all, education, reinforced by improved living conditions (and a generous measure of police repression), persuaded the Taiwanese to keep their political movements within the limits of the law. Japan might have achieved the goal of integration in the case of Taiwan had its colonial rule not been so abruptly terminated by its defeat in 1945. Political integration was never an immediate concern with regard to the Guandong Territory or the Pacific Islands, for Japan held no formal sovereignty over them.

■ ——Edward I-te Chen, "Japanese Colonialism in Korea and Formosa: A Comparison of the Systems of Political Control," *Harvard Journal of Asiatic Studies* 30 (1970). Nan'yōchō, ed, *Nan'yōchō shisei jūnen shi* (1932). Ōkurashō, ed, *Nihonjin no kaigai katsudō ni kansuru rekishiteki chōsa*, 35 vols (1947). Takumushō, ed, *Takumu tōkei, 1939* (1941). Yanaihara Tadao, *Nan'yō guntō no kenkyū* (1935). Edward I-te CHEN

Colonization Office → Kaitakushi

Combined Fleet, Imperial Japanese Navy

(Teikoku Kaigun Rengō Kantai). The Combined Fleet's origins can be traced to the founding of the standing fleet in 1889. It was composed of various units, including battleships, cruisers, aircraft carriers, destroyers, submarines, and airplanes, and it formed the foundation for the ocean-going fleet. The Combined Fleet was proud of its reputation for invincibility until the middle of World War II, when it lost its power and initiative as a result of defeats suffered at the Battle of MIDWAY and in the Solomons Campaign in 1942. YAMAMOTO ISOROKU was the commander in chief of the Combined Fleet at the outbreak of the war in the Pacific in 1941.

ICHIKI Toshio

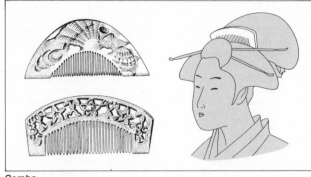

Combs

Ornamental combs of the Edo period. The drawings are of combs in the Suntory Museum of Art, Tōkyō.

combs

(kushi). Traditional Japanese combs, in addition to being functional, were often products of fine craftsmanship. The earliest combs had long teeth for holding the hair. By the medieval period (13th to 16th centuries), gold lacquered and mother-of-pearl inlaid wooden combs were being made. In the Edo period (1600–1868), as the variety and complexity of HAIRSTYLES increased, ornamental combs were manufactured in a profusion of designs, differing according to the social class or age of the wearer. Materials such as wood, bamboo, tortoiseshell, ivory, and metal were used. During the Meiji period (1868–1912), the spread of occidental hairstyles throughout the country diminished the demand for traditional combs.

HASHIMOTO Sumiko

comic magazines

The flourishing of a "comic culture" is one of the significant features of mass culture in present-day Japan. This culture is reflected in the enormous circulation of comic magazines and the large number of stories these magazines carry. Comic magazines fall into four categories: boys' comics *(shōnen komikku)*, girls' comics *(shōjo komikku)*, youth comics *(seinen komikku)*, and adult comics *(seijin komikku)*. Comic magazines are published weekly, biweekly, and monthly.

Boys' and girls' comics average around 400 pages, and a given issue usually contains some 15 serialized stories. Serials run for at least three to six months, and especially popular ones may continue for 10 years. Total combined weekly circulation of the major boys' comic magazines is about eight million, and it is estimated that two-thirds of all boys aged 5 to 18 read these magazines on a regular basis. More than one-sixth of Japanese girls in the same age bracket are regular readers of girls' comics.

Youth and adult comics average about 250 pages and contain about 10 serialized "story cartoons" and 5 "nonsense cartoons" in each issue. The serials run about the same number of months as in the children's comics. If so-called vulgar *(zokuaku)* comics are included, 40 to 50 different youth and adult comic magazines are published. There are no reliable statistics on circulation.

It once was exceptional for young women to continue reading comic books after the age of 20, but in recent years female readership of adult comics has increased. Serialized comics aimed at teenage and adult women are, for the most part, carried in women's weekly magazines along with other material, such as scandal stories and popular novels.

The popularity of comic magazines began in 1959 with the publication of *Shōnen sandē* and *Shōnen magajin*. Other children's comics appeared in rapid succession, and a large number of talented comic artists emerged to meet the demand. By around 1965, the explosive popularity of these magazines came to be known as the *manga būmu* (comic boom). Youth and adult comics attracted former readers of children's magazines in the late 1960s, and the quality of story cartoons *(sutōrī manga)*, realistic cartoons *(gekiga)*, and girls' comics has improved considerably. This diversification and improvement of quality appear to have been the major factors sustaining the popularity of comic magazines. See also MAGAZINES.

SOEDA Yoshiya

coming-of-age ceremonies → gempuku

Comintern 1927 Thesis

Resolution concerning the status of the communist movement in Japan adopted on 15 July 1927 in Moscow by the presidium of the Communist International (Comintern). Among the Japanese representatives invited to discussions of the resolution were TOKUDA KYŪICHI, WATANABE MASANOSUKE, and FUKUMOTO KAZUO. The thesis was subsequently adopted by the JAPAN COMMUNIST PARTY (JCP) as its first formal platform.˙ Noting the threat posed by Japanese imperialism, the thesis prescribed a two-stage process for what was considered an inevitable revolution: an initial bourgeois democratic revolution that would quickly develop into a socialist revolution. Declaring the need for a Communist Party based on a broad proletarian organization, the thesis denounced Fukumoto's ideas as intellectually elitist and rejected the doctrine of YAMAKAWA HITOSHI, who considered left-wing activity within the labor movement and the formation of a legal political party for workers more effective vehicles than the Communist Party. The thesis also expressed unreserved opposition to social democracy and disparaged the significance of the autocratic power of the emperor system. Though not as thoroughgoing as the COMINTERN 1932 THESIS, it was important in that it provided the JCP with a basic political strategy.

MATSUO Takayoshi

Comintern 1932 Thesis

Policy statement concerning the Japanese communist movement issued in May 1932 by the executive committee of the Communist International (Comintern). KATAYAMA SEN, NOSAKA SANZŌ, and Yamamoto Kenzō (1895–1942) contributed to preliminary discussions, but the thesis itself was based on a report by O. V. Kuusinen (1881–1964) criticizing the Trotskyist content of the 1931 draft thesis of the JAPAN COMMUNIST PARTY (JCP) that declared that the inevitable revolution would be a single-step proletarian revolution broadly embracing a simultaneous bourgeois revolution. The 1932 Thesis reverted to the policy of the COMINTERN 1927 THESIS by prescribing a two-stage process through which bourgeois democratic revolution would lead to general socialist revolution. The more exhaustive 1932 Thesis also emphasized the importance of agrarian revolution and outlined the unique significance of the emperor system in its relationship with monopolistic capitalism and a semifeudal system of land tenure. Consequently, the thesis regarded the overthrow of the emperor system as the first task of the revolution. The thesis formed the basis of subsequent JCP policy and influenced intellectuals outside the party as well.

MATSUO Takayoshi

Commercial Code

(Shōhō). The legal framework that defines the nature and operation of commercial entities and the essential features of commercial relationships in Japan. The Commercial Code establishes rules for the regulation of all commercial activities and is central to the operation of the Japanese economy, underlying all domestic and international economic activities.

Commercial Law in Japan's Industrial Economy——The evolution of increasingly complex legal rules has been a common feature in the development of all modern industrial economies. Japan is no exception, and its formal commercial law system is not significantly different from those of the other major "free enterprise" (as contrasted with centrally planned) economies. The Western observer, whether from a common law or civil law country, usually has little difficulty in understanding the structure of the legal rules governing commercial entities or commercial relationships in Japan. However, misunderstandings often arise over the actual interpretation and application of these formal legal rules in Japan's distinctive commercial environment.

The development of Japan's commercial law system since the Meiji Restoration (1868) has taken place during a period of rapid and fundamental commercial law reform in Europe and the United States. The past 100 years have seen the development of the LIMITED LIABILITY COMPANY as the most important vehicle for commercial activity; the adaptation of the rules of contract to the demands of an industrial and consumer economy; the evolution of increasingly sophisticated legal mechanisms for facilitating and regulating commercial credit; a widespread recognition that the private-enterprise economic system must be monitored by governments and, where necessary, regulated to prevent economic abuses;

and the creation of extensive administrative structures to implement regulatory systems in areas such as the control of unfair trade practices and monopolization, the protection of consumers, and the control of dealings in commercial securities. Japan has been directly influenced by these developments.

Although Japan is now unquestionably a major economic power, its commercial law system has contributed little to the worldwide evolution of commercial law, with the exception of prewar developments in its former colonies, Korea and Taiwan, and its contribution to law in Nationalist China. Japan's formal legal system is largely derivative, and its commercial practices are not readily exportable to other countries. The results of recent movements to reform Japan's commercial law system, particularly the important debate over the best method of imposing some measure of social responsibility and accountability on the activities of large commercial entities, may signal a new era in which Japan may for the first time have an influence on the development of commercial laws in other countries.

In view of the pervasive influence of the practice of ADMINISTRATIVE GUIDANCE in Japan, there has been a tendency to deemphasize the importance of formal legal rules in the management of the Japanese economy. A formal commercial law system does exist and it is very detailed. It affects every commercial transaction, from the sale of a bus ticket in Tōkyō to multimillion dollar contracts for the supply of oil from the Middle East, from a savings bank deposit in Ōsaka to a letter of credit to effect payment for a jumbo jet, from the relationship between partners in a souvenir stall in Kyōto to the rights of minority shareholders in a dispute with the directors of one of the great Japanese trading houses. The well-known debates about the "law consciousness" of the Japanese and the willingness or otherwise of Japanese to resort to litigation to settle disputes assume great importance for overseas businesses dealing with Japanese business entities, particularly when subject to Japanese commercial law. Even if in the long term litigation is unlikely, foreign businesses must be able to gauge the extent to which Japanese corporations' responses to problems will be based on the principles set out in Japanese commercial laws.

The Development of a Commercial Code —— As in other areas of Japan's social, political, economic, and legal development, the commercial law system since the Meiji Restoration has been subject to three major formative influences: Japan's own traditional legal system, and more particularly the commercial system of the late Edo period (1600–1868); the influence of Western ideas throughout the Meiji period (1868–1912); and the particular influence of the United States in the period after 1945.

By the end of the Edo period Japan had developed a sophisticated commercial system that provided a basis for rapid economic development in the latter half of the 19th century. No detailed set of national commercial laws had evolved, but rules and institutions had developed within the commercial structure that could have been formalized in modern legislation if the Meiji government had so desired. The concepts of group organizations were highly developed in the guilds (ZA); principles governing the sale and distribution of goods were quite sophisticated; and a system of credit had long operated. In the event, the draftsmen of the new commercial law system chose to look outside Japan for their inspiration.

The Meiji government was heavily influenced by German law in the early drafts of the Commercial Code, which were prepared by Karl Friedrich ROESLER, a leading German adviser. The draft also included concepts drawn from French and English law, but ultimately fell victim to the code revision debate in 1892. Some sections of the code dealing with corporations were enforced soon afterward, but a revised code, prepared by a committee consisting of UME KENJIRŌ, Tanabe Kaoru, and OKANO KEIJIRŌ, was not adopted until 1899.

This new code consisted of five books. Book 1 dealt with general concepts, Book 2 with corporations, Book 3 with commercial transactions, Book 4 with bills of exchange and checks, and Book 5 with maritime law. In 1934 Japan acceded to international conventions on bills of exchange and checks prepared by the civil law countries, and Book 4 was deleted from the code. The present law on bills of exchange and checks is set out in the Bills and Notes Law (Tegata Hō) and the Checks Law (Kogitte Hō). In 1938 a new type of company, corresponding to the English private company, was provided for in the Limited Liability Company Law. This basic structure remains today.

A new dimension was added to Japan's commercial law system during the OCCUPATION period (1945–52). Although controversy surrounds their activities, the Occupation authorities considered that their mandate to encourage democratic tendencies in Japan could be carried out only by extensive restructuring of the Japanese economy, including the system of commercial laws which regulated that economy. Significant amendments were made to the corporations section of the Commercial Code, particularly to strengthen the powers of shareholders; and new laws to regulate unfair business practices, monopolistic practices, and dealings in corporate securities were introduced, based on American regulatory systems. There have been no fundamental changes to the Commercial Code since 1951, although there were important amendments to details in 1955, 1966, 1974, and 1981. In contrast, the alien concepts embodied in the ANTIMONOPOLY LAW and the SECURITIES EXCHANGE LAW have been altered significantly. The administrative arrangements under both laws now also differ markedly from the original American models.

The Commercial Code and Other Commercial Laws —— Apart from the Commercial Code there are other important sources of commercial law. CUSTOMARY LAW, special legislation, and case law all play important roles.

The Commercial Code preserved the possibility of incorporating Edo-period commercial customs into the new system. Article 1 of the code prescribes that, where there is no specific provision in the Commercial Code covering a particular problem, resort may be made to customary law, and if customary law provides no answer, then an answer may be sought in the CIVIL CODE. Article 1, however, has not resulted in any significant role for customary law. Article 1 may also be used to incorporate into the legal framework modern commercial customs that command general acceptance.

Article 1 also establishes an important role for the Civil Code in all commercial situations. The Civil Code sets out the general framework for the law of CONTRACTS, the law of TORTS, and the law of PROPERTY RIGHTS, all of which are of great importance to the operation of the commercial law system. For example, questions concerning the contractual capacity of corporations are not covered in the Commercial Code, and so the lawyer must consult Book 1 of the Civil Code. Again, while Book 3 of the Commercial Code deals with most of the specific aspects of commercial transactions, the general principles of contract law, including such important matters as the principles of liability for nonperformance and the principles governing damages for breach of contract, are covered in the Civil Code.

A great many important areas of commercial life have long been covered by specific legislation. From early in the Meiji period important legislation was enacted covering such matters as the banking and insurance industries and Japan's commercial transactions with other countries. In the postwar period the volume of specific commercial legislation has increased, including legislation already mentioned covering monopolies, unfair business practices, and transactions in commercial securities, and more recently, the regulation of the supply and distribution of petroleum and the introduction of price controls.

The importance of judicial decisions in Japan cannot be underestimated. The courts appear to play a more important role in developing law in Japan than in some other civil law countries. It is impossible to understand commercial legislation in Japan without also being familiar with the relevant judicial decisions that have interpreted that legislation. There are also cases where the courts have developed principles that are not covered by legislation, for example, the development of a form of commercial security described by John Haley in "The Preliminary Contract for Substitute Performance," *Law in Japan* 7.33 (1974), which was later given a legislative basis.

Commercial Entities —— Any individual in Japan may engage in commercial activities, but the more economically important transactions are usually conducted by entities created by law. The Commercial Code establishes three types of commercial entity, the LIMITED PARTNERSHIP COMPANY, the UNLIMITED PARTNERSHIP COMPANY, and most important the JOINT-STOCK COMPANY. The Limited Liability Company Law, adopted in 1938, provides a fourth commercial entity. These commercial entities are called *kaisha*, in contrast to noncommercial entities created by law which are usually called HŌJIN. All individuals who are engaged in commercial activities as a continuing business and all commercial entities will be regarded as "merchants" or "traders" (*shōnin*) for the purposes of the Commercial Code.

Commercial Transactions —— There are quite important distinctions between the principles governing the 13 types of contractual relationship that may be established under the Civil Code and the contractual relationships covered in Book 3 of the Commercial Code. In any contractual situation it will always be important to know which code applies.

The classification of transactions turns partly on the nature of the parties and partly on the nature of the transaction. Commercial entities created by law will be regarded as *shōnin,* as will individuals who carry on business. All transactions in which a *shōnin* is a participant will be classified as commercial transactions, and it is not necessary that both parties be merchants for the commercial principles to apply. On the other hand, anyone who enters into any of the transactions spelled out in articles 501–503 of the code will be deemed to be engaged in a commercial transaction. An example of the importance of the distinctions between commercial and noncommercial transactions is that *shōnin* are expected to inspect goods as soon as they are received and to report any complaints about quality to the seller within a prescribed period. If a complaint is not made in time, the buyer will not be able to complain later.

Japanese Attitudes toward Commercial Contracts —— Since it is often remarked that Japanese do not seem to rely on formal written contracts in their commercial transactions, it is important to note that, so long as the basic prerequisites for a contractual relationship do exist, the Commercial Code and the Civil Code provide quite specific answers to most problems that may arise during the course of the contract. Although many provisions of the codes can be overridden if the parties choose to adopt contrary concepts, it is likely that most Japanese with a legal education have been persuaded by their university studies of the codes that the principles set out in the codes provide the most rational and scientific solutions to commercial problems. So long as judicial interpretations do not introduce uncertainties into the operation of the code provisions, legally trained Japanese are likely to rely on the codes once they have satisfied themselves that a contractual relationship has been established. The vast majority of law graduates enter commerce and industry or government rather than the legal profession in Japan, and law graduates exercise great influence at all levels of commercial life.

Widespread acceptance of the code provisions governing commercial transactions, coupled with fairly uniform interpretation and application of the principles by both businessmen and the courts, may provide one explanation for the popular view that Japanese rely on their "word" or their "honor" rather than on written contracts in their business dealings. Again, the extent to which the Japanese economy is based on transactions within groups of related enterprises would reduce the potential area of contractual dispute (see ENTERPRISE GROUPS). It is not surprising that different attitudes prevail in international contracting, where the Japanese cannot assume that the foreign party has a similar approach to the law or to business relationships.

■ —— Shin'ichirō Michida, "The Legal Structure for Economic Enterprise: Some Aspects of Japanese Commercial Law," in Arthur Taylor von Mehren, ed, *Law in Japan: The Legal Order in a Changing Society* (1963). Rex Coleman and John O. Haley, *An Index to Japanese Law: A Bibliography of Western Language Materials 1867–1973* (1975), entries under "commercial law"; and updated by entries in *Law in Japan: An Annual* (1967–). Malcolm D. SMITH

commercial paper

(tegata; kogitte). The Japanese Bills and Notes Law (Tegata Hō) and Checks Law (Kogitte Hō), both in effect since 1934, are based upon the international Convention providing a Uniform Law for Bills of Exchange and Promissory Notes of 1930 and the Convention providing a Uniform Law for Checks of 1931. The substance of both Japanese laws is almost the same as that of the international Uniform Laws.

The Bills and Notes Law primarily governs bills and notes of exchange, with many of its provisions applying to promissory notes. A large portion of the bills and notes used within Japan are promissory notes. Even when a bill of exchange is used, for example, when the buyer in a sales contract undertakes a bill of exchange and delivers it to the seller, the seller will record his own name on the receipt entry of the bill and will also sign as the issuer of the bill. Since 1966, bills and notes that are to be paid at a bank must be printed on a standard form issued by the Federation of Bankers Associations of Japan (Zenkoku Ginkō Kyōkai Rengō Kai). While a bill or note that is executed on something other than the standard form is effective as a bill or note under the Bills and Notes Law, paying banks generally agree by contract with their customers not to pay such bills or notes.

A severe sanction called a trade suspension disposition *(torihiki teishi shobun)* is imposed by clearing houses on the guarantor of a bill of exchange or the drawer of a promissory note that has not been paid at maturity at the bank where payment is due. Clearing houses and participatory banks have a duty not to advance credit or allow checking transactions to a person who has twice dishonored a bill or note within a six-month period. This suspension, under clearing house rules rather than the law, lasts two years. As a result, a person who has been subject to a trade suspension disposition cannot obtain credit or a checking account at any bank whatsoever. This disposition system poses problems because it imposes extremely harsh sanctions on merchants, but in view of the bad effects of delinquent bills or notes on the entire economy, case precedent has upheld the legality of this sanction. This system also applies to drawers of checks.

One special feature of the Japanese Bills and Notes Law is that many times a signatory seal will be used as a substitute for the signer's own personal signature. Article 82 of the Bills and Notes Law and article 67 of the Checks Law provide that "the word signature includes seals." This use of the seal, without limiting signatures to personal signatures, signifies that a person participates in many documentary transactions. The inclusion of a seal as a signature is based on an understanding reached at the Uniform Convention Conference.

The widespread use of blank notes and bills is also a special feature of Japanese law. Of the bills or notes that have a fixed day of payment, bills or notes with a blank date of issue or payee make up about half the bills or notes in circulation. When a bank, by agreement with its customers, is charged with the collection of bills or notes with a fixed day of payment and blank spaces for the date of issue or the payee, it is an established principle that the bank will present the bill or note for clearance without filling in the blank space. Even though this kind of transaction may cause trouble, the bank does not bear responsibility. Also, when this type of blank bill or note has been presented to a bank for payment, the bank agrees to pay without informing its customer. With a note or bill with a fixed date of payment, the practice of not recording the date of issue is widespread, because this is not necessary to fix the legal relationships of the bill or note, but legally a bill or note which does not mention the date of issue is incomplete. For this reason, where payment of such a bill or note is refused, the holder cannot seek redress for the delay from previous holders of the bill or note.

The Checks Law is also based on the Uniform Law but contains several provisions that employ Japanese reservations to the convention. The Uniform Law treats checks that have no indication of the place of payment as payable at the payer's principal place of business, while the Checks Law treats them as payable at the place where they are drawn (art. 2, para. 3). The Uniform Law has no provisions for a time period during which the drawer must have funds with which to clear his checks, while the Checks Law regulates this (art. 3). The Uniform Law restricts the issue of self-addressed checks to cases where the check is addressed from one business office of the drawer to another business office of the drawer, while the Checks Law recognizes the practice in a great many cases (art. 6, para. 3). The Uniform Law fixes the presentation period at 8 days, while the Checks Law fixes it at 10 days. The Checks Law does not recognize the check payable in account of article 39 of the Uniform Law. The Checks Law provides regulations regarding warranties of payment (arts. 57–62); however, it also provides that banks, by the terms of their checking account agreements, make no warranty of payment. KAWAMOTO Ichirō

Commission on the Constitution

(Kempō Chōsakai). Commission created by an act of the Diet in 1956 to investigate the origins, operation, and possible amendment of the 1947 CONSTITUTION of Japan. It was made up of Diet members and scholars and was chaired by TAKAYANAGI KENZŌ, former professor of law at Tōkyō University. The socialists boycotted the group, charging that its organization violated constitutional provisions concerning the amendment of the constitution and that the conservative majority had already made up its mind in favor of amending the document. The proceedings and reports of the commission are notable for the massive quantity of factual data on the formulation of the constitution and the great variety of opinion held concerning its enactment and correct interpretation. A majority of the members believed that the postwar constitution had been imposed on Japan by the Allied OCCUPATION authorities and that the document should be altered to make the emperor head of the state and to permit explicitly defensive armament. During the existence of the commission, which was abolished in 1965, the LIBERAL DEMOCRATIC PARTY, many of whose members favored constitutional revision, suffered a decline in electoral support and Diet representation. This made it very unlikely that the commission's work would soon lead to changes in the basic law. See also CONSTITUTIONAL PROBLEMS STUDY GROUP; CONSTITUTION, DISPUTE OVER REVISION OF.

Theodore McNelly

Committee of Seven to Appeal for World Peace

(Sekai Heiwa Apīru Shichinin Iinkai). Committee of seven prominent Japanese; founded in 1955 to campaign for world peace. To realize the goal of permanent world peace, the committee has advocated the banning of nuclear weapons and the establishment of a world federation of nations. During times of international stress, such as the Suez Crisis in 1956 and the Berlin Crisis in 1961, the committee launched appeals through letters and newspapers for the peaceful settlement of such disputes. Its first members were its organizer, SHIMONAKA YASABURŌ, former president of Heibonsha, Ltd, Publishers, and six other scholars and social leaders: former Minister of Education MAEDA TAMON; the physicists YUKAWA HIDEKI and KAYA SEIJI; the president of the Japan YWCA, UEMURA TAMAKI; the president of Japan Womens' University, Jōdai Tano (b 1886); and the feminist HIRATSUKA RAICHŌ. At one time KAWABATA YASUNARI, TOMONAGA SHIN'ICHIRŌ, and others served as members of this committee. Any vacancy in the committee caused by a member's death is filled by a new person selected by the remaining members.

commoners → heimin

common-law marriage

(naien). Common-law marriage, that is, cohabitation of a man and a woman, having all the outward characteristics of a marriage but lacking legal sanction, is not uncommon in Japan. A marriage is not considered legally valid under Japanese law until it is formally registered with the proper public authority.

There are various reasons for not registering a marriage. Often couples neglected to register simply because they attached greater significance to the traditional marriage ceremony and were unfamiliar with the registration requirement. In the past, the strict legal regulation of familial matters tended to discourage registration. For example, under the Civil Code of 1891, until its revision in 1948, formal marriage required the consent of the family head. Furthermore, especially in rural areas, it was fairly common not to register a marriage until after a "trial period," often lasting until the birth of the couple's first child.

Over the years the law has gradually come to recognize certain features of common-law marriage as legally binding and has provided these relationships with a certain measure of legal protection.

1. Persons who unilaterally break off a common-law marriage relationship without a valid reason have an obligation to compensate the other party for tangible and intangible damages. Compensation was first awarded in a court case before the Court of Cassation in 1915, on the legal fiction that the person had made a promise to marry, which was not carried out. In recent years, however, compensation has been recognized under a theory of tort liability.

2. In the area of social legislation there are several situations in which a common-law wife is treated the same as a formally married wife, primarily in connection with survivors' benefits paid to families of males injured in work-related accidents. This is first found in the FACTORY LAW OF 1911 and can also be seen in the postwar Labor Standards Law (see LABOR LAWS) and laws on WORKERS' COMPENSATION.

3. There are, in addition, precedents where the allocation of marital costs has been applied to common-law couples, and in the event of a dissolution of common-law marriage, the distribution of property is sometimes made as in a divorce.

There are, however, distinctions between formal and common-law marriages. For example, children of common-law marriages are not considered legitimate, and a common-law spouse does not have inheritance rights as a spouse or a familial relationship with his or her spouse's blood relations.

In recent years, because the legal restrictions which once discouraged registration have been abolished, common-law marriages have been decreasing. Some young couples, rejecting conventional views of marriage, have refused to register as a matter of principle. See also MARRIAGE.

Bai Kōichi

communion → naorai

Communist Party → Japan Communist Party

communists, public trial of (1931–1932)

A special open trial of leaders of the JAPAN COMMUNIST PARTY who were accused and found guilty of having violated the PEACE PRESERVATION LAW OF 1925 (Chian Iji Hō). During the 1920s political leaders and conservative bureaucrats were shocked by the spread of communist ideas and the illegal establishment of the Japan Communist Party. The government responded with the enactment of the harsh Peace Preservation Law of 1925 and a nationwide roundup of suspected party members and their supporters on 15 March 1928 (see MARCH 15TH INCIDENT). Other arrests followed, with thousands of suspects apprehended. Faced with the problem of what to do with these dissidents, the Japanese state reacted in a manner unlike that of some other nations that have perceived a serious internal threat: there was no mass application of terror, no deportations or forced labor brigades, and no category of "nonpeople." Instead, a remarkable system that emphasized TENKŌ (recantation of communist ideology coupled with rehabilitation) was designed to reform communists and other "thought criminals" and reintegrate them into society. A basic reason for this softer Japanese approach was the feeling that all Japanese were brothers under the emperor and that no "thought offender" was beyond salvation.

The special open trial at the Tōkyō District Court (108 sessions from 25 June 1931 to 2 July 1932, with sentencing on 29 October) was carefully staged by the Ministry of Justice to expose the inner workings of the Communist Party and to reeducate those who had slipped into the heresy of communism. Other reasons for the trial were that nearly 300 individual trials would have choked the courts, and a unified trial of party leaders would give the best picture of the party and its tactics. The defendants cooperated because they wanted to use the courtroom for propaganda purposes.

Among the communists on trial were key leaders: SANO MANABU, chairman of the party Central Committee; Nabeyama Sadachika (1901–79), Central Committee member; Kokuryō Goichirō (1902–43), Central Committee member and member of the labor union department; TOKUDA KYŪICHI, Central Committee member until 1927; ICHIKAWA SHŌICHI, who headed the party in 1927 while other leaders were in Moscow; SHIGA YOSHIO, chief editor of the journal *Marukusu shugi* (Marxism); and Takahashi Sadaki (1905–35), a leader of the Communist Youth League. Fuse Tatsuji (1880–1953) and other skillful lawyers represented the defendants. For this important case, the government selected Chief Justice Miyagi Minoru of the Tōkyō Appeals Court and "thought prosecutors" (shisō kenji) Hirata Susumu and Tozawa Shigeo.

Chief Justice Miyagi thoroughly prepared for the trial by reading books on communism and closely analyzing foreign and domestic trials of communists. The judge reviewed every aspect of the procedure in detail, even the order in which the defendants were to enter and depart from the courtroom. Since Miyagi's chief concern was to maintain the dignity of his court and to conduct the trial quickly and smoothly, he reached a compromise with party leaders. As long as they prevented disruptions among the defendants, the trial would remain open. Since the defendants badly wanted an open trial, Miyagi's carrot-and-stick strategy was effective.

Throughout the trial the communists insisted that they were political prisoners and that their testimony would not only show the repressive nature of the government but also present the public with a true picture of the party. Despite demonstrations outside the courtroom and sensational details in the leftist press, the trial progressed smoothly. Unfortunately for the defendants, however, the courtroom drama was quickly overshadowed by the greater drama in Manchuria, where fighting broke out in September 1931 (see MANCHURIAN INCIDENT). The courtroom was filled with denunciations of the "imperialistic" war and other antiwar slogans, but the communists misunderstood the public mood, and their antiwar campaign backfired. All the defendants were found guilty.

The prosecution asked for stiff punishment: imprisonment for five years for party members, and additional time for those engaged in party activities. Extra-heavy penalties were requested for defendants who refused to express remorse. Attorney Fuse and others denied that their clients had violated the provisions of the Peace Preservation Law and accused the prosecution of playing politics. Miyagi sentenced Nabeyama, Sano, and Ichikawa to life imprisonment; Takahashi and Kokuryō were sentenced to 15 years and Shiga and Tokuda to 10 years. It was made clear to the defendants that by renouncing the party they would become eligible for a reduced sentence. Those who cooperated, like Sano and Nabeyama, had their terms reduced, but die-hards like Tokuda and Shiga had their sentences confirmed by the Tōkyō Court of Appeals.

The message of this sensational trial was that those who violated the Peace Preservation Law would be severely punished. Miyagi's decision to execute no one was shrewd, since without blood there could be no martyrs. Judge Miyagi was rewarded for his services with a silver medal and an appointment to the Great Court of Cassation.

One startling result of the trial was the sensational recantation (tenkō) of Sano and Nabeyama, which, because of their prestige, prompted many other imprisoned communists to follow suit.

■■——Richard H. Mitchell, *Thought Control in Prewar Japan* (1976). Odanaka Toshiki, "San'ichigo yon'ichiroku jiken: Chian iji hō saiban to hōtei tōsō," in Wagatsuma Sakae, ed, *Nihon seiji saiban shi roku, 4, Shōwa-zen* (1970).   *Richard H. MITCHELL*

community centers

(kōminkan). Multipurpose community facilities built and operated by cities, towns, and villages. The Ministry of Education introduced the community center concept to Japan after World War II as part of its community education (shakai kyōiku; literally "social education") revitalization program which aimed in part at encouraging the democratic rebuilding of communities by providing facilities for bringing the citizens of a community closer together and making available to them opportunities for learning cultural and practical skills. Concrete plans for the operation, staffing, and management of the kōminkan were systematized by the 1949 Community Education Act (Shakai Kyōiku Hō). Community centers rank with libraries and museums in Japan as important community education facilities.

Community centers offer various educational, technical, recreational, and cultural programs for the layperson. They conduct special lecture series for youth and women and sponsor a variety of demonstrations, technical courses, physical education, and recreational activities as well. Kōminkan also lend books and are available for community meetings.

Each community center is staffed by a full-time director and several assistants. There are no fixed qualifications for these positions, but the staff is expected to be knowledgeable about and experienced in various aspects of community education. Advisory boards are set up to help the center director. As of 1978 there were 16,452 kōminkan in Japan with 11,649 full-time employees. See also COMMUNITY EDUCATION.   *KURAUCHI Shirō*

Community Chest

(Kyōdō Bokin). Organization of citizens and private social welfare organizations to raise funds for the benefit of the less fortunate. The first attempts to organize a community chest in Japan occurred in Nagasaki Prefecture in 1921. Fund-raising activity was heightened in 1947 to assist the many persons suffering from the severe social and economic dislocations in the immediate postwar period, as Occupation policy forbade public assistance to private welfare agencies.

The Community Chest continues to conduct an annual fund drive today, giving red-feather pins (akai hane) to donors. In 1980, total donations to the Community Chest drive totaled over ¥18 billion. Of this amount, the largest share came from individual contributions, followed by corporate contributions. These donations are shared by organizations and individuals engaged in providing services to the needy.

Other funds are obtained through the sale of special donation-included postcards for exchanging New Year's greetings and through the large-scale annual year-end fund drive sponsored by Japan's public broadcasting corporation (NHK). However, such efforts are hampered by the lack of a cultural disposition toward public charity since the family and the work group have traditionally been expected to take care of their own members. See also SOCIAL SECURITY PROGRAMS; SOCIAL WELFARE.   *Hiroki SHIOJI*

community education

The term "community education," a free translation of the Japanese *shakai kyōiku*, literally "social education," refers to various educational activities outside school education. *Shakai kyōiku* is a unique Japanese term, roughly equivalent to the adult education, *Volksbildung, éducation populaire,* or continuing education of the European countries and the United States. As a legal concept, community education was defined as "organized educational activities mainly for youths and adults (including physical and recreational activities), other than those provided in school courses," in the Community Education Law (Shakai Kyōiku Hō) of 1949. In a 1971 report dealing with the problems of community education and rapid social change, the Ministry of Education's Community Education Deliberative Committee (Shakai Kyōiku Shingikai) stated that "in the future community education should be considered to include all types of activity intended to raise educational levels in all areas of study in every possible place and at every possible opportunity in the lives of the people."

History—— Following the Meiji Restoration of 1868, preparations were rapidly completed for both laws and systems related to school education, but provisions for community education lagged behind. As part of the creation of a modern society, various campaigns for enlightenment and cultural programs for the general public were carried out under the name *tsūzoku kyōiku* (popular education). Throughout the late 19th and early 20th centuries, *tsūzoku kyōiku* activities were gradually expanded. In 1921 the term *shakai kyōiku* was adopted by the government in place of *tsūzoku kyōiku*. Community education facilities and groups as well as adult education and youth education programs came under the jurisdiction of a single administrative body responsible for all aspects of community education, creating a pattern which has continued to the present day. However, community education was still considered as no more than a supplementary activity in a system which was centered on school education. The years of World War II saw an abrupt increase in educational indoctrination of the people by the government, and community education groups came under strict government control and took on a wartime character.

After the war, the first of the UNITED STATES EDUCATION MISSIONS TO JAPAN issued a report on adult education which emphasized the importance of establishing libraries and museums, making school facilities available for use by the public, and encouraging group discussions. Following these recommendations, the Community Education Law of 1949, the Library Law (Toshokan Hō) of 1950, and the Museum Law (Hakubutsukan Hō) of 1951 were enacted, along with various measures encouraging the people to create active and autonomous community education programs. Major developments included the establishment of kōminkan (COMMUNITY CENTERS) as comprehensive facilities for community education, the organization of parent-teacher associations in each school, and the promotion of independent study group activities in communities and workplaces. Community use of school facilities for extension classes and lectures was also encouraged. After the enactment in 1953 of the Law for Promotion of Youth Classes (Seinen Gakkyū Shinkō Hō), youth classes providing general education, information, and skills in vocations and homemaking for working youth became widespread.

In the 1960s, with changes in Japan's rapidly advancing industrial structure, new developments in science and technology, and the general rise of educational levels, the problem of adapting community education to new social conditions was brought to public attention. Also, because of the increase in the average age of the Japanese population, enrichment of the lives of the elderly through education became a prominent issue.

System and Present Conditions—— As of 1978, Japan's community education facilities included 16,396 community centers, 1,218 libraries, 504 museums, 343 youth centers, and 19,835 physical education and recreation facilities. Both boards of education and community education facilities employ professional personnel for planning and implementing community education programs and providing guidance for students. In 1978 there were 5,963 such community education officers attached to boards of education throughout the country, as well as 7,622 kōminkan officers, 3,289 librarians and assistant librarians, 1,083 museum curators and assistant curators, and 1,181 guidance personnel at youth education facilities. A National Training Institute for Community Education (Shakai Kyōiku Kenshūjo) has been established as a training center for professionals in the field.

Public education administrative bodies and educational organizations offer a wide range of community education lectures and classes, including women's classes, domestic education classes, youth classes, adult education lectures, and classes for the elderly. In the one-year period between April 1974 and March 1975, classes and lectures sponsored by boards of education numbered 51,865, and those sponsored by kōminkan 59,184; approximately 7,200,000 persons took advantage of these study opportunities.

According to the Ministry of Education's *Survey on the Conduct of Lifelong Education* (1976), 1.8 times as many women as men attended these classes. Classified by age, those between the ages of 36 and 45 made up the highest percentage of participants, followed by those between 26 and 35. Classes related to art, the performing arts, and hobbies were attended by the highest number of students, followed by those related to homemaking and everyday life, culture, vocations, and physical education and sports.

There are also many private groups active in community education projects. These include groups for youth, women, and adults, as well as parent-teacher associations, sports and music groups, and groups involved in correspondence education or audio-visual education. Some of these organizations are local in scale and some are national.

Future Issues——With the rising interest in learning at every age level, a need has arisen for a wide variety of courses conducted at a high level. This in turn has created a need to see community education as an integral part of the larger educational system and to carefully consider its role in relation to those of school and home education, educational activities in the workplace, and educational activities of the mass media. Today, in all large cities of Japan, newspaper companies, broadcasting stations, and department stores engage in a wide range of community education programs and cultural activities. Some universities have started to accept adults under new special programs, and many people continue their education through study programs on television. TAKAMURA Hisao

community education officers

(*shakai kyōiku shuji*). Specialists in COMMUNITY EDUCATION (*shakai kyōiku;* literally "social education") employed by prefectural and municipal boards of education. They offer technical advice to citizens engaged in community education work and also plan and administer lectures, seminars, and recreation programs sponsored by education boards. They are chosen from among people experienced in educational or community work and are required to complete a special seminar held by the Ministry of Education before assuming their posts. KURAUCHI Shirō

commuting

Commuting to work, called *tsūkin,* and commuting to school, *tsūgaku,* are a daily problem faced by Japanese workers and students as a result of industrialization and urbanization. Residential districts have spread away from the inner city to outlying suburbs, and since transportation facilities and road maintenance and expansion have not kept up with demand, public transportation is often severely overcrowded. In Japan 53.1 million people are in the work force and 7.4 million people age 15 and over attend school, for a total of 60.5 million potential commuters. Of this number, 44.6 million, or 39.9 percent of the total population, commute to work or to school, and those people who commute long distances from their homes constitute 30.1 percent of the total number of commuters. However, in the case of big cities, the figure runs higher, particularly in Tōkyō, with 51.1 percent, and in Ōsaka, with 50.6 percent. This figure has risen rapidly in recent years, and long-distance commuting to work and school is on the increase. According to a 1975 survey conducted by NHK (Japan Broadcasting Corporation), the daily average time used in commuting to work was one hour and 11 minutes and for commuting to school one hour. In larger urban areas, of course, more time is required. Average daily commuting time on a weekday in Tōkyō is one hour and 40 minutes, and in Ōsaka one hour and 20 minutes.

The national rates for various types of commuting were 29.0 percent by train, 23.4 percent on foot, 15.1 by bicycle or motorbike, 14.6 by public bus, 14.5 by private car, 2.4 by company bus, and 1.0

by taxi or other means. In larger urban areas the rate of train use is higher, 63.1 percent in Tōkyō and 50.5 percent in Ōsaka. Transportation fares are in large measure borne by the employers; companies with 1,000 or more employees pay 97.7 percent of their employees' commuting expenses, and even small businesses with 30 to 99 employees pay 90.1 percent. KURITA Ken

company welfare system

Company welfare in Japan consists of the provision by employers of employee benefits and services other than wages and improved working conditions, in such areas as housing, health care, family support, recreation and leisure, education and training, and retirement. Some of these practices have a long history, going back to the early stages of Japanese industrialization and, since they were not legally required, have often been considered evidence of employer "paternalism" toward employees. In more recent years, especially since the end of World War II, they have become subjects of collective bargaining and joint consultation between unions and managements, as well as being regulated by law.

The Growth of Company Welfare——A main reason for the emergence of the company welfare system was the rapid transformation of the work force from rural agriculture to industrial labor beginning in the late 19th century. In this process, it was left largely to the individual employer to provide living and working conditions conducive to attracting and adapting workers to the discipline and requirements of industrial and urban life. There was little state planning in this regard, except in the "model" factories initially run by the Meiji government. Companies found it necessary to house and care for workers recruited from the countryside, especially in the case of the newly developing modern textile mills and shipyards for which large work forces needed to be assembled very quickly. Most of these recruits were in their early teens, and, notably in textiles and other light industries, many were young girls. In many cases the living and working conditions for workers were abysmal, but the more benevolent employers built dormitories, installed medical, recreation, and educational facilities, and provided meals. Other practices included withholding pay for remission directly to the parents of young workers or, in the case of the young females, accumulating their wages as dowries for marriages upon leaving employment and returning to their home villages (see LABOR MARKET).

In addition to the advantages to the enterprise in controlling the work force, no doubt many employers felt a responsibility to serve *in loco parentis.* Employers seemed to believe that they were carrying forward traditions long established in village and rural family life and in apprentice systems in the merchant houses and craft trades of feudal Japan. This belief became the basis for resistance by employers against government attempts beginning in the late 19th century to regulate industrial working conditions as the means for eliminating the worst abuses and exploitation of workers (see MANAGERIAL IDEOLOGY). The passage of the FACTORY LAW OF 1911 represented the first such regulation on a general scale, although this law was quite limited and did not take full effect until 1929. In the meantime, as the industrial labor force grew rapidly, company-provided welfare spread steadily throughout major enterprises, notably in the 1920s and 1930s when the practice of long-term employment of regular workers within individual firms was widely adopted. Since there was only a limited development of labor unionism in those years, employer welfare practices did not become subject to collective bargaining, although in many large companies employers established employee representation schemes for consultation about welfare matters as well as working conditions. With the establishment of branches of Sampō (Industrial Patriotic Association) at each major enterprise during the late 1930s as a part of the wartime mobilization effort, there was fortification of the company-based welfare systems with fewer distinctions between white-collar and manual workers throughout World War II.

Post-World War II Development——Company welfare grew in importance during the economic chaos of the early postwar period. Although wholesale labor law reforms and strong encouragement of labor unionism and collective bargaining gave the labor movement substantial institutional power, workers sought their economic and psychological security within their respective enterprises and therefore continued to expect to receive a wide range of benefits from employers to whom they had become regularly or permanently attached. Adoption of the Labor Standards Law of 1947 (see LABOR LAWS) and subsequent protective legislation furnished a minimum legal base for these company obligations toward employees for a wide range of working conditions and welfare benefits. In terms of legal requirements, this legislation brought Japan abreast of international standards at that time.

As a result, company welfare became an integral portion of the employee compensation system that has characterized postwar industrial relations in the large firms and government organizations. With the development of labor unions and collective bargaining at the enterprise level, the idea of career-long employment in one company was extended fully under union pressure from white-collar to blue-collar employees. An enterprise-level union typically embraced both groups in its membership so long as they were regularly, not temporarily, employed in the firm. See EMPLOYMENT SYSTEM, MODERN.

Along with long-term employment security came the practice of paying salaries and wages and money benefits primarily on the basis of length of service in the company, age, and level of formal education. Salaries and wages rose almost automatically from year to year under this system called *nenkō joretsu* (SENIORITY SYSTEM). For the most part, companies hired recruits to become regular employees upon their graduation from school, provided them with systematic training within the enterprise, promoted them to higher positions in a finely structured status hierarchy, and required retirement at the age of about 55.

Accordingly, with the expectation that most regular workers would be employed for their careers in a single organization, employers also provided various money allowances to meet individual life-cycle needs (for family, education, housing, etc) as well as nonmoney benefits for regular work force members as a whole. Company housing provides an example of meeting life-cycle needs: young, single employees are often housed in dormitories providing spare but comfortable facilities; married employees have access to heavily subsidized apartment dwellings, complete with shops and recreational areas; older employees have the opportunity to borrow funds at subsidized interest rates in order to purchase their own homes. A large percentage of the work force takes advantage of such opportunities. In addition, as the result of the new legal obligations under the postwar labor laws, a variety of insurance funds, with contributions from employers, employees, and government, were established principally in the form of enterprise-level societies for the purpose of providing for retirement, health and medical care, and layoff or unemployment.

It should be stressed, however, that this total system of company welfare applies only to large-scale organizations with 500 or more employees. The system applies far less or not at all to firms of smaller size, in which welfare benefits at the company level, if any, tend to be informal and unsystematized. Instead, government programs for old-age pensions, unemployment insurance, health care, and the like, with considerably lower benefit levels, cover workers in the small firms, often through interenterprise associations at the local, regional, or industrial level. It should be noted that, compared to large companies which have a high degree of labor unionization, workers in small firms tend to be loosely organized.

Development of company welfare as an integral portion of the total employment system among large-scale organizations has tended to decentralize relationships between employees and employers to the enterprise level. No doubt it has contributed to a strong sense of mutual identification and "enterprise-consciousness" among managers and workers in a particular organization. Sociologist Ronald P. Dore has labeled such self-contained arrangements as "welfare corporatism" (see INTERNAL ORGANIZATION OF JAPANESE COMPANIES).

The Level of Company Welfare—— Company welfare also has constituted a sizable component of labor costs for large-scale organizations. Depending on the method of calculation and size of firm, the cost of welfare on the average has tended to amount to 15 to 20 percent of the cash earnings of employees. This ratio is higher in large firms than in small; and because wages and salaries in big organizations usually average 25 to 35 percent higher than in the small, the value of the welfare benefits in money terms is of course considerably greater.

There is a computation problem in determining which items should be included in wages and salaries and which items in company welfare. The most important of these borderline items is the annual or semiannual BONUS paid to employees by almost all companies and organizations at the time of the Buddhist BON FESTIVAL in midsummer and/or at the NEW YEAR. These payments usually account for about one-third of the cash compensation which workers receive (and in some cases considerably higher) and originally were

thought of as a type of profit-sharing bestowed upon employees out of management beneficence. However, these bonuses have become subject to collective bargaining with labor unions and are now regarded far more as part of regular wage and salary payments than as welfare benefits.

The items clearly in the welfare category include legally required payments and voluntary or nonobligatory contributions to medical care, retirement pay, housing, food service, and recreation schemes, and health, pension, unemployment, and accident insurance programs. Another major category is severance pay for early retirements or discharges. Included also may be payments for education and vocational training, for services and goods in kind, recruitment, and various types of solatia. On the whole, depending on the method of calculation, voluntary payments tend to be almost double those required by law, the ratio being noticeably higher in large enterprises than in small. Because of improvements in the laws for social and employment security and for worker savings and loans, however, there has been a tendency in recent years for the legally required contribution to gain on the voluntary payments and costs (see SOCIAL SECURITY PROGRAMS).

Compared to other major market-oriented industrialized countries, company-provided, voluntary welfare expenditures as a percentage relative to cash wages and salaries tend to be among the highest. This is due in large measure to the virtually equal treatment of white-collar and blue-collar workers in Japanese companies, whereas in most other major nations benefits to white-collar workers are much higher. On the other hand, Japan is among the lowest compared to other countries in providing welfare through legal requirements. In the combination of mandatory and nonmandatory benefits, Japan stands somewhat below the average for the industrialized world.

Future of Company Welfare—— Although the company welfare system has become firmly entrenched, since the late 1960s there has been increasing debate in Japan over whether the government should assume a greater role in providing or regulating worker welfare. This has resulted largely from the lag in development of social services as Japan focused attention primarily upon increasing production during the era of rapid economic growth in the 1950s and 1960s. Since the economic slowdown that set in after the OIL CRISIS OF 1973, there has been mounting pressure for improving the "quality of life" through government programs. Social problems have been accentuated by a rapid demographic change with increasing proportions of the population at the upper age levels, for whom social security benefit levels and employment opportunities are considered by many as inadequate. The era ahead therefore may see reduced emphasis upon company welfare and greater reliance upon the welfare state.

——Ronald P. Dore, *British Factory–Japanese Factory: The Origins of National Diversity in Industrial Relations* (1973). Robert Evans, Jr, *The Labor Economics of Japan and the United States* (1971). Walter Galenson with the collaboration of Kōnosuke Odaka, "The Japanese Labor Market," in Hugh Patrick and Henry Rosovsky, ed, *Asia's New Giant: How the Japanese Economy Works* (1976). Japan Ministry of Labor, *Rōdōsha fukushi shisetsu seido tō chōsa hōkokusho* (annual). Japan Ministry of Labor, *Rōdō hiyō chōsa hōkoku* (annual). Japan Ministry of Labor, *Chingin rōdō jikan seido sōgō chōsa hōkoku* (annual). Koike Kazuo, "Kigyō no fukurihi no kokusai hikaku," in *Shosai no mado* (August 1977). Kazuo Ōkōchi, Bernard Karsh, and Solomon B. Levine, *Workers and Employers in Japan: The Japanese Employment Relations System* (1973). Fujita Yoshitaka, *Kigyō kankyō no hembō to shakai fukushi* (1977).   Solomon B. LEVINE

Comprehensive National Land Development Plan

(Kokudo Sōgō Kaihatsu Keikaku). A national plan for regional development adopted in October 1962 in conformity with the National Land Development Law (Kokudo Sōgō Kaihatsu Hō) of 1950. The plan was prepared by the government in an attempt to alleviate urgent demographic problems besetting the country. These problems centered on the overconcentration of population and industry in certain urban areas, primarily in the Tōkyō, Ōsaka, and Nagoya regions, a well as on the underpopulation of other areas.

Toward the solution of these problems, the plan established three regional categories and indicated developmental strategies for each. For congested regions suffering from excessive concentration of population and industry, the plan called for the prevention of further concentration through the dispersal of manufacturing plants and redevelopment in other directions. For the so-called auxiliary regions surrounding congested areas, such as the Kantō region around Tōkyō, the plan called for the improvement of industrial bases through the construction of new manufacturing plants. For regions lagging behind in development, such as Hokkaidō, the plan urged the establishment of strategic centers from which development would spread. To this end, 15 zones were designated as industrial development regions. However, the Japanese economy continued to expand during the 1960s in excess of the plan's expectations, with a continuing deterioration of the environment in the large urban areas and a population loss in the rural areas. The Comprehensive National Land Development Plan was expanded in 1969 and revised further in 1972. See also POPULATION REDISTRIBUTION.

KATŌ Masashi

compulsory education

(*gimu kyōiku*). The system of compulsory education in Japan was established by the EDUCATION ORDER OF 1872 and the Elementary School Order of 1886. The orders originally prescribed a period of four years; this was extended to six years in 1907. By 1905 the rate of school attendance had reached 90 percent. Since the end of World War II, compulsory education has been provided for and regulated by article 26 of the 1947 CONSTITUTION and article 4 of the Fundamental Law of Education. The prescribed period has become nine years, including three years of middle school.

SUGIYAMA Akio

computer industry

Japan has the second-largest data-processing industry in the world after that of the United States, with large-scale mainframe computer, minicomputer, peripheral equipment, and software subsectors. The value of total production in 1981 reached ¥1.48 trillion (US $6.7 billion), up 14.4 percent over the previous year and more than triple the level of 1972. Integrated vertically with the Japanese computer industry is one of the world's fastest growing electronic components sectors, with one-quarter of world semiconductor production in 1982 and growing rapidly. In some leading-edge electronic component sectors such as 64-K random excess memories, the global market share of Japanese producers exceeded 70 percent.

State of the Industry —— Japan is the largest computer market in the world outside the United States, and accounts for about 25 percent of all computer sets installed worldwide. Calculated in value terms, however, the Japanese share of the world market is only about 12 percent, reflecting the widespread use of small-scale business computers in Japan.

Alone among non-socialist countries other than the United States, Japan has a computer industry which controls over half its domestic market—55 percent in 1980. Twenty years ago, when the market was confined to large firms and Japan lacked a vigorous policy of support for computers, this ratio was 20 percent—comparable to levels in most other advanced nations. As the Japanese market broadened to include national government organizations and medium-sized firms, and then local governments and business enterprises, IBM and other foreign makers lost their market share to Japanese computer manufacturers, which concentrated on medium- and small-size computer systems rather than confront IBM head on. This pattern of Japanese strength in smaller computers is reflected in domestic producers' near 80 percent market share in the small- and medium-size computers category, nearly double their 42.6 percent share (1978) in very large systems (i.e., those costing over ¥500 million or US $2.4 million).

The Japanese computer market is not only relatively large but also relatively less mature than the US market, thus showing more potential for future growth. In June 1978 the annual growth rates for key sectors of the Japanese computer market (expressed in value terms) were: very small computers, 22.1 percent; small, 20.1 percent; medium, 9.6 percent; large, 15.8 percent. Total sales grew 18.2 percent in fiscal 1977 (through 31 March 1978), up from 12.1 percent in the previous year. Peripheral equipment production only overtook mainframe production in Japan in 1975, four years after the same event occurred in the United States, suggesting the relative immaturity of the Japanese market.

Because of rapidly expanding exports and stagnant or declining imports, Japanese computer production is expanding significantly more rapidly than the domestic market. Total domestic production in 1981 reached ¥1.48 trillion (US $6.71 billion), and exports

amounted to ¥193.6 billion (US $877.9 million) or 13.7 percent of total production, up from 2.5 percent of a much smaller base in 1973. Most of the computer exports consisted of peripheral equipment and small business computers, except in the case of North America, where central processing units (CPUs) are a major export item. The US share of Japan's computer exports has been rising sharply, from 16 percent in 1974 to 44 percent in 1978.

Japan in 1978 still had a ¥41.3 billion (US $195.3 million) trade deficit in computers, but this was less than half the 1973 level of ¥95.2 billion (US $351 million). The growth rate of the Japanese computer industry and its rapidly improving trade balance appeared to lend credibility to 1976 projections by the INDUSTRIAL STRUCTURE COUNCIL (Sangyō Kōzō Shingikai), an advisory organ for the Ministry of International Trade and Industry (MITI), stressing the strong export potential of the computer industry and its strategic contribution to industry growth. (The council forecast a 1974–85 average annual growth in Japanese computer exports of 30.4 percent, leading to growth in industry production averaging 14.1 percent through 1985 and an export share of total production reaching 15.8 percent in 1985.)

Behind the rise in Japanese export competitiveness has been steady improvement in the technical competitiveness of Japanese computers, as well as strengthening of the industry's international marketing network. By the early 1980s the Japanese computer industry had in many respects closed the 10-year gap in hardware sophistication which had existed in relation to IBM during the 1950s, although its software remained inferior in most applications. During the September 1980–June 1981 period, for example, six of the world's eight new large-capacity computer series were introduced by Japanese manufacturers.

Possible deterrents to continued rapid Japanese computer exports include: costs of financing leasing systems abroad; weakness in Japanese software (which, by many estimates, was roughly five years behind IBM in 1979); lack of adequate sales and service networks, and of the financial strength to develop them; and possible protectionist pressures, especially in Japan's largest market, the United States. The foregoing considerations have important implications for Japanese export strategy in computers. Japanese makers concentrate on exporting partial systems—items such as disk drives and peripherals, which require neither software nor extensive services. They are also striving to establish marketing joint ventures with foreign firms (such as the NEC–Honeywell, TRW–Fujitsū, Amdahl–Fujitsū, and Siemens–Fujitsū tie-ups) to compensate for the weaknesses of their foreign service and sales networks.

Structure of the Industry —— By international standards the Japanese computer industry is quite fragmented. In 1980 it included 240 peripheral and terminal equipment makers, 50 producers of process-control minicomputers, 45 specialized makers of small business computers, and six mainframe computer manufacturers making a more or less full line of equipment. (OKI ELECTRIC INDUSTRY CO, LTD, was until 1977 also a mainframer; it quit making large capacity CPUs to concentrate on peripherals, terminals, and telephone equipment.) The mainframers receive over 80 percent of the revenue going to Japanese suppliers.

In contrast to the US and European patterns, there are virtually no specialized computer makers in Japan, and none at all with a background in business machinery. Except for FUJITSŪ, LTD, where computers and data communications equipment constituted 69 percent of total sales in 1979, there is not a single major computer maker in Japan where computers provide over 35 percent of total sales. Three of the six major producers (Fujitsū, NIPPON ELECTRIC CO, LTD [NEC], and Oki), are telecommunications firms which diversified into computers; at NEC and Oki, computers average 30 percent of total sales. The other three computer firms (HITACHI, LTD, MITSUBISHI ELECTRIC CORPORATION, and TŌSHIBA CORPORATION) are general electronics firms which diversified into computers in the early 1960s. Their computer operations average only 7.9 percent of total sales.

The unusual composition of sales at Japanese computer companies makes them extremely flexible in the corporate strategy they may pursue toward the industry's development. It also reduces the pressure they feel to aggressively push development. The problem of this relatively weak sense of immediacy stemming from industry structure is compounded by the weakness of vested interests supporting computers in the political world and business leadership. As a new industry not employing large numbers of workers, nor assuming a major presence in any locality, nor having retired executives in key positions in the business world, it has had relatively little clout with either the ruling Liberal Democratic Party or KEIDANREN (Federation of Economic Organizations). For structural reasons, then, it has thus been the bureaucracy, which has been the constant initiator of policy on computers, rather than individual firms (as in the auto industry, petrochemical industry, or steel industry) or the political world (as in the shipping industry).

Another major structural feature of the computer industry has been the central presence of IBM JAPAN, LTD. With 27.6 percent of the domestic market in 1981, it is the largest computer manufacturer in Japan after Fujitsū. Like Fujitsū, but unlike the other makers, IBM is primarily a computer manufacturer, with the organizational concern for industry development which that implies. IBM's presence in Japan is also helpful to the country's balance of payments. The firm's 1981 export sales were an estimated ¥100 billion (US $453 million), accounting for 51 percent of the country's computer export sales in that year. Another major implication of IBM's presence has been to increase the leverage of MITI vis-à-vis the domestic industry by creating a threat to that industry. The presence of Texas Instruments's components manufacturing subsidiary has played an analogous role. The ability of both firms to blend into the Japanese social context has been aided by management selection policies. Both firms have Japanese chief executive officers; the head of Texas Instruments is a former high-level MITI bureaucrat. IBM includes retired officials of MITI, the Ministry of Finance, and even the Bank of Japan on its staff, to ensure that relations with the government go smoothly.

The Role of Government—— The formal framework of relations between the Japanese computer industry and government is determined by the Special Measures Law concerning Promotion of the Specialized Machine and Information Industry (Tokutei Kikai Jōhō Sangyō Shinkō Rinji Sochi Hō) passed in 1978. This act provides for government formulation of industrial policy objectives in the computer area, a council to ensure government and industry communications, the establishment of channels for financial assistance to computer manufacturers, and the selective exemption by MITI of any portion of the computer industry from the ANTIMONOPOLY LAW. The Special Measures Law is essentially a revision of the Electronic Industry Development Provisional Law of 1957, changed slightly to take into consideration technological advances in the industry. There is a substantial extralegal dimension to business-government relations in computers, but the legal framework is important because it defines the major points of leverage, which government may use to elicit private-sector cooperation in broader spheres.

Controls over foreign imports and investments have historically been an important form of government involvement in the Japanese computer industry. In the early 1970s, however, Japan began to liberalize its restrictions on the import of computer equipment. Import duties, raised sharply during the early 1960s, were lowered beginning in 1972 and had reached 10.5 percent for mainframes and 7.5 percent for peripherals by 1979. At the MTN negotiations, further reductions were agreed upon, which will bring duties on mainframes to 4.9 percent and on peripherals to the range of 3.7–6.0 percent, by 1 January 1987. Since December 1975 mainframe computer imports have not been under quantitative restriction. Control over capital investment in the computer industry has also been formally liberalized, but the government has continued to watch market trends closely to ensure that domestic producers secure an appropriate share.

Direct government assistance to the computer industry has taken the following forms.

1. *Japan Electronic Computer Company (JECC)*. To facilitate the marketing of hardware produced by domestic firms, MITI established JECC, a government-sponsored computer-leasing company, in 1961. JECC buys and leases the computers of Japan's top six domestic makers (Fujitsū, Hitachi, NEC, Tōshiba, Oki, and Mitsubishi), purchasing over half their total production. It also sells computers returned to JECC to their original producer. JECC's loans outstanding only grew 5 percent during the five years following the first oil shock (1974–79), partly because of the disengagement of the highly liquid Hitachi from involvement with it. However, the institution remains important for cash-short, rapidly growing makers such as Fujitsū and NEC.

MITI has no direct ownership in JECC, whose ¥59.7 billion (US $282 million) capitalization is subscribed by the major private computer firms. Several of its retired officials serve in key administrative positions within JECC, however, and the government-owned Japan Development Bank, where MITI influence is strong, provided over 40 percent (roughly ¥560 billion of ¥1305 billion in 1978) of the funds lent by JECC for purchases of domestic computers.

2. *Information Technology Promotion Agency (IPA)*. Established in 1970, the IPA's function is to promote development of the software industry. It purchases software packages having a high degree of public interest, together with their accompanying copyrights, and guarantees loans for businesses involved in the development of software packages.

3. *Research and development projects*. Between April 1972 and March 1977 the government provided 50 percent of the expenses incurred by Japan's top six makers in producing mainframe and peripheral equipment competitive with IBM's 370 series computer. The total government subsidy to these companies came to $195.9 million. During 1976–80, the government also provided ¥30 billion (US $132 million) of the ¥70 billion (US $307 million) required to support the Very Large-Scale Integration (VLSI) program for developing circuitry for the next generation of computers. To develop software, peripherals and terminals to complement the new fourth-generation hardware developed under the VLSI program, MITI in April 1979 inaugurated a new five-year program of subsidies for the development of operating systems. The subsidy budget for this 1979–83 project is ¥22.3 billion (US $99 million). A ten-year (1971–80) pattern-recognition project involving MITI's Electrotechnical Laboratory and 5 mainframe makers has also received a total of ¥21.9 billion (US $83.7 million) in subsidies. This project aims at developing a new-generation system capable of inputting, recognizing, and processing pattern information such as Japanese characters, drawings, shapes of objects, and even human voices.

The character of Japanese government R&D assistance to computers has been somewhat different historically from that of the United States. US manufacturers receive aid, often in amounts more substantial than that received in Japan, as a by-product of government projects designed primarily for governmental end-use, especially in the defense and aerospace sectors. Japanese makers receive aid, often in the form of direct subsidies, for direct commercial purposes, although the amounts are relatively modest by international standards.

4. *Hardware and software incentives*. Under the terms of 1978 legislation, facilities used in the production of newly developed technologies may be depreciated in the first year by 30 percent of the initial book value of the facilities, in addition to normal depreciation. Special accelerated depreciation provisions encourage the purchase of new computer-related equipment. Since April 1979 special 20 percent first-year depreciation has been provided to users of entire systems of on-line complex equipment where computers are connected with intelligent terminals, including both hardware and software. Users are eligible for the depreciation regardless of whether the equipment is manufactured in Japan by Japanese firms, by foreign firms, or imported.

Aside from specific measures of support for computers, the general techniques of MITI support for computers are also noteworthy. Strategic technologies, such as the bubble memory in the case of the VLSI project, are constantly targeted, and singled out for special assistance, both at the development and production stages. Synergistic relationships among various elements of computer-related systems are also exploited, as in the integrated development of data-processing and telecommunications systems.

Although MITI is the main Japanese government entity concerned with computer industry development, the Ministry of Posts and Telecommunications (MPT), as well as Nippon Telephone and Telegraph (NTT), and Kokusai Denshin Denwa (KDD) also have a significant relationship to the industry. The MPT approves the entry of private firms into the teleprocessing and time-sharing business, and NTT and KDD are the common carriers for domestic and international telecommunications respectively. NTT also coordinates computer R&D projects related to teleprocessing and time-sharing; both NTT and KDD have played an important role in optical-fiber development. Since these institutions, which have little involvement in international affairs, have generally been more protectionist than MITI, and independent of it, their involvement in the administration of computer policy has often complicated access by foreign firms to Japanese computer markets.

History—— Although Ōsaka University launched Japan's first computer development program in 1947, the nation's first electronic digital computer was not constructed until 1956, 10 years after Sperry Rand developed the first electronic computer in the United States. Following the first exports of American computers to Japan in 1954, MITI organized a Research Committee on the Computer to coordinate computer industry development. But the committee's initial 1955 budget was only ¥675,000 (US $1,875). Computers did not attain urgent priority in Japanese industrial policy until the mid-1960s.

The major role of foreign-affiliated firms in the Japanese computer industry dates from 1960. In that year IBM, after an extremely lengthy negotiation, was granted permission to manufacture computers in Japan, as well as foreign exchange remittance guarantees, in return for licensing basic patents to all interested Japanese manufacturers. Thirteen Japanese firms immediately entered cross-licensing agreements with IBM. In 1963 Sperry Rand also made arrangements to manufacture in Japan through a 51–49 Japanese-controlled joint-venture arrangement with Oki Electric. Between 1961 and 1964 RCA, TRW, Honeywell, and GE, in addition to IBM and Sperry, all entered technical assistance agreements with Japanese makers.

The Japanese government's vigorous promotion of the computer industry dates from 1964, although the legal framework for bureaucratic guidance had been established seven years previously. In 1964 IBM introduced its system 360, the third generation of computers, an event which graphically demonstrated to the Japanese political and business worlds the strategic potential of computers. The IBM system 360 was particularly visible because it was utilized at the Tōkyō Olympic Games in October and introduced nationwide into a number of major banks. Also in 1964, GE purchased the largest French computer manufacturer, Machines Bull, demonstrating the inability of Europe to sustain an independent computer industry in the face of American competition. Japan, with its computer production of less than $100 million, distributed among seven small domestic firms plus IBM, looked equally vulnerable.

In Japan these two events galvanized a consensus within the ruling Liberal Democratic Party and the Keidanren in favor of accelerated development of domestic technology, especially large-system software, and rectification of the industry's small scale and fragmentation, through either formal consolidation of producers or increased joint activity and formal organization of the market. Computers had become, by general recognition, a strategic industry, whose fate held profound implications for Japan's economic future.

In the light of the new consensus, MITI's Heavy Industry Bureau stimulated preparation of the Electronics Industry Deliberation Council Report of 1966, often called the most important document in the industry's history. It stressed the importance of independent technical excellence, increased market share within Japan for domestic producers, and a gradual rise in profitability of domestic producers. To attain these goals, it proposed a joint government–private sector project to build a large new computer, strengthening of JECC, rationalizing production of peripheral equipment, and accelerated training of systems analysts. Virtually all the programs proposed were implemented. Epitomizing the new priority given to computers, government R&D subsidies by 1967 were four times 1960 levels, and Japan Development Bank loans to JECC were five times the levels of only four years before.

The 1970s were a period of enhanced cooperative relationships in the computer industry, stimulated by the dictates of technological development in the face of foreign competition. In 1971, under MITI aegis, the six mainframe makers organized three specialized R&D groups to develop computers capable of competing with IBM's 370 series. Four years later, an additional two groups were formed, to develop a new generation of computers utilizing VLSI technology by 1980. These cooperative research ventures, together with others in software, and production cartels in the peripheral equipment field, were intended to offset the effect of fragmented industry structure on competitive performance vis-à-vis foreign firms.

The 1970s also witnessed substantial redefinition of the Japanese computer industry's relationships to the world outside Japan, as both production processes and markets became increasingly internationalized. By 1975 all quantitative restrictions on imports of foreign computers into Japan had been liberalized, as well as restrictions on foreign capital investment in Japanese firms. The MTN negotiations also sharply slashed tariffs on computer imports into Japan. These actions created prospects for expanded exports and capital flow to Japan, provided issues of market access and administrative procedure could be resolved. By the early 1980s several foreign makers were taking advantage of these changes to set up marketing and production operations in Japan. Japanese makers were also assembling computers and producing components in the United States, Ireland, Spain, and elsewhere.

Rising Japanese international competitiveness in computers created the need for marketing tieups with foreign firms, oriented toward selling Japanese computers abroad, which could supplement the technical tieups that evolved during the 1960s. Fujitsū has since the early 1970s been selling large- and medium-scale computers in the United States and Canada through a joint venture (29 percent Fujitsū equity) with Amdahl, with the scope of cooperation broadened in 1976 to include Europe; in late 1978 Fujitsū also arranged an international marketing agreement with Siemens, and has subsequently concluded major marketing and service agreements with TRW. NEC supplies machines and components to Honeywell Information Systems (HIS) outside the United States, and Hitachi has, since 1977, been linked worldwide with Itel. See also COMPUTER TECHNOLOGY.

📖——*Japan Fact Book: Guide to Japan's Electronics Manufacturers and Industry* (annual). Japan Information Processing Center, *The Computer White Paper* (annual). Eugene J. Kaplan, *Japan: The Government-Business Relationship* (1972). Kimizuka Yoshirō, *Compyūtā gyōkai* (1979). Minamisawa Noburō, *Nihon compyūtā hattatsu shi* (1978). Nihon Denshi Keisanki Kabushiki Kaisha, *Compyūtā nōto* (annual). Nihon Jōhō Shori Kaihatsu Kyōkai, *Compyūtā hakusho* (annual). Nippon Yunibakku Kōhō Shitsu, *Compyūtā kanren shiryō* (annual). Tsūshō Sangyō Shō Kikai Jōhō Sangyō Kyoku, ed, *Sofutouea gyō no genjō to tembō* (1979).   Kent E. CALDER

computer technology

The computer industry was established in Japan 10 years later than in the United States. There are only two examples of the prototype manufacture of the vacuum tube computer in Japan. Okazaki Bunji of Fuji Photo Film Co designed and completed the first in 1956, which was used in lens design. The Okazaki computer, which was the first computer manufactured for practical use in Japan, is preserved in the National Science Museum. The other vacuum tube computer, called TAC, was assembled on a trial basis by Tōkyō University with the assistance of the TOSHIBA CORPORATION between 1951 and 1959.

Since it was a decade behind its American counterpart, the Japanese computer industry did not spend time in the development of vacuum tube computers and instead concentrated on the manufacture of both transistor and parametron computers. In the early stages of the transistor computer's development, the ELECTROTECHNICAL LABORATORY (ETL) of the MINISTRY OF INTERNATIONAL TRADE AND INDUSTRY (MITI) was an important influence. ETL completed the first relay computer, the ETL MARK-I, in 1952. Its design was based on the theories of Gotō Mochinori, a director of ETL, and the Nakajima-Hanazawa theory, which created a new design principle for relay circuits through the application of Boolean algebra.

In March 1954, a unique logical element, called the parametron, was invented by Gotō Eiichi, a graduate student at Tōkyō University. The parametron is a kind of resonance circuit that consists of ferrite cores, coils, and a capacitor and operates according to the principle of parametric excitation. It had amplification, memory, and logical functions. The price of the element was low and its action was quite stable. The development of the parametron computer was accomplished through the cooperation of Tōkyō University, the Electrical Communication Laboratory (ECL) of the NIPPON TELEGRAPH AND TELEPHONE PUBLIC CORPORATION (NTT), and the laboratory of the KOKUSAI DENSHIN DENWA CO, LTD (KDD).

The ETL MARK-II, an improved version of MARK-I, was completed in 1955. In developing transistor computers, ETL completed a point contact transistor computer, ETL MARK-III, in 1956, which was followed by a junction transistor computer, ETL MARK-IV, in 1957. Several major electronics companies entered into the development and manufacture of commercial transistor computers under ETL's guidance, using MARK-IV technology. This is regarded as the real beginning of the Japanese computer industry.

The model NEAC 2201 of NIPPON ELECTRIC CO, LTD (NEC), one of the first transistor computers developed, was shown in 1959 at the exhibition of the First International Information Processing Conference (AUTOMAS) in Paris, gaining attention as the world's first public demonstration of a transistor computer.

In March 1958 the first prototype parametron computer, the MUSASHINO-1, with a memory capacity of 256 words, was completed by the ECL. Utilizing the MUSASHINO-1 as a model, several major electronics firms started to develop and manufacture a commercial version of the parametron computer under the guidance of Tōkyō University, ECL, and KDD. HITACHI, LTD, manufactured the HIPAC 101; NEC, the NEAC 1101; FUJITSŪ, LTD, the FACOM 202; OKI ELECTRIC INDUSTRY CO, LTD, the OPC-1, among others. Hitachi's HIPAC 101 was successfully demonstrated at the AUTOMAS exhibition in Paris.

The parametron computer, the first commercial computer produced in Japan, was noted for its stable performance and ease of handling. Its advanced design made a significant contribution to the Japanese computer industry, but the parametron computer was on the market for only a few years. Because of such drawbacks as its slow operating speed and high power consumption, it was replaced by the transistor computer. However, some parametron computers manufactured in the 1950s were still in use in the early 1980s.

Relations with IBM —— IBM has maintained a position of technological superiority in the Japanese computer industry into the early 1980s. Accordingly, all Japanese companies wishing to manufacture computers and related equipment used IBM's basic patents. Fifteen related companies in Japan, including six mainframe makers, concluded a basic patent license agreement with IBM in December 1960. The contract, which is renewable every five years, was still valid in the 1980s.

Technical licenses are not included in the IBM patent license agreement. The Japanese mainframe manufacturers saw that a great gap existed between them and US companies in such matters as design and manufacture of hardware, development of software technology, and marketing. From 1961 to 1964 five mainframe companies concluded technical license agreements with several US mainframe manufacturers. Hitachi entered into a contract with RCA in May 1961. The initial product was the HITAC 3010, which corresponded to the RCA 301. The contract was continued until September 1971, when RCA withdrew from mainframe computer manufacturing. MITSUBISHI ELECTRIC CORPORATION entered into a contract with TRW in February 1962. The initial product was the MELCOM 1530, which corresponded to the TRW 530. The computer division of TRW was acquired by Bunker Ramo and then by General Electric (GE). NEC entered into a contract with Honeywell Information Systems, Inc (HIS), in July 1962. The initial product was the NEAC 2200, which corresponded to Honeywell's H200. HIS acquired GE's computer division in April 1970; GE's computer technology was included in the sale and became part of the contract between HIS and NEC. The technology transfer license with HIS was discontinued at the end of 1979. Oki Electric established a joint venture, Oki–Univac Co, in cooperation with Sperry Rand Corp in September 1963. The initial products were the OUK 1004 and 1050, which corresponded to the UNIVAC 1004 and 1050. This joint venture company was still operating in the 1980s. Tōshiba concluded a contract with GE in October 1964. The initial product was the TOSBAC 5400, which corresponded to the GE 400.

As a result of the acquisition of the GE computer business by HIS in 1970, the contract between Tōshiba and GE was combined into the contract between NEC and HIS, prompting new cooperation between NEC and Tōshiba. In all the above cases, the initial products manufactured by these licensed companies were almost the same as the American models, although the Japanese firms rapidly added their own technologies.

National Projects Guided by MITI —— To achieve rapid advancement in domestic computer technologies, several priority projects were undertaken nationally through MITI's leadership. MITI provided a limited subsidy for each project, and the remaining expenses for the projects were borne by the participating industries. All of these projects achieved a good degree of success.

The FONTAC project, aimed at strengthening the development of computers to reduce the technological gap relative to the US, was undertaken from 1962 to 1964 by Fujitsū, Oki Electric, and NEC. (The acronym is derived from the initial letters of the names of these companies.) This was the first prototype manufacturing project of a general purpose large-scale computer system in Japan. The performance target was 3 microseconds (μsec) or less for adding speed and 20 kilowords or more for memory capacity.

Another project aimed at prototype manufacture of a super-high-performance computer system was undertaken from 1966 to 1972. Later in the 1970s the project was expanded to develop a system capable of outperforming the IBM 360. ETL was in charge of the basic design of the system and eight manufacturers, including Hitachi, NEC, and Fujitsu, participated in the project. The project developed such technologies as LSI (large scale integration) manufacturing, a large-capacity memory file for a maximum of two million words, a time-sharing system, and improved software. By the early 1980s the project had expanded beyond its initial target area into several allied areas.

The research and development for the pattern information processing system was undertaken from 1971 to 1980. The project aimed at developing a modern system that could directly input, recognize, and process pattern information, such as characters, figures, substances, and voices. The project consisted of basic research and development of devices and materials: trial manufacturing and evaluation of pilot models of recognition equipment for characters, figures, substances, and voices; and trial manufacturing and testing of the whole system. Nine manufacturers, including NEC, Fujitsū, Hitachi, and Tōshiba, participated in the project.

The VLSI (very large scale integration) research and development project was undertaken from 1976 to 1979. It attempted to realize the development of the next generation's computer system, which is expected to be able to emulate IBM's so-called Future System. VLSI technology is regarded as the most important key to those new systems. The major targets of the project were development of a very fine processing technique for an order of 1 to 0.1 micron and establishment of manufacturing technologies for logic and memory devices for the next generation utilizing the above-mentioned technique.

The five participating companies, NEC, Tōshiba, Fujitsū, Hitachi, and Mitsubishi Electric, jointly organized the VLSI Technology Research Association and established three laboratories: the cooperative laboratory, responsible for research on basic technologies; NTIS laboratory, jointly organized by NEC and Tōshiba; and CDL laboratory, jointly organized by Fujitsū, Hitachi, and Mitsubishi Electric. The NTIS and CDL laboratories are responsible for development of applied technologies.

The ETL has offered cooperation and guidance in the project. NTT has already started a similar VLSI research and development project for future telecommunication systems in cooperation with NEC, Hitachi, and Fujitsū.

The research and development of the fourth generation of computers, which took place from 1979 into the early 1980s, made significant progress in software architecture and in high-speed logistics crucial to high-capacity memories. Plans for the next generation of computer technology center on creating humanlike machines of higher intelligence through improved software. In the forefront of this research is the Computer System Basic Technology Research Association formed by eight computer manufacturers (Oki Electric, SHARP CORPORATION, MATSUSHITA ELECTRIC INDUSTRIAL CO, LTD, and the five companies that participated in the VLSI project).

Background of the Japanese Mainframe Makers —— There are notable differences in background between the six mainframe manufacturers in Japan and those in the US. Of these six companies none specializes in business machinery production, as many American computer companies do. NEC, Fujitsū, and Oki Electric are the three biggest manufacturers of telecommunications equipment in Japan. Hitachi, Tōshiba, and Mitsubishi Electric are the three biggest manufacturers of general electrical and electronics equipment in Japan. All six companies have divisions for the development and manufacture of semiconductor devices and integrated circuits, and they rank among the world's top producers.

These companies are also the six major suppliers for NTT, which has a monopoly on public telecommunications under the Law of Public Telecommunications.

Since almost all of the telephone networks were destroyed during World War II, NTT executed successive 5-year construction programs over a 25-year period with many productive technological research and development projects undertaken by ECL. Many manufacturers offered to participate in NTT's construction programs during these years. Through joint activities they made significant technological advances in the research, development, and manufacture of telecommunications equipment, electronic devices, components, and materials. These cooperating manufacturers are now mainframe computer makers. In 1970 NTT started such data processing services as sales and inventory management, and science and technical computing for nonspecified general subscribers. Then NTT proceeded to develop a large-scale computer, DIPS, which was to be used for expansion of these services under joint cooperation with Hitachi, NEC, and Fujitsū. In December 1973 the first model, DIPS-I, was completed and put into commercial use, soon to be followed by an improved model, DIPS-II.

Toward Computers and Communications —— The Japanese computer industry is placing a strong emphasis on telecommunications in its plans for future development. Computer and communication technologies will doubtless come closer together in the future. Kobayashi Kōji, chairman and chief executive officer of NEC, emphasized this concept of computer and communication (C&C) in a keynote speech presented at the third US–Japan computer conference in San Francisco in October 1978 (see figure). In the speech he

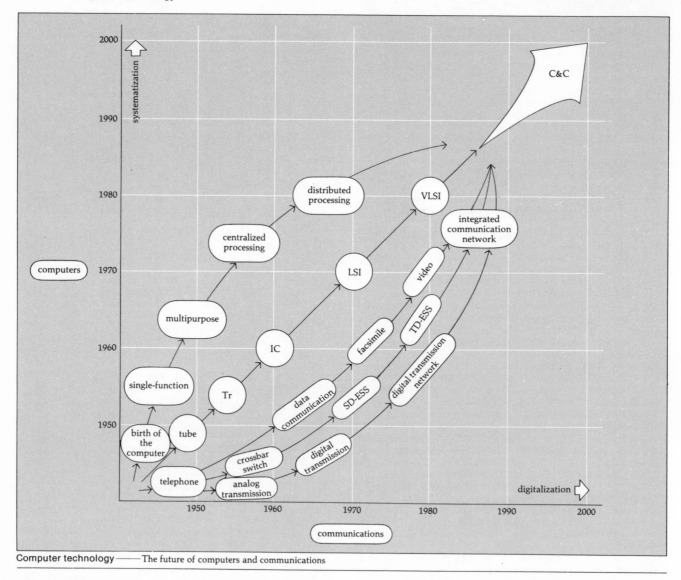

Computer technology ———The future of computers and communications

predicted that the technical progress of transistors and integrated circuits will play an important role in the development of the computer and communication industries. As computer technology progresses toward systematization, and communication technology toward digitization, there will be a mutual exchange of technologies, and a higher-level single C&C system will be formed at some time in the future.

As the figure shows, there has been progress in semiconductor-device technology, where there have been advances from discrete transistor to integrated circuits, LSI, and VLSI. Both computer and communication technologies are advancing with this as their basic technology. All mainframe manufacturers in Japan have their own powerful semiconductor divisions. They can thus develop and produce the necessary semiconductor devices themselves, having already achieved stronger technological ability by participating in the VLSI national project.

Trends in computer technology are indicated in the upper line of the figure, starting from a single-function system to a multi-function system. From about 1965 there has been production of such family-series systems as NEC's NEAC 2000, Fujitsū's FACOM 230, Hitachi's HITAC 8000, Tōshiba's TOSBAC 5000, Mitsubishi Electric's 3100, and Oki–Univac's OKU 9000.

In centralized processing by a large computer, however, there is deterioration in flexibility, reliability, and maintainability because of the enlarged scale of the hardware and the growing sophistication of the software. One solution for these problems is the development of a distributed processing system or a system network architecture that would introduce communication technology to the computer system. In 1976 and 1977 the mainframe manufacturers in Japan developed their own respective distributed processing systems.

Even though NTT was not a manufacturer, it developed its own system, called DCNA (Data Communication Network Architecture), with the cooperation of NEC, Hitachi, Fujitsū, and Oki Electric.

In 1971 the Law of Public Telecommunications was revised and the public telephone network of NTT partially opened to the public, an indication of the increased progress in the merging of computer technology with communication technology.

Trends in communication technology, as indicated in the lower section of the figure, are divided into three areas: terminal equipment, switching systems, and transmission systems. For many years the telephone set had been the most common terminal equipment. Initially the input voice was of the analog type, but as systems were improved digital data signals were introduced. These have become increasingly important, especially for integration into transmission networks. Switching systems have also developed correspondingly. For many years, step-by-step and cross-bar switching systems were common in Japan. Then the stored-program type was developed in successive stages. The first stage was the space-division electronic switching system (SD-ESS), so called because electromagnetic relays were used as its voice channel. In the late 1970s time-division ESS (or TD-ESS) progressed rapidly through the digitization of input signals. In the third area, the transmission system has progressed from data communication to fascimile and later to video signals.

Similar progress has been made in cable carrier communication and microwave communication systems. In both, the amplitude modulation or frequency modulation of analog signals has already been in use for a long time. Pulse-code modulation has been introduced, and its digitization is also rapidly expanding.

The three systems—terminal equipment, switching, and transmission—have been progressing toward systematization and digitization through different processes. To avoid technical discrepancies, NTT has initiated the Integrated Communication Network System (ICNS) to totally integrate all digital technology into a single unique system. Among the functions to be incorporated into the ICNS are switching systems; carrier transmission systems, including telephone lines, telephones, microwaves, and satellites; data information; telephone and pattern (TV or video) information; and other forms of computer signal information. Completion of this integrated system, in which manufacturers of computer mainframes, major terminals, and peripherals are working in conjunction with NTT, may not be completed until the mid-1990s.　　　　　TAKEDA Yukimatsu

conciliation

(chōtei). A procedure in Japanese law by which the parties to a civil dispute resolve their differences through mutual agreement before a conciliation committee established by the court. If conciliation is effected, the substance of the agreement as set forth in the written record has the same validity as a final judgment by a court. There are two types of conciliation of civil disputes: civil conciliation and family affairs conciliation. Civil conciliation is optional, but a suit or trial of a family affairs case cannot begin until conciliation measures have been exhausted.

A conciliation committee is composed of a judge and two private citizens. In practice, the private citizens are the principal members of the committee, and they are expected to bring a sound grasp of common sense and legal values to bear on their conciliation proposals. The civilian members are appointed by the Supreme Court. All committee members receive remuneration from the state. In general the procedures are simpler and less costly than litigation. See DISPUTE RESOLUTION SYSTEMS OTHER THAN LITIGATION.

　　　　　　　　　　　　　　　　KOJIMA Takeshi

In labor law, conciliation is called assen and is conducted by conciliators appointed by LABOR RELATIONS COMMISSIONS. Assen (sometimes translated as "good offices") is the least formal of three LABOR DISPUTE RESOLUTION PROCEDURES. The next level is chōtei (translated as "conciliation" above but usually called "mediation" in Western labor law), which is more formal and involves the development of settlement proposals by the mediation committee. The third level is arbitration (chūsai), which produces a binding decision; it is commenced only with the consent of both parties.

　　　　　　　　　　　　　　　　John JUNKERMAN

Concordia Society

(Kyōwakai). An organization for mass political mobilization in Manchuria after its occupation by the Japanese GUANDONG (KWANTUNG) ARMY in the MANCHURIAN INCIDENT of September 1931. Founded by Japanese civilian residents of Manchuria, or MANCHUKUO, as the puppet state created by the Guandong Army was called, the association endeavored to gather support among the other resident ethnic groups for a permanent Japanese presence there by espousing pan-Asian doctrines of racial harmony (minzoku kyōwa).

Although the Kyōwakai was originally intended by its founders to be a single mass political party by which Manchukuo would be governed after separation from China, it never achieved this status. It was preempted as an administrative organ by a regular Manchukuo government structure, containing hundreds of Japanese bureaucrats freshly arrived from the homeland, that conformed closely to guidelines set by the Guandong Army staff. Thus the principal functions of the Kyōwakai were confined in practice to counterinsurgency pacification in partnership with the Guandong Army and to providing cadres for the creation of grass-roots organizations that gave political and economic support to the regular Manchukuo regime.

The genesis of the Kyōwakai can be traced principally to the Manshū Seinen Remmei (Manchurian Youth League), founded in November 1928 by SOUTH MANCHURIA RAILWAY Company employees. The Manshū Seinen Remmei pursued agitation and lobbying efforts to alert Japanese to the dangers of the rising movement in China to recover full sovereignty in Manchuria. Colonel ISHIWARA KANJI's budding pan-Asian political notions were encouraged by his contact with this group, which advocated an independent Manchuria based on interethnic cooperation. Colonels Ishiwara and ITAGAKI SEISHIRŌ recruited members as civilian auxiliaries to create local self-governing bodies in the areas seized by the Guandong Army.

In April 1932 members of the Manshū Seinen Remmei joined with members of various Manchurian farmers' and businessmen's

associations, together numbering about 2,600, to form the Kyōwatō (Concordia Party). In July 1932 this was reorganized as the Kyōwakai in deference to the antiparty feelings expressed by powerful figures in the Japanese military and bureaucracy. From 1937 to 1945 the Kyōwakai became virtually an arm of the Manchukuo government, launching many social, economic, and political mobilization programs. The association expanded to reach 3.5 million members before the end of the war. The khaki uniform worn by members of the Kyōwakai was later adopted in the Japanese homeland as the wartime civilian uniform.

■──Hirano Ken'ichirō, "Manshūkoku Kyōwakai no seijiteki tenkai," Nihon seijigaku nempō (1972). Manshūkoku Shi Hensan Kankōkai, ed, Manshūkoku shi (1970). Yamaguchi Jūji, Manshū kenkoku no rekishi: Manshūkoku kyōwakai shi (1973).

　　　　　　　　　　　　　　　　David G. EGLER

Conder, Josiah (1852–1920)

British architect, urban planner, and teacher. Conder was the leading foreign designer of public and private buildings in late-19th-century Japan; to him more than any other individual may be attributed the progressive, eclectic appearance of Meiji period (1868–1912) Tōkyō. Whatever its inspiration—Gothic, Renaissance, Tudor, or Moorish—this architecture was characteristically red brick with white stone trim.

As a government-employed professor of architecture, from 1877 to 1888, and later through his own firm, Conder gave the Japanese their first and most extensive training in Western architecture. His pupils, including TATSUNO KINGO, Sone Tatsuzō (1853–1937), and Katayama Otokuma (1854–1917), formed the first generation of Western-style architects and laid the foundation for Japan's 20th-century architectural achievement.

Born in London and a graduate of the Royal British Institute of Architects where he was a pupil of William Burges, Conder came to Japan in 1877 at age 25. He served concurrently as professor of architecture at the government's Kōbu Daigakkō (later Tōkyō University) and as consultant for the Ministry of Engineering. Even after leaving service in 1888, he continued to advise the government and was awarded several imperial decorations.

Between 1878 and 1907 Conder designed over 50 major Western buildings in Tōkyō that served both as practical models and symbols of the Westernizing Meiji state. They include the Tōkyō Imperial Museum (1881), the ROKUMEIKAN pleasure palace (1883), and the Navy Ministry building (1895). He also designed and executed residences for prominent Meiji officials and sumptuous mansions for the Mitsubishi Company's Iwasaki family.

Conder's buildings were often part of his urban development plans, either government ordered, as in the case of the Hibiya government offices, or ordered by big business, as in Mitsubishi's build-up of the Marunouchi area of Tōkyō (1892–1905), Japan's first large-scale private development.

An early contributor to Western understanding of Japan, Conder published a number of books, including Landscape Gardening in Japan (1893). Among his surviving Tōkyō buildings are Nikolai Cathedral (1891), Prince Shimazu House (1915), and two Iwasaki mansions (1896 and 1908). The Mitsubishi office buildings in Marunouchi were completely demolished in the 1960s.　　Dallas FINN

condolence gifts

(kōden; literally, "incense money"). Monetary or material gift given to the family of a deceased person. Today, kōden is almost invariably in the form of money, which is used to defray part of the cost of the funeral, including the banquet, and to purchase return gifts (kōdengaeshi) which are about one-half to one-third the value of the kōden and are distributed after the funeral. Some families have done away with the custom of distributing return gifts and instead donate an equivalent amount of money to a charitable cause, announcing this by mail or by a notice in the newspaper.

For kōden, as for all other money gifts, crisp, clean paper money is placed in a special envelope designed for this purpose. The envelope is tied with a decorative string (MIZUHIKI) dyed one-half of its length in white and the other half in black, gray, or yellow—color combinations that symbolize mourning. A less expensive envelope has the mizuhiki imprinted on it. It is customary to write the amount enclosed on the back.

In the past, and until very recently in rural Japan, such staples as rice and soy sauce were common condolence gifts given by close relatives and fellow villagers, and these were cooked for meals served at the banquet after a funeral.

When death occurs in a family from which one has received *kōden* in the past, the receiver is morally obliged to reciprocate by giving *kōden* of the same amount to that family. 　*Harumi* BEFU

confections

Japanese confections *(wagashi)* were developed to be enjoyed with green tea, which has a somewhat astringent taste. They are made entirely of natural ingredients such as fruit, nuts, seeds, beans, and grains.

One of the principal ingredients in Japanese confections is *an* (sweet bean paste), which is made of boiled, blanched red adzuki beans or white bush beans which have been heated and mashed to a paste with sugar and a small amount of water. In addition to various kinds of bean paste and bean flours, grains are also used, especially wheat flour and rice in the form of granules or flour.

In Japanese confections, neither dairy products nor vegetable oils are used. Instead, sparing use is made of such ingredients as walnuts, peanuts, or sesame seeds, which have their own natural oil. Artificial flavoring agents are not added, and even natural flavorings with strong aromas are avoided. Ingredients such as *yuzu* (citron), *shiso* (beefsteak plant; *Perilla frutescens crispa*), poppy seeds, and sesame seeds are favored for their mild aromas.

Designs are based on natural forms and motifs associated with the four seasons. Flowers, plants, trees, birds, the moon, snow, water—all elements from nature—are represented in stylized shapes and designs and in colors to please the eye. The custom of enjoying these small confections and becoming aware of the beauty of nature was influenced and encouraged by the spirit of the TEA CEREMONY.

Mizuame, a thick sweet syrup made from rice or millet, is thought to have been produced in prehistoric times. Gradually it was replaced with sugar, which was initially imported from China. In the 7th century, 8 different kinds of confections and 14 varieties of *kapei* (processed foods made from wheat or rice flour) were imported from China. A number of them are still eaten today: *mochi,* hot steamed rice which is pounded into a doughlike cake; *dango,* small balls of *mochi* on bamboo skewers, four or five to a stick; *kashiwa mochi, mochi* filled with bean paste, steamed, then wrapped in a folded oak leaf and eaten on 5 May, Children's Day; and *sembei, mochi* which is rolled into thin sheets, cut into circular shapes, flavored with soy sauce, and roasted on both sides.

Green tea, also imported from China, was introduced to Japan during the 7th century. Eventually the tea ceremony was developed, reaching a high point in the 15th century. At the same time, confections were created to enhance the taste of the green tea. A number of representative Japanese confections eaten today were devised during the 15th century: *yōkan,* a jellylike confection made by cooking agar-agar and bean paste, pouring it into a rectangular box, and chilling it until firm; *manjū,* a round cake made from bean paste enclosed in leavened wheat dough and steamed until it rises; *rakugan,* a confection made from rice or bean flour mixed with sugar, and pressed into carved wooden molds of various shapes; and *zenzai,* a bean jam made by stewing adzuki beans with sugar, to which pieces of *mochi* are added.

In the 16th century, with the beginning of trade with European countries such as Portugal and Spain, confections from these countries were brought to Japan. The following items, with names reminiscent of southern Europe, are enjoyed by the Japanese today: *pan* (bread, from Portuguese *pão*), *bisuketto* (biscuits or crackers, from Portuguese *biscauto*), *aruheitō* (taffy, from Portuguese *alfeloa*), *kompeitō* (sugar candy, from Portuguese *confeito*), *kasutera* (sponge cake, from the Portuguese pronunciation of the Spanish place name Castilla), and *karumera* (caramel, from Portuguese *caramelo*).

When contact with foreign countries was suspended during the Edo period (1600–1868), many of these imported confections were integrated with traditional Japanese forms and made into uniquely Japanese confections; the technique of making such confections reached an artistic level.

During the Meiji period (1868–1912), European and American confections were imported. In 1875 the Japanese were making a cookie-like confection in Tōkyō, and in 1878 they brought in machinery from the United States to make crackers and hard candies, going into large-scale production.

After the end of World War II in 1945, eating habits became Westernized and European and American confections became popular. Both the manufacture and sales of these confections developed rapidly in the 1960s. By the end of the 1970s, Western-style confec-

tions such as chocolates, cakes, and candy accounted for 70 percent of Japanese production, while traditional Japanese varieties accounted for 30 percent. 　*KANEKO Yoshimasa*

confession

(jihaku). In criminal cases in Japan, confession, as the statement of a person with first-hand experience of a crime, has been traditionally treated as an important form of evidence. The use of torture was permitted to obtain confessions up to the early part of the Meiji period (1868–1912) because the defendant could not be found guilty without a confession. With the establishment of a modern legal system, confessions came to be treated equally with other forms of evidence. Nonetheless, in practice, the former sense of the necessity of a confession was not entirely eradicated, and easy fact-finding through confession was hard to avoid. After World War II, strict evidentiary controls were imposed through the new constitution and Penal Code.

When a confession has been obtained by force, torture, or intimidation, or after an unduly long period of detention, in sum, if there is any doubt as to its voluntary nature, it is not admissible as evidence. This rule has been adopted in order to prevent findings from being based on false confessions, to protect the defendant's human rights, and thus to ensure proper interrogation procedures. Under the Case Law, confessions made in reliance on a promise not to prosecute, or obtained during an investigation conducted while the defendant was still in manacles, or elicited after the defendant was deceived into believing that his accomplice had confessed are all inadmissible as evidence. Moreover, where a confession is the only incriminatory evidence against the defendant, a verdict of guilty cannot be made. Other corroborative evidence is necessary. In investigation and trial, other forms of evidence are given priority over confessions in order to avoid a mistrial in the event reliance on the confession proves to have been unwarranted. Therefore, whether a confession has been made extra-judicially or in court, the rule of corroboration is applicable.

Confession in civil cases consists of the acknowledgment of the truth of assertions by the accuser which are unfavorable to the accused. Since the Code of Civil Procedure adopts the adversary system, findings based on evidence are unnecessary if a judicial confession is obtained, and the court must take the confession as the basis for its decision. Once a confession is made, it cannot be withdrawn, and it binds the confessing party on appeal as well. Where a party does not clearly dispute his opponent's allegations, he is deemed to have made a "constructive confession." Testimony by a party acknowledging an opponent's allegations operates as a waiver or admission of the cause of action, thus terminating the litigation, and should be distinguished from both evidence and confession.

　TAMIYA Hiroshi

conflict resolution

Conflict resolution is usually translated into Japanese as *funsō shūketsu* (conflict termination) or *funsō kaiketsu* (conflict settlement), although *funsō shori* (conflict management) may be preferred, since in Japan conflict is usually channeled and controlled rather than actually eliminated. Although conflict is ubiquitous in Japan, as elsewhere, sensitivity to it and well-developed techniques of conflict management sometimes make it a less obvious phenomenon than in some other societies.

Marxist arguments that social conflicts arise internally from conflicts of interest over the possession of the means of economic production or over authority, as Ralf Dahrendorf has theorized, do not in themselves provide a guide to the frequency or severity of overt conflict in Japan. It is not uncommon for individuals with deeply conflicting interests to be bound together in intimate, emotionally charged social relationships in which conflict is carefully avoided or obscured. Conversely, persons with fewer apparent conflicts of interest may engage in bitter, nearly uncontrollable conflict. Internal sources of conflict in Japan can best be understood as the interaction between conflicts of interest and the institutions that have been developed to manage or control them.

Types of Conflict—— *Vertical conflict.* Japanese society has relatively strong vertical integration and relatively weak horizontal integration (see VERTICAL SOCIETY). Hierarchical relations between subordinates and superordinates tend to be interdependent and close, while relations between equals tend to be competitive and distrustful. Although the mutual interdependence of subordinate and superordinate obscures conflicts of interest between them, it gives rise to a different type of conflict when a failure of mutual trust occurs. Such conflicts become especially sharp and painful because the emotional sense of betrayal and broken harmony is combined with a new awareness of the previously obscured conflict of interest. Status conflicts in which such status inferiors as BURAKUMIN (a former class of social outcasts) women, or students seek to alter their subordinate relationships are an important form of conflict emerging in contemporary Japan.

Factional conflict. Conflicts between relatively equal parties are exacerbated by the generally weaker horizontal integration of Japanese society, whether they occur within groups or between groups. Those within groups are far more complex and troublesome, however. Virtually all group activity requires the cooperation of persons who are related horizontally as fellow group members, rather than vertically in an acknowledged authority relationship. Most Japanese groups try to strengthen the horizontal integration among members by emphasizing each member's interest in the group as a whole, and requiring consensus for group action. This system is effective to the extent that it engages each member's efforts toward the prevention or avoidance of conflict. If a dispute arises despite these efforts, there are neither rules nor structures to surmount the failure of consensus. The group quickly divides into factions on the basis of pre-existing relationships that tend in turn to be based on the stronger vertical alliances (see BATSU). Some factional conflicts are resolved by the destruction of the original group, while others continue indefinitely as internal struggles. Factional conflicts are the most bitter and intractable of all conflicts in Japan. They involve some of the sense of betrayal that is experienced in status conflict, in this case, the feeling that the interest of the group as a whole, and oneself as a member, has been violated by the opposing faction. Factional conflicts organize opposing groups on the basis of vertical relationships, the strongest social ties, leaving only horizontal relationships, the weakest ties, as the basis for reconciliation.

Conflict between groups. Conflict between horizontally equal but unrelated groups is the most acceptable form of conflict in Japan, since it involves only the weakest social ties and does not violate important emotional commitments. Such intergroup conflict is often encouraged as a way of reducing internal group conflict. It is easily channeled into fierce but impersonal competition for an external prize, as when sports teams or companies compete. Common interests among parallel but unrelated groups often lead to the mutual acknowledgment and observance of territorial boundaries, market shares, rank orders, or other forms of prize division. These agreements are tenuous and unenforceable; when circumstances change, they are quickly trampled in the heat of renewed competition. When conflict between two apparently unrelated groups is unusually intense, there often turns out to be some historical connection between the two groups; conversely, when independent organizations coalesce as factions in a new group, their disputes tend to have the cooler emotional tone of conflicts between unrelated groups.

Individual versus group. A final characteristic form of conflict in Japanese society is that between individual and group. The mutuality of vertical relations and the efforts expended on group interests ensure that some part of each individual's needs are met, but there are inevitably times when people are obliged to act against their own interests in the service of others. On such occasions, the same elements that normally meet individual needs, the strength of vertical relations and the emphasis on overriding group interests, make it particularly difficult for individuals to assert their personal interests. The conflict is exacerbated by the norms of group participation and consensus, which ensure that the group's response to an errant member will be to exert further pressure to conform, rather than simply allowing the person to withdraw. Conflicts of this type are not overt, but they certainly occur as frequently and absorb as much energy as the other types.

Conflict-Resolution Processes——Regardless of the source or scale of conflict, the experience of direct, face-to-face confrontation between individuals is regarded as extremely unpleasant. By contrast, expressing direct conflict in a large solidary group is less traumatic and may even occasionally be a satisfying experience. This strong aversion to direct interpersonal confrontation implies a high sensitivity to the potential for conflict and a willingness to expend considerable energy to avert unpleasant incidents. The range of conflict-resolution processes commonly used in Japan may be understood in terms of these cultural preferences.

A major technique for anticipating and preventing conflict in Japan is the extensive use of prior consultation, or *nemawashi* (literally, "binding the roots"). Well before any decisions are made or meetings called to discuss solutions to a problem, all involved parties are consulted individually about the matter. The purpose of the consultation is to find out how each person feels about the problem and any proposed solutions, so that potential conflicts can be identified and accommodated in some way. *Nemawashi* is a delicate combination of salesmanship, vote-counting, fact-finding, problem-solving, and horse-trading. Much energy is invested in the development and cultivation of good interpersonal relations in Japanese society. *Nemawashi* both depends on such relations and reinforces them. Skill in conducting *nemawashi*, an essential quality of leadership in Japan, requires sensitivity, patience, and flexibility.

A closely related technique for anticipating and preventing conflict is the use of go-betweens to perform the necessary consultations. While *nemawashi* is used among group members or associates, go-betweens are utilized most often when the parties who wish to negotiate are not yet in a direct personal relationship, such as when marriage arrangements or business contracts between independent firms are proposed. The go-between insulates the parties from the possibility of direct conflict due to misunderstanding or differences in expectations, and also permits them to withdraw from the negotiations without the withdrawal becoming further cause for conflict. Go-betweens are also used when an existing relationship is threatened by imminent conflict. This may occur informally, when a friend, coworker, or family member negotiates on behalf of someone else, or it may be part of a formal or legal proceeding. Mediation, using a court-appointed go-between, is widely used in Japanese divorce proceedings as well as in labor relations.

Associated with the cultural preference for avoiding direct interpersonal conflict is a relatively high tolerance for unexpressed or ambiguous conflict. Conflict between individuals may be unacknowledged and quietly tolerated by one or both parties for a very long period of time. The parties may even tacitly cooperate to prevent the conflict from being expressed openly. Conflict that is suppressed or ignored in this fashion is often expressed indirectly with the aim of inducing guilt in the offending party.

Institutionalized Conflict-Resolution Procedures——Several different types of conflict-resolution procedures have been developed in Japan to handle situations of recurrent conflict. All serve to remove conflict from direct confrontations between individuals and to make resolution the responsibility of a larger and more neutral body.

The most general conflict-resolution procedure used in Japan is consensus decision making, a method for decision making that encourages the suppression and avoidance of conflict. The rules require that all decisions be made with the agreement of all participants; until everyone consents, no decision has been reached. In order to achieve a consensus, the participants must carefully avoid polarization while discussing the issue. They must search for common ground and work to meet the objections of any individual who is reluctant to consent. At the same time, each participant is placed under increasing pressure to accept the growing consensus, regardless of private objections. Personal relations and differences in power may also affect the ability of individuals to express their objections. Consensus decision making is usually combined with extensive prior consultation (*nemawashi*). It is the routine procedure for most decision-making bodies, with the notable exception of the Diet, which uses Western-style parliamentary procedure and individual votes.

A variant of consensus decision making, the so-called *ringi* system (see MANAGEMENT), is used by bureaucratic organizations for administrative decisions that are made by different units and levels over a period of time, rather than in a joint meeting. A written document (*ringisho*) containing a proposal is circulated in a fixed order to all units and individuals who should participate in accepting it. After internal discussion, the head of each unit signifies agreement by affixing his personal stamp to the document. The document may be delayed temporarily, and the stamp may be placed upside down to indicate some reservations, but eventually it must be approved. Here, too, prior consultation is an essential element in the process. As the document moves upward in the bureaucracy, it acquires the force of a growing consensus, although the person ultimately in charge has the formal authority not to act on the proposal.

Consensus decision making and the *ringi* system are procedures for making a decision within a single group or organization. Failure to achieve consensus is a sign of conflict so deep that it threatens the survival of the group, since there are no established procedures for this contingency.

The weakness of horizontal integration makes it difficult for equal but separate units of a bureaucratic organization or independent organizations to work together. It has been pointed out that a common procedure for conflict resolution in such situations is to create a joint consultative body containing representatives of the units involved. Such bodies are not always effective, but they are sometimes able to create a new unit with sufficient internal agreement to reach decisions and sufficient power to have them accepted by their respective constituencies.

Still another institution for conflict resolution is the use of third-party bodies, such as the courts, to help resolve conflicts between individuals or groups. Japanese courts rely extensively on mediation and conciliation procedures, and favor settlements that avoid polarization of the conflicting parties or clear establishment of a guilty and an innocent party (see DISPUTE RESOLUTION SYSTEMS OTHER THAN LITIGATION). Despite this, some scholars have shown that Japanese tend to avoid use of the legal system to settle private disputes precisely because of its polarizing, conflict-laden character. Others have argued that the courts are used in Japanese labor disputes not as a last resort, but early in the conflict as a means of legitimizing a union's bargaining position. Somewhat similarly, the courts have been used in pollution cases to legitimize the grievances of private citizens against powerful companies, particularly when the companies have refused to follow traditional rituals for the settlement of conflict and thereby precipitated a breakdown of trust.

Just as the formal institution of consensus decision making relies heavily on the informal practice of nemawashi for its success, so are the formal legal processes of conflict resolution supported by informal means of achieving out-of-court settlements. Professional specialists in achieving such settlements are called jidan'ya (compromise-brokers). It has been pointed out that the interplay between the formal (tatemae) or "front-stage" (omote) procedures and rituals and the informal (honne) or "back-stage" (ura) negotiations is essential to successful conflict resolutions (see TATEMAE AND HONNE).

Ritualization of Conflict——Confrontation rituals are sometimes staged by organized groups to permit anger and frustration to be vented and in some cases to set the stage publicly for serious private negotiations. Such collective rituals are often extremely aggressive, hostile, and violent, in stark contrast to the delicate conflict-avoidance behavior exhibited by Japanese as individuals. The annual spring labor offensive, or SHUNTŌ, is a relatively controlled confrontation ritual through which unions demonstrate their power with a brief strike before settling down to negotiations. Mass demonstrations are a similar form of confrontation ritual, with the important difference that they are generally staged by groups without bargaining rights or other means of affecting decisions. Both strikes and demonstrations are ritualized, controlled, and rule-bound events, although the rules may permit a great deal of spontaneous behavior as well as deliberate law-breaking and violence.

A somewhat more personalized confrontation ritual is taishū dankō (mass bargaining), in which officials considered to be responsible for some injustice are called upon to attend a mass meeting at which the audience presents demands and insists upon a public explanation and self-criticism. The officials experience an awesome combination of direct personal conflict, public degradation, and psychological pressure to confess and repent, while the audience experiences the catharsis of venting rage on a symbolic enemy with some protection of anonymity. Taishū dankō are employed in vertical status conflicts, where they epitomize the failure of trust and consequent rejection of old role relations between subordinate and superordinate.

Quite different from confrontation rituals are conflict-resolution rituals symbolizing the formal end of a conflict. Conflict-resolution rituals all involve some form of apology, which requires acceptance of responsibility for the conflict and signals a willingness to end it. Interpersonal conflicts may be settled by simple apology. Minor traffic violations or misdemeanors often require the writing of a formal apology called shimatsusho. The task of writing the document and rewriting it until it satisfies the appropriate official is imposed in lieu of a fine or other sentence. TENKŌ (ideological recantation) is a specialized form of conflict-resolution ritual used by persons who have been involved in ideological or political conflict with the state.

Serious conflict, particularly situations in which a company or institution has transgressed against individuals, is frequently settled by a formal apology from the responsible official. Such an apology requires that the official take personal responsibility for the transgression, even though it may have been accidental and completely beyond personal control. Often the apology is accompanied by the official's resignation, as well as an announcement of some compensation for the victims. See also COLLECTIVE BARGAINING RIGHT; LABOR DISPUTE RESOLUTION PROCEDURES.

■——Dan Fenno Henderson, Conciliation and Japanese Law (1965). Kawashima Takeyoshi, ed, Funsō kaiketsu to hō, 2 vols (1972). Fred N. Kerlinger, "Decision-Making in Japan," Social Forces 30 (1951). Ellis Krauss, Thomas Rohlen, and Patricia Steinhoff, ed, Conflict in Japan (forthcoming). Yasuyuki Owada, Alan H. Gleason, and Robert W. Avery, "Taishū Dankō: Agency for Change in a Japanese University," in Takie Sugiyama Lebra and William Lebra, ed, Japanese Culture and Behavior (1974). Herbert Passin, "The Sources of Protest in Japan," The American Political Science Review 56.2 (June 1962). Tsuchiya Moriaki and Tominaga Ken'ichi, ed, Kigyō kōdō to konfurikuto (1972). Ezra F. Vogel, ed, Modern Japanese Organization and Decision-making (1975). Nitagai Kamon, Ōmori Wataru, and Nagai Susumu, ed, Chiiki kaihatsu to jūmin undō: shakaiteki konfurikuto no bunseki (1976).

Patricia G. STEINHOFF

Confucianism

A tradition of Chinese origin said to have been known in Japan since the 5th century AD. Confucianism has religious aspects, but is mainly a philosophical, ethical, and political teaching. In Japan it has exercised a formative influence especially in the areas of education and ethical and political thought and conduct. It assumed particular importance during the 6th to 9th centuries and during the Edo (1600–1868), Meiji (1868–1912), Taishō (1912–26), and early Shōwa (1926–ca 1945) periods.

Confucius and the Tradition in Ancient China——Confucianism owes its basic orientation largely to Kong Qiu (K'ung Ch'iu), a teacher and philosopher of the Zhou (Chou) dynasty (1027–256 BC). Confucius, the name he is known by in English, is a latinized form of Kong Fuzi (K'ung Fu-tzu), in which Fuzi means Master; in China he is popularly known by the abbreviation Kongzi (K'ung-tzu; J: Kōshi). Confucius wished to restore the hierarchical but harmonious feudal society he believed to have existed at the beginning of the Zhou dynasty. This concern gave the tradition a generally conservative orientation, an element of protest at contemporary society, and an intense interest in political power and office. Confucianism has thus tended to appeal to ruling elites and to reflect their mentality and interests. Confucius believed that the ideal social order should be achieved, not by the enforcement of law, but by the moral example of those in authority, by proper ritual conduct, and by the observance by individuals of the norms of conduct appropriate to the status they occupied. The ruler should delegate power to officials chosen not on the basis of hereditary privilege but for their moral and intellectual capacities. Confucius was thus also concerned with the education and moral training of the individual. The source of morality lay in filial piety, a child's respect for and obedience to its parents, in practice mainly to the father, for the tradition concerned itself rather little with women. Emphasis on the family as a hierarchically ordered unit was to remain common to all Confucians and to inspire a detailed ideology of kinship. Confucius taught further that men should study and cultivate themselves to become "superior men" (zhunzi or chun-tzu; J: kunshi). This ideal, held to be an end in itself, was characterized by knowledge of classical songs, ritual, and music and by such virtues as loyalty, uprightness, and moderation. Most important, however, was ren (jen; J: jin), a kind of benevolence or altruism. The humanism that these concerns suggest was reflected in Confucius' lack of interest in metaphysical or religious questions and in the rational temper of his thought. Such religious concern as the tradition retained was most conspicuous in state rituals, ancestor worship, and the cult of Confucius himself that developed several centuries after his death.

Confucius called himself "a transmitter, not a creator" and did not write original works. Tradition, however, ascribes to him the editing of the following texts: Yi jing (I ching; Book of Changes), basically a manual of divination; Shu jing (Shu ching; Book of Documents), a collection of historical works; Shi jing (Shih ching; Book of Songs), an anthology of early song texts; Li (Ritual), a ritual text no longer extant; Chun qiu (Ch'un ch'iu; Spring and Autumn Annals), a brief history of Confucius' own state of Lu. With these were later grouped the Lun yu (Lun yü; Analects), a collection of sayings by Confucius and his disciples; the Xiao jing (Hsiao ching; Classic of Filial Piety); and a number of commentaries and ritual compendia including the influential Li ji (Li chi; Record of Ritual). These texts constituted the Confucian canon, and their study was a basic commitment of Confucians in all times and places.

In the two centuries following Confucius' death his teachings were elaborated by his followers. Mencius (Mengzi or Meng-tzu; popular name of Meng Ke or Meng K'o; 371–289 BC), whose writings were given canonical status during the Song (Sung) dynasty

(960-1279), developed the application of benevolence to government. He believed that kingship was a moral charge from Heaven to be exercised paternalistically and benevolently for the benefit of the people. Its abuse would result in Heaven transferring its mandate to another who would replace the delinquent by force of arms. Mencius' theory of justified revolt was employed to explain changes of dynasty in China, but was to be less readily acceptable to the Japanese political tradition. Mencius also developed Confucian ideas on the psychology and self-cultivation of the individual. His belief that human nature was fundamentally good was to influence the thought of the medieval Neo-Confucian revival. Confucius' emphasis on filial piety was meanwhile developed in a tradition associated with his disciple Zengzi (Tseng-tzu; popular name of Zeng Can or Tseng Ts'an; 505–ca 436 BC). Filial piety became an all-embracing dedication to the material and psychological welfare of the parents and, after their deaths, to the ritual care of their spirits. Confucius' interest in ritual institutions was pursued by Xunzi (Hsün-tzu; popular name of Xun Kuang or Hsün K'uang; ca 298–233 BC), who argued that men required the restraint of ritual institutions for society to function harmoniously.

The Confucian school suffered persecution under the despotic Qin (Ch'in) dynasty (221-206 BC), whose centralized administrative organization and dependence on the tradition known as Legalism (Fajia or Fa-chia) left a permanent mark on the Chinese state. Under the succeeding Han dynasty (206 BC–AD 220) Confucianism entered its long ascendancy in China. The principle of Confucian meritocracy was institutionalized in 124 BC when a state college staffed by doctors of the Confucian classics and a system of written examinations for appointment to the state bureaucracy based on the classics were established. Also during the Han Confucius himself became the object of a state cult of sacrifices and worship. At the same time the tradition underwent an important development which reflected its new status as the ideology of a centralized empire and determined the form in which it first came to the attention of the Japanese. A detailed cosmology was developed according to which the universe was seen as an organic structure under the control of Heaven and composed of the two forces of yin (negative) and yang (positive) and the five elements. Man, particularly the ruler, played a pivotal role as mediator between Heaven and the natural order. It was the ruler's function to instruct his subjects to conform to Confucian precepts and, according to his success or failure, Heaven responded with auspicious events, portents, or visitations. This system gave rise to a school of divination and a body of literature which dealt with directional taboos and calendrical superstitions. Known as yinyang jia (yin-yang chia; J: OMMYŌDŌ), this system was only tenuously Confucian and indeed contrary to the rational spirit of Confucius' teaching, yet it exercised great influence on the lives of the Chinese and later of the Japanese.

The influence of Confucianism on the Han state was perpetuated in later Chinese dynasties and was expressed on a particularly impressive scale in the institutions of the Sui (589–618) and Tang (T'ang; 618–907) dynasties. It was thus as the ideology of a powerful, centralized bureaucratic state that the tradition first became the subject of serious and sustained interest in Japan.

Confucianism in Ancient Japan —— Confucianism was transmitted to the kingdoms of Korea during the course of the 4th century AD. Tradition claims that from there it was introduced to Japan with the arrival from the Korean state of PAEKCHE (J: Kudara) in 404 and 405 respectively of the Korean scholars who are known in Japan as Achiki and WANI. This tradition reflects the influence of Korea in the early history of Japanese Confucianism, an influence that was to recur in its later history. A similar debt to the peninsula is reflected in records of the arrival from Paekche from 513 of doctors of the Five Classics.

The increasing centralization of Japanese society from the late 6th century created a climate particularly favorable to Confucianism. From the reign of the empress Suiko (r 593–628), the tradition is closely linked with the development of the Japanese state. It was not, however, its exclusive official ideology, for the Japanese court, like its Chinese model, remained ideologically pluralist. Thus the SEVENTEEN-ARTICLE CONSTITUTION of Prince SHŌTOKU (574–622) promulgated in 604, a landmark in the centralization of the Japanese state, employs Chinese Legalist and Buddhist as well as Confucian ideas to promote a harmonious, hierarchical political structure centered on the institution of the emperor. But its use of moral exhortation is Confucian, and the text quotes widely from the Confucian classics.

The opening of diplomatic relations with the Sui dynasty and its successor the Tang dynasty created a more direct path for the trans-

mission of Confucianism to Japan. From 608, students were included in the Japanese missions to China, and men such as MINABUCHI NO SHŌAN (fl early 7th century) and the scholar-monk SŌMIN (d 653), who spent many years in China, spread Confucian ideas on their return. Some were closely involved in the Taika coup of 645 and the ensuing reform, and there is little doubt that their Confucian ideas played an important role in these events.

The decades following the coup witnessed a sustained attempt by the Japanese court to emulate the style and institutions of the centralized bureaucracy of Tang China. To the extent that the latter was a Confucian state, therefore, the conduct and institutions of government in Japan now also assumed a Confucian coloring. Though the Tang Confucian state ritual program was apparently not adopted in full, Japanese emperors adopted the Confucian stance of moral responsibility for the welfare of their subjects, enjoined Confucian values on their officials, and issued decrees proclaiming the importance of ritual propriety for the maintenance of social order. The RITSURYŌ SYSTEM of administration (the word ritsuryō refers to penal and administrative codes) established during this period also shows Confucian influence in its underlying assumption that government was moral in purpose. Such institutions as the ministries and bureaus staffed by officials chosen for their merit and the handen system (see HANDEN SHŪJU SYSTEM) of equal land distribution also derive from Confucian ideals. More conspicuous Confucian influence can be seen in the fields of divination, kinship, historiography, and education.

The Japanese of the ritsuryō period inherited the Han-dynasty Confucian belief in portents and divination. The ON'YŌRYŌ (Bureau of Yin and Yang) set up under the Taihō code of 701 was charged with augury and prognostication of events, particularly as they affected administration. Before long, however, ommyōdō, whose highest claim would be that it monitored the effect of man's moral conduct on the natural world in accordance with Confucian beliefs, seems to have become little more than superstition. After mid-Heian times, it was absorbed by esoteric Buddhism and Shintō, eventually passing into the realm of folk belief. Yet it has never, even in modern times, altogether lost its traditional association with the Book of Changes and, though peripheral to the main tradition, must be accounted an enduring influence of Confucianism in Japan.

In the field of the kinship system and the ethics associated with it, the codes again embodied Confucian principles. Provision was made for rewarding Confucian conduct such as filial piety and chastity. Conversely, the state prescribed punishments for un-Confucian conduct, and the penal code enforced the respect for senior members of the family that was a basic Confucian value. At the same time, the ritsuryō lawmakers appear to have balked at full-scale implementation of the Confucian family system as embodied in their Tang model. Thus though a mourning system on the Confucian pattern was introduced, it was reduced in scope. The Confucian prohibition against marriage with another of the same surname appears also to have been dropped. These departures from the Chinese model suggest that even in this Sinophile period the full-scale Confucianization of Japanese society was not considered desirable. In view, also, of the probably limited enforcement of the codes, it is safe to conclude that the Japanese were likely to have been at most superficially Confucianized at this period. Indeed, despite this and later attempts at Confucianization, Japan was to retain a kinship system characterized by a less rigorous adherence to the agnatic principle; greater tolerance of endogamy; a tendency to "unigeniture" rather than the joint fraternal inheritance accepted as ideal by many Chinese Confucians; and a generally less extensive or hierarchical family structure than either the Confucian ideal or the Chinese practice.

The writing of history was a central Confucian activity whereby events were recorded, judged in the light of Confucian assumptions, and made to yield lessons in statecraft and morality. By contrast with a lack of much originality in Confucian canonical scholarship in ancient Japan, history writing was a field of Confucian intellectual endeavor that called forth creativity from leading scholars of the period such as SUGAWARA NO MICHIZANE (845–903). The codes provided for the continuous compilation of records, but the official histories were the product rather of ad hoc commissions. The best-known work is the NIHON SHOKI or Nihongi (720; tr Annals of Japan, 1896), an official history from earliest times to AD 697, which projected back into the past the Confucian view of the state and the imperial institution. Former emperors are presented as Confucian stereotypes, yet the work also preserves the indigenous myths concerning the divine descent of the imperial line. The resulting synthesis of native tradition with elements of the Confucian view of sovereignty was destined to become one of the most potent ideological influences in the history of the Japanese state. Five official histories, constituting with the *Nihongi* the RIKKOKUSHI (Six National Histories), followed, covering the years 697–886.

The most conspicuous and sustained Confucian influence in the ancient period was in the field of state-sponsored education. Here the Japanese attempted to reproduce the Chinese system of metropolitan and provincial schools and state examinations designed to provide Confucian educated personnel for the bureaucracy. There are grounds for believing that a metropolitan university was founded around a group of Korean immigrants about AD 670. Certainly Korean influence was initially strong, though as time passed the Tang model assumed greater importance. Though always far smaller than its Chinese counterpart, this university was similarly centered on Confucian studies. The importance of Confucius was symbolized by the observance there of the spring and autumn *sekiten* (Ch: *shidian* or *shih-tien*) service in honor of the Sage and his disciples from 701. This Chinese ceremony, which involved animal or in later times often vegetable offerings, became the main public manifestation of the religious dimension of Confucianism in Japan and the history of its observance reflects the standing of the tradition among Japanese.

As established under the *ritsuryō* codes, the DAIGAKURYŌ, a university, was a department of the Shikibushō (Ministry of Ceremonial). Its academic staff included one doctor and two assistant doctors of the Confucian classics. Four hundred students were prescribed for the main course of Confucian studies, largely chosen from among families of the fifth court rank and above and the descendants of immigrant scribes. Members of families of sixth to eighth rank and graduates of provincial schools could be admitted on petition. The curriculum was devoted to the Confucian classics and followed the Tang model. Students selected from a list of seven classics with prescribed commentaries by Han or post-Han Chinese scholars, grouped according to size and, in addition, all studied the *Analects* and the *Classic of Filial Piety*. Study appears to have been rigidly formalized and to have stressed memorization. Internal examinations were held regularly. A student graduated when he answered correctly a certain proportion of questions on the classics he had elected to study. He would then proceed to the Ministry of Ceremonial and take the state examination for admission to court rank and office. Outside the capital, *kokugaku* (provincial schools) modeled on the metropolitan university were officially prescribed for each province. Their students, whose numbers varied from 20 to 50 according to the size of province, were drawn from the families of provincial officials or, if recruitment from that source was insufficient, from commoners. The curriculum probably resembled that of the university. Graduates could proceed to the university for further study or take the state examinations in the Ministry of Ceremonial.

Success in the state examinations conferred one of several degrees. Most prestigious was *shūsai* ("outstanding talent"), only 65 passing during the years 704–935. This examination involved answering two essay questions in Chinese. The *myōgyō* ("canonical knowledge") degree required exposition of passages from elected classics and their prescribed commentaries. The *shinshi* ("recommended scholar") degree required success at completion tests on Chinese literary texts together with essays in Chinese on questions of contemporary government policy. Candidates were awarded classes according to performance. Generally, only the first two classes in each degree entitled the holder to immediate court rank and office.

Such, in outline, were the institutions of Confucian learning prescribed under the early 8th-century codes. Had they functioned ideally, they might have made Confucian learning the basic qualification for bureaucratic office and realized the principle of Confucian meritocracy. From the beginning, however, there were serious obstacles. First, it was a long time before the university or the provincial schools even began to approach their prescribed strength. Second, the restricted social basis for admission effectively excluded a truly meritocratic standard of recruitment to the bureaucracy through the system. Indeed, even within the limited stratum of society admitted to Confucian studies, the hereditary principle proved more powerful than the meritocratic. Sons of men of fifth court rank and above were automatically entitled to court rank higher than would have been achieved by the most brilliant examination results, and they enjoyed better prospects for promotion. Confucian education, therefore, did not become in Japan, as it did in Tang China, an important path to highest office. The university, therefore, rather functioned to train middle- and lower-ranking officials whom birth normally denied high rank and office.

Third, the Confucian emphasis of the university curriculum was fairly quickly diluted with a technical and more particularly a linguistic and literary emphasis. The creation of a special Chinese literary course in 728 in particular reflects both the great prestige of Chinese belles lettres at the Japanese court and the need, since Chinese was the official language of the bureaucracy, for linguistically qualified personnel to fill lower posts. Certainly, as indeed was the case also in Tang China, from this time on Chinese literary studies grew in prestige within the university at the expense of the more narrowly Confucian curriculum. Finally, in Japanese society at large, Confucianism never seriously challenged Buddhism as the dominant religious or intellectual persuasion. It was mainly to Buddhism that the Nara government looked for ideological support, and even officers of the Confucian Daigakuryō seem to have embraced it as their private faith.

The century and a half following the establishment of the new capital in Kyōto in 794 was a period of relative prosperity for the state education system. Its finances were made more secure, and the Confucian curriculum expanded. There were some signs of genuine intellectual controversy within the community of Confucian scholars. It seems, too, that from around the second decade of the 9th century almost every province had a school. At the same time, however, there was also an intensification of trends further subverting the Confucian character of state education. The tendency to value literary skill and to a lesser extent also history over Confucian studies increased. Attempts were made to restrict access to the university and, particularly, to the prestigious literature course, to the higher aristocracy. The public, meritocratic ideal of Confucian education was also undermined by the growth within the university of semiprivate *bessō* (separate halls) devoted to the interests of particular families (e.g., the KANGAKUIN of the Fujiwara family), and hereditary occupation of academic office began to appear within the university itself.

By the beginning of the 10th century, the general decay of the *ritsuryō* system was well advanced. Confucianism, its congruity with the social order lost, cut off from the stimulus of contact with the Chinese mainland by the decision of 894 to abandon missions to the Tang and as yet shallowly rooted in Japan, rapidly declined into a remote and formal pursuit. Hereditary occupation of academic office became established, and from the 11th century, university posts were virtually monopolized by a few court families. Confucian scholarship became increasingly privatized. Academic families developed their own variations on the system of diacritical markings used to construe Chinese texts and transmitted them privately and eventually even in secrecy. Buddhism also increasingly penetrated the university. From the mid-10th century the *sekiten* service was observed only in abbreviated form. The standard of examination, believed hitherto to have been high, also declined. Examination questions were leaked, and from the 11th century students might be permitted to pass merely on the recommendation of an unqualified dignitary. The financial position of the university also became insecure. In the provinces, too, decline had set in from the beginning of the 10th century, and by the end of the 11th the provincial schools vanish altogether from the records. In 1177 the university burned to the ground and was not rebuilt. Though academic offices, examinations, and ceremonies were perpetuated, they seem to have become a meaningless formality.

The Heian period thus closes with the failure of the *ritsuryō* state along with its state-sponsored Confucian institutions and the ideals on which they were based, and with the triumph of Buddhism over Confucianism as the dominant religious and intellectual persuasion. Nonetheless this first period of Confucian influence left important legacies. However flouted in practice, the Confucian ideal of sovereignty as appropriated by the imperial line and compounded with indigenous myth was to remain an important influence in Japanese political thought. While Confucian education had failed in its main purposes, it had been the means for familiarizing at least the upper classes of Japanese society with Confucian ethical concepts and lore. However, the course of rejecting a radical Confucianization of Japanese society was, generally speaking, to be followed in later periods. Japan was to remain much less Confucianized than its neighbor, Korea.

Confucianism in Medieval China: The Neo-Confucian Revival

The state-sponsored Confucianism of the Tang dynasty and of ancient Japan had tended to stress the institutional and ritual aspects of the tradition. During the Song (Sung) dynasty (960–1279) in China, however, Confucianism underwent a revival and development known as Neo-Confucianism, and it was in this form that it was destined to become most widely studied in Japan from the 13th or 14th century. This revival shifted much of the emphasis of the tradition from institutions and formal education to the spiritual and ethical concerns of the individual. It was distinguished by a systematized method of self-cultivation and by elaborate and precise metaphysical and cosmological ideas, for much of which it was indebted to its rivals, Buddhism and Taoism. There were two main schools of Neo-Confucianism. The more important is known as the Cheng-Zhu (Ch'eng-Chu) school from three of its leading figures, the Cheng brothers: Cheng Hao (Ch'eng Hao; 1032–1085); Cheng Yi (Ch'eng Yi; 1033–1107); and Zhu Xi (Chu Hsi; 1130–1200). In Japanese it is usually referred to as SHUSHIGAKU (the Zhu Xi school). This was a dualistic system of thought centered on the concepts of "principle" (*li*; J: *ri*) and "ether" or "material force" (*qi* or *ch'i*; J: *ki*). Principle was the organizing, rationally accessible category that governed the properties of things and the course of events. It was permanent, good, and unchanging and was endowed in man as his nature. This nature, however, could be obscured by the quality of the material force, the physical component of man's makeup and of the world. It was man's task to purify his *qi* by a number of techniques including objective study of principle itself and subjective introspection. The system, though puritanical and contemplative in tendency, retained the Confucian commitment to social objectives and had much to recommend it to an established government as an ideology. Its doctrine that the natural and human orders were based on unchanging natural principles would inhibit radical change, and the view that self-cultivation of the individual held the key to social harmony was admirably suited to a conservative, bureaucratic order. Zhu Xi Neo-Confucianism was established as the official orthodoxy in China, having become the basis for the civil service examinations by 1314.

The second school of Neo-Confucianism reached maturity only in the Ming (1368–1644) dynasty. It is usually known in Japan as the Yangming (J: Yōmei) school (see YŌMEIGAKU) after the cognomen of its leading thinker Wang Yangming (1472–1529). Wang deplored what he considered the unpractical and academic emphasis of the Zhu Xi system. He reformulated Neo-Confucian doctrine as a monistic idealism in which the mind contained all things and was itself principle *(li)*. Wang thus rejected the objective study of principle and substituted subjective intuition as the standard of moral action. His thought was endowed further with a dynamic, activist character by an epistemology that proclaimed the mutual interdependence of knowledge and action. Wang's system, on account of its activism, subjectivity, and concern with internal motivation rather than adherence to external norms, held a potential appeal for those dissatisfied with the status quo and in times of rapid change.

Confucianism in Medieval Japan

The date of the arrival of Neo-Confucian doctrines in Japan is uncertain, but it was in the Zen Buddhist community (see GOZAN) rather than among the traditional Kyōto court Confucian families that they first took root. Zen monks saw in Neo-Confucianism a useful secular complement to their own religious teachings, of particular value in their relations with political leaders. This eclecticism set the tone for the Confucianism of the Kamakura (1185–1333) and Muromachi (1333–1568) periods, and there came into being a type of Buddhist-Confucian monk known as a *jusō* (Confucian monk). An early example is the Chinese expatriate Lanxi Daolong (Lan-hsi Tao-lung; J: RANKEI DŌRYŪ; 1213–78), who instructed the fifth Hōjō regent Tokiyori (r 1246–56) on matters relating to self-cultivation and administration in essentially Confucian language. Of the hundred or so Zen monks of the Kamakura period who visited China or were themselves Chinese, some 12 are known to have spread Neo-Confucianism in this way.

Doctrines consciously exploited by men whose commitment lay in a different direction were likely to play a restricted role in society. For a brief while at the end of the Kamakura period, however, Confucian ideas exerted influence at the center of national political life. It is clear that many of the leaders of the KEMMU RESTORATION (1333–36) of the emperor Go-Daigo (r 1318–39) were interested in Neo-Confucianism. Though the restoration quickly foundered, it left an influential legacy in the form of two Japanese works which revived and developed the fusion of national tradition, imperial ideology, and Confucian moral teaching expressed in the *Nihongi*. The JINNŌ SHŌTŌ KI (tr *A Chronicle of Gods and Sovereigns*, 1980) of KITABATAKE CHIKAFUSA (1293–1354), a history of the imperial house, is ostensibly more Shintō than Confucian, but it condemns insubordination, particularly vis-à-vis the emperor, and stresses the value of loyalty in Confucian terms. The TAIHEIKI (Chronicle of Great Peace, partial tr, 1959), a prose warrior tale, presented Go-

Daigo in a Confucian manner as a wise and virtuous ruler, and celebrated his warrior supporter KUSUNOKI MASASHIGE (d 1336) as the ideal of subject possessing the Confucian virtues of loyalty, wisdom, benevolence, and courage. This work, permanently popular in feudal Japan, both reflected and in turn furthered the assimilation and adaptation of Confucian values in Japanese warrior society. The intense belief in self-denying loyalty, particularly toward the emperor, found in both these works may derive in part from Song thought. But it owes even more to the indigenous feudal tradition of the bond of loyalty between a warrior and his commander. A tendency to place loyalty over other Confucian values including even filial piety was to become an important theme in the adaptation of Confucianism to Japan.

The first century of the Muromachi period saw a continuation of the activity of *jusō* and the subordination of Confucianism to Buddhism. A well-known example is GIDŌ SHŪSHIN (1325–88), a favorite of the third Ashikaga shōgun Yoshimitsu (r 1369–94), who used Confucianism as a device to lead his patron towards Buddhist truths. At the same time, syncretism between Neo-Confucianism and Shintō was also explored by such scholars as ICHIJŌ KANEYOSHI (1403–81) and YOSHIDA KANETOMO (1434–1511), who founded schools of thought that survived into the Edo period.

The growth of larger and better integrated territorial units from the late 15th century created conditions more receptive to Confucian ideology. Many *jusō*, dispersed from the capital by the destructive Ōnin War (1467–77), found employment with provincial *daimyō*. In the southwest, the Zen monk KEIAN GENJU (1427–1508) visited successively the domains of Iwami, Chikugo, and Hizen, where in 1477 he performed the *sekiten* service and lectured on Confucian texts. In 1478 he was invited to the Satsuma domain, where he laid the foundation of a school of Confucianism which is said to have contributed to the special quality of Satsuma warriors. In the Ōuchi domain centered in Yamaguchi, the daimyō ŌUCHI YOSHITAKA (1507–51) imported Confucian books from Korea and had refugee nobles from Kyōto lecture on Confucian texts. In Tosa, Minamimura Baiken (dates unknown) taught a Zen-Confucian syncretism which according to tradition was the origin of the school of Confucian learning (the NANGAKUHA) in the Edo period. As a result of such activity, Confucian ideas became increasingly prominent in the house laws of the 16th-century daimyō.

Only one Confucian institution of this period, however, the Ashikaga school (see ASHIKAGA GAKKŌ) in modern Tochigi Prefecture, appears to have achieved durability. Originally founded in the 12th century, it was reestablished by the scholarly military leader UESUGI NORIZANE (1411–66). The curriculum was at first confined to Chinese and largely Confucian books, with overwhelming attention paid to the *Book of Changes*. Evidently the school met a contemporary need, for students, mostly Zen monks, flocked from as far afield as the Ryūkyū Islands. At its height in the third quarter of the 16th century, they are said to have numbered over 2,000. However, insofar as it was largely staffed by Buddhists and was chiefly concerned with a peripheral aspect of the Confucian tradition, the Ashikaga school was not fully Confucian but exemplified the eclectic temper of its age.

The Edo Period: Official Patronage and Education

The establishment of the Tokugawa peace made the world-denying assumptions of Buddhism less attractive and heightened interest in questions of society and government. Confucianism was equipped to meet this concern at many levels. Its ideal society was in many respects congruent with the feudal order of Tokugawa Japan. It offered a potential legitimation to the shogunate and the daimyō for their political hegemony, and its belief in a permanent natural and social order was attractive to those who wished to preserve the status quo. Samurai, whom peace caused increasingly to assume the role of bureaucrats, could derive a moral raison d'être from the gentlemen-officials of the Confucian ideal. Privately many men were undoubtedly attracted by the rationality, humanism, and spiritual discipline of Neo-Confucianism, and by the challenge of the study of Chinese texts. Increased wealth, leisure, and use of printing made the tradition ever more widely accessible. Japanese Confucian scholarship and thought achieved genuine creativity, and the Edo period became the golden age of the tradition in Japan.

The diffusion of Confucianism was in part the result of the considerable activity of private teachers and popularizers throughout the period. It probably owed as much or more, however, to an official patronage at both shogunate and domain levels that reflects the continuing appeal of Confucianism to governing elites. This patronage, though not as consistent or extensive as sometimes suggested, illustrates how well, by the end of the period, Confucian teachings had become established in Japan. Early interest on the part of the shogunate is suggested by the tradition that Ieyasu (r 1603–05), the first Tokugawa ruler, attempted unsuccessfully to employ FUJIWARA SEIKA (1561–1619), the founder of Japanese Neo-Confucianism as a movement independent of Buddhism, as an adviser. Seika is said to have declined, but his more ambitious disciple, the Cheng-Zhu scholar HAYASHI RAZAN (1583–1657) was employed in that capacity from 1607. Ieyasu, however, appears to have had little sympathy for Razan's aims for Neo-Confucianism, and Razan does not appear significantly to have influenced the formation of the political institutions of the regime.

Confucianism was accorded greater official recognition during the reign of the third Tokugawa shōgun, Iemitsu (r 1623–51). In 1630 Razan was given land and money to found a school in Edo (now Tōkyō). This was, however, his private academy and did not correspond to the ancient Daigakuryō. In 1632, a shrine to Confucius was constructed and, in 1633, the *sekisai* (Ch: *shizai* or *shih-tsai*), a version of the *sekiten* service, was performed. The shogunate also commissioned Confucian-style historical works from Razan, the best known being the *Honchō tsugan* (General History of Our State), which was finally completed in 1670.

The position of Confucianism was further improved under the fifth shōgun, Tsunayoshi (r 1680–1709), himself a keen student of the tradition. In 1690, the Confucian shrine and Hayashi school were moved to a larger site and the endowment of the school was also increased (see SHŌHEIKŌ). During the reigns of the next two shōguns, however, the Hayashi family were eclipsed as Confucian advisers by the great scholar and historian ARAI HAKUSEKI (1657–1725). Hakuseki certainly influenced shogunate policy in a Confucian direction, but on a personal rather than an institutional basis. The eighth shōgun Yoshimune (r 1716–45) encouraged diffusion of Confucian teachings among the nonsamurai urban population. He also employed Confucian advisers such as MURO KYŪSŌ (1658–1734) and the brilliant OGYŪ SORAI (1666–1728).

Shogunate patronage of Neo-Confucianism underwent an important development during the period of KANSEI REFORMS (1787–93). Ideological uniformity was imposed on the Hayashi school in 1790 by prohibiting all but Cheng-Zhu teachings (the so-called Kansei prohibition on heterodoxy). In the next few years the school was reorganized and an official college known as the Shōhei-zaka Gakumonjo, designed to train shogunal administrators, was founded alongside it. Examinations based on a Cheng-Zhu syllabus were now conducted every three years (from 1818 every five years). During 1798–99, the Confucian shrine was lavishly rebuilt to symbolize the new importance of Confucian learning. The college also published some 200 titles, mostly Confucian, between the years 1799 and 1867 and was the scene of a major Confucian historical project, the compilation of the *Tokugawa jikki* (Veritable Record of the Tokugawa), completed in 1849. There is no doubt that this expansion and revitalization of the Hayashi school influenced the climate of administration for the remainder of the Edo period. For the first time since the failure of the ancient Daigakuryō, Confucian learning could be considered a formal preparation for government service. In the late Edo period the shogunate also established special schools for commoners in shogunal lands and supported lectures by representatives of popular religious movements, such as SHINGAKU, which had a strong Confucian component.

In the daimyō domains, where the shogunate made few direct attempts to impose ideological uniformity, it was, particularly early in the period, the inclination of the individual ruler that largely determined the extent of Confucian influence. Though no domain tried a thoroughgoing Confucianization of its institutions, some daimyō such as IKEDA MITSUMASA (1609–82) in Okayama and HO-SHINA MASAYUKI (1611–72) in Aizu were dedicated followers of the tradition and tried to exemplify it in their rule. Many Confucian-minded daimyō employed Confucian scholars *(jusha)* as advisers on questions of ritual and as tutors for their families. The status of these men varied; rarely high, it tended to fall as the period progressed. Most domain professional Confucian scholars were lower middle samurai.

The most conspicuous Confucian institutions of the Edo period were the official domain schools *(hankō)*. These were at first founded intermittently: up till 1689 only 8 domains had them; in the next decade 7 more were founded. Another increase took place in the last three decades of the 18th century. Thereafter, an even pace was maintained until by 1865, 73 percent of the daimyō had such schools in their domains. These schools were usually the center for the veneration of Confucius in the domains. Some 59 domains possessed a separate building for this purpose, and in the case of the richer, these were often quite elaborate. The *sekiten* was observed twice annually in 88 of these schools, and a further 110 performed it or similar ceremonies at least once annually. The majority of the staff of the domain schools were Confucian scholars, and the curriculum placed great weight on the study of Confucian texts. Usually, from the age of 8 to 10 (Japanese reckoning) at which a boy enrolled until about 15 he learned the conventional Japanese readings for the Chinese text. From 15 he proceeded to the content, and lectures and group readings were held. Schooling continued into the twenties. Particularly toward the end of the period examinations similar to those of the shogunal college were conducted. Many domain schools, like the shogunal college, also published Confucian texts. During the Edo period 1,394 Confucian titles and a further 763 Chinese historical works are said to have been published in this way.

Samurai who did not attend domain schools might go to private institutions, often run by a single Confucian scholar who usually employed the Confucian classics as his texts. By 1870 there were some 1,400 such schools in Japan. The nonsamurai classes were less well provided with the opportunity for Confucian study by the authorities than the samurai. Some 17 domains, however, are known to have admitted commoners into their domain schools. Many domains also supported lectures for commoners by members of movements such as Shingaku. Finally Confucian ethics, particularly filial piety, were an element in TERAKOYA (village school) education, whose main purpose was the inculcation of basic literacy among commoners. By 1870 there were about 11,000 of these schools in Japan. It has been estimated that by 1868, some 43 percent of boys and 10 percent of girls attended some form of school. All of these would probably have been exposed at least to the main Confucian ethical concepts.

The effect of this wide diffusion of Confucian teaching is difficult to gauge. It is clear, however, that there were important limitations to the penetration of Confucianism in Tokugawa Japan, when compared with Buddhism in particular, or with Shintō. Confucianism was institutionally weak; the number of men professionally engaged in the study and teaching of the tradition remained much smaller than their Buddhist counterparts, and Buddhism still received a greater share of official patronage. Religious practices remained largely Buddhist or Shintō, and the number of Buddhist publications greatly outnumbered the Confucian. Moreover, the standards of Confucian learning even among samurai were probably not very high, nor did Confucian studies monopolize school curricula; other subjects including military training and later in some schools Japanese and Dutch medical studies were taught. Nor, it seems probable, was the basic structure of Japanese society radically modified by Confucianism. Confucian meritocracy made undramatic progress against the predominantly hereditary occupation system; as in ancient Japan, Confucian learning, even in the last decades of Tokugawa rule, was never an established path to the highest administrative office, though it could perhaps be argued that the Confucian principle of meritocracy was one inspiration behind the activities of discontented samurai during the Restoration movement. Nor were the samurai dissuaded from their martial values by Confucian civilian ideals. The Japanese kinship system remained to a large extent unaltered by Confucian norms. The system of ethical values, too, though many of its concepts assumed Confucian names, retained much or most of its indigenous character, as exemplified by the widely accepted preference for loyalty over filial piety. That said, however, the conservative, hierarchical, and harmonistic emphases of Confucianism must certainly have exerted an integrating and stabilizing influence at many levels and in many areas of Edo-period life. Much of the credit for the achievements in Tokugawa education, probably the highest of any premodern Asian society, must be given to Confucianism. Some Confucian influence can even be seen in the arts, and particularly in literature. It is, however, in the vigorous intellectual life of the period that Confucian influence can be most clearly documented.

Confucian Thought in the Edo Period —— Confucianism provided most of the metaphysical and ethical categories and ideals by which Tokugawa thinkers interpreted and judged their world. To a considerable extent, indeed, the development of Confucian thought determined the intellectual history of the period. This thought derived its vitality and variety from the urge of Confucian thinkers, themselves representing different classes and interests, to relate their Chinese inheritance to their own changing experience and conditions. Their views are preserved in a vast volume of commentaries, tracts, correspondence, biographies, lectures, essays, memorials, diaries, and other material. These men shared the defining commitments of the tradition to the study of Confucian texts; veneration of the Chinese past; belief in the ideal of a harmonious, hierarchical society, commonly expressed in terms of a fourfold division into the occupational groups of SHI-NŌ-KŌ-SHŌ (samurai, peasant, artisan, and merchant); paternalistic, benevolent government; education; and, though usually within well-defined limits, the meritocratic principle. Most saw themselves as moralists, dedicated to the improvement of society, or at least lamented the failings of their age. However, most also accepted the basic dispositions of Tokugawa feudal society as broadly congruent with their ideals, though the position of the shōgun, anomalous from the Confucian point of view, occasioned increasing difficulty. Beyond this, however, there were important differences over metaphysics; the nature, function, and importance of moral self-cultivation; choice of Confucian texts for emphasis; and the relation of Confucianism to indigenous religions and political institutions.

Traditional accounts divide Tokugawa Confucianism into schools of thought, appropriately insofar as most Japanese students studied the tradition through the interpretation of a seminal thinker who mediated between the Chinese tradition and Japanese experience. Each school perpetuated and sometimes developed or reinterpreted the ideas of its founder. Tokugawa Confucian thought thus tends to be both conservative and cumulative in character. At the same time, long-term developments occurred that are not necessarily directly related to the history of the schools. Four phases may usefully be distinguished.

The first phase spans the 17th century but its ideas found adherents also throughout the remainder of the period. Its dominating assumption was that the Neo-Confucianism of the Song and Ming was broadly congruent with the realities of Japanese society. In the Cheng-Zhu tradition two schools are important. The Kyōgakuha (Kyōto school), founded by Fujiwara Seika, originated in Kyōto. Its most prominent scholar was Hayashi Razan, whose own thought derived its ideological cast partly from his proximity to the center of the political power. Razan was among the first Confucian thinkers of the period to develop the medieval tradition of syncretism between Neo-Confucianism and Shintō. Contrasting with the rather broad-minded approach of this school was that of the extensive Kimon Gakuha (Yamazaki school) founded by YAMAZAKI ANSAI (1618–82). Ansai brought to Japanese Neo-Confucianism a narrow and almost religious intensity. He particularly emphasized the Confucian ethical value of "reverence" (kei; see TSUTSUSHIMI), and his emphasis on the loyalty owed by subjects to their ruler, itself increasingly typical of Japanese Confucianism, was to exert an influence on the imperial loyalists of the Meiji Restoration of 1868. The first committed exponent of the doctrines of Wang Yangming in Japan was NAKAE TŌJU (1608–48), the founder of the Yōmei Gakuha (school of Wang Yangming). Tōju explored the inner, subjective aspect of man's nature, believing that men were endowed with a faculty analogous to conscience which guided them in their daily conduct. His teachings possessed a simplicity and religious feeling that gave them lasting appeal. Tōju's most influential disciple was KUMAZAWA BANZAN (1619–91), whose extensive writings on economic and administrative questions, rational and humanitarian in spirit, laid the foundation for much of the Confucian social and economic thought of the Edo period.

The second phase begins around the third quarter of the 17th century, when thinkers began to find an incongruity between what they felt to be the static, contemplative emphasis of Neo-Confucianism and their own experience and sense of the needs of contemporary society. These men rejected much of the Neo-Confucian system of metaphysics and self-cultivation and advocated a return to what they held to be pristine Confucianism. They are often grouped together under the name of Kogakuha (School of Ancient Learning; see KOGAKU). The earliest major figure in this tradition is YAMAGA SOKŌ (1622–85), who advocated regulation of society less by self-cultivation in the manner of orthodox Neo-Confucianism than by the external restraints of rituals and codes of conduct. His detailed prescriptions for samurai in the latter field became known as BUSHIDŌ (the Way of the warrior). Another major critic of Neo-Confucianism was the townsman ITŌ JINSAI (1627–1705) who taught that men were endowed with a predisposition to do good which they cultivated by the pursuit of moral ideals rather than by the recovery of a static nature and endowed within themselves. Jinsai's rejection of Neo-Confucianism was consolidated and developed in a political direction by Ogyū Sorai, the most

original of the Japanese Confucians. Sorai argued that the Confucian way consisted of the institutions created by the ancient sage-kings of China. It was the duty of Confucians to comprehend these institutions through rigorous philological study of the classics and to provide a basis for their adaptation to their own times. His argument that Confucian institutions were relative, human creations rather than, as many of the Song Neo-Confucians had believed, a part of the unchanging order of nature, weakened the sanctions of the traditional Confucian ethical and political order. Sorai's thought resulted in a subtle liberalization of the spirt of Confucian studies that influenced the remainder of the period. It opened the way for new intellectual developments including KOKUGAKU (National Learning) and has been seen as facilitating Japan's acceptance of new institutions and of Western thought during the second half of the 19th century.

The third phase of Tokugawa Confucian thought, which spans the 18th century and beyond, is complex and even confused. Several trends can be identified. A tendency toward rationality and empiricism is seen in a number of thinkers mainly in the Cheng-Zhu tradition, such as KAIBARA EKIKEN (1630–1714), who wrote on botany among other subjects, the historian and statesman Arai Hakuseki, and the speculative philosopher MIURA BAIEN (1723–89). An eclectic temper is demonstrated by a group of scholars who reacted against the sectarian spirit that had been occasioned by Sorai's radical attack on the Cheng-Zhu system. This group, known as SETCHŪ-GAKUHA (Eclectic school), drew on Han and Tang commentarial scholarship, the exegesis of the Song and Ming, and the philological approach of Jinsai and Sorai. Overlapping this movement was another known as the Kōshō Gakuha (Textual school), chiefly concerned with textual criticism and bibliography, an approach influenced both by Sorai and by contemporary Chinese scholarship. At the same time, there was a revival of Cheng-Zhu Neo-Confucianism related to the Kansei prohibition on heterodoxy of 1790. The Cheng-Zhu school remained popular, particularly in the domain schools, more than half of which based their curricula on it by the end of the period. It also formed the conceptual basis for early Japanese attempts to understand Western science. Yet another trend was the reformulation of Confucian doctrines syncretically with Shintō and Buddhism. This syncretism was an important vehicle for the diffusion of Confucian ethical concepts among townsmen and peasants. The popular Shingaku (Heart Learning) movement founded by ISHIDA BAIGAN (1685–1744) exemplifies the development largely in the cities. Its rural counterpart, the Hōtoku (Repayment of Virtue) movement led by the peasant teacher NINOMIYA SONTOKU (1787–1856), flourished in the 19th century.

The final phase of Edo Confucian thought coincides with the quickening of intellectual life that took place against the background of the challenge of the West and the decline of shogunal power. One theme is an increased, if largely private, interest in the teachings of Wang Yangming, whose combination of activism and subjectivity was attractive in a time of intellectual and political turbulence. The most conspicuous trend, however, was the reemergence, with an intensified element of national feeling, of the ancient synthesis of Confucianism, Shintō, and imperial ideology. This movement had its main origin in the Mito domain, where a loyalist tradition had been associated with the compilation of the DAI NIHON SHI (History of Great Japan), begun under the daimyō Tokugawa Mitsukuni (1628–1700). In the first half of the 19th century the Mito Gakuha (MITO SCHOOL) created a fresh synthesis from several traditions, including the emphasis on status relationships of the Song historian and thinker Sima Guang (Ssu-ma Kuang; 1019–86), the administrative thought of Kumazawa Banzan, Shintō nationalism, and the emphasis on loyalty, particularly toward the emperor, that had been characteristic of the Kimon school. A similarly loyalist and nationalist feeling was expressed in the popular Nihon gaishi (Unofficial History of Japan) by the Confucian historian RAI SAN'YŌ (1781–1832). Proimperial, antiforeign rhetoric deriving from these ideas spread among elements of society hitherto denied a political voice. It inspired imperial restoration activitists such as YOSHIDA SHŌIN (1830–59), who finally resolved the longstanding tension between loyalty to the shōgun and to the emperor decisively in favor of the latter. Not all Confucian thinkers of the time, however, accepted the antiforeign views of the Mito school. Men such as SAKUMA SHŌZAN (1811–64), a military scientist and Cheng-Zhu thinker, and YOKOI SHŌNAN (1809–69) tried to assimilate the implications of Western science and civilization within a Confucian metaphysical framework.

Confucianism in Modern Times —— From one point of view the Meiji Restoration of 1868 and the establishment of the new bureaucratic state may be interpreted as a long-delayed realization of Confucian meritocracy. For many Japanese, however, the opening of Japan to massive Western influence must have shattered the cogency and integrity of the traditional Confucian world view. After a brief initial period during which the restorationists attempted to model the Japanese state on the Confucian-inspired institutions of the early 8th century, a reaction took place. The shogunal college and most of the domain schools were refounded as Western-style institutions or abolished within a few years of the Restoration, and regular observance of the *sekiten* service was abandoned. Confucianism, however, had by now become so well established that it was likely to persist, even if only in fragmented form. That it reasserted itself so soon was in no small degree due to the influence on the Meiji emperor (r 1867–1912) of his Confucian preceptor MOTODA NAGAZANE (1818–91), and to the advocacy of the philosopher and educationalist NISHIMURA SHIGEKI (1828–1902), who attempted a synthesis of Confucian metaphysics with Western thought. The culmination of their efforts, the influential IMPERIAL RESCRIPT ON EDUCATION of 1890, expressed a combination of Shintō tradition concerning the imperial dynasty with a Confucian view of the duties of his subjects. In this way, the survival into modern times of the Mito fusion of Confucian ethics with national tradition was secured. In one sense, the long process of diffusion of Confucianism in Japan was complete. Confucian ethics, particularly loyalty, which was by now usually interpreted to subsume filial piety, became a basic part of the elementary-school curriculum. This, however, was the ethical element of the tradition detached from its intellectual background and original element of protest, wedded to beliefs concerning the divine character of the Japanese imperial institution and reinterpreted in the service of national objectives which came to include the acquisition of a colonial empire. This fragmentation did, nonetheless, enable the tradition to survive Japan's emergence into the modern world as a force in national life. It also helps to explain how, in contrast to China, Confucianism in Japan, freed from much of the deep cultural conservatism of the tradition as a whole, could be a positive force in modernization by promoting harmony and national solidarity.

After Motoda's death Confucianism became temporarily less conspicuous in government. At a popular level, however, the volume of Confucian publications remained high. Nor did the tradition lack articulate spokesmen, such as the philosopher INOUE TETSUJIRŌ (1855–1944), for example, who attempted to work out new underpinnings for it and to adapt it to the needs of the Japanese state. Institutionally, too, Confucianism soon began to revive. In 1907 regular observances of the *sekiten* service at the old Confucian shrine at the Shōheikō in Tōkyō were restarted by a society organized for that purpose, and in 1918 several Confucian organizations were refounded as the Shibunkai (Confucian Association) with support from government and business. This society's aims were to combat what was seen as the materialist spirit of the West, social unrest, and the decline of public morals. It endeavored to influence education by promoting the study of Chinese and, particularly, Confucian texts.

The deterioration of both the domestic and the international situation by the early 1930s provided a receptive atmosphere for the synthesis of nationalism with Confucian ethics that had by now become orthodox. From about 1933, the promotion of Confucianism became both domestic and foreign policy. Domestically, Confucian ideas were seen as a means for achieving the ideological mobilization of the nation. The most famous example of this use of the tradition is the KOKUTAI NO HONGI (Cardinal Principles of the National Entity of Japan) of 1937, which, within six years, had achieved a circulation of just under two million copies. This tract is primarily a Shintoist exposition of the national polity of Japan, but it also presents the emperor as a ruler in the Confucian style and enjoins loyalty, filial piety, harmony, and the proper performance of their occupations on the Japanese people.

Abroad, Confucianism was seen by Japanese nationalists as a unifying force in Japan's expansion on the Korean peninsula and the mainland. In Korea, a country more deeply Confucianized than Japan, in the year following the annexation by Japan in 1910, the old Confucian college in Seoul was refounded and *sekiten* services were restarted. The association of the Japanese administration with Confucianism continued throughout the occupation. In Manchuria, where the Japanese established the state of MANCHUKUO in 1932, Confucianism was also used to justify Japan's continental mission, and the Japanese depicted themselves as restorers of Confucian tradition. Confucian classics were taught in schools, rewards given for

Confucian conduct, and Confucian shrines restored. In China, where the Japanese set up a provisional government over the northern provinces in 1937, a political party called the Xinmin Hui (Hsinmin Hui; Society for the Renovation of the People) dedicated to the revival in China of Confucian cultural values was founded.

Following defeat in World War II, the Japanese once more turned their backs on their Confucian heritage. In recent years, however, there have been signs of a modest revival of interest. Popular editions on the Confucian classics continue to be published and the *Analects* are still quoted in speeches on graduation day and such occasions. Though echoes of prewar Confucianism may still occasionally be heard, this new interest in the tradition seems usually to be free from explicitly nationalist sentiments.

Exposure to Confucianism over more than a millennium and a half has left a complex legacy on present-day Japan which is hard to assess concisely. Possibly the most important influence remains in the field of education, where the sophistication of the tradition and the value it placed on rationality and on learning as a rounded and disciplined program still indirectly contribute to Japan's present high standards. Japanese politics and administration may still owe something to Confucian ideals of paternalism and integrity. Undoubtedly also the Confucian emphasis on loyalty, hierarchy, and harmony within family and society has contributed to the discipline and solidarity with which the Japanese people still confront the problems of the modern world. But the picture should not be overdrawn. It can be argued that neither the Japanese kinship system nor the political structure owes any very profound debt to Confucian influence. Nor, despite its Confucian conceptual dress, is the Japanese value system necessarily in substance the product of Confucian influence. Self-denying loyalty, for instance, whether to state or enterprise, to which many ascribe Japan's success, may be consonant with Confucianism. In Japan, however, loyalty also had peculiarly strong indigenous roots which determined its precise form and relative importance.

📖 ———Ashikaga Enjutsu, *Kamakura Muromachi jidai no jukyō* (1932). Robert L. Backus, "The Kansei Prohibition of Heterodoxy and Its Effects on Education," *Harvard Journal of Asiatic Studies* 39 (1979). Robert L. Backus, "The Relationship of Confucianism to the Tokugawa Bakufu as revealed in the Kansei Educational Reform," *Harvard Journal of Asiatic Studies* 34 (1974). W. G. Beasley and E. G. Pulleyblank, ed, *Historians of China and Japan* (1961). Bitō Masahide, *Nihon hōken shisōshi kenkyū* (1961). Ronald P. Dore, *Education in Tokugawa Japan* (1965). John Whitney Hall, "The Confucian Teacher in Tokugawa Japan," in David S. Nivison and Arthur F. Wright, ed, *Confucianism in Action* (1959). Hisaki Yukio, *Daigakuryō to kodai jukyō* (1968). Kasai Sukeharu, *Kinsei hankō ni okeru gakutō gakuha no kenkyū*, 2 vols (1969–70). Kasai Sukeharu, *Kinsei hankō no sōgōteki kenkyū* (1960). Masao Maruyama, *Studies in the Intellectual History of Tokugawa Japan*, tr and ed by Mikiso Hane (1974). Minamoto Ryōen, *Tokugawa gōri shisō no keifu* (1972). Sagara Tōru, *Kinsei no jukyō shisō* (1966). Seki Giichirō and Seki Yoshinao, ed, *Kinsei kangakusha denki chosaku daijiten* (1943). Shibunkai, ed, *Nihon kangaku nempyō* (1977). Warren W. Smith, Jr., *Confucianism in Modern Japan: A Study of Conservatism in Japanese Intellectual History* (1959). John Joseph Spae, *Itō Jinsai: A Philosopher, Educator and Sinologist of the Tokugawa Period*, Monumenta Serica Monograph XII (1948, repr 1967). Ryūsaku Tsunoda, Wm. Theodore de Bary, and Donald Keene, comp, *Sources of Japanese Tradition* (1958). Tokugawa Kō Keisō Shichijūnen Shukuga Kinenkai, ed, *Kinsei Nihon no jugaku* (1939). Wajima Yoshio, *Nihon sōgaku shi no kenkyū* (1962). Wajima Yoshio, *Chūsei no jugaku* (1965). James McMULLEN

"Conquer Korea" debate → Seikanron

consanguinity

(shinzoku). A legal relationship between persons arising as a result of blood or marital ties. The Japanese Civil Code establishes provisions concerning three types of such relations: (1) a blood relation within the sixth degree of kinship; (2) spouse; and (3) a marriage relation within the third degree of kinship (art. 725). In addition to these three classifications, there are four generally recognized means of categorizing consanguinity: direct line (*chokkei;* including ancestors and descendants), collateral line (*bōkei;* parallel descendants from the same ancestor), ascendants (*sonzoku;* persons of preceding generations), and descendants (*hizoku;* persons of succeeding generations).

Relationships of consanguinity arise as a result of birth, marriage, adoption, or acknowledgment of paternity, and are dissolved by death, dissolution of marriage, or nullification of adoption. The effects of consanguinity extend in many directions. Certain relationships of consanguinity give rise to obligations for support (Civil Code, arts. 877–881) and rights of inheritance (Civil Code, arts. 887–890). Marriage between persons of close consanguineous relationship is prohibited (Civil Code, art. 734). Cases in which the operation of criminal law is affected by consanguinity include an increase in the penalty for a lack of proper care of the deceased bodies of direct relations (Criminal Code, art. 218 [2]) and a waiver of penalty for theft from consanguineous relations who are also cohabitants (Criminal Code, art. 244).　　　　　　　*Ono Kōji*

Conscription Ordinance of 1873

(Chōheirei). Law making military service compulsory for all males; enacted in January 1873, it went into effect in April. After the Meiji Restoration of 1868, the new government did not immediately organize a national army but depended instead on the military forces of the powerful southwestern domains, such as Satsuma (now Kagoshima Prefecture) and Chōshū (now Yamaguchi Prefecture), that had played a leading role in the overthrow of the Tokugawa shogunate. The government found, however, that it could not deal effectively with the successive peasant uprisings and rebellions by discontented former *samurai* (see SHIZOKU), and so it decided to organize an army under its direct control. Opinion was divided as to whether service should be voluntary or compulsory. ŌMURA MASUJIRŌ and YAMAGATA ARITOMO of the Chōshū domain overrode all opposition and forced the adoption of a conscription system. They argued that—as proven by the success of irregular militia (KIHEITAI) in Chōshū—an army drawn from all classes of society would be more effective than one composed of samurai and that the conscription systems already adopted by the advanced nations of Western Europe had proven both militarily and financially advantageous. After the abolition of the domains and the establishment of the PREFECTURAL SYSTEM in 1871, the government was able to consolidate both its political and fiscal position and decided to institute conscription. On 28 December 1872 the National Conscription Edict was issued, and on 10 January 1873 the Conscription Ordinance was passed, to become effective in April.

Under the ordinance, all males who had reached the age of 20 were required to serve for three years. At first, however, exemptions were made for several categories, such as government officials, students at government schools, heads of households, only sons, and those who paid proxy money in the amount of ¥270. In this respect, the Conscription Ordinance was far from universal; rather it resembled the old feudal corvée (BUYAKU), and again the burden was borne by the peasantry, who made up more than half of the population. Throughout 1873 peasant uprisings (KETSUZEI IKKI) sprang up in all parts of the country.

Nonetheless, the government's successful suppression of the SATSUMA REBELLION (1877), a large-scale revolt by former samurai of that domain, proved the value of conscription, and steps were taken toward a more efficient and fairer system. In 1883 the proxy system was abolished, and six years later the exemption system was abolished as well. Through these and other reforms, the principle of universal conscription was finally established. Following extensive revisions in April 1927, the Conscription Ordinance was replaced by the Military Service Law (Heieki Hō), which was abolished in November 1945 during the OCCUPATION of Japan.

■——Matsushita Yoshio, *Meiji gunsei shi ron* (1956). E. H. Norman, *Soldier and Peasant in Japan: The Origins of Conscription* (1943). Yamagata Aritomo, *Rikugunshō enkaku shi* (1905).

　　　　　　　　　　　　　　　　　　Kuroda Nobuyuki

conservation

Conservation as a conscious movement aimed toward the protection of nature so as to ensure adequate supplies of natural resources and provide a wholesome environment for future generations is relatively new in Japan. The beginnings of the modern conservation movement lay, for the most part, in the Meiji period (1868–1912). By the start of the 19th century, the diminution of resources and destruction of the natural environment that accompanied the Industrial Revolution had already given an impetus to conservation movements in Europe. Although early attempts at various forms of conservation in Japan can be traced back several centuries, it was

only in the latter part of the 19th century that several individuals emerged to lead a fledgling conservation movement.

Toward the end of the Meiji period, MIYOSHI MANABU, a professor of botany at Tōkyō University who had studied in Germany and was impressed with the conservation efforts he witnessed there, began a campaign to awaken public opinion about the need for implementing conservation programs in Japan. From this came the first conservation laws in Japan. The Association for the Preservation of Historic Sites, Places of Scenic Beauty, and Natural Monuments was founded in 1911, and a Law for the Preservation of Historic Sites, Places of Scenic Beauty, and Natural Monuments (Shiseki Meisho Tennen Kinembutsu Hozon Hō) was enacted in 1919. During the same period, the American National Parks Law attracted attention in Japan, and a movement sprang up in 1912 to make NIKKŌ a national park. However, it met with little initial success. In 1927 the National Parks Association of Japan was established, leading to the passing of the National Parks Law (Kokuritsu Kōen Hō) in 1931.

These movements concentrated mainly on the protection of rare natural phenomena or places prized for their historical import or exceptional scenic beauty. Conservation movements in the truly contemporary sense of the term actually began in the 1950s, when Japanese post–World War II industrial development began to affect the environment profoundly. In 1950 the Diet passed the Comprehensive National Land Development Law (Kokudo Sōgō Kaihatsu Hō; see COMPREHENSIVE NATIONAL LAND DEVELOPMENT PLAN) and the Law for the Protection of Cultural Properties (Bunkazai Hogo Hō; see CULTURAL PROPERTIES LAW). The next year, 1951, saw the establishment of Japan's first natural conservation group, the Nature Conservation Society of Japan. This was followed by the passage of the Natural Parks Law (Shizen Kōen Hō) in 1957, which established strict regulations concerning the development of national parks and the so-called quasi-national parks. It placed stringent controls on the hunting of animals and the gathering of plants in these areas. It also called for the better use of natural scenic sites. The Nature Conservation Society of Japan played a major role in helping this bill gain passage. This group became an incorporated foundation (*zaidan hōjin*; literally, "juristic person") in 1960 and began regular publication of a society journal entitled *Shizen hogo*, dedicated to spreading the ideals of nature conservation.

The 1960s were a period of rapid economic development in Japan. Under the Comprehensive National Development Plan, land development programs were instituted in many parts of Japan (see LAND RECLAMATION). This was accompanied by the reclamation of coastal areas and the large-scale felling of forests. Around this time the conservation movement in Japan underwent a transformation. Up to this point, the ranks of conservationists had mainly been filled by scholars, educators, and a small number of concerned individuals from the general public. Following the reclamation of shoreline lands and the erection of giant oil-refining complexes, however, residents in the areas affected rose in protest. This swelled the ranks of the conservation movement (see CITIZENS' MOVEMENTS).

This movement continued into the 1970s, when pollution and environmental destruction in Japan became ever more visible. Damage attributed to photochemical smog became a serious public issue in 1970; this prompted the unification of 77 of the nation's conservation groups under the umbrella of the Japan Union of Nature Conservation in 1971. During that same year the government, recognizing the need for a government agency that would deal exclusively with environmental problems, established the ENVIRONMENT AGENCY. At the time of its inception, the Environment Agency took a positive stance toward promoting conservation and betterment of the environment. In 1972 its director-general attended the United Nations Conference on the Human Environment held in Stockholm and presented a report on environmental conditions in Japan. That same year the Diet passed the Natural Environment Preservation Law (Shizen Kankyō Hozen Hō). This bill distinguished between "wilderness areas" and "nature conservation areas." The former came under stiff protective measures, but the latter was further subdivided into two types of areas: those that required the express permission of the director-general of the Environmental Agency for their development and those that merely required notification of intent to develop.

The oil crisis of 1973 resulted in a setback in land development plans. This might have seemed a welcome state of affairs from the standpoint of the conservation movement. However, in some sectors of society and in the Environment Agency itself, restrictions on development and environmental pollution tended to slacken in order to gain relief from the economic recession brought on by the oil crisis. This led to confrontations between the Environment Agency and citizens' groups behind the conservation movement. The basic question is whether the government should impose stiff controls to protect the natural environment or strive to maintain past levels of economic prosperity. There is apparently no simple solution. See also ENVIRONMENTAL QUALITY; NATURAL MONUMENTS AND PROTECTED SPECIES.

——Fukushima Yōichi, ed, *Shizen no hogo* (1975). Nihon Kagakushi Gakkai, ed, *Seibutsu kagaku,* in *Nihon kagakushi taikei,* vol 15 (1965). Shinshū Daigaku, ed, *Shizen hogo o kangaeru* (1973).

Suzuki Zenji

consolidated financial statements

(renketsu zaimushohyō). In recent decades an intensification of economic competition among Japanese corporations has resulted in the increasing prevalence of enterprise groups as a means of securing profits, spreading risks, and stabilizing management. Consolidated financial statements are formulated and made public in order to disclose the operating results and financial condition of these groups. Such statements are based upon the individual financial statements of member companies of the industrial groups and are formulated through a consolidating procedure. In Japan, an official statement of concepts and principles govern actual formulation and disclosure requirements for consolidated financial statements. All consolidated accounting practices are based on this statement.

The first step in formulating consolidated financial statements is to determine the scope of consolidation. In Japan, a corporation controlling more than 50 percent of another company's voting stock is referred to as a parent company. The company whose stock is held by the parent company is referred to as a subsidiary company. The parent company and all subsidiary companies should in principle be included in the consolidated financial statement. The statement consists of a consolidated balance sheet, a consolidated income statement, and a statement of consolidated surplus. The balance sheet is formulated by applying an elimination process to the parent company's investment account and the subsidiaries' capital account as well as to the intercompany debits and credits. The income statement is formulated by applying the same elimination process to intercompany sales among the consolidated subsidiaries, intercompany profits in inventories, fixed assets and other intercompany accounts. For subsidiaries and affiliated companies outside the scope of consolidation, the equity method is applied. Before being made public, consolidated financial statements are subjected to auditing for their fairness in reflecting the financial conditions and operating results of the industrial group involved.

Wakasugi Akira